The Living and the Dead in Islam
Studies in Arabic Epitaphs II

The Living and the Dead in Islam

Studies in Arabic Epitaphs

II
Epitaphs in Context

by

Marco Schöller

2004

Harrassowitz Verlag · Wiesbaden

Publication of this book was supported by a grant of the Deutsche Forschungsgemeinschaft.

Bibliografische Information Der Deutschen Bibliothek:
Die Deutsche Bibliothek verzeichnet diese Publikation in der Deutschen Nationalbibliografie; detaillierte bibliografische Daten sind im Internet über http://dnb.ddb.de abrufbar.

Bibliographic information published by Die Deutsche Bibliothek:
Die Deutsche Bibliothek lists this publication in the Deutsche Nationalbibliografie; detailed bibliographic data is available in the internet at http://dnb.ddb.de.e-mail: cip@dbf.ddb.de

For further information about our publishing program have a look at our website http://www.harrassowitz.de/verlag

Printed on permanent/durable paper.
Printing and binding: Memminger MedienCentrum AG
Printed in Germany
ISBN 3-447-05083-7

حَيَاةٌ وَمَوْتٌ وَانْتِظَارُ قِيَامَةٍ * ثَلَاثٌ أَفَادَتْنَا أُلُوفَ مَعَانِ

*Living, dying and expecting a resurrection: * three things which taught us many a thousand thoughts.*

(al-Maᶜarrī, *al-Luzūmīyāt*)

I was told that Abū l-ᶜAlāᵓ Ḥasan b. Aḥmad al-Hamaḏānī al-ᶜAṭṭār was seen after his death in a dream. He stood in a town whose walls were entirely made of books. Countless books were piled up around him and he was busy with studying them. When he was asked, 'What about all those books?', he replied 'I asked God that He may let me continue in the hereafter what I was doing all my life, and He granted me that.'

(Ibn al-Ǧawzī, *Kitāb al-Muntaẓam*)

Though criticism has been cultivated in every age of learning, by men of great abilities and extensive knowledge, till the rules of writing are become rather burdensome than instructive to the mind; though almost every species of composition has been the subject of particular treatises, and given birth to definitions, distinctions, precepts and illustrations; yet no critic of note that has fallen within my observation has hitherto thought sepulchral inscriptions worthy of a minute examination, or pointed out with proper accuracy their beauties and defects.

(Samuel Johnson, *An Essay on Epitaphs*)

General Introduction

Aim and scope

The present studies aim at reconstructing the place, impact and importance of epitaphs – i.e. funerary inscriptions[1] – and related funerary structures within the culture, society, and intellectual and religious history of the Islamic lands. On the basis of the edited epigraphic material and the available literary sources[2] we cannot hope to present an all-encompassing study comparable to what has been published in regard to funerary epigraphy and connected issues in non-Islamic areas of research. None the less, we feel that the present studies will fill a gap in a hitherto neglected field in the wider realm of Arabic and Islamic studies. They will also contribute to the deepening of our understanding of Islamic attitudes towards death, burial, mortuary cult and memory, as well as afterlife and the relations between the worlds of the living and the dead.

This complex matter, well-researched in the greater European and Mediterranean context,[3] has been summarised as follows in a recent monograph dealing with the place of the dead in the European Late Medieval and Early Modern societies; the passage is worth being quoted here and may well apply to the present volumes:

1 In our studies, the term "epitaph(s)" only refers to funerary inscriptions as found on tombstones and other tomb-markers or funerary structures. It does not denote the "literary epitaph", being a purely poetical genre, nor the speech pronounced at the funeral; *cf.* also Volume II, Chapter 4.

2 Here as elsewhere the term "literary sources" refers to every written source in the form of books, treatises, anthologies etc., in order to distinguish them from written documentary sources such as epigraphy and epistolography.

3 It must suffice to mention the major studies, above all the general monographs Ariès: *Essais* and *Western Attitudes*; Assmann: *Tod als Thema*; Illi: *Begräbnis und Kirchhof*; Jupp/Howarth: *Changing Face of Death.* Much research has been done concerning the European Middle Ages. See Binski: *Medieval Death*; Braet/Verbeke: *Death in the Middle Ages*; Borst/Graevenitz: *Tod im Mittelalter*; Geary: *Living with the Dead*; Ohler: *Sterben und Tod im Mittelalter*. Other studies deal with the Ancient Near East (Jonker: *Topography of Remembrance*) or the ancient Mediterranean (Morris: *Burial and ancient society*). Of special interest to our subject are works which analyse practices and discourses of remembrance as well as funeral poetry from a general European perspective (Petrucci: *Writing the Dead*) or are related to specific periods and places such as ancient Greece (Prinz: *Epitaphios Logos*; Sourvinou-Inwood: *'Reading' Greek Death*), the European Middle Ages (D'Avray: *Memorial Preaching*; Geary: *Phantoms of Remembrance*; Lemaitre: *Mémoire des morts*) or the early modern period (Gordon/Marshall: *Place of the Dead*; Houlbrooke: *Death in England*; Ström: *Funeral Poetry*). Finally, literature dealing with funerary epigraphy in European languages has been taken into account in Volume II, Chapter 4.

"The theme of 'the place of the dead' is a highly multivalent one, and provides a means of gaining new and unexpected access to a wide range of themes and problems current in a number of apparently discrete historiographies. Yet this is far from implying that we can approach it merely as a shorthand method of expressing and exposing fixed and underlying societal 'structures'. The [. . .] cultural significance of the dead was never a 'given', something taken for granted and unimpeachable. Rather it was the product of a matrix of social, religious and economic relations which had to be enacted and articulated anew with each generation that passed away. That most reflective and past-minded of activities, the remembrance and commemoration of the dead, is in every age a remarkable contemporary testimony."[4]

The cultural significance of the dead is, in a larger sense, indeed the main focus of the present studies, exemplified in Arabic funerary epigraphy and related material. None the less, there is little originality on the pages to follow, and we tried to let the sources speak for themselves. It is without doubt necessary to know first what we are confronted with in the realm of the Arabo-Islamic culture before venturing upon gross generalisations and grand theories. As Timothy Reuter put it in a different context, "there is still an immense amount of positivist establish-the-facts-spadework to be done".[5]

In order to cope with the vast amount of material produced by the culture of Islam, our studies have been restricted in time and subject matter. As to time, we limited ourselves to the pre-modern period of Islamic culture, that is, roughly the time from the beginnings of Islam up to the end of the twelfth century H(iǧrī). Features belonging to the modern and contemporary period have been occasionally touched upon. However, this period clearly demands a study of its own, not only for its rich and widely scattered source material but also for the sizeable and growing influence of non-Islamic, Western elements since the thirteenth century H (nineteenth century CE). As to subject matter, the present studies deal mainly with epitaphs and relevant literary sources composed in the Arabic language.

In Volume I it is the epitaphs themselves, i.e. epitaphs seen as texts, which are to the fore. Additionally, non-epigraphic sources – Qurʾān, Ḥadīṯ, letters of condolence and various literary sources – are cited in order to enlarge the basis of research, determine the phraseological conventions and to better elucidate the religious, mental and social background to funerary epigraphy. Apart from Arabic epitaphs, in some sections of this volume epitaphs written in Hebrew or Turkish have also been taken into account for the sake of comparison with the Arabic material.

Volume II deals with the social and material aspects of Islamic burial sites and funerary monuments insofar these provide the wider context of Arabic funerary epigraphy. Moreover, all kinds of literary sources, including the important genre of Arabic visitation and cemetery guides, have been given ample attention. The use made of literary sources allows for the research into the importance of epitaphs in

4 Gordon/Marshall: *Place of the Dead* p. 16 (Introduction).

5 *The New Cambridge Medieval History. Volume III, c.900–c.1024,* ed. by Timothy Reuter, Cambridge 1999, p. 12.

Arabic literature and the uses to which funerary inscriptions were put in different discourses. The volume also comprises a catalogue of epitaphs and epitaph-poems cited in Arabic literary sources.

Given the fact that Arabic was the dominant language within the culture of Islam during the pre-modern period, particularly in the realm of devotion and piety, the geographical area covered in both studies reaches far beyond the actual Arabic-speaking countries and includes Anatolia, Iran, Afghanistan, Central Asia, Pakistan, India, Ceylon (Sri Lanka) and China. For our purposes, Spain and Portugal (al-Andalus), as well as Sicily and southern Italy, have also been considered an integral part of the pre-modern Arabo-Islamic world.

Method

The method adopted in both studies might be described as a phenomenological approach which aims at reconstructing a substantial segment of pre-modern Islamic culture, its specific discoursivity and the mental outlook that generated it and was generated by it; another term which fittingly describes our procedure is "anatomy", in the sense it has acquired in other fields of study.[6]

In general, this method rests on some basic assumptions about how to make sense of a cultural system and follows a theoretical framework which has been elaborated elsewhere.[7] This involves close attention to detail and the use of language, as well as the perusal of the greatest number of sources possible. Only after the reconstruction of the extensions, limits and intersections of Islamic discourses pertaining to death, burial and funerary epigraphy, will a feasible picture of the whole emerge and only then can its interpretation be attempted. This is especially true of the discourse of funerary epigraphy, which depends on and is influenced by a range of other more or less related discourses (e.g. Ḥadīṯ, epistolography including letters of condolence, ascetic and religious poetry, panegyric poetry, non-funerary epigraphy, biographical and hagiographical literature) and Qurʾānic diction.

Reconstructing the discourse of funerary epigraphy and the discourses related to it means discovering the mentalities underlying them and the respective *Sinnwelten* which they reflect and constitute at the same time. *Sinnwelten*, a term coined by the egyptologist Jan Assmann,[8] structure the cultural memory and provide the semantic and symbolic means to fill out this structure. *Sinnwelten* enable the members of a given culture to create a world of their own and to cope with it, to express themselves according to a complex and dynamic, but ultimately limited and thus usable system of concepts and images. The importance of discourses and the *Sinnwelten* they entail seems, to our mind, paramount for the analysis of a culture, all the more so in view of the fact that few cultural achievements in human history have been so language- and discourse-centred as the culture of Islam.

6 See Kemp: *Ancient Egypt*, especially the instructive introductory chapter.

7 For details, see Schöller: *Methode und Wahrheit*.

8 Assmann: *Ägypten* p. 17 and passim.

The discourses themselves are language-centred, and therefore will be the prime vehicles in our quest for understanding as Arabists. As mentioned, the discourses analysed in our research span some 1200 years in time and cover a wide geographical area. Synchronically, they yield the structural features of a given culture, while taken diachronically they contain elements of development and change. Together, they allow us to perceive, it is hoped, how things appear, or are made to appear, at a certain point in time and space, but they also guide us towards the appraisal of how things came to be and how they have evolved in time and space.

The reconstruction of a culture on the basis of its discourses leads to a multi-faceted approach, which foregoes any attempt to adopt a normative perspective, i.e. trying to show what is a "correct" Islamic usage or belief and what is not. It also seems appropriate to generate a holistic view, which stresses continuities and discontinuities at the same time. This does not mean that it is the disruptive force of post-modern discourse analysis that we are looking for, rather, the analysis of the relevant discourses should result in the contrary, that is, in a reconstruction of the immensely rich, internally contrastive and yet externally coherent heritage which Islamic culture has left behind. This procedure may seem disruptive only to those who desire, for whatever reason, to depict Islamic culture in historically biased forms, narrowed down by ideology and present-day political considerations.

It might be of relevance to stress once again the elementary fact that, although people and their mental outlook are shaped by the world they live in, the very human contribution to that world is its conceptualisation, interpretation and evaluation according to a specific cultural code and its complex symbolic system. This human perception of the world will also have repercussions upon the way the world really is, resulting in the dialectical process of Man being shaped by the world and shaping it at the same time. The latter process is mainly the outcome, in the broadest sense, of intellectual efforts which find their most thorough and rich expression in the wide variety of literary forms and language-related modes, especially in Islamic culture.

Sources

Discourse analysis necessitates the largest number of sources possible and the inclusion of a great variety of different genres. Of course, this premise was already made in a number of preceding studies,[9] though we are confident that we have gone some way beyond that which has been achieved up to now.

The most important genre and the basic source material for our purposes is Arabic funerary epigraphy as far as it has been edited by modern scholars. Collecting nearly everything which has been published in this regard was an arduous task in itself, especially as many publications are not easily accessible. This material is of primary importance in Volume I, while literary written (non-epigraphic) sources are prevalent in Volume II. Some older publications have been inaccessible; however,

9 See e.g. Smith/Haddad's introduction to their *Islamic Understanding of Death*.

their number is limited. It is also worth mentioning that considerably more sources have been perused than are cited in the bibliographies. Thus the bibliography of epigraphic sources in Volume I does not aim at completeness but is confined to those works which proved relevant; the same, though to a lesser degree, applies to the literary sources used in Volume II.

The role of the Qurʾān in the funerary discourse, and hence in the discourse of epitaphs, cannot be overestimated. Not only are the basic eschatological concepts of Islam embodied in it, but it also deeply influenced form and style of epigraphic texts. However, Qurʾānic quotations in general tend often to become so conventional that they do not convey specific messages any longer.

No less important is Ḥadīṯ, viz. Tradition. Quite independent of the question of the authenticity of single traditions, legitimate as it is in other fields of research, the Ḥadīṯ material directly reflects the religious and social attitudes and concepts of early Muslim society. In addition, it is our main source for certain eschatological concepts which are not found in the Qurʾān.

Much attention has also been given to Arabic poetry. Since in pre-modern Arabic culture poetry was the most cherished and most highly evolved means of expressing emotions, sentiments, beliefs, convictions and shared values, no part of this culture can be properly understood without recourse to poetry. Concepts and images couched in poetical and other literary forms of expression are in themselves important elements for every "anatomy of culture", though only a detailed analysis and comparison with other evidence will show how far they genuinely reflect historical and social realities.[10]

In our studies, poetry is significant in two respects. On the one hand, poetry is a source material in itself insofar as it is cited in epitaphs, thus being an integral part of the discourse of Arabic epitaphs; in literary sources, very often only the poetical elements of epitaphs are quoted, which again proves the paramount importance attached to poetry. On the other hand, poetry has been cited by us from various other sources in order to elucidate certain concepts found in the epigraphic discourse or as parallels to epitaph-poetry. This method is all the more legitimate and appropriate as epitaph-poetry often goes back to, or is influenced by, poetry which is cited in literary sources (mostly ascetic poetry, i.e. *zuhdīyāt*, and mourning poetry, i.e. *marāṯī*) and attributed *there* to individual poets. Even though the authors of many epitaph-poems still remain unknown to us, we have reason to believe that the authorship of at least a certain amount of hitherto anonymous poems will be identified in due time.

Technical features

Throughout these studies, dates are in general given according to Hiǧrī years. This has been done mainly because the Islamic calendar provides a chronological scheme of its own which allows a detachment of the periodisation of pre-modern Islamic

10 See Schöller: *Methode und Wahrheit* p. 80.

culture from the periods of European history. For the sake of clarity, however, "H" has been added to all Hiğrī dates, while the Christian or Common Era, where applicable, has been indicated by "CE".

The Qurʾān has been rendered in English chiefly on the basis of Arberry's translation, though minor changes were introduced in a number of cases in which Arberry's version proved too distant from the original wording for our purposes. Passages in rhymed prose have been marked by / and ||, with the single stroke indicating the internal divisions and the double stroke indicating the end of groups of cola which share the same rhyme. Quotations from epitaphs are given by numbers whenever possible. Reference to numbers is mostly by the numbers alone, in certain cases marked with "N^{os}" or "n^{os}" for clarity's sake. References to pages are always preceded by "p.". Cross-references between the two volumes are simply given as "Vol(ume) I" and "Vol(ume) II", followed by the page number. In Volume II, bold numbers refer to the catalogue of epitaphs in the fourth chapter.

In view of the different scopes of the two volumes, each of them has been assigned its own bibliography. We feel that the bibliographies contain much information on the sources and the approaches followed, being themselves a kind of paratext of some importance for the reader. The separation of the bibliographies also stresses the fact that both volumes are, after all, two different books by two different authors; each of us is responsible for his volume only. However, we fruitfully collaborated and our common interest proved to be both pleasant and inspiring.

As for the indices, we thought it best suited the readers to create indices common to both volumes. These indices are contained in the third volume.

Cologne, 2004

Werner Diem
Marco Schöller

Acknowledgements

Many persons and institutions have provided valuable help during our work on the two volumes.

Prof. Hartmut Bobzin (Erlangen) gave us permission to copy some of the source volumes; Prof. Mordechai A. Friedman (Jerusalem) provided information on Jewish letters of condolence preserved in the Genizah; Prof. Claude Gilliot (Aix-en-Provence) photocopied books on epigraphy in the possession of Prof. ém. Solange Ory (Aix-en-Provence) which otherwise would have been inaccessible; Friedrich Kaltz (Cologne) read proofs and contributed valuable observations; Dr. Franz-Christoph Muth (Mainz) drew our attention to particular Arabic epitaphs; Dr. Friedrich Niessen (Cambridge University Library) gave details on Genizah letters of the Taylor Schechter Collection; Dr. Helga Rebhan of the Bayerische Staatsbibliothek Munich supplied us with various rare books; Prof. Reinhard Weipert (Munich) put at our disposal editions of classical poetry which were inaccessible in German libraries but are part of his personal collection of Classical Arabic literature.

A good stock of the basic epigraphic publications was at our disposal in the library of the Max Freiherr von Oppenheim-Foundation at the Oriental Institute of the University of Cologne. The curators of the foundation also provided means for acquiring additional epigraphic works. Many recent as well as older publications in the field, unavailable in Cologne, were obtained through the Cologne University Library from other German State and University Libraries, particularly those in Bamberg, Bonn, Göttingen, Halle, Jena, Munich, and Tübingen.

A considerable part of the research concerning the Prophet's tomb, its veneration and the relevant Arabic poetry and treatises (see Volume II, Chapter 1) was made possible thanks to a post-doctorate scholarship granted by the Deutsche Forschungsgemeinschaft (German Research Council) in 1998 to the author of Volume II. The Deutsche Forschungsgemeinschaft also generously financed the publication of the three volumes.

As we are not native speakers of English, a final version of the text was read by Mrs Katherine Maye-Saïdi (Cologne) and Professor Michael Carter (Oslo). Both of them considerably improved the English wording of the text, and we were able to discuss with them difficult points of English style, especially regarding the translation of Arabic terms. Professor Carter also made valuable observations of a technical nature.

To all these persons and institutions we extend our sincere thanks.

Contents of Volumes I–III

Contents

Introduction

General remarks and contents

Epitaphs need to be looked at, they are made to be noticed or read by someone. Their scope is manifold but, above all, they fulfil a communicative and commemorative function.[1] They keep alive the memory of persons who have passed away; they either tell us about the deceased and his destiny or they express that which the deceased is no longer able to utter: his last wishes, his hope for the hereafter, his admonition of the living. In short, little else in the history of culture is so exclusively designed to deliver a message as funerary inscriptions. Via funerary inscriptions, the dead communicate with the living. The study of epitaphs and their context, therefore, also raises the subject of the visitation of tombs and cemeteries (*ziyārat al-qubūr*) which in numerous cases also includes the veneration of graves.

The first chapters of this second volume of Studies in Arabic Epitaphs take their origin from these and similar considerations. Chapter 1 deals therefore with the visitation of tombs and cemeteries in pre-modern Islamic culture and the various practices connected with it. Chapter 2 dwells upon the material aspects of the tomb in so far as these are relevant for the study of Arabic funerary epigraphy. Put simply, both chapters deal with the social and some material aspects of burial sites in Islamic culture, that is, why and in what way people visit tombs and how these appear, or should appear, to the visitor. Given the communicative function of epitaphs, their existence and significance presuppose on the one hand that there are people who visit tombs, yet on the other that the tombs visited are equipped with tomb-markers and funerary inscriptions. The social and material aspects of Islamic burial sites may thus be said to form the wider context of Arabic funerary epigraphy.

Chapter 3 contains a short overview of pre-modern Arabic visitation and cemetery guides. This literary genre is the outcome of the general importance of the visitation of tombs and cemeteries in Islamic culture and can thus be considered the textual link which mediates between the social and material context of burial sites and the

1 It is astonishing, and perhaps also reveals a deep psychological insight, that not a few Arabic scholars claimed that the reading of epitaphs (*qirāʾat ʾalwāḥ*, or *kitābāt*, *al-qubūr*) will ruin the character and lead to forgetfulness (IĞawzīḤaṯṯ p. 18; ṢafĠayṯ I p. 410; QalNawādir p. 154; for further sources, see WKAS II p. 1711, s.r. *lwḥ*). This is also referred to in a late sixth-century treatise on the methods of teaching, see Ibrāhīm b. Ismāʿīl: *Šarḥ Taʿlīm al-mutaʿallim li-z-Zarnūǧī*, Cairo: Muṣṭafā al-Bābī al-Ḥalabī 1342, p. 43. However, it is not mentioned in an eleventh-century treatise on forgetfulness and the remedies against it (= NābNisyān, see bibliography).

literary and scholarly discourses that relate to the mortuary cult and connected issues. The writings pertaining to this genre are interesting in their own right, but in the present context their importance is mainly due to the fact that some of them provide rich material for Arabic funerary epigraphy.

Chapters 4 and 5 deal with Arabic epitaphs as cited in literary sources. Chapter 4 studies the quotation of funerary inscriptions in Arabic literary sources and is more closely concerned with the textual framework (which I avoided calling the "textual context") of Arabic epitaphs. This entails the analysis of the role epitaphs fulfil in Arabic literary sources and especially the varied uses to which funerary inscriptions were put in a number of different discourses and literary genres. In addition, Chapter 4 contains a catalogue of some 237 epitaphs and epitaph-poems as cited in Arabic literary sources (1st – 12th centuries H), together with an edition, translation and commentary of their wordings and variant readings; an Arabic "reader" of the respective epitaph-poems is provided at the end of the present volume (see Appendix). Chapter 5 attempts to show, by way of a particularly illustrative example, the intertextual relations which underlie the text of a single Arabic epitaph.

A note on the sources

As for the range and nature of the relevant sources used, nothing needs to be added here to what has already been said in the general introduction to both volumes. However, a point of special interest for the present volume is the fact that the social and material aspects of Islamic burial sites were at all times subjected to the tension between theory and practice, or put differently, between the prescriptive and descriptive tendencies in Islamic orthopraxy, learning and scholarship.

In general, theoretical views about basic cultural features as shaped and expressed by persons who represent and share that culture often aim at establishing a model for ideal behaviour or condemn deviations from that model, although at the same time they might still acknowledge the existence of different views. This strand of thought is often dubbed "normative", but also the term "theoretical" fittingly characterises the intellectual activity we are dealing with in Islamic culture, quite close to the original meaning of the term if we understand "theory" as "contemplation" or "doctrine", without reference to practice or practical needs in the first place.

The main area of that kind of theory in Islamic learning was jurisprudence (*fiqh*) and legal studies (*ʿilm al-furūʿ*), and legal literature is thus our most important source for theoretical views that pertain to questions of the visitation of tombs, the outer shape of grave monuments, the setting up of tombstones and the inscription of epitaphs. Some of these theoretical discussions were taken over into exegetical literature (*tafsīr*), but Qurʾān commentaries are in general a less promising source for funerary customs and structures because burial and related features are, apart from some minor details, not mentioned or alluded to in the Qurʾān.[2]

2 *Cf.* EQ I pp. 263-5 (J.E. Campo), *s.v.* "Burial". The Qurʾānic passage most closely relating to the

On the other hand, Muslim legal experts were themselves well aware of the fact that their field was mainly theoretical, at least in principle. In order to bridge the gap between theory and practice one took recourse to *ʾiftāʾ*, that is, the drafting of legal opinions or fatwas (*fatwā*, pl. *fatāwā* or *fatāwī*) which were and still are provoked by specific questions that most often (but not necessarily) had a practical background. It was especially in later times, during the Mamluk period and beyond, that fatwas increasingly became a comfortable pretext for drawing up very theoretical and abstract discussions of a specific argument. However, fatwas are in general an important source for both theory and practice.

The third substantial source for theory is the Islamic "Tradition" as preserved in Ḥadīṯ literature.[3] This claim might seem strange at first sight given the fact that what is reported in Ḥadīṯ collections is said to be historical facts or events, or at least a close reflection of those. Yet much of what we find there is not scrupulously authenticated or reliable as to its historicity by our standards. In many cases we lack the proper means to ascertain which report might be reliable and which might not, though research methodologies have become increasingly refined in recent years.[4] Essentially, the reports transmitted in Ḥadīṯ literature and anthologies of Tradition provide the core material for the arguments of the jurists and their legal reasoning. It was here that these reports fully acquired their significance, and the constraints of legal reasoning inevitably exercised some influence on the origin and shape of Traditions.[5] Joseph Schacht called this process, with good reason, the "transformation of legal propositions into pseudo-historical information. (...) We find new traditions at every successive stage of doctrine".[6] The Ḥadīṯ material – the Islamic Tradition – is thus in view of its intended use mainly theoretical.

Since the present study is not meant to assess the historicity of single Traditions stemming from the first century H, it must be stressed that on the following pages the reference made to reports as transmitted in Ḥadīṯ literature does not entail a close analysis of their textual history or of their transmitters (as might be necessary in other contexts). What is important here are the ideas and concepts conveyed, whatever their exact provenance and origin. These studies are mainly a quest for the "common" and, as it were, "largely shared" Islamic views, and thus it suffices for our purposes to be able to ascribe a Tradition roughly to a certain period and place.

mortuary cult, especially to the erection of tomb-mosques and mausolea (see below Chapter 2), is Q 18:21, concerning the "Seven Sleepers": *When they were contending among themselves of their affair then they said, "Build over them a building; their Lord knows of them very well"*; see also the detailed discussion of the implications of this verse in Leisten: *Architektur für Tote* pp. 18-23.

3 In this volume, "Tradition(s)" (with capital letter) renders the term *ḥadīṯ* (pl. *ʾaḥādīṯ*), no matter whether it denotes "the Tradition" (i.e. the corpus of all Traditions, seen as a field of knowledge) or "a Tradition" (i.e. a single Tradition or report handed down and studied as part of the corpus of Traditions).

4 The state of the art is well represented in the papers collected in Motzki: *Biography of Muḥammad*.

5 See my *Exegetisches Denken*, chapter III. *Cf.* also Grütter: *Bestattungsbräuche* pp. 150f.

6 Schacht: *Revaluation* p. 151.

Even the question of forgery loses much of its importance if seen in this light, because the very existence of a report proves its relevance and significance.

As to the pre-modern practice concerning the visitation of tombs in Islamic culture we depend on what the textual sources at our disposal tell us about it. Since information about practice, in contrast with theory, is not limited to a certain field of knowledge, there is no specific literary genre dealing with this theme; the genre which most substantially relates to practice are treatises which deal with the so-called *bidaʿ wa-l-ḥawādiṯ*, "innovations and novelties". As to the shape of funerary structures we must primarily have recourse to the objects and monuments that have been preserved. Being a different field of research from the one pursued here this was not attempted in the present study, but I have referred to the studies of art historians and archaeologists wherever necessary or fitting. However, many monuments have been destroyed or disappeared over the course of time, so we therefore also have to look for further evidence in literary sources.

The last thing to mention in this context is the simple question: what do the sources tell us? There is no ready-made answer to this question, above all in the vast field of Arabic learning and literature which is an array of the most diverse ways imaginable of transmitting and preserving information. In the best scenario, we find information that can be made use of without further ado or we might read successfully between the lines. In the worst case, we are confronted with passages such as the following, written by Ibn Ḥağar al-ʿAsqalānī (d. 852 H) with regard to a certain judge: "Some of our teachers said that he came to Egypt where the story in the Qarāfah (cemetery) happened to him. But this is not correct, because the person involved in that story in the cemetery happened to be somebody else".[7] Here we are *not* told (a) the exact identity of the source, (b) which story (*qiṣṣah*) was said to have happened, (c) why the story did not happen as said and (d) to whom the story did happen if not to the afore-mentioned judge. Obviously, this passage is useless to us as long as we possess no additional evidence which provides more details.

On the whole, however, the student of Arabic and Islamic history, compared with scholars in other fields of study, is in a privileged position due to the sheer mass of sources and valuable information. There will be no end to research for generations to come thanks to the admirable and immensely productive efforts of Arabic scholars to preserve the major and most minor details of their culture for posterity. I remember reading the following wish in the introduction to a learned Arabic treatise: "May God have mercy upon those who prefer the burden of knowledge to the affliction of ignorance!"

The significance of death and the hereafter in Islam

Death, afterlife and the hereafter play a dominant role in Islamic imagery. This soon becomes clear to anybody even vaguely familiar with the central traits of

7 IḤağRafʿ p. 174.

Islamic culture, and exactly this has been stressed over and over by the Muslims themselves. The extraordinary success of the poetry of Abū l-ᶜAtāhiyah (see **17**) is a good case in point, but also the sermons depicting the mortal fate of Man and delivered by the famous preacher Ibn Nubātah (d. 374 H)[8] or Ibn al-Ǧawzī's (d. 597 H) *Kitāb at-Tabṣirah*, "The Book of Enlightenment", some 850 pages of admonitory preaching (*waᶜẓ*) on topics mainly concerned with death and afterlife. Below on page 136 one will find a hortatory sermon by ᶜAlī b. Abī Ṭālib which contains a veritable *summa* of the concepts and topoi regarding the conditions of this and the world to come as they were circulated and shared by many in the formative centuries of Islam. Even modern reformist Muslims in Indonesia chose to call their creed *agama kuburan dan ganjaran*, "the religion of the grave and the reward (*or* retribution)".[9] Not forgetting also that we are dealing, in the Arabic realm, with a culture where people could bear names like Yamūt, "the One who is Bound to Die", or Abū l-Mawt, "Father of Death".[10] Moreover, a third-century traditionist from Baghdad was commonly known as *al-mayyit*, "the Dead".[11]

As with other Near Eastern monotheistic religions, there is a strong current of otherwordliness in Islam. It finds its expression in Qurʾānic passages such as the following: *fa-mā matāᶜu l-ḥayāti d-dunyā fī l-ʾāḫirati ʾillā qalīlun* (Q 9:38, "Yet the supplies of this present life, compared with the world to come, are but little"). Often, this has also been formulated programmatically in non-Qurʾānic Tradition, e.g. in a report from the Prophet, saying "The present world is the prison of the believer, the tomb is his fortress and towards the Garden (of Paradise) leads his way. The present world is the Garden of the unbeliever, the tomb is his prison and towards the Fire (of Hell) leads his way",[12] or put differently: "The sweetness of the present world is the bitterness of the hereafter, and the bitterness of the present world is the sweetness of the hereafter".[13] Yet there has never been any ready-made set of convictions and beliefs in Islam as to death, afterlife and the hereafter. Many different, also conflicting ideas and discourses existed side by side, and the pages of Volumes I and II provide ample evidence for this fact.

For the present purpose it may suffice to record that there were several literary discourses which expound the Islamic concept of death, afterlife and the nether realms. Most important among these discourses was the genre of the so-called "Books of Death" which has its origins in the third century H, most notably with some writings by Ibn Abī d-Dunyā (*Kitāb al-Mawt*, *Kitāb al-Qubūr*). Later writings,

8 Cited in IḪallWaf III pp. 156f. and *Wāfī* XVIII pp. 388f.

9 Woodward: *Islam in Java* p. 122.

10 For the latter, see MaqrMuq I p. 203.

11 TB III p. 283. For a 12th-century scholar known as "Ibn al-Mayyit", see GALS II p. 444.

12 DaylFird I p. 394 (*ad-dunyā siǧnu l-muʾmini wa-l-qabru ḥiṣnuhū wa-ʾilā l-ǧannati maṣīruhū wa-d-dunyā ǧannatu l-kāfiri wa-l-qabru siǧnuhū wa-ʾilā n-nāri maṣīruhū*); also abridged in IMandahFaw I p. 326. Further versions of this report appear in SuyBušrā p. 6.

13 ṮaᶜālTamṯīl p. 171 (*ḥalāwatu d-dunyā marāratu l-ʾāḫirati wa-marāratu d-dunyā ḥalāwatu l-ʾāḫirah*).

today lost, include the *Kitāb al-Qubūr* by Ibn Šākir al-Ḫarāʾiṭī (Muḥammad b. Ǧaᶜfar, d. ᶜAsqalān 327 H),[14] the *Kitāb Ḏikr al-mawt* by Abū Ḥafṣ Ibn Šāhīn (ᶜUmar b. Aḥmad, Baghdad 297–385 H), the treatise of the same title by Abū Isḥāq Ibrāhīm b. Muḥammad b. al-Azhar al-Marandī (fourth cent. H) and the *Kitāb Qabḍ rūḥ al-muʾmin wa-l-kāfir* ("Treatise Concerning the Seizing of the Soul of the Believer and the Unbeliever") by the Imamite scholar Ibrāhīm b. Sulaymān Ibn Ḥayyān an-Nihmī from Kūfah.[15] This first group of eastern Islamic works was then, from the sixth century H onwards, taken up by Andalusian[16] and North African scholars. Of their writings, the *Kitāb al-ᶜĀqibah* ("The Book of Result") by Ibn al-Ḫarrāṭ al-Išbīlī (d. 581 H) stands out as the first example of its kind; the writing is heavily influenced by the work of al-Ġazālī (d. 505 H), above all his *ʾIḥyāʾ ᶜulūm ad-dīn*. The *Kitāb at-Taḏkirah* ("The Memorandum") by al-Qurṭubī (d. 671 H) belongs to the next century and is in many ways the epitome of western Islamic learning on eschatological matters. As it turned out, it was to have the greatest success with later generations who contributed further treatises on this basis, thus creating the Mamluk genre of "Books of Death".[17]

Apart from the genre of "Books of Death", which is meant to cover all aspects of Islamic eschatology and afterlife, there were other literary discourses of a different or a more limited scope. One of these is the genre of consolation books, a genre which flourished during the Mamluk period, when the Black Death devastated the eastern and central Islamic lands decade after decade.[18] Other genres include treatises written by physicians, e.g. *al-Maqālah fī ḍarūrat al-mawt* ("Treatise on the Necessity of Death") by Rašīd ad-Dīn Abū Ḥalīqah (born 591 H) or *ar-Risālah ʾilā baᶜḍ ʾiḫwānihī fī l-istihānah bi-l-mawt* ("Epistle to Some of his Brethren, Concerning the Disdain of Death") by the famous Ibn al-Ǧazzār (Aḥmad b. Ibrāhīm, d. 369 H).[19] The question of whether someone could possibly have died a Muslim before the actual revelation of Islam aroused strong interest among religious scholars and traditionists. The most noteworthy example for that are the many treatises written about the fate of the Prophet's mother (see below pp. 17f.), while others researched whether the Pharaoh (*firᶜawn*), an important figure in the Qurʾān, had died a Muslim.[20]

14 *Cf.* QurṭTaḏk p. 80 and YāqIršād VI p. 464.

15 YāqIršād I p. 64. For the author, see ḤillīRiǧāl p. 15 (no. 22).

16 "Andalusian" indicates here and in the following chapters "Andalusī" or "Hispano-Arabic".

17 The most important authors of later centuries include Ibn Raǧab, Ibn Ḥaǧar al-ᶜAsqalānī and as-Suyūṭī. For a survey of those writings, see Thomas Bauer: *Islamische Totenbücher. Entwicklung einer Textgattung im Schatten al-Ġazālīs*, in: *Studies in Arabic and Islam. Proceedings of the 19th Congress, Union Européenne des Arabisants et Islamisants, Halle 1998*, edd. S. Leder *et al.*, Leuven – Paris 2002, pp. 421-36.

18 A number of consolation books have been used in Vols. I and II. For a general survey, see also Giladi: *Consolation Treatises*.

19 See IAUṣaybᶜUyūn pp. 482 and 597.

20 See e.g. the small *Risālah fī mawt Firᶜawn ᶜalā l-ʾIslām* by Ǧalāl ad-Dīn Muḥammad b. Asᶜad aṣ-Ṣiddīqī ad-Dawwānī (d. 908 H) (Maḫṭūṭāt Dār al-Kutub I p. 424). The question hinges on

Finally, we also know of Abū ᶜUmar Aḥmad b. ᶜAfīf Ibn Maryuwāl al-Umawī (Córdoba, 348–420 H), a washer of the dead in al-Andalus who wrote a substantial – though now lost – treatise about his profession.[21]

The significance of tombs and cemeteries

The tomb itself was a highly significant place throughout Islamic history; the first three chapters of the present volume are dedicated to this phenomenon. In keeping with the above-mentioned otherwordliness, many Muslims during their lifetime devoted much care to their final dwellings. Over the centuries, several persons would dig their own grave, like Abū Sufyān b. al-Ḥāriṯ (d. 20 H) in Medina (three days before his death),[22] as-Sayyidah Nafīsah (Mecca 145 – Cairo 208 H),[23] the fourth-century Malikite scholar al-Aṣīlī (ᶜAr. b. Ibr.),[24] the Andalusian judge Muḥammad b. Sulaymān al-Mālaqī al-Mālikī (d. 500 H),[25] the eighth-century Hanafite scholar Ǧalāl ad-Dīn al-Ḫuǧandī (Abū Ṭāhir A. b. M., d. Medina 802 H),[26] or the Moroccan mystic Aḥmad b. ᶜAlī al-Bū-Ṣaᶜīdī as-Sūsī (d. Marrakech 1046 H),[27] to mention but a few. Others would even "test" their tomb by stepping down into it and stretching out there some time before their actual death, like the famous Hanbalite Ibn Raǧab (d. 795 H), who was then buried in the Damascene Bāb aṣ-Ṣaġīr cemetery.[28] The physician Burhān ad-Dīn al-Ǧaᶜbarī (Ibr. b. Miᶜḍād, d. Cairo 687 H) fell ill towards the end of his life and was carried to the tomb which he had prepared for himself; he addressed it affectionately with *yā-qubayr*, "O (my) dear little tomb!"[29]

Some of the bigger cemeteries in the cities of the Islamic lands soon came to acquire a special significance for popular piety as well as for the complex history of thought in Islam. The main reason for this development lies in the fact that people desired to be buried near the tombs of individuals who were famous for their learning, for their piety, or for both. The underlying mentality has been well expressed by ᶜAbd Allāh b. Aḥmad (d. 290 H), the son of Ibn Ḥanbal, who reportedly said, "I

what is related in Q 10:90-2, viz. that towards the end of his life Firᶜawn professed to be a believer in God (i.e. a Muslim) but God refused to accept his conversion.

21 IBaškṢilah I p. 39.

22 FāsīᶜIqd VI p. 290; SamWafāʾ III p. 911.

23 For her mausoleum in Cairo, see Yūsuf Rāġib: *al-Sayyida Nafīsa, sa légende, son culte et son cimetière*, in: Studia Islamica 44 (1976), pp. 61-86.

24 ᶜIyāḍTartīb IV p. 648.

25 NubQuḍātAnd 132.

26 IḤaǧḎaylDK pp. 83f.; SaḫTuḥfLaṭ I pp. 147-53; ŠḎ VII p. 16; GAL I p. 265.

27 al-Marrākušī: *Iᶜlām* II p. 113. Other stories of people who dug their own grave: IBaškṢilah II p. 500; ᶜAynīᶜIqd IV p. 373; ŠaᶜrṬab I p. 47.

28 INāṣRadd p. 190; IMibrḎayl p. 40. For another "tomb-tester", see DK II p. 429.

29 MaqrMuq I p. 321; ITaġrManh I p. 178.

prefer the company[30] of a prophet to the company of my father",[31] meaning that he would rather be interred near the shrine of a saintly person than at his father's side (albeit his father was later to become something of a saintly person in the eyes of many Muslims). "Sainthood" is considered here to override family bonds, a custom roughly comparable to the former Christian practice of burial *ad sanctos*.[32] In the course of time, therefore, more and more graves clustered together around venerated tombs, and "cemeteries develop around shrines of holy men", with the surrounding mausolea "scattered like jewels" (Yolande Crowe).[33]

Among the most important Sunnite burial grounds, mention must be made of the Ḫayzurān, Bāb Ḥarb and aš-Šunayzīyah cemeteries in Baghdad,[34] the first situated near the shrine of Abū Ḥanīfah (d. 150 H) and in later centuries the burial place of many Hanafite scholars,[35] the second grouped around the tombs of Bišr al-Ḥāfī and Aḥmad Ibn Ḥanbal (d. 241 H, see **25**) and thus the favourite graveyard of Hanbalite scholars,[36] and the third containing the much-visited tombs of the mystics as-Sarī as-Saqaṭī (d. 251 H) and al-Ǧunayd (d. 298 H); apart from those, there are also the shrine of the mystic ᶜAbd al-Qādir al-Ǧīlānī (d. 561 H)[37] and the Shiite mausolea of al-Kāẓimayn. In Cairo, mention must be made of the Bāb an-Naṣr cemetery (north of the city) and the Qarāfah cemetery, which is divided into two areas, the "Greater" and the "Lesser" Qarāfah. These burial grounds contain a number of much-venerated shrines, for example the mausolea of aš-Šāfiᶜī (**36**), the second-century jurist al-Layṯ b. Saᶜd (d. 175 H), the seventh-century mystical poet Ibn al-Fāriḍ (d. 632 H)[38] and many others. In Damascus, the (al-)Bāb aṣ-Ṣaġīr and Bāb al-Farādīs cemeteries were frequently visited over the centuries and since the Umayyad period have remained cherished burial places;[39] in addition to this, there are numerous tombs and mausolea in the Ṣāliḥīyah quarter on the slopes of the Qāsiyūn mountain north of Damascus, with the mausoleum of the mystic Ibn ᶜArabī (d. 643 H), restored in the tenth century H, and many graves of Hanbalite scholars.

Several famous cemeteries are known from the western Islamic lands (e.g. in

30 Lit. "neighbourhood" (*ǧiwār*).

31 Cited in IAYaṬab I p. 188.

32 *Cf.* Ariès: *Western Attitudes* pp. 15-7.

33 EI² VIII p. 1034. *Cf.* also Hillenbrand: *Islamic architecture* pp. 266f. and Leisten: *Funerary Structures* pp. 467-72 (concerning the Caliphal tombs in ar-Ruṣāfah).

34 For the great cemeteries in Iraq and Syria, see also Geoffroy: *Proche-Orient.*

35 *Cf.* EI² III p. 699. The shrine around the tomb of Abū Ḥanīfah was erected in 459 H under Abū Šuǧāᶜ ᶜAḍud ad-Dawlah Alp Arslān (d. 465 H).

36 *Cf.* EI² I p. 273. See also the annotated translation of the relevant section of al-Ḫaṭib's *Tārīḫ Baġdād* (TB) in Lassner: *Topography of Baghdad*, ch. 13.

37 Geoffroy: *Le mausolée de ᶜAbd al-Qādir*.

38 *Cf.* Homerin: *Domed Shrine* and *Ibn al-Fāriḍ*.

39 See HarIšārāt p. 14; IAHawlFaḍ pp. 51f.; Moazz: *Cimetières Damas* pp. 79f.

Fez,[40] Marrakech, Córdoba and Granada[41]) or the southern Arabian peninsula (e.g. in Zabīd, Taʿizz and Tarīm). Further to the East, we find the giant necropolis of Tatta on the Makli hills (between Karachi and Hyderabad) and the important Šāh-i Zindā graveyard in Samarqand.[42] Iraq and Persia are strewn with the most widely known Shiite cemeteries around the Imamite mausolea in Baghdad, as-Samarrāʾ, an-Naǧaf, Karbalāʾ and al-Mašhad (Ṭūs);[43] in Ardabīl, the mausoleum of sheikh Ṣafīy ad-Dīn, eponymous ancestor of the Ṣafawid dynasty, and other members of his family acquired prominence from the eighth century H onwards.[44]

Finally, the largest cemeteries of Mecca and Medina, known respectively as *maqburat (Bāb) al-Maʿlāh* and *maqburat Baqīʿ al-Ġarqad* (or simply *al-Baqīʿ*), must be considered the most important funeral areas in the Islamic world, for both Sunnites and Shiites alike. This is due less to their size than to the fact that they contain a great number of tombs of the Prophet's children, wives, relatives and companions. Their visitation is even today frequently combined with the pilgrimage to Mecca and the visit to the Prophet's sepulchre in Medina, although little remains of their superstructures as a result of the destruction carried out by the Wahhābites in modern times.

Conclusion

The experience of death and loss, as well as the strategies for reducing their impact on the soul, are of course not specific to the Islamic world and there is much there which is shared by other cultures. For all the differences in detail, there is a strong current of common images and thoughts pertaining to this subject, thus many images and concepts that appear on the following pages will also remind the Western reader of his own culture. It is here that we reach the liminal zone between what is generated culturally – and therefore not easily shared by others who are foreign to that given culture – and what transcends the boundaries of any specific culture or system of thought; it is here that a particular culture loses its mind-shaping force and common human experience takes its place.

This experience, shared by all human beings, often lights up in literature and poetry where the specific ways and possibilities of expression within a culture, and a given language, render it explicit. Compare, in conclusion, how the fifth-century H Syrian poet Abū l-ʿAlāʾ al-Maʿarrī (see **111**) and the late eighteenth-century CE

40 *Cf.* EI² VI pp. 123f. (K.L. Brown).

41 For the Andalusian cemeteries, see the excellent (though somewhat dated) survey in Torres Balbás: *Cementerios* pp. 136f. and 163ff.

42 *Cf.* EI² VIII pp. 1034-6.

43 See al-Ǧalālī: *Mazārāt ahl al-bayt* and al-Ḫalīlī: *Mawsūʿat al-ʿatabāt* I; Kriss: *Volksglaube* I pp. 241-3; Schober: *Heiligtum ʿAlīs* (with further literature). A short list of the shrines of the Imams is also provided in Falaturi: *Zwölfer-Schia* pp. 75f.

44 Donaldson: *Shiʾite Religion* pp. 262-4; Gronke: *Derwische*, esp. pp. 51-7.

German man of letters Jean Paul (J.P. Richter) transformed the experience of death into verbal sentiment:

كَأَنَّ دُعَاءَ المَوْتِ بِاسْمِكَ نَكْزَةٌ * فَرَتْ جَسَدِي وَالسَّمُّ يُنْفَثُ فِي أُذْنِي

"As if death's calling your name was a (serpent's) bite * that cut my body lengthwise, while the poison was spat into my ear" (al-Maᶜarrī).[45]

*

"Du Arme! nun rollte sich der Schmerz zusammen und tat den erzürnten Schlangensprung an deine Brust und drückte alle seine Giftzähne hinein".[46]

"Poor thing! now the pain coiled itself up, launched the angry assault of a serpent at your breast and thrust all its poison-fangs into it" (Jean Paul).

45 ŠSiqṭZand II p. 931 (no. 41 v. 36); in English translation in Smoor: *Poems on Death* p. 55 note 18.

46 Jean Paul (J.P. Richter): *Sämtliche Werke. Abteilung I, vierter Band (Leben des Quintus Fixlein aus funfzehn Zettelkästen gezogen)*, ed. N. Miller, Munich – Vienna [4]1988, p. 59.

1 "Approach the Dead, Greet Them and Pray for Them!" *The Visitation of Tombs and Cemeteries*

1. *Introduction*

The veneration of tombs and their visitation, as well as the mortuary cult in general, must be considered one of the most important and wide-ranging features of Islamic devotion and piety. This holds true for more than a thousand years of pre-modern Islam and for the contemporary period, though many modernist and neo-Hanbalite groups across the Islamic lands are trying to do away with this phenomenon.

Among the Sunnites, we find the veneration of tombs and the accompanying rites or customs prevalent in the Islamic West and in Egypt, but there is hardly a region devoid of it.[1] In the eastern lands, it was chiefly the Shiites who fostered the mortuary cult linked to the tombs of the Imams.[2] Still further to the East, in Afghanistan and the realm of Indo-Muslim culture (Pakistan, India), the veneration of tombs has more than anywhere else become associated with Sufism and the burial places of mystics, ascetics and saintly men (*ʾawliyāʾ*).[3] To many Sunnite scholars, who incessantly (though often in vain) tried to make their views prevail about which rites should be followed and what these should look like, the question of visiting tombs has never ceased to be the *shibboleth* of their endeavours.

In regard to the visitation of tombs there has always been a certain gap between theory and practice, in broad terms comparable to what we will see below in Chapter 2 concerning the construction of mausolea and the outward appearance of graves. However, one cannot claim that both theory and practice were as a rule

1 *Cf.* Kriss: *Volksglaube* I pp. 53-129 and Mayeur-Jaouen: *Égypte* and *Intercession*; for popular Egyptian visitation sites, see Abu-Zahra: *Pure and Powerful* and Biegman: *Egypt*; for Morocco, see Dermenghem: *Culte des saints* and Andezian: *Maghreb*; for Syria, see Gonnella: *Heiligenverehrung*. Indispensable for the various regions of the Islamic world are the contributions in Chambert-Loir/Guillot: *Culte des saints*.

2 Nakash: *Shiʿis of Iraq*, ch. 6. Further literature is cited below pp. 29f.

3 *Cf.* Einzmann: *Ziarat und Pir-e-Muridi* and his *Volksbrauchtum*; Currie: *Muʿīn al-Dīn Chistī*; the papers in Troll: *Muslim Shrines*; Merklinger: *Tombs at Holkonda*; Matringe: *Pakistan*.

diametrically opposed to each other, not least because Sunnite scholars were, in regard to popular usage, rather divided over which theoretical approach to practice should be adopted. In any case, there was seldom, as a matter of principle, outright opposition to the custom of visiting tombs and many efforts were made to reconcile the claims of theory with the norm-like forces of practice. The so-called *ʾādāb az-ziyārah* or *šurūṭ az-ziyārah*, "the customs *or* rules to be followed during visitation", namely the visitation of the more famous shrines and cemeteries, were largely accepted; hence, many treatises contain a chapter dealing with these customs in great detail.[4]

The following pages are meant to set out the main features and aspects relating to the practice of visiting tombs and cemeteries in Islam. This will include elements which, though lesser known, are interesting in themselves. Of course, the general veneration of "saints" or "saintly persons" and their burial places in Islam is an outstanding phenomenon in that context, and probably the issue most thoroughly researched by modern scholarship. In the present chapter, this vast field cannot be covered in its entirety. It has been taken into consideration insofar as it can tell us something about why people actually visit a tomb or shrine, about what this visit looks like (or should look like) and about how the visitors behave when standing in front of it. In addition, the ramifications of legal theory and the wider disputes about the general feasibility of the visitation of tombs will be given ample attention.

Less emphasis than in other studies has been laid on elements linked with contemporary forms of popular piety, because these have already been treated elsewhere in detail and are relatively well-known.[5] Rather, I tried to give much attention to all branches of learned literature and belles-lettres (including poetry and *ʾadab* literature), especially in view of the breathtaking richness of the material preserved. It is hoped that this will open up new insights and make some additional details come to the fore that are likely to shape our views on the whole. Moreover, it will be seen that the attitudes of the learned élite – scholars, scribal officials, poets and men of letters – often relate to practice and might have been less remote from the attitudes of "the people", or in any case shaped and reflected them more than is often assumed.

Finally, even though all forms of the visitation of tombs, drawn from both Sunnite and Shiite sources, and the most diverse funeral sites have been taken into

4 It should also be noted that in general little difference was made whether *ziyārat al-qubūr*, "the visitation of tombs", meant visiting graves of a more private character (e.g. those of parents or other close relatives) or the visitation of tombs and shrines which were widely venerated, and thus had gained "public" attention and significance. Since in the latter case the practices linked to their visitation were much more visible and pronounced, and hence possibly at variance with the precepts of Islam as laid down by the learned élite, they were bound to arouse criticism more easily than the visits to "private" graves. The visitation of such tombs of "public interest", with the tomb of the Prophet being the most prominent example, therefore occupies a good deal of the space devoted to this argument in the available sources.

5 *Cf.* also al-ʿAffānī: *Sakb* II pp. 191ff., a compilation of numerous contemporary fatwas on all matters regarding the visitation of tombs.

consideration, it will be found that most attention has been devoted to the sepulchre of the Prophet in Medina. This is due to the fact that, with the Prophet and his role being of prime importance in Islam, the visitation of his tomb was the most outstanding example of its kind and thus over the centuries the most eagerly discussed practice, having by far the greatest impact on literature and poetry, and consequently on both mentalities and belief. The only sites to rival seriously the importance of the Prophet's tomb are those of the Imams in the realm of Shiism.

2. *Muslim Theory*

2.1. Reports from the Prophet

There are several widely-cited reports handed down from the Prophet which concern the visitation of tombs and cemeteries. Some of them have a rather negative ring or explicitly prohibit every form of visitation and mortuary cult, yet the majority of these Traditions clearly either allow or even support such practices.[6] This interpretation of the sources at our disposal, obvious as it may seem, is today likely to be obscured by the emphasis many contemporary Sunnite scholars and pamphleteers lay on those reports which disapprove of or condemn the practices connected with the visitation of graves and the usage as such.

2.1.1. Prohibition: "sitting down on / at the grave"

Among the Traditions censuring the visitation of tombs (and their veneration) appears a passage which is part of a longer report. It simply says that the Prophet prohibited, among other things, "the sitting down (*qᶜd* I, as verbal noun or verb, and in another version *ǧls* I)[7] on the grave".[8] The rather equivocal expression "sitting on / at the grave" (*al-ǧulūs ᶜalā l-qabr*) invites further interpretation, and hence the Muslim scholars were in dispute over what this exactly means.

The majority of jurists, among them Ibn Ḥanbal (d. 241 H)[9] and aš-Šāfiᶜī (d. 204 H), saw this as a general verdict and took "sitting" as a general synonym for "staying". It remains unclear, however, whether *ᶜalā* denotes literally "upon the grave" or rather "at the grave", "near the grave" or "in front of the grave". The first alternative clearly imposes a much more restricted meaning upon the Prophet's

6 *Cf.* also Leisten: *Architektur für Tote* pp. 6-12.

7 Both terms were considered synonymous, see HarMirqātMaf I p. 198.

8 ᶜARazMuṣ 6488 (III p. 504); IAŠayMuṣ III p. 218 (*ǧanāʾiz* 137); *Muwaṭṭaʾ* I p. 233 (*ǧanāʾiz* 11); ᶜAynīᶜUmdah VII p. 102; NawŠMusl VII pp. 37f. (*ǧanāʾiz* 94ff.) and NawRiyāḍ 1757 (p. 605, *bāb* 342); ADāʾūd III pp. 293f. (*ǧanāʾiz* 76f.); TirǦāmiᶜ II p. 257 (*ǧanāʾiz* 56); NasSunan IV p. 78; ḤākMust I p. 370; KU 42571 and 42574f. (XV p. 650). *Cf.* also IḤanbMusnad XV p. 241; IMāǧah I p. 499; MuwMuršid I p. 35; IḤaǧAḥwāl pp. 19 and 48; ŠāmīSubul VIII p. 385; HarMirqātMaf IV p. 69; Krawietz: *Ḥurma* p. 167; al-Muᶜallimī: *ᶜImārat al-qubūr* pp. 268-76.

9 IQudMuġnī II pp. 507f.; ManbTasl (C) pp. 102f. / (M) p. 98.

verdict and it seems that not a few scholars took it in this limited sense. However, in the sources there is nowhere an explicit discussion of what *ʿalā* means in this context. The Shafiites considered "sitting" = "staying on the grave" not only as abominable, but even as forbidden (*ḥarām*).[10] This also comes close to the view adopted by Hanbalite and Ẓāhirite scholars.[11] Some further Traditions discourage "sitting at" or "stepping upon" (*wṭʾ* I *ʿalā*) a believer's tomb,[12] yet we are not told how to understand this exactly.

Mālik b. Anas (d. 179 H) and the majority of his followers, on the other hand, understood "sitting" here as limited to the specific act of urinating or defecation,[13] and thus allowed sitting or stepping on the tomb under certain circumstances,[14] taking *ʿalā* and the expression "to sit (up)on" in the most literal sense. According to Abū l-Walīd Ibn Rušd (d. 520 H) and the Hanafite jurist Badr ad-Dīn al-ᶜAynī (d. 855 H), who makes a strong case for it, this view had also been endorsed by Abū Ḥanīfah (d. 150 H) and his pupils.[15] This specific interpretation does seem more far-fetched than it really is because defecating on burial sites must have been a constant problem; after all, there are various Traditions condemning it.[16]

In the biographical accounts we read that a man relieved himself (*ġwṭ* V) on the tomb of al-Ḥasan b. ᶜAlī (d. 50 H or after) in the Medinan Baqīᶜ cemetery and, as a consequence, became insane and started to bark like a dog. He died soon after and was heard howling in his tomb.[17] In his famous collection *Relief after Hardship*, at-Tanūḫī (d. 384 H) relates an anecdote from a man who had come in conflict with the Abbasid functionary ᶜAǧīf b. ᶜAnbasah in the time of al-Mutawakkil: the poor man was first captured and maltreated by ᶜAǧīf and thus peed into his trousers for fear. Later, however, after ᶜAǧīf had been killed for treachery by the caliph al-Muᶜtaṣim, his former victim peed upon ᶜAǧīf's provisional tomb, yet without knowing that the spot he was sprinkling was in effect the grave of his malefactor.[18] During the Almoravid period, when Seville was quickly expanding, "letrinas y cloacas descubiertes y construcciones parásitas se habían instalado entre las

10 NawŠMusl VII p. 37, NawRawḍah II p. 139; ArdabAnwār I p. 124; Ašraf: *al-Qabr* p. 25.

11 IQaylġāṭah I pp. 174, 181 and IQayZād I p. 526; ManbTasl (C) p. 102 / (M) p. 98; ᶜAynīᶜUmdah VII p. 102; MF XXXII p. 245; Wafā: *Aḥkām al-ǧanāʾiz* p. 264; al-Muᶜallimī: *ʿImārat al-qubūr* p. 195.

12 See e.g. IḤanbMusnad XV p. 241 and MunḏTarġīb IV pp. 373f.

13 *Cf.* BāǧīMunt II p. 24; IRušdBid I p. 244; NawŠMusl VII p. 37; MuwMuršid I p. 35; IǦuzQaw p. 114; ᶜAynīᶜUmdah VII p. 103; QasṭIršād II p. 370; RamlīNih III p. 11; ZurqŠMuw II p. 70; MF XXXII p. 245.

14 Namely when either the tomb was not elevated (*musannam*) any longer or when there was no other way around it, see Wafā: *Aḥkām al-ǧanāʾiz* p. 263.

15 IRušdBid I p. 244; ᶜAynīᶜUmdah VII pp. 102f. *Cf.* also QasṭIršād II p. 370 and ZurqŠMuw II p. 70.

16 *Cf.* ᶜARazMuṣ 6493 (III p. 506); HarMirqātMaf IV pp. 70 and 117. For the custom of urinating in graveyards *cf.* also IADunyāQubūr (A) p. 206 and MuᶜāfāǦalīs I pp. 437f.

17 TMD XIII p. 305; MunKawākib I p. 141.

18 See story no. 157 in TanFaraǧ II pp. 26-8. There is a German translation of this tale in *Ende gut, Alles gut. Das Buch der Erleichterung nach der Bedrängnis. Auswahl, Übersetzung aus dem Arabischen und Nachwort von A. Hottinger*, Zurich 1979, pp. 49-51.

tumbas".[19] In Damascus, people who felt strong aversion of the famous mystic Ibn ᶜArabī (d. 638 H) and his teachings would enter his shrine and urinate upon his tomb.[20] Of course, the problem of urinating upon or between tombs was not limited to the realm of the Islamic culture: in ancient Latin epitaphs, e.g., we often find phrases like *Ne quis hic urinam faciat* or *Qui hic mixerit aut cacarit habeat deos superos et inferos iratos.*[21]

Limiting the expression "sitting down on the grave" to some specific act (like defecation) and not taking it as a general synonym for "staying at the tomb" or "visiting the grave" was clearly meant to diminish the impact of the above-quoted report: "Do not sit on / at the grave!" That this was done primarily by Malikite scholars, who are often blamed for their rigorism, is especially noteworthy. However, apart from the report presently under discussion, there is at least one other Tradition which less equivocally expresses the Prophet's aversion of the visitation of tombs. He is reported to have pronounced: "Whosoever visits graves is not one of us".[22] This report did not find wide acceptance and is rarely cited.

2.1.2. Abrogation and permission

A third Tradition transmitted from the Prophet includes the following utterance: "I used to forbid you to visit the graves, but (now I tell you:) Do visit them!" (*ʾinnī kuntu nahaytukum ʿan ziyārati l-qubūri fa-zūrūhā*),[23] a wording sometimes changed into a less positive and encouraging message, for example in the Ḥadīṯ anthology of an-Nasāʾī (d. 303 H) and in many later sources where we read: "(The Prophet said) 'I did forbid you to visit the graves, but (now I tell you:) Whosoever desires to visit (them) may do so'" (*... fa-man ʾarāda ʾan yazūra fa-l-yazur*).[24] Many versions of this Tradition also contain the final part *fa-ʾinna fīhā ʿibratan*, "because in them (*sc.* the tombs) you have a (warning) example!"

Here we encounter the problem of abrogation (*nasḫ*), because the reports condemning the practice of visiting graves, among them those which refer especially to women, were said to have been superseded by this very Tradition.[25] There is also a

19 Torres Balbás: *Cementerios* p. 160. *Cf.* also IᶜAbdūnTraité p. 57: "On y a aménagé des latrines et des cloaques à ciel ouvert dont le contenu se déverse au-dessus des morts".

20 ŠaᶜrṬab I p. 188. Others tried to burn his cenotaph, see Gramlich: *Wunder* p. 236.

21 Geist: *Grabinschriften* 628f.

22 ᶜARazMuṣ 6705 (III p. 569); ᶜAynīᶜUmdah VII pp. 101f. (*man zāra l-qubūra fa-laysa minnā*).

23 ᶜARazMuṣ 6708 (III p. 569); IAŠayMuṣ III p. 223 (*ğanāʾiz* 145); NawŠMusl VII p. 46 (*ğanāʾiz* 107); ADāʾūd III p. 296 (*ğanāʾiz* 81); NasSunan IV p. 73; ḤākMust I pp. 374ff.; IḤazmMuḥ V pp. 160f.; ḤāzIᶜtibār p. 101; DaylFird II p. 372; IḪarrāṭᶜĀqibah p. 118; MuwMuršid I p. 25; MunḏTarġīb IV p. 357; SaḫTuḥfAḥbāb p. 7; KU 42557 (XV p. 646). *Cf.* also IMāğah I pp. 500f.; IŠāhNāsiḫ 307 (p. 373); SuyŠṢudūr p. 408; ŠāmīSubul VIII p. 384; HaytTuḥfMuḥt III p. 199; HarMirqātMaf IV p. 111; al-Albānī: *Aḥkām al-ğanāʾiz* pp. 178f.

24 NasSunan IV p. 73; ḤākMust I p. 376; IḪarrāṭᶜĀqibah p. 118; QurṭTaḏk p. 16; IQaylġāṯah I p. 185. For another wording, see ITayMağm XXVII p. 119 and HarMirqātMaf IV p. 112.

25 ḤākMust I p. 374; ᶜIyāḍŠifāʾ (B) II p. 71 / (Š) II p. 84 = HarŠŠifāʾ II p. 149; HarMirqātMaf IV pp. 112 and 117.

report on the authority of ᶜĀʾišah (cited below p. 36) which has the Prophet first prohibiting but then permitting the visitation of tombs. Interestingly, the ninth-century scholar al-ᶜAynī tried to take this as a reflection of the course of events and thus develops a historical perspective, though he was by no means the first to do so:

> "The significance of the prohibition of visiting tombs was especially great in the first years of Islam, because the Muslims were still near to the period when idols were worshipped and tombs were taken as places of worship. However, after the (creed of) Islam had established itself and become strong in the hearts of the people, and after the worshipping of idols and the prayer to them could be safeguarded, the prohibition of the visitation of graves was abrogated because it (*sc.* visitation) reminds us of the hereafter (i.e. it serves as a *memento mori*) and teaches renunciation (*tuzahhidu*) in this world".[26]

To the Traditions encouraging (or at least permitting) the practice of staying in cemeteries and visiting tombs belongs, ultimately, a widely-quoted report that contains the Prophet's saying on the occasion of visiting the tomb of his mother: "I asked my Lord that I may visit her tomb and He granted me that. I further asked that I may beg forgiveness for her, but He did not grant me that".[27] There are different versions of this Tradition, the longer of which have significant additions: "Therefore, do visit the graves because it reminds (you) of death (*tuḏakkiru l-mawta*, or in another version, said of the hereafter: *tuḏakkiru l-ʾāḫirata*)"[28] or also "... because it softens the heart and makes the eye weep"; another version of this report has the following addition: "but do not overdo their visitation" (*wa-lā tukṯirū ziyāratahā*).[29]

26 ᶜAynīᶜUmdah VI p. 435. A very similar (though shorter) passage is cited from al-Qāḍī ᶜIyāḍ in WanšMiᶜyār I p. 321; from an-Nawawī in al-Albānī: *Aḥkām al ǧanāʾiz* p. 179. *Cf.* also MunḏTarġīb IV p. 357; QurṭTaḏk pp. 12f.; HarMirqātMaf IV p. 112 and HarŠŠifāʾ II p. 150 (where other similar passages are cited).

27 ᶜARazMuṣ 6714 (III pp. 572f.); IAŠayMuṣ III p. 224 (*ǧanāʾiz* 145); ISaᶜd I p. 117; WāḥAsbāb p. 268 (*ad* Q 9:113); BayDal I p. 189; ĠazDurrah p. 42 and ĠazIḥyāʾ (B) IV p. 485 / (C) IV pp. 412 and 416; ŠarŠMaq I p. 176; IḪarrāṭᶜĀqibah p. 118; NawŠMusl VII pp. 45f. (*ǧanāʾiz* 105f.); QurṭTaḏk p. 15; MuwMuršid I p. 25; IRaǧAhwāl p. 176; ManbTasl (C) p. 104 / (M) p. 100; ᶜAynīᶜUmdah VI p. 434; QasṭMaw I p. 92; ŠāmīSubul VIII p. 384; IDaybaᶜḤad I p. 149; KU 42586 (XV p. 652). *Cf.* also AYūsĀṯār 996 (p. 225); ḤākMust I pp. 374ff.; IĞawzīWafā pp. 114f.; DimSīrah pp. 37f.

28 Still other versions of this report have the similar wordings *fa-ʾinnahā* (sc. *ziyārata l-qubūr*) *tuḏakkirukumu l-mawta* (or *al-ʾāḫirata*) and ... *tuḏakkiru bi-l-mawt*; sometimes, the wording also employs the nouns *taḏakkur* or *taḏkirah*.

29 The versions of this report are found in: ᶜARazMuṣ 6714 (III p. 573); IAŠayMuṣ III pp. 223f. (*ǧanāʾiz* 145); ADāʾūd III p. 296 (*ǧanāʾiz* 81); TirĞāmiᶜ II p. 259 (*ǧanāʾiz* 60); NasSunan IV p. 74; IMāǧah I pp. 500f.; QNuᶜmDaᶜāʾim I p. 239; ḤākMust I pp. 375f.; BayDal I p. 190; IḤazmMuḥ V p. 161 (and *cf.* Adang: *Women's Access* p. 90); ŠīrMuhaḏ I p. 138; ĠazIḥyāʾ (C) IV p. 416; ḤāzIᶜtibār p. 101; IQudMuġnī II p. 566; ŠarŠMaq I p. 175; IḪarrāṭᶜĀqibah p. 118; MuwMuršid I p. 26; MunḏTarġīb IV p. 357; IQaylġāṯah I pp. 184f.; ŠīrŠadd p. 5; IRaǧAhwāl pp. 175f.; SaḫTuḥfAḥbāb p. 7; SuyŠṢudūr p. 32. *Cf.* also IŠāhNāsiḫ 307f. (pp. 373f.); ZamRabīᶜ IV p. 179; ĠazIḥyāʾ (C) IV p. 412; QurṭTaḏk p. 11 and 13; IbšīhīMust II p. 442 (ch. 81); QasṭIršād II p. 327; HarMirqātMaf IV pp. 113 and 116; MF XXXII p. 252; al-Albānī: *Aḥkām*

According to the mystic aš-Šaᶜrānī (d. 973 H), who also quotes this last addition, this was said because frequent visits either lead to the *meditatio mortis* (*al-iᶜtibār*) losing its impact "since everything done too much has little importance to it", or because people will then suffer from "the death of the heart" (*mawt al-qalb*), i.e. they will lose their courage, due to the constant vision of the dead and their burial places.[30]

2.1.3. The tomb of the Prophet's mother and related issues

The report mentioned before ("I asked my Lord that I may visit her tomb and He granted me that" etc.) refers to the Prophet's visit to the tomb of his mother Āminah bint Wahb. She had died an unbeliever many years before the call of Muḥammad as Prophet. Her tomb lies most probably at the spot where she died, in al-Abwāʾ between Mecca and Medina.[31] There it was visited by the Prophet either in the year 6 H or after the conquest of Mecca (during the so-called "farewell pilgrimage" in 10 H), thus shortly before the Prophet's death.[32] According to various sources, the Prophet's father ᶜAbd Allāh (who died either before Muḥammad's birth or some months after) was also buried in al-Abwāʾ,[33] a fact which was to acquire some importance for the discussions of later times (see below).

In itself, the story of the Prophet visiting his mother's grave is plausible enough, but nevertheless gave rise to a vigorous discussion among Muslim scholars. The reason is that there exists another famous (or rather ill-famed) report which says (according to its best-known wording): "The Prophet said, 'I went to the tomb of my mother Āminah and asked God, my Lord, that He may raise her (from the dead). He did bring her back to life and then she believed in me (i.e. she became a Muslim, thus being spared the fate of the unbelievers on the Last Day). Eventually, God restored her to her former condition'".[34] This report was first circulated by both Ibn Šāhīn (d. 385 H, see below) and al-Ḫaṭīb al-Baġdādī (d. 463 H); it was further acknowledged by as-Suhaylī (d. 581 H) in the West, and the Meccan scholar Muḥibb ad-Dīn aṭ-Ṭabarī (d. 694 H) edited an abridged version of it.[35] Nevertheless, this report met with strong opposition, especially because it is contrary to explicit

al-ǧanāʾiz pp. 187f.; al-Munayyar: *Tasliyah* p. 46; al-ᶜAffānī: *Sakb* I p. 642. What this *memento mori* was seen to mean for the emotional state of the visitor is explained in ĠazIḥyāʾ (C) IV p. 418. *Cf.* also Reintjens-Anwari: *Tod aus islamischer Sicht* p. 174.

30 ŠaᶜrAnwārQudsīyah p. 894.

31 ISaᶜd I pp. 116f.; IĞawzīMawḍ I p. 284; IDaybaᶜḤad I p. 30; ŠāmīSubul II pp. 120f. Knowledge of the exact site of her tomb was soon lost and thus no *ziyārah* of it has been possible, see MaġlBihār C p. 222. Others have her tomb at Mecca, more exactly in the Dār ar-Rāʾiᶜah, see IĞamMuḫt p. 26; FīrūzQāmūs III p. 31 (*rwᶜ*) = QasṭMaw II p. 88; ŠāmīSubul II p. 126; SinğManāʾiḥ I p. 443; *cf.* also below pp. 218 and 303.

32 DimSīrah p. 37; HarMirqātMaf IV pp. 113f.

33 MuġIšārah p. 63. *Cf.* also IĞamMuḫt p. 27.

34 QurṭTaḏk p. 15; ŠāmīSubul II p. 122; IDaybaᶜḤad I p. 148 (abridged).

35 As cited in QasṭMaw I p. 89 and IDaybaᶜḤad I pp. 148f.; *cf.* also ŠāmīSubul II p. 122.

Qurʾānic passages: *But God shall not turn towards those who do evil deeds* (...) *neither to those who die disbelieving* (Q 4:18) and *It is not for the Prophet and the believers to ask pardon for the idolators, even though they be near kinsmen, after that it has become clear to them that they will be the inhabitants of Hell* (Q 9:113). Bringing back to life or resurrecting the Prophet's mother (who died a pagan) in order that she may become a Muslim posthumously is thus not easy to reconcile with the Qurʾānic wording which is not lacking clarity in this point.[36]

Strangely enough, most works of *tafsīr* avoid the subject when discussing Q 4:18 and 9:113. What is more, they do in general not indicate any connection between these verses and the above-mentioned report; some refer instead to Abraham and his father, while others name Abū Ṭālib on whose behalf the Prophet was said to have invoked mercy.[37] Yet the connection between Q 9:113 and the story of the Prophet's mother is by no means arbitrary because a number of sources contain a report according to which verse 9:113 was revealed after the Prophet had visited the tomb of his mother.[38] In many Qurʾān commentaries and related works we find, however, the following: When the Prophet said, "Would I only know what fate awaits my parents!", verse 2:119 was revealed: *Thou shalt not be questioned touching the inhabitants of Hell*,[39] an interpretation rejected by others.[40]

In view of these reports, it is clear that there was no straightforward way out of this dilemma, but at least different paths could be tried:[41] in order to safeguard the report about Āminah's resurrection (to whom the Prophet's father was soon added who was said to have been buried in the same place) one could either propose a case of abrogation or stress the unique status of the Prophet which puts him above the Qurʾānic message. In the first case, one could claim that the above-quoted utterance of the Prophet – "I asked my Lord that I may beg forgiveness for my mother, but He did not grant me that" – was later nullified by the fact that God resurrected the Prophet's mother. This was put forward by Ibn Šāhīn[42] and others, but it could only account for the differences between the various reports and did not resolve the conflict with the Qurʾānic wording. In the second case, one could argue that Āminah having been restored to life was part of the Prophet's *ḫaṣāʾiṣ* ("peculiarities" or "special features") which were bestowed upon him alone; the report does thus not stand in contrast with what we read in the Qurʾān. This was the view of al-Qurṭubī (d. 671 H), the author of the highly influential treatise on eschatology

36 For the same reason, and with explicit reference to Q 9:113, an-Nawawī prohibits in general to invoke mercy for an unbeliever, no matter one's own personal relation to that person, be they father or mother, see NawFat p. 52.

37 WāḥAsbāb p. 268 *ad* Q 9:113; Ṯaʿālṭafsīr II p. 79 *ad* Q 9:113; ŠāmīSubul II pp. 429f. According to some spurious Traditions, Abū Ṭālib was also resurrected by God in order to become a Muslim, see QurṭTaḏk p. 15.

38 WāḥAsbāb pp. 268f.; BayDal I p. 190; IĞawzīWafā p. 116; ŠāmīSubul II pp. 125f.

39 IĞuzTashīl I p. 83 *ad* Q 2:119; see also WāḥAsbāb pp. 42 f. *ad* Q 2:119; QurṭTaḏk p. 15; ŠāmīSubul II pp. 123-5.

40 E.g. ṮaʿālTafsīr I pp. 109f. *ad* Q 2:119.

41 Indispensable for the understanding of the following are the lengthy expositions of the argument in QasṭMaw I pp. 88-96 and ŠāmīSubul II pp. 120-8.

42 IŠāhNāsiḫ 307f. (pp. 373f.) = QurṭTaḏk p. 15.

known as *at-Tadkirah* ("the Memorandum").[43] However, we look in vain for that report in comprehensive writings dealing with the *ḫaṣāʾiṣ* of the Prophet such as Ibn al-Mulaqqin's *Ġāyat as-sūl*, al-Ḫayḍarī's *al-Lafẓ al-mukarram* or as-Suyūṭī's *al-Ḫaṣāʾiṣ al-kubrā*.

Alternatively, one could discard the report about Āminah's resurrection altogether and declare the respective Tradition(s) forged. This was done, for example, by al-Qurṭubī's presumed teacher Ibn Diḥyah al-Kalbī (d. 633 H) – for the reason that the report contradicts the Qurʾān[44] – and by Abū Ḥayyān (d. 745 H) who presented the report in question as the opinion of the Shiites.[45] Authors of *sīrah* literature, like Ibn Ǧamāʿah (d. 767 H, see **158**), would mention the Prophet's visit to his mother's tomb but pass over her presumed resurrection in silence.[46] Ibn al-Ǧawzī (d. 597 H) included this report in his collection of forged Traditions entitled *Kitāb al-Mawḍūʿāt*,[47] something for which he earned the bitter wrath of as-Suyūṭī who criticised Ibn al-Ǧawzī especially in this point.[48]

Up to the ninth century H, the debate concerning the reports about the Prophet visiting his mother's tomb was conducted in the realm of Tradition and related fields (e.g. the biography of the Prophet). As far as I am aware, it was only with a writing by Šams ad-Dīn Ibn al-Ǧazarī (d. 833 H) that the problem became the subject of a monograph and thus gave origin to a literary sub-genre of its own.

In the following centuries, a number of scholars contributed further monographs expounding the issue to its furthest ramifications. The list in the following offers a short (although probably incomplete) inventory of these writings:

(1) *ar-Risālah al-bayānīyah fī ḥaqq ʾabaway an-nabī*, by Šams ad-Dīn Abū l-Ḫayr M. b. M. (Ibn) al-Ǧazarī (Damascus 751 – Šīrāz 833 H). The ms. is preserved: GAL II p. 203; EI^2 III p. 753b.

(2) *Ǧuzʾ fī ʾiḥyāʾ ʾabaway an-nabī*, by as-Saḫāwī (d. 902 H). This treatise is mentioned by the author himself in one of his works, see Āl Salmān/aš-Šuqayrāt: *Muʾallafāt as-Saḫāwī* p. 80 (no. 118). It seems that as-Saḫāwī in his writing tended to view the matter as ultimately not resolvable.

(3) Ǧalāl ad-Dīn ʿAr. b. Abī Bakr as-Suyūṭī (Cairo, 849–911 H): On the specific question of the Prophet's parents' temporary resurrection (and its refutation by Ibn al-Ǧawzī) as-Suyūṭī wrote six (or seven, see below) diverse monographs[49] in support of their having been called back to life: (a) *Masālik al-ḥunafā fī (ʾislām) wāliday al-Muṣṭafā* (see bibliography), as-Suyūṭī's longest and most elaborate treatise; (b) *al-Maqāmah as-sundusīyah fī ḫabar wāliday Ḫayr al-barīyah*, see GAL II p. 147 and GALS II p. 183; (c) *ad-Daraǧ al-munīfah fī l-ʾābāʾ aš-šarīfah*, his third and shortest monography on the subject (printed in SuyRas pp. 27-43); (d) *at-Taʿẓīm wa-l-mannah fī ʾanna wāliday al-Muṣṭafā* (or *ʾabaway rasūli llāh*) *fī l-ǧannah*: written in 887 H; this treatise (printed in

43 QurṭTadk pp. 15f. = ŠāmīSubul II pp. 123f.

44 As cited in QurṭTadk pp. 15f.; QasṭMaw I p. 90; ŠāmīSubul II p. 123. This is also discussed in Ignaz Goldziher: *Die Ẓāhiriten. Ihr Lehrsystem und ihre Geschichte*, Leipzig 1884, p. 175f.

45 Quoted in QasṭMaw I p. 92.

46 IǦamMuḫt p. 27.

47 IǦawzīMawḍ I pp. 283f. (he calls this report "without doubt invented", *mawḍūʿ bi-lā šakk*); *cf.* also ŠāmīSubul II p. 123.

48 *Cf.* ŠāmīSubul I p. 258, citing from SuySubul p. 170.

49 Not all of them seem to have been current among later scholars. Thus al-Harawī (d. 1014 H), who opposed as-Suyūṭī's opinion in a monograph of his own – see the list above, entry no. 9 –, knew of only three relevant treatises by as-Suyūṭī, see HarMawrid p. 26.

SuyRas pp. 119-64) was criticised by Burhān ad-Dīn Ibr. b. M. an-Nāǧī ad-Dimašqī (Damascus, 810–900 H), see SuyNaẓmᶜIqyān p. 27; (e) *Našr al-ʿalamayn al-munīfayn fī ʾiḥyāʾ al-ʾabawayn aš-šarīfayn*, a monograph of about 16 pages in modern print (see bibliography); (f) *as-Subul al-ǧalīyah fī l-ʾābāʾ al-ʿalīyah*, his sixth and (as as-Suyūṭī himself explained) last writing on the subject (see bibliography); (g) *ad-Durar al-kāminah fī ʾislām as-sayyidah ʾĀminah*, a writing quoted by as-Suyūṭī's pupil Šams ad-Dīn aš-Šāmī (ŠāmīSubul II p. 128) whose text has (to my knowledge) not yet come to light.

(4) *Risālah fī ʾabaway an-nabī*, by Zayn ad-Dīn M. Šāh Çelebi b. M. al-Fanārī (d. Aleppo 926 H): mentioned by title in ḤḪ I pp. 841f. According to Ḥāǧǧī Ḫalīfah, the author in this treatise supported the thesis that both parents of the Prophet eventually died as believers (*mātū ʿalā l-ʾīmān*).

(5) *Risālah fī tafṣīl mā qīla fī ʾabaway ar-rasūl* (also known as *Risālah fī t-takallum ʿalā ʾabaway al-Muṣṭafā*, see GAL II p. 669), by Šams ad-Dīn A. b. Sul. Ibn Kamāl Pasha (d. Istanbul 940 H). This short treatise is preserved in a number of mss., see GAL II p. 450 and 669; Loth: *Indian Office* 178 (p. 288); Mingana Collection 1868 (IV p. 346). In at least one ms., the treatise is followed by as-Suyūṭī's monograph *as-Subul al-ǧalīyah* (see above no. 3f).

(6) *Manāhiǧ as-sunnah fī kawn ʾabaway an-nabī fī l-ǧannah*, by M. b. ᶜAlī Ibn Ṭūlūn ad-Dimašqī aṣ-Ṣāliḥī (Damascus, *c.*880–953 H). The writing is mentioned by the author himself among his works in IṬūlFulk p. 134. As with other works by Ibn Ṭūlūn, it is likely to have been a more or less close adaptation of one of as-Suyūṭī's works on the issue. The title indicates that Ibn Ṭūlūn advocated the temporary resurrection of the Prophet's parents.

(7) *Risālah fī ḥaqq ʾabawayhi*, by Burhān ad-Dīn Ibr. b. M. al-Ḥalabī (d. Istanbul 956 H, the author of *Multaqā l-ʾabḥur*): GAL II p. 432.

(8) *al-ʾAqwāl al-manqūlah ʿan al-lāʾimah fī ʾabawayhi*, by Šihāb ad-Dīn A. b. M. Ibn Ḥaǧar al-Haytamī (Maḥallat Abī l-Haytam 909 – Mecca 973 H): Mingana Collection 1867 (IV p. 346).

(9) *Risālah fī kufr wāliday al-Muṣṭafā* (also entitled *Risālah fī ʾabaway an-nabī*, see GAL II p. 395), by ᶜAlī b. Sulṭān al-Qāriʾ al-Makkī al-Harawī (d. Mecca 1014 H). According to MuḥḪul III p. 186, al-Harawī composed this treatise in order to prove that the Prophet's parents did actually die unbelievers and will remain so until the Last Day.

(10) *Mawrid aṣ-ṣafā bi-ʾabaway al-Muṣṭafā*, by M. ᶜAlī b. M. ᶜAllān al-Bakrī aṣ-Ṣiddīqī (Mecca, 996–1057 H): GAL II p. 391. This writing is quoted as *Mawrid aṣ-ṣafā fī mawlid* (!) *al-Muṣṭafā* in *Ḏayl* ḤḪ II p. 605.

(11) *Risālah fī naǧāt ʾabaway al-Muṣṭafā*, by Awḥad ad-Dīn ᶜAbd al-Aḥad an-Nūrī (d. Istanbul 1061 H): GAL II p. 662. As the title indicates, the treatise is written in support of the resurrection of the Prophet's parents.

(12) *Manẓūmat Durrat aṣ-ṣafā li-ʾiḫwat* (or *ʾuḫūwat*) *al-wafā fī ʾīmān ʾabaway al-Muṣṭafā*, by M. b. M. as-Saqqāf al-Bā-ᶜAlawī: GAL II p. 403 and GALS III p. 1296. Written in 1095 H.

(13) *Birr wāliday Ḫayr al-warā*, by Ǧamāl ad-Dīn ᶜUmar Maḥmūd b. M. aš-Šayḫūnī (d. 1119 H): GALS III p. 1285. The title gives no clear hint as to whether the treatise indeed deals with the death and subsequent resurrection of the Prophet's parents.

(14) *Risālah fī mā yataʿallaq bi-ʾabaway an-nabī*, by M. Sāǧaqlīzādeh al-Marᶜašī (d. 1150 H). A short treatise of only 5 folios length, see GALS II p. 498; Mingana Collection 1864 (IV p. 345).

(15) *Ḥadīqat aṣ-ṣafā fī wāliday al-Muṣṭafā*, by Murtaḍā az-Zabīdī (M. b. M., d. 1205 H), the author of the well-known dictionary *Tāǧ al-ʿarūs*: *Ḏayl* ḤḪ I p. 398.

From the very beginning of this controversy (which still awaits closer analysis), many scholars had reached the conclusion that the problem could not be resolved and took the matter with humour; those who argued against the resurrection of the

Prophet's parents often lost their patience and gave in to their sturdy opponents. Ibn Nāṣir ad-Dīn ad-Dimašqī (d. 842 H), also author of a consolation book, wrote a little poem expressing his resignation in this point. Its closing line runs (*wāfir*):

فَسَلِّمْ فَالقَدِيمُ بِذَا قَدِيرٌ * وَإِنْ كَانَ الحَدِيثُ بِهِ ضَعِيفَا

"Therefore surrender, because what is told of old has much standing in this matter,[50]
* even if the Tradition which tells us about it is weak (i.e. poorly authenticated)".[51]

2.1.4. Hortatory value and *meditatio mortis*

In a report traced back to the Prophet and cited above on page 16 we have seen that the transmitted wording often contains the final passage: "Do visit graves because it reminds (you) of death!" This hortatory or, as it were, paraenetical value of the visitation of tombs and cemeteries was an important factor in all periods of pre-modern Islamic culture, but it is necessary to underline that this is already a recurring element in widely-known Prophetic Traditions. Moreover, the Tradition mentioned before is not the only one which includes the seminal *memento mori* or *meditatio mortis*-motif, because, according to another report, the Prophet said: "Approach your dead, greet them and pray for them, for in them you will have an admonitory example (*ītū mawtākum fa-sallimū ʿalayhim wa-ṣallū ʿalayhim fa-ʾinna lakum fīhim ʿibratan*)".[52]

Besides all that, there is a number of Traditions linking the visitation of tombs to its possible (or even probable) result, viz. the "softness of the heart" (*riqqat al-qalb*) or the softening of the hard-hearted. Not all of these Traditions are traced back to the Prophet himself, but the following is: "When a man came to the messenger of God and lamented his own hardness of heart (*qaswat* or *qasāwat al-qalb*), the Prophet told him 'Go to the tombs and reflect upon the Day of Resurrection!'"[53] According to other reports, ʿĀʾišah told a man (or a woman) who deplored his (or her) hard-heartedness to attend funerals and to meditate upon death.[54] The afore-mentioned Prophetic Tradition is also alluded to in al-Ḥarīrī's (d. 516 H) eleventh Maqāmah (called *as-Sāwīyah*) where he has his hero al-Ḥāriṯ say: "I was aware of hardness of the heart while I sojourned at Sāwah. So I betook

50 There is a wordplay (*tawriyah*) here with *qadīm*, "old" or also "eternal". Given the second meaning of *qadīm*, the first hemistich could also be translated as follows: "Therefore surrender, because the Eternal (i.e. God) has the power to do so, i.e. to resurrect the dead temporarily". Probably we have to take *ḥadīṯ* in the second hemistich either as "Tradition" or as "the created, *or* temporal (= Man)", viz. *muḥdaṯ*, thus the second hemistich would also yield the meaning: "even if Man is not able (lit. too weak) to do so".

51 Cited in QasṭMaw I p. 95.

52 ʿARazMuṣ 6711 (III p. 570); IQaylĠāṭah I p. 185; HarMirqātMaf IV p. 112; *cf.* ḤākMust I p. 375; al-Albānī: *Aḥkām al-ǧanāʾiz* p. 179.

53 As cited in ZamRabīʿ IV p. 203 and KU 42999 (XV pp. 761f.).

54 ŠarŠMaq I p. 175; ḤurRawḍ p. 28; al-Qināwī: *Fatḥ ar-raḥīm* p. 176.

myself to the Tradition handed down (*al-ḫabar al-maʾṯūr*) that its cure is by visiting the tombs".[55] In the *Daʿāʾim* of al-Qāḍī an-Nuʿmān (d. 363 H), the well-known Fatimid jurist, we find that ʿAlī did not approve of a father putting his dead child into the tomb, because this could "cause the softness of his heart" (*ḫawfan min riqqati qalbihī ʿalayhi*).[56] "Softness of heart" is here seen as something menacing or, put in contemporary terms, as something causing emotional disorder, while in the examples cited above "softness of heart" is a positive concept, softening the "hard-heartedness" of those unmoved by the experience of human frailty and transitoriness.[57]

This attitude towards tombs and cemeteries – which were seen as places of meditation, reflection and attrition – must have been widespread from the formative period of Islam, as we also see from what is reported about the early ascetics and world-renouncers. Further below (p. 27) we also will learn about an old woman whose story, quoted by Abū Ḥāmid al-Ġazālī (d. 505 H), contains her saying: "The heart of the hard-hearted (...) will be softened only by the signs of decay (*rusūm al-bilā*)".

2.2. Historical information and the legal debate

Returning to the discussion about the visitation of tombs as conducted by Sunnite scholars we find among the historical (or seemingly historical) reports stemming from the period of nascent Islam that the second caliph ʿUmar (r. 13-23 H) visited the tomb of his father al-Ḫaṭṭāb,[58] and some women from the family of the Prophet are known for having regularly visited tombs in Medina (see below p. 36). Many more examples of people visiting tombs or cemeteries during the first centuries of Islam are collected below in section 4.

Based on the sayings transmitted from the Prophet which encourage the visitation of tombs, and notwithstanding the fact that there were reports to the contrary, this practice was in general seen as permitted by later Sunnite scholars, with some of them even promoting it. Others claimed that there was general agreement (*ʾiǧmāʿ*) that the visit must be considered recommended (*mandūb*) for men only.[59] The traditionist at-Tirmiḏī (d. 279 H) summed up the *opinio communis* of his time, or so he claims: "The actual position of the scholars is that they do not see any harm in the

55 ŠarŠMaq I p. 175 / (Chenery) I p. 164.

56 QNuʿmDaʿāʾim I p. 237. On the contrary, in ṬūsīMabsūṭ I p. 187 we read that a father should not participate actively in burying his son, nor approach his tomb, because "this causes hardness of heart" (*yuqassī l-qalb*), i.e. hardness against God who took his child away.

57 We might understand this concept better with the help of the following anecdote: the Umayyad caliph ʿAbd al-Malik b. Marwān (r. 65-86 H) described himself to Saʿīd b. al-Musayyab by saying "O Saʿīd, I have grown into someone who, if doing good, is not delighted by it and, if doing bad, is not grieved by it". Whereupon Saʿīd told him, "Now the death of your heart is complete" (*al-ʾāna takāmala fīka mawtu l-qalbi*: IṬiqFaḫrī p. 122).

58 ʿAynīʿUmdah VI p. 435.

59 HaytTuḥfMuḥt III p. 199. *Cf.* also below p. 38.

visitation of tombs. This concords with the opinion of Ibn al-Mubārak (d. 181 H), aš-Šāfiʿī, Aḥmad (Ibn Ḥanbal) and Isḥāq (probably Ibn Rāhūyah, d. 238 H)".[60] However, this question could not be decided on the sole basis of reports going back to the Prophet, because some of those reports clearly forbid visitation, while others encourage it openly.[61] It seemed, therefore, only right that some clear criterion was needed in order to decide which Prophetic report was actually relevant for practice.

The fourth-century traditionist al-Ḥākim an-Nīsābūrī (d. 405 H), who also defended the practice of setting up inscribed tombstones (see below p. 273), declared the visitation of tombs a valid practice (*sunnah*): "I thoroughly examined (the Traditions) urging the visitation of graves, with the result that perfoming those visitations must be considered a firmly established practice (*sunnah masnūnah*) because of its effect of bringing about the desire (for good actions) and because it makes those who covet (material gain in this world) aware of their sinful behaviour".[62] This defense of the visitation of tombs stresses above all the moral value of doing so, while others, such as the Malikite Ibn al-Ḫarrāṭ al-Išbīlī, underlined the religious merits of visiting the dead: "Know that the tombs of the righteous are not devoid of blessing (*barakah*) and that those who visit them, greet them, recite the Qurʾān for them and invoke mercy for them will receive only good and increase their (later) reward".[63]

The Sunnite traditionists and legal scholars were in this overt approval often in accordance with many ascetics and mystics who already before had claimed, like the fourth-century mystic from Ḫurāsān Abū ʿAbd Allāh aš-Šaǧarī, that "visitations of the tombs of the saintly (*al-ʾawliyāʾ*)" belong to "the most useful things for the novice (*murīd*) to do".[64] Though this utterance does seem to refer to the visitation of certain tombs and not to the visiting of tombs as such, it might also be read as a general approval of the practice of visitation.

In later centuries the Hanbalite Ibn Qayyim al-Ǧawzīyah (d. 751 H) likewise deemed visiting tombs "a *sunnah* which the Prophet rightfully imposed upon his community" (*sannahā li-ʾummatihī wa-šaraʿahā lahum*).[65] This statement proves, if proof is needed, that the Hanbalites in some cases endorsed the visitation of tombs[66] though one of their chief representatives, the neo-Hanbalite and teacher of Ibn al-Qayyim, Ibn Taymīyah (d. 728 H), has become known as the most fierce

60 TirǦāmiʿ II p. 259 (*ǧanāʾiz* 60) = ʿAynīʿUmdah VI p. 434.

61 Therefore, there is no consensus among the scholars on questions regarding the tomb and the visitation of tombs, apart from the fact that it is considered obligatory to bury the dead; see the relevant section in IMunḏIǧmāʿ pp. 30f.

62 ḤākMust I p. 377.

63 IḪarrāṭʿĀqibah p. 129.

64 ŠaʿrṬab I p. 100.

65 IQayZād I p. 526.

66 *Cf.* also IQudMuġnī II pp. 565f. and CIA Égypte II p. 65, n. 4. However, IQudʿUmdah p. 122 is less positive: "there is nothing wrong with (*lā baʾs bi-*) the visitation of tombs by men", which actually is expressed rather discouragingly.

opponent of the various practices connected to the visitation of tombs and shrines (see below). Nevertheless, in other writings Ibn al-Qayyim polemicised heavily against the visitation of tombs and calls it, with a subtle wordplay, *fitnat al-qabr*, "the allure of the tomb", meaning by this the seductive force of the mortuary cult which entices people to unbelief and superstition.[67] Before Ibn Taymīyah and Ibn al-Qayyim, the Hanbalite Ibn al-Ǧawzī had already given proof of his positive attitude towards the visitation of tombs in his hagiography of Ibn Ḥanbal, inserting two chapters that deal with "the merit (*faḍīlah*) of visiting his tomb" and "the merit of seeking his (protective) neighbourhood (*muǧāwarah*)", i.e. visiting and staying at his sepulchre.[68]

Another Sunnite authority to have called the visitation of tombs a *sunnah* was none less than al-Ġazālī who in that context wrote the following passage: "Visiting the tombs is recommended (*mustaḥabbah*) in general, for it makes people think and reconsider (*li-t-taḏakkuri wa-l-iʿtibār*). Visiting the tombs of the righteous is (likewise) recommended, because of the blessing and the reminder of death it yields".[69] Reflection about one's own mortality, the *meditatio mortis*-motif, is thus again seen as the main benefit to be gained from the visitation of tombs.[70]

The blessing involved in doing so was due to both the visitor and the visited. Ḥātim al-Aṣamm (d. Balḫ 237 H), himself a noted member of "the Khorasanian school of asceticism",[71] said: "Whosoever visits a cemetery and neither reflects about himself nor invokes blessings upon the dead, betrays himself and the dead also".[72] This comes close to the teaching of Ḥātim's spiritual guide and fellow countryman Šaqīq al-Balḫī (d. 194 H): "The gate of (God's) merciful help is closed to men (...) if they bury their dead without being prompted (by their aspect) to reconsider".[73] The "betrayal of the dead", on the other hand, is paradoxically conceptualised in the following dictum which stresses the fact that the living must care for the dead, in short, that there must be a certain interaction between the dead and

67 IQayIġāṯah I p. 171. Commonly, *fitnat al-qabr* was understood to mean the Trial of the Grave, being more or less synonymous with the term *ʿaḏāb al-qabr* ("Chastisement of the Grave"); for further details, see Volume I, Chapter 2.

68 IǦawzīManIbnḤanbal pp. 481-4. For his own report of visiting Ibn Ḥanbal's shrine in 574 H, see IǦawzīMunt X pp. 283f.

69 ĠazIḥyāʾ (C) IV pp. 416.

70 In Christian Europe, similar arguments were voiced, see e.g. the passage in John Weever's *Ancient Funerall Monuments* (1631 CE): "The frequent visiting, and advised reviewing of the Tombes and monuments of the dead (but without all touch of superstition) with the often reading, serious perusall, and diligent meditation of wise and religious Epitaphs and inscriptions, found upon the tombes or monuments, of persons of approved vertue, merit, and honour, is a great motive to bring us to repentance" (cited in Franke: *Vers-Epitaph* p. 57).

71 Arberry: *Sufism* pp. 38f.

72 Cited in MunKawākib I p. 589.

73 Quoted in MunKawākib I pp. 321f. and Gramlich: *Vorbilder* II p. 55.

the living: "If there was not the living, the dead would perish (*law lā l-ʾaḥyāʾu la-halakati l-ʾamwāt*)".[74]

Finally, among all Sunnite scholars the one to have put forward the most extreme favourable position as to the visitation of tombs was without doubt the Andalusian Ẓāhirite authority Ibn Ḥazm (d. 456 H). He considered the visitation of graves not only recommended, but even an obligation (*farḍ*).[75] This clearly exceeds the claim made by most other Sunnite scholars that visiting tombs qualifies as an accepted *sunnah* in Islam.

2.2.1. A fatwa by Ibn Ḥağar al-Haytamī

The average Sunnite view regarding the visitation of tombs, as it had developed during almost ten centuries of intense study, has been summarised in a fatwa by Ibn Ḥağar al-Haytamī (d. 973 H). In this fatwa he defends the practice of undertaking journeys in order to perform such visitations,[76] notwithstanding the blameful practices (*bidaᶜ*, "innovations") that happened or were feared to happen on such occasions:

> "*Quaeritur*: Is it permitted to visit the tombs of saintly persons (*al-ʾawliyāʾ*) in a certain period and connected with a journey (*riḥlah*), although around these tombs many abominable things happen, such as the intermingling of women and men,[77] the kindling of many lamps and whatever else there is?
> *Respondeo*: The visit to tombs of saintly persons is a righteous deed (*qurbah*) that is desirable. The same holds true of the journey (to them),[78] though the sheikh Abū Muḥammad (i.e. al-Ğuwaynī, d. 438 H) said that the journey is only desirable if it leads you to the tomb of the Prophet[79] (whereas visiting other tombs or travelling to them was prohibited).[80] This opinion was rebutted by al-Ġazālī who argued that Abū Muḥammad saw here an analogy with the prohibition of visiting mosques other than the three mosques (of Mecca, Medina and Jerusalem),[81] yet the case is clearly different,

74 IRağAhwāl p. 174; SuyŠṢudūr p. 410.

75 IḤazmMuḥ V p. 160. *Cf.* FB III p. 191; QasṭMaw III p. 405; Adang: *Women's Access* p. 89.

76 The question of whether travelling to venerated tombs should be allowed or not was fiercely debated since the eighth century H. The idea behind this was that a journey being a costly, dangerous and long undertaking, the visitation of tombs could thus be seen as so important as to justify such an undertaking, something which in the eyes of many Sunnite scholars clearly exceeded the merit which was to be accorded to the practice of visitation. In defending travelling in order to visit tombs, Ibn Ḥağar opposes those scholars in a fatwa, in particular Ibn Taymīyah; see also below p. 75.

77 For the cemeteries as places of easy seduction, *cf.* also Torres Balbás: *Cementerios* p. 161 and below p. 43.

78 *Cf.* ŠubrḤāš III p. 35 and WanšMiᶜyār I p. 321: "The visit to the tombs of the righteous and the learned is allowed, no matter whether the journey (to them) is long or short". The same is said some lines before with regard to the graves of parents and relatives.

79 *Cf.* also ŠirwḤāš III p. 199.

80 This is cited from al-Ğuwaynī in KarKawākib p. 163.

81 *Cf.* FB III p. 83 (*faḍl aṣ-ṣalāh fī masğid Makkah* 1); WanšMiᶜyār I p. 320; ᶜUlaymīUns I pp. 230f. See also below p. 75 with notes 406f.

because apart from these three all mosques are of equal standing and thus there is no benefit in visiting any of them especially.[82] Saintly persons, on the contrary, differ in their closeness to God, and the visitors (to their tombs) will benefit according to the open and secret knowledge they possessed. Thus, travelling to them (individually) has its benefit. (...) As to the innovations (*bidaᶜ*) or forbidden acts (...), I say that righteous deeds (such as visiting tombs) should not be given up for that reason. It rather obliges everybody to perform (such deeds) and to combat the innovations, yea to abolish them if one is able to do so. (...) Therefore, the visit should be undertaken, but staying separated from the women and condemning everything that seems forbidden, or even doing away with it if possible. (...) Of course, performing the visit during a time when there are no such abominable things happening is preferable".[83]

Ibn Ḥağar al-Haytamī then goes on to justify the intermingling of men and women by the fact that it would also happen during most of the pilgrimage rites, "but since none of the foremost scholars ever prohibited any of these rites on the ground that men and women would intermingle, (...) this *a fortiori* applies in this case". And it certainly shows how tired a tenth-century scholar must have been of opposing common use and practice, when we read that al-Haytamī offers as an astonishing conclusion of his fatwa that not every innovation (*bidᶜah*) as such was prohibited. On the contrary, there were innovations that are not only recommended but obligatory.[84]

In another context, al-Haytamī, taking up a concept elaborated already during the seventh century H by ᶜIzz ad-Dīn Ibn ᶜAbd as-Salām (d. 660 H), divides "innovations" into five classes, ranging from "obligatory" to "prohibited", thus being parallel to the normal rulings or "judgments" (*ʾaḥkām*) applied in legal matters. As an example for an "obligatory innovation" al-Haytamī mentions the study of grammar which was not yet known at the beginning of Islam but helps to understand Qurʾān (and Tradition) and is therefore to be welcomed.[85] This classification of innovations goes quite beyond the usual division of "innovations" into those "commendable" (*mustaḥsan*) and those "disapproved of" (*mustaqbaḥ*), or in the terms of aš-Šāfiᶜī, "laudable" (*maḥmūd*) and "blameworthy" (*maḏmūm*).[86]

2.2.2. Arguments against the visitation of tombs

The general consensus invoked by many a Sunnite scholar concerning the visitation of tombs was not generally accepted and sometimes voices were raised against it. Take, for example, what Ibn Ḥağar al-ᶜAsqalānī (d. 852 H) had to say on this point: "(The Shafiite authority) an-Nawawī (...) stated that 'there is general agreement that visiting tombs is permitted for men without exception'.[87] This might be contested,

82 *Cf.* also WanšMiᶜyār I p. 320 and QasṭMaw III pp. 405f.

83 HaytFatFiqh II p. 24.

84 HaytFatFiqh II p. 24.

85 HaytFatḤad p. 150.

86 See AŠāmahBāᶜiṯ p. 12; *cf.* also Masud: *Definition of Bidᶜa* and Gronke: *Missbräuche*.

87 *Cf.* ᶜAynīᶜUmdah VI p. 434; SaḫTuḥfAḥbāb pp. 7f.; QasṭIršād II p. 327; HaytTuḥfMuḥt III p. 199.

though, for Ibn Abī Šaybah (d. 235 H)[88] and others reported (...) that visiting graves is reproachable without exception (i.e. for men and women alike), and aš-Šaᶜbī (d. 110 H) even went so far as to say 'Had the Prophet not prohibited doing so, I would have visited the tomb of my daughter'".[89]

The Medinan authority Mālik b. Anas seems also to have been little inclined towards the visitation of tombs. Though he did not see anything wrong with men undertaking such visits – in his words: *lam ʾara bi-ḏālika baʾsan*[90] – and though his later followers tried to explain away the Prophet's prohibition "to sit on / at tombs" (see above p. 14), he reportedly disliked visiting cemeteries if spiritual exercise and contemplation (*iᶜtibār*) was hoped for: "When Mālik was told, '(The cemetery is a place) for contemplation', he rebutted 'What is there to contemplate? One sees nothing but dust!'"[91] A similar anecdote is told by a companion of Abū Ḥāzim al-Aᶜrağ (Salamah b. Dīnār, d. 140 H): when Abū Ḥāzim stood in a cemetery at the edge of a tomb and was asked what he was seeing, he said "I see a dry pit and stone-deaf rocks!"[92]

In other sources we find that Mālik hated someone saying "I visited the tomb of the Prophet", though the later adherents to his legal tradition tried to belittle Mālik's verdict either by arguing that he merely disliked the use of the expression "to visit" – thus it boils down to a purely semantic question, known as *karāhat al-ism* – or because "the word *ziyārah* is also used when people visit each other and thus he disliked putting the visit of the Prophet on the same level as the people visiting each other, preferring instead expressions which are reserved (for the visit of the Prophet's sepulchre), e.g. 'we saluted the Prophet' (*sallamnā ᶜalā n-nabī*)".[93] Others claimed that Mālik "disliked someone saying this because it shows bad manners, not because he disapproved of visiting the Prophet's tomb as such";[94] still others held that Mālik merely disliked the Medinans' greeting the Prophet in his tomb, though the foreigners were free to do so.[95]

The critical attitude towards the visitation of tombs clearly conflicts with some utterances reported from the Prophet (see above). Moreover, the critical stance was not to the liking of many later scholars, e.g. al-Ġazālī, who defended the visiting of tombs for the very reason of its spiritual dimension and tried to support this view by the following report (which is, by the way, not an explicit, but surely an implicit rebuttal of Mālik's above-mentioned dictum): "An old lady was living with ᶜAbd al-Qays' clan. She was very pious and (...) during the day used to visit the graves. When she was reproached for her frequent visits to the cemetery, she replied 'The

88 *Cf.* IAŠayMuṣ III p. 226 (*ğanāʾiz* 146).

89 FB III p. 191 (*ğanāʾiz* 31). The saying of aš-Šaᶜbī also appears in ᶜARazMuṣ 6707 (III p. 569) and IAŠayMuṣ III p. 226 (*ğanāʾiz* 146). *Cf.* ᶜAynīᶜUmdah VI p. 435.

90 QasṭIršād II p. 327. *Cf.* also BāğīMunt II p. 24.

91 WanšMiᶜyār I p. 324.

92 Quoted in ZamRabīᶜ IV p. 206 and IRağAhwāl p. 181.

93 ᶜIyāḍŠifāʾ (B) II pp. 71f. / (Š) II p. 84 = HarŠŠifāʾ II pp. 149f.; MarğBahğah II p. 398; *cf.* SubkīŠifāʾ pp. 74-6.

94 FB III p. 85 (*faḍl aṣ-ṣalāh fī masğid Makkah* 1). *Cf.* also ITayMağm XXVII p. 26; ITayZiy pp. 20 and 23; KarKawākib p. 154.

95 ZarkAḥkām p. 271.

heart of the hard-hearted (...) will be softened only by the signs of decay (*rusūm al-bilā*). I visit the tombs and when I look around it seems that (the dead) come forth from their (underground) layers and I seem to see those dust-covered faces, those decomposed (*mutaġayyirah*) corpses, those swollen eyelids. Verily, what a sight!'"[96]

After the time when the practice of visiting tombs in Islam had given rise to different usages which could be easily marked as abominable "innovations" (viz. the lighting of candles, touching or kissing the tomb, circumambulating the shrine, etc.), later scholars and preachers found still more reasons than the early authorities why the visitation of tombs should be severely condemned. In Ramaḍān 1132 H, al-Ǧabartī reports, a Turkish preacher in the Cairene Muʾayyad-Mosque publicly condemned "what the people of Cairo were doing at the shrines of the 'saints' (*ḍarāʾiḥ al-ʾawliyāʾ*), as well as the lighting of candles and lamps upon their tombs and the kissing of their thresholds. He said that doing so was unbelief; thus the people are obliged to stop this and the men in charge of public affairs must try to abolish it".[97]

Few scholars, however, went as far as aš-Šawkānī (d. 1250 H) who saw in the visitation of tombs "the wicked stratagems of Satan" at work and ceaselessly denounced the heathen-like aberrations of perverted "tombers" (*al-qubūrīyūn*), as he calls them, "who reached extremes in their belief in the dead as it was never reached by the polytheists with their belief in their idols".[98] In this vein aš-Šawkānī also produced, among much else, the following outburst:

> "The fool, whose eye falls upon a tomb of those above which a mausoleum (*qubbah*) rises, will enter it and look at the graves covered with precious drapings and at the glimmering candle-lights, with the braziers of incense filling the air around him.[99] There is no doubt and no uncertainty that his heart will be filled with awe at the spectacle of such a tomb and that his mind will shrink so as to become incapable of forming a (correct) idea about the rank of the deceased.[100] He will be overwhelmed by a thrilling sense of devout veneration due to the satanic creed which was implanted in his heart, this being from among the most potent machinations (*makāyid*) of Satan against the Muslims and his most effective means of leading astray the servants (of God). It will rock him away from Islam step by step, until he asks from the deceased in that tomb what nobody except God – praise be to the Lord! – has the power to do, and eventually he will become one of the unbelievers".[101]

In linking the veneration of shrines to idol worship and the pernicious influence of

96 ĠazIḥyāʾ (C) IV p. 418; IĞawzīṢafwah II p. 518; ŠarŠMaq I p. 175. With a similar wording also in IḪarrāṭʿĀqibah p. 129.

97 ĞabʿAǧāʾib I p. 92.

98 ŠawkDurr p. 35.

99 For this practice, *cf.* Dermenghem: *Culte des saints* pp. 123f.

100 I.e., the buried person's rank will always be modest inasmuch he was but a mortal being.

101 ŠawkŠṢudūr p. 72 (the passage goes on for a while and is worth reading; the respective passages in ŠawkDurr pp. 11f. and 19f. exhibit similar verve and are also of interest).

Satan, aš-Šawkānī comes close to what already Ibn Qayyim al-Ǧawzīyah[102] (who is often cited approvingly by him) and Ibn Kaṯīr (d. 774 H) had to say on the matter. The latter wrote with regard to the Cairene mausoleum of as-Sayyidah Nafīsah:

> "Until the present day, the common people show extreme veneration for the shrine of as-Sayyidah Nafīsah and those of others. Above all, it is the common people of Cairo who use expressions about her which are loathsome and foolish and will eventually lead to unbelief and polytheism, and many other terms as well which they should know to be not feasible. (...) One must not put one's faith in as-Sayyidah Nafīsah unless in the manner that befits all pious women, and the origin of idol worship lies in the excessive veneration of tombs and their occupants. The Prophet had ordered the levelling of the graves and their effacement, while the excessive veneration toward (mere) human beings is forbidden".[103]

Nevertheless, aš-Šawkānī went beyond the rhetoric of the eighth-century scholars and tried to produce empirical evidence of the futility of putting one's hopes in the powers and *barakah* of a certain tomb or shrine. Thus he writes about the tomb of al-Muʾayyad bi-llāh Yaḥyā b. Ḥamzah (d. *c.*747 H): "He was buried in Ḏamār (Yemen) and his tomb is today a famous place, visited by many people. Word has spread widely that a man who enters his tomb with a piece of iron will not be harmed by fire ever again. I tried that out, but it had not that effect".[104] However, to present empirical evidence was to little avail in that discussion, because such evidence could also attest to the opposite, as for example in the case of the tenth-century scholar al-ʿUlaymī who reports his positive experiences at the shrine of Abraham in al-Ḫalīl (Hebron).[105] Moreover, if the prayers uttered at a specific tomb were not fulfilled, there were plenty of other burial sites one could turn to. The Egyptian mystic al-Burhān al-Matbūlī thus gave the following advice: "If someone among you asks a favour from God, then implore intercession (*wsl* VI *bi-*) first (at the tomb) of al-Manūfī (ʿAl., d. 749 H). If (your plea) is not fulfilled, then turn to (the tomb of) Šaraf ad-Dīn al-Kurdī in al-Ḥusaynīyah; if (your plea) is not fulfilled there, turn to (the tomb of) aš-Šāfiʿī; if (your plea) is not fulfilled there, then you may still turn to (the tomb of) Nafīsah".[106]

2.3. The visitation of shrines in Shiite Islam

In Shiism, the question concerning the visitation of tombs and cemeteries has never brought about the same heated discussion as among the Sunnites, largely because there was little disagreement that it belonged to the accepted or even principal elements of Shiite Islam. From the very beginning, the mortuary cult connected with

102 IQaylġāṯah I pp. 170f. and *passim*; II pp. 165, 179 and 188.

103 BN X p. 262.

104 ŠawkBadr II p. 333 = Gramlich: *Wunder* p. 229.

105 ʿUlaymīUns II pp. 56f. For the mausoleum, see Leisten: *Architektur für Tote* pp. 174f. (no. 1).

106 MunKawākib III p. 46.

the burial places of members of the ᶜAlid family (*ʾāl al-bayt*, *ʾahl al-bayt*),[107] of persons from among the offspring of an Imam (*imāmzādagān*, *ʾawlād al-ʾaʾimmah*) and especially of the Imams themselves formed an integral part of Shiite belief[108] and has thus been dubbed by Richard Yann a "specifically Shiite devotion".[109]

The veneration of those sites was already noted by European travellers in Ṣafawid Iran, and the Shiite mortuary cult also included the visitation of the burial sites of former prophets and of persons of non-ᶜAlid descent, e.g. the tombs of Salmān al-Fārisī ("the Pure", d. 36 H) and al-Ḥuḏayfah b. al-Yamān (d. 36 H) in al-Madāʾin,[110] or those of Bilāl al-Ḥabašī (d. 20 H) and Abū Ḏarr al-Ġiffārī (d. 31 H or later) in Damascus.[111] Apart from those important and widely venerated tombs (known in Persian as *ziyāratgāh*) it was also considered "desirable to visit the graves of the believers, in particular those of the learned and the righteous, and especially those of parents and relatives",[112] what amounts to nothing less but a general encouragement to visit any kind of tomb that may be of significance for the respective visitor. A contemporary account of the principles of the Shiite-Imamite faith provides a neat summary of the issue:

> "Visiting the graves of Muslims, in particular, those of relatives and friends, is an established practice in Islam, one which brings about positive effects. For instance, the very witnessing of the stillness of the graveyard (...) is a moving experience and contains a lesson for those willing to learn. Such persons may say to themselves: This transient life, whose end is to lie hidden beneath shovels of earth, is not worth wasting through unjust acts. They then might take a fresh look at their own lives and reform their spiritual and mental attitudes. The Holy Prophet said: 'Visit the graves, for truly this will remind you of the hereafter.'
>
> In addition, the visiting of the graves of great personages in our religion is a kind of propagation both of the faith and of the holy sites. The attention paid by people to the graves of these great souls strengthens the idea that it is the spirituality of these great ones that gives rise to this desire, on the part of others, to visit their graves; whilst those

107 For these places, see the excellent survey in al-Ǧalālī: *Mazārāt ahl al-bayt*.

108 *Cf.* KulKāfī IV pp. 569-87; ṬūsīTahḏ VI pp. 20-95; ŠarMurtRas I p. 291; ᶜĀmilīWas III pp. 293-463; al-Amīn: *Miftāḥ* II; Donaldson: *Shiʾite Religion*, esp. chs. 24f.; Falaturi: *Zwölfer-Schia* pp. 75f.; Richard: *Iran* (with further literature); Nakash: *Shiᶜis of Iraq* ch. 6; Ḥasan b. Makkī al-Ḫuwaylidī: *Ziyārat al-Ḥusayn. ʾAsrāruhā, maqāṣiduhā, ʾādābuhā*, Beirut 1423/2003.

109 Richard: *Shiʾite Islam* p. 8. See also Ayoub: *Redemptive Suffering* pp. 180-96 and Nakash: *Visitation of the Shrines*.

110 Another shrine (*mašhad*) of Salmān existed at Azdūd; see its foundation inscription RCEA 4600 (667 H). The relation of Ibn Diḥyah al-Kalbī's (d. 633 H) visit to the shrine of Salmān in al-Madāʾin has been preserved in MaqqNafḥ (C) VII p. 43.

111 For Bilāl's epitaph, see Volume I p. 83. For Abū Ḏarr, "a typical representative of the proto-Shiʾite hero" (Y. Richard), see Richard: *Shiʾite Islam* pp. 23f.; Alan J. Cameron: *Abû Dharr al-Ghifârî, an examination of his image in the hagiography of Islam,* London 1973. Abū Ḏarr's hagiography has been compiled by Shiite authors (see ZA II p. 140) and some Ismailite scholar (Ivanow: *Ismaili literature* p. 78); the location of his tomb is uncertain, though many reports state that it lies in ar-Rabaḏah, between Medina and Mecca (DabMaᶜālim I p. 90).

112 al-Amīn: *Miftāḥ* II p. 271.

who possessed great power and wealth, but were devoid of spirituality, are simply buried in the earth and nobody pays them any attention. (...)
In books of Hadith, visiting the graves of the saints and religious authorities is given as a strongly recommended practice (*mustaḥabb muʾakkad*); and the Imams of the *ahl al-bayt* always visited the grave of the Prophet and the graves of the Imams preceding them, inviting their followers to do likewise".[113]

Visitation of the sepulchres of the Imams will guarantee their intercession on behalf of the believers on the Day of Accounting,[114] and the avoidance of visiting their tombs could be seen as a negligence towards the precepts of Islam, as a breach of obligation (*farḍ*) and as a general lack of faith,[115] the result of which is damnation to Hell.[116] In contrast with Sunnite writings, Shiite works are therefore replete with lengthy litanies and quotations of what has to be pronounced by the visitors to certain tombs and shrines (including the martyrs' tombs, *qubūr aš-šuhadāʾ*, in Medina); the very word for "visitation" (*ziyārah*) has thus become a synonym for "tomb" or "shrine",[117] and hence of "litany" or "prayer recited during the visit", such as are amply cited in the relevant sources or have been collected in the form of monographs (*ziyārat-nāmah*). Typically Shiite is also the practice of compiling huge collections of mourning poems on al-Ḥusayn and his descendants (e.g. aṭ-Ṭurayḥī's *al-Muntaḫab fī ǧamʿ al-marāṯī wa-l-ḫuṭab*, see bibliography).

Apart from the known sites of the Imams' tombs (*mazārāt*)[118] in Medina, Iraq and Persia, this favourable attitude is best demonstrated by the array of shrines over the tombs of lesser members of the ʿAlid family which adorn the streets of Cairo and were chiefly built – or renovated[119] – under the Fatimids (4th–6th centuries H);[120] the Fatimid caliphs also used to visit the better known tombs of the Qarāfah cemetery and the local mosque built there in 366 H.[121]

Even though Shiism (of the Ismailite branch) vanished in Egypt with the end of the Fatimid rule between 555 and 567 H, visiting these shrines remained an important element of local piety; some of

113 Sobhani: *Doctrines of Shiʿi Islam* pp. 174f. (article 134: Visiting Graves).

114 KulKāfī IV p. 567; ṬūsīTahḏ VI pp. 79 and 93; MaǧlBiḥār C pp. 116f.; Richard: *Iran* pp. 152-6.

115 See IQūlKāmil pp. 193f.; ʿĀmilīWas III pp. 333-6 and 345f.

116 IQūlKāmil p. 193; ʿĀmilīWas III p. 337.

117 *Cf.* also RCEA 5208 (706 H).

118 This term (*mazār*, pl. *mazārāt*) means "place of visitation" and hence "(visited) shrine".

119 In 516 H, the so-called "seven shrines" in the Qarāfah were renovated and "what had been demolished of them was restored. At every shrine (*mašhad*) a marble was affixed, bearing its name and the date of its restoration": IMuyassarAḫbār p. 91 = IMaʾmūnAḫbār p. 35.

120 There is a list of the relevant sites in IZawlFaḍMiṣr pp. 43-6 and 51-3; IǦubRiḥlah (B) pp. 21f. *Cf.* also Kessler: *Funerary Architecture* p. 258; Rāġib: *Mausolées Fatimides*, *Sanctuaires* and *Deux monuments*; Bannerth: *Wallfahrtsstätten Kairos* pp. 3, 5f., 13-5 and 19-48; Williams: *The Cult of ʿAlid Saints*; Taylor: *Reevaluating the Shiʿi Role*; Behrens-Abouseif: *Islamic Architecture in Cairo* pp. 74-6; al-Ǧalālī: *Mazārāt ahl al-bayt*; Leisten: *Architektur für Tote* pp. 28f.

121 IṬuwNuzhah pp. 222f.; MaqrḪiṭaṭ I p. 491; Gayraud: *Qarāfa al-Kubrā* pp. 452ff.

these Fatimid monuments survived the vicissitudes of time and range today among Cairo's most ancient preserved buildings from the entire Islamic period. Many Sunnite scholars of later times did not hesitate to acknowledge the practice of visiting these shrines and no Sunnite ruler ever seriously tried to do away with it.[122] (The differences between Sunnism and Shiism in Islam never played much of a role for the common people when visiting famous shrines was at stake. After all, throughout the Muslim world there are also a number of shrines visited by Muslims, Jews, Christians and Hindus alike).[123] Furthermore, the construction of larger funerary architecture within and outside the city of Cairo may well have been fostered in general under Fatimid rule,[124] which is in itself a token of the strong Shiite influence on Sunnite practices between the fourth and sixth centuries H. In the words of Christel Kessler: "It seems (...) that the major impulse for the growth of a monumental type of funerary architecture had come from the Shīᶜīs whose veneration of the Imams and their descendants made it a pious duty to give their tombs special attention. The archaeological evidence of Cairo indeed suggests such an assumption, for all early funerary monuments surviving date back to the period of the Shīᶜī Fāṭimīs".[125] If nothing else, this evidence is – also chronologically – paralleled in other, rather different fields, e.g. in the realm of poetry in praise of the Prophet which among eastern Sunnites likewise seems to be partly an offshoot of the preceding Shiite poetry in praise of the Prophet's family and the Imams (*cf.* also below p. 71).

The fact that eleven out of the twelve Imams of the Imamite ("Twelver") branch of Shiism met a violent death and thus were reckoned as martyrs (whose intercession on behalf of the believers was taken for granted) further enhanced the development of an intense mortuary cult, coupled with the deeply rooted sentiment of "suffering" and "sharing in the fate of the Imams" typical of the main branches of Shiism.[126] This has led one Western scholar to speak of "the gloomy Shīᶜa",[127] notwithstanding the fact that modernist theologians have tried to purge Shiism of some of the elements connected with visitation rites and the sentiment of suffering.[128]

The regard for the burial sites of the Imams and other persons of their family among the Shiites in the East brought about a different, more caring attitude towards tombs and cemeteries in general: Shiite graveyards have even today an appearance much more similar to the well-tended cemeteries of Christian Europe, especially if

122 Strangely enough, it is often the Shiite visitation guides (see Ch. 3) which regularly neglect or omit to mention the Cairene mausolea of members of the ᶜAlid family. If nothing else, this seems to demonstrate the historically-grown eastern perspective of Arabic Shiite literature and the fact that Egypt after the Fatimid epoch was a faraway place for most Shiites.

123 See Ayoub: *Cult and culture*; Dermenghem: *Culte des saints* pp. 125f.; Currie: *Muᶜīn al-Dīn Chistī* p. 117-9. *Cf.* also de Jong: *Cairene Ziyāra-Days* pp. 28 and 35; M. Voinot: *Pélerinages judéo-musulmans du Maroc*, Rabat 1948 (Institut des Haute Études Marocaines: Notes et documents 4; I have not seen the book myself).

124 The erection of mortuary complexes and mausolea goes back to the pre-Fatimid period, but nothing of them has survived to the present day.

125 Kessler: *Funerary Architecture* p. 258. Arguing to the contrary Taylor: *Reevaluating the Shiᶜi Role*, esp. p. 2; *cf.* also Sayyid: *al-Qāhira et al-Fusṭāṭ* pp. 643ff.; Shoshan: *Popular culture* p. 95, n. 161.

126 *Cf.* Ayoub: *Redemptive Suffering*, esp. ch. I; Jafri: *Origins and Early Development* pp. 211-6; Halm: *Schia* pp. 177f.; Richard: *Shiʾite Islam* pp. 11-4 and 97-106.

127 Rypka: *Iranian Literature* p. 83.

128 Falaturi: *Zwölfer-Schia* p. 69 with note 2.

contrasted with Sunnite cemeteries.[129] The construction of larger funerary monuments (see Chapter 2) as well as the growing importance of the *ziyārat al-qubūr*, which marks the steady growth of Sunnism in the central Islamic lands from the sixth century H onwards, was influenced and at least partially caused by practices current among the Shiites. This observation will be taken up again below on page 70.

Among the Sunnites, the general importance of the *Gräberkult* in Shiite circles was often criticised, especially vehemently by Ibn Taymīyah, who in his controversy with the Shiite scholar al-ʿAllāmah al-Ḥillī (d. 728 H) did not fail to point out the "pernicious" influence of Shiite practices on Sunnite customs:

> "What the Shiites show of extremism, polytheism and (blameworthy) innovations is found among many of those who profess to be Sunnites, because many of them venerate their sheikhs in an extreme manner, treat them as demi-Gods and have brought on ways of devotion (*ʿibādāt*) which are not lawful. Many of them also visit the tomb of somebody they have strong confidence in, either to ask him (*sc.* the deceased) for something or that he may ask God on their behalf, and some also think that praying at somebody's tomb will have a greater effect than (praying) in mosques. Others among them consider the visitation of their masters' tombs more valuable than the pilgrimage itself, and still others profess at the tombs they glorify amiability and submissiveness such as they do not profess in mosques, houses and elsewhere, quite like the Shiites use to do. What is more, they relate forged sayings of the type current among the Shiites, such as (...) the dictum 'If wordly affairs (*al-ʾumūr*) make you weary, then turn towards the inhabitants of the tombs (*ʾaṣḥāb al-qubūr*)' or also 'The tomb of N.N. is a proven antidote (*or* remedy: *at-tiryāq al-muǧarrab*)'".[130]

2.4. Times of visitation

As the most appropriate time of visitation, the Muslim scholars – Sunnites and Shiites alike – opted for Friday (the whole day, that is including the night from Thursday to Friday)[131] and Saturday morning (until sunrise).[132] The reason is that the souls of the dead were believed to be present in or near the graves between Thursday afternoon and Saturday morning[133] and thus were capable of knowing who came to visit them.[134] Reportedly, the Prophet himself used to visit the tombs in the Medinan Baqīʿ cemetery on Thursday evening[135] and the martyrs' tombs[136] on

129 *Cf.* Wirth: *Orientalische Stadt* p. 426.

130 ITayMinhāǧ I pp. 132f. For the term *at-tiryāq al-muǧarrab*, see below p. 86.

131 There are reports discouraging the visit of cemeteries at night in general, see below p. 155.

132 ĠazIḥyāʾ (C) IV pp. 416f.; AfricDescr II p. 509; SuyNūrLum p. 217; HaytFatḤad p. 6 and HaytFatFiqh II p. 8 (quoting from al-Qurṭubī); MunKawākib III p. 36 (from al-Yāfiʿī).

133 MuwMuršid I p. 54; ŠubrḤāš III p. 36; ŠirwḤāš III p. 200.

134 IADunyāQubūr (A) p. 203; ĠazIḥyāʾ (C) IV p. 417; IAYaṬab II p. 26; MuwMuršid I p. 34; IRaǧAhwāl pp. 111f.; ManbTasl (C) p. 103 / (M) p. 98; SuyBušrā p. 59; SuyḤāwī II p. 170; SuyNūrLum p. 217; SuyŠṢudūr pp. 272f.

135 ŠīrŠadd pp. 12f.; al-Amīn: *Miftāḥ* II pp. 273f.

136 Viz. of the Muslim combatants killed in the battle of Uḥud.

Saturday. This was explained by the ingenious hypothesis that on Fridays the Prophet could not leave the town because he was busy (with leading the prayer, communal affairs, etc.).[137]

The Prophet's daughter Fāṭimah visited the tomb of Ḥamzah every Friday[138] – in later times it was common to visit his tomb on Thursdays[139] –, and Friday was in general seen as the most appropriate day for visiting tombs.[140] This day was considered suitable for visiting the bigger "public" shrines which attracted many people, but also for approaching "private" tombs, following the Tradition of the Prophet who said: "Whoever visits the tomb of his parents or that of one of them every Friday will be forgiven (his sins)".[141]

On Saturdays, people visited the tomb of the ascetic Maᶜrūf al-Karḫī (d. 199 or 200 H) in Baghdad,[142] and the same day was asigned to the visitation of the so-called "seven tombs" in the Cairene Qarāfah cemetery.[143] Other days which were considered suited for the visitation of tombs were Thursday and Monday, with Thursday offering the advantage that the visit did then not clash with the noon-prayer on Fridays. The ascetic Mālik b. Dīnār (d. 131 H) used to visit cemeteries on Thursdays (see below p. 164), and Thursday was also the visitation-day of the martyrs' tombs in Medina[144] as well as of the famous shrine of Ḫwāğah ᶜAbd Allāh al-Anṣārī (d. 481 H) in Harāt during the Tīmūrid period.[145] In contrast, the tomb of Ibn Ḥanbal in Baghdad and the shrine of Fāṭimah an-Nabawīyah Bint al-Ḥusayn in Cairo were visited on Mondays.[146] The tomb of Ibn Ḥağğūn al-Qināʾī (ᶜAbd ar-Raḥīm b. A., d. Qinā 592

137 ŠubrḤāš III p. 36; ŠirwḤāš III p. 200.

138 ᶜARazMuṣ 6713 (III p. 572) and 6717 (III p. 574); BayDal III p. 309; SamWafāʾ III p. 932; SuyŠṢudūr p. 281. *Cf.* also IRağAhwāl p. 111 and QNuᶜmDaᶜāʾim I p. 239. – KulKāfī III p. 228 and IV p. 561 (= al-Amīn: *Miftāḥ* II p. 273), ᶜĀmilīWas III p. 279 and MağlBihār C p. 216 have Fāṭimah visiting the tombs of the martyrs (of Uḥud) every Friday. According to them, she was so grieved after the death of the Prophet that she spent even more time in the martyrs' cemetery (MağlBihār XLIII p. 155). See also below p. 36 with note 162.

139 DiyTārḪamīs II p. 176. For his tomb, see also IĞubRiḥlah (B) p. 173 and **168**.

140 The Ayyubid ruler al-Malik al-Kāmil (r. 615–35 H) thus decreed Friday to be the official day for visiting tombs, see Schimmel: *Sufismus* p. 282.

141 *man zāra qabra ʾabawayhi ʾaw ʾaḥadihimā kulla ğumᶜatin ġufira lahū*: SuyNūrLum p. 216; HaytFatḤad p. 271; HarMirqātMaf IV p. 116. The same Tradition is known among the Shiites concerning the tomb of al-Ḥusayn, see ᶜĀmilīWas III p. 374. *Cf.* also TurkLumaᶜ I p. 316 and al-Albānī: *Aḥkām al-ğanāʾiz* p. 258.

142 IAYaṬab I pp. 288f. For the mausoleum, see Leisten: *Architektur für Tote* p. 116 (no. 22).

143 IẒuhFaḍMiṣr p. 193 (*cf.* below p. 31 with note 119).

144 DiyTārḪamīs II p. 176.

145 Subtelny: *Cult of Anṣārī* p. 387.

146 IAYaṬab I pp. 288f.; de Jong: *Cairene Ziyāra-Days* p. 31.

H or before) was commonly visited on Wednesdays, because the people had found out, or so they claimed, that on this day the prayers at his tomb were fulfilled.[147] Wednesday was also considered a good "visitation day" for the Cairene Qarāfah.[148]

However, there were people who visited certain tombs – especially tombs of purely private relevance – every day or every week, for example Muḥammad b. an-Naṣīr al-Anṣārī ad-Dimašqī (634–720 H) who went daily to the grave of his father;[149] also, ᶜAlī is said to have visited the tombs of Fāṭimah and the Prophet once a week.[150] In bigger cities, there were so many shrines that over the centuries a time-table was developed, assigning each day to the visitation of one or several tombs.[151] In addition, according to other Traditions, the Prophet as well as the first caliphs visited the martyrs' tombs at the beginning of each year,[152] a practice not attested for later centuries. Finally, there are several other days on which the visitation of tombs is considered recommended, such as certain days after the burial (after three days, then after 15 and 40 days) as well as on festive days (at ᶜĀšūrāᵓ, during the Ramaḍān, during the night of *an-niṣf min Šaᶜbān*,[153] etc.).[154]

Strangely enough, in some cases only rather elaborate time-tables of visitation were said to result beneficial to the visitor: thus somebody visiting the tomb of Abū ᶜAbd Allāh al-Ḥusayn b. Aḥmad al-Bayṭār (d. 363 H) first on three Saturdays which follow each other (*mutawāliyah*), then on three Saturdays which do not follow each other (*mutafarriqah*), would obtain "the fulfillment of his needs".[155] Prayers are heard, we are told, at the tomb of the mystic Abū Ǧaydah b. Aḥmad al-Yazġīšanī (d. after 360 H) if it is visited on four (or forty) consecutive Wednesdays.[156]

147 UdfṬāliᶜ p. 300 = Gramlich: *Wunder* p. 401.

148 IZayKawākib p. 30.

149 DK V p. 46. For another case, see YāfNašr p. 20.

150 AṬālibAmālī p. 87.

151 See de Jong: *Cairene Ziyāra-Days* pp. 35-9 (with a detailed discussion of the reasons of why certain days were established as visitation-days in Cairo); for the weekly visitation schedule of shrines in Algiers, see Dermenghem: *Culte des saints* p. 125, n. 1; for the visitation-days in an-Naǧaf and Karbalāᵓ, see Nakash: *Visitation of the Shrines* pp. 163f.

152 ᶜARazMuṣ 6716 (III pp. 573f.); ᶜAynīᶜUmdah VI p. 435; SamWafāᵓ III p. 932; SuyŠṢudūr p. 281. *Cf.* also WāqMaġ I pp. 312f.; BayDal III p. 308; DimSīrah pp. 274f.

153 At mid-Šaᶜbān, religious festivities and exercises are held in the night preceding the 15th. Praying for the dead during that night will bring them, according to popular belief, the forgiveness of sins. In addition, on this night God is said to descend to the lowest Heaven; for further details, see EI² IX p. 154 (A.J. Wensinck) and IRaǧLaṭāᵓif pp. 142ff.

154 See the detailed listing of such days in al-Albānī: *Aḥkām al-ǧanāᵓiz* pp. 258f.

155 ŠīrŠadd p. 105.

156 al-Marrākušī: *Iᶜlām* I p. 186.

2.5. Visitation of tombs by women

2.5.1. The legal debate

In view of the debate concerning the visitation of tombs by men, what, then, was said about women visiting the cemeteries? A good overview of the problems involved in this question is provided by the detailed exposition by Ibn Ḥağar al-ᶜAsqalānī on whose broad learning we already have relied upon before:

> "As to women, opinions are in conflict. Most (scholars) held the opinion that women must be included in this permission (to visit tombs) which is valid universally (...). This view is based on the argument that the Prophet did not reproach a certain woman sitting at a tomb, thus his implicit agreement proves the point made.[157] Another to have understood the permission to be valid for both men and women was ᶜĀʾišah (...) who was seen visiting the grave of her brother ᶜAbd ar-Raḥmān.[158] When she was asked 'Did not the Prophet prohibit this?' she replied 'Yes, he had prohibited this, but then he (changed his mind and) firmly recommended the visitation of tombs'.[159] Others held that the permission is valid only for men, whereas women are not allowed to visit graves. This was the conviction of Abū Isḥāq (aš-Šīrāzī, d. 476 H) (...) who relied upon a report from ᶜAbd Allāh b. ᶜUmar (d. 73 H) (...) that contains the passage: 'May God curse the women who visit the graves!'[160] (...) But al-Qurṭubī said, 'This curse refers only to those women who are excessive in their visits'".[161]

The case of ᶜĀʾišah visiting the tomb of her brother ᶜAbd ar-Raḥmān (b. Abī Bakr, d. 53 H) served commonly as an argument for scholars promoting the visits of women to graves. Moreover, we also hear that Fāṭimah frequently went to the tomb of the Prophet's uncle Ḥamzah b. ᶜAbd al-Muṭṭalib (d. 3 H).[162] On the other hand, a negative dictum reported from the Prophet and referred to by Ibn Ḥağar says that he cursed the female visitors of tombs.[163]

Known in different versions (though always with the same wording of the main part), the only point of uncertainty was the Arabic term for "female visitors", either *zāʾirāt (al-qubūr)*[164] or *zawwārāt (al-qubūr)*. The second term seems to indicate,

157 *Cf.* also KirmŠBuḫ VII p. 79; IḤağAḥwāl p. 49; SaḫTuḥfAḥbāb p. 8.

158 *Cf.* also ᶜARazMuṣ 6711 (III p. 570); IḤazmMuḥ V p. 161; IᶜABarrIst II p. 401; ĠazIḥyāʾ (C) IV p. 416; IQudMuġnī II p. 570; MuwMuršid I p. 26; IḤağIṣābah II p. 408; ᶜAynīᶜUmdah VI p. 435; HarMirqātMaf IV p. 82; al-Albānī: *Aḥkām al-ğanāʾiz* p. 181.

159 For this report, see also TirĞāmiᶜ II p. 260 (*ğanāʾiz* 62); IMāğah I p. 500; ḤākMust I p. 376; ĠazIḥyāʾ (C) IV p. 416; ᶜAynīᶜUmdah VI p. 435. *Cf.* also above p. 15.

160 This report is also quoted in IḤāğğMadḫ I p. 251; for further sources, see below note 164.

161 FB III p. 191 (*ğanāʾiz* 31).

162 ᶜARazMuṣ 6713 (III p. 572); ḤākMust I p. 377; ĠazIḥyāʾ (C) IV p. 416; MuwMuršid I p. 26 and 62; ᶜAynīᶜUmdah VI p. 435. This report is severely criticised in ḎahTalḫ I p. 377.

163 ᶜARazMuṣ 6704 (III p. 569); TirĞāmiᶜ II p. 259 (*ğanāʾiz* 61); IMāğah I p. 502; IŠāhNāsiḫ 304-6 (pp. 371f.); ḤākMust I p. 374; ŠīrMuhaḏ I p. 138; ḤāzIᶜtibār p. 101; IQudMuġnī II p. 570; MunḏTarġīb IV p. 358; IQayZād I p. 526; TurkLumaᶜ I p. 218; ᶜAynīᶜUmdah VI p. 434; ŠaᶜrAnwārQudsīyah p. 894; HaytTuḥfMuḥt III p. 201. *Cf.* also HarMirqātMaf IV p. 83.

164 IAŠayMuṣ III pp. 225f. (*ğanāʾiz* 146); IḤanbMusnad III p. 324; ADāʾūd III p. 297 (*ğanāʾiz*

according to the rules of Arabic derivation as understood by most scholars, that only those women are meant who visit cemeteries often, that is, women who are excessive in their visits[165] and, by implication, those who are excessive in their lamentation (*an-nawḥ*).[166] This would then give the report a different turn as not women in general, but rather the frequency of their visitations of tombs and cemeteries was condemned.

Scholars in this case pointed again to the problem of abrogation (*cf.* above p. 15), saying that the dictum might not have been valid any longer after the Prophet had given his general permission to visit tombs: "Some among the scholars hold the opinion that the prohibition (for women) belongs to the period before the Prophet allowed the visitation of tombs. So when he did allow that, the permission was valid for both men and women alike".[167] According to the Hanafite scholar al-ᶜAynī, visiting tombs is therefore allowed in general, no matter whether the visitor was male or female.[168] Before that, al-Ġazālī and other Shafiites, e.g. an-Nawawī,[169] had stressed that visiting tombs was a *sunnah* and so women should also have their part in it, at least given that "a woman visits the cemetery in a decent dress which shields her from the eyes of men".[170] The Hanbalites did not arrive at a uniform opinion, because divergent interpretations were transmitted on the authority of Ibn Ḥanbal, either discouraging the visits of women or considering them as indifferent and identical to visits performed by men.[171]

Women were of course not barred from visiting the Prophet's sepulchre, as al-Qasṭallānī (d. 923 H) notes, rather it was judged *mandūb* ("recommended"), and long before him the Malikite scholar al-Qāḍī ᶜIyāḍ (d. 544 H) had remarked that the wording of the most important report in that context, viz. "who visits my (*sc.* the Prophet's) tomb etc.",[172] must be taken as generally valid (*muṭlaq*), with the implication that it applies to men and women alike;[173] the same might, in analogy, also apply to the tombs of the prophets and other saintly persons (*al-ʾawliyāʾ*).[174]

82); ḤākMust I p. 374; MundTarġīb IV p. 358; ᶜAynīᶜUmdah VI p. 434; KU 42986 (XV pp. 758f.); ŠawkDurr p. 11 and ŠawkŠṢudūr p. 70.

165 This was the opinion of al-Qurṭubī (see above) and al-ᶜAynī, see ᶜAynīᶜUmdah VI p. 435; QasṭIršād II p. 327; RamlīNih III p. 36; al-Albānī: *Aḥkām al-ǧanāʾiz* pp. 185-8; al-Muᶜallimī: *ᶜImārat al-qubūr* p. 156.

166 HarMirqātMaf IV p. 112. For lamentation at burials, see below p. 174.

167 ḤāzIᶜtibār pp. 101f. *Cf.* TirǦāmiᶜ II p. 259; MundTarġīb IV p. 358; QurṭTadk p. 12; ᶜAynīᶜUmdah VI p. 434; HarMirqātMaf IV p. 117.

168 ᶜAynīᶜUmdah VI p. 433. *Cf.* also INuǧNih II p. 210; QasṭIršād II p. 327 and QasṭMaw III p. 405; HarMirqātMaf IV p. 112.

169 According to HarMirqātMaf IV p. 112.

170 ĠazIḥyāʾ (C) IV p. 416.

171 IQudMuġnī II p. 570; ManbTasl (C) pp. 104f. / (M) pp. 100f.

172 For this report, see below p. 46.

173 ᶜIyāḍŠifāʾ (B) II p. 71 / (Š) II p. 84 = HarŠŠifāʾ II p. 149.

174 QasṭIršād II p. 327. *Cf.* also RamlīNih III p. 36.

Nevertheless, the Sunnite scholars did not reach a unanimous position and the differences between the individual legal traditions, and even within those traditions, persisted. The Shafiite scholar an-Nawawī detected three major positions concerning visits to tombs by women: (1) This being forbidden (*harām*) because of the known Tradition "May God curse the female visitors, etc.", (2) its being merely disliked (*makrūh*) and (3) its being indifferent (*mubāḥ*) as long as the women behave properly and do not seduce the men (that is, as long as there is no *fitnah*). Together with the majority of the Shafiites,[175] an-Nawawī himself seems to have taken to the middle position,[176] while other Shafiite authorities before and after him had pronounced the visits of women to be prohibited.[177] (The same opinions were put forward, by the way, with regard to hermaphrodites).[178] Those among the Shafiites who considered visits by women forbidden saw here an analogy with the Prophet having prohibited the participation of women in funeral processions and burials, as some Traditions have it.[179] A similar strand of thought we also find in a Syrian sixth-century treatise on the duties of the market inspector (*muḥtasib*). There we read accordingly that the "*muḥtasib* must stop women from visiting graves, because the Prophet said 'May God curse the women who visit graves'. (...) The most important thing, however, is to prohibit women from attending the burial".[180]

In Shiite literature, the question of women visiting tombs and cemeteries appears much less disputed. Little is said about their visiting "private" graves (i.e. tombs of relatives and the like), because it probably met with no sizeable opposition. It is certainly the case that Shiite women are as much involved in local pilgrimages and the visitation of shrines than their Sunnite counterparts,[181] yet with the difference that this form of "funeral piety" is in general seen positively by Shiite theologians and scholars. In regard to their visitation of the tombs of the Imams, there is wide agreement that this must be considered, in any case, as "desirable" (*mustaḥabb*).[182] In one early Shiite source we even read that "the visitation of al-Ḥusayn's tomb is obligatory for men and women", because it is "a duty imposed by God incumbent on every Muslim" (*farīḍatun mina llāhi wāğibatun ʿalā kulli muslim*).[183]

175 *Cf.* QasṭMaw III p. 405; HarMirqātMaf IV p. 112; RamlīĠāyah p. 152; RamlīNih III p. 36.

176 NawŠMusl VII p. 45 and NawRawḍah II p. 139; TurkLumaʿ I p. 218 (quoting, as it seems, from either ʿIzz ad-Dīn Ibn ʿAbd as-Salām or Ibn Daqīq al-ʿĪd); HaytTuḥfMuḥt III p. 201.

177 ŠīrMuhaḏ I p. 138; *cf.* also ŠaʿrAnwārQudsīyah p. 894.

178 HaytTuḥfMuḥt III p. 200; RamlīNih III p. 36.

179 FB III pp. 186f. (*ğanāʾiz* 29); NawŠMusl VII p. 2; IMāğah I pp. 502f.; IŠāhNāsiḫ 309f. (p. 375). *Cf.* also IḤāğğMadḫ I p. 268. However, if a women had died in child-bed or of intestinal ailment, other women were allowed to be present at the burial, in order to determine whether the deceased woman was pregnant or not; see IḤağIṣābah IV p. 397.

180 ŠayzḤisba p. 127.

181 *Cf.* Betteridge: *Shrines in Shiraz*.

182 ʿĀmilīWas III pp. 339f.

183 IQūlKāmil p. 122.

2.5.2. The peculiar role of the Malikites

Fierce attacks on the right of women to visit tombs and cemeteries are known from a number of Malikites, especially from the eighth-century Egyptian scholar Ibn al-Ḥāǧǧ (d. 737 H), a contemporary of Ibn Taymīyah. In his *Kitāb al-Madḫal* he devotes considerable space (and rhetoric) to this issue:[184]

> "Women must be prohibited from leaving their homes and visiting tombs, even the tombs of their relatives,[185] according to the rulings laid down in the Tradition (*sunnah*) (...). Nevertheless, scholars have put forward three different claims as to women visiting (the cemeteries): first its being prohibited, as said before; second its being allowed on the condition that they observe what is requested by the law (*aš-šarᶜ*), that is, to cover themselves and to behave reservedly; third its being allowed for older women, but prohibited for the younger ones.[186] But you need to know that the said difference of the scholars' opinions only referred to the women of their times (...). With regard to women visiting (the cemeteries) in our days, God forbid that there is anyone from among the learned or virtuous or showing zeal in religious matters to pronounce it allowed! In case it is unavoidable (for women to visit the cemetery), then the legal rules for covering themselves up must be strictly followed, as said before, and they must not take to those vicious manners as we know they show in general".[187]

In the following, Ibn al-Ḥāǧǧ not only deploys a wide range of arguments why access to burial sites, including those of the nearest kin, should be barred to women but he also describes in detail how their visits appeared to him in practice:

> "Let us now speak of women and their conduct when visiting the graves! They ride to and fro on donkeys, and the muleteers touch them and lay their arms around them when they mount or get off. He will put his hand on her leg and she will lay her hand on his shoulder, both her hand and wrist being uncovered and unveiled. (...) It also happens that the woman gossips with the muleteer and speaks to him as if he were her husband or somebody else of her family. What a wondrous thing, then, that her husband or somebody else in charge of her either witnesses this scene directly or knows that it happens when they are not present![188] (...)
> When the women arrive in the cemetery, things become even worse and more disgusting, because their presence leads to numerous scandalous acts, such as women who during their visit walk together with men at night, that is, being hidden from view (by the darkness) and there are many buildings easy to disappear in; the women will uncover their faces and other parts, quite as if they were with their husbands in privacy. Moreover, they will converse with unacquainted men, they will jest and play, they will laugh and

184 The following passages are also analysed in Zepter: *Friedhöfe* pp. 80-3; *cf.* also Berkey: *Culture and society* p. 389.

185 *Cf.* RamlīNih III p. 36.

186 The reason for this being the danger of young women getting involved with the opposite sex, *cf.* IᶜAbdūnTraité p. 59, condemning the presence of young men in the cemetery: "On n'y laissera pas non plus les jeunes gens, les jours de fêtes, se placer dans les allées, de façon à se trouver sur le passage des visiteuses".

187 IḤāǧǧMadḫ I pp. 250f.

188 *Cf.* also TurkLumaᶜ I p. 214.

sing a lot, and all this in a place of humility, contemplation (*iᶜtibār*) and submissiveness! For, truly, this place (i.e. the cemetery) is the first abode (lit. house) of the hereafter and thus it rather requires sadness and fear, contrary to the way those visitors behave. (...) Therefore, whosoever visits such a place is obliged to abstain from jokes and games.[189] If women visit (the cemeteries) in this manner during daylight, one could justly fear that they might commit 'the most abominable act' (*al-mafsadah al-kubrā*, i.e. sexual intercourse or adultery), now please imagine what happens at night![190] (...) Yet it is also prohibited for women to visit (cemeteries) during the day, nay especially at daylight when their beautiful attire shows forth more obviously and the eyes (of the men) will catch sight of their uncovered parts. All this happens without any sign of shame!

Then look – may God have mercy upon me and you! – how the women organise their visitation (of the cemeteries) which they have brought about to serve their own interests! For every shrine they have fixed a certain day, first Friday and then other days as well, in order to find a means to put their wicked intentions into action on more than one day (a week). Thus (in Cairo) they assemble at the shrine of as-Sayyid al-Ḥusayn on Monday, at the shrine of as-Sayyidah Nafīsah on Tuesday and Saturday; on Thursday and Friday they visit the Qarāfah, e.g. the mausoleum of aš-Šāfiᶜī and others, and (the tombs of) their own dead relatives as well".[191]

Not all Malikites, however, shared this hardly conciliatory attitude. Some time before the eighth century H, that is, before the question of the visitation of tombs (*masʾalat ziyārat al-qubūr*) had become such a fashionable topic, the Andalusian Malikite jurist Ibn ᶜAbd al-Barr (d. 463 H) had declared: "The permission (*ʾibāḥah*) to visit tombs is valid for everybody in the same way as before the prohibition was valid for all without exception".[192] This also accords with the view of the Ẓāhirite Ibn Ḥazm[193] and was later taken up by al-Qāḍī ᶜIyāḍ (see above p. 37). As a scholar, Ibn ᶜAbd al-Barr felt first attracted to Ẓāhirism, but ultimately adhered to the Malikite tradition, though not without harbouring great sympathy for the Shafiites. His opinion as to whether women should visit cemeteries, if juxtaposed with the opinion of Ibn al-Ḥāǧǧ, shows the problem we face when speaking about the Malikites, because,

189 Similar invectives were voiced by a seventh-century Hanafite scholar: "In our days, people turned the visitation of tombs into playful amusement (*malᶜabah*) and recreation (*manzahah*) (...), with women intermingling with men, dancing and playing the drum and the lute. They forget about death and their reflection about the hereafter and the Last Day is but little" (TurkLumaᶜ I p. 214).

190 The problem did not only pertain to women but there are also reports that men used the lonely corners of cemeteries (e.g. mausolea in the Cairene Qarāfah) as a convenient place for (homo)sexual intercourse, see SuyŠṢudūr p. 277. In another case, or so we are told, the mystic Abū l-Ḥasan b. aṣ-Ṣāʾiġ as-Sikandarī (d. in the seventh century H) cried out from his tomb when a man and a young boy entered his mausoleum (the text has *maqburah*, but clearly the mausoleum is intended) in order to have sexual intercourse, see ŠaᶜrṬab I p. 162.

191 IḤāǧǧMadḫ I pp. 267-9; *cf.* also Langner: *Historische Volkskunde* p. 22.

192 Cited in ᶜAynīᶜUmdah VI p. 434. *Cf.* also SaḫTuḥfAḥbāb p. 8.

193 IḤazmMuḥ V pp. 160f.; Adang: *Women's Access* p. 89.

notwithstanding the notoriety they have gained for putting forward strict and narrow opinions, this holds true only for a limited number of Malikites.

If we consider the rulings which pertain to aspects of burial and funerary monuments as they are transmitted from Mālik himself, we find him frequently either deviating from other legal traditions or supporting less rigorous claims. Thus, to take up examples already cited on previous pages or still to follow, Mālik is said (1) to have disapproved of the burial within a mosque or the construction of mosques on or around a tomb, with the exception, however, that a mosque could be built in a graveyard not in use any longer; (2) to have advocated the raising or making a mound over the tomb; and (3) to have understood "sitting on /at the grave" only in the specific sense of "defecation" or "urination", but not as a generic synonym for "staying at the tomb" or "visiting the grave". Another facet showing the relative "liberality" of the Malikite tradition can be seen in the discussion whether women should be barred from the funeral and the funeral procession. This was affirmed, on the basis of reports traced back to the Prophet, by a number of Shafiites and the Hanafites,[194] but rejected by Mālik b. Anas[195] and Ibn Ḥazm.[196]

In view of this, it seems difficult to sustain the following interpretation which reflects a common misconception: "The Islamic world west of Egypt is effectively a dead letter so far as the history of medieval mausolea is concerned. It is hard to avoid the conclusion that this – like the virtual absence of book painting – has something to do with the dominance of the Maliki *madhhab* in the area, for that law school took a hard line on the breaches of orthodox practice which these particular visual arts entailed".[197] Of course, hard-liners within the Malikite tradition did exist, with Ibn al-Ḥāǧǧ being the best example, but it is significant that he was living in Egypt and right at the time when the topic of visiting graves and the construction of mausolea was on the agenda of Sunnite scholars, mainly due to the relentless efforts of Ibn Taymīyah. How influential the teachings promoted by a legal tradition really were might be deduced from the fact that the Shafiites and, in part, the Hanbalites were every bit as assiduous in opposing these practices as were the most fanatic among the Malikites, though the region dominated by both Shafiism and Hanbalism – mainly Egypt, Syria and Iraq – is certainly not "a dead letter so far as the history of medieval mausolea is concerned". Thus the link between legal concepts and their architectural expression is not as straightforward as it might seem at first glance.

We possess a number of clear examples of Malikites being extremely supportive of and engaged with regard to the mortuary cult, the veneration of tombs in general and the various practices entailed by doing so. Thus we hear that the Malikite Abū ʿImrān al-Fāsī (d. 430 H) even went so far as to pronounce visiting the Prophet's tomb obligatory (see p. 47). Another Malikite authority resident in Tunis declared it permitted to take earth from a tomb (for blessing), to lay one's hand on it and then to rub one's face at the gravestone.[198] Thus the modern view of the Malikites as a

194 INuǧBaḥr II p. 207.

195 SaḥMudaw I p. 188.

196 IḤazmMuḥ V p. 160; Adang: *Women's Access* p. 89.

197 Hillenbrand: *Islamic architecture* p. 271. For a more complex view of the Malikites and their attitude towards funerary architecture, see Leisten: *Attitudes* p. 17.

198 DabMaʿālim III p. 212.

particularly rigorous and scripturalist legal tradition, largely comparable to the Neo-Hanbalites and their modern followers, is something of a myth, though within the Malikite legal tradition different forces were continously struggling with one another, possibly to a much higher degree than in the remaining legal schools.[199]

Returning to the question of women's visitation of tombs, we soon realise that the Malikite Ibn al-Ḥāǧǧ was by no means the only one in his time to condemn this harshly, and the matter was also of some interest to the secular authorities in Egypt. For example, we are told of Ibn al-Ḥāǧǧ's contemporary al-Amīr ᶜAlāᵓ ad-Dīn aṭ-Ṭabars al-Manṣūrī al-Maǧnūn (d. 708 H) that he "was an upright and pious person (...), notwithstanding (!) the austerity he showed in dealing with women. During festivities he went to the Qarāfah cemetery and punished them severely. Women could not leave their homes under his regime except when they had valid reasons for doing so, such as visiting the public bath or similar things".[200]

The custom of women visiting the Qarāfah cemetery provoked countermeasures starting as early as 253 H when Muzāḥim b. Ḫāqān, the police prefect of Fusṭāṭ, "barred women from attending baths and cemeteries and put the effeminates and (female) mourners into prison";[201] in 402 H, women were again "barred from the visitation of tombs, and thus not a single woman was to be seen in the cemetery during the festivities".[202] Further prohibitive measures of this kind are known from Mamluk times, e.g. from the year 793 H[203] and from the first half of the ninth century H.[204] Other authorities made subtle distinctions, e.g. that women should visit graves only when they had reached a certain age, were married or stayed together, segregated from men.[205] At any rate, they should not overdo their visits, first in order "not to infringe upon the rights (*ḥuqūq*) of their husbands" (that is, by too often staying away from home), and second because "they are prone to crying and screaming and other abominable behaviour".[206]

2.5.3. The character of women and their behaviour

An allegedly specific character of women had been brought up already by the traditionist at-Tirmiḏī who cites another scholar who disliked women visiting the cemeteries "because they show little patience and much anxiety".[207] In another context, women are seen as pernicious elements "messing up" funerary and related practices. Thus the Egyptian historiographer al-Maqrīzī (d. 845 H) relates:

199 A modern Malikite defence of the visitation of tombs, the practices related to it and the efficacy of intercession is contained in al-Marrākušī: *Iᶜlām* I pp. 178-215.

200 MaqrSulūk II p. 51 and NZ VIII p. 230 = Shoshan: *Popular culture* p. 69. *Cf.* also Zepter: *Friedhöfe* p. 80.

201 MaqrḪiṭaṭ I p. 313 = Shoshan: *Popular culture* p. 69.

202 MaqrḪiṭaṭ II p. 287 = Shoshan: *Popular culture* p. 69.

203 IQŠuhbTārīḫ I p. 383; IḤaǧInbāᵓ III p. 76; IFurTārīḫ IX p. 266.

204 See Shoshan: *Popular culture* p. 69 (with further sources).

205 QurṭTaḏk p. 12; ᶜAynīᶜUmdah VI p. 435.

206 ᶜAynīᶜUmdah VI p. 435.

207 TirǦāmiᶜ II p. 259; *cf.* also IQudMuġnī II p. 570; ḤāzIᶜtibār p. 102; ᶜAynīᶜUmdah VI p. 434; QasṭIršād II p. 327; HarMirqātMaf IV p. 117.

> "In the mausoleum (of al-Layṯ b. Saᶜd)[208] the reciters gathered every Saturday night in order to recite the noble Qurᵓān in a beautiful way and they even managed to finish with it in a single nocturnal session.[209] A number of people were attracted to spend the night with them and to gain the blessing conveyed by the recitation. After a while, though, the company started to become indecent when women appeared, together with (abominable) innovations and clamour. It all changed into a very disagreeable performance and nobody would listen anymore to the recitation nor would they pay attention to the sermons".[210]

It was a widespread attitude towards the role of women in society and everyday life which is reflected in the following and similar statements: "Nothing is better for a woman than to remain in the abode of her home, shielded from public view.[211] Many scholars already declared the practice abominable that women leave their houses for prayer, so just imagine if they head for the cemeteries!"[212] And some lines further: "What all this discussion (about women visiting graves and cemeteries) boils down to is nothing other than the verdict that the visiting of tombs by women is disapproved of, nay it is rather forbidden in our times, especially if one keeps in mind the women of Cairo! When they set out for the cemetery, it always leads to immorality (*fasād*) and seduction (*fitnah*)".[213] Seduction in the graveyard was, by the way, a real threat at all times and places, and well-known in that context was the story of Ibn Ḥazm who fell in love during a funeral in a Córdoban cemetery.[214] Ibn al-Ǧawzī relates that a noble of Baghdad noticed a beautiful girl, dressed black in mourning, in a cemetery and felt so attracted by her that he eventually composed some verses in her praise.[215]

As already in the case of Ibn al-Ḥāǧǧ and elsewhere, the comparison between former times and the present led many scholars to choose to overrule legal opinions as they were transmitted from earlier authorities. In other words, the impact of practice tended to influence theoretical views considerably, though practice did not, according to the most widespread accounts, have a place among the sources from which legal rulings and orthopraxy were to be deduced. This point certainly merits further study. Needless to add that to the present day women are among the most

208 For this mausoleum, see MuwMuršid I pp. 408ff.

209 For this practice, see also FāsīᶜIqd II p. 272 and below p. 154.

210 MaqrḪiṭaṭ II p. 463. Similar events are discussed in Langner: *Historische Volkskunde* p. 44.

211 Lit. "than sticking to the (deepest) abyss of her home" (*luzūmu qaᶜri baytihā*). This expression is common to indicate permanent seclusion from the company of people and society in general, see e.g. ISaᶜd VII p. 142 (regarding an ascetic): *kāna yalzamu qaᶜra baytihī* and IMandahFaw II p. 92 (in a report from the Prophet, regarding a woman): *fī qaᶜri baytihā*; *cf.* also WaṭwāṭĠurar p. 463 and WKAS II p. 553 (s.r. *lzm*).

212 ᶜAynīᶜUmdah VI p. 434.

213 ᶜAynīᶜUmdah VI p. 435, anonymously cited in QasṭIršād II p. 327. The word *fitnah* denotes in this context specifically the physical attraction exercised by women upon men.

214 IḤazmṬawq p. 104 and ḌabbīBuġ pp. 100f.; Torres Balbás: *Cementerios* p. 161.

215 Cited in IQaylIthāf p. 443.

frequent of visitors to cemeteries,[216] a fact that still arouses much dismay among Sunnite Muslims of a more severe attitude.[217]

2.6. Summary

The average Sunnite position seems to have been to consider men's visitation of tombs as recommended or desirable, while the visits of women were seen, in many instances, rather negatively. This comes hence close to the view of the Hanafites[218] and Shafiites,[219] whereas fierce attacks on the right of women to visit tombs and cemeteries are especially known from a (limited) number of Malikites and Hanbalites. In Shiism, the visitation performed by both men and women was in general seen as desirable, which sometimes was understood to be on the brink of actually being a religious obligation (especially if the shrines of the Imams were concerned).

Little difference was made in the legal debate whether the visitation led the believers to tombs of a private character (e.g. the graves of parents or relatives) or to tombs which had become the object of an established *ziyārah* and thus had some "public" standing. The visitation of "public" shrines (and in particular the practices this involved) offered more points of criticism than visiting tombs which mattered only to few people, mainly the relatives of the deceased; and in the former case it was rather the accompanying practices which provoked criticism, not the visitation as such. Nevertheless, there were always Sunnite scholars, stemming especially from Malikite and Hanbalite circles, who harshly condemned any form of visitation of tombs. Their most important mouthpiece was the rebellious neo-Hanbalite Ibn Taymīyah whose fervour led him to recall even the beneficial effects of the visitation of the Prophet's sepulchre in Medina into question.

The dispute which Ibn Taymīyah generated and which was to occupy the activity of eighth-century scholars and generations to come will be treated further below. The first decades of the eighth century H were the period during which the question of visitation (*mas'alat ziyārat al-qubūr*) had reached the utmost importance in Sunnite Islam and the peak of the scholars' attention. The controversies about this question could even lead to violent clashes. This struggle over the *ziyārah* continued, albeit less vigorously, for several centuries, generating a whole literary genre *sui generis*, though from the beginning the endeavour of Ibn Taymīyah and his followers was a lost cause. As Christopher Taylor correctly remarked, Ibn Taymīyah was not "the ardent spokesman for the cultural and religious elite", but "the persecuted champion of a minority position among his colleagues".[220]

That the opponents of visitation were fighting a battle that eventually could not

216 *Cf.* Wirth: *Orientalische Stadt* p. 425.

217 *Cf.* Mabrūk: *Bidaʿ*, *passim*.

218 INuğBaḥr II p. 210.

219 *Cf.* ŠirMuhaḏ I p. 138; NawRawḍah II p. 139; INaqʿUmdah p. 241; ArdabAnwār I p. 124; QasṭIršād II p. 327 and QasṭMaw III p. 405; RamlīNih II p. 35.

220 Taylor: *Vicinity of the Righteous* p. 222.

be won becomes clear from the reports, told in various biographical accounts, about the much-attended funeral of Ibn Taymīyah – "nothing of his shroud was left when the corpse reached the cemetery", i.e. many people had successfully grasped a piece of it – and the scenes of devotion witnessed later at his tomb.[221] Yet his was not the only known case in which the teaching of a devout Hanbalite was belied at the moment he was deposited in his tomb. Much more striking is the case of ᶜAbd Allāh al-Anṣārī, the patron-saint of Harāt, who "although strictly opposed to any form of saint worship on account of his Hanbalite convictions, (...) ironically became the focus of a veneration cult".[222] Likewise, so many people gathered at the tomb of Ibn Ḥanbal after his burial, that "the sultan (*sic*) sent his forces of order who occupied the site and barred the visitors, for fear of public uproar (*fitnah*)". However, the crowd which materialised at that site was so large that access to Ibn Ḥanbal's tomb was only possible one week after the burial, or so we are told in Ibn Ḥanbal's hagiography.[223]

In practice, many Muslims never ceased to visit tombs and cemeteries regularly; the well-off and the powerful never ceased to build sumptuous mausolea or to have tomb-mosques constructed. Nor did the Muslims abstain, as called for by Ibn Taymīyah and his pupils, from approaching the shrines of saintly men (and women) or to ask the Prophet's intercession (*šafāᶜah, wasīlah*) and to visit his sepulchre.

3. *The visitation of the Prophet's sepulchre in Medina*

Of all tombs visited and venerated throughout the Islamic world, the sepulchre of the Prophet in Medina has always been, from the first centuries of Islam and for obvious reasons, of primary importance to the Muslim community.[224] It is commonly called *al-ḥuǧrah aš-šarīfah*, "the noble apartment", *al-qabr aš-šarīf*, "the noble tomb", or simply *ar-rawḍah*, "the garden" (see below).

The Prophet's grave is also the "Holy Sepulchre", *la sacra tomba* par excellence; Lisān ad-Dīn Ibn al-Ḫaṭīb, to mention but him, called it in a poem *al-qabr al-muqaddas*

221 For the general religious and cultural significance of public funerals of famous scholars and other known indiduals, see Zaman: *Funeral processions*.

222 Subtelny: *Cult of Anṣārī* p. 378 and *passim* for the detailed description of how this cult was organised in the Tīmūrid period.

223 IǦawzīManIḤanbal p. 418.

224 One of the best pre-modern descriptions of the tomb and its surroundings offers IǦubRiḥlah (B) pp. 168-73 and 177-81 (fully quoted in ŠarŠMaq II pp. 151-4); the most detailed account, covering the entire history of the complex up to the beginning of the tenth century H, is found in the second volume of SamWafāʾ.

("the sanctified tomb" or "the sacred tomb"),[225] whereas in one of his *Kunstbriefen* he refers to it as *at-turbah al-muqaddasah* ("the sacred mausoleum").[226]

3.1. General remarks

More than any other tomb in the Islamic world, the Prophet's sepulchre is considered a source of blessing for the visitor. In a famous report, attributed to the Prophet himself and edited by ad-Dāraquṭnī (d. 385 H) and many others, we read: "He who visits my grave will be entitled to my intercession" (*man zāra qabrī wağabat lahū šafāʿatī*) or, according to a different version: "I will intercede for those who have visited me, *or* my tomb" (*man zāranī*, or *man zāra qabrī, kuntu lahū šafīʿan*).[227] Another Tradition says that paying the Prophet a visit after his death will be like having paid him a visit during his lifetime", viz. *man zāranī baʿda mawtī* (var. *wafātī, mamātī*) *fa-kaʾannamā* (var. *kāna ka-man*) *zāranī fī ḥayātī*,[228] sometimes with the significant addition: "And who dies in one of the *ḥaramayn* (i.e. in Mecca or Medina) will be (...) among the true believers safe from the Fire (*al-ʾāminīna*) on the Day of Accounting".[229] They will also be entitled to the Prophet's intercession.[230]

All these reports are shared by Sunnites and Shiites alike, though the ways of transmission differ. It is noteworthy that in very early sources, e.g. the *Muṣannaf* by ʿAbd ar-Razzāq aṣ-Ṣanʿānī, we read only the following: *mān zāranī – yaʿnī man ʾatā l-Madīnata – kāna fī ğiwārī*, "Who visits me – i.e. who comes to Medina –

225 IḪaṭDīwān I p. 347; MN II p. 38 (v. 39). For the Shiites, the tomb of al-Ḥusayn is also a "holy sepulchre" (*ḍarīḥ muqaddas*), see al-Amīn: *Miftāḥ* II p. 283.

226 IḪaṭIḥāṭah IV p. 526; IĞubRiḥlah (B) pp. 168-72 calls it *ar-rawḍah al-muqaddasah*, "the sacred Garden (of Paradise)", *al-qabr al-muqaddas* and *at-turbah aṭ-ṭāhirah al-muqaddasah*. However, the expression *ar-rawḍah al-muqaddasah* was also applied to the tombs of mystics, see ŠīrŠadd pp. 88f. and RCEA 5172f. (703 H, Iranian, on the tomb of M. b. Bakrān).

227 DīnMuğāl I p. 440; IQūlKāmil pp. 11 and 13f.; IBābManLā II p. 338; KulKāfī IV p. 548; BaySunan V p. 245; ṬūsīTahḏ VI p. 4; ĠazIḥyāʾ (C) IV p. 417; ʿIyāḍŠifāʾ (B) II p. 71 / (Š) II p. 83 = HarŠŠifāʾ II p. 149; IĞawzīWafā p. 817; INağDurrah p. 397; ŠarŠMaq II p. 151; ṬabQirā p. 627 and 682; SubkīŠifāʾ pp. 5-20 and 29-36 (the most detailed entry); MarğBahğah II p. 378; ḤurRawḍ pp. 354f.; INāṣMağlis p. 28; QasṭMaw III p. 404; DiyTārḪamīs II p. 174; HaytTuḥfZuw p. 30 (with a similar report from ʿAlī) and p. 67; ʿĀmilīWas III p. 263; MağlBihār C p. 140; KU 12371 (V p. 135) and 42583 (XV p. 651).

228 IQūlKāmil p. 13; BaySunan V p. 246; ʿIyāḍŠifāʾ (B) II p. 71 / (Š) II pp. 83f. = HaytTuḥfZuw pp. 29f. = HarŠŠifāʾ II p. 149; IĞawzīWafā p. 816; INağDurrah p. 397; ṬabQirā pp. 627f.; ṬūsīTahḏ VI p. 3; SubkīŠifāʾ pp. 20-7; MarğBahğah II p. 378; ḤurRawḍ p. 355; DiyTārḪamīs II p. 174; ʿĀmilīWas III p. 260 and 263; KarKawākib pp. 150f.; MağlBihār C pp. 140, 143 and 159; KU 12368 (V p. 135) and 42582 (XV p. 651); al-Amīn: *Miftāḥ* II p. 9. Told of al-Ḥusayn in ʿĀmilīWas III p. 453. *Cf.* also Donaldson: *Shiʾite Religion* p. 147.

229 DīnMuğāl I p. 444; BaySunan V p. 245; ʿIyāḍŠifāʾ (B) II p. 79 / (Š) II p. 93 = HarŠŠifāʾ II p. 166; ṬabQirā pp. 628, 654 and 683; SubkīŠifāʾ pp. 30-2; QasṭMaw III p. 404.; HaytTuḥfZuw p. 31. Very similar KulKāfī IV p. 548, parallel on p. 558.

230 *Cf.* IQūlKāmil p. 13; IBābManLā II p. 338; TMD LII p. 33; MağlBihār C p. 139 and 142; KU 12371-3 (V pp. 135f.); Memon: *Ibn Taimīya's Struggle* p. 289; al-ʿAffānī: *Sakb* I p. 77.

will be under my protection".[231] This wording, which does not mention the Prophet's death, would refer rather to those who came to him *during his life*, with the Prophet granting them his protection, as for example in the case of pagan Meccans who had fled to Medina. Only a detailed analysis of this complex material from Tradition could show whether these Traditions did not at all refer to the visitation of the Prophet's tomb initially, but rather to visiting his person while alive, or whether the visitation of his sepulchre was intended from the very beginning.

The Prophet's tomb was also a major element in dreams or visions. This is well illustrated by a story told by the jurist Abū Ḥanīfah and cited in later sources: he saw himself in a dream digging up (*nbš* I) the Prophet's tomb and when he asked Muḥammad Ibn Sīrīn (the famous interpreter of dreams) about its meaning he was told: "Nobody from among the people of our age should have had that dream. (...) But if you are right in that you will be the one to revive the *sunnah* of your Prophet".[232] Not surprisingly, this vision of opening the Prophet's tomb reappears in Arabic monographs about dreams. There we read accordingly that anybody digging up the Prophet's tomb will renew (or revive) his *sunnah*, whereas the motif in general – opening somebody else's tomb – was interpreted to mean that the person in question will follow, or desires to follow, the way of life (*ṭarīqah*) of the buried person.[233]

That visiting the Prophet's tomb (*ziyārat qabr an-nabī* or simply *az-ziyārah*) was permissible or even to be encouraged was claimed to be unanimously agreed upon by all Muslims (*ʾiğmāʿ al-ʾummah*),[234] including the Shiites. One fifth-century Malikite scholar, viz. Abū ʿImrān al-Fāsī, even went so far as to pronounce visiting the Prophet's tomb "obligatory" for every believer,[235] a statement quite close to what Ibn Ḥazm had to say about the visitation of tombs in general and purportedly backed by an utterance of Mālik according to which it is obligatory to travel to the tomb of the Prophet.[236] The attitude of Mālik remains, however, ambiguous, because he is reported as having disapproved of someone saying "I visited the tomb of the Prophet etc." (see above p. 27).

Others, e.g. al-Qāḍī ʿIyāḍ, termed the visitation of the Prophet's sepulchre merely a unanimously accepted *sunnah*[237] or, like Ibn Taymīyah, did not consider it at all a practice in compliance with Islamic precepts and therefore unnecessary (see below). However, scholars who had come to stay at Mecca during the lifetime of Ibn Taymīyah but did not visit the Prophet's sepulchre in Medina were criticised for

231 ʿARazMuṣ 17166 (IX p. 267); *cf.* MarğBahğah II p. 378.

232 IḤamdTaḏk IX p. 311; slightly different and abridged in ḤurRawḍ p. 203. A similar story is also told about the Malikite jurist Saḥnūn, see DabMaʿālim II pp. 103f.

233 ẒāhIšārāt p. 245; NābTaʿṭīr II p. 139.

234 ʿAynīʿUmdah VI p. 435.

235 SubkīŠifāʾ p. 68; IʿAHādīṢārim p. 254; QasṭMaw III p. 403; HaytTuḥfZuw p. 65.

236 One tried to belittle this "obligation" by saying that Mālik meant "the obligation in the sense of its being preferable" (*wuğūb nadb*), not "the obligation in the sense of compulsion" (*wuğūb farḍ*), see ʿIyāḍŠifāʾ (B) II p. 72 / (Š) II p. 84 = HarŠŠifāʾ II p. 150.

237 ʿIyāḍŠifāʾ (B) II p. 71 / (Š) II p. 83 = QasṭMaw III p. 404 = HaytTuḥfZuw p. 59 = HarŠŠifāʾ II p. 149; SubkīŠifāʾ p. 65.

this by their colleagues.[238] For later adherents to the basic doctrines of Ibn Taymīyah, such as the twelfth-century Indian traditionist Walīy Allāh ad-Dihlawī, the sepulchre of the Prophet remained an important place nevertheless, possessing a deep spiritual dimension, though the visitation of tombs in general was seen by him less positively.[239]

The Shiites almost universally upheld the belief in the beneficial effects of the visitation of the Prophet's sepulchre (rewarding the visitor with Paradise)[240] and thus declared it "desirable" (*mustaḥabb*) without restrictions.[241] Among the Shiites, this was often combined with extolling the visit to the tombs of members of his family. Reportedly, the Prophet told al-Ḥusayn (or, in some versions, al-Ḥasan): "My dear son, whosoever comes to visit me during my life or after my death or visits your father or your brother or yourself: I will truly be obliged to visit him on the Day of Resurrection in order to take away his sins".[242]

3.1.1. "A garden of the gardens of Paradise"

Visiting the sepulchre of the Prophet was for the visitor not only an important (or even the only necessary) step towards Paradise, but the tomb itself had been brought into direct connection with Paradise.

As a famous report – cherished by Sunnites and Shiites alike and widely quoted – has it, the Prophet's tomb, or more specifically the zone between the tomb (*qabr*, *huğrah* or *bayt*) and the pulpit in the Prophet's mosque, is a *rawḍatun min riyāḍi l-ğannah*, "a garden of the gardens of Paradise".[243] This Tradition was later also to become a common element in poetry in praise of the Prophet.[244] The distance between the pulpit and the tomb is given, on the authority of early sources such as

238 As e.g. by Nağm ad-Dīn al-Iṣbahānī (d. 721 H), see ŠḎ VI p. 55.

239 *Cf.* Sirriyeh: *Sufis and Anti-Sufis* pp. 5-8.

240 ᶜĀmilīWas III p. 429.

241 *Cf.* ᶜĀmilīWas III p. 260.

242 IBābManLā II p. 345; KulKāfī IV p. 548 (and a similar report on p. 579, addressed to ᶜAlī); ṬūsīTahḏ VI p. 4 and 40; ᶜĀmilīWas III p. 256-8; MağlBihār C pp. 140-2.

243 FB III p. 90 (*faḍl aṣ-ṣalāh fī masğid Makkah* 5); IV p. 123 (*faḍāʾil al-Madīnah* 12); XI p. 568 (*riqāq* 53); IQūlKāmil p. 16; KulKāfī IV pp. 549-52; ANuḤilyah III pp. 26 and 264; ANuAḫbIṣf II p. 276; BaySunan V pp. 246f. (*bāb fī r-rawḍah*); TB IV p. 403; ṬūsīMiṣbaḥ p. 493 and ṬūsīTahḏ VI pp. 7f.; (very detailed:) ᶜIyāḍŠifāʾ (B) II pp. 74 and 78f. / (Š) II pp. 87 and 91f. = HarŠŠifāʾ II pp. 154 and 164f.; IĞawzīWafā p. 259; NawŠMuslim IX pp. 161f.; IĞubRiḥlah (B) p. 170; INağDurrah pp. 362f.; QazwĀṯār p. 108; ṬabQirā pp. 681f.; SubkīŠifāʾ p. 74; ZarkAḥkām p. 251; ḤurRawḍ p. 355; IḤağRafᶜ pp. 448f.; QasṭMaw III p. 416 and 420; ŠāmīSubul X p. 387; ᶜĀmilīWas III pp. 270f.; MağlBihār XLIII p. 185 and C p. 146; al-Amīn: *Miftāḥ* II p. 26. For the term *rawḍah*, see also Torres Balbás: *Cementerios* p. 133. The area called *rawḍah* in the Prophet's mosque is believed to include also the tomb of Fāṭimah, see ᶜĀmilīWas III pp. 288f. and below p. 505.

244 IḪaṭIḥāṭah III p. 113 (from a poem by Ibn Marzūq at-Tilimsānī, *sarīᶜ*: *wa-rawḍatu l-ğannati bayna rawḍatin wa-minbarin*); MN I p. 382 (from a poem by al-Buraᶜī: *ʾilā rawḍatin mā*

Ibn Zabālah's *History of Medina*, as 53 cubits (*ḏirāᶜ*).[245] The scholars were uncertain whether this report actually intended to say that the tomb as such will once be brought into the garden of Paradise, whether the sepulchre actually is already part of the Paradise or whether the expression must be understood metaphorically, thus meaning that whoever cares about it or visits it will be rewarded with Paradise.[246] In addition, the Shiites saw here a connection with the fact that Fāṭimah was allegedly buried in that area, hence the Prophet is said to have called the space between his tomb and the pulpit a garden merely because Fāṭimah was buried there.[247]

That the report *qabrī rawḍatun* etc. did not go unquestioned in early Muslim scholarship is shown by the fact that Ibn Qutaybah (d. 276 H) in his treatise on problematic reports devotes considerable space to this very Tradition:

> "The opponents say, 'A Tradition which belies speculation and observation and goes against other reports and the Qurʾān. You transmit the utterance of the Prophet: *This pulpit of mine rests on a canal opening of the canal openings of Paradise, and the space between my tomb and my pulpit is a garden of the gardens of Paradise* (...), yet you transmit other reports that the Paradise is in the Seventh Heaven, thus there is a difficulty and a contradiction'.
>
> Abū Muḥammad (i.e. Ibn Qutaybah) replies: We argue that there is no difficulty and no contradiction here. The reason for that is that the Prophet in his utterance *The space between my tomb and my pulpit is a garden of the gardens of Paradise* did not intend to say that this area is a garden in the real sense (*bi-ᶜaynihī*), but only that prayer at that spot (...) leads into Paradise and thus is part of it. (...) [Ibn Qutaybah now quotes the following Tradition] from Ǧābir b. ᶜAbd Allāh al-Anṣārī who reported that the Messenger of God came forward to them and said, 'Pasture in the gardens of Paradise!', but they asked 'Where are the gardens of Paradise, O Messenger of God?' He replied, '(They are) the gatherings where His name is mentioned (*maǧālis aḏ-ḏikr*)!'. (...) Thus in the same manner the gatherings where His name is mentioned lead to the gardens of Paradise and therefore they are part of it. The same is true of the utterance of ᶜAmmār b. Yazīd: 'Paradise is under the swords and under the shadow of the swords'. He intends to say that *ǧihād* leads to Paradise (...).[248] Some people also preferred the following wording: *The space between my tomb and my pulpit is (on earth) opposite of a garden of the gardens of Paradise (in Heaven)* (...), thus they made it part of Paradise inasmuch there was on earth something corresponding to what is in Heaven. The first wording is preferable in my view, and God knows best".[249]

bayna qabrin wa-minbarin); MN I p. 532 (from the *Tāʾīyah* of Bahāʾ ad-Dīn as-Subkī, *ṭawīl*: *wa-ʾaṣbaḥa bayna l-qabri wa-l-minbari llaḏī * yalīhi mina l-ǧannāti ʾaᶜẓamu rawḍatī*); NawāǧīMaṭāliᶜ p. 190 (*ḫafīf*): *mā bayna ṯarā minbarī š-šarīfi wa-qabrī * min bābi ǧinānin tafūḥu rawḍatu ġufrān*).

245 FB IV p. 125; IDaybaᶜḤad II p. 933.

246 See the discussion of these points in FB IV p. 125; NawŠMuslim IX pp. 161f.; INaǧDurrah p. 363; IAĞamrBahǧah I pp. 464 and 466f.; ZarkAḥkām pp. 251f.; IDaybaᶜḤad II p. 933.

247 IBābManLā II p. 341.

248 These arguments are also voiced in later writings, e.g. FB IV p. 125.

249 IQutTaʾwīl pp. 82f.

The *rawḍah* area around the Prophet's tomb, viz. *ar-rawḍah al-kubrā*, "the Greater Garden",[250] became a favourite place of study during the Mamluk period, especially for such important prophetological books as al-Qāḍī ʿIyāḍ's *aš-Šifā bi-taʿrīf ḥuqūq al-Muṣṭafā* which had already been introduced to the Ḥiǧāz around 600 H, some two generations after the author's death in 544 H. Although we have evidence of the practice of studying at the Prophet's sepulchre from the early Ayyubid period onwards,[251] it only became a widespread phenomenon during the ninth century H when Medina was on the verge of rivalling Cairo as the most important centre of Sunnite scholarship. The motif of the Prophet's tomb being a "garden of Paradise" also developed into a major theme of Sunnite poetry in praise of the Prophet (*madḥ an-nabī*).

3.1.2. Tombs and cemeteries as a "garden"

Apart from what was said about the Prophet's sepulchre, there are Traditions which describe every tomb of a pious Muslim as being a "garden of the gardens of Paradise", often with the significant addition "or a pit of the pits of the Fire (of Hell)";[252] another report, transmitted solely by Ibn Mandah, has the divergent wording: "The believer in his tomb is in a green garden".[253] This concept is based on the idea that even during his stay in the grave the deceased person, on the condition that he led a pious and God-pleasing life, will enjoy the Bliss of Paradise,[254] though this was only with difficulty harmonised with the idea of the "Chastisement of the Grave" which affects every deceased.[255] On preserved epitaphs, we therefore find the wish that "God may make this tomb a garden of the gardens of Paradise".[256] The concept of the garden also provides the common link to other current poetical images: the tomb, a blossoming garden, emanates fragrance, and sprinkling the grave was like a

250 E.g. in a verse by Ibn Hilāl aṣ-Ṣafadī (A. b. Yūsuf, d. Cairo 738 H): MaqrMuq I p. 757.

251 E.g. MaqrMuq V p. 696 and DāʾūdīṬab II p. 151 about aš-Šāṭibī, staying at Medina as early as 617 H: *samiʿa (min fulānin) bayna qabrihī wa-minbarihī*.

252 ṮaʿālṮimār p. 696; IĞawzīṢafwah II p. 150; TMD XLII p. 497 (as said by ʿAlī); MundṮarġīb IV p. 238; TurkLumaʿ I p. 482; ṬabMiškāh p. 305; IZayKawākib p. 172; ManbTasl (C) p. 207 / (M) p. 200; ḤurRawḍ p. 118; SuyBušrā pp. 31, 35 and 42; MaʿbIstiʿdād p. 27; MaǧlBihār VI pp. 214, 218, 267 and 275; al-ʿAffānī: *Sakb* I p. 661; KU 42109 (XV p. 546) and 42397 (XV p. 603). al-Qazwīnī cites the following Tradition from the Prophet, concerning Samarqand: "There is a fountain of the fountains of Paradise (*al-ǧannah*), a tomb of the tombs of the prophets and a garden of the gardens of Paradise (*rawḍatun min riyāḍi l-ǧannah*)" (QazwĀṯār p. 510). *Cf.* also Leisten: *Architektur für Tote* pp. 80f.

253 *al-muʾminu fī qabrihī fī rawḍatin ḫaḍrāʾa*, cited in SuyBušrā p. 43.

254 *Cf.* ŠirŠadd p. 12.

255 For details, see Volume I, Chapter 2.

256 RCEA 82 (192 H, Upper Egypt), 93 (197 H, Egypt), 96 (198 H, Egypt), 121 (202 H, Egypt), 200 (215 H, Egypt), 204 (216 H, Fusṭāṭ), 207 (216 H, Egypt), 223 (218 H, Upper Egypt), 249 (221 H, Fusṭāṭ), 260 (224 H, Egypt), 361 (239 H, Fusṭāṭ), 3646 (605 H, Central Asia), 5172 (703 H, Iranian), 5177 (704 H, Damascus) and 797 017 (Akšehir); see Volume I pp. 149ff.

beneficial rainshower; the practice of putting flowers upon tombs also contributed to the concept of the grave as a garden.

All these notions, most of which going back to pre-Islamic times, loom large in Islamic thought and literature; they are dealt with in more detail in Chapter 2. For the time being, it must suffice to cite only three illustrative examples of how these images could appear in poetry. The first example stems from a poem, composed by Diᶜbil b. ᶜAlī al-Ḫuzāᶜī (*c.* 148–244 H), mourning the death of al-Ḥusayn (*kāmil*):

مَا رَوْضَةٌ إلاَّ تَمَنَّتْ أَنَّهَا * لَكَ مَضْجَعٌ ولَخَطِّ قَبْرِكَ مَوْضِعُ

"There is no garden that does not wish * to be your deathbed[257] and the spot where your tomb is traced out!"[258]

The second example, much richer in images and conceptual power, is two verses which are part of a poem by Abū l-Qāsim al-Biǧāʾī al-Qaṣṣār from Alexandria, mourning the death of the Mamluk sultan an-Nāṣir Muḥammad (d. 741 H) (*kāmil*):

فَغَدَا بِهِ القَبْرُ الَّذِي قَدْ حَلَّهُ * رَوْضاً يَفُوحُ كَنَشْرِ مِسْكٍ عَاطِرِ
وَكَأَنَّهُ مُذْ حَلَّ فِيهِ رَوْضَةٌ * مَمْطُورَةٌ قَدْ نُمِّقَتْ بِأَزَاهِرِ

"Thus the tomb in which he has settled became through him * a garden that emanates perfume like sweet-smelling musk that lingers (in the air),
It is as if the tomb, ever since he settled in it, has been a garden, * showered by rain, which was adorned with flowers".[259]

In these lines almost all notions are present which are commonly associated with the binary concept "tomb = garden", yet the poet does not simply reiterate the known concepts but adapts them in a particular way and thus gives an important twist to the message: instead of the tomb being a garden because it is the gateway to Paradise for the deceased one, it is the deceased who, by his outstanding qualities, transforms his tomb into a perfumed garden, sprinkled by rain and adorned by flowers. However, this reversal of the metaphor was nothing new in Mamluk times, because Yaḥyā b. Ziyād al-Ḥāriṯī (d. 207 H) had already composed the line (*ṭawīl*):

وَطَابَ ثَرًى أَصْبَحْتَ فِيهِ وَإِنَّمَا * يَطِيبُ إذَا كَانَ الثَّرَى لَكَ مَضْجَعَا

"The moist earth, in which you came (to be buried), does emanate fragrance, but it only * scents inasmuch the moist earth is *your* (death-)bed!"[260]

257 *maḍǧaᶜ*: for this term, see below p. 345 with note 117 and p. 366.

258 BaṣrīḤam (B) I p. 201 / (C) II p. 30; ṬurayḥīMunt p. 211 and 483 (var. *maḍǧaᶜun*: *turbatun* and *qabrika*: *ǧanbika*). The verse is missing in DiᶜbilDīwān.

259 NuwIlmām IV p. 156. Note also that the much more famous contemporary of al-Biǧāʾī, Ibn Nubātah al-Miṣrī, speaks in one of his mourning poems of the *rawḍatu laḥdin*, "the garden of the burial niche" (INubDīwān p. 74).

260 WriǦurzah p. 107; BaṣrīḤam (B) I p. 235 (var. *ʾaṣbaḥta fīhī*: *ʾafḍā ʾilayka*) / (C) II p. 112. In verses like this we also perceive the strong connection between mourning poetry and panegyrical

The third example is taken from a poem by Šaraf ad-Dīn Ibn ᶜUnayn (M. b. Naṣr Allāh, d. 630 H), mourning the young son of an Ayyubid ruler (*kāmil*):

فَسَقَى ضَرِيحَكَ كُلُّ دَانٍ مُسْبِلٍ * مُتَوَاصِلِ الإبْرَاقِ وَالإرْعَادِ
حَتَّى تُرَى عَرَصَاتُ قَبْرِكَ رَوْضَةً * مَوْشِيَةً كَوَشَائِعِ الأَبْرَادِ

"May every approaching downpour water your grave, * incessantly accompanied by lightning and thunder,
Until the spacious site of your tomb is seen as a garden * embellished like the weaver's spools of garments!"[261]

With lines like these we come close to the notion of the tomb being a garden in connection with and caused by the beneficial watering of the grave. This is studied in further detail in Chapter 2.

Among the Shiites, the *rawḍah*-concept was particularly transferred to the tomb of al-Ḥusayn,[262] to the tomb of Fāṭimah in Medina,[263] and to the town of Kūfah (which was said to contain the tombs of Abraham and Noah as well as of 370 other prophets and 600 trustees of the faith, *ʾawṣiyāʾ*).[264] In the eastern Islamic lands, the term *rawḍah* (viz. Persian *rouẕeh*) soon acquired the general meaning of "shrine" or "venerated tomb" as well as "lamentation" or "mourning dirge" recited at those shrines, with the latter meaning originating from the title of a known tenth-century book recited at shrines, namely the *Rawḍat aš-šuhadāʾ* ("Garden of the Martyrs").[265]

A considerable number of graveyards (or single shrines and tombs) were named *rawḍah* by the Sunnites; in Egypt, the term *rawḍah* was in recent times also conferred to guest facilities provided by well-off Sufi orders and in general attached to some shrine that attracts a sizeable number of non local visitors.[266] The older use of the term *rawḍah* in the sense of "cemetery" (or also "mausoleum", "shrine", or "tomb") seems first to have become current in the Islamic West. The following examples, collected from literary sources and preserved epitaphs, are meant to illustrate this fact (from West to East):

poetry. The latter abounds in lines like the following (*wāfir*): *wa-ʾanta ʾiḏā waṭiʾta turāba ʾarḍin * yaṭību ʾiḏā mašayta bihā t-turābū* ("If you set your foot on the earth of the ground, * the earth emanates fragrance since *you* walked on it": *Aġānī* XII p. 235).

261 Cited in IWāṣilKurūb IV p. 223. The comparison of the second verse is between the rich colouring of precious garments and the colour of the flowers blossoming forth upon the tomb; note also the *taǧnīs* between *wšy* and *wšᶜ*.

262 IQūlKāmil p. 112; KulKāfī IV p. 588; ṬūsīMiṣbaḥ p. 509 and ṬūsīTahḏ VI p. 72; ᶜĀmilīWas III pp. 324 and 400f.; ṬurayḥīMunt p. 72.

263 IBābManLā II p. 341; ṬūsīMiṣbaḥ p. 494; MaǧlBihār VI p. 232 and C pp. 192-6.

264 ᶜĀmilīWas III p. 301. *Cf.* also IQūlKāmil pp. 28f. and MaǧlBihār C p. 389. Parallel Traditions among the Sunnites state that there are 99 prophets buried in Mecca between the corner of the Kaᶜbah and the Zamzam well, see ṬabQirā p. 654.

265 *Cf.* also EI² VIII p. 465 (P. Chelkowski, *s.v.* "Rawḍa-ḫwānī").

266 See Chih: *Rawda*, esp. pp. 58f.

AL-ANDALUS. The jurist and traditionist Abū ᶜAbd Allāh Muḥammad b. Yūsuf b. Saᶜādah al-Mursī (Murcia 496 – Šāṭibah [sp. Játiva] 555 H) was buried "in the *rawḍah* named after Abū ᶜUmar Ibn ᶜAbd al-Barr", that is, the cemetery around the tomb of the famous traditionist and Malikite scholar (d. 463 H);[267] in Córdoba, there was a cemetery called *rawḍat aṣ-ṣulaḥā'* ("Garden of the Righteous");[268] in Seville we hear of the *rawḍat 'Abī Muḥammad aš-Šantarīnī*; in Murcia someone was buried in the *rawḍat Ibn Farağ*;[269] from Almería, we hear of a *rawḍat Banī Ḫāṭimah*,[270] and from Málaga of the *rawḍat Banī Yaḥyā*[271] and the *rawḍat al-Qāḍī 'Abī ᶜAbd Allāh b. al-Ḥasan*.[272]

MAGHRIB. The shrine of Mūlāy Idrīs in Fez has often been called *ar-rawḍah*,[273] and in Fez we hear of the cemetery known as *rawḍat aš-šurafā'* ("Garden of the Nobles")[274] as well as of the *rawḍat al-walīy 'Abī ᶜAbd Allāh Muḥammad b. al-Ḥusayn*, located outside Bāb al-Ğīsah;[275] in Marrakech we know of the cemeteries called *rawḍat al-'umarā'*, *rawḍat aš-šuyūḫ*,[276] and *rawḍat as-Saᶜdīyīn* (the mausoleum of the Saᶜdid rulers; *cf.* **115**). Moroccan literary sources use the term *rawḍah* for either "mausoleum" or "cemetery";[277] the term (with the meaning "tomb") also appears in Moroccan epitaphs, e.g. on a marble slab from Miknās dated 1110 H.[278] In the sense of "tomb", *rawḍah* is used in an early eighth-century writing from Tunisia,[279] and al-Qāḍī ᶜIyāḍ has a passage about "the construction of mausolea and shrines upon tombs" (*binā' … al-qibābi wa-r-rawḍāti ᶜalā l-qubūr*).[280] Until today, *rōḍa* is in Moroccan Arabic used as a generic term for "cemetery".

EGYPT and ḤIĞĀZ. The whole of the Cairene (southern) Qarāfah cemetery has been referred to as *ar-rawḍah*,[281] and Ibn Ğubayr called the tombs of the Qarāfah cemetery summarily *rawḍāt*;[282] one should also recall that, fittingly, the nearby Nile was seen as one of the rivers of Paradise. Certainly unusual, but probably also referring to the Qarāfah cemetery is al-Maqrīzī's expression when he writes that Sirāğ ad-Dīn al-Urmawī (A. b. Maḥmūd, d. 667 H) was buried "in the *rawḍah* underneath the Citadel" (*dufina bi-r-rawḍati taḥta Qalᶜati l-Ğabal*).[283] The shrine of al-Ḥusayn's head in Cairo: Ibn Ğubayr mentions that above the shrine (which is said to contain al-Ḥusayn's head)[284] stylised

267 IAbbTakm II p. 36; MaqqNafḥ (C) II p. 359.

268 *Cf.* also Lévi-Provençal: *Espagne musulman* p. 209, n. 2, and *Historia de España (dir. par Ramón Menéndez Pidal) IV: España musulmana hasta la caída del califato de Córdoba (É. Lévi-Provençal)*, Madrid [5]1982, p. 91, for the death of the caliph ᶜAbd ar-Raḥmān (d. 172 H): "Fué enterrado en una capilla sepulcral (*rawda*) del Alcázar de los emires".

269 IAbbTakm II pp. 86 (Córdoba), 181 (Seville) and 111 (Murcia).

270 IQāḍīDurrah II p. 88.

271 EI[2] VI p. 221.

272 NubQuḍātAnd p. 159.

273 Dermenghem: *Culte des saints* p. 115.

274 al-Marrākušī: *Iᶜlām* II p. 113; ZA I p. 181.

275 IQāḍīDurrah II p. 222; ŠN I p. 286.

276 IAbbTakm II p. 75 and 304; al-Marrākušī: *Iᶜlām* IV p. 378 has *ğabbānat aš-šuyūḫ*.

277 Ibn Zaydān: *Itḥāf* I pp. 174, 209 and *passim*; al-Marrākušī: *Iᶜlām* II pp. 194, 233 and *passim*.

278 Ibn Zaydān: *Itḥāf* I p. 175.

279 ITawSabk p. 116.

280 ᶜIyāḍMad p. 301.

281 MuwMuršid I p. 13 (in a poem).

282 IĞubRiḥlah (B) p. 20 and 22.

283 MaqrMuq I p. 658.

284 For the controversy whether al-Ḥusayn's head was indeed brought by the Fatimid vizier aṣ-

apples of gold were appended, "giving it the semblance of a garden (*rawḍah*)"; afterwards, he repeatedly calls the area around the shrine *ar-rawḍah*. Later on, he refers to different mausolea in the Medinan Baqīᶜ cemetery as a *rawḍah*, thus making this word almost synonymous in use with *qubbah* or *mašhad*.[285] The very first example of the use of *rawḍah* in the sense "tomb" and employed in funerary epigraphy stems from Egypt (RCEA 631: 259 H), see Volume I p. 148f.

SYRIA and ANATOLIA. The Hanbalite cemetery in aṣ-Ṣāliḥīyah around the mausoleum of Muwaffaq ad-Dīn Ibn Qudāmah was called *ar-rawḍah* or *rawḍat al-ǧabal*, with reference to the Qāsiyūn mountain (north of Damascus);[286] *rawḍah* also appears as a name for an area in the Marǧ ad-Daḥdāḥ cemetery (i.e. the Bāb al-Farādīs area) in down-town Damascus.[287] In a large number of seventh and eighth-century H epitaphs from Anatolia the tomb is frequently referred to as a *rawḍah*.[288]

IRAN. The cemetery around the tomb of Abū ᶜAbd Allāh Muḥammad b. Ḫafīf "aš-Šayḫ al-kabīr" (d. 371 H) in Šīrāz was called *ar-Rawḍah al-Kabīrīyah*. Likewise in Šīrāz, we hear of the mausoleum of al-Bayṭār (d. 363 H) as *rawḍat aš-šayḫ Ḥusayn al-Bayṭār*, used synonymously with *mazār aš-šayḫ Ḥusayn*.[289]

It is worth pointing out that the term *rawḍah* was, for its multiple connotations, a first choice for the titles of works dealing with graveyards or single shrines. In particular, we know of the following books: (1) *ar-Rawḍah al-ʾanīsah bi-faḍl mašhad as-Sayyidah Nafīsah*,[290] (2) *ar-Rawḍah fī ʾasmāʾ man dufina bi-l-Baqīᶜ* (also *ar-Rawḍah al-firdawsīyah wa-l-ḥaḍīrah al-qudsīyah* or *Rawḍat al-firdaws*), (3) *ar-Rawḍah ar-rayyā fī man dufina bi-Dārayyā* and (4) *ar-Rawḍāt fī mazārāt Tabrīz*. These works will be dealt with in detail in Chapter 3.

3.2. Poetry in praise of the Prophet

In Arabic poetry in praise of the Prophet (*madḥ an-nabī*), the tomb of Muḥammad and the pleasant fragrance emanating from it have been often invoked and the visitation of the Prophet's sepulchre was in practice often combined with the rites of the pilgrimage, the pilgrims first performing the *ḥaǧǧ* in Mecca and afterwards passing on to Medina (but not *vice versa*).[291] This procedure is reflected in the expression *al-ḥaǧǧ wa-z-ziyārah*, "pilgrimage and visitation (of the Prophet's tomb)",

Ṣāliḥ Ṭalāʾiᶜ (d. 556 H, the founder of the famous mosque at the Cairene Bāb Zuwaylah) from ᶜAsqalān (Ascalon) to Cairo, see MunKawākib I pp. 148f.

285 IǦubRiḥlah (B) p. 19 (Cairo) and 174 (Medina); also quoted in SamWafāʾ III p. 918.

286 IRaǧḎayl II p. 320; al-ᶜAffānī: *Sakb* I p. 333; *cf.* also IQŠuhbTārīḫ I pp. 13 and 207; IMibrḎayl pp. 17, 25, 52, 54f. and *passim*.

287 MurSilk IV p. 246; MiknāsīIḥrāz pp. 233f.

288 See RCEA 3667 (607 H), 4696 (673 H), 5217 (707 H), 4996 (694 H), 5038 (696 H), 5118 (700 H), 5220 (707 H), 5298 (711 H), 5404 (718 H), 5463 (721 H), 5658 (734 H), 5695 (736 H), 5715 (737 H), 5954 (742 H), 5982 (745 H), 6058 (748 H) and 780 011; *rawḍah* for "tomb" appears also in a poem inscribed on the wall of an Aleppine mausoleum, see al-Ġazzī: *Nahr aḏ-ḏahab* II p. 205.

289 ŠīrŠadd pp. 38 and 106f.

290 Var. *az-Zawrah al-ʾanīsah* etc., see SaḫǦawāhir III p. 1275.

291 *Cf.* SubkīŠifāʾ pp. 27-9 and 38f.

typical of western sources from the third century H onwards and later adopted in the writings from the Islamic East.[292]

The custom of visiting the Prophet's tomb after the pilgrimage was supported by a known (though heavily disputed) report from the Prophet which says: "Who performs the pilgrimage and does not visit me, has shunned me" (... *man lam yazur qabrī*[293] *fa-qad ǧafānī*).[294] Visiting the Prophet's tomb after the pilgrimage was, by the majority of Sunnite legal scholars, considered recommened (*mustaḥabb* and *mandūb*).[295] Some Shiites, who were on their way to the Ḥiǧāz, left graffiti in sixth-century Fatimid Egypt asking God for "the pilgrimage towards the sacrosanct House of God (i.e. the Kaᶜbah) and the visitation of the Prophet's sepulchre".[296]

The common practice of combining visitation of the Prophet's tomb in Medina and pilgrimage to Mecca led to the adaption of that motif in poetry; during the Mamluk and Ottoman periods it was also common to welcome people after their return from the visitation of the Prophet's sepulchre with poems composed for the occasion. Advice to the contrary, i.e. not to undertake the travel to Medina, was rare and left as good as no mark in literature. Thus the sites in Medina connected to the Prophet, including his sepulchre, already loom large in al-Qāḍī ᶜIyāḍ's ascetic poems (*zuhdīyāt*) which exhibit a strong affinity to the related poetical genre expressing the desire to visit Medina and to perform the pilgrimage,[297] a genre flourishing in the distant West during the fifth to seventh centuries H. However, the theme as such had been known since centuries, as is shown by a poem by the Malikite scholar ᶜAbd al-Malik Ibn Ḥabīb (d. 238 or 239 H) which deals with the visit to Medina and the Prophet's sepulchre;[298] Ibn Ḥabīb was an Andalusian, but he studied in Egypt and Medina.

292 This and similar expressions, linking the *ḥaǧǧ* to the *ziyārat qabr an-nabī*, appear in IᶜAdīmZubdah p. 409; YāfRawḍ pp. 312f. and 377; NuwIlmām IV p. 31; IḤiǧTam p. 301; ḤurRawḍ p. 42; FāsīᶜIqd II p. 325; ḎL VII p. 194 and XI p. 106; SuyḤusnMuḥ II p. 21; IDaybaᶜBuġ p. 208; ᶜUlaymīUns II p. 246; ŠḎ IV p. 86; MuḥḪul III p. 440; Padwick: *Muslim Devotions* p. 144. There is a work by Ibn Musdī (M. b. Yūsuf, d. Mecca 663 H) bearing the title *Kitāb al-Bašārah bi-ṯawāb al-ḥaǧǧ wa-z-ziyārah*: MaqrMuq VII p. 516 and FāsīᶜIqd II p. 435.

293 Var. *man lam yazurnī*.

294 INaǧDurrah p. 397; ṬabQirā p. 627; ITayMaǧm pp. 25, 29 and 35; ITayZiy pp. 19f. (here the report is qualified as an outright lie); Memon: *Ibn Taimīya's Struggle* p. 305; SubkīŠifāᵓ pp. 65-8; MarǧBahǧah II p. 378; ḤurRawḍ p. 355; DiyTārḪamīs II pp. 174 (with a slightly different wording); HaytTuḥfZuw pp. 29f.; HarŠŠifāᵓ II pp. 149f.; KarKawākib p. 150; KU 12369 (V p. 135). In Shiite sources we find the following: "On the Day of Resurrection I will shun those who came to Mecca on pilgrimage and did not pay me a visit in Medina" (IBābManLā II p. 339; KulKāfī IV p. 548; ṬūsīTahḏ VI p. 4; ᶜĀmilīWas III p. 261; MaǧlBihār C p. 140; al-Amīn: *Miftāḥ* II pp. 8f.).

295 See HaytTuḥfZuw p. 77.

296 RCEA 3097f. (534 H).

297 The known poems have been edited in al-ᶜUmarī: *al-Qāḍī ᶜIyāḍ*.

298 Cited in MaqqNafḥ (C) I pp. 55f.

3.2.1. The journey to the Prophet's sepulchre

The obvious place to insert the poetical rendering of the journey to the Prophet's tomb and its eventual visit into a larger composition was the so-called "camel-section" or "travel-section" (*raḥīl*, lit. "setting out"), which could be the middle part of a classical qaṣīdah poem.[299] As in secular praise poetry and panegyrics, the *raḥīl* was stylised to portray the journey of the poet to the person praised. In poetry in praise of the Prophet this journey was consequently adapted for depicting the travel of the poet to the sepulchre of the Prophet and thus to the person praised.

The first example of a fully worked-out *raḥīl* leading to the Prophet's sepulchre in Medina was composed by the Syrian scholar and poet al-Amīn al-Ḥalabī (d. 643 H).[300] He composed only a single known poem in praise of the Prophet, and it was mainly for his wine poetry (*ḫamrīyāt*) that ʿAbd al-Muḥsin had became famous. However, this was in no way seen detrimental to his reputation as a Ḥadīṯ scholar and encomiast of the Prophet. Fittingly the later historian Ibn Kaṯīr – no friend of earthly pleasures as far as we know – wrote about the situation in Damascus in the year 643 H: "Wine was flowing and viciousness was everywhere".[301]

The *Maǧmūʿah* of an-Nabhānī contains al-Amīn al-Ḥalabī's long qaṣīdah poem in praise of the Prophet, commonly known as *al-Qaṣīdah al-lāmīyah fī madḥ an-nabī*.[302] Of 140 verses length, the poem takes its inspiration from the widely known "Mantle Ode" (*Qaṣīdat al-burdah*) by the Prophet's contemporary Kaʿb b. Zuhayr:[303] Being a traditional qaṣīdah, al-Ḥalabī's poem begins with a rather lengthy *nasīb* (i.e. the traditional introductory section of amatory verses) of about 35 verses, which is followed by the *raḥīl*. This "camel-section" terminates in Yaṯrib, that is Medina (*cf.* v. 52), and, more exactly, at the Prophet's tomb (v. 68). The actual praise of the Prophet then starts, after a short laudatory description of the grave itself (vv. 69-73), with verse 74. The remainder of the poem, roughly half of the whole, deals with different aspects of Muḥammad's prophethood, but almost never departs from a somewhat abstract and rhetorically refined level of panegyric style, exhibiting few references to actual episodes of the Prophet's life. Though poems in praise of Muḥammad had been composed before, al-Amīn al-Ḥalabī's insertion of a *raḥīl* leading to the Prophet's tomb in Medina was quite original and had, as far as I know, no antecedents.

3.2.2. Yearning for "the noble sepulchre"

The *raḥīl* towards the Prophet's tomb must be seen in close connection with the related sentiment of "longing for Medina" (*at-tašawwuq ʾilā l-Madīnah*), frequently expressed in eastern Shiite religious poetry from the fourth century H onwards – e.g. in a number of poems by aš-Šarīf ar-Raḍīy – and subsequently in Sunnite

299 For the poetical *raḥīl* in general, see Jacobi: *Camel-Section*.

300 Abū l-Faḍl ʿAbd al-Muḥsin b. Maḥmūd (Ḥammūd) b. ʿAbd al-Muḥsin b. ʿAlī al-Ḥalabī at-Tanūḫī (570–643 H): ḎahʿIbar V p. 177 and ḎahTaḏk IV p. 1432; KutFawāt II pp. 393-6; NZ VI p. 353; GAL I p. 257; GALS I p. 457; ZA IV p. 295.

301 BN XIII p. 167.

302 MN III pp. 36-47.

303 Also known, for its *incipit*, as *Bānat Suʿād*, *cf.* the editions in IHišSīrah IV pp. 147-56; IMaymMunt I pp. 72-85; ISayNāsMinaḥ pp. 257-62; MN III, 1-8. For the poem as such, see Schimmel: *Messenger* pp. 179f. and Ḥusayn: *Burdah* pp. 17-45.

poetry in praise of the Prophet.[304] In the Islamic West, where this theme was adapted by Sunnite poets much earlier than in the East and seems to have been felt more deeply, it was clearly related to the literary tradition, important in the Islamic West from early Islamic times, of lamenting the great distance that divided the North African and Andalusian Muslims from Medina and thus from the Prophet's tomb. Parallel to that, there are also many poems which dwell on the theme of longing for Mecca or the Kaᶜbah, though these are more explicitly connected to the pilgrimage.[305]

A telling example of the poetical employment of the concept "of longing for Medina" in the West are two lines by the famous traveller Ibn Ǧubayr (Valencia 539 or 540 – Alexandria 614 H) who himself came repeatedly to Medina (*mutaqārib*):

إذا بَلَغَ المَرْءُ أرْضَ الحِجَازِ * فَقَدْ نَالَ أفْضَلَ مَا أمَّ لَهْ
وَإنْ زَارَ قَبْرَ نَبِـــيِّ الهَـدْيِ * فَقَدْ أكْمَلَ اللَّهُ مَا أمَّلَهْ

"When someone reaches the land of Ḥiǧāz, * then he has reached the best he ever had set out for,
And if he visits the tomb of the Prophet of right guidance, * then God has fully satisfied what He had given him hope of".[306]

Other famous verses expressing "the yearning for the noble sepulchre" (*at-tašawwuq ʾilā ḍ-ḍarīḥi š-šarīf*) were composed by the eminent western philologist and man of letters Ibn al-Abbār (d. 658 H), nick-named *al-Faʾr* ("the Mouse").[307]

The concept of "yearning for Medina" (and, in general, for the Prophet's tomb) was taken up by eastern Sunnite poets during the seventh century H and soon became a central theme of eastern *madḥ an-nabī* poetry.[308]

To give just one example, "longing for Medina" was one of the most dominant themes in the poetry of the blind Hanbalite and mystic aṣ-Ṣarṣarī (Ṣarṣar near

304 *Cf.* EI² VII p. 377. The "longing for the Ḥiǧāz" as such has an old tradition in Arabic poetry, furthered especially by the Ḥiǧāzī style of poetry (during the Umayyad period) and the people of Medina themselves, but this kind of poetry did not yet show the religious undertone of later compositions or the strong and explicit connection with the Prophet and his sepulchre.

305 Examples include a poem by Ibn Sīd al-Baṭalyawsī (Abū M. ᶜAl. b. M., 444–521 H), quoted in IḪāqQal pp. 230f.

306 Cited in MaqqNafḥ (C) III p. 245 = al-Marrākušī: *Iᶜlām* III p. 92. Note the sylistical device known as *ǧinās mafrūq malfūf* ("distinct rounded *ǧinās*") in *mā ʾamma lah* / *mā ʾammalah*. For another poem by Ibn Ǧubayr extolling the status of Medina, see al-Marrākušī: *Iᶜlām* III pp. 90-2 (rhyme *-ārā*).

307 Abū ᶜAl. M. b. ᶜAl. b. Abī Bakr al-Quḍāᶜī al-Balansī (d. in Tunis), see MarrḎayl VI pp. 253-75; *Wāfī* III pp. 355-8; ĠubrᶜUnwān pp. 309-13; ḎahᶜIbar V p. 249; KutFawāt III pp. 404-7; NZ VII p. 92; MaqqNafḥ (C) III pp. 346-50; ŠN p. 195; GAL I pp. 340f. and GALS I pp.580f.; Nykl: *Hispano-Arabic Poetry* pp. 332f.; ZA VII p. 110. For the verses mentioned, see IAbbDīwān pp. 444f. (10 verses) as well as MaqqAzhār III p. 225 (7 verses, with the lines 3, 5 and 10 of the *Dīwān* missing) and MaqqNafḥ (C) III p. 350.

308 Yet not as late as with Ibn Daqīq al-ᶜĪd (d. 702 H), as claimed, albeit with some reserve, in Schimmel: *Messenger* p. 189.

Baghdad 588 – Baghdad 656 H), whose everlasting fame rests on his numerous poems in praise of the Prophet, which are said to have filled twenty volumes.[309] His poems derive their distinctive tone from the poet's longing for the Ḥiğāz, the abode of the beloved Prophet. In this context, aṣ-Ṣarṣarī uses motifs of the traditional "camel section" (*raḥīl*)[310] and evokes the land of the Ḥiğāz by mentioning its typical plants or certain Medinese place-names.[311] Having himself visited the Ḥiğāz in 651 H[312] – in contrast with many poets of the distant western lands who never set foot in the Arabian peninsula –, aṣ-Ṣarṣarī often addresses the people leaving Iraq for Arabia and more than once stresses his own distance from the Beloved (*kāmil*):

عَجَباً لِجِسْمٍ بَالعِرَاقِ مُخَلَّفٍ * وَفُؤادُهُ مَغْرًى بِطَيْبَةَ مُولَعُ

"A wondrous thing indeed! A body that stays behind in Iraq * while his heart is seduced by Medina (*aṭ-Ṭaybah*), burning with passion!"[313]

In another of his poems we read the lines (*munsariḥ*):

أَيُّ خِدَاعٍ يُزَخْرِفُ الحُلُمُ * يُصْغِي إِلَيْهِ ذُو الفِطْنَةِ الفَهِمُ
يُدْنِي مِنَ المُعْرِقِ الحِجَازَ وَكَمْ * بَيْنَهُمَا لِلرِّجَالِ طُلَّ دَمُ
وَأَيْنَ مِنْ صَرْصَرٍ وَحَاضِرِهَا * وَعْرُ الفَلا وَالعِضَاهُ وَالسَّلَمُ

"Which deception[314] that renders beautiful a dream, * to which the wise and reasonable lends his attention,
Brings the Ḥiğāz near to someone rooted in Iraq, and how many * a man has shed his blood on the way between them (*sc.* between the Ḥiğāz and Iraq)!
How far are from Ṣarṣar and its inhabitant[315] * the roadless desert, the thorny bushes and the *salam*-trees!"[316]

309 Ğamāl ad-Dīn Abū Zak. Ya. b. Yūsuf al-ᶜIrāqī az-Zarīrānī aḍ-Ḍarīr: ᶜUmMas XVI pp. 123f.; ḎahᶜIbar V p. 237 and ḎahTaḏk IV p. 1439; ṢafNakt pp. 308f.; KutFawāt IV pp. 298-319; BN XIII p. 211; IRağḎayl II pp. 262f.; NZ VII pp. 66f.; GAL I p. 250; GALS I p. 443; ZA IX pp. 225f. Ibn Rağab visited aṣ-Ṣarṣarī's tomb on his way to the Ḥiğāz in 749 H.

310 See, for example, MN I pp. 114 and 404, II p. 107, III p. 265.

311 Ḥiğāzī plants often named by aṣ-Ṣarṣarī include the moringa-tree (*al-bān*) and the *rand*-tree, while among the place names, al-ᶜAqīq (a valley in Medina) and Salᶜ (a hill near Medina) are present in virtually every poem; Kāẓimah, well-known from the second line of al-Būṣīrī's *Burdah*-poem, also appears in some verses (*cf.* MN I p. 406, IV pp. 36 and 183).

312 See MN IV p. 67. He also composed two poems about the way the Iraqi pilgrims take for the Ḥiğāz, see MN I pp. 393-98 (81 verses) and pp. 494-504 (144 verses).

313 KutFawāt IV p. 304 (v. 14). In other poems, aṣ-Ṣarṣarī deals especially with his passion for Medina, see e.g. MN II pp. 405f. and III pp. 239-46.

314 I.e. the appearance of the beloved person, as e.g. in dream or fancy.

315 I.e. the poet himself.

316 MN IV p. 59 (vv. 1-3); *cf.* also MN I p. 113 (vv. 1-4) and II p. 111 (vv. 9-11).

3.3. Not visiting the Prophet's sepulchre: reward and punishment

Notwithstanding the importance of visiting the Prophet's tomb in the Sunnite world from at least the sixth century H onwards (and before that in the Islamic West),[317] there were from early on individual voices which offered alternative, more rewarding ways of pleasing God. I know of no better illustration of that fact than the anecdote of Buhlūl b. Rāšid al-Maġribī (Kairouan 128–83 H, a pupil of Mālik b. Anas)[318] and Muᶜattib b. Rabāḥ, though it is not only the visitation of the Prophet's tomb but also the repetition of the pilgrimage which is at stake here:

> "Muᶜattib b. Rabāḥ came to see Buhlūl in his mosque, and the latter asked him 'Abū Aḥmad, what's up with you?' He replied, 'Abū ᶜAmr, I have decided to perform the pilgrimage this year'. 'Abū Aḥmad, have you not already performed the pilgrimage?' 'Yes, I performed it, but I feel strong desire to go to the sacrosanct House of God (i.e. the Kaᶜbah) and the tomb of the Prophet – blessing and peace be upon him!' 'How much money do you plan to spend?' 'A hundred dinars.' 'So what do you think if you give them to me and I will spend them for various purposes, and I guarantee you will attain with God the Exalted ten pilgrimages which He accepts?'
>
> Muᶜattib hurried off and returned with the sum (which he planned to spend for his travel). Buhlūl stored it under the leather mat he was sitting upon, then he had Muᶜattib sit down beside him. To every man who entered (the mosque) Buhlūl would hand over some of the money, to this one five dinars, to that one eight dinars, to a third one ten dinars. There was one he addressed with the words: 'Spend it on your marriage and take the rest for living', to another one he said 'Be generous with it towards your family and your children', and to a third man he spoke 'Cover with it your face'.[319] After both had been sitting for a little while, all the money was given away.
>
> In a quarter of Kairouan a righteous man was living, called Abū Sulaymān the blind, a pious and virtuous person (*min ʾahli d-dīni wa-l-faḍl*). (...) This Abū Sulaymān reported that he had been visited[320] by somebody the night after and was told 'Abū Sulaymān, go to Muᶜattib b. Rabāḥ and let him know that God the Exalted – may He be blessed! – has fulfilled the promise which was guaranteed to him by Buhlūl'. But Abū Sulaymān was overtaken by sleep, until a second person appeared to him, saying 'Abū Sulaymān, go now to Muᶜattib before the morning rises and let him know that God the Exalted has made what Buhlūl promised him come true'. So Abū Sulaymān went off immediately and knocked on the door of Muᶜattib's house. Muᶜattib showed up before him and asked 'Abū Sulaymān, what's up with you at this time?', and Abū Sulaymān answered 'I was sent to you in order to tell you that God the Exalted has fulfilled for you the promise which Buhlūl made to you on His behalf'".[321]

317 There is certainly some link between the dominance of the Malikite legal tradition in the Islamic West and the importance attributed to Medina and the Prophet's sepulchre in particular.

318 For him, see AᶜArabṬab pp. 124 and 126-38; ḪušṬab p. 81; Marzolph: *Buhlūl* p. 6, n. 26.

319 I cannot say whether this is to be taken literally or rather as a metaphorical expression whose significance is unknown to me; it might mean: "Lead a respectful life!"

320 Probably in a dream.

321 MālRiyāḍ I pp. 208f.

In some way connected to this and similar stories are others which stress that failing to visit the Prophet's sepulchre was neither detrimental nor indicative of lack of faith. Particularly famous in this regard is the story of Abū l-ᶜAtīq as-Saksakī al-ᶜUyānī (Abū Bakr b. Yaḥyā, d. 628 H): he performed the pilgrimage in 580 H, but was for some unknown reason not able to visit Medina and the Prophet's tomb. Therefore he remained much preoccupied and worried, until the Prophet in person appeared to him in a dream, saying "O Abū Bakr, since you have not visited us, we came to visit you (*lammā lam tazurnā zurnāka*)".[322]

Here, as often in Islam, intention (*niyyah*) is seen to override action.[323] If an intended or planned visitation could not be carried out, both Shiites and Sunnites took recourse to what might be called "substitute-visitations", that is, not having visited or having been able to visit the Prophet's sepulchre could be made up for by visiting another shrine. Among the Sunnites, tombs of pious persons (see **75**) could be substituted for that purpose, or also the tomb of a former prophet. Thus the Prophet is reported to have said repeatedly: "Who is not able to come to visit me (i.e. my tomb) may visit the tomb of my father Abraham (...)" (*man lam yumkinhu ziyāratī fa-l-yazur qabra ᵓabī ᵓIbrāhīma l-Ḫalīli ᵓalayhi s-salām*).[324] Among the Shiites, a visitation of almost every shrine of the venerated Imams was (and still is) considered to equal one or more pilgrimages including the visitation of the Prophet's sepulchre (see also **75**). However, prescriptions of that sort conflict with some reports from the Prophet, such as the following: "Who performs the pilgrimage and does not visit me, has shunned me" (see above).[325]

On the basis of this and similar Traditions, being unable to visit the Prophet's sepulchre could thus indeed be taken as a sign of sinfulness and indicate a lack of faith of the respective person. Arguably the best-known case in this context is that of the Andalusian mystic and philosopher Ibn Sabᶜīn (d. 669 H).[326] He enjoyed largely the reputation of a heretic, in many respects comparable to that of his more famous fellow countryman Ibn ᶜArabī, and exchanged polemics with his contemporary Quṭb ad-Dīn al-Qasṭallānī (d. 686 H) in Mecca. Ibn Sabᶜīn spent some time in the cave of Mt. Ḥirāᵓ (once the Prophet's place of retreat), in the hope that there the divine revelation (*al-waḥy*) would come down on him "according to his perverted belief that prophethood is an acquired quality (*muktasabah*) and nothing but an

322 ḪazrᶜUqūd I p. 49; IFahdItḥāf II p. 552.

323 According to the much-debated Tradition: "The intention of the believer is better than his (actual) doing" (*niyyatu l-muᵓmini ḫayrun min ᶜamalihī*), see IᶜASalāmQaw I p. 333.

324 SubkīŠifāᵓ p. 39; ᶜUlaymīUns I p. 56. According to another version, the report runs: "He who visits me (i.e. in my sepulchre) and the tomb of my father Abraham within one year is guaranteed (entry into) Paradise", a wording classified as forgery by an-Nawawī, see ZarkAḥkām p. 296 and MarǧBahǧah II p. 378.

325 *Cf.* also INaǧDurrah p. 397 = SubkīŠifāᵓ p. 36: "If someone from my community has the means (*or* the possibility) but does not visit me, he will have no excuse".

326 Abū M. ᶜAbd al-Ḥaqq b. Ibr. b. M. b. Naṣr ... al-Maqdisī (Murcia 614 – Mecca, Šawwāl 669 H): BN XIII p. 261; FāsīᶜIqd V pp. 5-9; ŠḎ V pp. 329f.; EI^2 III pp. 921f.

emanation which takes hold of every pure soul".[327] Now, this "eccentric Ibn Sabᶜīn" (F. Rosenthal), for all his vices in the eyes of his less open-minded contemporaries,

> "was (already) in the present world subjected to chastisement (*ʿaḏāb*), and his chastisement in the hereafter will be doubled. A Maġribī told me that from among his chastisement in this world was the fact that Ibn Sabᶜīn went to visit (the sepulchre of) the Prophet, but when he had reached the portal of the Prophet's mosque, he started to bleed heavily, like a menstruating woman, thus he went away and washed himself. When he returned to enter (the mosque), the blood started again to stream, forcing him to occupy himself with its removal, but eventually it prevented him from visiting the Prophet".[328]

The Meccan historian al-Fāsī, who relates this story, adds that his grandfather aš-Šarīf ᶜAlī, together with some of his friends, set out for the tomb of Ibn Sabᶜīn and tore out (*qlᶜ* I) the tombstone from his grave, for the reason that "ignorant foreigners were assiduously visiting his tomb". Once the tombstone had been removed, the location of Ibn Sabᶜīn's grave was no longer known.[329]

3.4. Writing letters to the tomb of the Prophet

From the sixth century H onwards, the impossibility for many a Muslim of the distant western lands to reach the Prophet's tomb in person gave rise to various practices in order to overcome this difficulty and to establish some sort of contact with the Prophet's sepulchre without being physically present there. In this context one must remember that the West, in particular al-Andalus, was in general seen as the remotest corner of the Islamic world. This is apparent in the following Tradition which has the Prophet addressing the townsfolk of Medina: "Invoke blessings upon me, because your blessing will reach me from wherever you are; you and those in al-Andalus are entirely equal (in this respect)" (*wa-ṣallū ʿalayya fa-ʾinna ṣalātakum tabluġunī ḥayṯumā kuntum mā ʾantum wa-man bi-l-ʾAndalusi ʾillā sawāʾ*),[330] meaning that the distance from Medina had no effect upon the efficiency of the blessing.

In order to bridge the distance between al-Andalus and the location of the Prophet's sepulchre one could ask somebody who was about to travel to the Ḥiǧāz to utter a salute or certain phrases on one's own behalf at the Prophet's tomb.[331] On the other hand, one could put the respective utterance down in writing and hand it

327 BN XIII p. 261 = (abridged) FāsīᶜIqd V p. 9.

328 I do not know whether there is any connection between that story and what we read in EI² III p. 922 about Ibn Sabᶜīn: "He possessed a restless temperament, racked by a nervous distemper which led even to the vomiting of blood, according to the reports of some of his biographers".

329 FāsīᶜIqd V p. 9.

330 Cited in IQaylġāṯah I p. 178. For other versions of that report which do not mention al-Andalus, *cf.* ᶜIyāḍŠifāʾ (B) II p. 68 / (Š) II p. 80; BayḤayātAnb pp. 30-2; HaytFatḤad p. 279; Donaldson: *Shiʾite Religion* p. 143.

331 See e.g. the story told in MālRiyāḍ II pp. 443f.

over to somebody performing the pilgrimage who in this case would act as a personal courier and deliver the letter in Medina. Given the specific features of Arabic culture, this usage of drafting letters, addressed to the Prophet and meant to be taken to his tomb, soon became a literary genre of its own. The subject matter of this literary genre was of course closely related to the "yearning for the noble sepulchre" as employed in poetry, and the plea for intercession almost always played a prominent part in the message. Formally, the genre consisted of *Kunstbriefe* (*rasāʾil*) which were addressed to the Prophet's tomb (or formally to the Prophet himself) and composed in a mixture of rhymed prose and verses.

Though not called a "letter" or "epistle" (both in Arabic either *kitāb* or *risālah*), the first example of its kind might be a piece in artificial prose (*ʾinšāʾ*) composed by Abū l-Qāsim Ibn al-Ǧadd "al-Aḥdab" (d. 515 H)[332] and "written as uttered by someone (*ʿalā lisān man*) returning from the sacrosanct house of God (i.e. the Kaʿbah) and the visit to the tomb of His Prophet". This testifies again to the common combination of pilgrimage and the visitation of the Prophet's sepulchre. The main arguments of the letter are the prayer for the Prophet's intercession and the hope for a return to the Ḥiǧāz.[333]

However, the earliest known example of a genuine "letter to the Prophet" stems from the Andalusian vizier and man of letters Ibn Abī l-Ḫiṣāl. During the following centuries, up to the ninth century H, a number of similar "letters (addressed) to the Prophet" or, more exactly, "to the sepulchre of the Prophet", were composed by poets and scholars of the Islamic West:

(1) "Letter to the Prophet" (*Kitāb ʾilā n-nabī*), by Ibn Abī l-Ḫiṣāl (d. 540 H).

Abū ʿAl. M. b. Masʿūd b. (Ṭayyib b.) Farağ al-Ġāfiqī aš-Šāqūrī, Ḏū l-Wizāratayn (Farġalīṭ near Šāqūrah [sp. Segura] in 463 or 465 – Córdoba 540 H): ŠantḎaḫ III pp. 784-809; IḪāqQal pp. 199-206; IDiḥMuṭrib pp. 187-90; IAbbMuʿǧṢadafī pp. 144-49; ḌabbīBuġ 121; ʿUmMas XIII pp. 39f.; IḪaṭIḥāṭah II pp. 388-418; al-Marrākušī: *Iʿlām* III p. 5-9; GAL I pp. 368f.; Nykl: *Hispano-Arabic Poetry* pp. 259f.; ZA VII 316; Vizcaíno: *Vida y obra de Ibn Jayr* p. 336; Penelas/Zanón: *Nómina de ulemas andalusíes* p. 174; al-Makkī: *Madāʾiḥ* pp. 122-24; CHAL *Andalus* p. 195.

Ibn Abī l-Ḫiṣāl had embarked on a career as a state functionary in Granada, Córdoba and Seville. His interests focused on stylistics and rhetorics (*balāġah*), belles-lettres and history. He earned his fame mainly for his epistolography of refined rhymed prose; the encyclopaedist al-ʿUmarī (d. 749 H), who certainly knew what he was talking about, called him "the foremost *Staatssekretär* of the West" (*kātibu l-maġribi muṭlaqan*).[334] Unfortunately, Ibn Abī l-Ḫiṣāl's letter does not seem to have been preserved in full. The ninth-century historian of Medina, as-Samhūdī, who calls it simply *Kitāb ʾilā n-nabī*, cites only the verses and the accompanying story:

332 M. b. ʿAl. b. al-Ǧadd, vizier and secretary in Seville under the son of al-Muʿtamid Ibn ʿAbbād and later under the Almohad ruler ʿAlī b. Yūsuf (r. 500–537 H), died in Liblah (sp. Niébla) in 515 H: IḪāqQal pp. 123-9; ŠantḎaḫ III pp. 285-322; MarrMuʿǧib p. 237; ZA VI p. 228.

333 For the text of the letter, see ŠantḎaḫ III pp. 286-8.

334 ʿUmMas XIII p. 39.

"Abū Muḥammad al-Išbīlī said in his book about the merit of the pilgrimage (*fī faḍl al-ḥaǧǧ*) that a man from Granada was afflicted by an illness which the doctors were unable to cure and so they had given him up. The vizier Abū ᶜAbd Allāh Muḥammad b. Abī l-Ḫiṣāl then composed in his name a letter to the Prophet in which he asked for his being cured of the disease and rescued from what had befallen him. This letter contained some verses [*quoted in the following, 11 lines in all*].[335] At the moment the caravan reached Medina and the verses were read at (*ᶜalā*) the Prophet's tomb the man back home was cured. When the person who had been charged (with reciting the letter) returned he found the man as if no evil had ever befallen him".[336]

(2) "An Epistle which he Addressed to the Sanctified Sepulchre" (*Risālah katabahā ʾilā l-qabr al-muqaddas*), by al-Qāḍī ᶜIyāḍ (d. Sabtah 544 H), quoted in GALS I p. 632 from a manuscript kept at St Petersburg. The preposition *ʾilā* is in GALS given as *ᶜinda*, hence the title would translate as "An Epistle which he Wrote *at* the Sanctified Sepulchre". Yet this is highly improbable, especially because al-Qāḍī ᶜIyāḍ never actually went to Medina nor performed the pilgrimage. Nothing else is known about this epistle. I have not seen the ms. by myself.

(3) Though not called properly "epistle" or "letter", and thus not unlike the composition by Abū l-Qāsim Ibn al-Ǧadd (see above), a qaṣīdah poem in praise of the Prophet is worth mentioning here. It was sent to the Prophet's sepulchre by the governor of al-Mahdīyah (modern Tunisia), Abū ᶜAlī ᶜUmar b. Abī Mūsā (born in 573 H), an older contemporary of Ibn al-Abbār. This poem is, rather unusually, referred to as "a word" or "an address" (*kalimah*) which the author sent to the tomb of the Prophet. It was carried there, on his behalf, by the mystic Ibn ᶜArabī.[337]

(4) "The Epitome of Merits, Based upon the Book of (the Prophet's) Features" (*ᶜUnwān al-faḍāʾil ᶜalā muḍamman Kitāb aš-Šamāʾil*), by the Andalusian poet, prose writer and jurist Abū l-Ḥasan al-Wādī Āšī al-Ġassānī (d. 609 H).

Abū l-Ḥasan ᶜAlī b. A. b. M. b. Yūsuf b. Marwān b. ᶜUmar al-Ġassānī al-Wādī Āšī al-Mālikī (born in a little village near Wādī Āš [sp. Guadix] 547 – Wādī Āš 609 H): IBaškṢilah IV pp. 125f.; IAbbTakm III p. 225; IḪaṭIḥāṭah IV pp. 181-3; IFarDībāǧ pp. 302-4 (double entry!); ZA V pp. 61f.; Penelas/Zanón: *Nómina de ulemas andalusíes* p. 101.

The work in question, today no longer extant, has been described by Ibn Farḥūn as "a writing in verse (*naẓm*) about the features of the Prophet".[338] If this refers to at-Tirmiḏī's *Šamāʾil an-nabī*, which had been introduced in al-Andalus only towards

335 From the second verse we learn that the person had been paralysed and could only communicate by gestures (... *fa-lam yastaṭiᶜ ʾillā l-ʾišārata bi-l-kaffi*).

336 SamWafāʾ IV p. 1387 = HaytTuḥfZuw pp. 123-5 and abridged in al-Marrākušī: *Iᶜlām* III p. 9. This letter of Ibn Abī l-Ḫiṣāl is not cited or mentioned in the collection of his works, viz. IAḪiṣālRas.

337 IAbbḤullah II pp. 284f. (with extracts of the poem, amounting to 15 verses).

338 IFarDībāǧ p. 303. In the Ottoman period, Abū l-Futūḥ M. b. Muṣṭafā al-Bakrī produced an abridgement of at-Tirmiḏī's *Šamāʾil* entitled *ᶜUnwān al-faḍāʾil fī talḫīṣ aš-Šamāʾil* (*Ḏayl* ḤḪ II p. 128), which may, or may not, have been inspired by al-Wādī Āšī's writing. The similarity in the titles is striking.

the beginning of the sixth century H, then al-Wādī Āšī's work must be considered the first (though only partial) adaptation in verse of an earlier writing from the field of *sīrah* and related scholarship in Arabic literature. However, it cannot have been a versification in the proper sense of the word, because Ibn al-Ḫaṭīb describes it thus: "al-Wādī Āšī composed *ʾadab* works, both (in the form of) poems (*manẓūmāt*) and epistles (*rasāʾil*), and they are known to everybody. (...) In addition, he produced a versification (*naẓm*) of the *šamāʾil* of the Messenger of God, a splendidly eloquent epistle (*risālah badīʿah*) which includes parts in verse (*naẓm*) and prose (*naṯr*). He sent the writing to the noble tomb (of the Prophet)".[339] From this description it becomes apparent that al-Wādī Āšī's *naẓm* was less a versification similar to later works called, for example, *naẓm as-sīrah*,[340] than a *Kunstbrief* in rhymed prose with passages in bound speech. As such it would count as the fourth example of the western fashion to draw up letters which are preceded by a poem and formally addressed (and subsequently delivered) to the Prophet's sepulchre.

(5) "Epistle to the Sepulchre of the Prophet" (*Risālah ʾilā ḍarīḥ an-nabī*), by the poet and encomiast of the Prophet al-Fāzāzī (d. 627 H).

Abū Zayd ʿAr. b. Abī Saʿīd Yaḫlaftan b. A. b. Tanfalīt al-Qurṭubī al-Andalusī (d. Fez 627 H): IAbbMuqt pp. 185f. and IAbbTakm III pp. 47f.; *Wāfī* XVIII pp. 302f.; IḪaṭIḥāṭah III pp. 517-22; SuyBuġ II p. 91; MaqqNafḥ (C) VI pp. 211f.; GAL I p. 273; GALS I pp. 482f.; ZA IV p. 118; EI^2 II p. 874 (C. S. Colin); Penelas/Zanón: *Nómina de ulemas andalusíes* p. 73; FāzĀṯār pp. 7-15.

This letter contained in the Leiden manuscript is edited in FāzĀṯār pp. 37-9. In modern print it fills a mere three pages and opens with a hymnic poem of 13 verses addressing Muḥammad, followed by the actual letter composed in rhymed prose. After greeting the Prophet, al-Fāzāzī explicitly states that he wrote his *risālah* "because between myself and the kissing of your Prophetic dust, between myself and the vision of your Muḥammadan splendour, there lie deserts without end (*mafāwiz*) which are only crossed by those who could purify their dirty clothes with the water of repentance (...) Alas, I was turned down every time I sought repentance and when I approached the gate, it was shut in my face".[341] Thus excusing himself for not having visited Medina, al-Fāzāzī then asks for the Prophet's intercession on his behalf. At the end of the letter, he "signs" with his full name and takes up a concept which we also encounter in his poetry: "This was written by your servant who has laid hold of Your most firm bond, unbreaking" (*al-mustamsiku bi-ʿurwatika l-wuṯqā*, *cf.* Q 2:256). The *risālah* of al-Fāzāzī must be seen, notwithstanding the earlier examples, as an important model for similar later writings in rhymed prose.

(6) "Epistle Concerning the Noble Rank of the Chosen (i.e. the Prophet)" (*Risālah fī šaraf al-Muṣṭafā*), by the Andalusian man of letters Ibn al-Ǧayyān (d. *c.*655 H).

339 IḪaṭIḥāṭah IV p. 182. The relevant entry in IFarDībāǧ p. 304 runs instead: "... a versification of the *šamāʾil an-nabī* and (!) a splendid epistle..."!

340 *Cf.* Arberry: Sîra *in Verse*.

341 FāzĀṯār p. 38.

Abū ᶜAl. M. b. M. b. A. al-Anṣārī al-Mursī (d. Biǧāyah *c*.655 H): IḪaṭIḥāṭah II pp. 348-59; MaqqNafḥ (C) X pp. 270-98; ŠN pp. 193f.; Penelas/Zanón: *Nómina de ulemas andalusíes* p. 170.

The text of Ibn al-Ǧayyān's letter *fī šaraf al-Muṣṭafā* has been preserved in MaqqNafḥ (C) X pp. 276-8. Actually, the letter as such is not addressed to the Prophet's sepulchre, but merely dedicated to Muḥammad. However, in both style and content it closely resembles the known letters formally addressed to the sepulchre of the Prophet and may thus be said to fall within this literary genre. Ibn al-Ǧayyān's *Kunstbrief* is an exquisite example of an *ʾinšāʾ* text (highly stylised rhymed prose). It proceeds from a general praise of Muḥammad's virtues to invoking many of his better known miracles (the night-journey, the splitting of the moon, the love of the palm trunk, the poisoned lamb speaking to the Prophet, etc.), in order to return then to his meritorious qualities and his beneficial intercession on behalf of the believers.

(7) "Epistle to the Holy Mausoleum" (*Risālah ʾilā t-turbah al-muqaddasah*), by Lisān ad-Dīn Ibn al-Ḫaṭīb (Abū ᶜAl. M. b. ᶜAl., 713 – Fez 776 H).

Nothing needs to be said here about Ibn al-Ḫaṭīb, this most accomplished of all Andalusian men of letters, "une des dernières figures attachantes de l'humanisme andalou" (M. Arkoun)[342] and the "bright star in the pleiad of great minds of his age" (A. Knysh).[343] The letter was written in the name of the Naṣrid ruler Abū l-Ḥaǧǧāǧ Yūsuf I (see **92d**) and addressed "to the holy mausoleum"; according to Ibn al-Ḫaṭīb, the letter belongs to his earliest poetical writings.[344]

(8) "Epistle to the Sepulchre of the Messenger of God" (*Risālah ʾilā ḍarīḥ rasūli llāh*), by Ibn al-Ḫaṭīb. According to the author himself, the letter was written in the name of the Naṣrid ruler Muḥammad V (r. 755–60 and 763–93 H) "at the beginning of the year 771" (some manuscripts have "761").[345]

(9) as-Saḫāwī tells us in two of his writings that the Shafiite jurist and preacher Ibn al-Fālātī (d. 870 H)[346] had drafted a letter in prose and verse (*risālatan min naẓmihī wa-naṯrihī*) addressed to the Prophet.[347] Shortly before his death he had given it to as-Saḫāwī to deliver it during his stay in Medina at the sepulchre of the Prophet and indeed as-Saḫāwī was able to do this, although, as he says himself, not

342 Arkoun: *Pensée arabe* p. 86.

343 For his biography and achievements, see MaqqNafḥ (C); al-Marrākušī: *Iᶜlām* III pp. 352-69 and IV pp. 2-20; Arié: *Ibn al-Khaṭīb*; CHAL Andalus pp. 358-71 (A. Knysh).

344 Its text is quoted in IḪaṭIḥāṭah IV pp. 526-35, IḪaṭRayḥ I pp. 55-62 and MaqqNafḥ (C) IX pp. 58-64. The initial poem of 33 verses is also cited in MN IV pp. 94-7.

345 IḪaṭDīwān I pp. 156f. and IḪaṭIḥāṭah IV p. 536. Its text has been preserved in IḪaṭIḥāṭah IV pp. 536-60, IḪaṭRayḥ I pp. 62-80 and MaqqNafḥ (C) IX pp. 64-83. The introductory poem (54 verses in the metre *ṭawīl*) is also cited in IḪaṭDīwān I pp. 156-9 = MN I pp. 443-7. The poem as edited in the IḪaṭIḥāṭah is missing lines 15, 40 and 46 of IḪaṭDīwān, while in MaqqNafḥ (C) verses 7-8 are lacking.

346 Šams ad-Dīn Abū l-Faḍl M. b. ᶜAlī ad-Dimašqī al-Qūṣī (Cairo 824–870 H), see SaḫWaǧīz II pp. 776f. and ḌL VIII p. 197-9; IlyāsBad II p. 440; ŠḎ VII p. 311.

347 *ʾarsalahā ... li-sayyidi l-ʾawwalīna wa-l-ʾāḫirīn* (*Waǧīz*); ... *li-l-ḥaḍrati n-nabawīyah* (ḌL).

during the lifetime of the author. Five lines that were part of that *risālah* are quoted by as-Saḫāwī, the first two of which running (*ṭawīl*):

أُكَرِّرُ تَسْلِيمِي مَدَى الدَّهْرِ إنَّهُ * شِفَاءٌ لِقَلْبِي مِنْ أَلِيمِ فِرَاقِهِ
وَأُهْدِي إلَى القَبْرِ الشَّرِيفِ تَحِيَّةً * عَلَى قَدْرِ حَالِي فِي عَظِيمِ اشْتِيَاقِهِ

"I will repeat my greeting for time eternal because it is * a cure for my heart from the pain of being separated from him (i.e. the Prophet).
I render to the noble tomb a salute * corresponding to my inner state of utmost longing for him."[348]

This late example of a letter addressed to the Prophet's tomb is important because it shows not only that the practice of composing such letters had not been abandoned during the ninth century H, but also that this custom was not limited to the Islamic West and al-Andalus in particular. However, writing epistles in prose and verse to the Prophet was never popular in the Islamic East. Eastern scholars and men of letters preferred to compose "conventional" poems in praise of the Prophet (*qaṣāʾid nabawīyah*) – or entire collections of those – and recite them, or have them recited, at the Prophet's sepulchre. For this practice, attested from the sixth century H onwards, see page 103 below.

The letters discussed so far are artistic compositions of rhymed prose and poetry drafted by more or less famous men of letters, mostly of Andalusian or North African origin. But the practice of writing letters to the Prophet's tomb was not a prerogative of men of letters. This is best illustrated by a fragmentarily preserved letter from fifth-century Egypt which has been published by Werner Diem. In this letter we hear from a woman who had returned from the "little pilgrimage" (*al-ʿumrah*) to Egypt. In the Ḥiǧāz, she had visited both Mecca and Medina ("those *mašāhid*") and, as she says in the letter, "I gave the letters (*riqāʿ*) to the servants (at the Prophet's mosque) at the appointed time, so you were in the presence of the Messenger of God",[349] that is, the woman had delivered the letters of persons who had remained in Egypt at the Prophet's sepulchre and this was seen as a substitute for being personally present.

This Egyptian letter is interesting in our context for two reasons. First, the term *riqāʿ* (unlike the terms *kitāb* or *risālah*) accentuates rather the material aspect of the letter, namely that the woman delivered some sheets of paper, probably quite similar to those which until the present day are often left at venerated shrines. Those letters *en miniature* often contain personal wishes, vows and pleas for intercession. Second, the letter of this woman stems from fifth-century Egypt and thus antedates the first known epistles addressed to the sepulchre of the Prophet by poets and men of letters. This is likely to signify that the practice of addressing and sending letters to the Prophet had been current for some time among Muslims before it was taken up

348 SaḫWaǧīz II p. 777 and ḌL VIII p. 199.

349 Diem: *Arabische Briefe* 69 ll. 4-5 (p. 228).

by members of the learned élite. By doing so they transformed a popular custom into a literary genre.

The practice of writing letters to the dead is also known from Ancient Egypt.[350] Here, such letters were inscribed on pottery, textiles or papyrus, and subsequently deposited in the tomb. Regarding this pratice "va riconosciuta la credenza (...) che i morti possano ancora interessarsi e intervenire, benevolmente o malevolmente, nelle cose terrene e negli affari dei viventi; come ai vivi assenti si scrivevano lettere, mediante lettere si poteva comunicare coi morti nell'altro mondo".[351] This sounds familiar to every student of the Islamic mortuary cult, and the fact that the earliest letter addressed to the Prophet's sepulchre stems from Egypt might suggest that there was some continuity of the practice of writing letters to deceased persons from pre-Islamic times into the Islamic period.

3.5. The dispute of the eighth century H and its aftermath

At the beginning of the eighth century H the issue of the visitation of tombs and cemeteries had entered the agenda of Sunnite scholars;[352] again, the visitation of the tomb of the Prophet was in this context seen as the exemplary practice and thus shifted to the centre of attention. At stake were questions of whether visits to graves, including the sepulchre of the Prophet, were in any way meritorious or even permissible and whether doing so, together with the specific forms of veneration connected with it, conformed to the precepts of Islam if understood properly.

As often in the Arabo-Islamic culture, we can easily assess the importance of a given issue if we look at the literature that was produced about it. In the present case, the eighth-century debate about visiting tombs, and visiting the sepulchre of the Prophet in particular, was prepared for by some influential Sunnite writings from the fifth century onwards. It is to these writings that we must now turn.

3.5.1. The visitation of the Prophet's tomb in writings before the eighth century H

The practice of visiting the Prophet's sepulchre was debated by Muslim scholars from the very first centuries, mainly in writings belonging to the spheres of law and Tradition or dealing with the "proofs of prophethood" (*dalāʾil an-nubuwwah*) and the biography of the Prophet (*sīrah*). Yet there were no independent monographs on this subject nor was it deemed important enough to be singled out within larger writings, for example as a chapter or section of its own.

Among the first to do so, however, were the polymath Ibn Abī d-Dunyā (d. 275 H) and his contemporary, the Shiite genealogist and scholar Abū l-Ḥusayn Yaḥyā b. al-Ḥasan al-ʿAqīqī (d. 277 H).[353] Ibn Abī d-Dunyā's treatise entitled *Kitāb Ziyārat al-qubūr* is quoted by al-Marǧānī with the remark that it contains a chapter on the

350 *Cf.* A.H. Gardiner/K. Sethe: *Egyptian Letters to the Dead*, London 1928; J. Janák: *Revealed but Undiscovered: A New Letter to the Dead*, in: Journal of Near Eastern Studies 62 (2003), 275-77 (with further literature).

351 Bresciani: *Antico Egitto* p. 32; *cf.* also Parkinson: *Voices from Ancient Egypt* pp. 142-5.

352 For the background of that debate, see Chodkiewicz: *Sainteté et les saints.*

353 as-Sayyid aš-Šarīf Abū l-Ḥusayn Ya. b. al-Ḥasan al-Ḥusaynī al-ʿAqīqī al-ʿUbaydalī (Medina 214 – Mecca 277 H): SubkīŠifāʾ p. 38; *Ḏarīʿah* I p. 349; GAS I p. 273; ZA VIII pp. 140f.

visitation of the Prophet's sepulchre (*bāb ziyārat qabr an-nabī*),[354] yet this writing is spurious and nothing of it is known in other sources nor has it been preserved.[355] The genealogist al-ᶜAqīqī, a Medinan by birth, wrote one of the earliest histories of that town, and his *ʾAḫbār al-Madīnah* is cited by Taqīy ad-Dīn as-Subkī with the comment that it contains a "chapter about what has been said concerning the visitation of the Prophet's tomb" (*bāb mā ǧāʾa fī ziyārat qabr an-nabī*).[356] In the course of the next century, we find that the widely-travelled scholar and traditionist Ibn as-Sakan (d. 353 H)[357] included a chapter about the reward due to the visitor to the Prophet's sepulchre (*bāb ṯawāb man zāra qabr an-nabī*) in his collection of Traditions entitled *Kitāb as-Sunan aṣ-ṣiḥāḥ* (or also *al-Muntaqā aṣ-ṣaḥīḥ*),[358] more exactly at the end of the section about the pilgrimage (*kitāb al-ḥaǧǧ*). It is again as-Subkī who provides us with that notice and he adds that this chapter did contain but a single report, assecuring the intercession of the Prophet for those who have visited his sepulchre (see above).[359]

During the fifth century H the issue was taken up by Abū Bakr b. al-Ḥusayn al-Bayhaqī (d. 458 H) who is also the author of the most influential pre-modern treatise on the so-called "proofs of prophethood" (= BayDal). In his great collection of Traditions, the *Sunan al-kubrā*, al-Bayhaqī devoted a little chapter of its own to the visitation of the Prophet's tomb (*bāb ziyārat qabr an-nabī*).[360] Though it does only amount to little more than half a page in modern print, it is nevertheless noteworthy for its very existence. In later writings dealing with the visitation to the Prophet's tomb this chapter is often quoted specifically, and as-Subkī remarked that the fact that al-Bayhaqī included this chapter in his book is enough support for those arguing in favour of the practice of visitation.[361]

The next steps in establishing the visitation of the Prophet's sepulchre as a subject of its own standing were made in the Islamic West. The visitation of the Prophet's tomb is amply dealt with in al-Qāḍī ᶜIyāḍ's (d. 544 H) *Kitāb aš-Šifā bi-taᶜrīf ḥuqūq al-Muṣṭafā*. This work features a lengthy section about visiting the Prophet's tomb and the merit for those who perform the visit and salute the Prophet.[362]

354 MarǧBahǧah II p. 383.

355 The work is not listed in GAS. *Cf.* also Weipert/Weninger: *Ibn Abī d-Dunyā*.

356 SubkīŠifāʾ p. 39. I presume that the *ʾAḫbār al-Madīnah* by Abū l-Ḥasan al-ᶜAqīqī is referred to in SaḫIᶜlān p. 129 (= Rosenthal: *Historiography* p. 475) where a history of Medina is ascribed to a certain "aš-Šarīf an-Nassābah", though Yaḥyā b. al-Ḥasan al-Ḥasanī (*sic*) is mentioned some lines below as the author of a book dealing with the *faḍāʾil al-Madīnah*.

357 Abū ᶜAlī Saᶜīd b. ᶜUṯmān b. Saᶜīd al-Baġdādī al-Miṣrī al-Bazzār, Ibn as-Sakan (294 – Egypt 353 H): ḎahTaḏk III pp. 937f. and TI XXVI pp. 88f.; *Wāfī* XV p. 242; NZ III p. 338; ŠḎ III p. 12; GAS I p. 189; ZA III p. 98.

358 See the sources in the preceding note; the work is not mentioned in GAS.

359 SubkīŠifāʾ p. 20.

360 BaySunan V pp. 245f.

361 SubkīŠifāʾ p. 20.

362 ᶜIyāḍŠifāʾ (B) II pp. 71-6 / (Š) II pp. 83-9.

A generation later, the well-known Córdoban Malikite scholar Ibn Baškuwāl (Abū l-Qāsim Ḫalaf b. Abī Marwān ʿAbd al-Malik, d. 578 H) introduced this issue at a conspicuous point in one of his writings: in his monograph about the merits of invoking blessing upon the Prophet (*aṣ-ṣalāh ʿalā n-nabī*) entitled *al-Qurbah ʾilā rabb al-ʿālamīn* ("The Nearness[363] to the Lord of the Worlds"), the very last chapter is devoted to the reports about visiting the Prophet's sepulchre (*mā ǧāʾa fī ziyārati qabri n-nabī*).[364] Here, the visitation of the Prophet's tomb is presented as a meritorious deed, and Ibn Baškuwāl stresses that the intercession of the Prophet will be certain for those who have come to visit his tomb.

During the late sixth and early seventh centuries H, interest in the subject of visiting the Prophet's sepulchre intensified in the Islamic East, most notably among the Hanbalites. Here it was first Ibn al-Ǧawzī (see **26**) who in his history of Mecca entitled *Muṯīr al-ʿazm as-sākin ʾilā ʾašraf al-ʾamākin* ("Arouser of the Dormant Will to [Visit] the Most Noble Place") inserted a chapter about the visitation of the Prophet's tomb.[365] In his monograph on the proofs of prophethood, he likewise has a little section dealing with the high rank of the Prophet's sepulchre[366] which also contains the most widely known reports about the merit of visiting the Prophet's tomb. Another important contribution seems to have been the chapter on the visitation of the Prophet's tomb in the legal manual called *Kitāb al-Mustawʿab (fī l-fiqh)* by Ibn Sunaynah as-Sāmarrī (d. 616 H),[367] another Hanbalite scholar. This chapter is explicitly quoted in later monographs.[368] Finally, the 16th chapter in Ibn an-Naǧǧār's (d. 647 H) *History of Medina* (= INağDurrah) is entirely devoted to the visitation of the Prophet's sepulchre.[369]

In the second half of the seventh century H, the first monograph on the visitation of the Prophet's sepulchre was composed by Abū l-Yumn Ibn ʿAsākir (d. Medina 687 H).[370] A pious man and panegyrist of the Prophet, and reportedly the outstanding authority in the Hiǧāz during his lifetime, he wrote something about the sandals of the Prophet[371] and a ground-breaking treatise concerning the visitation of the Prophet's

363 Lane (*s.r.*) gives the exact meaning of that term though his explanation is much too incumbent to be used in translation: "*Nearness of station,* or *grade,* or *rank*", or also "*A thing* [*such as prayer,* or *any righteous deed* or *work,*] *whereby one seeks nearness, to bring himself near, to draw near,* or *to approach, unto God;* or *to advance himself in the favour of God*".

364 IBaškQurbah pp. 120-3.

365 As cited in SubkīŠifāʾ p. 67; *cf.* also IʿAHādīṢārim p. 254.

366 IǦawzīWafā p. 816.

367 Nāṣir ad-Dīn M. b. ʿAl. as-Sāmarrī al-Ḥanbalī (Sāmarrāʾ 535 – Baghdad 616 H): IRağḎayl II pp. 121f.; ʿUlaymīManh II pp. 353f.; ŠḎ V pp. 70f.; GALS I p. 689; ZA VI p. 231.

368 E.g. SamWafāʾ IV p. 1376 and 1391.

369 INağDurrah pp. 397-401.

370 Amīn ad-Dīn Abū l-Yumn ʿAbd aṣ-Ṣamad b. ʿAbd al-Wahhāb Ibn ʿAsākir ad-Dimašqī aš-Šāfiʿī (Damascus 614 – Medina 686 H): BN XIII p. 311; KutFawāt II pp. 328-30; ŠḎ V pp. 395f.

371 *Timṯāl an-naʿl aš-šarīf*, see SaḫIʿlān p. 91 = Rosenthal: *Historiography* p. 401; SuyMunǧam p. 231.

sepulchre.[372] This treatise has recently been published, but unfortunately I have not yet seen a copy of it.[373] It was an important source for the account by Taqīy ad-Dīn as-Subkī who claimed to possess an autograph of that book.[374]

With Ibn ᶜAsākir's monograph, the subject had won a respectable place in the wider discoursivity of Islamic scholarship. It is of course not by accident that this happened in the course of the seventh century H when, under the aegis of the Ayyubid rulers, the growth of Sunnism was under way. The specific form of Sunnism propagated during this period is much centred on the person of the Prophet and his veneration, and as such it was mainly accomplished in the Islamic East by *c.*700 H. But as in related cases, the development of interest in the visitation of the Prophet's tomb shows that the growth of Sunnism would not have been possible without previous impulses from the Islamic West and the further East (Iran).

In the first region, the long and deeply felt relationship with the distant East had created a strong bond with the holy sites in the Ḥiǧāz which culminated in the veneration of the Prophet's home town and his tomb. In the East (and less so in Fatimid Egypt) the influence of Shiism, together with the veneration of the *ʾahl al-bayt* and their burial places, was considerable during the third to fifth centuries H.[375] At any rate, it is worth noting that one of the first attempts to single out the visitation of the Prophet's sepulchre as scholarly topic was made by a Shiite scholar. Also the Hanbalites in sixth- and seventh-century Baghdad felt attracted by that subject and thus contributed to the continuous spread of the practice of visiting the Prophet's tomb. The subject, however, was always a disputed one, and around the beginning of the eighth century H, time was ripe for the show-down between the opponents and supporters of the practice of visitation.

3.5.2. The role of Ibn Taymīyah

Setting the scene for this show-down of prime importance was principally the work of Ibn Taymīyah (Ḥarrān, Rabīᶜ I 661 – Damascus, Ḏū l-Qaᶜdah 728 H).

Taqīy ad-Dīn Abū l-ᶜAbbās Aḥmad b. aš-Šihāb Abī l-Maḥāsin ᶜAbd al-Ḥalīm al-Ḥarrānī ad-Dimašqī al-Ḥanbalī: IĞazḤaw II pp. 306-10; ṢafAᶜyān I pp. 66-72 and *Wāfī* VII pp. 15-33; ḎahMuᶜǧam pp. 25-7, ḎahMuᶜǧŠuyūḫ pp. 41f. and ḎahTaḏk IV pp. 1496f.; KutFawāt I pp. 74-80; BN XIV pp. 135-40 and *passim*; IRağḎayl II pp. 387-408; INāṣRadd, *passim*; MaqrSulūk II pp. 304 and MaqrMuq I pp. 454-79; IḤağTarǧITaym and DK I pp. 154-70; ITaġrManh I pp. 358-62; KarKawākib; ŠḎ VI pp. 80-6; GAL II pp. 100-5; GALS II pp. 119-26; Laoust: *Schismes* pp. 266-73; ZA I pp. 140f.; Memon: *Ibn Taimīya's Struggle* p. 333 note 1 (with further literature); EI² III pp. 951-5 (H. Laoust).

372 *ʾItḥāf az-zāʾir wa-ʾiṭrāb al-muqīm li-s-sāʾir fī ziyārat an-nabī* (sic?), see SaḫIᶜlān p. 129 = Rosenthal: *Historiography* p. 475.

373 Ed. Ḥusayn M. ᶜAlī Šukrī, Beirut: Dār al-Arqam 2001.

374 SubkīŠifāʾ p. 6.

375 Parallel to the changes in the Sunnite mortuary cult, which were influenced by and at the same time reacted against Shiism, we note a similar "transformation" in Islamic art and architecture caused by the competition with Shiism. For further details, see Tabbaa: *Transformation.*

Ibn Taymīyah was not the only one among his contemporaries to be intrigued by the question of the visitation of tombs. He not only spoke against the widespread custom, which had reached a peak in the second half of the seventh century H, of visiting the tombs of popular saints and prophets, but also against the visiting of the tomb of the Prophet himself. The impact of Ibn Taymīyah has been already well-researched in modern scholarhip, and there are at least three major studies which analyse in some detail the debate about the visitation of tombs as it was generated by Ibn Taymīyah and his adherents.[376] The following pages will therefore add little to what is already known; they are merely meant to summarise some of the main points and to assess the place and importance of that eighth-century debate about the practice of visitation.

As said above, the growing importance of the *ziyārat al-qubūr* and the related mortuary cult is one of the many features which accompany the growth of Sunnism in the central Islamic lands from the Ayyubid period onwards.[377] In Arabic literature and scholarship this development is reflected in the massive spread of poetry in praise of the Prophet during the seventh century H in the eastern lands, and in the composition of visitation and cemetery guides from the sixth century H onwards (see Chapter 3). These aspects were heavily influenced and in part caused by similar and earlier developments in Shiism under the aegis of both the Būyids and the Fatimids.

Visiting tombs and shrines as well as other practices relating to the mortuary cult had been well prepared in regions dominated by Shiism, mainly in Iraq and further to the East. Thus a work called "The Ceremonies of the Pilgrimage (!) to the Shrines" (*Manāsik ḥaǧǧ al-mašāhid*), composed by a certain al-Mufīd Ibn an-Nuᶜmān, was heavily attacked by Ibn Taymīyah and his pupil Ibn Qayyim al-Ǧawzīyah. The latter writes in an almost Calvinistic spirit:[378]

> "The matter (of visiting tombs) stylised did eventually lead those misguided polytheists to legalise (*šrᶜ* I) pilgrimage to the tombs and lay down its ceremonies (*manāsik*), until one of the extremists among them (*baᶜḍ ġulātihim*) compiled a book about it and called it *Manāsik ḥaǧǧ al-mašāhid*, thus comparing the visitation of tombs with that of the Kaᶜbah (*al-bayt al-ḥarām*). It is obvious that this means parting with the precepts of the Islamic religion and entering the religion of the idolaters".[379]

Ibn al-Qayyim's teacher and spiritual mentor Ibn Taymīyah in his *Minhāǧ as-sunnah* has roughly the same notice:

376 Kabbani: *Heiligenverehrung*; Olesen: *Culte des saints*; Taylor: *Vicinity of the Righteous*.

377 On the growth of Sunnism during the fifth and sixth cent.s H, see now Nagel: *Heilszusage*. The term "growth" is meant to indicate, unlike the term "Sunni Revival" (or the like) used in recent literature (see e.g. Tabbaa: *Transformation*, ch. 1), that we are not dealing here with a simple revival of a worldview of the past, but rather with an unprecedented phenomenon that was fashioned by its protagonists to continue the Islamic thought of the formative years. The actual history of thought, however, does not corroborate this alleged continuity.

378 It is worth the effort to read the treatise against the cult of relics by John Calvin (*Traité des reliques*, Geneva 1543) while studying the writings by Neo-Hanbalites such as Ibn Taymīyah or Ibn Qayyim al-Ǧawzīyah and their later adherents like aš-Šawkānī. One then realises that many arguments put forward sound astonishingly similar.

379 IQaylġāṯah I p. 182.

"Their (*sc.* Shiite) sheikh Ibn an-Nuᶜmān, known among them as 'al-Mufīd', the teacher of al-Mūsawī and aṭ-Ṭūsī, wrote a book entitled *Manāsik al-mašāhid* in which he maintains that the pilgrimage towards the tombs of (ordinary) mortals equals the pilgrimage towards the Kaᶜbah, the sacrosanct house of God that God erected for mankind (...), yet He did not command any other pilgrimage than to the Kaᶜbah. It is also known with certainty from the Islamic creed that the Prophet did not command that which they claim about visiting sites of veneration (*mašāhid*), nor did he establish for his community ceremonies (*manāsik*) to follow at the tombs of the prophets and the righteous, nay this all is nothing but the creed of polytheists".[380]

The work referred to – *Manāsik* (*ḥaǧǧ*) *al-mašāhid* – does not seem to be extant nor could I find it mentioned in GAL and other bibliographies or catalogues. The title must certainly arouse suspicion as to its correct citation in Ibn Taymīyah's and Ibn al-Qayyim's accounts, since the term *ḥaǧǧ* was also among the Shiites, as far as I know, reserved for the pilgrimage to Mecca.[381] Moreover, by Ibn Taymīyah and in aš-Šawkānī's citation from Ibn al-Qayyim the title is rendered simply as *Manāsik al-mašāhid*.[382]

The identity of the named author "Ibn an-Nuᶜmān" is not entirely beyond doubt: aš-Šawkānī says that the person referred to as "Ibn an-Nuᶜmān" was *Ibn* al-Mufīd,[383] which in itself is problematic because the scholar thus named would be the Imamite author Muḥammad b. Muḥammad b. an-Nuᶜmān al-ᶜUkbarī (Baghdad, 336–413 H), who is known as "(aš-Šayḫ) al-Mufīd" or "Ibn al-Muᶜallim", yet not as "Ibn al-Mufīd". This, in turn, would be corroborated by Ibn Taymīhah's description, but no treatise bearing the title *Manāsik* (*ḥaǧǧ*) *al-mašāhid* has been attributed to al-Mufīd.[384] Yet the name "Ibn an-Nuᶜmān" also recalls Abū ᶜAbd Allāh Muḥammad b. an-Nuᶜmān (Kairouan 340 – Cairo 389 H),[385] supreme judge in Cairo after 374 and son of "the founder of Ismaili jurisprudence"[386] al-Qāḍī an-Nuᶜmān (d. 363 H). No work by him entitled *Manāsik al-mašāhid* is known either, but the Jewish convert and Fatimid official Ibn Killis (Yaᶜqūb b. Yūsuf, d. 380 H) wrote about the same time a treatise entitled *Mansak al-ḥaǧǧ al-kabīr*,[387] which might suggest that the term *ḥaǧǧ* had in Fatimid circles more than one meaning and that writings of that kind were produced after all. The title of the work in question is similar to that of many later books dealing with the ceremonies of pilgrimage, viz. *Manāsik al-ḥaǧǧ*. In Sunnite *manāsik al-ḥaǧǧ*-writings, the visitation of the Prophet's tomb was often included and its rites were called *manāsik* (if not *ʾādāb* or *šurūṭ*), though of course not *manāsik al-ḥaǧǧ*. In some Shiite legal manuals the question of *ziyārat al-qubūr* (including that of the

380 ITayMinhāǧ I p. 131; *cf.* also ITayMaǧm XXVII p. 162.

381 There is, however, one Arabic passage that uses the term *ḥaǧǧ* in the sense of "pilgrimage to a tomb", albeit not referring to an Islamic practice. The passage is found in MaqrMuq III p. 351 and says: "Is it thus that the Christians behave towards the Apostles? Nay, they rather turned every single tomb of them into visitation-sites for pilgrimage and devotion (*bal ǧaᶜalū qabra kulli wāḥidin mazāran li-ḥaǧǧin wa-ᶜibādatin*)".

382 ŠawkDurr p. 40.

383 ŠawkDurr p. 40. *Cf.* also Memon: *Ibn Taimīya's Struggle* p. 363, n. 320.

384 *Ḏayl* ḤḪ II p. 558 lists a writing entitled *Manāsik al-Mufīd* (without further details).

385 For him, see Stern: *Ismāᶜīlī Movement* p. 445.

386 Halm: *Fatimids* p. 41.

387 See Ivanow: *Ismaili Literature* p. 41 (no. 107).

Prophet) is treated within the chapter about the pilgrimage,[388] in others we find it as part of the chapter on death and burial[389] or as a chapter of its own.[390] The Hanbalite Ibn al-Qayyim accused some people (whom he does not specify) of "carrying out their *manāsik ḥağğ al-qabr*" with certain practices he goes on to mention, but it does not become clear what exactly he had in mind when using this expression.[391]

Seen from a modern perspective, the fact that in his writings Ibn Taymīyah time and again denounced the Shiites for promoting the visitation of tombs and cemeteries is not without some historical justification as to their actual role in that process.[392] It is worth noting, however, that this subject, viz. the visitation of tombs and shrines as well as the mortuary cult in general, is not dealt with in any particular way in Ibn Taymīyah's major writings directed against Shiism, e.g. his voluminous *Minhāğ as-sunnah*. On the contrary, his struggle is fiercely aimed at attacking the opinions and practices of his fellow Sunnite co-religionists.

Ibn Taymīyah condemned the visitation of tombs and the accompanying practices in a number of small treatises (*rasāʾil*) and fatwas.[393] This included, as said before, the prohibition or at least the inappropriateness – Ibn Taymīyah was careful not to pronounce himself too clearly on the matter – of visiting the sepulchre of the Prophet in Medina,[394] a fact that to later scholars appeared as "one of the most repulsive teachings handed down from Ibn Taymīyah, (...) because visiting the Prophet's tomb is a most laudable deed (...) and its lawfulness is established by an *ʾiğmāʿ* (i.e. consensus) which has never been challenged by anyone".[395] What is more, also the reports according to which the visitors of the Prophet's tomb would gain his intercession were summarily declared forgeries by Ibn Taymīyah.[396]

On the other hand, we possess compelling evidence that Ibn Taymīyah did not categorically intend to ban the visitation of tombs, because in one of his fatwas we read, after all, that "visiting the tombs of the (Medinan) Baqīʿ cemetery and of the martyrs of Uḥud is desirable (*yustaḥabb*)".[397] Ibn Taymīyah's stance in the dispute about the *ziyārah* that ultimately led to his death in prison can thus not be reconstructed

388 *kitāb al-ḥağğ*: KulKāfī IV pp. 548-89 (*ʾabwāb az-ziyārah*); ʿĀmilīWas III pp. 251-470 (*ʾabwāb al-mazār*).

389 *kitāb al-ğanāʾiz*, e.g. KulKāfī III pp. 228-30.

390 *kitāb al-mazār* or *az-ziyārāt*: ṬūsīTahḏ VI pp. 2-119; MağlBihār C p. 101ff.

391 IQaylġāṯah I p. 180. Similarly, al-Albānī: *Aḥkām al-ğanāʾiz* p. 260 condemns people who call themselves *ḥāğğ* after having performed the visitation of tombs (without further details).

392 For another polemical passage against the Shiites, see also IQaylġāṯah I pp. 180f.

393 ITayMağm XXVII pp. 5-38; 64-124; 137ff. Some of his writings on the visitation of tombs have been published separately as *Kitāb az-Ziyārah*, Beirut 1980.

394 ITayZiy pp. 19ff. *Cf.* also Shoshan: *Popular culture* p. 68.

395 FB III p. 85 (*faḍl aṣ-ṣalāh fī masğid Makkah* 1) and the remark in HarŠSifāʾ II p. 151: "to declare forbidden what the scholars unanimously consider as desirable would amount to unbelief (*kufr*)".

396 ITayMağm XXVII pp. 29f., 35f., 118f., 130-4 and *passim*.

397 ITayMağm XXVII p. 22.

with certainty and remains elusive. Perhaps there is no consistent position to be expected from an irascible and pugnacious, though impressively learned and astute man like Ibn Taymīyah. The main arguments Ibn Taymīyah marshalled for his cause consisted in his repeated claim that the Prophet as well as the first-generation Muslims (*as-salaf*) did not care about the visitation of tombs (but rather thought it a polytheist and hence abominable practice) and that reports to the contrary were either wrongly attributed or invented or both.

That Ibn Taymīyah's line of thought, or that of his pupil Ibn al-Qayyim, did not necessarily reflect the tradition of mainstream Hanbalism becomes clear from the fact that the Hanbalites Ibn al-Ǧawzī or Ibn Rağab did not hesitate to mention the practices of veneration witnessed at certain tombs and their own visits to others.[398] Their attitude becomes manifest when Ibn al-Ǧawzī in one of his sermons exhorts the believers to visit the shrine of Ibn Ḥanbal and "the tombs of the righteous".[399] However, Ibn Taymīyah's followers, e.g. al-Karmī, claimed that much had been attributed to Ibn Taymīyah which actually did not represent his views: "The abuse of the sheikh grew stronger and stronger, he was incorrectly quoted and people reported from him what he never said, thus the result was a conflict (*fitnah*) whose sparks were emitted everywhere and the matter worsened increasingly".[400]

Of all his numerous writings and pamphlets, Ibn Taymīyah's main work on the subject seems to be a treatise called "The Question of Visitation (i.e. of the tombs)" (*Masʾalat az-ziyārah*), alternatively entitled "The Visitation of the Tombs and the Appeal to the Buried for Help" (*Ziyārat al-qubūr wa-l-istinǧād bi-l-maqbūr*) or "The Refutation of al-Iḫnāʾī, Concerning the Question of Visitation" (*ar-Radd ʿalā l-ʾIḫnāʾī fī masʾalat az-ziyārah*), written in 709 or 710 H following various incidents which had happened in Cairo in 709 H.[401] The main events can be summarised as follows:

While still in Damascus, Ibn Taymīyah had aroused the wrath of the Shafiite chief judge Ibn aṣ-Ṣaṣrī (d. 723 H).[402] Both were summoned to Egypt and arrived in

398 IǦawzīṢafwah I p. 582 (he more than once visited the tomb of Abū ʿAlī ad-Daylamī in Baghdad, "situated just behind the shrine of Maʿrūf al-Karḫī with only some graves between them"). The Hanbalite authority Ibn Rağab visited the tomb of the encomiast of the Prophet, aṣ-Ṣarṣarī (see above note 309).

399 IǦawzīTabṣ II p. 284.

400 KarKawākib p. 148.

401 The treatise appeared for the first time in print in Cairo, as part of a *Maǧmūʿat ar-rasāʾil* (Maṭbaʿat al-Ḥusaynīyah 1323/1906). Only a comparison of the mss. will show whether this treatise is similar or even identical to another by Ibn Taymīyah entitled *al-Ǧawāb al-bāhir fī ziyārat* (var. *zawr*) *al-maqābir* and preserved in Damascus (GALS II p. 125). This work was also glossed by one of Ibn Taymīyah's followers called al-Ǧamāl ʿAbd Allāh b. Yaʿqūb al-Iskandarī "Ibn al-Ardabīn" (or "Ibn Ardus") who died in aṣ-Ṣāliḥīyah/Damascus in 749 or 754 H, see DK II p. 414; IQŠuhbTārīḫ II pp. 589f.; INāṣRadd p. 184.

402 Naǧm ad-Dīn Abū l-ʿAbbās A. b. al-ʿImād M. (655–723 H): IṢuqTālīWaf p. 190; BN XIV pp. 106f.; DK I pp. 280-2; ITağrManh II pp. 97-9 and NZ IX p. 258; IṬūlṮağr pp. 84f.; ŠḎ VI pp. 58f.

Ramaḍān 705 H. A tribunal was set up in order to investigate Ibn Taymīyah's case, as a result of which he was put in prison and later transferred to Alexandria. Released in early 709 H, Ibn Taymīyah returned to Cairo and polemicised against the Sufis, his most prominent opponent being the mystic Ibn ᶜAṭāᵓ Allāh as-Sikandarī (d. 709 H).[403] Thus Ibn Taymīyah encountered new trouble and was again imprisoned, though released already in Šawwāl 709 H. During that period, obviously while in prison, Ibn Taymīyah wrote something in a somewhat derisory manner and directed it against Taqīy ad-Dīn al-Iḫnāᵓī al-Mālikī (see below) "in a book he had composed about the *ziyārat al-qubūr*", and as a consequence he was prohibited in Ǧumādā II 709 H from publishing further writings.[404] Thus, if the date is correct, Ibn Taymīyah composed his above-mentioned writing about the visitation of tombs in 709, though other sources mention the year 710 H.[405] Towards the end of Ibn Taymīyah's life the "question of visitation" brought about a new crisis in 726 H:

> "The reason for that was that Ibn Taymīyah had published a fatwa to the effect that no journeys should be undertaken except to visit 'the three mosques',[406] according to the known Tradition,[407] and further, that no journey should be undertaken to visit the tombs of the prophets, such as the tombs of our father Abraham (Ibrāhīm al-Ḫalīl), of the Prophet and of others from among the prophets and the righteous.[408] At the same time it happened that (Ibn Taymīyah's pupil) aš-Šams Muḥammad (Ibn al-Qayyim) Imām al-Ǧawzīyah went to Jerusalem and (...) in a sermon he held there mentioned the question (of the *ziyārah*), saying 'I will return from here (to Damascus) and I shall not visit the tomb of Abraham (in Hebron)', thus demonstrating bad manners towards him (*sc.* Abraham)'.[409] Then he went to Nāblus where a session was held for him. In his sermon,

403 *Cf.* ITaġrManh II p. 121 and Northrup: *Mamlūk sultanate* pp. 267f.

404 IǦazḪaw II pp. 263f.; BN XIV p. 134. *Cf.* also MaqrMuq I pp. 463f.

405 *Cf.* GALS II p. 124. I am not sure whether this work is the same as that mentioned by IQay-MuᵓallbnTay p. 30 by the title *ad-Durr al-manṯūr fī ziyārat al-qubūr*.

406 I.e. in Mecca, Medina and Jerusalem (al-Aqṣā mosque); *cf.* above p. 25. How important the concept of these three mosques was might be gleaned from the fact that the Marīnid sultan Abū l-Ḥasan (r. 731–49 H) wrote three copies of the Qurᵓān with his own hand and had them sent to those three mosques (IḪaldᶜIbar VII pp. 265f. = MaqqNafḥ (C) VI pp. 135f.).

407 For this Tradition (*lā tušaddu r-riḥālu ᵓillā ᵓilā ṯalāṯati masāǧida ...*), see FB III p. 81 (*faḍl aṣ-ṣalāh fī masǧid Makkah* 1) and 90 (*faḍl* etc. 6); IV p. 89 (*ǧazāᵓ aṣ-ṣayd* 26); IV p. 302 (*ṣawm* 67); ᶜIyāḍŠifāᵓ (B) II pp. 76f. / (Š) II pp. 89f. = HarŠŠifāᵓ II pp. 158f.; HaytTuḥfZuw pp. 72-6. *Cf.* ITayMaǧm XXVII p. 5 and *passim*; ḤurRawḍ p. 355; KarKawākib pp. 150-2; al-Albānī: *Aḥkām al-ǧanāᵓiz* pp. 224-31; Memon: *Ibn Taimīya's Struggle* pp. 15 and 261. The background of this Tradition is analysed in Kister: *Three Mosques*.

408 For this fatwa, see also MaqrMuq I p. 467.

409 Ibn Taymīyah often polemicised against visiting that tomb in particular, see ITayMaǧm XXVII pp. 8f., 20f., 32 and 107-11. For its veneration and visiting, see ᶜUlaymīUns II pp. 56-8. That the attack of Ibn Taymīyah against this popular shrine also had an enormous political impact is obvious, the more as the sultan al-Malik an-Nāṣir Muḥammad himself had visited Hebron in 717 H (IIyāsBad I p. 449). According to az-Zarkašī, the veneration of Abraham's shrine in Hebron was unheard of before the conquest of Jerusalem in 583 H by Ṣalāḥ ad-Dīn, see ZarkAḥkām p. 296.

Ibn al-Qayyim spoke in detail about the question until he said 'The tomb of the Prophet must not be visited as his mosque should'.[410] At this point, the people rose against him and he had to be protected by the governor of Nāblus".[411]

As a result of this conflict, Ibn Taymīyah (together with Ibn al-Qayyim) was locked up in prison in Šaᶜbān 726 H in Damascus and did not leave it again until his death in Ǧumādā II 728 H. He had been forbidden to publish further fatwas and write or read anything in prison; even his books, writing-paper and pens were confiscated.[412]

3.5.3. Attacking and defending Ibn Taymīyah

The dispute over the question of visitation as it raged during the first half of the eighth century H gave rise to a large corpus of writings which either criticise this practice or defend it. Most of these writings are meant to react against the challenge of Ibn Taymīyah. Ibn Ḥaǧar al-ᶜAsqalānī quotes his contemporary al-Kirmānī (whom he otherwise shunned and heartily despised) with the words: "Concerning this question, many debates arose in our time in the Syrian lands and both sides (i.e. opponents and defendants: *aṭ-ṭarafayn*) composed treatises on the matter".[413]

Eighth-century writings

No systematic attempt has been made so far to reconstruct the range of literature known to pertain to the subject. In order to support further research, I will list in the following those literary sources (both extant and lost) which are of relevance to the question of the *ziyārat al-qubūr*, especially the visitation of the Prophet's sepulchre. The majority of those writings take a critical stance towards Ibn Taymīyah, defending the common practice against his invectives.

(1) "The Accepted Way of Visiting the Messenger (of God)" (*al-ᶜAmal al-maqbūl fī ziyārat ar-rasūl*) by Ibn az-Zamlakānī (d. 727 H).

al-Kamāl Abū l-Maᶜālī M. b. al-ᶜAlāʾ Abī l-Ḥasan ᶜAlī ... b. Ḫālid b. Abī Duǧānah Simāk b. Ḫarašah al-Anṣārī aš-Šāfiᶜī (Damascus 666/7 – Bilbays 727 H): IǦazḤaw II pp. 230-35; ḎahMuᶜǧam pp. 165f. and ḎahMuᶜǧŠuyūḫ p. 540; *Wāfī* IV pp. 214-21; BN XIV pp. 131f.; KutFawāt IV pp. 7-11; SubkīṬab IX pp. 190-6; IMulᶜIqd pp. 421f.; INāṣRadd pp. 107-9; MaqrSulūk II p. 290 and MaqrMuq VI pp. 315-8; DK IV pp. 192-4; NZ IX pp. 270f.; SuyḤusnMuḥ I p. 277; ŠḎ VI pp. 78f.; ŠawkBadr II pp. 212f.; GAL II p. 71; ZA VII p. 175; *cf.* also Shoshan: *Popular culture* p. 129 note 17.

Ibn az-Zamlakānī's treatise counters the teaching of Ibn Taymīyah and is therefore often called *ar-Radd ᶜalā bn Taymīyah.* Unfortunately, although mentioned in a

410 It is hard to see what this phrase was intended to mean in practice, since the Prophet's sepulchre and his mosque are virtually part of the same building complex. Most probably the intention (*niyyah*) of the visitor was at stake, that is, whether he visited that place for the mosque or for the tomb in the first place.

411 IǦazḤaw II p. 111. *Cf.* also ṢafAᶜyān I p. 67.

412 BN XIV p. 134; *cf.* also Shoshan: *Popular culture* pp. 68f.

413 FB III p. 85 (*faḍl aṣ-ṣalāh fī masǧid Makkah* 1). For the reverberations of this conflict in modern Egypt, see Bannerth: *Wallfahrtsstätten Kairos* pp. 90-3.

number of sources, the work has not been preserved as far as I know. Ibn az-Zamlakānī was at first a fervent supporter of Ibn Taymīyah, but later changed his mind and became one of his better known adversaries.[414]

(2) "The Clear Statement and the Triumph: The Visitation of the Selected Prophet" (*al-Bayān wa-l-intiṣār fī ziyārat an-nabī al-muḫtār*) by Dā'ūd aš-Šāḏilī (d. 733 H).

aš-Šaraf Abū Sul. Dā'ūd b. ar-Rukn ʿUmar b. Ibr. aš-Šāḏilī al-Sikandarī (al-Iskandarānī) al-Mālikī (Alexandria, 690–715 or only 732/3 H): DK II p. 191; SaḫTuḥfLaṭ I pp. 328f.; SuyBuġ I p. 562; ŠN p. 204.

In his biographical dictionary of Medinan people, as-Saḫāwī describes the work as a "refutation of the opponents of this practice (...), a long book, in two volumes, well-done".[415] The work is not, as it seems, extant any longer. In Medina, it was transmitted by the family of the historian as-Samhūdī (d. 911 H), from the author himself,[416] and as-Samhūdī quotes it in his history of Medina.[417]

(3) "The Exquisite Gem: A Refutation of the Opponents of Visitation" (*at-Tuḥfah al-muḫtārah fī r-radd ʿalā munkirī* [or *man ʾankara*] *z-ziyārah*) by Tāğ ad-Dīn (Ibn) al-Fākihānī (d. 734 H).

Abū Ḥafṣ Tāğ ad-Dīn (Sirāğ ad-Dīn) ʿUmar b. Abī l-Yumn ʿAlī b. Sālim al-Laḫmī al-Iskandarī al-Mālikī (Alexandria, 654 or 656 – 731 or 734 H): IĞazḤaw III pp. 704f.; BN XIV p. 168; IFarDībāğ pp. 286f.; DK III pp. 254f.; SuyBuġ II p. 221 and SuyḤusnMuḥ I p. 381; IQāḍīDurrah III pp. 197-9; ŠḎ VI pp. 96f.; ŠN pp. 204f.; GALS II p. 15; ZA V pp. 217f.

The work, which has not been preserved, is mentioned by title in several of the sources cited. Ibn al-Fākihānī was a fervent advocate of the veneration of the Prophet, though he also composed a work critical of the celebrations held in occasion of the Prophet's birthday, entitled *al-Mawrid fī l-kalām ʿalā ʿamal al-mawlid*. Moving is the story of his visit to Damascus in Ramaḍān 731 H: "at-Tāğ al-Fākihānī went to Damascus in order to visit the sandal of the Messenger of God that is kept there in the Dār al-Ḥadīṯ al-Ašrafīyah. (...) When he saw the blessed sandal, he uncovered his head, kissed it and rubbed his face on it. Tears were flowing down his cheeks and he recited (*ṭawīl*):

فَلَوْ قِيلَ لِلمَجْنُونِ لَيْلَى وَوَصْلَهَا * تُرِيدُ أَمِ الدُّنْيا وَمَا فِي طَوَايَاهَا
لَقَالَ غُبَارٌ مِنْ تُرَابِ نِعَالِهَا * أَحَبُّ إِلَى نَفْسِي وَأَشْفَى لِبَلْوَاهَا

If al-Mağnūn is told 'Do you desire Laylā[418] and to be united in love with her * or do you crave for the world with all its designs?',

414 *Cf.* also MaqrMuq I p. 469.

415 SaḫTuḥfLaṭ I p. 329.

416 SaḫTuḥfLaṭ II p. 52.

417 SamWafā' IV p. 1385 (*qāla ʾAbū Sulaymāna fī muṣannafihī fī z-ziyārah* ...) = HaytTuḥfZuw p. 120.

418 The poet refers here to al-Mağnūn and Laylā, one of the most popular love couples in Arabic poetry and literature.

Then he would respond 'The dust particles sticking at her sandals * are more lovable to my soul and better suited to heal its affliction'".[419]

(4) "The Slaying Sword: A Refutation of Ibn as-Subkī (Concerning the Visit of the Prophet)" (*aṣ-Ṣārim al-munkī fī r-radd ʿalā bn as-Subkī* [*fī ziyārat an-nabī*]) by Ibn ᶜAbd al-Hādī (d. 744 H).

Šams ad-Dīn Abū ᶜAl. M. b. al-ᶜImād A. ... b. Qudāmah al-Maqdisī al-Ǧammāᶜīlī aṣ-Ṣāliḥī al-Ḥanbalī (Damascus, between 704 and 706 – 744 H): DahTadk IV p. 1508; *Wāfī* II pp. 161f.; BN XIV p. 210; ḤusDayl pp. 49f.; IRaǧDayl II pp. 436-9; INāṣRadd pp. 63-5; MaqrSulūk II pp. 659f.; DK III pp. 421f.; SuyBuġ I pp. 29f.; IṬūlQal pp. 313-6; ŠD VI p. 141; ḤḪ II p. 1070; GALS II p. 128; ZA VI p. 222.

This text, repeatedly printed,[420] counters the treatise by at-Taqīy as-Subkī (see below no. 6) in which he attacked Ibn Taymīyah. Ibn ᶜAbd al-Hādī thus defends his former teacher,[421] and Ibn Ḥaǧar later commented: "In this treatise, Ibn ᶜAbd al-Hādī sides with Ibn Taymīyah (...), and the book is famous among us".[422]

(5) "The Refutation of Ibn Taymīyah, Concerning the Question of Visitation" (*ar-Radd ʿalā bn Taymīyah fī masʾalat az-ziyārah*) by Taqīy ad-Dīn (Ibn) al-Iḫnāʾī (d. 750 H).

at-Taqīy Abū l-ᶜAl. M. b. Abī Bakr b. ᶜĪsā as-Saᶜdī al-Miṣrī al-Mālikī (*c.*658 – 750 H), Malikite chief-judge in Egypt for many years and belonging to the close entourage of al-Malik an-Nāṣir Muḥammad: IFarDībāǧ p. 413; DK IV pp. 27f.; NZ X p. 247; SaḫWaǧīz I p. 490; SuyḤusnMuḥ I p. 392; ŠN p. 187; Escovitz: *Office of Qāḍī* pp. 49f. and 102-4.

It was presumably this work which prompted Ibn Taymīyah to respond with a treatise of his own (see above); not extant.

(6) "The Healing of the Sick: The Visitation of the Best of Mankind" (*Šifāʾ as-siqām* [or *al-ʾasqām*] *fī ziyārat Ḫayr al-ʾanām*) by Taqīy ad-Dīn as-Subkī (d. 756 H).

at-Taqīy Abū l-Ḥasan ᶜAlī b. az-Zayn Abī M. ᶜAbd al-Kāfī al-Ḫazraǧī aš-Šāfiᶜī:[423] DahTadk IV p. 1507; ḤusDayl pp. 39f.; SubkīṬab X pp. 139-338; BN XIV p. 252 and *passim*; IMulᶜIqd pp. 413f.; MaqrSulūk III pp. 22f.; DK III pp. 134-42; ITaġrManh VIII pp. 106-9 and NZ X pp. 318f.; SaḫWaǧīz I p. 82; SuyḤusnMuḥ I pp. 277-82; IṬūlṮaġr pp. 101-3; ŠD VI pp. 180f.; ḤḪ II p. 1049; GAL II pp. 86-8; GALS II pp. 102-4; ZA V p. 116; EI^2 IX p. 744 (no. 6).

As as-Subkī himself says towards the beginning of his treatise, its title initially ran "The Launch of an Attack against those who Oppose the Journey of the Visitation" (*Šann al-ġārah ʿalā man ʾankara safar az-ziyārah*) and was then changed, for

419 IFarDībāǧ pp. 286f. = IQāḍīDurrah III p. 199.

420 Cairo 1319; Hyderabad n.d.; Beirut 1405 = IᶜAHādīṢārim (see bibliography).

421 He also wrote his biography: *al-ʿUqūd ad-durrīyah min manāqib Ibn Taymīyah*, ed. M. Ḥāmid al-Fiqī, Cairo: Maṭb. Ḥiǧāzī 1356/1938 (and repr. in Beirut).

422 FB III p. 85 (*faḍl aṣ-ṣalāh fī masǧid Makkah* 1).

423 He must not be confounded with his great-cousin, likewise known as Taqīy ad-Dīn as-Subkī (al-Adīb Abū l-Fatḥ M. b. ᶜAbd al-Laṭīf b. Ya.: 704 or 705 – Damascus 744 H): ḤusDayl pp. 51f.; DK IV pp. 144f.; ŠD VI pp. 141f.; EI^2 IX p. 744 (no. 2).

unknown reasons, to the present title.[424] The treatise by as-Subkī (who visited the Prophet's tomb himself in 716 H) was to prove the most influential and widely known among those attacking the teaching of Ibn Taymīyah; it did not only provoke counter-attacks (see above no. 4), but was deemed important enough to being abridged by a later scholar;[425] it was printed repeatedly.[426] The text was read by aṣ-Ṣafadī with the author himself,[427] and Ibn Ḥağar in his scholarly curriculum provides a chain of transmission for the book.[428] The work was of prime importance for the chapter on visiting the Prophet's tomb in as-Samhūdī's history of Medina, who relies heavily on as-Subkī's text and once cites it as *ar-Radd ᶜalā bn Taymīyah fī mas'alat az-ziyārah.*[429]

(7) "The Edited Traditions that Mention the Visitation of the Tomb of the Prophet" (*al-'Aḥādīṯ al-wāridah fī ḏikr ziyārat qabr an-nabī*) by aṣ-Ṣalāḥ al-ᶜAlā'ī (Ibn Kaykaldī) (d. 761 H).

Ṣalāḥ ad-Dīn Abū Saᶜīd Ḫalīl b. Kaykaldī al-Maqdisī aš-Šāfiᶜī (Damascus 694 – Jerusalem 761 H): ṢafAᶜyān I pp. 361-4 and *Wāfī* XIII pp. 410-6; ḤusḎayl pp. 43-6; BN XIV p. 267; IQŠuhbahTārīḫ III pp. 167-9; SubkīṬab X pp. 35-8; IMulᶜIqd p. 430; INāṣRadd pp. 173f.; MaqrSulūk III p. 55; DK II pp. 179-82; ITaġrManh V pp. 282-5 and NZ X p. 337; SaḫWağīz I pp. 108f.; ᶜUlaymīUns II pp. 106f.; ŠḎ VI pp. 190f.; ZA II pp. 369f.

The work is mentioned by title in several of our sources. Though the text has been lost, it may be safely assumed that its material consisted of those Traditions which affirm or otherwise support visiting the Prophet's sepulchre. The author was on intimate terms with other scholars who attacked the views of Ibn Taymīyah in writings of their own: al-ᶜAlā'i's most important teacher for many years was al-Kamāl Ibn az-Zamlakānī (see above no. 1), who gave him the permission to issue fatwas in 724 H, and Taqīy ad-Dīn as-Subkī (see no. 6) compiled his academic curriculum (or list of teachers and works studied: *al-mašyaḫah*).

Later treatises

Works about the *ziyārat al-qubūr*, which were produced after the eighth century H and sometimes only indirectly relate to the dispute brought about by Ibn Taymīyah, include the following:

(1) "Condemning (*or* Dispraising) the Visitation of Tombs" (*Ḏamm ziyārat al-qubūr*) by Ğalāl ad-Dīn as-Suyūṭī (d. 911 H). This title is cited by al-Kattānī among

424 SubkīŠifā' p. 4. *Cf.* also ḤusḎayl p. 40 and SubkīṬab X p. 308.

425 *Iḫtiṣār Kitāb Šifā' as-siqām* by Šams ad-Dīn as-Sayyid aš-Šarīf Abū ᶜAl. M. b. al-Ḥasan aš-Šāfiᶜī al-Wāsiṭī al-Ḥusaynī (d. 776 H); for his biography, see DK IV p. 41; ŠḎ VI p. 244; GAL II p. 34 and 87; GALS II p. 30. The writing, whose text has been preserved (*cf.* GAL II p. 87), was completed in 765 H.

426 Būlāq 1319; Beirut 1411 = SubkīŠifā' (see bibliography).

427 SubkīṬab X p. 5.

428 IḤağMuᶜğam p. 397.

429 SamWafā' IV p. 1404.

the writings of as-Suyūṭī,[430] although nothing is heard of this work in other sources or bibliographical reference books.

(2) "The Gem of the (frequent) Visitors to the Tomb of the Selected Prophet" (*Tuḥfat az-zuwwār ʾilā qabr an-nabī al-muḫtār*) and "The Well-Strung Jewels:[431] The Visitation of the Venerated Prophetic Noble Tomb" (*al-Ǧawhar al-munaẓẓam fī ziyārat al-qabr aš-šarīf an-nabawī al-mukarram*) by Ibn Ḥağar al-Haytamī (d. 973 H).[432] Both works are extant and printed; they stress the merits of visiting the Prophet's tomb and must be seen, in the wake of as-Subkī's treatise (see above no. 6), as the most accomplished monographs propagating the practice of visitation.

The ascription of the first work (= HaytTuḥfZuw) is not entirely beyond doubt: the title does not appear in any source known to me apart from the manuscript itself, and on the title-page of the ms. (used for the published version) the author's name is only given as "Šihāb ad-Dīn Aḥmad b. Ḥağar aš-Šāfiᶜī", while at the beginning of the text, the author is introduced as "al-Ḥāfiẓ Ibn Ḥağar" (p. 23). The colophon at the end is dated Ǧumādā II 1050 H (p. 210). Given the content of the treatise (see the following) the authorship of Ibn Ḥağar al-Haytamī seems, however, possible because al-Haytamī's name-sake Šihāb ad-Dīn Aḥmad Ibn Ḥağar al-ᶜAsqalānī cannot be the author, since the text quotes substantially from later authorities. The date mentioned at the end of the text may well be the date when the treatise was copied in later times without being stated explicitly; this is not uncommon in Arabic manuscripts.

Both writings by al-Haytamī are far from identical. The first, shorter treatise (= HaytTuḥfZuw) is actually nothing but a reworking of the long chapter on the visitation of the Prophet's tomb which closes as-Samhūdī's history of Medina.[433] Though the order of some of the material taken from as-Samhūdī's treatise has been changed, the overall structure – preface, four chapters, closure – was copied by al-Haytamī; there is almost no additional material, but substantial parts of as-Samhūdī's account were left out. It is therefore hard to consider this work as an original contribution to the field. None the less, it is a neat summary of the issue.

The second, longer text (= HaytǦawhar) is al-Haytamī's main contribution to the literature about the visitation of the Prophet's sepulchre. As he says in the preface, he was prompted to compose it after visiting the Prophet's tomb in Šawwāl 956 H (p. 9). In eight chapters, al-Haytamī discusses all aspects of the visitation of tombs and the sepulchre of the Prophet in particular, thus making this treatise the most comprehensive coverage of the subject written after the eighth century H. Interestingly, more than half of the book deals less with the merit of visiting the Prophet's tomb – which is largely taken for granted – than with the behaviour and the rites which the visitor to Medina and the Prophet's mosque should follow. This aspect, centred on the practice of visitation, renders the treatise similar to many

430 al-Kattānī: *Fahras* II p. 1017.

431 *Munaẓẓam* means literally "well-ordered" and usually refers to pearls, or jewels, arranged on a string (e.g. in a necklace).

432 Šihāb ad-Dīn Abū l-ᶜAbbās A. b. M. as-Saᶜdī al-Makkī (Maḥallat Abī l-Haytam 909 – Mecca 973 H): ᶜAydNūr pp. 258-3; Bā-FaqīhŠiḥr pp. 380-2; ŠḎ VIII pp. 370-2; *Ḏayl* ḤḪ I p. 249; GAL II p. 388; GALS II pp. 527-9. ZA I p. 234.

433 SamWafāʾ IV pp. 1336-421.

Shiite visitation guides (see Chapter 3) that are replete with litanies and the description of the common rites at the individual shrines. It also shows that in the time between the eighth century and the middle of the tenth century H interest in the custom of visitation had shifted noticeably towards its practical side. This happened because the supporters of visitation had won the day with most scholars, and hence the visitation of the Prophet's sepulchre had during the ninth century H become an established and widely-accepted practice. Consequently, there was less need to defend it than was necessary during the turbulent eighth century H when the challenge of the Neo-Hanbalites was still virulent.

(3) "The Shining Pearl: The Well-Approved-Of Visitation" (*ad-Durrah al-muḍīyah fī z-ziyārah ar-raḍīyah* [or *al-Muṣṭafawīyah*]) by al-Qāriʾ al-Harawī (d. 1014 H).[434]

This little treatise about the visit of the Prophet's sepulchre in Medina covers some 15 folios and is extant in ms. 886 of the Bayerische Staatsbibliothek, Munich.[435] I have not seen the ms. myself. Looking at some comments by al-Harawī in his *Šarḥ aš-Šifāʾ*, it seems that he did not side with Ibn Taymīyah and his supporters, although al-Harawī was very balanced in his judgment:

> "What is known from aš-Šaᶜbī and an-Naḫaᶜī,[436] viz. that they pronounced the visitation of tombs disapproved of, is rather singular and their opinion is not taken into account because it conflicts with the consensus of all other scholars. Ibn Taymīyah of the Hanbalites went too far when he prohibited travelling to visit the Prophet's sepulchre – *taṣliyah* –, in the same manner as others who exaggerate when they claim that it was known with certainty (*bi-ḍ-ḍarūrah*) on the basis of the creed that the visitation (of the Prophet's tomb) is a meritorious action (*qurbah*) and that everybody who denies that must be considered an unbeliever. However, the second opinion is perhaps nearer to the truth because prohibiting that upon which the scholars agree in its being desirable (i.e. the practice of visitation) might indeed amount to unbelief".[437]

(4) "The Healing of the Hearts, Concerning the Visitation of Shrines and Tombs" (*Šifāʾ aṣ-ṣudūr fī ziyārat al-mašāhid wa-l-qubūr*) by al-Karmī (d. 1033 H).[438]

The work is extant, one manuscript being preserved in the Library of Ǧamīl Abī Sulaymān at-Taᶜlīmī as-Saᶜūdī in Tunis.[439] However, the work has not been edited yet, as far as I could establish, nor have I seen the ms. myself. Judging by the title, the treatise concerns the question of visiting tombs in general, not only the visit to the Prophet's sepulchre in Medina. Considering that al-Karmī was a faithful follower

434 al-Mullā ᶜAlī b. Sulṭān al-Qāriʾ al-Harawī al-Makkī al-Ḥanafī (d. Mecca 1014 H): ḤḪ I p. 743; MuḥḪul III pp. 185f.; GAL II p. 394-8; GALS II pp. 539-43; ZA V pp. 166f.

435 Aumer: *Staatsbibliothek* 886 (= p. 395); not mentioned in GAL(S).

436 See above p. 27.

437 HarŠŠifāʾ III p. 151.

438 Zayn ad-Dīn Marᶜī b. Yūsuf b. Abī Bakr al-Maqdisī al-Ḥanbalī (d. Cairo 1033 H): *Ḏayl* ḤḪ II p. 50; GAL II p. 369; GALS II pp. 496f.

439 See the editor's remarks in KarKawākib p. 25 (no. 47). The work is missing in GAL(S).

of the teachings of Ibn Taymīyah (whose biography he also wrote), it might be assumed that the work is largely critical of the usages connected with the visitation of tombs and the mortuary cult in general.

(5) "The Crème of Notions: The Visiting of the Lord of Mankind" (*Zubdat al-fikar fī ziyārat Sayyid al-bašar*) by ᶜAlī Ḫayrī al-Kūtāhīyeh-wī ar-Rūmī al-Ḥanafī (d. after 1037 H). This writing is mentioned only in *Ḏayl* ḤḪ I p. 612.

(6) "The Garden of Serenity: The Customs to Follow in Visiting the Chosen (Prophet)" (*Rawḍat aṣ-ṣafā fī ʾādāb ziyārat al-Muṣṭafā*) by Muḥammad b. ᶜAlī b. Muḥammad Ibn ᶜAllān al-Makkī (d. 1057 H), mentioned by Ḥāǧǧī Ḫalīfah.[440]

(7) "The Precious Pearl: What the Visitor to the Prophet Will Achieve if Coming to Medina"[441] (*ad-Durrah aṯ-ṯamīnah fī mā li-zāʾir an-nabī ʾilā l-Madīnah*) by the mystic Aḥmad b. Muḥammad ad-Daǧānī al-Qurašī (born 991 – d. Medina 1071 H).[442] According to az-Ziriklī, the work has been printed.

(8) "The Selected Treatise about the Prohibited Usages during the Visitation" (*ar-Risālah al-muḫtārah fī manāhī z-ziyārah*) by Ibrāhīm b. Sulaymān al-Azharī al-Ḥanafī. In this treatise, written *c.*1100 H and preserved in manuscript,[443] the author "shows that it is contrary to the law, when visiting graves, to touch or kiss them, or lie on them".[444]

(9) "Uncovering the Light from (i.e. Concerning) the Inhabitants of the Tombs" (*Kašf an-nūr ʿan ʾaṣḥāb al-qubūr*) by ᶜAbd al-Ġanīy Ibn an-Nābulusī (d. 1143 H).[445] This is one of several fatwas which he wrote in favour of the concept of intercession and in defence of the visitation of the tombs of saintly men, directed, among others, against the teachings of Ibn Taymīyah. According to the preface, Ibn an-Nābulusī wrote this *risālah* about "the appearance of miracle-like blessings (*karāmāt*) worked on behalf of the pious[446] after their death, about the ruling whether a building might be erected above their tombs and screenings be set up, apart from other things (...)".[447] This short work is preserved in various manuscripts,[448] but still awaits publication.

440 ḤḪ I p. 926.

441 The Arabic construction is ambiguous. It might also be translated as "What does expect the Visitor of the Prophet, *or* what happens to him".

442 MuḥḪul I pp. 343-6; GAL II p. 392; ZA I p. 239.

443 GAL II p. 315.

444 Ahlwardt no. 2694 = EI^2 I p. 821.

445 *Ḏayl* ḤḪ II p. 369.

446 The *karāmāt al-ʾawliyāʾ* are sometimes, albeit incorrectly, called "miracles of the saints".

447 *fī ẓuhūri karāmāti l-ʾawliyāʾi baʿda mawtihim wa-ḥukmi rafʿi l-bināʾi ʿalayhim wa-taʿlīqi s-sutūri ʾilā ġayri ḏālika* (cited in Maḫṭūṭāt Dār al-Kutub II p. 259).

448 Cairo, Dār al-Kutub no. 19117b (Maḫṭūṭāt Dār al-Kutub II p. 259); Damascus, Ẓāhirīyah ms. 1377, ff. 30a-41b, see Chodkiewicz: *Sainteté et les saints* p. 26; *cf.* also Gramlich: *Wunder* p. 364.

4. *Practice: common motives for visiting tombs and cemeteries*

4.1. General remarks

There are several reasons why, in Islamic culture, people set out to visit tombs and cemeteries. This development of a mortuary cult and its accompanying practices was not primarily, or even exclusively, the outcome of the believers being "deeply affected by the mystical side of Islam".[449] Though indeed numerous shrines visited today belong to Sufi saints, especially in the eastern parts of the Islamic world as well as on its western fringes and in sub-Saharan Africa, historically it seems that the spread of organised Sufism followed the growth of the practice of *ziyārah* which can be observed among the Sunnites from the sixth century H onwards.

On the other hand, the visitation of tombs was not always in accordance with the precepts laid down by Sufi brotherhoods, in particular during the twelfth and thirteenth centuries H, a period which saw the rise of a number of important Sufi movements that fought against those allegedly "popular" or even "decadent" forms of religion and ritual.[450] More than by Sufism, the Sunnite mortuary cult seems to have been influenced by Shiite Islam (see above p. 70) which was spreading from Iraq and the eastern lands and later towards Syria and Egypt. The Fatimid interlude in Egypt was less important in this process than might be imagined at first glance, notwithstanding their important contribution to the development of larger burial monuments and tomb-sanctuaries.[451] In North Africa there have always been indigenous forms of a mortuary cult, though these exerted, as it seems, little influence on nearby al-Andalus and even less so on the central and eastern Islamic lands with the notable exception of Egypt.

Western practices were carried from al-Andalus and the Maghrib into Egypt and mingled with local or other imported customs, contributing to that extraordinary funerary culture we witness there. In some sense, Gérard de Nerval was thus unwittingly right when he wrote in his travel journal: "L'Égypte est un vaste tombeau".[452] Nerval was prompted to his remark by the remnants of pharaonic Egypt, and the customs of the ancient Egyptians relating to death and burial[453] are a long way from what we find in the Islamic culture. In Islam, no importance in any way comparable to ancient Egypt has been attached to the tomb as such, its inner decoration or its outward appearance (see Chapter 2), nor to the material remains of the body or its conservation; there are no grave offerings nor were objects relating to the future life

449 Rippin: *Muslims* I p. 98.

450 Thus the Moroccan Tiǧānīyah order explicitly prohibited its members from visiting the tombs of dead Sufi "saints", see Sirriyeh: *Sufis and Anti-Sufis* p. 18.

451 *Cf.* Lapidus: *Ayyūbid Religious Policy* pp. 280f. and Taylor: *Reevaluating the Shiʿi Role*, esp. pp. 4-6. See also below p. 217.

452 Gérard de Nerval: *Voyage en Orient*, edd. J. Guillaume and C. Pichois, with an introduction by André Miquel, Paris 1998 (^{1}1851), p. 144.

453 *Cf.* Assmann: *Tod und Jenseits* and Assmann: *Tod als Thema*, esp. pp. 17f. and 27.

of the deceased ever buried with the dead;[454] even information about the dead at their respective burial sites, e.g. in epitaphs, was reduced to a minimum or lacking at all.[455] Nevertheless, Nerval's dictum applies to Islamic Egypt as well. The reason for that is that the presence of the dead was chiefly the work of the mind and hence articulated mainly by words, both oral tradition and literary texts, either by the deceased themselves (who appear in dreams or visions) or by the living. This is why, as we will see further below, continuous contact with the dead and the verbal communication between the dead and the living was of outstanding importance. This also fits into the picture of a wholly language-centred culture such as the pre-modern Islamic culture was.

The importance of tombs and their visitation is frequently depicted, by modern non-Muslim and Muslim scholars alike, as an element of popular religion and piety which is contrary to the precepts of Islam as laid down in Qurʾān and Tradition and embraced by the learned élite. This in some sense is true, because if somewhere in the Sunnite Islamic world criticism was raised against the practice(s) of visitation, it normally stemmed from the learned who were eager to portray these practices either as an aberration of the ignorant, bereft of faith and reason, or as a pernicious adaptation of Shiite customs. However, in another sense this is utterly untrue, and far too much attention has been given to those scholars who, like Ibn Taymīyah and his followers, voiced this criticism.

As will appear from the following pages, visiting tombs and cemeteries (with all this entails) was a cherished practice among the common people and the learned élite alike. Support of that usage among many scholars and men of religion was genuine enough from the early days of Islam. What is more, no distinction could be made between the visitation of tombs of a "private" character – the tombs of relatives and the like – and of those of a "public" character – the shrines of saintly men and women, or the Shiite Imams –, because this difference is blurred in most sources. This is the result to be drawn from a vast range of pre-modern sources. Here the conclusion reached by Boaz Shoshan in his *Popular culture in medieval Cairo* can be referred to:

> "Despite the existence of cultural division (if one is to avoid the notion of hierarchy) (...) there has been in most cultures, at a given point in time, a common cultural domain consisting of shared practices and meanings, the very links between high and low cultures. The Cairene case was no exception: in medieval Cairo the cult of saints created a cultural common ground for the people and the elite".[456]

454 Exceptions were made for objects which in themselves have little material value but were considered to possess immense personal or "eschatological" value for the deceased, like single hairs of the Prophet, pieces of earth from a sacred shrine, or books and ascetic poems.

455 For details, see Volume I, especially Chapter 1. The relative lack of autobiographical texts on Islamic funerary monuments and tombs, notwithstanding those few epitaphs which seem to belie this, can be seen as one of the major contrasts with the ancient civilisation of Egypt. For the relationship between texts and funerary monuments in pharaonic Egypt, see Assmann: *Der literarische Aspekt*.

456 *Popular culture* p. 78. Moreover, the following remark of Jonathan Berkey should be recorded

The pre-modern Arabic literary sources, embracing the most diverse genres, are replete with notices relating to the practices of visitation of both private tombs and commonly venerated shrines. It is curious to see, therefore, that modern scholars have often neither sufficiently acknowledged[457] nor even realised that richness of source material which allows us to reconstruct many facets of the pre-modern Islamic mortuary cult and the practices of visitation.

The practice of praying for the deceased (*aṣ-ṣalāh ʿalā l-ʾamwāt*) or invoking blessings on their behalf has not been singled out in the following pages as an independent motive of visiting tombs. That this practice must be seen as one of the most important reasons for visiting tombs of a "private" character is obvious; yet there is little to say about this practice apart from the simple fact that people went to a tomb and uttered prayers for the benefit of the deceased.

This practice was unanimously acknowlegded as desirable and accepted by even the most strict scholars.[458] Ibn Taymīyah acknowledged doing so and saw in it the only lawful justification for the visitation of tombs (*az-ziyārah aš-šarʿīyah*, as opposed to *az-ziyārah al-bidʿīyah*).[459] His pupil Ibn al-Qayyim called it, fond of rhetoric as he always was, the "visitation in the manner of the faithful" (*ziyārat ʾahl al-ʾīmān*).[460] None the less, this only applied to private prayers – performing the ritual prayer on cemeteries was categorically (*muṭlaqan*) ruled out by Ibn al-Qayyim and others[461] – if and as long as the benefit of the deceased and not that of the visitor was intended.[462] According to popular belief, praying for the deceased would illuminate their tombs.[463]

4.2. Healing and intercession

The most common reason for visiting tombs, especially if the deceased were considered pious and saintly persons, was (and still is) the hope for their intercession and succor. Much polemic against the overall feasibility of intercession (*šafāʿah, wasīlah*), above all that of the Prophet himself, and its invocation (*tawassul, tašaffuʿ, istiʿānah, istiġāṯah*) is known from the Neo-Hanbalites;[464] its refusal has been made a cornerstone of the ideology of the modern Wahhābite movement and many contemporary Islam-

here: "The cultic visitation of tombs (...) brings together the various social strata in a practice which demonstrates the diversity and fluidity of late medieval Egyptian culture" (Berkey: *Culture and society* p. 411). *Cf.* also Chamberlain: *Knowledge and social practice* p. 119.

457 See e.g. Leisten: *Architektur für Tote* p. 64: "Erstaunlich wenige Berichte beziehen sich auf Handlungen, die im Zusammenhang mit dem Begräbnis oder dem Totenbesuch von Hinterbliebenen oder Pilgern in Mausoleen stattfanden".

458 On the merits of the *duʿāʾ ʿalā l-ʾamwāt*, see HarMirqātMaf IV pp. 81f. *Cf.* also Gräf: *Auffassungen vom Tod* p. 136 and Kinberg: *Interaction* pp. 305f.

459 ITayMaǧm XXVII pp. 119f.; ITayZiy pp. 23ff.; *cf.* Memon: *Ibn Taimīya's Struggle* p. 18.

460 IQaylġāṯah I pp. 184-7.

461 IMandahFaw II p. 122; IQaylġāṯah I pp. 172 and 176; *cf.* FB III p. 263 (*ǧanāʾiz* 66) and Leisten: *Architektur für Tote* p. 7.

462 *Cf.* IQudʿUmdah p. 122.

463 See e.g. Basset: *Contes* III p. 382 (episode no. 229).

464 ITaylstiġ esp. I pp. 268ff. and II pp. 424ff.; Memon: *Ibn Taimīya's Struggle* pp. 265-97; IQaylġāṯah I pp. 201-6; al-Albānī: *Aḥkām al-ǧanāʾiz* p. 264 and *passim.*

ists.[465] However, it is hard to see how the possibility of intercession can be ruled out categorically in Islam, especially as we read in the Qurʾān: *If, when they wronged themselves, they had come to thee* (i.e. the Prophet) *and prayed forgiveness of God, and the Messenger had prayed forgiveness for them, they would have found God turns, All-compassionate* (Q 4:64), and *Ask forgiveness for thy sin, and for the believers, men and women* (Q 47:19).[466] These two verses, whose wording is not open to discussion, have always been the most important Qurʾānic evidence for those arguing in favour of intercession.[467]

The general plea for intercession could include asking for healing, viz. the removal of physical or psychical suffering, or help in bringing about the desired outcome in a wide range of worldly affairs (arranging or avoiding marriages, success in business, etc.); in cases, people might also want to express gratitude for help received. Thus one often spoke of "a tomb where prayers are heard (i.e. fulfilled)".[468] Put more succinctly, one called such a site "a proven tomb" (*qabr muǧarrab*), which was taken to mean that its visitation in many cases had had the desired effect. The people dubbed a tomb of that sort also "a proven antidote" (*tiryāq* or *diryāq muǧarrab*)[469] against all sorts of evils. Reports about somebody being cured or helped in various ways after visiting tombs and shrines abound in the sources and could easily fill another book. We even hear of tombs where not human beings, but wild beasts (e.g. hyenas) and birds were cured or otherwise aided.[470] The most remarkable story in this regard is told by al-Munāwī in the biography of Yūsuf al-ʿAǧamī al-Kūrānī (d. Cairo 768 H), featuring a "saintly" dog which was approached and later buried by the people, while his fellow-dogs bewailed him at his death and then took on the habit of visiting his grave.[471]

The practices connected to visits within the scope of intercession and succor are numerous, but it is mainly direct physical contact with the tomb (or more specifically the cenotaph) which was believed to bring about the desired result. Touching the tomb, in one way or another, is an age-old usage, which many legal scholars did not become tired of condemning: "It is detestable to see how the visitors to (the tombs

465 *Cf.* Gaborieau: *Cult of Muslim Saints*. For that argument in general, see Schimmel: *Messenger* pp. 84-91; an excellent discussion of the Arabic terms of relevance in that dispute is provided by ŠawkDurr pp. 2ff. and *passim*; *cf.* also Mayeur-Jaouen: *Intercession.*

466 *wa-law ʾannahum ʾiḏ ẓalamū ʾanfusahum ǧāʾūka fa-staġfarū llāha wa-staġfara lahumu r-rasūlu la-waǧadū llāha tawwāban raḥīman* (Q 4:64); *wa-staġfir li-ḏanbika wa-li-l-muʾminīna wa-li-l-muʾmināti* (Q 47:19).

467 *Cf.* SubkīŠifāʾ pp. 81ff.

468 E.g. *al-qabr al-mašhūr bi-stiǧābat ad-duʿāʾ*, *al-qabr al-maʿrūf bi-ʾiǧābat ad-duʿāʾ ʿindahū* or *ad-duʿāʾ yustaǧāb ʿinda qabr fulān*; *cf.* also Taylor: *Vicinity of the Righteous* pp. 52f.

469 IǦawzīṢafwah I p. 529; QušRis p. 427 and Memon: *Ibn Taimīya's Struggle* p. 270 (in both places said of the tomb of Maʿrūf al-Karḫī in Baghdad), *cf.* also Gramlich: *Wunder* p. 400; IḤallWaf V p. 232; MuḥḪul II p. 210; al-Marrākušī: *Iʿlām* I p. 186 (concerning the tomb of Mūsā al-Kāẓim). Ibn Taymīyah discusses these and similar expressions in ITayMaǧm XXVII p. 115; *cf.* also IQayIġāṯah I p. 200; al-Albānī: *Aḥkām al-ǧanāʾiz* p. 261; Zepter: *Friedhöfe* p. 75. The Arab doctors thought theriac one of the most potent remedies, especially the variant known as *tiryāq al-fārūq*, "viper-theriac", see ʿAydNūr p. 124 and SiggelGifte p. 182 (from Ǧābir b. Ḥayyān's *Kitāb as-Sumūm wa-dafʿ maḍārrihā*).

470 IZayKawākib p. 79; SaḫTuḥfAḥbāb p. 184; ʿUlaymīUns II p. 146 (outside Jerusalem); Schober: *Heiligtum ʿAlīs* p. 72.

471 MunKawākib III p. 111.

of) saintly persons commonly knock on the cenotaphs or cling to them and whatever else they use to do".[472]

al-Ḥusayn b. ᶜAbd Allāh b. ᶜAbd Allāh b. al-Ḥusayn, "when he felt pain, used to remove the pebbles from the stone (*al-ḥağar*: tombstone?) which was in the house of Fāṭimah 'the Virgin', right behind the wall of the Prophet's tomb, and rub (his back?) against it".[473] In Damascus people reportedly "pressed their aching back on the column which is at the head of the tomb of (the Umayyad caliph) Muᶜāwiyah";[474] similarly, after kissing the tomb of ᶜAlī people should press their cheeks against it;[475] touching the tombstone with one's hand was beneficial at the grave of Abū l-Ḥasan al-Ḫaraqānī (d. 425 H), according to his own testimony.[476] From a certain venerated tomb in Jerusalem – the so-called "Tomb-Of-We-Found" (see below p. 281) –, the people carried away the stones (*ʾaḥğār*) that were lying upon the tomb but the next morning the stones were as many as they had been the day before.[477]

A rather peculiar practice, without parallel in other sources that I know of, is reported from Kairouan. Here the people actually used to scrape the tombstone (a white or brightly shining column, probably of marble: *ʿamūd ʾabyaḍ*) of Abū ᶜAlī Šuqrān b. ᶜAlī al-Hamdānī (d. 186 H) and mix the particles with *kuḥl* (antimony), for the obvious reason of obtaining blessing from the resulting powder. This led to the tombstone becoming hollowed out or "perforated" (*nqb* II), though the chronicler Ibn Nāğī at-Tanūḫī (d. 839 H) remarked that "in our times this practice has been given up, maybe because of a fatwa condemning it".[478] Another practice included the mutual hand-shaking of the visitors at a certain tomb in Cairo.[479]

Individual burial sites or cemeteries were often chosen as places appropriate for performing the prayer for rain (*ṣalāt al-istisqāʾ*) or prayers for the removal of plague (*ad-duʿāʾ bi-rafʿ al-wabāʾ*), especially in the Islamic West, in Egypt and in the Sudan, regions largely dominated by the Malikite legal tradition.[480] In this case, it was not the well-being of an individual, but the benefit of the community as a whole that was aimed at; "cemeteries were the scenes of public supplication in time of calamity".[481] Nevertheless, these practices were harshly condemned by Ibn Taymīyah and his later followers.[482]

472 ŠubrḪāš III p. 12. For touching and kissing the cenotaph, see below p. 236.

473 SaḫTuḥfLaṭ I p. 292.

474 ITayMağm XXVII p. 113.

475 IQūlKāmil p. 40; ṬūsīMiṣbaḥ p. 514; al-Amīn: *Miftāḥ* II p. 296; *cf.* MağlBihār C p. 134.

476 Gramlich: *Wunder* p. 400.

477 ᶜUlaymīUns II p. 152.

478 DabMaᶜālim I p. 287.

479 IZayKawākib p. 77 = SaḫTuḥfAḥbāb p. 177.

480 For cases of rain-prayer in cemeteries and near burial sites, see MaqrSulūk II p. 55 (on the Cairene Qarāfah in the year 709 H); IQŠuhbTārīḫ III p. 431 (in 778 H); NZ XIV p. 97 (in 823 H); *cf.* also Lecker: *Burial of Martyrs* p. 45 and Abu-Zahra: *Pure and Powerful*, ch. 1.

481 Goitein: *Mediterranean Society* V p. 185.

482 Memon: *Ibn Taimīya's Struggle* pp. 268f.; Haja: *Mort et Jugement Dernier* p. 37.

In Nīsābūr, the prayer for rain was performed at the tomb of the renowned traditionist Abū Bakr Ibn Fūrak (d. 406 H);[483] in Baghdad, the tomb of Maʿrūf al-Karḫī was known for being a favourable place for performing the *istisqāʾ*;[484] in al-Ḥīrah, rain was invoked at the grave of Abū ʿUṯmān al-Ḥīrī (Saʿīd b. Ism. ar-Rāzī, d. 298 H);[485] in Sudan, the rain-prayer was performed at the tombs of Ṣuġayyirūn or Ṣaġīrūn (M. b. Sarḥān al-ʿAwdī, eleventh c. H, buried in al-Qūz) and his uncle ʿAbd ar-Raḥmān b. Ǧābir;[486] in Kairouan, the people assembled – not without success as we are told – at the tomb of Ṣadaqah aḍ-Ḍarīr (d. 335 H) for the rain-prayer;[487] in Marrakech, rain was invoked at the tomb of the mystic Abū l-ʿAbbās b. al-ʿArīf (A. b. M. aṣ-Ṣanhāǧī, Almería ? – Marrakech 536 H);[488] in Córdoba, rain-prayers were performed at the tomb of Yaḥyā b. Yaḥyā al-Layṯī (d. 233 or 234 H).[489] In Ramaḍān 748 H, the people gathered in the Northern Qarāfah in Cairo to pray for the end of the plague;[490] in 822 H, Sultan al-Muʾayyad Šayḫ (r. 815–824 H) summoned the people of Cairo there for the same reason.[491] On all these occasions, the mausolea of former Mamluk sultans were frequently taken as prayer places or for the performance of other rites, e.g. slaughter sacrifices.

Among the authors of legal writings attention to the practices of seeking healing or aid and pleading intercession is often rather secondary or completely absent – with the exception of those condemning these practices, though of course, as is known, many of them did themselves visit tombs and shrines for the sake of receiving help and blessing (*barakah*).[492]

4.2.1. Taking dust or earth from the tomb

Apart from touching the tomb or performing other rites, the dust or earth covering the tombs of saintly persons was often taken away – a practice declared disapproved at least by some scholars[493] – because it was considered curative or beneficial in other ways.

In Damascus, dust was collected from the tomb of the mystic Ibn ʿArabī;[494] in Mawṣil, people took the earth from the tomb of Fatḥ al-Mawṣilī (d. 220 H) to their homes, for its blessing;[495] in Zabīd, the mystic aš-Šihāb aṭ-Ṭabandāwī (A. b. aṭ-Ṭayyib, d. 948 H) once a week visited the cemetery, collected the earth from various venerated tombs in a vessel, mixed it with water and drank it, claiming that this is a "proven antidote" (*tiryāq muǧarrab*);[496] in Cairo, people carried away

483 QazwĀṯār p. 297.

484 ŠaʿrṬab I p. 72; Gramlich: *Wunder* p. 400; Gronke: *Derwische* p. 354 n. 93.

485 IDiḥIbtihāǧ p. 146. For Abū ʿUṯmān, see MunKawākib I pp. 623-5.

486 IḌayfṬab p. 238 and 252.

487 MālRiyāḍ II p. 129; DabMaʿālim II p. 334; *cf.* also *ib.* III p. 165.

488 MaqqNafḥ (C) IV p. 214 = al-Marrākušī: *Iʿlām* I p. 175.

489 MaqqNafḥ (C) II p. 217.

490 ŠaʿrṬab II p. 2.

491 NZ XIV pp. 78-80.

492 For the concept of *barakah*, see Taylor: *Vicinity of the Righteous* pp. 47ff. and Wha: *Baraka*.

493 IMuflĀdāb III p. 288.

494 IṬūlMufāk p. 347.

495 AzdīTārMawṣil p. 247 = Gramlich: *Wunder* p. 400.

496 ʿAydNūr p. 207.

the earth from the tomb of the mystic Ḏū n-Nūn, "because to take away the earth of his tomb in order to have one's problems solved by it is a tried and tested fact, and a great number of Egyptians are doing so";[497] in the Libyan village Ġānīmah the people took the earth from the tomb of a locally venerated jurist, so his grave had to be reshaped over and again;[498] in Tunis, the local mariners collected earth from the tomb of the mystic Muḥriz b. Ḫalaf (d. 413 H) in order to throw it on the waves when they were out in their ships and the stormy sea endangered their lives;[499] in Kairouan, the people crowded at the burial of Abū ʿAbd Allāh ad-Dabbāġ (M. b. ʿAlī, d. Šaʿbān 618 H) "until they broke the bier" and afterwards they took away the earth (*turbah*) from his tomb.[500] In Aġmāt (Morocco), Ibn ʿAbd aṣ-Ṣamad, the court poet of al-Muʿtamid Ibn ʿAbbād (see **1**), prostrated himself upon the latter's tomb and kissed its earth.[501]

The earth of widely-venerated tombs, as well as that taken from the Prophet's sepulchre (see below), was used in powdered form especially for the treatment of eye-diseases. Abū l-ʿAbbās Ibn Ḥiǧǧī (d. 816 H) relates in his academic curriculum from as-Sirāǧ ʿAlī b. ʿAbd al-Karīm al-Baṭāʾiḥī al-Mizzī:

> "He told me a strange story, for he said: When I was a boy, a sister of mine was stricken with an eye-disease (*ramad*). As we strongly believed in Ibn Taymīyah – he was a colleague of my father and often used to visit him –, it entered my mind to take some earth from Ibn Taymīyah's grave in order to make an eye powder (*kuḥl*) for my sister. Yet her eye-disease remained unaltered and the eye powder had no effect on her. Thus I went again to the grave, and there I found someone from Baghdad who had collected bags full of earth. I asked him 'What are you going to do with this?', and he replied 'I am taking it to use it for eye-disease, for I make of it an eye powder for some of my children.' I rejoiced, 'But do you find it effective?' 'Yes', and he added that he had experienced its effect. Hearing this, I felt reassured about my intention and took some earth from the tomb. I put the powder on my sister's eyes while she was sleeping, and soon she was cured (from the disease)."[502]

In Cairo, it was not only the earth taken from specific tombs that was considered curative but the entire ground of the Qarāfah cemetery at the slopes of the Muqaṭṭam Hill. Thus in the year 796 H, a woman who had for a long time been suffering from an eye-disease (*ramad*) saw the Prophet in a dream. He ordered her to take white pebbles from the slopes of the Muqaṭṭam Hill, to grind them into little pieces and to put this as *kuḥl* upon her eyes after the pulverisation. Since the woman was cured instantly the matter became famous and the people followed her example. However,

497 IZayKawākib p. 233. A number of other cases where earth was taken away from tombs has been collected, from the Cairene cemetery guides, in Taylor: *Vicinity of the Righteous* pp. 53f. *Cf.* IZayKawākib pp. 119, 126, 197 (earth curative against magic spells) and p. 201.

498 TiǧRiḥlah p. 317.

499 ZA V p. 284. For his tomb, see also MiknāsīIḥrāz pp. 322f.

500 DabMaʿālim III p. 212.

501 IḪāqQal p. 34; ŠantḎaḫ III p. 58 = Dozy: *Loci de Abbadidis* I p. 307 and II p. 180; MaqqNafḥ (C) V p. 355; al-Marrākušī: *Iʿlām* II p. 321; Dozy: *Historia de los musulmanes* IV p. 223; Nykl: *Hispano-Arabic Poetry* p. 153. For further details, see below p. 102.

502 INāṣRadd p. 136.

after a while the practice was abandoned.[503] I should like to add here that in other cases earth brought from the slopes of Muqaṭṭam Hill was put for its blessing in or upon tombs (*fī l-qabr*) or in burial niches (*fī l-laḥd*).[504]

The motif of "taking away the earth from a grave" also entered Arabic mourning poetry. In a poem by Ibn Bassām (ʿAlī b. M., d. 302 H), mourning the death of ʿAlī b. Yaḥyā al-Munağğim (d. 275 H), we read the following famous verse (*kāmil*):

وَلَوِ اسْتَطَعْتُ حَمَلْتُ عَنْكَ تُرَابَهُ * فَلَطَالَمَا عَنِّي حَمَلْتَ نَوَائِبِي

"If only I could I would take away its (i.e. the tomb's) earth from you, * for how often did you take my calamities away from me!"[505]

"Taking away the earth" has here more than one meaning. In the first place, the poet seems to refer to the concept of "making the earth light for the deceased" (see Vol. I pp. 131ff.), that is, the less earth that was heaped upon the tomb the lighter one imagined the suffering of the buried there to be; "taking away the earth" might thus mean "relieving the deceased from his suffering in the grave". Moreover, the first hemistich might also intend to say, in a more general sense, "If only I could I would free you from the tomb", i.e. bring you back to life. Still, the wording *ḥml* I *at-turāba ʿanhu* is also typically said of "taking away the earth from the grave for the sake of its blessing", so that the poet would again benefit from the deceased as he benefitted from him during his life-time ("you took my calamities away from me").

The fragrance of the tomb's earth

In many cases, the fragrance of the earth of tombs – or the earth of a whole burial ground – was likened to perfume or, more specifically, to musk (*misk*). Musk was considered "the most sweet-smelling perfume" (*ʾaṭyab aṭ-ṭīb*),[506] and it was also said to emanate from the earth of Paradise.[507] The notion of a tomb perfumed with musk puts it thus in direct connection with Paradise itself, or rather it portrays the tomb as a part of Paradise.

The perfume of musk was said to emanate from the grave of Ibn ʿAbbās in aṭ-Ṭāʾif[508] as well as from that of the Zaydite Imam al-Mahdī Aḥmad b. al-Ḥusayn (killed in Yemen in 656 H).[509]

503 IḤağInbāʾ III p. 217. *Cf.* also IQŠuhbTārīḫ I p. 522.

504 Thus both Kaʿb al-Aḥbār and the caliph ʿUmar II b. ʿAbd al-ʿAzīz reportedly expressed the last wish that earth from that place should be "spread" (*frš* I) in or upon their respective tombs, see IZawlFaḍMiṣr p. 96; IẒuhFaḍMiṣr p. 109; NuwIlmām III p. 278; IZayKawākib p. 13; SuyḤusnMuḥ I p. 111.

505 Cited in ḤuṣZahr (M) III p. 726 / (Ṭ) II p. 79; IBuḥtUns p. 87; YāqIršād V pp. 465f.; ŠayMağānī III p. 43. Yāqūt names a certain ʿAlī b. Sulaymān as author of the poem.

506 NawŠMusl XV p. 8.

507 NuwIlmām V p. 96.

508 ʿUğIhdāʾ p. 65.

509 ḪazrʿUqūd I p. 124.

According to a famous Tradition, Adam – shortly after his being created – addressed the Muqaṭṭam Hill (above the Cairene Qarāfah cemetery) with the words: "O mountain upon which mercy lies, on your slopes is the Garden (of Paradise) and your earth is musk in which the brides of the Garden are buried!"[510] In al-Munāwī's commentary on the *Kitāb aš-Šamā'il* we find the following eulogy referring to its author at-Tirmiḏī: "May God make his tomb a garden whose fragrance is sweeter than the aromatic musk!" (*ǧaʿala llāhu qabrahū rawḍatan ʿarfuhā ʾaṭyabu mina l-miski š-šaḏī*).[511]

The musk-scented earth also provided an important "poetical" link between the image of the tomb, whose earth is perfumed, with its common characterisation as a garden (*rawḍah*, see pp. 50ff. above). This becomes clear from two verses by Ibn al-Muʿtazz in which he describes not a tomb, but a real garden (*basīṭ*):

يُضَاحِكُ الشَّمْسَ أَنْوَارُ الرِّيَاضِ بِهَا * كَأَنَّمَا نُثِرَتْ فِيهَا الدَّنَانِيرُ
وَتَأْخُذُ الرِّيحُ مِنْ دُخَانِهَا عَبَقاً * كَأَنَّ تُرْبَتَهَا مِسْكٌ وَكَافُورُ

"The lights (i.e. the blossoming flowers) of the meadows in it jest with the sun * as if (golden) dinars were strewn all over it,
And the breeze takes (its) fragrance from its vapours * as if its earth was musk and camphor".[512]

A second link was provided by the notions of "sprinkling the tomb" and "putting plants upon the tomb" (see Chapter 2). Thus we find the following verse in a mourning poem of the pre-Islamic poet Aws b. Ḥaǧar (*basīṭ*):

لاَ زَالَ مِسْكٌ وَرَيْحَانٌ لَهُ أَرَجٌ * عَلَى صَدَاكَ بِصَافِي اللَّوْنِ سَلْسَالِ

"May musk and fragrant plants, of pleasant perfume, continue * (to grow) upon your buried body, together with (*or* nurtured by) limpid (water), of clear colour!"[513]

As seen above, it was also tempting to collect earth from burial sites, and in many cases such earth allegedly turned out to be musk or emanating its fragrance: Mālik b. Dīnār had taken earth (*turāb*) from the grave of Abū Firās ʿAbd Allāh b. Ġālib al-Ḥuddānī (in Baṣrah) and then realised that it was musk.[514] According to Abū Nuʿaym, "the people after his burial took earth from his tomb as if it were musk and impregnated their clothes with it". This story soon became famous for the fact that the people were so enticed (*futina*) by what had happened that Mālik sent some men to the tomb and had it levelled, evidently, in order to make it disappear and thus

510 NZI p. 30. *Cf.* also MasMurūǧ II p. 66.

511 MunŠŠam I p. 2.

512 IMuʿtDīwān 854 vv. 5-6 (II p. 297) = *Wāfī* XVII p. 465.

513 AwsDīwān (G) ٣٢ v. ١٦ (p. ٣٢: var. *ʿalā ṣadāka*: *yaǧrī ʿalayka*) / (N) 40 v. 21 (p. 105); *Aġānī* XI p. 73; IMaymMunt II p. 225.

514 Two versions have *wa-ʾiḏā huwa misk*, whereas Abū Nuʿaym's version (see the following note) has only "that he scented the perfume of musk" (*rīḥ al-misk*); *cf.* also (abbreviated) MunKawākib I p. 346.

prevent the people from crowding there.[515] When ᶜAbd Allāh b. Ġālib was seen in a dream, he was asked why the scent of musk (*rāʾiḥat al-misk*) lingers upon his tomb and replied, "This is the scent of recitation and desire (lit. thirst)".[516]

Another, closely related motif appears in other reports, e.g. in the story about the burial of the Kūfan ascetic Muḥammad b. an-Naḍr al-Ḥāriṯī (d. 174 H). There, myrtles (or fragrant plants: *rayḥān*, see Chapter 5) were found spread out in his burial niche (meaning that the deceased had been rewarded by God with the Bliss of Paradise), and therefore someone descended into the tomb and collected a part of them. He kept it at his home where the *rayḥān* remained fresh for 70 days and "there was such a crowd of people to see this that the local emir was afraid of unrest and took the myrtles away from the man".[517]

Somebody else took a handful of earth from the tomb of the Prophet's companion Saᶜd b. Muᶜāḏ – who was killed during "the Battle of the Trench" and reportedly replied from his tomb to greetings[518] –, and by the time he had come home the earth had turned into musk;[519] in any case the scent of musk was emanating from the earth of his grave.[520] Abū ᶜAbd Allāh ad-Dabbāġ (whose burial was mentioned before) went one day to the tomb of Ibn al-Qābisī (ᶜAlī b. M., d. 403 H) and later told his disciples that "after I had laid my hand on its earth, the strong perfume of musk adhered to my hand. It remained there for days and days, so that I kept my hand hidden so that the people were not led to think that I had perfumed my hand".[521] What is more, the fragrance of musk at certain tombs was not necessarily a constant feature, but could be limited to certain times or days. Thus we hear of the tomb of the Yemenite jurist Abū l-Ḥasan al-Aṣābī (ᶜAlī b. al-Ḥusayn, 577–658 H) that "the visitor finds at his grave the fragrance of musk, especially during Friday night".[522]

Another effect of the pleasant smell of the earth at the burial site of a blessed or otherwise venerated person[523] was that it could lead to its being rediscovered, after people had lost knowledge of its location.[524] This was in general seen positively, yet in cases this could produce the contrary effect. An unknown poet – perhaps Muslim b. al-Walīd – therefore said (*ṭawīl*):

أَرَادُوا لِيُخْفُوا قَبْرَهُ عَنْ عَدُوِّهِ * فَطِيبُ تُرَابِ القَبْرِ دَلَّ عَلَى القَبْرِ

515 ANuḤilyah II p. 258; IḪarrāṭᶜĀqibah pp. 129f.; IĞawzīṢafwah II p. 203; SaḫTuḥfAḥbāb p. 9.

516 *tilka rāʾiḥatu t-tilāwati wa-ẓ-ẓamaʾ*: IRağLaṭāʾif pp. 170f. Ibn Ġālib's answer refers probably to his reciting the Qurʾān in the tomb and his longing for the encounter with God; the term *ẓamaʾ* means lit. "thirst", yet also "being thirsty for s.th.", i.e. "longing for s.th, *or* desiring s.th.", see Lane *s.r.*

517 MunKawākib I p. 438.

518 SuyḪaṣ I p. 364.

519 IRağAhwāl p. 93; ŠāmīSubul X p. 379.

520 MubKāmil (C) IV p. 102; SuyḪaṣ I p. 363; ŠāmīSubul X p. 379.

521 Cited in DabMaᶜālim III p. 212.

522 ḪazrᶜUqūd I p. 129. For a similar case from Cairo, see IZayKawākib p. 233.

523 *Cf.* also ŠīrŠadd p. 238; al-ᶜAffānī: *Sakb* I p. 295 and 583. For other cases in which the odour of musk was emanating from tombs, see IZayKawākib p. 295 and IRağAhwāl pp. 92f.

524 *Cf.* Schober: *Heiligtum ᶜAlīs* p. 61.

"They wished to conceal his tomb from his enemy, * but the fragrance of the earth of the tomb led the way to the tomb".[525]

This famous verse is cited – or adapted to other contexts[526] – in a number of writings; the English reader may also recall a poem by Tomas Carew (1594/5–c. 1640 CE) which contains the verses: *And here the precious dust is layd; / Whose purely temper'd Clay was made / So fine, that it the guest betray'd.* It was considered one of the "plagiarisms" (*sariqāt*) of al-Mutanabbī that he took up the above-cited verse ascribed to Muslim b. al-Walīd and composed in a panegyrical poem the following line; the verse alludes to the ancestors of the praised (*wāfir*):

وَمَا رِيحُ الرِّيَاضِ لَهَا وَلَكِن * كَسَاهَا دَفْنُهُمْ فِي التُّرْبِ طِيبَا

"The (perfumed) breeze of the gardens is not scented by (its passing over) them,[527] but because * their[528] having been buried in the earth vested them (i.e. the gardens) with perfume".[529]

Moreover, even the more natural odour of the tomb, which may be anything other than fragrant but rather the result of a decaying corpse, has found its way into the poetical imagery of the Arabs, albeit mainly in satirical or jest poetry. One such example is found in a poem by ar-Raffāʾ (d. after 360 H) in which he describes an invitation to dinner and wine[530] during a very hot night. Unfortunately, apart from the heat, they were served an awful dish which was heaped again and again upon their plates until the morning rose, and "when the (morning) breeze wafted over it, it smelled as if * the breeze had passed over dead corpses whose (covering) earth it had blown away".[531]

Finally, the motif of the fragrant earth, or earth scented with musk, was not reserved for the perfume of the soil as found in or upon tombs, but could be applied to other sites as well. The soil most famous for its pleasant odour was said to be the

525 Cited in ʿAskMaʿānī II p. 523; *Aġānī* XIX p. 34; ṮaʿālYat I p. 149 (var. *ʿan*: *min*); RāġibMuḥaḍ IV p. 528 (line 5); IRašʿUmdah II p. 836 (with further sources in note 5); MutanDīwān (U) I p. 154; ZawzḤam I p. 222; NuwNih V p. 177; INubMaṭlaʿ p. 327.

526 *Cf.* the version in ʿĀmKaškūl I p. 89: "After Laylā had died, al-Maǧnūn came to her tribe and asked for her tomb, but they would not lead him to it. Thus he started to sniff at the earth of every tomb he passed and when he finally smelled the earth of her tomb, he recognised it and said: *ʾarādū li-yuḫfū qabrahā ʿan muḥibbihā * wa-ṭību turābi l-qabri dalla ʿalā l-qabrī*". In TMD XIV p. 245 and BN VIII p. 203, we hear that a bedouin from the Banū l-Asad found the tomb of al-Ḥusayn by collecting handfuls of earth and smelling at them. After he had hit upon the tomb, he said: *ʾarādū li-yuḫfū* etc.

527 Since for gardens it is natural to emanate a pleasant fragrance.

528 I.e. the ancestors of the praised.

529 MutanDīwān (U) I p. 154 / (W) p. 295; ṮaʿālYat I p. 149.

530 ar-Raffāʾ was a connoisseur in that field, see van Gelder: *God's Banquet* p. 46.

531 ṮaʿālYat II p. 154.

earth of Iṣfahān, described in a poem "as a paste of musk" (*miskun ʿağīnun*),[532] and though this seems to lead us away from our subject, we are brought back to it by Yāqūt ar-Rūmī. In his topographical dictionary he first mentions the good climate and the healthy air of Iṣfahān. Then he goes on to say that "the dead do not decay in its earth (*fī turbatihā*), (...) and it may happen that one digs a pit there and hits by chance upon a tomb that is thousands of years old, and the buried person will be found in his former condition, not altered (by decomposition)".[533]

The earth of the Prophet's tomb

The earth taken from the Prophet's grave was seen as the most precious earth or dust. Among the Shiites, also the earth from the tombs of ʿAlī, Mūsā al-Kāẓim[534] and al-Ḥusayn was highly venerated; in the latter case the common word for "earth" is "clay", ar. *ṭīn* or pers. *gil*, though *turbah* is used too.[535] As is well-known, the Shiites also consider it recommended to put a small piece of clay from Karbalāʾ into the tomb.[536]

According to one reliable source, the Prophet's tomb had been surrounded by a wall on the order of ʿĀʾišah because people were taking the earth away from it,[537] and the people in Medina would not dust off their hands after they had been in contact with the Prophet's tomb.[538] As is further known, Mālik b. Anas[539] only walked around in Medina on foot, never mounting a riding animal there, because he could not bear its hooves trampling on the earth (*turbah*) which contained the sepulchre of the Prophet.[540] The Prophet's daughter Fāṭimah reportedly grasped a handful of earth from her father's tomb shortly after the burial, inhaled its fragrance and put it on her eyes (see also below).[541] This belief in the quasi-holiness of the earth from the Prophet's sepulchre was spread by the Muslims wherever they took

532 From a poem by the man of letters Muḥammad b. A. ad-Dawāʾī, cited in IṣfḪar (I) I p. 188.

533 YāqBuldān I p. 207 (*s.v.* Iṣfahān).

534 Donaldson: *Shiʾite Religion* p. 201 (quoting from al-Mağlisī).

535 IQūlKāmil pp. 274-86 (very detailed) = (abridged) ʿĀmKaškūl I p. 267; IBābManLā II p. 362 (*bāb faḍl turbat al-Ḥusayn ʿalayhi s-salām wa-ḥarīm qabrihī*); KulKāfī IV pp. 588f.; ṬūsīMiṣbaḥ pp. 509-11 and ṬūsīTahḏ VI pp. 74-6; ʿĀmilīWas III p. 402 and 411-6; BaḥrKaškūl III p. 389. *Cf.* also Donaldson: *Shiʾite Religion* pp. 90f.; al-Albānī: *Aḥkām al-ğanāʾiz* p. 253; Schober: *Heiligtum ʿAlīs* p. 97. For the beneficial effects of different types of *ṭīn* in general, see IMuflĀdāb III pp. 26 and 71 (where soil taken from tombs, however, is not mentioned).

536 *Cf.* ṬūsīMabsūṭ I p. 186.

537 SamWafāʾ II p. 544.

538 SaffĠiḏāʾ II p. 262; see also SuyḪaṣ II p. 487 and MunKawākib I p. 69.

539 He was in this context often confounded with Anas b. Mālik, a Companion of the Prophet.

540 ŠaʿrṬab I p. 53.

541 IĞawzīWafā p. 819; ZawzḤam I p. 196 and INāṣBard (A) p. 63 / (C) p. 59 = SuyBard p. 143 (with two verses); IBuḥtUns p. 79; INağDurrah p. 387 and INāṣMağlis p. 25 (again with both verses); IAḤağSulwah p. 73; ZarkAḥkām p. 273; QasṭMaw III p. 400; DiyTārḪamīs II p. 173; HaytTuḥfZuw pp. 22f. (with both verses); *cf.* also IʿARabʿIqd (Ğ) II pp. 153f. / (M) III

their creed. No wonder, then, that in Java the tombs of the kings of the Mataram dynasty at Imo Giri were "believed to have been sanctified by soil brought from the prophet Muḥammad's grave".[542]

In the first half of the sixth century H, al-Qāḍī ᶜIyāḍ was to affirm that the earth of the Prophet's tomb ranked higher than the Kaᶜbah itself (!),[543] and according to as-Samhūdī this claim had become a consensus (*ʾiǧmāᶜ*) among scholars.[544] The tenth-century scholar aš-Šāmī went one step further and stated that "the spot where he is buried ranks higher (*or* is nobler) than the Kaᶜbah and the Throne (of God)";[545] the addition "nobler than the Throne of God" was purportedly introduced by Taqīy ad-Dīn as-Subkī on the authority of Ibn ᶜAqīl al-Ḥanbalī.[546] This fits well into a story circulating among scholars (cited by Ibn al-Ǧawzī and later authors in two versions, one of them attributed to Kaᶜb al-Aḥbār) according to which Jibril and many other angels, "came down and took the earth of our Master from the place where Muḥammad's tomb would be (*fa-ʾaḫaḏū turbata sayyidinā ṣlᶜm min mawḍiᶜi qabrihī*)" and then ascended with it to Heaven. In Kaᶜb's version we read: "Jibril and the angels of Paradise (*al-firdaws*) (...) descended, and he took a handful of earth (*turbah*, var. 'clay', *ṭīnah*) from the place of the tomb of the Messenger of God (*or* of the Noble Tomb, *al-qabr aš-šarīf*), whose earth is shining white and radiant". Once brought to Heaven, the earth was then soaked in the Salsabīl-spring (or, in the second version, in the water of Tasnīm[547]) and immersed in all the rivers of Paradise, until its immensely bright light reappeared. Then it was shown around in Heaven and on Earth so that the whole creation acknowledged the primordial prophethood of Muḥammad. Finally, "God the Exalted took care of it and put it to the right of His Throne, until He created Adam. (...) While creating Adam, He put a handful (of earth or clay) of the Messenger of God in his back".[548]

Apart from mystical speculation according to which "the primal man was moulded from the crystallised light of Muhammad and took the corporeal personality of Adam"[549] – a concept also

p. 238; MuwMuršid I p. 37; ᶜĀmKaškūl II p. 366; ṬurayḥīMunt p. 34 (various verses); al-Munayyar: *Tasliyah* p. 31 (quotes the verses without the detail concerning the earth).

542 Woodward: *Islam in Java* p. 175.

543 Quoted in ITayMaǧm XXVII p. 38; *cf.* also IᶜAHādīṢārim p. 244. ᶜIyāḍ himself writes in his *Šifāʾ*: "There is no discord that the place of his (*sc.* the Prophet's) tomb is the noblest spot on earth", see ᶜIyāḍŠifāʾ (B) II p. 78 / (Š) II p. 91 = HarŠŠifāʾ II p. 163.

544 SamWafāʾ I p. 28 = MunŠŠam II p. 217.

545 ŠāmīSubul X p. 335 (*bi-ʾanna buqᶜata llatī dufina fīhā ʾafḍalu mina l-kaᶜbati wa-mina l-ᶜarš*).

546 SamWafāʾ I p. 28.

547 *Cf.* Q 83:25-8 and below **90** (epitaph-poem).

548 IǦawzīWafā p. 27 = ŠāmīSubul I pp. 68f.; IAǦamrBahǧah I p. 465 = QasṭMaw I p. 34. The story is also found in the popular work BakrīAnwār p. 12. This book was much scorned upon, e.g. by Ibn Taymīyah (see ITayᶜIlmḤadīṯ pp. 491-3) and as-Suyūṭī who pronounced its lecture forbidden as it contains too much nonsense, see SuyḤāwī I p. 369. In Shiism, many details of this story were linked to al-Ḥusayn's tomb, see ṬurayḥīMunt pp. 62f. and 70f.

549 Schimmel: *Messenger* p. 126.

immortalised by the Egyptian Sufi poet Ibn al-Fāriḍ (d. 632 H)[550] in his *ḫamrīyah* or "Wine-Ode" in praise of the Prophet[551] – there is a famous report, known in different wordings asserting that Muḥammad was a Prophet "when Adam was still nothing but a piece of clay" or, put in the mouth of the Prophet himself: I was a Prophet "when Adam was between body and spirit" (*wa-ʾĀdamu bayna r-rūḥi wa-l-ǧasad*).[552] This means, according to most scholars, that God had formed Adam's body, but had not yet breathed unto him his spirit.[553]

The earth of the Prophet's tomb as a motif in poetry

In the wide realm of Arabic poetry in praise of the Prophet, flourishing from the fifth century H onwards in the Islamic West and after the sixth century H in the East, the earth of the Prophet's grave as well as the earth surrounding his body developed into a favourite motif of the poets[554] who frequently likened it to musk[555] or spoke generally of the perfume (*nasīm*, *ʿarf*, *ʾarağ*) of the Prophet's tomb.

Perhaps the most famous (though not the earliest known) verse in this regard is a line from the *Burdat al-madīḥ* ("Mantle Ode") by al-Būṣīrī (d. *c.*696 H) (*basīṭ*):

لا طِيبَ يَعْدِلُ تُرْباً ضَمَّ أَعْظُمَهُ * طُوبَى لِمُنْتَشِقٍ مِنْهُ وَمُلْتَثِمِ

"No fragrance equals the earth which encloses his bones: * good fortune to the one scenting and kissing it (*sc.* the earth)".[556]

The precious earth of the Prophet's sepulchre was also considered a remedy against various diseases or at least, metaphorically, "a healing of the hearts".[557] More specifically, its earth was believed to cure eye-diseases (*ramad*) or even blindness;[558] it has already been mentioned above that Fāṭimah took earth from the Prophet's

550 For his shrine, see Homerin: *Domed Shrine* and *Ibn al-Fāriḍ*.

551 IFāriḍDīwān II pp. 186f., vv. 23-26.

552 TirǦāmiʿ V pp. 244f.; BayDal I pp. 83-5 and II p. 130; IMandahFaw II p. 50; SuhrAwārif p. 448; IǦawzīWafā pp. 25f.; BakrīAnwār p. 7; SuyḪaṣ I pp. 7f. and SuyḤāwī II pp. 100f.; ŠāmīSubul X p. 274.

553 See the detailed discussions of this in QasṭMaw I pp. 28-40 and ŠāmīSubul I pp. 77-84.

554 For the argument, *cf.* Schimmel: *Messenger* pp. 191-4.

555 *Cf.* also IRašUnmūḏaǧ p. 108.

556 BūṣDīwān p. 194. The verse is also quoted in QasṭMaw III p. 416 and MN IV p.7 (v. 58). In his letter dedicated to the visitation of the Prophet's sepulchre, Ibn al-Ǧadd al-Aḥdab (see above p. 62) says: "And I begrime my cheek in the sacredness of your earth" (*wa-ʾuʿaffiru ḫaddī fī muqaddasi turbika*), cited in ŠantḎaḫ III p. 287.

557 *wa-mā turbuhā ʾillā šifāʾu qulūbinā*, in a poem cited in MurSilk III p. 146.

558 In other cases, e.g. in Kairouan, rain water which had assembled upon or beside a tomb was brought in contact with eyes in order to cure diseases: DabMaʿālim III p. 104; for earth from a tomb against other kinds of injuries, see Gramlich: *Wunder* p. 400.

sepulchre and put it on her eyes.[559] In the case of the blind encomiast of the Prophet, aṣ-Ṣarṣarī, this concept has been clearly expressed in one of his poems (*basīṭ*):

تُرَابُ[560] مَرْبَعِهِ الرَّحْبِ المُنِيرِ بِهِ * شِفَاءُ عَيْنِي إذا مَا شَفَّهَا الرَّمَدُ

"The earth of his wide mansion illuminated by him[561] * is the remedy of my eye whenever it is befallen by blinding disease".[562]

Another poetical example of the beneficial effects of the earth from the Prophet's sepulchre, including its being a remedy against eye-diseases, occurs in a poem in praise of the Prophet by Ibn Saʿīd al-Maġribī (d. 685 H or before).[563] This lengthy composition, a splendid example of a seventh-century H western poem in praise of the Prophet,[564] was written in Alexandria in 639 H during Ibn Saʿīd's pilgrimage. It begins with the common invocation of the poet's distance from the Prophet's tomb and addresses those travelling to Medina, before shifting to the actual praise of the Prophet. The parallel with aṣ-Ṣarṣarī's verses becomes obvious in lines 13-15 (*kāmil*):

يَا لَيْتَنِي بُلِّغْتُ لَثْمَ تُرَابِهِ * يَزْدَادُ سَعْداً مَنْ بِذَلِكَ يُسْعَدُ
فَهُنَاكَ لَوْ أُعْطَى مُنَايَ مَحَلَّةٌ * مِنْ دُونِهَا حَلَّ السُّهَى وَالفَرْقَدُ
عَيْنِي شَكَتْ رَمَداً وَإِنَّ شِفَاءَهَا * مِنْ دَائِهَا ذَاكَ الثَّرَى لا الإِثْمِدُ

1 *yazdādu saʿdan man bi-ḏālika: yazādu saʿdan man bi-niʿmā* (MaqqNafḥ). – **3** *wa-ʾinna šifāʾahā: wa-ʾanta šifāʾuhā* (MaqqNafḥ).

"O were it possible for me to kiss the earth of his (tomb)! * Those who are given such good fortune (*sc.* by standing before his tomb) acquire increased happiness.
For were my desire granted a place there, * the farthest stars and the brightest suns would shine up above it.
My eye suffered from blindness, and its cure * from its illness is that moist earth (from his grave), not powdered antimony!"[565]

A third famous episode which concerns the healing effect of visiting the Prophet's

559 See above p. 94. Another case of the visitation of the Prophet's sepulchre curing an eye-disease, though not applying its earth, is recorded in ITaġrManh VI pp. 340f. (the biography of Ṣardāḥ b. Muqbil al-Ḥasanī, d. Cairo 833 H). Sometimes the Prophet appeared to blind people in dreams and told them a remedy in order to regain their sight, see IQŠuhbTārīḫ I pp. 217f.

560 I read تراب instead of يراب

561 I.e. the Prophet's tomb, or also the whole town of Medina.

562 MN II p. 18 (v. 8).

563 Abū l-Ḥasan ʿAlī b. Mūsā [b. M.] b. ʿAbd al-Malik b. Saʿīd al-Mudliǧī [al-Maḏḥiǧī] al-Qalʿī al-Ġarnāṭī: IḪaṭIḥāṭah IV pp. 152-8; IFarDībāǧ pp. 301f.; ITaġrManh VIII pp. 228f.; SuyBuġ II pp. 209f.; MaqqNafḥ (C) III pp. 29-135; ŠN pp. 197f.; GAL I pp. 336f. and GALS I pp. 576f.; Nykl: *Hispano-Arabic Poetry* p. 361; Arié: *España Musulmana* pp. 401f.; Penelas/Zanón: *Nómina de ulemas andalusíes* p. 113; CHAL *Andalus* p. 120.

564 MaqqNafḥ (C) III pp. 78-81 (53 vv.) = MN II pp. 51-5 (52 vv.).

565 MaqqNafḥ (C) III p. 79 = MN II p. 52.

sepulchre and kissing or applying its earth for those suffering from eye-diseases is known from Ibn Rušayd al-Fihrī's (d. 721 H)[566] travel journal and biographical dictionary *Mil' al-ʿaybah*. Ibn Rušayd performed the pilgrimage in 684 H together with Ḏū l-Wizāratayn (Ibn) al-Ḥakīm,[567] and during this journey they met with important poets and scholars; they even left graffiti in mausolea they visited, e.g. in Tilimsān (Tlemcen).[568] Ibn Rušayd describes their arrival in Medina as follows:

> "When we reached Medina in the year 684, I was in the company of my fellow, the vizier Abū ʿAbd Allāh b. Abī l-Qāsim b. al-Ḥakīm, who was suffering from an eye-disease (*kāna 'armada*). After we had come to Ḏū l-Ḥulayfah[569] or near there we dismounted the camels. The desire to approach the visitation site (*mazār*, i.e. the Prophet's tomb) was growing within him, thus he got off and hurried away on foot, as a sign of esteem for the place / and to extol the one who had lived in that space ||.[570] As a consequence he felt cured (from his disease), and he composed the following verses describing his condition [*ṭawīl*]":

وَلمَّا رَأَيْنَا مِنْ رُبُوعِ حَبِيبِنَا * بِيَثْرِبَ أَعْلاَماً أَثَرْنَا لَنَا الحُبَّا
وَبِالتُّرْبِ مِنْهَا إذْ كَحَلْنَا جُفُونَنَا * شُفِينَا فَلاَ بُؤساً نَخَافُ وَلا كَرْبَا (...)
نَسُحُّ سِجَالَ الدَّمْعِ فِي عَرَصَاتِهَا * وَنَلْثِمُ مِنْ حُبٍّ لِوَاطِئِهِ التُّرْبَا

3 *fī ʿaraṣātihā*: *fī ʿaraṣātihī* (QasṭMaw, one ms. of MaqqNafḥ).

"When we saw the outlines of the quarters of our Beloved * in Yaṯrib (i.e. Medina), they made us overwhelmed with love,
And by their earth, at the moment we rubbed our eyelids (with it), * we were cured, thus we fear neither calamity[571] nor sorrow. (...)
We pour out buckets of tears in its courtyard (i.e. at the Prophet's tomb, *or* in his mosque) * and we kiss the earth, for love of him who once trod upon it".[572]

The last example to be presented here, likewise from the West, stems from the *Dīwān* of the Jewish convert and poet Ibn Sahl al-Andalusī. He composed a qaṣīdah poem in praise of the Prophet[573] which Abū Ḥayyān praised as follows: "When I

566 Abū ʿAl. [Abū Bakr] M. b. ʿUmar b. M. al-Mālikī (Sabtah [sp. Ceuta] 657 – Fez 721 H), see IḪaṭIḥāṭah III pp. 135-43; IFarDībāǧ pp. 400f.; MaqrMuq VI pp. 432f.; DK IV pp. 229-31; SuyBuġ I pp. 199f.; al-Marrākušī: *Iʿlām* III pp. 250-5; GAL II pp. 245f.; ZA VI p. 314. *Cf.* also CHAL *Andalus* p. 366.

567 Abū ʿAl. M. b. ʿAr. ar-Rundī al-Laḫmī (Rundah 660 [sp. Ronda] – Granada 708 H), see IḪaṭIḥāṭah II pp. 444-76; MaqqNafḥ (C) VIII pp. 13-20; ZA VI p. 192.

568 MaqqNafḥ (C) VII p. 149.

569 A village some six or seven miles from Medina.

570 *iḥtisāban li-tilka l-'āṯār / wa-'iʿẓāman li-man ḥalla tilka d-diyār*.

571 The edited text has *ba'san* instead of *bu'san*.

572 Quoted from Ibn Rušayd in IḪaṭIḥāṭah II pp. 462f. = QasṭMaw III p. 407 = MaqqNafḥ (C) III pp. 378f.; see also MN I pp. 436f. The lines cited above are vv. 1-2 and 5 of the poem.

573 ISahlDīwān 94 (pp. 207-12). Incomplete versions of the poem are quoted in MN II pp. 321f.

came across it, I realised that it belongs to the most skillful (*ʾabdaʿ*) compositions ever produced in that field".[574] The poem was current among men of letters and scholars of later centuries as is shown by the fact that it was several times enlarged and rewritten in stanzaic form (*taḫmīs*).[575]

The motifs found in Ibn Sahl's poem are familiar from earlier western poetry in praise of the Prophet, the dominant themes being the yearning for distant Medina and the fragrant breeze (*nasamah*) which comes forth from Medina and lures the pilgrimage caravan, notwithstanding the hardships of desert travel, towards the Prophet's home town and his sepulchre. Two particularly attractive verses play with the well-known Tradition about the odour of musk that was said to emanate from the Prophet while alive.[576] This is taken up by Ibn Sahl when he says that Medina is transformed into a garden and permeated by the fragrance of musk by the people's talk about Muḥammad and their confidential conversation with the Prophet (at his tomb).[577] This specific motif – the scent of musk emanating from the Prophet's body and speech while alive – must be seen as complementary to the motif of the fragrance of musk that emanates from the earth of his tomb. In Ibn Sahl's poem, both motifs are joined, and indeed the one cannot be appreciated while the other is neglected.

4.3. Ties to the past

4.3.1. The recitation of poetry

Over the centuries of pre-modern Islam members of the learned élite, scholars and men of letters, but also common people, used to gather in cemeteries to recite poetry (or in cases also rhymed prose) in front of somebody's tomb. The verses spoken had sometimes been composed by the deceased himself, often shortly before his death, and were meant to be recited before or during the ceremony of mourning, as we know it for example of the Syrian poet Abū l-Maǧd al-Maʿarrī (d. 523 H);[578] as such, this practice is related to the custom of composing one's own funerary

(eleven lines); KutFawāt I p. 21 (nine lines); ʿĀmKaškūl I pp. 47f. (18 lines). The *incipit*s are given in *Wāfī* VI pp. 7f. and ITaġrManh I p. 68.

574 Quoted in MaqqNafḥ (C) V p. 70.

575 al-Makkī: *Madāʾiḥ* pp. 130f.

576 The fragrance surrounding the Prophet, often said to resemble musk, is mentioned in all treatises concerning the features (*šamāʾil*) of the Prophet. The best illustration of this Tradition is the account of a vision, quoted by Padwick: *Muslim Devotions* pp. 149f. from as-Suyūṭī: "One night I fulfilled the number of blessings of the Prophet and I fell asleep. I was dwelling in a room and, lo, the Prophet had come to me in through the door, and the whole room was lighted up by him. Then he moved towards me and said 'Give me the mouth that has blessed me so often that I may kiss it'. And my modesty would not let him kiss my mouth, so I turned away my face, and he kissed my cheek. Then I woke trembling from my sleep and my wife who was by my side awoke, and lo the house was odorous of musk from the scent of him, and the scent of musk from his kiss remained on my cheek about eight days. My wife noticed the scent every day".

577 ISahlDīwān 94 vv. 10f. (pp. 208f.). A similar adaptation of the motif of the Prophet's scent appears in a line of Ibn al-Fāriḍ which runs: "The perfume of musk is wafted abroad whenever my name is mentioned" (Schimmel: *Messenger* p. 281, n. 68 = IFāriḍDīwān I p. 232, *ḫafīf*: *yaʿbaqu l-misku ḥayṯumā ḏukira smī*).

578 M. b. ʿAl. b. M. (Maʿarrat an-Nuʿmān 440 – Ḥamāh 523 H): IṣfḪar (Š) II p. 32. For a similar

inscription before dying (see below p. 328). Often, however, the poetry recited during the mourning ceremony was composed by somebody else who would also perform the recitation, or the verses were taken from the œuvre of a famous poet and then adapted to the occasion.

Reciting poetry at graves was mainly done if the deceased was either a personal acquaintance or a distinguished individual, e.g. a pious man or woman, a famous poet or also an "unlucky ruler", that is, a person fitting the topos of the wise potentate who met a cruel fate or was otherwise wronged by destiny, like Ibn ᶜAbbād (**1**). In the first case – personal acquaintances – the recitation was in general performed during the burial or soon after, whereas in the second case – distinguished individuals – the tomb approached could well belong to a person who died many centuries before.

The poetry composed for these occasions resembled in style both traditional mourning poetry (*riṯāʾ*)[579] and panegyrical poetry (*madḥ*), resulting in that particular interweaving of styles[580] which also characterises the verses we find in many epitaphs of men of letters or secular rulers. For obvious reasons, there has always been a strong relationship between elegy and praise in Arabic mourning poetry, or put in European terms, between the *oratio funebris* and the *laudatio funebris*.[581] Thus Abū l-Fatḥ al-Bustī (ᶜAlī b. M., d. 400 H) in one of his verses called mourning poetry "the praise of the dead" (*madāʾiḥuhum wa-hunna marāṯin*),[582] and Ibn Nubātah al-Miṣrī says in one of his poems that "in every verse of praise there is the voice of a mourner" (*fī kulli baytin li-ṯ-ṯanāʾi ṣawtu nāʾiḥin*).[583] Arguably the most famous verse regarding this theme stems from the second-century poet Ašǧaᶜ b. ᶜAmr as-Sulamī (*ṭawīl*):

لَئِنْ حَسُنَتْ فِيكَ الْمَرَاثِي وَذِكْرُهَا * لَقَدْ حَسُنَتْ مِنْ قَبْلُ فِيكَ الْمَدَائِحُ

"If the mourning poems about you, and their recitation, fit you (now) * so did fit you before the poems said in your praise".[584]

event, see MaqdīšNuzhah II p. 404: *wa-raṯāhu tilmīḏuhū (...) bi-marṯiyatin ṭawīlatin qaraʾahā ᶜinda sarīri naᶜšihī qabla ṣ-ṣalāti ᶜalayhi.*

579 For an ample survey of secondary literature dealing with Arabic mourning poetry, see Smoor: *Poems on Death*; for a Tradition condemning *marāṯī*, see KU 42446 (XV p. 615).

580 *Cf.* the remarks in ḤuṣZahr (M) IV p. 999 / (Ṭ) II p. 307 and IRašᶜUmdah II p. 831. A typical poem combining the themes of both panegyrical and mourning poetry are the lines by al-Ḥusayn b. Muṭayr al-Asadī (d. *c.*170 H), cited in BaṣrīḤam (C) II p. 47.

581 *Cf.* Rhodokanakis: *Trauerlieder* pp. 74ff. and D'Avray: *Memorial Preaching* p. 15.

582 ZawzḤam I p. 257; *cf.* also IBuḥtUns p. 78. This also concords with the Islamic precept that nothing but good shall be said about the dead, *cf.* ManbTasl (C) pp. 121ff. / (M) pp. 119ff.

583 INubDīwān p. 99.

584 MarzḤam II p. 859; ŠantŠḤam I p. 474; BaṣrīḤam (C) II p. 43; IḤamdTaḏk IV p. 216; IbšīhīMust II p. 456 (var. *fa-qad*); BaġdḪizānah I p. 269; WriĞurzah p. 112. I also remember having read this line in other sources. Parts of the same poem, which is famous enough, are cited in ᶜĀmKaškūl II p. 490.

The practice of reciting poetry at someone's tomb, rather often referred to in the literary sources, was commonly called *al-qirāʾah ʿalā l-qabr* (which in this case did not mean the recitation of the Qurʾān, but of poetry) or *al-ʾinšād ʿalā* (or *ʿinda*) *l-qabr*.

Historical evidence

Early instances of poetry being recited at a grave – I leave out those episodes which go back to pre-Islamic times[585] – include the verses which ʿĀʾišah recited at the tomb of her brother ʿAbd ar-Raḥmān[586] as well as those which Ibn ʿUmar, the son of the second caliph, uttered at the grave of his brother ʿĀṣim (d. 70 H).[587]

Many other examples include the following: ʿAlī recited poetry at the tomb of Fāṭimah after her burial.[588] The Umayyad caliphs Sulaymān b. ʿAbd al-Malik (r. 96–99 H) and Yazīd b. ʿAbd al-Malik recited some lines at the grave of Sulaymān's son Ayyūb[589] and at the tomb of the Medinan singer Ḥabābah, respectively.[590] The Syrian Umayyad poet Abū l-Miqdām Bayhas b. Ṣuhayb al-Ǧarmī (*fl.* late 1st cent. H) recited a nine line-poem at the tomb of his beloved Ṣafrāʾ;[591] the poet al-Farazdaq pronounced some verses at the tomb of an-Nawār[592] and at that of Bišr b. Marwān;[593] the Ḥiǧāzī poet Kuṯayyir (b. ʿAbd ar-Raḥmān, d. 105 H), famous for his unfulfilled love of ʿAzzah, later stood at her tomb in Egypt and composed some verses at that occasion;[594] likewise in Egypt, somebody stood at the tomb (*waqafa ʿalā qabr*) of Abū Muḥammad Ibn Ṭabāṭabā (ʿAl. b. A., d. 348 H) and recited a verse, with the result that the deceased appeared to him in a dream;[595] Qays b. Ḏarīḥ (d. *c.*68 H) recited poetry at the tomb of his beloved Lubnā;[596] Abū l-ʿAtāhiyah recited a poem while standing at the tomb (*ʿalā qabrihī*) of ʿAlī b. Ṯābit;[597] the poet Faḍl ar-Raqāšī (d. *c.*200 H) recited verses at the tomb of al-ʿAbbās b. Muḥammad al-Barmakī in ar-Ruṣāfah (Baghdad);[598] the caliph al-Maʾmūn spoke some verses, which were not of his own composition, at the tomb of his brother Abū ʿĪsā (d.

585 E.g. at the tomb of ʿAmr b. Ḥumamah ad-Dawsī, see ḤuṣZahr (M) IV pp. 1129-31 / (Ṭ) II pp. 428-30; verses by Quss b. Sāʿidah at the tomb of his brothers: ṬurṭSirāǧ p. 21 and BaṣrīḤam (C) II p. 63; two verses by aḏ-Ḏalfāʾ bt. al-Abyaḍ at the grave of Naǧdah b. al-Aswad: YāqIršād VI pp. 295f. and IBuḥtUns p. 77.

586 Quoted in MubKāmil (C) IV pp. 30f.; *Aġānī* XV p. 309 and XVII p. 361; IʿABarrIst II p. 401; IḤamdTaḏk IV p. 249; ŠirŠadd p. 9; FāsīʿIqd V p. 35.

587 DabMaʿālim I p. 164.

588 IʿABarrBahǧah II p. 359. For further details, see below pp. 113f. with note 682.

589 Cited in MubKāmil (C) IV p. 53; INāṣBard (A) p. 61 = SuyBard p. 141. *Cf.* also IḤamdTaḏk IV p. 243 and IBuḥtUns pp. 79 and 91.

590 SarrāǧMaṣ I p. 120; BaṣrīḤam (C) II p. 603; ʿĀmKaškūl II pp. 413f. The verses were not of his own composition but by the known poet Kuṯayyir; see also what follows above.

591 *Aġānī* XXII pp. 138f.

592 ĠazIḥyāʾ (B) IV p. 487; IḤarrāṭʿĀqibah p. 114.

593 TMD X p. 262.

594 Cited in ḤuṣZahr (M) II p. 525 / (Ṭ) I p. 429; SarrāǧMaṣ I p. 126; ʿIṣāmīSimṭ III p. 167.

595 *Wāfī* XVII pp. 42f.

596 *Aġānī* IX p. 219.

597 AʿAtāhDīwān p. 491. For the verses, see also below note 664.

598 *Aġānī* XVI p. 247.

209 H);[599] two verses by Abū Nuwās were recited by the Córdoban vizier Abū Ḫālid Hāšim b. ᶜAbd al-ᶜAzīz (d. 273 H) at the tomb of the Andalusian Umayyad ruler Muḥammad I (r. 238–273 H);[600] the mystic Abū Bakr aš-Šiblī (d. Baghdad 334/5 H) spoke verses at the tomb of al-Ǧunayd.[601]

From later centuries we know of a lengthy mourning poem at the grave of Abū Isḥāq aṣ-Ṣābiʾ (d. 384 H);[602] Ibn al-Aqfāṣī al-Mawṣilī wept for the death of the vizier Ǧalāl ad-Dawlah Ibn Ṣadaqah (d. 522 H) in Baghdad, "entered his mausoleum" (*daḫala ... ʾilā qabrihī*) and pronounced a mourning poem;[603] seventy mourning poems were recited at the tomb of Abū l-ᶜAlāʾ al-Maᶜarrī (d. 449 H);[604] Abū Bakr b. Sawār al-Ušbūnī (i.e. from Lisbon) recited poetry at the tomb of the Almoravid ruler Yūsuf b. Tāšufīn (d. 500 H);[605] the vizier Abū l-ᶜAlāʾ Ibn Azraq spoke a verse at the tomb of Ibn Ṭāhir (nick-named *ar-Raʾīs al-ʾAǧall*, d. 508 H) in Murcia;[606] many mourning poems were also recited at the tomb of Ibn Šuhayd (see **73**).[607]

Further examples, likewise from the West, are the verses which Ibn al-Ḫaṭīb pronounced at the tomb of Ibn ᶜAbbād (**1**) in Aġmāt in 761 H, some 280 years after Ibn ᶜAbbād's court poet Ibn ᶜAbd aṣ-Ṣamad had delivered his own mourning poem which made the people weep "until they had wet their garments";[608] before that, Ibn ᶜAbd aṣ-Ṣamad had circumambulated the tomb, prostrated himself and kissed the earth upon it (see above); Ibn al-Ḫaṭīb recited a mourning poem at the tomb of his teacher Ibn al-Ǧayyāb (d. 749 H), five days after his burial,[609] and he composed a number of poems when visiting the tomb of the Marīnid sultan Abū l-Ḥasan (r. 731-49) in Marrakech.[610] In Medina, the man of letters Abū ᶜAbd Allāh Muḥammad b. ᶜAlī al-Ġarnāṭī (aš-Šāmī, Granada *c.*690 – Medina 715 H) pronounced a long poem at the tomb of Ḥamzah b. ᶜAbd al-Muṭṭalib (**168**) in the Baqīᶜ cemetery.[611] In Granada, verses were recited at the graves of the philologist Ibn al-Faḫḫār (M. b. ᶜAlī, d. 754 H)[612] and of aš-Šarīf Abū l-Qāsim Muḥammad b. Aḥmad al-Ḥasanī (d. 761 H), by their common pupil Ibn Zumruk.[613] The secretary of state Muḥyī d-Dīn Ibn ᶜAbd aẓ-Ẓāhir composed a mourning poem upon the death of al-Malik aẓ-Ẓāhir Baybars (d. 676 H) in 678 H and sent it to his mausoleum in Damascus in order to be recited there.[614]

599 IḤamdTaḏk IV p. 219.

600 IAbbḤullalı I p. 138.

601 TMD LXVI p. 75.

602 ṮaᶜālYat II pp. 311f.

603 YāqIršād V p. 128.

604 ŠayMaǧānī VI p. 313.

605 IᶜIḏBayān IV p. 47.

606 Nykl: *Hispano-Arabic Poetry* p. 205.

607 ŠantḎaḫ I pp. 335f.

608 IḪaṭAᶜmāl pp. 191-7 (= Hoenerbach: *Islamische Geschichte Spaniens* pp. 337f.) and IḪaṭIḥāṭah II p. 120 (= al-Marrākušī: *Iᶜlām* II p. 323); MaqqNafḥ (C) V p. 355; al-Marrākušī: *Iᶜlām* II p. 321 (for the poem of ᶜAbd aṣ-Ṣamad); ᶜAzzām: *Ibn ᶜAbbād* pp. 104f.; *cf.* also IḪāqQal pp. 34f.; ŠantḎaḫ III pp. 57f.; Nykl: *Hispano-Arabic Poetry* p. 153.

609 MaqqNafḥ (C) VII pp. 364-7.

610 IḪaldᶜIbar VII p. 334 = MaqqNafḥ (C) VIII p. 322.

611 MaqqNafḥ (C) III pp. 415f. The first verses of the poem are also cited in SaḫTuḥfLaṭ II p. 548.

612 MaqqNafḥ (C) VII pp. 300f.

613 MaqqNafḥ (C) VII pp. 120-3 = IZumrDīwān pp. 74-7.

614 IFurTārīḫ VII pp. 143f. For other examples of poetry recited at someone's tomb, see IḪāqQal

A topos frequently encountered in literary sources is that of women (often referred to as "Arab women") reciting poetry at the tombs of their beloved, be they their father or their son.[615]

Reciting poetry at the tomb of the Prophet

Even the sepulchre of the Prophet was often chosen for the recitation of verses or larger poetical compositions. The earliest attested example that I know of (from Sunnite circles) is the qaṣīdah poem in praise of the Prophet recited by the Syrian poet Ibn Rawāḥah al-Ḥamawī (d. 585 H)[616] "while standing in front of the Prophet's sepulchre". Unfortunately, only a few lines of his composition have been preserved which do not allow a detailed study.[617] Another example would be the poetry of Abū ᶜAlī ᶜUmar b. ᶜĪsā b. Abī Ḥafṣ al-Ḥafṣī (d. 646 H). He was, according to his contemporaries, a brillant poet and collected a large *dīwān* of his own composition. This he sent, from Seville, to the sepulchre of the Prophet.[618]

However, the earliest specimen of Sunnite poetry in praise of the Prophet which proved influential with later generations and was recited in front of the Prophet's sepulchre is the collection of the so-called "seven qaṣīdahs" (*al-qaṣāʾid as-sabᶜ*) by ᶜAlam ad-Dīn as-Saḫāwī (Saḫā 558/9 – Damascus 643 H).[619] His poetry became known in Egypt as early as 590 H, yet the last of his seven eulogies was not composed until 624 H.[620] The second of these, dealing with the miracles of the Pro-

p. 284 (by Abū Bakr Ibn al-Labbānah ad-Dānī, d. 507 H); MarzNūr p. 162; MuᶜāfāĞalīs II pp. 250-2; al-ᶜAffānī: *Sakb* I p. 658 (anon.); *cf.* also Goldziher: *Trauerpoesie* p. 326.

615 E.g. IQutᶜUyūn II pp. 325 and 340; IDāūḏZahrah p. 362; IMandahFaw I pp. 357f. (several stories, mostly related from al-Aṣmaᶜī); IᶜABarrBahğah II pp. 352f.; ĠazIḥyāʾ (B) IV p. 487; SarrāğMaṣ I p. 216; IĞawzīṢafwah II pp. 78f.; IĞawzīḤaṯṯ pp. 48f.; IĞawzīNisāʾ pp. 115 and 177; MuġulṭāyWāḍiḥ pp. 90 and 199; IBuḥtUns pp. 72, 86 and 88; IQaylthāf pp. 356 and 359; IZayKawākib p. 151; ḤurRawḍ pp. 30 and 34; al-Qināwī: *Fatḥ ar-raḥīm* pp. 176f.

616 Abū ᶜAlī al-Ḥusayn b. ᶜAl. b. Rawāḥah b. Ibr. al-Anṣārī al-Ḥamawī aš-Šāfiᶜī (Ḥamāh, Ṣafar 515 – Acre 585 H): IṣfḪar (Š) I pp. 481-96; MunḏTakm I p. 116; IMulᶜIqd p. 325; MaqrMuq III pp. 517-20; ZA II p. 242. The poet stemmed, as he boasted himself, from the progeny of ᶜAbd Allāh b. Rawāḥah, a known poet and companion of the Prophet. He studied in Damascus, *inter aliis* with Abū l-Qāsim Ibn ᶜAsākir (d. 571 H), and travelled to Alexandria where he met Abū Ṭāhir as-Silafī (d. 576 H). During his ship passage back to Syria he was taken captive and deported to Sicily. After a long imprisonment, he was released and returned to Ḥamāh as a professor of Shafiite law. He died as a martyr outside ᶜAkkā (Acre) in 585 H.

617 IᶜAdīmZubdah pp. 419f. Four of his verses in praise of the Prophet are cited in MaqrMuq III p. 518, some eight lines in IWāṣil Kurūb II p. 301.

618 TiğRiḥlah p. 364. For the author, see also ZA V p. 58.

619 Abū l-Ḥasan ᶜAlī b. M. al-Hamdānī aš-Šāfiᶜī. He was a pupil of the specialist in Qurʾānic readings aš-Šāṭibī and first studied and taught in Cairo; later, he moved to Damascus where he held lessons for over 40 years, among his pupils being also the known historian Abū Šāmah. For as-Saḫāwī's biography, see AŠāmahTar p. 177; YāqIršād V pp. 414f.; ḎahTaḏk IV p. 1432; BN XIII p. 170; ĞazṬab I pp. 568-71; NZ VI p. 354; IṬūlQal p. 238; ŠḎ V pp. 222f.; GAL I pp. 410f. and GALS I pp. 727f.; ZA IV pp. 332f.

620 For the text, see SaḫQaṣāʾid. The full title is given in ĞazṬab I p. 570 as *Kitāb al-Qaṣāʾid as-sabᶜah* (!) *fī madḥ Sayyid al-ḫalq Muḥammad – taṣliyah.*

phet, was the first as-Saḫāwī had written. He recited it during his first pilgrimage in 590 H at the tomb of the Prophet, in the presence of a big crowd that was moved to tears by his verses.[621] The fifth and sixth poems stem from the year 598 H and were also recited at the Prophet's sepulchre by the author himself.[622] His last poem, the fourth in the collection, was composed in 624 H in Damascus. However, being unable at that time to visit Medina in person, as-Saḫāwī sent it with the pilgrimage caravan to Medina in order to be recited there at the Prophet's tomb.[623]

Particular fame was achieved by *al-Qaṣīdah at-tāʾīyah (fī madḥ an-nabī)*, i.e. the "Qaṣīdah Poem with the Rhyme Letter *Tāʾ* (in praise of the Prophet)", a poem which for centuries seriously competed with the renown of al-Būṣīrī's *Burdah* (the so-called "Mantle Ode"). Bahāʾ ad-Dīn as-Subkī (see **160**), "visited the Prophet's tomb"[624] and recited his poem in front of it, "standing upright and his head covered".[625]

The tenth-century polymath Ibn Ṭūlūn correctly mentions al-Bahāʾ as-Subkī as the author,[626] while the poem is wrongly attributed to his father Taqīy ad-Dīn as-Subkī in GAL II p. 88 and missing from the EI² entry on Bahāʾ ad-Dīn; there is also a commentary on the poem by Ǧalāl ad-Dīn M. b. A. as-Samannūdī (d. *c.*838 H, see GAL II p. 88). The poem is cited and commented upon, alongside al-Būṣīrī's *Burdah*, in Nūr ad-Dīn al-Ḥalabī's three-volume biography of the Prophet entitled *ʾInsān al-ʿuyūn*, in individual verses throughout the text (according to the matter treated).

Other verses of some renown, which were composed to be recited in front of the Prophet's sepulchre, include a qaṣīdah poem by Ibn Bint al-Aʿazz the Younger (d. Cairo 695 H):[627] "He performed the pilgrimage and visited the tomb of the Prophet. There he recited in the 'noble apartment' (*al-huǧrah aš-šarīfah*, i.e. the tomb area) a splendid qaṣīdah with the rhyme consonant *dāl*".[628]

However, it was not before the ninth century H that the practice of sending poems in praise of the Prophet to his tomb in Medina was to become widespread. In this century we see a number of celebrated poets who took much care to present their verses to the Prophet, e.g. Ibn Kumayl al-Manṣūrī (M. b. A., d. Cairo 848 H)[629]

621 SaḫQaṣāʾid f. 71a.

622 SaḫQaṣāʾid ff. 73b and 74b.

623 SaḫQaṣāʾid f. 73a.

624 ITaġrManh I p. 411.

625 SaḫTuḥfLaṭ I p. 224.

626 IṬūlFulk p. 40.

627 Taqīy ad-Dīn Abū l-Qāsim ʿAr. b. Tāǧ ad-Dīn Abī M. ʿAbd al-Wahhāb b. Ḫalaf al-ʿAlāʾī aš-Šāfiʿī al-Miṣrī: BN XIII p. 346; SubkīṬab VIII pp. 172-5; IMulʿIqd p. 174; ITaġrManh VII pp. 188-91 and NZ VIII pp. 82f.; Escovitz: *Office of Qāḍī* pp. 62, 67-9 and 115. For his father, a Malikite chief judge and likewise known as "Ibn Bint al-Aʿazz", see Jackson: *Two-Tiered Orthodoxy* pp. 72ff.

628 NZ VIII p. 83 and ITaġrManh VII pp. 190f. Unfortunately, the poem does not seem to be extant, apart from the two lines quoted by Ibn Taġrī Birdī and the four lines in SubkīṬab VIII pp. 173f.; a short notice of this event also appears in SuyḤusnMuḥ II p. 157.

629 He composed a number of poems in praise of the Prophet and recited them by himself at the Prophet's tomb (*fī l-ḥuǧrah an-nabawīyah*), see SaḫWaǧīz II p. 597.

and aš-Šihāb al-Manṣūrī (A. b. M. Ibn al-Hāʾim, d. 887 H).[630] The poet most assiduously offering his verses to the Prophet was Šams ad-Dīn an-Nawāǧī (M. b. al-Ḥasan, d. 859 H). Between the years 830 and 858 H, he composed one qaṣīdah poem every year to be sent to the Prophet's sepulchre in Medina (*ʾilā l-ḥuǧrah aš-šarīfah*), where it was recited and "presented unto his noble ears" (*fa-ʿuriḍat ʿalā masāmiʿihī š-šarīfah*).[631] Only once, in 833 H, did he perform the pilgrimage himself. On this occasion he recited the poems he had sent so far in front of the Prophet's sepulchre; an-Nawāǧī's poems of later years, which have also been collected in a *dīwān*, were taken to Medina by some of his friends.

4.3.2. Scholars visiting tombs

Among scholars and men of letters we often find the desire to "approach" their predecessors by visiting their tombs. If we cast a glance, for example, into biographical dictionaries or travel accounts we find in a number of instances the authors describing how they visited the grave of certain famous persons; thus Ibn Raǧab's dictionary of Hanbalite scholars or al-Maqqarī's monumental *Nafḥ aṭ-ṭīb* contain frequent references to the authors' visits to the tombs of distinguished scholars.

These visits were obviously undertaken for two reasons. First, in order to strengthen the ties to the past, one of the most forceful motives underlying Arabo-Islamic learning and literature in general;[632] and second, in order to invoke mercy upon the deceased. The latter practice was deemed important enough to attract attention in a scholar's biography which fills merely a page in modern print, namely in the case of Abū Ǧaʿfar an-Nīsābūrī (M. b. Ṣāliḥ, d. 340 H). Although the report cited in the following concerns his funeral and is thus not a proper case of "visitation", we read in his biography that "(his companion) Abū ʿAbd Allāh Ibn al-Aḫram al-Ḥāfiẓ[633] recited the death prayer (for him). After his burial, he stood at his tomb, invoked mercy upon him (*taraḥḥama ʿalayhi*) and praised him".[634] Worth mentioning in a biography was also the opposite case, namely that after the death of a person "there were few people who invoked mercy upon him" (*qalla man yataraḥḥamu ʿalayhi*).[635]

The practice of visiting scholars' tombs, which in some ways is very reminiscent of the romantic *Grabeskult* of the 19th century CE and shows an essential understanding of the *genius loci* of burial sites, has been common throughout all centuries

630 as-Saḫāwī relates that he "performed the pilgrimage and praised the Prophet – *taṣliyah* – in a number of qaṣīdah poems, one of which he recited in front of his tomb (*bayna yadayhi*)", see ḌL II p. 150; *cf.* also GAL II p. 19. His poems are edited in MN.

631 NawāǧīMaṭāliʿ p. 78.

632 For this argument, see also Chamberlain: *Knowledge and social practice* pp. 119f.

633 M. b. Yūsuf an-Nīsābūrī (d. 344 H).

634 NawMuḫt p. 207.

635 IQŠuhbTārīḫ I p. 364. This phrase was often used generically in order to indicate that nobody felt sad or unhappy about the death of somebody, especially if the person deceased belonged to the ruling class and had a reputation for ruthless and violent behaviour.

and regions, but particularly so in the Islamic West. In some writings we find such visits portrayed in great detail – e.g. the visit of al-Maqqarī to the tomb of Lisān ad-Dīn Ibn al-Ḫaṭīb in Fez[636] – and there are at least three other instances worth taking into account here. The first story involves Abū Rāfiᶜ, the son of the well-known Ẓāhirite scholar Ibn Ḥazm. He went to the cemetery of Córdoba in the company of some of his colleagues and strolled around between the tombs there, saying:

> "The one who is buried here – and he indicated the tomb of Abū l-Walīd Yūnus b. ᶜAbd Allāh (b. Muġīṯ) b. aṣ-Ṣaffār (Córdoba, 338–429 H) – transmitted to me from the one who is buried here – and he indicated the tomb of Abū ᶜĪsā (al-Layṯī) – on the authority of the one who is buried here – and he indicated the tomb of ᶜAbd Allāh[637] (b. Yaḥyā) – from the one who is buried here – and he indicated the tomb of his father Yaḥyā b. Yaḥyā (d. 233 or 234 H) – from Mālik b. Anas al-Madīnī".[638]

The continuous chain of transmission was in that way manifested by the physical presence of the dead transmitters, visibly symbolised by their tombs. The pupil of Abū Rāfiᶜ, the Malikite scholar Abū Ǧaᶜfar al-Biṭrawšī, therefore added the final remark about this "cemetery tour": "Everybody who was present approved of this".

Some hundred years later, the famous Andalusian biographers and men of letters Ibn Baškuwāl (d. 578 H) and Ibn Ḫayr al-Išbīlī (d. 575 H)[639] set out to visit Ibn Abī l-Ḫiṣāl's tomb in Córdoba. For this event they had made the special arrangement that in front of Ibn Abī l-Ḫiṣāl's grave his qaṣīdah poem in praise of the Prophet entitled *Miᶜrāǧ al-manāqib*[640] would be recited to them. When this was done, they uttered blessings upon Ibn Abī l-Ḫiṣāl and addressed him with the words: "Peace be upon you, O ornament of Islam! (*yā-zayna l-ʾislām*)".[641]

Finally, at the tomb of Ibn al-Ḫarrāṭ al-Išbīlī (d. 581 H) in Biǧāyah, students would sit around his grave and recite his writings. His biographer al-Ġubrīnī himself studied Ibn al-Ḫarrāṭ's treatise on eschatology (entitled *al-ᶜĀqibah*, see bibliography) at his tomb, together with his teacher Abū ᶜAlī al-Arkušī who transmitted the work and could boast a chain of transmission for the work reaching back to the author.[642]

636 MaqqNafḥ (C) VII p. 83.

637 Or rather "ᶜUbayd Allāh"?

638 YāqBuldān I p. 447 (*s.v.* "Biṭrawš").

639 Abū Bakr Muḥammad b. Ḫayr al-Išbīlī: for his biography as well as his important bibliography known as *al-Fahrasah*, see now the exhaustive study by Vizcaíno: *Vida y obra de Ibn Jayr*.

640 Fully entitled *Miᶜrāǧ al-manāqib wa-minhāǧ al-ḥasab aṯ-ṯāqib fī nasab rasūli llāh (wa-muᶜǧizātihī wa-manāqib ʾaṣḥābih)*, a long poem of 366 lines, see IDiḥMuṭrib p. 188; GAL I p. 369 and GALS I p. 629. Parts of it are quoted in KalIktifāʾ I pp. 32-37 (121 verses) and IAḪiṣālRas pp. 627-37. *Cf.* also al-Makkī: *Madāʾiḥ* p. 124.

641 IAbbMuᶜǧṢadafī p. 146; al-Marrākušī: *Iᶜlām* III p. 6.

642 ĠubrᶜUnwān p. 44.

4.4. Communicating with the dead

4.4.1. General remarks

Another reason for scholars, ascetics and other people to visit tombs and cemeteries was their desire to communicate with the dead. This possibility to enter directly into contact with the netherworld – something which for the common people often constituted one of the major reasons why cemeteries should be avoided at night[643] – was very attractive to many among the learned and pious, or so it seems from the sources at our disposal.[644] To converse with the deceased and to be addressed by them was, especially in the formative period of Islam and again during the Mamluk and Ottoman periods, a widespread phenomenon.[645]

To give just two illustrations: the eminent Yemeni mystic and historian al-Yāfiʿī (d. 768 H, see **159**) reported from the Meccan scholar al-Muḥibb aṭ-Ṭabarī (d. 694 H) that he once stayed in the cemetery of Zabīd with the mystic and jurist Ismāʿīl b. Muḥammad al-Ḥaḍramī (d. 676 or 678 H).[646] The latter asked Muḥibb ad-Dīn, "Do you believe that the dead speak (*ʾa-tuʾminu bi-kalāmi l-mawtā*)?" and al-Muḥibb replied, "Yes, I do", whereupon Ismāʿīl said, "Look here, the one who is buried in this tomb tells me: 'I am from the stuff of Paradise' (*ʾanā min ḥašwi l-ǧannah*)".[647]

The same Ismāʿīl also had another, quite remarkable dialogue with a deceased person as we learn again from the account of al-Yāfiʿī:

> "One day, he walked around in a cemetery in the company of many people. There he burst out into tears, but then suddenly started to laugh. When he was asked for the reason, he answered 'I saw how the people (buried) in this cemetery are chastised and thus I became very sad. Then I asked God that I may intercede on their behalf and He granted me that. At this point the inhabitant of that tomb' – and he indicated a tomb that had been dug recently – 'said, I also belong to them, O faqīh Ismāʿīl! I am fulānah (i.e. N.N.), the singing girl. That is why I had to laugh and I told (her), (Yes,) you also belong to them'. He called the undertaker (in order to prove the veracity of his words) and said 'Whose tomb is that?', and the undertaker replied 'This is the tomb of *fulānah*, the singing girl'".[648]

643 After all, there is an utterance of the Prophet that explicitly forbids to visit cemeteries during the night, see ZamRabīʿ IV p. 179; a similar report from ʿAlī in IbšīhīMust II p. 442 (ch. 81). On the other hand, the Prophet is reported to have visited the Medinan cemeteries at night (*zāra laylan*), see IḤanbMusnad VII p. 140.

644 *Cf.* also Goldziher: *Culte des saints* p. 80.

645 I am not concerned here with the appearance of the dead in dreams, except when this took place at the very burial site; see below p. 117.

646 Quṭb ad-Dīn aš-Šāfiʿī, see ŠḎ V pp. 361f.; ZA I p. 324.

647 Quoted in ŠīrŠadd p. 21, YāfRawḍ pp. 182f. and SuyŠṢudūr p. 276. The story also appears in YāfNašr p. 17, with a different wording that seems somehow corrupt.

648 YāfNašr p. 17 and YāfRawḍ p. 182 = Gramlich: *Wunder* p. 358; SubkīṬab VIII p. 131. Slightly abbreviated, the story is also quoted in ŠḎ V p. 362 (who adds that the episode took place in the cemetery of Zabīd).

Conversing with the dead, as common occurrence, was not limited to certain groups of people, e.g. the ascetics, nor to specific cemeteries, e.g. the vast burial grounds of Cairo or of Mecca and Medina,[649] but it happened elsewhere as well. In Munastīr, for example, Abū ṭ-Ṭāhir Ismāᶜīl ar-Rakrākī (d. 662 H) would go to the tomb (*rawḍah*) of sheikh Abū ᶜAbd Allāh al-Kūmī and sit there. "He talked to him and the sheikh replied from his tomb, with words clearly audible to all present".[650]

We know of numerous other reports that the dead were heard speaking from inside their tombs, e.g. the legal authority aš-Šāfiᶜī (see **35**), the Egyptian "saint" Aḥmad al-Badawī (see below p. 142), Ibn ᶜAbbās,[651] the mystic Sahl at-Tustarī[652] or an unknown youth.[653] In the case of pious and saintly persons, their capacity to address the living from the tomb was also reckoned as one of the many kinds of "miracle-like blessings" (*karāmāt*) granted to them by the grace of God.[654] Even the Prophet himself is said to have addressed the believers from his tomb in Medina:[655] he did that sometimes in rhymed speech,[656] and on other occasions the call to prayer was heard from his tomb.[657] When a bedouin had come to the Prophet's sepulchre to implore mercy and intercession, a voice was heard from inside the tomb, saying "God has forgiven you!"[658] In other cases, the Prophet in his grave was addressed by a believer, but the answer came forth from the adjacent tomb of ᶜUmar b. al-Ḫaṭṭāb.[659]

Talking with the dead was believed to require a special attitude that is described by the mystic Muḥammad b. Ḥasan Ibn ᶜInān aš-Šāfiᶜī al-ᶜĀrif bi-llāh (d. 922 H) as follows: "He who wishes to hear the dead speak in their tombs must be a keeper of secrets, because the inability to keep secrets is an obstacle to hearing their voices".[660]

In any case, the subject of speaking with the dead and its implications belong among the most important facets of Islamic eschatology. This might be gleaned from as-Suyūṭī's little treatise *al-Lumᶜah fī ʾağwibat al-ʾasʾilah as-sabᶜah* ("The Gleaming of Answers to Seven Questions") which contains replies to the following questions: (1) Do the dead realise when the living are coming to visit them? (2) Are the dead acquainted with the deeds and vicissitudes of the living? (3) Do the dead hear the speech of the living? (4) Where do souls dwell (after death)? (5) Do souls

649 *Cf.* ḌL I p. 174: the visit of al-Burhān al-Abnāsī (Ibr. b. Mūsā, *c.*725–804) to the Baqīᶜ cemetery in Medina.

650 ITawSabk p. 116.

651 ᶜUğIhdāʾ p. 66.

652 Gramlich: *Wunder* p. 358.

653 SarrāğMaṣ II p. 41.

654 *Cf.* YāfNašr pp. 17ff. and MunKawākib I p. 15.

655 *Cf.* also *Wāfī* XII p. 350 (the scene described is part of a dream, though); Gramlich: *Wunder* pp. 87 and 359.

656 ᶜAydNūr p. 30.

657 INağDurrah p. 400; TI XXXII p. 193; MarğBahğah II p. 406; SuyInbāʾAḏk pp. 48f. (quoting from Abū Nuᶜaym), SuyḪaṣ II p. 491 and SuyŠṢudūr pp. 282f.; QasṭMaw III p. 414. Other persons could as well pronounce the *ʾaḏān* from their tombs, see IAYaṬab I p. 407.

658 NuwIlmām III pp. 15f.

659 MālRiyāḍ II pp. 443f.

660 ŠḎ VIII p. 117. Ibn ᶜInān was among the teachers of aš-Šaᶜrānī, see for his biography and teachings ŠaᶜrṬab II pp. 117-21.

meet and see each other? (6) Is the martyr subjected to the Interrogation in the tomb? (7) Is a child subjected to the Interrogation in the tomb?[661] As can be seen, questions relating to the communication between the living and the dead occupy a prominent place, and as-Suyūṭī at the beginning of his writing stresses the importance of these issues by saying that "these are important problems to solve", not without adding, as is typical for him, "that only a few people have contributed anything truly helpful in their regard".[662]

4.4.2. The silence of the tombs

The silence of the tombs and death as exhortation

Before we proceed any further we must note that, as far as the tomb and its inhabitant are concerned, discourses of different origins existed side by side in pre-modern Islam. Sometimes those discourses did indeed intermingle, but in many cases they remained separate from each other and did not exert mutual influence. If they did intermingle, though, the resulting inconsistencies were preserved – as it seems deliberately – and no efforts were made to reach a uniform whole.

On one hand, the dead were supposed to communicate with the living, and the tomb was by no means considered a place of silence. This view reflects, by and large, what theologians and Ḥadīṯ scholars were putting forward according to the Islamic Tradition. On the other hand, the tomb was portrayed as a place of utter silence, and death meant above all being silenced. This motif is equally widespread in pre-modern Islamic culture and its continuity was ascertained by its presence in *ʾadab* literature and poetry. As such, the second motif had its origins less in the monotheist tradition inherited and continued by Islam, but rather in the old Arabic bedouin world-view and in concepts being part of that post-Hellenistic melting pot which the Middle East was when the Muslims entered the scene up to the borders of Byzantine Anatolia and Sasānid Iran during the seventh and eighth centuries CE.

It might, therefore, be no accident that we encounter the motif of death as silencer of the living in a tradition about Alexander the Great. As recorded in many *ʾadab* anthologies, Aristotle (d. 323 BCE) is said to have mourned his royal patron after his death by saying: "Yesterday he exhorted us by his words and today he exhorts us by his silence" (*kāna ʾamsi yaʿiẓunā bi-kalāmihī wa-huwa l-yawma yaʿiẓunā bi-sukūtihī*).[663] Abū l-ʿAtāhiyah was inspired by this dictum and composed the widely-quoted line (*wāfir*):

661 SuyḤāwī II pp. 169-75.

662 SuyḤāwī II p. 169.

663 ZamRabīʿ IV p. 188. This motif appears, though often differently expressed, in many other *ʾadab* and poetry anthologies, e.g. ANuwDīwān II p. 164; ǦāḥBayān I pp. 81 and 407; MubKāmil (C) II p. 11; ṮaʿālTamṯīl p. 176; MasMurūǧ II p. 10; RāġibMuḥāḍ IV p. 485; ḤuṣZahr (M) III p. 729 / (Ṭ) II p. 81; IBuḥtUns pp. 65, 76 and 106; IbšīhīMust II p. 466 (ch. 83); *cf.* also MarzḤam II p. 881.

وكَانَتْ فِي حَيَاتِكَ لِي عِظَاتٌ * فَأَنْتَ اليَوْمَ أَوْعَظُ مِنْكَ حَيَّا

"There were in your life lessons for me (to learn), * but you are today (i.e. after your death) teaching a better lesson than while you were alive".[664]

This version of the *memento mori* motif, familiar in all cultures, was often connected to the fate of rulers and holders of power. In the Mamluk period, the motif could thus reappear in an "actualised" form, e.g. in a verse by the Egyptian poet Šams ad-Dīn Ibn Nubātah (d. 768 H) (*ṭawīl*):

كَفَى بِبَنِي أَيُّوبَ لِلنَّاسِ وَاعِظاً * وَإِنْ صَمَتَتْ أَفْوَاهُهُمْ فِي الضَّرَائِحِ

"Suffice the Ayyubids for the people as an exhorter,[665] * although their mouths have become silent in the tombs".[666]

Particularly suitable for demonstrating the contrast between the discourse of *ʾadab*, which took the finality of death and the silent tomb as sufficient exhortation, and the Islamic religious discourses, which rather stress the transient nature of death and the hortatory value of the hereafter,[667] are two verses by Abū Bakr Muḥammad b. al-Ḥasan az-Zubaydī (d. 379 H) (*sarīʿ*):

لَو لَمْ تَكُنْ نَارٌ وَلا جَنَّةٌ * لِلْمَرْءِ إلاَّ أَنَّهُ يُقْبَـرُ
لَكَانَ فِيهِ وَاعِظٌ زَاجِرٌ * نَاهٍ لِمَنْ يَسْمَعُ وَيُبْصِرُ

"If there was neither a Fire nor a Garden (i.e. neither Hell nor Paradise) * for man except (the fact) that he gets buried,

664 This line is quoted in the accounts of al-Ǧāḥiẓ, al-Mubarrad, ar-Rāġib, al-Ḥuṣrī and al-Ibšīhī (all as given in n. 663); further in AʿAtāhDīwān pp. 491f.; MasMurūǧ (P) IV p. 382; ṬurṭSirāǧ p. 14 (var. *fī*: *min*); BaṣrīḤam (C) II p. 198; IBuḥtUns p. 76; IAḤaǧSulwah p. 142.

665 Or "to teach them a lesson".

666 INubDīwān p. 100. The related dictum *kafā bi-l-mawti wāʿiẓan* ("death suffices as exhortation!") – alternatively as *kafā bi-d-dahri wāʿiẓan* (KU 42115 = XV p. 547) – appears in the religious discourse and was attributed, among others, to the Prophet (MundTarġīb IV p. 240) or to Abū d-Dardāʾ (d. 32 H), see IRaǧLaṭāʾif p. 102; MunKawākib I p. 118; KU 42794 (XV p. 699). In a poem by Bišr b. Abī Ḫāzim, this is taken up as follows (*wāfir*): *ṯawā fī mulḥadin lā budda minhū * kafā bi-l-mawti naʾyan wa-ġtirābā* (BišrDīwān p. 48; YāqBuldān III p. 41 = al-Ǧubūrī: *Muʿǧam* p. 108, *s.v.* "ar-Raddah", with the var. *mulḥadin*: *maḏǧaʿin*), "He settled in a burial niche that is inevitable; * death suffices as remoteness and estrangement!" In a poem by ʿAdī b. Zayd we read: *kafā wāʿiẓan li-l-marʾi ʾayyāmu dahrihī*, "The days of his destiny (i.e. his Fate) suffice as an exhorter for man", see al-Lawāsānī: *Kaškūl* p. 19; the wording is not beyond doubt, however, see ʿAdīDīwān p. 104 (no. 23 v. 16, var. *wāʾiẓan*: *zāǧiran*). *Cf.* also QurṭTaḏk p. 20 (*wa-kafā bi-l-mawti fa-ʿlam wāʿiẓan*). In IHuḏaylMaq p. 118 there is the saying: "Fate suffices as educator, and reason as guide!" (*kafā bi-d-dahri muʾaddiban wa-bi-l-ʿaqli muršidan*).

667 See, however, ManbTasl (C) pp. 204f. / (M) p. 199 where different "Islamic solutions" mediating between the finality of death and the hereafter are presented.

This would then do as a forcible exhortation, * prohibitive for those who hear and see".[668]

In a verse attributed to Abū Nuwās we encounter the same thought, yet now not formulated as a hypothesis but as a statement of conviction (*sarīʿ*):

مَا صَحَّ عِنْدِي مِنْ جَمِيعِ الَّذِي * يُذْكَرُ إلاَّ المَوْتُ وَالقَبْرُ

"In my opinion, there is no truth in all that * is mentioned except death and the grave" (Kennedy's translation).[669]

As is obvious, this is contrary to what the adherents of Islam commonly profess. It reminds one rather of those blasphemious utterances ascribed to the Umayyad caliph Muʿāwiyah (r. 41-60 H) who in a poem of his – if ascribed correctly – ruled out any encounter after death (*fa-laysa lanā baʿda l-mamāti talāqiyan*) and dubbed the belief in Resurrection mere "fables of amusement that puts the heart at ease" (*ʾasāṭīru lahwin yağʿalu l-qalba sāhiyan*).[670]

Beside the discourses of *ʾadab* literature and poetry, the motif of the silent tomb also found its way into discourses of a somewhat more religious significance, chiefly funerary epigraphy and ascetic poetry. For one thing, we often find this motif in epitaphs, both in those preserved and in those cited in literary sources (see **14**, **43**, **87** and **192**). On the other hand, the motif soon entered ascetic poetry (*zuhdīyāt*) and the field of hortatory preaching or exhortation (*waʿẓ*). Both fields were to an exceptional degree pervaded by ancient (pre-Islamic) or common Near Eastern concepts which were continuously and successfully transmitted in the *ʾadab* discourse. In the wider realm of Islamic culture, poetry in this context can thus be seen as a vehicle for the "pessimistic" counterpart to what the academic and scholarly discourses were offering on religious and eschatological matters. How pervasive that motif of the silent tomb and of the dead being unable to speak was, can be seen from two verses recited by none less than Abū Ḥanīfah himself, at a newly-dug tomb (*munsariḥ*):

كَمْ مِنْ أَخٍ لِي قَدْ كَانَ يُؤنِسُنِي * فَصَارَ تَحْتَ التُّرَابِ مُنْجَدِلاَ
لاَ يَسْمَعُ الصَّوْتَ إنْ هَتَفْـــتَ بِهِ * وَلا يَرُدُّ الجَوَابَ إنْ سُئِـــلاَ

"How many a brother of mine did comfort me with his company * and then were thrown down into the earth:
He will not hear the voice if you call to him * and he will not return an answer if he is asked".[671]

668 Cited in ṮaʿālYat II p. 71 and MaqqNafḥ (C) VI p. 74 (who adds: "He was right in that – may God the Exalted have mercy upon him!").

669 MarzMuw p. 427; TB VII p. 442 (var. *taḏkuruhū*); TMD XIII p. 444 (var. *tuḏkaru*); Kennedy: *Wine Song* p. 134.

670 Cited in BaḥrKaškūl III p. 31.

671 Quoted in IḤağRafʿ p. 26.

Similarly, Ibn al-Muᶜtazz in a verse described the wailers as crying out at the dead, adding that "they do not notice him (because they cannot hear) and are silent to him" (*wa-hum ġāfilūna ʿanhu ṣumūtun*).[672] After the battle of Badr, Qutaylah, the sister (or daughter?) of an-Naḍr b. al-Ḥāriṯ aṯ-Ṯaqafī, mourned him in a poem that contains the famous line (*kāmil*):

هَلْ يَسْمَعَنِّي النَّضْرُ أَنْ نَادَيْتُهُ * أَمْ كَيْفَ يَسْمَعُ مَيِّتٌ لَا يَنْطِقُ

"Will an-Naḍr hear me when I call to him? * But how will a dead person hear that does not speak (any longer)?"[673]

In a verse by the Andalusian poet Ibn Ḫafāğah we read (*ṭawīl*):

أَلَا صَمَّتِ الأَجْدَاثُ عَنِّي فَلَمْ تُجِبْ * وَلَمْ يُغْنِنِي أَنِّي رَفَعْتُ لَهَا صَوْتِي

"Lo! The tombs were deaf to me; thus they did not respond, * and it was of no use to me that I raised my voice (shouting) at them!"[674]

When Ḥusayn b. aḍ-Ḍaḥḥāk (Baṣrah *c.*162 – Baghdad 250 H) walked with Abū l-ᶜAtāhiyah across a cemetery he saw a woman weeping at the tomb of her son. This sight prompted him to compose the following line (*wāfir*):

تُنَادِي حُفْرَةً أَعْيَتْ جَوَابًا * فَقَدْ وَلِهَتْ وَصَمَّ بِهَا صَدَاهَا

"She addresses a pit which fails to answer * thus she became mad with grief and her echo became dumb with her".[675]

The famous preacher Ibn Nubātah al-Ḫaṭīb (d. in Mayyāfāriqīn 374 H or before), put it thus in one of his fiery sermons: "The dead do not tell whereto they proceed, yet if they could speak, they would do so. (...) God, who (once) made them utter, has now made them silent (*ʾaskatahum*)".[676]

672 IMuᶜtDīwān 1152 v. 13 (III p. 17).

673 The ways of transmission and the respective wordings of this verse differ in the fields of *sīrah* literature and poetical anthologies. The wording reported above stems from *sīrah* works, viz. IHišSīrah III p. 45, MaġrSīrah I p. 564, KalIktifāʾ II p. 36, ISayNāsᶜUyūn II p. 337 and ŠāmīSubul IV p. 63. In poetical anthologies and other writings, the verse is reported as *fal-yasmaʿanna n-Naḍru ʾin nādaytuhū * ʾin kāna* (var. *ʾam kayfa*) *yasmaʿu mayyitun ʾaw* (var. *lā*) *yanṭiqū*, see IRašᶜUmdah I p. 73; MarzḤam II p. 965; ŠantŠḤam I p. 602. See also IAUṣaybᶜUyūn p. 170 and Wagner: *Dichtung* I p. 120 (in German). The obvious implication being that there is no dead person that is capable of hearing or speaking.

674 IḪafDīwān p. 61. For the expression *ṣammati l-ʾağdāṯu*, see also **14**.

675 *Aġānī* VII p. 210. The expression (as used here) *ṣamma bihā ṣadāhā*, "her echo became dumb", is normally intended to mean "she perished, *or* was made to perish" (see Lane *s.r.*). However, the literal meaning of the expression is important in that verse because it clearly refers to the first hemistich – the tomb not answering, i.e. "echoing" the woman's voice –, and as a consequence of this her echo becomes dumb, i.e. she perishes (of grief).

676 Cited in IḪallWaf III pp. 156f. and *Wāfī* XVIII pp. 388f.

These and similar phrases really remind one of the many verses expressing this concept in the poetry of Abū l-ᶜAtāhiyah, but they were also stock-in-trade of the early Islamic ascetics and world-renouncers, e.g. the Baṣran Mālik b. Dīnār (d. between 123 and 131 H).[677] We know some of his verses which describe how he went out to the cemeteries and spoke to the tombs, "but the tombs remained silent to me" (*wa-lākinna l-qubūra ṣamatna ᶜannī*).[678] On another occasion, the Baṣran al-Fuḍayl (or al-Faḍl) ar-Raqqāšī went to a cemetery and shouted at the dead. After he had come back, he said: "Not a single group (*firqah*) of them responded. By my life, even if they did not respond by words, they did respond by their being a (warning) example (*ʾin lam yakūnū ʾağābū ğawāban laqad ʾağābū ᶜtibāran*)".[679] In the same vein, the Baṣran al-Ḥāriṯ b. Nabhān (Abū M. al-Ğarmī, d. after 160 H) relates: "I used to go out to the cemeteries (*ğabbānāt*), praying for mercy upon the inhabitants of the tombs, meditating and reflecting (about their fate). I would look at them: they are silenced and do not speak, they are neighbours and do not visit each other".[680] Muḥammad b. al-Munkadir (d. 130 H) circulated the following Tradition: "I was told that Adam said after the death of his son: 'O Eve, your son has died', and she asked 'Lo! What does "dying" mean?' Adam replied, '(It means:) He does not eat, he does not drink, he does not rise, he does not walk and he will not speak ever again'".[681]

ᶜAlī is said to have approached the tomb of Fāṭimah where he recited, his eyes full of tears, the following verses (*kāmil*):

مَا لِي وَقَفْتُ عَلَى القُبُورِ مُسَلِّماً * قَبْرَ الحَبِيبِ فَلَمْ يَرُدَّ جَوَابِي
أَحَبِيبُ مَا لَكَ لا تَرُدُّ جَوَابَنَا * أَنَسِيـــتَ بَعْدِي خُلَّةَ الأَحْبَـــابِ

"Why am I standing among the tombs, greeting * the tomb of the beloved one, but there was no reply?
My beloved, what has befallen you that you do not reply to us? * Did you forget, after becoming separated from me, the friendship of the loved ones?"

677 For his life and teachings, see Gramlich: *Vorbilder* I pp. 59-121, esp. pp. 74ff.

678 IQutᶜUyūn II p. 328; ANuḤilyah II p. 373; ŠirŠadd p. 28; Gramlich: *Vorbilder* I p. 77 (in German translation). *Cf.* also TurkLumaᶜ I p. 222 and Mālik's verses cited in ŠarŠMaq I p. 176; ḤurRawḍ p. 31; al-Munayyar: *Tasliyah* p. 58. From a poem by al-Ḥusayn, composed when he visited the martyrs' tombs in Medina, we have the line (*kāmil*): *nādaytu sukkāna l-qubūri fa-ʾuskitū * wa-ʾağābanī ᶜan ṣamtihim turbu l-ḥaṣā*, "I called to the inhabitants of the tombs, but they were made silent, * and the earth and pebbles (upon their tombs) gave me the answer as to their silence" (BN VIII p. 209; al-ᶜAffānī: *Sakb* II p. 535; with a different wording in IDāʾūdZahrah p. 365).

679 Quoted in al-ᶜAffānī: *Sakb* I p. 668. For Fuḍayl, see ANuḤilyah III pp. 102f. and IĞawzīṢafwah II p. 127.

680 TurkLumaᶜ I p. 222; ḤurRawḍ p. 34. A very similar passage is attributed to Ṯābit al-Bunānī in ḤurRawḍ p. 30 and al-Qināwī: *Fatḥ ar-raḥīm* p. 176 (*wağadtu ʾahla l-qubūri ṣamūtan lā yatakallamūna wa-furādā lā yatazāwarūna*).

681 ANuḤilyah III p. 148.

Then he heard a voice pronouncing these lines (*kāmil*):

قَالَ الحَبِيبُ وَكَيْفَ لِي بِجَوَابِكُمْ * وَأَنَا رَهِينُ جَنَادِلٍ وَتُرَابِ
أَكَلَ التُّرَابُ مَحَاسِنِي فَنَسِيتُكُمْ * وَحُجِبْتُ عَنْ أَهْلِي وَعَنْ أَصْحَابِي

"The beloved said, 'How could I reply to you * while I am held in pledge by stones and earth?
The earth did swallow up my beautiful features, so I forgot about you, * and I was secluded from my family and my companions'".

These verses exist in many different versions; not all of them are said to have been recited by ᶜAlī.[682] On another occasion, ᶜAlī was asked why he was staying in the cemetery so often and replied: "I find them the best neighbours to confide in (*ḫayru ǧīrāni ṣidqin*), they hold their tongues and remind me of the hereafter!"[683] A similar phrase is transmitted by Mālik b. Anas, from a cemetery-dweller in Medina.[684] The poetess Laylā al-Aḫyalīyah (first cent. H) was reproached by someone as to why she would not stop at the tomb of her lover Tawbah b. al-Ḥumayyir (d. 85 H) and greet him. She said: "I cannot bear that he does not return my greetings".[685]

Alternative discourses

The discourse presented so far – centred on the finality of death and symbolised by the motif of the silent tomb – seems to stand in contrast with what was put forward in the religious discourses proper which stress the transitional nature of death and the salvatory role of the afterlife according to the message of Islam; both discourses may thus be labelled "alternative discourses". However, this is not to say that they were mutually exclusive, rather they should be viewed as complementary aspects and discoursive formations of one and the same conceptualisation of death. What we are dealing with here is a question of emphasis: stressing the finality of death might thus be seen to emphasise the this-wordly aspect, whereas stressing the transitional nature of death emphasises the other-wordly aspect.[686]

Jan Assmann, who in his study of the Ancient Egyptian concepts of death dif-

682 Cited in ŠirŠadd p. 29 and YāfRawḍ p. 401. Other versions of these lines show often a different wording and additional verses; it would be worthwhile to collect them all from the various sources. The versions known to me appear in: ALL (B) I p. 325 (136rd night) / (C) II p. 135; ḤurRawḍ p. 29; FanSirāǧ p. 182; BaḥrKaškūl III p. 185; al-Qināwī: *Fatḥ ar-raḥīm* p. 176; ŠayMaǧānī IV p. 34; al-ᶜAffānī: *Sakb* II pp. 534f.. In other sources, completely different verses of ᶜAlī, pronounced at Fāṭimah's tomb, are quoted: MubKāmil (C) IV p. 30; IḤamdTaḏk IV p. 237; NuwNih V p. 164; INāṣBard (A) p. 62 / (C) p. 58 = SuyBard p. 142 (rhyme *-īlū*).

683 Cited in ŠarŠMaq I p. 175 and KU 42989 (XV pp. 759f.).

684 IᶜABarrBahǧah II p. 341 (*ʾinnahum ǧīrānu ṣidqin ... wa-lī fīhim ʿibrah*).

685 IBuḥtUns p. 87; *cf.* LaylāDīwān p. 111. However, it remains unclear in this case whether Tawbah would not return the greeting because he had been repudiated by the father of Laylā when he once had approached her, or because of his being dumb-in-death. See also p. 373.

686 *Cf.* D'Avray: *Memorial Preaching* pp. 222f.

ferentiates between (a) death seen as an enemy, (b) death seen as a return and (c) death seen as a mystery, interprets these seemingly conflicting concepts as "komplementäre Aspekte ein und derselben Todeskonzeption".[687] Transferred to the Islamic realm, the finality of death might be said to parallel the Ancient Egyptian concept of death seen as an enemy, while its transitional nature and the role of the hereafter parallels the concept of death seen as a return. Taken together, both represent the Islamic conceptualisation of death and closely depend on each other. As said before, the word "alternative" should not indicate that both concepts were mutually exclusive or logically inconsistent with one another, but that for the individual, one individual on a certain occasion or a group of individuals the choice was left open in principle which conceptualisation meant more to him (or them) and which discourse was to be followed by them.[688]

The complementary aspect of both discourses in Islamic culture – the finality of the silent tomb vs. the transitional nature of death and the salvatory message of Islam – is visible even in Tradition. Here we observe that the seemingly un-Islamic motif of the silent tomb as the most forceful and unique exhorter of mankind, which marginalises the role of creed and the impact of the salvatory message of Islam, was not kept outside the religious discourse of Tradition, but one tried to safeguard this motif and combine, or even to reinforce it, with the basic tenets of the Islamic faith. This comes to the fore in the following report from the Prophet who said: "I left among you (i.e. the community of believers) someone speaking and someone silent".[689] This was understood to refer to the "eloquent" Islamic message ("the speaking Qur'ān") and to the finality of "taciturn" death ("the silent tomb"), each of which representing one of the before-mentioned "alternative discourses".

4.4.3. Asking the dead for hidden knowledge or advice

The motif of the "silent tomb" successfully entered, but never wholly dominated, the larger Islamic discourses which were centred around questions of theology and eschatology. These larger Islamic discourses, clearly distinguishable from the discourses of *'adab* and many branches of poetry, were mainly shaped by the material found in the numerous collections of Tradition. Many Muslim scholars tried hard to push the motif of the "silent tomb" (the finality of death or death seen as enemy) aside or at least to weaken its impact. Nor did this motif replace the popular belief that communication with the dead was in fact possible and that the tombs were anything but places of forced silence, and thus of irreversible non-existence.

It was a widespread practice to stroll around in cemeteries, alone or, more often

687 Assmann: *Tod als Thema* pp. 18f.

688 *Cf.* Assmann: *Tod als Thema* p. 38: "Trotzdem stehen sich nun aber diese beiden Todesbilder, der Tod als Feind und der Tod als Heimkehr, (...) nicht im Sinne alternativer Lösungen gegenüber, sondern gehören zusammen und entfalten erst in ihrer komplementären Verbindung ihre ganze kulturfundierende Bedeutung".

689 IḪarrāṭʿĀqibah p. 38 and MaʿbIstiʿdād p. 10 (*taraktu fīkum* [added in IḪarrāṭʿĀqibah: *wāʿiẓayni*] *nāṭiqan wa-ṣāmitan*).

than not, in company, in order to hear the "speech of the deceased in their graves" (*kalām al-mawtā fī qubūrihim*). Until today, as it was during the pre-modern period, this phenomenon has been known as "the tomb speaking" (*al-qabr yatakallam*), although this expression bears, according to the context, two different meanings: either the visitor is addressed from within the tomb (in which case it is actually the deceased who is speaking), or the tomb as such will speak to its occupant, e.g. when greeting and addressing the deceased immediately after his burial.[690]

One of the many gains to be had from talking to the dead was the knowledge of things hidden or unknown. The obvious advantage of such communication between the dead and the living was expressed by a dead person speaking from his tomb and addressing his visitor: "Alas, you act but you do not know, and we know but have no power to act",[691] that is, the dead possess knowledge that could be used by the living who are still able to act if only they could acquire the necessary knowledge. A rather special case of the "powerless" dead delivering information to the living is known from the biography of the Syrian mystic Abū Bakr al-Bālisī (d. 658 H): one day, he sauntered about in a cemetery and the spirits of the dead appeared to him. After they had offered their greetings, a young lad with a beautiful face spoke to Abū Bakr and informed him that he had been assassinated. He then indicated his murderers, who came from a village nearby, and thus their crime became known.[692]

The idea that the dead know or perceive things unknown to the living must have been fairly popular. This is well illustrated by the famous and widely-quoted story about the first-century Baṣran Abū ᶜAbd Allāh Muṭarrif b. ᶜAbd Allāh (d. after 87 H). Muṭarrif was living in the countryside, but on Fridays he mounted his riding animal and came to attend the Friday prayer in town. When he passed a graveyard, he stopped and took a nap. Then he saw (in his dream?) the buried (*ʾahl al-qubūr*) standing at the openings of their tombs, saying to each other "That one (i.e. Muṭarrif) is on his way to the Friday prayer". The startled Muṭarrif asked, "How is that? Are you able to distinguish the Friday from other days?" They answered, "Of course we are! We even know what the birds are saying in the lofty air". "What are they saying, then?" "They say: 'Greetings of peace, greetings of peace for a blessed day (*salāmun salāmun li-yawmin ṣāliḥin*)'".[693]

But of course, contacting the dead for information (as in other cases one turned to the djinns who were likewise thought to possess hidden knowledge) had also another and even more "practical" side. The information desired could, up to the

690 *Cf.* IADunyāQubūr (A) pp. 56-61; IĞawzīTabṣ I p. 349 (*muḫāṭabat al-qabr*); IRağAhwāl pp. 31-4; SuyŠṢudūr pp. 153-8 and 203; al-ᶜAffānī: *Sakb* I pp. 659-67.

691 IADunyāQubūr (A) p. 208; IḪarrāṭᶜĀqibah p. 115; SuyŠṢudūr pp. 285f. and 409f.; similar versions appear in BayDal VII p. 40; ŠīrŠadd p. 14; MaᶜbIstiᶜdād p. 30.

692 MunKawākib II p. 347. For another episode of a deceased naming his murderers, see Gramlich: *Wunder* pp. 358f.

693 IĞawzīṢafwah II p. 133; MunKawākib I p. 449. Different versions of this story appear in IADunyāQubūr (A) p. 204 = SuyŠṢudūr p. 303; IQutᶜUyūn II p. 342; ANuḤilyah II p. 205; YāfRawḍ p. 178 (told of Ṣāliḥ al-Murrī); BN VI p. 278; IRağAhwāl p. 112; SuyNūrLum p. 217.

present, be stimulated by the interest in material profit, e.g. in the case of a treasure-hunt.[694] The dead were in this case in a privileged position, not only for their superior knowledge, but also because tombs were among the favourite places where people tended to hide their riches.[695] Finally, the dead were approached in order to seek advice, mainly with regard to questions of private nature.

Sleeping at a tomb

In order to assure that the communication with the dead took place the person seeking advice or information would often stay at a tomb (or inside a mausoleum) and sleep there. In dream, then, one or more from among the deceased would appear, giving suggestions and the desired advice or information.[696]

A vivid discussion was conducted among Muslim scholars whether sleeping in a cemetery or inside a mausoleum was permissible or not;[697] the Hanafites were especially known for their firm rejection of that practice[698] and there are some stories to the effect that the deceased is "hurt" by somebody sleeping at his tomb.[699] However, numerous episodes tell us about people sleeping near tombs or inside venerated shrines (e.g. the mausoleum of aš-Šāfiᶜī, see below).[700] The earliest, though altogether peculiar, instance that I know of concerns Fāṭimah. She stretched down beside (or upon?) the Prophet's tomb (*ḍǧᶜ* VIII *ᶜalā qabr an-nabī*), but when the Prophet "stepped out to her" while she was sleeping she believed this to be an evil vision enticing and tempting her (*ftn* I), so she did not do that again.[701] A particularly long and detailed story is transmitted from al-Ḥāriṯ b. Nabhān who slept "in the shadow of a mausoleum (*qubbah*)" and had a dream in which the occupant of the

694 See e.g. Ibrāhīm ᶜAbd al-ᶜAlīm ᶜAbd al-Barr: *Kašf as-sitār ᶜan fatḥ al-kunūz wa-l-ᵓāṯār*, Cairo 1420/2000.

695 For thieves frequenting those mausolea which were not looked after and whose doors had been taken off the hinges, see IḤāǧǧMadḫ II p. 18; for professional tomb-robbers looking for riches, see below p. 206. Local Arabs in Yemen believed that someone buried in a coffin would hide treasures with him (Niebuhr: *Reisebeschreibung* p. 402).

696 The encounter of the souls of the living with those of the dead in dreams, insofar this is not connected to a burial site, is a broad subject in its own right and cannot be covered here. For further details, see MuwMuršid I pp. 50-3; SuyŠṢudūr pp. 357-91; Smith/Haddad: *Islamic Understanding of Death* pp. 51f.; Gramlich: *Wunder* pp. 344-9; Schimmel: *Träume* pp. 198-229; Kinberg: *Interaction* esp. pp. 290-307.

697 ᶜAynīᶜUmdah VII p. 102; *cf.* also ĠazIḥyāᵓ (C) IV p. 418; MuwMuršid I pp. 50f.; IḤāǧǧMadḫ I p. 252; Kriss: *Volksglaube* I p. 48.

698 INuǧBaḥr II p. 209; HarMirqātMaf IV p. 69; MF XXXII p. 246.

699 See e.g. IḪarrāṭᶜĀqibah p. 128.

700 *Cf.* also IADunyāQubūr (A) pp. 53f., 59 and 126; YāfRawḍ pp. 178 and 305; IRaǧAhwāl pp. 169f.

701 ISaᶜdṬab II pp. 313f.

tomb, cruelly chastised, appears. Eventually all ends well and the deceased is relieved of his pains.[702]

Among mystics, we hear of persons who fell asleep beside the tombs of their masters and then communicated with them in their dreams, e.g. Abū Isḥāq Ibrāhīm b. Šaybān al-Qarmīsīnī (d. 303 H) who slept at the tomb of Abū ᶜAbd Allāh al-Maġribī.[703] In Baghdad, a jurist went to the tomb of a colleague and recited the entire Qurᵓān there. Then he slept at this tomb and saw the deceased in his dream, thus he was able to ask him some questions on legal matters.[704] Finally, people were also sleeping at the sepulchre of the Prophet, for example the Fatimid vizier Abū Muḥammad al-Ḥasan b. ᶜAlī al-Yāzūrī (d. 450 H)[705] or the mystic Abū l-Ḫayr at-Tīnātī (d. Cairo after 340 H) who fell asleep behind the pulpit near the tomb and in his dream saw the Prophet offering him a loaf of bread, one half of which he ate, and, in his words, "when I woke up, I held the other half in my hand".[706]

One of the sites often chosen as sleeping places was (and still is) the Cairene mausoleum of aš-Šāfiᶜī. Though there is evidence that in Egypt the practice of sleeping at shrines or venerated sites was known from pharaonic times,[707] in the Islamic period this was done mainly for making contact with the deceased and only rarely, as it had often happened in Ancient Egypt, in order to be cured instantly (see above p. 85). Thus in the year 1007 H it so happened that the famous jurist Ḫayr ad-Dīn ar-Ramlī (993–1081 H)[708] visited the mausoleum of aš-Šāfiᶜī. He did that for the following reason:

> "Ḫayr ad-Dīn refused to follow his (elder) brother (Šams ad-Dīn ᶜAbd al-Ġanīy) in entering the Hanafite *maḏhab*, and his brother refused to study Shafiite law. That is why they approached one of the important scholars at al-Azhar who suggested that Ḫayr ad-Dīn should write the details of the matter on a piece of paper, in order to put it then on the tomb of aš-Šāfiᶜī and to sit down beside it. Ḫayr ad-Dīn wrote it down, set off and laid the piece of paper (on the tomb).[709] After having sat down, he soon fell asleep and in his dream Imam aš-Šāfiᶜī appeared, saying 'We all are on the right path'. Ḫayr ad-Dīn returned and reported the dictum to the person who had suggested (the visitation of aš-Šāfiᶜī's tomb). The man told him, 'The Imam gives you the permission

702 TurkLumaᶜ I pp. 223-7.

703 *Adab al-mulūk* p. 17 = GramlLebensweise p. 43.

704 IZayKawākib p. 162.

705 See the story told in MaqrMuq III p. 408.

706 YāfRawḍ pp. 126f.; ŠaᶜrṬab I p. 109; HaytTuḥfZuw p. 117. The same story is also told from Abū ᶜAbd Allāh Ibn al-Ǧalāᵓ (d. 306 H), see QušRis p. 371; MarǧBahǧah II p. 406; ḤurRawḍ p. 356; Gramlich: *Wunder* p. 346.

707 Strabo of Amasya: *The Geography*, ed. and tr. Horace L. Jones, 8 vols., London – Cambridge (Mass.) 1923–35 (Loeb Classical Library), XVII, I, 17 (= VIII p. 62-5): "Canobus is a city situated at a distance of one hundred and twenty stadia from Alexandria (...). It contains the temple of Sarapis, which is honoured with great reverence and effects such cures that even the most reputable men believe in it and sleep in it – themselves on their own behalf or others for them".

708 See GAL II p. 314.

709 This was commonly done until modern times (*cf.* Bannerth: *Wallfahrtsstätten Kairos* p. 55) and resembles the practice, known from many shrines, of leaving scraps of paper with messages or vows (Ar. *naḏr*, pl. *nuḏūr*, or Pers. *niyāz*) or veritable letters at a venerated tomb.

(*ʾiǧāzah*) to follow your brother in studying the law according to the *maḏhab* of Abū Ḥanīfah'. Therefore, Ḫayr ad-Dīn gave in and seriously took up studying (...) until he had surpassed his brother (in learning)".[710]

The dead know less than the living

The idea that the dead possess knowledge of things hidden from the living was not undisputed in Islamic learning. In any case, this idea blatantly contradicts that what we read in the Qurʾān, e.g. in Q 27:65 *Say: 'None knows the Unseen in the heavens and earth except God'*, with *al-ġayb*, "the unseen",[711] being the favourite term for the kind of information that was asked from the deceased. The following passage by Ibn al-Ḥāǧǧ shows that some scholars tried to keep to the Qurʾān and denied that the deceased would help in knowing the unknown, quite on the contrary:

> "It has been prohibited to stay overnight at the tombs (*al-mabīt fī l-qubūr*) since one must fear the disclosure of the secrets of the dead (*kašf ʾasrār al-mawtā*), and God the Exalted has veiled that from us[712] as a sign of His mercy. Thus the person who stays there will inevitably subject himself to the loss of this wise state (*ḥikmah*) because he will see things which take away his faculty of reasoning".[713]

However, in order to harmonise the afore-mentioned Qurʾānic passage with the growing importance of "knowledge of the unseen" among ascetics and mystics, some scholars argued, on the basis of Q 27:65 and the following verse, that the term *al-ġayb* only referred to the time of the Last Day, but not to "the unseen" or to "things hidden" as such.[714] The possibility to converse with the dead, or to see the deceased appear in dreams or visions, was therefore called "a sort of disclosure" (*nawʿ min al-kašf*),[715] the term *kašf* being commonly used in order to indicate the way(s) towards the knowledge of hidden things, possessed by both the living (e.g. saintly persons, *ʾawliyāʾ*) and the dead.[716]

Even the Prophet himself, although he was unanimously believed to have predicted during his lifetime a number of events and elucidated matters "hidden from mankind" (*al-ġāʾibāt* or *al-ġuyūb*),[717] was not granted the possibility of an increase in knowledge after his death: "My knowledge after my death is like my knowledge in life" (*ʾinna ʿilmī baʿda mawtī*[718] *ka-ʿilmī fī l-ḥayāh*, or *fī ḥayātī*), as a famous Tradition has it;[719] yet this also intends to say, after all, that the Prophet had *not lost* his

710 MuḥḪul II p. 136.

711 *Cf.* the well-considered discussion of that term in HaytFatḤad pp. 311f.

712 I.e. He protected us from knowing what the dead know, according to their condition.

713 IḤāǧǧMadḫ I p. 252.

714 IǦuzTashīl II p. 135; ṮaʿālTafsīr II p. 504 (*ad* Q 27:65).

715 ŠīrŠadd p. 24; YāfRawḍ p. 181; SuyBušrā pp. 44f.

716 For the tomb as a place for "being told the unseen" (*al-ʾiḫbār bi-l-ġayb*), see also MaʿarrīLuzūm II p. 207.

717 IḤazmǦaw p. 10; ʿIyāḍŠifāʾ (B) I pp. 249-58 / (Š) I pp. 325-46 = HarŠŠifāʾ I pp. 677-708; IǦawzīWafā pp. 308-24. *Cf.* also IǦuzTashīl II p. 135 (*ad* Q 27:65).

718 Var. *wafātī*.

719 IMandahFaw II p. 31; SuyInbāʾAḏk p. 47; HaytTuḥfZuw p. 41; ḤalInsān II p. 180.

former knowledge and that the believers could still approach him for guidance and information. All the more startling, however, is another Tradition from the Prophet of his praise of Abū Bakr: "Whosoever wishes to see a dead man walking on the face of the earth may behold Abū Bakr", which was understood to mean that Abū Bakr had been granted "manifest knowledge such as the common believers will reach only after their death".[720]

Criticism of the idea that the dead exceed the living in knowledge was rarely voiced, but there are many reports which indirectly point to the fact that the dead actually know less than the living and thus depend for their part on gaining information from them. For example, the dead will ask the visitors coming to their tombs for news of their relatives,[721] and therefore people used to converse with their dead parents in order to keep them abreast of affairs.[722] Some reports say that the caliphs ᶜUmar and ᶜAlī went to the Medinan cemeteries and informed the dead buried there of what had happened to their belongings, their families and the Islamic community in general since they had died.[723] If no recourse to information from the living was possible, the dead in a burial area had to wait for "newcomers". Thus, when a recently deceased person enters his tomb, those already dead could ask him for news of the living,[724] being curious, e.g., to know who had married in the meantime.[725]

From Ibn ᶜAsākir and al-Ḥākim an-Nīsābūrī, as-Suyūṭī relates the following, as told by Saᶜīd b. al-Musayyab:

> "Together with ᶜAlī b. Abī Ṭālib we went to the cemetery of Medina. He called, 'O ye inhabitants of the tombs! Peace be upon you and the mercy of God! Will you tell us your news, or should we tell you ours?' We heard a voice saying 'Peace be upon you and the mercy of God and His blessings, O Prince of the Believers! Tell us what happened after our death!' ᶜAlī said, 'Your wives have remarried, your belongings have been divided, your children have been gathered among the orphans and the edifice you had firmly built (*šyd* II) has been occupied by your enemies. So this is the news we know of, and what is the news known to you?' One from among the dead replied: 'The shrouds have been burnt, the hair has fallen out, the skin has burst open, the pupils have flown down the cheeks and the nose drips with rotten pus. We found what we had prepared (for ourselves during our lives) and what we left behind we have lost. We are but pledges of our deeds'".[726]

720 SuhrᶜAwārif p. 538.

721 IADunyāQubūr (A) pp. 212f.; the whole section is also taken up in IRağAhwāl.

722 SuyŠṢudūr p. 279.

723 QurṭTaḏk p. 12; SuyŠṢudūr pp. 279f.

724 IQutᶜUyūn II p. 342; DīnMuğāl III, p. 228; IRağAhwāl pp. 35-8. *Cf.* also Horten: *Gedankenwelt* pp. 300f. and Smith/Haddad: *Islamic Understanding of Death* p. 54.

725 IRağAhwāl p. 36; SuyḤāwī II p. 170; HaytFatFiqh II p. 29. *Cf.* also ZamRabīᶜ IV pp. 179f.

726 SuyḪaṣ I p. 113. I could not trace that passage in TMD, although the central part, spoken by ᶜAlī, is contained in one of his sermons, see TMD XLII p. 499.

The dead are acquainted with the deeds of the living

There was general belief that the dead are affected by the deeds of the living. They rejoice for the virtuous conduct of their relatives still alive, while if these behaved differently the dead are believed to say: "O our God, do not let them die until You lead them on the right path, as You did lead us" (*allāhumma lā tumithum ḥattā tahdiyahum kamā hadaytanā*).[727] According to as-Suyūṭī, who quotes some Traditions in support, the dead are informed of the deeds of their living relatives every night between Thursday and Friday, or every Friday.[728] Another Tradition states that the spirit of a dead person is "revolved around (*dīra bihī*) his house for a month and around his tomb for a year, before being lifted to the *sabab* (i.e. the place, *or* gate, of ascent of the Heaven?)[729] where he will meet the spirits of the living and the dead".[730] According to Shiite belief the dead visit their living relatives once in a while in the guise of birds and thus remain informed about their relatives' lives and doings.[731]

In the Sufi manual of as-Suhrawardī we read that "the souls (of the deceased) wander about in limbo (*barzaḫ*) and look down on what happens in the world (of the living), and the angels in Heaven speak about the state of men (*ʾaḥwāl al-ʾādamīyīn*)".[732] However, the Malikite scholar Ibn al-Ḥāǧǧ was a little more cautious when he discussed that question:

> "Every believer who is taken to the hereafter knows about the condition (*ʾaḥwāl*) of the living, at least in most cases. (...) It is also probable that there is a special period in which they get acquainted with the deeds (*ʾaʿmāl*) of the living, yet it is likewise probable that things are different because these facts are hidden from us. However, the Trustworthy (i.e. the Prophet) tells us about their being acquainted with the deeds (of the living) and thus there is no doubt that it does take place, but the exact manner (in which this happens) is not known. God knows best about it".[733]

Two fatwas by Ibn Ḥaǧar al-Haytamī are concerned with the question of whether the dead know about what is going on among the living. In the first fatwa, his answer runs as follows: "Yes, they do know that, though it is uncertain at which

727 SuhrʿAwārif p. 447; ŠīrŠadd p. 11; IRaǧAhwāl p. 116; SuyḤāwī II p. 170. *Cf.* also Kinberg: *Interaction* pp. 304-7 and below p. 122.

728 SuyNūrLum p. 217. *Cf.* also DaylFird I p. 90; ŠīrŠadd p. 11; HarMirqātMaf III p. 238 (who leaves open the exact days when this happens).

729 *Cf.* Lane *s.r.* where he explains the term *ʾasbāb as-samāʾ*: "*The places of ascent of the heaven,* or *sky:* or *the tracts,* or *regions, thereof:* or *the gates thereof*".

730 DaylFirdaws II p. 364.

731 KulKāfī III pp. 230f.; MaǧlBihār VI pp. 257f.

732 SuhrʿAwārif p. 447 = ŠīrŠadd pp. 9f. (The citation diverges from the original wording in one point, but it seems to make more sense and has thus been adopted).

733 IḤāǧǧMadḫ I p. 259. On the concept, important to Muslim scholars, of accepting human ignorance as far as eschatological matters are concerned, see Gräf: *Auffassungen vom Tod* pp. 127 and 144f. See also Volume I p. 151.

period they learn of it, in contrast with what was said by those who mention a fixed time".[734] In the second fatwa, the *responsio* says:

> "Yes, on the basis of the report (...) according to which 'your works are presented to your relatives and kinsfolk among the dead, and if (these works) are good the dead will rejoice, and if they are not they will say: *O our God, do not let them die until you lead them on the right path, as You led us*'. From this we learn that the righteous dead are acquainted (with the deeds of the living). (...) al-Ḥakīm at-Tirmiḏī quoted another report to the effect that the deeds (of the living) are presented to God on Monday and Thursday, and to the prophets and the fathers and mothers on Friday".[735]

4.4.4. Are the dead able to hear?

Notwithstanding the manifold testimonies which affirm that the dead are not only able to hear and speak but also exceed the living in knowledge, the concept that the dead hear (and speak) was not undisputed and not seldom it was met with incredulity. This incredulity is, in all probability, due to the influential motifs of the "silent tomb" and of death as the "silencer of the living" both of which have been described above. There it was said that these concepts were primarily shaped by ancient pre-Islamic Near Eastern ideas, and from the beginning they were present in the nascent Islamic culture as well. With good reasons, and in view of what in later centuries was to become the mainstream of Sunnite (and Shiite) belief, these concepts might even be called "Qur'ānic" rather than "Islamic".

The Qur'ānic wording

For the motif of the dead being incapable of hearing and speaking to the living we possess considerable evidence from Arabic mourning poetry, ranging from the formative period of Islam until later centuries. But for their incapacity to hear, there are also some passages in the Qur'ān which rather explicitly seem to deny the possibility of the dead being able to hear the living: *Not equal are the living and the dead. God makes to hear whomsoever He will; thou canst not make those in their tombs to hear* (Q 35:22),[736] and: *Thou shalt not make the dead to hear, neither shalt thou make the deaf to hear the call when they turn about, retreating* (Q 27:80 = 30:52).[737] This Qur'ānic wording also found its way into poetry, especially the passage *wa-mā 'anta bi-musmi'in man fī l-qubūr* (Q 35:22), e.g. in a verse by Ibn Ḫafāğah (*kāmil*):

يَا أَيُّهَا النَّاعِي وَلَسْتَ بِمُسْمِعٍ * سَكَنَ القُبُورِ وَبَيْنَنَا أَسْدَادُ

734 HaytFatFiqh II p. 29. *Cf.* also ŠīrŠadd pp. 6 and 10f.

735 HaytFatFiqh II p. 29. This report is also cited in Suhr'Awārif p. 447 and ŠīrŠadd pp. 10f. See also above p. 33 with note 134.

736 *Cf.* IRağAhwāl p. 103 and ManbTasl (C) pp. 224f. / (M) pp. 214f.

737 *Cf.* also Smith/Haddad: *Islamic Understanding of Death* p. 51.

"O you who laments,[738] though you will not make to hear * the inhabitants of the tombs because there are barriers between them and us".[739]

In the Qurʾānic passages mentioned, the "normal" situation of the deceased is without doubt equated with that of the deaf, viz. their being not able to hear. This is further confirmed by the phrase "not equal are the living and the dead" which contrasts their condition with that of the living among whom the capacity to hear is the normal condition and its absence a deficiency.

Thus we read in BayḍTafsīr IV p. 121 (*ad* Q 27:80): The unbelievers are "likened to the dead because they are not enjoying the capacity to hear what is spoken to them, and thus they are in the following also likened to the deaf", or rather their condition is "like that of the dead who have lost the faculty of hearing",[740] being "bereft of their senses".[741] It was hard to distinguish between the literal and metaphorical understandings of the relevant verses. If taken metaphorically, Q 30:52 could be glossed with the words: "He (i.e. God) compared the unbelievers with the dead, because since the dead do not hear the call (*nidāʾ*), so the unbelievers do not listen to the call (*duʿāʾ*) when they are called to the (right) belief".[742] In regard to Q 27:80, *Thou shalt not make the dead to hear*, we read instead: "As you are not able to make the dead hear, so you cannot instruct the Meccan unbelievers",[743] and Q 35:22 was paraphrased as "Not equal are the discerning and the ignorant. God instructs whomsoever He wills; you are not able to instruct the dead, i.e. the unbelievers";[744] as in this example, the living and the dead were often likened to believers and unbelievers, respectively.[745]

However, the main problem persisted, namely that the Qurʾānic verses mentioned do in fact depict the dead as being incapable of hearing (or of being made to hear), notwithstanding whether this was understood in its literal sense or metaphorically. We see therefore the Muslim scholars struggling with the impact these Qurʾānic verses unmistakably had when confronted with what was otherwise known from numerous reports and widespread belief. The eighth-century Andalusian scholar Ibn Ǧuzayy tried to tackle this problem in his Qurʾān commentary, being one of the few commentators to attempt this seriously:

> "It was said that this verse (*sc.* Q 35:22) means that the inhabitants of the tombs (*ʾahl al-qubūr*) – referring to those really dead (i.e. not understood metaphorically) – do not hear and thus 'you are not able to make them hear. Rather, you were sent to the living'. ʿĀʾišah took this verse as a proof that the dead are truly not able to hear and refuted by it what is reported as part of the Prophet's speech to those (unbelievers) killed at Badr who were buried in the Pit (*al-qalīb*).[746] However, it is possible to reconcile what she claimed and what the (mentioned) report says, because if the dead in the tombs are

738 The edited text has النائي (which would also make sense, yet it seems somewhat less probable to me in the given context). If we read *an-nāʾī* we have to continue with *wa-lastu* etc.

739 IḪafDīwān p. 90.

740 ZamKaššāf II p. 151 *ad* Q 27:80.

741 IǦuzTashīl II p. 170 *ad* Q 30:52.

742 SamTafsīr III p. 17; *cf.* also ṮaʿālTafsīr II p. 548 *ad* Q 30:52.

743 SamTafsīr II p. 592 *ad* Q 27:80.

744 SamTafsīr III p. 98 *ad* Q 35:22.

745 BayḍTafsīr IV p. 181; IǦuzTashīl II p. 215; SuyǦal p. 456, all *ad* Q 35:22.

746 The report in question, together with the criticism of ʿĀʾišah, is cited below p. 127.

given their souls (*ʾarwāḥuhum*) back to their bodies they will hear, yet as long as the souls are not given back they will not hear".[747]

This explanation seems to develop an argument which al-Qurṭubī had hinted at in his *Taḏkirah*: "It is conceivable that they (i.e. the dead) are able to hear at some moments and under some circumstances".[748] Others preferred to leave the question open, e.g. Ibn Sayyid an-Nās (d. 734 H) who in his biography of the Prophet merely contrasts the differing views and does not offer a solution of his own:

> "Qatādah said (concerning the report about the unbelievers buried at Badr), 'God did restore them to life so that they could hear the speech of the Messenger of God, as a rebuke for them'. This clearly takes the report at its face value. But we are told from ᶜĀʾišah that she gave an interpretation of this report and said, 'The Prophet intended merely to show that they (i.e. the dead) were now aware that "what I say to them is the truth"', then she recited: *Thou shalt not make the dead to hear*".[749]

This passage is – almost verbatim and slightly abbreviated – taken over from al-Buḫārī's *Ṣaḥīḥ*, though the statements of Qatādah and ᶜĀʾišah are there assigned to different reports and have been re-arranged by Ibn Sayyid an-Nās.[750] Telling as it is, this example mainly serves to illustrate two points. First, the Qurʾānic wording – in this case Q 27:80 – was seen by some as a valid proof that the dead are indeed "dumb-in-death", notwithstanding reports or beliefs to the contrary. Second, the problem defied any easy solution and was never resolved to full satisfaction.

Strangely enough but supporting what has been said so far, we find in an Egyptian epitaph (al-Fusṭāṭ, 221 H) that God is implored to deliver to the buried person the greetings of the living: *wa-ʾabliġhu minnā taḥīyatan wa-salāman* (RCEA 249). This obviously implies that the dead are *not* able to hear the greetings of the living.

Two fatwas

We possess a couple of fatwas concerning this matter and are thus able to form a better idea of what was considered permissible in this point. It will also be seen that the basic beliefs put forward by many scholars did not take into account the relevant passages of the Qurʾān cited above, but present a completely different view of the problem. The first fatwa was drafted by ᶜIzz ad-Dīn Ibn ᶜAbd as-Salām (d. 660 H):

747 IĞuzTashīl II p. 215 (*ad* Q 35:22). Some hundred years or so later, Ibn Ḥağar in FB VII p. 386 (*maġāzī* 8) also tried to harmonise between the differing claims. Yet he does not argue, as does Ibn Ğuzayy, on the basis of possibilities (which are in principle not refuted by reason or logic), but he sticks to the very wording of the reports and straightens out the differences by careful shifts of interpretation and subtle distinctions.

748 QurṭTaḏk p. 37 = AšḫŠBahğah I p. 187.

749 ISayNāsᶜUyūn I p. 307. *Cf.* also ŠāmīSubul IV p. 55 and SuyḤāwī II pp. 12 and 174f. (a short fatwa, in the guise of a poem, about the capacity of the dead to hear and the conflict between the Qurʾānic wording and the report about the events at the Pit, *al-qalīb*).

750 *Cf.* FB VII pp. 382f. (*maġāzī* 8).

"*Quaeritur*: Does the deceased (in his grave) experience (the presence) of the one who visits him or not? (...)
Respondeo: It is obvious that the deceased recognises the visitors, because we were ordered to greet them (i.e. the dead) and the law does not command us to address someone who does not hear.[751] (...) Moreover, one scholar declared that the spirits of the dead linger above the mouths (*ʾafniyah*) of the tombs[752] and we are told from the Messenger of God that they are chastised in their tombs. To stand at the head of the deceased person and to pray for his being forgiven (by God) is lawfully correct. But God knows best".[753]

The second fatwa was composed, some 300 years later, by Ibn Ḥağar al-Haytamī:

"*Quaeritur*: Does the dead person know who is visiting his grave and does he rejoice in it?
Respondeo: Ibn Rağab mentioned a report edited by (Abū Ğaᶜfar) al-ᶜUqaylī. It says that the dead are able to hear the greeting (of the visitors), but are unable to reply".[754]

Ibn Ḥağar refers here to a Tradition stating that the dead are unable to reply to the living. This report stands, on the one hand, in marked contrast with what we find in the Qurʾān (according to which the dead are not even able to hear, see above), and on the other it contradicts many Traditions and testimonies according to which the dead recognise their visitors and at the same time return the greetings.[755] The Tradition propagated by al-ᶜUqaylī and relied upon by Ibn Ḥağar was probably identical or similar to the reported utterance of the Prophet which has him addressing the deceased and contains the remarkable passage: "But no! The dead, if they were allowed to reply, would say (...)".[756] This obviously means what it says, namely that the dead in general do not or cannot reply to the living.

The idea of the dead being able to hear but not to speak must have been fairly old. We already find it in the *sīrah* account of Ibn Isḥāq.[757] The Baṣran ascetic Muṭarrif b. ᶜAbd Allāh put forward a theological explanation, which restricts the silence of the dead to the act of returning the greetings, but does not deny their general capacity to speak: "In a dream I saw myself descending to the dead

751 A clever argument indeed, *mā ʾaḥsana l-bayān*! In his *Qawāᶜid*, Ibn ᶜAbd as-Salām specifies that the living are to greet the dead because their souls "linger above the mouths of the tombs" (*cf.* the following note), i.e. they are present to the visitors and thus cannot be ignored, see IᶜASalāmQaw II p. 383.

752 For this expression – *ʾarwāḥu l-mawtā ᶜalā ʾafniyati l-qubūr* –, see IᶜASalāmQaw II p. 383; IRağAhwāl pp. 148-52; IḤağĞawKāfī p. 40. This does not hold true for the souls of martyrs, which dwell permanently in Paradise (HaytFatḤad p. 6).

753 IᶜASalāmFat pp. 100f.

754 HaytFatFiqh II p. 9. This reference to al-ᶜUqaylī is also cited in IRağAhwāl pp. 101 and 108; SuyŠṢudūr pp. 271f. = HarMirqātMaf IV p. 116.

755 *Cf.* IADunyāQubūr (A) pp. 201-9; ĠazDurrah p. 43; MuwMuršid I p. 37; IḪarrāṭᶜĀqibah p. 118; IRağAhwāl pp. 108-11; SuyBušrā p. 58, SuyḤāwī II p. 170; SuyŠṢudūr pp. 271-4; QasṭMaw III p. 413; HaytFatḤad p. 6; HarMirqātMaf III p. 238, IV pp. 114 and 116. See also KulKāfī III p. 228.

756 ZamRabīᶜ IV p. 180; *cf.* also KU 42983 (XV p. 756).

757 IHišSīrah II p. 639, cited below p. 127.

and I saw them sitting (upright in their tombs). I greeted them, but none of them returned the greeting. So I asked them about this and they replied, 'Returning the greeting is a meritorious deed (*ḥasanah*), but we are no longer able to add to our meritorious deeds'".[758] Some scholars also came out with the opinion that the dead recognise and address their visitors only between Thursday day and Saturday morning,[759] which is held to be the most appropriate time for visiting tombs (see p. 33 above). Others claimed that the fact that a person did not leave a will in his lifetime would lead to his being not able to utter sounds once he was dead and buried.[760]

The dead hear and recognise the living

The capacity of the dead to hear (if not to speak) was never seriously questioned in the religious and eschatological discourses proper, notwithstanding the Qurʾānic wording. Here we might refer to a passage, which neatly summarises the argument and much else of what has been said so far, written by the eleventh-century scholar Nūr ad-Dīn al-Ḥalabī:

> "After its separation from the body, the soul (*rūḥ*) will preserve a strong link (*taʿalluq*) with it or with what remains of it (...). The soul does not perish, even though the body dwindles away, being swallowed up by the earth, by wild animals, by birds or by fire. Thanks to this strong link (between body and soul), the dead person is able to know who visits him and enjoys his company. Thanks to this, he will also be able to return the greeting if he is greeted, as we know for certain from Traditions. In the majority of cases, this strong link will not bring the dead person back to life, in the sense of the life in the present world, but it will make him something in between (*mutawassiṭ*) being alive and being dead, with 'dead' meaning here that no such strong link between his soul and his body exists any more. This link may even become so strong that the dead becomes *like* someone alive in the present world, even if he lacks the capacity to perform acts according to his will".[761]

The widespread belief in the capacity of the dead to hear is also shown by a famous (though disputed) Tradition involving the Prophet. The report has it that on the day of the battle of Badr the Prophet addressed the unbelievers killed on the battlefield, whereupon his companions asked him "O Messenger of God, they are dead, so why do you call to them?", and he replied "They hear better than you do!"[762]

This takes up the earliest preserved *sīrah* account, namely a passage from Mūsā b. ʿUqbah's (d. 141 H) *Kitāb al-Maġāzī*, where we read: "Some of the Prophet's companions told him, 'O Messenger of God, are you (really) calling out to dead men?', and he answered 'You cannot hear what I say better than they'".[763] In ano-

758 ŠaʿrṬab I p. 34. The same story is ascribed to Maysarah b. al-Ḥusayn (from al-Maṣṣīṣah), cited via al-Awzāʿī in ḤurRawḍ pp. 33f.

759 IRaǧAhwāl pp. 111f.; SuyḤāwī II p. 170 and SuyŠṢudūr pp. 272f.

760 IRaǧAhwāl pp. 122f.; SuyInbāʾAḏk p. 56 and SuyŠṢudūr p. 356.

761 ḤalInsān II p. 180.

762 As cited in MaǧlBihār VI p. 207.

763 Cited from Mūsā b. ʿUqbah in FB VII p. 410 (*maġāzī* 12); BayDal III p. 117; IQŠuhbahMaġMūsā p. 69. The last-mentioned source is a ms. containing some fragments of Mūsā b. ʿUqbah's *Maġāzī*. Edited for the first time by Eduard Sachau in 1904, there is an English translation of

ther early *sīrah* version, that of Ibn Isḥāq, we find correspondingly: "(...) the Muslims said, 'O Messenger of God, do you call to decayed people?', and he replied 'You cannot hear what I say better than they, but they are not able to answer me'".[764] If compared with the version of Mūsā b. ᶜUqbah, the addition of the last sentence (which limits the faculty of the dead to hearing, excluding speech) is significant and was to prove helpful to later scholars.[765]

However, Ibn Isḥāq's account includes another version of the same story. His version is more elaborate and also mentions the known criticism of ᶜĀʾišah (see p. 123). The final part of this second version starts with the Prophet's words addressed to the dead warriors who were buried in the Pit (*qalīb*): "'O people of the Pit, have you found that what your Lord promised is true?[766] As for me, I have found that what my Lord promised me is true'. His companions asked him, 'O Messenger of God, are you speaking to dead people?' He replied that they knew that what their Lord had promised them was true. ᶜĀʾišah said, 'People claim that he said, They have heard what I said to them, but what the Messenger of God (really) said was: They knew (i.e. what I said to them)'".[767]

In later *sīrah* literature, the story of the Prophet addressing those killed at Badr is frequently quoted from Ibn Isḥāq, also without giving his name.[768] Some others, such as al-Wāqidī, concocted reports of their own of what they found in previous sources and confused the single Traditions;[769] others varied the wording, e.g. Ibn Ḥibbān al-Bustī (d. 354 H), who has the Prophet reply to his puzzled companions, "If you did hear my words, so did they (i.e. the dead), too!";[770] finally, in yet other *sīrah* accounts, the report is conspicuously absent.[771] The critical attitude of ᶜĀʾišah towards the capacity of the dead to hear was given some standing outside the *sīrah* tradition, because the relevant Tradition was incorporated in al-Buḫārī's *Ṣaḥīḥ* and thus could not escape further attention. In al-Buḫārī's *Ṣaḥīḥ* there is also another version of the story[772] which did not become popular in the *sīrah* tradition apart from some later writings:[773] In this version, it is ᶜUmar who expresses his astonishment: "O Messenger of God, how is that? Speaking to bodies without souls?", after which the Prophet replied "By God, you cannot hear what I say better than they can". Another, closely

the above-cited passage in IHišLife p. xliv (no. 5). KalIktifāʾ II p. 33 and DiyTārḪamīs I p. 385 hint at Mūsā b. ᶜUqbah's version but do not quote it.

764 IHišSīrah II p. 639 = IHišLife p. 306; SuyḪaṣ I pp. 328f.

765 We find this addition chiefly preserved in the "western strand" of the *sīrah* tradition, viz. in IᶜABarrDurar p. 71 and ISayNāsᶜUyūn I p. 306 (who quotes, however, from Ibn Ǧarīr aṭ-Ṭabarī), probably because this passage had been also included in Muslim's *Ṣaḥīḥ* (see NawŠMusl VI p. 234), which was popular with western scholars and more relied on than al-Buḫārī's collection. *Cf.* also FB III p. 297 (*ǧanāʾiz* 86) and VII p. 386 (*maġāzī* 8); DiyTārḪamīs I p. 385.

766 *Cf.* Q 7:44; see also below p. 281, n. 813.

767 IHišSīrah II p. 639 = IHišLife p. 305.

768 KalIktifāʾ II p. 32; IDaybaᶜḤad II pp. 506f.; DiyTārḪamīs I p. 385; ḤalInsān II pp. 179f.

769 See WāqMaġ I p. 112.

770 BustīSīrah p. 179. For other wordings, see ŠāmīSubul IV pp. 55f.

771 E.g. in IḤazmǦaw p. 86.

772 FB VII p. 382 (*maġāzī* 8).

773 ᶜĀmBahǧah I pp. 186f.; SuyḪaṣ I pp. 338f.; ŠāmīSubul IV p. 55 and X p. 16; DiyTārḪamīs I pp. 385f.; ḤalInsān II p. 179.

related story has the Prophet approaching the tomb of Umm Miḥǧan and addressing her in her tomb. When she replies, the people present on the scene are astonished and the Prophet tells them, "You cannot hear better than she can" (*mā ʾantum bi-ʾasmaʿa minhā*).[774]

Summing up what we find in *sīrah* and Ḥadīṯ writings with regard to this story, we can conclude that the capacity of the dead to hear was not in general, with the exception of the report transmitted from ʿĀʾišah, called into doubt, while there are a number of voices which deny the dead being able to actively make conversation. In other sources it was often stressed (in support of the belief that the dead hear and recognise the living) that the dead were capable of noticing who washed and buried them; they were also capable of hearing the funeral rites and litanies.[775]

Yet also the ability of the dead to speak was acknowledged by more than a handful of scholars. The deceased had to speak somehow at the moment when after the burial they were questioned by the death-angels in the tomb (*suʾāl al-qabr*). In epitaphs from early Islamic Egypt we find therefore the wish expressed: *allāhumma ... ṯabbit ʿinda l-musāʾalati manṭiqahū* ("O God, ... make his elocution persist during the Interrogation").[776] Thus, the incapability to speak could be restricted merely to the deceased not being able to address the living, but also this was often denied while the capacity of the dead to at least greet the living was affirmed.

This was all well and good for most scholars since it was commonly believed that the Prophet in his tomb would always return the greeting and was able to hear those addressing him, in line with the famous report *mā min ʾaḥadin yusallimu ʿalayya ʾillā radda llāhu ʾilayya*[777] *rūḥī ḥattā ʾarudda ʿalayhi s-salām* ("Nobody greets me unless God restores my soul to me so that I may return the greeting").[778] The capacity of the Prophet to hear the greetings and prayers of his community was also considered among his "peculiarities" (*ḫaṣāʾiṣ*) as a prophet.[779] However, the

774 SuyḪaṣ II p. 112; ŠāmīSubul X p. 16.

775 DaylFird II p. 364; IRağAhwāl pp. 114f.; SuyBušrā pp. 31f., SuyḤāwī II p. 171; SuyŠṢudūr pp. 127-31 and 277f.; HaytFatFiqh II p. 29; HarMirqātMaf I p. 198; MunKawākib I p. 426. *Cf.* also Kinberg: *Interaction* p. 304 and Schimmel: *Träume* pp. 218f.

776 RCEA 96 (198 H), 121 (202 H), 164 (209 H), 221 (218 H), 268 (225 H), 292 (228 H), 307 (230 H) and 991 (306 H, Fusṭāṭ). For further details, see Volume I pp. 120ff.

777 Var. *ʿalayya*.

778 BayḤayātAnb p. 30 and BaySunan V p. 245; ʿIyāḍŠifāʾ (B) II p. 66 / (Š) II p. 79; IḪarrāṭʿĀqibah p. 119; INağDurrah p. 398 = HaytTuḥfZuw p. 39; ITayZiy p. 20; SubkīŠifāʾ pp. 41f.; MarğBahğah II p. 390; INāṣMağlis p. 29; SuyInbāʾAḏk pp. 45, 53, 55 and SuyḪaṣ II p. 490; ḤalInsān II p. 182. *Cf.* also MarğBahğah II p. 403 (the father of al-Marğānī, M. b. ʿAbd al-Malik, is greeted by the Prophet during his visitation in 751 H) and SuyNaẓmʿIqyān p. 163 (the Prophet returns the greeting to Nūr ad-Dīn an-Nuwayrī); ŠaʿrṬab II p. 147 (Ṣadr ad-Dīn al-Bakrī, d. 918 H, himself heard the Prophet returning the greetings); MunKawākib IV p. 147 (Abū l-ʿAbbās al-Maġribī al-Marīnī was greeted by the Prophet and talked to him). There is another famous Tradition of the Prophet saying: "Whosoever utters blessings upon me at my tomb I will hear" (*man ṣallā ʿalayya ʿinda qabrī samiʿtuhū*, cited in QasṭMaw III p. 413 and SuyḪaṣ II p. 489).

779 ŠāmīSubul X pp. 338f.

same was said about the martyrs killed in the battle of Uḥud and buried in the so-called "martyrs' tombs" (*qubūr aš-šuhadā'*).[780] Some later scholars and mystics extended this belief to include all "saintly men" (*'awliyā'*): "If somebody visits the tomb of a *walīy*, he will recognise him, and if somebody greets him he will return the greeting";[781] others maintained that the dead reply to the living generally, at least if they belong to the Muslim community.[782] Even Ibn Ḥağar al-Haytamī, whose fatwa was discussed above, did at some point revise his opinion that the dead would not speak and thus produced another fatwa about the same question (viz. "Do the dead experience the visit of the living, and what is their condition?"). Now he arrived at the conclusion that they not only are able to recognise their visitors, but also to greet them.[783]

As further evidence we might add a couple of reports as found in al-Bayhaqī's seminal writing on the proofs of prophethood.[784] The first is told about an aunt of al-ᶜAṭṭāf b. Ḫālid al-Maḫzūmī. She visited the tombs of the martyrs at Uḥud and afterwards described her experience thus: "Only two lads were staying with me and took care of my riding-animal. Then I greeted them (i.e. the dead), and they returned the greeting, saying 'By God, we know you well as we know each other!' At this point I shuddered and cried out, 'Young boy! Get me my mule!', then I rode away". In another version of the same story,[785] the following detail is added: "I heard how the greeting was returned to me, coming out from under the ground (*yaḫruğu min taḥti l-'arḍ*)". In a second report, this time taken over by al-Bayhaqī from al-Wāqidī,[786] we hear the following from Fāṭimah al-Ḫuzāᶜīyah, who stayed with one of her sisters between the martyrs' tombs (at Uḥud) after night had fallen: "I told her, 'Come with me, let's greet the tomb of Ḥamzah!', and she agreed. Thus when we reached his tomb, I said 'Peace be upon you, O uncle of the Messenger of God!' Then we heard a response addressed to us, 'Peace be upon you, and the mercy of God'. There was nobody else to be seen around us".

Among the mystics, the belief was current that masters would, after their death, continue to teach their adepts by talking to them from their respective tombs, "and some of them proved more beneficial to their adepts in death than during their lives".[787] In other cases, teachers who died before they had completed the lecture of a book, e.g. al-Buḫārī's *Ṣaḥīḥ*, would continue listening to their pupils from the tomb and correct them if necessary.[788]

780 SuyḪaṣ I p. 363.

781 ŠaᶜrṬab II p. 72.

782 KU 42556 (XV p. 646) and 42601f. (XV p. 656).

783 HaytFatFiqh II p. 29 and HaytTuḥfZuw pp. 37-9. *Cf.* also Kinberg: *Interaction* pp. 303f.

784 BayDal III pp. 307-9.

785 Also cited in BN IV p. 45.

786 WāqMaġ I p. 314.

787 ŠaᶜrṬab II p. 73. *Cf.* also Gramlich: *Vorbilder* I p. 576.

788 ŠīrŠadd pp. 23f.

Taking off one's shoes in the cemetery

The last point to take into account of in the present context – viz. are the dead able to hear? – regards the practice of taking off one's shoes when entering the cemetery. Two Traditions from the Prophet have become particularly famous in that regard. The first tells us that the Prophet was walking across a graveyard when he saw somebody going in there with his sandals on. The Prophet shouted at him: "O fellow wearing the *sibtayni* (or *sibtīyatayni*),[789] woe betide you! Take them off!" The man was startled, but when he recognised the Prophet, he took off his sandals and threw them away.[790] In this story, the connection between wearing sandals in the cemetery and the capacity of the dead to hear is not made explicit, and Muslim scholars were not at all unanimous as to why the Prophet ordered the man to take off his sandals, as we will see in a moment. In a second Tradition, however, this connection is quite explicit, for Muḥammad is reported to have said: "When the servant (of God, i.e. a human being) is deposited in his grave and his comrades leave the site, then he will hear the footfall (*qarᶜ*, in some versions: *ḫafq*) of their sandals (on the ground)".[791]

The Hanbalites considered taking off one's shoes in cemeteries as desirable – or, like Ibn al-Ǧawzī, they left the decision open[792] –, and be it only as a sign of humility (*ḫušūᶜ*) and as a noble gesture towards the dead. Exceptions would only be made for tracts of land too dirty or muddy to walk on barefoot or covered with thorny plants.[793] The Persian judge Abū Hammām Isrāʾīl b. Muḥammad used to take off his shoes before entering a cemetery,[794] and the Ẓāhirite scholar Ibn Ḥazm, sticking closely to the wording of the above-mentioned report, "ventured the absurd opinion" (*ʾaġraba*, lit. "he went far astray") that cemeteries might be trodden upon in shoes, though not in those of the *sibtīyah* type (because the above-cited report from the Prophet mentions only these specifically); this opinion was later dismissed by Ibn Ḥaǧar as "tremendous obstinacy" (*ǧumūd šadīd*).[795] Others, however, like the Baṣrans al-Ḥasan and Muḥammad Ibn Sīrīn, walked around between the tombs

789 *sibt* is the tanned skin of a oxen, very smooth and with no hairs left on the surface. The term is also used for sandals made of this expensive material, see MuwMuršid I p. 35; RamlīNih III p. 11; SaffĠiḏāʾ II pp. 263f.

790 ADāʾūd III p. 295 (*ǧanāʾiz* 78); al-Albānī: *Aḥkām al-ǧanāʾiz* pp. 136f., 199; shorter versions in IAŠayMuṣ III p. 269 (*ǧanāʾiz* 199); NasSunan IV p. 79; IMāǧah I p. 500; MuwMuršid I p. 28; IQudMuġnī II p. 564; FB III p. 265 (*ǧanāʾiz* 68).

791 FB III p. 264 (*ǧanāʾiz* 67) and p. 298 (*ǧanāʾiz* 86); ADāʾūd III p. 295 (*ǧanāʾiz* 78); NasSunan IV p. 79; DīnMuǧāl I p. 327; IᶜABarrDurar p. 71; DaylFird I p. 120; IQudMuġnī II p. 564; MuwMuršid I p. 27; IRaǧAhwāl pp. 16 and 102; ᶜAynīᶜUmdah VII p. 55; KU 42379 (XV p. 600); HarMirqātMaf I p. 198. *Cf.* also Seidensticker: *Rūḥ* p. 144.

792 Quoted in FB III p. 265 (*ǧanāʾiz* 68). *Cf.* also al-Albānī: *Aḥkām al-ǧanāʾiz* p. 200 note.

793 IQudMuġnī II p. 564.

794 IǦawzīṢafwah II pp. 277f.

795 FB III p. 265.

without taking their shoes off.[796] This foreshadows the opinion later put forward by Shafiite scholars: "There is no objection against walking around between graves wearing shoes".[797] According to the tenth-century scholar Šams ad-Dīn ar-Ramlī, this opinion did not conflict with the order transmitted from the Prophet to take off *sibtīyah* sandals in the cemetery. He supposed the Prophet to have said so either because he considered them too luxurious for a place like a cemetery or because they had been dirty on that particular day.[798]

4.4.5. The "life" of the dead in their tombs

In marked contrast with certain pre- or non-Islamic beliefs that saw death as the undeniable and irrevocable end of life it was commonly believed that the dead somehow continue to "lead a life" in their tombs.[799]

In the context of eschatology, death was commonly (but often metaphorically) spoken of as "the life of the hereafter" (*ʿayš al-ʾāḫirah*),[800] and we also hear about "the life in the tomb" (*al-ḥayāh allatī fī l-qabr*), for example in a passage by the seventh-century scholar Ibn Abī Ǧamrah (d. *c.*695 H) where he comments a widespread Tradition about the Interrogation in the tomb and the Chastisement of the Grave:

> "In this Tradition we find evidence for the fact that the souls are given back to the bodies in the tombs, because the Chastisement can only affect the living. The dead one, on the other hand, cannot possibly be chastised, because he is neither capable of understanding nor thinking nor feeling pain or well-being.[801] This life, which is in the tomb, and the death (*mawtah*), which comes afterwards (i.e. after the Interrogation),[802] are one of the two lives and the two deaths about which He, the Exalted, informs us in His Book, saying: *Our Lord, Thou hast caused us to die two deaths and Thou hast given us twice to live* (Q 40:11)".[803]

796 IAŠayMuṣ III p. 269 (*ǧanāʾiz* 199); IQudMuġnī II p. 564.

797 NawRawḍah II p. 136; ArdabAnwār I p. 124. This was also the opinion of al-Baġawī, cited in MuwMuršid I pp. 28f. and HarMirqātMaf I p. 198.

798 RamlīNih III p. 11; *cf.* also MuwMuršid I pp. 29 and 35.

799 For this topic in general – i.e. to what extent the deceased are "alive" in their tombs and in what manner and at what time are their souls present in the body? –, see SuyŠṢudūr pp. 273-5 and 299-301; ḤalInsān II p. 182. *Cf.* also IḪarrāṭʿĀqibah pp. 144ff.; YāfRawḍ pp. 183f.; MaġlBihār C p. 131; Smith/Haddad: *Islamic Understanding of Death*, ch. II; Gramlich: *Wunder* pp. 355f.; John MacDonald: *The Preliminaries to the Resurrection and Judgment (Islamic Eschatology IV)*, in: Islamic Studies 4 (1965), pp. 137-63, esp. pp. 155ff.

800 E.g. MunKawākib I p. 415.

801 This seemingly common-sense thought did not meet with the approval of all scholars. Some argued that the body feels the pain also after the soul has departed (*mufāraqat ar-rūḥ*) from it (ŠaʿrDurar p. 58). *Cf.* also SuhrʿAwārif pp. 448f.; ManbTasl (C) pp. 224ff. / (M) pp. 214ff.

802 According to as-Suddī "the dead are given life (a second time) in the tomb for the Interrogation, then they die again" (cited in ṮaʿālTafsīr III p. 91 *ad* Q 40:11).

803 IAĞamrBahǧah I p. 172. In the same manner, al-Ġazālī equated the "second death" (*al-mawtah aṯ-ṯāniyah*) with the Raising on the Day of Judgment, see ĠazDurrah p. 56. *Cf.* also SuyInbāʾAḏk

Accordingly, given that the dead are somehow "alive" in their tombs, we frequently encounter the concept that the deceased converse with each other in their graves. They would also visit each other[804] and therefore are in need of a respectable shroud covering them, as a famous Tradition has it.[805] After the Kūfan ascetic Kurz b. Wabrah (who settled finally in Ǧurǧān and was buried there)[806] had died, "a man in his dream had a vision of the deceased (*ʾahl al-qubūr*) sitting upon their tombs, dressed in new garments. When they were asked, 'Why is that?', they answered that the dead had been given new dresses because Kurz was coming to them (i.e. joining them in the cemetery)".[807] Others even held the opinion, one much criticised by most Muslim scholars, that the dead would eat and drink in their tombs.[808] Some, like Šams ad-Dīn ar-Ramlī, added that the martyrs and dead prophets (on both see below) did not only eat and drink in the hereafter, but that they were also obliged to fast, pray and perform pilgrimages; it only remained disputed whether they would marry or not.[809]

The idea that the dead are living in their tombs was, as seen above, further supported by the concept of the Chastisement of the Grave which necessitates a kind of feeling on the part of the deceased who thus were believed to be somehow alive. As Kaᶜb al-Aḥbār reportedly said: "The pain of death does not leave the dead as long as he stays in his tomb".[810] The common notion of the dead speaking to the living as

p. 54 and Reintjens-Anwari: *Tod aus islamischer Sicht* p. 179; for the concept of the "second death" in ancient Egyptian culture, see Assmann: *Tod als Thema* pp. 26f. The "Second Death" (*mors secunda*) in the Christian tradition was generally interpreted as the damnation on the Last Day, following *Revelation* 20:14; as such it also appears in Dante's *Commedia* (Inf. I, 117: *che la seconda morte ciascun grida*). Curiously, but without eschatological connotations, the Andalusian Ibn al-Ḫaṭīb became known as *Ḏū l-Maytatayni wa-Ḏū l-Qabrayni* ("possessing two deaths and two graves"), because he was first strangled to death and buried; after having been exhumed, his final remains were burned and interred a second time (see al-Marrākušī: *Iᶜlām* III pp. 353 and 361; see also EI² VIII, 399, for the Algerian mystic *Abū Qabrayni* M. b. ᶜAbd ar-Raḥmān al-Ġaštulī, d. 1208 H). In a non-theological context, the "second death" was sometimes understood as the physical death of a person, whereas the "first death" was equated with reaching old age (*aš-šayb*), see e.g. IAṯīrMaṯal p. 198.

804 See QurṭTaḏk p. 70; IRaǧAhwāl pp. 97-9; SuyBušrā pp. 56-8; SuyḤāwī II pp. 173f., SuyInbāʾAḏk p. 56; SuyŠṢudūr pp. 258-62, 277 and 356; MaǧlBihār VI p. 234; Smith/Haddad: *Islamic Understanding of Death* p. 51; Schimmel: *Träume* p. 219.

805 IRaǧAhwāl pp. 97f.; SuyBušrā pp. 53f. *Cf.* also Smith/Haddad: *Islamic Understanding of Death* p. 54.

806 NawMuḫt p. 452.

807 IǦawzīṢafwah II p. 72. With a similar wording also in QušRis p. 372. The same was told about the burial of Bišr b. al-Ḥāriṯ al-Ḥāfī in Baghdad, see TB I p. 122.

808 This view was put forward by M. b. Ya. b. ᶜAlī al-Ḥanafī az-Zubaydī (d. 555 H), see YāqIršād VII p. 134 and SuyBuġ II p. 263. *Cf.* also MaǧlBihār VI p. 234. Others tried to limit this to martyrs alone, see SuyInbāʾAḏk pp. 50f.; see also Smith/Haddad: *Islamic Understanding of Death* p. 55.

809 Quoted from ar-Ramlī in ḤalInsān II p. 181.

810 Cited in MunKawākib I p. 409.

well as the fact that they were often heard praying or reciting the Qurʾān in their tombs (see below p. 151) could likewise support that idea. In addition, the striking parallels between the present world and the World to Come, as they were often depicted by the Muslim scholars (see below p. 159), fostered the concept of the "living dead".

Particularly famous stories in that regard are the following. Abū Saʿīd al-Ḫarrāz (d. 277 H) said: "In Mecca, I once passed the gate of the Banū Šaybah[811] and saw there a young man, dead but with a beautiful face. When I looked at him, he smiled at me and said, 'O Abū Saʿīd, didn't you know that persons beloved (by God) are alive even though they have passed away? In death they are merely transferred from one abode to another'".[812]

Abū Yaʿqūb (Yūsuf b. Ḥamdān) as-Sūsī[813] (third cent. H) said: "In Mecca, a novice (*murīd*) came to me and told me, 'O master, tomorrow at noon I will die, so take that dinar and spend half of it on digging my tomb and buy a shroud for me with the other half!' The next day, at noon, he set out to circumambulate the Kaʿbah, then he stopped and died. I washed him, shrouded him and put him in the burial niche. Suddenly, he opened his eyes and I exclaimed, 'Lo! Is there life after death?!' He answered, 'I am alive, as every God-lover (*muḥibb allāh*) is alive'".[814]

According to Sunnite belief, there are two "categories" of the dead which are commonly believed to possess an exceptional status compared to the other deceased, namely martyrs and prophets. As to the martyrs, the Qurʾān is quite explicit: *Count not those who were slain in God's way as dead, but rather living with their Lord, by Him provided* (Q 3:169), and this concept passed uncontested into Islamic Tradition.[815] Similarly, the prophets are considered alive and praying in their tombs,[816] and in Shiism the Imams were added to their number.[817] Though the prophets, including the Prophet Muḥammad, are alive in their tombs they do not need to eat or drink,[818] being in that similar to the angels.[819] In contrast with the other deceased, their

811 For this gate, see below p. 307 with note 82.

812 QušRis p. 311 = YāfNašr p. 18 and YāfRawḍ pp. 184f.

813 Var. as-Sanūsī (!).

814 Both stories are taken from ŠīrŠadd p. 18 = Gramlich: *Wunder* p. 357; see also YāfRawḍ p. 185. A different version of the second episode is found in QušRis p. 309 (where the authority is given as Abū Yaʿqūb Isḥāq an-Nahrağūrī, d. 330 H). On the same page, there is another story which has the deceased utter the same phrase, though the context varies; this time Abū ʿAlī (A. b. M.) ar-Rūḏbārī (d. 322 H, **43**) is quoted as authority for the story.

815 *Cf.* also WāḥAsbāb p. 134 (*ad* 3:169) and SuyInbāʾAḏk p. 50.

816 ANuAḫbIṣf II p. 328 and ANuḤilyah III p. 352 (the prophet Moses); BayḤayātAnb pp. 23-25 (prophets in general), 25-28 (Moses); DaylFird I p. 74 and 133; SuyḪaṣ II p. 490, SuyḤāwī II pp. 152f., SuyInbāʾAḏk pp. 45-7 and 51f. (Moses), SuyŠṢudūr pp. 252f. and 425-9; QasṭMaw III p. 413; HarMirqātMaf III pp. 241f.; MağlBihār VI p. 207.

817 ŠarīfMurtRas I p. 280.

818 In contrast with the martyrs who will eat and drink (and possibly marry) also in the hereafter, though not out of necessity, but as an honour to and a delight for them, see ḤalInsān II pp. 180f. Others took these material aspects metaphorically but clearly this concept was due to the very wording of the "martyrs' verse Q 3:169 "... by Him provided" which was understood to mean their nourishment (in the widest sense).

819 HarMirqātMaf III p. 238.

corpses are not subject to decay because "the earth does not swallow up (*blw* IV or *ʾkl* I) the bodies of the prophets".[820]

The concept of the prophets living in their tombs is a subject in its own right and cannot be covered here in detail. In any case, the intricacies of this issue gave rise to a whole literary genre. The earliest independent treatise seems to be al-Bayhaqī's *Ḥayāt al-ʾanbiyāʾ fī qubūrihim*, which was later adapted and largely supplemented in as-Suyūṭī's *ʾInbāʾ al-ʾaḏkiyāʾ* (for both, see bibliography) and amply commented upon by Nūr ad-Dīn al-Ḥalabī.[821] Other treatises on the issue, which are less widely known, were composed by Ibn ʿAbd al-Hādī al-Ḥanbalī (d. 744 H) and al-Kawākibī (d. 1096 H). Ibn ʿAbd al-Hādī, a Damascene Hanbalite traditionist and ardent supporter of Ibn Taymīyah (see above p. 78), compiled "a fascicle" (*ğuzʾ*) about "the Traditions concerning the life of the prophets in their tombs" (*ʾaḥādīṯ ḥayāt al-ʾanbiyāʾ fī qubūrihim*),[822] nothing of which is known except its title. In the eleventh century H, *ar-Risālah fī ḥayāt an-nabī fī qabrihī* was composed by the Hanafite scholar al-Kawākibī (M. b. Ḥasan, Aleppo 1018–1096 H),[823] dealing exclusively with the "life" of the Prophet in his sepulchre. It is preserved in manuscript, but has not been edited yet (GAL II p. 315).

4.4.6. Isolation of the dead from each other

As already in other cases, we find different concepts regarding the "life" of the dead in their tombs and their behaviour which are in conflict with each other within the wider culture of Islam and its specific discoursivity. These concepts have never been successfully reconciled but used to exist side by side, without the one threatening to oust the other.

In the present context, the concept to run heavily counter to the beliefs put forward by many traditionists and scholars is the view of the tomb as a place of utter solitude and forlornness (*waḥdah, waḥšah*),[824] with the essential condition of the deceased person being his separation or isolation (*infirād, inqiṭāʿ*) from the other deceased (and the living as well). This concept has been expressed chiefly by poets as well as in the larger realm of exhortation (*waʿẓ*) and pious thought.

As for poetry, the question of whether the dead do visit each other in their tombs or converse among each other has been answered by two famous and often-quoted verses by the third-century poet Ibn al-Muʿtazz (*ṭawīl*):

وَسُكَّانِ دَارٍ لاَ تَوَاصُلَ بَيْنَهُمْ * عَلَى قُرْبِ بَعْضٍ فِي التَّجَاوُرِ مِنْ بَعْضِ
كَأَنَّ خَوَاتِيماً مِنَ الطِّينِ فَوقَهُمْ * فَلَيْسَ لَهَا حَتَّى القِيَامَةِ مِنْ فَضٍّ

820 Quoted from the *Ziyādāt* ("additions of") Yūnus b. Bukayr to the *Kitāb al-Maġāzī* of Ibn Isḥāq in IQayIġāṯah I p. 188 and SuyInbāʾAḏk p. 51. See also IĞawzīWafā p. 825; NuwIlmām IV p. 194; ḪayḏLafẓ pp. 124 and 391f. The bodies of prophets are not devoured by beasts: SuyḪaṣ II p. 489.

821 ḤalInsān II pp. 180-2.

822 IRağḎayl II p. 439; ITūlQal I p. 315.

823 MuḥḪul III pp. 437-9; GAL II p. 35; ZA VI p. 90.

824 See Volume I pp. 137ff. *Cf.* also TurkLumaʿ I p. 325.

1 *wa-sukkāni dārin*: *wa-ǧīrāni ṣidqin* (IᶜABarrBahǧah, IRaǧAhwāl);[825] *tawāṣula*: *tazāwura* (IᶜABarr-Bahǧah, ŠantDaḫ, ḤuṣZahr, ŠarŠMaq, IRaǧAhwāl); *ᶜalā*: *siwā* (IRaǧAhwāl); *fī t-taǧāwuri*: *fī l-maḥallati* (ŠantDaḫ, ḤuṣZahr, IRaǧAhwāl).

"How many inhabitants of a house (i.e. a tomb) have no contact among each other,
* even though the one is the close neighbour of the other!
'Tis as if there were seals of clay over them, * and they will not be broken open until the (Day of) Resurrection".[826]

As to exhortation, take for example what ar-Raqqāšī – either the ascetic Yazīd b. Abān or his nephew al-Faḍl b. ᶜĪsā – had to say about the dead in their tombs (while he went about between the graves): "They have no contact among each other (*lā yatawāṣalūna*) as brothers use to have, and they do not visit one another (*lā yatazāwarūna*) as neighbours do.[827] Decay has pulverised them crushingly, and the stones and the moist earth have swallowed them up".[828]

The Shiite view becomes clear from an utterance attributed to Imam Ǧaᶜfar aṣ-Ṣādiq: "(When you visit the tombs), the deceased will be happy about your company, and if you leave them, they are left in loneliness (*fa-stawḥašū*)".[829] According to similar statements that we find in Sunnite sources,[830] the dead not only hear the speech of the living, but "are heartened by their loved ones visiting them and they benefit when the Qurʾān is recited for them and when prayers are uttered on their behalf".[831] Therefore, a deceased person whose tomb was regularly visited on Fridays by one of his friends appeared to him in a dream and uttered verses of reproach after he once had not shown up as he used to do.[832] This also explains the attitude of al-Manṣūr Ibn Abī ᶜĀmir (d. 392 H, see **170**) who, after the conquest of Santiago de Compostela (in 387 H), found nobody in the town apart an old monk sitting at the tomb of St James. When Ibn Abī ᶜĀmir asked him why he was staying there, the monk said "I keep James company (*ʾūnisu Yaᶜqūba*)", and thus Ibn Abī ᶜĀmir ordered to let him go.[833]

825 This variant is not trivial, because the term *ǧīrānu ṣidqin* was often used when extolling the dead buried in the cemetery, see e.g. IᶜABarrBahǧah II p. 341 and ŠarŠMaq I p. 175; *cf.* above p. 114 with note 684.

826 IMuᶜtDīwān 1294 (III p. 164) = IᶜABarrBahǧah II p. 341 = ŠantDaḫ I p. 334 = ḤuṣZahr (M) III p. 829 / (Ṭ) II p. 171 = ŠarŠMaq I p. 176 = IRaǧAhwāl p. 204. The expression *yafuḍḍu ḫawātīma(n)* recurs also in IMuᶜtDīwān II p. 22.

827 For a parallel utterance by al-Ḥāriṯ b. Nabhān, see above p. 113.

828 As cited in IᶜARabᶜIqd (Ǧ) II p. 153 / (M) III p. 236; ḤuṣZahr (M) III p. 859 / (Ṭ) II p. 197.

829 KulKāfī III p. 228, with a similar utterance from his son Mūsā on the same page; MaǧlBihār VI pp. 256f.; al-Amīn: *Miftāḥ* II p. 272; *cf.* also IQūlKāmil p. 321. For the motif itself, see Kinberg: *Interaction* p. 305.

830 ŠīrŠadd p. 8; HaytFatFiqh II p. 29; MunKawākib I p. 277.

831 ŠīrŠadd p. 6.

832 QušRis p. 373. *Cf.* also **221**.

833 MaqqNafḥ (C) I p. 393. For this event, see CHAL Andalus p. 92 and Makki: *History of al-Andalus* p. 43.

Sometimes, the topos of the "isolation of the dead" was countered by reports like the following from Abū l-Ḥusayn an-Nūrī (d. 295 H, see **20**) who witnessed the death of a young man in the wilderness:

> "I raised him from the earth, kissed him between the eyes and said, 'O Lord, a boy forlorn in a strange country (*šābb ġarīb*), separated from his loved ones and his mates! So have mercy upon his being far away from home (*ġurbah*) and make his forlornness (*waḥšah*) comfortable!'[834] Suddenly, the boy was smiling in my face and uttered 'How? Do you pity me, although I am dear to God the Exalted?' I cried out, 'O my friend, is there life after death?', and he replied 'The friends (*ʾawliyāʾ*) of God the Exalted do not die, but they are rather transferred from one abode to another'".[835]

The most impressive exhortation taking up the concept of isolation stems from a famous sermon in rhymed prose about the transitoriness of the world by ᶜAlī b. Abī Ṭālib. This sermon contains so many of the topoi and concepts which concern the condition of the dead in general that it is necessary to quote the major part of it in full; much of what the sermon says is also found, in the same or similar words, in a great number of epitaphs as well as in ascetic poetry (*zuhdīyāt*). The following text is taken from the *Nahǧ al-balāġah*, with some additions (in square brackets) from the version in Ibn ᶜAsākir's *History of Damascus*:

> *wa-ʿlamū ʿibāda llāhi ʾannakum wa-mā ʾantum fīhi min hāḏihī d-dunyā ʿalā sabīli man qad maḍā qablakum mimman kāna ʾaṭwala minkum ʾaʿmārā / wa-ʾaʿmara diyārā / wa-ʾabʿada ʾāṯārā* || *ʾaṣbaḥat ʾaṣwātuhum hāmidah / wa-riyāḥuhum rākidah / wa-ʾaǧsāduhum bāliyah / wa-diyāruhum ḫāliyah / wa-ʾāṯāruhum ʿāfiyah* || *fa-stabdalū bi-l-quṣūri l-mušayyadah / wa-n-namāriqi l-mumahhadah* || *aṣ-ṣuḫūra wa-l-ʾaḥǧāra l-musnadah / wa-l-qubūra l-lāṭiʾata l-mulḥadah*[836] || *allatī qad buniya bi-l-ḫarābi fināʾuhā / wa-šuyyida*[837] *bi-t-turābi bināʾuhā* || *fa-maḥalluhā muqtarib / wa-sākinuhā muġtarib* || *bayna ʾahli maḥallatin mūḥišīn / wa-ʾahli farāġin mutašāġilīn* || *lā yastaʾnisūna bi-l-ʾawṭān / wa-lā yatawāṣalūna tawāṣula l-ǧīrān* || *ʿalā mā baynahum min qurbi l-ǧiwār / wa-dunūwi d-dār* || *wa-kayfa yakūnu baynahum tazāwurun wa-qad ṭaḥanahum bi-kalkalihī l-bilā / wa-ʾakalathumu l-ǧanādilu wa-ṯ-ṯarā* || [*fa-ʾaṣbaḥū baʿda l-ḥayāti ʾamwātā / wa-baʿda ġaḍārati l-ʿayši rufātā* || *fuǧiʿa bihimu l-ʾaḥbāb / wa-sakanū t-turāb / wa-ẓaʿanū fa-laysa lahum ʾiyāb* ||] *wa-kaʾan qad ṣirtum ʾilā mā ṣārū ʾilayhi* [*mina l-waḥdati wa-l-balāʾi fī dāri l-mawtā*] *wa-rtahanakum ḏālika l-maḍǧaʿ / wa-ḍammakum ḏālika l-mustawdaʿ* || *fa-kayfa bikum law* [*qad*] *tanāhat bikumu l-ʾumūr / wa-buʿṯirati l-qubūr /* [*wa-ḥuṣṣila mā fī ṣ-ṣudūr* || *wa-ʾūqiftum li-t-taḥṣīl / bayna yadayi l-maliki l-ǧalīl* || *fa-ṭārati l-qulūb / li-ʾišfāqihā min sālifi ḏ-ḏunūb* || *wa-hutikat ʿankumu l-ḥuǧubu wa-l-ʾastār / wa-ẓaharat minkumu l-ʿuyūbu wa-l-ʾasrār*][838]

834 This phrase appears also in QušRis p. 309.

835 ŠīrŠadd p. 19. Clearly, the story seems to be a concoction of elements found in similar episodes, e.g. that quoted above p. 133 (from Abū Saᶜīd al-Ḫarrāz) and another in QušRis p. 309.

836 This vocalisation is preferable (see also WKAS II p. 289, s.r. *lḥd*), while NB (Ḥ) has ... *musannadah* / ... *mulaḥḥadah*.

837 Var. *šīda*.

838 NB (B) IV p. 81 / (Ḥ) III pp. 83f. The version in TMD XLII pp. 500f. is longer than that in

"You must know, servants of God, that you, and your condition in the present world, are equal to those who were before you, those whose lives were longer than yours, / whose houses were more peopled (than yours) / and whose vestiges will outlast (yours). || But their voices have become extinct, / their breathing has stopped, / their bodies are decaying, / their houses are empty / and their traces are effaced! || They exchanged lofty castles / and smooth cushions || for rocks and stones tightly set / and for flattened tombs provided with a burial niche, || (tombs) whose courtyard was built with debris / and whose edifice was plastered with earth ||, their location is near / but those who dwell in them are far, || being in a peopled place they are utterly forlorn, / craving for something to do among people whose lot is idleness, || they find no company in homelands / and have no contact among each other as neighbours use to have || although they stay in neighbouring closeness / and their houses (i.e. the tombs) are near to each other! || But, how could they pay visits among each other while the mill of decay has ground them (to pieces) / and the stones and the moist earth have devoured them? || [Thus they became dead after being alive / and mere remains after the freshness of life, || the loved ones were struck with grief by them, / they settled in the earth / and they departed, and there will be no return for them! ||] It is as if you have already come to what they came to [(namely) a state of loneliness and affliction in the house of the dead], as if that bed[839] has (already) taken you in pledge / and (as if) that receptacle has enclosed you! || How will you fare when your matters come to an end / and the tombs are dispersed (i.e. on the Day of Resurrection), / [when that which the hearts harbour is taken account of || and you are stationed for the Reckoning / before the Sublime Ruler (i.e. God)? Then hearts will beat heavily / from anxiety over the sins committed previously, || the veils and coverings will be torn away from you / and (all) your vices and secrets will come to light!]"

In epitaphs, the solitary condition of the deceased is often expressed with the terms *waḥdah* ("solitude"), *waḥšah* ("forlornness"), *infirād* ("loneliness, seclusion", also "isolation") and *ġurbah* ("estrangement, solitariness", or also "being far away from home").[840] These terms also entered the religious discourse, especially the field of hortatory preaching (*waʿẓ*).[841]

There is little discussion in the sources whether the "isolation" or "loneliness" of the deceased in his tomb might be reduced or avoided if buried together with another person, or more persons, in one grave. In any case, though not being the rule, this happened in a number of instances, and in general either father and son,[842]

the NB and some of its additions are cited above. However, in Ibn ʿAsākir's version there are important words missing whose absence is likely to distort the meaning; what is more, some other additions in TMD – not cited above – interrupt individual cola of the rhymed prose and thus seem to be later insertions, while in other cases more or less synonymous terms have been substituted for those found in the *Nahǧ al-balāġah*.

839 I.e. the tomb, see below **2** (with note to the first line).

840 See below **1** (note to verse 1).

841 E.g. the passage quoted in ŠarŠMaq I p. 175.

842 *Cf.* FāsīʿIqd II p. 82 and V p. 42; IQŠuhbTārīḫ I p. 252. Indicated in epitaphs: az-Zaylaʿī: *Amirate of Mecca* 70 lines 9f. (p. 430).

brothers,[843] teacher and pupil,[844] or warriors killed at the same spot[845] could be interred together in one tomb; there could also be a considerable distance in time between the first occupant of a grave and his later companion.[846]

The usage of burying more than one person in a tomb was dealt with in legal literature, with the result that this must be avoided except for serious reasons, e.g. if there was not sufficient space for digging more than one tomb.[847] However, burial in one tomb was considered forbidden categorically if the persons buried were not of the same sex.[848] Married persons and lovers,[849] or mother and son, should thus not be interred together, but this (debated) restriction was not always observed in practice: from the Cairene Qarāfah cemetery we know an epitaph for a mother and her son (**42**), and in another case it is said that a man and his wife were buried in one tomb (*wa-qīla ᵓanna zawǧatahū maᶜahū fī qabrihī*).[850] When the Tīmūrid ruler Ḫalīl Sulṭān b. Mīrān Šāh of Samarqand was poisoned in 814 H, his wife committed suicide with a dagger and was afterwards buried with her husband "in one grave" (*fī qabr wāḥid*). However, being buried together in one tomb was often not seen as the best solution, as in the case of ᶜAbd Allāh b. ᶜAmr who was killed at Uḥud and buried with another one or two warriors,[851] yet his son Ǧābir b. ᶜAbd Allāh said that "my soul did not find peace (*lam taṭib*) until I had him (i.e. his father) exhumed and buried in a grave of his own (*ᶜalā ḥidatin*)", six months after his first burial.[852]

In any case, it is difficult to discover in the sources cases of more than one person being buried in one tomb. If so, it must be stated clearly in the sources that

843 An epitaph common to two brothers is quoted in IZayKawākib p. 141; there is also a famous story of three brothers who were living far away from each other but were eventually buried in one tomb (*fī qabrin wāḥidin*): IQŠuhbTārīḫ I p. 408; the two brothers of Muḥammad b. Ibr. known as "Ibn aš-Šahīd", Maǧd ad-Dīn and Naǧm ad-Dīn, both died in 793 H and were buried in one tomb, "after having been separated for long" (*wa-dufinū* [sic]*fī qabrin wāḥidin baᶜda š-šatāti ṭ-ṭawīli*: SaḫWaǧīz I p. 300).

844 E.g. NawMuḫt p. 148; IḤiǧṮam pp. 208f.; FāsīᶜIqd V p. 58.

845 This is the famous case of Ḥamzah b. ᶜAbd al-Muṭṭalib (see **168**), who was buried either with Musᶜab b. ᶜUmayr or ᶜAbd Allāh b. Ǧaḥš "in one tomb", see FB III p. 271 (*ǧanāᵓiz* 73); FāsīᶜIqd III p. 442; SamWafāᵓ III p. 936; *cf.* also KU 42917 (XV p. 733). After the reconquest of Alexandria in 767 H, a mass grave was dug for the fallen warriors (NuwIlmām II pp. 151 and 221f.). For an early Islamic "Sammelgrab" from Yazd, see Leisten: *Architektur für Tote* p. 279; for mass graves excavated in al-Fusṭāṭ, see Gayraud: *Qarāfa al-Kubrā* pp. 459ff.

846 *Cf.* the story reported in IZayKawākib pp. 121f.

847 IQāsimFatḥ p. 220.

848 *Cf.* Lane: *Manners and Customs* p. 515: "If males and females be buried in the same vault – which is not commonly the case – a partition is built to separate the corpses of one sex from those of the other".

849 *Cf.* SarrāǧMaṣ I p. 111 and IĞawzīNisāᵓ p. 110.

850 IZayKawākib p. 126.

851 IᶜABarrIst II p. 339; ISayNāsᶜUyūn II p. 32; IḤaǧIṣābah II p. 350; ᶜĀmBahǧah I p. 207.

852 SamWafāᵓ III p. 937. *Cf.* also below p. 207.

two (or more) persons were buried in one single grave, e.g. *fī qabr wāḥid.*[853] Expressions like *dufina fī qabri fulān* do normally *not* indicate that someone was buried in the tomb of another person, but rather indicate that he was buried at his side, in the plot of his tomb, or in his mausoleum. Cases in which somebody stipulated to be buried at the side of another person are legion. One moving story in that regard is known from the poet Ibn Huḏayl at-Tuǧībī (Ya. b. A., d. 753 H): he was very grieved at the death of his wife and wished to be buried by her side. He expressed that wish to Ibn al-Ḫaṭīb, who was later able to put it into effect, in a poem beginning with the following verses (*ṭawīl*):

إذَا مِتُّ فَادْفِنِّي حِذَاءَ حَلِيلَتِي * يُخَالِطُ عَظْمِي فِي التُّرَابِ عِظَامَهَا
وَلاَ تَدْفِنَنِّي فِي البَقِيعِ فَإِنَّنِي * أُرِيدُ إِلَى يَوْمِ الحِسَابِ الْتِزَامَـــهَا

"When I have died bury me at the side of my wife * so that my bones mingle with her bones in the earth,
And do not bury me in the open field[854] because I * desire to stay close to her until the Day of Accounting!"[855]

Another concept which stands in relation to the motif of the deceased being isolated in their tombs (or not) is also found in numerous stories about pious or saintly persons whose burial in certain cemeteries "set free" those already buried there, or "makes them rejoice". This was well expressed by a Yemenite sheikh who said (after his death, appearing in a dream) that he had been "imprisoned" since his burial, but when a certain famous jurist died and was interred in his vicinity, "he invoked mercy on us and thus we were set free. All those buried in the cemetery were forgiven for the blessing of the arrival of that man (in the graveyard)"[856] (see also **190**). In this vein, the deceased interred in a common burial ground were seen as some sort of company or group whose fate was interrelated. The same holds true for the conviction, often attested in the sources, that the vicinity of a deceased person of ill reputation, or impiety, would have a negative influence on those buried around him (*cf.* below p. 210).

4.4.7. Signs of afterlife

The dead – if they were not prophets or martyrs – were not "alive" in the literal sense of the word, though nevertheless they could regain lifelike manners and appearances on special occasions or for a limited period of time.

Events of that kind were normally reported under the heading *man ʿāša baʿda*

853 *Cf.* also KU 42372 (XV P. 599).

854 A reference to the Medinan Baqīʿ cemetery seems unlikely in the present context.

855 Cited in MaqqNafḥ (C) VIII p. 12.

856 ḪazrʿUqūd I p. 156.

l-mawt, "people alive after death".[857] The stories which circulated about such occurrences would include either the appearance of a deceased person after his death, his ability to speak to the living or to smile at them, to make gestures towards them or to touch a living person; in rare cases it was not even possible to decide whether someone had really died or not because there seemed no visible difference.[858] In contrast with the "life in the tomb", those and similar things did, as a rule, not happen in the grave but outside it, or before or during the burial. Many a story reporting such an event is reminiscent of ghost stories and gothic novels known from the European tradition, and we find many comments in the Arabic sources such as: "After this had happened, my hair stood on end!"

Gesturing by the deceased and physical contact

A great number of stories, mainly from the seventh to tenth centuries H, are known about persons gesturing or moving after their death. The belief in such occurrences is clearly related to the motif of death silencing the living, which means that the deceased was only left with physical ways of expressing himself in some way or another while he was prevented from raising his voice. To give an example: a pious scholar had met his death outside Cairo, and his friends carried his body to town. At their arrival at the city gate, they were barred from entering together with the dead man, and it was only when the finger of the dead man's hand was seen rising that the people let them pass.[859] In other cases, deceased persons moved their bodies, opened their eyes or gestured with the fingers, chiefly during the funeral[860] or when grave-robbers tried to open their tombs.[861]

There are at least two known instances of a dead person somehow indicating that a ring had been forgotten. First, this happened in the case of Abū l-Farağ Ibn al-Maġribī (M. b. Ğaᶜfar, d. Cairo 478 H) who "had stipulated in his last wish that a ring in his possession be put on his finger, but his family had forgotten. When he was undressed for the washing his finger remained raised to the amazement of the washer (...)".[862] Second, we know of the mystic ᶜImrān b. Dāᵓūd al-Ġāfiqī (d. in Cairo) that he had asked his family to put his ring on his finger after his death, but

857 For this argument, see al-ᶜAffānī: *Sakb* I pp. 709-13 and Ibn Abī d-Dunyā: *Man ᶜāša baᶜda l-mawt*, ed. ᶜAbd Allāh M. Darwīš, Beirut: ᶜĀlam al-Kutub 1406/1986.

858 QušRis pp. 403f. and Gramlich: *Wunder* p. 361. See also the various cases reported in Rāġib: *Faux morts*.

859 SuyŠṢudūr p. 276. Other deceased who moved their fingers during the burial include the mystics Ḏū n-Nūn al-Miṣrī and Sahl at-Tustarī (d. 283 H), see Gramlich: *Wunder* p. 357.

860 IĞawzīMunt X p. 90; MaqrMuq V p. 227. In the ninth century H, al-ᶜĀrif bi-llāh ᶜAlī after his death covered his pudendum when the washer of the dead had torn away the cloth (*ḫirqah*) that was covering it (IḤanbDurr I p. 281).

861 See esp. the story in ŠirŠadd p. 24 according to which a grave-robber fell dead on the spot when he was shouted at by a dead person after having opened his tomb. For another story (with a happy end), see Gramlich: *Wunder* p. 358.

862 MaqrMuq V p. 503 (the latter part of the story is not well-preserved in the ms.).

"when he died they forgot about that. After washing the corpse the washer set about wrapping him in the shroud, but his finger suddenly raised and the washer told his family, 'How is that? I see the sheikh raising his finger!'" However, the matter was quickly resolved as his family members remembered about the ring. In this case, the ring even bore the following inscription which was clearly considered important for the deceased and his fate in the hereafter: "A sinful servant, a merciful Lord" (*ʿabdun mudnibun wa-rabbun ġafūrun*).[863]

Many more stories about deceased persons moving or gesturing were also collected by the eighth-century scholar Muʿīn ad-Dīn aš-Šīrāzī in the introduction to his cemetery-guide *Šadd al-ʾizār*.[864] The most moving of those stories I found to be the following, which aš-Šīrāzī quotes from al-Yāfiʿī, from Maḥmūd al-Warrāq:

> "There was a black man called Mubārak, who (...) had never married. Every time we told him 'O Mubārak, why don't you marry?', he replied 'I ask God that he will marry me to the black-eyed virgins (in Paradise)'. Later, we fought together in some raids (*maġāzī*) and when the enemy pressed upon us, Mubārak was killed in combat. We found him, his head in one place and his body in another. He lay prostrated on his stomach, with his hands under his chest. We stood around him and said, 'O Mubārak, how many black-eyed virgins have been awarded to you in marriage?' His hand moved forth from under his breast and three fingers were stretched out".[865]

Apart from moving or gesturing, the deceased could also feel the need for physical contact with the living[866] and try to touch them, e.g. by gripping their hand or one of their fingers (often the thumb) or even the beard. In more extreme cases, the deceased would rise and slap or severely beat the people around him, especially during the washing.[867] The grip of the hand could be witnessed also in the case of the deceased being buried long before, e.g. when a hand was stretched out from within the tomb (or cenotaph). Famous examples of such occurrences are known from the mausoleum of aš-Šāfiʿī, who would speak from his tomb and stretch out his hand. Take for example the story of Zayn al-ʿĀbidīn, son of the better known ʿAbd ar-Raʾūf al-Munāwī (d. 1031 H):

> "He had visions of outstanding character and it was reckoned among his miracles (lit. breaches of the natural order of things, *ḫawāriq*) that Imam aš-Šāfiʿī addressed him from within his tomb. In one instance, he even stretched out his hand from the tomb

863 IZayKawākib p. 251. Interestingly, these words on the ring take up an inscription which the Prophet reported to have seen in Paradise, viz. *ʾummatun mudnibatun wa-rabbun ġafūrun*, "a sinful community, a merciful Lord", see ʿUfīTarāǧim p. 141.

864 ŠīrŠadd pp. 14-20. *Cf.* also Gramlich: *Wunder* p. 353.

865 ŠīrŠadd p. 17. *Cf.* also Maher Jarrar: *The Martyrdom of Passionate Lovers. Holy War as a Sacred Wedding*, in: A. Neuwirth *et al.* (eds.): *Myths, Historical Archetypes and Symbolic Figures in Arabic Literature. Towards a New Hermeneutical Approach*, Beirut 1999 (Beiruter Texte und Studien 64), pp. 87-107.

866 *Cf.* IADunyāQubūr (A) p. 60 = SuyŠṢudūr p. 280.

867 *Cf.* ŠīrŠadd p. 15.

and handed something over to him.[868] The latter (i.e. Zayn al-ᶜĀbidīn) said: 'When I visited (aš-Šāfiᶜī's tomb) one day, I saw at his mausoleum (*ᶜinda qubbatihī*) two streams (pouring forth), on one of them there was a white dove and on the other a red dove'(?). In addition, (az-Zayn) saw his ancestor aš-Šaraf Yaḥyā al-Munāwī sitting (upright) in his tomb, clothed in black. Yaḥyā not only spoke to him, but enjoyed his company and invoked blessings on his behalf".[869]

Physical contact with famous dead also happened elsewhere, although the belief that the dead touch the living was especially widespread in Egypt. The Lower Egyptian "saint" Aḥmad al-Badawī spoke from his tomb to the well-known mystic ᶜAbd al-Wahhāb aš-Šaᶜrānī and, as he himself relates, "his noble hand came forth and gripped mine".[870] In Qinā (Upper Egypt), the hand of Ibn Ḥağğūn (d. 592 H or before) was stretched out from under the cenotaph and grasped the palm of a stunned visitor.[871]

In Yemen, likewise a region not devoid of unwavering beliefs regarding the afterlife of the dead, the mystics Muḥammad b. Abī Bakr al-Ḥikamī and Abū l-Ġayṯ b. Ğamīl al-Yamanī (d. 651 H) were approached by fellow Sufis after their death who desired their companionship (*ṣuḥbah*); so the latter stretched out his hand from his tomb in order to accept their discipleship by hand-shaking.[872] Mainly in Shiite sources we also learn that the hand (or both hands) of the Prophet himself was seen to show from his tomb.[873] To the famous mystic ar-Rifāᶜī (Aḥmad b. ᶜAlī, 500–78 H) it happened that he recited two lines of poetry in front of the Prophet's sepulchre. As a result of this, "his noble hand came out from the tomb and he (*sc.* ar-Rifāᶜī) kissed it".[874] Finally, bodily movements of the dead did not exclude their being able to utter sounds at the same time: the mystic as-Sayyid al-ᶜĀrif Aḥmad al-Buḫārī al-Ḥusaynī (d. Istanbul 922 H) reportedly turned himself towards the direction of prayer when he was put in the grave and uttered blessings upon the Prophet.[875]

868 Until here, this passage is also cited in Gramlich: *Wunder* p. 363.

869 MuḥḪul II pp. 194f. Šaraf ad-Dīn himself had been addressed from within the tomb of aš-Šāfiᶜī (see MunKawākib I p. 15).

870 ŠaᶜrṬab I p. 186; MunKawākib II p. 389. The veneration of Aḥmad al-Badawī has never ceased to be very popular in Egypt (for his veneration, see Mayeur-Jaouen: *Intercession*). This provoked the following outburst of the ninth-century scholar and mystic Abū l-Ġayṯ b. Katīlah from Maḥallah when he saw the people in Būlāq frenetically celebrating al-Badawī's birthday: "What a scene! If only the people cared as much for the visitation of their Prophet as they care for Aḥmad al-Badawī!" (ŠaᶜrṬab p. 187).

871 UdfṬāliᶜ p. 300 = Gramlich: *Wunder* pp. 362f.

872 YāfRawḍ p. 182; ŠirŠadd p. 22.

873 MağlBihār VIII p. 44; Gramlich: *Wunder* pp. 361f.

874 MunKawākib II p. 220; NābDīwān p. 104.

875 ŠḎ VIII p. 107.

Deceased speaking after their death

Some cases of people speaking after death have already been cited above page 133. As seen likewise above, the concept of the dead speaking met with some scholarly opposition, but was at all times more or less widely accepted. However, there are stories which either have a more religious significance than the above-mentioned cases or whose impact is much reminiscent of "gothic tales".

Some of these stories go right back to the formative period of Islam, e.g. the following: the brother of Ribᶜī b. Ḫirāš al-ᶜAbsī, a certain Rabīᶜ (d. 104 H), had died, and "while we stood around him and had sent someone to buy a shroud, he uncovered his face and said 'Peace be upon you!'" He then reported his death and his encounter with the Lord. This exceptional event was corroborated by ᶜĀʾišah who had heard the Prophet say "A man from my community will speak after death".[876] In the same manner, though, people killed in the 'Wars of Apostasy' and during the conflict with the "false prophet" Musaylimah would speak.[877] Several other persons, like Zayd b. Ḫāriğah, would speak after their death and utter testimonies to the veracity of Muḥammad's prophethood.[878] In another instance, Ibrāhīm b. Adham (d. 161 H or the year after)[879] stood in front of a tomb which suddenly cracked open (*šqq* VII): its inhabitant had been brought back to life by God in order to address Ibn Adham, and afterwards the tomb closed again.[880] From the tomb of the ascetic Ṯābit al-Bunānī a poem was heard recited although his body had miraculously vanished from the burial niche immediately after the burial (as we understand, he had been transferred to God).[881]

In later centuries, a deceased person would often raise his voice when the Qurʾān was recited at his tomb. Thus the mystic Ibn ᶜAṭāʾ Allāh as-Sikandarī (d. 709 H), who is buried in the Cairene southern Qarāfah cemetery, called from his tomb to someone who had come to visit him and was reciting the surah *Hūd*.[882] As another instance we hear that once, during the recitation of the surah *al-Kahf* in the Cairene mausoleum of as-Sayyidah Zaynab, the reciter got the wording wrong and a voice was crying out from the tomb correcting him;[883] several pious men were also addressed by as-Sayyidah Nafīsah from within her grave.[884] When someone recited the surah *al-Baqarah* at the tomb of Abū ᶜUmar Ibn Qudāmah (d. 607 H) in Damascus, "'the sheikh replied to me from his tomb. Fear befell me and I started to quiver and tremble and ran away'. This reciter died some days after that event, and

876 ANuḤilyah IV pp. 367f.; ŠāmīSubul X p. 114: Two slightly different versions of the same story, one of which is also quoted in IĞawzīṢafwah II p. 21 and ŠīrŠadd pp. 17f.; *cf.* also Gramlich: *Wunder* p. 360 (with further sources).

877 BayDal VI p. 58; IRağAhwāl pp. 25f.

878 BayDal VI pp. 55-7; IḤağIṣābah I p. 565.

879 For his tomb (whose location is disputed), see Gramlich: *Vorbilder* I pp. 279-82.

880 MunKawākib I p. 199; Gramlich: *Vorbilder* I p. 232. For other stories of dead persons (or, in some cases, dead animals) being restored to life, see YāfNašr pp. 14-7; Gramlich: *Wunder* pp. 349-52. For the "resurrection" of the Prophet's mother, see already above pp. 17ff.

881 ḤurRawḍ p. 90.

882 MunKawākib III p. 10.

883 SaḫTuḥfAḥbāb p. 199. A similar story is reported from Nağm ad-Dīn al-Iṣfahānī (d. Mecca 721 H) who heard a dead person speaking from his tomb, see FāsīᶜIqd IV p. 426; V p. 100.

884 MunKawākib I p. 724.

all that is a famous story. On another occasion, someone recited the surah *al-Kahf* at al-Muwaffaq Ibn Qudāmah's tomb and then heard a voice from within the grave: 'There is no God but God!'"[885] At his tomb in Baghdad, Ibn Ḥanbal was heard continuing the recitation of the Qurʾān when one of the visitors who were reciting forgot the wording.[886]

Other stories have decapitated heads speaking, e.g. it was said that the head of al-Ḥusayn in Damascus was heard uttering sounds whenever the Qurʾān was recited.[887] Often, it was the heads of pious people decapitated by unjust rulers (or the Christian enemy) which are reported to have recited Qurʾānic verses or confessions of faith.[888] On rare occasions, a deceased person could appear ghost-like to the living and address them outside burial areas, although there is no clear border to be drawn between such events and visions proper: the tenth-century mystic aš-Šaʿrānī invoked the help of Sīdī Abū l-ʿAbbās al-Ḥarīṯī (d. Dimyāṭ 945 H), "and I saw him leave his tomb, walking from Dimyāṭ (...) until he approached me for about five cubits and said 'You need to be patient'; then he disappeared".[889] In his biography of the mystic Yūsuf al-ʿAǧamī al-Kūrānī (d. Cairo 768 H), al-Munāwī has the following story:

> "A man came to visit his (*sc.* al-Kūrānī's) tomb and left his donkey at the door of the *zāwiyah* (ascetic lodge), then entered and performed his visitation. Upon leaving, he could not find his donkey; so he re-entered saying to the deceased 'I came to pay you a visit and you made me lose my donkey!?' Now the tomb cracked open and the deceased left the building and went into the surrounding countryside. He then returned with the donkey and said, 'Next time you come to my place tie your donkey up so that you don't bother me again! If not, then better stay away!'"[890]

Notwithstanding these and similar stories, the appearance of the deceased in visible form – as ghosts or haunting spirits – has never acquired in Islam an importance comparable to that, for example, in Christian Europe or in the classical Chinese culture.

Finally, a very special case is reported from Alexandria. Here, the deceased was not heard speaking from his tomb but his message would appear in written form upon the grave. The story is told by the historian of Mecca, al-Fāsī:

> "Abū l-ʿAbbās, the son of the Imam, the eminent mystic Abū l-Ḥasan aš-Šāḏilī – may God have mercy upon him! – often related the following: 'I used to visit the tomb of Sīdī Abū Muḥammad ʿAbd ar-Razzāq (d. 595 H), the companion of Abū Madyan (d.

885 IRaǧḎayl II p. 60.

886 ŠīrŠadd p. 23.

887 MunKawākib I p. 148 = Gramlich: *Wunder* p. 359.

888 SuyŠṢudūr pp. 283f. and 296f. *Cf.* also Gramlich: *Wunder* p. 365 (the story of the decapitated ʿAyn al-Quḍāh al-Hamdānī who walked to the cemetery with his head under his arm).

889 ŠaʿrṬab II p. 171. The intimacy of aš-Šaʿrānī with the dead is also discussed in Arberry: *Sufism* pp. 126-8, with more illustrative examples. For other cases of dead leaving their tombs (and sometimes even chasing away robbers), see Gramlich: *Wunder* p. 364.

890 MunKawākib III p. 111.

594 H).[891] Every time I was in need of something, I would come to his tomb. Once I was in urgent need of something and thus I went to his tomb, recited a part of the Qur'ān and explained the matter to him. Then I turned towards the grave, which was covered by sand (*ramal*), and I saw written there: *Aḥmad's matter has been resolved*".[892]

4.5. Institutions of learning and burial sites

Apart from the phenomena and features discussed so far, there were still other and somewhat more mundane reasons to visit, as it were *en passant*, cemeteries, tombs or mausolea. The most important of those reasons was connected with the fact that in the central Islamic lands from around the late fourth century H onwards – and not much later also in the Islamic West[893] – *zāwiyahs* (ascetic lodges), colleges (madrasahs) and Sufi hospices (*ribāṭ*, pl. *rubuṭ*) were founded either as part of larger funerary structures or beside them, in any case being situated on larger burial areas or in the vicinity of tombs. In order to proceed to their places of study and class-rooms, or to their living quarters, many students, scholars and Sufis thus had to traverse or enter burial areas, and some of them even settled there (see below p. 163).

4.5.1. Institutions of learning in cemetery areas: the case of Cairo

The foundation of institutions of learning and Sufi hospices is attested in almost all major cities in the central Arabo-Islamic world, but the best documented example for that is once again Cairo with its numerous buildings in both the southern and northern Qarāfah cemeteries.[894] With more and more "public" buildings being erected in that area, the number of people frequenting the cemetery area inevitably rose in the course of time, and therefore al-Maqrīzī could write about the small congregational mosque beside the mausoleum of aš-Šāfiʿī: "This congregational mosque (*ǧāmiʿ*) was a small mosque (*masǧid*), but when the people staying in the Lesser Qarāfah had increased in number (*fa-lammā kaṯura n-nāsu bi-l-qarāfati ṣ-ṣuġrā*) after (the Ayyubid ruler) Ṣalāḥ ad-Dīn (...) had founded his madrasah near the tomb of aš-Šāfiʿī (...), al-Malik al-Kāmil Muḥammad b. ʿĀdil (...) enlarged the afore-mentioned mosque".[895]

The earliest known example of an institution of learning founded in a Cairene cemetery is the Ṣalāḥīyah madrasah (also known as an-Nāṣirīyah) beside the mauso-

891 For him, see Cornell: *Abū Madyan*.

892 FāsīʿIqd II p. 327 (*'Aḥmadu quḍiyat ḥāǧatuhū*).

893 *Cf.* Torres Balbás: *Cementerios* p. 134. The Andalusian scholar Abū ʿAl. M. b. ʿUmar al-Kātib (d. 596 H) was buried inside a *ribāṭ* in Fez, see IAbbTakm II p. 77. The first madrasahs, however, appeared in the Islamic West not before the eighth century H.

894 *Cf.* Gayraud: *Qarāfa al-Kubrā*, passim; Nedoroscik: *City of the Dead* pp. 18ff.; Sayyid: *al-Qāhira et al-Fusṭāṭ* pp. 643ff.; Taylor: *Vicinity of the Righteous*, ch. 1.

895 MaqrḪiṭaṭ II p. 296, quoted (rather freely) in MacKenzie: *Ayyubid Cairo* p. 134; *cf.* also Lapidus: *Ayyūbid Religious Policy* p. 286, n. 10, and Gayraud: *Qarāfa al-Kubrā* pp. 452ff.

leum of aš-Šāfiʿī in the southern (or "Lesser") Qarāfah, constructed under Saladin (Ṣalāḥ ad-Dīn Yūsuf b. Ayyūb, al-Malik an-Nāṣir). This building was for centuries to come one of the centres of Egyptian scholarship and during its history housed a large range of top professors; unfortunately, important as it was, the madrasah has not survived to the present day.[896] However, this madrasah was to be the only Ayyubid foundation in the Qarāfah area,[897] and the practice of building institutions of learning in that quarter only started to gain pace during the Mamluk period, especially during the ninth century H.

By that time, close bonds between institutions of learning and burial sites had developed. This fact is accurately described by Jonathan Berkey: "Indeed, so great was the connection in the public mind between institutions of learning and places of burial that the terms madrasa and *turba* (tomb) could be conflated. Several institutions in late medieval Cairo were known as 'turbas,' but functioned as schools".[898] As Berkey further notes, Kāfūr aš-Šiblī aṣ-Ṣarġitmišī (d. 830 H) built a mausoleum (*turbah*) outside Cairo, and this was commented upon by Ibn Taġrī Birdī with the words that "he" – i.e. aṣ-Ṣarġitmišī – "had (also) another madrasah", thus the terms *turbah* and *madrasah* were used more or less synonymously.[899]

Apart from institutions of learning, there were other buildings (combined with mausolea or not) constructed in the Cairene cemeteries. Among the earliest of these were the various "monasteries" (sg. *ribāṭ*) founded during the Fatimid period,[900] later the *zāwiyah*-mausoleum of Ibrāhīm al-Ǧaʿbarī (d. 687 H) in the Bāb an-Naṣr cemetery (north to the Fatimid city),[901] the Sufi hospice (*ḫānqāh*) of Qūṣūn founded in the southern Qarāfah in 735 H,[902] and another founded by Arġūn al-ʿAlāʾī (who was married to the mother of al-Malik aṣ-Ṣāliḥ Ismāʿīl and killed in Cairo in 748 H).[903]

4.5.2. The combination of mausoleum and madrasah

Conversely, tombs could be established in madrasahs or madrasah-like institutions which were not situated in cemeteries, but within the boundaries of towns themselves. The result of this practice was the development of that specific type of architectural complex that has been called "tomb-college".[904] Being mostly endowments, each of these complexes contained the tomb of the founder and a madrasah proper.

The earliest example of burial in an institution of learning, as far as I am aware

896 For the madrasah, see MaqrḪiṭaṭ II pp. 400f.; SuyḤusnMuḥ II pp. 224-6; MacKenzie: *Ayyubid Cairo* pp. 111 and 134; Behrens-Abouseif: *Islamic Architecture* p. 128; Lev: *Saladin* p. 82.

897 For the Ayyubid madrasahs founded in the greater Cairo area, see Lapidus: *Ayyūbid Religious Policy* pp. 283f.

898 Berkey: *Transmission of Knowledge* p. 144.

899 NZ XV p. 143; SaḫWaǧīz II p. 497; Berkey: *Transmission of Knowledge* p. 144.

900 MaqrḪiṭaṭ II p. 454; Berkey: *Transmission of Knowledge* pp. 173f.; Lev: *Saladin* pp. 122f.; *cf.* also Taylor: *Vicinity of the Righteous* p. 33.

901 ŠaʿrṬab I p. 204.

902 IlyāsBad I p. 471; SuyḤusnMuḥ II p. 230.

903 DK I p. 376.

904 Little: *Mamluk Madrasahs*, esp. pp. 17f.; Leisten: *Architektur für Tote* pp. 41-4.

and though the wording of the source text is open to discussion, is the Shafiite scholar Abū Sahl aṣ-Ṣuᶜlūkī (M. b. Sul., d. 369 H) from Nīsābūr who "was interred in the gathering place where he used to teach".[905] Other early but more explicitly known instances are the burial of the mystic al-Qušayrī (d. 465 H) and his son Abū Saᶜīd (d. 494 H) in their madrasah in Nīsābūr;[906] the interment of Muǧāhid ad-Dīn Bihrūz b. ᶜAbd Allāh al-Ġiyāṯī (d. Baghdad 540 H) in his *ribāṭ* on the banks of the Tigris;[907] the interment of the mystics ᶜAbd al-Qādir al-Ǧīlī (d. 561 H) and ᶜAbd al-Qāhir as-Suhrawardī (d. 563 H), who died in Baghdad and were buried in the madrasahs they had each founded.[908] Another case, from Syria, would be the madrasah-mausoleum of the Zangid ruler Nūr ad-Dīn (d. 569 H) in Damascus.[909]

In Cairo, the first example of that kind might be seen in the decree by sultan Ṣalāh ad-Dīn to place "a teaching circle" (*ḥalqat tadrīs*) right in front of the "tomb" inside the shrine of al-Ḥusayn's head (*al-mašhad al-Ḥusaynī*),[910] though here an already existing mausoleum was equipped with learning faculties and not the other way round. The first full-scale mausoleum-madrasahs inside the town of Cairo were erected by sultan al-Manṣūr Qalāwūn (d. 689 H) almost a hundred years later, viz. the tomb-college of Umm Ṣāliḥ (finished as early as 683 H)[911] and his own tomb-college called "al-qubbah al-Manṣūrīyah", "one of the most impressive and splendid royal buildings".[912] These were only the first of a great number of such and similar complexes founded by many Mamluk sultans or powerful emirs until the beginning of the tenth century H, either in the town itself or to the south of it (but not in the actual area of the southern Qarāfah), or in the Northern Qarāfah commonly known as "the Desert" (*aṣ-Ṣaḥrāʾ*).

In other Islamic lands, secular rulers, for example the Rasūlid rulers in Taᶜizz (Yemen), were customarily buried in madrasahs or tomb-colleges they had founded from the seventh century H onwards.[913] About the same time, mystics resident in Cairo or Qūṣ were buried in the *zāwiyah*s they had founded, e.g. the famous Ḫiḍr al-Mahrānī al-ᶜAdawī (d. 676 H), the personal spiritual master of

905 *dufina fī l-maǧlisi llaḏī kāna yudarrisu fīhi* (NawMuḫt p. 204; IḪallWaf IV p. 205 = Leisten: *Architektur für Tote* p. 209; DāʾūdīṬab II p. 155).

906 NawMuḫt pp. 484 and 490; Leisten: *Architektur für Tote* p. 209 (no. 3).

907 IǦawzīMunt X p. 117.

908 IǦawzīMunt X p. 219 and 225; ŠaᶜrṬab I p. 140; Leisten: *Architektur für Tote* p. 137.

909 Kessler: *Funerary Architecture* p. 259; IḪallWaf V p. 187 = Leisten: *Architektur für Tote* p. 157 (no. 12).

910 MaqrḪiṭaṭ I pp. 427f. = MacKenzie: *Ayyubid Cairo* p. 112 (he inserts the term *madrasah* in the quoted passage, while al-Maqrīzī speaks only of a *mašhad*). *Cf.* also Lapidus: *Ayyūbid Religious Policy* p. 283 who simply but erroneously has "the *madrasa* in the Mashhad al-Ḥusayn", and Lev: *Saladin* pp. 136f.

911 MaqrḪiṭaṭ II p. 394; Williams: *Islamic Monuments* pp. 122f.

912 MaqḪiṭaṭ II p. 380; IᶜAẒāhirTašrīf pp. 55f. and 179f. *Cf.* Behrens-Abouseif: *Islamic Architecture in Cairo* pp. 95-100.

913 See IDaybaᶜBuġ pp. 81ff.; *cf.* also Finster: *Islamic Religious Architecture* pp. 142f. (with material for the later Ottoman period).

sultan Baybars I.[914] The practice of erecting tomb-colleges had first become widespread in seventh-century Baghdad and in eighth-century Egypt, but it is worth noting that this type of complex, in contrast with the *zāwiyah*-mausoleum, was never adopted in the Islamic West.

4.5.3. Visitation of tombs and cemeteries by Mamluk rulers

Visiting tombs or mausolea was part of the Mamluk court and state ritual because "such visits provided both an opportunity for a public display of piety as well as the chance to highlight for personal political purposes a connection to a respected deceased sultan, especially when the visitor was himself a reigning sultan whose grip on the government was weak".[915] The tradition of visiting the mausolea of former rulers in particular seems to have been inherited by the Mamluks from both the Fatimids and the Ayyubids.

The Fatimids are known for having visited the mausolea of preceding rulers. Thus al-Muᶜizz li-Dīn Allāh (r. 341–65 H) visited the tomb of the Iḫšīdid ruler Kāfūr (**31**) in 362 H,[916] and the tombs of the Fatimid rulers in their palace in Cairo soon became a site of veneration for their successors.[917] In contrast, the Ayyubid rulers, in order to stress the Sunnite character of their governance, used to visit the tombs of the former Umayyad caliphs, e.g. Ṣalāḥ ad-Dīn who visited in 584 H the grave of ᶜUmar b. ᶜAbd al-ᶜAzīz (d. 101 H) in Maᶜarrat an-Nuᶜmān;[918] three years later, Ṣalāḥ ad-Dīn's son al-Malik aẓ-Ẓāhir Ġāzī (r. in Aleppo 582–613 H) was likewise to pay a visit to that tomb.[919] In Mamluk Cairo, the mausolea of former sultans were to serve much the same purpose. Especially important among those mausolea proved to be that of al-Manṣūr Qalāwūn: his son, al-Malik al-Ašraf al-Ḫalīl (r. 689–93 H) visited the mausoleum three times in 690 H, before and after the fall of Acre;[920] newly appointed officers (*ʾumarāʾ*) would celebrate their installation by a procession towards the *qubbah al-Manṣūrīyah* and a visitation thereof.[921]

Yet it was not only the tombs or mausolea of predecessors that were approached by Mamluk rulers, but also the shrines of famous Sunnite scholars and "saints". The Ayyubid al-Malik al-Kāmil visited some burial sites in the Qarāfah,[922] and in Rabīᶜ II 796 H sultan Barqūq (second reign 792–801 H) "with all his entourage headed for the mausoleum of Imam aš-Šāfiᶜī, visited it and gave alms to the poor so abundantly as to be beyond belief. Then he moved on to the mausoleum of as-Sayyidah Nafīsah (*al-mašhad an-Nafīsī*), visiting it also. There, and on his way (through the

914 IFurTārīḫ VII p. 103; ITaġrManh V p. 220; for Qūṣ, see e.g. UdfṬāliᶜ p. 195.

915 Berkey: *Transmission of Knowledge* p. 146.

916 IMuyassarAḫbār p. 161 = MaqrḪiṭaṭ I p. 470.

917 For the mausoleum of the Fatimid rulers in Cairo, see below p. 217 with note 342.

918 IWāṣilKurūb II p. 270.

919 al-Ġazzī: *Nahr aḏ-ḏahab* III p. 93.

920 IFurTārīḫ VIII p. 111; MaqrḪiṭaṭ II p. 381 and MaqrSulūk I p. 774; IIyāsBad I p. 368.

921 MaqrḪiṭaṭ II pp. 380f.

922 MuwMuršid I p. 608.

Qarāfah), he again donated lavishly".[923] In the same manner, the later sultan al-Malik aẓ-Ẓāhir Ǧaqmaq (r. 842–57 H) visited the Qarāfah in Ḏū l-Qaʿdah 845 H.[924] In Ottoman times, it was the leading state officials, such as Ibrāhīm Bey Ṭannān (d. 1192 H), who toured the most famous shrines of the Qarāfah, especially on Fridays.[925]

However, the Mamluk rulers not only paid visits to famous burial sites in and around Cairo, which, after all, were easily accessible, but they were also eager to visit venerated shrines and tombs during their travels, e.g. in Syria. There is an interesting passage in Ibn Šaddād's topography of Syria which might illustrate this:

> "When in the year 669 I travelled to Damascus in the company of our master, sultan al-Malik aẓ-Ẓāhir (Baybars, r. 658–76 H) – may God make his rule last eternally! –, and at the service of our master aṣ-Ṣāḥib Bahāʾ ad-Dīn ʿAlī b. Muḥammad b. Sulaym – may God make his days last forever! –, he (*sc.* the sultan) was eager to visit the blessed places that are widely venerated and so he asked in every town and village he entered who was buried there from among the noble and the righteous (*al-ʾakābir wa-ṣ-ṣāliḥīn*) and which blessed places there were, in order to visit them and give alms to the poor and the displaced (*al-fuqarāʾ wa-l-munqaṭiʿīn*)".[926]

4.5.4. The recitation of the Qurʾān

The construction of tomb-colleges was considered beneficial "because both the dead and the living benefit from the recitation of the Qurʾān that takes place there. In addition, it serves to distinguish the status of the deceased buried there from others".[927]

If the mausoleum was not part of a madrasah or tomb-college of Qurʾān reciters, one could nevertheless bring the reciters to the dead, for example by founding madrasahs or colleges of Qurʾān reciters in burial areas. A number of such buildings are known from the Cairene Qarāfah, in particular "the reciters' mosque" (*ǧāmiʿ al-qurrāʾ*).[928]

923 NZ XII p. 54; the same notice also in MaqrSulūk III pp. 807f. and ITaġrManh I p. 253.

924 SaḫTuḥfAḥbāb p. 137. For further examples of Mamluk sultans visiting either the big Cairene cemeteries or mausolea *intra muros*, see Berkey: *Transmission of Knowledge* pp. 145f. An interesting parallel to the practice of Mamluk rulers are the frequent official visits of the tenth- and eleventh-century Moghul rulers to Indian Muslim shrines, see Currie: *Muʿīn al-Dīn Chistī* pp. 99-110 and Moini: *Rituals and Customary Practices* pp. 60f., n. 3.

925 ǦabʿAǧāʾib II p. 57.

926 IŠadAʿlāq II (Damascus) pp. 187f.

927 HaytFatFiqh II p. 16.

928 ŠaʿrṬab II p. 120.

Reciting the Qur'ān at a tomb

In general, albeit with the notable exception of some Malikites[929] and notwithstanding a number of reports to the contrary,[930] reciting the Qur'ān at tombs or even when entering a cemetery[931] was considered beneficial for the deceased and thus not only allowed but even encouraged, e.g. by Ibn Ḥanbal and later Hanbalites like ᶜAbd al-Ġanīy al-Maqdisī (d. 600 H).[932] Others, like Ibn ᶜUmar – the son of the caliph –, had stipulated in their will that certain passages of the Qur'ān be recited at their tombs, and Ibn ᶜUmar also invoked the similar practice of the Prophet in that point.[933] In inscriptions in mausolea, we find endowment rules laid down for the future recitation of the Qur'ān at the tombs.[934] According to Shiite Traditions, Qur'ānic passages should be recited at tombs while laying the hand on them.[935] However, reciting the Qur'ān at tombs could also have the contrary effect, namely in producing harmful consequences for the person buried. Ibn Iyās reports about the tomb of Aḥmad b. Ṭūlūn (see **39**) that a learned sheikh was reciting the Qur'ān at his tomb every day, but then had to stop that practice because Ibn Ṭūlūn appeared to him in a dream, asking him to discontinue the recitation.[936]

The question of whether reciting the Qur'ān at tombs was beneficial for the deceased was disputed for centuries, and thus Ibn Ḥağar al-ᶜAsqalānī could write in this regard: "This is a famous problem (*mas'alah*) and I have compiled a booklet on it.[937] Summing up (what I arrived at in the booklet), the majority of the early authorities argued that it (*sc.* the recitation of the Qur'ān at tombs) is beneficial and the position to be taken towards this problem is to refrain from giving a definitive judgment, though it is desirable to perform it (i.e. reciting the Qur'ān), even in large measure".[938] Centuries before that, the famous Shafiite scholar ᶜIzz ad-Dīn Ibn ᶜAbd as-Salām had been known for his rebuttal of the view that reciting the Qur'ān was in any way beneficial for the dead. Still, when after his death he appeared to one of his pupils in a dream he reportedly said, "What misery! I found the matter different from what I had believed it to be".[939] In general, therefore, the majority of Sunnite

929 IḤāğğMadḫ I pp. 266f.; *cf.* also Haja: *Mort et Jugement Dernier* p. 37.

930 al-Albānī: *Aḥkām al-ğanā'iz* pp. 191-4; Wafā: *Aḥkām al-ğanā'iz* pp. 266-8.

931 *Cf.* ŠirŠadd pp. 31f.; IṬūlQal II p. 474; HarMirqātMaf IV p. 82; al-Amīn: *Miftāḥ* II pp. 271 and 273-5.

932 ĠazIḥyā' (C) IV p. 418; NawRawḍah II p. 139; IQudMuġnī II p. 566; MuwMuršid I pp. 38 and 40f.; QurṭTaḏk pp. 14 and 72f.; ManbTasl (C) pp. 199f. / (M) p. 193; WanšMiᶜyār I p. 320; SuyŠṢudūr pp. 416-21; HaytFatFiqh II p. 16; MF XXXII p. 255.

933 ŠirŠadd p. 31.

934 Inschriften Syrien 210 (after 640 H, aṣ-Ṣāliḥīyah).

935 KulKāfī III p. 229.

936 IIyāsBad I p. 168.

937 I could not find this booklet mentioned in the lengthy and probably near to complete list of Ibn Ḥağar's works in SaḫDurar II pp. 659-96.

938 IḤağĞawKāfī p. 41.

(and Shiite) scholars strongly endorsed the practice of reciting the Qurʾān at a tomb or in cemeteries, though in the Tradition they found relatively little material to support their view.[940]

In order to defend the practice of recitation at tombs, many scholars drew a parallel with the custom of placing fresh palm fronds upon tombs (see p. 251): if doing so is beneficial, they argued, so is the recitation of the Qurʾān.[941] Others either put reciting the Qurʾān on one plane with the giving of "purifying alms" (*ṣadaqah*)[942] or insisted that the beneficial effect of the recitation might be seen in practice: when the mystic Ibn ᶜInān was told that a deceased person in the cemetery was heard every night crying out from his tomb, he went there and recited the Qurʾān and uttered blessings, after which no signs of torment were heard anymore.[943]

It was also believed that the deceased themselves recite the Qurʾān in their tombs, especially on Fridays,[944] and Ibn ᶜAbbās confirmed that every dead person is given a copy of the Qurʾān (*muṣḥaf*) in order to recite from it.[945] Abū ᶜAlī aṭ-Ṭūmārī told his friends of the following vision he had had: "I saw (the reciter) Abū Bakr Ibn Muǧāhid[946] as if he was reciting (the Qurʾān), and I appeared to ask him, 'My master, you are dead and yet you recite?' It seemed that he replied, 'At the end of every ritual prayer and every time I completed the recitation of the Qurʾān (in my lifetime) I asked (God) that he may put me among those who recite in their tombs, and now I *am* among those who recite in their tombs'".[947]

Other examples include the following: ᶜAbd Allāh b. ᶜAmr, the father of the traditionist Ǧābir b. ᶜAbd Allāh (*cf.* above p. 138), was heard reciting the Qurʾān in his tomb;[948] the Baṣran ascetic Ṯābit al-Bunānī dug his own tomb and prayed in it,[949] and after his death he was heard reciting the Qurʾān in his tomb[950] as well as praying there.[951] Šihāb ad-Dīn al-Ġazzī (A. b. ᶜAl., d Mecca 821 H) was

939 Cited in YāfRawḍ p. 177 and ŠīrŠadd p. 33.

940 Several other stories stressing the beneficial effect of Qurʾān recitation for the dead are collected in ŠīrŠadd pp. 32-6 and YāfRawḍ pp. 177f.

941 TurkLumaᶜ I p. 229.

942 ŠīrŠadd p. 32.

943 ŠaᶜrṬab II p. 118.

944 IAYaṬab I p. 407; BayDal VII p. 41; IRaǧAhwāl pp. 52-4; SuyBušrā pp. 46-9; SuyŠṢudūr pp. 253-7 and 275f. *Cf.* also ŠīrŠadd p. 21; YāfNašr p. 21 and YāfRawḍ pp. 180f.; Gramlich: *Wunder* p. 360. The jurist A. b. M. Ibn Abī s-Suᶜūd aṭ-Ṭūsī (d. 654 H) was often heard reciting the Qurʾān in his tomb on Friday night (ḪazrᶜUqūd I p. 122); *cf.* also SuyḪaṣ p. 364.

945 IRaǧAhwāl p. 54; SuyŠṢudūr pp. 255 and 257.

946 A. b. Mūsā al-Muqriʾ (d. Baghdad 324 H).

947 TB V p. 148; NawMuḫt p. 370.

948 SuyḪaṣ I p. 364 and II p. 112.

949 ZamRabīᶜ IV p. 201. However, digging one's tomb before death was not seen by all scholars as desirable, see al-Albānī: *Aḥkām al-ǧanāʾiz* pp. 160f. and 257.

950 ANuḤilyah II p. 322; MarǧBahǧah II pp. 402f.; IRaǧAhwāl p. 52; SuyŠṢudūr p. 253; Gramlich: *Vorbilder* I p. 44.

951 ANuḤilyah II p. 319 = SuyBušrā pp. 45f.; ŠaᶜrDurar p. 58 and ŠaᶜrṬab I p. 36. Ṯābit

heard reciting the surah *Yā-Sīn* in his tomb.[952] The second-century ascetic Ḍirār b. Murrah aš-Šaybānī from Kūfah "dug his grave 15 years before his death. He used to stay in it and completed there the recitation of the Qurʾān"; others added that the grave had been dug in his very house,[953] something which is also reported of the first-century ascetic ar-Rabīᶜ b. Ḫuṯaym[954] and of as-Sayyidah Nafīsah.[955] The caliph Hārūn ar-Rašīd had, during his last illness, dug his tomb and ordered reciters to step down into it and recite the whole Qurʾān there.[956] The mystic Aḥmad ᶜAbd al-Ḥaqq ar-Rudawlī (d. 836 H or later) dug his grave, entered it, covered it and stayed in it for six months, until he had successfully completed the stages of the Sufi path.[957]

From Ibn ᶜAsākir's *History of Damascus*, Yāqūt quotes the following story, concerning the burial of al-Ḫaṭīb al-Baġdādī in 463 H:

> "As Abū Bakr al-Ḫaṭīb al-Baġdādī was nearing death, he stipulated that he should be buried beside (the tomb of) Bišr b. al-Ḥāriṯ (al-Ḥāfī) – may God have mercy upon him! Yet the place beside (the tomb of) Bišr was already occupied by a tomb Abū Bakr Aḥmad b. ᶜAlī aṭ-Ṭurayṯīṯī (*sic*) had dug for himself. He used to come to that place reciting the entire Qurʾān and uttering prayers; he had been doing this for several years. After al-Ḫaṭīb had died, Aḥmad was asked whether al-Ḫaṭīb might be buried on that spot, but he refused and said, 'This is my tomb which I dug by myself and in which I completed numerous recitations of the Qurʾān! Nobody else can be interred in it, that is completely out of the question!'[958] The dispute became known to my father[959] – may God have mercy upon him! –, so he spoke to Aḥmad, 'O sheikh, if Bišr b. al-Ḥāriṯ al-Ḥāfī were still among the living and you and al-Ḫaṭīb were coming before him, which of you would he have sit down at his side, you or al-Ḫaṭīb?' Aḥmad replied,''Not me, of course, but al-Ḫaṭīb!' My father said, 'And this is how it must be done even now that Bišr is dead, because al-Ḫaṭīb is more entitled (to be at Bišr's side) than you are'. Now Aḥmad gladly withdrew his claim and accepted that al-Ḫaṭīb should be buried in that spot, and so it was done".[960]

Apart from being beneficial for the deceased, reciting the Qurʾān at a tomb could also be intended to have beneficial results for the reciter himself, like a specific form of prayer or plea for intercession or help. Thus we read about the tomb of the mystic Ibn Ǧābār al-Ǧurǧānī (Abū ᶜAl. M., d. 361 or 362 H) who was buried in the Cairene Qarāfah: "Some people who often visit the cemetery say that the recitation of the verse *Say: He is God, One* (Q 112:1) at the tomb of Ibn Ǧābār, repeated

reportedly said: "If ever I offered a prayer to someone in his tomb, then offer me a prayer in my tomb" (ISaᶜdṬab VII p. 233); similarly MarǧBahǧah II p. 402 and SuyBušrā p. 46.

952 ᶜĀmBahǧNāẓ p. 129.

953 IǦawzīṢafwah II p. 68. This notwithstanding the report from the Prophet: "Do not turn your houses into tombs" (see below p. 214).

954 MunKawākib I p. 282.

955 MunKawākib I p. 724.

956 AFidāʾMuḫt II p. 18; ᶜIṣāmīSimṭ III p. 300.

957 Gramlich: *Wunder* p. 187.

958 *hāḏā mimmā lā yutaṣawwar.*

959 I.e. the father of Abū l-Barakāt Ismāᶜīl b. Abī Saᶜd aṣ-Ṣūfī, who related this story.

960 TMD V pp. 34f. = YāqIršād I p. 247.

eleven times and coupled with a prayer to God the Exalted to make something happen, will lead to the fulfillment of that prayer. It has been proved in practice".[961] After the death of ᶜAbd Allāh b. Ibrāhīm as-Sukkarī al-Maġribī al-Mālikī (d. Jerusalem 829 H), the Prophet was seen in a dream, saying "He who recites the *Fātiḥah* to sheikh ᶜAbd Allāh as-Sukkarī will enter Paradise". This dictum soon became widely known and the people flocked from the towns, and those who had not encountered as-Sukkarī during his life went to his tomb and recited the *Fātiḥah* to him.[962]

Organised recitation

It was customary to recite the whole Qurᵓān at the tombs of persons recently buried. Doing so was called "performing the *ḫatmah*", that is, "the completion (of recitation)" of the entire Qurᵓān. Such *ḫatmah*-sessions (pl. *ḫatamāt*) could well be organised by friends and relatives when a member of the family had died, but more often than not those recitations took place at the tombs of famous individuals.

At the tomb of aš-Šarīf Abū Ǧaᶜfar ᶜAbd al-Ḫāliq b. ᶜĪsā (411–70 H), who was buried beside Ibn Ḥanbal in Baghdad, "the people gathered continuously and stayed there the whole night of Thursday (to Friday) each reciting the *ḫatmah*; vendors would come and sell fruit and other food.[963] (...) This went on for some months until winter set in and the cold made the people stay at home. However, it was said that during that period ten thousand *ḫatmahs* were recited at his tomb".[964] At the head of the tomb (*ᶜalā raᵓsi qabrihī*) of Abū Manṣūr al-Ḫayyāṭ (d. 497 H or after), likewise buried in Baghdad, no less than 221 *ḫatmahs* were performed in less than ten days after his death.[965] After the death of Ibn ᶜIzz al-Quḍāh (Ism. b. ᶜAlī, d. Cairo 689 H), "the people recited the Qurᵓān around him and pronounced numerous *ḫatmahs* at his tomb".[966] After the burial of the famous mystic Ibn ᶜAṭāᵓ Allāh as-Sikandarī (d. Cairo 709 H) "the people thronged to visit his tomb, hoping for blessing. In the night of eleventh Ǧumādā I of every year they organise a meeting in order to recite the Qurᵓān and eat there, but vile elements are present which bring up various kinds of objectionable practices. They continue to do so (i.e. to gather at his tomb) to the present day".[967] After the death of Ibn Kaṯīr (d. 774 H), the Shafiites of Damascus visited his grave for days on end in order to complete the recital of the Qurᵓān several times and to recite lengthy mourning poems; some had outstanding visions at his grave.[968] In Cairo in 893 H, the Qurᵓān reciters beleaguered (*nwb* VIII) the tomb of a sheikh for an entire week.[969] The practice of reciting the complete Qurᵓān seems to have been introduced in al-Andalus in 399 H when, according to al-Qāḍī ᶜIyāḍ, the colleagues and disciples of

961 IZayKawākib p. 128; MaqrMuq V p. 476. In another case, known from early fifth-century Toledo, surah 112 was to be recited regularly ten times in front of a certain tomb, following the last wish of the buried person (see IBaškṢilah I pp. 90f.).

962 ᶜUlaymīUns II p. 246.

963 Many scholars disapproved of eating in the cemetery.

964 IRaǧḎayl I pp. 23f.

965 IRaǧḎayl I pp. 97.

966 ITaġrManh II p. 409.

967 MaqrMuq I pp. 597f. Ibn ᶜAṭāᵓ Allāh's mosque-mausoleum in the Lesser Qarāfah is still a place of veneration and has been recently restored (or, rather, rebuilt).

968 INāṣRadd p. 166.

969 SaḫWaǧīz III p. 1033.

Ibn al-ᶜAṭṭār al-Qurṭubī (Abū ᶜAl. M. b. A.) stayed at his tomb for days and recited the entire Qurʾān more than once: "This had never happened before in al-Andalus".[970]

Among secular rulers, it had become common practice to pay for Qurʾān recitation at certain venerated tombs and to see to it that the endowment stipulations for their respective mausolea provided for the payment of professional reciters performing those recitations continuously and without time limits.

The first recorded case seems to be the fact that Ibn Ṭūlūn in 270 H had four tents (or open galleries, *ʾarwiqah*) erected over the tomb of Muᶜāwiyah in Damascus; he instituted a Qurʾān recitation there and lit candles at the grave.[971] In later times, organised recitation of the Qurʾān was a common phenomenon in mausolea and endowed tomb-colleges of Mamluk rulers,[972] e.g. at the Damascene mausoleum of sultan Baybars, where sixteen reciters were at work "day and night, two of them for three hours at a time, and every reciter was to receive 25 dirhams (monthly)".[973] In Cairo, the tomb-college of al-Manṣūr Qalāwūn maintained a permanent group of Qurʾān scholars and reciters,[974] and the later sultan al-Ašraf Barsbāy saw to the equipment of his own mausoleum (in the Northern Qarāfah) with a sufficient number of reciters.[975] It was also possible to organise *ḫatmahs* for other members of the rulers' families, especially for their children or parents. For example, Qurʾān reciters were stipulated for the tomb of the mother of the Ayyubid ruler al-Malik al-Kāmil in the mausoleum of aš-Šāfiᶜī;[976] every Friday night a *ḫatmah* was performed at the tomb of sultan an-Nāṣir's son Ānūk b. Muḥammad b. Qalāwūn (723–40 H), on the instigation of his mother;[977] sultan Barqūq had arranged for continuous recitation at the grave of his father Anaṣ (d. 783 H).[978]

Organised recitation took place in other Cairene mausolea as well which had no connection with the ruling secular élite, for example the widely-attended *ḫatmah*-sessions held regularly in the mausoleum of aš-Šāfiᶜī[979] and of Imam al-Layṯ b. Saᶜd (see above p. 43); aš-Šāfiᶜi himself was said to have inaugurated the custom of reciting the Qurʾān at the tomb of al-Layṯ every Friday night.[980] From the Islamic East we hear that the Tīmūrid ruler Ḥusayn (b. Manṣūr, r. 873–911 H) appointed "an imam (...) with specific instructions to recite one complete portion (*sī pāra*) of the Koran every day at the tomb of (Abū ᶜAbd Allāh) Anṣārī".[981] In general, it was the ruling class, viz. the secular and military élite, which was responsible for financing organised recitation either at widely visited shrines, or at their own mausolea.

A practice closely related was the public performance of preaching sessions

970 ᶜIyāḍTartīb IV p. 656.

971 NZ II p. 47.

972 *Cf.* Berkey: *Transmission of Knowledge* p. 145.

973 IŠadMalẒāhir p. 227.

974 MaqrḪiṭaṭ II pp. 380f.

975 ITaġrManh III p. 276.

976 MaqrḪiṭaṭ I p. 174.

977 DK I p. 447.

978 MaqrDurar II p. 517.

979 *Cf.* Schimmel: *Sufismus* p. 283.

980 ᶜUlaymīUns I p. 294.

981 Subtelny: *Cult of Anṣārī* p. 391.

(*maǧālis waʿẓ*) and the public reading of religious texts in burial grounds or near the mausolea of famous dead. This seems to have been a widespread practice, especially in sixth-century Baghdad where the most famous of all preachers, Abū l-Faraǧ Ibn al-Ǧawzī, regularly summoned the people to the shrine of Maʿrūf al-Karḫī; others would rally the believers at nearby mausolea, e.g. at the tomb of Ibn Ḥanbal.[982]

Circles of study were held near a tomb or in a mausoleum, e.g. for lectures on legal manuals such as Faḫr ad-Dīn ar-Rāzī's *Ḥāwī*.[983] In Naṣrābād, the *Ṣaḥīḥ* was read in public at the tomb of its author Muslim b. al-Ḥaǧǧāǧ in 530 H.[984] In Cairo, a certain ʿAbd ar-Raḥmān al-Ḫawāṣṣ was known as "the cemetery-preacher",[985] and lectures on Tradition were held at the tomb of Ibn Abī Ǧamrah (d. 695 H): "He was the one who collected the sound (*ṣaḥīḥ*) Traditions from the Messenger of God – *taṣliyah* – which are read at his tomb on the first day of every year. The people gather there and initiate the year by visiting his tomb and listening to the noble Traditions he collected".[986] A pupil of Ibn Ḥaǧar al-ʿAsqalānī reports that in 834 H he studied with him the *Kitāb Manāqib al-Layṯ* (*b. Saʿd*) and the *Kitāb Manāqib aš-Šāfiʿī* – books dealing with the laudable achievements of these scholars – at their respective burial sites.[987]

4.6. Living in the cemetery

In the Arabo-Islamic culture, cemeteries were looked upon in two different ways: as gloomy and unhealthy places on the one hand, and as blessed and "attractive" places on the other. Both these points of view continued side by side throughout the centuries and dominate the perception of cemeteries until the present day.

4.6.1. Cemeteries as haunted places

As haunted and unsanitary sites, cemeteries often ranged on a par with ruins, toilets and other squalid or isolated places. The problem of dirt and lack of hygienical conditions was discussed earlier, and this is why some first-generation Muslims found it abominable to dig a pond or well (*rukayyah*, *biʾr*) on a funeral site for either drinking or ablution, "because the graves are submerged (and overflow) when there is heavy rain".[988]

Another point often made when speaking about graveyards was the notion of desolation and seclusion: "It is considered reprehensible to stay (overnight or for a longer period) in the cemetery (*al-mabīt bihā*) without excuse, as is obvious because

982 IRaǧḎayl I p. 85.

983 ŠīrŠadd p. 72.

984 NawMuḫt p. 260. For the study of Muslim's *Ṣaḥīḥ* at a tomb, see IAbbTakm II p. 295.

985 *wāʿiẓ al-maqburah*, see IZayKawākib p. 43.

986 IlyāsBad I p. 390.

987 SaḫǦawāhir III pp. 1141f.; *cf.* also *ib.* pp. 997 and 1043.

988 ʿARazMuṣ 6496 (III p. 507); IAŠayMuṣ III p. 269 (*ǧanāʾiz* 200).

it is a place dominated by solitariness (*waḥšah*).[989] But if it is considered recommended, if the lack of desolation can be guaranteed and the sole aim is the *meditatio mortis* (*taḏakkur al-mawt*) (...), then it does not seem far-fetched either".[990] The commentator of this passage, ar-Ramlī, indeed had the right impression when he wrote:

> "In this statement the author seems to imply that it is not disapproved of to stay (even) in an isolated mausoleum (*al-qabr al-munfarid*). al-Isnawī said that this has some likelihood to it and he distinguished between a tomb situated in wasteland (*bi-ṣaḥrā'*) or in an inhabited house.[991] This distinction is valid, because many mausolea (*turab*) are inhabited like houses.[992] (...) As to the desolation, it yields a motive for the disapproval (of staying in the cemetery) if someone is alone (*munfarid*). But if there is a group of people – as it happens often in our times when people meet to stay overnight (*mabīt*) on Fridays in order to recite the Qur'ān and or to visit (the tombs) – then it is not disapproved of".[993]

The desolation typical of cemeteries was thus in principle acknowledged, although with the intensification of the mortuary cult more and more people gathered in burial areas and the danger of remaining truly alone was indeed negligible; therefore one could argue that it was better to be buried in a cemetery than somewhere else (e.g. in a private house or in the wilderness), because the many visitors and passers-by in the cemetery procure much blessing by their prayers (*du'ā'*).[994] As a consequence, it seems that the motif of the "solitary graveyard" – which is closely related to the motif of the dead utterly isolated in the tomb (see above p. 134) – soon became little more than a literary motif going back to former centuries and no longer truly relevant during the Mamluk period, at the latest. If at all, after centuries of a highly developed urban culture, the nearest a report stemming from the formative period of Islam would come to the reality of later times was a Tradition from the Prophet such as the following, stressing the forlornness of the cemetery but giving it a "cultural turn": "He who stays with the bedouins / will become coarse ‖ and the inhabitants of villages / are like the inhabitants of tombs" (i.e. utterly ignorant and far from being civilised).[995]

Nevertheless, the desolation of graveyards and burial sites proved to be a topos impossible to eradicate from the common imagery because it was firmly rooted in

989 This phrase occurs verbatim also in ŠīrMuhaḏ I p. 138.

990 HaytTuḥfMuḥt III p. 193.

991 *Cf.* IQudMuġnī II pp. 508f. Being buried in a house (*dār*), possibly within the city limits, was and is in general considered disapproved of, see al-Albānī: *Aḥkām al-ǧanā'iz* p. 138, MF XXI p. 9 and below pp. 212ff.

992 The author took this distinction probably from 'Izz ad-Dīn Ibn 'Abd as-Salām, who ruled that the mausolea of scholars and righteous persons (*mašāhid al-'ulamā' wa-'ahl aṣ-ṣalāḥ*) were to be considered as private houses (*buyūt*), see I'ASalāmFat p. 130.

993 RamlīNih III p. 29 = ŠirwḤāš III p. 193.

994 HaytTuḥfMuḥt III p. 193 and MF XXI, p. 9; see also **9**, **32**, **34**, **85**, **88**, **174** and **188**.

995 IẒuhFaḍMiṣr p. 3 (*man badā / fa-qad ǧafā ‖ wa-sukkānu l-kufūr / ka-sukkāni l- qubūr*).

the Arabic narrative tradition (ʾ*adab)* and poetry.[996] In this vein, the city of Toledo, after it had been devastated by caliphal forces, was described by the Córdoban poet Abū l-Qāsim ᶜAbbās b. Firnās (d. 274 H)[997] as follows (*kāmil*):

تُرِكَتْ بِلاَ أَهْلٍ تُأَهِّلُهَا * مَهْجُورَةَ الأَكْنَافِ كَالقَبْرِ

"It was left without people inhabiting it, * its quarters deserted like a tomb".[998]

The idea of the cemetery as a deserted and haunted place was further reinforced by the connection in people's minds between graveyards and all sorts of snakes and scorpions[999] or, more importantly, of demons and evil spirits, mainly the djinns (pl. *ğinn* or *ğānn*), which has been always strong, both in pre-modern times and today.[1000] Famous is the story that in 433 H the Cairene Qarāfah cemetery was haunted by evil spirits who came down at night from the Muqaṭṭam Hill, snatching away little children and digging up the tombs in order to devour what they found therein.[1001]

Moreover, graveyards were one of the favourite dwelling places of the so-called

996 See also the famous verse which stresses the forlornness of a tomb even phonetically (*rağaz*): *wa-qabru Ḥarbin bi-makānin qafrū * wa-laysa qurba qabri Ḥarbin qabrū* ("The tomb of Ḥarb [b. Umayyah] is in a place desert * and there is no tomb near the tomb of Ḥarb"), cited in ŠTalḫīṣ I p. 99 = MehrenRhetorik p. 16 and IAṯīrMaṯal p. 179. The verse was reportedly uttered by djinns (ĞāḥḤay VI p. 207); *cf.* also Fück: *Arabiya* p. 65. The wordplay *qafr / qabr* appears also in a verse by the Umayyad caliph Sulaymān b. ᶜAbd al-Malik (r. 96–99 H) upon the grave of his son Ayyūb (*ṭawīl*): *waqaftu ʿalā qabrin muqīmin bi-qafratin* (cited in MubKāmil (C) IV p. 53; IḤamdTaḏk IV p. 243, with the var. *wuqūfun ʿalā*); INāṣBard (A) p. 61 = SuyBard p. 141); for the term *muqīm cf.* Bravmann: *Spiritual Background* pp. 288-95 and Homerin: *Death and Afterlife* p. 167.

997 It might be interesting for the reader to learn that Ibn Firnās was an aviation pioneer, though his efforts eventually proved futile: "He conceived a method to make his body fly, and so he covered himself with feathers and fixed two wings. He flew in the air a long distance, but his technique did not work well during landing and he hurt his buttocks. He forgot to consider that a bird merely touches down upon its tail (*zimikk*), and he had not constructed a tail for himself" (MaqqNafḥ [C] IV pp. 345f.; *cf.* also ISaᶜīdMuġrib I p. 333; Arié: *España musulmana* p. 416, based upon Elías Terés: *Sobre el "vuelo" de ʿAbbās Ibn Firnās*, in: al-Andalus 29 [1964], pp. 365-9). The problem of the missing tail was also the reason for the failure of a similar attempt by an English aviation pioneer, viz Oliver of Malmesbury, an astrologer and mechanician who was an old man in 1066 CE: "He is said by William of Malmesbury (...) to have fitted wings to his hands and feet and to have attempted to fly off a tower with the help of the wind; he fell and broke his legs. He attributed his failure to the lack of a tail" (George Sarton: *Introduction to the History of Science, Vol. I: From Homer to Omar Khayyam*, Baltimore 1927 [repr. 1962], p. 720. My thanks are due to Friedrich Kaltz for this information).

998 Cited in MaqqNafḥ (C) I p. 153.

999 *Cf.* MaqrMuq III p. 424.

1000 For the cemetery as a place of demons and ghosts in Europe, see Ariès: *Essais* pp. 123-31 and Jean-Claude Schmitt: *Ghosts in the Middle Ages: The Living and the Dead in Medieval Society*. tr. by T. Fagan, Chicago – London 1998.

1001 MaqrḪiṭaṭ II p. 445 = Taylor: *Vicinity of the Righteous* p. 22; IlyāsBad I p. 468.

"unseen callers" (*ḥātif*, pl. *ḥawātif*) who could either be djinns or demons or, in some cases, the spirits of the dead themselves.[1002] These "callers" frightened people by announcing imminent cases of death or other tragic events of the future.[1003] In less disturbing cases, they simply provided a *memento mori*, a reminder of mortality.[1004] Another kind of rumour and shouting, equally frightening, was produced by those among the dead who were cruelly chastised in their graves[1005] – including the Jews[1006] –, and the traditionist Yaḥyā b. Maᶜīn (d. 233 H) was told by the undertaker of the cemetery of his town that he often heard a groaning (*ʾanīn*) from the tombs, "resembling the groaning of ill people".[1007] Similarly, when the emir al-Faḫr ᶜAbd al-Ġanīy al-Armanī, a cruel tyrant hated by everyone, was buried in Šawwāl 821 H in the mausoleum of his tomb-college in Cairo,[1008] "a number of Sufis and other people heard him crying out loud in his tomb. This event was soon on the lips of everybody".[1009] Ibn al-Ḫarrāṭ al-Išbīlī relates the following from a Sevillan scholar called Abū l-Ḥakam b. Barǧān (?):

> "When they had buried somebody in their village to the east of Seville they sat down near the tomb and talked to each other. A donkey (lit. 'riding animal', *dābbah*) was grazing nearby. Suddenly it rushed towards the tomb and laid its ears upon it as if it was listening, then it turned quickly away. Yet it approached the tomb again and laid its ear upon it as if it was listening, then it turned away as before. The donkey continued to do so again and again, and Abū l-Ḥakam – may God have mercy upon him! – added that this had reminded him of the Chastisement of the Grave and the saying of the Prophet: 'Verily, they (*sc.* the dead) will be chastised by a Chastisement which the beasts are able to hear!'"[1010]

The pitiful state of many a cemetery and the common disregard for the upkeep of funerary structures (*cf.* below p. 288) contributed to the perception of cemeteries as places of desolation. This has been poetically expressed by Ibn Ḫafāǧah (*ṭawīl*):

وَقَدْ دَرَسَتْ أَجْسَامُهُمْ وَدِيَارُهُمْ * فَلَمْ أَرَ إلاَّ أَقْبُراً وَيَبَابَا

1002 *Cf.* MuwMuršid I pp. 15f. and IRaǧAhwāl pp. 169f.

1003 *Cf.* IADunyāQubūr (A) pp. 51-4; IĞawzīTabṣ I p. 270; IḪallWaf III p. 470; HarMirqātMaf IV p. 105.

1004 IADunyāQubūr (A) pp. 56f. and 154f.; IBuḫtUns p. 71; ŠīrŠadd pp. 30f.; IRaǧAhwāl pp. 187-9; SuyŠṢudūr pp. 289-92.

1005 IADunyāQubūr (A) pp. 93-100; IRaǧAhwāl pp. 49f., 63f. and 87; IḤaǧAḥwāl p. 24; SuyŠṢudūr p. 283; ŠaᶜrṬab I p. 127; HarMirqātMaf I pp. 202f.; Smith/Haddad: *Islamic Understanding of Death* p. 45.

1006 FB III pp. 308f. (*ǧanāʾiz* 87); IḪarrāṭᶜĀqibah pp. 145f.; KU 42543 (XV p. 644) and 42947 (XV p. 742).

1007 IAYaṬab I p. 407; SuyBušrā p. 45.

1008 *Cf.* Williams: *Islamic Monuments* p. 146.

1009 NZ XIV p. 153; for similar events in Ardabīl, see Gronke: *Derwische* p. 86 with note 63. *Cf.* also Kinberg: *Interaction* p. 293.

1010 IḪarrāṭᶜĀqibah pp. 162f. For the Tradition "Verily, they will be chastised ...", see FB XI p.

"Their bodies and houses have already been effaced, * and thus I saw nothing but tombs and devastation".[1011]

However, the image of destruction and desolation could also be applied *vice versa*: a town whose cemetery seemed to outrank the settlement could become the fitting metaphor for the utmost degree of forlornness and Godforsakenness. The Syrian jurist al-Awzāʿī (d. Beirut 157 H) relates: "In Beirut, I once had the pleasure of strolling around the local graveyard and found a black woman sitting among the tombs. I asked her 'Where are the inhabitants?', and she replied 'If you look for the inhabitants, they are here', pointing to the tombs, 'but if you look for ruins (*al-ḫarāb*), they are just in front of you', pointing towards the town".[1012]

4.6.2. Cemeteries as blessed places

The negative attitude towards burial areas could not, on the other hand, prevent cemeteries from being seen either as an integral part of the everyday world or even as blessed places; people were in general aware of the presence of the dead, something which resulted in a certain coexistence of the living and the dead. This ambivalent notion of the cemetery runs roughly parallel to the ambiguous attitudes towards the tomb and death in general. Even in dreams, seeing cemeteries and mausolea could be considered a positive omen.[1013]

Parallels between the present world and the hereafter

The "life" of the dead in their tombs, their "presence" and the way they deserved to be treated were often likened to the society of the living.[1014] This concept could be expressed in phrases such as the following: "The present world and the World to Come are equal as far as souls are concerned" (*ad-dunyā wa-l-ʾāḫiratu ʿinda l-ʾarwāḥi sawāʾ*),[1015] or "The rulings (*ʾaḥkām*) in the hereafter underlie the principles of the law (*ʾuṣūl šarʿīyah*) which are valid in this abode, i.e. in this life (*fī hāḏihī d-dār*)".[1016]

There is a famous saying by the Prophet which draws a parallel between the graveyard and the market-place,[1017] and according to another report "the Prophet called the cemetery (*mawḍiʿ al-qubūr*)

208 (*daʿwāt* 37); NawŠMuslim V p. 86 (*masāǧid* 125); MundTarġīb IV p. 361; QurṭTaḏk pp. 134f.

1011 IḪafDīwān p. 52.

1012 Quoted in NābḤaqīqah p. 247. A parallel for this imagery appears in IADunyāQubūr p. 114.

1013 ISīrMunt pp. 47f.; ẒāhIšārāt pp. 243f.; NābTaʿṭīr II p. 139; as-Suṭūḥī: *Maqābir al-Hū* pp. 108-10.

1014 QurṭTaḏk p. 14; ZurqŠMuw II p. 70.

1015 SuhrAwārif p. 447.

1016 IAĞamrBahğah I p. 175. A similar phrase occurs also on p. 590 (*ḥukmu l-ḥayāti mustaṣḥabun fī l-mamāt*).

1017 IMāğah I p. 499; IQudMuġnī II pp. 508 and 565; HarMirqātMaf IV p. 117; MF XXXII p. 246; a more detailed wording in IAŠayMuṣ III p. 219 (*ğanāʾiz* 138).

a *dār*, because the dead gather there as the living do in their homes (*diyār*)".[1018] Moreover, when Muḥammad had ordered that the deceased should not be buried in the vicinity of an evil-doer (*ǧār as-sūʾ*), he was asked "O Messenger of God! Does the righteous neighbour (*al-ǧār aṣ-ṣāliḥ*) help in the hereafter?" He replied "Does he help in the present world, then?", and when this was affirmed he said: "It is the same in the hereafter".[1019]

Parallels between the "settlements of the dead" and the "settlements of the living" were commonly drawn by the world-renouncers also, for example by the second-century Baṣran ascetic Yazīd b. Abān ar-Raqāšī.[1020] Every person approaching a tomb should address the deceased facing him "because while visiting him it is as if you are speaking to somebody who is alive, and when you speak to a living person, you also turn towards his face".[1021] The mystic Abū l-Mawāhib aš-Šāḏilī explained this theme as follows: "When transferred from abode to abode, saintly men (*ʾawliyāʾ*) possess the same inviolability (*ḥurmah*) after their death as during their lives. Behaviour towards them (*al-ʾadab maʿahum*), once they are dead, must be the same as the behaviour shown to them when they were alive".[1022] In general, the bodies of the deceased were considered to possess the same *ḥurmah* as those of the living,[1023] and the most famous Tradition in this regard says: "Breaking the bones of a Muslim (*or* of a believer, *muʾmin*) after his death is like breaking them while he is alive" (a saying directed mainly against the digging up of tombs).[1024] The dead should therefore be buried "in the midst of righteous people (*wasṭa qawmin ṣāliḥīna*), because the vicinity (lit. neighbourhood) of an evil-doer harms the deceased, just as the living are harmed by the vicinity of an evil-doer".[1025]

However, the parallels between the conditions of the present world and those of the afterworld, the latter thought to prevail in burial areas, cannot be pushed too far, because, even though it was considered permissible to stay overnight in a tomb-mosque, activities such as eating, drinking and trading were in general discouraged

1018 Quoted in HarMirqātMaf IV p. 114.

1019 Cited in ZamRabīʿ IV p. 179 and IbšihīMust II p. 442 (ch. 81); *cf.* also KU 42371 (XV p. 599) and 42916 (p. 733).

1020 ISaʿdṬab VII p. 245 (short notice); IADunyāQubūr (A) p. 114; IʿARabʿIqd (Ǧ) II p. 153 / (M) III p. 236.

1021 MuwMuršid I p. 36. *cf.* also HarMirqātMaf IV p. 115 (*ziyāratu l-mayyiti ka-ziyāratihī fī ḥāli ḥayātihī*).

1022 Quoted in ŠaʿrṬab II p. 72.

1023 ŠīrŠadd p. 13. See also the analysis in Krawietz: *Ḥurma* pp. 116-68, esp. pp. 127-31.

1024 *Muwaṭṭaʾ* I p. 238 (*ǧanāʾiz* 15) = SuyTanwīr p. 246; ISaʿdṬab VIII p. 481 (here ascribed to ʿĀʾišah); MunḏTarġīb IV p. 375; IAǦamrBahǧah I p. 590 (with a different wording); IḤāǧǧMadḫ III p. 20; ŠīrŠadd p. 14; IbšihīMust II p. 445 (ch. 81); KU 42694 (XV p. 677); al-Albānī: *Aḥkām al-ǧanāʾiz* p. 233. *Cf.* also DabMaʿālim III pp. 20f. (the story of a mystic who lived in terror until his death because he had dug a pit near a cemetery, hit erroneously a tomb and broke the bones of a dead woman).

1025 DaylFird I p. 68; IḪarrāṭʿĀqibah p. 130; KU 42371 (XV p. 599) and 42916 (p. 733); for the argument *cf.* Taylor: *Vicinity of the Righteous* pp. 47-9.

in graveyards.[1026] That is, a sense of awe or "other-worldliness" was felt to be appropriate in burial sites. The invectives of strict scholars like Ibn al-Ḥāǧǧ, who strongly condemned the lack of solemnity and the desire for "entertainment" exhibited by many visitors to cemeteries, have already been cited above. After all, there is also a report – poorly authenticated – saying that a certain man once laughed in the cemetery and as a consequence his teeth fell out (*ʾanna raǧulan ḍaḥika fī maqburatin fa-tanāṯarat ʾasnānuhū*),[1027] and according to another Tradition cited in a Shiite source the Prophet had forbidden laughing while in the vicinity of a burial site.[1028]

More important is what we read in the Qurʾān: *Not equal are the living and the dead* (Q 35:22), a phrase not easily misunderstood and certainly not supporting the parallels between the present world and the hereafter that were often drawn. As a result, there were also some – rather few – voices which tried to separate both spheres, e.g. by saying that the cemetery was no place for worldly affairs or business, "because it belongs only to the hereafter" (*al-maqābiru ʾinnamā hiya ʾamru l-ʾāḫirah*).[1029] In the same vein, Ibn Ḥaǧar al-ʿAsqalānī wrote: "Some regard (the deceased's knowledge of who is coming to visit them) as very unlikely, assuming it to be based on a (false) analogy between those who are accustomed to the conditions of this life, whereas in fact the conditions in limbo (*barzaḫ*) are clearly different".[1030]

The predominant Islamic attitude towards cemeteries – not only among the common people, but among the learned élite alike – considered them integral parts of the present world, with the hereafter being rather more "here" than "after". Therefore, J. Nedoroscik is right when he writes with regard to the Cairene cemeteries:

> "Historically, Egyptians refuse to see the graveyard as a dark, evil and forbidden place. No atmosphere of fear or danger surrounded the cemetery. The cemetery has always been an active part of the community. Only in recent times have more Western views of cemeteries pervaded Egyptian attitudes. Indeed, it appears that it was not until the French occupation (from 1798 to 1801) that the idea of a strict separation between tombs and houses was introduced into Egyptian culture. This view was reinforced under British occupation. Today, those living in the cemeteries are ostracized from mainstream society".[1031]

1026 See ĠazDurrah p. 44 and IʿASalāmFat p. 83. *Cf.* also IʿAbdūnTraité pp. 57f., with regard to the cemetery of Seville: "Ce qui se passe de plus choquant dans le cimitière de cette ville (...) c'est qu'on y tolère que des individus viennent s'installer sur des tombes pour boire du vin et parfois même pour s'y livrer à la débauche. (...) L'un des devoirs les plus importants du cadi – qu'Allah l'assiste! – est donc d'ordonner la démolition des constructions élevées de nouveau dans le cimetière et d'expulser les marchands des boutiques qu'on y a bâties et dont l'emplacement doit être réservé aux visiteurs qui stationnent dans les allées réservées entre les tombes". And again on page 59: "Il importe de ne tolérer aucun vendeur dans les cimetières, car ils pourraient voir les femmes en deuil le visage découvert".

1027 Quoted in ZawzḤam I p. 264.

1028 QNuʿmDaʿāʾim I p. 239.

1029 IMuflĀdāb III p. 306.

1030 IḤaǧĞawKāfī p. 41.

1031 Nedoroscik: *City of the Dead* p. 6.

Similar observations made by A. Marcus (who refers to Syria, Lebanon and Palestine) are also worth quoting here:

> "It would be wrong to conclude that this society lacked respect for the dead and their resting places. It was rather that people were relatively relaxed and casual in the way they related to graveyards. Their sense of respect for the dead was not accompanied by inhibiting taboos or an attitude of joyless solemnity toward the cemeteries. What fear or uneasiness they felt about them appears to have been limited largely to night hours, when harmful spirits were believed to haunt them. Entering a cemetery in the dark was regarded as an act of personal courage".[1032]

Cemetery-dwellers

By many Muslims, especially mystics, ascetics and other pious people, burial sites and cemeteries were frequently seen as the most appropriate places to retreat to from this world and its mundane preoccupations. It seems that throughout the Islamic world this phenomenon was far more widespread than, say, in Christian Europe, although one knows of – yet rarely imitated – persons like the desert hermit St Antony who had "retired to live in a tomb within reach of his village. Then, as he attracted growing numbers of sightseers, he withdrew to a ruined fortress on the edge of the desert".[1033]

The main reason for withdrawing into desolate areas such as cemeteries was well explained by an ascetic upon being asked why he spent his time "among the tombs". He said: "In the cemetery my neighbours are people who do not harm me when I am present and who do not slander me when I am absent" (*ʾuǧāwiru qawman ʾin ḥaḍartu lam yuʾḏūnī wa-ʾin ġibtu lam yaġtābūnī*).[1034] A different explanation was reportedly given by ᶜAlī. When he was asked "Who counts as an ascetic (*zāhid*) in the present world?", he replied "One who does not forget about the cemetery and decay, (...) one who counts himself among the dead".[1035] Another ascetic, the "wise fool" Abū ᶜAlī b. al-Muġīrah, who was likewise asked where he usually lived, answered: "(I live) in a house where the mighty and the lowly are equals". Then he was asked "Where is this house?", and he replied "It is the cemeteries (*al-maqābir*)". They further asked "But don't you feel lonely (there) in the darkness of the night?", and he replied "I imagine the darkness of the burial niche and the solitariness therein, then the darkness of the night seems of little importance to me". They persisted saying, "But what if you see something horrible in the

1032 Marcus: *Funeral and Burial Practices* p. 103.

1033 Lawrence: *Medieval Monasticism* p. 5.

1034 YāfNašr p. 333. With this or a slightly different wording this sentence has been ascribed to various persons, e.g. al-Ḥasan al-Baṣrī (IRaǧAhwāl p. 179) or Buhlūl (IǦawzīṢafwah I p. 645; MunKawākib I p. 568; ᶜĀmKaškūl I p. 7; al-Munayyar: *Tasliyah* p. 58; Basset: *Contes* III p. 343 [episode 205]).

1035 IᶜABarrBahǧah II p. 319.

cemetery?", and he answered "Maybe, but the fear of the hereafter is likely to distract me from the fear of the cemetery".[1036]

This attitude towards cemeteries and solitary places was over the centuries regarded as typical of ascetics and austere mystics. When, therefore, the eighth-century Yemenite scholar al-Yāfiᶜī set out to defend the ascetics and their way of life in his *Našr al-maḥāsin*, including the more extreme and unorthodox forms, he devoted an entire chapter to the question of "why some of them roam the countrysides and deserts and why some of them stay in the cemeteries (*fī l-maqābir*) and amidst the ruins (*fī l-ḫarabāt*)".[1037] The passages cited above provide the most common answers to those questions.

Among ascetics – and even among monks[1038] – the search for solitude could thus either lead to frequent visits to cemeteries or even to staying permanently in burial areas. In the latter case, funerary structures and cemeteries were not only seen as places of temporary retreat, but some people chose to spend their entire lives in graveyards. Paradoxically, the attraction of ascetics to cemeteries and other deserted areas led to the "peopling" of those areas, and instead of becoming places of retreat from the present world and of meditating about the hereafter, they often became mundane places that were anything but deserted. During the centuries of nascent Islam, however, most Muslim cemeteries were not yet truly inhabitated places, and the bulk of information about assiduous cemetery-dwellers stems from the first two centuries H:

> The first-century ascetic Abū Yazīd ar-Rabīᶜ b. Ḫuṯaym aṯ-Ṯawrī, a resident of Kūfah, used to go to the cemeteries when night had fallen and when he was in despair at the people's negligence (*ġaflah*) towards God and their religious duties.[1039] Among the tombs he started shouting: "O ye grave dwellers, we have been and you have been!"[1040] At dawn he returned "and it seemed as if he was resurrected from a grave".[1041] Other early ascetics who reportedly spent time in cemeteries – some of them entire nights and days – were ᶜAṭāʾ as-Sulamī (or as-Salīmī, d. after 140 H),[1042] ᶜUtbah b. Abān,[1043] ᶜAmr b. ᶜUtbah b. Farqad (1st cent. H, Kūfan)[1044] and Abū Bišr Ṣāliḥ al-Murrī (d. 172 H or 176): the latter "remained completely aghast for two or three days after he had seen a cemetery and he would not reason, talk, eat, or drink. He had heard the speech of the dead (*kalām al-mawtā*), he had talked to them and they talked to him".[1045] The Kūfan ascetic Dāʾūd b. Nuṣayr aṭ-Ṭāʾī (d. 162

1036 YāfNašr p. 333 and YāfRawḍ p. 187; IĞawzīṢafwah I p. 646 (with a different wording).

1037 YāfNašr pp. 332ff.

1038 YāfRawḍ pp. 224f.

1039 For the term *ġaflah*, see Gramlich: *Vorbilder* I pp. 634f.

1040 This intends to say, as I understand it, that the living are as good as dead though still alive.

1041 IĞawzīṢafwah II p. 35; MunKawākib I p. 282. The anecdote is also told, slightly abbreviated, in ZamRabīᶜ IV p. 186.

1042 ĠazIḥyāʾ (C) IV p. 413; IĞawzīṢafwah II p. 199; Gramlich: *Vorbilder* I pp. 125-7.

1043 IĞawzīṢafwah II p. 228 (he dug his own grave in his mansion); ŠaᶜrṬab I p. 47.

1044 ANuḤilyah IV p. 158; IĞawzīṢafwah II p. 40 (he rode on his horse at night to the cemeteries and addressed the dead) = MunKawākib I p. 386.

1045 ŠaᶜrṬab I p. 46; MunKawākib I p. 329.

or 165 H)[1046] once strolled around among tombs: "When he heard a woman saying 'O my love! If I only knew which of your cheeks will be the first to decay? The right one or the left?', he lost consciousness".[1047] The early Baṣran traditionist and ascetic Mālik b. Dīnār, who also collected epitaphs and transmitted them, used to mount his donkey on Thursdays and pass the day in cemeteries;[1048] looking at the newly buried, he frequently lost his consciousness and had to be carried home by his friends.[1049] Around the same time, the caliph ᶜUmar b. ᶜAbd al-ᶜAzīz, also renowned for his piety in Sunnite circles, went to visit the cemetery and cried at the sight of the tombs of his ancestors,[1050] as the third caliph ᶜUṯmān had done before him.[1051] As to later centuries, we hear of the Iraqi mystic Abū l-Ḥusayn Aḥmad b. Muḥammad an-Nūrī (d. 295 H, see **20**). He "stayed among ruins and avoided all human settlements (*wa-stawḥaša mina l-ᶜumrān*): for years he did not enter a town except on Fridays"; it was certainly cemeteries which are meant by the term "ruins" (*ḫaribāt*).[1052] Abū l-ᶜAbbās al-Ḫarrār (A. b. Abī Bakr, seventh century H), who lived near the southern Qarāfah of Cairo, often went at night to the graveyard in order to inquire whether the dead were enjoying the grace of God or were subjected to the Chastisement of the Grave.[1053] Many other stories about a number of people living in the second century H – prominent among them Buhlūl[1054] and Mālik b. Dīnār as well as the Baṣrans Ṯābit al-Bunānī (d. after 123 H)[1055] and al-Ḥasan al-Baṣrī – who used to spend time in cemeteries have been collected by Ibn Abī d-Dunyā, Abū Nuᶜaym, Ibn al-Ǧawzī, Ibn al-Ḫarrāṭ, al-Yāfiᶜī, Ibn Raǧab, as-Suyūṭī, al-Munāwī, Richard Gramlich and others.[1056]

The persons mentioned so far were no regular cemetery-dwellers, but rather visited burial sites more or less often, for a number of reasons. However, as said above, there were also people living in cemeteries (who would sometimes hear voices reciting from the nearby tombs at night).[1057] Those persons who permanently settled in cemeteries belong to yet another category than the ascetics mentioned before.

For the permanent occupants, graveyards seem to have provided comfortable space for living, especially those around greater cities like Medina and Cairo, as

1046 For his life and teachings, see Gramlich: *Vorbilder* I pp. 283-324.

1047 IǦawzīṢafwah II p. 78; *cf.* also IQutᶜUyūn II p. 325.

1048 IQutᶜUyūn II p. 327. *Cf.* also MuwMuršid I pp. 15f.; IRaǧAhwāl p. 178; MaᶜbIstiᶜdād p. 27.

1049 IǦawzīṢafwah II p. 169; Gramlich: *Vorbilder* I pp. 76 and 79.

1050 IǦawzīTabṣ I p. 171; IBuḥtUns p. 67. He also pronounced three verses about the moral value of visiting cemeteries, see ŠarŠMaq I p. 176.

1051 ŠarŠMaq I p. 176; ŠaᶜrṬab I p. 19; MunKawākib I pp. 92f.

1052 *Adab al-mulūk* p. 32 = GramlLebensweise p. 71 and Gramlich: *Vorbilder* I p. 382.

1053 IZayKawākib p. 154; MunKawākib II p. 349.

1054 See Marzolph: *Buhlūl* pp. 35 (no. 11), 41 (no. 46), 46f. (nos. 70 and 73), 60-3 (nos. 106 and 108), 65f. (no. 121) and 68 (no. 127); see also **202**.

1055 On him, see ANuḤilyah II pp. 318-33; IǦawzīṢafwah II, pp. 157-9; ŠaᶜrṬab I p. 36; Gramlich: *Vorbilder* I pp. 37-50. Ṯābit dug his own tomb and prayed in it (ZamRabīᶜ IV p. 201; MunKawākib I p. 244), and after his death he was heard reciting the Qurᵓān in his tomb as well as praying (*cf.* above p. 151).

1056 Esp. IADunyāQubūr (A) pp. 51-61 and 93-115; IǦawzīṢafwah I p. 454; YāfRawḍ pp. 187ff.; IRaǧAhwāl pp. 176-85; SuyŠṢudūr pp. 279-89. See also IᶜARabᶜIqd (Ǧ) II p. 153 / (M) III p. 237.

1057 IǦawzīTabṣ I p. 270.

e.g. in the case of Abū Sa^c^īd Kaysān al-Layṯī (d. 100 H) and his son Sa^c^īd (d. 123 H), a transmitter of many reports and pupil of Abū Hurayrah. Both were known as "al-Maqburī", the son "because he settled in the Baqī^c^ cemetery, (...) (or) because of a cemetery near which he had his house".[1058] Likewise, the habits of a man called Sābiq in the western Iranian town Mihriǧān Qaḏḏaf had little to do with the homiletic or religious significance of cemeteries. He was "an insane person, bereft of reason and with brutish manners, who used to dwell in ruins, thickets and cemeteries",[1059] yet notwithstanding his strange appearance and disturbed personality he was approached by many people for his wise sayings and pious utterings. This accords with the common reverence shown in Islamic culture towards the *maǧnūn*, the "wise fool", or the *maǧḏūb*, the "possessed", or rather the "lunatic by the grace of God", the best expression, however, being the German *Gottesnarr* ("divine fool") as used by Richard Gramlich.

By far the most populated cemetery in pre-modern Islamic history (and until today) is the Cairene Qarāfah cemetery. The social life of this burial ground began as early as the Fatimid period[1060] when "the people were eager to dwell there since they preferred that place to living in town".[1061] The later adoption of this site as a place for learning and study (see above p. 145) and as a common dwelling-place during the Mamluk period further enhanced that situation; canals were dug across the Qarāfah area and the population increased steadily.[1062]

During the Mamluk period and beyond, a number of people became known for having settled in the Qarāfah, e.g. Šihāb ad-Dīn Aḥmad b. Muḥammad al-Miṣrī Ibn an-Nāṣiḥ, nazīl al-Qarāfah, "the Qarāfah-dweller", (d. 804 H)[1063] or the Malikite jurist Badr ad-Dīn Muḥammad b. Yaḥyā al-Qarāfī, i.e. "the Qarāfah-man" (d. 1008 H);[1064] others had some other connection with that graveyard, such as ^c^Uṯmān Ibn Ḫaṭīb al-Qarāfah (d. after 760 H).[1065] Arguably the most famous bearer of the nisbah "al-Qarāfī" did not himself stem from or live in the cemetery: Šihāb ad-Dīn al-Qarāfī (A. b. Idrīs, d. Cairo 682 or 684 H), author of the *Ḏaḫīrah* (a compendium of Malikite law), took his *nisbah* from the Qarāfah yet he had his home elsewhere.[1066] Other interesting cases are those of Abū ^c^Alī at-Takrūrī (d. 871 H) who only in old age came to live in the Qarāfah where he cared for the tombs,[1067] and of the mystic Nūr ad-Dīn aš-Šūnī (d. 944 H). The latter stayed for long years first in the

1058 MālRiyāḍ I p. 123; DabMa^c^ālim I p. 178; NZ I p. 290; SaḫTuḥfLaṭ I p. 403. For the related nisbah "al-Maqābirī", see IAYaṬab I p. 387.

1059 IĞawzīṢafwah II p. 277; MunKawākib I p. 298.

1060 *Cf.* Lev: *Saladin* pp. 123f. and Taylor: *Vicinity of the Righteous* pp. 18-20.

1061 IlyāsBad I p. 476.

1062 *Cf.* MaqrḪiṭaṭ II p. 445 and MaqrSulūk I p. 174; IlyāsBad I p. 376; for the Qarāfah and its place in urban geography, see Taylor: *Vicinity of the Righteous* pp. 56-61. A short description of the Qarāfah from the year 1762 CE can be found in Niebuhr: *Reisebeschreibung* p. 130.

1063 ŠḎ VII p. 42.

1064 MuḥḪul IV pp. 258-62; ḪafRayḥ pp. 259f.; GALS II p. 436; ZA VII p. 141.

1065 DK II p. 461.

1066 This is explicitly said so in ITaġrManh I p. 232, in contrast with what we read in EI^2 IX p. 435 that "he grew up in the Qarafah"; *cf.* also ZA I pp. 94f.

1067 SaḫTuḥfAḥbāb p. 156.

mausoleum (*turbah*) of sultan Barqūq, then in the mausoleum of Ṭūmānbāy in the northern Qarāfah; he only came to live in the city and to marry there when he was ninety.[1068]

Finally, it must be remarked that cemeteries and mausolea were not always chosen as dwelling-places or as sites to visit voluntarily, but could be also approached in cases of forced retreat. As such they protected people in the case of war or gave shelter to the oppressed. Burial sites in general also functioned as a refuge, a practice attested for a number of different regions throughout the Islamic lands, mainly Morocco, Egypt, Sudan and Iran.[1069]

This practice left its traces also in the realm of poetry, there being at least two cases of renowned poets who took refuge at tombs. The first instance is known of al-Kumayt b. Zayd (Kūfah *c.*60 – 126 H or after) who sought protection (*ǧwr* X) at the tomb of Muᶜāwiyah b. Yazīd (d. 64 H) when he was in conflict with the Umayyad caliph Hišām (r. 105–25 H) because he had been told that Hišām used to visit Muᶜāwiyah's tomb once a week, always on the same day. So al-Kumayt, in order to gain the caliph's pardon, pitched his tent (*ḍrb* I *al-binā*ᵓ) on that very day at the tomb of Muᶜāwiyah. Hišām arrived and when his eye fell on al-Kumayt's tent he ordered him to be killed. Only the intercession of Hišām's son Maslamah could prevent this as he told his father "that behaving treacherously towards the dead (*ᵓiḫfār al-ᵓamwāt*) is a shame for the living", and Hišām "was so much distressed by that matter that he finally offered protection to al-Kumayt".[1070]

A second instance we know of is the story of Ḥammād ᶜAǧrad (a contemporary of Baššār b. Burd, *cf.* below p. 321) who had offended the Abbasid emir of Baṣrah, Muḥammad b. Sulaymān al-Hāšimī (d. 173 H), in one of his poems, with the result that the latter openly called for revenge and Ḥammād had to flee from Baṣrah. He turned to the tomb of the emir's father Abū Ayyūb Sulaymān b. ᶜAlī, in order to seek refuge, and hence composed the following lines (*ḫafīf*):

غَيْرَ أَنِّي جَعَلْتُ قَبْرَ أَبِي أَيُّـ * ـوبَ لِي مِنْ حَوَادِثِ الدَّهْرِ جَارَا
وَحَقِيقٌ لِمَنْ يُجَاوِرُ ذَاكَ الْـ * ـقَبْرَ أَنْ يَأْمَنَ الرَّدَى وَالعِثَارَا
لَمْ أَجِدْ لِي مِنَ الأَنَامِ مُجِيراً * فَاسْتَجَرْتُ القُبُورَ وَالأَحْجَارَا

2 First hemistich: *wa-ḥarīyun mani staǧāra bi-ḏāka l-* (*Aġānī*). – **3** *mina l-ᵓanāmi*: *mina l-ᶜibādi* (*Aġānī*); *al-qubūra*: *at-turāba* (*Aġānī*).

1068 ŠaᶜrṬab II p. 171. A number of mystics who are somehow connected to the Qarāfah are also treated in the first chapter of Shoshan: *Popular culture*; for *maǧḏūb*-mystics of the tenth century H who regularly stayed in the Qarāfah, see ŠaᶜrṬab II pp. 144f.

1069 Dermenghem: *Culte des saints* pp. 168f.; Kriss: *Volksglaube* I p. 132; Gramlich: *Wunder* pp. 235f.; Gronke: *Derwische* p. 113; Zepter: *Friedhöfe* p. 21; Grandin: *Nord-Soudan oriental* p. 89. In Persia, venerated shrines functioning as a refuge are known as *bast*, see EI² I p. 1088 (*s.v.*). For this tradition in Christian Europe, see Ariès: *Western Attitudes* pp. 23f.

1070 *Aġānī* XVII p. 19. Another story of somebody putting himself under the protection of the Umayyad caliph ᶜAbd al-Malik by taking refuge at the tomb of his father Marwān (d. 65 H) is told in TMD IX p. 197.

"Except that I made the tomb of Abū Ay- * yūb become my neighbour (protecting me) from the accidents of fate
– And anyone staying in the neighbourhood (i.e. under the protection) of that * tomb truly deserves to be safe from destruction and perdition! –,
I did not find for myself among mankind a protector, * thus I sought protection with the tombs and the stones".[1071]

I should like to add that also the tomb of the poet Farazdaq's (d. *c.*112 H) father Ġālib b. Ṣaʿṣaʿah was a place for those seeking protection and asylum: whosoever sought refuge and protection (*ǧwr* X) at that tomb was helped and protected by Farazdaq.[1072] In contrast, in at least one case a burial site was chosen for the execution of capital punishment.[1073]

5. *Concluding remark, concerning the history of Islamic thought*

What then, about the significance of the material collected in this chapter for the history of Islamic thought? Different aspects of the grave and the merits of visiting it stand in contrast with each other, different discourses yield contradictory claims about the nature of death and the "life" of the dead in the hereafter; there is no single master narrative providing a common frame. Yet, although they are alternative ways of conceptualisation, these different discourses clearly complement each other if seen in historical perspective. It would therefore be unwise to point to certain aspects or certain discourses in order to single them out as the "truly Islamic" ones and thus the only representative ways of conceptualisation. Rather, it is exactly the variety of concepts and approaches in pre-modern Islamic culture which intrigues the observer, especially if he considers that this variety of contrasting concepts and claims never led to a disruption of that culture but seems, paradoxically, to have been the very reason for its ultimate unity.

The same holds true for the conflict between theory and practice. Annemarie Schimmel wrote that cemeteries as such do not play an important role in Islam, because the Prophet is said to have disapproved of the vistation of tombs,[1074] the words "as such" being meant to indicate that a certain conflict between theory and practice did exist and was never eventually resolved. Yet again, this is not in itself

1071 Quoted in IMuʿtṬab p. 67 and *Aġānī* XIV p. 377. In the version of IMuʿtṬab, the sequence of the verses is 3-1-2. However, also the present sequence, taken from the *Aġānī*, does not seem the best solution. I rather prefer the sequence 1-3-2. More poems on this event are found in *Aġānī* XIV pp. 378f.

1072 See MubKāmil (C) II pp. 86-8.

1073 The bandits who attacked and killed the philosopher al-Fārābī somewhere in Syria were crucified at his tomb, see ẒāhirḤukamāʾ p. 34.

1074 Schimmel: *Träume* p. 213 ("Friedhöfe spielen im Islam an sich keine wichtige Rolle, denn der Prophet soll Grabesbesuche mißbilligt haben").

surprising, but the truly astonishing fact is that this continuous conflict of approaches, concepts and practices was in general accepted and, in its entirety, considered an integral part of Islamic culture. The incoherences of concepts on the lower levels ultimately guaranteed, when seen as constituent parts of the wider frame of Islamic culture, the coherence and overall integrity on the higher level.

To my mind, we are dealing here with an attitude very similar to Judaism, where "there is no conflict of authority in [the] conflict of interpretations, because it is the whole dialogue which is authoritative, not just the isolated interpretations that emerge from it".[1075] In Judaism as well as in Islam, the individual approaches and interpretations were open to re-interpretation, because "multiple meanings coexist; it is a way of thinking in which the example is not the mere particularization of a concept but in which the example holds together a multiplicity of meanings".[1076] Put simply, one did not try, in Islamic culture, to reduce the natural multiplicity of meanings and the constant ambiguities of the present world and the hereafter to a uniform and outwardly coherent picture, devoid of inner conflicts and uncertainties: life and death, the relations between the present world and the afterworld are not things easily understood and reduced to simple ideas. Both theory and practice as related to the visitation of tombs and cemeteries provide a good example of what this attitude amounted to in the wider Islamic cultural framework during the pre-modern period.

1075 Gerald L. Bruns: *Midrash and Allegory: The Beginnings of Scriptural Interpretation*, in: Robert Alter/Frank Kermode (eds.): *The Literary Guide to the Bible*, London 1987, pp. 625-46, here: p. 632.

1076 Emmanuel Levinas: *Nine Talmudic Readings*, tr. Annette Aronowicz, Bloomington 1994 (= *Quatre lectures talmudiques*, Paris ^{1}1968 and *Du sacré au saint: cinq nouvelles lectures talmudiques*, ^{1}1977), p. 60.

2 “You Shall not Build upon the Tomb nor Write upon it!” *Funerary Monuments and Epitaphs in Islamic Theory and Practice*

1. *Introduction*

Together with epitaphs, funerary structures of all sorts – tombstones, cenotaphs, mausolea – represent in many cases the only lasting visible vestiges of a person’s former existence in this world. Therefore, if one carries out research in the vast field of Arabic epitaphs and their setting, one important question that comes to mind, after having tackled those of accessability and significance of the tombs and cemeteries (Chapter 1), regards the place of funerary inscriptions both within the larger framework of the Islamic culture in general and as part of the Islamic concepts of death, burial and the mortuary cult in particular.

1.1. General remarks

The aspect which has been singled out in this chapter concerns the (mainly pre-modern) Islamic attitudes towards tombs, tomb-mosques, tombstones and epitaphs. The continuous interest in this subject, which we witness in many different Islamic discourses and above all in the legal discourse, led the learned not only to the tricky discussion of how Muslim tombs should be fashioned and marked at all, but also what role tomb-markers and epitaphs fulfil in doing so. Moreover, from what has been said so far it is clear that funerary inscriptions are often an integral part of larger funerary structures (cenotaphs, mausolea, tomb-mosques, etc.) and cannot be dealt with independently of these structures.

The erection of funerary constructions, ranging from simple tombstones and cenotaphs to domed mausolea and larger funerary complexes, has never ceased to be severely criticised by many Sunnite scholars and traditionists,[1] and it is thus the Sunnite views which the following pages discuss, though not exclusively. The same goes, albeit to a lesser degree, for epitaphs as such. Strangely enough, and in marked contrast to what happened with regard to the practice of visiting tombs and cem-

1 *Cf.* EI^2 VI pp. 651ff. For a typical contemporary perspective, see Mabrūk: *Bidaʿ*.

eteries, these questions never prompted the pre-modern Muslim scholars to compose monographs dealing with that issue nor did they ever generate a literary sub-genre devoted to it. The only pre-modern monographic treatment I know of, a treatise of a mere 14 pages in modern print, was written by the Zaydite scholar aš-Šawkānī (d. 1250 H), entitled "Delight of the Hearts: The Prohibition of Erecting Tombs" (*Šarḥ aṣ-ṣudūr fī taḥrīm rafʿ al-qubūr*, see bibliography); yet the achievement of this man must be seen to stand at the very brink of an indigenous Islamic modernity, and thus his writing does not really provide an exception to the rule that there were no pre-modern treatises on the subject but rather confirms it. Admittedly, many pre-modern works dealing with the visitation of tombs and cemeteries, and even a number of eschatological and consolation books, devote some space to the question of the outer shapes of tombs and also supply useful material in this regard. However, this question is then of secondary importance (if not intrusive to the matter as a whole) and clearly seen as dependent on or connected to other, more significant issues.

Anyone familiar with burial sites in Islamic countries is aware of the fact that the restrictions put forward by Muslim scholars over the centuries have had little impact on practice: "In the presence of the considerable number of richly decorated tombs found in all Muslim countries, it must be admitted that there are few areas where the divorce between theory and practice was so marked".[2] In another pointed remark, referring to larger funerary monuments, it has been said that in this case "the religious law was both constantly violated and constantly venerated".[3]

1.2. Aspects of theory and practice

In the following pages those aspects will be analysed which are connected to the various ways of designing the surface of a tomb, marking it as such or distinguishing it from others, e.g. by applying signs of identification or inscriptions. That is, the topics dealt with in the following concern the appearance and shape of the surface or enclosure of tombs (section 2), the construction of cenotaphs and larger funerary monuments upon or around graves (section 3) and finally, and most importantly in our context, the application of tomb-markers, the setting up of tombstones and the use and function of epitaphs (section 4).

This chapter mainly sets out topics that might be said to fall under the general heading of "theory", but it also contains much more information relevant to practice.[4] Both theory and practice are inseparable, because theory might (or might not) react to practice and practice may (or may not) follow theory. Therefore, aside from the emphasis on theory, on which our sources offer plenty of material, much information pertaining to practice(s) will be presented in this chapter. Still, practice as known through archaeological evidence and preserved monuments does not constitute the

2 EI² IV p. 355 (Y. Linant de Bellefonds).

3 Kessler: *Funerary Architecture* p. 267.

4 For a detailed view of what "theory" and "practice" mean in this context, see above pp. 2f.

main topic in the following pages as there is already a quantity of secondary literature dealing with the material vestiges of Islamic funerary architecture.

Practice and popular customs were often invoked by the Muslim scholars either to support a given opinion (and thus assenting to it) or to refute it. In the majority of cases, however, they tended to stress theoretically established rulings against the deviations in practice, viz. the so-called "blameworthy innovations" (*bidaᶜ*). The memorable dictum by Ibn Masᶜūd – or some other early authority; the sources do not agree – "What is considered agreeable (*or* good: *ḥasan*) by Muslims, is considered so by God"[5] was neither meant nor understood to license all kinds of practice as they developed over the centuries. Rather, it was generally understood to refer only to the points agreed upon by the Muslim scholarly community (*al-ʾiǧmāᶜ*), a rare event in both theory and practice.[6]

2. *The shape and outward appearance of the tomb*

In theory, the outer features of the Islamic tomb in its simplest form as sanctioned by the law, according to the most widely-accepted interpretations, consist of little else but a small heap of pebbles or earth, if at all. The question most debated among scholars in this context hinges on whether graves should be flat in order not to rise over the surrounding terrain or whether a certain elevation of the tomb, the exact height of which also disputed, was permissible.

The first possibility was known as *tasṭīḥ* or *taswiyat al-qabr* ("flattening" or "levelling the grave"), while the second was called *tasnīm al-qabr* or, more rarely, *rafᶜ al-qabr* ("mounting" or "raising the grave").[7] In practice, this theoretical debate boiled down to the question of whether graves should be left without a tumulus (or mound) that rises noticeably above ground level or whether they should be marked by a mound or (walled) enclosure, a question of principle which also bears upon the use of cenotaphs and other, still higher funerary structures and monuments.

2.1. Pre-Islamic customs

Due to the lack of sources it cannot be resolved whether graves covered by mounds were in general characteristic of pre-Islamic Arabian usage though it seems that

5 MuwMuršid I p. 39; MF XXXIII p. 250.

6 *Cf.* IᶜASalāmFat p. 29.

7 Or rather, making them appear "like the hump of the camel", *cf.* KirmŠBuḫ VII p. 160; ŠirwḤāš III p. 173; HarMirqātMaf IV p. 68; MF XXXII p. 248; Grütter: *Bestattungsbräuche* p. 170. The term *rafᶜ* was in later times generally understood to mean the construction of larger funerary structures upon or around the grave, e.g. a mausoleum.

they were.[8] A line by the famous *Muʿallaqah*-poet Ṭarafah b. al-ʿAbd, already referred to by a number of modern scholars,[9] may indicate this (*ṭawīl*):

تَرَى جُثْوَتَيْنِ مِن تُرَابٍ عَلَيْهِمَا * صَفَائِحُ صُمٌّ مِنْ صَفِيحٍ مُنَضَّدِ

"You see two tumuli of earth upon which there are * layers (*or* slabs) of massive stone,[10] regularly and compactly set against each other".[11]

The word used by Ṭarafah for "tumulus" or "mound", *ǧuṯwah* (pl. *ǧuṯan*), frequently recurs in later works[12] and was also used to describe the "tombs of the martyrs" (*qubūr aš-šuhadāʾ*) as well as the Prophet's sepulchre in Medina.[13]

Likewise of interest for the shape of pre-Islamic burial sites is a verse, similar to that of Ṭarafah, by the Christian poet Abū Zubayd Ḥarmalah b. al-Munḏir aṭ-Ṭāʾī (d. Raqqah *c.*61 H), who was born towards the end of the sixth century CE (*ḫafīf*):

فِي ضَرِيحٍ عَلَيْهِ عِبْءٌ ثَقِيلٌ * مِنْ تُرَابٍ وَجَنْدَلٍ مَنْضُودِ

"In a tomb upon which there is a heavy load * of earth and stones compactly set".[14]

The panegyrist of the Prophet, Ḥassān b. Ṯābit, describes in a mourning poem the tomb of Ḥamzah b. ʿAbd al-Muṭṭālib (*kāmil*):

أَشْكُو إِلَيْكَ وَفَوْقَكَ الـ * ـتُّرْبُ الْمُكَوَّرُ وَالصَفَائِحْ
مِنْ جَنْدَلٍ نُلْقِيهِ فَوْ * قَكَ أَذْ أَجَادَ الضَّرْحَ ضَارِحْ
فِى وَاسِعٍ يَحْشُونَهُ * بِالتُّرْبِ سَوَّتْهُ الْمَمَاسِحْ

"I complain to you while stratified (?) earth * and layers of stone cover you, of
The stones we put above * you, when the gravedigger dug the grave-pit well
In a wide space, which they filled * with earth carefully smoothed (lit. levelled)".[15]

8 For funerary structures among the pre-Islamic Arabs in general, see Wellhausen: *Reste* p. 180; Goldziher: *Culte des ancêtres* pp. 161ff.; Abdesselem: *Thème de la mort* pp. 89-92; Smith/Haddad: *Islamic Understanding of Death* pp. 149-51; Homerin: *Death and Afterlife*; Leisten: *Attitudes* pp. 13f. and pp. 19f., n. 24; Leisten: *Architektur für Tote* pp. 5f.; Hoyland: *Arabia* pp. 174f.

9 CIA Égypte II p. 64 note 2; Abdesselem: *Thème de la mort* p. 91; Rāġib: *Structure de la tombe* p. 401 note 75.

10 For the term *ṣafāʾiḥ*, see p. 435, n. 409.

11 Line 64 of his *Muʿallaqah*, see ṬarafDīwān (B) p. 48 / (P) p. ٣١; AnbŠQaṣ p. 200; ZawzŠMuʿall p. 53 = al-Ḥašrūm: *Ġurbah* p. 299. The expression *ṣafāʾiḥu ṣummun* also appears in a poem that addresses the tomb of a stranger (*yā-ṣāḥiba l-qabri l-ġarībi* ...) in SarrāǧMaṣ II p. 140.

12 For the term, see MarzḤam II pp. 823f. and below p. 180.

13 SamWafāʾ II p. 557; see also below p. 192.

14 AḫfIḫt p. 520; ŠayŠuʿarāʾNaṣr p. 88.

15 IHišSīrah III p. 162 = IHišLife p. 418 = MaġrSīrah II p. 655 = ŠāmīSubul IV p. 236 = ḤassānDīwān I p. 452 (no. 278, vv. 36-8).

Moreover, the seventh-century Andalusian scholar al-Qurṭubī, author of the *Taḏkirah*, explicitly states that "it is forbidden to raise the mound of the tomb too much, for that is what the Arabs during the *ǧāhilīyah* used to do. They heightened the mounds considerably and erected constructions upon the graves, both as a sign of honour and as glorification". Though al-Qurṭubī, given his remoteness in time and space, might seem a dubious authority on pre-Islamic matters, he nevertheless quotes five lines of poetry (without indicating thc author) that support his statement.[16] As becomes clear from a passage in al-Maqrīzī's *Ḫiṭaṭ*, these verses were composed by the Andalusian poet Yaḥyā b. Ḥakam al-Ġazāl (156–250 H).[17] They thus reflect one possible attitude towards burial monuments in the later formative period of Islam, which was still under the spell of ancient pre-Islamic concepts; the first two lines go (*wāfir*):

أَرَى أَهْلَ القُصُورِ إذا أُمِيتُوا * بَنَوْا فَوْقَ المَقَابِرِ بِالصُّخُورِ
أَبَوا إلاَّ مُبَـاهَاةً وَفَـخْراً * عَلَى الفُقَرَاءِ حَتَّى فِي القُبُـورِ

1: *al-quṣūri ʾiḏā ʾumītū*: *aṯ-ṯarāʾi ʾiḏā tuwuffū* (MaqrḪiṭaṭ); *fawqa*: *tilka* (MaqrḪiṭaṭ). – 2: *mubāhātan*: *al-mubāhāta* (QurtTaḏk, does not fit the metre); *wa-faḫran*: *wa-tīhan* (MaqrḪiṭaṭ).

"I see that the lords[18] of the palaces, when they are made to perish, * build upon the burial sites with solid stones.
Thus they could not refrain from boasting with vainglory and pride * towards the poor, even in their tombs".[19]

If, on the contrary, there was no difference between the graves of the rich and the poor, one took this as a sign of true nobility. Thus ʿAbd Allāh b. az-Zibaʿrā (d. after 13 H) proudly said in a poem which he composed after the battle of Uḥud (*ramal*):

وَالعَطِيَّاتُ خِسَاسٌ بَيْنَهُمْ * وَسَوَاءٌ قَبْرُ مُثْرٍ وَمُقِلْ

"Gifts are mean among them, * and equal are the graves of the rich and the poor".[20]

As is known, the Islamic debate concerning funeral rites and burial sites often stresses the fact that Muslims should not follow the customs of either Jews, Christians or pre-Islamic Arabs (the polytheists). A good example for that attitude would be that the construction of tomb-mosques was discouraged by the Prophet by pointing to Jewish and Christian usage and declaring it to be in conflict with the divine law (see below p. 240). Another example is found in the following Tradition: "The Prophet used not to sit down until the body was deposed in the burial niche (*laḥd*),

16 QurṭTaḏk p. 86.

17 For him, see IDiḥMuṭrib pp. 133-51; ISaʿīdMuġrib II pp. 57f.; ḌabbīBuġ pp. 485f.; ZA VIII p. 143.

18 Lit. "inhabitants".

19 QurṭTaḏk p. 86; MaqrḪiṭaṭ II p. 380. For the wordplay on *quṣūr* / *qubūr*, see below pp. 397ff.

20 IHišSīrah III p. 143 = IHišLife p. 408 = MaġrSīrah II p. 642; anonymously cited in TMD X p. 265 (var. *ḫisāsun*: *ḫišāšun*).

but remained standing at the head of the grave together with his companions. A Jew said, 'That is how we do it (when we bury) our dead'. So the Prophet sat down and told his companions, 'Do not behave like the Jews!'"[21] Finally, we also know of the Prophet's instruction to not slaughter camels at graves[22] – a common pre-Islamic Arab custom called *al-ʿaqr* – nor to bewail the dead in public because "this conforms to the usage in pre-Islamic times" (*hāḏā min ʿamali l-ǧāhilīyah*, or in another version: *min ʾamri l-ǧāhilīyah*).[23]

According to a widespread belief, bewailing the deceased (*nawḥ*, *niyāḥah*) and weeping for the dead (*al-bukāʾ*) resulted in harm coming to them and in increasing their Chastisement,[24] but also the wailing woman (*nāʾiḥah* or *nawwāḥah*, *naddābāt*) was harming herself, following an utterance of the Prophet: "The wailing woman who does not repent before her death will be resurrected on the Last Day, wearing a garment of tar and a cuirass of scabies (*ǧarab*)".[25] Yet notwithstanding this and other discouraging verdicts by the Prophet, wailing women frequently attended Islamic funerals. In Abbasid Baghdad, they were often seen in court circles and formed part of the accepted funeral customs;[26] in the Arabic mourning poetry of that period, *nawḥ* is commonly mentioned or alluded to, and often the wailing women are addressed directly, e.g. in a line by Muḥammad b. Abī ʿUyaynah (*fl.* c.150 H) mourning his brother Dāʾūd (*wāfir*): *ʾa-nāʾiḥata l-ḥimāmi*[27] *qifī fa-nūḥī * ʿalā Dāʾūda rahnan fī ḍarīḥī*, "O mourner of the mortal fate, stop and bewail * Dāʾūd as he lies as a pledge in his tomb".[28] The usage of *nawḥ* (also known as *naʿy*), utterly un-Islamic as it was from an orthodox Sunnite point of view, never disappeared from funeral customs and in Arabic mourning poetry until the Ottoman period; clearly, we are dealing here with conflicting discourses and practices which were preserved side by side in the various realms of Arabo-Islamic culture (*cf.* above pp. 114f.). Again and again, people tried to prevent others from bewailing them after their death, as for example

21 INuǧBaḥr II p. 206; ŠāmīSubul VIII p. 365; HarMirqātMaf IV pp. 62f. *Cf.* Grütter: *Bestattungsbräuche* pp. 176f.

22 *Cf.* ManbTasl (C) pp. 119-21 / (M) pp. 116-8; Hoyland: *Arabia* p. 175.

23 IMāǧah I p. 504; NawŠMuslim VI p. 235; MuwMuršid I p. 62; MundTarġīb IV pp. 350f.; IQayZād I p. 528; *Wāfī* XI p. 191. *Cf.* also IQudMuġnī II p. 571 and IQudʿUmdah p. 122; QurṭTaḏk p. 17; NuwIlmām IV p. 202; IḤaǧAḥwāl pp. 34f. and 58-60; KU 42434 (XV p. 612); HarMirqātMaf IV pp. 89f.

24 See *Muwaṭṭaʾ* I p. 234 (*ǧanāʾiz* 12) = SuyTanwīr p. 243; IḤanbMusnad I pp. 231, 262, 280f. etc., VIII pp. 43, 48f.; FB VII p. 382 (*maġāzī* 8), *cf.* also FB III pp. 206 (*ǧanāʾiz* 33) and 227 (*ǧanāʾiz* 45); NawŠMuslim VI pp. 228-35; IḪarrāṭʿĀqibah pp. 123ff.; DaylFird II p. 380; MundTarġīb IV p. 348; MaqdʿUddah pp. 122f.; INāṣBard (A) p. 58 / (C) p. 54 = SuyBard pp. 138f.; IḤaǧAḥwāl p. 60; SuyŠṢudūr pp. 397-400; KU 42413ff. (XV pp. 608ff.); Smith/Haddad: *Islamic Understanding of Death* pp. 59f. For the custom of *nawḥ* (in practice and as reflected in literature), see ManbTasl (C) pp. 50ff. / (M) pp. 50ff.; Lane: *Manners and Customs* p. 508; Goldziher: *Trauerpoesie*, esp. section III; Wensinck: *Weinen* pp. 31f.; Abdesselem: *Thème de la mort* pp. 97ff.; Grütter: *Bestattungsbräuche* pp. 153f.; Anawati: *Mort en Islam* pp. 195f.; Gilʿadi: *Consolation Treatise* p. 377; Zepter: *Friedhöfe* pp. 46f.; Reintjens-Anwari: *Tod aus islamischer Sicht* pp. 185-90; Davidson: *Lamentations*; Mokri: *Pleureuses professionnelles*.

25 NawŠMuslim VI pp. 235f. (*ǧanāʾiz* 29); RāġibMuḥāḍ IV p. 506; TurkLumaʿ I p. 216; NuwIlmām VI p. 63; KU 42440 (XV p. 613); HarMirqātMaf IV p. 89; al-Munayyar: *Tasliyah* p. 34. Some versions have "a cuirass of sulphur"; see also the sources listed in the preceding note.

26 See e.g. *Aġānī* VII p. 306.

27 The edition has *al-ḥamāmi*.

28 *Aġānī* XX p. 102.

the Prophet's companion Qays b. ᶜĀṣim who instructed in his last wish that his children were not to bewail him, thus following the example of the Prophet.[29] In a sixth-century treatise on public order it is said that the market inspector (*muḥtasib*) "must oversee the funeral ceremonies and the graveyards and if he hears any woman wailing or lamenting he should chastise and prevent her, because lamenting is unlawful".[30] This notwithstanding, wailing women at funerals seem to have been so common that a seventh-century scholar from Isnā (Upper Egypt) felt obliged to stipulate in his testament that no such women should appear at his burial,[31] and centuries before that ᶜAmr b. al-ᶜĀṣ had uttered the same wish before his death;[32] others decreed that their body should be taken to the tomb accompanied by tambourines and flutes, i.e. without signs of lamentation.[33] In Shiite devotion, the litanies and poems mourning the fate of the martyr Imams, often solemnly delivered at their tombs and including the dirges of the djinns,[34] are known as *nawḥāt*, "lamentation dirges".[35] The Shiites share the Sunnite view that excessive mourning – such as striking or scratching oneself, cutting off one's hair and loud wailing – is forbidden, though tearing apart of clothes is allowed in the case of one's father or brother dying.[36]

Still, it seems questionable to look for a similar motive – that is, that the Muslims should not follow the customs of either Jews, Christians or pre-Islamic Arabs – behind the Islamic precept to level the graves; at least the sources at our disposal do not suggest that. Mounds and raised funerary structures were often rejected either because their aesthetic function as embellishment (*zīnah*) was seen unsuitable for funeral sites, or because they were considered signs of *superbia* or vainglory (*mubāhāh*) in view of human mortality and the omnipotence of God.[37]

Robert Hillenbrand writes in that context that the "levelling of the tombs (...) symbolised the equality of all believers in death as in life".[38] This concept (well-known from the Christian tradition) only rarely appears in this guise in the Islamic sources when discussing questions of burial and the shape of the tomb, although most Muslim scholars would have certainly agreed. There are some known (albeit not universally acknowledged) Traditions expressing that concept, e.g. the following: "Justice in the hereafter begins with the tombs, where the noble is not distinguished from the lowly" (*ʾawwalu ᶜadli l-ʾāḫirati l-qubūru lā yuᶜrafu šarīfun min waḍīᶜin*),[39] a thought recurring in poetry as *lam yuᶜrafi l-mawlā mina l-ᶜabdi*, "(in the grave)

29 ISaᶜdṬab VII p. 37; IḤağIṣābah III p. 253.

30 ŠayzḤisba p. 127.

31 *Wāfī* XIX p. 70. *Cf.* also Goitein: *Mediterranean Society* V p. 163.

32 ŠīrŠadd p. 8. The absence of the testamentary stipulation not to have wailing-women present at one's funeral amounted, according to some jurists, to having stipulated that wailing-women *should* accompany the funeral, see NawFat p. 51.

33 DK IV p. 108; MunKawākib III p. 93.

34 See IQūlKāmil p. 938.

35 *Cf.* Wensinck: *Weinen* p. 30; Pinault: *Zaynab bint ᶜAlī*, esp. pp. 83-93.

36 ṬūsīMabsūṭ I p. 189.

37 *Cf.* HaytFatFiqh II p. 16.

38 Hillenbrand: *Islamic Architecture* p. 253. *Cf.* also Wagner: *Dichtung* II pp. 126f.

39 DaylFird I p. 38.

the patron cannot be distinguished from the servant",[40] or as *fa-ʾinna l-mawta ʾātin ʿalā l-maḫdūmi minnā wa-l-ḫadīmi*, "truly, death comes upon those who are served among us and those who serve".[41] In the same vein, Ibn al-Ǧawzī has the "wise fool" Abū ʿAlī say about the cemetery: "This is the abode where the mighty and the lowly are equals" (*dārun yastawī fīhā l-ʿazīzu wa-ḏ-ḏalīl*).[42]

Similar are the famous verses by the Baṣran ascetic Mālik b. Dīnār (*mutaqārib*):

أَتَيْتُ القُبُورَ فَنَادَيْتُهَا * فَأَيْنَ المُعَظَّمُ وَالمُحْتَقَرْ

وَأَيْنَ المُدِلُّ بِسُلْطَانِهِ * وَأَيْنَ العَزِيزُ إِذَا مَا افْتَخَرْ

"I went to the tombs and called to them: * 'Now where lies the glorious and where the despised?
Where the one who boasted his power * and where the mighty with his (haughty) pride?'"[43]

In an epitaph from Almería (undated) we read towards the end of the text: *bi-dārin yusāwī l-ʿabdu fīhā maʿa l-ḥurri*,[44] "in an abode (*or* house) in which the servant is an equal to the free man", and similar lines are known from epitaphs cited in literary sources. Epitaph **218** contains a poem of which the last line goes: "Destruction (i.e. death) has made us all equal, for it made us settle at a place * where there is no difference between the served and the servant".

It is interesting to point out in this regard that the Muslim legal scholars – in contrast with the poets – almost never took recourse to theological arguments;[45] also the prohibition to erect larger funerary structures and mausolea, voiced in Tradition, was never part of the "principles of the faith" (*uṣūl ad-dīn*) as is claimed by Thomas Leisten.[46] Rather, the Muslim jurists refused to enter what they saw as the domain of theology viz. *kalām* (dialectical theology), such as Ibn Nuǧaym (d. 970 H), who stopped short of following the argument concerning the Interrogation of the deceased in his tomb by saying: "This problem (*masʾalah*) is not a legal one (*fiqhīyah*), but rather a theological one (*kalāmīyah*). Therefore, we will not deal with it".[47] This distinction between the spheres of law and theology comes close to what some Christian scholars put forward in scholastic literature,[48] though many others argued on theological grounds, a fact unparalleled in pre-modern Islam, against the

40 Cited anonymously in IʿABarrBahǧah II p. 340.

41 Quoted in ṢafAʿyān II p. 117.

42 IǦawzīṢafwah I p. 646.

43 Quoted in IQutʿUyūn II p. 326 (with the variants *fa-nādaytuhā fa-*: *fa-nādaytuhunna* and *al-ʿazīzu*: *al-muzakkā*); ĠazIḥyāʾ (B) IV p. 487; IḪarrāṭʿĀqibah p. 114 (var. *mudillu*: *muḏillu*); ŠarŠMaq I p. 176; TurkLumaʿ I pp. 221f.; ḤurRawḍ p. 31; al-Qināwī: *Fatḥ ar-raḥīm* p. 177; ŠayMaǧānī IV pp. 27f. Perhaps *mudillu* has to be read here as *muḏillu*, which also would yield a good sense.

44 Arabic Inscriptions (Caskel) XIII = Inscripciones Almería 12.

45 *Cf.* also Leisten: *Attitudes* pp. 14f.

46 Leisten: *Architektur für Tote* p. 8.

47 INuǧBaḥr II p. 211.

48 *Cf.* Le Goff: *Naissance du Purgatoire* p. 235.

construction of sumptuous mausolea.[49] In general, the pervasiveness of dogmatic and, for that matter, theological arguments in Christendom sets it well apart from the Islamic approach,[50] and the question of funeral customs and burial structures is a good case in point.

2.2. Reports from the Prophet

The arguments put forward in legal treatises rely heavily on Traditions which report sayings or actions of the Prophet, his nearest kin or companions.

However, Traditions about the Prophet's sayings concerning the design of the upper tomb-structures are very rare. The only truly relevant reports are two Traditions, the first of which contains the following utterance of the Prophet: "If one of your brothers dies, level the earth on his grave".[51] The second Tradition is cited by the Yemenite traditionist ᶜAbd ar-Razzāq aṣ-Ṣanᶜānī (d. 211 H): "A man died in the time of the Prophet. The latter came to attend the funeral, saying 'Ease the burden of your companion'. What he meant was that they should not put a huge amount of earth on his grave".[52] Still, a tiny amount of earth upon the tomb is not objectionable, because the Prophet himself dispersed a three handfuls of earth upon the grave of his companion ᶜUṯmān b. Maẓᶜūn.[53]

Besides that we are left with little material as to the Prophet's actual practice, apart from his utterances and advice. One of the most important and widely-cited reports in that regard is the Tradition, transmitted by Sunnites and Shiites alike, that the Prophet levelled the tomb of his son Ibrāhīm who died in the year 10 H, just short of being two years old.[54] Moreover, the Prophet is said to have levelled the earth upon the tomb of Saᶜd b. Muᶜāḏ who died during the conflict with the Jewish Banū Qurayẓah and was then buried in the Medinan Baqīᶜ cemetery.[55]

2.3. Historical information

Next to the reports which are transmitted from the Prophet or contain an account of his practice, the Muslim scholars eagerly looked for historical information, that is, for the actions of the Prophet's companions, including the first caliphs.

49 Le Goff: *Naissance du Purgatoire* p. 53.

50 For this argument, see van Ess: *Prémices*, esp. chapter 1.

51 ĠazIḥyāʾ (C) IV p. 418; IQayZād I p. 523; *cf.* also IRaǧAhwāl p. 33 and Rāġib: *Structure de la tombe* p. 401.

52 ᶜARazMuṣ 6492 (III p. 505); *cf.* also al-Muᶜallimī: *ᶜImārat al-qubūr* p. 123 (with a report to the contrary) and 126. In early third-century epitaphs we thus find the wish expressed that God shall remove the earth from the deceased's body, see Vol. I pp. 131ff. and above p. 90.

53 ŠāmīSubul VIII p. 380; *cf.* also QNuᶜmDaᶜāʾim I p. 238.

54 ŠāfUmm I p. 458; ŠīrMuhaḏ I p. 138; KulKāfī III p. 263; IḤazmĞaw p. 31; IQudMuġnī II p. 505; MuwMuršid I p. 65; KirmŠBuḫ VII p. 161; HarMirqātMaf IV p. 68. *Cf.* also Rāġib: *Structure de la tombe* p. 400; see also below p. 195. For the tomb of Ibrāhīm, with a white cupola, see IĞubRiḥlah (B) p. 174.

55 HarMirqātMaf I p. 210; MaǧlBihār VI p. 220.

Not a small number of the companions was of the opinion that not marking the grave by mounds or huge heaps of earth (or raised enclosures) was preferable and in concordance with Muḥammad's views on the matter. Thus we hear that the third caliph ᶜUṯmān (r. 23–35 H) had all graves levelled to the ground,[56] and his successor ᶜAlī b. Abī Ṭālib (d. 40 H) explicitly claimed the authority of the Prophet for doing so and likewise gave the order that elevated graves had to be levelled.[57]

In another case, the Arabic commander-in-chief during the conquest of Rhodes, Faḍālah b. ᶜUbayd al-Anṣārī (d. 53 H or later),[58] gave the order that the grave of a comrade should be levelled, because Faḍālah had heard of an instruction from the Prophet to do so.[59] Later scholars, in order to reason away the implications of this report, claimed that levelling (*taswiyah*) did not in this case refer to the tomb being truly levelled to the ground, but to its being configured in a proper way, i.e. putting its stones together and straightening the heap of earth: "the repair and maintenance of graves" (*ʾiṣlāḥu l-qubūri wa-ʾibqāʾuhā*).[60]

The grandson of the second caliph Abū Bakr, Abū Muḥammad al-Qāsim b. Muḥammad (d. 108 or 109 H), told his son "Pour dust upon me[61] and level my grave!"[62] The companion of the Prophet Abū Zamᶜah ᶜUbayd al-Balawī (d. 34 H), who was buried in Kairouan with three hairs from the Prophet's head – one each in his hands and the third upon his tongue –, likewise ordered his fellows to "level the earth upon his tomb".[63]

This was not the only case of that sort because after Ibn Ḥinzābah (see **45**) had died "three hairs from the Prophet's hair, which he had acquired for an immense sum, were put in his mouth. He used

56 IAŠayMuṣ III p. 222 (*ǧanāʾiz* 143); IŠabAḫbār II p. 132; KU 42927 (XV p. 735). The verdict is formulated less strictly in ᶜARazMuṣ 6489 (III p. 504).

57 ᶜARazMuṣ 6487 (III p. 504); IAŠayMuṣ III p. 222 (*ǧanāʾiz* 143); NawŠMuslim VII p. 36 (*ǧanāʾiz* 93); ADāʾūd III p. 291 (*ǧanāʾiz* 72); TirmĞāmiᶜ II p. 256 (*ǧanāʾiz* 55); NasSunan IV p. 73; ḤākMust I p. 369; IQudMuġnī II p. 504; QurṭTaḏk p. 86; IQayIġāṯah I p. 181 and IQayZād I p. 524; IMuflFurūᶜ II p. 271; ManbTasl (C) p. 203 / (M) p. 197; QasṭIršād II p. 390; ŠāmīSubul VIII p. 381; HarMirqātMaf IV p. 68; ŠawkŠŠudūr p. 70; al-Muᶜallimī: *ᶜImārat al-qubūr* pp. 165-81. *Cf.* also Ašraf: *al-Qabr* p. 25 and MF XXXII p. 249.

58 *Cf.* ANuḤilyah II p. 17; MālRiyāḍ I p. 80; IḤaǧIṣābah III p. 206. For his tomb in Damascus, see IŠadAᶜlāq II (Damascus) pp. 184f.

59 IAŠayMuṣ III p. 222 (*ǧanāʾiz* 143); FB III p. 329 (*ǧanāʾiz* 96); NawŠMuslim VII pp. 35f. (*ǧanāʾiz* 92); ADāʾūd III p. 291 (*ǧanāʾiz* 72); NasSunan IV pp. 72f.; BaySunan III p. 411; IᶜABarrIst III p. 197; IMuflFurūᶜ II p. 271; IQayIġāṯah I p. 181; SamWafāʾ II p. 557; QasṭMaw III p. 401; ŠāmīSubul VIII p. 381; HarĞamᶜWas II p. 219; al-Albānī: *Aḥkām al-ǧanāʾiz* p. 208; al-Muᶜallimī: *ᶜImārat al-qubūr* pp. 108-14. *Cf.* KU 42387 (XV p. 601) and 42991 (p. 760).

60 HarĞamᶜWas II p. 219.

61 *snn* I *ᶜalayya t-turāba (sannan)*: for this expression, see also ḤumĞuḏwah p. 136; DabMaᶜālim III pp. 16 and 18; ŠirŠadd p. 8; ŠāmīSubul VIII p. 379; KU 42921 (XV p. 734); *cf.* also ISaᶜdṬab VII p. 494 and Lane s.r. *snn*: According to common understanding, the reference is here to the custom of covering the body in the burial niche with a thin layer of dust or earth, *cf.* al-Albānī: *Aḥkām al-ǧanāʾiz* pp. 152f.

62 IĞawzīṢafwah I p. 387.

63 AᶜArabṬab p. 77; MālRiyāḍ I p. 84; DabMaᶜālim I p. 98 with note 1; *cf.* al-Kinānī: *Takmīl* p. 3.

to keep them in a golden drawer lined with musk and stipulated that they be put in his mouth after his death, and so it was done".[64] However, it was not considered desirable to be buried together with such precious relics, thus Ǧamāl ad-Dīn Abū ᶜAbd Allāh Muḥammad al-Muršidī (Mecca 763 – Medina 829 H) had met a pious man in Jerusalem "who was in the possession of six hairs that were ascribed to the Prophet – *taṣliyah*. When his death had drawn near, he handed each of them over to different persons, six in all, and al-Muršidī was one of them".[65] Another, pre-Islamic custom, which survived into early Islamic times, was the placing of women's hair upon a tomb, e.g. in the case of Ḫālid b. al-Walīd b. al-Muġīrah (d. 21 H) after whose death "all the women of the Banū Muġīrah put their curls upon his grave, i.e. they cut their hair and laid it upon his tomb (*ᶜalā qabrihī*)".[66]

Finally, the Umayyad caliph ᶜUmar II b. ᶜAbd al-ᶜAzīz (d. 101 H), who was generally known for his pro-Sunnite views, saw in flattening the tomb (*tasṭīḥ al-qabr*) a practice typical of the Shiites since the Prophet's time.[67] Nevertheless, as he reportedly said, "this does not matter because an accepted practice (*sunnah*) is not given up just because of blameworthy innovators (*ʾahl al-bidᶜah*, i.e. the Shiites) following it, too";[68] eventually, ᶜUmar's own tomb was levelled as well.[69]

The question whether an established *sunnah* should be followed even though groups with, according to the Sunnite view, heretical reputation (e.g. the Shiites) share it was a topic debated over the centuries. Around the middle of the seventh century H, the famous Shafiite jurist ᶜIzz ad-Dīn Ibn ᶜAbd as-Salām (d. 660 H) wrote in one of his fatwas, using a classical *a fortiori* argument: "It is not permitted to abandon accepted customs (*sunan*) just because the innovators are also following them. The reason for this is that truth is not given up in exchange for error, and the righteous scholars never stopped following the *sunan* though they knew that the innovators were doing the same. Thus, if truth is not given up in exchange for error, how could the truth then be given up because somebody shares in it?"[70]

On the other hand, historical reports concerning the practice of the Prophet's companions yielded no uniform trend that could be helpful in settling the question once and for all. The obvious next step for the Muslim scholars was therefore to investigate what the tombs had really looked like during the first centuries H. This could be done in accordance with the commonly accepted idea that the first-generation Muslims (*as-salaf*) had still known and followed the correct use as they had not yet been "corrupted" nor "deviated from the right path", as it were, like the succeeding generations. In this case, eye-witness evidence was brought into play against inform-

64 MaqrMuq III p. 47.

65 ḌL VII p. 184.

66 *Aġānī* XVI p. 196. *Cf.* also Wellhausen: *Reste* pp. 181f.

67 *Cf.* MuwMuršid I p. 65 and HarMirqātMaf IV p. 68. For the Shiite traditions concerning the levelling of the tomb, see MaǧlBihār VI pp. 220 and 277. However, some Shiites shared with the Sunnite scholars the conviction that the grave should be raised about four fingers above the ground, see ṬūsīMabsūṭ I p. 187 and below p. 194 with note 184.

68 QasṭIršād II p. 390; HaytTuḥfMuḥt III p. 173. *Cf.* also ŠīrMuhaḏ I p. 138; IQudMuġnī II p. 505; IMuflFurūᶜ II p. 271.

69 NZ I p. 247.

70 IᶜASalāmFat p. 23. The same dictum is reported from Abū ᶜAlī aṭ-Ṭabarī (al-Ḥasan b. al-Qāsim, born 263 – d. Baghdad 350 H) as cited in MuwMuršid I p. 65.

ation taken from literary sources,[71] thus providing arguments against the numerous reports condemning the placing of mounds over tombs. Take for example the report from an unknown transmitter who testified to having seen the tomb of Ibn ᶜUmar covered by a mound[72] or the report from the late first-century traditionist aš-Šaᶜbī (d. 103 H) who claimed: "I saw the tombs of the martyrs (who died in the battle) of Uḥud: these are tumuli (*ǧuṯan*) covered by intense green (*naḍir*), that is, by plants".[73]

2.3.1. Growing plants on tombs and burial sites

The growing of plants (i.e. flowers, bushes or trees) – or their spontaneous growth – upon graves was in general seen as a blessing and thus tolerated or even encouraged. An argument voiced in modern times – I do not know a pre-modern parallel to it although it has been ascribed to Ǧalāl ad-Dīn as-Suyūṭī – even has it that plucking plants and herbs from tombs is disapproved of because "they praise God and make company for the deceased".[74] In contrast with this, other modern Muslim writers consider it forbidden to put flowers on tombs "because this resembles the Christian usage".[75]

Nevertheless, tombs in the realm of Sunnite Islam are often adorned with plants or flowers and regularly looked after,[76] although there is a marked difference between the respective Sunnite and Shiite attitudes. By some later Sunnite legal scholars (including the Wahhābites),[77] the custom of adorning the grave with flowers or plants is rejected, mostly because they detect here a parallel to the construction of mausolea and the affixing of epitaphs.[78] Scholars arguing the contrary refer to a famous Tradition, according to which the Prophet put fresh palm fronds upon two graves in order to lessen the Chastisement of their occupants, and took this as a hint that any plant or tree upon the tomb would have a beneficial effect.[79]

In addition to palm fronds (*or* risps, boughs: *ǧarāʾid*) and other plants which

71 For the role of the eye-witness in Arabic historiography and beyond, see Rosenthal: *Historiography* p. 60 and Schöller: *Exegetisches Denken* pp. 61f.

72 IAŠayMuṣ III p. 215 (*ǧanāʾiz* 130); al-Muᶜallimī: *ᶜImārat al-qubūr* p. 122.

73 IŠabAḫbār I p. 85; IAṯīrNih I p. 170. ᶜARazMuṣ 6490 (III p. 505) and IAŠayMuṣ III p. 215 (*ǧanāʾiz* 130) have instead "raised tumuli" (*ǧuṯan musannamah*), only *musannamah* in the report quoted in KU 42932 (XV p. 736); *cf.* also al-Muᶜallimī: *ᶜImārat al-qubūr* pp. 118f. and 142. A different wording also in IAŠayMuṣ III p. 223 (*ǧanāʾiz* 143).

74 Krawietz: *Ḥurma* p. 168; al-Albānī: *Aḥkām al-ǧanāʾiz* p. 201; Wafā: *Aḥkām al-ǧanāʾiz* p. 275.

75 Haja: *Mort et Jugement Dernier* p. 36. For the prohibition of putting flowers on graves, as voiced in modern South Asian fatwas, see Masud: *Definition of Bidᶜa* p. 73.

76 *Cf.* Wirth: *Orientalische Stadt* p. 423. The related custom of putting plants or herbs within the tomb itself or in the burial niche (*laḥd*) cannot be discussed here, but *cf.* FB III pp. 274f. (*ǧanāʾiz* 76) and Grütter: *Bestattungsbräuche* pp. 173f.

77 See Krawietz: *Ḥurma* p. 168 with note 37.

78 IḤāǧǧMadḫ III p. 280; ArdAnwār I p. 124. Arguing the contrary: RamlīNih II p. 35. *Cf.* also below p. 274.

79 TurkLumaᶜ I p. 229 and below p. 252.

were temporarily placed upon tombs but not properly planted, flowers or even trees could grow permanently on the surface of tombs. Thus (Ibn) al-Qifṭī saw "mallows broken forth and dried up" during his visit to the tomb of al-Maᶜarrī in Maᶜarrat an-Nuᶜmān (Northern Syria),[80] and Egyptian tombs could be covered by aloe plants.[81] On the tomb of the Persian poet Ǧāmī in Harāt (Afghanistan), a tree grew from the grave, something which is, according to Donaldson, "not infrequent at the tombs of poets".[82] A distich by Ibn al-Muᶜtazz alludes to the custom of growing plants upon tombs (*ṭawīl*):

مَرَرْتُ بِقَبْرٍ زَاهِرٍ وَسْطَ رَوْضَةٍ * عَلَيْهِ مِنَ الأَنْوَارِ مِثْلُ الشَّقَائِقِ
فَقُلْتُ لِمَنْ هَذَا فَقَالَ لِي الثَّرَى * تَرَحَّمْ عَلَيْهِ إِنَّهُ قَبْرُ عَاشِقِ

"I walked by a luminous[83] tomb in the middle of a garden,[84] * upon which there were blossoms such as (red) anemones,
Thus I said, 'Whose (tomb) is that?', and I was told by the moist earth: * 'Have mercy upon him, it is the tomb of a lover!'"[85]

The fact that there were red anemones on the grave clearly hints at two things. First at the tears which are shed for the deceased one at his tomb, because tears were in poetry often compared to drops of blood;[86] second at the idea that dying for love was considered a kind of martyrdom, with the red anemones "emblematically" indicating the martyr's blood, i.e. his "violent" death.[87]

Since there is a strong connection in poetical and eschatological imagery between the tomb and the garden (*rawḍah*) as *loecus amoenus* (see above p. 50 and Vol. I pp. 112f.), we often find a combination of both, which sometimes also includes the cemetery as such. The fifth-century Andalusian poet Ibn al-Labbānah, famous for

80 QifṭīInbāh I pp. 70f. For the mausoleum of al-Maᶜarrī, see below p. 292 and **111**.

81 Winkler: *Volkskunde* p. 226.

82 Donaldson: *Shiʾite Religion* p. 269. The category "tombs of the poets" is interesting in itself. In a quarter of Tabrīz called "Surḫāb" there was, from the fifth century H onwards, a "cemetery of the poets" to which a modern monograph has been devoted (Saǧǧādī: *Surḫāb*, see bibliography).

83 In the sense of "covered by blossoms", as becomes clear from the second hemistich: *ʾanwār* = "blossoms, flowers", or also "lights".

84 This refers probably to a real garden; for the later use of *rawḍah* in the sense of "cemetery", see above p. 52.

85 IMuᶜtDīwān 1089 (II pp. 561f.) = SarrāǧMaṣ I p. 130 (var. *zāhirin*: *mušriqin*) and p. 301 (var. *mina l-ʾanwāri miṯlu*: *mina n-nuwwāri ṯawbu*; *fa-qāla lī*: *fa-ǧāwabanī*) = Schoeler: *Naturdichtung* p. 262 (in German translation).

86 See below p. 187 for an example; anemones in particular were compared to blood-like tears, see the verse by Ibn Huḏayl in IKattTašb p. 153 = IKattVergleiche p. 142. The Arabic language facilitates the equation of blood and tears by the phonetic similarities between *dam* ("blood") and *damᶜ* ("tear"), thus offering a tempting opportunity for wordplay.

87 *Cf.* Schoeler: *Naturdichtung* p. 263.

his relation to the Sevillan prince-poet al-Muᶜtamid Ibn ᶜAbbād (see above p. 103 and **1**), has the following verses in one of his mourning poems (*mutaqārib*):

سَقَى قَبْرَهُ وَاكِفٌ يَنْهَمِي * وَظَلَّلَهُ وَارِفٌ يَرْطَبُ
وَلَا بَرِحَتْ فَوْقَهُ رَوْضَةٌ * بِأَزْهَارِ رَحْمَتِهِ تَعْشَبُ

"May trickling rain that flows down pour forth upon his tomb * and may verdant plants that are moistened (*or* succulent) shade it!
May the blooming meadow upon it never cease to grow, * freshly covered with the blossoms of His mercy!"[88]

The Sevillan poet Ibn Šiblāq[89] (d. 413 H) saw in a dream "as if I stood in a graveyard covered with blossoming flowers (*ḏātu ᵓazāhīra wa-nawāwīr*). There was a tomb surrounded by much *rayḥān* (i.e. fragrant plants, see Chapter 5) and people had gathered around it for a bacchanal".[90] The Egyptian poet an-Nawāǧī (d. 859 H), in a poem in praise of the Prophet, composed the following verse in which he took up this imagery of a garden in bloom and turned it into metaphor, with the words (*ṭawīl*):

نَبِيٌّ لَهُ قَبْرٌ شَرِيفٌ وَرَوْضَةٌ * حَدَائِقُهَا بِالنُّورِ لَا النَّوْرِ تُزْهِرُ

"(He is) a Prophet who possesses a noble tomb and a garden * whose meadows[91] shine forth by light, not by flowers".[92]

As is known, the Prophet's tomb and the adjacent space were commonly known as *ar-Rawḍah* (see above p. 48), but the metaphor could be applied to other tombs as well, or to the tomb as such. Ibn Nubātah in his anthology *Maṭlaᶜ al-fawāᵓid* quotes a revealing verse from the sixth-century poet Ibn Sanāᵓ al-Mulk (*ṭawīl*):

وَيَا قَبْرَهُ لَا شَكَّ أَنَّكَ رَوْضَةٌ * وَلَكِنْ بِهَا مِنْ أَدْمُعِ الخَلْقِ أَنْهَارُ

"O tomb of his: no doubt that you are a garden * but one in which rivulets flow from the tears of creation (shed about your death)".[93]

Not without practical intent, a mound of earth (*turāb*) covered by grass (*ḥašīš*) could also be carefully piled up in order to camouflage a tomb, as in the case of the ᶜAlīd pretender Zayn b. ᶜAlī, the grandson of al-Ḥusayn who died in Kūfah in 121

88 Cited in IṣfḪar (M) II p. 132. The verse is not among the poetry edited in HadjIbnLabb.

89 Or "Ibn Šibrāq", Abū l-Muṭarrif ᶜAr. b. ᶜAl.

90 Cited in IBaškṢilah II p. 325 and ḤumǦuḏwah p. 274.

91 *ḥadāᵓiq*, lit. "gardens of trees, *or* bushes".

92 NawāǧīMaṭāliᶜ p. 131 (v. 33) = MN II p. 222 (v. 32); the poem was composed in 840 H and subsequently sent to the Prophet's sepulchre. Playing with the root *nwr* was a favourite device of many Arabic poets, giving them ample possibilites of *taǧnīs* with a number of seminal terms (*nūr* "light", *nār* "fire", *nawr* "flowers").

93 INubMaṭlaᶜ p. 350.

or 122 H. The device eventually proved futile because Zayd's tomb was discovered and his body exhumed, crucified and burned.[94]

The visitation of cemeteries by careless visitors not seeking inner elevation and meditation was likened by the Hanbalite scholar Ibn ᶜAqīl to strolling happily through a garden (*wa-lā farqa ʿindaka bayna l-qubūri wa-l-basātīni maʿa l-furǧah ...*),[95] which shows that the image of the garden was also resorted to in a negative sense.[96] His Hanbalite companion al-Manbiǧī condemned the planting of "different kinds of fragrant plants" (*ʾanwāʿ ar-rayāḥīn*) upon tombs as a "detestable innovation".[97] This aspect is also attested in Arabic poetry, where we find verses which stress that there were no flowers or plants upon graves, e.g. in a verse by aš-Šarīf ar-Raḍīy.[98]

Concerning the vegetation in graveyards there is little information in most literary sources, although we may suppose that there were often plants or trees in them, according to the conditions of the terrain. For obvious reasons, the cultivation of crops in public graveyards was considered forbidden though in many cases cemeteries were in use as pasture ground for sheep and goats.[99] One of the oldest examples of vegetation in cemeteries is the name of the famous Medinan cemetery *Baqīʿ al-Ġarqad* which simply means "tract of land with *ġarqad*-trees" (a species of large thorny plants).[100] Other graveyards, whose names go back to the local vegetation, were the "palm-cemetery" (*maqburat an-naḫīl*) in Seville[101] and the so-called *mašhad an-nāranǧ* (the "orange-tree-visitation site") in Damascus near the tomb of the Umayyad caliph Muᶜāwiyah b. Abī Sufyān.[102]

In the Islamic West, we sometimes hear of olive-trees or palms growing among the tombs,[103] and the tomb of the Sevillan ruler and poet al-Muᶜtamid Ibn ᶜAbbād in Aġmāt (see **1**) was shaded by a lote-tree (*sidrah*, lat. *spina Christi*);[104] in Biǧāyah (Algeria), a cemetery was famous for a giant tree which was growing there.[105] In addition, in Morocco (as well as in Egypt, Palestine, Syria and Iraq)

94 MasMurūǧ IV p. 43.

95 As cited in IMuflĀdāb III p. 287.

96 It might be significant that Ibn ᶜAqīl uses the simpler term *bustān* (pl. *basātīn*), not *rawḍah*.

97 ManbTasl (C) p. 203 / (M) p. 197.

98 ŠarīfRaḍDīwān I p. 386 (*ǧadaṯun ʿalā ʾan lā nabāta bi-ʾarḍihī * waqafat ʿalayhī maṭālibu r-ruwwādī*) = INubMaṭlaᶜ p. 340 (with the variant *waqfun*); *cf.* also ŠTalḫīṣ III p. 466.

99 *Cf.* below pp. 204ff. with note 256; *cf.* also Wirth: *Orientalische Stadt* p. 423.

100 SamWafāʾ III p. 892; HarMirqātMaf IV p. 115. The name "al-Baqīᶜ" remained over the centuries even though there were no such trees left in the area since they had been removed already during the Prophet's lifetime.

101 IAbbTakm II pp. 39 and 181.

102 IMunlāMutᶜah I p. 86 (with the editor's note). *Cf.* also IŠadAᶜlāq II (Damascus) p. 184.

103 Torres Balbás: *Cementerios* pp. 135f. The famous Jewish convert Kaᶜb al-Aḥbār was buried in Ḥimṣ among olive-trees (Lecker: *Burial of Martyrs* p. 40 n. 13; *cf.* also MunKawākib I p. 411 and EI² III p. 402); however, Kaᶜb's tomb was also recorded in al-Ǧīzah (IǦubRiḥlah [B] p. 30) and Damascus (IŠadAᶜlāq II p. 184; MiknāsīIḥrāz pp. 166f.; RCEA 1543).

104 IḪaṭAᶜmāl p. 191. A lote-tree – which evokes the Seventh Heaven according to the Qurʾānic eschatological imagery (*cf.* Q 53:14) – was also known from the Bāb Ḥarb cemetery in Baghdad, see IǦawzīMunt X p. 164.

105 ĠubrᶜUnwān p. 74.

we find the phenomenon of *arbres consacrés* in the vicinity of shrines.[106] For the eastern lands, however, notices of the vegetation on graves and in cemeteries are not very numerous. In 921 H, a large walnut-tree standing in (or near) a cemetery in Damascus was cut down and sold in order to build a new precinct for the graveyard with the money;[107] the twelfth-century scholar (Ibn) an-Nābulusī (d. 1143 H) witnessed during his travels through Lebanon, Syria and Egypt a number of tombs which were either adorned by flowers[108] or had *maysah*-trees planted upon or beside them;[109] in ᶜAkkā (Acre), the presumed mausoleum of the prophet Ṣāliḥ was surrounded by fig- and olive-trees.[110] There was a palm-grove (*naḫīl*), or at least a single palm, near or beside the mausoleum of the Prophet's son Ibrāhīm in Medina.[111]

Due to more favourable climatic conditions, the Islamic cemeteries in Anatolia[112] and Rumelia frequently have the aspect of gardens, with high grass and leafy trees or cypresses; the same holds true for many burial sites in the eastern and South Asian Islamic lands, e.g. in Afghanistan and Indonesia.[113] For many centuries, the appearance of graveyards in Ottoman Turkey shaped the imagination of the West, as can be seen from the following passage in a nineteenth-century CE treatise: "The Mohammedans generally bury their dead outside the city (...) Their immense graveyards present a strange and gloomy appearance, their white marble columns, surmounted by turbans, shimmering like ghosts through and above the groves of cypresses that always mark the last repose of the Moslem sleepers".[114]

As a part of the Isrāʾīlīyāt – the "Jewish lore" in Islamic Tradition – al-Yāfiᶜī relates a story, on the authority of Kaᶜb al-Aḥbār, that in the time of the Banū Isrāʾīl God created the first evergreen cypress (*sarw*) upon the tomb of a sinner who had come to live in the company of twelve ascetics. They buried him on the bank of a river after they had washed him in its waters, and overnight God made twelve cypresses grow upon his tomb.[115] Quite romantic appears, to our eyes, what is said of the tombs of the poet ᶜUrwah b. Ḥāzim and his beloved ᶜAfrāʾ (mid-first century H), who were buried side by side north of Ṣanᶜāʾ. As a visitor reports, "the trunk of a tree came forth from each grave and both trunks grew into one (*ʾlf* VIII) roughly

106 See Dermenghem: *Culte des saints* pp. 136-41; Kriss: *Volksglaube* I pp. 20f., 82-5 (on "holy trees" in Cairo), p. 87 (a *nabq* or lote-tree shading a mausoleum), pp. 186f. and 242 (trees venerated at the shrine of al-Ḥusayn in Karbalāʾ); Haja: *Mort et Jugement Dernier* p. 37. For "sacred" trees in India, see Currie: *Muᶜīn al-Dīn Chistī* p. 9; for those in Turkey (near Istanbul): Laqueur: *Friedhöfe Istanbul* p. 50 with note 309.

107 IṬūlMufāk p. 312.

108 NābTuḥfah p. 93 (in Ṭarābulus).

109 NābḤaqīqah p. 186 and NābTuḥfah p. 94. For this kind of trees (*celtis australis*), see Kriss: *Volksglaube* I pp. 20 and 147f.

110 NābḤaqīqah p. 295. *Cf.* also above n. 103.

111 INağDurrah p. 404, corrected by SamWafāʾ III p. 896.

112 *Cf.* Laqueur: *Friedhöfe Istanbul* pp. 5, 21 and 111.

113 Chambert-Loir/Guillot: *Indonésie* p. 240 (on sacred trees, mainly fig-trees, in cemeteries). Here as in many other cases, pre- or non-Islamic beliefs influenced Muslim practice. From the learned Islamic point of view, venerating trees is clearly to be ruled out, *cf.* ŠawkDurr p. 9 and al-Albānī: *Aḥkām al-ğanāʾiz* p. 261.

114 Kippax: *Churchyard Literature* pp. 23f.

115 YāfRawḍ pp. 292f.

at the height of a man. Local people therefore used to say, 'They were in harmony with each other (*ʾlf* VI) in life, and so they are in death'".[116]

Likewise of interest in the present context is the historical notice that in the first half of the eleventh century H in the mausoleum (*turbah*) of an Ottoman governor in Tripoli "a sprig of grapevines (*ġarsatu karmin*) was planted, thus giving the place a friendly atmosphere and an air of splendour".[117] From pre-Islamic times onwards, grapevines, and also wine in general, had been connected to burial sites. This is best illustrated by a famous and influential line of the poet Abū Miḥǧan aṯ-Ṯaqafī (Mālik b. Ḥabīb, d. after 16 H) (*ṭawīl*):

إذَا مِتُّ فَادْفِنِّي إلَى جَنْبِ كَرْمَةٍ * تُرَوِّي عِظَامِي بَعْدَ مَوْتِي عُرُوقُهَا

"After my death bury me by a grapevine * whose roots after my death may slake (the thirst of) my bones".[118]

According to al-Hayṯam b. ʿAdī, the grave of Abū Miḥǧan (probably located somewhere in the Islamic East) was indeed adorned with three flourishing grapevines and his tomb bore the simple inscription: *hāḏā qabru ʾAbī Miḥǧanini (ṯ-Ṯaqafīyi)*.[119] Further examples of poets expressing their desire to be interred near a grapevine are cited in the note to epitaph **193**.

2.3.2. "Sprinkling" the tomb with water

The growing of plants, especially of flowers or fragrant plants, upon or among tombs was closely connected with the commonly accepted idea of "watering" or "sprinkling" the tomb (*aṣ-ṣabb* or *ar-rašš ʿalā l-qabr*).[120]

In poetry and biographical accounts

The concept of "sprinkling the tomb" is a familiar and widely-used motif in Arabic poetry.[121] One of the better known and often imitated verses which combine the

116 SarrāǧMaṣ I pp. 212 and 264. For another Yemenite story of a pair of lovers buried together and whose tomb was afterwards covered by plants, see Schönig: *Jemenitinnen* p. 152.

117 IĠalbTiḏkār p. 153.

118 IQutŠiʿr p. 253; IBuḥtUns p. 85; ʿĀmKaškūl II p. 546; Kennedy: *Wine Song* p. 21; Heine: *Wein und Tod* p. 119 (in German translation); Wagner: *Dichtung* II p. 37 (in German). The verses are also quoted in the *Aġānī*, namely in XVIII p. 374 (var. *ʿiẓāmī*: *mušāšī*) and XIX pp. 7, 10 and 13 (var. *ǧanbi*: *ʾaṣli*). A number of similar verses by later poets are cited from an-Nawāǧī's *Ḥalbat al-kumayt* in Heine: *Wein und Tod* pp. 119-21.

119 As quoted in *Aġānī* XIX p. 13 (with the bracketed part) and FāsīʿIqd VI p. 318. For the discourse of a friend at the tomb of Abū Miḥǧan, see IHuḏaylMaq p. 68.

120 *Cf.* ʿARazMuṣ 6481-3 (III pp. 501f.); MasMurūǧ I p. 76; IḤāǧǧMadḫ III p. 280. Many of the Arabic terms for the irrigation, watering and sprinkling of tombs, as well as for several sorts of rain, are discussed in De Haas: *Moisture*.

121 *Cf.* ḤuṣZahr (M) III pp. 721f. / (Ṭ) II pp. 75f.; Abdesselem: *Thème de la mort* pp. 105f., 192 and 244; Smith/Haddad: *Islamic Understanding of Death* p. 149; Seidensticker: *Rūḥ* pp. 148.

concept of "watering" with that of herbs growing on the tomb was composed by an-Nābiġah aḏ-Ḏubyānī (*ṭawīl*):

سَقَى الغَيْثُ قَبْراً بَينَ بُصْرَى وَجَاسِمٍ * بِغَيثٍ مِنَ الوَسْمِيِّ قَطْرٌ وَوَابِلُ
وَلاَ زَالَ رَيْحَانٌ وَمِسْكٌ وَعَنْبَرٌ * عَلَى مُنْتَهاهُ دِيمَةٌ ثُمَّ هَاتِلُ

"May rainfall irrigate a tomb between Buṣrā and Ğāsim, * with rainfall as in spring, (now) dripping and (now) a showering downpour,
May a fragrant plant,[122] musk and amber not cease (to grow) * on his last mansion; a continuous rainfall, then a flood-like torrent!"[123]

These verses are undoubtedly among the most influential lines by an-Nābiġah; they have been imitated by many Arab poets, e.g. by the panegyrist of the Prophet, Ḥassān b. Ṯābit (d. 40 H or after).[124] Centuries after, the first verse was copied almost verbatim in a mourning poem by Sirāğ ad-Dīn Ibn al-Ġamr al-Qūṣī (d. after 533 H).[125] Another typical example of a mourning poem playing upon the concept of "sprinkling the tomb" are two verses composed by al-Ḥakīm Abū Muḥammad b. Ḫalīfah al-Miṣrī on the death of Abū l-Faḍl Muḥammad b. ᶜAbd al-Wāḥid al-Baġdādī (d. Toledo 455 H) (*ṭawīl*):

سَقَى اللّهُ قَبْراً حَلَّ فِيهِ أَبُو الفَضْلِ * سَحَاباً يَسُحُّ المُزْنُ وَبْلاً عَلَى وَبْلِ
وَكَيْفَ يُسَقِّي المُزْنُ قَبْراً يَحِلُّهُ * وَفِي طَيِّهِ بَحْرُ المَكَارِمِ وَالفَضْلِ

"May God irrigate the tomb which Abū l-Faḍl occupies[126] * with clouds bursting forth with one heavy rainfall after another!
But how could the rainclouds ever irrigate a tomb which *he* inhabits, * given that it encloses the sea of noble traits and excellence?"[127]

The image of the buried person being a "sea" or an "ocean" (*baḥr*) – a metaphor for plenty and abundance – of noble attributes which renders the sprinkling of his tomb, or the beneficial rainfall, either superfluous or of little impact, had already been used (and made familiar) by Abū Tammām,[128] Ibn al-Muᶜtazz[129] and others.[130]

122 For *rayḥān*, "fragrant plant", see below Chapter 5.

123 NābiġahDīwān p. 93 (vv. 26f.).

124 *Aġānī* XVIII p. 161. The variants of the poem are listed in detail in ḤassānDīwān 345 (I pp. 506f.). Given the similarity to the line by an-Nābiġah, Ḥassān's verses have also been attributed to the older poet, see e.g. YāqBuldān II p. 14 (*s.v.* Tubnā).

125 See *Wāfī* XIII p. 229; similar lines also appear in IMuᶜtDīwān 1189 v. 1 (III p. 67) and 1207 v. 4 (*op. cit.* p. 90).

126 The wording of this first hemistich is very conventional in Arabic poetry, see e.g. a line by Mutammim b. Nuwayrah mourning his brother Mālik, cited in YāqBuldān III pp. 307 and 461 (and many other sources): *saqā llāhu ʾarḍan ḥallahā qabru Mālikin*, etc.

127 Cited in DabMaᶜālim III p. 196 (note the wordplay on "Abū l-Faḍl" and *faḍl*, "excellence").

128 ATamDīwān IV p. 84 (v. 27) = ᶜAskMaᶜānī II p. 525 (*ṭawīl*): *wa-kayfa ḥtimālī li-s-sahābi ṣanīᶜatan * bi-ʾisqāʾihā qabran wa-fī laḥdihī l-baḥrū.*

However, according to al-Mutanabbī, who liked to run counter to conventional images and traditional concepts, the buried person is the last to benefit from both fragrant herbs and rainfall. He addressed the dead mother of his patron in the following verse (*wāfir*):

تُحَجَّبُ عَنْكِ رائِحَةُ الخُزَامَى * وَتُمْنَعُ مِنْكِ أَنْدَاءُ الطِّلالِ

"The perfume of lavender is now veiled from you, * and the (refreshing) moisture of the gentle showers is denied to you".[131]

In poetry, the concept of "watering the tomb" could also be taken metaphorically, e.g. in a verse by the fourth-century poet Ibn Hāniʾ al-Andalusī (*ramal*):

إنَّ فِي الجَوْسَقِ قَبْراً تُرْبُهُ * مِنْ دَمِ البَاكِينَ إضْرِيجٌ جَسَدْ

"There is a tomb in the palace whose earth * has become stained by the blood of those weeping (at it) with saffron-like redness".[132]

Moreover, the wish for a beneficial rainfall is occasionally expressed in epitaphs.[133]

In poetry, the "sprinkling of the tomb" mainly refers to rainfall, and thus it is the forces of nature, not man, that provide for irrigation. We encounter this important concept also in biographical accounts where the natural "sprinkling of the grave" by rain appears as a sign of heavenly approval.

Two examples may serve to illustrate this point. In the first case, we hear of the funeral of the Baṣran Harim b. Ḥayyān al-ᶜAbdī (first century H): "Harim died on a very hot summer day. After his grave had been closed, a cloud drifted by and stopped right over his grave. The raincloud was neither longer nor shorter than the (enclosure of the) tomb. Rain poured forth and sprinkled (the grave) until it was watered, then the cloud disappeared". The traditionist Qatādah (d. 118 H) added: "The grave of Harim b. Ḥayyān was rained upon on the very day (of his burial), and from that day on it was covered by plants".[134] In the second case, the funeral of the famous Syrian traditionist Abū l-Qāsim Ibn ᶜAsākir (d. 571 H) in Damascus is described as follows: "The rain had been very scarce that year, but it absolutely poured down (*fa-darra wa-saḥḥa*) when his bier was lifted, quite as if the

129 IMuᶜtDīwān 1173 v. 2 (III p. 43) = ḤuṣZahr (M) III p. 721 / (Ṭ) II p. 75 = *Wāfī* XIX p. 374 (*ḫafīf*): *lastu mustasqiyan li-qabrika ġayṯā * kayfa yaẓmā wa-qad taḍammana baḥrā*; *cf.* also IMuᶜtDīwān 1207 v. 5 (III p. 90).

130 E.g. the verse by al-Marwānī, quoted in IKattTašb p. 273 = IKattVergleiche p. 225.

131 MutanDīwān (U) III p. 17 / (W) p. 392 (v. 24) = ŠayMaǧānī VI p. 237 = Winter: *al-Mutanabbī's Elegies* p. 331.

132 IHāniʾDīwān p. 119 (v. 29). The metaphor of blood for bitter weeping and tears was later to have extraordinary success with Persian poets, see for some examples Reintjens-Anwari: *Tod aus islamischer Sicht* pp. 187-9; see also above n. 86.

133 *Cf.* Inscriptions Ẓafār-Ḏī Bīn pp. 9f.; Inscriptions Espagne 112 = Inscripciones Almería 66 (*saqā llāhu turbata qabrihī*, *c.*520 H.); RCEA 5040 (697 H?), and (in epitaphs cited in literary sources) **1**, **62**, **127**, **139** and **158**.

134 ISaᶜdṬab VII pp. 133f.; ANuḤilyah II p. 122; IĞawzīṢafwah II p. 128. *Cf.* Grütter: *Bestattungsbräuche* p. 181.

sky was weeping tears of both heavy and fine rain upon him, / and soaked the ground with its watering (*as-samāʾu bakat ʿalayhi bi-damʿi wablihī wa-ṭašših / wa-ballati l-ʾarḍa bi-rašših*)".[135]

Legal arguments and historical evidence

Notwithstanding what we know from poetry and biographical works, water was not in every case seen as beneficial. There were some legal scholars who condemned the growth of plants on the tomb because this would lead to the moistening of the earth and therefore be "detrimental to the proper decomposition of the corpse" that should lie in dry soil.[136] The Muslim jurists also discussed the effects of waste-water seeping into the soil of burial sites and considered this a valid reason for disinterring and transferring the dead. But the problem not only concerned the dead, but the living as well: waterlogged cemeteries were likely to contaminate sources of water or wells and to create considerable hygiene problems.[137] In any case, too much moisture or water could be "harmful" to the deceased: after Ṭalḥah b. ʿUbayd Allāh (d. 36 H) had been buried at the bank of a river in Baṣrah, he appeared to one of his clients in a dream and said, "Come and rescue me, because I drown in water!" So a house was bought for him in Baṣrah, for some 10.000 dinars, and his body was transferred there.[138]

As mentioned earlier, "watering the tomb" was not only caused by rain (or depicted so in poetical imagery and biographical accounts), but also by the tomb being "sprinkled" artificially, a pre-Islamic custom and in many cases carried out immediately after the burial had taken place. The Sunnite legal scholars – apart from their known objections to that practice[139] – tried to discover some practical purpose in the custom of "sprinkling the tomb" and thus saw it either as a method of marking the grave "in order that its traces may not vanish"[140] or as a way to level the earth on it;[141] others stressed that it served to hold the mound together.[142] Given that the concept of "sprinkling" and "watering" the tomb was a pre-Islamic element

135 IṣfḪar (Š) I p. 278. For the topos that much rain on the day of burial was seen as a good omen, *cf.* also YāqIršād III p. 163.

136 IḤāǧǧMadḫ III p. 280 (this passage is treated in more detail below pp. 254ff.).

137 A pressing problem especially in modern times, see Krawietz: *Ḥurma* p. 165 and Zepter: *Friedhöfe* p. 25. For the contamination of water near cemeteries in Andalusian (formerly Islamic) towns, see Casey: *Early Modern Spain* pp. 32f.

138 ZamRabīʿ IV p. 211; Krawietz: *Ḥurma* p. 163; Leisten: *Architektur für Tote* pp. 12, 38 and 140f. (with further sources). For his tomb, famous in Baṣrah, see ŠaʿrṬab I p. 21.

139 The Hanafite scholar Abū Yūsuf disapproved of the watering of the tomb because it resembled, in his eyes, its plastering with gypsum or clay (on this practice, see below p. 258), *cf.* INuǧBaḥr II p. 209; according to Abū Ḥanīfah himself, "there is no objection" to sprinkling the tomb (al-Albānī: *Aḥkām al-ǧanāʾiz* p. 205).

140 ŠīrMuhaḏ I p. 138; MuwMuršid I p. 65; RamlīNih III pp. 34f. Others, on the contrary, held that sprinkling the tomb was likely to make its traces disappear quickly, as happened at the grave of al-Ḥusayn, see BN VIII p. 203. *Cf.* also below p. 190.

141 INuǧBaḥr II p. 209.

142 IQudMuġnī II p. 504; IḤāǧǧMadḫ III p. 264.

that had passed with full force into the mainstream of Islamic culture, without being very compatible with "orthodox" Islamic views on the subject, there were often attempts to minimise its theological implications. This becomes evident in a passage by Yāqūt ar-Rūmī (d. 626 H): "When the poets speak about the watering (*istisqā*ʾ) of tombs – even though the dead do not benefit from this – they mean that people 'drop in on him' (i.e. the deceased, *or* his tomb), i.e. they go to that tomb and invoke mercy upon the deceased".[143]

In a Shiite source we find a more explicit reference to theological arguments, viz. "the Chastisement (of the Grave) will be spared him (*sc.* the deceased) as long as there is moisture in the earth", and here the fact is added that the Prophet imprinted his palm on the freshly sprinkled earth of the tombs of his family members.[144] In another treatise we read that after the burial those "who wish doing so" may "lay their hand on the tomb, spread their fingers and leave their imprint on it", a practice accompanied by prayer for the deceased; we also learn that the sprinkling of the tomb (*ṣbb* I) should "begin from its head, then all around the other sides of the grave until one reaches the former point at the head, and if some water remains it should be poured on the centre (*wasaṭ*) of the tomb".[145] However, the popular belief that a husband, who had re-married, should irrigate the tomb of his former wife in order to "cool the heat of her jealousy", found no favour with the scholars.[146]

The tomb of the Prophet was "sprinkled"[147] – with cold water, a fact that al-Munāwī does not fail to mention (see below)[148] –, but the first time this practice is said to have been applied in Islam was, according to the historian az-Zubayr b. al-Bakkār (d. 256 H),[149] when Muḥammad's son Ibrāhīm was interred.[150] Afterwards also the tombs of the Prophet's companions Saᶜd b. Muᶜāḏ and ᶜUṯmān b. Maẓᶜūn[151] as well as the graves of Shiite Imams were sprinkled;[152] the army leader ᶜAmr b. al-ᶜĀṣ (d. 43 H) expressed the last wish for the earth upon his tomb to be "sprinkled".[153] Outstanding seems the case of the grave of Fāṭimah, because it was sprinkled in order to make its exact location disappear: "Forty graves (around her tomb) were sprinkled so that her tomb was no longer recognisable

143 YāqBuldān II p. 14 (*s.v.* Tubnā).

144 KulKāfī III p. 200.

145 ṬūsīMiṣbāḥ p. 35 and ṬūsīMabsūṭ I p. 187.

146 See al-Albānī: *Aḥkām al-ǧanāʾiz* p. 262.

147 ISaᶜdṬab II p. 306; IᶜABarrIst I p. 36; INağDurrah p. 386; QasṭMaw III p. 400. *Cf.* BaySunan III p. 410. To perform the sprinkling was Bilāl b. Rabāḥ (d. 32 H), see BayDal VII p. 264 = DiyTārḪamīs II p. 172; HarĞamᶜWas II p. 218 and HarMirqātMaf IV p. 77.

148 MunKawākib I p. 69.

149 As cited in DiyTārḪamīs II p. 146.

150 ŠīrMuhaḏ I p. 138; BaySunan III p. 411; IᶜABarrIst I p. 46; MuwMuršid I p. 65; DimSīrah p. 51; SamWafāʾ III p. 891; ŠāmīSubul VIII p. 381; RamlīNih III p. 34; HarMirqātMaf IV p. 68 and 76; Wellhausen: *Reste* pp. 182f.; MF XXXII p. 249; Grütter: *Bestattungsbräuche* p. 181; al-Muᶜallimī: *ᶜImārat al-qubūr* p. 120. *Cf.* also KulKāfī III pp. 199f.

151 QNuᶜmDaᶜāʾim I p. 239; ŠāmīSubul VIII p. 378; HarMirqātMaf I pp. 76 and 83; MF XXXII p. 249. On Ibn Maẓᶜūn, see below p. 255.

152 KulKāfī III p. 140.

153 IRağAhwāl p. 111.

among the other graves".[154] A similar practice was observed after the death of the Abbasid caliph Abū Ǧaᶜfar al-Manṣūr in Mecca in 158 H: he was buried in the Maᶜlāh cemetery,[155] and "in that night they dug forty graves for him, so that his actual tomb would not be known".[156] The account of aṭ-Ṭabarī is somewhat different, but more detailed: "A hundred graves were dug for al-Manṣūr and they were all filled in so that the position of his tomb, which was obvious to the people, was not (any longer) known, and he was buried in a different tomb because of fear for him. This was done with the tombs of the caliphs of the Abbasid family and no one knew the whereabouts of their tombs".[157] When al-Mutawakkil had the tomb of al-Ḥusayn destroyed in 236 H (see below p. 290), the site of his former tomb was not only sprinkled, but the soil was ploughed and plants grown on it.[158]

For the sprinkling of tombs, cold water was preferred.[159] The use of rose-water was rejected by an-Nawawī as a waste of money[160] but defended by others:

> "It is not forbidden, at least given that people do it with proper intentions, either to honour the deceased or to welcome (lit. receive) visitors with the pleasant odour of the site (...) . If somebody were to pronounce it forbidden, he could well put forward good arguments, but my opinion is backed by as-Subkī who said that using it moderately does no harm, especially if one desires the presence of the angels because they love the pleasant smell".[161]

The use of rose-water for sprinkling, on the other hand, is often attested among the ruling classes with their tendency to overt luxury. This motif is also encountered in poetry, e.g. in a verse by Abū l-Ḥakam al-Maġribī (ᶜUbayd Allāh b. al-Muẓaffar al-Marīnī, d. Damascus 549 H), mourning the Atābak Zangī b. Āqsunqur (d. 541 H), in the metre *ḫafīf*:

فَاسْكُبُوا فَوْقَ قَبْرِهِ مَاءَ وَرْدٍ * وَانْضِحُوهُ بِزَعْفَرَانٍ وَمِسْكِ

"Pour rose-water upon his tomb * and sprinkle it with saffron and musk!"[162]

Near the mausoleum of an early eighth-century Mamluk official and scholar in the Cairene Qarāfah cemetery there was, according to al-ᶜUmarī's first-hand report cited by al-ᶜAynī, "an elementary school (*maktab*) for orphans, who copied the

154 MaǧlBiḥār XLIII p. 183. See also below p. 196, n. 209.

155 According to MasTanbīh p. 295 he was buried in the *ḥaram* of Mecca, but this might also mean the wider area of the town and its surroundings.

156 SinǧManāʾiḥ II p. 102.

157 ṬabHistory XXIX p. 167.

158 MaqrMuq III p. 616.

159 RamlīNih III p. 35; HarMirqātMaf IV p. 76.

160 NawRawḍah II p. 136. *Cf.* also MF XXXII p. 250; al-Albānī: *Aḥkām al-ǧanāʾiz* p. 253; Haja: *Mort et Jugement Dernier* p. 37.

161 RamlīNih III p. 35. In Northern Pakistan and India, the tombs of Sufis are sprinkled with perfume or "washed" with rose-water (*ġusl al-qabr*): see Einzmann: *Ziarat und Pir-e-Muridi*, plates after p. 177; Moini: *Rituals and Customary Practices* pp. 65 and 71; Desai: *Major Dargahs* p. 80 (washing the tomb with sandalwood paste and scented water); for the South Asian custom of sprinkling the tombs in Muḥarram, see Masud: *Definition of Bidᶜa* p. 73.

162 IṣfḪar (M) I p. 297.

Qurʾān on small boards (ʾ*alwāḥ*). Whenever they wanted to erase (what they had written on) their boards, they washed them with water and poured it upon his tomb. I asked them about this and was told that it had been stipulated by the founder of the *waqf* (to which that school belonged). This is a laudable intention and betrays right belief".[163]

The idea of "watering" or "irrigating" the grave could also, at least in early Abbasid times, be associated with the idea of boon companionship (*munādamah*) and thus with wine.[164] Of course, there is an obvious connection between sprinkling the tomb with wine and taking the trouble to plant a grapevine upon it or in its vicinity (mentioned above). The most famous example, whose attestations are scattered widely in the sources, of boon-companions sitting at a tomb and sprinkling it with wine, is the case of two Arabs from the Banū Asad who had befriended a Persian noble in Rāwand (or, according to other versions, in nearby Qāšān). When later one of the Asadīs died, the remaining two friends met at his tomb, downed two cups and poured out a third over the grave of their friend (*wa-yaṣubbāni ʿalā qabrihī kaʾsan*); when finally only one friend had survived, he went to his friends' tombs (which were located side by side, as appropriate for intimates) and recited a last poetical farewell which contains the line (*ṭawīl*):

أَصُبُّ عَلَى قَبْرَيْكُمَا مِنْ مُدَامَةٍ * فَإِنْ لَمْ تَذُوقَاهَا أَبُلُّ ثَرَاكُمَا

"I pour old (i.e. precious) wine upon your tombs * so that, even if you cannot (any longer) taste it, I (at least) moisten your earth with it".[165]

Roughly the same story is also told about the second-century poet Abū l-Hindī Ġālib b. ʿAbd al-Quddūs (d. *c.*180 H), who lived in Persia (see **193**). A third, less closely related story is told by Yāqūt. He has it that ʿĪsā b. Yazīd Ibn Daʾb al-Layṯī al-Kinānī (d. 171 H), who hailed from the Ḥiǧāz, was once asked by the caliph al-Mahdī, who felt ill after a night of drunken conversation, to entertain him. ʿĪsā then told him a story about some wine-traders of the Kinānah tribe who had come to Syria. When one of their companions died there, they sat down at his tomb and started drinking; there was also a poem recited at that occasion.[166] A poem by Abū Nuwās, in which he adresses a wine-trader, begins with the words: "Drink at (*or* upon) the tomb of ʿAwn ...!" (ʾ*išrab ʿalā qabri*

163 ʿAynīʿIqd IV p. 476.

164 *Cf.* Heine: *Wein und Tod* pp. 118f. Surprisingly, the argument is not dealt with in Kathryn Kueny: *The Rhetoric of Sobriety. Wine in Early Islam*, Albany 2001.

165 MarzḤam 289 v. 4 (II p. 877) = IḪallWaf I p. 95; *Aġānī* XV p. 249 (where the second hemistich runs: *fa-ʾillā taḏūqā ʾarwī minhā* etc.); MaʿarrīŠḤam 288 v. 5 (I p. 528: *fa-ʾillā taḏūqāhā turawwi* etc.); MuʿāfāĞalīs I p. 563 (same variants as *Aġānī*); YāqBuldān III p. 20 (*s.v.* Rāwand, with the variant *fa-ʾillā taḏūqāhā turawwi* etc.); BaṣrīḤam (C) II p. 64 (var. *turawwī*); BaġdḪizānah II p. 74 (var. *fa-ʾillā tanālāhā turawwi ǧuṯākumā*) and p. 76 (var. *fa-ʾillā taḏūqāhā turawwi*), for interesting parallels see also *op. cit.* pp. 69f.; Wellhausen: *Reste* p. 183; Homerin: *Death and Afterlife* p. 184. The story with the accompanying poem is also cited in BalFutūḥ pp. 454f. and ŠantŠḤam 321 (I pp. 534f.), yet the above-quoted verse is missing there. A similar story is reported in al-ʿAffānī: *Sakb* I pp. 517f.

166 YāqIršād VI p. 107 = Heine: *Wein und Tod* p. 118.

ʿAwnin).[167] Finally, a story is told about a man in Baṣrah who used to sit at a tomb in the courtyard (*mağlis*!) of his house and drink many a cup beside it. He called that tomb "my drinking-companion" (*nadīm*); moreover, he also fell prostrate upon that tomb and was only brought back to consciousness by a servant who poured water over his face.[168]

Most interesting in our context are, to conclude with, two lines quoted anonymously in an-Nuwayrī's *ʾIlmām*, especially as they contain a reference to an epitaph (*ḫafīf*):

أَسْقِيَانِي حَتَّى أَمُوتَ مَكَانِي * وَادْفِنَانِي فِي طِينِ رُوسِ الدِّنَانِ
وَاكْتُبُوا مِنْ دَمِي عَلَى لَوْحِ قَبْرِي * رَحِمَ اللّٰهُ مَيِّتاً سَكْرَانْ

"You two, pour wine in my cup until I die on the spot * and bury me in the clay stoppers of wine-jugs!
Write with my blood upon my tombstone: * 'May God have mercy upon one who died a drunkard!'"[169]

2.3.3. The tomb of the Prophet as a model

From the second century H onwards, scholars tried to find evidence for settling the question of erecting a mound over the tomb (or not) by taking the shape of the Prophet's sepulchre as a model.

There was no unanimity as to what the Prophet's tomb looked like, whether flattened or raised above the ground. There seems to be a certain tendency, noticeably increasing in the course of time, to describe the Prophet's tomb neither as wholly levelled nor as truly raised. This was not only because in view of the uncertainty as to the correct usage, the jurists did not want to assign the Prophet's grave to one of the two categories, but it was also the result of their strong interest in that tomb, so that conflicting reports multiplied.

Various people reported that the Prophet's tomb was either wholly levelled[170] or elevated for only about one span (*šibr*) or two spans (*šibrayn*),[171] measures later taken up by the Shafiites and other legal traditions (see below), but that at its rear side it was raised (*musannam*) somewhat more, yet without curvature.[172] Others stressed that the entire tomb was somewhat raised above the ground (*musannam*) or had a true mound over it,[173] a description to which others objected by pointing out

167 ANuwDīwān III p. 241 (no. 298, 1).

168 SarrāğMaṣ I p. 27.

169 NuwIlmām III p. 304 = WKAS II p. 1711 (s.r. *lwḥ*, only the second verse).

170 YaʿqTārīḫ II p. 114; IʿABarrIst I p. 36; BayDal VII pp. 263f.; DiyTārḪamīs II p. 172; HarMirqātMaf IV p. 68; MunKawākib I p. 69. *Cf.* Rāğib: *Structure de la tombe* p. 400.

171 INağDurrah p. 386; QurṭTaḏk p. 86; SamWafāʾ II p. 557; QasṭMaw III p. 400; KU 42924 (XV p. 735); HarĞamʿWas II p. 218; al-Albānī: *Aḥkām al-ğanāʾiz* p. 154.

172 ʿARazMuṣ 6484 (III pp. 502f.). A different wording appears in HaytTuḥfMuḥt III p. 173. These reports are also cited in ISaʿdṬab II pp. 292-4.

173 FB III p. 326 (*ğanāʾiz* 96) = INağDurrah p. 386; ISaʿdṬab II pp. 306f.; BayDal VII p. 264; MuwMuršid I p. 65; SamWafāʾ II pp. 556f.; QasṭMaw III p. 400; DiyTārḪamīs II p. 172;

that the elevation was not made until the levelled original construction was replaced under the caliph ᶜUmar II b. ᶜAbd al-ᶜAzīz (*cf.* below)[174] or under al-Walīd b. ᶜAbd al-Malik by a new one.[175]

A typical report showing the tendency to arrive at some intermediate position is a Tradition from ᶜĀʾišah to the effect that the Prophet's tomb as well as those of Abū Bakr and ᶜUmar were "neither elevated (*mušrifah*) nor wholly flat (*lāṭiʾah*), (with their surface) levelled (*mabṭūḥah*, or in other versions: *masṭūḥah* or *musaṭṭaḥah*) with smooth red pebbles from the courtyard",[176] though others stressed that the tombs of Abū Bakr and ᶜUmar had mounds or were "raised" (*musannamah*).[177] The aforesaid pebbles are probably referred to in a Tradition which states that *naqal*, "little stones", had been strewn on the graves of the Prophet, Abū Bakr and ᶜUmar,[178] but this, it was claimed, had nothing to do with their having mounds or not. Moreover it was argued that the "flatness" (*tasṭīḥ*) of the tomb did not refer to its being flat or low in the literal sense, but to its being merely well-kept, that is, with its surface evened or smoothed.[179] Following the presumed model of the Prophet's tomb, however, the practice of scattering pebbles on the grave's surface should only be performed on graves wholly levelled;[180] the pebbles should serve to keep the loose earth of the mound together,[181] to prevent the tomb from being opened by wild animals, or as a sign to mark it as a burial place.[182]

In time, scholars devoted entire monographs to the question of the shape of the Prophet's sepulchre, for example Abū Bakr al-Āǧurrī (d. 360 H) who "adduces in

HarǦamᶜWas II p. 218 and HarMirqātMaf IV p. 67 and 79. *Cf.* AYūsĀṯār 397 (p. 80); IAŠayMuṣ III pp. 215f. (*ǧanāʾiz* 130 and 132); al-Albānī: *Aḥkām al-ǧanāʾiz* p. 154.

174 FB III p. 329 (*ǧanāʾiz* 96); QasṭMaw III p. 401.

175 FB III p. 328; QasṭIršād II p. 390 and QasṭMaw III p. 401; SamWafāʾ II pp. 556f.; HaytTuḥfMuḥt III p. 173; HarMirqātMaf IV p. 68. *Cf.* also ITayMaǧm XXVII pp. 140f.; Hillenbrand: *Islamic Architecture* p. 253.

176 FB III p. 328; ADāʾūd III p. 292 (*ǧanāʾiz* 72); MasTanbīh p. 251; ḤākMust I pp. 369f.; BayDal VII p. 263; IQudMuġnī II p. 504; INaǧDurrah pp. 386 and 392; QasṭIršād II p. 390 and QasṭMaw III p. 401; SamWafāʾ II pp. 551f., 554 and 556; HarǦamᶜWas II p. 219; al-Muᶜallimī: *ᶜImārat al-qubūr* pp. 115, 118 and 134-7. *Cf.* also ᶜARazMuṣ 6485 (III p. 503); ŠīrMuhaḏ I p. 138; BaySunan III p. 411; IQayZād I p. 524; DiyTārḪamīs II p. 172; HarMirqātMaf IV pp. 68 and 78f.; CIA Égypte II p. 66; WKAS II p. 682 (s.v. *lāṭiʾ*); MF XXXII p. 249; al-Albānī: *Aḥkām al-ǧanāʾiz* p. 154. Similar, though shorter in KulKāfī III p. 201.

177 HarǦamᶜWas II pp. 218f.; al-Muᶜallimī: *ᶜImārat al-qubūr* p. 116.

178 ᶜARazMuṣ 6717 (III p. 574). *Cf.* also SamWafāʾ II p. 555.

179 HarǦamᶜWas II p. 219. Pebbles (*al-ḥaṣā* or *al-ḥaṣbāʾ*) were also strewn on the grave of the Prophet's son Ibrāhīm, see SamWafāʾ III p. 891 and ŠāmīSubul VIII p. 381.

180 BaySunan III p. 411; NawRawḍah II p. 136; ArdAnwār I p. 124; MF XXXII p. 249; al-Muᶜallimī: *ᶜImārat al-qubūr* pp. 120, 137 and 143.

181 IMuflFurūᶜ II p. 271; MF XXXII p. 250.

182 HarMirqātMaf IV p. 76. *Cf.* also RamlīNih II p. 35 and Grütter: *Bestattungsbräuche* pp. 170f. For similar practices of putting pebbles on tombs in modern Egypt and North Africa, see Winkler: *Volkskunde* p. 227 (with further literature in the note).

his book 'The Shape of the Prophet's Tomb' (*Kitāb Ṣifat qabr an-nabī*) a report from (...) ᶜUṯaym b. Nisṭās al-Madīnī (*or* al-Madanī) who said, 'I saw the tomb during the caliphate of ᶜUmar b. ᶜAbd al-ᶜAzīz and it was elevated (*murtafiᶜan*) (above ground level) a measurement of about four fingers'".[183] This measure, viz. four fingers or four fingers and a half, was largely adopted in legal and Ḥadīṯ literature (and also accepted by Shiite scholars) as the standard height of the mound.[184]

Other reports from the second century H indicate that the Prophet's tomb or the burial niche – the wording is ambiguous – was covered by unburnt bricks (*libn*).[185] It might be interesting to note in this context that az-Zamaḫšarī (d. 538 H, see **94**) in a poem in praise of the Prophet says: *li-llāhi maytun bi-l-Madīnati qabruhū qaṣrun mašīdun*, "How good is a dead one in Medina (i.e. the Prophet) whose tomb is a tall palace!"[186]

The concession that the grave could be elevated to a certain degree was probably motivated, at least in part, by the very reports describing the Prophet's tomb. But there were, for all the theoretical aspects of the discussion, practical considerations as well. For that reason, aš-Šāfiᶜī argued as follows: "I disapprove of the raising of the grave over the height necessary to mark it as such, and in order to prevent somebody from stepping upon or sitting down on it".[187] This was taken up and supplemented by the tenth-century scholar Ibn Ḥağar al-Haytamī who stated: "The tomb is to be raised for one span only – or approximately –, if there is no danger of its being destroyed by an unbeliever, a heretic or a thief. It also serves to identify it and in order to be visited and revered".[188]

2.4. The legal debate

In view of the conflicting information found in Tradition and the historiographical sources, it comes as no surprise that the legal experts, as in many other cases, did not arrive at a unanimously shared opinion. The basic dichotomy, namely levelling

183 FB III p. 328 (*ğanāʾiz* 96; the name of ᶜUṯaym is here erroneously rendered as "Ġunaym b. Bisṭām"); SamWafāʾ II pp. 552f.; QasṭMaw III p. 401; al-Muᶜallimī: *ᶜImārat al-qubūr* pp. 117 and 140.

184 IAŠayMuṣ III p. 216 (*ğanāʾiz* 132); MasTanbīh p. 251; KulKāfī III pp. 140, 199 and 201; ṬūsīMiṣbāḥ p. 35 and ṬūsīMabsūṭ I p. 187; INuğBaḥr II p. 209; Grütter: *Bestattungsbräuche* p. 171; four fingers and a half: ḤaḍrMuq p. 103; HaytMinhāğ p. 103. Larger measures, for example ten spans, were not tolerated, see WanšMiᶜyār I p. 318.

185 IAŠayMuṣ III p. 214 (*ğanāʾiz* 129); IĞamMuḫt p. 148; DiyTārḪamīs II p. 172; HarĞamᶜWas II p. 218. Different reports are cited in Rāġib: *Structure de la tombe* p. 398.

186 MN II p. 135 (v. 45). The meaning of *mašīd* is "high rising, lofty", especially if said of a palace or castle (see Lane *s.r.*), and with this meaning the word is used in Q 22:45 (Arberry translates "a tall palace"). For a similar verse, see IĞawzīTabṣ II p. 238; *cf.* also ANuḤilyah III p. 289 and IMuᶜtDīwān 1156 v. 10 (III p. 21: *ʾayna l-quṣūru llatī šayyadtahā*).

187 TirmĞāmiᶜ II p. 257 (*ğanāʾiz* 55); NawRawḍah II p. 136. This was also the view of Abū Ḥanīfah, see AYūsĀṯār 399 (p. 81). See also above p. 13.

188 HaytTuḥfMuḥt III p. 173. Practical reasons are also alluded to in IMuflFurūᶜ II p. 270. *Cf.* also IQudMuġnī II p. 504.

the grave vs. erecting a mound over it, was fully preserved in the field of law and has not been truly resolved since. Ibn Ḥağar al-ᶜAsqalānī wrote:

> "Some scholars, for example Mālik, Abū Ḥanīfah, Aḥmad (b. Ḥanbal),[189] al-Muzanī and a great number of Shafiites, held the conviction that piling up mounds was desirable (*mustaḥabb*);[190] the judge Ḥusayn even claimed the unanimity of the (Prophet's) companions in that regard. On the other hand, the majority of the first generations of Shafiites regarded the levelling (of the grave) as desirable, a rule laid down by aš-Šāfiᶜī himself, al-Māwardī and others".[191]

As stated by Ibn Ḥağar, aš-Šāfiᶜī himself as well as many representatives of the Shafiite legal tradition appear indeed to have been adherents of the more severe interpretation, namely that marking the grave by a mound was not permissible and therefore to be avoided.[192] Clearly, aš-Šāfiᶜī considered this proceeding to be correct, basing his opinion upon a Tradition about the Prophet's practice: "The tomb has to be levelled (*yusaṭṭaḥu*), in keeping with what we are told from the Prophet, namely that he levelled the tomb of his son Ibrāhīm".[193] Which is not to say that aš-Šafiᶜī was entirely consistent in this matter for he also stated that "it is desirable that the tomb rises not more than a span (*šibr*) or nearly so above ground level".[194] That is, he did not exclude that the surface of a tomb (or its enclosure) might be elevated somewhat, and many later Shafiites, following their main authority, arrived therefore at the following conclusion: "The tomb may be raised for one span (above the ground), except in regions of war, but levelling it (*tasṭīḥuhū*) is preferable".[195] The measure of "one span" or "two spans", used conventionally for the measure of tombs, appears in Arabic poetry, too.[196]

Many Malikites, on the other hand, considered "setting a mound over the grave" or "marking the grave with a mound" (*tasnīm al-qabr*) the proper solution,[197] though

189 *Cf.* IQudMuġnī II p. 505; MuwMuršid I p. 65; HarMirqātMaf IV p. 68. Other Hanbalites, however, did more often than not discourage the elevation of the tomb above ground level, see IMuflFurūᶜ II p. 271.

190 *Cf.* MF XXXII p. 248; al-Albānī: *Aḥkām al-ğanāʾiz* p. 204. According to NawRawḍah II p. 137, only al-Ġazālī and a few other Shafiite authorities opted against levelling the grave.

191 FB III p. 328 (*ğanāʾiz* 96) = HarĞamᶜWas II p. 219, anonymously cited in QasṭIršād II p. 390 and QasṭMaw III pp. 400f. *Cf.* also ITayMağm XXVII p. 121.

192 *Cf.* IQāsimFatḥ p. 218; IᶜASalāmFat p. 87; IQudMuġnī II p. 505; ArdAnwār I p. 124; KirmŠBuḫ VII p. 161; HarMirqātMaf IV p. 68; MF XXXII p. 249.

193 ŠāfUmm I p. 458; QasṭIršād II p. 390. See also above p. 177.

194 ŠāfUmm I p. 463. *Cf.* also BaySunan III pp. 410f.; NawŠMuslim VII p. 36; IMuflFurūᶜ II p. 271; HaytTuḥfMuḥt III p. 173; HarMirqātMaf IV p. 68; ŠawkŠṢudūr p. 70; al-Muᶜallimī: *ᶜImārat al-qubūr* p. 115.

195 ŠīrMuhaḏ I p. 138; NawRawḍah II p. 136; INaqᶜUmdah p. 240 (*ğanāʾiz* 5); ArdAnwār I p. 124; HaytTuḥfMuḥt III p. 173; MF XXXII p. 249.

196 BaṣrīḤam (C) II p. 61 (*ʾiᶜğab li-qabrin qīsa šibran* [var. *qadra šibrin*] *qad ḥawā* etc.); ṬurṭSirāğ p. 18 (*man kāna baynaka fī t-turābi wa-baynahū * šibrānī* ...).

197 Cited from al-Qāḍī ᶜIyāḍ in NawŠMuslim VII p. 36; QurṭTaḏk p. 86; WanšMiᶜyār I p. 31;

there are other reports found in Malikite works which seem to point to the contrary.[198] The Hanafites, as already indicated by Ibn Ḥağar al-ᶜAsqalānī (see above), generally held the belief that placing a mound over the grave was preferable, with individual scholars among them even considering it obligatory.[199] According to a saying transmitted from Abū Ḥanīfah, the raising of the tomb above ground level should mainly serve to mark the grave as such so that nobody steps or tramples upon it.[200] The Hanbalites more or less followed the view of the Shafiites.[201] Very typically and in agreement with a general trend in Hanbalite scholarship, they tried to harmonise between the different views put forward in other legal schools: they saw the tomb best levelled towards its borders, but raised towards the middle.[202] Some of them also argued that the amount of earth on the grave (that is, the mound) should consist of nothing more than what was excavated when digging the grave, an opinion also accepted by other Sunnite legal traditions[203] and the Shiites.[204]

In any case, levelling the tomb – as with sprinkling its surface[205] – could also be carried out in order to make the site of a tomb disappear, e.g. when it was feared that people could unearth the corpse,[206] or in order to prevent its becoming a site of worship, as in the case of ᶜAbd Allāh b. Ġālib (see above p. 91).

In another instance, Abū Ayyūb Ḫālid b. Zayd al-Anṣārī, who was buried near Constantinople in the year 52 H (or after), expressed as his last wish that his tomb be levelled (*swy* II) on purpose, by horses and soldiers trampling upon it, thus flattening it until no trace would be left.[207] However, this must not have been done satisfactorily because al-Wāqidī (whose trustworthiness as to reports like the following, however, is not beyond doubt) relates that Abū Ayyūb's tomb was "adopted" by the Byzantines who also had erected a mausoleum (*qubbah*) upon it; they visited the tomb frequently and performed the rain-prayer.[208] In yet another instance, we are told that the tomb of Fāṭimah in Medina was levelled (*swy* II), reportedly by ᶜAlī, in order to make its traces disappear.[209]

MF XXXII p. 249; Rāġib: *Structure de la tombe* p. 400; al-Muᶜallimī: *ᶜImārat al-qubūr* p. 122; *cf.* also MuwMuršid I p. 65.

198 *Cf.* SaḥnūnMud I p. 189; IĞuzQaw p. 113.

199 *Cf.* MarġHid I p. 114; INuğBaḥr II p. 209; HarMirqātMaf IV p. 79.

200 AYūsĀṯār 399 (p. 81) = al-Muᶜallimī: *ᶜImārat al-qubūr* pp. 122f.

201 *Cf.* IQudMuġnī II p. 505; IQaylġāṯah II p. 179.

202 IMuflFurūᶜ II p. 271. *Cf.* also al-Muᶜallimī: *ᶜImārat al-qubūr* p. 133.

203 IQudMuġnī II p. 504; IQaylġāṯah I pp. 181f.; al-Muᶜallimī: *ᶜImārat al-qubūr* pp. 199f.; for the Malikite opinion: DabMaᶜālim III p. 16. *Cf.* also ŠāmīSubul VIII pp. 380f.; Rāġib: *Structure de la tombe* p. 400; al-Albānī: *Aḥkām al-ğanāʾiz* p. 205.

204 KulKāfī III p. 202; QNuᶜmDaᶜāʾim I p. 239; ṬūsīMiṣbāḥ p. 35 and ṬūsīMabsūṭ I p. 187.

205 See n. 140 above.

206 See the story cited in IQaylġāṯah I p. 188.

207 TMD XVI p. 58 = Lecker: *Burial of Martyrs* p. 44.

208 Cited in IĞawzīṢafwah I p. 196.; *cf.* also TMD XVI pp. 61f. According to others, Abū Ayyūb's tomb was only rediscovered by a vision after the Ottoman conquest of Constantinople, see Kriss: *Volksglaube* I pp. 315-8; Laqueur: *Friedhöfe Istanbul* p. 25. *Cf.* also Memon: *Ibn Taimīya's Struggle* p. 269.

209 MağlBihār XLIII pp. 183, 193 and 215. When some women went out to dig up the tombs to

To sum up, there was no unanimity among Muslim scholars and jurists as to whether graves should be levelled, with their surfaces more or less flattened, or whether they should be marked by a mound or even a tumulus. It was certainly not the case that the overwhelming majority of scholars opted for levelling as claimed by an-Nawawī (who in general was fond of invoking the *communis opinio* or the *ʾiǧmāʿ* in order to support his own arguments).[210] However, as will have become clear from what Ibn Ḥaǧar and many others had to say on this point, there was no discussion of which practice was allowed and which forbidden, but what was at stake was the question which of the two practices was preferable: "The point of conflict here is not which of the two ways is allowed, but which of them is preferable".[211]

As we know from innumerable shrines, mausolea and cemeteries throughout the Islamic world, the practice as to the shape of tombs and larger funerary structures has always been markedly different from the theory. This was also recognised by the Muslim scholars who, over the centuries, tried to reach theoretical positions closer to reality. Ibn Ḥaǧar al-ʿAsqalānī, to mention but one, had recourse to that spirit of compromise which is typical of much pre-modern Islamic learning and many other facets of pre-modern Islamic culture, notwithstanding all the niceties of the academic debate: "If the tomb is raised with good intent (*li-ġaraḍ ṣaḥīḥ*) and not with the intention (to satisfy) vainglory, it is permitted".[212]

However, how distant from each other the extremes of the Islamic attitudes with regard to funerary structures were becomes evident if we contrast Ibn Ḥaǧar's opinion with the attitude of a companion of the Malikite scholar Saḥnūn, Abū ʿAbd Allāh Muḥammad b. Abī Ḥumayd as-Sūsī (d. 293 H), who purportedly used to say: "Once I have died, throw rubbish (*kunāsah*) upon my tomb!"[213] A seventh-century scholar from Egypt, Ibrāhīm al-Qulaybī, stipulated in his will that his tomb be obliterated after his burial.[214] Yet another scholar, the Andalusian Abū Yaʿqūb al-Ḫaššāb, who was buried on the Isle of Djerba (modern Tunisia), ordered the obliteration (*taʿmiyah*) of his tomb because he feared that the Christians would conquer the island and thus he did not want his tomb exposed to the unbelievers.[215] Equally outspoken, to conclude, was the point of view of the mystic Aḥmad al-Buhlūl (d. Cairo 928 H). The words expressing Aḥmad's last wish as to his own burial are a veritable epitome of the strictest view imaginable and clearly do not reflect the common practice in the Islamic lands. It is worthwhile quoting them here in full:

see which was the tomb of Fāṭimah, ʿAlī rushed there, sword in his hand, and prevented them from doing so, see *op. cit.* p. 212.

210 NawRawḍah II p. 137.

211 FB III p. 328 (*ǧanāʾiz* 96); QasṭMaw III p. 401.

212 FB III p. 287 (*ǧanāʾiz* 81).

213 DabMaʿālim II p. 251.

214 MaqrMuq I p. 164 (*wa-ʾawṣā ʾan yuṭmasa qabruhū fa-ṭumisa*).

215 TiǧRiḥlah p. 261. His fear was well-justified for Djerba had been occupied by the Normans of Sicily from 1135 to 1160 CE. Between 1284 and 1335 CE and again from 1383 to 1392 CE the island was then in the hands of the Aragonese rulers of Sicily.

"Sīdī Aḥmad al-Buhlūl used to say, 'Do not bury me anywhere but outside the Qarāfah Gate in the street (*fī š-šāriʿ*) and do not put a tombstone on my grave! Gather cattle and mules so that they may trample upon me (i.e. upon my tomb, in order to wipe out every trace)! Beware that they do not put a cenotaph or a cover (of cloth) upon my tomb, lest I should not find peace in the tomb with everybody passing me by and knocking on my cenotaph!' When his companions told him 'But we already prepared a tomb for you in the Baṭīḫah-Mosque', he replied 'If you are able to take me there, then do it'. And indeed, when (after his death) they tried to move with the bier (*naʿš*) towards the mosque, they were not able to do so, but when they turned towards the Qarāfah they proceeded easily".[216]

2.5. Practice: funerary monuments

In view of common practice we must conclude that the legal discussion of whether a tomb should have a mound over it or be levelled proved rather academic, not to mention futile. For as long as there is no mausoleum or another roofed funerary structure, many graves in Islamic countries tend indeed to be covered by low heaps of earth (also called *ʾasnimat al-qubūr*, literally "humps of the graves" and hence "elevated parts of the tombs")[217] or slabs until the present day, not at all dissimilar to the Christian graves of middle and northern Europe, that is to say, "plain" graves.

Very often we also find or read about cenotaphs (of stone or wood) or low enclosure-walls of the grave recinct made of bricks, stone, marble or, occasionally, wood of about 20-30 cm height,[218] sometimes with uncut or carved stones or other ornamental objects marking the four corners or at least the foot and the head;[219] such stones are therefore simply called *raʾs* ("head") among the bedouins of Egypt.[220] If, however, there was a cenotaph (or for that matter, a whole mausoleum) erected

216 ŠaʿrṬab II p. 145. The motif of a deceased person not being able to be transported to a certain place (or not even lifted at all from the ground) is a known topos in Sufi hagiography and biographical literature, e.g. (a) the case of Abū Turāb an-Naḫšabī (d. 245 H) in MunKawākib I p. 547; (b) the case of aš-Šihāb A. b. Mūsā al-Ḥanafī (d. Cairo 703 H), as reported in ITaġrManh II p. 237; *cf.* also Gramlich: *Wunder* p. 354 and *Vorbilder* I p. 332; Lane: *Manners and Customs* pp. 510f. This topos is also known in the European cultures, see Ariès: *Western Attitudes* p. 17 and Lawrence: *Medieval Monasticism* p. 64: The English missionary Boniface "had chosen Fulda to be his place of burial. After his martyrdom in Frisia (...), local enthusiasts tried to retain his body. But it was well known that the will of the saints was as impossible to frustrate after death as it was in life; the bier became immovable until they placed it on a barge to carry it up the Rhine on the first stage of its journey to Fulda".

217 *Cf.* IĞubRiḥlah (B) p. 24.

218 E.g. as described in ŠawkŠṢudūr pp. 70f.

219 Kriss: *Volksglaube* I p. 17; for al-Andalus, see Torres Balbás: *Cementerios* pp. 139ff. Such enclosures resemble sepulchral mounds as they are also known from ancient Roman tombs (often made of bricks, *tegulae*); *cf.* Peral Bejarano: *Excavación y estudio* pp. 26f. and 30. For the similarities between ancient (and Sasānid) tomb structures and later Islamic practices, see also Kervran: *Cimetières islamiques* p. 71 with note 14.

220 Winkler: *Volkskunde* p. 315.

above the grave, this was seen rather to fall under the prohibition not to construct burial monuments of any kind and has little to do with the surface of the grave being flattened or having a mound over it (see below).

The pre-modern literary sources, for all their profusion, are of little help in reconstructing the shape of tombs. Very often, they contain no information at all about their outer appearance, which makes most of them rather disappointing for art historians and archaeologists. In those rare cases where we do find some information, we merely read that someone's tomb was "built", without being told exactly how, or we hear, as for example in the occasional remarks by the twelfth-century biographer al-Murādī, that somebody's grave was provided with "beautiful stone-work" (*ʿalā qabrihī taḥǧīrun laṭīfun*),[221] whatever this may have looked like.

In the same vein, al-ʿUlaymī describes a mausoleum as *qabrun ʿalayhi bināʾun ʿaẓīmun*, "a tomb upon which there is a great building", or he says, in another passage, *wa-banā ʿalā qabrihī masṭabatan kabīratan bi-bināʾin muḥkamin*, "and over his tomb he had constructed a large *masṭabah* – a rectangular structure resembling a bench –, in the form of a solid building".[222] Similarly little concrete evidence is provided in the information about the tomb of Ibn al-Ḥaddād (M. b. A., d. 344 H) in Cairo: "on the outside of its enclosure[223] there had been a marble slab (*ruḫām*), but it was torn out (*fa-quliʿa*)".[224] Very often we simply read that "a beautiful building" (*bunyān ḥasan*)[225] or "a beautiful shrine" (*mašhad ḥasan*)[226] had been erected upon somebody's tomb.

On the basis of these and many other comments in the sources, we are unlikely to get any clear idea of the exact shape and form of a building if it has not been preserved to posterity; hence we are not in a position to compare the material vestiges with the vague description offered in the sources. The only exception among the literary sources are the two Cairene cemetery guides by Ibn az-Zayyāt and as-Saḫāwī (on both, see Chapter 3). Here we find indeed a relatively detailed terminology concerning funerary monuments, since many architectural features of those monuments have been noted by the authors. We also see that here some development had taken place: two centuries before, al-Muwaffaq Ibn ʿUṯmān in his cemetery guide *Muršid az-zuwwār* had not yet possessed the refined terminology – nor, as it seems, the interest – to describe the funerary monuments in detail; he merely speaks of tombs and mausolea as *qabr*, *turbah* or *qubbah* and adds little else besides. However, the attitude towards funerary monuments commonly found in most literary sources is probably part of the wider significance of architectural items and aesthetic elements and their rendering in pre-modern Arabic works, especially during the Mamluk period:

221 MurSilk IV p. 102; see also III p. 161 and IV p. 265. By *taḥǧīr*, probably a little wall around the sides of the grave is meant; *cf.* Dozy: *Supplément* I p. 250.

222 ʿUlaymīUns II pp. 151 and 241. "Solid" in the sense of being made of stone or bricks.

223 *ʿalā ẓāhir ḥuǧratihī*, or rather *ḥaǧratihī*: "of its side"?

224 MaqrMuq V p. 258.

225 E.g. IFuwaṭīḤaw p. 181.

226 E.g. IFurTārīḫ VII p. 108.

> "Aside from mentioning how large or tall or strange a building was, or listing particular expensive materials in its construction, or indicating that a certain surface was ornamented using a certain complicated technique, formal or spatial qualities of the buildings were passed over in silence. (...) Formal and architectural investigations seem to have been outside the intellectual curiosity or scholarly training of Mamluk authors. Because of that handicap, they do not seem to have developed the techniques and terminology to carry out such examinations, and it shows in their texts".[227]

Still less concrete and much more generic is the depiction, if we can call it thus, of funerary monuments in poetry. In pre-Islamic poetry stone-work tombs are mentioned or alluded to (see above p. 172), and Durayd b. aṣ-Ṣimmah (d. 8 H) in a mourning poem speaks of the *bunyān al-qubūr*, "the (solid) building of the tombs".[228] In a verse by Usāmah b. Munqiḏ (mourning his son Abū Bakr) – as well as in other Arabic mourning poetry – we find the generic mention of "earth and stones" (*turbun wa-ʾaḥǧārun*) heaped or put upon a tomb, but it is impossible to conclude from this anything in particular regarding the outer shape of the grave (*basīṭ*):

أَزُورُ قَبْرَكَ مُشْتَاقًا فَيَحْجُبُنِي * مَا هِيلَ فَوْقَكَ مِنْ تُرْبٍ وَأَحْجَارِ

"I visit your tomb longing (for you), but I am secluded (from you) * by what was heaped upon you of earth and stones".[229]

3. *Larger funerary structures and cemeteries*

The question of placing a mound over the grave also bears upon the problem as to whether larger funerary constructions should be erected, e.g. a cenotaph (*tābūt*, *ṣundūq*, seldom *tarkībah* or *nuṣb*[230]) or a (roofed or domed) mausoleum (*qubbah* or *turbah*).[231] Thus one could argue *a fortiori* that solid constructions over graves were disapproved of or at least not preferable, by analogy with the doctrine that there

227 Rabbat: *Architecture in Mamluk Sources* pp. 158f. See also Jarrar: *Al-Maqrizi's Reinvention*.

228 *Aġānī* XV p. 98.

229 IMunqiḏDīwān 511 v. 1 (p. 300). See also below p. 352.

230 E.g. FāsīʿIqd III p. 24 (*wa-buniya ʿalā qabrihī nuṣb*).

231 For the confusing and imprecise terminology used in the Arabic sources for all types of funerary architecture, see Leisten: *Architektur für Tote*, esp. pp. 67-77 and *passim*; Badr: *Styles of Tombs* p. 349; Behrens-Abouseif: *Qubba*; Marcus: *Funerary and Burial Practices* p. 102; Hillenbrand: *Islamic Architecture* pp. 255ff. Though *qubbah* literally means "dome" or "cupola", it was in general used in the wider sense of "mausoleum" or "shrine", sometimes also in the sense of a certain type of "Sufi foundation" or "ascetic lodge" (*zāwiyah*). The more restricted meaning of "dome" was emphasised, however, by Ibn Ḥazm who differentiated between erecting a *qubbah* and a non-domed, "stable construction" (*bināʾ qāʾim*) upon the tomb, see Wafā: *Aḥkām al-ǧanāʾiz* pp. 264f. In the eastern lands (Anatolia, Persia, Central Asia), we often find the term *marqad*, "resting place", said of a mausoleum.

should be no mounds.[232] On the other hand, one could also argue that the fact that graves as such should not be covered by mounds does not *per se* mean that there should be no funerary constructions erected above them, as long as the surface of the grave as such remained levelled or low above the ground. However, the problem was much more complex than that.

3.1. Reports from the Prophet and the legal debate

If we look, as the Muslim jurists did, to what is transmitted or reported from the Prophet, we find the famous and widely-quoted interdiction "to build upon the grave" (*nahā ... ʾan yubnā ʿalayhi*).[233] This very unspecific wording leaves large room for speculation as to what exactly is intended by "building upon the grave" (often rendered as *al-bināʾ ʿalā l-qabr*): did it mean either not to build anything on the upper surface of the grave and its recinct as such (the so-called *ḥarīm al-qabr*), for example heightening it in order to prevent its being stepped on, or did it amount to a general prohibition of building larger funerary structures above or around the grave, for example a *turbah*, a madrasah or a tomb-mosque?[234]

Understandably, many legal scholars opted for the second possibility because "just four square stones[235] put around the grave (...) are not called 'building' (*bināʾ*) in common linguistic use (*ʿurfan*)".[236] Malikite scholars therefore considered it a matter of indifference (and thus not forbidden from a legal point of view) to raise the tomb in the form of a building (*tasnīmuhū bi-l-bināʾ*) and to surround the grave recinct by a wall or enclosure, – without, however, constructing a roof or cupola above it –, in order to distinguish it from neighbouring graves or to prevent its violation or destruction.[237] In later centuries, the cenotaphs commonly erected on saints' tombs were likewise not seen as falling under the verdict "not to build upon the grave".[238] Thus, the scholars in general understood the verdict by the Prophet as pertaining merely to the construction of tomb-chambers and (roofed or domed) mausolea.

As in the case of placing a mound over the grave, aš-Šāfiʿī was opposed to these and similar structures: "(It is desirable) that the tomb is neither built (of stone *or*

232 This argument was put forward by the Malikite scholar Saḥnūn, see Leisten: *Attitudes* p. 17.

233 ʿARazMuṣ 6488 (III p. 504); IAŠayMuṣ III p. 218 (*ğanāʾiz* 137); NawŠMuslim VII p. 37 (*ğanāʾiz* 94); ADāʾūd III p. 293 (*ğanāʾiz* 76); TirmĞāmiʿ II p. 258 (*ğanāʾiz* 57); NasSunan IV pp. 71f.; IMāğah I p. 498; ḤākMust I p. 370; BaySunan III p. 410; IḤağAḥwāl p. 48; KU 42920 (XV p. 734); HarMirqātMaf IV p. 69; ŠawkŠŠudūr p. 70; al-Albānī: *Aḥkām al-ğanāʾiz* p. 204; al-Muʿallimī: *ʿImārat al-qubūr* p. 229 and *passim*.

234 *Cf.* SuyZahr IV p. 71; RamlīNih III p. 34; ŠirwḤāš III p. 198.

235 That is, not simple pebbles or gravel (*ḥaṣan*), but cut stones, see ŠirwḤāš III p. 199.

236 HaytTuḥfMuḥt III p. 198. *Cf.* also IMuflFurūʿ II p. 272 and RamlīNih III p. 32.

237 WanšMiʿyār I pp. 317f. *Cf.* IĞuzQaw p. 113.

238 ŠubrḤāš III p. 34.

bricks, etc.) nor whitened with gypsum plaster (*taǧṣīṣ*)".[239] Yet here, too, it remains pretty unclear what exactly is meant, though it seems that aš-Šāfiʿī had in mind any structure built upon or above a grave, be it a simple enclosure made of stones or a full-scale mausoleum. This lack of clarity is due to the ambiguous use of the Arabic term *qabr*, which could either mean "grave" (that is, the grave in the ground as such) or rather "tomb" in the sense of "tomb-chamber" or "mausoleum" of which the actual grave is only a part.[240]

The Malikites, as said above, tended to view the construction of low enclosures around the grave as legitimate, while they rejected larger funeral structures, especially if roofed. Thus Ibn Rušd wrote fatwas to the effect that all larger funerary constructions were to be torn down and that nothing was to be left but little walls around the grave recinct in order to mark the tomb as such and to prevent casual unearthing;[241] al-Qāḍī ʿIyāḍ quotes from the fatwa of an earlier Malikite scholar who had to decide whether a newly built mausoleum (in front of a tavern) had to be torn down or not: "The destruction of the building (*bunyān*) which has been erected upon the tomb is obligatory, and building upon tombs is (in general) disapproved".[242]

The Hanbalite position has been summarised by Ibn Qayyim al-Ǧawzīyah: "It is contrary to the (right) guidance of the Prophet to raise tombs, to build them using baked bricks (*ʾāǧurr*), stones or unbaked bricks (*libn*), to plaster them, to cover them with clay or to erect domes (*or* mausolea: *qibāb*) over them.[243] Every such practice is nothing but an abominable innovation (*bidʿah*) contrary to the (right) guidance of the Prophet. (...) He forbade us the whitening of the tomb (with gypsum), to build upon it or to apply an inscription".[244] This opinion has been endorsed by the Wahhābites during the last two centuries, though of late their scholars have been arriving at a less uncompromising attitude.[245] In Shiite sources, we read that "plastering the tomb with gypsum and erecting a building over it in these places where this is (in principle) allowed, is unanimously considered disapproved (i.e. it should be avoided if possible)".[246]

239 ŠāfUmm I p. 463. *Cf.* also ŠīrMuhaḏ I p. 138; IQāsimFatḥ p. 218; INaqʿUmdah p. 241; Mabrūk: *Bidaʿ* pp. 34f. The same from Mālik in SaḥnūnMud I p. 189.

240 *Cf.* also Hillenbrand: *Islamic Architecture* p. 257.

241 WanšMiʿyār I p. 318. *Cf.* also QurṭTaḏk p. 86 and MF XXXII p. 251.

242 ʿIyāḍMaḏ p. 301.

243 In IQayIġāṯah I p. 170, he speaks of such mausolea derogatorily as "temples" (*hayākil*).

244 IQayZād I p. 524, very similar (though shorter) in IQayIġāṯah I p. 181. *Cf.* also IMuflFurūʿ II p. 272; al-Albānī: *Aḥkām al-ǧanāʾiz* pp. 218f.; Wafā: *Aḥkām al-ǧanāʾiz* p. 261.

245 See the treatise al-Muʿallimī: *ʿImārat al-qubūr*.

246 ṬūsīMabsūṭ I p. 187 (*taǧṣīṣu l-qubūri wa-l-bināʾu ʿalayhi* [sic] *fī l-mawāḍiʿi l-mubāḥati makrūhun ʾiǧmāʿan*).

3.2. Tombs in public cemeteries and private property

As can be seen from the preceding quotation, building upon a grave as such was not in all cases considered forbidden (*harām*) by the majority of legal scholars, but the not doing so was judged preferable.[247]

The later Shafiite legal tradition introduced in this context the important distinction between private and public property. Thus building a mausoleum was considered disapproved of (*makrūh*) or even indifferent (*mubāḥ*) if the grave recinct lay within the land owned by the builder (and, sometimes, the future occupant),[248] whereas it was judged forbidden (*ḥarām*) if the tomb was situated in a communal cemetery; these conditions were also seen as valid for tomb-mosques which, consequently, had to be torn down if erected on communal ground.[249]

3.2.1. Communal cemeteries

By "communal cemetery" (*al-maqburah al-musabbalah*)[250] a burial area is meant whose sole purpose to serve as a cemetery to the population was fixed and inalienable, thus being similar (but not equal) to an endowment (*waqf*). Literally, the term should probably be rendered as "designated *or* appointed cemetery",[251] and the idea parallels what in European sources is called "municipal cemetery".[252] For our purposes, however, the term *maqburah musabbalah* – in cases also *maqburah muḥabbasah*[253] – is best translated by "communal cemetery" for reasons that will become clear below.

The tying of the ground (that is, its revenue or the use it may be put to) to a certain purpose – hence its "appointment" – was called *tasbīl*, with the analogous expression *sabbalta šay'an* being explained as "making a thing lawful for someone to receive, as if you provided for it a trodden path", that is, determining for it a fixed purpose or employment.[254] A burial ground which was "tied" or "appointed" in that way was therefore called *musabbal*, meaning that it was designated for the community in order to serve as a graveyard.[255] Thus Ibn Ḥağar al-Haytamī could write in a related context that "it is not permitted to raise crops on communal cem-

247 *Cf.* Leisten: *Attitudes* p. 16.

248 *Cf.* also MF XXI p. 9; Wafā: *Aḥkām al-ğanā'iz* p. 261; Leisten: *Architektur für Tote* p. 12.

249 HarMirqātMaf IV p. 69.

250 NawŠMuslim VII p. 37 and NawRawḍah II p. 136; MuwMuršid I p. 66; ArdAnwār I p. 124; HaytFatFiqh II p. 17; *cf.* also Leisten: *Attitudes* pp. 18f.; Zepter: *Friedhöfe* pp. 33f. For the Hanbalite view: IMuflFurūᶜ II pp. 272f. and MF XXXII p. 251.

251 *Cf.* E.R. Hardy Ivamy: *Mozley and Whiteley's Law Dictionary*, London – Sydney [10]1990, p. 29: "Appointment (...) is specifically used of the appointment (...) limiting an estate or interest in lands or other property for the benefit of some person or persons".

252 *Cf.* the articles in Jupp/Howarth: *Changing Face of Death.*

253 SuyḤusnMuḥ I p. 112.

254 IAṯīrNih II p. 156.

255 See n. 296 below.

eteries, even if it has no influence on the decay of the corpses buried there (!), because the ground must not be used for anything except burials".[256]

Waqf *ground and private property*

The further distinction between a *maqburah musabbalah* and *waqf* land was introduced by the scholars because communal cemeteries could include *waqf* land as well as land not possessed or claimed by anyone (*mawāt*),[257] but in no case private property.[258] Others understood the term *musabbal* as simply meaning "wasteland" or "unspecified *waqf* land", which in practice it often was.[259]

The distinction between a communal cemetery and other burial areas, e.g. these on privately owned land, was relevant for legal interpretation. For one thing, the scholars urged people to bury their dead not in private land or in houses but rather in communal cemeteries, especially because putting the tomb on private property was seen as a material loss for the heir(s),[260] and this is why, in their opinion, wills or last wishes to that effect were not to be executed. On the other hand, everybody was free to buy the land for his future tomb during his life time.[261] Another reason for distinguishing between communal land and private property becomes clear from a fatwa again written by Ibn Ḥağar al-Haytamī: "It is forbidden to build a tomb (permanently, as a funerary construction: *binā*ʾ *al-qabr*) in communal cemeteries, that is, graveyards commonly used by the inhabitants of a town for burial.[262] The same is valid for *waqf* land".[263] In order to support this ruling, al-Haytamī neither refers to a report from the Prophet or to some legal authority, but rather tries to justify his verdict with practical reasons:

> "The reason for the prohibition of building upon graves is that its *ratio legis* (*ʿillah*) is permanent, namely the stone-work of (or above) the surface of a grave after the decay of the deceased, for in most cases the construction remains after the decomposition (of the corpse) and people are reluctant to open a (strongly) built tomb. Therefore, (strongly

256 HaytTuḥfMuḥt III p. 198; ŠubrḤāš III p. 34. This assertion by al-Haytamī seems, in practical terms, largely superfluous because most cemeteries were established on arid or waste land in the first place, in order not to waste ground which was suitable for agricultural use, *cf.* Wirth: *Orientalische Stadt* p. 423. However, in IŠadAʿlāq II (Damascus) p. 186 we read that the cemetery (*ğabbānah*) in Damascus was used for raising crops (*ḥuriṯat wa-zuriʿat*) for about 100 years; see also below p. 290.

257 *Cf.* RamlīNih III p. 34. Others instead saw the case of burial sites and mausolea on *mawāt* land as different from the cemeteries termed *musabbalah*, see HaytFatFiqh II pp. 16 and 18.

258 *Cf.* HaytTuḥfMuḥt III p. 198.

259 IMuflFurūʿ II p. 272.

260 Because it prevented the heir(s) from using the land for other purposes which might provide sources of income.

261 IQudMuġnī II p. 510.

262 *Cf.* HaytFatFiqh II p. 17.

263 *Cf.* also WanšMiʿyār I p. 318. However, not every grave has *waqf* or *ḥabs* status by its very nature, as might be understood from a passage in IĞuzQaw p. 113.

built) tombs narrow the space in the cemetery with the result that the people cannot any longer use it properly, and thus it has been forbidden".[264]

Obviously, the distinction between tolerating the construction of burial monuments on private property while prohibiting it in communal cemeteries was not easily reconciled with the Prophet's general verdict "not to build on graves". Some scholars consequently opposed this distinction, for example the seventh-century Shafiite Šihāb ad-Dīn al-Aḏraʿī[265] who argued that prohibiting the erection of funerary monuments was valid without exception, no matter whether it concerned private property or communal land, first because the Prophet did not specify the prohibition as to its exact application, and second because the erection of funerary monuments leads to the waste of money for an abominable purpose and demonstrates nothing but extravagance (*saraf*) and futile vainglory in the style of unjust rulers and unbelievers.[266]

However, in view of the fact that many mausolea *were* constructed on private ground, the afore-mentioned distinction made by other Shafiites remained valid with most legal scholars and was also taken up by many (though not all) Malikites[267] and the Hanbalites. The Malikite Ibn al-Ḥāǧǧ therefore simply stated, referring to the Qarāfah cemetery in Cairo that was considered a "communal cemetery" with *waqf*-like status: "When the Prince of the Believers ʿUmar b. al-Ḫaṭṭāb – may God be pleased with him! – appointed it for (*ǧaʿalahū li-*) the burial of the Muslim dead (...) he thus prohibited the building of (funerary monuments) in that area".[268]

The digging up of tombs

Funerary constructions of stone were often erected in order to prevent the re-opening of the tomb for another burial before the deceased had decayed.[269] Otherwise, as suggested by Ibn Ḥaǧar (see above p. 204), a tomb might have been dug up soon after burial in order to gain space in a "crowded" cemetery. Especially for the construction of the Mamluk mausolea in Cairo corpses were unearthed and tombs destroyed (see also below p. 290), much to the dismay of scholars such as as-Suyūṭī, who refers first to some seventh-century critics of this practice and then goes on to

264 HaytFatFiqh II pp. 24f. *Cf.* also *ib.* pp. 16 and 18; IMuflFurūʿ II p. 273; SuyḤusnMuḥ I p. 112; RamlīNih III p. 34; Leisten: *Attitudes* p. 18.

265 Abū l-ʿAbbās A. b. Ḥamdān al-Ḥalabī (d. 783 H), see IʿIrāqīḎʿIbar II pp. 528-30; IḤaǧInbāʾ II pp. 61-3.

266 Cited in HaytFatFiqh II p. 16.

267 WanšMiʿyār I p. 318 (funerary constructions on private property are considered like private houses and therefore not prohibited); *cf.* also Leisten: *Attitudes* p. 17.

268 IḤāǧǧMadḫ I p. 253 = SuyḤusnMuḥ I pp. 112f.

269 See ŠirwḤāš III p. 196. In early modern Europe "immigration to the industrialising towns and cities (with their great mortality rate), resulted in overcrowded, urban burial grounds in the metropolis which rapidly degenerated into public health hazards. (...) Corpses were buried in shallow graves and often disinterred after a brief period, usually in a state of semi-decay, to make room for others" (Jupp/Howarth: *Changing Face of Death* pp. 122f.).

comment: "If that was the scholarly opinion in their times, before they (*sc.* the Mamluk rulers) exaggerated the construction (of tombs), their artful embellishment and the opening of tombs for that reason, and before the emptying of the toilets upon the tombs of deceased nobles, scholars, pious people and others from among the Muslims (became feasible), – so how then in our time?"[270]

Digging up tombs was also the work of professional tomb robbers (*nabbāšūn*) who were looking for treasures and valuables.[271] In some cases, as they reported afterwards, they witnessed such awful scenes in the tombs they opened – as a result of the "Chastisement of the Grave" – that they repented and turned away from their former practice.[272] The opposite topos is also frequent, viz. that unearthed corpses were found unaltered, a prodigious fact not easily reconciled with the concept of the Chastisement of the Grave, which was chiefly thought to be a physical torment from which nobody, with the exception of the Prophet and some women of his company, would escape.[273]

In other cases, deceased had reportedly vanished from their tombs, a fact discovered after their graves were opened, for some reason or other, following the burial. Such was the case of al-ᶜAlāᵓ ᶜAbd Allāh b. al-ᶜImād al-Ḥaḍramī (d. during the caliphate of ᶜUmar): he was killed in combat and buried at the spot, but somebody warned his companions that in this place the earth would "spit out" (*lfẓ* I) the dead, so they had better taken him to a place a mile or two away where the earth "accepts" (*qbl* I) the dead. So his companions opened his tomb, but they found the burial niche empty and beaming with light.[274]

270 SuyḤusnMuḥ I p. 112.

271 The relatively frequent appearance of tomb robbers in the sources must appear surprising because grave goods are virtually unknown in Islam, although secular rulers could be buried with insignia of their power, such as the Ayyubid Ṣalāḥ ad-Dīn (Saladin) who was interred with his sword (ᶜIṣāmīSimṭ IV p. 10). However, some people also hid their riches in tombs or burial areas, and thus there might have been treasures to discover, after all: in Baghdad in 641 H, for example, a tomb was prepared in the Bāb Ḥarb cemetery and the gravediggers found two jars filled with dirhams from older times (IFuwaṭīḤaw p. 184); likewise in Baghdad, 600.000 dinars were found in a tomb in an Abbasid mausoleum (*turbah*), see AFidāᵓMuḫt II p. 74; in Cairo, the third-century ruler Aḥmad b. Ṭūlūn and his entourage hit upon a tomb while hunting in the countryside and found some 1.000.000 dinars in it, which were spent to build a mosque in the Qarāfah cemetery and other public buildings, see NZ III p. 10. Sometimes, tombs were dug up for less precious objects, e.g. drapes and clothings. Thus the funeral of the Venetian consul in Cairo in 1762 CE was performed in secrecy for fear that bedouins would exhume his body and plunder his grave (Niebuhr: *Reisebeschreibung* pp. 363f.).

272 IḪarrāṭᶜĀqibah p. 163; IRağAhwāl p. 89; TurkLumaᶜ I p. 334; Langner: *Historische Volkskunde* pp. 183f.; for what was found in the tombs of Umayyad rulers when they were unearthed, see MasMurūğ IV p. 44; RāġibMuḥāḍ IV p. 535; TMD LIII p. 127; *cf.* also IᶜAdīmZubdah p. 38.

273 See IHağĞawKāfī p. 41; MağlBihār C p. 131; al-Marrākušī: *Iᶜlām* II p. 113. *Cf.* also Kinberg: *Interaction* p. 293; Gramlich: *Vorbilder* II pp. 92f.

274 SuyḪaṣ II p. 111. The topos that somebody's corpse is not found in his grave – which implies that he had been taken away to God – is rather frequent in biographical dictionaries and pious literature, but it also appears in historiographical writings (e.g. ḪazrᶜUqūd II p. 77).

Sometimes corpses were disinterred from their tombs and their remains burned, dismembered[275] or, in cases, crucified as a form of posthumuous punishment or revenge.[276] Tombs of people who had made themselves enemies during their lives had therefore to be "shielded" or "guarded" (*ḥfẓ* I) in order to prevent malicious disinterment,[277] and the early Abbasid caliphs had their graves effaced for the same reason (see above p. 190). A particularly illustrative case from Egypt is related by Jonathan Berkey:

> "In the late twelfth century [CE], a Shāfiᶜī jurist and poet named Abū ᶜAbdallāh al-Kīzānī, who had a reputation for anthropomorphic beliefs, died and was buried next to the Imām al-Shāfiᶜī. Three years after his death, an indignant Ashᶜarī theologian named Najm al-Dīn al-Khabūshānī dug up the poet's bones and scattered them about, shouting that 'a righteous believer (*ṣiddīq*) and a heretic (*zindīq*) should not be buried in the same place!'"[278]

One Hanbalite scholar in Baghdad, initially buried in a cemetery frequented by Sufis, was unearthed and after five days transferred to another cemetery by his fellow Hanbalites who argued: "What has that Hanbalite to do at a Sufis' place?"[279] Likewise, in Baghdad, the Hanbalite preacher Abū Ṣāliḥ Naṣr b. Abī Bakr (d. 633 H), a great-grandson of ᶜAbd al-Qādir al-Ǧīlī, was initially buried in the mausoleum (*dikkah*) of Ibn Ḥanbal, but the caliph disapproved of this and ordered his transfer (*taḥwīl*); thus Abū Ṣāliḥ was exhumed at night and buried at a spot nearby.[280]

Several people were, over the centuries, buried, exhumed and re-buried more than once. The earliest instance seems to be the father of the first-century Medinan traditionist Ǧābir b. ᶜAbd Allāh, who was exhumed by his son, for different reasons, three times over a period of forty years.[281] Another memorable story is that of the Abbasid vizier Abū ᶜAlī Ibn Muqlah (d. 326 or 328 H) who was unearthed twice and buried no less than three times: first in the caliphal complex (*dār al-ḫilāfah*) of Baghdad, then – at the request of his relatives – in his own house, and finally in another house.[282] Similarly, the emir of Mawṣil, Mawdūd b. Altūntakīn (d. 507 H), was first buried in a mausoleum in Damascus, then carried to Baghdad and buried in the vicinity of Abū Ḥanīfah, then brought to Iṣfahān and interred there.[283]

For more pious motives, a corpse could be exhumed from its former burial site when in the meantime a mausoleum had been constructed; this was in general the

275 As it happened when the Marīnid ruler Abū Yūsuf (r. 656–85 H) had the tombs of the last Almohad rulers opened in 674 H, see MaqrDurar I p. 133; *cf.* also TMD LIII p. 127.

276 E.g. MasMurūǧ (P) IV p. 43; IḪaṭIḥāṭah III p. 331; DK I p. 418.

277 *Cf.* IǦawzīMunt X p. 162.

278 Berkey: *Culture and society* p. 402.

279 IRaǧḎayl I p. 305.

280 IFuwaṭīḤaw p. 87. There is no mentioning of that fact in Abū Ṣāliḥ's biographies in ḎahMuḫt-Dub p. 366 and IRaǧḎayl II pp. 189-92.

281 See for details SamWafāᵓ III p. 938; *cf.* also FB III p. 275 (*ǧanāᵓiz* 77) and IḤaǧIṣābah II p. 350; Wellhausen: *Reste* p. 180.

282 HamdTakm p. 110; AFidāᵓMuḫt II p. 85; IDawKanz V p. 367; NZ III p. 268.

283 IAṯīrKāmil X p. 497 = Leisten: *Architektur für Tote* p. 24 note 202.

case with the deceased of the ruling classes.[284] It was also considered a valid reason for unearthing a corpse if no washing (*ġusl*) and no death-prayer had been performed before the first burial, so it was necessary to exhume the deceased, perform those rites and bury him again.[285] In a Shiite treatise we read that if the deceased was buried in ground that was subsequently sold, the buyer is allowed to exhume and transfer the corpse, although it was deemed preferable to leave the tomb untouched.[286] If, on the other hand, a tomb was to be opened for less pious motives or "illegally" one could expect divine interference. Thus the eighth-century Mamluk emir Qarāqūš was unable to excavate a tomb because when he tried to do so his hand was immobilised by someone within the grave.[287]

Quite exceptional is the case of ᶜAbd ar-Raḥīm Ibn Šuqayšiqah (Damascus, 1083–1173 H) whose tomb was re-opened in order to put one of his books in his grave. This was done because the deceased scholar had appeared to his daughter in a dream, informing her that God was curious to see the book he had written. Therefore his tomb was opened and ᶜAbd ar-Raḥīm was found with his hand outstretched "like someone who desires to grasp something, as if he needed to get the book".[288]

Books, single leaves (containing poems, prayers, litanies etc.) or also copies of the Qurʾān were among the more common "grave goods" in pre-modern Islamic culture. Especially scholars and gifted writers desired to be buried with one of their works, e.g. the Andalusian traditionist Ibn al-Ḥaḏḏāʾ (M. b. Ya., Córdoba 347 – Zaragoza 416 H) who expressed the last wish to be buried together with one of his books entitled *al-ʾInbāʾ ʿalā ʾasmāʾ Allāh*. So the binding of the book was undone and the pages were put between his shirt and the shroud.[289] The famous eighth-century poet Ibn Abī Ḥağalah at-Tilimsānī (d. Cairo 776 H) "ordered shortly before his death that his treatise (attacking the mystical poems of Ibn al-Fāriḍ) be placed together with him in his coffin (*or* on his bier: *fī naʿšihī*), nay that it be buried with him in his tomb".[290]

In theory, however, opening a (Muslim's) grave was considered forbidden either unconditionally[291] or at least before the decay of the deceased was completed,[292] except when there were legally valid reasons for doing so; those reasons are set out in detail in Sunnite and Shiite legal manuals, fatwa collections or Ḥadīṯ anthologies and there is no need to repeat them here.[293] In a Shiite manual we read that "it is not

284 E.g. IQŠuhbTārīḫ I p. 572; see also below p. 229 and Vol. I pp. 78-80.

285 See e.g. IᶜIrāqīḎᶜIbar II p. 449; MaqrSulūk III p. 282.

286 ṬūsīMabsūṭ I p. 188. *Cf.* also MāwAḥkām p. 338.

287 SaḫTuḥfAḥbāb p. 115.

288 MurSilk III p. 11.

289 IBaškṢilah II p. 507.

290 SaḫWağīz I p. 211.

291 *Muwaṭṭaʾ* I p. 238 (*ğanāʾiz* 15) = SuyTanwīr p. 246.

292 See NawRawḍah II p. 140; ṬūsīMabsūṭ I p. 188; IQudMuġnī II p. 511; ArdAnwār I p. 124; ḤaḍrMuq p. 103; RamlīFat II p. 39. *Cf.* also Goldziher: *Culte des saints* pp. 88f. and Marcus: *Funerary and Burial Practices* p. 100.

293 See ṬūsīMabsūṭ I pp. 188f.; MāwAḥkām p. 338; MunḏTarġīb IV p. 152; NawFat p. 51; al-Albānī: *Aḥkām al-ğanāʾiz* pp. 235f.; Krawietz: *Ḥurma* pp. 164-7.

permitted to open a grave in order to bury another deceased there, except under the strain of necessity, but if there is another possibility and sufficient space available, it is not permitted for whatever reason".[294]

It is finally worth mentioning that, as far as I can see, the practice of unearthing the dead left no trace whatsoever in the texts of Arabic epitaphs, that is, there are no references to this practice known from pre-modern funerary inscriptions. In the European context, such references have been found in ancient Latin epitaphs (for example *Fossor, parce, hic iam cubat*, i.e. "O gravedigger, leave it! Somebody already rests here") as well as in those from later epochs, e.g. the famous epitaph of William Shakespeare in Stratford-upon-Avon: *Good Frend for Iesus sake forbeare, / To digg the dust encloased heare: // Bleste be ye Man* [*tha*]*t spares thes stones, / And curst be he* [*tha*]*t moves my bones*. However, invocations that God should be "the opposing party" of those who "change" the tomb or the mausoleum, altering its present shape and appearance, do sometimes occur in extant Arabic epitaphs.[295]

Overcrowded public cemeteries

Insufficient space was mainly a problem in the larger communal cemeteries which were held in great esteem, e.g. the burial area on the slopes of the Qāsiyūn mountain in the Ṣāliḥīyah quarter to the north of Damascus or the Baqīᶜ graveyard in Medina. Other famous communal cemeteries were the necropolis to the south of Cairo (al-Qarāfah)[296] and the well-known graveyards of Mecca, Baghdad and Karbalāʾ.

In the case of those "noble tracts (of land)" (*al-biqāᶜ aš-šarīfah*) serving as cemeteries it were not only the larger funerary constructions which restricted the space available, but very early on the sheer quantity of graves had become a problem, because "it is desirable to be buried in cemeteries where many righteous persons and martyrs lie, in order to enjoy their blessing".[297] Three examples illustrate the problems that this attitude led to:

(1) A companion of ᶜĀʾišah, ᶜĀmirah bt. ᶜAbd ar-Raḥmān "said to one of her relatives, 'Make the place of my tomb in a walled enclosure (*ḥāʾiṭ*)' – and they (*sc.* her relatives) possessed a walled enclosure adjacent to the Baqīᶜ area – 'for I heard ᶜĀʾišah herself say that breaking the bones of the dead is like breaking the bones of someone alive'".[298] According to another version, ᶜĀmirah had told her relatives,

294 ṬūsīMiṣbāḥ p. 35; *cf.* also ṬūsīMabsūṭ I p. 187.

295 For some examples, see Volume I pp. 102f.

296 MuwMuršid I pp. 5f. and 67: on p. 6 he explicitly says that this area "had been appointed (*subbilat*) as a cemetery for the Muslims", and on p. 67 he mentions the caliph ᶜUmar as the one who "appointed" (*sbl* II) the area at the slopes of the Muqaṭṭam Hill, "though the term 'appointing' (*tasbīl*) does not appear in a document (*kitāb*) there is no doubt as to its historicity"; as-Suyūṭī writes accordingly that the Qarāfah was a *waqf* instituted by ᶜUmar for the Muslim dead (SuyḤusnMuḥ I p. 112). *Cf.* also IZawlFaḍMiṣr p. 96; IẒuhFaḍMiṣr pp. 108f.; Leisten: *Attitudes* p. 22 note 85.

297 IQudMuġnī II p. 509. *Cf.* also MF XXI p. 9.

298 For this report, see above p. 160.

"Assign me a little tract of your land in which I might be buried because I heard ᶜĀᵓišah say, etc.".[299] The implication of this wish is, obviously, that somebody's grave in an enclosure or a tract of land privately owned was not at a risk of being touched afterwards, as was common on communal or public graveyards.

(2) ᶜUrwah (b. az-Zubayr) disliked being interred in the Medinan Baqīᶜ cemetery, not because the place in itself was undesirable but because there was not a single place left in the whole area without somebody buried beneath it. Therefore he was very unwilling to be buried there, because it would have meant removing the bones of another person in order to gain space for his own tomb. Yet if this deceased was a sinner, ᶜUrwah felt no desire to be buried in his vicinity (i.e. in his former grave), and if the deceased was a righteous person, he felt bad about having to excavate his bones for his own sake.[300]

(3) For the cemetery in the Ṣāliḥīyah quarter (Damascus), Ibn Ṭūlūn relates:

> "There is no place left without a tomb. Once, I saw a marvellous thing happen there, for while digging a new grave we hit upon a burial niche (*laḥd*) and I told the gravedigger: 'Go a little deeper!', but when he had worked himself downwards there was another niche below. We told him 'Go deeper!', but when he had dug still deeper there appeared another niche. Thus there were three graves in all, one under another".[301]

However, there were always less favoured public cemeteries where lack of space presented no problem. One such burial ground was the so-called *maqburat aš-šuhadāᵓ*, "the martyrs' cemetery", in Jerusalem: "This is a beautiful cemetery because only few people desire to be interred there".[302]

A very peculiar case of an "occupied" tomb being re-used is known from Fatimid Egypt, though this was not due to lack of space. Rather, we are told that the vizier Ṣadaqah b. Yūsuf al-Falāḥī, a converted Jew, was to be executed in the Cairene dungeon *Ḫizānat al-bunūd* in Muḥarram 440 H. When in office, he had executed his former colleague Abū l-Ḥasan ᶜAlī Ibn al-Anbārī in 436 H, who had then been buried in the said dungeon, but now, before the execution of al-Falāhī, a pit was dug for him in the same dungeon. Suddenly a head appeared in the earth and was recognised as that of Ibn al-Anbārī. Nevertheless, al-Falāhī was to be buried in that very pit and thus he said, "It is I who killed him (*sc.* Ibn al-Anbārī), and I had him buried in that spot! Then he recited (*ḫafīf*):

رُبَّ لحْدٍ قَدْ صَارَ لحْداً مِرَاراً * ضَاحِكاً مِنْ تَزَاحُمِ الأَضْدَادِ

'Many a burial niche has become a burial niche repeatedly, * (thus) mocking the rivalry of opposites!'"[303]

299 ISaᶜdṬab VIII p. 481.

300 *Muwaṭṭaᵓ* I p. 232 (*ǧanāᵓiz* 10) = BāǧīMunt II p. 23. *Cf.* also ZurqŠMuw II p. 69; al-Albānī: *Aḥkām al-ǧanāᵓiz* p. 235.

301 IṬūlQal II p. 592. Concerning a cemetery in Seville, IᶜAbdūnTraité p. 58 offers a very similar description: "il (*sc.* le cimetière) est encore utilisé aujourd'hui, mais on y enterre les cadavres les uns par-dessus les autres, tant il est devenu exigu".

302 ᶜUlaymīUns II p. 64 (*wa-hiya maqburatun laṭīfatun li-qillati man yaqṣidu d-dafna fīhā*).

303 This verse was composed by al-Maᶜarrī, see ŠSiqṭZand III p. 976 (var. *ḍāḥikin*). What is meant is that two persons of opposite traits of character, e.g. one virtuous and one malicious, share the same burial niche.

After that, al-Falāḥī was executed and buried in the pit together with the final remains of Ibn al-Anbārī.[304]

The location of public cemeteries

Public cemeteries qualified as *musabbalah* ("appointed" or "communal" cemeteries) were normally situated outside the towns (*extra muros*) and not infrequently in the vicinity of a city gate. In a number of major Islamic cities, public or "communal" cemeteries are thus named after the adjacent gate.

Examples are known from Aleppo (Bāb al-Farağ, Bāb al-Maqām), Alexandria (Bāb al-Maḥrūq), Almería (Bāb Baǧǧānah), Baghdad (Bāb Abraz, Bāb at-Tibn, Bāb Ḥarb, Bāb aš-Šām and others), Baᶜlabakk (Bāb Saṭḥā), Biğāyah (Bāb Amsiyūn, Bāb al-Marsā), Cairo (Bāb Naṣr), Córdoba (Bāb ᶜĀmir al-Qurašī), Damascus (Bāb al-Farādīs, Bāb Kaysān, al-Bāb aṣ-Ṣaġīr and others), Fez (Bāb al-Futūḥ, Bāb al-Ǧīsah, Bāb al-Maḥrūq), Granada (Bāb Ilbīrah), Ḥimṣ (Bāb ad-Durayd), Jerusalem (Bāb Arīḥā, Bāb ar-Raḥmah), Kairouan (Bāb Nāfiᶜ, Bāb Salm, Bāb Tūnis), Manbiğ (Bāb al-Kūfah), Marrakech (Bāb Aġmāt, Bāb Tāġzūt), Mecca (Bāb Šubaykah), Murcia (Bāb Ibn Aḥmad), Nīsābūr (Bāb Maᶜmar, Bāb ᶜUrwah), Seville (Bāb Qarmūnah), Tilimsān (Bāb al-ᶜAqabah), Valencia (Bāb Biṭālah), Zabīd (Bāb al-Qurtub, Bāb Sihām) and Zaragoza (Bāb al-Qiblah). – Sometimes, it would work the other way round and a burial ground provided the name for a city gate, e.g. in the Upper Egyptian town of Qūṣ where we know of a *Bāb al-Maqābir*.[305]

In general, Muslim graveyards were meant to be reserved for deceased Muslims only; Christians and Jews possessed burial grounds of their own. In the particular case that a Christian woman, who was married to a Muslim, had died while bearing a child in her womb, it was not easy to decide where the woman was to be interred because the child was considered a Muslim, yet the mother was not. In a fatwa, an-Nawawī offers the following deliberations on the subject:

> "The most correct thing to do is to bury her between the tombs of the Muslims and those of the unbelievers. Others maintained that (she must be interred) at the wayside in a Muslim graveyard (*fī ṭuruq maqābir al-muslimīn*). Still others claimed that she is to be handed over to the people of her religion who will see to her washing and burial in a Christian cemetery. However, when buried she must be turned with her back towards the direction of prayer, because the face of the embryo faces the back of his mother".[306]

The use of an area as a communal cemetery was either determined by tradition or, in some cases, by decree. In many places, e.g. al-Andalus and Syria, this followed ancient, pre-Islamic traditions and was often perceived as contrasting with the Christian usage of burying the dead within the city walls or around the (parish) churches.[307]

304 IMuyassarAḫbār p. 8 = MaqrḪiṭaṭ I pp. 424f.

305 UdfṬāliᶜ p. 85; IFurTārīḫ VII p. 137.

306 NawFat p. 51.

307 The Roman pattern of cemeteries *extra muros* was given up in Christianity from around the fifth century CE onwards in favour of graveyards in or near parish churches *intra muros* (Laqueur: *Cemeteries in Orient and Occident* p. 4 and *Friedhöfe Istanbul* pp. 62f.). Large municipal extramural cemeteries in Christian countries were reintroduced during the 19th

Thus Cervantes in his *Don Quijote* could write about a person who wished to be buried outside the city walls that "he had laid down in his testament to be interred in the countryside, as if he was a Moor" (... *que le enterrasen en el campo, como si fuera moro*).[308] In Persia, older burial sites continued to be used after the Islamic conquest, for example in the Šāhanbūr cemetery in Nīsābūr.

There are many graves, both famous and much-visited or also little known, graves which are not part of cemeteries at all, but situated somewhere outside settlements or even in the wilderness, more often than not far away from any settlement and not easily accessible.[309] On the other hand, settlements could arise around famous shrines, as in the case of the sixth-century Iraqi mystic Šayḫ Ǧākīr who was buried in the desert near Samarrāʾ. At that site, "the people then founded a village, because in doing so they hoped for blessing (*barakah*)".[310] In many other cases public burial grounds grew either around the tomb of a venerated person or around clusters of graves belonging to a single family or tribe. That is also why a great number of ancestral cemeteries throughout the Islamic lands are known as *maqburat Banī (Fulān)*, "cemetery of members of the tribe So-and-So".

Burial in houses and mosques

However, not all burial places throughout the Islamic lands were as a rule outside the towns[311] and we know of a considerable number of individuals – from all over the Islamic world and predominantly between the fourth and fifth-centuries H – who were buried in their houses. As Thomas Leisten correctly stated, "für die ersten 600 Jahre islamischer Zeitrechnung gehört die Bestattung innerhalb von Wohnhäusern zur Normalität".[312]

The Arabic expression for describing burial in houses is *dufina fī dārihī* ("he was buried in his house") or, more rarely, *fī manzilihī* ("in his dwelling"); the term *dār*, however, not only indicates the house as such but also the adjoining courtyard and the surrounding area.[313] In most cases, the house would be that of the deceased's

century CE when the steady growth of major cities had made the closing of many intramural graveyards necessary (Jupp/Howarth: *Changing Face of Death* p. 123; Laqueur: *Cemeteries in Orient and Occident* pp. 4-7).

308 Cervantes: *Don Quijote* I, ch. 12 (I p. 128) = Torres Balbás: *Cementerios* p. 132. However, the said person – called Grisóstamo – had stipulated in his will to be buried where he had first met his love; thus there were no religious motifs behind his last will. For cemeteries *extra muros cf.* also Laqueur: *Cemeteries in Orient and Occident* p. 4 and *Friedhöfe Istanbul* pp. 6f.; Zepter: *Friedhöfe* pp. 24f.

309 The Muslim scholars stress that burials should only take place in cemeteries and not outside of or far from them, see al-Albānī: *Aḥkām al-ǧanāʾiz* p. 137.

310 ŠaʿrṬab I p. 150.

311 *Cf.* Grütter: *Bestattungsbräuche* pp. 185f.; Taylor: *Reevaluating the Shiʿi Role* p. 4 (about burial sites in the settled areas of Kūfah); Wirth: *Orientalische Stadt* pp. 250 and 423.

312 Leisten: *Architektur für Tote* p. 13.

313 E.g. ʿAl. b. ʿAmr b. al-ʿĀṣ (d. *c.* 65 H), buried in Egypt: *dufina fī dārihī* (TMD XXXI p. 242); Abū M. Yūsuf b. Yaʿqūb b. Ḥammād (d. Baghdad 297 H): *dufina fī dārihī* (ʿIyāḍTartīb

family and one of his former possessions, but it seems that sometimes a house was purchased for the purpose of burial, e.g. in the case of the philologist al-Mubarrad (d. *c*.285 H) who was interred in the Bāb al-Kūfah cemetery "in a house (*dār*) that had been bought for him".[314] In Baghdad, Bahāʾ ad-Dīn Aḥmad b. ᶜUṯmān al-Burūǧirdī (d. 676 H) was "buried in a mausoleum (*turbah*) which he had built for himself in his *dār* in the Darb al-Fālūḏaǧ".[315] This shows that the term *dār* could be applied to larger housing complexes because we must presume that the said *turbah* was not inside the living area of that *dār*, but rather adjoined to its outer walls or in the courtyard. However, Islamic burial in houses never entailed, as far as we know, the placement of tombs directly "under the floor" and thus within the very building, as commonly done in ancient Mesopotamia; there seems to be no continuity here between the pre-Islamic and the Islamic periods, not even in Iraq where one might expect the preservation of this ancient usage.

One of the earliest Arabic testimonies for the practice of burial in private houses or palaces, or at least in their immediate vicinity, is a line by Abū l-Maᶜālī b. ᶜAbd al-Qāhir b. al-Munḏir who had a palace constructed for himself, but died shortly after its completion. He stipulated that he should be buried in his *dār* (*sarīᶜ*):

وَمَنْزِلٍ أَمَّلْتُ عُمْرَانَهُ * أَصْبَحَ فِي جَانِبِهِ رَمْسِي

"Alas, a dwelling which I had hoped would be prosperous (*or* thriving with people) * has become flanked by my tomb".[316]

Although burial in private houses or courtyards seems to have prevailed during the formative period of Islam up until the fourth and fifth centuries H, we also have evidence of that practice stemming from later times, from such distant places as Egypt, Persia and Yemen. The first instance that I know of relates to the death of the chief-judge in Damascus, Ǧamāl ad-Dīn al-Miṣrī, who was also a gifted poet.

III p. 187); the Shafiite scholar Ibn an-Naqqāš (Abū Bakr M. b. Ḥasan, d. Baghdad 351 H): *dufina fī dārihī* (TB II p. 205; NawMuḫt p. 189, YāqIršād VI p. 496); Abū ᶜAl. M. b. Ḥasan aṣ-Ṣiqillī (d. Cairo 363 H): *dufina fī dārihī* (MaqrMuq V p. 535); aṣ-Ṣāḥib Ibn ᶜAbbād (d. Rayy 385 H): *dufina min ġadin fī dārihī* (YāqIršād I p. 69); the Hanafite chief-judge Ibn Abī l-ᶜAwwām (A. b. M., Cairo 349–418 H): *dufina fī dārihī* (*ib*. I p. 606); Abū l-Ḥazm Ǧawhar b. M. (d. Córdoba 435 H): *dufina bi-dārihī* (IBaškṢilah I p. 131); the Ismailite judge ᶜAbd al-Ḥakam b. Saᶜīd (d. Cairo 435 H): *māta ... fa-ṣulliya ᶜalayhi fī dārihī wa-dufina fīhā* (IḤaǧRafᶜ p. 208); Abū l-Qāsim ᶜAr. b. M. al-Labīdī (d. Kairouan 440 H): *dufina fī dārihī* (ᶜIyāḍTartīb IV p. 708); M. b. M. al-Ḫalamī (d. Karḫ 547 H): *dufina fī dārihī* (IǦawzīMunt X p. 150, and other instances from Baghdad: pp. 146, 151). Apart from those mentioned above, persons in Baghdad and Nīsābūr were often buried in their houses, sometimes before being finally taken to a public cemetery (see ᶜIyāḍTartīb IV p. 588; TB III pp. 99, 247 and 403; IV pp. 156, 377; V pp. 80, 382; IǦawzīMunt X pp. 34, 97, 109, 160, 247; NawMuḫt pp. 217, 277, 294, 314 and 349; BN XI p. 330; Leisten: *Architektur für Tote* pp. 110ff.).

314 MarzNūr p. 333 (It remains unclear whether the house had been bought during his lifetime or after his death, though the latter seems more likely).

315 IFuwaṭīḤaw p. 395.

316 Cited in IBuḥtUns p. 90; *cf.* also two verses cited in TMD LIII p. 446f.

He was buried in his house (*dufina fī dārihī*), and this was taken up, somewhat sarcastically, in a distich by Šaraf ad-Dīn Ibn ᶜUnayn (d. Damascus 630 H) (*sarīᶜ*):

مَا قَصَّرَ المِصْرِيُّ فِي حُكْمِهِ * إذْ صَيَّرَ التُّرْبَةَ فِي دَارِهْ
فَخَلَّصَ الأَحْيَاءَ مِنْ رُحْمِهِ * وَخَلَّصَ الأَمْوَاتَ مِنْ نَارِهْ

"al-Miṣrī did not fail in his judgment * when he fashioned the mausoleum in his house:
He saved the living from pitying him[317] * and he saved the dead from his Fire!"[318]

Further instances of burial in houses *after* the sixth century H include the following: in Cairo, the sheikh Sayf ad-Dīn Ibn Yūnus was buried in his house in 706 H (*dufina fī dārihī*);[319] in Persia, the man of letters Bahāᵓ ad-Dīn al-ᶜĀmilī (d. 1031 H) died in Iṣfahān and was then carried to Ṭūs where he was buried in his house (*fa-dufina bihā fī dārihī*);[320] in Yemen, the mystic Ḥātim b. Aḥmad al-Ahdal (d. 1013 H) was buried in his house (*dufina fī baytihī*) in al-Muḫā.[321] From this we can deduce that burial in houses, and in any case not in proper cemeteries, was a constant practice throughout pre-modern Islamic history. This in itself is not surprising, but it is worth noting that there are some widely-transmitted Traditions from the Prophet which do condemn this practice.

The most commonly known Tradition says: "Do not take your houses as tombs!" or "Do not turn your houses into cemeteries!", viz. *lā tattaḫiḏū buyūtakum qubūran* or *lā tağᶜalū buyūtakum maqābira*, respectively.[322] The most probable interpretation of these sayings is that they are meant to ban burial in houses, and indeed there are other reports which stress that Muslims should be buried in cemeteries and nowhere else. This most plausible interpretation was, of course, acknowledged by Muslim scholars, e.g. by Ibn Ḥağar who said that this report prohibits the conversion of houses into graves wherein the dead are buried.[323] But if we compare this interpretation with historical practice we find that burial in houses was never given up in Islamic culture, and therefore it is interesting to see that not a few scholars tried to reason away the obvious implications of the above-cited Tradition. In the accounts of Ibn Ḥağar and al-Harawī we find an array of earlier scholarly opinions to that effect, for

317 Nobody would pass by, and hence see, his tomb because it was situated in his house, unlike tombs in the open.

318 I.e. from suffering al-Miṣrī's torture in the tomb, since it was commonly believed that a buried person who underwent the Chastisement of the Grave was likely to affect those buried around him. The verses are cited in IWāṣilKurūb IV p. 173.

319 ᶜAynīᶜIqd IV p. 438.

320 MuḥḪul III p. 454.

321 ᶜAydNūr p. 161.

322 See FB I pp. 696f. (*ṣalāh* 52); BayḤayātAnb p. 30; ᶜIyāḍŠifāᵓ (B) II p. 67 / (Š) II p. 80 = HarŠŠifāᵓ III p. 144; al-Albānī: *Aḥkām al-ğanāᵓiz* p. 191; *cf.* also SubkīŠifāᵓ p. 47.

323 FB I p. 697.

example by Abū Sulaymān al-Ḫaṭṭābī (d. 386 H or after) who argued that since the Prophet himself had been buried in his house this cannot be prohibited for his community. Others stressed that the phrase "Do not turn your houses into cemeteries" actually means that one should pray in one's house regularly in order to avoid "turning them into graves because the dead do not pray in their tombs".[324] In a Shiite source we find the following:

> "Burial in the cemetery is better than burial in the house (*fī l-bayt*),[325] because the Prophet licensed (*ǧwz* IV) to his companions (burial in) the cemetery. Yet regarding burial in the house, this is permissible (*ǧwz* I) also. It is further recommended that a person possesses a burial ground (*maqburah*) privately owned, in which his family and his relatives are interred".[326]

If seen from a general perspective, the fact is significant that many scholars, with regard to practice, tried to interpret the relevant Prophetic reports in such a way as not to run counter to actual practice; they rather preferred to twist the wording of reports or their intended messages.

By and large, the same holds true for burial in or near mosques.[327] Islamic tombs have been found (dating to the late Umayyad and early Abbasid period) attached to the outer *qiblah* wall of a mosque in al-Baḥrayn, thus resembling the Christian practice of burying the dead around the churches;[328] during the fights with the Qarāmiṭes, people were buried in the *masǧid al-ḥaram* in Mecca;[329] in 676 H, somebody was buried in Tabūk "close to a local mosque" (*dufina ǧiwāra masǧidin hunāka*).[330] Noteworthy in this context is also the tomb-mosque of Ibn ᶜAbbās in aṭ-Ṭāᵓif, where "the number of graves steadily grew until half of the mosque's courtyard was occupied by them, and were it not for the prohibition of further burials there, announced by aš-Šarīf Zayd b. Muḥsin (Ibn Abī Numayy, d. 1077 H), the remaining open space would have completely vanished and the whole area would have been turned into a cemetery".[331] In 910 H, somebody was interred in a mosque in Ṣanᶜāᵓ.[332] In al-Mawṣil, we know of a *maqburat al-ǧāmiᶜ al-ᶜatīq*, "the cemetery at, *or* around, the Old Mosque"[333] which seems not only to indicate that there was a burial ground beside a mosque, but also that this cemetery must have been quite old and dating from the early Islamic centuries; in fifth-century

324 As seen in Chapter 1, the dead were believed to pray and recite the Qurᵓān in their tombs – another clash of discourses here. None the less, this interpretation seems rather far-fetched.

325 *Cf.* also MundTarġīb IV p. 152.

326 ṬūsīMabsūṭ I p. 188.

327 For this phenomen in general, see Leisten: *Architektur für Tote* pp. 44f. and 177.

328 See Kervran: *Cimetières islamiques* pp. 58-60 and 69; for tombs situated behind the *qiblah* wall in Yemen, see Finster: *Islamic Religious Architecture* p. 143; for a tomb (dated 688 H) at the outer *qiblah* wall (lit. "behind the *miḥrāb*") of a cemetery-mosque in Šīrāz, see ŠīrŠadd p. 139.

329 AFidāᵓMuḫt II p. 74.

330 IFurTārīḫ VII p. 113. For another case of somebody buried "near a mosque", see MaqrMuq V p. 601.

331 ᶜUǧIhdāᵓ p. 76.

332 ŠawkBadr II p. 214.

333 ᶜUlaymīManh II p. 324.

Baghdad, there were the *maqburat ǧāmiᶜ al-madīnah* and the *maqburat ǧāmiᶜ al-Manṣūr.*[334] The well-known poet aš-Šarīf ar-Raḍīy (d. Baghdad 406 H) was "buried in his house in the Mosque of the Anbārīs" (*dufina fī dārihī bi-masǧidi l-ᵓanbārīyīn*: TB II p. 246). The man of letters and philologist Abū ᶜAlī al-Kūfī (Ibr. b. M. ... b. ᶜAlī b. Abī Ṭālib) died in 466 H aged 66 and was buried in Kūfah *bi-masǧid as-Sahlah.*[335] However, this usage was not limited to the Arabian Peninsula or Iraq, as is shown by the burial of the jurist al-Awzāᶜī (d. 157 H) "in the *qiblah* of the mosque" (*wa-huwa madfūnun fī qiblati l-masǧid*) in Ḥantūs (Beirut)[336] and by the widespread custom in al-Andalus of burying people in a mosque or courtyard of a mosque, obviously also *intra muros.*[337] There, the indigenous Christian culture might have exerted some influence upon the location of Muslim burial sites, though this must remain a matter of speculation, since such an influence is clearly ruled out for the Arabian peninsula where we witness the same phenomenon.

From the third century H onwards, several mausolea in the Islamic East, mainly in Northern Syria and Persia, were constructed as independent buildings *intra muros*,[338] and from the sixth century onwards often as part of larger complexes situated *intra muros* (madrasahs, mosques, sufi hospices; *cf.* above p. 146). One of the earliest preserved examples of its kind in the Islamic East is the mausoleum erected in 592 H over the tomb of Ṣalāḥ ad-Dīn in Damascus, followed some decades later by the mausoleum of another Ayyubid ruler, namely al-Malik aṣ-Ṣāliḥ Naǧm ad-Dīn (r. 637–47 H), in the heart of Cairo.[339] In the last quarter of the seventh century H, the custom of burying secular rulers *intra muros* had become so compelling that al-Malik as-Saᶜīd Barakah (r. 676–78 H), the son and successor of the Mamluk ruler al-Malik aẓ-Ẓāhir Baybars I, overruled the latter's testament (which stipulated his burial outside Damascus near Dārayyā) and had him interred in town, "thus following the examples of other sovereigns (*mulūk*) who had been buried inside the town of Damascus".[340]

334 Mentioned in al-Ḫaṭīb's *Tārīḫ Baġdād*, e.g. TB II p. 338; III pp. 103 and 336; IV p. 294.

335 YāqIršad I p. 319.

336 IḪallWaf III p. 127 = Leisten: *Architektur für Tote* p. 177; see also below p. 283.

337 E.g. the case of the commander ᶜAl. b. ᶜAbd al-ᶜAzīz ar-Rabaḍī "al-Ḥaǧar" (d. 393 H) who was buried in Lérida (ar. Lāridah), "in the mosque of that town" (*wa-qabruhū fī masǧidihā*: IAbbḤullah I p. 220); the case of Ibn Ṭālib (A. b. ᶜAl. at-Tamīmī, d. Córdoba 467 H): *dufina bi-ṣaḥni masǧidi Ġizlāna s-Sayyidati dāḫila l-madīnati wa-huwa ᵓawṣā ᵓan yudfana bihī* (IBaškṢilah I p. 64). In another case, a scholar in Córdoba was buried in 441 H in the courtyard of a ruined mosque outside the city walls, see *ib.* I p. 93; the scholar ᶜAbd al-Malik b. Ḥabīb (d. 238 H) was buried in the Umm Salamah cemetery of Córdoba *fī qiblati masǧidi ḍ-ḍiyāfah* (ᶜIyāḍTartīb III p. 47). For cemeteries *intra muros* in Ottoman Istanbul, see Vatin/Yerasimos: *Cimetières Istanbul.*

338 Leisten: *Architektur für Tote* p. 56. The Hamdānid ruler Sayf ad-Dawlah (d. 356 H) "died in Aleppo, was carried to Mayyāfāriqīn and buried in the mausoleum (*turbah*) of his mother which is located within the town (*daḫila l-balad*)" (NZ IV p. 18).

339 *Cf.* Kessler: *Funerary Architecture* pp. 258f.; Behrens-Abouseif: *Islamic Architecture in Cairo* pp. 90f.; MacKenzie: *Ayyubid Cairo* p. 151; Berkey: *Transmission of Knowledge* pp. 143f. See also above p. 147.

340 IŠadMalẒāhir p. 224. IFurTārīḫ VII p. 97, ITaġrManh III p. 462 and NZ VII p. 176, where we have roughly the same notice, say explicitly *dāḫila s-sūr*, "*intra muros*".

In the Islamic West, fewer buildings than in the East have been preserved and hence we depend mainly on literary sources. Ibn Baškuwāl preserves the notice that the judge and vizier Abū l-Muṭarrif Ibn Fuṭays (ᶜAr. b. M., d. Córdoba 402 H) "was buried (...) in the mausoleum (*turbah*) of his forefathers, at the gate of their living quarter and close to their mosque",[341] which probably must be taken to mean that it was situated within the city limits. Nonetheless, burial within the town did not include the development of larger public graveyards but remained confined to single tombs and mausolea. The later burial of most Naṣrid rulers in the rear area of the Alhambra may be likewise said not to be a case of burial *intra muros*. Theirs is a case parallel to the Fatimids who were buried in their eastern palace in the Fatimid city properly called "al-Qāhirah" (more specifically, in the quarter called *Bayn al-Qaṣrayn*). At that time, Cairo was still a palace-town with little residential aspect, and thus the Fatimid burial site (known variously as *Turbat az-Zaᶜfarān, at-Turbah al-Muᶜizzīyah*, or *Turbat al-ᵓAᵓimmah*) can only with reserve be dubbed *intra muros*, though it practically was;[342] the same is likely to apply to persons buried "in their house" during the Fatimid epoch.

3.2.2. Theory and practice

Arguments in favour of funerary constructions

Against the general trend to view funerary constructions as either disapproved or even forbidden, some Sunnite scholars adduced several practical reasons for various cases in which a proper building (*bināᵓ*) or, for that matter, the erection of tents were not to be opposed, namely the danger of the tomb being dug up maliciously by men[343] or animals. In al-Andalus, therefore, the market inspectors were required to make sure that "the gravediggers dig out the tombs to considerable depth so that the odour of the deceased does not come forth and wild animals and dogs cannot unearth them. Further, that they cover what is visible of the bones of the deceased in the earth and put them out of sight".[344] The forces of nature were no less harmful than wild animals, when tombs were opened by strong winds[345] or washed away by floods or strong torrents as frequently happened in Mecca and in Baghdad.[346]

341 IBaškṢilah I p. 312.

342 *Cf.* IMaᵓmūnAḫbār p. 40 = MaqrḪiṭaṭ I pp. 407; Leisten: *Architektur für Tote*.p. 214 (no. 5). The Fatimid tombs, together with the palace complex, were destroyed under Ayyubid rule. Thomas Leisten (in *Funerary Structures* pp. 473ff.) stresses that the Fatimid tombs, notwithstanding their location in the palace area which was not accessible to all, were public places, having "a highly visible presence in a central, public and administrative area". However, he is forced to admit that the visitation of the Fatimid mausoleum was not permitted to the people in general.

343 *Cf.* BāǧīMunt II p. 23 and above p. 206.

344 SaqaṭīḤisbah p. 68.

345 IADunyāQubūr (A) p. 117; ṬurṭSirāǧ p. 13; IRaǧAhwāl pp. 88 and 94.

346 IRaǧAhwāl p. 89; IĞawzīMunt X p. 65 (the tomb of Ibn al-Ğanāzah, M. b. ᶜAl. [d. 530], was

The tomb of Ibn az-Zayyāt (M. b. ᶜAbd al-Malik, d. 233 H), vizier under the Abbasid caliphs al-Muᶜtaṣim (r. 218–27 H) and his successors al-Wāṯiq and al-Mutawakkil, was not deep enough and thus opened by wild dogs that devoured the body of the deceased.[347] The Būyid vizier Faḫr al-Mulk (Abū Ġālib M. b. ᶜAlī, d. 407) was interred in Ahwāz, yet "he was not buried deep enough, thus dogs scratched up his tomb and devoured him".[348] (The bodies of saintly men, however, who were left unburied for several days, were unlikely to be approached by beasts).[349] – Floods were frequent in Baghdad, most drastically perhaps in 569 H, when the Bāb Ḥarb cemetery was completely flooded: "It seemed as if the tombs were turned upside down, and the water had amassed a giant pile of bones and a pile of tombstones (*ʾalwāḥ al-qubūr*)".[350] In 614 H, a great flood of the Tigris that lasted for one week drowned Baghdad and "the water rose until it came level with the tombs except for two fingers's height".[351] In 646 H, the tombs of the caliphs in ar-Ruṣāfah, a suburb of Baghdad, were flooded.[352] In Kairouan, parts of the corpses could reappear on the surface of tombs after heavy rainfall.[353] In Mecca, the tomb of the Prophet's mother was said to have been put under water by a giant torrent in the time of al-Maʾmūn, probably by the flood later known as "the torrent (*sayl*) of Ibn Ḥanẓalah".[354]

From the sixth century H onwards, the construction of mausolea and tomb-mosques above or around the burial places of saintly persons was increasingly favoured and sometimes openly encouraged by many scholars, for example by al-Ġazālī.[355] The reasons normally adduced for supporting that view were the preservation and marking of the tomb,[356] the blessing received from the deceased (*at-tabarruk*) and the intention to honour his memory (*al-ʾikrām*). From the point of legal theory based on the known Traditions, this attitude could hardly be sustained seriously, but here again we find the scholars, with an air of slight resignation, pointing to historical practice. This is what the Shafiite scholar Ibn ar-Rafᶜah (d. 710 H, see **63**) – who does not appear from the sources to have been a whole-hearted supporter of burial monuments[357] – had to say on the matter:

> "There is no doubt that mausolea and tomb-mosques have existed all over the Islamic world, from former times up to our own. It is not known of any learned or righteous person or of those responsible for religious affairs that they opposed this usage, be it by

effaced by a flooding); HaytTuḥfMuḥt III p. 196; HarMirqātMaf IV p. 72. *Cf.* also IAŠayMuṣ III p. 216 (*ǧanāʾiz* 131); Rāġib: *Structure de la tombe* p. 402 n. 81f.; Gronke: *Derwische* p. 31.

347 IḪallWaf V p. 102. *Cf.* also al-Ḫašrūm: *Ġurbah* p. 300. This was a constant problem in Europe as well, e.g. in sixteenth-century Seville: there were complaints of "dogs often disinterring the bodies and eating at them" (Casey: *Early Modern Spain* p. 34).

348 IḪallWaf I p. 126 = Leisten: *Architektur für Tote* p. 101.

349 See the case reported in MālRiyāḍ I p. 250.

350 IǦawzīMunt X p. 245.

351 BN XII p. 75.

352 IFuwaṭīHaw p. 233.

353 DabMaᶜālim III p. 13.

354 IǦawzīWafā p. 116; SinǧManāʾiḥ II p. 150.

355 *Cf.* HaytFatFiqh II p. 16.

356 *Cf.* Leisten: *Attitudes* p. 17.

357 See SuyḤusnMuḥ I p. 112.

word or deed, though there is likewise no doubt that they would have had the means to do so".[358]

Much later, during the Ottoman period, the following voice was raised: "The fore-bearers (*or* first-generation Muslims: *as-salaf*) had declared it indifferent to build (funerary constructions or mausolea) on the tombs of the foremost authorities (*al-mašāyiḫ*) and famous scholars, in order that the people might pay them a visit and find relaxation in staying with them".[359] In that context it is interesting to see that some scholars, for example Šaraf ad-Dīn al-Anṣārī, invoked the historical past and the practice of former generations in order to emphasise that mausolea even on communal cemeteries (e.g. the Cairene Qarāfah) should be tolerated: "The first-generation Muslims (*as-salaf*) witnessed the Greater and Lesser Qarāfah cemeteries from early times onwards. Though mausolea (*turab*) and houses were constructed in that area, nobody from among the learned of that time opposed this fact, neither by word nor deed".[360] The silent consensus of the scholars thus served as a legal argument, overriding the theoretical precepts laid down in legal literature.

Still, even the recourse to past practice did not solve the problem because, like theory, practice yielded manifold and conflicting evidence. Take for example the statement of aš-Šāfiʿī: "I saw certain governors (*wulāh*) destroying funerary structures in Mecca, but I did not notice any of the jurists raise his voice against it".[361] Others therefore tried to uphold the rulings as laid down in theory, at least in respect of the prohibition of building funerary structures in communal cemeteries: "It is an established opinion that (...) (funerary) constructions are forbidden in communal cemeteries. Those existing have to be destroyed. There is no difference between the tombs of righteous and learned persons and other tombs".[362]

The mausoleum of aš-Šāfiʿī

The prohibition of erecting any kind of funerary monument or construction in communal cemeteries (or even as a matter of principle) was often taken very seriously; doing so had repeatedly been pronounced strictly forbidden (*ḥarām*) by the Shafiites and the adherents to other legal traditions.[363] Now and again, the rulers were called upon to put that verdict into action, though they tended to act only if there was no danger of public unrest breaking out as frequently happened when rigorous scholars tried to do away with customs which were firmly rooted in popular piety .

In order to demonstrate the gravity of the matter, many Shafiites opposed the new Ayyubid mausoleum (*qubbah*) erected above the tomb of their highest authority in Cairo: "It is obligatory for those in power to destroy the buildings in communal

358 Quoted in HaytFatFiqh II p. 16.

359 HarMirqātMaf IV p. 69.

360 Cited in HaytFatFiqh II p. 16.

361 ŠāfUmm I p. 464. *Cf.* also NawŠMuslim VII pp. 37f. and below p. 291.

362 HaytFatFiqh II p. 17.

363 *Cf.* also al-Albānī: *Aḥkām al-ğanāʾiz* pp. 218f.

cemeteries. A number of leading Shafiite scholars therefore officially advised (*ʾaftā*) the tearing down of the mausoleum of aš-Šāfiᶜī, notwithstanding the fact that for its construction thousands of dinars were spent, for the reason that it had been built in a communal cemetery".[364] The mausoleum of aš-Šāfiᶜī (in its present shape) was built on the initiative of al-Malik al-Kāmil (r. 615–35 H), one of "the major Ayyubid benefactors to al-Qarafa",[365] in the year 608 H.[366] However, according to everything we know of aš-Šāfiᶜī, his later followers certainly would have obtained his approval when they tried, albeit in vain, to prevent the construction of his mausoleum.

Testamentary stipulations

Another famous person likewise buried in the Cairene Qarāfah cemetery, the third-century mystic D̲ū n-Nūn al-Miṣrī (T̲awbān b. Ibrāhīm, d. 245 H or after), took steps in his lifetime to prevent the construction of a mausoleum over his tomb. This is apparent from what is said towards the lower end of his still extant epitaph: "He stipulated in the testament which has come down to us that his tomb shall not be 'built' and that there shall be no mausoleum (*qubbah*) upon it",[367] and in literary sources we read that he "ordered that his tomb must be made plain with the ground" (*ʾan yuǧᶜala qabruhū maᶜa l-ʾarḍ*).[368]

How efficient both the Shafiite scholars as well as D̲ū n-Nūn were in impeding the construction of mausolea may be judged from the fact that many such buildings (including that of aš-Šāfiᶜī and D̲ū n-Nūn)[369] are still extant. In fact, as as-Suyūṭī

364 HaytFatFiqh II p. 25. *Cf.* also *op. cit.* p. 17 and HaytTuḥfMuḥt III p. 198; ŠubrḤāš III p. 34; MF XXXII p. 250. Others, like ᶜIzz ad-Dīn Ibn ᶜAbd as-Salām, argued that aš-Šāfiᶜī's mausoleum would not fall under this verdict as it was not upon communal land, but "within the *dār* of Ibn ᶜAbd al-Ḥakam" (quoted in Leisten: *Architektur für Tote* p. 12 and *Attitudes* p. 19).

365 MacKenzie: *Ayyubid Cairo* p. 151.

366 MaqrḪiṭaṭ II p. 462; RCEA 3682f. For the building, see IḪallWaf V p. 81; IǦubRiḥlah (B) pp. 22f.; Kriss: *Volksglaube* I pp. 60f.; Kessler: *Funerary Architecture* p. 259; Bannerth: *Wallfahrtsstätten Kairos* pp. 52-6; Behrens-Abouseif: *Islamic Architecture in Cairo* pp. 85-7; MacKenzie: *Ayyubid Cairo* pp. 148f.; Williams: *Islamic Monuments* pp. 134-37.

367 CIA Égypte II p. 562; Rāġib: *Premiers monuments* p. 36; Leisten: *Attitudes* p. 20 note 29. It might be interesting to learn that Pliny (the Younger) in one of his letters refers to Frontinus, the known Roman architect, who likewise decreed that no funeral monument should be erected above his tomb, because "the necessary expenses are superfluous. We will be remembered by generations, if we have acquired merits in life", see C. Plinius: *Epistularum Libri X / Briefe*, ed. Helmut Kasten, Munich – Zurich [5]1984, pp. 520-2. *Cf.* also Vol. I p. 78.

368 ANuḤilyah IX p. 364.

369 For the tomb of D̲ū n-Nūn, see also MuwMuršid I pp. 377-87; *Wāfī* XI p. 24; IZayKawākib pp. 233-5; MaqrḪiṭaṭ II p. 461; MunKawākib I p. 614; the mausoleum (*mašhad*) was visited more than once by Ibn Ḫallikān (IḪallWaf I p. 318). The shrine of D̲ū n-Nūn was restored only a few years ago at the expense of the local population and with the financial aid of the Egyptian *waqf* ministry.

rightly observed, "the people of Egypt revered D̲ū n-Nūn's tomb after that", that is, immediately after his burial, which was accompanied by miraculous signs.[370]

Other persons, whose last wish not to have mausolea built upon their graves was ignored by posterity, include the army commander ᶜAmr b. al-ᶜĀṣ (see below p. 257), the Būyid state official Abū Ṭāhir aš-Šabāšī (d. 408 H),[371] the Ayyubid sultan al-Malik al-Muᶜaẓẓam ᶜĪsā (r. 615–24 H)[372] and the son of al-Malik al-Kāmil (r. 615–35 H), the Rasūlid al-Malik al-Masᶜūd Yūsuf (d. Mecca 626 H).[373] Divine intervention was sometimes claimed when the construction of a mausoleum was thwarted, e.g. in al-Andalus, where we know of a ruler in Zaragoza who intended to erect a domed mausoleum (*qubbah*) above the graves of two companions of the Prophet, but was dissuaded from his plan by a pious woman who told him that she had seen both of them in a dream telling her that there must be no monument raised above their tombs.[374] The most famous example, however, is the case of Ibn Ḥanbal as related by Ibn Baṭṭūṭah: "Above the tomb of the Imam Abū ᶜAbd Allāh Aḥmad b. Ḥanbal no mausoleum (*qubbah*) rises. The people say that more than once its construction had been attempted, but (again and again) it collapsed, caused so by the power of God the Exalted".[375] Also the mausoleum (*qubbah*) of the above-cited Abū Ṭāhir aš-Šabāšī, who tried to prevent its building by testament, did collapse shortly after its construction.

Testamentary dispositions to the contrary – that is, expressing the wish to have a mausoleum constructed above one's tomb – were in general considered invalid,[376] except when somebody decreed by will that a mausoleum should not be constructed upon his *own* tomb, but rather above that of another, saintly person.[377] However, this merely reflects the scholars' view, whereas other persons, especially if belonging to the ruling élite or the wealthy merchant class,[378] often stipulated burial at certain places, mainly in mausolea they had erected or in madrasahs they had founded during their lives. The scholars, on the other hand, often expressed the last wish to be buried in a certain cemetery or in the vicinity of the tomb of a person famous for his knowledge or piety, and sometimes for both.

The attitudes of a Mamluk ruler

The holders of power, especially secular rulers and their entourage, had quite different reasons for desiring to have mausolea of their own constructed.

Take for example the testament of the Mamluk sultan Baybars I (r. 658–76 H). He had decreed in his last will that "upon his burial site a building (*bināʾ*) shall be

370 SuyḤusnMuḥ I p. 421.

371 IĞawzīMunt VII p. 289; Leisten: *Attitudes* p. 20, n. 30.

372 Leisten: *Attitudes* p. 20, n. 30.

373 IḪallWaf V p. 84; see also below p. 257. According to ḪazrᶜUqūd I p. 42, he had stipulated burial among the "strangers" (*ġurabāʾ*) in Mecca. Some years after his death, a mausoleum (*qubbah*) was raised above his tomb by Qāymāz al-Masᶜūdī.

374 Torres Balbás: *Cementerios* pp. 137f.

375 IBaṭṭRiḥlah p. 240; see also **25**.

376 TurkLumaᶜ I p. 215; WanšMiᶜyār I pp. 317f.

377 According to al-Ad̲raᶜī, quoted in HaytFatFiqh II p. 16.

378 E.g. the Syrian merchant Ibn Rawāḥah (d. 622 H) who decreed by will to be buried in the madrasah he had founded (*Wāfī* XXVII p. 325).

erected which preserves his memory during the course of the times and whose visitors provide him with the forgiveness and clemency of God".[379] Hence future glory in the present world is aimed at, along with the hope for a merciful fate in the hereafter. Glory and a merciful fate mainly for his own person, that is, because Baybars himself was not always favourably inclined towards the mausolea of others: "He had arrived at the decision to tear down every building found in the Qarāfah", though his vizier pointed out to him that this could lead to unrest "for there (i.e. in the Qarāfah) are also the places (i.e. mausolea and charitable foundations) of the leading officers (*ʾumarāʾ*)". It was agreed to ask the learned for a fatwa on the matter, and indeed some famous scholars of the day supported the sultan's intention to clear the Qarāfah of all buildings in a fatwa. However, the vizier received the fatwa and protracted the matter; Baybars in the meantime had travelled to Syria where he eventually died and so nothing came of his plans.[380]

Ibn al-Ḥāǧǧ, from whom I took the report about this event, mentions among the scholars, who supported the sultan's decision to demolish the buildings in the Qarāfah, Ibn al-Ǧummayzī[381] and at-Tazmantī.[382] However, Ibn al-Ǧummayzī died already in 649 H and it is therefore impossible that he was active during the reign of Baybars. What is more, as-Suyūṭī quotes the gist of the story as if it had already happened under the Ayyubid ruler al-Malik aṣ-Ṣāliḥ.[383] Since this version is no less likely and as Ibn al-Ḥāǧǧ refers to the said scholars only in passing, I presume that the event did indeed take place under Baybars and Ibn al-Ḥāǧǧ is wrong in naming Ibn al-Ǧummayzī and at-Tazmantī. Their fatwas must in any case go back to the first half of the seventh century H, and it is worth noting that both adhered to the Šāfiʿite legal tradition (*cf.* above p. 220).

Notwithstanding his uncompromising attitude towards funerary constructions in the Qarāfah cemetery, Baybars had in general been no opponent of the mortuary and saint cult, nor of the practice of visitation. After his ascent to power "he showed much beneficence towards the sheikhs of the Lesser and the Greater Qarāfahs (*mašāyiḫ al-Qarāfatayn*)",[384] and his attachment to the ascetic Ḫiḍr (Ḫaḍir) – whose role has been compared to that of Rasputin – until the year 671 H is well-known.[385] Baybars visited a number of shrines in Cairo and other Egyptian cities (Alexandria, Burullus) and had a tomb (*ḍarīḥ*) constructed at the burial site of a venerated person called sheikh Abū l-ʿAbbās as well as tomb-mosques upon the graves of Noah in

379 IŠadMalẒāhir p. 224. *Cf.* also NZ VII p. 176 and above p. 216.

380 IḤāǧǧMadḫ I p. 253; Shoshan: *Popular culture* p. 69.

381 Abū l-Ḥasan Bahāʾ ad-Dīn ʿAlī b. Hibatallāh b. Salāmah b. al-Muslim al-Laḫmī aš-Šāfiʿī, Ibn al-Ǧummayzī (Cairo 559–649 H), an important transmitter of Ibn Isḥāq's *Sīrat an-nabī*: SubkīṬab VIII pp. 301-4; MaqrMuq V p. 307; NZ VII p. 24; SuyḤusnMuḥ I p. 348.

382 Either Sadīd ad-Dīn ʿUṯmān b. ʿAbd al-Karīm at-Tazmantī (605–74 H, see IŠadMalẒāhir p. 147 and SuyḤusnMuḥ I pp. 350f.) or, which is more probable, Ẓāhir ad-Dīn Ǧaʿfar b. Ya. al-Qurašī aš-Šāfiʿī at-Tazmantī (d. 682 H), a pupil of Ibn al-Ǧummayzī and teacher of Ibn ar-Rafʿah (**63**), see SubkīṬab VIII p. 139; IFurTārīḫ VII p. 287; MaqrMuq III p. 66 and MaqrSulūk I p. 721; SuyḤusnMuḥ I p. 352.

383 SuyḤusnMuḥ I pp. 112f.

384 IŠadMalẒāhir p. 271.

385 *Cf.* also Irwin: *Mamluk Sultanate* pp. 53-5 and above pp. 148f. with note 914.

Karak and the prophet Moses (in 668 H);[386] he also commissioned a tomb recinct (*ḥawš*) in the Qarāfah for the dead from among his military officers.[387] On other occasions, he restored the extant shrines of famous persons (e.g. of Ḫālid b. al-Walīd and Abū ᶜUbaydah Ibn al-Ǧarrāḥ) in Syria and endowed property for their future upkeep.[388]

This ambivalent attitude of Baybars and his brand of personal and political motifs – desire for mundane glory and mercy in the afterlife, acceptance of visitation practices together with the determination to put legal proscriptions into action – seem, in its complex whole, to embody the almost perfect combination of what was put forward in Islamic culture in the discourses of *ʾadab* and those of the religious realm, viz. in ascetic poetry and in the more rigorist legal traditions. This is not to say that, from the theoretical point of view, the Mamluk rule was an ideal Islamic regime, which it certainly was not.[389] But it is to say that the Mamluk rule was very representative of what practically had developed in the multi-faceted Islamic society, because that society had something which appealed to everyone, and rulers like Baybars could have their cake and eat it, too.

To have achieved that synthesis between differing, even contrasting tendencies may also explain the long-lasting success of the Mamluk phenomenon as a whole within the Arabo-Islamic world. In any case, it symbolises well the dual nature of what has been commonly (and justly) associated with the Mamluk rulers in general: glory on earth and bliss in Heaven for themselves and their class, but denied in the cases of others and bestowed again upon others such as pious persons and famous individuals of the past as a token of piety and beneficence. This fusion of motifs, easily reconcilable and mutually supportive in the Mamluks' worldview, was the main thrust behind the construction of numerous mausolea by rulers, state officials and influential faction leaders during the Mamluk period, who would advertise their piety by doing so. In his study of the role of religion in the Mamluk era, Donald P. Little has already drawn attention to that specific character of Mamluk rule. It is, for him, exemplified in the influence Ibn Taymīyah exerted upon his colleagues, upon the religious policy of the Mamluk rulers and upon the society at large:

> "It is Ibn Taymiyya's distinction that he opposed by word and deed almost every aspect of religion practiced in the Mamluk Empire. Whether it be the visitation of holy places, the erection of mausolea, the extreme beliefs and practices of Sufis, Muslim imitation of Christian rites, lenient treatment of Copts, the peril posed to Islam by the Mongols, the toleration of Shīᶜism, or, most importantly, deviations from Qurʾanic and traditional Islam, Ibn Taymiyya was militantly opposed and did not hesitate to articulate his views in public. (...) Nevertheless, also in dealing with Ibn Taymiyya the Mamluks proved to be ambivalent, for many of them admired him and supported his views and even though he was arrested, they allowed him access to visitors and five times freed

386 IŠadMalẒāhir pp. 351 and 356f.; NZ VII pp. 194 and 196; ᶜUlaymīUns I p. 102.

387 IŠadMalẒāhir p. 347.

388 IŠadMalẒāhir pp. 302 and 351; NZ VII p. 180.

389 *Cf.* Irwin: *Mamluk Sultanate* pp. 152ff., esp. p. 153; Northrup: *Mamlūk sultanate* pp. 265-71.

him. (...) In the last analysis, then, the Mamluks handled Ibn Taymiyya in much the same way they handled the caliphs, judges, lawyers, teachers, Sufis, dervishes, and Christians. Out of religious conviction and personal piety in some instances but also with an acute sense of their own welfare, the Mamluks strove to keep diverse religious forces in Egypt and Syria in a state of equilibrium. In such circumstances, Islam undeniably flourished".[390]

3.3. Other types of funerary constructions

In most legal literature, no difference was drawn between constructing any sort of mausoleum, e.g. a simple rectangular tomb chamber with a flat roof and opening towards a little courtyard in front of it (a structure commonly called *ḥawš*, especially in Egypt),[391] or building a domed mausoleum, that is, a tomb chamber covered by a cupola (*qubbah*), either standing for itself or as part of a larger building complex, e.g. a mosque or a madrasah.[392] As in both cases we are dealing with funerary constructions of either brick or stone, the jurists did not see the need to distinguish between both types insofar as the general prohibition to build over the tomb was concerned. However, the distinction between domed mausolea and other burial monuments was not unknown to legal scholars, not the least because it had already been formulated in Tradition, namely in connection with the pre- and early Islamic usage of pitching a tent upon the grave.

3.3.1. Pitching a tent upon the tomb

A tent pitched upon the grave was called *ḫaymah* or *fusṭāṭ* (both meaning "tent" in the proper sense), sometimes *miẓallah* ("sun-shade"), *ḫibāʾ* (pl. *ʾaḫbiyah*; "tents *or* places of hiding") or *qubbah* ("cupola, dome");[393] in at least two cases I know of such tents also being referred to as *bināʾ* ("building").[394] There are several reports in

390 Little: *Religion under the Mamluks* pp. 180f.

391 *Cf.* Badr: *Styles of Tombs* pp. 374ff. and Nedoroscik: *City of the Dead* p. 4.

392 *Cf.* MF XXXII p. 250. To date, there exists no monograph dealing with the various possible forms of tombs and mausolea throughout the Islamic world. The most extensive recent surveys of funerary architecture are Leisten: *Architektur für Tote* and Hillenbrand: *Islamic Architecture* pp. 253-330. For a typology of tombs as found in southern Syria, see Inscriptions Ḥawrān pp. 11ff.; for Aleppo, see Gonnella: *Heiligenverehrung* pp. 122-9; for Egypt, see Winkler: *Volkskunde* pp. 222-5 (with plates 60-9); for Baḥrayn, see Kervran: *Cimetières islamiques* pp. 63-66; for central Anatolia, see Güngör: *Stèles figurées* pp. 186f.; for al-Andalus, see Inscriptions Espagne I pp. XXII-XXV; Arabic Inscriptions (Caskel) pp. viii-x (on the so-called Almería-stelae and prismatic gravestones); Peral Bejarano: *Excavación y estudio* pp. 25-31 and the further articles in Acién Almansa/Torres Palomo: *Cementerios islámicos*; for Pakistan, see Zajadacz-Hastenrath: *Chaukhandigräber*; for Java (Indonesia), see: *Wali Songo Pilgrimage* (with numerous plates).

393 For this term in the meaning "tent" or "domed tent, cupola", see Esin: *Qubbah Turkiyyah* esp. pp. 281f. and Leisten: *Architektur für Tote* pp. 71f.

394 See *Aġānī* XVII p. 19 and below n. 398.

Tradition and biographical works about the use of those tents. As can be inferred from the term *miẓallah*, the aim was obviously to keep out heat and provide shade for persons staying at the grave,[395] e.g. in the case of the Prophet's wife Zaynab bt. Ǧaḥš (al-Asadīyah, d. 20 or 21 H) over whose tomb such a tent was erected for the first time, purportedly by ᶜUmar himself.[396]

Other tombs of well-known personalities above which tents were pitched include ᶜĀʾišah's brother ᶜAbd ar-Raḥmān b. Abī Bakr,[397] the famous commentator of the Qurʾān Ibn ᶜAbbās (whose tomb is in aṭ-Ṭāʾif)[398] as well as a grandson of ᶜAlī, al-Ḥasan b. al-Ḥasan (Abū M. al-Hāšimī, d. 97 H); in the latter case the tent, erected by his wife Fāṭimah bt. al-Ḥusayn, remained there for an entire year.[399] About the tomb of Ibn Saḥnūn (d. 256 H) in Kairouan we hear that after the burial "tents (*qibāb*) were pitched over (*ᶜalā*) his tomb for four months, night and day, until the onset of winter forced the people to leave the place";[400] al-Qāḍī ᶜIyāḍ provides a more detailed account of that event, giving it a political turn:

> "A tent (*qubbah*) was pitched over his tomb and other tents (*ʾaḫbiyah*) around it. People stayed there for many months, thus markets were set up around his grave for buying and selling, given the multitude of the people. This went on until Ibn Aġlab[401] became anxious about the situation and sent to the cousin of Ibn Saḥnūn known as Ibn Labdah,[402] and he dispersed the people".[403]

Some 150 years later tents (*ʾaḫbiyah*) were set up at the tomb of Ibn al-Qābisī (ᶜAlī b. M., d. 403 H), which were to remain there for an entire year; the Qurʾān was recited constantly during this period, with about 100 different mourning poems.[404]

This setting up of tents, which was not uncommon during the first centuries of Islam, was also tolerated by many legal scholars who argued that tents were not

395 For a palm-tree serving the same end, see below p. 253.

396 IAŠayMuṣ III p. 217 (*ǧanāʾiz* 133); BāǧīMunt II p. 23; ᶜAynīᶜUmdah VII p. 46; CIA Égypte II p. 66; Grütter: *Bestattungsbräuche* p. 175.

397 FB III p. 286 (*ǧanāʾiz* 81); BāǧīMunt II p. 23; MuwMuršid I p. 66; al-Muᶜallimī: *ᶜImārat al-qubūr* p. 257.

398 YaᶜqTārīḫ II p. 262; BāǧīMunt II p. 23; IᶜABarrIst II p. 352; ŠarŠMaq I p. 112; IḪallWaf III p. 64; DabMaᶜālim I p. 112; *Wāfī* XVII p. 232; ᶜAynīᶜUmdah VII p. 46; CIA Égypte II p. 66 note 9. In the relevant report in IAŠayMuṣ III p. 217 (*ǧanāʾiz* 133) this tent (*fusṭāṭ*) is called *bināʾ*, with the additional remark that it remained there for three days.

399 FB III p. 257 (*ǧanāʾiz* 61); ĠazIḥyāʾ (B) IV pp. 486f. / (C) IV p. 413; IḪarrāṭᶜĀqibah p. 113; ŠirŠadd pp. 27f.; *Wāfī* XI p. 418; INāṣBard (A) p. 15 / (C) p. 14 = SuyBard p. 90; ᶜAynīᶜUmdah VII p. 46; HarMirqātMaf IV p. 105; Goldziher: *Culte des ancêtres* p. 180; CIA Égypte II p. 67; al-Muᶜallimī: *ᶜImārat al-qubūr* pp. 153f.; Leisten: *Architektur für Tote* pp. 16f.

400 DabMaᶜālim II p. 136. A short notice of that fact already in MālRiyāḍ I p. 455.

401 Muḥammad II b. Aḥmad (r. 250–61 H).

402 Abū Ǧaᶜfar Aḥmad (d. 261 H).

403 ᶜIyāḍTartīb III p. 117.

404 DabMaᶜālim III p. 142.

reprehensible as long as "the shade relieves the living",[405] that is, as long as the "right intention" (*ġaraḍ ṣaḥīḥ*) prevailed and not the aim to relieve the deceased, because the dead person "will be shaded (i.e. protected) only by the good works which he performed during his life".[406] However, this reasoning also seems to imply that many people believed that providing the deceased with shadow was indeed of great benefit to them. The usually positive connotations of "shadow" in Arabic culture – i.e. "shadow" understood as cover, protection and source of plenty or bliss[407] – render it possible or even probable that "shading the deceased" was considered in popular Islam an act of piety towards the dead mainly aimed at their benefit while they were subjected to the Chastisement of the Grave.

The practical need for shading the living over a new grave becomes clear from the following report: "One usually considered it recommended to remain with the deceased for seven days, because they are tried and interrogated (by the death angels) in their graves for seven days",[408] or put differently: "The deceased in his home (*fī baytihī*, i.e. the tomb) sees the Fire for seven days".[409] Others, like Ibn Ḥabīb (al-Mālikī), considered it preferable to pitch a tent only upon the graves of women (in order to shield them against their being exposed to view when being buried)[410] or when there was the danger that the grave might otherwise – i.e. if unprotected – be desecrated.[411] Still others argued that tents were useful and hence allowed if they shaded the Qurʾān reciters at a tomb.[412] In later times, tents were set up with the intention that women visiting a tomb should be covered from men's sight, which in effect often led to increasing attraction between the sexes and the frequent intermingling between men and women.[413]

405 ŠirwḤāš III p. 197.

406 FB III pp. 286f.; ʿAynīʿUmdah VII p. 101; QasṭIršād II p. 370; TurkLumaʿ I p. 216. *Cf.* also Grütter: *Bestattungsbräuche* p. 174; Leisten: *Attitudes* p. 16 with note 43.

407 Islamic Tradition and Arabic poetry offer plenty of evidence for the positive symbolic value of shadow. Here it must suffice to cite but three examples, taken from (a) the Qurʾān, (b) the Tradition and (c) the introductory section of al-Ḥarīrī's *Maqāmāt*: (a) *Then We raised you up after you were dead, that haply you should be thankful. / And We outspread the cloud to overshadow you, and We sent manna and quails upon you* (Q 2:56f.: *ṯumma baʿaṯnākum min baʿdi mawtikum laʿallakum taškurūna * wa-ẓallalnā ʿalaykumu l-ġamāma wa-ʾanzalnā ʿalaykumu l-manna wa-s-salwā*); (b) "Verily, the sad one is 'in the shadow' of God" (MunḏTarġīb IV p. 339); (c) "O God, fulfil to us this wish; give us to attain to this desire: put us not forth of Thy large shadow, make us not a morsel for the devourer" (ŠarŠMaq I p. 9 / Chenery I p. 104).

408 ʿAynīʿUmdah VI p. 435; QasṭIršād II p. 327. *Cf.* also ANuḤilyah IV p. 11; IṣfḪar (Š) II p. 32; IRaǧAhwāl p. 149.

409 IḤaǧAḥwāl p. 52.

410 *Cf.* also MF XXI p. 16 and Grütter: *Bestattungsbräuche* p. 175.

411 BāǧīMunt II p. 23; ʿAynīʿUmdah VII p. 46.

412 HarMirqātMaf IV p. 69.

413 Torres Balbás: *Cementerios* pp. 161f. A Persian manuscript of the mid-9th century H shows a tent pitched above the deceased which is reserved for the female mourners, see Bağçi: *Mavi,*

However, not all Muslims shared that opinion, because many scholars, such as Ibn Ḥanbal or Ibrāhīm an-Naḫaʿī, vehemently opposed the putting up of tents[414] – with some of them pointing to the fact that it was a waste of money[415] –, and some Shiites also condemned "the shading of the tombs" (*at-taẓlīl ʿalayhā*),[416] which certainly refers to the practice of pitching tents over them. When ʿAbd Allāh b. ʿUmar (whose father had set up a tent on Zaynab bt. Ǧaḥš's tomb, see above) once saw such a *qubbah* (or, in another version, *fusṭāṭ*), he forbade its further use and had it removed immediately.[417] The traditionist Muḥammad b. Kaʿb al-Quraẓī (d. 118 H) called such tents "(abominable) innovations" (*muḥdaṯah*),[418] and the famous companions of the Prophet, Abū Hurayrah and Abū Saʿīd al-Ḫudarī, even expressed their last wish that tents (sg. *fusṭāṭ*) must not be pitched upon their graves.[419]

The hypothesis put forward by Ignaz Goldziher that those tents provided the model for the later construction of domed mausolea does not seem convincing, even if some Muslim scholars themselves drew an analogy between tents of that kind and cupolas made of brick or stones. Rather, to the eyes of Muslim scholars, the problem of pitching tents upon the graves was mainly connected with the prohibition against taking tombs as places of worship and veneration (see below p. 240).[420] New research has shown that, in the absence of an indigenous Arabic tradition, it must have been above all the monuments and *martyria* of Byzantine Syria which served as a model for funerary architecture in the nascent Islamic community.[421]

3.3.2. Cenotaphs and coffins

The same attitude as that towards larger funerary constructions (e.g. mausolea) was displayed towards the setting up of cenotaphs, that is, it was in general discouraged

mor ve siyah p. 164 and plate II, fig. 4. To tents of another kind in the cemetery, albeit also peopled by seductive women, refers IʿAbdūnTraité pp. 60f.: "Il faut défendre aux diseurs de bonne aventure et aux conteurs en plein air de s'isoler avec des femmes, pour leur parler, dans le tentes qu'ils dressent [pour exercer leur profession], car c'est là pour eux un moyen de les violenter ou une ruse pour les voler; d'ailleurs, ce ne sont que de femmes sans vergogne qui viennent les trouver".

414 IQudMuġnī II p. 507; IMuflFurūʿ II p. 272; IQaylIġāṯah I p. 182. *Cf.* also NawRawḍah II p. 136 and MF XXXII p. 251.

415 HarMirqātMaf IV p. 69.

416 ṬūsīMiṣbāḥ p. 35.

417 FB III p. 286 (*ǧanāʾiz* 81); BāǧīMunt II p. 23; MuwMuršid I p. 66; ʿAynīʿUmdah VII pp. 46 and 100; QasṭIršād II p. 370; HarMirqātMaf IV p. 69; Goldziher: *Culte des ancêtres* p. 180; MF XXXII p. 251; Wafā: *Aḥkām al-ǧanāʾiz* p. 265. *Cf.* also IMuflFurūʿ II p. 272.

418 IAŠayMuṣ III p. 217 (*ǧanāʾiz* 133).

419 IAŠayMuṣ III p. 216 (*ǧanāʾiz* 133); IQudMuġnī II p. 507; IQaylIġāṯah I p. 182; MF XXXII p. 251; al-Muʿallimī: *ʿImārat al-qubūr* p. 257. *Cf.* also BāǧīMunt II p. 23 (who adds Ibn al-Musayyab).

420 *Cf.* also ʿAynīʿUmdah VII p. 46.

421 Hillenbrand: *Islamic Architecture* pp. 254f. and *Turco-Iranian Elements* p. 148. For the development of domed mausolea in the East, see Esin: *Qubbah Turkiyyah* esp. pp. 296ff.

and considered forbidden. Here, the majority of scholars – at least up to the tenth century H – not only detected a clear parallel to the ruling "not to build upon the grave", but the unanimously acknowledged verdict not to bury the deceased in a coffin (*tābūt*, rarely *ṣundūq*)[422] was also considered of relevance,[423] probably because the term *tābūt* was used for both the coffin and the cenotaph without distinction (see also below).[424] All the more surprising therefore, given the prescriptions of the Muslim legal scholars, is that coffins were widely in use. The Arabic *tābūt* even found its way into European languages, e.g. into the dialects of Sicily in which the term *tab(b)uto* or *tabutto* is applied to the coffin to the present day.

The legal debate

In the discourse of eschatology, the use of a coffin was connected with Hell. There is a (weakly authenticated) Tradition saying that on Jugdement Day the evil-doers and their likes will be crammed into an iron coffin (*tābūt min ḥadīd*) and thrown into the Fire.[425] However, as in the case of larger funerary structures, the use of a *tābūt* (either a cenotaph or a coffin) in the present world was sanctioned under certain conditions, e.g. for the burial of women (a claim of the Hanafites)[426] or when there was the danger that the corpse of the deceased could be unearthed easily due to the softness or moistness of the ground, or if animals that would dig up the soil (e.g. hyenas) were present in the area.[427] The verdict of the Shiite scholar aṭ-Ṭūsī (d. 548 H or after) sounds somewhat stricter: "The use of the coffin is detestable according to scholarly consensus, yet if the tomb is moist it is allowed that a piece of teak wood or comparable material be spread in it".[428]

The same arguments were in general also adduced for the practice itself of burying human beings.[429] It was never disputed in Islam, as a matter of principle, that the dead should be buried in

422 *ṣundūq* in the sense of "coffin" appears e.g. in IFuwaṭīḪaw pp. 172f. For the term, see also below p. 238.

423 There is an *ʾiǧmāʿ* on this point, see ṬūsīMabsūṭ I p. 187; RamlīNih III p. 30; MF XXI p. 16 and XXXII p. 247. *Cf.* also Marcus: *Funerary and Burial Practices* p. 98 with note 1 and Goitein: *Mediterranean Society* V p. 162.

424 Sometimes the cenotaph (not the tombstone) was referred to as *ḥaǧar manqūš*, see IMuflFurūʿ II p. 270. The ambiguity of *tābūt* meaning both "coffin" and "cenotaph" appears in expressions such as *wuḍiʿa ʿalā qabrihī tābūt*, "a cenotaph was set upon his tomb" (e.g. MuḥḪul II p. 315). Strangely enough, *at-tābūt* was the nick-name of the Ḥanafite scholar Abū Kāmil al-Muẓaffar b. Yūsuf (d. 574 H), see *Wāfī* XXV p. 687 (alas, no reasons given!).

425 MunKawākib I p. 460. With a slightly different wording also in DaylFird I pp. 153f. ("a single coffin", *tābūt wāḥid*, instead of "a coffin of iron", *tābūt min ḥadīd*).

426 MF XXI p. 16.

427 *Cf.* INuğBaḥr II p. 209; HaytTuḥfMuḥt III p. 194; RamlīNih III p. 30; MF XXXII p. 247. However, if burial was impossible, e.g. during military expeditions on enemy territory, the unburied soldiers whose corpses were devoured by birds and beasts of prey were believed to obtain martyrdom, see Lecker: *Burial of Martyrs* p. 37 and 49.

428 ṬūsīMabsūṭ I p. 187.

429 *Cf.* also Krawietz: *Ḥurma* pp. 150-2.

the earth, following Q 5:31 and 77:25f.: *Then God sent forth a raven, scratching into the earth, to show him* (i.e. Cain) *how he might conceal the vile body of his brother. He said, 'Woe is me! Am I unable to be as this raven, and so conceal my brother's vile body?'* (Q 5:31), and *Made we not the earth to be a housing / for the living and for the dead?* (Q 77:25f.). However, in that context one also took recourse to less practical arguments: some Traditions from the Prophet claim that burying the corpse in the ground should prevent the living from hearing the voices of those chastised in their tombs.[430]

The use of coffins was considered permissible – at least by the majority of scholars[431] – when the deceased had to be carried from one place to another (a relatively frequent practice, especially among the ruling classes)[432] or from his home to the graveyard, though a bier (*naʿš* or *sarīr*,[433] rarely *ǧanāzah*[434] or also *ʾālah ḥadbāʾ*[435]) was preferred for shorter distances. According to Muslim scholars, the first deceased Muslim ever to be carried on a bier was either Umm Salamah Zaynab bt. Ǧaḥš, one of the Prophet's wives, or Fāṭimah;[436] some add that this custom had been adopted from the Ethiopians.[437]

Coffins were also in use for preserving the bodies of persons whose burial sites, e.g. mausolea, were still under construction, something which could take several years.[438] Thus members of the ruling classes were often interred temporarily (at their so-called *al-madfan al-ʾawwal*, their "first burial place") or not at all, a fact that is even mentioned in epitaphs.[439] In fourth and fifth-century Baghdad or Cairo, people were often interred in their houses before being transferred to regular cemeteries. The pompous funeral processions during which the bodies of rulers or high

430 IḤaǧAḥwāl p. 24. Notwithstanding the burial, though, some people were able to listen to the Interrogation of the dead, see IRaǧAhwāl pp. 26f. See also above p. 151.

431 *Cf.* also Krawietz: *Ḥurma* pp. 157-9.

432 *Cf.* Grütter: *Bestattungsbräuche* p. 187.

433 *sarīr* in the sense of "bier" is used in a Prophetical Tradition (FB III p. 235 = *ǧanāʾiz* 50), whereas in another (SuyḪaṣ II pp. 483 and 485) its exact meaning is doubtful; *sarīr* as "bier" also appears in ISaᶜdṬab VIII p. 229 (for the death of Arwā bt. Kurayz) and ṮaᶜlQatlā p. 155. The slightly redundant term *sarīr an-naʿš* and similar expressions appear in mourning poetry (e.g. TB IV p. 151 and ṢafAᶜyān II p. 79) and other sources (YaᶜqTārīḫ II p. 115: *ǧaʿalathā ʿalā s-sarīri naʿšan*). In rare cases, we also find the term *ǧanawīyah* used for the bier, e.g. MaqrMuq I p. 331; an anonymous riddle of the *naʿš* is quoted in BN XII p. 10.

434 E.g. TanFaraǧ III pp. 64f.

435 Literally "hunchbacked utensil", e.g. in a line of Kaᶜb b. Zuhayr's famous "Mantle-Ode" (*basīṭ*): *kullu bni ʾunṯā wa-ʾin ṭālat salāmatuhū * yawman ʿalā ʾālatin ḥadbāʾa maḥmūlū*, "And everyone born to woman, even if safe for long, * is one day borne upon a funeral bier" (for the translation *cf.* Ibn Kathīr: *The Life of the Prophet Muḥammad*, tr. by Trevor Le Gassick, vol. III, Reading 2000, p. 504).

436 *Cf.* Schöller: *Anfänge* p. 32.

437 YaᶜqTārīḫ II p. 115; BN VII p. 105; ḤalInsān III p. 321.

438 *Cf.* Leisten: *Architektur für Tote* pp. 24f.

439 E.g. in the epitaph of the Saᶜdid ruler al-Mahdī bi-llāh (d. 964 H, see **115a**): *ṯumma nuqila min madfanihī l-muqaddasi ʾilā laḥdihī l-mukarrami bi-r-rawḍati l-mušarrafah.* For more epitaphs, see Vol. I pp. 22 and 78-80.

officials were transported in coffins from the temporary burial sites to their final destinations were great events from the early centuries onwards and might well be said to have been veritable "state funerals", e.g. in the cases of the Fatimid vizier al-Afḍal al-Ǧuyūšī in 515 H[440] or of the Mamluk ruler al-Manṣūr Qalāʾūn, whose body was brought from the Citadel to his mausoleum in downtown Cairo in 690 H.[441] Some decades before, in Šaʿbān 640 H, the body of the caliph al-Mustanṣir was transferred from the "House of the Caliphate" (*dār al-ḫilāfah*) in Baghdad to the caliphal burial ground at ar-Ruṣāfah, and the vivid as well as detailed description of this event by Ibn al-Fuwaṭī is worth reading.[442]

Ibn al-Fuwaṭī's chronicle also contains a remarkable passage in which he describes the *taḥwīl at-tawābīt*, "the transfer of coffins", in Baghdad in 646 H.[443] He relates that Faḫr ad-Dawlah al-Ḥasan b. al-Muṭṭalib was to be transferred from his burial place (*madfan*) in the vault (*ʾīwān*) of his congregational mosque on the banks of the Tigris to the shrine of Mūsā b. Ǧaʿfar because a wall had collapsed in the mosque, but the jurists would not allow this because more than sixty years had passed since his death. However, in the year before, Ibn al-Fuwaṭī reports,

> "a wall had cracked (in two) in the mausoleum (*turbah*) of the caliph al-Mustaḍīʾ bi-Amr Allāh (r. 566–76 H), and so he was transferred from his burial place to a place in the afore-mentioned mausoleum (*turbah*)[444], and seven other coffins (*tawābīt*) were carried with him, containing his sister ʿĀʾišah, known as 'al-Fayrūzağiyah', her son Abū Manṣūr, the parents of aẓ-Ẓāhir (Abū Naṣr, r. 622–23 H) and aẓ-Ẓāhir's wife. Then they were transferred in this year to the mausolea (*turab*) in ar-Ruṣāfah, and (the following bodies) were also brought from the Ḥarīm aẓ-Ẓāhirī to ar-Ruṣāfah: al-Muʿtaḍid bi-llāh (r. 279–89 H), more than 350 years after his death; his son al-Muktafī (r. 289–95 H), 350 years after his death; al-Qāhir (d. 338 H), brother of al-Muktafı, after 300 years; the cousin of al-Qāhir, after 290 years; and al-Mustakfī (d. 338 H), after 320 years".[445]

Historical evidence

The use of coffins for transport was a common feature in Islam through all centuries and nearly everywhere. Some examples particularly illustrative of that fact, or concerning famous personalities, include the following:

440 See the detailed account of his funerary procession in IMaʾmūnAḫbār pp. 15-17.

441 MaqrḪiṭaṭ II p. 381.

442 IFuwaṭīḤaw pp. 171-3.

443 According to Ibn Kaṯīr this happened only in 647 H, see BN XIII p. 177. The damages reported in the following were due to the flooding of the Tigris, *cf.* above p. 218.

444 Here the text is not without ambiguity, but this must refer to the shrine of Mūsā.

445 IFuwaṭīḤaw p. 242. The latter years given by Ibn al-Fuwaṭī are not exact. The same notice appears abridged in BN XIII p. 177. Here, different caliphs are named, and Ibn Kaṯīr says that the transfer of the bodies had been carried out in order to avoid their being damaged by the flooding of the Tigris. However, as Ibn al-Fuwaṭī reports, the tombs of the caliphs in ar-Ruṣāfah were flooded after all, and the passage in his chronicle suggests that the necessary steps were taken only after the burial sites had been damaged.

Abū ᶜAbd Allāh al-Bāhilī (A. b. M., "Ġulām Ḫalīl") died in Baghdad in 275 H and was carried in a *tābūt* to Baṣrah, where he was buried and a *qubbah* erected over the tomb;[446] Ibrāhīm b. Aḥmad Ibn Aġlab (r. 261–89 H) was carried in a *tābūt* from Sicily to Kairouan (?);[447] the first Fatimid ruler of Egypt, al-Muᶜizz li-Dīn Allāh (d. 365 H), had the remains of his predecessors transferred in coffins (*tawābīt*) from their burial places in Tunisia to the newly-built mausoleum of the dynasty in Cairo;[448] the Fatimid caliph Nizār (r. 365–86 H) took the coffins of his ancestors with him while campaigning in Syria;[449] Muḥammad b. al-ᶜAbbās al-ᶜUṣmī al-Harawī (294–378 H), who died near Nīsābūr, stipulated in his last will that he was to be carried in a *tābūt* to his native town Harāt and buried there;[450] the coffin of Muḥammad b. ᶜUbayd Allāh (d. 385) was carried from Qāsān to Iṣfahān;[451] the *tābūt* of the Shafiite authority al-Bayhaqī was in 458 H carried from Nīsābūr to Bayhaq;[452] the wife of the Aleppine governor Qasīm ad-Dawlah Āqsunqur (d. 487 H),[453] who was killed by her husband in 481 H "while he stabbed towards her with a dagger as a sort of play and jesting and hit her heart", was carried to her burial place "in the East" in a *tābūt*;[454] Abū Muḥammad ᶜAbd Allāh b. ᶜAlī al-Muqriʾ (Baghdad, 464–541 H)[455] died in the chamber he had in the upper storey of his mosque, thus his body was put in a *tābūt* and lowered down from the roof of the mosque with the help of ropes;[456] the famous scholar Zakarīyāʾ al-Anṣārī (d. Cairo 926 H) was put in a coffin (or rather "on a bier"?, *ᶜalā tābūt*) and carried to the Ottoman governor Ḫayrbak so that he could pronounce the burial prayer over his body, because Ḫayrbak felt too weak to ride all the way to al-Anṣārī's final burial place in the southern Qarāfah.[457] In the same way, the body of aš-Šāfiᶜī was carried on a bier to the house of as-Sayyidah Nafīsah in order that she perform the burial prayer over him before he was taken to his tomb in the Qarāfah.[458]

Quite astonishing is the circumstantial detail that "beneath" (*taḥta*) the *tābūt* of the famous Mamluk emir Ilġāy al-Yūsufī (d. 775 H) red felt (*labbād ʾaḥmar*) had been put when his body was carried from the Nile (where he had drowned) to the mausoleum in his newly-built madrasah.[459] Employing red felt was perhaps just a sign of reverence, as in the related case of a wooden coffin "covered with something

446 TB V p. 80; IǦawzīMunt V p. 96 = Leisten: *Architektur für Tote* p. 140 (no. 2).

447 AFidāʾMuḫt II p. 50. Perhaps his coffin was brought to Palermo, see the discussion of the relevant notices in Amari: *Musulmani di Sicilia* II pp. 115f.

448 IMaʾmūnAḫbār p. 40 = MaqrḪiṭaṭ I p. 407.

449 NZ IV p. 121.

450 TB III p. 121; NawMuḫt p. 212.

451 ANuAḫbIṣf II p. 303.

452 BN XII p. 94.

453 Father of the first Zangid ruler ᶜImād ad-Dīn Zangī (r. 521–41 H). He had his father later exhumed and buried in a madrasah he had founded in Aleppo (IᶜAdīmZubdah pp. 301f.).

454 IᶜAdīmZubdah p. 223.

455 *Wāfī* XVII pp. 331f.; ĠazṬab I pp. 434f.

456 IǦawzīMunt X p. 122; IRaǧḎayl I p. 212.

457 ŠaᶜrṬab II p. 124. Transporting the dead on a bier (or in a coffin) to the Qarāfah cemetery could also be the subject of mourning poems, see AŠāmahRawḍ I pp. 126f.

458 IlyāsBad I p. 145.

459 ITaġrManh III p. 43. The madrasah is still extant today; *cf.* also Williams: *Islamic Monuments* pp. 91-3.

reddish resembling red felt'"[460] which was unearthed in Medina after 360 H at the shrine of al-Ḥasan b. ᶜAlī.[461] More probably, however, this practice had been adopted on the basis of reports according to which red velvet (*qaṭīfah ḥamrāʾ*) or, according to others, a piece of the purple cloth of his saddle (*qiṭᶜatu raḥlihī wa-kānat min ʾurǧuwān*)[462] had been put in the Prophet's tomb.[463] The scholars argued that the application of red velvet – or the disposal of any cloth in the burial niche – had been a prerogative of the Prophet and was not be imitated by later Muslims.[464] Ibn Saᶜd (d. 230 H) cites various explanations as to why a *qaṭīfah ḥamrāʾ* was put in the Prophet's tomb, viz. because the earth of his grave was considered too moist, because the Prophet's body would not decay in the sepulchre, or because nobody else should wear that *qaṭīfah* after the Prophet's death.[465]

It frequently happened that people who died on the way to Cairo were carried to the Qarāfah cemetery in order to be buried there,[466] and people who died in aṣ-Ṣāliḥīyah (Damascus) were often, though by no means always, carried to the greater Damascene cemeteries (or *vice versa*). Among scholars, state officials and nobles, Jerusalem[467] or the blessed cities of the Ḥiǧāz (Mecca and Medina) were sometimes chosen as places of burial, even though the bodies had to be carried there over hundreds of miles. Arguably the most famous and probably earliest case in this context is that of Ǧaᶜfar b. al-Faḍl Ibn Ḥinzābah (Baghdad 308 – Cairo 391 H, see **45**) who had bought a house in Medina attached to the wall of the Prophet's sepulchre and decreed by will to be buried there. When this had been conceded, his body was transported in a coffin (*tābūt*) from Egypt to the Ḥiǧāz and, before the burial, carried around in Mecca, the proper rites of pilgrimage being performed.[468]

A comparable, likewise remarkable case is that of the vizier Ǧamāl ad-Dīn Muḥammad b. Abī Manṣūr ᶜAlī al-Iṣfahānī al-Ǧawād (d. 559 H)[469] who had made a

460 *tābūtun min ḫašabin muġaššan bi-šayʾin ʾaḥmara yušbihu l-labbāda l-ʾaḥmar.*

461 QNuᶜmDaᶜāʾim I p. 237; SamWafāʾ III p. 909.

462 YaᶜqTārīḫ II p. 114.

463 *Cf.* also MasTanbīh p. 245; IǦamMuḫt p. 147.

464 ISaᶜdṬab II p. 299; SaḫǦawāhir II p. 960; SuyḪaṣ II p. 486.

465 ISaᶜdṬab II pp. 299f.

466 Even the poet Ṣalāḥ ad-Dīn al-Irbilī (570–631 H) was carried to the Qarāfah cemetery after he had been buried for five years in distant Edessa (ar-Ruhā), see MaqrMuq I p. 499.

467 *Cf. Wāfī* XVII p. 237; ZarkAḥkām p. 294 (*faḍl ad-dafn fī Bayt al-Maqdis*); FāsīᶜIqd II p. 186; ITaġrManh III pp. 127 and 474; ᶜUlaymīUns I p. 235. The most detailed research concerning burial in Jerusalem is found in MaqdMuṯīr pp. 246-9 and Gil: *History of Palestine* pp. 631-5. By an Ismailite scholar, ᶜAlī is quoted as saying: "Bury the corpses at the places where they met their fate (*fī maṣāriᶜihā*) and do not behave like the Jews who carry their dead to Jerusalem!" (QNuᶜmDaᶜāʾim I p. 238).

468 YāqIršād II pp. 408f.; IḪallWaf I p. 349; MaqrMuq III p. 48; ZA II p. 126; Leisten: *Architektur für Tote* p. 24 note 201 and p. 195 (no. 2).

469 He had spent a fortune during his lifetime on renovating and founding of buildings in Medina and Mecca, see IǦawzīMunt X p. 209; AŠāmahRawḍ I pp. 137f.; NZ V p. 365.

pact with his friend al-Malik al-Manṣūr Asad ad-Dīn Šīrkūh (an uncle of Ṣalāḥ ad-Dīn)[470] to the effect that whichever of them died earlier had to be carried by the other to Medina and buried there. Thus Šīrkūh after the death of al-Ǧawād provided for some mystics to bring al-Ǧawād in a coffin to Medina, together with reciters who would walk around the coffin and utter litanies ceaselessly. They carried al-Ǧawād to his burial place near the Prophet's sepulchre, yet not without having performed the rites of pilgrimage in Mecca (including the slaughter of a camel in his name) and having visited the sepulchre of the Prophet (*ar-rawḍah*) before that.[471] Only two years later, in 561 H, the coffin of the Zurayᶜid ruler of ᶜAdan ᶜImād ad-Dīn Abū Mūsā ᶜImrān b. Muḥammad Ibn al-Makram al-Hamdānī was carried around the pilgrimage sites of Mecca "because he was obsessed (*mašġūf*) with performing the pilgrimage", then he was laid at rest in the Maᶜlāh cemetery.[472]

The ninth-century historian al-Fāsī adds that Ibn Ḥinzābah and Ǧamāl ad-Dīn Ibn Abī Manṣūr were among the first ever to be carried in a coffin to Mecca, together with Ibn Ruzzīk,[473] the brother of the Fatimid vizier aṣ-Ṣāliḥ Ṭalāʾiᶜ b. Ruzzīk (d. 556 H), and the Yemenite queen al-Malikah al-Ḥurrah (d. 547 H, see **126**);[474] in 539 H, Ibrāhīm Rāmušt (Abū l-Qāsim al-Fārisī, d. 534 H) was brought in a coffin (*tābūt*) from Iraq to Mecca.[475] Some 120 years later, the philologist and traditionist aṣ-Ṣāġānī (al-Ḥasan b. M., d. Baghdad 650 H) had stipulated in his will that whoever would bring his body to Mecca would receive 50 dinars.[476] This was a meagre reward for such an undertaking, but he was eventually carried to Mecca in the latter half of the seventh century H and buried beside al-Fuḍayl b. ᶜIyāḍ (*cf.* **116**).

Others, from among the followers of Ibn ᶜArabī, expressed the last wish to be taken in a coffin to Damascus and buried beside their master.[477] Likewise, a huge number of Hanbalite scholars desired to be buried near the shrine of Ibn Ḥanbal[478] (as did many Shafiites and Hanafites who stipulated that they were to be interred near aš-Šāfiᶜī's or Abū Ḥanīfah's mausoleum) and drew up testaments to that effect. Abū l-ᶜAbbās aḍ-Ḍabbī (A. b. Ibr., d. Burūǧird 398 H) was therefore carried in his *tābūt* to Baghdad, and his son wrote in a letter to the Elder of the Hanafites that his

470 A general of the Zangid ruler al-Malik al-ᶜĀdil Nūr ad-Dīn Māḥmūd (r. 541–69 H) and first *de facto* Ayyubid ruler in Fatimid Egypt. He was known for visiting the tomb of aš-Šāfiᶜī (ᶜIṣāmīSimṭ IV p. 5) and performed the pilgrimage in 555 H. In Medina, he had founded a Sufi hospice and "stipulated in his last will to be carried there for burial after his death" (IFahdItḥāf II p. 522; ZA III p. 183).

471 IǦawzīMunt X p. 209; AŠāmahRawḍ I p. 137; IḪallWaf V pp. 145ff. = Leisten: *Architektur für Tote* p. 24 note 201; IFahdItḥāf II p. 527; ZA VI p. 278. The longest version of the story is in FāsīᶜIqd II pp. 310f.

472 IFahdItḥāf II p. 529. For similar cases, attested in extant epitaphs, see Vol. I p. 81.

473 EI^2 X pp. 149-51.

474 FāsīᶜIqd II p. 311.

475 IFahdItḥāf II p. 508; SinǧManāʾiḥ II p. 246; see also **124**.

476 IFuwaṭīḤaw p. 263; *Wāfī* XII p. 242; ITaġrManh V p. 123.

477 ŠaᶜrṬab I p. 203.

478 This could involve transport from Wāsiṭ to Baghdad, see IFuwaṭīḤaw p. 433; NZ IV p. 108; ITaġrManh VIII p. 166.

father had stipulated that he was to be buried in the *mašhad* of Abū Ḥanīfah. In order to carry out his father's last wish the son asked for the acquisition of a burial place (*turbah*) there and the Elder offered to buy a *turbah* for 5000 dinars, yet the Šarīf aṭ-Ṭāhir Abū Aḥmad, who was ultimately responsible for the matter, refused the sum and granted the mausoleum for free.[479]

In al-Andalus, many a deceased person was taken from other cities to be buried in either Córdoba or Granada. ᶜAbd Allāh b. Aḥmad Ibn Zaydūn (d. 405, a native of Córdoba) died in Ilbīrah (sp. Elvira) and was carried in a *tābūt* to his burial place in Córdoba;[480] the Almohad ruler Abū Yaᶜqūb Yūsuf I b. ᶜAbd al-Muʾmin (d. 578 or 580 H) was carried in a *tābūt* from Santarém (Šantarīn) to Seville, his final burial place;[481] the jurist and man of letters Abū Muḥammad Ibn Ḥawṭ Allāh al-Ḥāriṯī (ᶜAl. b. Sul., 541–612 H) died in Granada in Rabīᶜ II but was taken in a *tābūt* to Málaga where he was buried in Šaᶜbān.[482] The Andalusian traditionist and biographer al-Ḥumaydī (d. Baghdad 488 H) "had entrusted Muẓaffar b. Raʾīs ar-Ruʾasāʾ with the task of burying him near the tomb of Bišr al-Ḥāfī, but Muẓaffar ignored his last wish and interred him in the Bāb Abraz cemetery instead.[483] After a while, Muẓaffar saw al-Ḥumaydī in a dream "as if he was reproaching him for ignoring his will, so al-Ḥumaydī was (finally) transferred to the Bāb Ḥarb cemetery in Ṣafar 491 H and buried near the tomb of Bišr".[484]

In fact, carrying a deceased person away from the place where he died and burying him somewhere else was not considered, according to some reports, acceptable, but rather disapproved of[485] or even prohibited;[486] the market inspectors were held to prevent that practice.[487] Nevertheless, the practice was widespread in later centuries and it was soon argued that "the prohibition was valid only during the first years of Islam".[488] Some Sunnite reports state that the first to have been moved from one tomb to another (i.e. from Kūfah to Medina) in Islamic times was ᶜAlī b. Abī Ṭālib,[489] a claim rejected by the Shiites. The Sunnite scholars also discussed the question whether the soul of the deceased, in the case of his being moved from one place to another, would follow the body to the new burial place.[490]

479 YāqIršād I pp. 67f.; ZA I p. 86.

480 ᶜIyāḍTartīb IV p. 724.

481 IĠalbTiḏkār p. 95.

482 MaqqNafḥ (C) VI p. 67.

483 Others, such as Šams ad-Dīn al-Kirmānī (M. b. Yūsuf, 717–86 H), stipulated that they were to be interred in the Bāb Abraz cemetery (IQŠuhbTārīḫ I p. 152).

484 MaqqNafḥ (C) II p. 316.

485 *Cf.* also Leisten: *Architektur für Tote* pp. 23-5.

486 MunḏTarġīb IV p. 152: "The transport of the body to another place is prohibited, except in the vicinity of Mecca, Medina and Jerusalem".

487 IDaybaᶜḤisbah p. 83. His views regarding this point are based on MawAḥkām p. 338.

488 There is a long discussion in HarMirqātMaf IV pp. 72f.

489 TMD XLII pp. 566f.; NZ I p. 120; KU 42933 (XV p. 737).

490 See IḤaǧĞawKāfī p. 41.

The misgivings of many legal scholars about transporting a body in a coffin and unearthing a deceased person come to the fore in a most remarkable story from the tenth century H. The story concerns an ancestor of Muḥammad b. ᶜAbd Allāh b. ᶜUmar; the latter died in ar-Rawḥāᵓ (Yemen) in 1055 H and was commonly known, for his famous ancestor, as "Ibn al-Manqūl", "Son[491] of the Transferred One (i.e. from one grave to another)". The "Transferred One", a certain ᶜAbd al-Walīy b. Muḥammad, was a Yemenite jurist in the time of the Ṭāhirid ruler ᶜĀmir b. ᶜAbd al-Wahhāb (r. 894–923 H). Together with his brother ᶜUmar, ᶜAbd al-Walī first lived in Bayt al-Faqīh (Ibn ᶜUǧayl)[492] but had then married in Maḥall al-Aᶜwaṣ. After his death, however, he was buried in the mausoleum (*turbah*) of Ibn ᶜUǧayl and thus the problems started:

> "His brother (ᶜUmar) saw him in a dream as if he was saying, 'Transfer me to Maḥall al-Aᶜwaṣ!' The jurist ᶜUmar was alarmed by this and said (to himself): 'This was truly a vision in a dream, yet the transfer (of deceased) is forbidden according to the legal scholars and unearthing the dead counts among the gravest of wrongdoings'. But his brother appeared to him another night, then again a third time. He said to him, 'So far you haven't carried me away, and if it does not happen soon I will leave the tomb!' The jurist hurried to the tomb in order to transfer his brother's body. There he found him outside the tomb clothed in his shrouds, so they took him and he was carried to his actual tomb in Maḥall al-Aᶜwaṣ. This is the reason why he was called 'the Transferred One' (*al-manqūl*)".[493]

Among the Shiites it was often decreed by will to be buried in Karbalāᵓ, an-Naǧaf, Baghdad (Kāẓimayn cemetery) or al-Mašhad (near the Imams al-Ḥusayn, ᶜAlī, Mūsā al-Kāẓim and ᶜAlī ar-Riḍā, respectively), though this could entail the transport of the corpses over hundreds or even thousands of miles.[494] From the Būyid period onwards, when this practice of interment near one of the tombs of the Imams started to flourish increasingly, this led to the constant arrival of caravans carrying the corpses from far places to their destinations; further growth of the corpse traffic took place during the tenth century H and then again during the thirteenth century H. This so-called *naql al-ǧanāᵓiz*, "the transfer of the biers", notwithstanding the use of coffins, caused the air to be filled with the odour of corpses in a more or less advanced state of decay, a fact that aroused dismay among some Shiite scholars and

491 In the wider sense of "from the progeny of …".

492 The location was named after Abū l-ᶜAbbās A. b. Mūsā b. ᶜAlī b. ᶜUǧayl (d. 690 H, see GALS I p. 461). Around his tomb, a widely-venerated shrine, the village called "Bayt al-Faqīh (Ibn ᶜUǧayl)" had grown since *c.*700 H (Schuman: *History of the Yemen* pp. 10 and 64 with note 67). In 1763 CE, Carsten Niebuhr visited Bayt al-Faqīh and the tomb of Aḥmad b. Mūsā (Niebuhr: *Reisebeschreibung* pp. 316-8).

493 MuḥḪul IV pp. 27f.

494 *Cf.* Wirth: *Orientalische Stadt* p. 426.

secular reformers alike and caused them to condemn this practice as "detestable innovation" and thus not allowed.[495] Others, e.g. aṭ-Ṭūsī, were more lenient, stating that "it is disapproved to transfer the deceased from the spot where he died to another town, except if he is carried to one of the (Imamite) shrines (*mašāhid*) since this is recommended".[496]

The decomposition of corpses was a universal problem when transporting the dead. Take for example the case of the poet Abū s-Suᶜūd b. Muḥammad al-Kūrānī (d. 1056 H) who died of the plague outside Aleppo: he was carried back to the town for burial, but when he arrived "his body had already swollen and become putrid, and his appearance had changed".[497] Still more drastic seems the case of the governor of Egypt, Takīn, who died in Rabīᶜ I 321 H and was carried in a coffin (*tābūt*) to Jerusalem.[498] Since they had not been able to procure camphor for his embalming, rats ate the tips of his fingers and ants his eyes.[499] But there is one even more distasteful detail: according to a story reported by al-Yāfiᶜī, the mule which carried Takīn's coffin stumbled when it entered Jerusalem, so the coffin fell down and the mule urinated upon it.[500]

Touching and kissing the cenotaph

Other scholars accepted the existence of cenotaphs, at least in the case of tombs commonly venerated by Muslims, and sometimes even tried to justify the role they played during the visitation of the grave: "It is considered disapproved of (...) to kiss the cenotaph that is set upon the tomb as well as to kiss the grave (itself) or to touch it, nor should the thresholds be kissed when entering for the visit to (the tombs of) saintly persons. Nevertheless, if by kissing their tombs the intention is to gain blessing (*tabarruk*), it must not be considered detestable, as my father (Šihāb ad-Dīn ar-Ramlī) laid down in a fatwa".[501]

Some scholars, including al-Ġazālī, condemned the practice of touching or kissing the cenotaph and called it "Christian habits" (*min ᶜādati n-Naṣārā*).[502] Ibn Ḫallikān reports from Ibn ᶜAsākir that he had met Abū ᶜAbd Allah Ibn Ṣaffār from Asfarāʾīn (in Northeastern Iran) whose grandfather ᶜUmar used to kiss the threshold of the shrine (*mašhad*) of the Shafiite scholar Abū Isḥāq al-Asfarāʾīnī (Ibr. b. M., d. 418 H).[503] According to Shiite custom, the visitors should kiss the threshold of ᶜAlī's

495 For the modern debate, see Richard: *Shiʾite Islam* p. 9; Nakash: *Shiᶜis of Iraq*, ch. 7, esp. pp. 192ff.; Halm: *Schia* p. 178 and Halm: *Naql al-ǧanāʾiz*.

496 ṬūsīMabsūṭ I p. 187. A critical view concerning carrying the dead to burial sites near famous shrines was already expressed by ṬūsīMiṣbāḥ p. 35.

497 ᶜUrḍīMaᶜādin p. 270.

498 *Cf.* NZ III p. 211.

499 Gil: *History of Palestine* p. 635, n. 109.

500 Cited in SuyḤusnMuḥ I p. 422.

501 RamlīNih III p. 33; *cf.* also al-Albānī: *Aḥkām al-ǧanāʾiz* pp. 262f.; MF XXXII p. 256.

502 ĠazIḥyāʾ (C) IV p. 417; MuwMuršid I p. 37; HaytTuḥfZuw p. 20 (*al-mass wa-t-taqbīl min fiᶜl an-naṣārā wa-l-yahūd*); HarMirqātMaf IV p. 115. For the Malikites condemning the kissing of tombs, see DabMaᶜālim III p. 212.

503 IḪallWaf VI p. 394. However, Abū Isḥāq had died in Nīsābūr.

mausoleum in an-Nağaf as well as the cenotaph,[504] or the tomb, of al-Ḥusayn,[505] and some Sunnite scholars ventured the opinion that it was permissible (*lā ba's bihī*) to kiss at least the tomb of one's own parents.[506] However, the Shiites embraced that practice openly, quite in contrast with the Sunnite scholars: "It is not disapproved to kiss the cenotaphs, but it is rather a *sunnah* among us. If hiding the faith (*taqīyah*) is necessary, then it is best to do without kissing.[507] With regard of the kissing of thresholds, there is no authoritative report (*naṣṣ*) to refer to".[508]

Of course, most Sunnite scholars also declared it reprehensible to kiss or even to touch[509] the tomb of the Prophet in Medina, yet with the notable exception of Ibn Ḥanbal, Ibn ᶜUmar, al-Muḥibb aṭ-Ṭabarī and Ibn Ḥağar al-ᶜAsqalānī; in any case, there was no consensus (*'iğmāᶜ*) on this point.[510] On the other hand, kissing his tomb or the threshold of his mosque appears among the common motifs in poetry in praise of the Prophet. It is necessary for the visitor, the poet says, (*ṭawīl*):

لِيَلْثَمَ أَعْتَاباً لِمَسْجِدِكَ الَّذِي * بِهِ الرَّوْضَةُ الفَيْحَاءُ مِنْ جَنَّةِ الخُلْدِ

"That he kiss the thresholds of your mosque * in which there is the sweet-smelling garden[511] that belongs to the Garden of eternal bliss",

a verse by as-Sayyid Ḥusayn b. ᶜAlī al-Madanī (eleventh cent. H).[512] Similarly, in a verse by al-Witrī (d. 663 H) we read: *ṣabābatuhū hāğat li-taqbīli qabrihī*, "the loving desire he felt made him urge to kiss his (i.e. the Prophet's) tomb".[513]

The question of touching and kissing the cenotaph – together with taking away earth from the tomb (see above p. 88) – was once more on the agenda of scholars during the twelfth century H, that is, in a period when the concern for a reform of the modes and forms of piety was growing steadily. This often led to critical voices against the mortuary cult, in general much reminiscent of the arguments put forward

504 ṬūsīMiṣbāḥ p. 518; MağlBihār C pp. 295, 303, 306, 320, 332 and *passim*; al-Amīn: *Miftāḥ* II p. 296; Schober: *Heiligtum ᶜAlīs* pp. 128 and 133-5.

505 ṬūsīMiṣbāḥ p. 502.

506 HarMirqātMaf IV p. 115.

507 *Cf.* also Laoust: *Schismes* p. 411.

508 MağlBihār C p. 136.

509 AŠāmahBāᶜiṯ p. 70. *Cf.* also ᶜIyāḍŠifā' (B) II p. 72 / (Š) II p. 85 = HarŠŠifā' II p. 152: Mālik b. Anas (or Anas b. Mālik) approached the tomb of the Prophet, but he would not touch it with his hand; see ḤurRawḍ p. 357; SamWafā' IV p. 1402 = HaytTuḥfZuw p. 21; al-Albānī: *Aḥkām al-ğanā'iz* pp. 195 and 266. Among the Malikites, however, touching a venerated tomb with one's hand was disputed, see DabMaᶜālim III p. 212.

510 QasṭMaw III p. 416; DiyTārḪamīs II p. 175; KarKawākib p. 156, citing Ibn Taymīyah, e.g. ITayMağm XXVII pp. 79 and 91f.; al-Albānī: *Aḥkām al-ğanā'iz* pp. 195f. and 266.

511 I.e. the Prophet's sepulchre and the surrounding area, see above p. 48.

512 MN II p. 75 (v. 23). For another two verses on the same argument (i.e. *fī š-šawqi 'ilā laṯmi ᶜatabati sayyidi l-'anbiyā'*), see ᶜĀmKaškūl I p. 127.

513 Cited in MN II p. 283 (v. 19). *Cf.* also Bannerth: *Wallfahrtsstätten Kairos* p. 5.

by the Neo-Hanbalites in the eighth century H. The condemned practices often have some connection with the mystical elements of Islam in the Ottoman period and were called by Arthur Arberry, not without exaggeration, "the dark side of Sufism in its last phase".[514] Arberry also provides a nice example of such a critical voice, that is some verses by "one brave spirit of the eighteenth century", as he says, a certain Badr ad-Dīn al-Ḥiǧāzī:

"For they have forgotten God, saying 'So-and-so provides deliverance from suffering for all mankind.'
When he dies, they make him the object of pilgrimage, and hasten to his shrine, Arabs and foreigners alike:
Some kiss his grave, and some the threshold of his door, and the dust –
So do the infidels behave towards their idols, seeking thereby to win their favour".[515]

Practice

As for the use of cenotaphs (*tābūt* or *ṣundūq*,[516] also *tarkībah* or *nuṣb*) in Islamic culture, it seems certain that it followed models known since Antiquity and thus must have been current from the very beginning in all Islamic regions around the southern and eastern fringes of the Mediterranean. Such cenotaphs were in general either made of cut stones or plastered bricks, sometimes of precious metals, especially silver.[517] During the later Mamluk and Ottoman periods, wooden cenotaphs and cage-like shelters came increasingly into use – e.g. at the tomb of the prophet Yūnus near Ṣafad as witnessed by (Ibn) an-Nābulusī[518] – though they had been by no means unknown before that time. One of the earliest cases is probably the tomb (*sic*) made of wood for the poet D̲ū r-Rummah.[519]

In the sixth century H, a "gate-like framework[520] of engraved wood with bolts of brass" was erected on the tomb of the jurist Ibn al-Mannī al-Ḥanbalī (d. Baghdad 583 H) after the burial, obviously in order to prevent direct access to the grave.[521] A structure of teak wood (probably set up in 547 H) covered the tomb of Ibn ᶜAbbās in aṭ-Ṭāʾif, and in the same mausoleum, a drape-covered wooden cenotaph (*tābūt ḫašab*) was set upon the tomb of Muḥammad b. al-Ḥanafīyah.[522] Another wooden cenotaph is explicitly mentioned in the epitaph of the Syrian mystic Abū Bakr b. Qawām

514 Arberry: *Sufism* p. 122.

515 Arberry: *Sufism* pp. 121f. = Sirriyeh: *Sufis and Anti-Sufis* p. 2. Unfortunately, Arberry and Sirriyeh mention no source and I have been unable to trace the wording of these lines.

516 *Cf.* for the term *ṣundūq*: IḪallWaf VII p. 206; MuwMuršid I p. 15; *Wāfī* XXIX p. 136; IFuwaṭīḤaw p. 253 (*banā turbatan … wa-ᶜamila ḍarīḥan wa-ṣundūqan*); Ǧarǧūr: *Taslīṭ an-nūr* p. 28; RCEA 4318 (647 H); CIA Égypte II 592 (864 H).

517 IǦubRiḥlah (B) p. 19 (a *tābūt fiḍḍah* in the Cairene shrine of al-Ḥusayn's head). However, also the silver screening of the shrine might be referred to.

518 NābḤaqīqah p. 299. *Cf.* Kriss: *Volksglaube* I pp. 252f.

519 See *Aġānī* XVIII p. 45.

520 *malban*, see WKAS *s.r.*

521 *Wāfī* XXVII p. 81.

522 ᶜUǧIhdāʾ pp. 66f. and 69.

al-Bālisī (d. 658 H), as found in his Damascene mausoleum (RCEA 4633); according to literary sources, al-Bālisī had stipulated in his last wish to be buried in a coffin (*tābūt*), because he wished to be carried to Damascus after his initial burial in his native village.[523] The ascetic Muḥammad b. Sakrān (d. 667 H) was buried in his lodge in Baghdad where his tomb was covered by a mausoleum (*qubbah*) and a wooden cenotaph (*ḍarīḥun mina l-ḫašab*).[524] In the Southern Qarāfah cemetery in Cairo, the tomb of a certain sheikh ᶜAbd an-Nūr was in an open recinct (*ḥawš*) which contained "a wooden cenotaph (*tābūt ḫašab*) bearing his name and the date of his death.[525]

The somewhat larger tomb constructions in use in the Islamic West, about 80–150 cm long and commonly known as *mqābrīyah*,[526] occupy a sort of middle position, as they are higher than the enclosures found elsewhere, but could also be described as cenotaphs; the same holds true for the (mainly Egyptian) tombs known as "bench", *masṭabah* (or *mastabah*).[527]

As seen above page 197, the setting up of cenotaphs was not encouraged by the scholars who, on the contrary, regarded this custom as an abominable and dreadful innovation.[528] Yet in pre-modern Arabic terminology, there is not even a specific term for the cenotaph as such; usually it was simply named "coffin" or "box". On the other hand, these very terms subsumed everything which could, in practice, be "built upon" a tomb except mausolea or tomb-mosques. Cenotaphs were not considered lawful in theory, and therefore the legal scholars did not discuss their various shapes nor – apart from the usages of touching or kissing them – widespread practices, e.g. sprinkling them with perfume or covering them with a draping. Such

523 KutFawāt I p. 225. *Cf.* for wooden cenotaphs also Winkler: *Volkskunde* p. 315; Grütter: *Bestattungsbräuche* p. 173; Kriss: *Volksglaube* I pp. 24, 27, 93 (on portable wooden cenotaphs called *maḥmal*) and 228 (wooden cenotaphs upon the tombs of Bilāl b. Rabāḥ al-Ḥabašī – RCEA 3987 [625 H] – and Sukaynah bt. al-Ḥusayn – RCEA 3195 and 4717 – in Damascus [*tābūt min ḫašab*: al-Amīn: *Miftāḥ* II p. 263]); Rāġib: *Mausolées Fatimides* pp. 7-10); RCEA 4681 (inscribed wooden cenotaph on the tomb of Ǧalāl ad-Dīn ar-Rūmī, d. 672 H in Konya); RCEA 4778 (inscribed wooden cenotaph on the tomb of al-Malik al-Muẓaffar Maḥmūd, d. Ḥāmah 678 H); Behrens-Abouseif: *Islamic Architecture in Cairo* pp. 76 (mausoleum of Yaḥyā aš-Šabīh), 85 and 87 (mausoleum of aš-Šāfiᶜī); RCEA 3679: inscribed wooden cenotaph of the mother of al-Malik al-ᶜĀdil (d. 608 H) in the mausoleum of aš-Šāfiᶜī; RCEA 3092 (533 H): inscription on the wooden cenotaph in the Cairene mausoleum of as-Sayyidah Ruqayyah (*cf.* also Rāġib: *Mausolées Fatimides* p. 27).

524 IFuwaṭīḤaw p. 364.

525 IZayKawākib p. 321. The author adds that the cenotaph was then stolen and nothing but a "heap of earth" (*kawm turāb*) remained to be seen.

526 Torres Balbás: *Cementerios* pp. 140 and 148-56; Dermenghem: *Culte des saints* p. 121; *cf.* Inscriptions Espagne I p. XXV; Peral Bejarano: *Excavación y estudio* pp. 27ff. For the Tunisian tumulus tombs called *bazina*, which exhibit round stone enclosures, and their influence on Muslim burial structures, see Mahjoub: *Pérennité des structures* pp. 152ff.; for circular tombs surrounded by stones (sometimes covered by clay) in Egypt, see Winkler: *Volkskunde* pp. 224f. (with plate 62 no. 1) and Kriss: *Volksglaube* I pp. 17f. (with plate 46); in Sudan: Grandin: *Nord-Soudan oriental* p. 90.

527 *Cf.* SaḫTuḥfAḥbāb pp. 208, 211, 214f. and *passim*; ᶜUlaymīUns II p. 241; Badr: *Styles of Tombs*, esp. pp. 356ff.; Winkler: *Volkskunde* p. 223; Kriss: *Volksglaube* I p. 17.

528 ŠubrḤāš III p. 12.

drapings are called *kiswah,* "cover, vestiment", *sitārah* or *sitr*, "veil", or also *sanǧaq*, "banner".[529] By persons who possessed the necessary means, a cover (*kiswah*) was promised as a vow to the Prophet's sepulchre, and it was duly manufactured and sent to Medina after the desired result had been obtained.[530] However, in this case, too, we find persons who abhorred the prevailing practice and considered the covering or draping of the cenotaph not to be a decent custom. This is, for example, true of Ǧamāl ad-Dīn Abū l-Ḥasan ᶜAlī b. Yaḥyā al-Maḫramī (d. Baghdad 646 H) who stipulated that his cenotaph remain uncovered (*makšūf*), without any cover (*ġiṭāʾ*) or cloth (*ṯawb*) upon it.[531] To my knowledge, the earliest case of a tomb being covered was ᶜĀʾišah's tomb, upon which "a cloth" had been laid out (*madadnā ᶜalā qabri ᶜĀʾišata ṯawban*).[532] In an Ismailite source, the tomb of Ibn Maẓᶜūn is said to have been the first Muslim grave covered by a cloth (*wa-huwa ʾawwalu qabrin busiṭa ᶜalayhi ṯawbun*).[533]

3.4. Places of veneration and tomb-mosques[534]

3.4.1. Reports from the Prophet

The most famous among the reports handed down from the Prophet, or at least attributed to him, is undoubtedly the following Tradition: "May God fight against the Jews and the Christians, because they took the tombs of their prophets as places of prayer (*masāǧid*)".[535] As is clear, mosques in burial areas or tomb-mosques are hard to reconcile with the generally accepted Islamic notion that the ritual prayer must not be performed in cemeteries: "The building of mosques among burial sites (*maqābir*) is disapproved because he (*sc.* the Prophet) prohibited ritual prayer in cemeteries".[536]

529 The tomb of ᶜUṯmān b. ᶜAl. al-Maǧḏūb (d. Istanbul 1193 H) was covered with a drape or curtain (*kiswah*) resembling the Mawlawī cowl he had worn during his life (MuṛSilk III p. 161). A detailed description of the festive covering with silken drapes and red cloth at the (supposed) tomb of Moses provides ᶜUlaymīUns I p. 102. In a story related in SarrāǧMaṣ I p. 27, we hear of "a tomb covered by green cloth" (*qabrun ᶜalayhi ṯawbun ʾaḫḍaru*). *Cf.* also Leisten: *Architektur für Tote* p. 64.

530 IQŠuhbTārīḫ I p. 347.

531 IFuwaṭīḤaw p. 237.

532 ISaᶜdṬab VIII p. 80.

533 QNuᶜmDaᶜāʾim I p. 238.

534 The distinctive sign of a tomb-mosque, in contrast to a mausoleum, is the presence of the prayer-niche (*miḥrāb*), marking it thus as a place of prayer, see Kessler: *Funerary Architecture* p. 258 and Leisten: *Architektur für Tote* pp. 15-23.

535 ŠāfUmm I p. 465; IḤanbMusnad III p. 270; FB I p. 700 (*ṣalāh* 55); IᶜABarrDurar p. 204. *Cf.* also IAŠayMuṣ III p. 226 (*ǧanāʾiz* 146); IQudMuġnī II p. 508; MuwMuršid I p. 64; ITayMaǧm XXVII pp. 22f., 31, 62 and *passim*; IQayIġāṯah I p. 173; ŠawkDurr p. 11 and ŠawkŠṢudūr pp. 69f.; CIA Égypte II p. 66.

536 ZarkAḥkām p. 296. For the general prohibition of performing the ritual prayer in the cemetery, and the conditions under which this might be allowed, see MuwMuršid I pp. 63-5; TurkLumaᶜ

Another Tradition, on the authority of ᶜĀʾišah, conveys by and large the same message as the above-cited Tradition: some of the Prophet's wives had allegedly visited a church in Ethiopia, and when they praised its beauty and the icons found therein in the presence of the Prophet, he replied "If a righteous person from among them dies, these people will build a mosque on his tomb and apply such icons. But they are reckoned by God as wicked creatures".[537]

A third Tradition, again on the authority of ᶜĀʾišah, links the above-quoted Tradition condemning the construction of tomb-mosques to the sepulchre of the Prophet himself and is therefore worth citing here: "The Messenger of God said during the illness that led to his death, 'God curse the Jews and the Christians, because they took the tombs of their prophets as places of prayer'.[538] Had it not been for this, they would have 'shown forth' (*la-ʾabrazū*) his (*sc.* the Prophet's) tomb, but I was afraid that it could then be taken as a place of prayer (*masǧidan*)".[539]

The meaning of *brz* IV in this context is uncertain.[540] Ibn Ḥaǧar al-ᶜAsqalānī explains it as follows: "That is, the tomb of the Prophet would have been exposed, without anything hindering access to it.[541] What is meant is burial outside his house, and ᶜĀʾišah said this before the Prophet's mosque was enlarged. After it had been enlarged, her *ḥuǧrah* (i.e. her private area or apartment) was therefore shielded and divided into three parts (*or rather* constructed in the form of a triangle?), so that nobody could pray at the side of his tomb facing the *qiblah*".[542] The "exposure", which Ibn

I p. 216; MaǧlBihār C p. 128. However, there is the famous Tradition, saying "The whole earth is a place of prayer (*masǧid*), except the cemetery and the bath", cited in DaylFird I p. 76; ITayMaǧm XXVII pp. 34 and 159; IQaylġāṯah I p. 174. See also al-Albānī: *Aḥkām al-ǧanāʾiz* pp. 210-5 and below p. 245.

537 IAŠayMuṣ III p. 225 (*ǧanāʾiz* 146); ISaᶜdṬab II p. 239; FB III p. 267 (*ǧanāʾiz* 70); IQaylġāṯah I pp. 171f.; ᶜAynīᶜUmdah VII p. 65; QasṭIršād II p. 358; ŠawkDurr p. 11 and ŠawkŠṢudūr p. 69. *Cf.* also ITayMaǧm XXVII p. 155; CIA Égypte II p. 65; al-Albānī: *Aḥkām al-ǧanāʾiz* p. 218; al-Ašraf: *al-Qabr* p. 26; Leisten: *Architektur für Tote* p. 15.

538 *Cf.* also NasSunan IV p. 78; IQaylġāṯah I pp. 173f. and 178; TurkLumaᶜ I p. 216; KarKawākib p. 155; al-Albānī: *Aḥkām al-ǧanāʾiz* p. 216; Leisten: *Architektur für Tote* p. 16.

539 FB III p. 257 (*ǧanāʾiz* 61); ᶜAynīᶜUmdah VII p. 47; QasṭIršād II pp. 389f. and QasṭMaw III p. 400; IQaylġāṯah I pp. 173 and 179; KarKawākib p. 155; HarǦamᶜWas II p. 418; ŠawkŠṢudūr p. 70; al-Muᶜallimī: *ᶜImārat al-qubūr* p. 120. The same Tradition is quoted, with slight variation in wording, in FB III p. 326 (*ǧanāʾiz* 96); BayDal VII p. 264; SuyḪaṣ II p. 488. *Cf.* also IQudMuġnī II p. 508; CIA Égypte II p. 66; al-Albānī: *Aḥkām al-ǧanāʾiz* p. 216; Memon: *Ibn Taimīya's Struggle* p. 264; Leisten: *Attitudes* p. 17.

540 For the expression, *cf.* also ŠaᶜrṬab I p. 103 and Dozy: *Supplément* I p. 70 ("*rendre public, ouvrir ... au public*").

541 *Cf.* also KirmŠBuḫ VII p. 113 and ŠawkŠṢudūr pp. 69f.

542 FB III p. 258 (cited in QasṭMaw III p. 400 and HarǦamᶜWas II p. 418) and very similar ᶜAynīᶜUmdah VII p. 47; Memon: *Ibn Taimīya's Struggle* p. 292; *cf.* also Leisten: *Architektur für Tote* p. 7. This description is largely corroborated by what Ibn Ǧubayr saw at the Prophet's sepulchre, see IǦubRiḥlah (B) p. 168. In another case, the tomb of Ibn ᶜAbbās in aṭ-Ṭāʾif was shielded by wooden barriers in 1047 H, because some bedouin were seen performing the *ṭawāf* around it (ᶜUǧIhdāʾ pp. 69f.). In Cairo, people who were eager to perform the *ḥaǧǧ* to Mecca first circumambulated (*ṭwf* I) the tomb of an ascetic woman (called Fāṭimah al-Maw-

Ḥağar explains as "burial outside the house", refers quite probably to the fact that the Prophet's tomb was originally located in an area belonging to the *ḥuğrah* of ᶜĀʾišah's house[543] and was thus not open to the public. Ibn Taymīyah wrote: "They buried him (i.e. the Prophet) in the *ḥuğrah* of ᶜĀʾišah – in contrast with what they normally used to do, namely burying the dead in the open field (*fī ṣ-ṣaḥrāʾ*) – in order that the people might not pray at his tomb or take it as a place of prayer, turning his tomb into an idol".[544] His pupil Ibn al-Qayyim shared in principle the same ideas, but in another context (not with regard to the Prophet's sepulchre) he saw the "not being shown forth of a tomb" in close relation to its being "levelled", that is, its site being completely unknown and thus of no possible "seduction" (*fitnah*) to the people who might be inclined to venerate it.[545]

The severe attitude towards the construction of tomb-mosques, as it comes to the fore in these Traditions from the Prophet, was in later centuries adopted by most Sunnite scholars, though practice was often at variance from at least the seventh century H onwards. Put in the words of the Hanbalite Ibn Qayyim al-Ǧawzīyah, who himself takes to the wording of one of the Traditions quoted, this attitude might be summarised as follows: "The Messenger of God prohibited the use of tombs as places of prayer and the lighting of lamps (*suruğ*) upon them. He laid so much weight on this prohibition that he cursed everybody doing so".[546]

3.4.2. The use of candles and lamps

The eighth-century scholar Taqīy ad-Dīn as-Subkī (d. 756 H) wrote an entire treatise on this matter (as well as on a number of related subjects), entitled *Tanazzul as-sakīnah ʿalā qanādīl al-Madīnah* ("The Coming Down of the Tranquility of Mind: About the Chandeliers in Medina") and published as part of his fatwa-anthology.[547] In contrast with what the title suggests, however, the major part of the treatise deals with the use of lamps (and other things, e.g. drapings) in mosques and more especially in the Kaᶜbah-complex of Mecca. The sepulchre of the Prophet is treated only on pages 278ff.; as-Subkī clearly advocates the use of lamps and candles there (p. 278) though he is mainly preoccupied with the legal status of those

ṣilīyah) seven times and this, so they believed, would grant them the *ḥağğ* in the very same year (IZayKawākib p. 122). Carsten Niebuhr was told in Baṣrah that Ḥasan al-Baṣrī had appeared in a dream and asked that in his new mausoleum his head be buried near the wall, so that the people could not surround his tomb (Niebuhr: *Reisebeschreibung* pp. 595f.)

543 *Muwaṭṭaʾ* I p. 232 (*ğanāʾiz* 10) = SuyTanwīr p. 241; ISaᶜdṬab II p. 241; FB III pp. 326 and 329 (*ğanāʾiz* 96); SubkīFat I p. 278; HarMirqātMaf IV p. 117. For the *ḥuğrat ʿĀʾišah* and the exact location of the Prophet's tomb, see SamWafāʾ II pp. 540-50 and p. 594. *Cf.* also BayDal VII p. 262; HaytTuḥfMuḥt III p. 193; Leisten: *Architektur für Tote* p. 13 and *Attitudes* p. 17; al-ᶜAffānī: *Sakb* I pp. 126f.

544 Cited in KarKawākib p. 155.

545 IQayIġāṯah I p. 188.

546 IQayZād I p. 526 and again parallel or similar in IQayIġāṯah I pp. 175 and 182; II pp. 179 and 188. *Cf.* also IAŠayMuṣ III p. 225 (*ğanāʾiz* 146); IQudMuġnī II p. 508; TurkLumaᶜ I pp. 215 and 217; ŠawkŠŠudūr p. 70.

547 SubkīFat I pp. 264-84. The treatise is also cited by title in SamWafāʾ II p. 591.

objects insofar as they are presented as gifts or bought and sold.[548] His pupil Mağd ad-Dīn aš-Šīrāzī (al-Fīrūzābādī, d. 817 H)[549] wrote another treatise on the same topic, entitled *ar-Risālah fī ḥukm al-qanādīl an-nabawīyah fī ḏikr qanādīl al-Madīnah al-munawwarah min aḏ-ḏahab wa-l-fiḍḍah.* It stands to reason that this work (which has been preserved in manuscript)[550] is in some ways related to as-Subkī's treatise.

Notwithstanding the general prohibition reported from the Prophet, candles – and also incense (*baḫūr*) – have always been an important feature of the Islamic mortuary cult. The candles lit in the mausoleum of Abū Ayyūb al-Anṣārī could range among the earliest cases. He was buried under the walls of Byzantium and his tomb was subsequently venerated by the local Christian population.[551] One could argue that we are here still dealing with a Christian custom, even if the tomb belonged to a Muslim. However, the custom soon found widespread acceptance in the Islamic lands and some noteworthy examples of that are the following: the tomb of the Hanbalite Ibn al-Ǧawzī was lit after his burial by lustres and candles (*qanādīl wa-šumūʿ*) for the whole month of Ramaḍān,[552] and the famous poetess ʿĀʾišah al-Bāʿūnīyah (d. 922 H), known as a pious woman, sponsored the cenotaph (*tābūt*) for the tomb of a local saint in Damascus "and every Friday night lit a candle on his grave".[553]

At the Cairene tomb of Abū Zakarīyāʾ at-Taymī (Ya. b. Sallām, d. 200 H), a light (or in another version: two lustres, *qindīlān*) could be seen to light up miraculously every night;[554] in 743 H, the mother of sultan al-Malik aṣ-Ṣāliḥ Ismāʿīl (r. 743–46 H) donated a golden lustre (*qindīl ḏahab*) to the shrine of as-Sayyidah Nafīsah after her son had been cured from a chronic nosebleed.[555] In Šīrāz it happened that in the mausoleum of Rukn ad-Dīn Abū n-Naǧīb (d. 630 H) somebody was reciting

548 For the use of lamps and/or candles (*qanādīl*) at the Prophet's tomb in Medina as well as the practice as such, see also ʿIyāḍŠifāʾ (B) II p. 73 / (Š) II pp. 85f. = HarŠŠifāʾ II p. 152; IǦubRiḥlah (B) p. 172; MaqrDurar I p. 65; SamWafāʾ II pp. 576f. and 584-98; DiyTārḪamīs II p. 175; (critical:) Memon: *Ibn Taimīya's Struggle* pp. 263f. and al-Albānī: *Aḥkām al-ǧanāʾiz* pp. 232f. and 265; Kriss: *Volksglaube* I pp. 79f. (large wax candles formerly in the Cairene mausoleum of al-Malik an-Nağm Ṣāliḥ); Leisten: *Architektur für Tote* p. 64; for the Islamic West, see Dermenghem: *Culte des saints* p. 123.

549 For him see below pp. 302ff.

550 GALS II p. 235 (no. 9).

551 TMD XVI p. 62. See also above p. 196 with note 208.

552 IRağḎayl I p. 429 = al-ʿAffānī: *Sakb* I p. 587.

553 IṬūlQal II p. 531. Further examples: the use of lamps and candles at the shrine of the Shiite Imam Mūsā al-Kāẓim in Baghdad, see IḪallWaf V p. 310; the Cairene shrine of al-Ḥusayn, see IǦubRiḥlah (B) p. 19; lights (*ʾanwār*) at the Cairene shrine of the mystic Šaraf ad-Dīn al-Irbilī (d. *c.*700 H), see MunKawākib III p. 31.

554 AʿArabṬab p. 111; MālRiyāḍ I p. 191 = DabMaʿālim I p. 326. On another tomb, there was said to be seen "a kindled light, or something like it" (*miṣbāḥun ʾaw ka-l-miṣbāḥ*): MālRiyāḍ I p. 250. Ibn az-Zayyāt in his cemetery-guide mentions tombs whose occupants were unknown, but who had been given names referring to the fact that lights or candles were seen upon them at night (IZayKawākib p. 127: *qabru ṣāḥibi l-qindīl*; pp. 189 and 297: *qabru ṣāḥibi š-šamʿah*); *cf.* also Taylor: *Vicinity of the Righteous* p. 55.

the Qurʾān when he suddenly heard a crack from the lustre (*qindīl*) hanging above his head. A piece fell down, and the reciter discovered that it was a solid gold dinar.[556] In inscriptions of mausolea, *waqf* provisions for the future acquisition of lamp oil (*zayt al-qindīl*) and/or incense are often made.[557] The Fatimids donated golden and silver lamps to various Shiite shrines.[558]

Apart from all that it is interesting to see that the prohibition of lighting candles at tombs or in mausolea was connected by some scholars with the fact that fire – being primarily understood to symbolise the Fire of Hell – was seen as a bad omen (*tafāʾul radīʾ*) for the deceased.[559] This argument will return in the section dealing with the question whether a tomb might be constructed from burnt bricks (see below p. 259). On the more practical side, candles and lamps – and the presence of fire in general – often constituted a real danger to the funerary monuments. The mosque of the Prophet in Medina was more than once devastated by fire (*cf.* below p. 246), and the mausoleum of Maʿrūf al-Karḫī in Baghdad was destroyed by fire in 459 H "because the local warden prepared for himself a hot barley soup (...), then the fire (*sc.* from under the cooking pot) licked at the wood and the entire shrine went up in flames".[560] In Fatimid Egypt, a *tābūt* (coffin or cenotaph, possibly of wood) covered with drapings caught fire when candles were lighted in front of it.[561]

3.4.3. The legal debate and historical evidence

Similarly, as in the case of the outward appearance of tombs, it was the Shafiites who held the most uncompromising position among the Sunnites and who went further than the other legal traditions in condemning the practice of erecting tomb-mosques,[562] though some among them, for example al-Ġazālī, tried to defend the construction of tomb-mosques above or near the graves of saintly persons (*al-ʾawliyāʾ*).[563] The Shafiites advocating the mainstream attitude, viz. the prohibition of the erection of larger funerary structures, could point to good arguments supporting their view, because, as seen before, many widely-known Traditions from the Prophet exist, which are quite outspoken in this regard.

The main reason for condemning the construction of tomb-mosques must be seen in the initial Islamic aversion towards the mortuary cult and the Christian veneration of martyrs, as is also shown by the frequent references to Christian practice in the above-mentioned Traditions from the Prophet. Hence a similar practice

555 MaqrSulūk II p. 625.

556 ŠīrŠadd p. 89.

557 See e.g. Inschriften Syrien 210 (after 640 H, Ṣāliḥīyah) and 187 (1164 H, Damascus); *cf.* also IŠadMalẒāhir p. 227 (the provisions made for the mausoleum of sultan Baybars I).

558 IMaʾmūnAḫbār p. 40 = MaqrḪiṭaṭ I p. 408.

559 IḤāǧǧMadḫ I p. 252.

560 BN XII p. 95.

561 IMuyassarAḫbār p. 4.

562 *Cf.* INaqʿUmdah p. 241; ITayMaǧm XXVII p. 140.

563 See above p. 218 with note 355.

was, at least in theory, to be avoided by Muslims, in order to set off Islam against Christianity. Pre-Islamic pagan Arabic usages, on the contrary, are likely to have played a relatively insignificant role in shaping that attitude,[564] especially as the nascent Islamic community swiftly shifted its centre towards Christian Egypt and Syria and Jewish Iraq, increasingly leaving the Arabian heartlands in a cultural backwater and eventually rendering them marginal to the Islamic world by the later second century H. The Ḥiǧāz, with its main cities Mecca and Medina, was only to regain a truly important role from the middle of the seventh century H onwards and even more so during the Ottoman period.

But, on the other hand, scholars also argued against human *superbia* and the improper worship of human beings and their relics. This has been well expressed by aš-Šāfiᶜī who declared, "I disapprove strongly that a creature should be exalted so much that his tomb becomes a place of prayer (*ḥattā yuǧᶜala qabruhū masǧidan*), because I fear harm (*fitnah*) for him (i.e. worsening his condition in the tomb) and for the people of later generations".[565] This is an argument tied to theological considerations to a degree rarely reached by most later Muslim legal scholars. Not even the Hanbalite Ibn al-Qayyim expressed himself so explicitly when he stated that "it is contrary to the (right) guidance of the Prophet (...) to revere tombs, turning them into places of prayer, by praying near them or even being inclined towards them, or (turning them) into idols (*ʾawṯān*) and shrines with (regular) festivals (*ʾaᶜyād*)".[566]

The same applies, *a fortiori*, to the Prophet's sepulchre, which must not be worshipped, in accordance with the Prophet's sayings: "Do not turn my tomb into an idol that is worshipped" (*lā taǧᶜal qabrī waṯanan yuᶜbad*),[567] and: "Do not take my tomb as a festival (*ᶜīdan*)".[568] This attitude prompted ᶜĀʾišah to shield the Prophet's sepulchre from the visitors (see above p. 241), and the Sunnite scholars

564 Arguing to the contrary, Leisten: *Attitudes*.

565 Cited in ŠīrMuhad I p. 138; NawŠMuslim VII p. 38; MuwMuršid I p. 64; IQayIġāṯah I p. 176. *Cf.* also QasṭIršād II p. 358.

566 IQayZād I p. 526.

567 *Muwaṭṭaʾ* I p. 172 (*ṣalāt as-safar* 24) = SuyTanwīr p. 189; IAŠayMuṣ III p. 226 (*ǧanāʾiz* 146); ISaᶜdṬab II p. 242; IḤanbMusnad XIII pp. 87f.; ŠīrMuhad I p. 138; DaylFird II p. 414 (no. 7531); ᶜIyāḍŠifāʾ (B) II pp. 72 and 75 / (Š) II pp. 84 and 88 = HarŠŠifāʾ II p. 150 and 157; ITayMaǧm XXVII pp. 31, 160 and *passim*; IQayIġāṯah I p. 175 and II p. 179; TurkLumaᶜ I p. 216; ŠawkDurr p. 11; CIA Égypte II p. 66; al-Albānī: *Aḥkām al-ǧanāʾiz* p. 216. *Cf.* also IQayZād I p. 526. A parallel wording has "Do not take my tomb as a place of prayer (*masǧidan*)", cited in MuwMuršid I p. 64 and MaǧlBihār C pp. 138 and 190. This expression, rarely encountered in the sources, was certainly considered unfortunate by most scholars, especially as a mosque had actually been constructed around the Prophet's tomb.

568 IAŠayMuṣ III p. 226 (*ǧanāʾiz* 146); ISaᶜdṬab II p. 240; ᶜIyāḍŠifāʾ (B) II p. 75 / (Š) II p. 88 = HarŠŠifāʾ II p. 157; BayḤayātAnb p. 30; ITayMaǧm XXVII pp. 121 and 160; IQayIġāṯah I pp. 177f. and II p. 179; KarKawākib p. 155; ŠawkŠṢudūr p. 71; al-Albānī: *Aḥkām al-ǧanāʾiz* pp. 219f.; Memon: *Ibn Taimīya's Struggle* p. 260.

agreed that it was under no circumstances allowed to pray towards (*ᶜalā*) the tomb of the Prophet.[569]

As is known, the Prophet's sepulchre soon became part of a mosque which was continuously added to, enlarged or embellished. After the devastating fire in 654 H which destroyed much of the *ḥuǧrah aš-šarīfah* – parts of the wooden ceiling fell upon the Prophet's tomb –,[570] the Mamluk ruler Baybars I had the ceiling repaired and decorated with gold, and the walls of the edifice whitened.[571] Around the same time, Kamāl ad-Dīn ar-Rabaᶜī (A. b. ᶜAbd al-Qawīy, d. 686 H), the governor of Qūṣ (Upper Egypt), was responsible for the renovation of the Prophet's sepulchre and the cupola rising above it, and though his initiative was merely meant as a charitable deed, his activities were condemned by some pious-minded person (*baᶜḍu ʾahli ṣ-ṣalāḥ*) who complained that the *rawḍah aš-šarīfah*, the Prophet's burial place, was unnecessarily affected by the construction work and the workers' activities;[572] the role of sultan al-Manṣūr Qalāʾūn (r. 678–89 H) in that initiative is not wholly clear.[573]

Nevertheless, the opinion of Sunnite legal scholars was rather uniform on that point, viz. refusing tomb-mosques in theory, and might be said to have corresponded by and large to the explicit reports as transmitted from the Prophet. During the first centuries, some also turned that theory into practice, such as the Egyptian judge al-Ḥāriṯ b. Miskīn al-Umawī (*c.*154–250 H), said to adhere to the Malikite legal tradition, who had a mosque torn down which a person from Ḫurāsān had erected in a burial ground (*bayna l-qubūr*).[574] In view of this, the dictum by the second-century jurist Sufyān aṯ-Ṯawrī (as quoted by the traditionist ᶜAbd ar-Razzāq) is all the more remarkable: "If a tomb in Mecca is more than ten years old, do with it whatever you like, be it a house or a mosque or a field[575] or something else. However, in your towns you have to wait for twenty years".[576] This obviously takes the fact of tomb-mosques or mosques in burial areas for granted.[577]

In the course of time, the legal scholars also tried to justify or safeguard at least the existence of tomb-mosques which had become important visitation sites. The precursors of tomb-mosques in burial grounds were open places of communal prayer (sg. *muṣallā*) in or near cemeteries and congregational mosques in graveyards, e.g. the mosques built in the Cairene Qarāfah from the fourth century H onwards.[578]

569 See the discussion in ḪaydLafẓ pp. 123-5.

570 SamWafāʾ II pp. 598-601.

571 NZ VII p. 194. *Cf.* also IŠadMalẒāhir p. 300 and SamWafāʾ II pp. 604f.

572 UdfṬāliᶜ p. 89; ITaġrManh I p. 340.

573 *Cf.* Esin: *Qubbah Turkiyyah* p. 305. In any case, there is no mention of it in IᶜAẒāhirTašrīf.

574 IḤaǧRafᶜ p. 119. The expression *bayna l-qubūr* might well mean the Qarāfah cemetery, as explicitly in a passage *op. cit.* p. 174.

575 *Cf.* HaytTuḥfMuḥt III p. 198 (on the prohibition of raising crops on cemeteries).

576 ᶜARazMuṣ 6494 (III p. 506).

577 The reason for aṯ-Ṯawrī's dictum is not wholly clear. Perhaps it refers to the fact that the dead in the Meccan Maᶜlāh cemetery were said to decompose sooner than in other towns, due to the heat of the place, see IḤāǧǧMadḫ III p. 272 and Zepter: *Friedhöfe* p. 27 with note 5.

578 *Cf.* Lev: *Saladin* pp. 122-4.

After all, the construction of and the widely-felt need for tomb-mosques could hardly be avoided, because the mainstream Islamic cultural tradition was characterised by a steady intensification of the mortuary cult and of the custom of visiting tombs.[579]

The basis for such a development in legal theory, aiming at its reconciliation with common practice, might have been laid down already by Mālik, who is said to have disliked burial within a mosque[580] or the construction of mosques above or around tombs, the only exception being mosques built in graveyards no longer in use (*maqburah dāṯirah*), a view adopted also by the Hanbalites and Mālik's later followers.[581] That is, one did not rule out the construction of tomb-mosques categorically, another case in which the Malikites put forward a lenient ruling in absolute contrast with their common image as the strictest of all Sunnite legal traditions. Still more permissive seems to have been the attitude of the Shafiite al-Bayḍāwī (d. *c.*685 H):

> "After the Jews and Christians used to prostrate before the tombs of the prophets, thus exalting their rank (*taʿẓīman li-šaʾnihim*), and made them a direction of prayer (*qiblah*) towards which they turned, thus taking them as idols, the Prophet cursed them and prohibited the Muslims from doing the same. However, if a place of prayer (*masǧid*) is established in the vicinity of a righteous person (*bi-ǧiwāri ṣāliḥin*) with the aim of receiving blessing from being near to him (*bi-l-qurbi minhu*), without the intention to exalt him or to pray to him, then such practice does not fall under the afore-mentioned verdict".[582]

Later scholars of Mamluk and Ottoman times, taking practice into account, became more and more tolerant towards the fact that mosques were erected above or beside the tombs of saintly persons and arrived at the conclusion that this was not only not prohibited, but rather to be encouraged or even, in rare cases, desirable.[583]

On the basis of the literary sources at our disposal we must assume that the construction of mausolea and tomb-mosques goes right back to the formative period of Islam. We know of a passage in al-Wāqidī's (d. 207 H) *Kitāb al-Maġāzī* which explicitly says that during the lifetime of the Prophet a place of prayer was erected upon the tomb of Abū Baṣīr: *wa-banaw ʿalā qabrihī masǧidan,*[584] whatever the term *masǧid* exactly means in this context. During the first centuries of early Islam, a number of other mausolea and tomb-mosqes had already been built, e.g. in Ḥulwān (southern Iraq) upon the tomb of Mālik b. ʿAlī al-Ḫuzāʿī (d. 222 H) where "a domed

579 *Cf.* Leisten: *Architektur für Tote* p. 18.

580 *Cf.* also MF XXI p. 9.

581 ʿAynīʿUmdah VII p. 47; QasṭIršād II p. 358; MF XXI p. 9. The Hanbalites Ibn Taymīyah and Ibn al-Qayyim, however, did not adopt that view, see Memon: *Ibn Taimīya's Struggle* p. 264 and IQaylġāṭah I p. 174.

582 Cited in QasṭIršād II p. 358.

583 See the long passage in HaytFatFiqh II p. 16.

584 WāqMaġ II p. 629 = Rāġib: *Premiers monuments* pp. 22f. and Taylor: *Reevaluating the Shiʿi Role* p. 4.

mausoleum (*qubbah*) containing his grave was built at the wayside".[585] As to the preserved monuments, "the earliest surviving Islamic mausoleum", Robert Hillenbrand records, "is generally agreed to be the Qubbat al-Sulaybiya [aṣ-Ṣulaybīyah] at Samarra, datable to the mid-ninth century [CE]. In comparison with the surviving evidence as to mosques, palaces, (...) this is indeed a late beginning".[586]

Ever since, the Muslims have been erecting large funerary structures such as shrines, domed mausolea and tomb-mosques, notwithstanding the theoretical disapproval or prohibition of doing so. Some lavish examples of that sort range among the most impressive creations of Islamic architecture. At times, rather strange buildings were the outcome, such as the mausoleum of Abū l-Ḥasan ᶜAlī al-Harawī (d. 611 H, see **5**) in Aleppo, resembling the cubic form of the Meccan Kaᶜbah,[587] or the tomb of Nāẓir al-Haram (an-Nāṣir Abū l-Faḍl M. b. ᶜUmar al-Ḥanbalī, d. 711 H) in Cairo which "was covered with a mound (*musannam*), and in shape resembled a pyramid".[588] What is more, in the Cairene Qarāfah cemetery there was an assembly hall (*ǧawsaq*) – apparently not serving as a mausoleum – built in the form of the Kaᶜbah (*ʿalā hayʾati bināʾi l-kaʿbah*) where people would meet during festivals in order to listen to professional Qurʾān-reciters; on such occasions incense was burnt and amber-perfumed candles were lit.[589]

3.4.4. Mausolea and tomb-mosques in Shiite Islam

Though in Shiism the attitude towards the visitation of tombs and the mortuary cult differs greatly in many respects from the attitude prevalent in Sunnism, we also find the outspoken prohibition to construct tomb-mosques in Shiite sources pertaining to the matter.[590] However, a considerable number of Shiite scholars, who certainly

585 *Aġānī* XIX p. 114. Notices about other early Islamic funerary monuments are collected in Grabar: *Commemorative Structures* and Rāġib: *Premiers monuments*.

586 Hillenbrand: *Islamic Architecture* p. 254. *Cf.* also Rāġib: *Premiers monuments* pp. 21 and 34-6; Taylor: *Reevaluating the Shiʿi Role* p. 1; Leisten: *Attitudes* p. 12; Wirth: *Orientalische Stadt* p. 250 with the illustration on p. 251. The most detailed survey to date is Leisten: *Architektur für Tote*, esp. pp. 253-5 dealing with the Qubbat aṣ-Ṣulaybīyah.

587 See also the inscription at the site: *hāḏihī t-turbah ʿalā miṯāli l-kaʿbah* (CIA Alep 131); *cf.* also al-Ġazzī: *Nahr aḏ-ḏahab* II p. 221. It is not clear to me what the deeper significance of fashioning a burial monument in the form of the Kaᶜbah could be, though it seems that this could symbolise its being a place of veneration and visitation, or a sacred place in general, analogous to the Meccan sanctuary. In view of the fact that the Kaᶜbah is the "House of God" (*baytu llāh*) this could appear as an almost blasphemous analogy. However, the metaphorical likening of a venerated tomb to the Kaᶜbah is known from biographical dictionaries, e.g. IḌayfṬab pp. 268, 323, 329 and 374, where such tombs are, for example, described as *qabruhū ẓāhirun yuzāru bal kaʿbatun maḥǧūǧatun* ("his tomb is [still] visible and visited, nay it is a Kaᶜbah to which pilgrimage is made").

588 SaḫTuḥfAḥbāb p. 163; Taylor: *Vicinity of the Righteous* p. 41.

589 IZayKawākib p. 74.

590 KulKāfī III p. 228; ṬūsīMabsūṭ I p. 188 (who invokes a consensus in this point); Leisten: *Architektur für Tote* pp. 18f.

formed the majority, saw nothing wrong with constructing tomb-mosques and mausolea, especially if the tombs of the Imams were concerned. They transmitted various Traditions from the Prophet to that effect[591] and, consequently, considered the solid "building" (*al-binā᾿*) of the Imams' tombs as desirable.[592] The Shiite sources include a report from the Prophet according to which those building mausolea (sg. *turbah*) on tombs were among the blessed on Judgment Day, as if they were assisting Solomon in his construction of Jerusalem.[593] Until the present day, monumental funerary architecture is a widely-accepted element in Shiite Islam, and Iran, though only a stronghold of Shiism since the tenth century H, has always been a region where the veneration of burial sites and the erection of burial monuments were important elements of religion, popular belief and, not the least, statecraft.[594]

Zaydite scholars likewise seem to have been in favour of funerary constructions (and their subsequent veneration), such as al-Mu᾿ayyad bi-llāh Yaḥyā b. Ḥamzah (d. 745 H), who explicitly states that "there is nothing wrong with mausolea and shrines over the tombs of the distinguished" (*lā ba᾿sa bi-l-qibābi wa-l-mašāhidi ᶜalā qubūri l-fuḍalā᾿*). The twelfth-century Yemenite scholar aš-Šawkāni, who quotes this passage, is much at pains to belittle this opinion and to characterise it as isolated and in contrast with everything else that was ever pronounced on the matter.[595]

3.5. Concluding remarks

Looking at the course of Islamic history in the central lands, the sixth and early seventh centuries H, at the latest, seem to have been the turning point towards the general spread of funerary architecture on a grand scale and the growth in both size and splendour of what was constructed.[596] Although the Fatimids had shown a strong interest in the mortuary cult inasmuch as this concerned members of the ᶜAlīd family (see above p. 31), it was only the growth of Sunnism, brought about first by the Seljuqs and then by the Ayyubids, which contributed to the wider diffusion and acceptance of funerary architecture. Around the same time, the caliphs of Baghdad were continuously constructing or renewing burial sites and shrines, and the resurgence of Hanbalism in that period led to a strong interest in the widely

591 MağlBihār C pp. 120-2.

592 MağlBihār C pp. 136f.

593 ᶜĀmilīWas III p. 298; MağlBihār C p. 121.

594 For a more detailed discussion, see Gierlichs: *Imāmzādagan*; Hoffmann: *Das Mausoleum Khomeinis*; Jean Calmard: *Shiᶜi Rituals and Power II: The Consolidation of Safavid Shiᶜism: Folklore and Popular Religion*, in: Charles Melville (ed.): *Safavid Persia. The History and Politics of an Islamic Society*, London – New York 1996, pp. 139-90. Another article focuses on the frequent visits of Ṣafawid rulers to Shiite shrines in Persia, see Charles Melville: *Shah ᶜAbbas and the Pilgrimage to Mashhad*, in: Melville, *op. cit.* pp. 191-229.

595 ŠawkŠṢudūr pp. 66f.

596 *Cf.* Wirth: *Orientalische Stadt* p. 250.

venerated sepulchre of Ibn Ḥanbal. In 574 H, the shrine's interior was renovated and a new inscription was set up (see **25**), and in 633 H even the opening of a new receptacle for cool water (*muzammalah*) near the shrine under al-Mustanṣir was amply celebrated by the public and commemorated by the poets of the day.[597]

Once this development towards a greater significance and acceptance of monumental funerary architecture had set in, it was fostered during the seventh and eighth centuries H by the spread of Sufism on the one hand,[598] and by the increasing ideological value that funerary architecture tended to acquire under the Mamluks, for both the rulers and their entourage, on the other. One of the greatest poets of the Mamluk period, Ibn Nubātah al-Miṣrī (d. 768 H), could therefore without further ado credit the Mamluk rulers with "erecting the shapes of the tombs into lofty heights".[599] This development was paralleled in the Islamic West where the dynasties of the Marīnids in Morocco and the Naṣrids in Granada likewise encouraged the construction of large funerary monuments.[600]

It comes as no surprise, then, that the most heavy onslaught on funerary architecture and the mortuary cult connected with it was led by Ibn Taymīyah in the first quarter of the eighth century (see above p. 70), right at the moment when the practice concerning burial monuments and the mortuary cult in general was for the first time felt to have substantially changed the ways of Islamic culture. Yet, as is known, his struggle eventually proved futile during the pre-modern period and the opposite view was backed by a large number of scholars who were part of the intellectual establishment that adhered largely to the Hanafite and Shafiite legal traditions. The aftermath of that struggle largely consisted in the occasional reappearance of the question of funerary architecture and the visitation of tombs, though without the debate ever again reaching the intensity it had had before.[601]

Nevertheless, erecting cenotaphs or mausolea over graves was considered disapproved of by the large majority of Muslim scholars or, under certain conditions, even forbidden, as long as there were no practical reasons for a more solid construction of the tomb.[602] Yet "there were never any consistent blocks of supporters and opponents of funerary architecture identified with the *madhāhib*; no particular position for any of them can be definitely determined".[603] The same holds true for the combination of burial site and place of prayer, for example by building a mosque upon,

597 IFuwaṭīḤaw pp. 91f.

598 *Cf.* Blair: *Sufi Saints and Shrine Architecture*.

599 INubDīwān p. 99 (*ʿammara bi-l-ʿulyā rusūma ḍ-ḍarāʾiḥī*).

600 Undoubtedly, though, the most exquisite works of funerary architecture belong to the non-Arab Islamic East, especially India; *cf.* Schimmel: *Ausdrucksformen* pp. 276f.

601 The obvious exception, in the modern period, being the Wahhābites who, during the 19th and early 20th centuries, put Ibn Taymīyah's views into action and destroyed almost all burial sites that they could lay hands on, including many shrines in southern Iraq and, most regrettably, in Mecca and Medina.

602 *Cf.* ŠirwḤāš III pp. 196f.

603 Leisten: *Attitudes* p. 17.

around or near a tomb, which was often vehemently disapproved of. Truly exceptional in this regard seems to have been the opinion of al-Ḥasan al-Baṣrī (d. 110 H) who tolerated without further ado the construction of mausolea – as well as the use of unburnt bricks (adobe) in order to close the burial niche (*loculus*)[604] or to set up a grave recinct –, without reference to practical needs or specific circumstances making this necessary.[605] On the other hand, al-Ḥasan was not simply a liberal defender of all kinds of funerary monuments, because he disliked, for example, the marking of the grave by a slab (*lawḥ*).[606]

4. *Tomb-markers and epitaphs*

4.1. Tomb-markers and tombstones

The custom of marking graves with tombstones or other material signs constituted another problem for the Muslim scholars, especially as the various Traditions handed down from the Prophet are, once again, in conflict with each other.

4.1.1. Reports from the Prophet and historical information

The Prophet is reported to have said: "Do not put *fī qabrī* a piece of wood or a stone". The expression *fī qabrī* would mean rather "in my grave" and not necessarily "upon my grave", more regularly expressed with *ʿalā qabrī*. Thus, *fī qabrī* might refer to the subterraneous space of the grave, that is, the burial niche (*laḥd*),[607] not to the surface of the tomb. Still, in many other Traditions *fī l-qabr* clearly means "upon the tomb" and not "in the tomb".[608]

Putting palm boughs and rayḥān *upon the tomb*

From Tradition we learn that the Prophet himself took a fresh or green palm bough – *ǧarīd(ah)*, in other versions *ʿūd*, "cane, twig",[609] *ʿasīb*, "palm bough, risp"[610] or

604 *Cf.* Kervran: *Cimetières islamiques* pp. 70f.

605 IAŠayMuṣ III p. 214 (*ǧanāʾiz* 129).

606 IAŠayMuṣ III p. 216 (*ǧanāʾiz* 131).

607 FB III p. 286 (*ǧanāʾiz* 81). A wooden board was found in a tomb in al-Baḥrayn protecting the body, see Kervran: *Cimetières islamiques* p. 66 with fig. 13; wooden planks are in use among Javanese Muslims to construct the burial niche, see Woodward: *Islam in Java* p. 161.

608 In various manuscripts of one text, as noted by the Muslim scholars, *fī l-qabr* and *ʿalā l-qabr* were also used interchangeably, with the result that it was uncertain whether "in(side) the tomb" or "upon the tomb" was meant, see FB III p. 286 (*ǧanāʾiz* 81). See also above p. 13 and n. 628 below.

609 *Cf.* FB III p. 310 (*ǧanāʾiz* 88).

610 TurkLumaʿ I p. 229.

ġuṣn, "twig"[611] –, broke it in two halves and stuck these onto the graves of two persons who were thought to be suffering from the Chastisement of the Grave (*ʿaḏāb al-qabr*), in order to ease their pain. This was supposed to be effective as long as the boughs did not dry up.[612] Interestingly, an eleventh-century scholar saw the beneficial effect of the palm bough (*ğarīdah*) as parallel to the usage of lighting candles on tombs.[613]

In some versions of this report, "fresh" (*raṭb*) or "green" (*ʾaḫḍar*) is not specified, though the later scholars clearly encouraged the use of fresh palm boughs.[614] In addition, the presence of grass or plants on the grave was not considered an adequate substitute for a *ğarīdah* nor could it increase the beneficial effect for the deceased.[615] According to Shiite Traditions, two fresh palm boughs should be attached to the body of the deceased before burying him.[616] The fact that here *two* palm boughs are mentioned might be connected with another, different version of the above-cited Tradition according to which the Prophet broke a palm bough (*ğarīdah*) in two, but ordered to put them upon a single grave, one bough at the head and the other at the foot.[617] However, this use of palm fronds, as it is described in the sources cited,[618] had originally little to do with marking the tomb (but see below), nor does it seem to be meant as a remedy against the physical desiccation of the buried corpse,[619] but the prime aim was to guard the deceased from the Chastisement of the Grave.[620]

The scarce historical evidence tells us that the placing of palm boughs (or boughs from other trees) upon a tomb was practised during the formative period of Islam. Undoubtedly the most famous and widely-quoted example for this is the case

611 BayDal VI p. 9 (here not applied to a palm, but to another type of tree; see what follows above).

612 FB I p. 427 (*wuḍūʾ* 56a), III p. 285 (*ğanāʾiz* 81), III p. 310 (*ğanāʾiz* 88) and X p. 575 (*ʾadab* 46); ʿAynīʿUmdah VII p. 103; NasSunan IV pp. 86f.; TB I p. 183; IḪarrāṭʿĀqibah pp. 158f.; IḤāğğMadḫ III p. 280; SuyŠŠudūr p. 420; HaytFatḤad p. 273; KU 42950–2 (XV pp. 742f.); HarMirqātMaf I p. 350. *Cf.* also Wafā: *Aḥkām al-ğanāʾiz* p. 275; Zepter: *Friedhöfe* p. 38; Leisten: *Architektur für Tote* p. 6.

613 ŠubrḤāš III p. 35. For this practice, see above p. 242.

614 HaytTuḥfMuḥt III p. 197 and RamlīNih II p. 35.

615 ŠubrḤāš III p. 34 and ŠirwḤāš III p. 197. *Cf.* also IĞawzīTabṣ II p. 217; TurkLumaʿ I p. 229; Horten: *Gedankenwelt* p. 296; Grütter: *Bestattungsbräuche* p. 173; Ašraf: *al-Qabr* pp. 23f.

616 KulKāfī III pp. 151-4 and MağlBihār VI pp. 215f. Not all versions are identical as to the exact wording.

617 BayDal VII p. 42.

618 According to still other versions, not a palm frond but twigs from unspecified trees had been used, see BayDal II p. 9.

619 *Cf.* Leisten: *Attitudes* p. 16.

620 "As long as the palm frond is green, the deceased one will benefit from the mercy of God", as told by an Egyptian in the first half of the 20th century CE, see Winkler: *Volkskunde* p. 226. This concept is largely corroborated in HaytFatḤad p. 274. In Egypt, the practice of putting palm boughs in or upon the tomb was pre-Islamic and had been practised from pharaonic times, see Zepter: *Friedhöfe* p. 39 (with further literature) and n. 631 below.

of Buraydah b. al-Ḥuṣayb al-Aslamī, a companion of the Prophet who died in distant Marw in 62 or 63 H.[621] He stipulated that two palm boughs (*ğarīdatāni*) be put on his grave, though again not for identification of the grave but for the beneficial qualities of that tree (*barakat an-naḫlah*).[622] Similarly, two wooden sticks or twigs taken from an olive-tree were put upon the tomb of ᶜAbd al-ᶜAzīz, the son of the caliph ᶜUmar b. ᶜAbd al-ᶜAzīz,[623] though here, as we understand from the passage, the aim seems indeed to have been that of marking the grave as such. Scholars critical of that and similar practices, however, stressed that nobody from among the Prophet's companions ever had palm boughs planted or set upon his tomb, apart from Buraydah. The palm fronds employed by the Prophet (see above) had, they maintained, a beneficial effect only insofar as they had been touched by the Prophet's hand, and thus "nobody followed him in doing so, (...) because if they had understood it differently they all would have hurried to imitate this usage and burial in gardens (*fī l-basātīn*) would be desirable".[624]

Another intriguing report is known from a Shiite source. It refers to the beneficial effect of the palm-tree upon or near a burial site, but gives it another turn. More importantly, it also stresses its value of marking the tomb, because it says: "Over the tomb of Ibrāhīm, the son of the Messenger of God, there was a palm-tree (*ᶜaḏq*)[625] which shielded the sun from it and slowly turned around, following the course of the sun. When this palm-tree had dried up, the traces of the tomb were wiped out, with nobody being left who knew its exact place".[626]

Apart from palm fronds, also sprigs of the myrtle-tree or basil (*rayḥān*) were put upon tombs,[627] as we learn from a fatwa drafted by Ibn Ḥağar al-ᶜAsqalānī:

> "(*Quaeritur*:) May the *rayḥān* and the palm frond be planted on (*ġrs* I *ᶜalā*) the surface (*matn*) of the tomb or on the nape (or closure?, *qāfiyah*)[628] of the burial niche, or what else is the procedure? (...) (*Respondeo*:) The precept for doing so is provided uncon-

621 On him, see NZ I p. 157; IḤağIṣābah I p. 146; in some cases his name is given as Buraydah b. Sufyān al-Aslamī (IĞawzīṢafwah I p. 192) though this seems incorrect. *Cf.* also Lecker: *Burial of Martyrs* p. 46. He also transmitted an important Tradition from the Prophet urging the visitation of tombs, see HarMirqātMaf IV p. 111 and above p. 15.

622 ISaᶜṬab VII p. 116; TB I p. 183 (here: Abū Barīzah al-Aslamī); FB III p. 285 (*ğanāʾiz* 81); ᶜAynīᶜUmdah VII p. 100; QasṭIršād II p. 370; SuyŠṢudūr p. 420; HaytFatḤad p. 274. *Cf.* also KirmŠBuḫ VII pp. 137f. (quoting from Ibn Baṭṭāl); al-Albānī: *Aḥkām al-ğanāʾiz* pp. 202f. (note). For the beneficial qualities associated with palm-trees, see Schöller: *Palmen* pp. 334f.

623 Rāġib: *Structure de la tombe* p. 402 note 76.

624 IḤāğğMadḫ III p. 280. *Cf.* also Wafā: *Aḥkām al-ğanāʾiz* pp. 275f.

625 *ᶜaḏq*, in contrast with the more common *ᶜiḏq* ("date-bush"), means simply "palm-tree", especially in the dialect of the Ḥiğāz, see SiğNaḫlah pp. 131 and 143; Schöller: *Palmen* p. 367.

626 KulKāfī III p. 254. However, the mausoleum or shrine (*mašhad*) of Ibrāhīm was in later centuries known in the Baqīᶜ cemetery in Medina, see below p. 256.

627 See Wafā: *Aḥkām al-ğanāʾiz* p. 275 and below Chapter 5.

628 HaytFatḤad p. 274 has *mā fīhi l-laḥd*, but this does not make much sense to me either.

ditionally in correct reports, thus the intended effect will in any case be achieved, no matter at which place of the tomb they are set (*ġrs* I)".[629]

Some 200 years later, al-Qāriʾ al-Harawī cited one Ibn Ḥağar, stating that "one of the Imams of later times, from among our own, issued the legal opinion (*ʾaftā*) that the practice of putting *rayḥān* plants and palm fronds (on the tomb) has the status of a *sunnah* on the basis of that Tradition (i.e. the report from Buraydah al-Aslamī)".[630]

It remains pretty unclear which "Ibn Ḥağar" is referred to by al-Harawī, because Ibn Ḥağar *al-Haytamī* also drafted a fatwa on the practice of putting palm fronds, *rayḥān* plants and unspecified trees (*ʾašğār*) upon the tomb, and its wording is roughly parallel to what Ibn Ḥağar *al-ʿAsqalānī* had already written. In contrast with al-ᶜAsqalāni, though, al-Haytamī twice considers the widespread usage worthy of attention because he explicitly mentions "the practice of the common people (*al-ʿāmmah*) of covering the tomb with palm leaves (*ḫūṣ*)".[631] On the other hand, he does agree with al-ᶜAsqalānī that the scholars who researched the matter did not specify at which place upon (or inside) the tomb the palm fronds or plants should be put; neither does the Tradition from the Prophet render any details, so that "the desired effect will be achieved independent from the exact place upon or within the tomb (*bi-ʾayyi maḥallin minhu*)", though according to another Tradition the Prophet put a palm risp (*ğarīdah*) at the head of the grave (*ʿalā raʾsi l-qabr*).[632]

Some Malikite authors, among them the indefatigable Ibn al-Ḥāğğ, strongly disapproved of that practice altogether:

"In the same manner beware of what some people have introduced, namely the planting of a tree or an Indian fig (*ṣubbārah*, *ficus indica*) or a myrtle (*rayḥān*) or similar plants at the grave.[633] They justify this with two arguments. First, because the angels would like to stay in a green place (...), and second, because the Prophet passed by two tombs (whose inhabitants were) being chastised and took a fresh palm bough, broke it in two and put one of them on each of both tombs (...). But this report yields no argument".[634]

According to Ibn al-Ḥāğğ, as he goes on to say, the law rather prescribes that the dead must be buried in dry ground, with the earth "drinking up" whatever liquids come forth from the corpses. If, on the contrary, plants were grown upon the tomb, this would lead to the tomb being watered and the earth thoroughly moistened, thus "it cannot take up (the liquids or the moisture) any longer and the deceased 'melts

629 IḤağĞawKāfī p. 39 and 41.

630 HarMirqātMaf I p. 351.

631 See the fatwa in HaytFatḤad pp. 273f. In 20th-century Egypt, people used to put stones or palm boughs at both ends of the mound, "in order to mark the place as a tomb" (as recorded in Aswān in the 1930s by Winkler, see his *Volkskunde* p. 225); see also as-Suṭūḥī: *Maqābir al-Hū* pp. 40f.

632 For modern fatwas rejecting the use of palm fronds, see Krawietz: *Ḥurma* p. 168.

633 See also TurkLumaᶜ I p. 215 who considers among the abominable innovations "their (*sc.* of the tombs) embellishment by jasmin or *rayāḥīn* (fragrant plants)". In the Qarāfah, there was a tomb known as *qabru l-Yāsmīnī* because jasmin was often found growing upon the tomb, see IZayKawākib p. 121.

634 Arguing to the contrary, TurkLumaᶜ I p. 229.

away' in his tomb as a consequence. Then it would make no difference between burying him in the soil or carving for him a niche in solid stone".[635]

In conclusion, the modern scholar al-Albānī offers another interesting statement on the question, with quite an intriguing argument, whose logical force is undeniable, towards the end:

> "It is not lawful to plant myrtles (*ʾās*) and similar fragrant plants (*rayāḥīn*) and roses on tombs, because this was not practiced by the first-generation Muslims, and if it were beneficial, they would have done so. (...) This is not contradicted by the Tradition that the Prophet broke two palm fronds [sic] into halves, put them upon two graves and said, 'I hope this will ease their pain as long as they are not dried up' (...), because this was peculiar to the Prophet, whereas his companions did not do so. (...) However, alleviating the Chastisement was due to his intercession and invocation, not to the fronds being moist (i.e. still fresh). (...) Another reason is that the mollifying effect of moisture on the Chastisement of the Grave is neither legally nor rationally established. Nay, were this the case, then those less chastised (in their graves) would be the unbelievers, as these are buried in cemeteries which much resemble gardens for their lush vegetation of flowers and trees!"[636]

Paradoxically, the placing of palm leaves and myrtles upon tombs, something much discussed by the scholars and often rejected, has even become a distinctive mark of Islamic cemeteries in the Western perception, possibly also because this usage indeed reminds one of the Christian practice; see e.g. the following description by a nineteenth-century CE author: "In the 'Cities of Silence' of Turkey, the graves are adorned with leaves of the palm tree, and marked by boughs of myrtle and cypress".[637]

Stones as tomb-markers

We know a Tradition to the effect that the Prophet put "a rock" (*ṣaḫrah*) or stones (*ḥağar*) at the head[638] of the grave of ᶜUṯmān b. Maẓᶜūn (d. 3 H),[639] the Prophet's fosterbrother and the first of the Meccan emigrants (*al-muhāğirūn*) to have been buried in the Baqīᶜ cemetery in Medina (though the actual location of his tomb was said by some to be outside the Baqīᶜ area).[640] The wording is important here, for the

635 IḤāğğMadḫ III p. 280.

636 al-Albānī: *Aḥkām al-ğanāʾiz* pp. 200f. (with note).

637 Kippax: *Churchyard Literature* p. 22.

638 The version that he put two stones, one at the head and the other at the foot (see SamWafāʾ III p. 893), is dismissed as a transmission error in HarMirqātMaf IV p. 78, though he acknowledges that this had become a *sunnah* among the Muslims.

639 IAŠayMuṣ III p. 215 (*ğanāʾiz* 130); IMāğah I p. 498 = ŠāmīSubul VIII p. 381; QNuᶜmDaᶜāʾim I p. 238; ŠīrMuhaḏ I p. 138; IᶜABarrIst III p. 86; IMuflFurūᶜ II p. 270; SamWafāʾ III p. 893; AnṣTuḥfah p. 86; HarMirqātMaf IV p. 77. *Cf.* also QasṭIršād II p. 370; CIA Égypte II p. 64 note 2; MF XXXII p. 251; al-Albānī: *Aḥkām al-ğanāʾiz* p. 155; Grütter: *Bestattungsbräuche* pp. 171f.; Wafā: *Aḥkām al-ğanāʾiz* p. 262.

640 IᶜABarrIst III p. 86; IĞawzīṢafwah I p. 187; *Wāfī* XIX p. 511; IḤağIṣābah II p. 464; SaḫTuḥfLaṭ I p. 176; HarMirqātMaf IV p. 76. On Ibn Maẓᶜūn, see also ANuḤilyah I pp. 102-6; MunKawākib I p. 183.

term *ṣaḫrah* ("solid stone, rock") implies a stone of a certain size and massiveness (especially as marking the grave must be durable, which only a large stone will ensure), whereas *ḥağar* does not.[641] Reportedly, the Prophet justified the putting up of the stone with these words: "By this the tomb of my brother shall be made known so that the deceased of my family (*ʾahlī*) may be buried at his side".[642] What is more, the tomb of ᶜUṯmān was also said to have been "sprinkled" (see above p. 189) and raised above ground level (*murtafiᶜ*).[643] It is important to quote here the account regarding the tomb of ᶜUṯmān as told by as-Samhūdī:

> "The Prophet himself prepared the burial niche for him (*laḥada lahū*). He put aside one stone from the masonry of the burial niche (*min ḥiğārati laḥdihī*), carried it himself and set it on the foot of the tomb. Later, when Marwān b. al-Ḥakam had become governor of Medina, he came across that stone and had it removed,[644] saying 'By God, there is no need for a stone upon the tomb of ᶜUṯmān b. Maẓᶜūn so that it (i.e. the grave) might be known!' However, somebody from the Banū Umayyah objected, 'What an evil deed you committed! You misappropriated a stone which was set up by the Prophet himself and had it removed. Truly, what an evil action, so go there and have (the stone) returned (to its place)!' But Marwān answered, 'By God, I had it removed, so it will not be set up again!'"[645]

The Prophet had also the grave of his son Ibrāhīm marked with a suitable object (whose nature is left undefined in the sources) serving as a "sign" (*ᶜalāmah*),[646] i.e. tomb-marker, yet there is no mention in Sunnite sources of his putting or planting a palm-tree upon the tomb (as cited above). It is noteworthy that the tombs of Ibrāhīm and ᶜUṯmān b. Maẓᶜūn were situated very close to each other and later developed into a joint complex known as *mašhad sayyidinā ʾIbrāhīm*,[647] thus there is the possibility that the reports (or some of their elements) concerning the tombs of ᶜUṯmān and Ibrāhīm have become confused in the process of Ḥadīṯ transmission.

641 HaytTuḥfMuḥt III p. 199. Quite unusual, on the contrary, is the term used in the account of Ibn Zabālah (as quoted in SamWafāʾ III p. 914), according to which the Prophet put "the lower part of a mortar" (*ʾasfal mihras*) upon the tomb of Ibn Maẓᶜūn, as a tomb-marker (lit. "sign": *ᶜalāmah*).

642 BaySunan III p. 412; MuwMuršid I pp. 66f.; SamWafāʾ III pp. 895f.; RamlīNih II p. 35; HarMirqātMaf IV p. 78; MF XXXII pp. 251f.; Haja: *Mort et Jugement Dernier* p. 36; al-Muᶜallimī: *ᶜImārat al-qubūr* pp. 119, 158 and 193. "Of his family" (*min ʾahlihī*) instead of "of my family" (*min ʾahlī*) in the versions of IQudMuġnī II pp. 505 and 509; "my relatives" (*qarābatī*) in QNuᶜmDaᶜāʾim I p. 238; still another wording in HarMirqātMaf IV p. 77.

643 IAŠayMuṣ III p. 216 (*ğanāʾiz* 132).

644 Lit. "he ordered it to be cast away".

645 SamWafāʾ III pp. 893f. According to other versions of the story, however, Marwān gave in and had the stone put back (*op. cit.* p. 914).

646 IᶜABarrIst I p. 46; DiyTārḪamīs II p. 146. This report is contested in BaySunan III p. 411. *Cf.* also Grütter: *Bestattungsbräuche* p. 171.

647 SaḫTuḥfLaṭ I p. 42; SamWafāʾ III pp. 892f.; HarMirqātMaf IV p. 78. *Cf.* also DiyTārḪamīs II p. 176.

Historical evidence

Not much different is the situation for the historical or, in cases, pseudo-historical information stemming from the first century H. Thus we hear that Fāṭimah put "a sign" (*ʿalam*) on the tomb of Ḥamzah b. ᶜAbd al-Muṭṭalib (an uncle of the Prophet) so that it may be recognised.[648]

However, contrary to what was related from the Prophet, the majority of historical reports (or, rather, reports in historical guise) seem to suggest that marking the grave by signs or similar objects was not encouraged. For example, in a report going back to the time of the caliph ᶜUmar, we learn of the funeral of the Yemenite ascetic Uways b. ᶜĀmir al-Qaranī, who had come to settle in Kūfah and who after his death was buried by his friends in a hurry in a tomb which had been miraculously dug, but when they returned to his grave in order to put a mark on it (*ʿlm* II), they were not able to find it anymore and there was no trace of the tomb.[649] The context of the whole story – which was condemned by some later scholars[650] – shows that it was probably seen due to divine intervention that the tomb disappeared before it could be marked, thus clearly implying that leaving the grave unmarked was preferable. This also becomes clear from what happened to the tomb of ᶜAbd Allāh al-Yamanī, a pupil of Uways: "A tomb was built over the grave, but it disappeared twelve years later. After his death one of the dervishes saw him in a dream and asked what God had done with him. He replied that God had accepted all his acts, and also prophesied that his tomb would be destroyed. For the dervish should be without name or trace in this world".[651] Another telling example for that attitude would be the view of ᶜAmr b. al-ᶜĀṣ who died in Egypt and decreed by will that no tombstone be put on his grave.[652]

Finally, a more general denial of marking graves, whether by signs or in other ways, is supported by a report from Abū ᶜAbd ar-Raḥmān b. Ṭāwūs who once was asked by Ibn Abī Šaybah whether a tomb should be whitened with gypsum. He started to laugh and replied, "God beware! It would be the best for you not to know the tomb, were it not for the fact that you might visit it in order to ask for forgiveness and to pray for the deceased. It has reached me from the Prophet that he prohibited building over the graves of Muslims, whitening them with gypsum or growing plants on them, thus the most blessed of your tombs are those which are unknown".[653]

648 ᶜARazMuṣ 6717 (III p. 574); SamWafāʾ III p. 932. For the tomb *cf.* SaḫTuḥfLaṭ I p. 43 and below **168**.

649 ANuḤilyah II pp. 83f.; IĞawzīṢafwah II p. 32; YāfRawḍ p. 169; ŠaʿrṬab I p. 28. The tomb of Uways is variously shown in Damascus, ar-Raqqah, Alexandria and other places, see IŠad-Aʿlāq II (Damascus) p. 185; SaḫWağīz III p. 991 (for his mausoleum, *turbah*, in Damascus). For the legends surrounding the life of Uways, see Baldick: *Imaginary Muslims* pp. 15ff.

650 *Cf.* MunKawākib I pp. 214f.

651 Baldick: *Imaginary Muslims* p. 62.

652 Goldziher: *Culte des ancêtres* p. 181. *Cf.* also above p. 221.

653 ᶜARazMuṣ 6495 (III p. 506).

This also accords with some Traditions adduced by Ibn Abī Šaybah which say that "it was generally disapproved of that a man should have his tomb marked".[654]

4.1.2. Plastering the tomb with gypsum or clay

As seen above page 202 (in the citation from aš-Šāfiᶜī), the plastering of the tomb with gypsum or lime mortar, a technique called *taǧṣīṣ* or *taqṣīṣ*, was considered disapproved of (*makrūh*) by most later scholars,[655] with the probable exception of Abū Ḥanīfah.[656] In Tradition we even find an outspoken prohibition against it attributed to the Prophet,[657] but among the Shiites – who likewise condemned the plastering of the tomb in principle[658] – reports were current that the Imam Mūsā al-Kāẓim (d. 183 H) had ordered the tomb of one of his daughters in Medina to be whitened (or plastered) with gypsum (*ǧṣṣ* II).[659]

It remains unclear whether the term *taǧṣīṣ* meant covering the outer features of the tomb or funerary structure by gypsum or whether the sole use of gypsum as construction material (*bināʾuhā bi-l-ǧiṣṣ*) inside or outside the tomb was intended, e.g. when closing the subterranean burial niche (*laḥd*) or when fixing the upper enclosure. In some cases, the first seems more likely,[660] though, in others, the second may be referred to. Quite outstanding, and without any parallel according to my knowledge, is the passage in a verse by aṣ-Ṣāḥib Ibn ᶜAbbād (d. Rayy 385 H) commanding that something be written, or inscribed, upon a tomb using gypsum (*fa-qultu ktubū bi-l-ǧiṣṣi min fawqi qabrihī ...*).[661]

Interestingly, the application of gypsum was, it seems, not always discouraged for its embellishment (*taḥsīn*, *tazyīn*)[662] or the fact that it highlights or marks the grave, as happens in the present day in the case of many tombs or shrines which are

654 IAŠayMuṣ III p. 215 (*ǧanāʾiz* 131).

655 AYūsĀṯār 425 (p. 84); SaḥnūnMud I p. 189; SamḪizānah I p. 127; ŠīrMuhaḏ I p. 138; NawŠMuslim VII p. 37 and NawRawḍah II p. 136; MuwMuršid I p. 66; IQāsimFatḥ p. 218; QurṭTaḏk p. 86; IMuflFurūᶜ II pp. 271f.; IQayIġāṯah I p. 181; ManbTasl (C) p. 203 / (M) p. 197; ArdAnwār I p. 124; HaytTuḥfMuḥt III p. 196; al-Muᶜallimī: *ᶜImārat al-qubūr* p. 122. For the topic, see also Rāġib: *Structure de la tombe* pp. 402f.; Wafā: *Aḥkām al-ǧanāʾiz* p. 260; Zepter: *Friedhöfe* p. 29.

656 IRušdBid I p. 244; IĞuzQaw p. 113.

657 ᶜARazMuṣ 6488 (III p. 504) and 6497 (III p. 507); IAŠayMuṣ III p. 218 (*ǧanāʾiz* 137); NawŠMuslim VII p. 37 (*ǧanāʾiz* 94) and NawRiyāḍ 1767 (p. 607, *bāb* 348); ADāʾūd III p. 293 (*ǧanāʾiz* 76); TirĞāmiᶜ II p. 258 (*ǧanāʾiz* 57); NasSunan IV pp. 71f.; IMāǧah I p. 498; ḤākMust I p. 370; BaySunan III p. 410; IḤaǧAḥwāl p. 48; ŠawkŠṢudūr p. 70; al-Muᶜallimī: *ᶜImārat al-qubūr* pp. 201-3.

658 ṬūsīMiṣbāḥ p. 35.

659 KulKāfī III p. 202.

660 *Cf.* SuyZahr IV p. 72; ŠirwḤāš III p. 196; Leisten: *Attitudes* p. 15.

661 Cited in AnbNuzhah p. 326; YāqIršād II p. 314; ZawzḤam I p. 249; WaṭwāṭĠurar p. 59; ṢafĠayṯ II p. 294.

662 *Cf.* IQāsimFatḥ p. 218; QurṭTaḏk p. 86; IMuflĀdāb III p. 306 and IMuflFurūᶜ II p. 270; ŠirwḤāš III p. 196; HarMirqātMaf IV p. 76; ŠawkŠṢudūr p. 72; MF XXXII p. 250; Wafā: *Aḥkām al-ǧanāʾiz* p. 260; al-Muᶜallimī: *ᶜImārat al-qubūr* p. 148.

widely visible for their white colouring. Thus aš-Šāfiʿī is cited with the statement that plastering the grave with clay (*taṭyīn al-qubūr*), which does not highlight the tomb as gypsum does, is unobjectionable (*lā ba's bihī*),[663] an opinion which, according to an-Nawawī, was shared by the vast majority of scholars except al-Ǧuwaynī and al-Ġazālī.[664] It was also adopted by Ibn Ḥanbal and the Hanafites[665] as well as, under certain conditions, by the Shiites.[666] The seeming inconsistency – plastering the grave with clay (*taṭyīn*) was considered acceptable but not with gypsum (*taǧṣīṣ*) – is explained by the tradionist Zayn ad-Dīn al-ʿIrāqī (d. 806 H) as follows: "Someone from among the learned mentioned that the rational principle (*ḥikmah*) behind the prohibition of whitening the tombs was the fact that gypsum (*ǧiṣṣ*) is very inflammable. Therefore, there is no harm in using clay instead, as set down by aš-Šāfiʿī".[667] Similarly, Zayd b. Arqam rejected the use of burnt bricks (*'āǧurr*) or gypsum when his son was being buried, saying "Nothing must be in his neighbourhood that has been touched by fire".[668]

This dictum shows that the use of inflammable materials or substances that have been in contact with fire were not regarded as suitable for use either for the outer tomb constructions or for the closure of the burial niche.[669] Most plausibly, this was a consequence of the widespread belief in the Chastisement of the Grave (*ʿaḏāb al-qabr*) and the existence of Hell, which are both basically related to the idea of a burning fire; at least this is insinuated by al-Bahā' al-Maqdisī: "Everything which has been touched by fire is disliked because it is a bad omen with regard to (Hell-) Fire (*li-t-tafā'uli bi-n-nār*)".[670] Less plausible seems the physical explanation put forward by modern scholars, namely that materials that had been in contact with fire could dry out the grave or "would accelerate the desiccation by sun and air".[671] The eschatological background not only explains why burnt or baked bricks (*'āǧurr*)

663 TirmǦāmiʿ II p. 258 (*ǧanā'iz* 57); MuwMuršid I p. 66; HarMirqātMaf IV p. 76.

664 NawRawḍah II p. 136; MF XXXII p. 250. In some Shafiite law manuals, the practice of *taṭyīn* is therefore judged disapproved of, see ArdAnwār I p. 124.

665 IQudMuġnī II p. 507; IMuflFurūʿ II p. 271; HarMirqātMaf IV p. 68; MF XXXII p. 250; Leisten: *Attitudes* p. 16; Wafā: *Aḥkām al-ǧanā'iz* p. 266. For plastering the (brick) walls of tombs with clay as it is practised in Egypt, see Winkler: *Volkskunde* pp. 222f.

666 KulKāfī III p. 201. Here we read: "Do not plaster the tomb with clay other than that taken from it (when digging it)". *Cf.* also ṬūsīMiṣbāḥ p. 35 and ṬūsīMabsūṭ I p. 187.

667 Cited in SuyZahr IV p. 71. *Cf.* also Wafā: *Aḥkām al-ǧanā'iz* p. 266.

668 IAŠayMuṣ III p. 218 (*ǧanā'iz* 137). *Cf.* also ZamRabīʿ IV p. 210; IQudMuġnī II p. 503 and IQudʿUmdah p. 121; IMuflFurūʿ II p. 270; IQaylġāṯah I p. 182; Rāġib: *Structure de la tombe* pp. 399f.; Leisten: *Architektur für Tote* p. 9. An exception was made for regions where "the soil is weak", i.e. where little else could be used except burnt bricks, see MF XXI p. 14.

669 *Cf.* Grütter: *Bestattungsbräuche* pp. 172f.

670 MaqdʿUddah p. 121. As is known, for the same reason it was considered forbidden in Islam to cremate the dead (*cf.* Krawietz: *Ḥurma* pp. 121-3). This argument was also adduced against the placing of candles upon tombs (see above p. 244) and the carrying of torches at funeral processions (IḤāǧǧMadḫ I p. 252; KU 42339 = XV p. 593).

671 Leisten: *Attitudes* pp. 15f.

were not considered suitable, but also why cane or reed (*qaṣab*) was preferred to wood, the first being less flammable than the second.[672] Others insisted that wood and burnt bricks, the most common construction materials, would fall under the verdict of "not to build upon the grave", thus diverting the debate from eschatological matters.[673] In line with this, the Andalusian poet Abū ᶜĀmir Ibn Šuhayd (d. 428 H, see **73**) stipulated that after his death "the earth shall be poured upon him, without (putting in his tomb) burnt bricks or wood, but this was ignored".[674] In any case, it was usual for tombs to be constructed with baked bricks (*ʾāğurr*, also *ṭūb ʾaḥmar* and *ṭūb ʾāğurr*) as becomes clear from the frequent mention of this material in Cairene cemetery guides.[675]

Those advocating the use of clay could point to a Tradition from the Prophet that he used a clod of earth or clay (*madarah*) to embellish the tomb of his son Ibrāhīm, saying "In itself, it is neither harmful nor useful, but it delights the eye of the living",[676] and a similar report is told about the burial of Muḥammad's daughter Umm Kulṯūm.[677] But in overt contrast to this report, the scholars stressed that even clay should not be used if it was mainly meant as an embellishment.[678] Moreover, the dead were barred from hearing the call to prayer (*ʾaḏān*) if their tombs were plastered.[679] (The same argument was also adduced when jurists condemned the practice of heaping earth upon the tomb, for this would lead to the dead not being able to hear the call to prayer and to see who was coming to visit them).[680]

In any case, the custom of whitening and/or plastering the tombs is certainly old and reaches back to the formative period of Islam, as is shown by the lively interest the jurists and traditionists took in it from the very beginning. We are told that the first grave in Egypt to be whitened (*byḍ* II) with gypsum was the tomb of Ibrāhīm b. Ṣāliḥ al-ᶜAbbāsī (d. 176 H), governor of Egypt under al-Mahdī.[681] Nor is the

672 *Cf.* AYūsĀṯār 398 (p. 80) and 425 (p. 84); IAŠayMuṣ III p. 219 (*ğanāʾiz* 137); SamḪizānah I p. 127; IQudMuġnī II pp. 503, 507 and IQudᶜUmdah p. 121; IMuflFurūᶜ II pp. 270f. Strangely enough, an-Nawawī did not condemn the use of burnt bricks, see NawRawḍah II p. 136. For the argument, *cf.* also Rāġib: *Structure de la tombe* pp. 398-400.

673 INuğBaḥr II p. 209.

674 ḤumĞuḏwah p. 136.

675 E.g. IZayKawākib pp. 67, 69, 71, 98 and 311. *Cf.* also Diem: *Amtliche Briefe* pp. 16f. (baked bricks for the restoration of a *turbah*).

676 ᶜARazMuṣ 6499 (III p. 508); KU 42401–3 (XV pp. 603f.); Rāġib: *Structure de la tombe* p. 398. *Cf.* also KulKāfī III p. 199.

677 BaySunan III p. 409. According to ŠāmīSubul VIII p. 379 the Prophet said, "It is of no use whatsoever but it does gladden the soul of the living". *Cf.* also IMuflFurūᶜ II p. 269.

678 IMuflFurūᶜ II p. 271; RamlīNih III p. 33. *Cf.* also INuğBaḥr II p. 209.

679 DaylFird II p. 429; IQudMuġnī II p. 507; Leisten: *Architektur für Tote* p. 9 and *Attitudes* p. 16; Wafā: *Aḥkām al-ğanāʾiz* p. 266.

680 DabMaᶜālim III p. 16 (as quoted from Abū l-Faḍl Yūsuf b. Naṣr, d. 325 or 326 H).

681 MaqrMuq I p. 180; CIA Égypte II p. 64 note 4. *Cf.* also IZayKawākib p. 56 and Lane: *Manners and Customs* pp. 514f.

information about the tomb of the famous man of letters aṣ-Ṣāḥib Ibn ʿAbbād in Iṣfahān without relevance in that context; al-Qifṭī writes that "his mausoleum is still there and in good shape. The descendants from his daughter's side purchase some lime (*kils*) from Iṣfahān from time to time and whiten the building with it".[682] Similarly, Carsten Niebuhr witnessed the whitening of local mausolea in Zabīd which were freshly painted before the beginning of Ramaḍān.[683]

4.1.3. The later legal debate

Notwithstanding the reports pointing to the contrary, the marking of the grave by objects (stones, wooden planks, panels, sticks, slabs and columns) is quite often seen positively in legal literature, in accordance with the Traditions about the Prophet's actions which more often than not seem to encourage such a practice.[684]

Thus the tenth-century Shafiite scholar Zakarīyāʾ al-Anṣārī wrote in the commentary on his own legal manual, expressing the mainstream opinion of his legal tradition:[685] "It is a *sunnah* to display a sign marking the tomb (*ʾiẓhāru ʿalāmati l-qabr*) which is made of bricks – that is, unfired bricks (adobe) – or other material – for example fired bricks, reed sticks and dry plants (*ḥašīš*) –, so that something of that material may be put at the head of the grave".[686] The Hanbalite Ibn Qayyim al-Ǧawzīyah put it thus, implying the permission to do so: "The Prophet used to mark the grave by a solid stone (*bi-ṣaḫratin*) when he considered its identification (*taʿarruf*) desirable";[687] other Hanbalites even declared it desirable to mark the tomb (*taʿlīm*) by stones, wood or other materials.[688]

Many Malikites likewise considered the use of stelae (sg. *ʿamūd*), cut or uncut stones and wooden objects as indifferent (and thus allowed without restrictions), as long as they served to mark the graves and as long as there was no inscription.[689] Muḥammad, the son of al-Qāḍī ʿIyāḍ, quotes a legal *responsio* issued by Abū l-Ḥasan Ibn al-Qābisī (d. 403 H):

> "When he was asked about someone who had stipulated in his last will that 100 dinars should be taken and kept back from his heritage in order to pay for the construction of

682 QifṭīInbāh I p. 202. For the whitening of tombs, *cf.* also Kriss: *Volksglaube* I p. 17.

683 Niebuhr: *Reisebeschreibung* p. 324.

684 *Cf.* MuwMuršid I p. 65; IMuflFurūʿ II p. 270; HaytTuḥfMuḥt III p. 199; HarMirqātMaf IV p. 78.

685 *Cf.* also ŠīrMuhaḏ I p. 138; NawRawḍah II p. 136; ArdAnwār I p. 124; RamlīNih II p. 35; MF XXXII p. 251.

686 AnṣTuḥfah p. 86. Putting another stone at the foot – a practice known from at least the fifth century H onwards and very popular in the later Ottoman period – was disputed among scholars (see HaytTuḥfMuḥt III p. 199), but reportedly encouraged by al-Māwardī (RamlīNih II p. 35 and MF XXXII p. 251).

687 IQayZād I p. 525.

688 IQudMuġnī II p. 504; IMuflFurūʿ II p. 270; MF XXXII p. 251.

689 BāǧīMunt II pp. 22f.; MF XXXII p. 251.

a small mausoleum (?, *ḥuğrah*) of stone, the application of lime upon his tomb and the tomb of his father and for the setting up of an engraved tombstone (*ḥağar manqūš*) at the head of both (their graves), he ruled: 'Carrying out this will is not considered acceptable because neither the present world nor the hereafter will derive benefit from it. However, the tombstone, which he stipulated to be set up at their heads, is less reproachable because it serves as a sign (*ʿalam*) which leads (the visitor) towards the tomb he looks for, and thus some scholars did tolerate this usage, having also a report (*ʾaṯar*) upon which they base their opinion".[690]

Some Malikites were less lenient, however, and the severe Ibn al-Ḥāğğ had the following to say on tombstones and objects serving as tomb-markers: "Beware of that (abominable) innovation which some people have established as a custom, namely putting marble on the tombs. This is a (detestable) innovation, a waste of money and a display of pride and haughtiness", and some lines further: "In the same manner it is forbidden to erect a column at the head of the deceased, even if there is no inscription upon it and no matter whether it is made of marble, stone, wood or other material, because that means nothing but a display of haughtiness and a waste of money".[691] Finally, and in contrast with other legal traditions, we hear from Abū Ḥanīfah that he and his teachers disliked the practice of setting up tomb-markers or objects serving as such (*ʿalāmah*).[692]

4.1.4. Pictorial representations and images

As to the use of images (*ṣuwar*), reliefs depicting persons and statues (*tamāṯīl*), we find in Tradition the harsh verdict transmitted by ʿAlī from the Prophet that there shall be no such things on tombs; any that are found should be effaced or taken away.[693] This verdict, wholly embraced by the later legal scholars, is one of the few cases in which theory was more or less in conformity with practice, because pictorial representations have indeed not become part of Arabo-Islamic funerary structures at any time. Rather, their application was confined to areas under Turkish influence,[694]

690 ʿIyāḍMaḏ p. 302.

691 IḤāğğMadḫ III pp. 272f.; *cf.* also Haja: *Mort et Jugement Dernier* p. 36.

692 AYūsĀṯār 425 (p. 84).

693 NawŠMuslim VII pp. 36f. (*ğanāʾiz* 93); TirĞāmiʿ II p. 256 (*ğanāʾiz* 55); IQudMuġnī II p. 504; IQaylġāṯah I pp. 171 and 181; II p. 179 and IQayZād I p. 524; IMuflFurūʿ II p. 271; ManbTasl (C) p. 203 / (M) p. 197; ŠāmīSubul VIII p. 381; HarMirqātMaf IV p. 68; ŠawkŠṢudūr p. 70; al-Muʿallimī: *ʿImārat al-qubūr* pp. 162-81. With a slightly different wording, regarding images in houses: ʿARazMuṣ 6487 (III p. 504) and NasSunan IV p. 73. *Cf.* also al-Ašraf: *al-Qabr* p. 25 and Zepter: *Friedhöfe* p. 31.

694 Symbolic and pictorial representations are known from Islamic gravestones and cenotaphs in western Iran, dating from the 13th century H (Mortensen: *Nomadic Cemeteries and Tombstones*) as well as from Pakistan (Zajadacz-Hastenrath: *Chaukhandigräber*; Schimmel: *Ausdrucksformen* p. 275; Rosiny: *Pakistan* pp. 271 with plates 8 and 60f.) and central Anatolia (Güngör: *Stèles figurées*; *cf.* also Laqueur: *Friedhöfe Istanbul* pp. 2-5); for the tombs of Ahlat, see Vol. I p. 344. In the later Ottoman period, tomb-stelae in Anatolia and other areas dominated by

clearly regions where pre-Islamic and later non-Islamic customs had been preserved more fully than in the central Islamic lands.

Quite exceptional is the case of the Upper Egyptian town al-Hū (or al-Hiw, near Nag Hammadi),[695] where we find painted cenotaph-like structures upon the graves. These constructions, which M. as-Suṭūḥī describes as "in the shape of camels", are made of mud bricks and show a large rectangular cenotaph often mounted by two stelae (sg. *šāhid*) which are rounded at the top: the stele at the head (often more than two metres high) rises to a height more than double that of the rear stele, thus the whole conveys the impression of a bulky camel whose neck and head are formed by the front stele and whose hump is marked by the rear stele. This scheme is reminiscent of the common practice of putting up two stelae (or columns) upon a tomb (see below), yet in al-Hū none of this stelae bears any inscription. Instead, the constructions are first completely whitened with lime and then covered with colourful paintings, mainly in brown, red and yellowish (earth) colours.[696] Most of the ornaments are geometrical, but there are also stylised depictions of plants and objects of daily use (walking-sticks, parasols, mirrors, clothes, pots, etc.); on the tomb of a young man, the camel-like shape of the tomb structure is evidenced by the fact that a draping with cords is depicted on the cenotaph and a saddle between the front and the rear stele. Interestingly, there are marked differences in ornament and depicted objects between the graves of adult men, women and young people.

A similarly intriguing case is reported from the Cairene Qarāfah cemetery. As the relevant cemetery guides tell us, one could see there the tomb of a certain *Ṣāḥib al-Ḥilyah* ("The Possessor of Pleasing Appearance, *or* Traits"), and "at the head (of his tomb) there was a column with a white face at the top (*wa-ʿinda raʾsihī ʿamūdun fawqa raʾsihī waǧhun ʾabyaḍ*)". According to al-Muwaffaq Ibn ʿUṯmān, the white face appeared when a friend of the deceased had said after the latter's death: "If only I knew what my friend's face looked like in his tomb!" So when the friend approached the tomb the next day, "he found upon the column a white face".[697] Though we are not told the details, we must presume either that a white face was somehow painted on top of the column, or that a white head, i.e. of marble and possibly dating from ancient times, was put on top of the column.

Of equal importance for funerary structures throughout the Islamic world is the general absence of sculptures, though the "pervasive Islamic distaste for figural sculpture" is not so much the outcome of religious observance based on Tradition. It rather reflects, as Robert Hillenbrand observed, the specific role of burial sites in Islamic culture, because "to argue that Muslims raised tombs because they would not raise statues is to miss the point. The typical Islamic mausoleum has a social and religious dimension perforce denied to a statue".[698] The only noteworthy example of a funerary sculpture I have come across, and a very peculiar one at that, stems

Turkish influence were commonly adorned with floral motifs, see e.g. Bacqué-Grammont: *Stelae Turcicae* II pp. 57-89 (with plates 1-48) and Laqueur: *Friedhöfe Istanbul* pp. 110-14 (with plates 14-6).

695 For the following, see the detailed study as-Suṭūḥī: *Maqābir al-Hū* (with many illustrations).

696 To judge by the description; the accompanying plates are all black-and-white.

697 MuwMuršid I pp. 358f. = IZayKawākib p. 243. Of course, the white face should indicate, on the basis of a known Qurʾānic verse (Q 3:106), that the deceased had been accepted by God and was to be among the inhabitants of Paradise.

698 Hillenbrand: *Islamic Architecture* p. 253.

from the fringes of the eastern Islamic world. It is related in the memoirs of Ǧahāngīr (r. 1014–37 H):

> "On Tuesday [in D̲ū l-Ḥiǧǧah 1015 H] camp was made at Jahangirpur. This spot is one of my favourite hunting grounds. In the vicinity is a tower erected at my order over the grave of an antelope named Hansraj, which was without equal in tame antelope fights and in trapping wild antelopes. On the tower Mulla Muhammad Husayn Kashmiri, the chief calligrapher of the age, had inscribed the following prose composition in stone: 'In this delightful open space came an antelope into the trap of the ruler of the world, the God-fearing Nuruddin Muhammad Jahangir. Within a month it had lost its wildness and become the chief of the royal antelopes.' On account of the rarity of the above-mentioned antelope, (...) I also commanded a gravestone made in the shape of an antelope and erected".[699]

4.1.5. Practice and terminology

Archaeological evidence shows that cut stones and stelae, either inscribed or not, had been in use as tomb-markers since the first century H and thus from the very beginning of Islamic culture.[700] In later times, tombstones, markers made of brick and columns became increasingly popular.

In general, the pre-modern Arabic sources up to the Ottoman period refer to the tombstone, whatever its shape, mainly as "(tomb)stone" (*ḥaǧar*)[701] and occasionally as "sign, *or* (tomb-)marker" (*ʿalāmah*, rarely *ʾišārah*).[702] Yet not every mention of a *ḥaǧar* indicates a tombstone, and any block of stone, especially if inscribed, could be termed *ḥaǧar*. An example of this generic use is the report of a stone (*ḥaǧarun ʿalayhi manqūš*) inscribed with three verses found in a pit in Mecca, though it was, as far as we know, not a tombstone.[703]

The term šāhid

In modern Arabic, stelae, slabstones and, especially since the Ottoman period, columns (which may also appear in semi-rounded or rectangular form)[704] are known as *šāhid* (pl. *šawāhid*), "witness".[705] As far as I can see, this term is not attested in this sense in literary sources until the ninth century H. If the related term *mašhad*, which in some cases signifies not, as it normally does, "mausoleum" or "shrine" but

699 *Jahangirnama* p. 69.

700 About the use of stelae in pre-Islamic times, see Leisten: *Attitudes* pp. 19f. note 24.

701 *Cf.* Grütter: *Bestattungsbräuche* p. 171. For the pl. we find the term *ḥiǧārat al-qubūr*, see HarǦamʿWas I p. 142.

702 E.g. IǦubRiḥlah (B) p. 65; ʿUlaymīUns I pp. 43 (*ʿalāmāt al-qubūr*) and 70 (*ʾišārah*); for the term *ʿalāmah*, see already above p. 261.

703 *Aġānī* XX p. 92.

704 Winkler: *Volkskunde* p. 223; Kriss: *Volksglaube* I p. 17.

705 *Cf.* Lane: *Manners and Customs* p. 515; Winkler: *Volkskunde* p. 224; Dermenghem: *Culte des saints* p. 121; Behrens-Abouseif: *Ottoman Rule* p. 243 (mausoleum of ʿUqbah b. ʿĀmir).

rather "tombstone" or "cenotaph" is not taken account of,[706] the first usage of *šāhid*, "tombstone", is in passages from Ibn az-Zayyāt's cemetery guide. There we read of a mausoleum (*turbah*) "most tombs of which have disappeared, there being no tombstones (*šawāhid*) left".[707] In another passage, concerning the tomb of Ḏū n-Nūn al-Miṣrī, we hear that "at the head (of his tomb) there was a tombstone (*šāhid*) bearing his name and the date of his death".[708] Since it is not clear whether these notices were taken by Ibn az-Zayyāt from an earlier source or not, the use of the term *šāhid* might well predate the ninth century H. Arabic dictionaries up to the 13th century H contain no material for the term *šāhid* in the sense of "tombstone" or "column erected, *or* standing, upon a tomb".[709]

Outside the literary genre of cemetery guides, the term appears for the first time – to my knowledge – in aš-Šaʿrānī's biographical dictionary of mystics. Here we are told that the last wish of the mystic Aḥmad al-Buhlūl (d. 928 H) was: "Do not put a tombstone on my grave (*lā tağʿalū li-qabrī šāhidan*)!"[710] In an anecdote attributed to Abū l-Farağ al-Iṣfahānī, *šāhid* signifies a certain room, or building, in a Christian monastery, certainly not a stele or a column (for it is said to have had a wall, *ḥāʾiṭ*); accordingly it has been translated as "martyrion".[711]

It remains a matter for speculation whether the term *šāhid*, which literally means "witness", was derived from *šahādah*, "profession of the creed" because the wording of the *šahādah* was often inscribed upon the tombstone.[712] However, the late occurence of the term *šāhid* and the general disappearance of credal statements inscribed upon tombstones after the fourth century H do not support the link between *šāhid* and *šahādah*. More likely, the literal meaning of the term, viz. "witness", may indicate the inscribed tombstone, as it does "bear witness" to who is buried in a certain place. The term *šāhid* could have had its origin in the language of administrative and notarial documents where legally binding or otherwise important texts are commonly attested or "witnessed to".

706 Tombstones or inscribed cenotaphs are frequently indicated by the term *mašhad* (pl. *mašāhid*) in DabMaʿālim, e.g. III pp. 164f. (*cf.* **104**). For other types of funeral stelae, chiefly in Southern Syria, the term *mašhad* is used, see Kriss: *Volksglaube* I p. 18; in the Syrian town Ḥiṣn al-Akrād, there was a cemetery known as "*al-Mašhad*" (ITağrManh VI p. 71). Dozy: *Supplément* I p. 794 (*s.r.*) lists *mašhad* as "piedra para sepoltura", similar to the term *šāhid.*

707 IZayKawākib p. 108.

708 IZayKawākib p. 233.

709 *Cf.* Dozy: *Supplément* I p. 794 (*s.r.*) who lists *šāhid* (as well as *šāhidah*) either as "indice, signe", or more specifically as "stèle ou pierre qu'on place perpendiculairement sur le tombeau", based on the information in Lane: *Manners and Customs* (see above n. 705).

710 ŠaʿrṬab II p. 145.

711 YāqIršād V p. 158 = IṣfStrangers p. 33.

712 *Cf.* Dozy: *Supplément* I p. 794 (s.r. *šhd* – *mašhad*). The use and function of the *šahādah* in Arabic epitaphs is amply dealt with in Vol. I pp. 115ff.

Other terms indicating material and shape

Somewhat more rarely, the shape or the material of tombstones (and other objects serving as such or bearing the epitaph) are indicated in literary sources, viz. its being a slab or a panel (*lawḥ* or *lawḥah*, pl. *ʾalwāḥ*, *lawḥāt*; also *balāṭah*), a slab of marble (*ruḫāmah*), a brick-marker (*labinah* or *libnah*) or a rounded column (*ʿamūd*, more rarely *sāriyah*); for the Qurʾānic term *ar-raqīm*, in general understood as an inscribed plaque made of lead, see below page 317. However, none of these terms was used exclusively in the context of burial sites or in order to indicate tombstones, since they could be applied to other objects as well of the appropriate size, shape or material.

lawḥ. The term *lawḥ*, "slab" (lit. "tablet") or simply "tombstone" in a wider sense, is the word commonly used in literary sources where the stones bearing the epitaphs are referred to; it is frequently attested in a wide range of texts and thus no further examples need be adduced here.[713] Such a *lawḥ* could also be affixed to the cenotaph, standing at its head, or at some point near the actual tomb, e.g. at the wall of a mausoleum.

ruḫāmah. For the term "marble (slab)" (*ruḫāmah*), see the following passages: "[...] is engraved on a marble slab on his tomb" ([...] *qad nuqiša fī ruḫāmatin ʿalā qabrihī*),[714] or also "What he wrote on a marble slab upon his tomb, under his head" (*mā katabahū fī ruḫāmatin taḥta raʾsihī fī qabrihī*).[715] Ibn Ǧubayr describes the tombstone on the grave of Hagar in Mecca and remarks that "its tomb-marker is a green marble slab" (*ʿalāmatuhū ruḫāmatun ḫaḍrāʾ*);[716] Ibn Baṭṭūṭah mentions "two marble slabs *or* tablets" (*lawḥāni mina r-ruḫām*) on a tomb in al-Ḫalīl (Hebron).[717] These examples stem from western sources, and most other occurrences of the term belong likewise to the Islamic West (Kairouan; Morocco)[718] as well as Egypt; the corpus of epitaphs in Chapter 4 contains some more occurrences of the term *ruḫāmah*. The term *ruḫāmah*, indicating a marble slab bearing the epitaph, is commonly used in the literary sources, especially in texts pertaining to burial monuments (see Chapter 3).

ʿamūd and *sāriyah*. Rounded columns on tombs are frequently mentioned as *ʿamūd* in the surviving ninth-century cemetery guides.[719] The description of the grave of ᶜAlī as-Saddār (d. 778 H), likewise in Cairo, contains the following passage:

713 One of the earliest attestations of the term *lawḥ* in a surviving epitaph may well be RCEA 77 (dated 190 H, al-Fusṭāṭ?).

714 IᶜIḏBayān II p. 301 (see also **170**).

715 IRašUnmūḏaǧ p. 197.

716 IǦubRiḥlah (B) p. 65.

717 IǦubRiḥlah (B) p. 77 and **97**.

718 WanšMiᶜyār I p. 319 mentions epitaphs on marble slabs; an epitaph on a *lawḥ min ar-ruḫām* in Kairouan: DabMaᶜālim I p. 99 (see also below p. 284).

719 E.g. SaḫTuḥfAḥbāb p. 194; IZayKawākib p. 87 = SaḫTuḥfAḥbāb p. 198. *Cf.* also IṬūlQal II p. 560.

"At the head of his tomb there is an upright column of marble (*ʿamūdun min ruḫāmin qāʾimun*)".[720] Various columns from second-century tombs in Kairouan have been specified by ad-Dabbāġ according to their colour; thus we hear of a blue column, various white columns and a red column.[721] It remains unclear, at least to me, whether this refers to the natural colour (or shading) of the material used or to its being painted. The funerary inscription on a marble column from al-Minyah refers to the column as *ʿamūd* (RCEA 4785, 679 H). Concerning the tomb of Ibn ᶜAbbās in aṭ-Ṭāʾif, we hear of a column (*sāriyah*) at the head of the grave (*ʿinda raʾsi ḍ-ḍarīḥ*) where prayers are answered;[722] a *sāriyah* served as tomb-marker upon the grave of Abū Zamᶜah (*ʿalamun ʿalā qabrihī*) in Kairouan, together with a column at the head of his tomb (*al-ʿamūdu ʿinda raʾsihī*);[723] finally, at the head of the tomb of the famous scholar Ibn Saḥnūn (d. 256 H) stood "a tall column" (*sāriyah ṭawīlah*).[724]

balāṭah. Less common is the word *balāṭah*, "flagstone" or "paving (of stone, especially marble)", also used in a general sense for any flat piece of stone or marble.[725] I have come across the following passages where that term is used for stones bearing epitaphs: Ibn ᶜAsākir writes that at the head of the tomb of Ibn al-Muᶜallim (M. b. ᶜAl., d. Damascus 412 H and buried on Mt. Qāsiyūn) "there is a *balāṭah* on which his name is made known";[726] Ibn Ḫallikān mentions "a marble flagstone" (*balāṭat ruḫām*) bearing an epitaph at the tomb of al-Murādī (d. Cairo 270 H, buried in the Lesser Qarāfah);[727] ad-Dabbāġ quotes from an inscribed *balāṭah* in al-Barqah;[728] the Malikite scholar Ibn al-Ḥāǧǧ uses the term *balāṭah* for a "flagstone" – in contrast with a wooden tablet – which bears a funerary inscription;[729] al-ᶜUlaymī mentions an epitaph from Jerusalem which was inscribed upon a *balāṭah* (see **32**); Ibn Ṭūlūn read the date of someone's death on a *balāṭah*;[730] finally, Ibn an-Nābulusī

720 MunKawākib III p. 61.

721 DabMaᶜālim I p. 263 (blue), I p. 287 and II p. 120 (white), and I p. 313 (red).

722 ᶜUǧIhdāʾ pp. 66 and 70.

723 DabMaᶜālim I p. 99. For similar, inscribed columns (also called *sāriyah*) on other tombs in Kairouan, see *op. cit.* III pp. 169 and 180.

724 DabMaᶜālim II p. 135.

725 A passage in BN XIII p. 75 describes the new "panelling" (*tablīṭ*), probably using marble, at the Umayyad mosque in Damascus which was finished in 614 H; the local governor came and fixed "the last panel with his own hand" (*waḍaʿa ʾāḫira balāṭatin minhu bi-yadihī*). In the dialects of Sicily, the word *balata* signifies a flagstone, such as might be used for paving the streets. *Cf.* also Amari: *Musulmani di Sicilia* I pp. 396f. with note 2.

726 TMD LIII p. 323: *wa-qabruhū bi-l-kahfi ʿalā raʾsihī balāṭatun maḏkūrun fīhā smuhū*.

727 IḪallWaf II p. 292.

728 DabMaᶜālim I p. 125.

729 IḤāǧǧMadḫ III p. 273 (the whole passage is also cited below p. 272).

730 ITūlQal II p. 535.

quotes the inscription from a *balāṭah* affixed to a mausoleum in ar-Ramlah.[731] In surviving epitaphs from Egypt, the expression *hāḏihī l-balāṭah* refers to the marble slabs bearing the inscriptions, see Stèles Musée arabe du Caire 3698 (end of the second cent. H.), RCEA 275 (third cent. H, Egypt), 1139 (= Stèles Musée arabe du Caire 1632: Upper Egypt, 319 H), RCEA 1829 (= Stèles Musée arabe du Caire 1930, 363 H).[732]

maǧdūlah. The use of this term is, as far as I can see, limited to visitation and cemetery guides, e.g. the important work by Ibn az-Zayyāt. As such, *maǧdūl(ah)*, "twisted", seems to refer to a twisted or rounded column, of slender shape; that is also why *maǧdūlah* is said, metaphorically, of a candle in a poem by Sulaymān b. Ḥassān an-Naṣībī[733] and of a woman in a verse cited by Ibn al-Ǧawzī.[734]

The term *maǧdūlu kaddānin*, "a tomb-column of tuff stone",[735] appears frequently in Ibn az-Zayyāt's cemetery guide.[736] In other passages we also read of a *maǧdūl ṭawīl*, "a long-stretched, *or* tall, column",[737] of a "marble column" (*maǧdūlu ruḫāmin*),[738] or of a *maǧdūlah* bearing the funerary inscription.[739]

In the absence of further information it is impossible to find out what exactly the shape of a *maǧdūl(ah)* was and which difference there was between a *maǧdūl(ah)* and other rounded tomb-markers (e.g. columns called simply *ʿamūd* or *sāriyah*). As a passive participle from *ǧdl* I we find *maǧdūlah* used in a verse by al-Mutanabbī:

يُقْعِي جُلُوسَ البَدَوِيِّ المُصْطَلِي * بِأَرْبَعٍ مَجْدُولَةٍ لَمْ تُجْدَلِ

"(The hunting dog) squats, like a bedouin who seeks the warmth (of the fire), * with four (paws) of solid twisting though untwisted".[740]

This is explained in the commentaries as follows: the dog sits on his rump like the bedouin who, squatting at the fireside and touching his buttocks with his heels, puts his knees in front of him in order that the heat of the fire may reach his body. *Maǧdūlah* is said to mean *maftūlah*, "twisted

731 NābḤaqīqah (C) p. 140.

732 *Cf.* for the term *balāṭ(ah)* also IĞubRiḥlah (B) pp. 36, 67 and *passim*; Kriss: *Volksglaube* I p. 143; ʿUlaymīUns I p. 236 (*al-balāṭah as-sawdāʾ* in Jerusalem).

733 Ṯaʿāl Yat I p. 425.

734 IĞawzīNisāʾ p. 188.

735 *kaddān*, or properly *kaḏḏān*, seems to refer to a sort of porous stone which Dozy explains tentatively as tuff stone ("pierre de tuf", "tuf calcaire", see his *Supplément* II pp. 450f. s.r. *kḏḏ*); similarly in WKAS I p. 90 (*s.r.*). In cemetery guides, *kaddān* is often used in order to indicate the material of the tombstone or the slab bearing the epitaph: *qabrun* ... *ʿalayhi lawḥu kaddānin ʿinda raʾsihī* (MuwMuršid I p. 405); *balāṭatu kaddānin* (IZayKawākib pp. 242 and 255); *ʿamūdu kaddānin* (*ib.* p. 320); *al-ḥaǧar al-kaddān* (sic, *ib.* p. 71).

736 IZayKawākib pp. 110, 119, 158, 197, etc.; *cf.* also SaḫTuḥfAḥbāb pp. 210 and 213.

737 IZayKawākib p. 208.

738 IZayKawākib p. 189.

739 IZayKawākib p. 97.

740 MutanDīwān (M) II p. 107 / (U) III p. 216 (v. 11) / (W) p. 203 (v. 11) = MehrenRhetorik p. 23 (in translation).

together *or* twined", as if the poet intended to say: With paws firm, *or* solid (*muḥkamah*), being made by God not by Man (*lam tuǧdal*, i.e. here: "not created"). al-Maʿarrī, however, sees a simple description here, and his interpretation seems more convincing: "As if they (i.e. the paws) were twisted but in reality they are not so". Lane in his dictionary renders *maǧdūl* as "slender, slim", or also "of firm, *or* compact, make", meaning "of beautiful compacture", and said of a leg: "well turned, *or* rounded" (*s.r.*). However, there is at least one passage in Ibn az-Zayyāt's cemetery guide where *maǧdūlah* cannot possibly refer to a column – assuming that the text is not corrupted: *fa-ʿalā bābi hāḏihī t-turbati lawḥun maktūbun ʿalayhi fī maǧdūlati ruḫāmin bi-l-qalami l-kūfī*, i.e. "at the entrance of this mausoleum there is a plaque upon which in a marble *maǧdūlah* is inscribed in Kufic letters".[741] From this passage one might deduce that the term refers to a marble medallion or something similar as it is said to have been applied to a tablet or slabstone. This, on the other hand, is not possibly the case in the other passages where the term *maǧdūl(ah)* must refer to something resembling a rounded or column-like tombstone.

labinah. Tomb-markers of brick are very rarely referred to in literary sources, at least in connection with actual graves. The few examples I know of are passages in Shiite treatises. There we read that at the head of tombs one should set up a *labinah* or a *lawḥ*.[742]

naṣībah. The tombstone bearing an epitaph is called in one source a *naṣībah*, in another *balāṭah* (see **32**). This term for tombstones is, as far as I can see, not attested in other texts. I presume that it refers to something like a column or a pillar, or an object made of stone which is erected above something, even though this would not match the term *balāṭah*. Perhaps the term *naṣībah* is a misspelling (or misprint) of *nuṣb*, "grave-monument" or also "cenotaph". There may also be some connection with the term *nuṣb* (or *naṣb*, pl. *ʾanṣāb*) as used by the pre-Islamic Arabs for holy stones erected upon or around tombs.[743]

ṣuwwah (pl. *ṣuwan* and *ʾaṣwāʾ*). It has been noted[744] that this term, which indicates a way marker or also a milestone, was applied to tombs as well. Ibn Manẓūr in his dictionary *Lisān al-ʿarab* reports that *ṣuwwah* refers to "a stone that serves as a road sign" (*ḥaǧarun yakūnu ʿalāmatan fī ṭ-ṭarīq*), or to any stone that indicates a direction or a way, in the form of erected (*manṣūbah*) and elevated (*murtafiʿah*) columns or slabs, or simply as heap of stones (a cairn) or earth. Therefore, tombs are also called *ʾaṣwāʾ* because "the tombs are likened to way markers (*ʾaʿlām*)".[745] However, it remains unclear whether tombs were so called because their mounds or upper enclosures resembled those way markers (and could also serve as such) or whether the tombs bore tombstones which more closely recorded the stones known as *ṣuwan* and *ʾaṣwāʾ*.[746]

741 IZayKawākib p. 146.

742 ṬūsīMiṣbāḥ p. 35 and ṬūsīMabsūṭ I p. 187.

743 Wellhausen: *Reste* p. 180 note 3 and p. 184.

744 CIA Égypte II p. 64 note 2.

745 LA XIV pp. 471f. (s.r. *ṣwy*); see alsoIAṯīrNih III p. 7 (*ṣwy*).

746 For disused milestones becoming the centre of a saint cult in India, see Currie: *Muʿīn al-Dīn Chistī* p. 13.

To judge from what we read in literary sources, slabstones (lit. "tablets", *ʾalwāḥ*) seem to have been the most common objects bearing epitaphs. It was only during the Mamluk and Ottoman periods that (rounded or rectangular) columns, sometimes adorned with the diverse forms of head-gear typical of Turkish stelae,[747] came into widespread use.[748] In other cases, the material of the tombstone is mentioned, which consisted, if found worth mentioning, mainly of marble (*ruḫām*), but we also hear of wooden panels.[749]

It is important to note that not a single source in which I found reports about marble tombstones, voices any critique of that practice, quite in contrast with some legal manuals or treatises whose authors railed against such "detestable innovations" (*bidaʿ makrūhah*).

4.2. Funerary inscriptions (epitaphs)

Among all the topics of relevance in the wider field of funerary structures, the question of epitaphs has only rarely, and often not at all, been touched upon by the scholars. The best example for this is the lengthy tirade launched by Ibn Qayyim al-Ǧawzīyah against the Shiites and other Muslims actively professing the mortuary cult. In that context, Ibn al-Qayyim dwells upon a number of points, but concerning inscriptions the only thing he has to say is the following: "The Prophet prohibited writing upon graves, according to the Tradition which Abū Dāʾūd and at-Tirmiḏī edited in their *Sunan*-works (see below). (...) And those people also put stones (*ʾalwāḥ*) upon the tombs and inscribe on them the Qurʾān and other things!"[750]

The main interest of Sunnite scholars, as reflected in their works, was therefore clearly directed to larger funerary constructions, and Robert Hillenbrand is right when he says that "inscribed stelae were venial sins when set against the gross violation of orthodox practice embodied in a mausoleum".[751] On the purely theoretical level, however, this is not the case, and epitaphs were seen by Muslim scholars often in analogy to funerary constructions such as mausolea and tomb-mosques. This has some plausibility, for if the latter were forbidden, it could be argued that also the former, which often were part of burial monuments or buildings, should likewise be prohibited.[752] What is more, the marking of tombs by objects, tombstones or buildings did not necessitate any inscription (*katb* or *kitābah*).

747 *Cf.* the typology of Ottoman tomb-stelae in Bacqué-Grammont: *Stelae Turcicae* II pp. 57-62 with plates 1-48; Laqueur: *Friedhöfe Istanbul* pp. 119-38 (with plates 4-13).

748 A beautiful example of such a rounded column with an epitaph is the gilded and painted stele at the tomb of the Mamluk ruler al-Farağ b. Barqūq (d. 815 H) in his mausoleum in the Northern Qarāfah in Cairo.

749 *Cf.* IḤağğMadḫ III p. 273 (*lawḥ min al-ḫašab*); SaḫTuḥfAḥbāb p. 100.

750 IQayIġāṯah I p. 181.

751 Hillenbrand: *Islamic Architecture* p. 254.

752 *Cf.* HaytTuḥfMuḥt III p. 197.

4.2.1. Reports from the Prophet and historical evidence

Epitaphs were in general considered disapproved of at best: "Putting an inscription on the grave is disapproved of, on the basis of its being prohibited (in a Tradition edited) by at-Tirmiḏī".[753]

The Tradition referred to, as quoted in the Ḥadīṯ collection of at-Tirmiḏī, runs as follows: "The Prophet prohibited the plastering of tombs with gypsum, writing upon them (*ʾan yuktaba ʿalayhā*), erecting buildings above them and stepping on them".[754] Moreover, this verdict is found not only in the collection of at-Tirmiḏī, but was included in the works of ʿAbd ar-Razzāq, Ibn Abī Šaybah, Abū Dāʾūd, Ibn Māǧah, an-Nasāʾī as well as many others.[755] The ruling was adopted in most later Sunnite legal treatises, especially among the Malikites and Shafiites.[756]

There are next to no reports of a more historical nature reflecting the practice with regard to epitaphs during the formative period of Islam. The only instance I could find, dating from the second century H, is a report telling us that the Shiite Imam Mūsā al-Kāẓim ordered the name of his daughter to be inscribed on a tombstone (*lawḥ*) and put upon her tomb in Medina.[757] Still, in view of the scarcity of evidence, the general verdict expressed by Jean-Claude Vadet, viz. that "les pierres et les inscriptions funéraires ne semblent pas avoir été d'un usage fréquent à l'époque du Prophète",[758] seems to depend chiefly on the Tradition quoted from the Prophet and the silence of the sources, though such an *argumentum ex negativo* is not without risks.

4.2.2. The legal debate

The silence of the sources as to the early Islamic period leaves us mainly with the debate among later legal scholars – and of course with the many epitaphs that have been preserved *in situ* (see Volume I). The rather unspecified wording of the Tradition cited above ("do not write upon them") was open to further discussion, at least as it was understood by Muslim scholars. In view of the common use of epitaphs in Islamic culture, they therefore tried to define more exactly which kind of inscription should be prohibited and which should not. It is far from the truth that the jurists

753 AnṣTuḥfah p. 86. The same verdict in INaqʿUmdah p. 241. *Cf.* also IQayZād I p. 524 and IMuflFurūʿ II p. 271.

754 TirmĞāmiʿ II p. 258 (*ǧanāʾiz* 57) = IQudMuġnī II p. 507 = ManbTasl (C) p. 203 / (M) p. 197; MuwMuršid I p. 66; QurṭTaḏk p. 86; KU 42576 (XV p. 650); HarMirqātMaf IV p. 76; MF XXXII pp. 251f.

755 ʿARazMuṣ 6497 (III p. 507); IAŠayMuṣ III p. 216 (*ǧanāʾiz* 131); ADāʾūd III p. 294 (*ǧanāʾiz* 76); NasSunan IV p. 71; IMāǧah I p. 498; ḤākMust I p. 370; ʿAyniʿUmdah VII p. 102. *Cf.* also IḤaǧAḥwāl p. 48; ŠawkŠṢudūr p. 70; al-Ašraf: *al-Qabr* 25.

756 BāǧīMunt II p. 23; ŠīrMuhaḏ I p. 138; NawRawḍah II p. 136; ArdAnwār I p. 124; WanšMiʿyār I p. 318; RamlīNih III p. 33; MF XXXII p. 251; Wafā: *Aḥkām al-ǧanāʾiz* p. 262.

757 KulKāfī III p. 202 (The report has *fī l-qabr*, but the context necessitates the meaning "on the tomb" which is normally rendered as *ʿalā l-qabr*; see also above p. 251).

758 Vadet: Review of Grütter: *Bestattungsbräuche* p. 202.

abhorred funeral inscriptions in general,[759] though they set up strict conditions concerning their application and content. As in many other cases, the Malikite Ibn al-Ḥāǧǧ had his say on this matter, and his account is one of the first, more detailed treatments of the questions of epitaphs in Arabic scholarship:

> "Beware of what some people are doing, namely inscribing the name of the deceased and the date of his death upon the tomb. It does not matter whether this (is done) towards the head of the dead on the tombstone (*ḥaǧar*) which marks his grave – even if the tombstone as such follows the precepts of the *sunnah* (...) –, whether the inscription is put on the building which they usually construct above the tomb – though building upon the tomb is forbidden (...) –, or whether this (is done) on an inscribed piece (of stone, *balāṭah*) or on a wooden tablet (*lawḥ min ḫašab*).[760] Worse than that, however, is (an inscription) put on a column made of marble or other material. Marble is the most detestable material,[761] yet even if (the inscription) is put on a wooden column it must be considered forbidden.
>
> Then look (...) what point has been reached by those who adopted the usage of inscriptions: they will write down verses from the Qur'ān which include a name of the names of God the Exalted or the name of the Prophet and whatever else there is protected (*lahū ḥurmah*) by the noble Law.[762] Then the mausoleum (*turbah*) in question will fall into oblivion and the memory of its people and their whereabouts will be lost; as a consequence, (the inscription or the epitaph) will fall to the ground. If it is then stolen,[763] the thief will sell it to someone who will put it to unsuitable places, e.g. on the threshold of a door or in the lavatory. Such a person will put the inscribed side (*nāḥiyat al-kitābah*) on the earth if he is a Muslim, without realising that doing so is a gross sin; if the thief sells it to a Christian or a Jew the matter is worse, because they intend the humiliation of everything which is exalted by the pure Muḥammadan Law. If, however, (the inscription or epitaph) is safeguarded from theft, it will stay at its place and be trampled upon by feet, which is likewise humiliating, until it will seem as if there was no reverence (*ḥurmah*) towards it. This is prohibited by the noble Law".[764]

Towards the end of the ninth century H, as-Suyūṭī delivers another succinct overview of that particular topic:

> "(Zayn ad-Dīn) al-ᶜIrāqī said, 'It might be that the prohibition refers to every (kind of) inscription (*kitābah*), such as writing the name of the deceased or the date of his death. Alternatively, it might refer to writing a passage from the Qur'ān or the names of God Almighty in the hope of blessing. In the latter case it could easily happen that somebody

759 *Cf.* Rāġib: *Structure de la tombe* p. 402: "Ces signes funéraires sont particulièrement recommandés par les juristes. Cependant, de pierre ou de bois, ils seront simples et nus, à savoir sans inscription ni décor. L'anonymat: aucun indice ne doit trahir la fortune ou le rang".

760 *Cf.* also al-Albānī: *Aḥkām al-ǧanā'iz* p. 262.

761 *Cf.* also Haja: *Mort et Jugement Dernier* p. 36.

762 See also TurkLumaᶜ I p. 215: "To the (abominable) innovations belongs the writings of the Qur'ān or something (*šay'an*) of the names of God the Exalted upon the tombs".

763 The edited text has "if it can be safeguarded from theft", though this is plainly impossible; see the passage which follows.

764 IḤāǧǧMadḫ III p. 273.

sets his foot on it or that it falls to the earth, ending up beneath the feet'. al-Ḥākim (an-Nīsābūrī) wrote in his *Mustadrak* after having edited the Tradition (that contains the prohibition uttered by the Prophet): 'The chains of transmissions (backing that Tradition) are correct, but in practice nobody acts accordingly (*laysa l-ʿamalu ʿalayhā*) and the foremost among the Muslim scholars in East and West have inscriptions put on their tombs. This custom was taken over by the later generations from the earlier generations (*as-salaf*)'.[765] In his abridgement (of al-Ḥākim's *Mustadrak*), aḏ-Ḏahabī severely criticised him for that statement, calling him a '(blameworthy) innovator' (*muḥdiṯ*); (he, i.e. aḏ-Ḏahabī, also defended the earlier generations by saying) that they had not heard of the prohibition yet".[766]

4.2.3. A tenth-century fatwa concerning funerary inscriptions

Some decades after as-Suyūṭī, the Meccan scholar Ibn Ḥağar al-Haytamī provides another lengthy discussion as to epitaphs in an interesting and detailed fatwa. His account is much more exhaustive than those of Ibn al-Ḥāğğ and as-Suyūṭī. The fact that al-Haytamī's fatwa is among the longest written by him regarding questions of burial seems to indicate that the display of epitaphs, a common practice in pre-modern Islam, was considered, at least by him, as a point of immense interest and relevance. The text of the fatwa, including the initial quaestio, is the following:

> "*Quaeritur*: Concerning the disapproval (*karāhah*) of inscriptions upon tombs (*al-kitābatu ʿalā l-qubūr*): Is it meant as a general rule including the names of God, the Qurʾān, the name of the deceased and what else might be written down, or does it refer in particular to some of the elements mentioned before, with clear definitions of what falls under the rule (and what does not)?
> *Respondeo*: The companions (of the Prophet) took the disapproval of inscriptions on tombs to be a rule generally valid, for the reason that the prohibition[767] is known from (a Tradition edited by) at-Tirmiḏī (*cf.* above) who stated that 'this is a correct report, there is no fault in it'. However, Abū ʿAbdallāh al-Ḥākim an-Nīsābūrī, the innovator (*al-muḥdiṯ*), challenged that view because in practice nobody acts accordingly and the foremost among the Muslim scholars in East and West have inscriptions put on their tombs. This practice was taken over by the later generations from the earlier generations.[768]

765 *Cf.* ḤākMust I p. 370 and the fatwa below. This passage is also cited in WanšMiʿyār I p. 318; al-Albānī: *Aḥkām al-ğanāʾiz* p. 206; MF XXXII p. 252.

766 SuyZahr IV p. 72. This is what ḎahTalḫ I p. 370 actually says: "We know of no companion (of the Prophet) who followed this practice, it rather was brought up (*ḥdṯ* IV) by members of the next generation (*at-tābiʿūn*) and later times who had not heard of its being prohibited". In contrast to aḏ-Ḏahabī, other scholars, e.g. the Syrian jurisprudent al-Birzālī (ʿAlam ad-Dīn al-Qāsim b. M., d. 739 H), took al-Ḥākim's statement at its face value and concluded that applying epitaphs was sanctioned by the consensus of the scholars, see HaytFatFiqh II p. 16.

767 Here, as in other cases, al-Haytamī does not always distinguish clearly between "disapproval" (lit. "detestation", *karāhah*) and "prohibition" (*taḥrīm*), though both categories are clearly distinct in legal theory. Nevertheless, the legal scholars often use expressions like *karāhatun tuḥmalu ʿalā t-taḥrīm* or similar, meaning "disapproval understood as prohibition" or "a disapproval to the same effect of, *or* having the same force as, a prohibition".

768 See n. 765 above.

Yet the objection of al-Ḥākim would be only allowable if all the foremost scholars of an age either had done so (that is, putting epitaphs upon their own tombs or on those of others) or did not declare it detestable though they knew (of the prohibition). What could be a stronger dismissal of the clear position of our (former) colleagues who opted for the disapproval (of funerary inscriptions) on the basis of the aforesaid Tradition!
Both as-Subkī and al-Aḏraʿī examined this problem thoroughly and in detail in the wider context of everything that has to do with indicating the (identity of the) deceased. The opinion of as-Subkī was, as we will see in a moment, that putting up an object which identifies the tomb is recommendable (*mustaḥabb*).[769] Thus, when an inscription is applied with this aim it must not be considered detestable, on condition that its content is limited to what is necessary for identification (*ʾiʿlām*).[770]
Instead, al-Aḏraʿī took the view that inscriptions (on tombs) are detestable, regardless of whether the inscription consists of the name of the deceased on a gravestone at the head (of the tomb) or of something else.[771] This (prohibition) was considered generally valid, and the obvious analogy is that writing down (parts of) the Qurʾān is forbidden (...), especially as (the text) would be exposed to the danger of being trampled upon, of being soiled or of being sullied with the unclean remnants of the dead as happens on communal cemeteries where exhumations are frequent.[772] As to other inscriptions, in verse or prose, it is likely that they are either disapproved of or forbidden, on the basis of (the Prophet) having prohibited them. As to writing down the name of the deceased, it has been argued that every object which identifies the tomb is preferable; thus if writing down (the name) provides that, it follows that it is likewise preferable, given that its content does not exceed what is necessary for identification. In this case, (an inscription) is not considered disapproved of, especially if on the tombs of saintly and righteous persons (*qubūru l-ʾawliyāʾi wa-ṣ-ṣāliḥīna*), because they could not be identified otherwise, in the course of so many years, unless by an inscription.[773] Then (al-Aḏraʿī) mentioned (the statement) of al-Ḥākim (an-Nīsābūrī) which has been quoted above, adding the following comment: 'As far as the writing down of the name of the deceased is concerned, and if it aims at identification (*taʿrīf*), the case is clear. The prohibition, however, concerns everything written for vainglory and embellishment, including hypocritical characterisations (of the deceased, e.g. in the case of the pompous epitaphs of rulers). It also concerns writing down (passages from) the Qurʾān and other texts'.[774]
The positions arrived at painstakingly by as-Subkī – namely that it is not detestable to write down the name of the deceased if this aims at identification – and al-Aḏraʿī – namely its being recommendable – show clearly that identification is only admitted if the deceased was either a learned or a righteous person and if there is the danger that

769 *Cf.* also MF XXXII p. 252.

770 *Cf.* WanšMiʿyār I p. 318. This comes close to the view of Abū Ḥanīfah, see Wafā: *Aḥkām al-ǧanāʾiz* p. 262.

771 *Cf.* HaytTuḥfMuḥt III p. 197; RamlīNih III p. 33; HarMirqātMaf IV p. 76. al-Aḏraʿī's claim is, however, belied by what follows below.

772 *Cf.* also RamlīNih III p. 33. To this the pernicious effect of rain might be added, see HaytTuḥfMuḥt III p. 197. See also above pp. 155 and 217f.

773 *Cf.* RamlīNih III p. 33 and MF XXXII p. 252.

774 The same distinction is made in IQudMuġnī II p. 507 and INuǧBaḥr II p. 209. *Cf.* also MF XXXII p. 252 and Haja: *Mort et Jugement Dernier* p. 36.

> (the site of) his tomb will be effaced or fall into oblivion in the course of many years, were it not for the name written on the tomb.[775] However, in all other cases inscriptions are prohibited, because the (general) wording of the Tradition (as edited by at-Tirmiḏī) allows the specification of its meaning which, in this case, is the need to identify (the deceased). This results from the analogy with the fact that it is considered recommended (*mandūb*) to display an object in order to identify the tomb – it even might be said to fall under this very ruling – or in order to preserve the memory of a scholar or pious person so that plentiful mercy can be invoked upon him and his blessing returns to those visiting (his grave).
> Moreover, al-Aḏraʿī's opinion about the prohibition of writing (parts of) the Qurʾān is largely correct, for even though trampling upon and sullying (the inscription) do not always and not necessarily occur in practice, something of that sort might happen as long as the widespread custom persists of digging up (graves) in (communal) cemeteries and of destroying (existing) tombs.[776] The concept of (writing down) the Qurʾān includes the names of the Almighty, in contrast with other texts in verse or prose whose (writing down) is considered detestable, but not forbidden;[777] however, one should do it only with reluctance. As to the harsh verdict pronounced by al-Aḏraʿī, I sometimes saw it considered disapproved of and sometimes (completely) prohibited. The prohibition refers either to writing down (parts of) the Qurʾān or the names of the Almighty, in contrast with other texts, or if an inscription aims at vainglory and embellishment".[778]

This is what a Sunnite Muslim scholar arrived at in the early Ottoman period, and as seen in al-Haytamī's fatwa, he took ample recourse to the opinions of authorities of the eighth century H and added little besides. Since the seventh century H, the impact of practice on legal reasoning had made itself felt more and more, at least in topics as heavily discussed as the construction of funerary structures and everything connected with them.

Nevertheless, no legal scholar I know of ever went so far as to sanction wholeheartedly the use of Qurʾānic verses or poetry in funeral epigraphy, even though a large number of, or perhaps most, Islamic epitaphs contain either Qurʾānic citations or expressions inspired by the Qurʾānic wording. Poetry as found on epitaphs, on the other hand, was much less commonly resorted to in funerary inscriptions than Qurʾānic citations or religious formulae. Yet poetry was very dear to many among the learned and men of letters (see Chapter 4), and al-Ġazālī in his *ʾIḥyāʾ* filled a whole page (in small modern print) with epitaph-poetry that had struck him as remarkable.

775 *Cf.* HarMirqātMaf IV p. 76.

776 WanšMiʿyār I pp. 318f.: "An inscription is only allowed if it is impossible to set your foot on it, for example on the marble slabs raised at the head side of the grave, but not on the surface of the tomb where there is the danger that somebody will step on it".

777 Similarly, it was considered forbidden or disapproved of, for reasons of reverence, to touch Qurʾānic verses written on walls (or even to write them on walls, including cenotaphs and the walls of mosques, see HarǦamʿWas I p. 142 and HarMirqātMaf IV p. 76) or to lean against them, see IʿASalāmFat p. 124. According to al-Harawī, the prohibition also concerns the names of the Prophet, see HarMirqātMaf IV p. 76.

778 HaytFatFiqh II p. 12. *Cf.* also MuwMuršid I p. 66.

4.2.4. Terminology

As said page 264 above, the old Arabic sources refer to the tombstone mainly as "(tomb)stone" (*ḥağar*) or, occasionally, as "(tomb-)marker" (*ʿalāmah* or also *ʿalam*). Otherwise they mention neither the tombstone nor the epitaph directly, using instead expessions such as "on the tomb was inscribed" (*kutiba ʿalā l-qabr*, *kāna ʿalā l-qabri maktūban*, *wuğida ʿalā l-qabri maktūban* and the like). If at all, epitaphs as such are indicated in literary sources simply as "inscription" (*kitābah* or, more rarely, *katb*),[779] while the term *kitāb* (in the sense of "inscription") appears in some surviving epitaphs.[780]

The employment of the word *taʾrīḫ* ("date") with the meaning "epitaph" or "inscribed tombstone" is attested in at least one surviving funerary inscription.[781] It seems natural to presume that this term was applied for the epitaph as such because in most cases the funerary inscription stated the name of the deceased and the date of his death. The use of the term *taʾrīḫ* in the sense of "epitaph" was dominant in the western Islamic lands, but it did not enter the terminology of the written sources on a large scale. Apart from the examples cited by Dozy,[782] I came across the following passages:

(a) The seventh-century western traveller Ibn Ğubayr mentions that he learned the names of those buried in the Cairene ʿAlīd shrines simply from "the inscribed tombstones fixed upon their tombs" (*ʾasmāʾu ʾaṣḥābi hāḏihi l-mašāhidi l-mubārakati ʾinnamā talaqqaynāhā mina t-tawārīḫi ṯ-ṯābitati ʿalayhā*).[783]

(b) Ibn az-Zayyāt in his cemetery guide has the following passage: "Ibn al-Ğabbās said, 'In their cemetery (i.e. the *maqburat al-Ġāfiqīyīn*) there were more than ten marble slabs (*ʾalwāḥ ruḫām*), but none of them has been preserved except for one marble slab in the lower wall (or the original part?) of the building (*fī ʾaṣli l-bināʾ*), upon which is written: *Yaḥyā al-Muqriʾ, mawlā of the Prince of the Believers ʿAlī b. Abī Ṭālib – may God honour his face!* This genealogy is written on most graves of this cemetery because they took pride in it'. The author (i.e. Ibn az-Zayyāt himself) then adds that 'this epitaph (*taʾrīḫ*) is no longer extant today'".[784] In another passage, Ibn az-Zayyāt writes: "I saw a marble slab bearing the following inscription in Kufic script: *This is the tomb of ʿĀʾišah bint Hišām b. Muḥammad b. Abī Bakr al-Bakrī*, but I do not know whether this is the epitaph of her tomb or not (*hal huwa*

779 DabMaʿālim III pp. 81 and 174.

780 RCEA 6 (*wa-kutiba hāḏā l-kitābu fī* ..., 31 H.); Stèles Musée arabe du Caire 3947 (*raḥima llāhu man qaraʾa hāḏā l-kitāba* ..., end of the 2nd cent. H.). For an epitaph dated 188 H, see Volume I p. 579.

781 Inscriptions Espagne 190 (= RCEA 2744: 477 H, Spain) and p. 184 with note 3. See also Dozy: *Supplément* I p. 17 (s.r. *ʾrḫ*); CIA Égypte I p. 422; doubtful is the meaning of *taʾrīḫ* in the building inscription of a mausoleum in Marrakech: RCEA 776 002 (line 4).

782 Dozy: *Supplément* I p. 17 (*s.r. ʾrḫ*).

783 IĞubRiḥlah (B) p. 21.

784 IZayKawākib p. 56.

ta'rīḫu qabrihā 'am lā), because I saw it at another place (i.e. not in the place where her tomb is supposed to be)".[785] Finally, Ibn az-Zayyāt describes the tomb of al-ᶜUmarī with the words "there is no *ta'rīḫ* upon it (*laysa ʿalā qabri l-ʿUmarīyī ta'rīḫ*)", which might mean "There is no engraved epitaph upon it" or "The death of al-ᶜUmarī is not indicated upon the tomb".[786]

The citations from the cemetery guide of Ibn az-Zayyāt are interesting for two reasons. First, because he uses the term *ta'rīḫ* as "epitaph", yet the funerary inscriptions cited do not mention the date of death (albeit they *could* have indicated it). This shows that the word *ta'rīḫ* had acquired the meaning of "epitaph" quite independently of whether the inscription actually provided the date of death. Second, because Ibn az-Zayyāt states that the inscription was done in Kufic writing (*bi-l-qalam al-kūfī*). Remarks about the script of funerary inscriptions in Arabic sources are largely confined to cemetery guides. Thus we find al-Muwaffaq Ibn ᶜUṯmān mentioning "the ancient script" (*ḫaṭṭ qadīm*) of a funerary inscription,[787] and Ibn az-Zayyāt more than once notes that an epitaph was written in Kufic letters.[788] Outside the realm of cemetery guides proper, the Meccan historiographers al-Fāsī and aš-Šaybī were interested in reporting the type of script they found on tombstones (see **119**, **123** and **126**); in some cases, al-Fāsī also took care to mention the names of the sculptors (see **135**). The seventh-century biographer al-Udfuwī mentions that he took some personal information from an epitaph inscribed in Kufic letters.[789]

However, in the majority of cases the actual tomb itself and not the tombstone or the inscription(s) it bears are referred to in Arabic literary sources. This stands in contrast with the usage in other cultures, e.g. in ancient Greece, where the grave-monument or the tombstone are mainly indicated verbally, while the terms for "grave" or "tomb" as such are rarely used.[790] This might reflect the lesser importance of grave-markers and tombstones in Islamic culture, where the symbolic value of the relevant tomb-marker or epitaph seems to have been of secondary interest when compared with the site of the tomb itself.

4.3. Tomb-markers and epitaphs in practice

4.3.1. The setting up of epitaphs

Apart from cut stones, stelae, slabs, columns or panels (see above p. 266), funerary inscriptions were also applied directly to the lower fringes of cenotaphs or, in the

785 IZayKawākib p. 79. *Cf.* also Taylor: *Vicinity of the Righteous* pp. 43f.

786 IZayKawākib p. 116.

787 MuwMuršid I p. 449.

788 See IZayKawākib pp. 98 (*ruḫāmatun bi-ḫaṭṭin kūfī*), 114 (*lawḥu ruḫāmin ... maktūbun fīhi bi-l-qalami l-kūfī*), 116 (*ʿamūd ... maktūbun ʿalayhi bi-l-kūfī*), 146 (*lawḥun maktūbun ʿalayhi ... bi-l-qalami l-kūfī*) and 189 (*maǧdūlu ruḫāmin maktūbun ʿalayhi bi-l-qalami l-kūfī*).

789 UdfṬāliᶜ p. 474 (*qara'tu nasabahū wa-wafātahū min lawḥin bi-l-kūfīyi ʿala qabrihī*).

790 See Sourvinou-Inwood: *'Reading' Greek Death*, chapter III.

Islamic West, on the *mqābrīyah*. In the case of mausolea and roofed structures, they were alternatively put above the entrance, on the threshold or on one of the inner walls, either engraved on stones or marble blocks or written upon the walls, sometimes also on wooden panels or fayence tiles.

We find next to no information in the sources about the practical aspects of tombstones and epitaphs, that is, about their manufacture and execution. In rare cases, the sculptor is named, or names himself, in the text of an epitaph (see **97**); in other cases, we know the sculptors from other sources. al-Maqrīzī quotes a passage from al-Quḍāᶜī in which he laments that the sculptors were often lacking knowledge of the correct names of the deceased and thus engraved wrong names upon the tombstones, e.g. by rendering "aṯ-Ṯaᶜālibī" erroneously as "al-Qitālī".[791] However, there is no information about the costs of tombstones and the accompanying epitaphs, nor are we told whether the execution of funerary inscriptions was seen as a specialist occupation or whether it was done by ordinary sculptors (sg. *naqqāš*) who would execute other inscriptions as well. The nearest we get to the personnel who made their living from burials are the occasional remarks about the washers of the dead (sg. *muġassil*), the bearers (sg. *ḥammāl*) and the gravediggers or undertakers (sg. *ḥaffār*). It is likewise unknown whether the sculptors used booklets or scripts which contained the most popular phrases and verses normally used in epitaphs, but the repetition of specific wordings and poems in geographically distant epitaphs seems to indicate that such booklets did exist.

The earliest surviving Arabic epitaphs belong to the first half of the first century H. From that time on, Arabic funerary epigraphy flourished, and though there are many examples of lengthy and beautiful inscriptions, only a small portion of Arabic epitaphs (as far as they are preserved in the original) mention personal details such as the name of the deceased, his genealogy, titles and profession, his date of death or, in some cases, his date of birth or the age, to say nothing of personal circumstances.[792] The remaining text of the epitaphs was generally reserved either for religious formulae and citations of Qurʾānic verses or, much more rarely, for lines of poetry. In many cases Arabic epitaphs amount indeed to nothing but what has been called, in another context, "a minimalist inscribed grave monument"[793] or "l'écriture minimale",[794] that is, bearing little else besides the name of the deceased and often lacking even his date of death.

4.3.2. Absence of epitaphs and anonymous tombs

Notwithstanding the large number of Arabic epitaphs (only a small part of which have been edited so far) there has always been, throughout the Islamic world, a

791 MaqrMuq V p. 445.

792 See Volume I, Chapter 1.

793 Sourvinou-Inwood: *'Reading' Greek Death* p. 279 note 691.

794 Labes: *Mémoire des tombes* p. 27.

great number of uninscribed tombs and anonymous mausolea,[795] thus making its occupants a frequent matter of speculation or guesswork. This also enabled the people to "re-discover" tombs or at least to declare new graves identical with the tombs of older, mainly famous or saintly personalities whose burial sites had by then become unknown or disputed (see also below);[796] this problem was even made the subject of monographs.[797] Especially noteworthy in this regard is the long account regarding the re-discovery of the tomb of Idrīs, the founder of Fez, in the year 841 H, as told in the chronicle of Muḥammad b. aṭ-Ṭayyib al-Ḥasanī al-Qādirī:

> "The tomb of the *imām* Idrīs had not [at one time] been visible or even known, that is it had not been known in which part of Masjid al-Shurafāʾ it was located. The cause for its disappearance had been the lack of concern for it by the Berbers (...), after the rulers of Fez, his descendants and successors had been defeated. (...) The [Berbers] neglected the noble tomb and did not grant asylum to those who sought refuge there,[798] and if they found anyone manifesting any signs of respect for it, they punished him severely. They continued thus until the tomb fell into ruins and no one remained who knew in what part of this *masjid* it was located. (...) When God the Exalted willed to reveal the tomb of the Prophet's flesh and blood, whose occupant is the protector of this city ([the foundation of] which was one of his pious deeds), as the stars are the protection of the heavenly beings, this happened as is written on the marble tablet next to it on the wall. The text of this reads:
>
> When the *imām* (that is the *imām* Idrīs, the founder of Fez) died, he was buried in their great, holy, famous city, in Masjid al-Shurafāʾ, but they were not able to locate the exact spot of his grave until God the Exalted chose to reveal it out of mercy and grace to his *umma*. It so happened that the left side of the base of the eastern wall was explored to examine it and see if it was in need of repair. The noble, pure tomb was then discovered. It was found that time had effaced its inscription, only a portion of which remained, but that his remains had not undergone any deterioration, as the termites had not been able to reach them. (...) It was agreed to write these lines on the wall parallel to the holy tomb to serve as a marker [*ʿalāmah*] and proof of it and for it to be known to all. This was all out of God's grace, charity, and unsolicited generosity to the present generation, since He preserved the material remains of the Noble Family

795 *Cf.* Hillenbrand: *Islamic Architecture* p. 264.

796 *Cf.* DabMaʿālim II p. 158; NZ IV p. 174; Gronke: *Derwische* p. 91. In Baghdad, there was often a mania for re-discovering tombs of early Shiite personalities, see IFuwaṭīḤaw pp. 373 and 404f.; Leisten: *Architektur für Tote* pp. 51-3. The phenomenon is well-known from European culture as well. The search for saints' tombs is often reported and many topoi are connected with such stories, viz. "the classical *mise-en-scéne*: the unsuccessful search for the graves, miraculous guidance to the spot (...)" (Lawrence: *Medieval Monasticism* p. 52).

797 E.g. the *Kitāb Dār (Darr) aṣ-ṣaḥāb fī bayān mawāḍiʿ wafayāt aṣ-ṣaḥābah* by aṣ-Ṣāġānī (al-Ḥasan b. M. al-Hindī al-Ḥanafī, d. 650 H), see Ahlwardt 9652 and GAL I p. 361. This deals with the localities where the companions of the Prophet had died and were buried; it is also cited as *Kitāb ʾAmākin wafayāt aṣ-ṣaḥābah* in FāsīʿIqd III p. 443.

798 *Cf.* above pp. 166f.

as an assurance of protection (...). The discovery of this tomb and the writing of these lines occurred in Rajab 841".[799]

On the other hand, the fact that tombs were only known by – often unreliable – hearsay or that burial sites of famous persons tended to multiply in the Islamic world, offered a convenient argument for those scholars who, like Ibn Taymīyah, vehemently attacked the practices of visiting tombs and cemeteries.[800]

Even the most popular graveyards, e.g. the Baqīᶜ cemetery in Medina, abounded in anonymous tombs and burial sites without proper identification. Take for example the so-called *mašhadu ʾummahāti l-muʾminīna ʾazwāği* (var. *zawǧāt*) *n-nabī*, the mausoleum (or shrine) of the "mothers of the believers, the wives of the Prophet", as it was found by a visitor of the ninth century H: "There are four tombs still visible (*or* distinguishable, *ẓāhirah*), but it is impossible to find out exactly which tomb belongs to whom.[801] It was said that Umm Ḥabībah Ramlah bt. Abī Sufyān (...) al-Umawīyah[802] is among them".[803] In the whole Baqīᶜ cemetery there were only nine tombs said to be known with certainty.[804]

Or take the so-called "tombs of the martyrs of Uḥud" (*qubūr aš-šuhadāʾ*): "The visitation starts with (the tomb of) Ḥamzah, the uncle of the Prophet, (...) then one visits the remaining martyrs, though not one of their tombs can be identified".[805] This is due to the fact that "the righteous first generation (of Muslims) refrained from exaggerating the aggrandizement of the tombs and plastering them (with gypsum), something which led to the obliteration of the vestiges of most of them, and thus no tomb of them is individually known, except in a limited number of cases".[806] In the Meccan al-Ḥağūn cemetery, Ibn Ǧubayr relates, "a multitude of the

799 Cited from *Muhammad al-Qadiri's* Nashr al Mathani: *The Chronicles*, ed. and transl. by Norman Cigar, London 1981, pp. 161f. (pp. 52-4 of the Arabic text).

800 See Memon: *Ibn Taimīya's Struggle* pp. 255-59 (from Ibn Taimīyah's *Kitāb al-Iqtiḍāʾ*); Zepter: *Friedhöfe* p. 88.

801 This is also quoted, from Ibn an-Naǧǧār, in SamWafāʾ III p. 917.

802 Umm Ḥabībah Ramlah bt. Ṣaḫr b. Ḥarb (d. Medina 42 or 44 H), one of the wives of the Prophet who reportedly married her while she was staying in Ethiopia in the year 6 H, see IᶜABarrIst IV pp. 303-6; IǦawzīṢafwah I pp. 356-8 and IǦawzīWafā p. 669; ṬabSimṭ pp. 162-9 and 362; ISayNāsᶜUyūn II pp. 373f.; FāsīᶜIqd VI pp. 388f.; IḤağIṣābah IV pp. 305-7; QasṭMaw I pp. 408f.; ZA VIII p. 33. Her epitaph is reported in various literary sources, in two different versions containing nothing but her name: (a) *qabru ʾUmmi Ḥabībata binti Ṣaḫri bni Ḥarbin* (IŠabAḫbār I p. 79 = SamWafāʾ III p. 912), and (b) *hāḏā qabru Ramlata binti Ṣaḫrin* (var. *binti ʾAbī Sufyāna*: IᶜABarrIst IV p. 306; INağDurrah p. 403; MarğBahğah II p. 431; SamWafāʾ III p. 912).

803 SaḫTuḥfLaṭ I p. 42. *Cf.* also MiknāsīIḥrāz pp. 259-61.

804 INağDurrah p. 401. A similar comment in ṬabQirā p. 685. The remark certainly refers to persons deceased during the lifetime of the Prophet, not to the dead of later centuries.

805 DiyTārḪamīs II p. 176. On the"martyrs' tombs", see also SamWafāʾ III pp. 932f.

806 SamWafāʾ III p. 916 (who quotes from al-Mağd al-Maṭarī).

Prophet's companions and their followers, of saintly and righteous men are buried, yet their blessed shrines fell into ruins and the local people forgot their names".[807]

Under these circumstances, the identification of unknown tombs was an important event. The Prophet himself is credited with the identification of the tomb of Abū Riġāl from the tribe of Ṯamūd, and the subsequent disinterment proved that he was right.[808] However, in another case, at the tomb of Umm Miḥǧan, a woman of black complexion, the Prophet was unaware of who was buried there and he had to ask.[809] That the local people were often the only ones who knew about a tomb is also shown in the following story reported by al-ᶜUlaymī:

> "Abū Zurᶜah[810] once sat at the tomb of Sarah (at Hebron) around prayer time. When a sheikh entered, he called upon him and asked, 'O sheikh, which of these tombs is that of Abraham?' The sheikh pointed with his hand to the tomb of Abraham – peace be upon him! – and left. When a young man entered, Abū Zurᶜah called him and asked the same question. The young man indicated the tomb of Abraham and went away. Then a boy came in, thus Abū Zurᶜah called him and asked the same question. The boy indicated the tomb of Abraham – peace be upon him! Abū Zurᶜah then said, 'I bear witness that this is the tomb of Abraham the Intimate (of God) – peace be upon him and the most excellent blessing! –, there is no doubt about it".[811]

al-ᶜUlaymī, who reports this story, has an even more remarkable tale to offer. It concerns a tomb in the Māmillā cemetery in Jerusalem which was known as "Tomb-Of-We-found" (*qabru waǧadnā*):

> "Someone was passing by that tomb on horseback and recited the word of the Exalted *And they shall find all they wrought present, and thy Lord shall not wrong anyone.*[812] (At that moment) came the reply from the tomb with His word: 'We found, we found (*waǧadnā waǧadnā*)!',[813] so that that man heard this utterance. This is a famous tomb and large stones (*ʾaḥǧār kibār*) are upon it, but the name of the deceased is not known, so it is simply called the "Tomb-Of-We-Found". Some people are wrong in thinking that it is the tomb of al-Wāsiṭī,[814] since this is not the case because al-Wāsiṭī's name is written upon his tomb, whereas the tomb under discussion bears no inscription (*laysa ᶜalayhi kitābah*)".[815]

807 IǦubRiḥlah (B) p. 87.

808 ṮaᶜālṮimār p. 136; BayDal VI p. 297. In pre-Islamic times, this grave was habitually stoned by the people.

809 SuyḪaṣ II p. 112; ŠāmīSubul X p. 16. *Cf.* also IḤaǧIṣābah IV p. 407.

810 Probably ᶜAbd Allāh b. ᶜAmr (d. Damascus 280 H).

811 ᶜUlaymīUns I p. 46. For the location *cf.* MiknāsīIḥrāz pp. 301-3.

812 Q 18:49 (*wa-waǧadū mā ᶜamilū ḥāḍiran wa-lā yaẓlimu rabbuka ʾaḥadan*).

813 Apart from being a response to what the passer-by was reciting, there is here a citation of Q 7:44, *The inhabitants of Paradise will call to the inhabitants of the Fire: 'We have found that which our Lord promised us true'* (*wa-nadā ʾaṣḥābu l-ǧannati ʾaṣḥāba n-nāri ʾan qad waǧadnā mā waᶜadanā rabbunā ḥaqqan*); *cf.* also ᶜŪfīTarāǧim p. 137.

814 ᶜUmar b. Ibrāhīm (d. 684 H).

815 ᶜUlaymīUns II p. 152.

However, in many cases tombs remained unidentified or even completely invisible, due to the obvious absence of written indications and other signs marking the tomb. The consequences of this widely-attested fact may be illustrated by the following incident: the Moroccan noble Aḥmad b. Muḥriz al-ᶜAlawī, who rebelled from 1084 to 1096 H against his uncle Ismāᶜīl b. Muḥammad I (the Filālī ruler, r. 1082–1139 H) and was eventually defeated by him, was killed and buried in Tārūdānt (near Agadir).[816] After some days, the local people decided to transfer him elsewhere for burial, so they set about excavating his tomb during the night. However, as they were uncertain which grave was his, they also unearthed one of Ibn Muḥriz's army leaders called al-Ġarnāṭī. Only when seeing the corpses they were able to recognise Ibn Muḥriz. They took his body away in a coffin (*tābūt*), but al-Ġarnāṭī, no longer of interest to them, was left behind unburied "on the edges of his pit" (*ᶜalā šafīri qabrihī*).[817] The absence of tomb-markers, on the other hand, led often to the involuntary digging up of former graves. Thus in Ḥamāh it happened that people were digging a grave for the deceased poet al-Maḥḥār al-Adīb (ᶜUmar b. Masᶜūd, d. 711 H), when they suddenly found bones and more than twelve skulls.[818]

Taking these various pieces of information together, we must conclude that tombs were often left without epitaphs or indications as to the name of the deceased or that these indications were not renewed and thus got lost over the centuries. Worse still, the locations of tombs were often completely forgotten, which explains why sometimes a grave was dug and people then found that somebody had been buried there before.[819] In some cases, however, the restoration or renewal of burial sites brought about the same effect, e.g. in a mausoleum in Cairo referred to in the following passage: "Most of the tombs in that mausoleum have fallen to pieces and there are no tombstones left, apart from those in the courtyard. New tombs were built (*ǧdd* V) inside and thus the whole arrangement (of the burial site) was changed".[820] In other cases the tomb-markers were extant, yet without any inscription, for example at the grave of Abū Yazīd Rabāḥ al-Laḫmī (d. 172 H) in Kairouan: "At the head of his tomb there is a blue column without inscription (*ᶜamūdun ʾazraqu laysa fīhi kitābah*) which is well-known to everybody in our town",[821] or upon the tomb of Abū ᶜAbd Allāh Muḥammad b. ᶜAbd Allāh al-Mālikī (d. 438 or 444 H), likewise

816 Ironically, Ibn Muḥriz was captured and killed by enemy troops after he had left his stronghold in order to visit the tombs of the righteous in its vicinity! *Cf.* also Abun-Nasr: *History of the Maghrib* pp. 231f.

817 al-Marrākušī: *Iᶜlām* II p. 122.

818 ITaġrManh VIII p. 325.

819 As in the case of Abū Zamᶜah al-Balawī in Kairouan, see MālRiyāḍ I p. 84; *cf.* also the examples cited above p. 210.

820 IZayKawākib p. 108; *cf.* Taylor: *Vicinity of the Righteous* pp. 43f.

821 DabMaᶜālim I pp. 262f. Other anonymous tomb-markers from Kairouan, a short column without inscription (*ᶜamūd ... laysa fīhi kitābah*) and a tall column (*sāriyah*) without letters upon it, are mentioned *op. cit.* II p. 330 and 345. In another instance, an inscription was found on a tomb but it proved to be illegible (*ib.* III p. 150).

situated in Kairouan: "At the head of his tomb there is an elegant column without inscription (*ʿamūdun laṭīfun laysa fīhi katb*).[822]

Until the present day, for example in the Cairene southern Qarāfah cemetery, a number of mausolea are known only by public hearsay, where tomb-markers are uninscribed or proper tombstones are lacking altogether. If this oral tradition was interrupted, the names of the sites would be irrevocably lost: "In the whole cemetery (i.e. the Qarāfah) there is not a single tomb of a companion (of the Prophet) whose site we know with certainty, except the tomb of ʿUqbah (b. ʿĀmir al-Ǧuhanī, d. 58 H) because in visiting it the later generations were guided by the former generations (*zārahū l-ḫalafu ʿani s-salaf*)".[823] Other interesting cases of anonymous tombs or persons, whose tombs were not known with certainty, include the following: Ibn Ḫallikān quotes from al-Quḍāʿī's *Kitāb Ḫiṭaṭ Miṣr* the passage: "About the tomb of ʿAbd Allāh b. Wahb there are different opinions, yet in the quarter of the Banū Miskīn (in Cairo) there is a small run-down tomb, known as 'the tomb of ʿAbd Allāh'. It is an old tomb and it seems as if it were that of Ibn Wahb".[824] Or take the story of the Syrian jurist al-Awzāʿī, likewise told by Ibn Ḫallikān: "His tomb is in a village at the entrance of Beirut called Ḥantūs whose inhabitants are Muslims. He is buried at the *qiblah* side of the (local) mosque, but the people of the village do not know this and say rather: 'This is (the grave of) a pious man on which the light descends'. The tomb is only known to the learned élite (*al-ḫawāṣṣ*) among the people".[825] How common anonymous tombs were can be gleaned indirectly from a treatise by the Córdoban scholar Ibn aṭ-Ṭaylasān which is entitled *at-Tabyīn ʿan manāqib man ʿurifa qabruhū min aṣ-ṣaḥābah wa-t-tābiʿīn wa-l-ʿulamāʾ az-zāhidīn*, "The Demonstration of the Virtues of those among the (Prophet's) Companions, Successors and Ascetic Scholars whose tomb is known".[826] From the title we might conclude, *ex negativo*, that the tombs of at least some, if not most, companions and scholars were *not* known any longer and had fallen in oblivion.

Many examples of anonymous and/or undated graves can be found in travel literature as well as in topographical works and cemetery guides.[827] The same applies to the numerous cases in which somebody was credited with two or more different burial sites, a fact which likewise points to the missing or at least inadequate identification of tombs. The phenomenon, well-known above all from the biographical literature, that the exact date or place of someone's death was not known or that there were a number of conflicting reports seems also to indicate that the authors either did not bother to consult epitaphs (which often do mention the date of death), or that there were no epitaphs. The analysis of the biographical literature (see Chapter 4) shows that often it might have been the lack of proper epitaphs which led to doubts or inaccuracies about the precise date or place of someone's death.

As a matter of fact, people were in general well aware that under these circumstances the exact location of a given tomb could easily be lost and the name of the

822 DabMaʿālim III p. 174.

823 NZ I p. 129.

824 IḪallWaf III p. 36. Ibn Wahb was a famous Malikite scholar, resident in Egypt.

825 IḪallWaf III p. 127.

826 For this work, see below p. 299.

827 HarIšārāt pp. 50 (in Alexandria) and 94f. (in Medina); IBaṭṭRiḥlah pp. 77 and 144 (in Medina); DabMaʿālim I p. 184 and II p. 184 (in Kairouan); SaḫTuḥfAḥbāb pp. 100, 102, 121, 138, 175, 196 (all in Cairo); Inscriptions Espagne I p. 72, quoting from a twelfth-century travel journal (in Toledo); anonymous cenotaphs in the mausoleum of Ibn ʿAbbās in aṭ-Ṭāʾif: ʿUǧIhdāʾ pp. 69f.

deceased and the burial site fade into oblivion. Neither could the miracle-like occurrence be relied upon that the deceased would call from his tomb in order to indicate its location, as it happened, reportedly, to Abū Tammām Ġālib b. Ḥasan al-Ḫuzāʿī (seventh cent. H) when he was looking for the tomb of Abū l-Ḥasan b. al-Ǧālūt.[828] So, even if there *was* an epitaph, one took recourse to additional precautionary measures in order to ascertain the future knowledge of the tomb. The most interesting case of that sort I found in DabMaʿālim III p. 81. Here, the ninth-century editor of this book, Ibn Nāǧī at-Tanūḫī (d. 839 H), speaks at length about the grave of Abū Muḥammad ʿAbd Allāh b. Hāšim b. Masrūr al-Qāḍī (d. 363 H) who was buried in the Bāb Salm cemetery in Kairouan:

> "At the head of his tomb there is a marble slab (*lawḥ min ruḫām*) upon which his name, his father's name, the date of his death and other things are inscribed, in beautiful letters the like of which we do not find a second time in the cemeteries of Kairouan. The inscription is actually on both sides (of the slab), and what is written on the front is repeated on the rear. So I said to our teacher Abū l-Faḍl al-Birzalī while we were standing in front of the tomb, 'It came to my mind that this was done because Ibn Masrūr was much revered by the people and they were afraid that the slab could fall down on one of its sides. (Supposing that the inscription was only on one side and the slab fell down with its blank side up, covering the inscription beneath it), somebody approaching (the tomb) after the slab had fallen down might think that there was no inscription (*katb*) at all on the stone, and then it will be trodden upon and covered with earth. Thus the knowledge of the tomb might be lost (lit. his tomb will be effaced), in the same manner as it happened to many of the scholars' tombs (*qubūr al-mašyaḫah*) because there were no inscriptions upon them'".[829]

In another instance, Ibn Nāǧī at-Tanūḫī again returns to the problem of anonymous tombs and the possible lack of inscriptions. The graves in question are the burial places of the judge Sulaymān b. ʿImrān (d. 270 or 277 H) and of Abū Muḥammad (ʿAbd Allāh b. Isḥāq) Ibn at-Tabbān (d. Kairouan 371 H). The passage is also worth quoting in full:

> "His (*sc.* Ibn at-Tabbān's) tomb is not visible any longer (*ġayr ẓāhir*). Therefore, when I came to that place (i.e. the cemetery) and we had reached the middle of the graveyard, I used to call with a loud voice: 'May God have mercy upon you, O Abū Muḥammad Ibn at-Tabbān!' For in the majority of cases the identity of a tomb is not preserved as long as there is no inscription (*kitābah*) upon its tombstone (*ʿalā mašhadihī*). If there is no inscription, it may still be widely-known, but then people will die of a plague and no one will remain from those who know about the tomb. In case there is an inscription

828 MaqqNafḥ (C) III p. 323.

829 This interesting passage also illustrates, among other things, a widespread attitude towards funerary monuments which is reponsible for so much deplorable decay throughout the Islamic lands: when something was in need of restoration or repair, people did not necessarily care to carry that out. Rather, as is clearly implied by the comment of Ibn Nāǧī who certainly knew what he was talking about, a fallen tombstone would just be left lying there and one could not even expect the people to turn it around in order to see whether anything was written on the other side.

(it is different), because even though an ignorant person may be unaware of the identity (or location) of a tomb, somebody else will stumble upon that burial place afterwards. When he has read the inscription, he will inform the others of it and thus the knowledge of it will spread among the people. Similarly, it happened that during our visit to the Bāb Salm cemetery (...) I was told by my paternal uncle Abū ᶜAbd Allāh Muḥammad – may God have mercy upon him! –, 'O my brother, you believe that in our days there is nobody in Kairouan who knows more about the tombs of our scholars than you. So tell me then, where is the tomb of Sulaymān b. ᶜImrān the judge?' I replied that his tomb was not known any longer, but he said that we already had found his tomb and that it was just in front of us, thus I looked at his tombstone (*mašhad*) and I noticed that upon it was inscribed: *This is the tomb of Sulaymān b. ᶜImrān the judge* (...). As a result of this, the location of his tomb soon became known to everybody".[830]

All this led Ibn Nāǧī at-Tanūḫī to the firm conviction that putting an inscription on tombs was desirable in order to safeguard the identity of burial sites, even though the existence of an inscription would not guarantee that the information on it would be correctly understood, either by being misread or because the wording was obscure to the general reader.[831]

To conclude, I cannot help quoting two anecdotes which somehow have to do with the lack of epitaphs.

(1) The first story, told on the authority of ad-Daylamī (author of the *Firdaws al-ʾaḫbār*), reports the miraculous appearance of an "epitaph": three persons travelling in Anatolia heard voices coming from some unburied bones, and when they approached these bones, they were told that the deceased had still to settle a debt of 15 dinars with his wife (because he had not yet fully paid her her dowry). The travellers offered their help and asked, "But how do we know what your name is, and where your home town and your wife are?", and the voice answered "Let one of you beat his hand on the earth". So one of the travellers hit the ground with his hand and an inscription (*manqūš*) appeared in the palm of his hand, giving the name of the deceased, his father's name and his village in writing which could not be wiped away. Only later, when the travellers had paid the debt of the deceased, did the writing disappear.[832]

(2) The second anecdote is taken from Ibn Ṭūlūn's *Qalāʾid* and stresses the importance of oral information when there was no inscription on a tomb: "When the eminent scholar Šaᶜbān al-Āṯārī came to aṣ-Ṣāliḥīyah (north of Damascus) in order to visit a certain tomb he was told, 'Nobody knows where it is except an

830 See also **104**. In DabMaᶜālim II p. 158, Ibn Nāǧī summarised the above-mentioned passage as follows: "The tomb of Sulaymān was not known to us, but then I was told about it by my uncle Abū ᶜAbd Allāh Muḥammad – may God the Exalted have mercy upon him! I think he was the first to make the site of Sulaymān's tomb known in our days, and in the following time his tomb became famous and a site of visitation (*mazār*), known to everybody among the learned and the common people".

831 DabMaᶜālim III p. 174.

832 ŠīrŠadd p. 25.

undertaker called Zaʿtar'. So he went and when he reached the burial area, he found someone who was about to bury a deceased person. He asked 'Who is this, O undertaker?',[833] and the man answered 'This is Zaʿtar'".[834]

4.3.3. Re-using and stealing tombstones

A strange incident involving the re-use of a tombstone is reported from Šīrāz. In a local cemetery, ʿImād ad-Dīn Abū Ṭāhir ʿAbd as-Salām b. Maḥmūd al-Ḥanafī, who died in Šaʿbān 661 H,

> "was buried (...) opposite aš-Šayḫ al-Kabīr.[835] It was said that on the tomb of the sheikh there was a tombstone (*ḥağar*), but it had been removed and another stone had been set up in its place. So Abū Ṭāhir took this stone for its blessing and stipulated that it should be put at the head of his own tomb, in a place which he had explicitly determined. Then he saw aš-Šayḫ al-Kabīr in a dream blaming him for doing so and saying, 'On whose authority do you claim to be the most outstanding Sufi and to have the most right to appropriate this stone to yourself alone?'"[836]

Another case is reported from Biğāyah (modern Algeria) where a tombstone was stolen from the grave of ʿAbd al-Ḥaqq al-Išbīlī, known as Ibn al-Ḫarrāṭ (d. 581 H).[837] His biographer al-Ġubrīnī tells the whole story: "The date of his death is written upon a marble slab (*ruḫāmah*) at his tomb. People say that a Christian took the slab away and brought it to his country. Later he returned it to its place because he regarded it as unlucky (*tašāʾama bihī*). However, afterwards it was stolen again and has not appeared since".[838] According to a story reported by Carsten Niebuhr from his stay in Yemen, the tombstone of a local sheikh was removed from the cemetery at the port of Zabīd after Niebuhr had begun copying the Kufic inscriptions there. The tombstone was found the next day in a hut and the local guardian told him that the saint himself had taken care of the stone.[839]

That the theft of tombstones was not infrequent, especially if they were made of such materials as marble, also becomes clear from a passage in the *Madḫal* of Ibn al-Ḥāğğ (quoted above p. 272). Sometimes tombstones were removed for other

833 I emended the text as edited من هذا الحفار to من هذا يا حفار.

834 ITūlQal I p. 531. For another anecdote involving an undertaker, see *Aġānī* XXIII pp. 73f.

835 Abū ʿAl. M. b. Ḫafīf aḍ-Ḍabbī, d. 371 H.

836 ŠīrŠadd p. 57.

837 Abū M. ʿAbd al-Ḥaqq b. ʿAr. al-Mālikī (Córdoba 510 or 514 – Biğāyah 581 H): IAbbTakm III pp. 120f.; IBaškṢilah IV pp. 4-7; ĠubrʿUnwān pp. 41-4; ḌabbīBuġ pp. 378f.; IʿAHādīṬab IV pp. 125-27; ḎahʿIbar IV pp. 243f. and ḎahTaḏk IV pp. 1350-52; KutFawāt II pp. 256f.; IFarDībāğ p. 277; NZ VI p. 100; SuyḤuffāẓ pp. 481f.; GAL I p. 371 and GALS I p. 634; ZA IV p. 52; EI^2 VIII p. 635; Penelas/Zanón: *Nómina de ulemas andalusíes* p. 66. ʿAbd al-Ḥaqq is mainly remembered for his legal treatise *al-ʾAḥkām* (in two versions, complete and abridged), his monograph on eschatology (*al-ʿĀqibah*, see bibliography), and two further treatises, one about the miracles (*muʿğizāt*) performed by the Prophet, the other on Prophetic medicine.

838 ĠubrʿUnwān p. 44.

839 Niebuhr: *Reisebeschreibung* pp. 322f.

purposes, for example by Marwān b. al-Ḥakam from the tomb of ᶜUṯmān b. Maẓᶜūn in Medina (see above p. 256), or because the deceased was not considered a worthy object of visitation, as with the Meccan mystic Ibn Sabᶜīn (d. 669 H, *cf.* above page 61). In his case, the removal of the tombstone served to obliterate the exact location of the grave and thus to make any visitation of it impossible.

Finally, it could conform to the last wish expressed by the deceased himself that the tombstone on his grave disappeared. A story of that sort is told by Ibn az-Zayyāt, concerning the tomb of Ibn al-Ašᶜaṯ (d. 296 H, see **40**); somebody related:

> "On Saturdays we went out to visit the cemetery and once we visited the burial ground of the Banū l-Ašᶜaṯ. There I saw the marble slab (tombstone, *ruḫāmah*) and examined it, but when I came the next day I could not find that tombstone any more. This made me sad and I slept badly that night, until in a dream I saw a person wearing beautiful clothes. I asked him, 'Who are you, may God have mercy upon you!' He said, 'I am ᶜAbd Allāh b. al-Ašᶜaṯ whose tomb you used to visit. I asked God to take that tombstone away from my tomb. However, if you come to visit me (again), then ask from God what you like at my tomb. I will intercede with God on your behalf, concerning that which you asked from Him".[840]

4.3.4. The destruction of tombs

Funerary inscriptions and tombs which today are lost or of unknown location can be recovered from written sources, yet the various sources, as said before, may not always be trustworthy as to the exact wording and their documentary value is inferior to that of surviving inscriptions. But as it is, much has been lost over the centuries, a fact already deplored by the Syrian traveller and author of a valuable visitation guide (see Chapter 3) Abū l-Ḥasan al-Harawī (d. 611 H):

> "The historians have already written about a number of the Prophet's relatives, his companions and the succeeding generation, about their murder or death in either Syria, Iraq, Ḫurāsān, the Maghrib, the Yemen or the Mediterranean Isles. In most of these places, however, I could not find anything of what the historians mention, for there is no doubt that the tombs of the aforesaid people have disappeared and their traces have vanished. But although their vestiges (*ʾāṯār*) are gone, information (*ʾaḫbār*) about them has been kept alive".[841]

Thus when the original monuments, e.g. tombstones, epitaphs or even whole mausolea, have disappeared we nevertheless may gather useful information about their whereabouts, shape, content and style from literary sources.[842] Many a cemetery guide, e.g. Ibn az-Zayyāt's *Kawākib*, seems an inventory of ruined or otherwise degraded funeral sites. Ibn az-Zayyāt, who often laments the collapse of mausolea or other funerary structures, says at one point: "We made it our duty to mention everybody

840 IZayKawākib pp. 77f.

841 HarIšārāt p. 2.

842 To my knowledge, there are no Arabic illustrated manuscripts showing details of funerary and/or burial practices and structures. There are, however, Persian and Ottoman miniatures which depict such scenes, see Bağçi: *Mavi, mor ve siyah.*

who was interred in these burial places, from the first to the last, because (the historian) al-Quḍāʿī mentioned many burial sites that have fallen into ruins and tombs that are no longer identifiable",[843] the implication being that, if Ibn az-Zayyāt did not mention all sites known to him, later generations would lack the information about many burial sites which by then would be in ruins or even have disappeared.

Those tombs and shrines that were preserved are often little cared for and convey, at least to the western observer, the impression of negligence or even, if put in a more positive light, of simplicity. In this vein, A.V. Williams Jackson concludes his description of the poor mausoleum of the fifth-century dervish poet Bābā Ṭāhir ʿUryān in Hamadān as follows:

> "Far be it from saying that the place 'might make one almost in love with death,' as Shelley said of the resting place of Keats in the Protestant Cemetery at Rome; but there was a marked simplicity in it all, suitable to the simplicity which characterized Bābā Ṭāhir's own verses. I mounted my horse and rode away, carrying with me these thoughts of the scene and living memories of the dervish quatrain-poet of nearly a thousand years ago".[844]

Unfortunately, though, the disappearance or destruction of tombs and other funerary structures (including the epitaphs once there) has always been a frequent phenomenon throughout the Islamic world, nothwithstanding the great importance of tombs and cemeteries in Islamic popular piety. Many tombs and mausolea were destroyed by natural phenomena (earthquakes or floods) or during the ravages of war. In addition, many other burial sites were deliberately demolished or removed. In the case of al-Andalus, cemeteries were discontinued or destroyed after the Christian conquest and funerary monuments were often torn down, their material being re-used for new constructions, mainly churches.[845]

The effects of the *Reconquista* in al-Andalus were often felt immediately, thus the reciter ʿAlī b. Ǧābir ad-Dabbāġ al-Laḫmī, who died in Seville in mid-Šaʿbān 640 H some eight days after the Christian conquest, was not taken to the cemetery but buried secretly in his house, and the hole "was hurriedly carved out with the use of knives".[846] Ibn al-Abbār, who reports this story, also writes about the preacher and traditionist Ibn Šarawīyah (Abū ʿĀmir M. b. Ǧaʿfar, d. Valencia 547 H) that "he was buried (in Valencia) outside the Bīṭālah Gate. His tomb was known there, with the people visiting it for its blessing, until the Christians took over Valencia for the second time towards the end of Ṣafar 636 and obliterated (*ṭms* I) his tomb and all other tombs of the Muslims".[847] — Spanish troops, who stayed in Tunis under the last Ḥafṣid ruler Abū ʿAbd Allāh Muḥammad VI b. al-Ḥasan (r. 981–2 H), dug up the tomb of the famous mystic and patron "saint" of the local mariners Sīdī

843 IZayKawākib p. 56; *cf.* also Taylor: *Vicinity of the Righteous* pp. 42f.

844 Jackson: *Tomb of Bābā Ṭāhir* p. 260. For Bābā Ṭāhir, see also Ehsan Yarshater (ed.): *Encyclopædia Iranica* III, London – New York 1989, pp. 296f. (L.P. Elwell-Sutton).

845 *Cf.* Torres Balbás: *Cementerios* pp. 189ff.

846 IAbbTakm III p. 240.

847 IAbbTakm II p. 13. However, there were exceptions such as the tomb of Abū r-Rabīʿ Sulaymān b. Ibr. b. Hilāl al-Qaysī (5th cent. H) whose grave in Toledo was venerated and visited by the Christian population (IBaškṢilah I p. 200).

Muḥriz b. Ḫalaf (d. 413 H), but they found nothing but sand in it.[848] The Cypriot soldiers who beleaguered and conquered Alexandria in 767 H destroyed a number of mausolea and individual shrines.[849]

The first recorded instance of tombs being removed on purpose by Muslims involves the Prophet himself who, shortly after his arrival in Medina, had a cemetery cleared in order to construct the first mosque in the area. Though the cemetery consisted of tombs of polytheists (making their removal less problematic than in the case of Muslim graves), the story is interesting all the same: "In that area were the tombs of the polytheists, some ruins[850] and some palms. The Messenger of God ordered the tombs to be excavated, the ruins to be torn to the ground and the palms to be cut down".[851]

In later times, it sometimes happened that the tombs or cemeteries of Jews, Christians and other non-Muslims were destroyed,[852] and it might, therefore, be not without historical background that the destruction of cemeteries is referred to in rabbinic pseudepigrapha which deal with the advent of the Muslims and the rise of Islam in Palestine and Syria.[853] Yet also the graveyards of Muslims were often not spared destruction; there are examples of this from all over the Arab-Muslim world:

ISLAMIC WEST. In fourth-century Sūsah (Sousse) it happened that a local ruler (whose exact identity is unclear in the sources) ordered ships to be constructed for the invasion of Sicily. So "the workmen destroyed the Muslim burial sites (*maqābir al-muslimīn*) and supported (*rfd* I) the ships

848 IADīnārMuʾnis p. 176.

849 NuwIlmām II p. 172.

850 The edited texts have *ḫirab,* explained as "ruins", though pre-modern scholars already had noted that different mss. showed other words instead (see FB, the following note).

851 FB VII p. 338 (*manāqib al-ʾanṣār* 46); NawŠMuslim V p. 7; IAĞamrBahğah I p. 589; IQayIġāṯah I pp. 174f.; al-Albānī: *Aḥkām al-ğanāʾiz* p. 237; Memon: *Ibn Taimīya's Struggle* p. 306. See also ZarkAḥkām p. 381 for the tombs of pagans destroyed in order to construct a mosque in the area.

852 E.g. by Ibn Ṭūlūn (r. 254–70, see **39**) when he took up construction work in his new quarter al-Qaṭāʾiʿ north of Fusṭāṭ in 265 H. In this case, Jewish and Christian cemeteries had been cleared by ploughing, see MaqrḪiṭaṭ I p. 315 and MaqrMuq I p. 421. After the conquest of Jerusalem in 583 H, tombs and mausolea belonging to Jews and Christians were destroyed around the Bāb ar-Raḥmah (IWāṣilKurūb II p. 230). In 694 H, a Christian mausoleum containing many tombs was destroyed in Baghdad and turned into a *ribāṭ* with preaching sessions (IFuwaṭīḤaw p. 484). Muslim soldiers opened and plundered tombs in Azerbaijan in 332 H (HamdTakm p. 141). Non-Muslims buried in the area of the *ḥaram* in Mecca were to be exhumed and interred somewhere else (ZarkAḥkām pp. 175 and 271). See also Goitein: *Mediterranean Society* II p. 285: "Since we have (...) a charter given to the Christians of Iraq that their ways of interring their dead would be respected (dated 1138 [CE]), we may assume that this malady of molesting the burials of non-Muslims was rampant. (...) The wording of the Iraqian charter might have been intended to grant protection from still another insult directed against the dead of the non-Muslims: the destruction of, or the prohibition to erect, tombstones and memorial monuments".

853 See Robert Hoyland: *Seeing Islam as Others Saw It. A Survey and Evaluation of Christian, Jewish and Zoroastrian Writings on Early Islam*, Princeton 1997, pp. 310 and 315.

with them.[854] An exception was made, however, for the tomb of Yaḥyā b. ᶜUmar (d. 289 H), because nobody dared to destroy it. Some of the black workers were then questioned about this and said that they saw upon it a great light which prevented them from destroying it".[855]

EGYPT. In 490 H, a mob stirred up by Shiite propaganda destroyed tombs of Sunnite "righteous men" (*ṣāliḥīn*).[856] In what is today the Southern Qarāfah cemetery in Cairo, the body of the mystic al-Kīzānī (M. b. Ibr., d. 562 H), who had been buried beside the tomb of aš-Šāfiᶜī, was unearthed[857] in 581 H and his grave destroyed, following an official order according to which his final remains (*rimmatuhū*) were to be thrown into the Nile. However, people did not carry out that last order and transferred his body to another tomb in the Qarāfah.[858] Again in the Qarāfah, the mausoleum (*qubbah*) containing the tombs of ᶜAmr b. al-ᶜĀṣ and Abū Baṣrah was destroyed by sultan Ṣalāḥ ad-Dīn (Saladin) Yūsuf in order to erect a new building on the site.[859] A few years later, in the year 608 H, work was completed at the Ayyubid mausoleum of aš-Šāfiᶜī,[860] and during the construction work "many bones were excavated from former tombs and buried in another area of the Qarāfah"[861] (or, according to other sources, they were brought to the mausoleum of as-Sayyidah Zaynab instead).[862]

ḤIĞĀZ. For the ᶜAlid tombs in the Medinan Baqīᶜ cemetery, as-Samhūdī relates the following: "The fact that the sites of the tombs of Fāṭimah – may God the Exalted be pleased with her! – and other first-generation Muslims are not known with certainty[863] has to do with the practice of that time not to build over the tombs or to plaster them. Moreover, the *ʾahl al-bayt* (i.e. the ᶜAlīds) – may God the Exalted be pleased with them! – met at all times the opposition of the (Meccan) governors. Thus al-Masᶜūdī mentioned that (the caliph) al-Mutawakkil ordered in the year 236 (...) the erasure of the place (*maḥwu ʾarḍihī*) of the tomb of al-Ḥusayn b. ᶜAlī, to destroy it and to leave no trace of it, further to punish those who were found in its vicinity".[864] (For sites in Iraq, see also below).

SYRIA and PALESTINE. The cemetery (*ğabbānah*) of Damascus was used for about 100 years to raise crops and "thus the local tombs are not any longer known".[865] Likewise in Damascus, a new mausoleum (*qubbah*) was constructed in 923 H above the tomb of Ibn ᶜArabī in Damascus and so

854 A modern commentator of this slightly obscure passage explains that the workmen took the slabs and marbles from the tombs in order to use them as ballast into the ship's hold. Interestingly, this very practice of using tombstones as ballast was also put forward in the contemporary debate about the earliest Islamic gravestones that were found in Java (Indonesia). According to one theory, these stones had reached the island in the hold of merchant ships, accidentally as it were, and thus cannot be claimed as evidence for the Islamisation of Java (personal communication from Peter Pink).

855 MālRiyāḍ I pp. 494f.; ᶜIyāḍTartīb I p. 363 and III p. 239.

856 IMuyassarAḫbār p. 65.

857 I read نبش instead of نشر.

858 MaqrMuq V p. 82.

859 NZ I p. 130 (quotes from al-Muwaffaq Ibn ᶜUṯmān).

860 *Cf.* also above p. 220. The description of his tomb before the Ayyubid re-construction, from al-Quḍāᶜī's *Kitāb Ḫiṭaṭ Miṣr*, is preserved in YāqIršād VI pp. 393f.

861 MaqrḪiṭaṭ II p. 462; *cf.* also MacKenzie: *Ayyubid Cairo* p. 149.

862 SaḫTuḥfAḥbāb pp. 199f.

863 For more details on the tomb of Fāṭimah, see Beinhauer-Köhler: *Fāṭima* pp. 270-86.

864 SamWafāʾ III p. 906; *cf.* also AFidāʾMuḫt II p. 68; NZ III p. 190; MaqrMuq III p. 616; ṬurayḥīMunt p. 7. The Mamluk caliphs, most notably al-Mutawakkil, also destroyed a number of other Shiite shrines in Iraq, see Rāġib: *Premiers monuments* p. 33.

865 IŠadAᶜlāq II (Damascus) p. 186 and above p. 246, n. 575.

they dug out a number of graves in order to build the foundation in their place. This was done at night because they were afraid of what the people would say.[866] The tomb of ᶜUbādah b. aṣ-Ṣāmit al-Anṣārī (d. 34 H) was no longer found in Jerusalem after the Christian occupation, together with other shrines at the Bāb Arīḥā.[867]

IRAQ. In Baghdad, ᶜUmar b. Bahlīqā aṭ-Ṭaḥḥān (d. 560 H) founded a mosque and for that purpose had bought some ground "upon which there were burial sites with many deceased (*turab fīhā mawtā*), so they were exhumed and the mosque was built". Ibn al-Ǧawzī, who reports this story, goes on to say that "when ᶜUmar died he was buried at the entrance gate of this mosque, distant from its wall.[868] Then his tomb was opened after some days, his body taken out and interred again (at a place) attached to the wall of the mosque, in order that it might become known to everybody that he was the founder of this mosque. A perspicacious contemporary was astonished by that fact and remarked, 'This man was quick to unearth a number of deceased persons, to have their bodies taken out and to turn their burial site (*turbatahum*) into a mosque, so he was condemned to be unearthed himself after his burial'".[869] Likewise in Baghdad, "Abū Ṣāliḥ al-Ǧīlī (d. 633 H) was buried by the side of Ibn Ḥanbal, nay it was even said: together with Ibn Ḥanbal, and this was taken care of by the mob and the common people. But those responsible for it were captured, punished and locked away; Abū Ṣāliḥ was exhumed at night and carried to another place after some days. His tomb was obliterated and nobody knew the site of his burial place".[870] A number of mausolea were destroyed by fire in Baghdad during the street-fights of the year 443 H.[871] In Kūfah, the caliph al-Manṣūr (d. 158 H) had a trench dug and for that purpose the people removed their buried dead from that site and interred them somewhere else.[872]

Imam aš-Šāfiᶜī witnessed the destruction of tombs in Mecca: "I saw some of the governors (*wulāh*) destroying funerary structures in Mecca, but I did not notice any of the jurists raise his voice against it".[873] The problem of whether tombs shall be destroyed or not was still virulent some 700 years after as becomes apparent from a fatwa issued by Ibn Ḥaǧar al-Haytamī:

> "*Quaeritur*: Given that the tomb of one of the companions of the Messenger of God is sheltered by a mausoleum (*qubbah*) and someone wishes to be buried beside it though there is not sufficient space to do so unless a small part of the (already existing) mausoleum is removed: is this removal permitted? If you consider it permitted, it will be done, but if you consider it forbidden, then how would that agree with what aš-Šāfiᶜī said, 'I saw the governors in Mecca ordering the destruction of funerary structures,[874] and the jurists did not raise their voice against them'?

866 IṬūlMufāk p. 373. *Cf.* also IṬūlQal II p. 537; ŠaᶜrṬab I p. 188; Geoffroy: *Proche-Orient* p. 51; Knysh: *Ibn ᶜArabi* p. 134 with note 117.

867 ᶜUlaymīUns I pp. 261 and 296; *cf.* also MaqdMuṯīr pp. 315f.

868 *al-ḥāʾiṭ*: I presume that the *qiblah* wall is meant.

869 IǦawzīMunt X p. 212.

870 *Wāfī* XXVII p. 73.

871 AFidāʾMuḫt II p. 171.

872 IADunyāQubūr (A) p. 91; IRaǧAhwāl pp. 88f. and 94f.

873 ŠāfUmm I p. 464 = MuwMuršid I p. 66. *Cf.* also NawŠMuslim VII pp. 37f.; Leisten: *Architektur für Tote* p. 11f. and *Attitudes* p. 18.

874 *Cf.* also IMuflFurūᶜ II p. 272.

Respondeo: If this mausoleum is built in an appointed (i.e. 'communal' *or* public) cemetery, as is normally the case with local burial sites, then the destruction is justified and everybody is entitled to do so. If, however, (the mausoleum is built) only upon a specific grave (i.e. on land privately owned) and not in a public cemetery, then nobody has the right to destroy it, for example if someone wishes to be buried beside it, as mentioned in the *quaestio*".[875]

In another fatwa, al-Haytamī arrived at the following conclusion: "It is not permitted to take (stones or bricks) from the wall of a mosque (in order to close a burial niche), even if the mosque is lying in ruins".[876] He likewise pronounces it forbidden to use stones taken from other tombs in order to close a burial niche or to build a new grave, except when the owner (of the existing tomb) gives his consent.[877] Existing tombs should thus not be demolished on purpose, e.g. by re-using their construction materials for new buildings. However, from a Shiite source we learn that once a burial monument had been destroyed or fallen into ruins, it was considered detestable to renovate (*ǧdd* II) or re-build the monument.[878] In eleventh-century Damascus it happened that a man had bought stones from aṣ-Ṣāliḥīyah for the construction of his father's tomb. When the stones were under way, the dead father appeared in a dream, saying that these stones must not be used for his tomb but returned to where they came from. Hence it was discovered that the stones had been removed from older graves in aṣ-Ṣāliḥīyah, so one put them back to their former sites and purchased a load of freshly cut stones instead.[879]

On other occasions, tombs and mausolea were not destroyed outright but kept in a delapidated condition that was bound to lead, over the centuries, to their total destruction. A particularly telling example of such negligence is found in the account of a visit to the tomb of the poet Abū l-ʿAlāʾ al-Maʿarrī (d. 449 H, **111**), as related by (Ibn) al-Qifṭī (d. 646 H):

"After I had entered the mosque of Maʿarrat an-Nuʿmān at prayer-time, (...) I noticed a man from al-Maʿarrah among the people. His name was Sāṭiʿ and I had met him before in Aleppo. When I asked him for the tomb of Abū l-ʿAlāʾ (al-Maʿarrī), I was shown the way and found the site in an open courtyard amidst the houses of his descendants. From the courtyard, we entered a door and inside there was the tomb, without any signs of ornament on the part of his family. On the tomb I saw mallows broken forth and dried up, and the whole room was in the outmost state of decay and negligence. I went around the cenotaph and recited the Qurʾān in front of it".[880]

The traveller at-Tiǧānī visited the cemeteries of Tripoli (Libya) at the beginning of the eighth century H and reports: "I visited all the cemeteries of Tripoli and I found

875 HaytFatFiqh II p. 7.

876 HaytFatFiqh II p. 23.

877 HaytFatFiqh II p. 25.

878 ṬūsīMabsūṭ I p. 187.

879 ĠazLuṭf I p. 215.

880 QifṭīInbāh I pp. 70f. The same account, though somewhat abbreviated, is given in IḪallWaf I p. 115.

that they were crammed with deceased persons (*banū ʾĀdam*). Their bones covered the surface of the earth, so you could not see a hand's breadth of soil without a skull or a bone lying upon it, especially in the northern part of the cemetery".[881]

Finally, we even hear that God himself made graves disappear, obviously as a sign of his grace. So it happened with the tomb of Uways al-Qaranī (see above p. 257). Another case is that of sheikh Zayn ad-Dīn ʿAbd ar-Raḥmān al-Kardabīsī al-Maġribī, a righteous man who died in Jerusalem before 800 H and was buried in the Māmillā cemetery. It belonged to the divine favours (or miracle-like blessings, *karāmāt*) granted to him by God that one day somebody who had acquired much faith in him, planned to construct a mausoleum (*qubbah*) over al-Kardabīsī's tomb, yet when he went there he could not find it any longer.[882] But here we enter the realm of the miraculous; the destruction of the vast majority of pre-modern funerary structures in Islam was due to human activity or the forces of nature.

In some rare cases, it was the epitaphs alone which survived the demolition or gradual collapse of funerary structures. Thus parts of al-Maʿarrī's epitaph (*cf.* **111**) can still be seen at his burial place, though his mausoleum, as described by (Ibn) al-Qifṭī (see above), has largely vanished. The same holds true for Abū l-Ḥasan al-Harawī's tomb in Aleppo, of which only the splendidly executed cenotaph (with inscriptions in floral Kufic) has been preserved, while the mausoleum itself was destroyed by the Mongols some centuries ago. Its remnants, including a great number of inscribed stone blocks, were then re-used for the crude walls which today surround the shrine, and the inscriptions they bear can today only be reconstructed with considerable difficulty (see Vol. I pp. 95ff.). In many other cases, however, even the epitaphs did not escape the vicissitudes of time, and often it is only by recourse to literary sources that we learn of their former existence and are able to reconstruct their shape and contents. Burial sites whose monuments have been preserved are often places of more or less continued veneration, but other sites have survived as well, depending on local conditions and notwithstanding the fact that some of these might be dubbed "secular mausolea", a characterisation which, however, makes little sense if applied to Islamic burial structures and funerary architecture in general.[883]

4.4. Summary

During the centuries of pre-modern Islam, epitaphs were often considered superfluous and declared disapproved of by the legal scholars. An exception was made for the tombs of saintly persons where the writing down of the bare name could help to ensure that the exact location of the tomb remained known. Otherwise, written information of any kind on tombs – as also in mausolea and tomb-mosques – was deemed unnecessary. This is due to the fact that the anonymity of graves did not

881 TiǧRiḥlah p. 267.

882 ʿUlaymīUns II p. 244.

883 *Cf.* Hillenbrand: *Islamic Architecture* p. 262.

diminish the benefit of visiting tombs or cemeteries, especially "if the purpose of the visit is nothing but a reminder of mortality (*taḏakkur al-mawt*) and (the contemplation of) the hereafter, because in this case it might be enough just to look at the tombs without knowing who is actually buried in them".[884] If nothing else, this divergence of legal discourse not only from common practice, but also from many other learned and/or literary discourses shows again that legal scholarship does not represent the unique, still less the exclusively valid Muslim way of looking at things.

Reconsidering the different theoretical positions arrived at by Muslim scholars, we can say that it was considered permitted or even desirable to mark the grave by mounds and tombstones (or similar objects serving as such), though not a few scholars regarded their absence as preferable and thus opted for the "levelling" or "flattening" of graves. Greater unanimity is found in respect of the construction of mausolea or tomb-mosques over and around burial sites: this was generally seen as disapproved of or even prohibited. There are relatively few prescriptions in legal literature and in Ḥadīṯ collections as to epitaphs, but a number of detailed fatwas from between the eighth and tenth centuries H exist. The opinions voiced in these sources do not encourage the display of inscriptions, but rather urge the contrary. If at all, epitaphs should be limited to bearing the name of the deceased in order to safeguard his tomb from oblivion, especially if the deceased was known for his piety and his tomb amply venerated. The use of Qurʾānic verses in epitaphs was unanimously rejected, at least in theory.

Strangely enough, the theoretical rule governing funerary inscriptions, although a marginal problem, seems to have had more impact on practice than any other of the theoretical rulings pertaining to the field of burial. Or put differently: the attitudes reflected by practice did match the attitudes expressed in theory more closely than in other cases. At least this is the conclusion to be drawn if one considers the high percentage of anonymous tombs, both as described in the sources and as witnessed in the reality. After all, many of the persons whose tombs were or are not (or only vaguely) known were not obscure figures but famous scholars, people of some standing or even members of the Prophet's family. Thus it seems that writing was resorted to less intensively in connection with burial sites than might be expected if one recalls what a dominant feature writing has been in Islamic culture. If one were to confine one's interest strictly to epitaphs, this startling fact might be said to be the most important result of the present study.

884 ŠirwḤāš III p. 200.

3 "Many Books have already been Composed ..." *The Arabic Literary Genre of Visitation and Cemetery Guides*

1. *Introduction*

The Arabic literary genre which is most closely connected with burial sites and hence with funerary epigraphy is visitation and cemetery guides. More than anywhere else, it is in works of this genre that epitaphs and their context are regularly dealt with in detail. For anybody interested in funerary epigraphy and related issues, works of that sort are a source of prime importance; a considerable number of the epitaphs collected and discussed in Chapter 4 are found in Arabic cemetery guides.

In view of the outstanding role of cemeteries and the general significance of the mortuary cult in its Islamic guise, it does not seem surprising that this gave rise, eventually, to a literary genre of its own. The purpose of that genre was, plainly, to provide guides for the visitation of the sites dealt with, though in many cases there is also a markedly historical interest in the persons buried in a certain place. Depending on whether the practical or rather the historical interest was paramount, these works concentrate either on the topographical and external features of the sites described or give ample space to the biographies of the persons buried in them. The Shiite guides, on the other hand, are replete with Traditions and litanies to be recited at the individual shrines, and are therefore best seen as devotional literature.

The great cemeteries were frequently visited for the *barakah* ("blessing") of their shrines as well as for a number of other reasons, since they were not considered places where everything is the reverse of life (see Chapter 1). Some people would also organise tours in order to visit the burial sites of a certain region, such as al-Yāfiʿī (who went round the shrines of Egypt and Palestine)[1] and the ninth-century Egyptian mystic Midyan b. Aḥmad al-Ašmūnī who undertook a journey to visit the shrines of the righteous in Syria (*as-safar ʾilā ziyārat aṣ-ṣāliḥīn bi-š-Šām*).[2] This, on the other hand, gave to the local inhabitants the opportunity to make their living

1 ITaġrManh VII p. 77.

2 ŠaʿrṬab II p. 101. The context makes it probable that no living colleagues of his were meant, but the wording in itself is ambiguous, see for comparison the passage in ITaġrManh II p. 479:

by showing visitors around the much-frequented graveyards. There is little information about such "tour-guides" in the literary sources, but we know at least of a person called Sāsī az-Zawwār who led people to the tombs of famous or pious persons and told them their stories and achievements in ninth-century Kairouan.[3]

Among orientalists, the literary genre of visitation and cemetery guides has been called, rather generically, "Pilgerführer", "guides à l'usage des pèlerins"[4] or pilgrimage guides.[5] However, this designation is misleading. First, because there is a marked difference between the Sunnite and Shiite works of that genre; second, because within this genre we have treatises that either deal with one particular cemetery or with sites in many different towns and regions; third, and most importantly, because the terms "pilgrim" and "pilgrimage" should be reserved for the actual pilgrimage, that is, the *ḥaǧǧ*.[6] I thus propose a division into the sub-genres of (1) "visitation guides" and (2) "cemetery guides". The first sub-genre comprises Sunnite works that deal with burial sites and shrines of various towns or regions – such as Abū l-Ḥasan al-Harawī's *Kitāb al-ʾIšārāt ʾilā maʿrifat az-ziyārāt* – as well as the Shiite *ziyārah*-books. The second sub-genre includes works that deal with a specific cemetery – such as aš-Šaybī's *aš-Šaraf al-ʾaʿlā fī ḏikr qubūr maqburat al-Maʿlā* – or with the burial ground(s) of a particular town, such as the Cairene cemetery guides.

2. *Visitation guides*

In Arabic Sunnite literature, we mainly come across cemetery guides, while visitation guides are rare. The most important among these is undoubtedly the treatise called "Indications to the Knowledge of Visitation Sites" (*Kitāb al-ʾIšārāt ʾilā maʿrifat az-ziyārāt*)[7] by Abū l-Ḥasan al-Harawī (d. 611 H)[8] who was "always restlessly travelling and used to scribble upon the walls. There is hardly a famous place (...) that does not bear his writing".[9] Abū l-Ḥasan provides in his treatise an exhaustive list

wa-kāna (...) kaṯīra z-ziyārati li-ṣ-ṣāliḥīna l-ʾaḥyāʾi minhum wa-l-ʾamwāt ("he often visited the righteous, both the living ones and the dead").

3 DabMaʿālim III p. 66.

4 Sayyid: *Genre de Khiṭaṭ* p. 90 and Rāġib: *Inventaire*.

5 *Cf.* Taylor: *Vicinity of the Righteous* p. 5 and *passim*.

6 In fact, visitation and cemetery guides never bear the term *ḥaǧǧ* (or derivatives) in their titles, because the visitation of every other place besides the Meccan Kaʿbah was not conceived of as "pilgrimage", but as *ziyārah*, "visitation".

7 Sometimes abbreviated as *Kitāb az-Ziyārāt* or *Kitāb fī maʿrifat az-ziyārāt*, e.g. in the Escorial ms. described in Casiri: *Bibliotheca* II p. 172.

8 ʿAlī b. Abī Bakr al-Ḥalabī aš-Šāfiʿī (d. Aleppo, mid-Ramaḍān 611 H). For his biography, see MunḏTakm II pp. 315f.; IMuḥKunūz I pp. 319-22; ḤḤ I p. 96; EI² III p. 178; SourdelLieux pp. xi-xxv; ZA IV p. 266. *Cf.* also **5** and Volume I pp. 95ff.

9 MunḏTakm II p. 315.

of cemeteries, mausolea and tombs scattered throughout the Islamic world between Morocco, Iraq and Yemen. His survey includes the larger cemeteries of Baghdad, Cairo, Damascus, Mecca and Medina as well as many lesser known sites in Anatolia, Sicily or Cyprus, though understandably he devotes special attention to Syria and Palestine. Hundreds of burial places and shrines are briefly described. Apart from Muslim graves we find many Jewish and Christian tombs listed, especially if these are connected with the great strand of monotheist salvation history (e.g. the Biblical prophets) and were thus also frequently visited by Muslim pilgrims.[10]

In his introduction, al-Harawī claims to have described in his guide book "the shrines I visited; the marvels, buildings and structures I saw by myself; the idols, ruins (*ʾāṯār*) and apotropaic signs I noticed in the inhabitated quarter and in the civilised zone (of this world)".[11] Some pages later, he again stresses the fact that he was widely travelled: "I visited places and travelled regions for many years. Most of what I saw I have forgotten, and what I witnessed with my own eyes has faded from my memory. No voyager or pious wanderer, nor the mere travellers and god-fearing strollers will ever attain what I have done, unless it is one who roams the globe on his own feet and can bear witness with soul and pen to the things I am about to describe (in my book)".[12]

In general, al-Harawī highly valued the importance of first-hand knowledge, that is, of having seen and inspected locations by himself. Yet on the other hand, he left no doubt that he considered information taken from written sources superior to the information possibly gained from the inspection of a site. This becomes clear in the introduction to his treatise where al-Harawī points out the importance of written information (as transmitted in books) in contrast with eyewitness evidence:

> "Historians have already written about a number of the Prophet's relatives, his companions and the succeeding generation, about their murder or death in either Syria, Iraq, Ḫurāsān, the Maghrib, Yemen, or the Mediterranean Isles. In most of these places, however, I could not find anything of what the historians mention, for there is no doubt that the tombs of the aforesaid people have disappeared and their traces have vanished, so that their vestiges (*ʾāṯār*) are gone, yet information (*ʾaḫbār*) about them is kept alive".[13]

10 For the widespread phenomenon of Near Eastern pilgrimage sites common to all three monotheist religions, see Ayoub: *Cult and culture* (with further literature). Visiting non-Muslim shrines was heavily disputed among scholars, though many defended this usage with the following argument: "If the visitation of tombs is made with the aim of contemplation and as a *meditatio mortis*, then this is recommended in all instances and all tombs are equally valid for that purpose" (ŠubrḤāš III p. 36, quoting as-Subkī).

11 HarIšārāt p. 1.

12 *Op. cit.* p. 3. In a biography of al-Harawī we read therefore that "he toured the world and ceaselessly moved from shrine to shrine, traversing the globe on land and sea, through the plains and over the mountains: every place was fine with him to arrive at" (IMuḥKunūz I p. 319). The melancholic passage cited from al-Harawī is reminiscent of the inscriptions in his mausoleum (in Aleppo) and upon his cenotaph that are dealt with elsewhere (see Volume I p. 108 and **5**).

13 HarIšārāt p. 2.

Nevertheless, in view of his favourable attitude towards travelling and visiting sites one should expect the author to have made much use of the information he found *in situ*, that is, mainly inscriptions and, in our case, epitaphs. However, this expectation is only partially fulfilled by the author, and it is certainly not the case, as claimed by M. Casiri, that in this work *multa virorum piorum Epitaphia referuntur*;[14] those few epitaphs mentioned or cited there report merely the name of the deceased and/or his date of death.[15] Thus al-Ḥarawī's treatise is similar to works of travel literature, e.g. Ibn Baṭṭūṭah's travel journal, which list many shrines but quote few epitaphs.[16]

The sub-genre of Arabic Shiite visitation guides (called *ziyārāt* for short)[17] precedes the Sunnite works, including the earliest cemetery guides, by at least two centuries. However, up to the thirteenth century H, those works mainly contain litanies and Traditions exalting the individual burial places of the Prophet, some of his companions and the later Imams, but they do not give historical or other information. We learn nothing of the actual location and shape of the shrines dealt with, and epitaphs are not quoted or alluded to. For the study of Islamic funerary epigraphy they are therefore without any serious value.

The earliest Shiite visitation guide may well be the *Kitāb az-Ziyārāt* compiled by al-Ḥasan b. ᶜAlī b. Faḍḍāl at-Taymī al-Kūfī (d. 224 H), which has not been preserved.[18] More influential are the guides produced during the fourth and fifth centuries H such as Ibn Qūlūyah's (Ǧaᶜfar b. M. al-Qummī, d. 367 H or after) *Kāmil az-Ziyārāt*, Ibn Dāᵓūd al-Qummī's (d. 368 H or after) *Kitāb al-Mazārāt al-kabīr*,[19] aš-Šayḫ al-Mufīd's (d. 413 H) *Kitāb al-Mazār* and aṭ-Ṭūsī's (d. 460 H) *Miṣbāḥ al-mutahaǧǧid*. Later works which gained some popularity are *al-Mazār al-kabīr* by as-Sayyid al-Murtaḍā and *Tuḥfat az-zāᵓirīn* by al-Maǧlisī ("a manual for attaining merits through pilgrimage").[20]

14 Casiri: *Bibliotheca* II p. 172.

15 E.g. the epitaph of ᶜUrwah b. Ṯābit on Cyprus, recently studied, on the basis of al-Harawī's writing, in Amikam Elad: *Community of Believers of 'Holy Men' and 'Saints' or Community of Muslims? The Rise and Development of Early Muslim Historiography*, in: Journal of Semitic Studies 47 (2002), pp. 241-308 (here: pp. 284-6).

16 For the tombs and venerated shrines mentioned in Ibn Baṭṭūṭah's writing, see the useful list in Wha: *Baraka* pp. 155-255.

17 *Cf.* Ayoub: *Redemptive Suffering* pp. 21f. and 254-8; Pinault: *Zaynab bint ᶜAlī*; *cf.* above p. 31.

18 IḤaǧLisān II p. 225; Rāǧib: *Inventaire* p. 259.

19 GAS I p. 544; Rāǧib: *Inventaire* p. 260.

20 This treatise is analysed in Donaldson: *Shiᵓite Religion* pp. 147-51. Popular modern visitation guides are the three-volume collection *Miftāḥ al-ǧannāt fī l-ᵓadᶜiyah wa-l-ᵓaᶜmāl wa-ṣ-ṣalawāt wa-z-ziyārāt* by as-Sayyid al-Amīn Muḥsin al-ᶜĀmilī al-Ḥusaynī as well as al-Qummī's *Mafātīḥ al-ǧinān* (see bibliography). Modern Shiite treatises dealing with the visitation of shrines in general are mentioned in Nakash: *Visitation of the Shrines* pp. 159-62.

3. *Cemetery guides*

The bulk of Sunnite works composed on the visitation of tombs and burial sites deals with specific towns or particular cemeteries. As such they are closely related to topographical, historiographical, hagiographical and biographical works which are each also often concerned with a single town; all these works share much the same material and their authors frequently rely upon each other. The devotional aspect is in no case paramount (and sometimes not even perceptible) in Sunnite cemetery guides. The earliest Sunnite cemetery guides were composed in the sixth century H. Their geographical distribution ranges from the Islamic West to Persia in the Islamic East.

3.1. The Islamic West

The first and earliest western literary work dealing with the burial sites of a town stems from the first half of the seventh century H and concerns, as far as we know, tombs located in Córdoba, being an "all-encompassing treatise (*taʾlīfuhū l-maǧmūʿ*) about the tombs of the righteous (*qubūr aṣ-ṣāliḥīn*) in Córdoba"[21] by the traditionist and reciter Abū l-Qāsim al-Qāsim (*sic*) Ibn aṭ-Ṭaylasān (Córdoba *c.*575 – Málaga 642 H).[22] His cemetery guide, known through a quotation by Ibn al-Abbār, has not come to light yet nor does it seem to have been preserved at all; Ḥāǧǧī Ḫalīfah adds that the work amounted to one volume, its abdrigement to one fascicle.[23]

The exact title of Ibn aṭ-Ṭaylasān's cemetery guide is not quoted by Ibn al-Abbār, but we know that the work was probably called *at-Tabyīn ʿan manāqib man ʿurifa qabruhū min aṣ-ṣaḥābah wa-t-tābiʿīn wa-l-ʿulamāʾ az-zāhidīn*, "Elucidation of the Merits of those Companions (of the Prophet), (their) Followers and Ascetic Scholars whose Tomb is Known"; ḤḪ I p. 343, on the other hand, renders the title as *at-Tabyīn ʿan manāqib man ʿurifa bi-Qurṭubah min at-tābiʿīn wa-l-ʿulamāʾ aṣ-ṣāliḥīn*, with قبره and بقرطبة being rather similar in the Arabic script. However, that the treatise dealt with tombs in Córdoba is clear from the afore-mentioned remark of Ibn al-Abbār, so the variant in the title is of little significance. Ibn aṭ-Ṭaylasān's treatise is also cited by the former title in a biography of his pupil Abū Muḥammad ʿAbd Allāh b. Aḥmad b. ʿUbayd Allāh an-Nifzī al-Qurṭubī (d. Sabtah 686 H).[24]

The second western work on burial sites and epitaphs was compiled around 915 H or little later by al-Ḥasan b. Muḥammad al-Wazzān az-Zayyātī al-Fāsī ("Leo Africanus").[25] In his *Descrittione dell'Africa*,[26] he speaks at length about the cemeteries

21 IAbbTakm III p. 231.

22 For him, see ĞazṬab II p. 23; *Wāfī* XXIV pp. 160f.; SuyBuġ II p. 261; DāʾūdīṬab II pp. 46f.; ŠḎ V pp. 215f.; ZA V p. 181. Neither author nor work(s) are listed in GAL(S).

23 ḤḪ I p. 343.

24 IQāḍīDurrah III pp. 67f.

25 Born in Granada between 894 and 901, d. in Tunis *c.*955 H, see GALS II p. 710; EI² V pp. 723f.; EAL II pp. 466f.

26 This work first appeared in print in the first volume of Giovan Battista Ramusio: *Navigationi et viaggi*, Venice 1550 CE, but it had been already completed in 1526 CE.

outside Fez, and in this context he does not fail to mention that "I took great care to collect all the epitaphs which I saw, not only in Fez, but in the entire Maghrib. I put them together in a little book and gave it as a gift to the brother of the present king who had succeeded (the throne) after their father, the old king,[27] had died".[28] This is further corroborated by another passage in his *Descrittione* where he describes the mausoleum of the Marīnid rulers in Chella: "I was inside that room and saw there 30 tombs of those rulers, and I wrote down all the epitaphs at that site. This happened in the year 915 of the Hiğrah".[29] As far as we know, this collection of epitaphs, copied from tombstones in Fez and other cities of the Maghrib, has not been preserved.

3.2. Egypt

When compared with the literary output of the West, nothing of which has survived, the range of cemetery guides produced in Egypt is impressive, a fact already noted by the Arab scholars: "Many books have already been composed about the persons buried in the Qarāfah".[30] A considerable number of these are extant and some three of them have so far been edited. The unusual size of the Cairene cemeteries, the impressive mass of funerary structures and monuments they contain, and the fact that for centuries they have been the privileged burial place for a great number of distinguished individuals easily explains the lively interest Muslim scholars took in those areas.

The works which may be properly said to belong to the literary genre of Cairene cemetery guides have already been researched in detail by Yūsuf Rāġib.[31] With minor exceptions, his findings are still valid. In the following, therefore, only those works are presented which have been made use of in the present volume.

(1) The first of these is the *Muršid al-zuwwār ʾilā qubūr al-ʾabrār* [or *al-ʾaḫyār*] ("The Guide of the Visitors to the Tombs of the Pious"), alternatively entitled *ad-Durr al-munaẓẓam fī ziyārat al-Muqaṭṭam* ("Pearls on a String: The Visitation of the Muqaṭṭam"),[32] by Muwaffaq ad-Dīn Ibn ᶜUṯmān (d. 615 H). This is the earliest cemetery guide to Cairo which has been preserved and edited.

27 I. e. the Waṭṭāsid ruler Abū ᶜAl. aš-Šayḫ Muḥammad I b. Ya. (r. 876–910 H).

28 "E io posi molta cura in raccoglier tutti gli epitaffi che io viddi, non solamente in Fez ma in tutta la Barberia: e questi ho ridotti in un piccolo volume, del quale feci dono al fratello del re che vive oggidì, quando morì il loro padre re vecchio" (AfricDescr [it.] 3:50) = "J'ai pris grand soin de recueillir toutes les épitaphes que j'ai vues non seulement à Fez, mais dans toute la Berbérie, et je les ai réunies dans un petit volume dont j'ai fait cadeau au frère du roi qui règne aujourd'hui lors de la mort de leur père, le vieux roi" (AfricDescr [fr.] I p. 231).

29 "Io fui in questa sala e viddivi trenta sepolture di quei signori, e scrissi tutti gli epitaffii che v'erano. Fu l'anno novecentoquindici di legira" (AfricDescr [it.] 3:10).

30 See MaqrḪiṭaṭ II p. 445. There is a similar remark in IẒuhFaḍMiṣr p. 193.

31 See especially his *Inventaire*. The monograph Taylor: *Vicinity of the Righteous* adds nothing new and depends largely on Rāġib's study.

32 E.g. in the ms. Bodleian Library 3049 (also cited by M. Muranyi in EI² VIII p. 829).

al-Muwaffaq Abū l-Qāsim ᶜAr. b. Abī l-Ḥaram Makkī[33] b. Abī ᶜAmr ᶜUṯmān al-Ḫazraǧī as-Saᶜdī[34] aš-Šāriᶜī aš-Šāfiᶜī:[35] MundTakm II p. 434; SaḫIᶜlān p. 105 = Rosenthal: *Historiography* p. 427; GAL II p. 34 and GALS II p. 30; Rāġib: *Inventaire* pp. 265-9; Taylor: *Vicinity of the Righteous* p. 229; Sayyid: *Genre de Khiṭaṭ* pp. 90f.

Among the other guides, al-Muwaffaq's proved to be the most influential and was taken up in a number of later guides,[36] but also in historiographical and topographical works, e.g. by Ibn Taġrī Birdī, al-Maqrīzī and others.[37]

(2) Some two hundred years later, the guide entitled *al-Kawākib as-sayyārah fī tartīb az-ziyārah fī l-Qarāfatayn al-kubrā wa-ṣ-ṣuġrā* ("The Planets: The Arrangement of the Visitation of the Greater and Lesser Qarāfah [Cemeteries]") was composed by Ibn az-Zayyāt (d. 805 or 814 H).

Šams ad-Dīn Abū ᶜAl. M. b. Nāṣir ad-Dīn M. b. Ǧalāl ad-Dīn ᶜAl. b. ᶜUmar al-ᶜAbbāsī al-Anṣārī al-Azharī[38] as-Suᶜūdī,[39] Ibn az-Zayyāt, an Egyptian scholar and mystic: MaqrSulūk III p. 1110 (records his death in 805 H); ḌL IX p. 231 (gives both dates); *Ḏayl* ḤḪ II p. 392; Mubārak: *Ḫiṭaṭ* X p. 89; GAL II p. 131 and GALS II p. 162; Rāġib: *Inventaire* pp. 275f.; ZA VII p. 44; Taylor: *Vicinity of the Righteous* pp. 230ff.; Sayyid: *Genre de Khiṭaṭ* p. 91.

This work, completed in Raǧab 804 H, was printed in Cairo in 1325/1907 and reprinted in Baghdad (see bibliography). Arguably, this is the most important and certainly the most substantial book on the burial sites of Cairo we have. Nūr ad-Dīn as-Saḫāwī called it "a well-known book" and took it as model for his own cemetery guide (see next item).

(3) Finally, we have, from the ninth century H, the *Tuḥfat al-ʾaḥbāb wa-buġyat aṭ-ṭullāb fī l-ḫiṭaṭ wa-l-mazārāt wa-t-tarāǧim wa-l-biqāᶜ al-mubārakāt* ("The Gift of the Beloved Ones and the Desire of the Knowledge-Seekers: The Districts, the Shrines, the Biographies and the Blessed Places") by Nūr ad-Dīn as-Saḫāwī (*fl.* end of ninth cent. H).[40] His treatise, printed for the first time in 1304 H, was modelled on the work of Ibn az-Zayyāt (see above) and depends mainly on him.

Seen in its entirety, the literary tradiṯion of Cairene cemetery guides cannot boast famous authors. Most of them did not leave any significant trace in the learned tradition of their times. The practice of composing cemetery guides seems to

33 On his and his son's tomb, see IZayKawākib p. 309 and SaḫTuḥfAḥbāb pp. 191f.; *cf.* also CIA Égypte II p. 204.

34 That is, his genealogy goes back to Saᶜd b. ᶜUbādah al-Anṣārī.

35 For his brother Ǧamāl ad-Dīn Abū ᶜAmr ᶜUṯmān b. Makkī (584–659 H), see NZ VII pp. 202 and 205; ŠḎ V p. 298.

36 It is cited by its title *Muršid az-zuwwār* etc. in IZayKawākib pp. 118 and 245. The title is also listed in ḤḪ II p. 1654; the author is mentioned in *Ḏayl* ḤḪ II p. 466.

37 NZ I p. 129; MaqrḪiṭaṭ II pp. 461 and 463; Rāġib: *Inventaire* pp. 268f.

38 MaqrḪiṭaṭ II p. 463 (referring to a *Kitāb fī z-ziyārah* by "Muḥammad al-Azharī"); SaḫTuḥfAḥbāb p. 15 ("Šams ad-Dīn al-Azharī").

39 This frequent *nisbah* refers to his lodging in the Cairene sufi hospice called *Saᶜīd as-Suᶜadāʾ*.

40 Nūr ad-Dīn Abū l-Ḥasan ᶜAlī b. A. b. ᶜUmar b. Ḫalaf b. Maḥmūd al-Ḥanafī as-Saḫāwī: GAL II p. 35; Rāġib: *Inventaire* pp. 277-9; Sayyid: *Genre de Khiṭaṭ* p. 92; *cf.* also *Ḏayl* ḤḪ I p. 238.

have been inspired by the Shiite custom of compiling works about the Cairene shrines of the "Nobles" (*al-ʾašrāf*, i.e. members of the ʿAlid line). Starting in the sixth century H, this must therefore count – like the Sunnite poetry in praise of the Prophet – as another of the many elements successfully adopted from Shiism by Sunnite Islam during that time.[41] The sources used in the Cairene cemetery guides do not belong to the core of the academic curriculum, with the exception of topographical works and mystical literature,[42] nor did the guide books themselves enter that curriculum. The people who felt most attracted to this kind of literature were probably sufi professionals, as is indicated by the fact that some of the ninth-century authors were members of the important Cairene sufi convent Saʿīd as-Suʿadāʾ.[43] Finally, the gap between the seventh and the ninth centuries H is noteworthy, for during the eighth century H no identifiable cemetery guide was produced and it is that period with coincides with the debate raging within the Islamic community about the visitation of tombs and cemeteries (see Chapter 1).

3.3. The Arabian peninsula

3.3.1. Mecca

The graveyards in Mecca and Medina have always been considered the most important Islamic burial grounds, for Sunnites and Shiites alike. Little needs to be said about the most important graveyard of Mecca, the (Bāb) al-Maʿlāh (المعلاة) cemetery.[44] (Some have called this place al-Muʿallā or al-Muʿlā / al-Maʿlā [المعلا or المعلى], but as the lexicographer al-Fīrūzābādī, who knew Mecca well, establishes its name as "al-Maʿlāh" in his famous dictionary, I follow his authority).[45] This burial ground to the north of the Ḥaram complex, especially its western part, is also known as al-Ḥağūn[46] cemetery, after the adjacent hill (and *wādī*) of the same name.[47] Many dis-

41 *Cf.* also Sayyid: *Genre de Khiṭaṭ* p. 90 ("cette littérature spécialisée ... était à l'origine spécifiquement chiʿite").

42 Thus, Ibn az-Zayyāt in his *Kawākib* cites numerous topographical and historical works (Ibn ʿAbd al-Ḥakam: *Futūḥ Miṣr*; al-Kindī: *Tārīḫ Miṣr* or *Kitāb Faḍāʾil Miṣr*; Ibn Muyassar: *Tārīḫ*; al-Quḍāʿī: *Tārīḫ* or *al-Ḫiṭaṭ*; Ibn Zawlāq: *Tārīḫ*; Abū Saʿid: *Tārīḫ Miṣr*; *Kitāb Tārīḫ Ifrīqiyā*), as well as a number of mystical and related writings (al-Qušayrī: *Risālah*; Abū Nuʿaym: *Ḥilyah*; Ibn al-Ğawzī: *Ṣifat aṣ-ṣafwah*; al-Yāfiʿī: *Kitāb Rawḍ ar-rayāḥīn*; Ibn al-Mulaqqin: *Ṭabaqāt al-ʾawliyāʾ*; *Kitāb al-ʿAṭāyā l-wahbīyah fī l-marātib al-quṭbīyah*; *Kitāb al-Kawkab al-munīr fī manāqib ʾAbī l-ʿAbbās al-Baṣīr*) and genealogical studies (aš-Šarīf Abū l-Ġanāʾim ʿAbdallāh b. al-Ḥasan al-Ḥusaynī an-Nassābah: *Kitāb Nuzhat ʿuyūn al-muštāqīn fī ʾansāb aṭ-ṭālibīn*; *ad-Durrah an-nafīsah fī tarğamat as-sayyidah Nafīsah*).

43 *Cf.* EI² VIII p. 861. See also above note 39.

44 See AzrMakkah II pp. 209-13; FāsīŠifāʾ I p. 284 and FāsīZuhūr pp. 128f.; EI² VI p. 168.

45 FīrūzQāmūs s.r. *ʿlw*; see also YāqBuldān V p. 158.

46 In many sources also vowelled as "al-Ḥağğūn" or "al-Ḥuğūn".

47 The second great cemetery of the town, *maqburat Bāb Šubaykah*, lies at its southern fringe.

tinguished individuals from all over the Islamic world are buried there. The Maᶜlāh burial ground also contains the alleged tomb of the first wife of the Prophet, Ḫadīǧah, and others even claimed the tomb of the Prophet's mother Āminah was located there;[48] however, none of the famous companions of the Prophet is known to be interred in that graveyard.[49]

It is impossible to list even the most prominent persons buried there. It must suffice to mention the second-century jurist Sufyān aṯ-Ṯawrī, the ascetic al-Fuḍayl b. ᶜIyāḍ (see **116**), Imām al-Ḥaramayn al-Ǧuwaynī (d. 478 H), Muḥibb ad-Dīn aṭ-Ṭabarī,[50] the mystic Muwaffaq ad-Dīn az-Zaylaᶜī (see **154**), the famous poet al-Burhān al-Qīrāṭī,[51] the eminent Shafiite scholars ᶜIzz ad-Dīn Ibn Ǧamāᶜah (d. 767 H, see **158**), al-Yāfiᶜī (d. 768 H, see **159**) and Bahāᵓ ad-Dīn as-Subkī (d. 773 H, see **160**), the members of the Ibn Abī Numayy clan (i.e. the later offspring of the Banū Qatādah and the rulers of Mecca for centuries),[52] ᶜAṭīyah b. Ẓuhayrah (d. 647 H, see **147**) and his descendants, the Ibn Ẓuhayrah clan, the members of the Nuwayrī clan, the Fāsī clan and the Ibn Fahd clan,[53] and finally aš-Šihāb Aḥmad aṭ-Ṭulūnī (d. 801 H), the architect of sultan Barqūq.[54] With good reason, therefore, the mystic Abū l-Qāsim an-Naṣrābādī (Ibr. b. M., d. 367 H) said to Abū ᶜAbd ar-Raḥmān as-Sulamī when he was looking at the Maᶜlāh cemetery, "O Abū ᶜAbd ar-Raḥmān, what blessedness for those whose graves are in this cemetery! I wish my grave were here also (*wa-layta qabrī kāna hunā*)!"[55] In fact, those buried in the Maᶜlāh cemetery were considered inhabitants of Paradise and thus not in need of the recitation of the Qurᵓān in order to promote their destiny; there were no "heretics" (*ᵓahl al-bidᶜah*) interred there, because the earth would not receive them.[56]

To this most important Meccan burial ground two cemetery guides have been devoted, and in the biographical dictionary of al-Fāsī its funerary inscriptions are constantly adduced as source texts. All three texts stem from the first decades of the ninth century H and were thus composed more or less at the same time.

(1) The first cemetery guide was produced by the famous linguist Maǧd ad-Dīn aš-Šīrāzī (Abū Ṭāhir M. b. Yaᶜqūb, Kāzarūn near Šīrāz 729 – Zabīd 817 H),[57] who in modern times has become known as "al-Fīrūzābādī". It had been his desire to be

48 SinǧManāᵓiḥ I p. 443.

49 *Cf.* FāsīŠifāᵓ I p. 285; EI² VI p. 168.

50 A. b. ᶜAl. al-Makkī aš-Šāfiᶜī (d. 694 H). For him and his offspring, see Bauden: *Ṭabariyya* and EI² X pp. 16f. (F. Bauden).

51 Ibr. b. ᶜAl. (Cairo 726 – Mecca 781 H): DK I p. 32 and IḤaǧInbāᵓ I pp. 312f.; IᶜIrāqīḎᶜIbar II pp. 488-90; FāsīᶜIqd III pp. 137-44; MaqrSulūk III p. 374; IQŠuhbTārīḫ I p. 12; ITaġrManh I p. 91 and NZ XI pp. 196-200; ŠḎ VI pp. 269f.; ZA I p. 43.

52 *Cf.* De Gaury: *Rulers of Mecca* pp. 91ff. and Peters: *Mecca* pp. 150ff.

53 For this family, see ar-Rašīd: *Banū Fahd*.

54 ITaġrManh II p. 284.

55 Cited in MaqrMuq I p. 287.

56 FāsīᶜIqd II p. 105, FāsīŠifāᵓ I p. 285 and FāsīZuhūr p. 128.

57 For his biography, see FāsīᶜIqd II pp. 425-31 (important entry); IḤaǧḎaylDK pp. 238-40, IḤaǧInbāᵓ VII pp. 159-63 and IḤaǧMaǧmaᶜ pp. 396-8; NZ XIV pp. 132-4; SaḫWaǧīz II p. 434 and ḌL X pp. 79-86; MaqqAzhār III pp. 48-52; ŠḎ VII pp. 126-31; ŠawkBadr II pp. 280-4; GAL II pp. 181f. and GALS II pp. 234-6; EI² II pp. 926f.; ZA VII pp. 146f.

buried in Mecca, yet this was denied him by fate because the path leading to the Maᶜlāh cemetery had been renewed and enlarged just in the year of his death. This "made access easier than before (...) thus attracting more people to pass here",[58] but in 817 H the restoration work blocked the street and, alas, al-Fīrūzābādī's body could not be carried to the Maᶜlah cemetery. His cemetery guide is entitled *ʾIṯārat al-ḥağūn ʾilā ziyārat al-Ḥağūn*, that is, "The Stirring Up of the Lazy for the Visitation of the Ḥağūn (Cemetery)".[59] The work is preserved at least in one manuscript (kept at Cairo),[60] and was printed in Mecca in 1332.[61] Taqīy ad-Dīn al-Fāsī, who knew al-Mağd al-Fīrūzābādī personally and had met him in his house in Minā, has the following to say about this treatise:[62] al-Fīrūzābādī

> "wrote something about the high rank of the Ḥağūn cemetery (*šayʾun fī faḍli l-Ḥağūn*) and about the companions (of the Prophet) buried there. However, I cannot see in the books that contain their biographies anything which guarantees that they were all buried in the Ḥağūn (cemetery), nor that all of those (mentioned by al-Fīrūzābādī) died in Mecca at all. Thus, if he bases his claim that they were buried in the Ḥağūn (cemetery) upon someone having said that they had merely settled in Mecca, then he (incorrectly) deduces from their settling there that they were all buried in the Ḥağūn (cemetery), yet people were also buried elsewhere, e.g. in the *maqburat al-muhāğirīn* (...) or possibly in their homes (*fī dūrihim*). God knows best".[63]

al-Fāsī himself[64] is the author of a history of Mecca entitled *al-ʿIqd aṯ-ṯamīn fī tārīḫ al-balad al-ʾamīn* ("The Precious Necklace: A History of the Honest Town[65]"), actually an immense biographical dictionary whose first volume is entirely devoted to the biography of the Prophet.[66] The remaining volumes, more than 2300 pages (in print), contain about 3200 entries of persons who had some connection with Mecca, up to the ninth century H. In 55 of these entries (if I counted correctly),

58 IFahdItḥāf III p. 522.

59 The title of the work is mentioned in Fāsīᶜlqd II p. 428; Saḫlᶜlān p. 133 = Rosenthal: *Historiography* p. 481; SinğManāʾiḥ I p. 244 (here as *ʾIṯārat aš-šuğūn* etc.); *Ḏayl* ḤḪ I p. 85 (here as *ʾIšārat al-ḥağūn* etc.). The title is a fine play with words, clearly concocted by an advanced philologist, in particular as the term *ʾiṯārah* might also be understood to mean "disinterment, exhumation" of something buried.

60 GALS II p. 236.

61 as-Sunaydī: *Muʿğam* p. 55. Unfortunately, this printed version was unaccessible.

62 He does not call al-Fīrūzābādī's treatise by its title here (see what follows above) and mentions the *ʾIṯārat al-ḥağūn* separately on the next page, but I presume that he is referring to the same work.

63 Fāsīᶜlqd II p. 427. For the burial in houses, see above pp. 212ff.

64 Abū ṭ-Ṭayyib Taqīy ad-Dīn M. b. A. al-Fāsī al-Makkī al-Mālikī (Mecca, 775–832 H): IFahdLaḥẓ pp. 291-7; IFahdItḥāf IV p. 47; ŠḎ VII p. 199; GAL II pp. 172f.; EI^2 II pp. 828f. (F. Rosenthal); ZA V p. 331. For his writings, see also al-ᶜAnqāwī: *al-Fāsī* and Millward: *al-Fāsī's Sources*.

65 *al-ʾamīn* is also a famous epithet of the Prophet from his early days.

66 The latter was published separately by the author with the title *al-Ğawāhir as-sanīyah fī s-sīrah an-nabawīyah*, *cf.* Saḫlᶜlān p. 89 = Rosenthal: *Historiography* p. 36; EI^2 II p. 829. It has been edited by M. Ḥāmid al-Fiqī (Beirut ^{2}1406).

al-Fāsī has no additional information other than the epitaphs he found and read in the Meccan Maᶜlāh cemetery. In another five cases, his information derives for its major part from epitaphs, and on about 35 occasions he refers to extant epitaphs in order to supplement or rectify information found in literary sources.

(2) Contemporary with the books by al-Fīrūzābādī and al-Fāsī is the cemetery guide by aš-Šaybī, a collection of epitaphs from the Maᶜlāh cemetery with much additional material. A diligent member of one of Mecca's old families, the Banū Šaybah,[67] Ǧamāl ad-Dīn aš-Šaybī went about copying and commenting on some 22 epitaphs he found in the Maᶜlāh cemetery.

Ǧamāl ad-Dīn Abū l-Maḥāsin M. b. Nūr ad-Dīn ᶜAlī[68] b. M.[69] b. Abī Bakr al-Qurašī al-ᶜAbdarī al-Makkī aš-Šaybī aš-Šāfiᶜī (Mecca, Ramaḍān 779 H – Rabīᶜ I or II 837 H)[70] had studied law with Ǧamāl ad-Dīn Ibn Ẓuhayrah and held an ʾiǧāzah from the foremost scholar of his age, Zayn ad-Dīn al-ᶜIrāqī (d. 806 H). He had travelled to Baghdad and Šīrāz and had lived for two years in Zabīd, and it is more than likely that he also met al-Fīrūzābādī. In 817 H (or only in 827?), he was appointed warden or "door-keeper" of the Kaᶜbah after the death of his uncle Faḫr ad-Dīn Abū Bakr,[71] a post (called *sidānat al-Kaᶜbah*) which he held until his death. Besides that, he was also in charge of the Meccan temenos (*nāẓir al-ḥaram*) and temporarily held the office of Shafiite judge in Mecca (in 830 H). The biographical sources mention his talent for composing poetry and his inclination towards *ʾadab* literature, and in fact aš-Šaybī compiled an abridgement (and a supplement to) ad-Damīrī's *Ḥayāt al-ḥayawān* and published a collection of proverbs. Moreover, he compiled a history of Mecca (*Tārīḫ Makkah*) which seems to be extant in manuscript though I was unable to find exact references as to the present whereabouts of the copy.[72] According to the biographical sources, this history dealt primarily with the events of his lifetime. In 837 H he was buried in the Maᶜlāh cemetery (see also below).

His work dealing with several epitaphs of the Maᶜlāh cemetery is commonly cited by the title *aš-Šaraf al-ʾaᶜlā fī ḏikr qubūr maqburat al-Maᶜlā* ("The Highest Honour: Mentioning the Tombs of the Maᶜlā Cemetery")[73] although aš-Šaybī at the beginning of his treatise does not call it thus, but simply says that "it occurred to me to collect in the following pages a part of what I read on the tombs of the distinguished

67 The Banū Šaybah were for centuries the wardens of the Kaᶜbah, see Peters: *Mecca* pp. 142f. and 280-2; EI² IX pp. 389f. Of particular prominence among the ancestors of Ǧamāl ad-Dīn was Maǧd ad-Dīn A. b. Daylam al-Makkī (642–712 H), himself for forty years warden of the Kaᶜbah (ITaġrManh I pp. 295f.).

68 ᶜAlī died in 815 H (ITaġrManh VIII pp. 156f.). He had followed ᶜAlī b. M. b. Abī Rāǧiḥ (d. 787 H) as warden of the Kaᶜbah (*ib*. VIII p. 157).

69 In some sources alternatively ᶜĪsā or Abū Bakr, but Muḥammad is correct.

70 For his biography, see FāsīᶜIqd II pp. 300f.; IḤaǧInbāʾ VIII pp. 322f.; NZ XV p. 186; MaqrSulūk IV p. 922; IFahdItḥāf IV p. 73; SaḫWaǧīz II pp. 531f. and ḌL VIII p. 182; ŠḎ VII pp. 223f.; ŠawkBadr II p. 214; GALS II p. 222 (with wrong year of birth); ZA VI pp. 287f. For his brother Abū l-Makārim A. (d. 808 H), see ITaġrManh I p. 402. The entries in FāsīᶜIqd and ḌL give his year of death as 827 H.

71 FāsīᶜIqd II p. 300 and IFahdItḥāf III p. 523.

72 *Cf.* as-Sunaydī: *Muᶜǧam* p. 100.

73 FāsīᶜIqd VI p. 382; SaḫIᶜlān p. 133 = Rosenthal: *Historiography* p. 481; GAL II p. 173. *Cf.* also Rosenthal: *ib*. pp. 126f., n. 5; as-Sunaydī: *Muᶜǧam* p. 185.

Meccan cemetery called 'al-Muᶜallā' "[74] (the various names of the cemetery have been discussed above). However, the proper title *aš-Šaraf* etc. certainly stems from the author himself because it is already cited by his contemporary al-Fāsī (who died five years before aš-Šaybī); its being mentioned by al-Fāsī also indicates that aš-Šaybī's treatise must have been completed (and circulated) some time before 832 H. Besides the incomplete Berlin manuscript (there are leaves missing after 9b, 10b, 22b and 27b; date of copy 1122 H) used in the present volume, the work is preserved in at least three further manuscripts which are actually kept in Tunis (al-Maktabah al-Waṭanīyah, *Maǧmūᶜah* 18325, 57 ff.), Medina (Maktabat ᶜĀrif Ḥikmet 130/900, 56 ff., date of copy 1231 H) and Mecca (Maktabat al-Ḥaram al-Makkī 3131f).[75] A critical edition of the text using all extant mss. is pivotal for further research; the following remarks are only based on the Berlin ms. and thus preliminary to a certain degree.

aš-Šaybī put together his collection of epitaphs, as he goes on to say on the first page, "because it makes their[76] fates and names immortal and helps to preserve their dates of death, but also because in this way one might pray for mercy upon them when standing (at their tombs)[77] and for the lesson to be learnt from their condition, together with other benefits, such as remarkable poetry (*šiᶜr ġarīb*) that deals with death and the (hortatory) warning of separation (i.e. death), and with the mention of passion (*tawaǧǧud*) towards the Abode of Encounter (i.e. the hereafter)". In these few lines, aš-Šaybī summarises what has been connected in Islamic culture with death and burial sites: aspects of human pride and glory (rendering the name immortal), of history (preserving biographical information), of piety (bestowing mercy upon the dead and providing counsel for the living), of poetry (putting the experience of loss into words) and of eschatology (visualising the hereafter). This interesting mixture makes aš-Šaybī's treatise an exceptional work, more complex than the common cemetery guides, and actually quite *sui generis*.

The obvious disadvantage of this manifoldness is that aš-Šaybī's treatise is, to put it mildly, not structured very well. Basically, its second part (beginning on fol. 10a) is ordered according to the epitaphs as the visitor comes across them; all of these, or so it seems, are located beside the tomb of al-Fuḍayl b. ᶜIyāḍ (**116**) or in its vicinity. The first, introductory part is a loose sequence of "unheard-of, but useful information" (*fawāʾid ġarībah*, 1b) – "*ġarīb*" is the favourite term employed by the author –, which does not contain any epitaphs and deals instead with the following arguments: the definition and nature of death (ŠaybīŠaraf 2a-3a), the question of who of mankind is the first and the last to die (3a-b), various events following death (3b), the question of whether digging one's own tomb during lifetime guarantees

74 ŠaybīŠaraf 1b.

75 as-Sunaydī: *Muᶜǧam* p. 185.

76 *Sc.* of the deceased.

77 Or "when encountering, *or* coming across, their names"?

that one will eventually be buried in it (3b-4a),[78] semantic remarks about relevant terms (such as *naʿš*, *ǧanāzah*, 4a-b), the throes of death (4b), persons "alive after their death" (*man ʿāša baʿda l-mawt*, 4b-5b) or brought back into life (5b), the speech of the dead and the Yemenite mystic Ismāʿīl al-Ḥaḍramī[79] (5b-6a), sudden death (6a), the fact that scholars died during sexual intercourse but never while preaching on the pulpit (6a), a Tradition transmitted from the Prophet (6a), general considerations relating to death and its acceptance (6a-7a), the different terms in Arabic for "grave" including other derivates from the root *qbr* (7a-b), Shafiite prescriptions for burial (7b-8a) and the diverse forms of the pit (8a-b) and the mound, levelling and sprinkling the tomb, together with other features of grave structure and burial (8b-9a), ways of behaving at tombs (9a-b) and finally the fact that putting more than one person in a common tomb or unearthing a corpse are not allowed (9b). The rest of the treatise is likewise distinguished by frequent digressions, here as elsewhere happily acknowledged by the author.[80]

These digressions concern chiefly arguments of philological, geographical and biographical interest which stray from the main theme, interluded with aš-Šaybī's own poetry or many chosen pieces from other, more or less famous poets (with additional information supplied about their work and life). In many ways, thus, aš-Šaybī's treatise resembles a *taḏkirah* or "memorandum" in which he put every interesting notice he found concerning death and burial in the first part, while in the second part his treatise deals with some epitaphs of the Maʿlāh cemetery. Here, the author added much information on the persons buried or on the related epitaph-poetry. It is, therefore, no exaggeration to say that, albeit much more modest in scope and size, aš-Šaybī's treatise resembles one of the most "digressive" and "stream-of-consciousness"-like books ever written by an Arab author, namely an-Nuwayrī al-Iskandarānī's (d. 775 H) *Kitāb al-ʾIlmām* (=NuwIlmām). Not surprisingly, an-Nuwayrī also inserted a lengthy chapter about everything concerning death, burial, eschatological matters, forms of consolation and mourning poetry in his treatise.[81]

The purpose for the composition of his treatise, as expressed by the author, does not tell the whole story. In fact, aš-Šaybī adduces a number of reasons (see above), but none of these are strictly personal or could be said to reflect his biography or family interest. Yet the epitaphs he included in his treatise are without exception all located near the tomb of al-Fuḍayl b. ʿIyāḍ, and it is exactly there that the Šaybī clan had its own mausoleum (*turbat Banī š-Šaybī*) in the Maʿlāh cemetery.[82] Therefore I assume that aš-Šaybī's treatise is somehow connected with that fact. Maybe he collected the epitaphs of that area because he spent so much time there, but more probable is that he intended to enhance the rank of his family's mausoleum by highlighting the noble tombs which were found in its vicinity. This would then count as

78 This was no merely academic question, but it did happen that somebody's tomb was occupied by someone else, see e.g. the case of M. b. Farağ al-Makkī (d. 827 H) in FāsīʿIqd II p. 337. *Cf.* also above p. 152.

79 About him, see above p. 107.

80 E.g. *wa-qad ṭāla l-kalāmu bi-mā laysa huwa min qaṣdinā* (ŠaybīŠaraf 3b).

81 NuwIlmām IV pp. 197-235.

82 ʿAydNūr p. 181. There was a gate leading to the area called *Bāb Banī Šaybah*, see Fāsī-ʿIqd II pp. 31 and 400, III p. 368, V p. 57; IFahdItḥāf II p. 535 and III p. 60; SinğManāʾiḥ II p. 256.

another of the many examples in Islamic scholarship where the main intention of a work has not been expressed overtly, but the message would not have been lost on his contemporaries, who knew perfectly well of the burial site of the Šaybī clan. But there is other evidence for the personal motives of aš-Šaybī, because al-Fāsī in his history of Mecca writes in the entry of Ḫadīǧah bt. Aḥmad an-Nuwayrīyah (d. Mecca 777 H), also known as Umm Ḫalīl aṣ-Ṣūfīyah:

> "Her grandson, our fellow the sheikh Ǧamāl ad-Dīn Muḥammad b. ᶜAlī aš-Šaybī al-Makkī, told me that she composed beautiful poetry which she exchanged in letters with sheikh Bahāʾ ad-Dīn as-Subkī. (...) Her grandson (...) aš-Šaybī also mentioned her in his book *aš-Šaraf al-ʾaᶜlā fī ḏikr qubūr maqburat al-Maᶜlā*, in his entry about sheikh Bahāʾ ad-Dīn (...) as-Subkī, and he heaped exaggerated praise upon her (*wa-ʾaṭnaba fī ṯ-ṯanāʾi ᶜalayhā*)".[83]

Everybody familiar with the conventions of Arabic prose will know that the verb *ṭnb* IV almost always bears negative connotations, and therefore its use here should doubtlessly convey the idea that aš-Šaybī was somewhat profuse in his work and biased with regard to members of his own family, extolling their merits beyond their due. Thus, al-Fāsī – although he introduces aš-Šaybī politely, another convention of academic prose – seems not to have thought very highly of aš-Šaybī's treatise.[84] Finally, the strong personal motives at work in the treatise of aš-Šaybī might become apparent from the fact that he chiefly cites the epitaphs of famous people. There was little interest in doing so for a historian, because there was much more, and superior, information about these persons in literary sources than their respective epitaphs.[85] Quoting the epitaphs of the famous, therefore, in Islamic scholarship had not always to do with an antiquarian, biographical or historical interest; it was rather a way of showing deference towards the famous, a way of venerating them and cherishing their memory, among other reasons. If a number of cherished persons, as in the case of aš-Šaybī, were buried around one's own mausoleum, all the better.

3.3.2. Medina

The most important cemetery of Medina, *Baqīᶜ al-Ġarqad*, is located towards the south-east area of the town. There are a number of Traditions exalting the Baqīᶜ cemetery and the visitation of the local tombs, and the first to be ever buried in the Baqīᶜ cemetery was ᶜUṯmān b. Maẓᶜūn (whose tomb is repeatedly dealt with in

83 FāsīᶜIqd VI p. 382.

84 This might be corroborated by the fact that al-Fāsī never mentions him (or quotes from his work) except in the passage presented above; he does not even refer to aš-Šaybī in those cases where he deals with the very persons whose epitaphs are included in aš-Šaybī's treatise, e.g. al-Fuḍayl b. ᶜIyāḍ (**116**) or the son of the mystic al-Qušayrī (**119**).

85 In fact, al-Fāsī adduces material from epitaphs only in the cases of little known or completely unknown persons, but never refers to funerary inscriptions where there was plenty of material to be had from books. The same holds true for the Cairene cemetery guides in which epitaphs are mainly cited if other information was lacking.

Chapter 2).[86] At all times, the Baqīᶜ cemetery was a revered place of burial, but especially so during the later Mamluk period when Medina had regained its former rank as an important centre of scholarship. One of the dominant figures of that period, Šams ad-Dīn as-Saḫāwī (d. 902 H), was laid to rest in the Baqīᶜ cemetery near the mausoleum of Mālik b. Anas (**167**),[87] thus symbolising the importance of Medina as a place of erudition after many centuries.

To my knowledge, only one pre-modern Sunnite cemetery guide was ever produced for the Baqīᶜ graveyard. It bore the title *ar-Rawḍah fī ʾasmāʾ man dufina bi-l-Baqīᶜ* ("The Garden: The Names of those Buried in the Baqīᶜ Cemetery")[88] and was composed in 718 H by Amīn ad-Dīn[89] al-Āqšahrī al-Aḫlāṭī.[90] This scholar of Turkish origin had widely travelled before settling in Medina, where he wrote his *Kitāb ar-Rawḍah* "about those buried in the most noble of all places" (*fī man dufina bi-ʾašrafi l-biqāᶜ*).[91] According to as-Saḫāwī, the book consisted of five chapters that dealt with (1) the rules for visiting the Prophet's sepulchre and the shrines of members of his family, (2) the family of the Prophet and the first caliphs, (3) the battles during the Prophet's life which led to the death of many of his companions, (4) the reports about the most famous companions and finally (5) those buried in Medina who were neither from the Prophet's family nor companions, but later scholars and mystics. In the second chapter, he mentioned 51 persons, while the fourth chapter listed 240 companions.[92] Until his death, the author transmitted his treatise personally in Medina and Mecca. It was known until the later ninth century H, but no copy of it seems to be preserved.

3.3.3. Yemen

Much information about the burial grounds of Yemen is contained in the local histories and biographical dictionaries. Yemen was also a region where, especially from the tenth century H onwards, many scholars and pious men rose to prominence

86 IMuḥKunūz II p. 62; SamWafāʾ III pp. 891f.; EI² I p. 957; Grütter: *Bestattungsbräuche* p. 184. According to others, though, the first person buried there was Asᶜad b. Zurārah (IMuḥKunūz II pp. 62 and 75) or Abū Umāmah al-Bāhilī (YāqBuldān IV p. 470, *s.v.* Kafr Naġd); the first of the Anṣār was Kulṯūm b. al-Hadam (IMuḥKunūz II p. 75).

87 IDaybaᶜFaḍl pp. 104f.

88 Alternatively entitled *ar-Rawḍah al-firdawsīyah wa-l-ḥaḍīrah al-qudsīyah* or simply *Rawḍat al-firdaws*, see ḤḪ I p. 928.

89 Or also "Ǧalāl ad-Dīn" or "Šams ad-Dīn".

90 Abū ᶜAl. or Abū Ṭaybah M. b. A. b. Amīn (Akšehir near Konya between 664 and 666 – Medina 731 or 739 H): FāsīᶜIqd II p. 8; DK III p. 398; MaqrMuq V p. 142; IFahdItḥāf III p. 218; SaḫTuḥfLaṭ II pp. 409-12 and SaḫIᶜlān p. 130 = Rosenthal: *Historiography* p. 476; ḤḪ I p. 928; ZA V p. 325.

91 A nice wordplay upon the shrines of the "nobles" (*ʾašrāf*) buried in the Baqīᶜ cemetery.

92 SaḫTuḥfLaṭ II p. 411. In view of this description the work was probably not similar to aš-Šaybī's collection of Meccan epitaphs (*cf.* Rosenthal: *Historiography* p. 127). It seems rather to have

and numerous venerated shrines came soon into existence. However, I do not yet know of a pre-modern cemetery guide for any Yemenite site.[93]

3.4. The Islamic East

The graveyards of eastern cities such as Damascus and Baghdad are among the most important burial sites in the wider Islamic world. In addition to this, the region possesses a huge number of mausolea and shrines in Jerusalem, Aleppo, Mawṣil,[94] Kūfah and lesser known locations, many of which are listed in al-Harawī's *Kitāb al-ʾIšārāt*. For the larger towns of the East several cemetery guides have been compiled over the centuries.

3.4.1. Syria and Lebanon

At least three (or four, see below) treatises specialising in Damascene mausolea and burial sites are known. The first is mentioned by the tenth-century polymath Ibn Ṭūlūn, who quotes a work written by his teacher al-Muḥyawī an-Naᶜīmī (an-Nuᶜaymī?) and bearing the title *al-Qawl al-ǧadīr fī man dufina min aš-Šāfiᶜīyah bi-Bāb aṣ-Ṣaġīr*.[95] According to the title, this was a dictionary of Shafiite scholars who were buried in the Damascene Bāb aṣ-Ṣaġīr cemetery. The second work was composed by the Shafiite scholar Maḥmūd b. Muḥammad al-ᶜAdawī (Ibn) az-Zūkārī (d. 1032 H)[96] whose *Kitāb az-Ziyārāt bi-Dimašq* (or *al-ʾIšārāt fī ʾamākin az-ziyārāt*) was printed in Damascus in 1956. The third work, also entitled *Kitāb al-ʾIšārāt ʾilā ʾamākin az-ziyārāt* was produced by the twelfth-century scholar Ibn al-Ḥawrānī (ᶜUṯmān b. A. as-Suwaydī) who completed it in 1117 H.[97] It deals with the visitation sites of Damascus and was printed in Damascus in 1302 H.[98] A fourth is possibly the *Risālat az-ziyārāt li-l-ʾawliyāʾ wa-ṣ-ṣāliḥīn allaḏīna lahum bi-Dimašq qubūr*

been a compilation of biographical material relating to those buried in the Baqīᶜ cemetery and for that reason it was listed among the town histories of Medina in SaḫIᶜlān.

93 The only treatise which may be said to fall vaguely within the field was written by Niẓām ad-Dīn Ibrāhīm Ibn Fuḍayl (d. 626 H). It bears the title *al-Iḥtiṣāṣ bi-ḏikr taǧdīd ʿimārat al-ǧabbānah allatī hiya muṣallā l-ʿīdayn fī muqaddam madīnat Ṣanʿāʾ wa-ʿimārat al-manāratayn fī l-masǧid al-ǧāmiʿ bi-Ṣanʿāʾ*, etc. To judge from the title it deals with, among other things, the restoration of a cemetery outside Ṣanᶜāʾ which was in use as an open place of prayer (*muṣallā*); the ms. is extant, see GALS I p. 570 and Sayyid: *Maṣādir tārīḫ al-Yaman* pp. 122f.

94 The preserved work *Manhal al-ʾawliyāʾ wa-mašrab al-ʾaṣfiyāʾ fī sādāt al-Mawṣil al-ḥadbāʾ* by M. Amīn b. Ḫayr Allāh al-ᶜUmarī (d. 1203 H), indicated in SourdelLieux p. xxxii, n. 3, as concerning the tombs and cemeteries of Mawṣil, seems to be rather a town history and biographical dictionary of Mawṣilīs (see GAL II p. 374 and GALS II, 501). However, more can be said only after an examination of the extant manuscripts.

95 IṬūlQal II p. 535.

96 ĠazLuṭf II pp. 642-4; MuḥḪul IV p. 322; GAL II p. 290 and GALS II p. 964 (no. 9); ZA VII p. 183; Abāẓah/Muṭīᶜ: *ʿUlamāʾ Dimašq* (q. 11) I pp. 375f.

97 ZA IV p. 203.

98 See GALS II p. 401 and note 1 by J. Sourdel-Thomine in HarIšārāt p. 3.

wa-maqāmāt by a certain Muḥammad Hibat Allāh ad-Dimašqī,[99] but nothing further is known to me about it.

Apart from Damascus, there is an eleventh-century treatise about the persons buried in Dārayyā, viz. *ar-Rawḍah ar-rayyā fī man dufina bi-Dārayyā* ("The Well-Irrigated Garden: People Buried in Dārayyā") by the judge and man of letters al-ᶜImādī al-Ḥanafī (d. 1051 H),[100] a pupil of al-Ḥasan al-Būrīnī and correspondent of al-Maqqarī; his work was printed in Damascus in 1408/1988. The town Dārayyā near Damascus was chiefly famous for the shrines of Abū Muslim al-Ḫawlānī and the ascetic Abū Sulaymān ad-Dārānī (d. between 215 and 235 H)[101] and the hagiographies of both persons make up the main bulk of al-ᶜImādī's treatise. The author discusses further the name of the town in detail and mentions briefly some of the Prophet's famous companions and other individuals of the first two centuries H who were said to have settled in Dārayyā. He concludes with seven Traditions (from the Prophet) which were transmitted "at the tomb (*ḍarīḥ*) of Abū Muslim". Summing up, al-ᶜImādī's booklet can only with considerable reserve said to be a cemetery guide, notwithstanding its (actually misleading) title. It more resembles the treatises of the *faḍāʾil*-type which dwell upon some of the famous persons connected with a certain village or town. There is no material about burial sites from later centuries nor are the tombs of the few protagonists (esp. Abū Muslim and Abū Sulaymān) described; there are no funerary inscriptions quoted either.

For burial sites in Lebanon, Syria and Egypt, ᶜAbd al-Ġanīy Ibn an-Nabulusī's and al-Miknāsī's travel journals yield much material, although they cannot be classified as cemetery or visitation guides. Though no proper cemetery guides either, a number of monographs were produced about figures whose shrines were venerated in Palestine, including the biblical prophets. Thus there is a book about the visitation of the tomb of the Prophet's companion Tamīm ad-Dārī[102] whose shrine is famous in Bayt Ǧibrīn. It was written by Ibn Zayd al-Ḥanbalī al-Mawṣilī ad-Dimašqī (A. b. M., d. 870 H) and is entitled *Tuḥfat as-sārī ʾilā ziyārat Tamīm ad-Dārī*.[103] As to the biblical prophets, there is a treatise about the visitation of Abraham's shrine in al-Ḫalīl (Hebron), composed in 814 H by the preacher of the local mosque Isḥāq b. Ibrāhīm at-Tadmurī aš-Šāfiᶜī (d. 833 H) and entitled *Muṯīr al-ġarām ʾilā* (or *fī faḍl*)

99 Cited in *Ḏayl* ḤḪ I p. 564.

100 ᶜAr. b. M. ad-Dimašqī (Damascus, 978–1051 H): MuḥḪul II pp. 380-9; ZA III p. 332; Abāẓah/Muṭīᶜ: *ᶜUlamāʾ Dimašq* (q. 11) I pp. 530-8. His work is mentioned in all the biographical sources as well as in *Ḏayl* ḤḪ I p. 594; GAL II p. 291 and GALS p. 402.

101 ᶜAr. b. A. b. ᶜAṭīyah al-ᶜAbsī: ANuḤilyah IX pp. 254-80; YāqBuldān II p. 431 (*s.v.* Dārayyā); ŠaᶜrṬab I pp. 79f.; MunKawākib I pp. 669-75; ᶜImādīRawḍah pp. 81ff.; ZA III pp. 293f.; *cf.* also Arberry: *Sufism* p. 43.

102 For him *cf.* MaqdMuṯīr pp. 318-23 and IḤaǧIṣābah I p. 184.

103 For author and work, see SaḫWaǧīz II p. 779 and ḌL II pp. 71f.; ŠḎ VII p. 310; ZA I p. 230. Ibn Zayd also wrote a known qaṣīdah-poem *fī t-tašawwuqi ʾilā Madīnati r-rasūli wa-ziyārati qabrihī*, i.e. "about the yearning for the Town of the Prophet (i.e. Medina) and the visitation of his sepulchre".

ziyārat al-Ḫalīl ʿalayhi s-salām, "The Stimulation of Desire towards the Visitation of 'the Intimate (friend of God, i.e. Abraham)', Peace be upon him".[104] Besides that, we know of some pages in which the Syrian polymath Ibn Ṭūlūn (d. 953 H) investigates the exact location of the tomb of Moses which was, as is well-known, never clearly identified. Merely four pages in the author's handwriting, the preserved ms. in Cairo bears the proud title *Risālah fī mawḍiʿ qabr Mūsā ʾalayhi s-salām.*[105] It may be an abstract of his somewhat longer work *Tuḥfat al-ḥabīb bi-ʾaḫbār al-katīb* which locates the tomb of Moses in Damascus and was read there publicly in 936 H.[106]

3.4.2. Iraq

In contrast with Egypt and Syria, Iraq offers little. I suppose that this is due to the fact that Sunnite cemetery guides generally did not appear before the sixth century H, and this is merely a hundred years before the sack of Baghdad by the Mongols. Thus it is not surprising that the known works date only from the sixth and seventh centuries H. In the case of Baghdad we are in the possession of information on at least two cemetery guides. The first is known from a quotation by Ibn Rağab, citing a *Kitāb Faḍāʾil maqburat ʾAḥmad* (i.e. the Bāb Ḥarb cemetery) which seems to have been composed by no less than Ibn al-Ğawzī.[107] A second work is referred to by aš-Šīrāzī as *(Kitāb) Maqābir Baġdād.*[108] Though he does not name its author, we know that its complete title ran *al-Maqābir al-mašhūrah wa-l-mašāhid al-mazūrah* ("The Famous Cemeteries and the Visited Shrines"), a work composed by Tāğ ad-Dīn Abū Ṭālib ʿAlī b. (al-)Anğab al-Baġdādī, commonly called Ibn as-Sāʿī (d. 674 H).[109]

3.4.3. Persia

The most important cemetery guide of a Persian town in Arabic is the *Šadd al-ʾizār fī ḥaṭṭ al-ʾawzār ʿan zuwwār al-mazār* ("The Strengthening of the Waist-Wrapper:[110] Putting Down the Burden from the Visitors to the Visiting Place") by Muʿīn ad-Dīn Abū l-Qāsim Ğunayd b. Maḥmūd aš-Šīrāzī (d. after 791 H).[111] His work is similar to

104 ḌL II p. 276; ŠḎ VII p. 203; ZA I p. 293; GAL II p. 131 and GALS II p. 162. The title is adapted from the *Muṯīr al-ġarām ʾilā ziyārat al-Quds wa-š-Šām* by Ibn Tamīm al-Maqdisī.

105 Maḫṭūṭāṭ Dār al-Kutub I p. 424.

106 GALS II p. 494 (the autograph is preserved at Leiden).

107 IRağḎayl I p. 247.

108 ŠīrŠadd pp. 12 and 23.

109 ITaġrManh VIII pp. 54f. (who lists a number of his writings but no cemetery guide) and pp. 62f. (double entry); ŠḎ V pp. 343f.; ḤḪ II p. 1778.

110 I.e. employing oneself vigorously in work ("rolling up one's sleeves"), or any undertaking. However, the word *ʾizār* was also used for the "shroud" (*kafan*), see SaḫĞawāhir III p. 1193.

111 ḤḪ II p. 1028 (with deviating title); GALS II p. 256; Storey: *Persian Literature* I, 2 p. 1123; see bibliography.

the Egyptian cemetery guides by al-Muwaffaq Ibn ᶜUṯmān and Ibn az-Zayyāt insofar as it is introduced by a lengthy chapter on the merit of visiting tombs in general. The entries are then ordered according to the location of the tombs, and the *mazārāt* are divided into seven areas so that they may be either visited during one week (one each day) or in seven weeks (going out only on Fridays or Saturday mornings). Unlike the Cairene guides, however, aš-Šīrāzī's treatise gives less emphasis to the actual topographical features of the graves, but accords more weight to the biographical material about the deceased; it resembles as such a biographical dictionary. According to Ḥāǧǧī Ḫalīfah, aš-Šīrāzī's work was later supplemented by the Persian treatise *Dustūr az-zā'irīn* by ᶜAbd al-ᶜAzīz b. M. al-Afḍal aš-Šīrāzī.[112]

In the biographical dictionary by al-Muḥibbī (d. 1111 H), we find a work quoted which bears the title *ar-Rawḍāt* ("The Gardens") and is described as dealing "with the shrines of Tabrīz" (*fī mazārāt Tabrīz*).[113] It is said by al-Muḥibbī to have been composed by a certain al-Ḥāfiẓ al-Ḥusayn al-Karbalā'ī al-Qazwīnī or at-Tabrīzī, who met Bahā' ad-Dīn al-ᶜĀmilī (d. 1031 H) in Damascus. However, I possess no other information regarding this book except the passage in al-Muḥibbī's dictionary. Apart from that, there are numerous works in Persian that deal with the *mazārāt* of Persian and Central Asian towns or regions, most notably Kirmān, Šīrāz, Buḫārā and Harāt, or with the Imamite shrines in Persia, Iraq and beyond.

Some modern Persian monographs about cemeteries in Iranian towns also exist, e.g. for Surḫāb-Tabrīz (Saǧǧādī: *Surḫāb*) and Iṣfahān (Mahdawī: *Taḏkirah*). The former assembles the biographies of poets who were buried in the so-called "cemetery of the poets" (*maqburat aš-šuᶜarā'*) from the fifth century H onwards, but derives its material almost exclusively from literary sources.[114] The second work concentrates on persons who died in the 20th century CE and is based on the actual tombs, though it adds much biographical material and, in many cases, a photograph of the deceased.

4. *Conclusion*

As a literary genre in Arabic literature, visitation and cemetery guides are closely connected with the revival of Sunnism during the sixth and seventh centuries H throughout the central Islamic lands. Their origin parallels the growth of the mortuary and saints cult during the same period. Although this process was in many ways linked with and influenced by practices prevalent in Shiism, this does not hold true for the visitation and cemetery guides, as they were composed by Sunnite authors. Here, the obvious genres which provided the models for those guides were biographical

112 ḤḪ I p. 754.

113 MuḥḪul III p. 443.

114 The Persian epitaphs quoted are likewise taken from literary sources, see Saǧǧādī: *Surḫāb* pp. 233 and 375.

dictionaries and topographical works, also books about the merits (*faḍāʾil*) of certain people or a certain place or town. The dominant role of litanies and prayer texts in Shiite visitation guides was never adopted in Sunnite Islam nor was it seen necessary to do so. Likewise, there is no evidence for a greater influence of Sunnite guides on Shiite visitation literature.

All known cemetery and visitation guides relating to individual Syrian towns stem from the Ottoman period, mainly the eleventh century H. If we compare this with the fact that virtually all cemetery guides of Cairo and the Ḥiǧāz belong to the Mamluk period (8th–10th cent.s H), it then becomes clear that this literary genre closely reflects the importance of a town during a certain period (as does also the related literary genre of biographical dictionaries). In fact, Damascus largely inherited the place of Cairo as the centre of Arabic Islamic scholarship and literature after the Ottoman conquest of the Near East. The picture is completed if we recall that among the earliest examples of cemetery guides are seventh-century works from al-Andalus and Baghdad, which is in keeping with the Sunnite resurgence of that period. Due to the ongoing *Reconquista* in Spain and the Mongol invasion of Iraq, the cultural elite from both regions was then forced to move to the centre, i.e. to Egypt, Syria and the Ḥiǧāz. There they continued to maintain Islamic scholarship and literature with doubled vigour. The result of that process was the extraordinary ambience of Mamluk Cairo and, from the eighth century H onwards, of Mecca and Medina.

On the whole, the literary genre of visitation and cemetery guides provides nothing less than a mirror of the course of Islamic cultural and intellectual history during the pre-modern period: when the living found the means and the time to produce books devoted to the abodes of their dead, this indicates with some certainty that they had achieved a truly flourishing culture.

4 "Upon his Tombstone I Found Inscribed ..." *Arabic Epitaphs in Literary Sources (1st–12th cent.s H)*

1. *Introduction*

For the history of Arabic funerary epigraphy and the collection of data, literary sources have hitherto been neglected, being used primarily to reconstruct the topography of cemeteries or architectural details of mausolea and other funerary structures. They have sometimes been consulted with the aim of identifying or verifying extant inscriptions as edited in the greater epigraphical collections such as CIA or RCEA, though to my knowledge no systematic effort has been made so far to collect epigraphic data from literary sources. What is more, literary sources, a huge number of which are currently edited and available, are not even mentioned among the possible sources for epigraphic texts in recent monographs that deal with that subject.[1]

According to their status and aesthetic or documentary value, and depending upon the discourse to which they belong, inscriptions are in literary sources either alluded to, briefly mentioned or quoted verbatim. As to their material base, the inscriptions that we encounter in literary sources can be divided into two groups, that is, inscriptions on portable objects (metalware, woodwork, tiles, rings and seals, armoury, etc.) and inscriptions on buildings or affixed to durable constructions. Clearly, epitaphs belong to the second category, though they are often inscribed on objects which in principle must be considered portable (slabs, panels, columns).

If we survey the general presence and importance of all kinds of epigraphy in literary sources, we find that a relatively large number of inscriptions cited actually belong to the first category, viz. inscriptions on portable objects. Many inscriptions of that kind, as with "literary" epitaphs, are quoted as "inscriptions", but were never actually inscribed on any object. Especially in the realm of Arabic poetry, whose material is scattered over a wide range of the most diverse literary sources, there is a huge number of verses which were composed to be written upon lamps, tiles and

1 Blair: *Inscriptions* (esp. ch. 15); Bierman: *Writing Signs*; Insoll: *Archaeology of Islam* (ch. 6).

carpets, saddles, swords and arches, cups, rings and seals, sticks and even nosebags.[2] As said before, those verses need not actually be inscribed on objects – although this could be done, in particular on swords, seals or signet rings –, but the actual practice of engraving something on objects of the sorts mentioned also offered a seductive pretext for poetic creativity. There are no formal criteria to differentiate between "common" or "regular" verses and such rhymed "inscriptions", but their status is chiefly determined by the accompanying paratext, e.g. when verses were preceded by a line saying "The following was written on a lamp", or "He composed the following inscription on a sword". Portable objects of some historical significance quite probably bore the wordings cited in the sources; there is, for example, a good deal of information about what was inscribed on the Prophet's seal[3] and on his white banner.[4] Given the fact that portable objects in general offered little space, the "inscriptions" were usually short and epigrammatic, not dissimilar in many ways from what is known in the European tradition as *emblemata* (though these were meant to accompany symbols, heraldry or images). Normally those "inscriptions" would not exceed one or two lines, and only a few, e.g. four verses which were intended to be inscribed on a bow,[5] are rather exceptional in length. In the same way, and for the same reason, many epitaph-poems do not in general exceed three to four verses.

As a second category we have those inscriptions which are said to have been found on architectural monuments or as part of durable structures and which are also quoted in literary sources; many of these inscriptions can be verified if they have been preserved. Though epitaphs belong to this category, they will be left aside for the moment, because they are dealt with in greater detail in the rest of the chapter. It is important, however, for a better understanding of the role epitaphs play in literary sources, to have some general idea of how inscriptions (in the wider sense, that is including "inscriptions" that were never really executed) are present in written works and what uses their wording was put to, or what value was accorded to them and what function they had in their context(s).

As to the uses of epigraphy in literary sources, three different tendencies can be detected in the texts at our disposition. This holds true, as we will see further below, for inscriptions in general as well as for funerary inscriptions in particular: inscriptions might thus be referred to – or quoted verbatim – in the sources (a) for their importance for the monotheist tradition in Islam, (b) for the aesthetic or paraenetical value they were considered to have, and (c) for the historical information they offer or seem to offer.[6] In a number of cases, more than one of these elements is present and it is often difficult to tell which feature aroused the author's interest in an inscription in the first place.

2 See e.g. IAYaṬab I p. 419.

3 AŠayḫAḫlāq p. 134; BaġAnwār II p. 542; HarĞamᶜWas I pp. 140-2; MunŠŠam I pp. 141f.

4 AŠayḫAḫlāq p. 155; BaġAnwār II p. 591.

5 IḪaṭIḥāṭah II p. 464; *cf.* also Schack: *Poesie und Kunst* I p. 233.

6 *Cf.* Grabar: *Graffiti* pp. 72f.

(a) Inscriptions on monuments were often seen of relevance for demonstrating the monotheist continuity of Islam which pursued and at the same time superseded the course of the older Jewish and Christian creeds. Thus, much material was taken over from the former monotheist traditions into the realm of Islamic learning and literature. Some items even entered the popular lore, e.g. the inscription of Solomon cited in *The Thousand and One Nights* (504th night), predicting the rise of Islam. Or, in another case, we hear of a plate of lead whose inscription gives the names of the "Seven Sleepers" and relates their story, in close connection to what we read in the Qurʾān: *Or dost thou think the Men of the Cave and* ar-raqīm *were among Our signs a wonder* (Q 18:9), with *ar-raqīm* commonly understood as a kind of inscription or inscribed plate.[7] The majority of inscriptions having a religious significance go back to the pre-Islamic period, or so we are told; most of these inscriptions, however, appear to be fictitious. On the other hand, inscriptions of this sort were referred to when pagan sites were claimed in the name of Islam, most notably in the case of the Meccan Kaᶜbah; al-Azraqī even cites inscriptions in that context which were said to have been executed by God Himself.[8] Widely known are the various inscriptions allegedly found on or near the Kaᶜbah before the prophethood of Muḥammad, one of them being "in Syriac" (*bi-s-suryānīyah*) and therefore unintelligible to the Meccan pagans until some Jews read and translated the wording.[9] As is obvious from this last example, the inscriptions cited as stemming from pre-Islamic times were not, as a rule, in Arabic nor written in Arabic letters; nevertheless, the sources seldom mention the original language (or writing) and never quote the wording in a language other than Arabic.[10]

(b) A large number of Arabic inscriptions are quoted in literary sources for their aesthetic or paraenetical value. Though of course it is not established from the outset that the aesthetic value of an inscription must go together with its paraenetical or, as it were, ethical or moral impact, the inscriptions deemed worthy to be cited in the sources normally possess both. More often it would have been rather impossible to draw a clear line between these aspects: an inscription, if set in metre, was considered to have a felicitous expression only if its content also matched its form, and no such inscription was seen worthy of consideration if its style and quality of expression did not equal its content. The majority of non-funerary inscriptions which fall into that category play on the concept of *vanitas*. The attitude they convey matches the mentality which Ján Rypka summarised as follows: "What was a human life? Thrones collapsed, persons came into prominence and then disappeared as they had come".[11] There was thus no particular Islamic religious significance attached to such inscriptions, but many of them were composed by holders of power

7 See IĞawzīTabṣ I pp. 366f.; Lane s.r. *rqm*; WKAS II p. 1710 (s.r. *lwḥ*).

8 AzrMakkah I pp. 78-80.

9 IHišSīrah I p. 196.

10 *Cf.* TMD LI p. 156.

11 Rypka: *Iranian Literature* pp. 83f.

and men of letters or poets close to court circles. Some of those inscriptions, many of which are clearly fictitious, actually make fun of religious customs or run counter to widely accepted conventions and convictions. The sources that cite those inscriptions mainly belong to the discourse of *ʾadab* literature or to the biographical genre; the monuments that reportedly bore those inscriptions were either palaces and the dwellings of the mighty, or – in accordance with their principal motif – the walls of ruined castles[12] and monasteries or, in cases, prison cells. In later times, even the walls of madrasahs and mosques were adorned with similar inscriptions. Establishing the authenticity of such inscriptions on the basis of the literary sources alone is notoriously difficult. But hardly any inscriptions have come to light so far which corroborate the texts as cited in literary sources.

(c) Citing inscriptions or referring to their content, with the purpose of making use of the historical or biographical information they yield, seems, at least from our point of view, the most straightforward reason for the interest in epigraphy. Thus on the basis of inscriptions one could determine the identity of a site, if it was uncertain by hearsay or in other ways, or the details of its foundation, construction and later history, if the site was commonly known. The books which often quote inscriptions for that reason include, as is obvious, topographical treatises and town histories. Other genres which occasionally dwell on inscriptions and exploit their content are travel accounts, biographical dictionaries and, though to a lesser degree, annals and works of historiography proper. The inscriptions normally of interest to the historians were foundation or restoration inscriptions and *waqf* stipulations, as found on mosques, minarets, madrasahs, Sufi hospices, mausolea, hospitals, city walls, gates, wells and fountains. From what appears, inscriptions of this kind are often more or less accurate citations of texts that were indeed inscribed on the objects mentioned and not merely "literary" inscriptions. As many of those inscriptions are today only known from literary sources, having disappeared *in situ* or altogether, their contents still form a precious source for the social and economic history of the Islamic world as well as for cultural and art history. Of course, the phenomenon is well-known and nothing else needs to be said here.

2. *Literary sources and the citation of epitaphs*

Arabic writings, either edited or in manuscript, are a rich source for all sorts of funerary epigraphy. Although written non-epigraphic sources will never replace original inscriptions in historical evidence and quantity, they are valuable sources nevertheless, especially as the literary transmission of inscriptions can often help in correcting or even in reading and understanding the inscriptions found *in situ*. A great number of otherwise lost epitaphs is either hinted at or even quoted verbatim in works belonging to a wide range of different literary genres.

12 *Cf.* Pieter Smoor: *Palace and Ruins, a Theme for Fāṭimid Poets?*, in: Die Welt des Orients 12 (1991), pp. 94-104.

2.1. Epitaphs in languages other than Arabic

The Arabic literary sources mention or cite a considerable number of epitaphs whose original language was not Arabic. In general, such epitaphs do not belong to the Islamic period, but stem from pre-Islamic times or go back, in our view, to legendary or semi-legendary times. Many of those epitaphs are fictitious, especially when they are attributed to the burial sites of persons who are not readily considered historical figures in the proper sense or whose historical existence is doubtful; on the other hand, truly historical inscriptions might have been misread and brought into connection with some better known "hero" of the mythical past. The main languages in which these epitaphs are said to have been drafted are Hebrew,[13] Greek,[14] ancient Persian[15] and Sabaean,[16] though often reference is made less to the foreign language as such, but to the non-Arabic characters of the inscription.[17] One of the richest sources for Ḥimyarite epitaphs is the section *al-Qubūrīyāt* in al-Hamdānī's *Kitāb al-ʾIklīl* where dozens of epitaphs from the tombs of Ḥimyarite kings, pre-Islamic prophets and Arabian heroes are cited.[18]

However, epitaphs of that sort are always quoted in Arabic translation, and also in later centuries, when there were more and more epitaphs composed partially in Persian or Turkish, the original wording was never reported in Arabic works as far as I am aware. The emphasis on the different writing systems, which is prevalent in the quotation of pre-Islamic epitaphs, shows that the value and function of those inscriptions in literary sources was above all symbolic. In fact, on one hand it was the message of such an epitaph that mattered – which was either of antiquarian or religious interest, e.g. when pre-figuring the rise of Islam –, but this could well be conveyed in Arabic without the need to refer to the original wording. On the other hand, the original writing of an inscription and its being found as an inscription at all was important because it served to underline the antiquity and veracity of the message conveyed, with the foreign characters functioning as icons which made the great age of those epitaphs and their message visible and unquestionable.

13 See IŠadAᶜlāq I (Aleppo) p. 129; IMuḥKunūz I pp. 96-8; IAHawlFaḍ pp. 34f. and 50; Grunebaum: *Islam im Mittelalter* p. 310.

14 IMuḥKunūz I pp. 96f.; IŠadAᶜlāq I (Aleppo) p. 128. For other Greek inscriptions, see IĞawzīTabṣ II p. 17. *Cf.* also Baffioni: *Filosofia islamica* p. 45.

15 ZamRabīᶜ IV p. 190; IĞawzīTabṣ I pp. 335f.; *cf.* also HamdIklīl pp. 170f.

16 IADunyāQubūr (A) pp. 160f.; *Aġānī* IV p. 218; AᶜArabṬab pp. 55f.; TMD IX p. 99; YāqBuldān I p. 157; QazwĀṯār pp. 17f.; MarğBahğah I pp. 153-6; IbšīhīMust II p. 467 (ch. 83); MaqrMuq III p. 695; BaḥrKaškūl I p. 353; ŠayMağānī IV p. 40. For the Ḥimyarite tombs, see also Smith/Haddad: *Islamic Understanding of Death* p. 150 and WKAS II pp. 1710f.

17 The South Arabian writing, *al-musnad*, is often mentioned. This term could be applied to hieroglyphs as well, but I do not know of any ancient Egyptian epitaph cited in Arabic sources.

18 HamdIklīl pp. 124-227.

2.2. Inscriptions on funerary monuments other than epitaphs

As just a number of non-Arabic epitaphs are quoted in literary sources, so we also read of Arabic inscriptions affixed to burial sites or inscribed upon funerary structures, e.g. the walls of a mausoleum, though these inscriptions were no epitaphs in the proper sense, but rather had a commemorative character or aimed at giving information about the erection (or the restoration) of the funerary monument. In the latter case, the inscriptions were similar in form and content to other building inscriptions, and therefore nothing else need be said here.

More interesting in our context, and much more rarely encountered in the sources, are those inscriptions on funerary structures which are neither epitaphs nor building inscriptions. In some instances, they clearly were meant to identify the monument and thus their function resembles that of epitaphs proper, as in the case of what al-Maqrīzī read on the door of the Cairene mausoleum of Abū Turāb "on a marble slab (*ruḫāmah*) on which several lines of Kufic characters were engraved".[19] In other cases, they had a distinct commemorative or paraenetical character. A good example would be the chronogram (*taʾrīḫ*) of three verses' length which Muḥammad b. Aflāṭūn composed upon the death of Aḥmad Pasha Walīy ad-Dīn al-Ḥusaynī (d. 902 H) and which he had written on the door of his mausoleum (*qubbah*).[20] In the same manner, the Syrian poet aṣ-Ṣanawbarī (A. b. M., d. 334 H) composed mourning poems about a daughter of his – six couplets in all –, then had a mausoleum (*qubbah*) built above her tomb and covered its walls with these verses.[21]

Certainly the most notable example of covering a funerary monument with commemorative or paraenetical inscriptions is seen in the inscriptions on the walls of the (no longer extant) mausoleum of the eccentric Aleppine scholar Abū l-Ḥasan ᶜAlī b. Abī Bakr al-Harawī (d. 611 H).[22] The mausoleum itself, which was constructed during al-Harawī's lifetime in 602 H as part of his madrasah but was partly destroyed only some decades later during the Mongol invasion,[23] seems to have been a curious monument, for it resembled the cubic form of the Meccan Kaᶜbah;[24] this is attested by an inscription found there that says: "This mausoleum (*turbah*) is modelled on the Kaᶜbah" (see also page 248).[25] There are other inscriptions extant which name al-Harawī as the founder of the mausoleum and give the year 602 H as date of its completion (see **5**).[26] According to Ibn al-Muḥaddiṯ, the walls of al-Harawī's *turbah*

19 MaqrḪiṭaṭ II p. 49.

20 ŠḎ VIII p. 13.

21 IŠadAᶜlāq I (Aleppo) p. 157. The verses are reported in A. b. M. aṣ-Ṣanawbarī aḍ-Ḍabbī: *Dīwān aṣ-Ṣanawbarī*, ed. Iḥsān ᶜAbbās, Beirut: Dār aṯ-Ṯaqāfah 1970, pp. 514f.

22 His pilgrimage guide *Kitāb al-ʾIšārāt* is dealt with in further detail above pp. 296f.

23 See IŠadAᶜlāq I p. 108 and al-Ġazzī: *Nahr aḏ-ḏahab* II p. 221. For photographs of what remains today of the building: CIA Alep II plates CXII-IV.

24 The mausoleum was visited by Ibn Ḫallikān, as he relates in his *Wafayāt* (IḪallWaf III p. 347). *Cf.* also EI² III p. 178.

25 CIA Alep 131. *Cf.* also the ground plan in CIA Alep II plate CXIa.

26 al-Ġazzī: *Nahr aḏ-ḏahab* II p. 222; CIA Alep 129f., 135 (fragment 7), 138; RCEA 3609–11.

were covered with wise sayings and religious exhortations (*ḥikam wa-mawāʿiẓ*) in verse and rhymed prose, some scattered fragments of which have been preserved. An ample reconstruction of these inscriptions is found in Volume I pp. 95ff.

Besides commemorative or paraenetical inscriptions, many a funerary monument was adorned with inscriptions comprising passages of the Qurʾān. This practice seems to have been so common (or so self-evident) that it was almost never commented upon or even mentioned in literary sources. The only instance to the contrary that I know of concerns the mausoleum (*turbah*) of Yūsuf b. Ibrāhīm al-Qifṭī in Aleppo (d. 646 H, the father of the bibliographer), as described by Ibn al-Muḥaddiṯ. In his acount we read that al-Qifṭī's mausoleum "is a beautiful dome (*qubbah*), firmly built, and on its outside (*ʿalā ẓāhirihā*) is written: *All that dwells upon the earth is perishing, / yet still abides the Face of thy Lord, majestic, splendid* (Q 55:26f.)".[27]

Finally, in various literary sources I have come across two other instances of inscriptions connected to burial sites which, however, do not fit any category and are unique; they are also wholly different from each other in character and thus deserve to be presented in the following.

The first case is a derogatory inscription scribbled on a tomb in Baṣrah.[28] The story is told by, among others, Ibn Ḫallikān and aṣ-Ṣafadī (although they differ as to the details): the poet Abū ʿAmr (or Abū Yaḥyā) Ḥammād ʿAǧrad (d. after 155 H)[29] was suspected for his heretical views and buried in Baṣrah. When the blind poet Baššār b. Burd (d. 167 or 168 H), likewise thought to have harboured unorthodox attitudes, was later killed by the caliph al-Mahdī, his body was carried to Baṣrah and buried aside Ḥammād.[30] An old enemy of Baššār, Abū Hišām al-Bāhilī, once came across their tombs and had written – at least according to Ibn Ḫallikān[31] – upon each of them the following lines (*sarīʿ*):

قَدْ تَبِعَ الأَعْمَى قَفَا عَجْرَدٍ * فَأَصْبَحَا جَارَيْنِ فِي دَارِ
قَالَتْ بِقَاعُ الأَرْضِ لا مَرْحَباً * بِقُرْبِ حَمَّادٍ وَبَشَّارِ

27 IMuḥKunūz I p. 430. This Qurʾānic passage, fitting as it is, was often inscribed upon funerary structures or tombstones. Most notably, it was part of the epitaph of Mālik b. Anas (**167**); see also below p. 410 with note 328.

28 According to Islamic belief the deceased must not be abused (*sabb al-ʾamwāt*, see IMandahFaw I p. 162; IAĞamrBahğah II pp. 1400f.; KU 42712ff. = XV p. 680). Some Traditions from the Prophet recommend that the merits (*maḥāsin*) of the deceased be extolled and their ugly deeds (*masāwī*) passed over in silence (cited in DaylFird I p. 70). However, the placing satirical or derogatory verses upon a tomb was not limited to the case presented above; *cf.* Schimmel: *Sufismus* pp. 287f.

29 On him, see also above p. 166.

30 *Cf.* BN X p. 114.

31 According to al-Iṣfahānī and aṣ-Ṣafadī, al-Bāhilī merely recited these verses at their tombs. Also following aṣ-Ṣafadī, Abū Hišām, like Baššār b. Burd, was blind and could not possibly have inscribed these verses by himself.

تَجَاوَرَا بَعْدَ تَنَائِيهِمَا * مَا أَبْغَضَ الجَارَ إِلَى الجَارِ
صَارَا جَمِيعاً فِي يَدَيْ مَالِكٍ * فِي النَّارِ وَالكَافِرُ فِي النَارِ

"Now the blind (i.e. Baššār) has followed the tracks of ᶜAğrad[32] * and both became two neighbours in one abode (i.e. the tomb, *or perhaps* the hereafter).
The spots of ground (where they are buried) said, 'No welcome * for the closeness of Ḥammād and Baššār!'[33]
Both have become neighbours after distancing themselves (i.e. after their death), * (and) how detestable the neighbour was to his neighbour![34]
Both are together in the hands of Mālik[35] * in the Fire, since the unbeliever stays in the Fire!"[36]

The second instance to be presented here is not a derisory inscription, but on the contrary a moving example of piety, – or, as some would say, of female submissiveness in a world dominated by male authority. The story, as related by Ibn al-Ğazarī, has it that the scholar and mystic Ibn Abī Ğamrah died in Ḏū l-Qaᶜdah 695 H in Cairo (where his mausoleum is still extant in the southern Qarāfah cemetery), and "his daughter kept him company (in his home) until he passed away (*quḍiya*). When this had happened, she wrote on a tablet (*lawḥ*): 'In the Name of God, the Merciful, the Compassionate. Come in to the sheikh, for he has passed away'. She put that tablet near the door and knocked on it until the servant appeared and opened the door. When he saw the tablet, he understood that the sheikh had died. All this was done in that way so that she did not have to speak to him and that nobody would hear her voice".[37]

2.3. The uses of epitaphs in literary sources

For the importance of epitaphs in literary sources much the same could be said as about inscriptions in general, with one exception: in the literary tradition Arabic epitaphs were not considered significant for the monotheist heritage of Islam, in contrast with other types of epigraphy and non-Arabic epitaphs (see above). However, like other inscriptions, epitaphs were referred to or cited in the sources either for their aesthetic or paraenetical value, or for the historical information they contain.

32 A very malicious hemistich: how could a blind person follow the traces of someone?

33 Slane translates: "How unwelcome to us is the neighbourhood of Hammâd and Bashshâr!" The verse intends to say that the earth received the bodies of both heretics only reluctantly. For the opposite case, *cf.* the first line of epitaph **190**.

34 Ḥammād ᶜAğrad and Baššār b. Burd had not been on friendly terms during their lives.

35 The angel of Hell.

36 The version of the verses follows *Aġānī* XIV p. 381; they are also quoted in IḪallWaf II p. 213 / (Slane) I p. 475 (missing line 3); *Wāfī* XIII pp. 143f.; Ḥusayn: *al-Adab al-ᶜarabī* II p. 269 (var. *tanāʾīhimā*: *tağāfīhimā*).

37 IĞazḤaw I p. 307.

According to different literary genres, the first or the second aspect was of paramount interest, and the respective points of view also determined in which way and to what degree epitaphs are cited verbatim in the sources. Of little surprise is that, if the aesthetic and paraenetical value of an epitaph was in fact of primary interest, only the verses contained in an epitaph would be cited; if the historical value stood in the foreground, only the name, the date of death and personal epitheta would be quoted.

Only rarely did it happen that both the aesthetic or paraenetical and the historical value of a funerary inscription were considered of interest in a literary source. This also explains why there are so few epitaphs cited completely in literary sources, that is, comprising the more formal elements (name, date, accompanying eulogies and epitheta, confessional statements, Qurʾānic passages) as well as, potentially, poetry. Even in those cases where we find the more or less complete wording cited, typical components of an epitaph (e.g. the *basmalah* or Qurʾānic verses) could be skipped because they were taken for granted and in any case of little informative value. In the catalogue of epitaphs quoted in literary sources (see below), the total number of epitaphs that may be said to be cited completely (including all formal elements) amounts to less than 2%.

The statistical evaluation of the catalogue yields another fact of great importance, namely that roughly two thirds of epitaphs quoted in literary sources only report the poetry.[38] This clearly shows that in most cases the "message" of an epitaph, especially if set in rhyme, was thought to be its most important element. In many literary genres – *ʾadab* literature and poetical anthologies, religious texts and eschatological works –, the number of instances where only verses are cited from epitaphs ranges from about 90% to 100%. In biographical works, the amount of poetry cited from epitaphs reaches some 75% of all epitaphs quoted, and even in historical works and cemetery guides the poetical parts of epitaphs make up almost half of all citations.[39] Still, in most Arabic cemetery guides and historical or biographical works the historical value of epitaphs is paramount, and sometimes funerary inscriptions were the only sources the historians could rely upon to establish the biographical data concerning a certain person (see below).

In medieval European chronicles most epitaphs cited do likewise not enhance our knowledge of historical or biographical facts, but offer a synthesis of somebody's achievement, character, or both. This holds true for such famous examples as the Latin verse epitaph composed by Rahewin for his teacher, the famous historian Otto of Freising (d. 1159 CE).[40] The importance of epitaphs which "digest" somebody's achievement or character in a few lines has a great tradition in the mediaeval and modern West and is in itself a token of the strong influence of the Greek and Roman tradition of

38 The many Meccan epitaphs cited in FāsīʿIqd, representing about one fifth of the total, are not included in the calculation, because he hardly ever quotes poetic material, and thus would unbalance the statistics.

39 These numbers again do not include FāsīʿIqd; see the preceding note.

40 Otto von Freising and Rahewin: *Die Taten Friedrichs oder richtiger Chronica (Gesta Frederici seu rectius Chronica)*, edd. A. Schmidt and F.-J. Schmale, Darmstadt [4]2000, pp. 542-6 (... *hoc epythaphium composui et tumulo seu cenotaphio eius inscribi feci*).

funerary inscriptions; the best way to grasp the mood of ancient (and also post-classical or Byzantine) Greek epitaphs is Book 7 of the so-called *Anthologia Graeca* (or *A. Palatina*), which comprises some 750 funerary inscriptions, most of them obviously fictitious and never inscribed upon real tombs.[41] An epitaph was thus often used as a purely literary form, without regard to its actual application in practice. This eventually became common in mediaeval and early modern Europe as well, and most epitaphs we find quoted in literary sources are merely poems clad in the form of an epitaph (see below). Moreover, the borders between the epitaph and the funerary discourse – both called *epitaphium*[42] – were fluid in the European tradition from ancient times. In the Arabic tradition, in contrast, epitaphs never did become an independent poetical genre. The idea that an epitaph was to condense the achievement or character of a person into a few memorable lines was but poorly developed in the Islamic realm.

The importance of epitaph-poetry as cited in Arabic literary sources is further enhanced by the fact that in a great number of cases the citations are not accompanied by any information about the deceased, which is why we are often left in the dark about the identity of the deceased and the actual location of his tomb. In more than half of the instances of quotations from epitaphs in religious and eschatological works we are not even told the date of death and are thus lacking concrete chronological evidence. Often the lifetime of the author of a given source, or the authority he happens to quote, must provide the *terminus ante quem* for an epitaph cited.

Interest in the historical content is relatively minor and the few instances where names and dates occur are confined to cemetery guides and chronicles. In contrast, the great mass of poetry quoted from epitaphs emphasises the aesthetic or paraenetical value of the inscriptions, which is heightened by being kept anonymous: the message was often completely unrelated to the one who had composed it or from the one upon whose tomb it was inscribed. The sole importance of the "message" becomes clear if we see how epitaphs are dealt with in religious, eschatological or *ʾadab* works. Here, they are normally grouped together, and their wordings are quoted without many details as to the location of the epitaph and the person buried. This is the case in the *ʾIḥyāʾ* of al-Ġazālī or also in the various works of Ibn Abī d-Dunyā, Ibn Rağab, as-Suyūṭī and others; in the realm of *ʾadab*, Ibn ʿAbd Rabbih has a chapter on "persons who mourned themselves and described their tombs, also what was written upon the tomb". Not surprisingly, however, poetical anthologies quote epitaphs only if they possess, or are considered to possess, poetical quality of some sort. This means that it is almost exclusively epitaph-poems, not entire epitaphs or the relevant prose parts, that are quoted in those books.

However, in many instances the deceased is duly identified in the sources, though only the poetical parts of his epitaph are quoted. This holds true especially if the verses were composed by the deceased himself (often as part of his last will, see below) or if the deceased was a personality of some standing and fame. In general, the practice followed depends on the literary genre. Thus biographical and historical

41 I consulted the chapter on funerary inscriptions in the German translation of the *Anthologia*, viz. *Die Griechische Anthologie in drei Bänden*, vol. II, Berlin 1991, pp. 7-202.

42 *Cf. Lexikon des Mittelalters* III: *Codex Wintoniensis bis Erziehungs- und Bildungswesen*, Munich 2002 (1999), pp. 2072-4, *s.v.* "Epitaphium".

sources normally name the deceased and the date of death if citing poetry from an epitaph – unidentified epitaphs in those sources amount to less than 5% –, while "message"-centred works (anthologies, eschatological treatises, etc.) do not. This also has had far-reaching consequences for the use made in modern scholarship of epitaphs quoted in literary sources: unidentified epitaphs, of which only the poetical passages are quoted, were considered of little or no value to the historian, yet they are of the utmost importance for the study of mentalities in the Islamic culture and our understanding of Islam as a cultural and religious system. In any case, the neglect of poetry in funerary inscriptions would deprive us of many a memorable line. On a more technical side, the versions of epitaph-poetry in literary sources are an invaluable help for the edition of epitaphs which are badly or only fragmentarily preserved.

That the poetical parts of epitaphs, which in general would contain the significant message, were considered their most precious component can be seen from a statement of Nūr ad-Dīn as-Saḫāwī who justly remarked that "people have written innumerable *mawāʿiẓ* on the tombs".[43] This shows the close connection between form and content because a *mawʿiẓah* (pl. *mawāʿiẓ*), a hortatory saying or thought, was, apart from its message, esteemed for its being set in verse or rhymed prose, or at least for being epigrammatical. As said above, the message of an epitaph could stand for itself in literary sources irrespective of the actual deceased, even if the epitaph cited – given that it was indeed inscribed upon a tomb and not mere literary fiction – did contain the name of the deceased and his date of death. In addition, a number of popular verses are said to have been found on more than one epitaph, and it seems to be no coincidence that verses which either appear in early literary sources or are cited in more than one source have also been found on preserved epitaphs (**2**, **11**, **72**, **86**, **195** and **202**). The combination of evidence from literary sources and preserved epitaphs easily shows that there were some truly famous verses which were known in almost every part of the Islamic world and frequently resorted to by the sculptors of tombstones. The existence of such "model-verses" is acknowledged in literary sources, for example when we read that Ayman b. Muḥammad (d. 734 H), an encomiast of the Prophet and thus called ᶜĀšiq an-nabī, "Lover of the Prophet", composed two verses which "are written on a number of tombs in the (Medinan) Baqīᶜ cemetery" (**169**).

As to the geographical distribution of Arabic epitaph-poetry, the evidence of literary sources confirms the general picture gained from preserved inscriptions, namely that from the second century H onwards epitaph-poems were employed in all regions of the Islamic world. On the whole, in the literary tradition there seems to be a slight dominance of the western lands after the fourth century H, and fewer examples than elsewhere are known from the East (Persia and beyond). However, the general literary impression might easily be misleading, because we depend on a limited number of sources which reveal either their place and time of origin and the limitations of the discourses they belong to, or the individual predilections of the

43 SaḫTuḥfAḥbāb p. 10.

author. Thus the vast majority of poetical epitaphs cited in *ʾadab* literature, poetical anthologies and eschatological treatises stem from Syria and Iraq, and more than a third of these go back to the first two centuries H (as far as we can say). Poetical epitaphs from the Islamic West are mainly found in biographical and historical works, and about 40% to 50% of these epitaphs belong to the fifth to the eighth centuries H. Of course, this does reflect the quality and quantity of the respective sources at our disposition more than the actual distribution of poetical epitaphs. At least the biographical literature in general indicates that poetry has been employed in the East, in particular in Syria, throughout all centuries up to 1200 H (and, of course, ever since, albeit with a growing distaste for funeral poetry in general and a noticeable tendency towards more "sober" and brief prose epitaphs in the contemporary period).

Finally, there remains one point of interest: was the poetical epitaph ever conceived of as a literary genre of its own in Islamic culture? For the European culture, this question must be answered positively from at least the fifteenth century CE, when the Humanist movement – inspired by ancient models – had engendered new interest in poetical funerary inscriptions which was then taken up in the vernacular literatures, ultimately leading to the flourishing of the poetical epitaph during the 16th to 18th centuries CE. By the late 16th century CE, various attempts were made to class epitaphs either as panegyric poems, as elegies, as epigrams, or as a combination of all three.[44] None of these categories were alien to Arabic literature, and indeed poe-

44 *Cf.* Franke: *Vers-Epitaph* pp. 48-71 and *passim*; Scodel: *Poetic Epitaph.* An important contribution for thc historical development of grave monuments and epitaphs (viz. memorial inscriptions) in Europe is chapter 11 in Houlbrooke: *Death in England.* – It seems worthwhile to quote here two early modern passages dealing with epitaphs: (a) from George Puttenham's *Arte of english Poesie* (1589): "An Epitaph is but a kind of Epigram only applied to the report of the dead persons estate and degree, or of his other good or bad partes, to his commendation or reproch: and is an inscription such as a man may commodiously write or engrave upon a tombe in few verses, pithie, quicke and sententious for the passer by to peruse, and iudge upon without any long tariaunce: So as if it exceede the measure of an Epigram, it is then (if the verse be correspondent) rather an Elegie then an Epitaph which errour many of these bastard rimers commit, because they be not learned" (cited in Franke: *Vers-Epitaph* p. 48 and Scodel: *Poetic Epitaph* p. 87); (b) from *Of the Antiquity and Selected Variety of Epitaphs in England* (1599/1600): "An epitaph is a monument of the dead; it is a kind of poem, though not perfect, but as an Italian calls it, a Mote, or Atome of poetry, *poeticus atomus.* Now as there is not any precise art or imitation required in such compositions, therefore they are not spoke of by Aristotle in his booke of poetry. And yet in this apish age, where so many imitators scribble poems, there are divers who prescribe rules for making epitaphs, allowing of none, except they contain as many parts as a demonstrative oration: such as the praise of the party buried – what a great loss or misse the world hath of him – and there upon a mournfull lamentation – then a comfort to the world – and lastly an exhortation to imitate his virtues. All these, say they, must be exprest shortly and clearly. Others will have the name of the defunct, together with his age, estate, deserts, gifts of body and mind, as also the time of his death sett forth; and so would have it a breif story or description of his life. – This forsooth should be the matter of an epitaph. For the form, they will have it of one peice, and as it were one maine conceit with the parts continued, chayned and depending: besides, it must not be verse, but a kind of metricall prose, seeming so

tical epitaphs do stand in some relation to panegyric poetry or mourning poetry, yet the obvious resemblance of funerary poetry as found in epitaphs is to ascetic poetry (*zuhdīyāt*) and related genres (e.g. *ḏamm ad-dunyā*). That most, albeit not all, epitaph-poems were epigrammatic in character was dictated by their being destined, at least theoretically, to find their place on a tombstone; some epitaph-poems, on the other hand, contain more than ten verses and in some cases even more (*cf.* **1** and **89**f.). Still, the European literary development of epitaphs towards a purely poetic "monument" of afterlife and thus a distinct literary genre without connection to an actual burial site,[45] does not seem to have occurred in the Arabic realm, although not every epitaph-poem reported in literary sources was indeed inscribed upon a particular grave.

In the literary sources at our disposal, we rarely find Arabic epitaphs quoted completely, and the nearest (but quite unique) attempt to treat epitaphs as a genre of its own is aš-Šaybī's collection of Meccan epitaphs (see Chapter 3). In addition, poetical epitaphs in Arabic literature were always bound up with an existing tomb, if not with an individual deceased. Furthermore, "anonymous" epitaphs were not depicted as purely literary fiction and thus only presented as "epitaph" for a commonly accepted convention of a literary genre, but always presented as if taken from or composed for an *actual* funerary inscription, that is, a possible epitaph. Moreover, literary sources do not cite, to my knowledge, Arabic epitaphs which play with human characteristics or social roles, similar to European compositions such as *Upon the grave of a beggar* or *Epitaph for a quarrelsome wife*; the Arabic epitaphs that come nearest to that might be the epitaphs for deceased physicians (**177** and **198**), yet they are still connected or ascribed to specific, or even famous, physicians. In European literature, on the contrary, composing "genre-epitaphs" was a convenient way of expressing general truths (or prejudices) about certain people or social classes, or of condensing the achievement of a famous personality in a few words (e.g. Pope's epitaph for Isaac Newton), and although the Arab poets attained great mastery in expressing similar thoughts and concepts, they never couched it in the form of an epitaph: there is many a biting verse about quarrelsome wives in Arabic literature, but it would be simply introduced by the paratext *So-and-so said about a quarrelsome wife*, yet not with *Upon the tomb of a quarrelsome wife was written*.

by the strange transposition of the words; which must likewiese taste nothing of the moderne, but be all 'antiche'; I speak not this, as if I lov'd not antiquities, which were ever venerable; I reverence them, as I would revere Adam, if he were alive; but I speak it for honor of our English epitaphes, notwithstanding they are not cutt out according to the aforesaid measure, but as they are divers, so have their divers formes; and yet none of them are without an especial grace. The only rule that is observed in them, is that which is required in an epigram, viz. witt and brevity; conformable to the opinion of Plato, who, in his commonwealth, requireth, that an epitaph should not consist of above four lines" (quoted in Franke: *Vers-Epitaph* p. 54).

45 With epitaphs being fictitious from the outset and thus completely "literary" this also meant that the shortness of expression, a necessary requirement for actual epitaphs, lost much of its importance. Literary epitaphs in the Western tradition tended to become longer over the centuries to the extent that they could no longer be inscribed upon real graves (save those of formidable size and costs).

Most importantly, there are as good as no humorous poetical epitaphs in Arabic literature, though some verses reported as funerary inscriptions are rather sarcastic or witty (**111**, **193**, **196**, **221** and **229**). Satirical or humorous epitaphs can be considered the most obvious examples of the purely fictional epitaph in the European tradition, because they were not, as a rule, composed for actually being written upon a tomb.[46] This particular genre is lacking in Arabic literature, and likewise the related genre of satirical mourning poems was never very popular. However, humorous mourning poems did exist, e.g. the compositions of Abū l-Ḥakam al-Bāhilī aṭ-Ṭabīb al-Andalusī[47] who was not only famous for playing the lute, but also for his poetry: "He made fun of his contemporaries and often composed mourning poems about persons who were actually alive". Some of these humorous elegies "in the guise of a mourning poem" (*ʿalā sabīli l-marṯiyah*) are quoted in biographical works.[48] Another man of letters who produced humorous mourning poems was Abū š-Šibl ʿĀṣim b. Wahb, for example about an imbecile physician (who was, of course, still alive), about a broken oil lamp and a stolen paper.[49]

2.4. Testamentary stipulations

A peculiar type of epitaphs in Arabic literature is verses said to have been composed by someone shortly before his death, together with the last wish to have them inscribed upon his tomb.[50] This is often reported in literary sources and seems to have been more widespread in the Islamic culture than, for example, in Europe. All instances of such "testamentary" epitaphs quoted in literary sources have been included in the catalogue of epitaphs (see below) because they provide important evidence for the history of mentalities and the textual history of Arabic funerary inscriptions, notwithstanding the fact that in most cases we do not know whether the verses were then indeed engraved upon the tomb or the tombstone or not.

Some of the more famous instances of "testamentary" epitaphs include the lines which the famous poets al-Muʿtamid Ibn ʿAbbād (**1**), Ibn Munīr aṭ-Ṭarābulusī (**3**), Abū Nuwās (**14**f.), Abū l-ʿAtāhiyah (**17**f.), Ibn Maṭrūḥ (**55**), al-Qālī (**72**), Ibn Šuhayd (**73**), al-Būrīnī (**80**), al-Luqaymī (**82**), al-Maʿarrī (**111**), Ibn Šarīf ar-Rundī (**175**), aš-Šilbī (**178**) and Ibn az-Zaqqāq (**188**) composed for their respective epitaphs, or those which the famous Hanbalite traditionist and preacher Ibn al-Ǧawzī stipulated

46 See e.g. the anthologies by Giovanni Francesco Loredano (*Il Cimiterio cioè epitaffi giocosi*, Venice 1654) and Hans Aßmann von Abschatz (*Schertz-Grabschrifften*, 1704).

47 ʿAbd Allāh b. al-Muẓaffar, born in Yemen and died in Damascus 549 H.

48 IAUṣaybʿUyūn p. 625; *Wāfī* XVII pp. 623-5.

49 See *Aġānī* XIV pp. 195 and 204-10. For mourning poems on animals, see **237**.

50 The Arabic verb commonly used in this context is *wṣy* IV *bi-* or *ʾan*. Unfortunately, this can either mean "to stipulate in the last will that ..." or "to decree by will that ...", which presupposes a written testament of some sort, or "to express the last wish that ...", which does not. It is thus not clear in the sources whether a certain person stipulated something and included this in his will or whether he expressed his last wish only orally.

by will to be written on his tombstone (**26**). In the latter half of the ninth century H, the Egyptian scholar Ibn al-Ūğāqī sent two verses to his younger colleague and friend, the biographer Šams ad-Dīn as-Saḫāwī, so that he could write them on his tombstone after his death (**69**). Though we do not know whether as-Saḫāwī actually had this done, he outlived Ibn al-Ūğāqī and quoted the verses in his biographical dictionary.

In other cases, it remains ambiguous in the sources whether such "testamentary" epitaphs were composed by the deceased himself or merely selected by him (e.g. **94**f.) and only occasionally do we find the former or the latter practice explicitly stated in the sources (e.g. **23**, **65**, **84**, **103**, **171** and **178**). In one of the few instances where we learn that a "testamentary" epitaph was duly carried out, we do not know its wording: Ibn ᶜAbd Rabbih says in his anthology that somebody "requested in his will that certain verses be written upon his tomb and they were indeed written upon it *(fa-kutibat)*".[51] Unfortunately, these verses are, as it seems, lost for ever.

That the interest in poetry – when referring to or quoting from (projected or actual) epitaphs – was paramount in a number of literary genres, especially in poetical anthologies and biographical dictionaries, we may infer from the fact that often verses of similar style and content are cited which were, however, not meant to be written on tombstones. Rather, they were to accompany the dead in his grave and be thus buried with him. A good example of this practice is the case of al-ᶜAlāʾ Abū l-Ḥasan Ibn aš-Šiḥnah (756–831 H),[52] who asked his cousin Muḥibb ad-Dīn Abū l-Faḍl to have two lines written and "thrown" into his grave (*ʾawṣāhu bi-ʾilqāʾihimā fī qabrihī*);[53] Abū l-Ḥasan's cousin duly fulfilled this last wish as he did not fail to remark. A similar story is known from the Alexandrian traditionist and jurist Abū l-Iḫlāṣ Ibn at-Tinnisī (after 780–853 H), who during the plague year of 847 H "composed" some verses in a dream and decreed by will that they be buried with him (see below page 379). Others stipulated that verses of their own should be written upon their shroud, e.g. the man of letters and poet Ṣalāḥ ad-Dīn al-Irbilī:[54] he composed two verses which were to be written "with saffron" upon his shroud (*ᶜalā ʾakfānihī*).[55]

2.5. Epitaphs as historical evidence

In biographical, topographical and historiographical literature the historical value of epitaphs was often considered the most important aspect. It is only in later, more "belletristic" historiographies that epitaphs are cited for their inherent message – and thus as an entertainment or admonition for the reader – even though there was

51 IᶜARabᶜIqd (G) II p. 161 / (M) III p. 248.

52 ᶜAlī b. Muḥammad b. Muḥammad b. Maḥmūd al-Ḥalabī, a Hanafite judge in Aleppo.

53 As cited in IŠamQabas I p. 529.

54 Aḥmad b. ᶜAbd as-Sayyid (Irbil 570 or 572 – ar-Ruhā 631 H).

55 MaqrMuq I p. 501.

no need to cite them as a historical document; this is, for example, the case with the epitaph of Abū Nuwās quoted by Ibn Iyās (see **15**).

It is also worth noting that the use made of epitaphs in the biographical literature cannot be assessed in general, that is, by speaking about this genre as a whole. Much depends on the single author, and there have been scholars who show no interest in epitaphs at all although they seem to have been very interested in burial sites and the location or structure of tombs. An example of this attitude would be the book containing the biographies of grammarians and philologists by the seventh-century Aleppine scholar (Ibn) al-Qifṭī. Nonetheless, the seventh century H was very much one of the periods when interest in funerary inscriptions – and epigraphy in general – flourished among Arabic scholars. This is attested in a number of biographical dictionaries and town histories of that epoch. Of course, interest in epitaphs did entail making visits to cemeteries and taking notes of the inscriptions, and the seventh century H is a time which is marked by a strong propensity towards travelling and inspecting places in general. In the centuries before, cemeteries were largely visited for the hortatory value of doing so, and some authors who collected the biographies of early ascetics therefore also strolled around in cemeteries, e.g. Abū Nuᶜaym (d. 430 H) in Nīsābūr.[56]

In the Mamluk period, that is from the late seventh-century H onwards, a more "bookish" approach came to prevail in much of the biographical literature as a result of the increasing quantity of learned literature. If we take the example of aṣ-Ṣafadī (in his *Aᶜyān* and *Wāfī*) we can see that he was not particularly interested in epigraphy nor in epitaphs; he cites almost no funerary inscriptions except those which he found mentioned in earlier literary sources or those which are "testamentary epitaphs" (and are also reported in literary sources or poetical anthologies). He certainly had no "archaeological" spirit like the authors of the seventh century H, and thus aṣ-Ṣafadī never uses expressions such as "I saw on ...", "I noticed at ..." or the like. This bookish approach, which depends almost entirely on literary sources and not on personal investigation or "sightseeing", was to dominate the entire Mamluk period, with only a few exceptions (e.g. al-Fāsī's biographical dictionary of Meccans). Ibn Ḥaǧar al-ᶜAsqalānī, to take another example, in his *Durar* (containing more than 5200 biographies) does not once, as far as I can see, quote an epitaph, nor does he refer to one in order to settle dates of death. Instead, he and many of his colleagues in numerous cases consulted only literary sources, even though these are often in disagreement with each other. The same holds true of the dictionary of Hanbalite scholars by Ibn Raǧab: he mentions only the epitaph of Ibn al-Ǧawzī (**26**) yet this was already known from previous literary sources. Šams ad-Dīn as-Saḫāwī, towards the end of the ninth century H, is a little more inquisitive and cites in his biographical works a handful of epitaphs, though their number is likewise limited if one considers the quantity of the material he offers.

Looking at Mamluk historiographies and town histories we again become aware of the fact that funerary inscriptions were not seen as such an important source,

56 ANuḤilyah X p. 244 = Gramlich: *Vorbilder* II pp. 191f.

after all. Ibn Qāḍī Šuhbah in his *Tārīḫ*, for example, never refers to or cites from epitaphs, nor does he use them as a source of information. His entire approach is wholly "bookish" although he often provides very detailed information as to the actual location of someone's tomb. Similarly, the *Qalāʾid* by the tenth-century scholar Ibn Ṭūlūn, covering the history and monuments of aṣ-Ṣāliḥīyah (Damascus), is noteworthy for its neglect of epitaphs: although the author writes for many pages about mausolea and funerary structures, he almost never mentions or cites from epitaphs, with only four exceptions throughout the entire treatise.[57] On the other hand, he quite often indicates the position of single tombs, which means that he probably had seen them.

A special interest in epitaphs can be observed in the Islamic West. From the fifth century H onwards, many epitaphs are cited in the biographical and historiographical literature stemming from western scholars, up to the *ʾIḥāṭah* by Lisān ad-Dīn Ibn al-Ḫaṭīb. It is also important to note in that context that stylistically refined and lengthy epitaphs were, especially from the seventh century H onwards, a common feature at the tombs of rulers in the Islamic West, e.g. of the Naṣrids in Granada or of the Moroccan dynasties (the Marīnids and Saʿdids). In the Mamluk East we find nothing of that sort and not a single tomb of a Mamluk ruler was equipped with an epitaph comparable to those of the Islamic West. This has certainly to do with the fact that the Mamluk rulers and their entourage, without exception of Turkish or Circassian origin, were promoters, but never part, of Arabic culture, in contrast with the rulers in the Islamic West, whose interest and proficiency in Arabic belles-lettres and poetry is well-documented.

However, in most cases the wording of epitaphs is only cited in western biographical literature when it consisted of poetry or when it offered a hortatory message. In the case of a funerary inscription only mentioning the name of the deceased and his date of death, we often find that the authors would only say that they had read an epitaph and taken up the information it offered. Thus the wording of the inscription is not quoted, but the relatively frequent recourse to funerary inscriptions in western biographical literature is a noteworthy feature, and it further attests to the fact that the scholars were moving around and possessed some kind of "archaeological" spirit, or rather a feeling for the *genius loci* of burial sites. The following passages from western biographical works document what has been said so far:

Abū ʿUmar Aḥmad b. Yūsuf al-Anṣārī (born in Toledo): "It was found on his tomb (*wuǧida ʿalā qabrihī*) in the Umm Salamah cemetery (of Córdoba) that he died in Šaʿbān of the year 479".[58]

Abū l-Walīd Mālik b. ʿAbd Allāh al-ʿUtbī as-Sahlī (Córdoba, 437–507 H), buried in the Mosque of Yūsuf b. Basīl: "I read the date of his death upon his tomb in the said mosque, after I had asked for it some of his companions who did not know it despite the fact that he had not died long before that".[59]

57 IṬūlQal I pp. 341f. and II pp. 535, 537 and 542.

58 IBaškṢilah I p. 69.

59 IBaškṢilah II p. 621.

Aḥmad b. Ḫālid al-Asadī, known as Ibn Abī Hāšim: "He died on Wednesday 6th Šawwāl 368. I read this date on an inscribed slab on his tomb".[60]

ᶜAbd al-Ḥaqq Ibn al-Ḫarrāṭ (d. Biǧāyah [fr. Bougie] 582 H): "I read this (date of death) on the marble slab which stands at his tomb",[61] and in another source: "The date of his death was written upon a marble slab (*ruḫāmah*) at his tomb (*ᶜinda qabrihī*)".[62]

Abū Zakarīyāᵓ Yaḥyā b. ᶜAlī b. Ġānīyah aṣ-Ṣaḥrāwī (d. in Granada in Šaᶜbān 543 H): "On his tomb there is a marble tombstone (*lawḥun min ar-ruḫām*) indicating the date of his death".[63]

Abū Muḥammad ᶜAbd Allāh b. Hāšim b. Masrūr al-Qāḍī (d. 363 H): "At the head of his tomb there is a marble slab upon which his name, his father's name, the date of his death and other things are inscribed, in beautiful letters the like of which we do not find again in the cemeteries of Kairouan".[64]

However, one cannot say that epitaphs are not taken into consideration in eastern biographical literature. This is, in any case, not true of works stemming from the seventh century H (see above), yet even in these, as in other works, we find time and again an author referring to an epitaph he had witnessed or read about, though without actually citing the wording of the inscription:

Abū ᶜAlī Yaḥyā b. Abān: he "was buried in Aleppo in the cemetery of the Qurayšites, his tomb is there and it bears an inscription".[65]

Abū Muḥammad ar-Rabīᶜ b. Sulaymān al-Murādī (a pupil of aš-Šāfiᶜī), died in Cairo in 270 H and was buried in the Lesser Qarāfah: "On the head of his tomb there is a tile (*balāṭah*) indicating his name and the year of his death".[66]

al-Qāḍī al-Fāḍil (Abū ᶜAlī ᶜAbd ar-Raḥīm, ᶜAsqalān 529 – Cairo 596 H): "He was buried in his mausoleum (...) on the slopes of the Muqaṭṭam Hill in the Lesser Qarāfah. I visited his tomb more than once and read the date of his death on the marble enclosure (*muḥawwiṭ*) around his tomb which can still be found there".[67]

Hišām b. ᶜUrwah (d. in Baghdad between 145 and 147 H): "He was buried in the Ḫayzurān cemetery on the eastern side (of the town), though others claimed that his tomb lies on the western side outside the market near the Bāb Quṭrabbul, behind the trench at the graves of Bāb Ḥarb cemetery. Indeed, it (*sc.* his tomb) can still be seen there and is generally known; upon it, there is an inscribed tombstone (*lawḥ manqūš*) saying that this is the tomb of Hišām b. ᶜUrwah. Those who state that his tomb is on the eastern side reply that the tomb on the western side belongs to Hišām b. ᶜUrwah al-Marwazī, the companion of ᶜAbd Allāh b. al-Mubārak (d. 181 H or after, see **101**). God knows best".[68]

60 IFarTārīḫ I p. 47.
61 IAbbTakm III p. 121.
62 ĠubrᶜUnwān p. 44.
63 IḪaṭIḥāṭah IV p. 347.
64 DabMaᶜālim III p. 81.
65 INadFihrist p. 160.
66 IḪallWaf II p. 292.
67 IḪallWaf III p. 162 = Lev: *Saladin* p. 23.
68 IḪallWaf IV pp. 80f.

Ibn al-Mibrad comments, when discussing the different dates proposed for the death of Zayn ad-Dīn Ibn Rağab (d. 795 H): "The tomb of Ibn Rağab is known in the Bāb aṣ-Ṣaġīr cemetery, and upon it is written that he died in the year (7)95".[69]

Finally, it does not seem an unreasonable idea to turn to the extant cemetery guides hoping that these will offer plenty of material on epitaphs, or so it would seem natural from our perspective. Unfortunately, this hope is ill-founded because epitaphs do not play a prominent role in this literary genre (see Chapter 3) nor do the authors seem to have been particularly keen on preserving their wording for posterity. Of course, the number of epitaphs cited or alluded to in cemetery guides varies according to the aim of every individual work: among the Cairene guides, al-Muwaffaq in his *Muršid* rarely refers to epitaphs as historical evidence and sees their wording rather as potential exhortation, and that is also the reason why he quotes so much anonymous epitaph-poetry in the introduction of his treatise. The later guides by Ibn az-Zayyāt and Nūr ad-Dīn as-Saḫāwī do take funerary inscriptions into account, though in doing so they limit themselves mainly to short epitaphs which give the name and, maybe, the date of death. Here, the function of epitaphs is clearly the identification of particular tombs and they are thus seen primarily as historical evidence. Finally, aš-Šīrāzī in his *Šadd al-ʾizār* lays much stress on the life and achievement of the buried, yet he quotes over many hundred pages (in modern print) merely one epitaph verbatim, and only the verses at that (see **180**). In two further passages he refers to funerary inscriptions he had seen himself but does not cite them.[70]

Without doubt the most important cases in which epitaphs are resorted to as historical evidence are the following: (a) if there is no other information about a person except his funerary inscription, or (b) if the information as given in someone's epitaph does not correspond to what is known from other sources and may thus help to verify the actual "historical" truth.

The first case – viz. the funerary inscription being the only information about a person – is attested in a number of biographical dictionaries, e.g. in the dictionary of Meccans by al-Fāsī (see **118**, **122**, **134** and **141**) or in the dictionary of Upper Egyptian personalities by al-Udfuwī.[71] The second case – the use of epitaphs in combination with literary sources in order to correct one of them – is well illustrated by a passage in as-Saḫāwī's ninth-century dictionary *aḍ-Ḍawʾ al-lāmiʿ*. There, in his entry on the Egyptian jurist and traditionist Burhān ad-Dīn al-Abnāsī (Abū Isḥāq Ibr. b. Mūsā, *c.*725–802 H), as-Saḫāwī refers to an epitaph in order to correct the information on the origin of the mausoleum in which al-Abnāsī was said to be buried according to al-Maqrīzī. The scholar in question, al-Burhān al-Abnāsī, had died in Muḥarram while returning from the pilgrimage[72] near al-Muwayliḥah on the

69 IMibrḎayl p. 41.

70 ŠīrŠadd pp. 180 and 295.

71 UdfṬāliʿ p. 474.

72 The pilgrimage of the year 801–802 H was a disastrous event since the heat was unbearable and the camels of the pilgrims died on the way, see MaqrSulūk III p. 980.

northwestern coast of the Arabian peninsula, but his coffin was carried to ᶜUyūn al-Qaṣab (al-ᶜAynūn), a town some 50 km to the north of al-Muwayliḥah:

> "(al-Maqrīzī said ...,) His (i.e. al-Abnāsī's) tomb is frequently visited by pilgrims for its blessing and a mausoleum (*qubbah*) was erected (above it). However, I say, once I went there and discovered that the origin of that mausoleum is connected with Bahādur al-Ǧamālī an-Nāṣirī, the emir in charge of the annual pilgrimage (*ʾamīr al-ḥaǧǧ*), as I read on his tombstone (*ʿalā lawḥ qabrihī*). It also states that he died on return from the pilgrimage in D̲ū l-Ḥiǧǧah 736, quite in accordance with what we know about his (i.e. Bahādur's) life. Before entering the mausoleum, there is another site (*makān*) which I think to be the actual burial place of the sheikh (i.e. al-Abnāsī), yet there is no mausoleum rising above it".[73]

Here, the visit of a burial site serves to correct information found in a literary source. In other cases, the wording of wrong funerary inscriptions was amended or their message corrected by recourse to facts known from literary sources. Thus Ibn Ḥaǧar in his dictionary of Egyptian chief judges has a passage about an incorrectly attributed tomb in the Qarāfah cemetery,[74] and Nūr ad-Dīn as-Saḫāwī in his cemetery guide discusses incorrect epitaphs in a number of instances.[75] The most widely-known example in that context is probably Ibn Ḫallikān's treatment of the epitaph of the historian aṭ-Ṭabarī (224–310 H) which he had found in the Cairene Qarāfah cemetery: "I saw (there) a venerated tomb at the head of which there was a tombstone bearing the inscription: *hād̲ā qabru bni Ǧarīrini ṭ-Ṭabarīyi*. The people say that this is the author of the *History* but this is not correct since he is actually buried in Baghdad".[76]

On the other hand, some scholars simply ignored the conflict between epigraphic evidence and what was known from literary sources. This is, for instance, the case with the presumed epitaph of Umm Ǧaᶜfar Zubaydah bt. Ǧaᶜfar b. al-Manṣūr (wife of the caliph ar-Rašīd – as well as his cousin – and mother of the caliph al-Amīn, d. Baghdad 216 H)[77] in aṭ-Ṭāʾif: according to al-Marǧānī,[78] her epitaph was inscribed upon one of three tombs situated inside the mausoleum of ᶜAbd Allāh b. ᶜAbbās;[79]

73 ḌL I p. 174 = IŠamQabas I p. 109 (with slight variation in wording). However, in the biographies (or obituaries) of al-Abnāsī as found in MaqrDurar I p. 123 and MaqrSulūk III p. 1024 there is no mention of a mausoleum. The rivalry between al-Maqrīzī and Ibn Ḥaǧar al-ᶜAsqalānī, inherited by the latter's pupil as-Saḫāwī, is well-known, and in his numerous works as-Saḫāwī misses no opportunity to point out the presumed mistakes found in al-Maqrīzī's writings.

74 IḤaǧRafᶜ p. 441.

75 SaḫTuḥfAḥbāb pp. 128, 133f., 140 and 144.

76 IḪallWaf IV p. 192 / (Slane) II p. 598.

77 IḪallWaf II pp. 314-7; ŠarŠMaq II pp. 244f.

78 MarǧBahǧah II p. 267.

79 For his tomb, see ᶜUǧIhdāʾ pp. 61-7. The mausoleum in its present shape was built in 547 H, as appears from an inscription "written on wood" (probably on the teak wood cenotaph of the grave itself), but some pages further (p. 74) al-ᶜUǧaymī says that "Raḍīy ad-Dīn Abū Ḥāmid M. b. A. (...) al-ᶜUmarī al-Makkī found inscribed on the tomb of the noble mosque – that is, the mosque of ᶜAbd Allāh b. ᶜAbbās", that it was built only in 592 H; another renovation took place in 1071 H. *Cf.* also Gaube: *Taif* pp. 21 and 24.

she had also sponsored the reconstruction of the so-called "Mosque of the Prophet" in aṭ-Ṭāʾif in 192 H, as we know from an inscription quoted in literary sources.[80] However, she had died in 216 H during the caliphate of al-Maʾmūn, and this clearly contradicts that what we read in her presumed epitaph, namely "This is the tomb of Zubaydah. She was taken (to God) in Ǧumādā II of the year 365". This is passed over by al-Marǧānī without further comment.

Summing up, it can be said that comparing information from extant epitaphs with literary sources – or even correcting the literary information on the basis of funerary inscriptions – was not a frequent practice among Muslim scholars. The nature of their system of learning, and of their personal attitudes as well, was too much centred on books and literary sources and thus did not permit funerary epigraphy to become a source of information to be commonly and constantly relied upon.

2.6. Difficulties and ambiguities of citation

There are a number of particular features connected with the quotation of epitaphs in Arabic literary sources. They all attest to the peculiar role epitaphs have played in the wider realm of Arabic discoursivity.

First of all, in not a few cases verses are cited both as epitaphs (or epitaph-poems) and as "literary" poems mourning a death (*cf.* **4**, **30**, **76**, **166**, **180**, **190**, **192**, **195**, **212**, **219** and **225**). This shows that there was no clear-cut boundary between these two formal genres, and indeed mourning poems could well be inscribed upon tombs quite as epitaphs may also have been recited as a poem (*cf.* **21**), notwithstanding the fact that most poems in epitaphs belong to the genre of ascetic poetry. Since many Arabic epitaphs are rather "impersonal" insofar they do not contain biographical elements of the deceased's vita[81] they could easily be transferred from one context to the other. Often it would suffice to change just one word in the verse, e.g. by inserting a name, in order to turn a literary poem into an epitaph-poem (see **4**, **62**, **180** and **198**). After all, an epitaph-poem is not defined by its content and character, for example by addressing the tomb (*yā-qabru …*) or its visitor (*yā-zāʾira l-qabri …*), and there is almost nothing in epitaph-poems which we do not also find in mourning and ascetic poetry, the only exception being references to the condition of the deceased uttered in the first person, which obviously only make sense if written upon a tomb. However, in the majority of cases an epitaph-poem is made such by its setting, i.e. by being actually inscribed on a tombstone or by being said to have been found inscribed on a tombstone. Even very personal epitaphs which allude to certain biographical data of the deceased (e.g. **109**) may be cited in the sources as lines which somebody uttered before his death, but not as his funerary inscription. Thus if a certain text, or poem, is described in the sources both as an epitaph and a mourning or ascetic poem, we cannot be sure whether this text was

80 ʿUǧlhdāʾ p. 60 and RCEA 84 (both quote from al-Fāsī); Gaube: *Taif* pp. 19f.

81 The elements shedding light upon life and professions of the deceased as far as they appear in extant epitaphs are dealt with in Volume I, Chapter 1.

ever inscribed upon a tomb, or whether it was first conceived as an epitaph-poem or as a "literary" mourning poem. On the other hand, nothing speaks against the fact that mourning or ascetic poems were first composed as purely literary pieces of poetry and afterwards adapted as a funerary inscription; it also happened that epitaph-poems became famous over the centuries and were then recopied somewhere else. Finally, there were some very popular epitaph-poems that recur over the centuries in rather distant places (**2**, **11**, **86**, **173**, **195** and **202**).

The variants in the wordings of quoted epitaphs and epitaph-poems are familiar from the transmission of Arabic literary texts and poetry; particularly the poetical texts may in some cases have a high degree of diversity – due to both mistakes in the process of transmission and to deliberate change of the wording or word order –, according to the sources and the difficulty of the wording. More about this and related issues will be said in the technical remarks that precede the catalogue of epitaphs further below.

The sources themselves are often not reliable when they report that such-and-such was inscribed upon the tomb of N.N. as becomes clear from the fact that many epitaph-poems are otherwise quoted as purely literary poems. On the other hand, we lack independent, archaeological evidence because almost none of the epitaphs cited in literary sources has been preserved, with the notable exception of the epitaphs of some Naṣrid rulers in Granada (**92a-d**), the epitaphs of the Moroccan Saᶜdid rulers (**115a-c**) and two epitaphs in Mecca (**139**) and Toledo (**186**). In a few other cases, only the epitaph-poems are attested in literary sources as well as on extant tombstones (e.g. **195**), albeit not on those tombstones which the literary sources say they are on.

Especially difficult to deal with are the cases in which more than one epitaph is ascribed in the sources to one and the same person, often a gifted poet or a person famous in other ways. Without further information we are then not able to decide whether in the course of the centuries different funerary inscriptions were put upon his tomb and thus gave rise to seemingly conflicting reports (see e.g. **14–16**, **93–95**), or whether only one of the reported epitaphs was ever inscribed upon the tomb and, if so, which. The opposite case is likewise encountered, namely that one epitaph is ascribed to several persons (**3**, **4** and **177**). Here we face basically the same problem as that indicated before: as long as there is no independent evidence, we are not in a position to judge which person the quoted epitaph can be ascribed to in the first place as long as there are no intrinsic reasons why a certain epitaph could not possibly belong to a certain person. In the absence of those reasons, there always remains the possibility that the same epitaph was put on the tombstones of several people, although in the case of famous persons this is unlikely because there is a notable tendency in the sources to credit them with very distinctive funerary inscriptions. The only way to establish probabilities in this regard is to look at the transmission and attestation(s) of a specific epitaph ascribed to several persons. When, for example, somebody is credited in five sources unanimously with a certain epitaph and only one source mentions another version, we are inclined to accept the version which is better and more widely attested. But also this may be fallacious.

3. *Catalogue of Arabic epitaphs cited in literary sources*

3.1. Introductory and technical remarks

The literary sources offering most material as to epitaphs are the guides to Cairene cemeteries, aš-Šaybī's collection of Meccan epitaphs and the dictionary of Meccans (*al-ʿIqd aṯ-ṯamīn*) by al-Fāsī. A number of anonymous funerary inscriptions in verse are reported in the eschatological treatises by Ibn Abī d-Dunyā, Ibn al-Ḫarrāṭ and Ibn Rağab.[81] Although these works were taken into account for the present catalogue, each of them clearly deserve a study of its own. From other sources only those epitaphs which are quoted completely or in considerable detail have been included, that is, citing *more than merely the name of the deceased and / or his date of death.* Hence a number of epitaphs quoted verbatim in Ibn az-Zayyāt's *Kawākib* were not included in the catalogue because they only contain the name and/or the date of death.

Not included in the present catalogue are also epitaphs only reported in works dating from the 13th century H or after, such as al-Anṣārī's *Nafaḥāt* (Tripoli), al-Ġazzī's *Nahr aḏ-ḏahab* (Aleppo), al-Mubārak's *Ḫiṭaṭ* (Cairo), al-Kinānī's *Takmīl* (Kairouan) or al-Marrākušī's *ʾIʿlām* (Fez and Marrakech). These works are referred to only as secondary evidence. Likewise *not included* are epitaphs cited by modern editors of pre-modern texts[82] or those that are quoted in pre-modern literary sources but preserved *in situ* and hence edited in epigraphic corpora, as e.g. the epitaphs of the Naṣrid rulers of Granada or the epitaphs of the Moroccan Saʿdids. An exception has been made, however, for several Naṣrid epitaphs (**89–91**, **114**), due to their extraordinary importance and the fact that the epitaph-poems have so far not been edited and/or translated.

All entries are ordered according to location and, within one location, according to date (if known) or source. Epitaphs of more than one known location have been inserted according to the location whose initial letter comes first in the alphabet; for the location *only the information from literary sources* was considered relevant, not that of preserved epitaphs. Epitaphs of unknown location are cited according to the sources that quote them, in chronological order. The names of locations are given according to the versions current in Western languages, except in those cases where no such name exists or where the Arabic name diverges considerably. The dates are either those mentioned in the epitaphs themselves *or those of the death of the deceased as reported in literary sources.* If the epitaph is *known* to be posterior to the date of the death of the person buried, the date of the making of the epitaph is given in the heading. If the epitaph cited is merely a testamentary disposition of the deceased, his date and place of death have been relied upon notwithstanding whether the epitaph was ever carried out.

81 IRağAhwāl pp. 190f. contains some one-line epitaphs that are not reported elsewhere, but the deplorable quality of the edited text does not permit use of them without further evidence from other sources.

82 E.g. ŠawkBadr I p. 255 note 1 and II p. 326 note 1.

In the case of preserved epitaphs that parallel those known from literary sources, the main wording cited follows, as a rule, the literary version; variants between different literary versions (or also between these and the extant epitaph) have been added in small print. Variants of one wording in literary sources might either go back to the manuscripts themselves or to the work of the modern editors and/or type-setters.[83] To facilitate "browsing" the material, the epitaph-poems contained in this catalogue have been added in Arabic script in the Appendix.

A special problem present the biographical entries in the history of Mecca (*al-ʿIqd aṯ-ṯamīn*) of al-Fāsī which are often abstracted from epitaphs which the author had deciphered in Meccan cemeteries. Alas, al-Fāsī does not quote the epitaphs, but composes a biographical notice on the basis of what he had read. In these cases, I tried to reconstruct the original epitaph, as in the following example:

> "[This is the tomb of] the blissful, the martyr + Naǧm ad-Dīn Abū ʿAbd Allāh + Muḥammad, son of + the jurist, the martyr + Raḍīy ad-Dīn Muḥammad b. ʿAbd Allāh b. ʿUṯmān al-ʿAsqalānī al-Makkī. + He was taken (to God) on Monday second Ḏū l-Qaʿdah in the year 588".

This epitaph has been reconstructed from al-Fāsī's biographical account of Naǧm ad-Dīn al-ʿAsqalānī (**135**). In order to show how the wording is actually reported by al-Fāsī, I should like to quote the complete biographical entry of Naǧm ad-Dīn al-ʿAsqalānī in the following; the passages which are part of the cited epitaph are set in italics:

> "*Muḥammad b. Muḥammad b. ʿAbd Allāh b. ʿUṯmān al-ʿAsqalānī al-Makkī*, his patronym is *Abū ʿAbd Allāh* and his honorific name *Naǧm ad-Dīn b. Raḍīy ad-Dīn. He was taken (to God) on Monday second Ḏū l-Qaʿdah in the year 588* and buried in the Maʿlāh cemetery. I copied his genealogy and the date of his death from his tombstone, which is in the writing of Muḥammad b. Barakāt b. Abī Ḥaramī.[84] He styled him (*tarǧamahū*) *the blissful, the martyr*, and he styled his father *the jurist, the martyr*".

On the basis of this entry it is easy to reconstruct the entire epitaph. The only addition made is the introductory epitaph-formula "This is the tomb of" (most probably *hāḏā qabru*, maybe also *hāḏā ḍarīḥu* or the like), which is often omitted in literary sources. However, we cannot tell from al-Fāsī's account whether the epitaph contained other elements as well, e.g. verses of the Qurʾān.

3.2. Catalogue of Arabic epitaphs

1

LOCATION. Aġmāt (southern Morocco). DATE. 487 or 488 H.

PERSON BURIED. The ʿAbbādid ruler and poet al-Muʿtamid (ʿalā llāh) Ibn ʿAbbād (Abū l-Qāsim Muḥammad II, born in 431 or 432, r. in Seville 461–84, d. exiled in Aġmāt 487 or 488 H): IḪāqQal pp. 4-35; ŠantḎaḫ III pp. 41-81;

83 It is often impossible to tell, without recourse to the manuscripts, to what degree the modern editors have tampered with the wording. Different editions of a source have been used whenever accessible to reduce the impact of mistakes in the printed versions to a minimum.

84 This information is certainly also taken from the epitaph. Yet in this case, it is hard to say how the writer, i.e. sculptor, names himself in the text. What we would expect is something like *wa-ʿamala(hū) fulān*, "N.N. did (it)", or *kataba(hū) fulān*, "N.N. wrote (it)". Conventionally, such information, if given, is found at the end of epitaphs.

IṣfḪar (M) II pp. 25-43; IAbbḤullah II pp. 52-68; MarrMuᶜǧib pp. 158-224; IḪallWaf V pp. 21-39; TI XXXIII pp. 264-74; IḪaṭAᶜmāl pp. 183-97 and IḪaṭIḥāṭah II pp. 108-20; NZ V p. 157; MaqqNafḥ (C) V esp. pp. 344-59, 372-6 and *passim*; al-Marrākušī: *Iᶜlām* II pp. 312-27; Dozy: *Historia de los Musulmanes* IV pp. 113ff. and *passim*; Nykl: *Hispano-Arabic Poetry* pp. 134-53; Khalis: *Vie litteraire* pp. 91-150; Arié: *España musulmana* pp. 391f.; ZA VI p. 181; EI^2 VII pp. 766-8 (É. Lévi-Provençal/R.P. Scheindlein); ᶜAzzām: *Ibn ᶜAbbād*; Kennedy: *Muslim Spain* pp. 152f. and 162-4; Raymond P. Scheindlin: *Form and Structure in the Poetry of al-Muᶜtamid Ibn ᶜAbbād*, Leiden 1974.

SOURCES. MuᶜtamidDīwān p. 96; ŠantḎaḫ III p. 57 = Dozy: *Loci de Abbadidis* I p. 307; MarrMuᶜǧib p. 222 = Emilio García Gómez: *Qasidas de Andalucía puestas en verso castellano*, Madrid 1940, pp. 97-107 (with Spanish translation);[85] IḪaṭAᶜmāl p. 191 and IḪaṭIḥāṭah II pp. 119f.; al-Marrākušī: *Iᶜlām* II pp. 320f.; ᶜAzzām: *Ibn ᶜAbbād* pp. 105f.; ᶜAlī Adham: *al-Muᶜtamid Ibn ᶜAbbād*, Beirut: Dār al-Quds 1974, p. 328; Riḍā as-Sūwaysī: *Malik ʾIšbīliyah aš-šāᶜir: al-Muᶜtamid b. ᶜAbbād 431–488 h / 1040–1095 m. Dirāsah wa-taḥqīq*, Tunis: Dār Bū-Salāmah 1985, pp. 336f. – Translations in other languages: Dozy: *Loci de Abbadidis* I p. 342 (Latin, according to ŠantḎaḫ); Nykl: *Hispano-Arabic Poetry* p. 136 (English); Hoenerbach: *Islamische Geschichte Spaniens* pp. 336f. (vv. 1, 3, 5f. and 10 in German, according to IḪaṭAᶜlām); Ridha Souissi [Riḍā as-Sūwaysī]: *Al-Muᶜtamid Ibn ᶜAbbād et son oeuvre poétique. Étude des Thèmes*, Tunis 1977, p. 196 (vv. 1-3), p. 215 (v. 5), pp. 208 and 220 (v. 10, French), p. 249 (vv. 2-4 in partially wrong transcription; v. 4 also on p. 247); *La poesia de al-Muᶜtamid: Rey-poeta de Sevilla*, traducción, introducción y notas de Miguel J. Hagerty, Barcelona 1979, pp. 120f. (no. 160, Spanish); Maria T. Mascari: *al-Mùtamid, un principe poeta della Spagna musulmana*, Mazara del Vallo 1981, pp. 46f. (Italian); *Al-Muᶜtamid Ibn ᶜAbbād: Poesías*, antología bilingue por María Jesús Rubiera Mata, Madrid 1982, pp. 62-4 (cites only the Spanish translation by E. García Gómez, see above); *cf.* also EI^2 VII p. 768.

DESCRIPTION. "When he felt his death approaching, he mourned himself with these verses and stipulated in his last will that they be written upon his tomb: [...]" (MuᶜtamidDīwān and most other sources); "He mourned himself with the following verses and ordered that they be written on his tomb: [...]" (IḪaṭIḥāṭah; al-Marrākušī: *Iᶜlām*); Nykl called these verses Ibn ᶜAbbād's "last adieu to the world".[86] – Ten verses in the metre *basīṭ*:

85 Verses 2 and 4 also in: al-Andalus 10 (1945), p. 292 (in Spanish translation).

86 In 761 H, Ibn al-Ḫaṭīb visited the tomb and gave the following description: "The tomb is situated in the cemetery of Aġmāt on elevated ground and shaded by a lote-tree (*or* surrounded by lote-trees). Beside it, there is the tomb of Iᶜtimād, his favourite concubine and client of Rumayk. Above both tombs lingers the loneliness of estrangement (i.e. the deceased being buried far away from their home town Seville) and the affliction of obscurity after their reign had come to an end, and thus the eye of someone looking at their graves cannot withhold tears", see IḪaṭAᶜmāl p. 191 = MaqqNafḥ (C) V p. 237 = Dozy: *Loci de Abbadidis* II pp. 222f. = ᶜAzzām: *Ibn ᶜAbbād* pp. 106f. = Hoenerbach: *Islamische Geschichte Spaniens* p. 337; *cf.*

*qabra l-ġarībi saqāka r-rā*ʾ*iḥu l-ġādī * ḥaqqan ẓafirta bi-*ʾ*ašlā*ʾ*i bni* ʿ*Abbādī*
*bi-l-ḥilmi bi-l-*ʿ*ilmi bi-n-nu*ʿ*mā* ʾ*iḏā ttaṣalat * bi-l-ḫiṣbi* ʾ*in* ʾ*ağdabū bi-r-riyyī li-ṣ-ṣādī*
*bi-ṭ-ṭā*ʿ*ini ḍ-ḍāribi r-rāmī* ʾ*iḏā qtatalū * bi-l-mawti* ʾ*aḥmara bi-ḍ-ḍirġāmati l-*ʿ*ādī*
*bi-d-dahri fī niqamin bi-l-baḥri fī ni*ʿ*amin * bi-l-badri fī ẓulamin bi-ṣ-ṣadri fī n-nādī*
*na*ʿ*am huwa l-ḥaqqu ḥābānī bihī qadarun * mina s-samā*ʾ*i fa-wāfānī li-mī*ʿ*ādī*
wa-lam ʾ*akun qabla ḏāka n-na*ʿ*ši* ʾ*a*ʿ*lamuhū ** ʾ*anna l-ğibāla tuhādā fawqa* ʾ*a*ʿ*wādī*
*kafāka fa-rfuq bimā stūdi*ʿ*ta min karamin * rawwāka kullu qaṭūbi l-barqi ra*ʿʿ*ādī*
yabkī ʾ*aḫāhu llaḏī ġayyabta wābilahū * taḥta ṣ-ṣafīḥi bi-dam*ʿ*in rā*ʾ*iḥin ġādī*
*ḥattā yağūdaka dam*ʿ*u ṭ-ṭalli munhamiran * min* ʾ*a*ʿ*yuni z-zuhri lam tabḫal bi-*ʾ*is*ʿ*ādī*
*wa-lā tazal ṣalawātu llāhi dā*ʾ*imatan ** ʿ*alā dafīnika lā tuḥṣā bi-ta*ʿ*dādī*

2 om. ŠantḎaḫ; IḪaṭAʿmāl and IḪaṭIḥāṭah. – **3** second hemistich: *bi-l-ḫiṣbi* ʾ*in* ʾ*ağdabū bi-r-riyyī li-ṣ-ṣādī* (ŠantḎaḫ, IḪaṭAʿmāl). – **4** om. ŠantḎaḫ, IḪaṭAʿmāl, IḪaṭIḥāṭah. – **5** *ḥābānī bihī*: *wāfānī bihī* (ŠantḎaḫ, MuʿtamidDīwān, IḪaṭAʿmāl), *fāğa*ʾ*anī* ʿ*alā* (IḪaṭIḥāṭah, al-Marrākušī: *I*ʿ*lām*); قدر: القدر (IḪaṭAʿmāl);[87] *li-mī*ʿ*ādī*: *bi-mī*ʿ*ādī* (al-Marrākušī: *I*ʿ*lām*). – **6** ʾ*a*ʿ*wādī*: ʾ*aṭwādi* (!, IḪaṭAʿmāl). – **7-9** om. ŠantḎaḫ, IḪaṭAʿmāl and IḪaṭIḥāṭah. – **8** ʾ*aḫāhu*: ʾ*aḫan* (ʿAzzām). – **10** *wa-lā*: *fa-lā* (IḪaṭAʿmāl and IḪaṭIḥāṭah); *wa-lā tazal ṣalawātu llāhi*: *wa-lā tazālu ṣalātu llāhi* (al-Marrākušī: *I*ʿ*lām*, ʿAzzām); *dā*ʾ*imatan*: *nāzilatan* (ŠantḎaḫ, IḪaṭAʿmāl and IḪaṭIḥāṭah, al-Marrākušī: *I*ʿ*lām*); بتعداد: يتعداد (IḪaṭAʿmāl).

"Tomb of the stranger, may the rain of the afternoon and of the morning pour forth upon you! * Rightfully you took possession[88] of the decaying corpse of Ibn ʿAbbād,
Of the clemency, of the knowledge, of the happiness when they were joined together, * of the fertility when the people suffered from barrenness, of the water stream for the thirsty,
Of the thrusting, the striking, the firing[89] when men raged in combat, * of death, blood-shedding, of the enemy lion,

also Dozy: *Historia de los Musulmanes* IV pp. 227f. and Schack: *Poesie und Kunst* I p. 344f.; Iʿtimād had died before Ibn ʿAbbād, *cf.* MaqqNafḥ (C) V pp. 342f. and VI pp. 8ff; Nykl: *Hispano-Arabic Poetry* pp. 138-41. In 1010 H, al-Maqarrī visited the tomb (MaqqNafḥ [C] V pp. 238 and 356f.). Today the site is in ruins, as can be seen from the photograph in ʿAzzām: *ib.* p. 3. For the tomb, see also al-Marrākušī: *I*ʿ*lām* I pp. 119f. and E. García Gómez: *El supuesto sepulcro de Mu*ʿ*tamid de Sevilla in Āgmāt* (sic), in: al-Andalus 18 (1953), pp. 402-11 (including a plan of the complex on p. 410 and photographs on plates 15-8).

87 Dozy changed his initial reading *al-qadaru* (*Loci de Abbadidis* I p. 307) into *qadarun* (*op. cit.* III p. 137).

88 Or "You overwhelmed, *or* conquered". The use of *ẓfr* I is common in mourning poetry although normally it is death or Destiny who overcomes a person, not the tomb, e.g. in a poem mourning the Barmakids (*ṭawīl*): *wa-qul li-l-manāyā qad ẓafirti bi-Ğa*ʿ*farin * wa-lan taẓfarī min ba*ʿ*dihī bi-musawwadī* (cited in IḤamdTaḏk IV p. 210 = NuwNih V p. 182).

89 This refers to Ibn ʿAbbād fighting with the lance, the sword and the bow.

Of fate (itself) in cases of vengeance, of the sea in matters of favour, * of the full moon in darkness, of the centre of the (courtly) gathering.
Yes, it is right, what was bestowed upon me by Destiny * from Heaven, thus it brought me to the appointed time,
And I did not, before (seeing) that bier, know * that the mountains could be assembled upon wooden boards.
Enough!, so kindly treat[90] what noble nature has been consigned to you! * Let every glowering flashlight, a roaring thunder, pour (its rain) upon you!
Weeping for his brother, whose heavy downpour[91] you did conceal * under the layer of stones, with a tear in the afternoon and in the morning;
Even the tear of dew may water you, (a tear) shed * by the eyes of the bright stars which have not been miserly with good fortune,
And may the blessings of God always continue to come down (like rain) * upon your tomb, innumerable beyond counting".[92]

NOTES. Ibn ᶜAbbād's epitaph is without doubt the Arabic funerary text most noted in Western scholarship and the most translated into Western languages. The tragic fate of this "princely poet" hit the nerve of many whose conception of poetry was influenced by the poetical heritage of Romanticism.

1. "Tomb of the stranger". The word *ġarīb* denotes the "stranger", the "loner" or the "estranged",[93] and to address a tomb (or its occupant) using the term *ġarīb* is also found in Arabic mourning poetry.[94] In the case of al-Muᶜtamid, the term called for a wordplay, because he was "a *ġarīb*, imprisoned in the land of the *Maġrib*" (referring to his exile in Aġmāt),[95] taking up a line composed by himself (*ṭawīl*):

غَرِيبٌ بِأَرْضِ المَغْرِبَيْنِ أَسِيرُ * سَيَبْكِي عَلَيْهِ مِنْبَرٌ وَسَرِيرُ

90 Addressing the tomb.

91 I.e. of generosities and favours. With some subtlety, Ibn ᶜAbbād is referred to as "brother" before because he was, like the beneficial forces of nature, a "rain of generosity".

92 The whole poem is strikingly similar (in diction, but also exhibiting the same rhyme and metre) to a mourning poem by Abū Bakr Ibn al-Labbānah ad-Dānī (d. Mallorca 507 H), see IḪāqQal pp. 25f. = Dozy: *Loci de Abbadidis* I pp. 59f.; ŠantḎaḫ III pp. 80f.; IṣfḪar (M) II pp. 110f.; MarrMuᶜǧib pp. 209-11; MaqqNafḥ (C) V pp. 345f.; Hoenerbach: *Islamische Geschichte Spaniens* pp. 338-40. For the poet, see IṣfḪar (M) pp. 107-39; al-Marrākušī: *Iᶜlām* II pp. 339-50; Khalis: *Vie litteraire* pp. 213-33; Arié: *España musulmana* p. 392; HadjIbnLabb.

93 Dozy's emendation *al-ᶜazīb* for *al-ġarīb* in the first line (see his *Loci de Abbadidis* III p. 137) is not possible in the present context.

94 See e.g. MuġulṭāyWāḍiḥ p. 180 (*yā-ṣāḥiba l-qabri l-ġarībi ...*); *cf.* also MubTaᶜāzī p. 182; IDāʾūdZahrah p. 366 (*saqā bi-l-Mawṣili l-qabra l-ġarībā*); below epitaphs **107** and **184**.

95 Ibn ᶜAbbād died in exile and thus "a stranger". Nevertheless, there are several mourning poems which refer to persons having died in Aġmāt (e.g. IḪafDīwān p. 73f.), and they all stress the concept of *ġurbah*, because Aġmāt was thought of as a forlorn and desolate place, far from "the civilised world" and on the outskirts of humanity.

"A stranger, imprisoned in the 'land of the two sunsets',[96] * bewailed by the pulpit and the reclining seat (*or* couch)".[97]

The Islamic concept of the "stranger" has already received some attention from modern scholars and its main features are well-known.[98] If one were to summarise the constituents of this concept in a few words, nothing could be more appropriate than the following anecdote told about Ibrāhīm al-Ḥarbī (d. 285 H), a traditionist from Baghdad: "Ibrāhīm asked his companions who were sitting around him 'Whom do you consider a stranger (*ġarīb*) in our times?', and one of them replied 'The stranger is the one who is far from his home'. Another said, 'The stranger is the one who is distant from his loved ones', and everybody contributed something. Then Ibrāhīm put an end to that, saying 'The stranger in our times is a righteous (*ṣāliḥ*) man living among righteous people'".[99] In an epitaph from Anatolia we find the passage: "Consider yourself a stranger in the present world and someone in passage, consider yourself to be one of the inhabitants of the tombs!" (RCEA 782 006), which almost verbatim takes up a Tradition from the Prophet.[100]

The concept of the "stranger" had also some relevance for the treatment of the dead: someone who died a stranger (*māta ġarīban*) was generally considered a martyr (*šahīd*). In greater cities public institutions would see to his burial, e.g. by procuring the necessary means for it. Endowments for the washing and burial of "deceased strangers" in Cairo were financed by various Mamluk rulers, e.g. Baybars I and al-Malik an-Nāṣir Muḥammad;[101] in seventh-century Tawzar (Tunisia), the

96 "Land of the two sunsets" (*cf.* Lane s.r. *ġrb*) is here said of the Maghrib. The expression is Qurʾānic (Q 55:17: *rabbu l-mašriqayni wa-rabbu l-maġribayni*) and not uncommon in poetry, e.g. in a line by Abū ʿAbd Allāh an-Nahaʿī al-Warrāq (*mutaqārib*): *wa-mā ziltu ʾaqṭaʿu ʿarḍa l-bilādi * mina l-mašriqayni ʾilā l-maġribayni*, "I never ceased to traverse the width of the regions * from 'the land of the two dawns' to 'the land of the two sunsets'" (cited in TawḥBaṣāʾir II p. 165 and IQutʿUyūn III p. 55, var. *al-bilād*: *al-falāt*). Ibn al-Ḫaṭīb commences a poem in praise of the Prophet as follows (*kāmil*): *daʿāka bi-ʾaqṣā l-maġribayni ġarību * wa-ʾanta ʿalā buʿdi l-mazāri qarību*, "A stranger in the farthest 'land of the two sunsets' invokes you, * and you are near although your shrine is far" (IḪaṭRayḥ I p. 62).

97 I.e. in the mosques and the courtly gatherings. Sources: MuʿtamidDīwān p. 98; IḪamdīsDīwān 152 v. 1 (p. 267); IḪāqQal p. 27 = Dozy: *Loci de Abbadidis* I pp. 62 and 145; ŠantḎaḫ III p. 75; see also Daʿdūr: *Ġurbah* pp. 92 and 94. Schack: *Poesie und Kunst* I p. 285. *Cf.* p. 370.

98 Rosenthal: *Stranger*; Schoeler: *Der Fremde im Islam*; Bauer: *Fremdheit*. For the concept of *ġurbah* in Arabic poetry, see al-Ḫašrūm: *Ġurbah* and Daʿdūr: *Ġurbah*. Interesting aspects are also found in Sarah Stroumsa: *Philosopher-King or Philosopher-Courtier? Theory and Reality in the* Falāsifa'*s Place in Islamic Society*, in: C. de la Puente (ed.): *Identidades marginales*, Madrid 2003 (Estudios onomásticos-biográficos de al-Andalus XIII), pp. 451f.

99 Cited in IĞawzīṢafwah I p. 579. Ibrāhīm's dictum intends to say that it is very rare to find a righteous man among righteous people, thus he is truly "a stranger" and hence "solitary" in society. As such, the dictum is obviously meant as a critique of Ibrāhīm's time. See also Bauer: *Fremdheit*, esp. pp. 95f.

100 FB XI pp. 280f. (*riqāq* 3): *kun fī d-dunyā ka-ʾannaka ġarībun ʾaw ʿābiru sabīlin*; IḪarrāṭʿĀqibah p. 94; TabMiškāh p. 304; IDaqŠArbaʿīn pp. 132f; YāfRawḍ p. 13; *Adab al-mulūk* pp. 28f. = GramlLebensweise p. 65 (with further sources for this report).

101 IŠadMalẒāhir p. 302; NZ VII p. 180; IIyāsBad I pp. 390 and 471. *Cf.* IFurTārīḫ VII p. 83.

local cemetery was equipped with a *dār* for the burial of strangers.[102] Often those strangers would also be interred in graveyards of their own which were then known as *maqburat al-ġurabāʾ*: Ibn al-Ḫaṭīb mentions such a *maqburat al-ġurabāʾ* in Granada from the eighth century H,[103] and comparable burial grounds were found in Ardabīl (the local *gūristān-i ġarībān*)[104] as well as in Aleppo (the local *maqābir* or *turab al-ġurabāʾ*).[105] The overall concept of the *ġarīb*, as it appears in funerary epigraphy and related discourses, is analysed in greater detail in Volume I pp. 143ff.

2. "The rain of the afternoon and the morning" (*ar-rāʾiḥu l-ġādī*). This motif is omnipresent in Arabic poetry, especially in panegyric and mourning poetry, and it goes well back to the pre-Islamic period. The concept is already attested, to name but one example, in a mourning poem by Aws b. Ḥağar, though the later common expression *ar-rāʾiḥu l-ġādī* is here rendered by the terms, largely parallel in poetical usage, *mumsā* and *muṣbaḥ*.[106] Sometimes it also appears, as in Ibn ʿAbbād's epitaph, in the very construction *saqāka r-rāʾiḥu l-ġādī*, e.g. in a verse by Diʿbil b. ʿAlī al-Ḫuzāʿī (d. 244 H or later).[107]

3. "Fertility" and "barrenness" (verse 2). This is likewise a frequent motif in Arabic panegyric and mourning poetry. In a pre-Islamic mourning poem by Bišr b. Abī Ḫāzim (d. *c.*600 CE), on the death of his brother Samīr (or Sumayr), we find the following line (*ḫafīf*):

كُنْتَ غَيْثاً لَهُنَّ فِي السَّنَةِ الشَّهْـ * ـبَاءِ ذَاتِ الغُبَارِ وَالإمْحَالِ

"You were a downpour for them (f.) in the year of * drought, (in a year) of dust and barrenness".[108]

4. "I did not, before (seeing) that bier, know ..." (verse 6, *wa-lam ʾakun qabla ḏāka n-naʿši ʾaʿlamuhū ...*). The "mountains" that are placed on wooden boards are a metaphor for the mighty ruler, or the hero, who is laid, after his death, upon the bier and carried to his place of burial.[109] This metaphor was commonly used in Arabic poetry. The structure of the whole verse is not without literary antecedents: compare for example the following verse in a poem by aš-Šarīf ar-Raḍīy (Abū l-Ḥasan al-Mūsawī), mourning the death of Abū Isḥāq aṣ-Ṣābiʾ (d. 384 H) (*kāmil*):

102 TiğRiḥlah p. 163.

103 Torres Balbás: *Cementerios* pp. 132 and 185f. (from IḪaṭIḥāṭah, but I was unable to verify the indicated passage).

104 Gronke: *Derwische* p. 57.

105 See CIA Alep I p. 382 and al-Ġazzī: *Nahr aḏ-ḏahab* II p. 342.

106 AwsDīwān (G) 32 v. 17 (p. ٢٣) / (N) 40 v. 22 (p. 106) = IMaymMunt II p. 225 (*yasqī ṣadāka wa-mumsāhū wa-muṣbaḥuhū*; Ibn Maymūn with the variant: *saqā* etc.).

107 DiʿbilDīwān p. 142 (no. 81 v. 1).

108 BišrDīwān p. 234 = IMaymMunt II p. 287. Similar ḪansāʾDīwān (B) and (Š) p. 65: *yā-Ṣaḫru kunta lanā ġayṯan naʿīšu bihī* (B with the less probable var. *ġayṯan*: *ʿayšan*).

109 *Cf.* Dozy: *Recherches* II p. 39 (where also verse 6 of Ibn ʿAbbād's epitaph is cited) and his *Loci de Abbadidis* I p. 342 note 93: "Vocabulo *montes* designantur *viri eximii et potentes*. Vocab. اعواد (pp. *ligna*) saepius *feretrum* indicat".

مَا كُنْتُ أَعْلَمُ قَبْلَ حَطِّكَ فِي الثَّرَى * أَنَّ الثَّرَى يَعْلُو عَلَى الأَطْوَادِ

"I did not know before you were put into the moist earth * that the moist earth can rise above the mountains".[110]

In any case, verse 6 of Ibn ᶜAbbād's epitaph also reminds one of two famous lines by al-Mutanabbī, from a poem mourning Muḥammad b. Isḥāq at-Tanūḫī (*kāmil*):

مَا كُنْتُ أَحْسِبُ قَبْلَ دَفْنِكَ فِي الثَّرَى * أَنَّ الكَوَاكِبَ فِي التُّرَابِ تَغُورُ
مَا كُنْتُ آمُلُ قَبْلَ نَعْشِكَ أَنْ أَرَى * رَضْوَى عَلَى أَيْدِي الرِّجَالِ تَسِيرُ

"I did not reckon, before your burial in moist earth, * that the stars would set in (*or* sink into) the earth;
I did not hope, before (seeing) your bier, that I would (ever) see * Raḍwā[111] moving along on the hands of men (i.e., like the deceased upon his bier during the funerary procession)".[112]

However, al-Mutanabbī was not the first to use this imagery, and the Arabic literary critics remarked accordingly that there were older verses expressing the same thought. The most remarkable of those verses had been composed by Ibn ar-Rūmī (I, *kāmil*) and Ibn al-Muᶜtazz (II, *sarīᶜ*):

(I) مَنْ لَمْ يُعَايِنْ سَيْرَ نَعْشِ مُحَمَّدٍ * لَمْ يَدْرِ كَيْفَ تُسَيَّرُ الأَجْبَالُ

"He who has not seen with his own eyes the bier of Muḥammad[113] moving along * did not (come to) know how the mountains are moved along".[114]

(II) هٰذَا أَبُو القَاسِمِ فِي نَعْشِهِ * قُومُوا انْظُرُوا كَيْفَ تَسِيرُ الجِبَالُ

"Here is Abū l-Qāsim[115] upon his bier: * rise and see how the mountains move along!"[116]

110 ŠarīfRaḍDīwān I p. 361 = ṮaᶜālYat II p. 307 (var. *ḥaṭṭika*: *dafnika*) = ᶜĀmKaškūl II p. 601.

111 A mountain.

112 MutanDīwān (W) p. 116 / (U) II p. 126 (no. 105 v. 4-5); also cited in ṮaᶜālYat I p. 229; NuwNih V p. 180; INubMaṭlaᶜ p. 337 (both with the variant *ʾaḥsibu*: *ʾaᶜlamu*). Strangely enough, the verse is attributed to Ṯaᶜlab in IḤamdTaḏk IV p. 218; see also ALL (Littmann) I p. 763 (106th night). See also Dozy: *Loci de Abbadidis* III p. 149.

113 I.e. Muḥammad b. Naṣr b. Bassām.

114 IRūmīDīwān 1526 v. 15 (V p. 1962). Also cited in MutanDīwān (U) II p. 126 and IWakīᶜMunṣif I p. 293.

115 ᶜUbayd Allāh b. Sulaymān (but the sources do not agree upon the identity of the one mourned).

116 IMuᶜtDīwān 1193 v. 2 (III p. 70, var. *kayfa tazūlu*). Also cited in MutanDīwān (U) II p. 127; IWakīᶜMunṣif I p. 293 (var. *ʾAbū l-Qāsimi*: *ʾAbū l-ᶜAbbāsi*); YāqIršād VI p. 511 (same var.; according to him, the poet was ᶜAlī b. Naṣr b. Bassām).

2

LOCATIONS. (a) Ahwāz. – (b) Wāsiṭ. – (c) Cairo, Dahlak, Kairouan and Tilimsān.

DATES. (a, b) Late second or third century H. – (c) 770 H.

PERSONS BURIED. (a) Unknown. – (b) Abū Hāšim al-Iyādī. – (c) Šamsah bt. Muʾmin az-Zawāġī (d. 770 H: RCEA 770 001) *et al.*

SOURCES. (a) IADunyāQubūr (A) p. 165; TMD IX p. 99; IḪarrāṭʿĀqibah p. 117; IRağAhwāl p. 189. – (b) IʿARabʿIqd (Ğ) II p. 161 / (M) III p. 249 (the first two lines only). – (c) Four extant epitaphs, see Volume I (Chapter 5), pp. 563f.

DESCRIPTION. (a) According to Ibn Abī d-Dunyā, Muḥammad b. ʿAlī aṭ-Ṭawīl was told by a man in Baṣrah that he had read on a tomb in Ahwāz the inscription quoted; Ibn al-Ḫarrāṭ and Ibn Rağab have no further details. The citation in TMD presents these lines as a Ḥimyarite epitaph inscribed on a silver plate. – (b) According to Ibn ʿAbd Rabbih, someone claimed to have seen the verses inscribed on the tomb of Abū Hāšim al-Iyādī in Wāsiṭ. – (c) The version reported in RCEA 770 001 is taken from the epitaph of Šamsah az-Zawāġī in Tilimsān. – Four verses in the metre *basīṭ*:

*al-mawtu ʾaḫrağanī min dāri mamlakatī * fa-t-turbu muḍṭağaʿī min baʿdi tašrīfī*
*li-llāhi ʿabdun raʾā qabrī fa-ʾaḥzanahū * wa-ḫāfa min dahrihī rayba t-taṣārīfī*
*hāḏā maṣīru banī d-dunyā wa-ʾin ʿamarū * fīhā wa-ġarrahumū ṭūlu t-tasāwīfī*
*ʾastaġfiru llāha min ʿamdī wa-min ḥanaqī * wa-ʾasʾalu llāha fawzan yawma tawqīfī*

1 *fa-t-turbu*: *fa-ḫtartu muḍṭağaʿī* (TMD), *fa-t-turābu* (IḪarrāṭʿĀqibah); *fa-t-turbu muḍṭağaʿī*: *wa-l-mawtu ʾaḍraʾanī* (IʿARabʿIqd), ... *maḍğaʿī* (IRağAhwāl, does not fit the metre); *baʿdi tašrīfī*: IADunyāQubūr has بين تنزيفي, but the editor admits not to have been able to read the words properly; *baʿda tatrīfī* (TMD). – **2** *li-llāhi ʿabdun raʾā qabrī fa-ʾaḥzanahū*: *li-llāhi ʿindahū ʾayyu qabrī fa-ʾaġbarahū* (!!, IḪarrāṭʿĀqibah); *fa-ʾaḥzanahū*: *fa-ʾaʿbarahū* (IʿARabʿIqd, IRağAhwāl); *rayba*: *rabba* (!, IḪarrāṭʿĀqibah, misprint?). – **3** Lines 3 and 4 are exchanged in Ibn Rağab's version, but Ibn Abī d-Dunyā's and the other versions, putting the *istiġfār* in the last verse, seem preferable; *hāḏā*: *hākaḏā* (IRağAhwāl); *ʿamarū*: *naʿimū* (IḪarrāṭʿĀqibah, IRağAhwāl); التساويف: التساويفي (!, IRağAḥwāl). – **4** *ʿamdī*: *ḏanbī* (TMD), *ğurmī* (IḪarrāṭʿĀqibah, IRağAhwāl); *min ḥanaqī*: *min zulalī* (TMD, IḪarrāṭʿĀqibah); *fawzan*: *ʾafwan* (TMD), *fawzī* (IRağAhwāl). – For the wordings of the extant epitaphs, see Vol. I pp. 563f.

"Death has exiled me from the palace of my kingdom, * and the earth is now my bed[117] after the time of my being honoured has passed.
How good is a servant (of God) who, on seeing my tomb, is grieved by it * and is seized by fear of the vicissitudes of his own destiny!
This is the way the children of this world must go, no matter whether they prospered

117 The related term *maḍğaʿ* (pl. *maḍāğiʿ*), in the sense of "deathbed", is an Qurʾānic expression (see Q 3:154). Both *maḍğaʿ* and *muḍṭağaʿ*, meaning "deathbed" and hence also "tomb", appear frequently in mourning and ascetic poetry. The terms are also used in eulogies, e.g. *barrada llāhu maḍğaʿahū*, "may God cool his deathbed (i.e. tomb)".

* in life and were deceived[118] by the lengthing of deferments (i.e., by reaching a great age, with death being postponed again and again).

I ask for God's pardon for my (wicked) intentions and my wrath, * and pray God to bestow upon me success on the day of my resurrection".[119]

NOTES. This epitaph is a good example of the versatiliy and widespread occurence of themes and topoi in pre-modern Arabic culture. Apart from being attested both in literary sources and upon several preserved tombstones, this epitaph appears, over a period of many centuries, in such distant places as Ahwāz and Tilimsān.

1. "Death exiled me" (verse 1, *al-mawtu ʾaḫrağanī*). The first line of the epitaph is very similar to the passage in a "mythical" epitaph recorded by Ibn al-Ğawzī. The story he quotes has it that David once met a monk (!, *rāhib*) who showed him the shrouded corpse of a dead man and indicated at the head of his grave a tombstone (*lawḥ*) bearing an inscription. David approached it and read the following:

> "I am *fulān*, the son of *fulān*, king of the kings. I lived a thousand years, I built a thousand towns and I defeated a thousand armies, I married a thousand women and I deflowered a thousand virgins. When I was still a king (*fī mulkī*), the angel (*malak*) of death came to me and exiled me from the state I was living in (*fa-ʾaḫrağanī mimmā ʾanā fīhi*). Now look what happened: the earth is my bed (*at-turābu firāšī*) and the worm is my neighbour!"[120]

2. "They prospered in life" (verse 3). For the expression of the third line one might also refer to a passage in the biography of the ascetic Abū Ḥāzim (Salamah b. Dīnār, d. 140). When he was brought before the Umayyad caliph Sulaymān b. ʿAbd al-Malik (r. 96–99), he was asked "O Abū Ḥāzim! How is it that we hate to die?", and replied "It is because you destroy your hereafter and only strive to prosper in the present world, thus you hate to be transferred from prosperity to destruction".[121]

3

LOCATIONS. (a) Aleppo (ar. Ḥalab). – (b) Bayt al-Maqdis (Jerusalem).
DATES. (a) 548 H or after. – (b) 843 H.

118 *Cf.* Q 45:35: *wa-ġarratkumu l-ḥayātu d-dunyā* ("and the present life deluded you").

119 *Cf.* also RCEA 4539 (663 H, Konya): *wa-ğaʿalahū yawma l-qiyāmati mina l-fāʾizīna*. The expression *fawz* denotes the Paradise in the Qurʾān, esp. the terms *al-fawz al-ʿaẓīm* (Q 4:13, etc.) and *al-fawz al-kabīr* (Q 85:11). For further details, see Volume I, Chapter 4.

120 IĞawzīTabṣ I p. 335. With a different wording also cited in IbšīhīMust II p. 465 (ch. 83); a related story appears in ṬurṭSirāğ p. 13.

121 Cited in MunKawākib I p. 219 (*li-ʾannakum ḫarrabtum ʾāḫiratakum wa-ʿammartumu d-dunyā fa-karihtum ʾan tunqalū mina l-ʿumrāni ʾilā l-ḫarāb*); with a slightly different wording in ḤurRawḍ p. 26. Very similar to this is a dictum of Yaḥyā b. Muʿāḏ ar-Rāzī (d. Nīsābūr 258 H; for his epitaph see **172**): "The present world is destruction, and most so the heart of the one who seeks prosperity in it. The hereafter is prosperity, and most so the heart of the one who craves it" (MunKawākib I p. 728).

PERSONS BURIED. (a) The poet Ibn Munīr aṭ-Ṭarābulusī (Abū l-Ḥusayn [Ḥasan] A. b. Munīr ar-Raffāʾ: Ṭarābulus 473 – Aleppo 548 H): AŠāmahRawḍ I p. 91; IʿAdīmBuġyah III pp. 144-57; IṣfḪar (Š) I pp. 76-95; IḪallWaf I pp. 156-60; TI XXXVII pp. 296-9; BN XII p. 231; MaqrMuq I pp. 692f.; ZA I p. 260; EI² X p. 216 (A. Schippers). – (b) The religious scholar Taqīy ad-Dīn Abū ṣ-Ṣidq Abū Bakr b. aš-Šams Abī ʿAbd Allāh Muḥammad b. al-Ǧamāl ʿAl. al-Ḥalabī al-Bisṭāmī aṭ-Ṭūlūnī (d. 843 H), see **32**.

SOURCES. (a) IʿAdīmBuġyah III p. 155; IḪallWaf I p. 159 / (Slane) I p. 141. – (b) ḌL XI p. 80; ʿUlaymīUns II p. 173.

DESCRIPTION. (a) Ibn al-ʿAdīm reports the following:

> "Ibn Munīr was buried outside the Qinnasrīn Gate near the mausoleum of Mušriq – that is, Mušriq b. ʿAbd Allāh the worshipper (*al-ʿābid*). I saw the tomb of Ibn Munīr to the south of the tomb of Mušriq, at some distance from it, and upon his tomb there are two verses of his poetry. I was told that he recited them when he was near death and stipulated in his last will that they be written upon his tomb, so they were engraved on the stones (*ʾaḥǧār*) of his tomb. They run: [...]. At the time when sultan al-Malik aẓ-Ẓāhir – may God have mercy upon him! – cleared the trenches of Aleppo and their earth was heaped upon the adjacent cemetery outside the Qinnasrīn Gate,[122] the superintendent Nāfiʿ b. Abī l-Faraḥ b. Nāfiʿ was afraid that the earth would also be heaped upon the tomb of Ibn Munīr. So he wiped it out and effaced its traces, exhumed the corpse, transferred his bones and moved (the site) of his tomb to the slopes of the Ǧawšan Hill in the vicinity of the shrine of al-Ḥusayn. This is where his tomb is located today".[123]

Ibn Ḫallikān visited Ibn Munīr's tomb in Aleppo and read the epitaph cited. – (b) "Of his own poetry (!, *min naẓmihī*) was also written upon his tomb: [...]" (both sources; for the remainder of the epitaph, see **32**). – Two verses in the metre *sarīʿ*:

*man zāra qabrī fal-yakun mūqinan * ʾanna llaḏī ʾalqāhu yalqāhū*
*fa-yarḥamu llāhu mraʾan zāranī * wa-qāla lī yarḥamuka llāhū*

1 *mūqinan*: *ʿāliman* (b); *ʾalqāhu*: *lāqaytu* (b). – **2** *fa-yarḥamu*: *fa-raḥḥama* (b); *imraʾan*: *fatan* (b).

"Whoever visits my grave must know for sure * that he will experience (*or* encounter) what I am experiencing (*or* encountering),
And God may have mercy upon the man who comes to visit me * and tells me 'May God have mercy upon you!'"

NOTES. It is interesting to see that 295 years separate these two, almost identical versions of this epitaph (a, b). However, the older version (a) was reportedly inscribed in Aleppo, and Abū ṣ-Ṣidq aṭ-Ṭūlūnī was himself, or at least on his family's side,

122 *Cf.* Gonnella: *Heiligenverehrung* 10 (p 164).

123 IʿAdīmBuġyah III pp. 155f. He goes on to report that Abū Ṭālib al-Qayyim and some of his companions went at night to the tomb of Ibn Munīr (who was ill-famed among the Sunnites for his open support of Shiism) and excavated it in order to see whether his corpse had turned into a pig, because the poet had insulted the caliphs Abū Bakr and ʿUmar during his lifetime. They found this indeed to be the case, so they tore the body out of the grave, burned it at the edge of the tomb, put it back into the pit and smoothed the earth over it.

from Aleppo. The fact that the sources describe the verses of his epitaph (b) as "from his own poetry" seems to indicate that the lines of (a) were not unduly popular or otherwise ascribed to a famous person. It would be interesting to know whether Abū ṣ-Ṣidq himself passed them off as verses of his own or whether this was only supposed by his biographers, being unaware of Ibn Munīr's epitaph as cited by Ibn Ḫallikān. However, the second part of Abū ṣ-Ṣidq's epitaph (**32**) has no antecedents.

1. The motif that someone standing before a tomb looks at his own destiny is frequent in surviving epitaphs as well as in those quoted in literary sources (*cf.* **83**, **88**, **183**, **213** and **218**). A short two-line poem which nicely expresses this concept is worth being cited here, though it was judged "mediocre" by aṣ-Ṣafadī. It was composed by Abū Muḥammad al-Baġdādī al-Muqriʾ (ʿAl. b. ʿAlī, d. 541 H, see above p. 231) (*ḫafīf*):

أَيُّهَا الزَّائِرُونَ بَعْدَ وَفَاتِي * جَدَثاً ضَمَّنِي وَلَحْداً عَمِيقَا

سَتَرَوْنَ الَّذِي رَأَيْتُ مِنَ المَوْ * تِ عِيَاناً وَتَسْلُكُونَ الطَّرِيقَا

"O those visiting after my passing away * a (certain) grave which did enclose me and a deep burial niche:
You will see what I have seen of dea- * th with (your own) eyes and you will take the (same) way!"[124]

2. The prayer for mercy is likewise one of the most common elements of Arabic funerary epigraphy (*cf.* **9**, **32**, **34**, **85**, **88**, **124**, **126**, **175** and **188**). However, a wording equal or close to the present prayer (verse 2) is only rarely encountered, e.g. in an epitaph that – incidentally or not – also stems from Aleppo: *raḥima {man} allāhu man qāla raḥimahū llāh* ("May God have mercy upon those who say 'May God have mercy upon him!'").[125] Invectives in mourning poems, on the other hand, could include the wish that the deceased may not enjoy the mercy of God.[126]

4

LOCATION. Aleppo. DATE. 587 H (but see below).

PERSON BURIED (?). The famous mystic and philosopher-scientist Šihāb ad-Dīn as-Suhrawardī (Yaḥyā b. Ḥabaš, Suhraward 549 – executed in Aleppo 587 H and therefore nick-named *aš-šayḫ al-maqtūl*), author of the treatise *Ḥikmat al-ʾišrāq*:

124 AnbNuzhah p. 403; *Wāfī* XVII p. 331; ŠayMaǧānī IV p. 40 (AnbNuzhah and ŠayMaǧānī with the variant: *wa-taslukūna ṭarīqā*).

125 CIA Alep 159 = RCEA 4413.

126 E.g. the verse (*kāmil*): *fa-lā raḥima r-raḥmānu turbata qabrihī * wa-lā zāla fīhā Munkarun wa-Nakīrū* (cited in IWāṣilKurūb I p. 167), *cf.* also ALL (Littmann) VI p. 634.

IAUṣaybᶜUyūn pp. 641-6; GAL I p. 437; EI² IX pp. 782-4; Gonnella: *Heiligenverehrung* 141 (p. 231).

SOURCES. IAUṣaybᶜUyūn p. 644; ṢafAᶜyān III p. 104; NZ V p. 204; al-Ġazzī: *Nahr ad-ḏahab* I p. 323.

DESCRIPTION. "Somebody from Aleppo told me that after the death of Šihāb ad-Dīn – may God have mercy upon him! – and his burial outside Aleppo the following was found written upon his tomb, and the verses are old: [...]" (IAUṣaybᶜUyūn). Following al-Ġazzī, however, these two lines were actually found inscribed on the tomb of Abū l-ᶜAlāʾ al-Maᶜarrī (**111**); aṣ-Ṣafadī quotes both verses simply as poetry, without further information. According to Ibn Kaṯīr, al-Ibšīhī and Ibn Taġrī Birdī, both verses were composed by Šibl ad-Dawlah Muqātil b. ᶜAṭīyah al-Ḥiǧāzī al-Bakrī (d. 506 H), mourning the death of the Seljuq vizier Niẓām al-Mulk (d. 485 H); it seems that these lines (see below) were later adapted for as-Suhrawardī's epitaph, with the wording being considerably changed in the first verse. – Two verses in the metre *basīṭ*:

*qad kāna ṣāḥibu hāḏā l-qabri ǧawharatan * maknūnatan qad barāhā llāhu min šarafi*
*fa-lam takun taᶜrifu l-ʾayyāmu qīmatahū * fa-raddahā ġayratan minhū ʾilā ṣ-ṣadafi*

1 *maknūnatan qad barāhā llāhu min šarafi*: *ġurran [fa-]qad ṣāġahā l-bārī* (!) *mina n-nuṭafi* (ṢafAyᶜān), *nafīsatan ṣāġahā r-raḥmānu min šarafi* (al-Ġazzī). – **2** فلم :تكن عزت فلم (ṢafAyᶜān, al-Ġazzī); *qīmatahū*: *qīmatahā* (ṢafAyᶜān, al-Ġazzī).

"The inhabitant of this tomb was once a well- * protected pearl[127] which God had created from red clay,[128]
Yet the days (i.e. his time = his contemporaries) did not recognise his value.[129] * So, being jealous of it, He returned it to the shell".

NOTES. Ibn Abī Uṣaybiᶜah explicitly says that these verses stem from earlier times (*aš-šiᶜr qadīm*) and were thus not composed for the occasion; as said above, the mourning poem by Muqātil al-Bakrī probably provided the model (*basīṭ*):

كَانَ الوَزِيرُ نِظَامُ المُلْكِ لُؤلُؤَةً * يَتِيمَةً صَاغَهَا الرَّحْمَنُ مِنْ شَرَفِ
عَزَّتْ وَلَمْ تَعْرِفِ الأَيَّامُ قِيمَتَهَا * فَرَدَّهَا غَيْرَةً مِنْهُ إِلَى الصَّدَفِ

1 – 2 *ᶜazzat wa-lam*: ... *fa-lam* (BN), *ʾaḍḥat wa-lā* (NZ).

"The vizier Niẓām al-Mulk was once a uniquely precious * pearl which the Merciful had created from red clay,

127 The Arabic text has literally "gem" or "jewel" (*ǧawharah*), but clearly a pearl is meant as is often the case in poetry; see also the examples quoted in the following.

128 Alternatively, *min šarafin* might also mean "of nobility", or here "as (a token of His) nobility" or "from honour".

129 The variant cited by al-Ġazzī (*qīmatahā*) would mean "its value", i.e. of the pearl.

It (*sc.* the pearl = the vizier) reigned with might, yet the days (i.e. its time) did not recognise its value. * So, being jealous of it, He returned it to the shell".

However, some decades later aṣ-Ṣafadī cites as-Suhrawardī's epitaph-poem as model for further lines fashioned after this epitaph and thus makes these verses appear to be the first of their kind. The two lines which aṣ-Ṣafadī quotes as being modelled on the epitaph were composed by a certain Šams ad-Dīn Muḥammad b. Dāʾūd, an elder contemporary of aṣ-Ṣafadī, upon the death of Ṣadr ad-Dīn Ibn al-Wakīl (M. b. ʿUmar, d. Cairo 717 H) who died at the age of 52. Two verses in the metre *basīṭ*:

مَا مَــاتَ صَدْرُ الدِّينِ لَكِنَّهُ * لمَّا غَدَا جَوْهَرَةً فَاخِـرَه
لَمْ تَعْرِفِ الدُّنْيَا لَهُ قِيمَةً * فَعَجَّلَ السَّيْرَ إِلَى الآخِرَه

"Ṣadr ad-Dīn died not; rather (it happened that) – * after he had become a splendid pearl –
The World did not recognise his value * and so he hastened the departure for the hereafter".[130]

The next dictum closest in meaning to the above-quoted epitaph – viz. death as a return of the pearl to its shell – was composed by Ibn Abī š-Šaḫbāʾ al-ʿAsqalānī al-Kātib (d. Cairo 482 or 486 H),[131] reportedly one of the masters of al-Qāḍī al-Fāḍil. In a poem about someone who had drowned, Ibn Abī š-Šaḫbāʾ takes to the pearl-metaphor although he does not mention the shell, but it is clear from the context that he is implying this very concept (*kāmil*):

فَكَأَنَّـمَا هُوَ دُرَّةٌ دُفِنَـــتْ * فِي حَيْثُـمَا وُلِدَتْ مِنَ البَحْرِ
وَتَنَزَّهَتْ عَنْ أَنْ يُصَافِحَهَا * تُرْبُ الصَّفِيحِ وَظُلْمَةُ القَبْرِ

"It were as if he was a pearl that was buried * down there where it had been born in the sea,
And thus it (i.e. the pearl) is much above being (ever) touched * by the earth of the ledger stone and the darkness of the tomb".[132]

That is, the pearl had returned to the bottom of the sea – its place of creation viz. birth – and thus it might be said to have "returned into the shell"; the fact that the mourned person died at sea conveys a double meaning to the pearl-metaphor which is missing in as-Suhrawardī's epitaph. In any case, a comparable dictum was pronounced upon the death of the Andalusian poet Ibn Sahl al-Isrāʾīlī (d. 659 H or before).[133] He drowned in the Mediterranean around the middle of the seventh cen-

130 ṢafAyʿān III p. 104.

131 Abū ʿAlī al-Ḥasan b. (M. b.) ʿAbd aṣ-Ṣamad, see: IḪallWaf II pp. 89-91; YāqIršād III pp. 200-15; *Wāfī* XII pp. 68-70; MaqrMuq III pp. 338f.

132 Cited in MaqrMuq III p. 338.

133 Abū Isḥāq Ibrāhīm b. Sahl al-Išbīlī al-Isrāʾīlī (a Jewish convert born in Seville 605 H; *cf.* p. 98): *Wāfī* VI pp. 5-11; ḎahʿIbar V p. 253; KutFawāt I pp. 20-30; ITaġrManh I pp. 67-74;

tury H and his tragic death was immortalised by the words: "The pearl returned to its homeland" (*ʿāda d-durru ʾilā waṭanihī*).[134]

In a more general sense, and explicitly referring to the image of the shell, the depiction of the grave as "shell" (*ṣadaf*, also "mother-of-pearl") and the deceased as the "pearl" – *durr(ah)* or also *ǧawhar(ah)* – is a common motif in Arabic funerary epigraphy known from literary sources (*cf.* **137**, last verse) and in mourning poetry.

In epitaph-poems, we find for example the following line, from the poem upon the tomb of Muḥammad Hilāl ar-Rāmḥamdānī[135] (d. 1147 H) in Aleppo (*basīṭ*):

إنَّ الَّذِي ضَمَّ هَذَا الرَّمْسُ جَوْهَرَةٌ * لاَ زَالَ إشْرَاقُهَا فِي الكَوْنِ مُتَّصِلاَ

"The one enclosed in this tomb is a pearl (*or* jewel): * may its radiance never cease to pervade the universe!"[136]

We also know the following line from an inscription in the mausoleum of as-Suhaylī (d. 581 H)[137] in Marrakech (*kāmil*):

إذْ صَانَ فِي الصِّيَانَةِ جَوْهَراً * فَرْداً سَنَاهُ بِالبَهَاءِ أَنِيقُ

"Given that it (i.e. the tomb) preserves in the guarding shell a pearl * unique whose splendour radiates with luminous beauty".[138]

One of the earliest examples from poetry that I am aware of is the following verse from a mourning poem composed by aš-Šarīf ar-Raḍīy (*ramal*):

لاَ تَقُلْ تِلْكَ قُبُورٌ إنَّمَا * هِيَ أَصْدَافٌ عَلَى غَيْرِ لآلِ

"Do not say 'These are graves!' Rather they * are shells though they do not contain (real) pearls".[139]

In a similar vein we read in a poem upon the death of the famous theologian Abū Bakr al-Bāqillānī (d. 403 H) (*basīṭ*):

أُنْظُرْ إلَى جَبَلٍ تَمْشِي الرِّجَالُ بِهِ * وَانْظُرْ إلَى القَبْرِ مَا يَحْوِي مِنَ الصَّلَفِ
وَانْظُرْ إلَى صَارِمِ الإسْلاَمِ مُغْتَمَداً * وَانْظُرْ إلَى دُرَّةِ الإسْـــــلاَمِ فِي الصَّدَفِ

GAL I pp. 273f.; Nykl: *Hispano-Arabic Poetry* pp. 344f.; ZA I p. 36; al-Makkī: *Madāʾiḥ* pp. 131f.; Penelas/Zanón: *Nómina de ulemas andalusíes* p. 17; CHAL *Andalus* p. 436.

134 IQāḍīDurrah I p. 34; Nykl: *Hispano-Arabic Poetry* p. 344.

135 See also Gonnella: *Heiligenverehrung* 160 (pp. 248-50).

136 al-Ġazzī: *Nahr aḏ-ḏahab* II p. 56.

137 For him, see IDiḥMuṭrib pp. 230-42. His tomb was repeatedly visited by al-Maqarrī in 1010 H, see MaqqNafḥ (C) IV pp. 370f.

138 Inscriptions Marrakech 39 (line 2).

139 ŠarīfRaḍDīwān II p. 201 (v. 61) = *Wāfī* XIX p. 87 (var. *ʾinnamā*: *ʾinnahā*; *ʿalā ġayri laʾālī*: *ʿalā durri l-laʾālī*).

"Behold a 'mountain'[140] that is carried away by men[141] * and behold the tomb, what pomposity it does embrace!
Behold the sharp (sword) of Islam put in the scabbard * and behold the pearl of Islam in the shell!"[142]

There is a poem by Usāmah b. Munqiḏ (d. 584 H), mourning the death of his son Abū Bakr, which contains a verse that certainly alludes to the nature of the pearl's enclosure which – like the tomb in the earth – offers little for the eye from the outside, but is covered inside by precious and shimmering mother-of-pearl (*basīṭ*):

فَمَا أَرَى غَيْرَ أَحْجَارٍ مُنَضَّدَةٍ * قَدِ احْتَوَتْكَ وَمَأْوَى الدُّرَّةِ الصَّدَفُ

"I see nothing (at your tomb) but stones neatly set * which did come to enclose you,[143] and (indeed) the lodging-place of the pearl is the shell".[144]

The Andalusian poet Ibn Zumruk (d. 791 H or after) – the famed author of many verses which adorn the walls of the Alhambra – has the following line in one of his mourning poems (*kāmil*):

كَمْ مِنْ سَرَاةٍ فِي الْقُبُورِ كَأَنَّهُمْ * فِي بَطْنِهَا دُرٌّ ثَوَى بِحِقَاقِ

"How many persons of high standing in their tombs are quite as if * they were in its belly[145] pearls lodged in cases".[146]

Ibn Maᶜṣūm (d. *c.*1020 H) composed a poem mourning the death of his aunt who had in the past taken care of the upbringing of his brother (*basīṭ*):

أَهَكَذَا دَوْحَةُ الْعَلْيَاءِ تَنْقَصِفُ * وَهَكَذَا الشَّمْسُ فِي الآفَاقِ تَنْكَسِفُ
وَهَكَذَا بَهْجَةُ الْعُلْيَا وَنَضْرَتُهَا * يُزْرِي بِمُشْرِقِهَا الإِظْلاَمُ وَالسَّدَفُ
وَهَكَذَا دُرَّةُ الْمَجْدِ الأَثِيلِ غَدَتْ * يَضُمُّهَا بَعْدَ حُسْنِ الْحِلْيَةِ الصَّدَفُ
لِلَّهِ أَيَّةُ رُوحٍ فَارَقَتْ جَسَداً * وَأَيُّ جُثْمَانِ عِزٍّ ضَمَّهُ جَدَفُ

140 I.e. a hero, see above p. 343.

141 I.e. during the funeral procession.

142 Cited in TB V pp. 382f.; IḪallWaf IV p. 270 / (Slane) II p. 672; SaḫĞawāhir III p. 1196; ŠayMağānī III p. 43.

143 This is an obvious reference to the visible shape of the grave on the surface, viz. some structure or recinct of cut stones.

144 IMunqiḏDīwān 515 v. 2 (p. 301) = IṣfḪar (Š) I p. 523.

145 The expressions *baṭn al-qabr, b. al-laḥd* or *b. aḍ-ḍarīḥ* etc. are common in mourning poetry and epitaph-poems (*cf.* **103**); *baṭn* may also be said of the belly of the earth, see **189**.

146 IZumrDīwān p. 76 = MaqqNafḥ (C) VII p. 122. The image of the "case" or "box" (*ḥuqqah*, pl. *ḥiqāq*) refers to small receptacles for pearls or jewellery, made from precious wood or ivory, such as are known especially from al-Andalus and Sicily.

"Is it thus that the wide-branching tree of loftiness is broken, * and that the sun is eclipsed on the horizons?
That the joy and resplendence of the upper (heaven) * are reviled in their splendour by darkness and dusk?
That the pearl of highborn glory has come * to be enclosed, after (it lost its) beauty of appearance, by the shell?
By God, what a soul left a body (with her)! * What a distinguished corpus (it is) that was enclosed by a (certain) grave!"[147]

For the pearl-metaphor, notice also a significant line in *The Thousand ond One Nights*[148] and the following anecdote concerning Saᶜīd al-Baġdādī (d. 417 H) who claimed that he could dictate a better book than the *ʾAmālī* by al-Qālī, if al-Manṣūr Ibn Abī ᶜĀmir (*cf.* **170**) so desired. Then Saᶜīd dictated a book which he called *al-Fuṣūṣ* ("The Pearls"), but it was found worthless and al-Manṣūr ordered it to be thrown into the river. A malicious poet said then, "*The Book of Pearls* was submerged in the river, and this is what happens to all things tedious!" To which Saᶜīd replied, "It only returned to its original abode, because pearls are found only in the deep sea!"[149]

5

LOCATION. Aleppo. DATE. 602/611 H.

PERSON BURIED. ᶜAlī al-Harawī (Abū l-Ḥasan b. Abī Bakr, born in Mawṣil, d. Aleppo 611 H): MundTakm II pp. 315f.; IḪallWaf III pp. 346-8; ZA IV p. 266; EI[2] III p. 178 (J. Sourdel-Thomine); see also above pp. 296f. and 320.

SOURCES. IMuḥKunūz I pp. 321f.; al-Ġazzī: *Nahr aḏ-ḏahab* II p. 222; CIA Alep 136 (with fig. 86 and plate CXIIIb). – Volume I pp. 95ff. (very detailed).

DESCRIPTION. "On his tomb (there is the inscription): [...]" (IMuḥKunūz). The inscription is also preserved as part of al-Harawī's extant epitaph; the small numbers in the text refer to that inscription (see note following the transcribed text):

[1]yā-ᶜazīzu rḥami ḏ-ḏalīla yā-qādiru rḥami l-ᶜāǧiza [2]yā-bāqī rḥami l-fāniya yā-ḥayyu rḥami l-mayyita [3]allāhumma ʾinnī ḍayfuka wa-nazīluka wa-fī ǧiwārika wa-fī ḥurmika wa-ʾanta ʾawlā man ʾakrama ḍayfahū wa-raḥima ǧārahū wa-ʾaᶜāna nazīlahū yā-rabbi yā-muġīṯ

According to CIA Alep 136 (where some words are only rendered fragmentarily or not at all) the inscription on the extant cenotaph contains other passages which name the deceased (twice) and the date of his death. A comparison with the preserved inscription shows that Ibn al-Muḥaddiṯ first quotes the passages from both long sides of the cenotaph (the northern side 1 and the southern side 2) and then the passage inscribed on the eastern side (3). However, he omits from the inscription on the eastern side the following introductory passage: *qāla sākinu hāḏihī t-turbati š-šayḫu ᶜAlīyu bnu ʾAbī Bakrini l-Harawīyu – raḍiya llāhu ᶜanhu wa-raḥimahū wa-raḥima ǧamīᶜa l-muslimīna – allāhumma ʾinnī ḍayfuka*, etc.

147 IMaᶜṣDīwān p. 622 (vv. 1 and 3-5 of the poem).

148 ALL (Mahdī) p. 624: ودرّة اودعت قبراً وكان لها * حشاى حرز فمن قص الثرا صدفا.

149 Adapted from Nykl: *Hispano-Arabic Poetry* p. 53.

"[1]O Mighty One, have mercy upon the forlorn, O Almighty One, have mercy upon the powerless, [2]O Everlasting One, have mercy upon the ephemeral, O Everliving One, have mercy upon the dead. [3]My God, I am Your guest and lodge with You, I am close to You and in Your shelter. You are the most likely to honour Your guest, to have mercy upon Your protégé and to support[150] those who lodge with You. O my Lord, O helper!"

NOTE. The concept of being "the guest of God" or "hosted by Him" is common in ascetic and mourning poetry as well as in epitaphs (see below **26**, **95**, **106**, **216** and **226**). The related expressions "to lodge (*nzl* I) with God" and "to be close to God" (lit. "to be in His protective neighbourhood, *or* vicinity", *fī ǧiwārihī*) are likewise frequent (see **216** and **235**).

6

LOCATION. Aleppo. DATE. 945 H.

PERSON BURIED. Muḥammad b. Aḥmad Ibn Mawlānā Ǧalāl ad-Dīn al-Ḫālidī al-Kaššī[151] as-Samarqandī al-Ḥanafī, known as "Munlā (Muḥammad) Šāh" al-ʿAǧamī (d. 945 H). He came to Aleppo in 945 H on his way to Mecca and died there after a short stay: IḤanbDurr II pp. 194-6; ĠazKawākib II p. 25; ŠḎ VIII pp. 263f.

SOURCE. IḤanbDurr II p. 196.

DESCRIPTION. "He was buried in the cemetery of the Righteous (*maqburat aṣ-ṣāliḥīn*).[152] Two verses, which I had composed to mourn him, were written upon his tomb, and I indicated in them the date of his death, saying [...]". – Two verses in the metre *kāmil*:

*māta l-ʾimāmu l-Ḫālidīyu fa-sāʾanā * yawmu n-nawā wa-l-ḥuznu ʿāda muḫalladā*
*wa-ʾuṣība fī l-ʿāmi llaḏī taʾrīḫuhū * qad ṭāba maṯwāhu r-raḥību wa-wuṭṭidā*
104 12 552 251 26 = 945

1 *al-ʾimāmu*: *ʾimāmunā* (var. in ms.); مخلدا: ملحدا (var. in ms.). – **2** ووطدا: وأوطدا (var. in ms.).

"The Imam al-Ḫālidī died, thus we were grieved * by the day of his absence and the affliction (for his death) became everlasting.[153]
He was struck (by Fate) in the year whose chronogram is as follows: * 'His spacious place of rest (i.e. his tomb) is pleasant and comfortable'".

NOTE. For chronograms (sg. *taʾrīḫ*) in epitaphs, see also the following entries and below **71**, **78** and **81**f. The use of chronograms was equally, or even more, widespread,

150 As above: *ʾaʿāna*, though other sources (e.g. al-Ġazzī: *Nahr aḏ-ḏahab* II p. 222) have *ʾaǧāra*, see Volume I p. 105 for further details.

151 In some sources البكشي.

152 *Cf.* Gonnella: *Heiligenverehrung* 17 (p. 167); *aṣ-ṣāliḥīn* is here misunderstood as a place name ("Ṣālḥīn").

153 *muḫallad* being a *taǧnīs* with the name of the deceased, *al-Ḫālidī*.

in Ottoman epitaphs from the tenth century H onwards. A huge number of Turkish chronograms from epitaphs is contained in the late eleventh-century guide to the mosques of Istanbul by Ḥüseyin al-Ayvānsarāyī (= AyvānGarden).

7

LOCATION. Aleppo. DATE. 949 H.

PERSON BURIED. Abū l-Faḍl Muḥibb ad-Dīn Maḥmūd b. Raḍīy ad-Dīn Muḥammad al-Ḥanafī al-Ḥalabī (d. 949 H), son of the author Ibn al-Ḥanbalī (d. 971 H), see his IḤanbDurr II pp. 466-71. He died at the age of 22.

SOURCE. IḤanbDurr II p. 466.

DESCRIPTION. "I pointed out the year of his death in (the lines) which I inscribed (*rqm* I) upon his tomb that is located in our mausoleum (*turbah*) outside the Bāb al-Maqām, and thus I said [...]". – Two verses in the metre *kāmil*:

*fī l-ḫaddi ʾuḫdūdun bihī ǧarati d-dimā * min faqdi man ḥāza ṭība muqāmī*
*waladī llaḏī taʾrīḫu ʿāmi wafātihī * kam nāla Maḥmūdun ṯawāba muqāmī*

"On the cheek is a furrow through which the drops of blood (i.e. the teardrops) trickle * for the loss of someone who had obtained a pleasant stay (on earth) (?).

(It is) my child whose year of death (gives the following) chronogram: * 'How much did *Maḥmūd / a laudable one* procure (to me) as a reward for my staying (alive while he died)!'"[154]

I am not sure about the translation of these two lines. Especially the terms *ṭīb* and *muqām* (or *maqām*) present difficulties of understanding for their multiple meanings, and almost certainly there is a wordplay here with "(Bāb) al-Maqām", the burial site of Ibn al-Ḥanbalī's son. In the first verse, we might also read *qad ḥāza ṭība maqāmin*, i.e. "he had reached goodness of rank (in the eyes of God), *or* of saintness"[155], or rather "he has gained the fragrance of a shrine" (implying that his tomb is venerated and its earth perfumed). In addition, I did not give the chronogram in Arabic numerals because the sum does not correspond to the year 949. According to my best arithmetic skills, the sum of the second hemistich – which contains the chronogram – only amounts to 929 (60 + 81 + 98 + 509 + 181); there is some fault in the wording.

The correct date *is* given by the chronogram if *muqām* is substituted in the second line by *saqām*, "illness". The second hemistich of verse 2 would then translate as "How much did *Maḥmūd / a laudable one* receive as reward for a certain illness (from which he died?)".

8

LOCATION. Aleppo. DATE. 952 H.

PERSON BURIED. aš-Šābb al-fāḍil Ṣadr ad-Dīn Muḥammad b. Masʿūd aš-Šīrāzī aš-Šāfiʿī, known as "Šāh Muḥammad" (d. 952 H): IḤanbDurr II pp. 99-101.

154 I.e. the son procured for his father a reward in the hereafter by dying before him; see Volume I, Chapter 3.

155 *Cf.* Dozy: *Supplément* II p. 427 (s.r. *qwm*).

SOURCE. IḤanbDurr II p. 101.

DESCRIPTION. "I recited when asked what was to be written upon his tomb: [...]", in the metre *ramal*:

*ḏā ḍarīḥun ḥalla fīhī fāḍilun * ṭāba min rayyā ʾayādīhi n-nasīm*
*māta fī l-ʿāmi llaḏī taʾrīḫuhū * kam li-Ṣadri d-Dīni min ʾarbā naʿīm*

60	324	95	90	213	170	= 952

1 *ḏā ḍarīḥun*: *yā ḍarīḥan* (var. in ms.). – **2** second hemistich: *kam li-Ṣadri d-Dīni min ʾağrin ʿaẓīm* (var. in ms., meaningful but impossible for the numerical values of the letters).

"This is a tomb in which a distinguished (person)[156] has settled * from whose fragrant hands the (perfumed) breeze took its perfume.
He died in the year whose chronogram is as follows: * 'How much gained (*or* possesses) Ṣadr ad-Dīn of Bliss most plentiful!'"[157]

9

LOCATION. Aleppo. DATE. 970 H.

PERSON BURIED. Abū Bakr b. Aḥmad an-Naqqāš al-Ḥalabī al-Ğallūmī (d. 970 H): IḤanbDurr I pp. 397-9.

SOURCE. IḤanbDurr I p. 398.

DESCRIPTION. An epitaph; two verses in the metre *ṭawīl*:

*ʾAbū Bakrini n-naqqāšu ʾaḥwağu sāʾilin * ʾilā raḥmatin tuqṣīhi ʿan mūğibi l-wazrī*
*fa-yā-ʾayyuhā l-muğtāzu naḥwa ḍarīḥihī * tamahhal qalīlan dāʿiyan li-ʾAbī Bakrī*

"Abū Bakr the sculptor (*or* the engraver) is the most needy of those who ask * for mercy which takes away from him what the sins would call for (i.e. his deserved punishment).
O you who pass towards his grave: * rest a little (while) and pray for Abū Bakr!"

10

LOCATION. Almería (ar. al-Marīyah). DATE. 485 H.

PERSON BURIED. The scholar and judge Ibn al-Murābiṭ (Abū ʿAl. M. b. Ḫalaf b. Saʿīd, d. 485 H), author of a commentary on the *Ṣaḥīḥ* of al-Buḫārī[158] and teacher of Abū ʿAlī aṣ-Ṣadafī (Ibn Sukkarah, d. 514): IBaškṢilah II pp. 557f.; *Wāfī* III pp. 46f.; GAS I p. 667; ZA VI p. 115; *cf.* also EI² VIII p. 707.

SOURCE. IBaškṢilah II pp. 557f.

DESCRIPTION. "I read in the hand-writing of our fellow Abū l-Walīd Sulaymān b.

156 *fāḍilun*: A wordplay on the deceased's epithet, *aš-šābb al-fāḍil*.

157 *Cf.* Q 16:92.

158 Not listed in GAS I.

ᶜAbd al-Malik: 'Upon the tomb of the judge Abū ᶜAbd Allāh Ibn al-Murābiṭ, on a marble slab (*ruḫāmah*) at the head of the tomb which is situated on the open street near the Baǧǧānah Gate, I read inscribed: [...]'".

hāḏā qabru l-qāḍī ʾAbī ʿAbdi llāhi bni l-Murābiṭi tuwuffiya – raḥimahū llāhu wa-naḍḍara waǧhahū – yawma l-ʾaḥadi li-ʾarbaʿin ḫalawna min Šawwālin sanata ḫamsin wa-ṯamānīna wa-ʾarbaʿimiʾah

"This is the tomb of the judge Abū ᶜAbd Allāh Ibn al-Murābiṭ. He was taken (to God) – may God have mercy upon him and make his face radiant![159] – on Sunday, four nights after the beginning of Šawwāl in the year 485".

11

Locations. (a) Near Anṭābulus (Pentepolis, in modern Libya) or Tripoli (Ṭarābulus or Aṭrābulus).[160] – (b) Kairouan. – (c) Naples.

Dates. (a) Second century H (?). – (b) 430 H. – (c) 473 H.

Persons buried. (a) Unknown (three brothers) – (b) Ṯābit b. Abī l-Qāsim al-Qalšānī al-ᶜAṭṭār. – (c) Muḥammad b. Abī Saᶜādah (not identified).

Sources. (a) IADunyāQubūr (A) pp. 166f. = IRaǧAhwāl pp. 191-3; TMD XXIV pp. 43-5 = ZabīdīŠIḥyāʾ X p. 357 (epitaphs I-III, but the texts of epitaph I and II exchanged in both works); YāfRawḍ pp. 202-4; SuyŠṢudūr pp. 391f.; ḤurRawḍ p. 27 (only epitaphs I and III); NuwIlmām IV p. 217 (only epitaph I); IRaǧLaṭāʾif p. 102 (first line of epitaph II, followed by the first line of epitaph I). – (b) Inscriptions Kairouan 342 (only epitaph I). – (c) Iscrizioni arabe Napoli V ll. 18-21 (p. 351) (only epitaph III) = Volume I pp. 183 and 571.

Description. (a) The epitaphs of three tombs (I-III) which were solidly built, of equal height and close to each other. The inscriptions are reported by ᶜAbd Allāh (or ᶜUbayd Allāh) b. Ṣadaqah b. Yazīd (or Mirdās) al-Bakrī, as personally witnessed by his father; al-Ḥurayfīš and al-Yāfiᶜī have no further comment; an-Nuwayrī and Ibn Raǧab (IRaǧLaṭāʾif) present these lines as if uttered by an unknown poet (*wa-li-baʿḍihim*: ...; *šiʿr*: ...). – (b) Epitaph I: inscribed on a preserved tombstone in Kufic letters. – (c) Epitaph III: inscribed on a tombstone, towards the end of the text. – Two verses each (*ṭawīl*):

Epitaph I:

*wa-kayfa yalaḏḏu l-ʿayša man huwa ʿālimun * bi-ʾanna ʾilāha l-ḫalqi lā budda sāʾiluh*
*fa-yaʾḫuḏu minhū ẓulmahū li-ʿibādihī * wa-yaǧzīhi bi-l-ḫayri llaḏī huwa fāʿiluh*

1 *man*: *li-man* (NuwIlmām, does not fit the metre); *huwa ʿālimun*: *kāna ʿāliman* (b), *kāna mūqinan*

159 For this expression, see note 663 below and Volume I p. 167.

160 The alternative is left open by Ibn ᶜAsākir and as-Suyūṭī. Ibn Abī d-Dunyā mentions only the former town, Ibn Raǧab the latter (though quoting from Ibn Abī d-Dunyā). The doubt is obviously due to writing mistakes in the process of transmission.

(IRağLaṭā'if); *'ilāha l-ḫalqi*: *'ilāha l-ḥaqqi* (NuwIlmām and epitaph b), *'ilāha l-ʿarši* (TMD XXIV p. 44). – **2** *minhū*: *min* (NuwIlmām); ظلمه: ظلمة (ḤurRawḍ); بالخير: بالخبر (!, IRağAhwāl, does not fit the metre); *wa-yağzīhi bi-l-ḫayri llaḏī huwa fāʿiluh*: *wa-ğazīhi* (sic) *bi-l-'amri llaḏī kāna fāʿilah* (b). See also Volume I p. 571.

"How does someone enjoy life knowing * that the God of Creation[161] will inescapably interrogate him (on Judgment Day)?
For He shall punish him for the injustice (committed) against His servants * and reward him for the good which he did (in life)".

Epitaph II:

wa-kayfa yaladdu l-ʿayša man kāna mūqinan[162] * *bi-'anna l-manāyā baġtatan sa-tuʿāğiluh*
*fa-taslubuhū milkan ʿaẓīman wa-bahğatan * wa-tuskinuhū l-bayta llaḏī huwa 'āhiluh*

1 *kāna mūqinan*: *huwa mūqinun* (TMD XXIV p. 43; SuyŠṢudūr, ZabīdīŠIḥyā'). – **2** *bahğatan*: *naḫwatan* (TMD XXIV pp. 43f., IRağAhwāl, SuyŠṢudūr, ZabīdīŠIḥyā'); *al-bayta*: *al-qabra* (TMD XXIV p. 43, YāfRawḍ).

"How does someone enjoy life being certain * that the throes of death will swiftly take him by surprise?
For they will snatch away from him great property and delight * and make him occupy the house which he (now) inhabits (i.e. the tomb)".

Epitaph III:

*wa-kayfa yaladdu l-ʿayša man kāna ṣā'iran * 'ilā ğadaṯin tublī š-šabāba manāziluh*
*wa-yaḏhabu wasmu l-waǧhi min baʿdi ḍaw'ihī * sarīʿan wa-yablā ğismuhū wa-mafāṣiluh*

1 *kāna ṣā'iran*: *huwa ṣā'irun* (TMD XXIV pp. 43 and 45, IRağAhwāl, SuyŠṢudūr, ZabīdīŠIḥyā', Iscrizioni arabe Napoli); second hemistich: *'ilā laḥdi qabrihī fīhi tablā šamā'iluh* (ḤurRawḍ, does not fit the metre); تبلي: يبلى (YāfRawḍ, Iscrizioni arabe Napoli; see also below); شتات (Iscrizioni arabe Napoli), the line in IADunyāQubūr (A) p. 167 and 171 runs: جدث تبلى التراب مناهله. – **2** *yaḏhabu*: *taḏhabu* (ZabīdīŠIḥyā'); *wasmu*: *ḥusnu* (TMD XXIV p. 43, SuyŠṢudūr, ZabīdīŠIḥyā'), *mā'u* (!, YāfRawḍ), *rasmu* (TMD XXIV p. 45, IRağAhwāl, ḤurRawḍ, Iscrizioni arabe Napoli); *ḍaw'ihī*: *ṣawnihī* (IADunyāQubūr [A] p. 167) and *ṣūratin* (IADunyāQubūr [A] p. 171), *bahā'ihī* (YāfRawḍ); *sarīʿan*: *qarīban* (ḤurRawḍ); *ğismuhū*: *li-ğismihī* (ḤurRawḍ, does not fit the metre); *mafāṣiluh*: *ma<w>āṣilah* (Iscrizioni arabe Napoli). The second hemistich is taken from SuyŠṢudūr because the text as edited in IADunyāQubūr (A) p. 167 (*wa-yablā minhu ğismuhū wa-mafāṣiluh*) falls short of the required metre. — Though the text of Iscrizioni arabe Napoli is not vocalised, the Italian translation which accompanies it shows that the verses were obviously read by the editor as follows: *wa-kayfa yaladdu l-ʿayša man huwa ṣā'irun * 'ilā ğadaṯin yablā š-šatātu manāzilah / wa-yuḏhibu rasma l-waǧhi min baʿdi ḍaw'ihī * sarīʿan wa-yublī ğismahū wa-ma<w>āṣilah.* However, as can be seen from the citation in the literary sources, the verse endings in epitaph III are

161 The version of epitaph (b) would translate as "the God of verity", or "of the true creed".

162 To this line compare the following verse in a homily by Zayn al-ʿĀbidīn ʿAlī b. al-Ḥusayn (d. 94 H) (*ṭawīl*): *wa-kayfa yaladdu l-ʿayša man huwa mūqinun * bi-mawqifi ʿadlin yawma tublā s-sarā'irū* (cited in TMD XLI p. 406 = BN IX p. 111; al-Lawāsānī: *Kaškūl* p. 342).

unlikely to have nouns in the accusative because the lines are strictly parallel in rhyme to the other two epitaphs cited and thus allow only for a noun in the nominative, viz. *manāziluh* and *mafāṣiluh*. Therefore, يبلى v. 1 must be changed into *tublī* (as much of the literary tradition has it), with *manāziluh* being the subject, and consequently only the readings *yaḏhabu* and *yablā* are possible in verse 2.

"How does someone enjoy life being on his way * to a tomb whose abodes (i.e. corners?) wear out the youth:
The facial traits shrink away, after they radiated (in life), * quickly and both his corpse and joints decay".

12

LOCATION. al-Aylah (Eilat) or al-Ubullah (al-Ablah?).[163]
DATE. Third century H (?).
PERSON BURIED. Unknown.
SOURCES. IADunyāQubūr (A) pp. 165f.; IRağAhwāl p. 190; IRağLaṭāʾif p. 285.
DESCRIPTION. An inscription "on a tomb in one of the cemeteries" (IADunyāQubūr); "On a tomb in al-Aylah could be read: [...]" (IRağAhwāl); cited as anonymous poetry in IRağLaṭāʾif. – Two verses in the metre *sarīʿ*:

*laysa li-l-mayyiti fī qabrihī * fiṭrun wa-lā ʾaḍḥan wa-lā ʿašrū*
*nāʾa ʿani l-ʾahli ʿalā qurbihī * kaḏāka man maskanuhū l-qabrū*

1 the first hemistich does not fit the metre; *ʿašrū*: *ʿayšū* (IADunyāQubūr). – **2** *man ... al-qabrū*: *maṣīrī* (!, IRağAhwāl).

"For the dead in his tomb * there is no fast breaking, no sacrifice and no 'ten-days period',[164]
He is distant from the people though he is near to them:[165] * such is the condition of those whose dwelling is the tomb".

NOTE. Compare with that the passage from epitaph RCEA 1279; *cf.* also Volume I p. 495. On the whole, the epitaph sounds similar to an utterance of the ascetic Abū Bakr aš-Šiblī who appeared on a festive day and said provocatively, "The people have fast breaking and celebration, yet I am lonely and on my own".[166]

163 The Arabic الابلة might be read, or misread, as الأبلة, الأُبلّة or as الأيْلة. *Cf.* also **101**.

164 *al-ʿašru* or also *ʾayyām ʿašr*: the ten days at the beginning of Ḏū l-Ḥiǧǧah, considered a sacred period and comprising *yawm ʿArafah* , "the Day of ʿArafah" (9th Ḏū l-Ḥiǧǧah) and *yawm an-naḥr*, "the Day of the Sacrifice" (10th Ḏū l-Ḥiǧǧah).

165 *Cf.* note to **13**.

166 Cited from Ibn al-Ǧawzī's *Talbīs ʾIblīs* in Gramlich: *Vorbilder* I p. 568.

13

LOCATION. al-Aylah (Eilat) or al-Ubullah (al-Ablah?).
DATE. Third century H (?).
PERSON BURIED. Unknown.
SOURCES. IADunyāQubūr (A) p. 162; IRağAhwāl p. 190.
DESCRIPTION. "I read upon a tomb: [...]". The chain of transmission mentions Abū Mālik Ḍayġam ar-Rāsibī who reported the inscription and added the remark: "Whenever this line comes to my mind, I cannot sleep" (IADunyāQubūr); "On a tomb in al-Aylah could be read: [...]" (IRağAhwāl). – One verse in the metre *basīṭ*:

*ʾanā l-baᶜīdu l-qarību d-dāri manẓaruhū * bayna l-ğanādili wa-l-ʾaḥğāri marmūsū*[167]

"I am the far away one whose abode is near, whose outward appearance * is buried between the rocks and stones".

NOTE. The expression "whose abode is near" obviously indicates the actual tomb, while "being far away" refers to the sojourn of the deceased in the hereafter and his separation from the world of the living; *cf.* also **12**, **166** and **211**. This dichotomy of the simultaneous closeness and distance of the deceased is a common motif in Islamic imagery.[168] It has been well expressed by the Baṣran ascetic ar-Raqqāšī who described the tomb as follows: "Its location is near, yet its inhabitant dwells in another sphere" (*maḥalluhā muqtaribun wa-sākinuhā muġtaribun*),[169] and the same expression we find verbatim in a sermon by ᶜAlī b. Abī Ṭālib (see above page 136). Similarly, in a poem it is said *kullu man taḥta t-turābi baᶜīd* ("everybody under the earth is distant").[170] The related wish "Do not go away!" (or "Do not become distant!") is often attested in pre-Islamic and later Arabic mourning poetry.[171]

In a famous and widely-quoted mourning poem, variously ascribed to the Baṣran ᶜAbd Allāh b. Ṯaᶜlabah al-Ḥanafī, Abū ᶜAbd Allāh Yaᶜqūb b. Dāʾūd as-Sulamī (d. Mecca 187 H) and others, we read as a description of the dead (*ṭawīl*):

هُمُ جِيرَةُ الأَحْيَاءِ أَمَّا جِوَارُهُمْ * فَدَانٍ وَأَمَّا المُلْتَقَى فَبَعِيدُ

ğīratu l-ʾaḥyāʾi: *ğīratu l-ʾamwāti* (IĞawzīṢafwah); *ğiwāruhum*: *maḥalluhum* (IḪallWaf), *mazāruhum* (IĞawzīṢafwah, IBuḥtUns), *qarāruhum* (IRağLaṭāʾif).

167 *marmūsū*: *marhūnū* (IRağAhwāl). This variant is not improbable; in a first-century mourning poem we find the corresponding line (*ḫafīf*): *rağaᶜa r-rakbu sālimīna ğamīᶜan * wa-ḫalīlī fī marmasin madfūnū* (*Aġānī* IX p. 51; TawḥBaṣāʾir VIII p. 201).

168 Apart from epitaph-poetry, this imagery is also present in amatory verses, see e.g. IDāʾūdZahrah pp. 140ff.

169 Quoted in ANuwDīwān II p. 166; IᶜARabᶜIqd (Ğ) II p. 153 / (M) III p. 236; (with changed word order) ḤuṣZahr (M) III p. 859 / (Ṭ) II p. 197; *cf.* also above p. 342 with note 96.

170 WriĞurzah p. 102.

171 *Cf.* Rhodokanakis: *Trauerlieder* pp. 60-2.

"They are the neighbourhood of the living: their neighbouring vicinity * is near at hand, but the place of encountering (them again) is far away".[172]

This poem also contains the famous line:

لِكُلِّ أُنَاسٍ مَقْبَرٌ بِفِنَائِهِمْ * فَهُمْ يَنْقُصُونَ وَالقُبُورُ تَزِيدُ

"All human beings have a place of burial at (*or* near) their domicile, * and they become fewer while the tombs grow in number".[173]

In a poem mourning the death of ᶜImrān, composed by his father Abū Muḥammad ᶜAbd al-Ḥaqq b. Muḥammad as-Sahmī al-Qurašī (a Sicilian, d. Alexandria 466 H), we find the following *incipit* (*ṭawīl*):

أَرَاكَ قَرِيباً وَاللِقَاءُ بَعِيدُ * وَجِسْمُكَ يَبْلَى وَالزَّمَانُ يُعِيدُ

"I see you near yet meeting (you) is far, * your body decays and time passes by".[174]

Finally, there is a passage in rhymed prose by Ḍiyāʾ ad-Dīn Ibn al-Aṯīr, actually part of a consolation letter mourning a woman and her deceased son, which contains the couplets: *qad nazalā bi-manzilin ᶜadīmi l-ʾīnās / wa-ʾin kāna maʾhūlan bi-ʾakṯari n-nās* || *fa-huwa l-qarību dāran / al-baᶜīdu mazāran* ("They have settled in a dwelling devoid of intimacy [with other persons] / even though it is frequented by most of the people.[175] || Truly, he [*sc.* the deceased] is near as to his abode, || yet he is far away as to seeing [*or* meeting] him again").[176]

14

LOCATION. Baghdad. DATE. *c.*198 H.

PERSON BURIED (?): The poet Abū Nuwās (al-Ḥasan b. Hāniʾ, near Ahwāz *c.*140 – Baghdad *c.*198 H): IMuᶜtṬab pp. 193-217; IQutŠiᶜr pp. 501-25; AnbNuzhah pp. 77-80; TB VII pp. 436-49; TMD XIII pp. 407-66; EI² I pp. 143f. (E. Wagner); GAS II pp. 543-50; ZA II p. 225; EAL I pp. 41-3.

SOURCES. (Version I:) ANuwDīwān II p. 171. – (Version II:) AᶜAtāhAnwār pp. 52f. and AᶜAtāhDīwān p. 92 = IQutᶜUyūn II p. 329 = MāwAdab (B) p. 141 / (C) p. 107 = ṬurṭSirāǧ p. 13 = QurṭTaḏk p. 95; IQutŠiᶜr p. 500; IMuᶜtṬab p. 233; MasMurūǧ (B) VI p. 340 / (P) IV p. 222; IṣfStrangers p. 50 (in English trans-

172 IQutᶜUyūn III p. 75; IᶜARabᶜIqd (Ǧ) II p. 153 / (M) III p. 236; MarzḤam II p. 891 = IḪallWaf VII p. 24 / (Slane) IV p. 357; IǦawzīṢafwah II p. 232; IBuḥtUns p. 93; IRaǧLaṭāʾif p. 351; ŠayMaǧānī III p. 44.

173 *Cf.* also ZamAsās p. 488 and QurṭTaḏk p. 85.

174 Cited in IQaṭṭāᶜDurrah p. 79 and ᶜIyāḍTartīb IV p. 776.

175 This takes up the common topos that the buried person in the tomb is in a state of desolation, even if his tomb is visited by many persons; *cf.* also below p. 397.

176 IAṯīrMaṯal p. 205.

lation); MarzŠḤam II p. 881 (first line, cited anonymously); IᶜABarrBahğah II p. 339; AnbNuzhah p. 79; TB VII p. 448; TMD XIII pp. 459 and 463; IBuḥtUns p. 67; al-ᶜAffānī: *Sakb* II pp. 409, 508f. and 525; Rescher: *Gesammelte Werke* II.3 p. 200; Smoor: *Poems on Death* p. 55 note 18 (vv. 1, 3 in English translation).

DESCRIPTION. The versions of this epitaph differ somewhat in the sources and are ascribed to several authors. – (Version I:) "I found those verses written upon his tomb: [...]" (ANuwDīwān). – (Version II:) "Abū l-Ḥasan ᶜAlī b. Muḥammad al-Ḫūzī al-Kaššī said, 'It has reached us that when Abū Nuwās was dying, he said, Write these verses on my grave: [...]'" (IṣfStrangers); "Abū Ğaᶜfar aṣ-Ṣāʾiġ reports that Abū Nuwās said when he was near his death, 'Write these verses upon my tomb: [...]'" (AnbNuzhah, TB, TMD XIII p. 463). However, version II has also been attributed by many to Abū l-ᶜAtāhiyah (e.g. by Ibn al-Muᶜtazz, Ibn Qutaybah, al-Masᶜūdī, al-Māwardī, Ibn ᶜAbd al-Barr, aṭ-Ṭurṭūšī and Ibn al-Buḥturī) and edited in his *Dīwān*. – Three verses in the metre *mağzūʾ al-kāmil*:

Version I:

*waʿaẓatka wāʿiẓatun ṣumut * wa-naʿatka nāʿiyatun ḫufut*
*wa-takallamat ʿan ʾaʿẓumin * tablā wa-ʿan ṣuwarin subut*
*wa-ʾaratka wağhaka fī t-turā- * bi wa-ʾanta ḥayyun lam tamut*

"Silent warners[177] have taught you a lesson * and inaudible voices[178] have announced death to you!
They spoke of bones * decaying and of facial features without motion;
They made you see your face in the * earth while you are (still) alive and not yet dead".

Version II:

*waʿaẓatka ʾağdāṯun ṣumut * wa-naʿatka ʾazminatun ḫufut*
*wa-takallamat ʿan ʾawğuhin * tablā wa-ʿan ṣuwarin šutut*
*wa-ʾaratka qabraka fī l-qubū- * ri wa-ʾanta ḥayyun lam tamut*

1 أجداث: أحداث (MasMurūğ); *naʿatka ʾazminatun*: *bakatka sākitatun* (MasMurūğ, al-ᶜAffānī: *Sakb* II p. 509), *wa-bakatka sākinatun* (IBuḥtUns); خفت: عفت (MarzŠḤam, AnbNuzhah). – **2** Lines 2 and 3 are exchanged in IᶜABarrBahğah; *ʿan ʾawğuhin*: *ʿan ʾaʿẓumin* (MasMurūğ, IBuḥtUns, al-ᶜAffānī: *Sakb* II p. 409; *cf.* version I); تبلى: تبكي (AnbNuzhah); وعن: ومن (MasMurūğ, some mss.); شتت: سبت (AᶜAtāhAnwār, IQutŠiᶜr, MāwAdab, ṬurṭSirāğ, QurṭTaḏk, MasMurūğ, AnbNuzhah, TMD, IBuḥtUns, al-ᶜAffānī: *Sakb* II pp. 508f.). Lines 2 and 3 are exchanged in al-ᶜAffānī: *Sakb* II p. 525. – **3** *qabraka*: *nafsaka* (QurṭTaḏk); *fī l-qubūri*: *fī l-ḥayāti* (AᶜAtāhAnwār and AᶜAtāhDīwān; MāwAdab, al-ᶜAffānī: *Sakb* II p. 508).

Here, as in Version I above, the vowelling of the verse endings (v. 1-2) is open to discussion, viz. in the case of صمت, خفت, شتت and سبت (including the variants). As in the transliteration above and

177 I.e. the tombs, see the commentary in ANuwDīwān II p. 172: "by *aṣ-ṣumut* he meant *al-ʾağdāṯ* (i.e. the tombs), and by *al-ḫufut* he meant *al-ʾazminah* (i.e. the turns of time, *or* destiny)"; see also Version II.

178 I.e. the calls of Fate, or Destiny (see the preceding note).

in a number of sources, the final ت is considered part of the root, the resulting form being thus *fuʿul(un)*, i.e. an adjective fem. pl. However, ت might as well indicate the 3rd person f. sing. perf. of the verb (also used for plural nouns), the resulting form being thus *faʿalat*. Since in our case the last root consonants of all verbs are weak, we get the following forms: *(wāʿiẓatun / ʾağdāṯun) ṣamat* (from *ṣmy*, "... that have come quickly, *or* that arrived hastingly, suddenly"), *(ʿan ṣuwarin) sabat* (from *sby*, either "... that have been captured [in the tomb]" or "... that were abducted, led away, *or* estranged") and *(ʿan ṣuwarin) šatat* (from *štw*, either "... that experienced barrenness, *or* dearth [i.e. lacking the freshness of life]" or "... that have become cold" [i.e. without life]). Problematic remains the form *ḫafat* (from *ḫfy*): it does probably mean *nāʿiyatun / ʾazminatun ḫafat* = "... which spoke in a low, soft tone"; also, it means "to hide, conceal" but is used only transitively, while the context clearly requires an intransitive verb meaning "to be hidden, concealed". The form *ḫafat* has been translated in this way,[179] though the correct Arabic form would be *ḫafiyat*. However, this device of alternative vocalisation was surely intended by the poet.

"Silent tombs have taught you a lesson * and inaudible turns of time have announced your death!
They spoke of faces * decaying and of scattered features;
They made you see your tomb among the * tombs while you were (still) alive and not yet dead".

Note. The concept that the deceased, though silenced, teach an eloquent lesson is often encountered in mourning poetry (*cf.* pp. 109f.) and epitaph-poems (see also **31** and **208**). The above-quoted lines were rather popular, at least to judge from the number of sources in which they appear, and firmly incorporated into the literary tradition and the *kulturelles Gedächtnis*. They served as models for many later poets, e.g. Lisān ad-Dīn Ibn al-Ḫaṭīb, who shortly before his death drafted a poem which was meant to be his obituary and is composed as if uttered by a dead man; one verse of it says (*mutaqārib*):

بَعُدْنَا وَإِنْ جَاوَرَتْنَا البُيُوتُ * وَجِئْنَا بِوَعْظٍ وَنَحْنُ صُمُوتُ

"We dwell far away even though the houses stand near from us (*or* in our vicinity), * and we bring an admonishing sermon even though we are mute!"[180]

The topos of the eloquent dead is not alien to many other cultures as well. As a telling specimen I should like to quote from Mark Twain's travel journal *The Innocents Abroad* in which he describes his visit to the grave of Carlo Borromeo in Milan: "Now we will descend into the crypt, under the great altar of Milan Cathedral, and receive an impressive sermon from lips that have been silent and hands that have been gestureless for three hundred years. (...) Dead Bartoloméo [!] preached

179 See e.g. MasMurūǧ (B) VI p. 340: "muettes et mysterieuses elles pleurent sur ton sort" (in the text: *wa-bakatka sākitatun ḫafat*).

180 IḪaldʿIbar VII p. 342; MaqqNafḥ (C) VII p. 39; IQāḍīDurrah II p. 273. *Cf.* the translation in Schack: *Poesie und Kunst* I p. 348: "Wohl weil' ich auf der Erde noch; allein ich glaube schon von ihr entfernt zu sein. Gelangt bin ich zum letzten Aufenthalt, wo nie ein Wort die Lippe ferner lallt".

his pregnant sermon, and its burden was: You that worship the vanities of earth — you
that long for worldly honor, worldly wealth, worldly fame — behold their worth!"[181]

15

LOCATION. Baghdad. DATE. *c*.198 H.

PERSON BURIED. The poet Abū Nuwās (see preceding entry).

SOURCES. (Version I:) ANuwDīwān II p. 174. – (Version II:) ANuwDīwān p. 166;
    ĞāḥBayān III pp. 199f.; MarzMuw p. 425 (only vv. 2-3); MuᶜāfāĞalīs I p. 385
    = TB VII p. 446; TMD XIII pp. 459f.; AnbNuzhah p. 79 (only v. 3); BN X p.
    228; IIyāsBad I p. 140.

DESCRIPTION. Here, as already in the preceding entry, the versions differ considerably
    so that it becomes almost meaningless to speak of them as variants of one and
    the same epitaph. – (Version I:) "It was said (...) that he ordered that upon his
    tomb be written: [...]" (ANuwDīwān II p. 174). – (Version II:) "Abū Nuwās
    said, [...]" (ANuwDīwān II p. 166 and ĞāḥBayān, similarly TMD); "Abū
    l-ᶜAtāhiyah said, 'I composed 20.000 ascetic verses, but I wish I had composed
    instead (only) those three verses which stem from Abū Nuwās: [...]'" (MarzMuw,
    BN). According to Abū Muslim al-Kātib, these verses were also inscribed
    upon the tomb of Abū Nuwās (MuᶜāfāĞalīs and TB); "On his tomb was seen
    written: [...]" (AnbNuzhah); "After his death it was written upon his tomb:
    [...]" (IIyāsBad).

Version I (*kāmil*):

*yā-ġāfira ḏ-ḏanbi l-ᶜaẓīmi bi-ğūdihī * iġfir li-ᶜabdika ḏanbahū mutafaḍḍilā*

"O pardoner of grave sin(s) through His generosity: * pardon Your servant his
sin(s), thereby showing Your grace!"

Version II (*ramal*):

*yā-Nuwāsīyu tawaqqar * wa-taᶜazzā wa-taṣabbar*
*sāᵓaka d-dahru bi-šayᵓin * wa-bi-mā sarraka ᵓakṯar*
*yā-kabīra ḏ-ḏanbi ᶜafwu l- * lāhi min ḏanbika ᵓakbar*

1 *tawaqqar*: *tafakkar* (ĞāḥBayān, TMD); تعزَّ: تعزَى (IIyāsBad);[182] *wa-taᶜazzā*: *wa-taġayyar* (BN).
– 2 The second verse has the wording in MuᶜāfāĞalīs and BN (and in TB the first hemistich): *ᵓin
yakun sāᵓaka dahrun * fa-la-mā sarraka ᵓakṯar*; *wa-bi-mā*: *wa-la-mā* (ĞāḥBayān), *ᵓinnamā* (TB);
bimā: *la-mā* (MarzMuw, TMD). – 3 *yā-kabīra*: *yā-kaṯīra* (MuᶜāfāĞalīs); *min*: *ᶜan* (AnbNuzhah).
TMD has a completely different wording of the third hemistich.

"O Nuwās, behave with dignity, * be patient and and show composure!
Destiny did wrong you sometimes, * but more often it did cheer you.

---

181   Mark Twain: *The Innocents Abroad. Roughing It*, ed. G. Cardwell, New York 1984, pp. 140f.

182   The form *taᶜazza* is the correct imperative, but it does not fit the metre; the other sources have
        taᶜazzā (poetic license).

O you who committed great sin(s): the forgiveness of * God, if compared to your sin(s), is greater!"

For the plea for God's forgiveness, a frequent feature of epitaph-poems, see also **2**, **9**, **34**, **44**, **55**, **82**, **116**, **199** and especially the note to epitaph **26**.

16

LOCATION. Baghdad. DATE. *c.*198 H.
PERSON BURIED. The poet Abū Nuwās (see **14**).
SOURCE. *Aġānī* VII p. 213.
DESCRIPTION. "al-Kawkabī told me from Abū Sahl b. Nawbaḫt, from ᶜAmr b. Bānah who said, 'When Abū Nuwās had died, Ḥusayn b. aḍ-Ḍaḥḥāk wrote upon his tomb: [...]'". – Two verses in the metre *munsariḥ*:

*kābaranīka z-zamānu yā-Ḥasanū * fa-ḫāba sahmī wa-ʾaflaḥa z-zamanū*
*laytaka ʾiḏ lam takun baqīta lanā * lam tabqā rūḥun yaḥūṭuhā badanū*

"Time did contend with me for you,[183] O Ḥasan, * yet my share (in that struggle) was the minor one and time did have the better end (i.e. was successful)!
If only, since you do not remain to us any longer, * no spirit (*or* soul) remained that is enclosed by a body!"[184]

17

LOCATION. Baghdad. DATE. 209/213 H.
PERSON BURIED. The poet Abū l-ᶜAtāhiyah (Ismāᶜīl b. al-Qāsim b. Suwayd, Kūfah or ᶜAyn at-Tamr 130 H – Baghdad between 209 and 213 H): IMuᶜtṬab pp. 228-34; IQutŠiᶜr pp. 497-501; MasMurūǧ (P) IV pp. 333-6; *Aġānī* IV pp. 1-112; IᶜAdīmBuġyah IV pp. 278-342; IḪallWaf I pp. 219-26; TI XV pp. 458-63; BN IX pp. 265f.; ZA I p. 321; GAS II pp. 534f.; EI² I pp. 107f. (A. Guillaume); EAL I pp. 27f.
SOURCES. AᶜAtāhAnwār p. 160 and AᶜAtāhDīwān p. 268; IᶜARabᶜIqd (Ǧ) II p. 160 / (M) III p. 248; *Aġānī* IV p. 111; TawḥBaṣāʾir VIII pp. 141f.; IᶜAdīmBuġyah IV p. 341; ZawzḤam I p. 218; al-ᶜAffānī: *Sakb* II p. 503.
DESCRIPTION. "When Abū l-ᶜAtāhiyah felt his death approaching, he stipulated in his last will that (the following verses) be written on his tomb: [...]" (AᶜAtāhDīwān and ZawzḤam, similarly TawḥBaṣāʾir and al-ᶜAffānī). According to al-Iṣfahānī, Abū l-ᶜAtāhiyah's son Muḥammad strongly rejected the claim that his father had ever stipulated to have verses of his own written on his tomb. However, Hārūn b. ᶜAlī b. Mahdī reported from ᶜAbd ar-Raḥmān b. al-Faḍl that he did read the four lines (as quoted below) on a tombstone (*ᶜalā ḥaǧarin*) near the

183 *Cf.* WKAS I p. 22 (s.r. *kbr* III).
184 I.e. if only all men had died with you.

grave of Abū l-ᶜAtāhiyah (*Aġānī* IV p. 112); "Ibrāhīm al-Baġawī said that he read on the tomb of Abū l-ᶜAtāhiyah: [...]" (IᶜAdīmBuġyah). – Four verses in the metre *maǧzūʾ al-ḫafīf*:

*ʾuḏna ḥayyin tasammaᶜī * ismaᶜī ṯumma ᶜī wa-ᶜī*
*ʾanā rahnun bi-maḍǧaᶜī * fa-ḥḏarī miṯla maṣraᶜī*
*ᶜištu tisᶜīna ḥiǧǧatan * fī diyāri t-tazaᶜzuᶜī*
*laysa zādun siwā t-tuqā * fa-ḫuḏī minhu ʾaw daᶜī*

1 *ḥayyin*: *ḥaqqin* (ZawzḤam); *ismaᶜī*: *wa-ḥfaẓī* (ZawzḤam); *ismaᶜī* etc.: *ṯumma ᶜī baᶜdahū wa-ᶜī* (TawḥBaṣāʾir). – **2** *maḍǧaᶜī fa-ḥḏarī*: *maṣraᶜī fa-ḥḏarū* (ZawzḤam). – **3** om. TawḥBaṣāʾir and ZawzḤam; *fī diyāri t-tazaᶜzuᶜī*: *ṯumma wāfaytu maḍǧaᶜī* (IᶜARabᶜIqd), *ṯumma fāraqtu maǧmaᶜī* (IᶜAdīmBuġyah). – **4** *zādun*: *šayʾun* (IᶜARabᶜIqd). – TawḥBaṣāʾir provides a different final line: *laysa maytun bi-rāǧiᶜin * kayfa mā šiʾti fa-ṣnaᶜī.*

"O ear of someone still alive, hark! * Listen well, and then remember again and again:
I am a pledge in my bed-like lodging (i.e. the grave), * but fear for yourself something not unlike my fatal end.
I lived for ninety pilgrimages (i.e. years) * in the abodes where everything is precarious;
There are no provisions (for the hereafter) apart from godliness, * thus take your share of it or leave it!"[185]

NOTES.

1. Ibn al-ᶜAdīm gives the following comment after having quoted the epitaph:

"These verses are not by Abū l-ᶜAtāhiyah, because they do not fit the dates of his birth and death. He did not live for 'ninety pilgrimages', and the verses stem from older times. I was told from[186] ... Muḥammad b. Abī l-ᶜAtāhiyah (the poet's son) who reported from Hišām al-Kalbī, from his father (M. b. as-Sāʾib al-Kalbī), from Abū Ṣāliḥ (d. 101),[187] from Ibn ᶜAbbās who said, 'In pre-Islamic times, a skull (*ǧumǧumah*) was found which bore the words inscribed:

*ʾuḏna ḥayyin tasammaᶜī * ismaᶜī ṯumma ᶜī wa-ᶜī*
*ʾanā rahnun bi-maḍǧaᶜī * fa-ḥḏarī miṯla maṣraᶜī'*

He (i.e. the son of Abū l-ᶜAtāhiyah) reported, 'I came to my father and told him about this, and he found it eloquent. Someone of our friends then added the line:

*laysa šayʾun siwā t-tuqā * fa-ḫuḏī minhu ʾaw daᶜī*'".[188]

2. This epitaph contains a number of notions and expressions well-known from mourning poetry and other epitaphs, e.g. the notion of "provisions" (*zād*, see **171**) for the hereafter or the motif of the deceased being a "pledge" (*rahn* or *rahīn*) in his tomb (*cf.* **55**, **103**, **177**, **211**, **223**, **232** and **234**). For the latter, largely conventional

185 There is also a German translation of these verses by Oskar Rescher, see his *Gesammelte Werke* V, part 1, p. 144.

186 Here follows a complete chain of transmission in the text.

187 Abū Ṣāliḥ Bāḏām (or Bāḏān) from Kūfah (d. 101 H), a much-criticised transmitter from Ibn ᶜAbbās to al-Kalbī, see Schöller: *Sīra and Tafsīr* p. 19 with note 3.

188 IᶜAdīmBuġyah IV pp. 341f.

concept we have a good example in two verses by Salm al-Ḫāsir (d. 186 H), pronounced after the death of the Abbasid caliph al-Manṣūr who died during his pilgrimage in Mecca in 158 H (*kāmil*):

حَجَّ الحَجِيجُ وَخَلَّفُوا ابْنَ مُحَمَّدٍ * رَهْناً بِمَكَّةَ فِي الضَّرِيحِ المُلْحَدِ
شَهِدُوا المَشَاهِدَ كُلَّهَا وَإِمَامُهُمْ * تَحْتَ الصَّفَائِحِ فِي الثَّرَى لَمْ يُشْهَدِ

"The pilgrims performed the pilgrimage and left the son of Muḥammad (i.e. al-Manṣūr) behind * as a pledge in Mecca in a tomb with vaulted niche.[189]
They had seen all the sites to visit, but their Imam * under the ledger stones in the moist earth was not visited".[190]

The early Abbasid poet al-ʿAbbās b. al-Aḥnaf (d. 192 H) in one of his love poems wishes for death as he is unable to bear the news that has reached him from his beloved (*munsariḥ*):

فَلَيْتَنِي قَبْلَ مَا سَمِعْتُ بِهِ * مِتُّ فَكُنْتُ الرَّهِينَ فِي اللَّحدِ

"If only I had died before I heard this (news) * thus (by now) I were a pledge in the burial niche!"[191]

Another example for the motif of the "pledge" render the verses quoted in ĞāḥBayān I p. 187 (*basīṭ*):[192]

قُومِي اصْبَحِينِي فَمَا صِيغَ الفَتَى حَجَراً * لَكِن رَهِينَةَ أَحْجَارٍ وَأَرْمَاسِ
قُومِي اصْبَحِينِي فَإِنَّ الدَّهْرَ ذُو غِيَرٍ * أَفْنَى لُقَيْماً وَأَفْنَى آلَ هِرْمَاسِ

"Come! give me a morning sip (of wine), for man has not been fashioned out of stone, * (though) he is a pledge to stones and the dust (of a grave).
Come! give me a morning sip, for Fate is full of changes; * it has destroyed Luqaym and destroyed Āl Hirmās".

189 Compare to this verse the first hemistich of a line by Aḥmad b. Darrāğ: *wa-ḫallafūhu ladayhi rahna malḥadatin*, "they left him behind there as a pledge of the burial niche" (IKattTašb p. 274 = IKattVergleiche p. 225).

190 Cited in SinğManāʾiḥ II p. 102. ṬabHistory XXIX pp. 147f. quotes from a funerary poem by Salm upon the death of al-Manṣūr, but not the verses cited above. The expression in the second line, لم يشهد, could also be read as *lam yašhadī* (with the possible rhyme *malḥadī* in the first verse). It would then translate as "he did not see – like the pilgrims – any of the monuments and sites of Mecca", or perhaps also as "(in this tomb) he does not bear witness to his creed", an important concept frequently expressed in epitaphs (*māta wa-huwa yašhadu ʾan* … or similar wordings, see **36**, **73** and **186**). In any case, the unvowelled wording is ambiguous and leaves room for diverse interpretations.

191 IAḥnafDīwān p. 121.

192 Also translated in Kennedy: *Wine Song* p. 87.

There is also a fine verse by the Andalusian poet and ascetic Ibn Abī Zamanīn (M. b. ᶜAl., d. Elvira *c.*400 H), mourning the by-gone generations (*basīṭ*):

سَقَاهُمُ الدَّهْرُ كَأْساً غَيْرَ صَافِيَةٍ * فَصَيَّرَتْهُم لِأَطْبَاقِ الثَّرَى رُهُنَا

“Fate made them drink a cup that held no limpid liquor * and turned them into pledges to the layers of moist earth”.[193]

In a passage in rhymed prose, announcing the death of a scholar, we read: “He cast away pen and scroll / and gave up the ghost when death told him ‘Skoal!’ ‖ He settled in the burial pit / firmly to his ancestors knit, ‖ thus he became talk of yesterday, / a pledge of the grave without delay”.[194]

17 bis

3. Ibn ᶜAbd Rabbih quotes a later “imitation” (*muᶜāraḍah*)[195] of epitaph **17** by an unknown poet: “Some poet emulated these verses and stipulated that they be also written upon his tomb, what indeed was done”. Nothing about the deceased and the location of his tomb is known. Four verses in the metre *mağzūʾ al-ḫafīf*:

أَصْبَحَ القَبْرُ مَضْجَعِي * وَمَحَلِّي وَمَوضِعِي
صَرَعَتْنِي الحُتُوفُ فِي الـ * ـتُّرْبِ يَا ذُلَّ مَصْرَعِي
أَيْنَ إِخْوَانِيَ الَّذِيـ * ـنَ إِلَيْهِمْ تَطَلُّعِي
مِتُّ وَحْدِي فَلَمْ يَمُتْ * وَاحِدٌ مِنْهُمُ مَعِي

“The tomb become my lodging bed, * my dwelling place and my resting site.
Death itself brought me down into the * earth, O what a disgraceful end of mine!

193 Cited in IBaškṢilah II p. 484; ḤumĞaḏwah p. 57; QurṭTaḏk p. 42 (*saqāhumu l-mawtu*, etc.); MaqqNafḥ (C) V p. 95; ŠayMağānī IV p. 30 (var. *saqāhumu l-mawtu*). See also the free translation in Nykl: *Hispano-Arabic Poetry* p. 64: “Fate made them drink a foul, poisoned cup, * Made of them dwellers of stone-lidded tombs!” Both motifs – the “pledge of the earth” and “the cup of death” (*kaʾs al-mawt*) – are present in Arabic mourning poetry from the very beginning, later also in funerary epigraphy (*cf.* **23**, verse 4) and in poetry in praise of the Prophet (see e.g. NawāğīMaṭāliᶜ p. 137 = MN I p. 465 [*basīṭ*]: *wa-l-mawtu kaʾsun bi-kaffi d-dahri dāʾiratun * tasqī l-warā wa-ğamīᶜu n-nāsi qad šaribū*). Already in the *Dīwān* of al-Ḫansāʾ we find expressions such as *rahīnu bilan, rahīnatu ramsin* and *rahnu ʾarmāsin*. As for *kaʾs*, we have the terms *kaʾsu manīyatin* and *kaʾsu ḥalāqin* (TMD LVI p. 220). For the common term *kaʾs al-mawt*, see also MuᶜāfāĞalīs I pp. 519f.; YāqBuldān III p. 168. MarzMuw p. 112, TMD LVI p. 220 and IḤağIṣābah IV p. 375: *al-mawtu kaʾsun fa-l-marʾu ḏāʾiquhū*, from a famous poem by Umayyah b. Abī ṣ-Ṣalt.

194 MurSilk IV p. 52: *fa-ramā l-qalama wa-l-qirṭās / wa-fāḍat nafsuhū ḥīna šariba min ḏālika l-kās // wa-sakana l-luḥūd / maᶜa l-ğudūd // wa-ṣāra ḥadīṯa ʾams / rahīna r-rams.* For the term *ḥadīṯu ʾamsi*, see also NZ V p. 202 (in a poem).

195 That is, a poem which adopts the metre, rhyme and subject matter of an already existing and usually well-known or even famous poem, see EAL II p. 534.

Where are my brothers who- * se company I strive for?
I died alone and not * one of them died with me!"[196]

18

LOCATION. Baghdad. DATE. 209 / 213 H.
PERSON BURIED. Abū l-ᶜAtāhiyah (see the preceding entry).
SOURCES. AᶜAtāhAnwār p. 136 and AᶜAtāhDīwān p. 237; TMD VII p. 59; IḪallWaf I p. 222 / (Slane) I p. 205; BN IX p. 266; Abū l-Faḍl Ibn ar-Riḍā: *Tarāǧim ar-riǧāl (Ǧild-i awwal az dah ǧild)*, Tehran 1372/1952, p. 155; Khawam: *Poésie arabe* p. 171 (in French).
DESCRIPTION. "He composed (the following verse) and had stipulated in his last will that it be written upon his tomb: [...]" (all sources except TMD); "Abū ᶜAlī al-Ḥasan b. Ḥabīb said that Abū l-ᶜAtāhiyah ordered that on his tomb be written: [...]" (TMD). – One line in the metre *ḫafīf*:

*ʾinna ʿayšan yakūnu ʾāḫirahū l-maw- * tu la-ʿayšun muʿaǧǧalu t-tanġīṣī*

"Verily, life whose outcome is dea- * th is a life spoilt in advance!"

NOTE. The topos that the enjoyment of life is "spoilt", as it were, by the fact that death is inevitably its final outcome – or as a poet has it, *laqad ʾafsada l-mawtu l-ḥayāta*, freely rendered as "Death spoils life from the very beginning"[197] – is well-known from Arabic literature and poetry (see also below **111** and note). In addition, there is a nice anecdote illustrating this concept: "The caliph al-Manṣūr told his vizier ar-Rabīᶜ (b. Yūnus), 'O Rabīᶜ, how pleasurable would be the present world, were it not for death!' (*mā ʾaṭyaba d-dunyā law lā l-mawt*), but ar-Rabīᶜ rejoiced, 'O Prince of the Believers, (on the contrary): The present world is only pleasurable because of death (*mā ṭābati d-dunyā ʾillā bi-l-mawt*)'. 'How is that?' 'If there were no death, you would not be sitting in that place you are now occupying!'"[198] The many panegyric poems from the early Abbasid period, mourning the late caliph and at the same time congratulating his successor,[199] demonstrate the obvious correctness of ar-Rabīᶜ's shrewd observation. For example, Marwān b. Sulaymān Ibn Abī Ḥafṣah (d. 181/2 H or after) mourned the late caliph al-Mahdī (d. 169 H) and congratulated his successor Mūsā (*ṭawīl*):

لَقَدْ أَصْبَحَتْ تَخْتَالُ فِي كُلِّ بَلْدَةٍ * بِقَبْرِ أَمِيرِ الْمُسْلِمِينَ الْمَقَابِرُ
وَلَوْ لَمْ تُسَكَّنْ بِابْنِهِ فِي مَكَانِهِ * لَمَا بَرِحَتْ تَبْكِي عَلَيْهِ الْمَنَابِرُ

196 IᶜARabᶜIqd (Ǧ) II p. 161 / (M) III pp. 248f. (and cited by the editor of AᶜAtāhAnwār p. 160 note 1) = ŠayMaǧānī II pp. 36f.; al-ᶜAffānī: *Sakb* II p. 503.

197 Cited anonymously in IBuḥtUns p. 82.

198 IBuḥtUns p. 82. A similar dictum is known from Buhlūl, see Marzolph: *Buhlūl* p. 53 (no. 98).

199 See e.g. the poems in BN X p. 165, NuwNih V pp. 216f. and those scattered through the pages of the *Aġānī*. *Cf.* also ṢafĠayṯ II p. 377.

"The cemeteries in every town have already begun to boast * of (having) the tomb of the Prince of the Muslims,[200]
And if the pulpits had not been calmed by his son taking his place (as caliph), they would have never stopped weeping for him".[201]

19

LOCATION. Baghdad. DATE. Third century H (?).
PERSON BURIED. Unknown (a slave-girl).
SOURCE. IᶜARabᶜIqd (Ğ) II pp. 161 and (repeated) 181f. / (M) III pp. 249 and (repeated) 280.
DESCRIPTION. "Upon the tomb of a slave-girl, beside the tomb of the poet Abū Nuwās (see **14**), three verses were to be found which were said to have been composed by Abū Nuwās: [...]". – Three verses in the metre *ṭawīl*:

*ʾaqūlu li-qabrin zurtuhū mutalaṯṯiman * saqā llāhu barda l-ʿafwi ṣāḥibata l-qabrī*
*laqad ġayyabū taḥta ṯ-ṯarā qamara d-duğā * wa-šamsa ḍ-ḍuḥā bayna ṣ-ṣafāʾiḥi wa-l-ʿafrī*
*ʿağibtu li-ʿaynin baʿdahā mallati l-bukā * wa-qalbin ʿalayhā yartağī rāḥata ṣ-ṣabrī*

"I speak to a tomb which I visited desiring to kiss it (?),[202] * 'May God pour forth the coolness of his forgiveness upon the woman in this tomb!'
Now that under the moist earth have been made disappear the moon of the gloomy night * and the sun of the bright morning, between layers of stone and dust:
I was amazed that an eye, after her passing away, became tired of weeping, * and that a heart, notwithstanding her loss, hopes for the comfort of composure!"

NOTES. This amazing epitaph is noteworthy for bringing together all the most important elements and motifs of Arabic mourning poetry in just three verses, though this also makes it, if seen as a whole, appear somewhat artificial. Anyhow, in the most

200 This line plays upon a concept otherwise known from the religious discourse, viz. that the cemeteries contend for a pious person to be buried in them. A prophetic Tradition to that effect says, "The cemeteries receive grace from the death of a believer, thus there is no tract of land that does not desire him to be buried in there" (cited in SuyBušrā p. 33).

201 *Aġānī* X p. 93; BaṣrīḤam (C) II p. 132; ʿIṣāmīSimṭ III p. 272 (var. *ʾamīrī l-muslimīna*: *ʾamīrī l-muʾminīna*; *fī makānihī*: *baʿda mawtihī*). The translation of both verses does not follow the word order of the original; the first verse means that the cemeteries have become boastful because someone like al-Mahdī has been buried in one of them, thus exalting their status. Ibn Wāṣil comments in that context that the combination of congratulation and consolation (*mazğ at-tahniʾa bi-t-taʿziyah*) in poetry was first introduced in al-Mahdī's time (IWāṣilKurūb IV p. 200).

202 *mutalaṯṯim* normally means "covering, concealing one's face with a veil" (WKAS *s.r.*; the present verse is among the quoted samples), though given the context one might rightly presume, as the editor of Ibn ʿAbd Rabbih's text does in note 1, that it signifies here "desiring to kiss it" or the like.

succinct way possible, Abū Nuwās – if he was the author – created here a little poetic encyclopaedia of almost all the features we regularly encounter in mourning poetry: addressing the tomb, visiting and, sometimes, kissing it; the beneficial rainfall upon it; the hoped-for coolness to be bestowed upon the deceased by God, and His forgiveness; the seclusion of the deceased under moist earth, combined with a metaphorical sun- and moon-setting; the stones of the grave and the dust therein (and upon its surface); the weeping for the deceased, and finally the concept of relieving patience or composure. Each of these elements looms large in mourning poetry and funerary epigraphy, and for virtually every phrase dozens of parallels could easily be adduced.

1. "The moon of the gloomy night" (verse 2). The fact that persons, in particular children, women and young men, were likened to the moon and/or the morning sun made it tempting, when describing their death, to resort to the metaphor of the moon or the sun setting below the horizon.[203] Among the earlier examples for this are two lines which al-Aṣmaʿī reportedly heard recited by a woman at the grave of her deceased child; these verses are also among the popular lines of poetry in *The Thousand and One Nights* and appear no less than four times in the older editions (*basīṭ*):

بِاللّٰهِ يَا قَبْرُ هَلْ زَالَتْ مَحَاسِنُهُ * وَهَلْ تَغَيَّرَ ذَاكَ المَنْظَرُ النَّضِرُ
يَا قَبْرُ مَا أَنْتَ لاَ رَوْضٌ وَلاَ فَلَكٌ * فَكَيْفَ يَجْمَعُ فِيكَ الشَّمْسُ وَالقَمَرُ

"By God, O tomb, have his charms vanished * and has that radiant appearance (of his) changed?
O tomb, you are neither a garden[204] nor a celestial sphere, * thus how do the sun and the moon come together in you?"[205]

The first verse of these popular lines is certainly influenced by one composed by the poetess al-H̱ansāʾ, whose mourning poetry was considered exemplary, together with the poems by Abū l-ʿAtāhiyah, through all the centuries of pre-modern Arabic culture. The verse by al-H̱ansāʾ runs as follows (*kāmil*):

203 As for the moon, also the image of a lunar eclipse was resorted to in this context.

204 I.e. not a real garden; *cf.* above p. 50f.

205 ḤurRawḍ p. 32 and ṢafAyʿān II pp. 199 and 273 (only v. 2; var. *yā-qabru mā ʾanta*: *mā ʾanta yā-qabru*; *fa-kayfa yağmaʿu*: *min ʾayna ğummiʿa*; *aš-šamsu*: *al-ġuṣnu*). The various passages in ALL also yield different versions of these verses, especially of the second hemistich: ALL (C) I p. 40 = Littmann I p. 89 (8th night) = Mahdī p. 120 (*yā-qabru yā-qabru hal zālat maḥāsinuhū * ʾam zāla minka ḍiyāka l-manẓaru n-naḍirū / yā-qabru mā ʾanta lā ʾarḍun* [var. *rawḍun*] *wa-lā falakun* etc.); (B) I p. 60 / (C) I p. 124 = Littmann I p. 273 (23rd night) = Mahdī p. 266 (… *yā-qabru lā ʾanta bustānun wa-lā falakun * fa-kayfa yağmaʿu fīka l-ġuṣnu wa-l-qamarū*); (B) I p. 325 (136th night: *yā-qabru mā ʾanta bustānun wa-lā falakun * fa-kayfa yağmaʿu fīka l-badru wa-z-zaharū*); (B) IV p. 1350 (840th night) = (C) VI p. 188 (841st night: *bi-llāhi yā-qabru hal zālat maḥāsinuhā * … / yā-qabru mā ʾanta lā rawḍun wa-lā ʾufuqun * fa-kayfa yağmaʿu fīka š-šamsu wa-l-qamarū*).

يُحْثَى التُّرَابُ عَلَى مَحَاسِنِهِ * وَعَلَى غَضَارَةِ وَجْهِهِ النَّضْرِ

"The earth is spread over his charms * and over the freshness of his radiant face".[206]

The sun- and moon-metaphors seemed particularly tempting when mourning the death of a learned person or scholar whose *laqab* was "Badr ad-Dīn" or "Šams ad-Dīn". The sun-metaphor could also be applied to life itself, that is, dawn = birth and sunset = death, as for example in a tenth-century mourning poem: *ka-šamsin ... ġāba fī maġribi l-qabri*, "Like a sun ... he went down in the *maġrib* of the grave".[207] Here, *maġrib* is not only "the place of the sunset", but this probably also alludes to the solitary state of the deceased (*al-ġurbah*), both based on the root *ġrb*.

For a good and representative example which illustrates what has been said so far it is best to quote two verses from a poem mourning the death of the Shafiite judge Afḍal ad-Dīn al-Ḫūnaǧī (M. b. Nāmāwār, d. Cairo 646 H), composed by his pupil ᶜIzz ad-Dīn al-Irbilī (d. 660)[208] (*ṭawīl*):

وَمَا كُنْتُ أَدْرِي أَنَّ لِلشَّمْسِ فِي الثَّرَى * أُفُولاً وَأَنَّ البَدْرَ فِي التُّرْبِ نَازِلُ
إِلَى أَنْ رَأَيْنَاهُ وَقَدْ حَلَّ قَبْرَهُ * قَضَيْنَا بِأَنَّ البَدْرَ فِي اللَّحْدِ حَاصِلُ

"I did not know that the sun in the moist earth * could set and that the full moon could descend into the earth
Until we saw him when he had settled in his tomb, * (and only then) we concluded that the full moon had sunk in the burial niche".[209]

The first verse is certainly influenced by that famous verse of al-Mutanabbī which has been already cited above page 344 (*kāmil*):

مَا كُنْتُ أَحْسِبُ قَبْلَ دَفْنِكَ فِي الثَّرَى * أَنَّ الكَوَاكِبَ فِي التُّرَابِ تَغُورُ

"I did not reckon, before your burial in moist earth, * that the stars could set in the earth".

Another good example for the use of the moon-metaphor is provided by two lines mourning the Egyptian scholar and jurist Badr (!) ad-Dīn Abū s-Saᶜādāt Muḥammad b. Muḥammad Ibn Raslān al-Bulqīnī aš-Šāfiᶜī (821–90 H), in the metre *ṭawīl*:

رَعَى اللَّهُ قَبْراً ضَمَّ أَعْظَمَ عَالِمٍ * بِتَحْقِيقِهِ حَاوِي الجَوَاهِرِ كَالبَحْرِ
فَمُذْ غَابَ فِيهِ أَظْلَمَ الجَوُّ بِلْوَرَى * وَكَيْفَ يُضِيءُ الجَوُّ مَعْ غَيْبَةِ البَدْرِ

206 Ḫansāᵓ Dīwān (B) p. 71 / (Š) p. 70.

207 MuḥḪul IV p. 224 and MuḥNafḥah III p. 75.

208 al-Ḥasan b. Muḥammad, not *vice versa* as in IAUṣaybᶜUyūn (see following note).

209 Cited in IAUṣaybᶜUyūn p. 587 (vv. 11f.) = IḤaǧRafᶜ p. 422 (only the first verse). The *incipit* of the poem is also quoted in ŠḎ V p. 237. See also ZawzḤam I p. 214, with a verse by Abū l-ᶜAtāhiyah (*munsariḥ*): *badrāni badrun ġadā bi-Baġdāda fī l- * ḫuldi wa-badrun bi-Ṭūsa fī r-ramsī* (not in AᶜAtāhDīwān).

"May God guard a tomb that contains the bones of a scholar[210] * who was by his accurate method of research a collector of pearls like the sea.[211]
Since he disappeared in it (i.e. the tomb) the sky has darkened for mankind * and, lo!, how can the sky gleam with light when the moon has disappeared (i.e. after the death of *Badr* ad-Dīn)?[212]

2. The expression "between layers of stones and dust" (verse 2) is common in mourning poetry and funerary epigraphy (*cf.* **85**, **97** and **211**). It appears most often as *bayna t-turbi / t-turābi wa-ṣafāʾiḥin / ṣ-ṣafāʾihi* or the like.[213] In a widely-quoted verse by the lover of Laylā al-Aḫyalīyah, Tawbah b. al-Ḥumayyir al-Ḫafāǧī (first cent. H), we find the prototypical use of that expression (*ṭawīl*):

وَلَوْ أَنَّ لَيْلَى الأَخْيَلِيَّةَ سَلَّمَتْ * عَلَيَّ وَفَوْقِي تُرْبَةٌ وَصَفَائِحُ

"And if (only) Laylā al-Aḫyalīyah would greet * me while I am covered by earth and layers of stones".[214]

20

LOCATION. Baghdad. DATE. 295 H.

PERSON BURIED. The mystic Abū l-Ḥusayn an-Nūrī, Ibn al-Baġawī (A. b. M., Baghdad *c.*226–95 H), a pupil of as-Sarī as-Saqaṭī: ANuḤilyah X pp. 249-55; IǦawzī-Ṣafwah I pp. 597f.; BN XI p. 106; ŠaᶜrṬab I p. 87; MunKawākib I pp. 522-6; EI² VIII pp. 139f. (A. Schimmel); Gramlich: *Vorbilder* I pp. 381-446; Knysh: *Mysticism* pp. 69-3.

SOURCE. *Adab al-mulūk* p. 32 = GramlLebensweise p. 71 und Gramlich: *Vorbilder* I p. 389 (in German translation).

210 One could also read: *ʾaᶜẓama ᶜālimin*, i.e. "the greatest scholar ever". See the note to **43**.

211 This mode of expression is conventional. The relevant terms were often used to indicate that someone was able to pick the choicest pieces (= the pearls) from a vast array of information (= the sea) and to arrange it by his accuracy (= *at-taḥqīq*) into an all-encompassing whole (= *al-ḥāwī*); the latter word, *al-ḥāwī*, is doubtless an allusion to the Shafiite legal manual *al-Ḥāwī (fī l-fiqh)* by al-Māwardī (d. 450 H) which Badr ad-Dīn al-Bulqīnī had reportedly studied with much thoroughness.

212 SaḫWaǧīz III p. 961 (var. *bi-l-warā*: *baᶜdahū*).and ḌL IX p. 100. For the mourned, see also SaḫḎRafᶜ pp. 322-42. For a similar poem, *cf.* ALL (Mahdī) p. 624 = Littmann II p. 497.

213 *Cf.* also above p. 172 and below p. 435, n. 409.

214 In different versions of the second hemistich, we have either *wa-fawqī turbatun wa-ṣafāʾiḥū*, *wa-fawqī ǧandalun wa-ṣafāʾiḥū* or *wa-dūnī turbatun/ǧandalun wa-ṣafāʾiḥū*, see LaylāDīwān pp. 66 and 111; IQutŠiᶜr p. 270; *Aġānī* XI p. 244; IDāʾūdZahrah p. 365; MuᶜāfāǦalīs I pp. 334-40; ṢafĠayṯ II pp. 43f.; MuġulṭāyWāḍiḥ p. 115; ᶜĀmKaškūl II p. 396; BaḥrKaškūl III p. 21; Abū ᶜUbayd Allāh M. Ibn al-Marzubān: *ʾAšᶜār an-nisāʾ*, ed. Hilāl Nāǧī and Sāmī Makkī al-ᶜĀnī, Beirut: ᶜĀlam al-Kutub 1415/1995, p. 43; Yūsuf b. Ḥasan Ibn al-Mubarrad al-Ḥanbalī: *Nuzhat al-musāmir fī ʾaḫbār Laylā l-ʾAḫyalīyah*, ed. M. at.Tanūḫī, Beirut: ᶜĀlam al-Kutub 1416/1995, p. 62. *Cf.* also ḤamTanzīl p. 63.

DESCRIPTION. "He died (...) in a ruined place (*ḫirbah* or *ḫaribah*) and was buried by al-Ǧunayd. The latter wrote[215] upon his tomb: [...]" (*Adab al-mulūk*).

hāḏā qabru ʾAbī l-Ḥusayni n-Nūrīyi ʿāšiqi r-raḥmān

"This is the tomb of Abū l-Ḥusayn an-Nūrī, lover of the Merciful".[216]

21

LOCATION. Baghdad. DATE. 363 or 364 H.

PERSON BURIED. The Monophysite (Jacobite) translator, philosopher and theologian Abū Zakarīyāʾ Yaḥyā b. ʿAdīy al-Manṭiqī at-Tikrītī (Tikrīt 280 or 281 – Baghdad 363 or 364 H), a pupil of al-Fārābī: INadFihrist p. 322; ẒāhirḤukamāʾ p. 97; IAUṣaybʿUyūn pp. 317f.; QifṭīTārīḫ pp. 361-4; GAL I p. 207 and GALS I p. 370; ZA VIII p. 156; EAL II p. 810.

SOURCES. IAUṣaybʿUyūn p. 318; BN XI p. 330.

DESCRIPTION. Abū ʿAlī Isḥāq b. Zurʿah said that "Yaḥyā b. ʿAdī – when his death had drawn near and he was staying at the church of Mār-Tūmā in Qaṭīʿat ar-Raqīq[217] – charged him in his will to inscribe the following two verses upon his tomb: [...]" (IAUṣaybʿUyūn). In BN, these verses are attributed to Abū l-Qāsim ʿĪsā b. al-Wazīr ʿAlī, Ibn al-Ǧarrāḥ al-Baġdādī (302–91 H). – Two verses in the metre *ḫafīf*:

*rubba maytin qad ṣāra bi-l-ʿilmi ḥayyan * wa-mubaqqin qad māta ǧahlan wa-ʿayyā*[218]
*fa-qtanū l-ʿilma kay tunālū ḫulūdan * lā taʿuddū l-ḥayāta fī l-ǧahli šayyā*

"Many a deceased has remained (after death) alive for his knowledge, * and (many a person) who continues in life has already died of ignorance and stammer.
Thus acquire knowledge so that you be granted eternal existence, * and consider a life spent in ignorance nothing!"

NOTE. These lines remind one of the pre-Islamic sage Luqmān who told his son, "God gives life to the hearts through the light of wisdom, like He gives light to the dead soil through rain from heaven". Franz Rosenthal refers in that context to Ibn Sīd al-Baṭalyawsī (i.e. from Badajoz, d. 521 H) who cites Luqmān's remark as an example of the metaphorical use of life and death for knowledge and ignorance.[219]

215 This must probably be understood as "The latter ordered to write (*or* be written) ...".

216 Or "infatuated with the Merciful". See also EI^2 VIII p. 139: "Al-Nūrī, who, according to ʿAṭṭār, was seen weeping along with the sad Iblīs, claimed to be a lover, *ʿās͟hik*, which led the Ḥanbalīs to declare him a heretic".

217 Misprinted in the ed. as الدقيق; a quarter in Baghdad, see YāqBuldān IV p. 377.

218 The more common form is *ʿiyy* (see Lane *s.r.*), but the rhyme necessitates *ʿayy*; BN has the var. *ġayyan*.

219 Rosenthal: *Knowledge Triumphant* p. 70 with note 2.

Closer to the above-cited epitaph than Luqmān's remark, however, are the famous and widely-quoted verses which Ibn Sīd himself composed on this matter (*ṭawīl*):

أَخُو العِلْمِ حَيٌّ خَالِدٌ بَعْدَ مَوْتِهِ * وَأَوْصَالُهُ تَحْتَ التُّرَابِ رَمِيمُ
وَذُو الجَهْلِ مَيْتٌ وَهْوَ مَاشٍ عَلَى الثَّرَى * يُظَنُّ مِنَ الأَحْيَاءِ وَهْوَ عَدِيمُ

"Who befriends knowledge is alive, everlasting, after his death * though his limbs have under the soil decayed.
But the ignorant is dead though he treads on moist earth; * he is thought to be of the living, yet he is inanimate (*or* non-existent)".[220]

Put into more religious, or mystical, terms this thought was expressed as follows by aš-Šarīf Ǧamāl ad-Dīn ʿAbd Allāh b. Muḥammad al-Ḥusaynī an-Nīsābūrī (d. 776 H). In addition, these verses are clearly inspired by Q 24:35, the "Light-Verse"[221] (*ḫafīf*):

إِنَّمَا النَّفْسُ كَالزُّجَاجَةِ وَالعَقْـ * ـلُ سِرَاجٌ وَحِكْمَةُ اللَّهِ زَيْتُ
فَإِذَا أَشْرَقَتْ فَإِنَّكَ حَيٌّ * وَإِذَا أَظْلَمَتْ فَإِنَّكَ مَيْتُ

"The soul is like nothing but glass, the faculty of * reason is a lamp and the wisdom of God is oil:
When the glass (= the soul) shines with light then you are alive * but when it has darkened then you are dead".[222]

220 Cited in IBaškṢilah I p. 293; IḪallWaf III p. 96 / (Slane) II p. 62; *Wāfī* XVII p. 570; BN XII p. 198; MaqqNafḥ (C) IV p. 213; ŠTalḫīṣ III p. 309 = MehrenRhetorik p. 58; ŠN p. 130. *Cf.* also the translations in Nykl: *Hispano-Arabic Poetry* p. 236 (English) and Schack: *Poesie und Kunst* I p. 236 (German). However, as-Subkī in his *ʿArūs al-ʾafrāḥ fī šarḥ Talḫīṣ al-Miftāḥ* attributes the verses mistakenly (?) to al-ʿAfīf al-Baṣrī. Yūsuf al-Baḥrānī in his anthology provides us with further verses of that kind, the first attributed to ʿAlī, the second anonymous (BaḥrKaškūl III p. 217); the verse of ʿAlī is also cited in IʿArabŠFākihah p. 153 (*ṭawīl*): *wa-fī l-ǧahli qabla l-mawti mawtun li-ʾahlihī * wa-ʾaǧsāduhum dūna l-qubūri qubūrū* ("Ignorance means death before dying for those who are ignorant, * and their corpses are tombs outside tombs (i.e. before they are actually interred)". Very similar is also a dictum reported by aṯ-Ṯaʿālibī: "The treasurers of material goods are dead though they are among the living, yet the treasurers of knowledge are alive though they are among the dead" (ṮaʿālTamṯīl p. 167: *māta ḫazanatu l-ʾamwāli wa-hum ʾaḥyāʾu wa-ʿāša ḫazanatu l-ʿulūmi wa-hum ʾamwātun*).

221 "God is the Light of the heavens and the earth; the likeness of His Light is as a niche wherein is a lamp, the lamp in a glass (*zuǧāǧah*), the glass as it were a glittering star kindled from a Blessed Tree, an olive that is neither of the East nor of the West whose oil (*zayt*) wellnigh would shine, even if no fire touched it; Light upon Light: God guides to His Light whom He will".

222 Quoted in IḤaǧInbāʾ I p. 119.

22

LOCATION. Baghdad (near the shrine of Mūsā b. Ǧaʿfar). DATE. 391 H.

PERSON BURIED. The poet Ibn (al-)Ḥaǧǧāǧ (Abū ʿAbd Allāh al-Ḥusayn b. A. aš-Šīʿī, Baghdad *c*.330–91 H): TB VIII pp. 14f.; IĞawzīMunt VII pp. 216-8; IḪallWaf II pp. 168-72; *Wāfī* XII pp. 331-7; TI XXVII pp. 252-4; BN XI pp. 329f.; ZA II p. 231; EI^2 III pp. 780f. (Ch. Pellat); GAS II pp. 592-4.

SOURCES. IḪallWaf II p. 171 / (Slane) I p. 449; AFidāʾMuḫt II p. 135; *Wāfī* XII p. 332.

DESCRIPTION. "Ibn al-Ḥaǧǧāǧ had stipulated in his last will to be buried at the feet of (the Shiite Imam) Mūsā (al-Kāẓim) b. Ǧaʿfar,[223] and that on his tomb be written: [...]" (all sources).

وَكَلْبُهُم بَاسِطٌ ذِرَاعَيهِ بِالوَصِيدِ

"And their dog is stretching its paws on the threshold" (= Q 18:18).

NOTE. The exaggerated submissiveness expressed by choosing this Qurʾānic passage for an epitaph is only known from this case. During his lifetime, Ibn Ḥaǧǧāǧ had mainly become famous for his *muǧūn* poetry, i.e. verses of obscene content.[224]

In 626 H, Ibn ʿAyyāš al-Ḥanafī (M. b. A., d. 616 H) appeared to aš-Šarīf al-Qāḍī ar-Rāzī al-Ḥanafī in a dream. The latter afterwards reported the following dialogue between the two: – "What did God do to you (in the hereafter)?" – "He forgave me." – "On what account?" – "On account of a relationship (*nisbah*) of mine to the Prophet." – "So you are a Šarīf?" – "No." – "Then what is the relation?" – "It is the relation of a dog to the shepherd".[225] In addition, some Shiite persons in the eastern part of the Islamic world bore the personal name "Kalb ʿAlī".

23

LOCATION. Baghdad. DATE. 413 H.

PERSON BURIED. The poet as-Sukkarī (ʿAlī b. ʿĪsā b. Sul. al-Fārisī, Baghdad 357–413 H): TB XII p. 17; IĞawzīMunt VIII pp. 10f.; TI XXVIII p. 325; BN XII p. 15.

SOURCES. IĞawzīMunt VIII pp. 10f.; BN XII p. 15.

DESCRIPTION. He was buried near the tomb of Maʿrūf al-Karḫī and had stipulated in his last will that the following verses, of his own composition, be engraved upon his tomb. – Seven lines in the metre *ḫafīf*:

*nafsu yā-nafsu kam tumādīna fī l-ġay- * -yi wa-taʾtīna bi-l-faʿāli l-maʿībī*
*rāqibī llāha wa-ḥḏarī mawḍiʿa l-ʿar- * -ḍi wa-ḫāfī yawma l-ḥisābi l-ʿaṣībī*
*lā taġurrannaki s-salāmatu fī l-ʿay- * -ši fa-ʾinna s-salīma rahnu l-ḫuṭūbī*

223 His shrine is situated in Baghdad.

224 *Cf.* for some examples ṢafĠayṯ II pp. 239-42 and ʿĀmKaškūl I pp. 158-60.

225 MaqrMuq V p. 292.

*kullu ḥayyin fa-li-l-manūni wa-lā yad- * -faʿu kaʾsa l-manūni kaydu l-ʾarībī*
*wa-ʿlamī ʾanna li-l-manīyati waqtan * sawfa yaʾtī ʿağlāna ġayra hayūbī*
*fa-ʾaʿiddī li-ḏālika l-yawmi zādan * wa-ğawāban li-llāhi ġayra kaḏūbī*
*ʾinna ḥubba ṣ-ṣiddīqi fī mawqifi l-ḥaš- * -ri ʾamānun li-l-ḫāʾifi ṭ-ṭalūbī*

1 *fī l-ġayyi wa-taʾtīna bi-*: *fī ṭalfi wa-tamšīna fī* (BN; regularly vowelled *ṭalaf*, but shortened to *ṭalf* in order to fit the metre). – **2** *mawḍiʿa*: *mawqifa* (BN). – **4** *kaʾsa*: *baʾsa* (IĞawzīMunt); *al-ʾarībī*: *al-ʾadībī* (BN). – **6** om. BN.; *aṭ-ṭalūbī*: *al-maṭlūbī* (IĞawzīMunt, does not fit the metre).

"Soul, O soul, how often do you persist in transgress- * ion and bring shameful deeds!
(But) fear God, beware of the place where (the doings) are exami- * ned[226] and be afraid of the Day of the crucial Accounting!
Let not your well-being in the (present) life deceive you, * for (also) someone enjoying well-being is a pledge of adverse circumstances (i.e. death):
Everybody alive is bound to succomb to fatal destiny and not (even) * the cunning of a wit will push back the cup of death![227]
Know that for the fate of death a time is fixed * that will come sooner than expected and without timid delay.
So prepare provisions for that day * and a (truthful) reply to God (in order to justify yourself), not the reply of a liar.
Verily, the love of the completey faithful will, when the Gathering takes * place, be a safeguard for the fearful, the one asking (for mercy) (?)".

24

LOCATION. Baghdad. DATE. After 560 H.
PERSON BURIED. The Jewish convert, philosopher and physician Abū l-Barakāt al-Baladī (Hibat Allāh b. Malkā al-Baġdādī, born Balad ? – d. Baghdad after 560 H), with the honorific title *ʾAwḥad az-zamān*, "the Unique of his Time": IʿIbrīMuḫt pp. 209f.; QifṭīTārīḫ pp. 343-6; IAUṣaybʿUyūn pp. 374-6; EI^2 I pp. 111-13 (S. Pines).
SOURCES. IʿIbrīMuḫt p. 210; QifṭīTārīḫ p. 345.
DESCRIPTION. "When he felt his death near, he bequeathed to those who would take care of his estate to inscribe the following upon his tomb: [...]" (both sources). Ibn al-Qifṭī reports from people who had seen the grave that the inscription had been made as desired by Abū l-Barakāt.

hāḏā qabru ʾAwḥadi z-zamāni ʾAbī l-Barakāti ḏī l-ʿibar / ṣāḥibi l-Muʿtabar

"This is the tomb of the Unique of his Time, Abū l-Barakāt, whose life serves as admonition, / the author of (the book called) *al-Muʿtabar*".[228]

226 Or lit. "where the doings are presented *or* submitted" (*ʿrḍ* I) to God.
227 See n. 193 above.
228 The *Kitāb al-Muʿtabar,* his main work, deals with logic, *naturalia* and metaphysics. That the

25

LOCATION. Baghdad. DATE. 574 H.

PERSON BURIED. The famous Imam and traditionist Aḥmad Ibn Ḥanbal (d. 241 H): ANuḤilyah IX pp. 167-233; IĞawzīManḤanbal; EI² I pp. 272-7 (H. Laoust). For his mausoleum, see Leisten: *Architektur für Tote* pp. 128f. (no. 87).

SOURCES. IĞawzīMunt X pp. 284f.; BN XII p. 300 (only the central passage).

DESCRIPTION. "At the beginning of Ǧumādā II (574 H) the Prince of the Believers (al-Mustaḍīʾ, r. 566–75) commissioned the making of a slab (*lawḥ*) which should be set up upon the grave of Imam Aḥmad b. Ḥanbal.[229] This was duly carried out, so the complete screening (*sitrah*) was torn down and re-built by square bricks, with two sides added. The new slab was put in its place, and on top of it was written: [...], and in the centre: [...]. The date of his death and the 'Throne-Verse' (Q 2:255) were inscribed around it (*ḥawla ḏālika*)" (IĞawzī-Munt, similarly but much abbreviated in BN).

[Top:] *hāḏā mā ʾamara bi-ʿamalihī sayyidunā wa-mawlānā l-Mustaḍīʾu bi-ʾamri llāhi ʾamīru l-muslimīna* [Centre:] *hāḏā qabru tāǧi s-sunnah / waḥīdi l-ʾummah / al-ʿālī l-himmah* || *al-ʿālimi l-ʿābidi l-faqīhi z-zāhidi l-ʾimāmi ʾAbī ʿAbdi llāhi ʾAḥmada bni Muḥammadi bni Ḥanbala š-Šaybānīyi — raḥimahū llāhu*

wāḥidi l-ʾummah: *wa-ḥabri l-ʾummah* (BN).

[Top:] "This work was ordered by our master and patron al-Mustaḍīʾ bi-Amr Allāh, Prince of the Believers". [Centre:] "This is the tomb of the diadem of the *sunnah*, / the one unique in the (Muslim) community, / the high-minded, || the learned, the worshipper, the jurist, the ascetic, the Imam Abū ʿAbd Allāh Aḥmad b. Muḥammad b. Ḥanbal aš-Šaybānī – may God have mercy upon him!"

26

LOCATION. Baghdad. DATE. 597 H.

PERSON BURIED. The famous Hanbalite traditionist and preacher Abū l-Faraǧ Ibn al-Ǧawzī (ʿAr. b. ʿAlī al-Qurašī al-Ḥanbalī, Baghdad 510–97 H): *Wāfī* XVIII pp. 186-94; EI² III pp. 751f. (H. Laoust).

SOURCES. AŠāmahTar p. 26; BN XIII p. 33; *Wāfī* XVIII p. 193; IRaǧḎayl I p. 430; ʿUlaymīManh II p. 282; al-ʿAffānī: *Sakb* I p. 292; IĞawzīḤaṯṯ p. 10 (editor's introduction).

DESCRIPTION. Ibn al-Ǧawzī stipulated in his last will that the verses quoted in the following be written upon his tomb. – Three verses in the metre *maǧzūʾ ar-ramal*:

life of Abū l-Barakāt serves as an admonition refers to the fact, as told by later biographers, that in his last years he was befallen by blindness, leprosy and grave illness "against which his medical skills were without effect and which neither his body nor his heart could bear".

229 *Cf.* also EI² I p. 273.

*yā-katīra l-ʿafwi ʿamman * katura d-danbu ladayhī*
*ǧāʾaka l-mudnibu yarǧū ṣ- * ṣafḥa ʿan ǧurmi yadayhī*
*ʾanā ḍayfun wa-ǧazāʾu ḍ- * ḍayfi ʾiḥsānun ʾilayhī*

1 عمّن كثر الذنـــــب: يا من كثرت ذنبي (BN).

"O You full of forgiveness for those * who heaped upon themselves much sinful behaviour:[230]
The sinner has come to You hoping for the par- * doning[231] of the sinful crimes his hands committed (during his life).[232]
(But) I am a guest, and to remunerate the * guest means treating him as one duly should!"

Notes. It is not known whether these verses were ever inscribed upon the tombstone of Ibn al-Ǧawzī. In any case, they are a good example of epitaph-poetry concerned with the presumed sinful behaviour of the deceased and expressing the hope that he will lodge with God (i.e. in Paradise) in the hereafter.

1. "Forgiveness" (verse 1). The first line of the epitaph is reminiscent of a famous verse by Abū Nuwās which was said to have been written on a piece of paper found under his bed after his death; the fact that the verse is also cited in a work by Ibn al-Ǧawzī himself shows that he knew the verse before composing his own epitaph (*kāmil*):

يَارَبِّ إنْ عَظُمَتْ ذُنُوبِي كَثْرَةً * فَلَقَدْ عَلِمْتُ بِأَنَّ عَفْوَكَ أَعْظَمُ

"O (my) Lord, though my sins have become great in number, * I know that your forgiveness is greater".[233]

The lines reportedly written upon the tomb of Abū Nuwās (**15**) are likewise very similar in style and content, and comparable verses were often chosen for an epitaph or written upon a piece of paper and buried with the deceased. The latter case is attested for Badr ad-Dīn Abū l-Iḫlāṣ Muḥammad b. Aḥmad as-Sikandarī Ibn at-Tinnisī, a Malikite judge and jurist (d. Cairo 853 H). He stipulated that the following two

230 I.e. whose sinful behaviour has been abundant.

231 *Cf.* Q 15:85: *wa-ʾinna s-sāʿata la-ʾātiyatun fa-ṣfaḥi ṣ-ṣafḥa l-ǧamīla* ("Surely the Hour is coming; so pardon thou, with a gracious pardoning").

232 Later sources have it that Ibn al-Ǧawzī indeed was forgiven his sins, as he himself stated in a dream.

233 ANuwDīwān II p. 173; IʿARabʿIqd (Ǧ) II p. 161 / (M) III p. 249; IʿABarrBahǧah II p. 375; TB VII p. 449; IǦawzīṮabāt p. 55; AnbNuzhah p. 80; TMD XIII p. 461; QazwĀṯār p. 328; BN X pp. 234f.; SuyŠṢudūr p. 389; MehrenRhetorik p. 146. The later sources have this and another two or three verses (as also in ANuwDīwān). See also a line by the Andalusian jurist and man of letters Ibn Ǧuzayy (693–741 H) which begins as follows (*basīṭ*): *yā-rabbi ʾinna dunūbī l-yawma qad katurat* (cited in DāʾūdīṬab II p. 87; MaqqNafḥ [C] VIII p. 30; IQāḍī-Durrah II p. 117). In addition, two very similar poems are cited in TanFaraǧ III p. 335 and WaṭwāṭĠurar p. 386 (their *incipit* being, respectively, *danbī ʾilayka ʿaẓīmun* and *ʾadnabtu danban ʿaẓīman*).

lines, written on a piece of paper, be buried with him; he had composed them "during a dream" at the time of the plague in 847 H. The verses struck a nerve with as-Saḫāwī since they are quoted in a number of his works (*wāfir*):

إلَهَ الخَلْقِ قَدْ عَظُمَتْ ذُنُوبِي * فَسَامِحْ مَا لِعَفْوِكَ مِنْ مُشَارِكْ
أَغِثْ يَا سَيِّدِي عَبْداً فَقِيراً * أَنَاخَ بِبَابِكَ العَالِي وَدَارِكْ

1 *ʾilāha l-ḫalqi*: *ʾilāha l-ḥaqqi* (SaḫḎRafᶜ). – **2** أغث: أعذ (SaḫTibr); ودارك: ودراك (SaḫTibr).

"O God of creation, my sins have been great, * so pardon what takes a share in your forgiveness.
Do help, O my Master, a poor servant * who (now) has taken abode at Your Sublime Porte and in Your House!"[234]

As for funerary inscriptions, we know an epitaph-poem from Aleppo (dated 897 H) which certainly takes its inspiration from the above-cited verse by Abū Nuwās and similar lines; the verses themselves stem from earlier centuries (*ṭawīl*):

تَعَاظَمَ بِي ذَنْبِي فَلَمَّا قَرَنْتُهُ * بِعَفْوِكَ رَبِّي كَانَ عَفْوُكَ أَعْظَمَا
وَلَمَّا دَنَتْ وَفَاتِي وَحَانَتْ مَنِيَّتِي * جَعَلْتُ رَجَائِي نَحْوَ عَفْوِكَ سُلَّمَا

"My sin(s) have been great with me, but after I had compared them * with Your forgiveness, my Lord, (I found that) Your forgiveness proved more enormous.
When my passing away had drawn near and the time of my fatal destiny had come * I made my hope a ladder[235] towards Your forgiveness".[236]

In Arabic theological and mystical literature, the – Qurʾānic – concept of God's forgiveness (*ʿafw*, also *maġfirah*) looms large.[237] One of the better known mystical texts, the *Kitāb al-Ḥikam* by Ibn ᶜAṭāʾ Allāh as-Sikandarī (d. Cairo 709 H), contains the following dictum closely related to the message of Ibn al-Ǧawzī's epitaph and the other passages quoted before: "Sin does not reach with you such a high degree which would turn you away from thinking the best of (*or* confiding in) God the Exalted, since the one who knows his Lord deems his sin little when compared with His magnanimity".[238] The binary concept of great sin and greater forgiveness was

234 SaḫḎRafᶜ p. 243, SaḫTibr p. 286, SaḫWaǧīz II p. 639 and ḌL VII p. 92 = IŠamQabas II p. 140.

235 I.e. a means of ascent. *Cf.* Q 6:35: *fa-ʾini staṭaʿta ʾan tabtaġiya … sullaman fī s-samāʾ* ("If thou canst seek out … a ladder in(to) heaven").

236 Quoted in al-Ġazzī: *Nahr aḏ-ḏahab* II p. 336 (var. *raǧāʾī*: *raǧāʿī*); see also IḪarrāṭᶜĀqibah pp. 90f. note and ĠazIḥyāʾ (B) IV p. 484. In TMD LI p. 430 and YāqIrṣād VI pp. 382f., the first verse and the 2nd hemistich of the 2nd verse are attributed to aš-Šāfiᶜī; the first verse is also attributed to Abū Nuwās in TMD XIII p. 458 and BN X p. 234. See also al-ᶜAffānī: *Sakb* II p. 483 (var. in v. 2: *wa-lammā qasā qalbī wa-ḍāqat maḏāhibī*), which again takes up a verse by aš-Šāfiᶜī (see TMD LI p. 430).

237 *Cf.* IDaqŠArbaᶜīn pp. 137ff.

238 IᶜAṭāʾḤikam p. 109 (no. 46) = RundīŠḤikam I p. 44 (*lā yaʿẓumu ḏ-ḏanbu ʿindaka ʿaẓamatan*

also part of invocations (*ʾadʿiyah*) and litany-like prayer texts (*ʾawrād*), e.g. as uttered by al-Fuḍayl b. ʿIyāḍ (see **116**): *allāhumma ʾinna ḏunūbanā qad ʿaẓumat wa-ǧallat wa-ʾanta ʾaʿẓamu minhā wa-ʾaǧall*, "O God, our sins have become great and mighty, but You are greater and mightier than they are".[239] Verses that implore God's forgiveness in general are legion in Arabic mourning and epitaph-poetry as well as in religious litanies.[240] This catalogue offers a number of other examples.

From the purely literary realm, an excellent, albeit largely conventional example, can be cited from a poem attributed to aš-Šarīf ar-Raḍīy (*ramal*):

رَبِّ فَاغْفِرْ لِيَ الخَطِيـ * ـئَةَ يَا خَيْرَ مَنْ غَفَرْ

"O my Lord, do pardon me (my) sin, * O best of those who pardon!"[241]

2. "I am a guest" (verse 2). The concept of the deceased being "a guest" who lodges with God is a constitutive element of the Islamic eschatological imagery.[242] After the death of Ǧamāl ad-Dīn Ibn Maṭrūḥ (see below **55**) a piece of paper was found on which was written the line (*kāmil*):

أَنَا مِنْ ضُيُوفِكَ قَدْ حُسِبْتُ وَإِنَّ مِنْ * شِيَمِ الكِرَامِ البِرَّ بِالأَضْيَافِ

"I am one of Your guests who has been already held to account, and among the * virtues of the noble is kindness towards the guests".[243]

This concept could also be transferred from God to the Prophet whose protected guest the believer will be (*man zāranī ... kāna fī ǧiwārī*, *cf.* above p. 46) when he calls upon him for mercy and intercession on the Last Day;[244] in Shiism, this is extended to the protection offered by Fāṭimah or one of the Imams.[245] It is especially in poetry in praise of the Prophet that Muḥammad is addressed as a protector

taṣudduka ʿan ḥusni ẓ-ẓanni bi-llāhi taʿālā fa-ʾinna man ʿarafa rabbahū staṣġara fī ǧanbi karamihī ḏanbahū).

239 NuwIlmām III p. 33 and VI p. 220. With a different wording: *allāhumma ʾinna ḏunūbanā ʿaẓīmatun wa-ʾinna qalīla ʿafwika ʾaʿẓamu minhā llāhumma ġfir lanā bi-qalīli ʿafwika ʿaẓīma ḏunūbinā* ("O our God, our sins are great but a little part of Your forgiveness is greater than they are, O God, pardon us with little of Your forgiveness the greatness of our sins!").

240 Translations of Arabic prayers and litanies contain Padwick: *Muslims Devotions* and Elmer H. Douglas: *Prayers of al-Shādhilī*, in: S.A. Hanna (ed.): *Medieval and Middle Eastern Studies in Honor of Aziz Suryal Atiya*, Leiden 1972, pp. 106-21.

241 Cited in NZ III p. 272 (not in ŠarīfRaḍDīwān).

242 See **5**, **95**, **106**, **216** and **226**; see also Volume I, Chapter 2.

243 Cited in IḪallWaf VI p. 261.

244 *Cf.* also IQūlKāmil p. 13; ṬūsīTahḏ VI p. 3; ʿIyāḍŠifāʾ (B) II p. 71 / (Š) II p. 83 = HarŠŠifāʾ II p. 149; IǦawzīTabṣ I p. 229; TurkLumaʿ I p. 225; ʿĀmilīWas III pp. 262f.

245 IQūlKāmil pp. 136f. For the general concept of the *muǧāwarah*, see EI^2 VII pp. 239f. (W. Ende).

(*muǧīr* or *ǧār*) whose intercession (*šafāʿah*) on the Last Day is seen as the ultimate hope for the believer.[246]

Of some interest in that context are two verses which are reported to have been found engraved upon "an old tomb" in the cemetery of the Prophet's companion al-Mundir al-Ifrīqī al-Yamānī[247] in Tripoli (Libya) (*kāmil*):

هِيَ فِي جِوَارِكَ يَامُنَيْذِرُ فَاحْمِهَا * وَمِنَ الْمُرُوءَةِ أَنْ يَعِزَّ الجَارُ
حَاشَى لِفَضْلِكَ يَارَفِيقَ مُحَمَّدٍ * مِنْ أَنْ تَمَسَّ مُجَاوِرِيكَ النَّارُ

"They (*sc*. the graves) are under your protection, O Munaydir, so do guard them, * since it is part of manliness that the protégé is honoured!
Far be it from your grace, O comrade of Muḥammad, * that the Fire will (ever) touch those which are (buried) in your protective neighbourhood!"[248]

27

LOCATION. Balaṭ (west of Mawṣil). DATE. 103 H.
PERSON BURIED. ʿUmar b. al-Ḥasan, the grandson of ʿAlī b. Abī Ṭālib (d. 61 H).
SOURCE. HarIšārāt p. 68.
DESCRIPTION. The inscription seems not to have been an epitaph in the proper sense, but rather the foundation inscription of a shrine (*maqām*), for al-Harawī says, "I read on a stone, which is set up at that place, the following: [...]".

basmalah. hādā maqāmu ʿUmara bni l-Ḥusayni bni ʿAlīyi bni ʾAbī Ṭālibin – raḍiya llāhu ʿanhum – wa-huwa ʾasīrun fī sanati ʾiḥdā wa-sittīna taṭawwaʿa bi-ʿimāratihī ʾIbrāhīmu bni l-Qāsimi l-Madāʾinīyu fī Ṣafarin sanata talātin wa-miʾatin wa-ḥabasa ʿalayhi ḫāna l-quṭni mina s-sūqi l-ʿatīqi bi-Balaṭ

"*Basmalah*. This is the shrine of ʿUmar b. al-Ḥusayn[249] b. ʿAlī b. Abī Ṭālib – may God be pleased with them! – who was made prisoner in the year 61. It was built[250] in Ṣafar of the year 103 by Ibrāhīm b. al-Qāsim al-Madāʾinī of his own will, and he stipulated for it(s upkeep the revenues of) the cotton storehouse in the old market of Balaṭ".

246 See e.g. MN II p. 139, III p. 251 (vv. 59f.), IV p. 304 (v. 40); *Wāfī* XXVII p. 204.

247 For him, see IʿABarrIst III p. 528; IḤaǧIṣābah III p. 465.

248 Cited in al-Anṣārī: *Nafaḥāt* p. 65. This epitaph was not included in the numbered catalogue because I know of no pre-modern source reporting its wording.

249 As Janine Sourdel-Thomine noted (SourdelLieux p. 151, n. 5), the correct name would be al-Ḥasan instead of al-Ḥusayn.

250 Or "restored" (but this is improbable in the present context).

28

LOCATION. al-Barqah. DATE. 53 H or after.

PERSON BURIED. The Prophet's companion Ruwayfiʿ b. Ṯābit al-Anṣārī (d. 53 H or after): MālRiyāḍ I pp. 81f.; DabMaʿālim I pp. 122-5; *cf.* ŠḎ I p. 55.

SOURCES. MālRiyāḍ I p. 82; DabMaʿālim I p. 125.

DESCRIPTION. "His tomb is known there.[251] After its traces had been lost, it was then rediscovered. At its head there is a tile (*balāṭah*) upon which is inscribed: [...]" (both sources).

hāḏā qabru Ruwayfiʿa bni Ṯābitini l-ʾAnṣārīyi ṣāḥibi rasūli llāhi – taṣliyah

ṣāḥibi rasūli llāhi taṣliyah: om. MālRiyāḍ.

"This is the tomb of Ruwayfiʿ b. Ṯābit al-Anṣārī, the companion of the Prophet – *taṣliyah*".

29

LOCATION. Baṣrah. DATE and PERSON BURIED. Unknown.

SOURCES. IADunyāQubūr (A) pp. 174f. = IRağAhwāl p. 189; IRağLaṭāʾif pp. 102 and 362.

DESCRIPTION. The following verses were found inscribed "upon a tomb in a cemetery of Baṣrah". In both passages of IRağLaṭāʾif, these verses are simply presented as anonymous poetry. – Four lines in the metre *basīṭ*:

*yā-ġāfila l-qalbi ʿan ḏikri l-manīyātī * ʿammā qalīlin sa-taṯwī bayna ʾamwātī*
*fa-ḏkur maḥallaka min qabli l-ḥulūli bihī * wa-tub ʾilā llāhi min lahwin wa-laḏḏātī*
*ʾinna l-ḥimāma lahū waqtun ʾilā ʾağalin * fa-ḏkur maṣāʾiba ʾayyāmin wa-sāʿātī*
*lā taṭmaʾinna ʾilā d-dunyā wa-zīnatihā * qad ḥāna li-l-mawti yā-ḏā l-lubbi ʾan yaʾtī*

1 عن: عند (IRağAhwāl; does not fit the metre); *sa-taṯwī*: *sa-talqā* (IRağLaṭāʾif p. 102). – **4** *ḥāna*: *ʾāna* (IRağLaṭāʾif p. 102).

"O you whose heart fails to think about the fate of death: * not long from now you will settle among dead people,
So think about the place where you will settle before you arrive there, * and turn to God in repentance for (your) trifle amusements and (wordly) pleasures!
For the fate of death a certain time is appointed, * so (start) thinking about calamities (which might befall you) every day and every minute!
Do not trust the (present) world and its splendour: * O man of understanding, the time when death will come has drawn near!"

NOTE. The last two lines of this epitaph are close, in both wording and content, to two verses by the Andalusian poet Ibn Abī Zamanīn (*basīṭ*):

251 The tomb of Ruwayfiʿ is also mentioned in YāqBuldān I p. 389, *s.v.* al-Barqah.

المَوْتُ فِي كُلِّ حِينٍ يَنْشُرُ الكَفَنَ * وَنَحْنُ فِي غَفْلَةٍ عَمَّا يُرادُ بِنَا
لاَ تَطْمَئِنَّ إِلَى الدُّنْيَا وَبَهْجَتِهَا * وَإِنْ تَوَشَّحْتَ مِنْ أَثْوَابِهَا الحَسْنَا

"Death unfolds the shroud at any time * and we are ignorant about our lot.
Do not trust the (present) world and its delight, * even if you wear one of the good garments that the world provides!"[252]

30

LOCATION. Baṣrah (?).
DATE and PERSON BURIED. Unknown.
SOURCES. *Aġānī* XVIII p. 346; AṬālibAmālī pp. 191f.; TMD XLII p. 527; IǦawzīTabṣ II p. 207; NubQuḍātAnd p. 44; IRaǧAhwāl p. 190; ṬurayḥīMunt p. 119 (only v. 1); al-ʿAffānī: *Sakb* II p. 527.
DESCRIPTION. "On a tomb was found the inscription: [...]" (IǦawzīTabṣ, al-ʿAffānī: *Sakb*); "On another tomb in Baṣrah could be read: [...]" (IRaǧAhwāl). According to the versions in the *Aġānī* and other sources, these popular verses are not taken from an epitaph. Rather, we are told – and al-Iṣfahānī cites "from the book of Ibn Abī d-Dunyā" – that Abū l-ʿAtāhiyah, when he was near death, asked for Muḫāriq b. Yaḥyā to come and to recite these lines to him; following the version of AṬālibAmālī, both verses are part of a five-verse poem by Aḥmad b. Yaḥyā; according to TMD and TurayḥīMunt, both lines are part of a poem pronounced by ʿAlī at Fāṭimah's tomb after her burial;[253] according to NubQuḍātAnd, these verses were often recited by al-Qāḍī ʿAbd Allāh b. ʿUmar b. Ġānim (d. 179 H). – Two verses in the metre *ṭawīl*:

*sa-tuʿriḍu ʿan ḏikrī wa-tansā mawaddatī * wa-yuḥdaṯu baʿdī li-l-ḫalīli ḫalīlū*
*ʾiḏā nqaṭaʿat yawman mina l-ʿayši muddatī * fa-ʾinna ġināʾa l-bākiyāti qalīlū*

1 *sa-tuʿriḍu*: *sa-yuʿriḍu/yuʿraḍu* (*Aġānī*, var. in ms. and edited text; AṬālibAmālī, TMD, IǦawzīTabṣ, NubQuḍātAnd, ṬurayḥīMunt, al-ʿAffānī); AṬālibAmālī and NubQuḍātAnd with exchanged verse order: 2-1. – **2** إذا انقطعت etc.: ما تقضت (IRaǧAhwāl), إذا ما انقضت عني من الدهر (*Aġānī*); *ʾiḏ inqaṭaʿat ʿannī* (AṬālibAmālī), *ʾiḏā nqaraḍat ʿannī* (NubQuḍātAnd); غناء: عناء (AṬālibAmālī, ms. of TMD); *al-bākiyāt*: *an-nākibāt* (!, TMD).

"You will abandon the thought of me and forget my loving friendship, * and after my death another friend will appear for the (former) friend.[254]
When one day the span of my life is brought to an end, * then the tune[255] of the wailing-women will be but little".

NOTE. The different contexts reported in the sources show that these lines, especially

252 QurṭTaḏk p. 42; MaqqNafḥ (C) V p. 95.
253 For further sources reporting this poem, see above p. 114, n. 682.
254 I.e. as a substitute for the friend that has died.
255 Or perhaps "the toil" (*ʿanāʾ*).

the first, were adapted for the most varied circumstances. In principle, they could be inserted in every poem of the metre *ṭawīl* and rhyming in *-(l)īlū/-(l)ūlū*, something not infrequent in Arabic poetry. Given that fact and their popularity, these verses might well have been actually inscribed upon a tomb. – For the topos of the deceased person being quickly forgotten by his friends and relatives, see note to **196**.

31

LOCATION. Bayt al-Maqdis (Jerusalem) (?). DATE. 357 H.

PERSON BURIED. The black eunuch Abū l-Misk Kāfūr (d. 357 H), powerful "grey eminence" and then nominal Iḫšīdid ruler of Egypt in 355-57 H: IḪallWaf IV pp. 99-105; TI XXVI pp. 149-52; *Wāfī* XXVI pp. 305-10; IIyāsBad I p. 184; ZA V p. 216; CHE I pp. 114-7.

SOURCES. IAṯīrKāmil VIII p. 581 (epitaph II); IḪallWaf IV p. 105 note 3 (epitaph II, in one ms.); TI XXVI p. 152 (epitaph I); BN XI p. 264 (epitaph II); NZ IV p. 10 (epitaphs I and II).

DESCRIPTION. (Epitaph I:) "It is said that upon his tomb was found engraved: [...]" (TI); "He was carried in a coffin to al-Quds and buried there. Upon his tomb was inscribed: [...]" (NZ). – (Epitaph II:) "al-Walīd b. Bakr al-ʿUmarī said that he found on the tomb of Kāfūr inscribed: [...]" (NZ); "It was written upon his tomb: [...]" (BN). According to Ibn Ḫallikān, aṣ-Ṣafadī and Ibn Iyās, however, Kāfūr was buried in the Cairene Qarāfah.

Epitaph I: Two verses in the metre *basīṭ*:

*mā bālu qabrika yā-Kāfūru munfaridan * bi-ṣ-ṣaḥṣaḥi l-marti baʿda l-ʿaskari l-laǧibī*

*yadūsu qabraka ʾāḥādu r-riǧāli wa-qad * kānat ʾusūdu š-Šarā taḫšāka fī l-kubabī*

2 *yadūsu*: *tadūsu* (TI); *ʿāḥādu*: *ʾafnāʾu* (TI); *ʾusūdu š-Šarā*: *ʾusūdu ṯ-ṯarā* (!, TI); *fī l-kubabī*: *fī l-kutubī* (both sources; does not make sense).

"Why is your tomb, O Kāfūr, forlorn * in destitute land of the barren desert[256] after (you were in the midst of) a tumultuous army?

Single men (now) tread upon (*or* treat with disdain) your tomb, while before that * (even) the lions of Šarā[257] did fear you in the crowds of combat".[258]

Epitaph II: Two verses in the metre *basīṭ*:

256 *al-mart*: desert land without vegetation and, especially, trees. See also ʿIṣāmīSimṭ III p. 332: "Nobody perishes with God unless his heart is as devoid of faith as the *mart*-desert is devoid of plants".

257 A proverbial expression indicating brave and courageous people, *cf.* YāqBuldān III p. 330 and Lane s.r. *šry*.

258 Or maybe also *fī l-kuṯubī*, "in the sand-hills"?

*unẓur ʾilā ʿibari l-ʾayyāmi mā ṣanaʿat * ʾafnat ʾunāsan bihā kānū wa-mā faniyat*
*dunyāhumū ḍaḥikat ʾayyāma dawlatihim * ḥattā ʾiḏā faniyat nāḥat lahum wa-bakat*

1 عبر: غير (IAṯīrKāmil, BN); *ʾunāsan*: *qurūnan* (BN); *wa-mā*: *wa-qad* (IAṯīrKāmil, var. in ms.). – 2 *dunyāhumū*: *diyāruhum* (IAṯīrKāmil, var. in ms.); *ʾiḏā faniyat*: *ʾiḏā nqaraḍū* (IAṯīrKāmil, var. in ms.); *nāḥat*: *nāḫat* (BN, NZ).

"Look at what the warning lessons[259] of Time were doing: * they annihilated people that lived in their time and were not themselves annihilated!
Their world laughed at the days of their rulership * until, once they (*sc*. the days of their rulership) were annihilated, it mourned them and cried".

32

LOCATION. Bayt al-Maqdis (Jerusalem). DATE. 843 H.

PERSON BURIED. The religious scholar and mystic Taqīy ad-Dīn Abū ṣ-Ṣidq Abū Bakr b. aš-Šams Abī ʿAl. Muḥammad b. al-Ǧamāl ʿAl. al-Ḥalabī al-Bisṭāmī āš-Šāfiʿī aṭ-Ṭūlūnī (748–843 H, see also **3**): ḌL XI pp. 80f.; ʿUlaymīUns II p. 173.

SOURCES. ḌL XI p. 80; ʿUlaymīUns II p. 173.

DESCRIPTION. He was buried in the Bisṭāmīyah grave-recinct (*ḥawš*) in the Māmillā cemetery. as-Saḫāwī reports that the verses cited in the following were found on a pillar (or pole, *naṣībah*) at the head of his tomb, written "on the outside" (the front?) of it; "the inside" (the back?) was adorned with the verses quoted above (**3**). al-ʿUlaymī says that this epitaph was inscribed upon a tile (*balāṭah*) at the head of his tomb, and the verses of **3** "were also written upon his tomb". Both authors agree, however, in that the epitaph was of aṭ-Ṭūlūnī's own composition, and that he had his tombstone prepared some time before his death. – Two verses in the metre *ramal*:

*raḥima llāhu faqīran * zāra qabrī wa-qarā*[260] *lī*
*sūrata s-sabʿi l-maṯānī * bi-ḫušūʿin wa-daʿā lī*

"May God have mercy upon a poor (servant) * who visits my tomb and recites to me
The surah of the seven *maṯānī*[261] * with humility, and prays for (mercy) on me!"

259 Or, according to some versions, *ġiyar*, "vicissitudes".

260 Poetic license for *qaraʾa lī*.

261 The so-called "seven *maṯānī*" are mentioned in Q 15:87 (*wa-laqad ʾataynāka sabʿan mina l-maṯānī wa-l-qurʾāna l-ʿaẓīm*, "We have given thee seven of the oft-repeated, and the mighty Koran") and, without number, in Q 39:23 (*allāhu nazzala ʾaḥsana l-ḥadīṯi kitāban mutašābihan maṯāniya*, "God has sent down the fairest discourse as a Book, consimilar in its oft-repeated"). However, the meaning of *maṯānī* is far from clear, and as Uri Rubin has shown, aṭ-Ṭabarī in his *Tafsīr* gives no less than 83 exegetic Traditions relating to verse 15:87. There is no single surah called "the seven *maṯānī*" but Muslim scholars refer to the surahs 20-26 as *al-maṯānī*. For this and further information, see Rubin: *Seven Mathānī*.

33

LOCATION. Near Bayt al-Maqdis (Jerusalem) in the hillside.
DATE. Second century H (?).
PERSON BURIED. Unknown.
SOURCE. IADunyāQubūr (A) pp. 161f.
DESCRIPTION. "I stopped at a tomb and when I looked at it, I noticed the writing: [...]". The chain of transmission mentions a man from the Banū Ḍamrah who read the inscription. – One verse in the metre *ramal*:

*ʾayyuhā l-wāqifu hawnan fa-ʿtabir * ʾinna fī l-mawti la-šuġlan fa-ddakir*

"O you standing there at ease (in front of my tomb) be warned: * death will bring trouble, bear that in mind!"

NOTE. In at least two epitaphs from Almería we find similar lines fragmentarily preserved: *yā-wāqifan bi-ʾizāʾi l-qabri muʿtabiran * qaddim li-nafsi* [*ka* ...] (Inscripciones Almería 66, *c*.520 H); *tā-llāhi yā-wāqifan bi-l-qabri muʿta*[*biran* ...] (67, *c*.520 H). A poem cited anonymously in IḪarrāṭʿĀqibah p. 102 begins with the hemistich: *ʾinna fī l-mawti wa-l-maʿādi la-šuġlan*.

34

LOCATION. Baza (ar. Basṭah). DATE. 694 H.
PERSON BURIED. Ibn Arqam al-Qāḍī, Abū Ḫālid M. b. A. b. M. an-Numayrī al-Wādī Āšī (Wādī Āš [sp. Guadix] – Basṭah 694 H): SuyBuġ I p. 42; ZA V p. 324.
SOURCE. SuyBuġ I p. 42.
DESCRIPTION. "On his tomb the following lines of his poetry were written: [...]". – Four verses in the metre *mutaqārib*:

*ʾataytu ʾilā ḫāliqī ḫāḍiʿan * wa-man ḫadduhū fī t-tarā yaḫḍaʿū*
*wa-ʾin kuntu wāfaytuhū muġriman * fa-ʾinniya fī ʿafwihī ʾaṭmaʿū*
*wa-kayfa ʾaḫāfu ḏunūban maḍat * wa-ʾAḥmadu fī zallatī yašfaʿū*
*fa-ʾaḫliṣ duʿāʾaka yā-zāʾirī * laʿalla l-ʾilāha bihī yanfaʿū*

"I came to my Creator submissively * – and he whose cheek lies in moist earth (easily) submits himself! –,
And even though I appear before Him as a sinner, * I still hope very much for His forgiveness.
How could I fear for sins that long have passed * when Aḥmad (i.e. the Prophet) intercedes on behalf of my lapses!?
So pray sincerely for me, O my visitor, * for maybe God will make good use of it (on my behalf)!"

35

LOCATION. Cairo (southern Qarāfah cemetery). DATE. Second century H (?).
PERSON BURIED. Ibn Šamāsah al-Mahrī.[262]
SOURCE. MuwMuršid I p. 447.
DESCRIPTION. Ibn ᶜUṯmān reports, while talking about the tomb of sheikh Abū l-Ḥasan Nūr ad-Dīn, that this tomb, according to hearsay, dates back to ancient times, having been originally the grave of Ibn Šamāsah. He further mentions that the lines quoted in the following were found upon the tomb (*wuǧida hāḏā ʿalā l-qabr*). – Four verses in the metre *sarīʿ*:

*yā-ʾayyuhā l-ġāfilu ǧadda r-raḥīl * wa-ʾanta fī l-lahwi wa-zāduk* (sic) *qalīl*
*law kunta tadrī mā tulāqī ġadan * la-ḏubta min faṭri l-bukā wa-l-ʿawīl*
*fa-ʾaḫliṣi t-tawbata taḥẓā bihā * fa-mā baqā* (!) *fī l-ʿumri ʾillā l-qalīl*
*wa-lā tanam ʾin kunta ḏā fiṭnatin * fa-ʾinna quddāmaka nawmun ṭawīl*

"O you[263] unmindful (of your destiny): departure comes quickly * while you are (immersed) in trifle amusement, your provisions (for the hereafter) are little!
If you knew what will happen to you tomorrow, * you would melt from breaking into tears and wailing!
So repent sincerely (and) you will attain good by it * since only little remains of life!
Do not sleep (now), if you have acumen, * because there is long sleep ahead of you!

NOTE. For many reasons – linguistic, formal and aesthetic – these verses cannot be said to be very satisfactory. Nonetheless, they constitute a good example of a typical epitaph-poem warning the reader that he will not escape Destiny (the common motif of *hodie mihi cras tibi,* see also **3**, **163** and **181**) and that he should reconsider his mortal existence. The last line of the poem uses the image of sleep in order to indicate death. This is remarkable, because the metaphor of sleep (for death) is not at all common in the Arabo-Islamic culture.[264]

36

LOCATION. Cairo (southern Qarāfah cemetery). DATE. 204 H.
PERSON BURIED. The legal authority and traditionist aš-Šāfiʿī (Muḥammad b. Idrīs, d.

262 This is his *nisbah* given in IZayKawākib pp. 18 and 67; MuwMuršid has "al-Mahdī". This rather obscure figure is counted by both authors among the generation following that of the Prophet's companions: Ibn ᶜUṯmān praises him as being "one of the foremost of distinguished traditionists" (MuwMuršid p. 447), and Ibn az-Zayyāt calls him "the sheikh, the jurist, the Imam" (IZayKawākib p. 67).

263 Addressing the visitor of the tomb.

264 However, the Arabs knew the metaphor of sleep as "the brother of death", see DaylFird II p. 378 and HarŠŠifāʾ III p. 144 (*fa-ʾinna n-nawma ʾaḫū l-mawti*). *Cf.* also Arberry: *Omar Khayyám* p. 130 (no. 244) with the note on p. 139.

204 H): ANuḤilyah IX pp. 63-167; BayManŠāf; TB II pp. 56-73; IḤağTawālī; ZA VI pp. 26f.; GAS I pp. 484-90; EI^2 IX pp. 181-5 (E. Chaumont); EAL II p. 702. For the mausoleum, see MuwMuršid I pp. 483ff., YāqIršād VI pp. 393f. and above pp. 219f.

SOURCES. BayManŠāf II pp. 300f. (versions I and II); TB II p. 70 (vers. II); MuwMuršid I p. 495 (vers. I). See also Volume I pp. 136 and 452.

DESCRIPTION. (Version I:) al-Bayhaqī quotes two more or less different (though clearly interrelated) versions of the epitaph. He cites the first version from two accounts, namely from Abū l-Faḍl b. Abī Naṣr as well as from a book (*kitāb*) by Abū l-Ḥasan Muḥammad b. al-Ḥusayn al-ᶜĀṣimī. The latter version is introduced by al-ᶜĀṣimī as follows:

> "I went to visit the tomb of Muḥammad b. Idrīs aš-Šāfiᶜī. It is situated in Cairo (*Miṣr*) in the local cemetery called 'al-Muqaṭṭam', in the cemetery of the Qurayšites among the graves of the Banī ᶜAbd Allāh b. ᶜAbd al-Ḥakam; 'al-Muqaṭṭam' is the name of a mountain towering over that cemetery. I saw his tomb raised, elevated (*musannaman murtafiᶜan*) over the ground with a height of two fingers or a little more,[265] and upon it two marble tombstones (*lawḥān ... min ruḫām*) were set up: one at its head and the other at the foot. On the slab at the foot his *nisbah* was inscribed, reaching back to Ibrāhīm Ḫalīl ar-Raḥmān (i.e. 'the intimate friend of the Merciful') – *taṣliyah*. On the slab at the head the following was carved in the stone: [...]".

The description of al-Muwaffaq Ibn ᶜUṯmān simply says "Upon the side of the tomb is written: [...]" (MuwMuršid). – (Version II:) This version is cited by al-Bayhaqī and al-Ḫaṭīb al-Baġdādī from Abū Aḥmad ᶜAbd Allāh b. ᶜAdīy al-Ḥāfiẓ (al-Ǧurǧānī, author of the *Kāmil*, d. 365 H). He reported, "I read upon the tomb of Muḥammad b. Idrīs aš-Šāfiᶜī in Cairo (*Miṣr*), on two slabs of stone (*ʿalā lawḥayni mina l-ḥiǧārah*), at its head and at its foot respectively, the following: [...]" (BayManŠāf, similarly TB).

Version I:

basmalah. hāḏā mā šahida bihī Muḥammadu bnu ʾIdrīsa bni l-ʿAbbāsi bni ʿUṯmāna bni Šāfiʿin ʾan lā ʾilāha ʾillā llāhu waḥdahū lā šarīka lahū wa-ʾanna Muḥammadan ʿabduhū wa-rasūluhū ʾarsalahū bi-l-hudā wa-dīni l-ḥaqqi bašīran wa-naḏīran wa-dāʿiyan ʾilā llāhi bi-ʾiḏnihī wa-sirāǧan munīran wa-yašhadu ʾanna l-ǧannata ḥaqqun wa-ʾanna n-nāra ḥaqqun wa-ʾanna l-mawta ḥaqqun wa-ʾanna llāha yabʿaṯu man fī l-qubūri ʿalā hāḏā š-šahādati ḥayiya Muḥammadu bnu ʾIdrīsa wa-ʿalayhā māta wa-ʿalayhā yubʿaṯu ḥayyan – ʾin šāʾa llāhu taʿālā – mina l-ʾāminīna llāhumma ġfir lahū ḏanbahū wa-nawwir lahū qabrahū wa-ḥšurhu maʿa nabīyihī Muḥammadin – taṣliyah – wa-ǧʿalhu min rufaqāʾihī ʾāmin yā-rabba l-ʿālamīna tuwuffiya Muḥammadu bnu ʾIdrīsa – raḥimahū llāhu – fī Raǧabin sanata ʾarbaʿin wa-miʾatayn

basmalah: om. MuwMuršid; *bihī*: om. MuwMuršid; *ibni l-ʿAbbāsi bni ʿUṯmāna bni Šāfiʿin*: om. MuwMuršid; *wa-ʾanna n-nāra ḥaqqun wa-ʾanna l-mawta ḥaqqun*: *wa-n-nāru ḥaqqun wa-l-mawtu ḥaqqun* (MuwMuršid); *ʿalā hāḏā š-šahādati*: *ʿalā ḏālika* (BayManŠāf); *ḥayiya Muḥammadu bnu*

265 For this detail, see above pp. 194f.

ʾIdrīsa: *ḥayiya* (BayManŠāf); *yubʿaṯu ḥayyan*: *yubʿaṯu* (MuwMuršid); *taʿālā*: om. MuwMuršid; *mina l-ʾāminīna*: om. BayManŠāf; *iġfir lahū*: *lahū* om. MuwMuršid; *nawwir lahū qabrahū*: *nawwir qabrahū* (MuwMuršid), *nawwir lahū fī qabrihī* (BayManŠāf, in one ms.); *maʿa nabīyihī Muḥammadin*: *maʿa nabīyihī* (MuwMuršid); *tuwuffiya ... miʾatayn*: om. MuwMuršid. – BayManŠāf mentions explicitly that according to Abū l-Faḍl b. Abī Naṣr the passages *ʾin šāʾa llāhu taʿālā* and *ʾāmin rabba* (sic) *l-ʿālamīna* were part of the text, whereas they do not appear in the version as given by al-ʿĀṣimī.

"*Basmalah*. This is what Muḥammad b. Idrīs b. al-ʿAbbās b. ʿUṯmān b. Šāfiʿ confesses: That there is no god but God, He is unique and without an associate,[266] and that Muḥammad is His servant and His Messenger. He sent him with the right guidance and the creed of truth[267] as a bringer of glad tidings, a warner, a summoner to God, by His permission,[268] and a shining lamp.[269] He (i.e. aš-Šāfiʿī) confesses (further) that the Garden (of Paradise) truly exists, that the Fire truly exists, that death truly exists and that God will raise up those who are in the graves.[270] According to that confession Muḥammad b. Idrīs lived, with that confession he died and with that confession he will be raised to life[271] – God willing[272] – among the peaceful. O God, forgive him his sin(s), illuminate his tomb for him, gather him together with His Prophet Muḥammad – *taṣliyah* – (on the Day of Resurrection) and make him one of his companions. Amen, O Lord of the Worlds. Muḥammad b. Idrīs – may God have mercy upon him! – was taken (to God) in Rağab of the year 204".

Version II:

hāḏā qabru Muḥammadi bni ʾIdrīsa š-Šāfiʿīyi wa-huwa yašhadu ʾan lā ʾilāha ʾillā llāhu waḥdahū lā šarīka lahū wa-ʾanna Muḥammadan ʿabduhū wa-rasūluhū wa-ʾanna l-ğannata ḥaqqun[273] *wa-ʾanna n-nāra ḥaqqun wa-ʾanna s-sāʿata ʾātiyatun lā rayba fīhā wa-ʾanna llāha yabʿaṯu man fī l-qubūri wa-ʾanna ṣalātahū wa-naskahū wa-maḥyāhu wa-mamātahū li-llāhi rabbi l-ʿālamīna lā šarīka lahū wa-bi-ḏālika ʾamara*[274] *wa-huwa mina l-muslimīna ʿalayhi ḥayiya wa-ʿalayhi māta wa-ʿalayhi*

266 *Cf.* Q 6:163.

267 *Cf.* Q 9:33 and 61:9. See also below **186**.

268 Or also "Calling unto God by His leave" (Arberry).

269 *Cf.* Q 33:45f.: *yā-ʾayyuhā n-nabīyu ʾarsalnāka šāhidan wa-mubašširan wa-naḏīran * wa-dāʿiyan ʾilā llāhi bi-ʾiḏnihī wa-sirāğan munīran* ("O Prophet, We have sent thee as a witness, and good tidings to bear and warning, * calling unto God by His leave, and as a shining lamp").

270 For this kind of "confession" or "testimony" (*šahādah*), see Watt: *Islamic Creeds*, and **73**.

271 The expression *yubʿaṯu ḥayyan* (not in MuwMuršid) reflects Q 19:33: *wa-yawma ʾubʿaṯu ḥayyan* ("and the day I am raised up alive").

272 *Cf.* Q 80:22: *ṯumma ʾiḏā šāʾa ʾanšarahū* ("then, when He wills, He sends him forth [from the grave]").

273 Here al-Bayhaqī remarks, "He did not mention the rest, but added the following: *wa-ʾanna ṣalātahū* etc.".

274 This is obviously mistaken, in both BayManŠāf and TB, for the correct formula *wa-bi-ḏālika ʾāmana*, attested from many Arabic epitaphs.

yubʿaṯu ḥayyan – ʾin šāʾa llāhu – tuwuffiya ʾAbū ʿAbdi llāhi li-yawmin baqiya min Rağabin sanata ʾarbaʿin wa-miʾatayn

aš-Šāfiʿīyi: om. BayManŠāf. – *wa-ʾanna n-nāra ḥaqqun ... man fī l-qubūri*: om. BayManŠāf.

"This is the tomb of Muḥammad b. Idrīs aš-Šāfiʿī. He confesses that there is no god but God, He is unique and without an associate, and that Muḥammad is His servant and His Messenger. He confesses (further) that the Garden (of Paradise) truly exists, that the Fire truly exists, that the Hour (of Judgment Day) will come, no doubt of it, that God will raise (from the dead) those who are in the graves and that his prayer, his devotion, his coming into life and his coming to death are directed towards God (*or* in the hand of God), the Lord of the worlds who has no associate. This he did command[275] and he was one of the believers. According to that (confession) he was living, with that (confession) he met his death and with that (confession) he will be resurrected to life – God willing. Abū ʿAbd Allāh died one day before the end of Rağab in the year 204".

NOTE. As seems obvious, this second version is an abridged form of version I, with some different wording in the latter part. However, this overall similarity led al-Bayhaqī to the following conclusion: "It seems as if they (i.e. the various persons reporting the epitaph) memorised what they had read inscribed upon the tomb, but then they tampered with the text (by commenting upon it) and so some of the wording slipped from their memory. God knows best".[276] – For another inscription (possibly) at the tomb of aš-Šāfiʿī, see below **220**.

37

LOCATION. Cairo (southern Qarāfah cemetery). DATE. 252 H (?).

PERSON BURIED (?). Muḥammad b. al-Muṯannā aṣ-Ṣadafī. Ibn az-Zayyāt describes him as "of great standing, of exalted rank, one of the great scholars and traditionists". This without doubt refers to the famous traditionist and teacher of Muslim (as well as al-Buḫārī), Muḥammad b. al-Muṯannā b. ʿUbayd al-ʿAnazī (167–252 H) who, however, is generally said to have died in Baṣrah.[277] The biographical material about him yields no evidence of his ever having come to Egypt, and the *nisbah* "aṣ-Ṣadafī" remains particularly difficult to explain.[278] The most plausible hypothesis, therefore, is that a certain Muḥammad b. al-Muṯannā aṣ-Ṣadafī was by later generations wrongly identified with the famous Ibn al-Muṯannā, inspiring an epitaph to that effect.

SOURCE. IZayKawākib p. 104.

275 Or rather in its correct form "in this he did believe" (see the preceding note).

276 BayManŠāf II p. 301.

277 NZ II p. 336; ŠḎ II p. 126; ZA VII p. 18.

278 The possibility of its being misread from "al-ʿAnazī" can be ruled out because the tomb is found in an area with a number of tombs of Ṣadafīs (*mina ṣ-Ṣadafīyīn*).

DESCRIPTION. Near the mausoleum of the legal authority al-Layṯ b. Saᶜd, there was a marble slab (*ruḫāmah*) bearing the inscription: [...].

Muḥammadu bnu l-Muṯannā ṣ-Ṣadafīyu šayḫu l-ʾimāmi Muslim

"Muḥammad b. al-Muṯannā aṣ-Ṣadafī, teacher of the Imam Muslim".

38

LOCATION. Cairo (southern Qarāfah cemetery). DATE. *c*.250 H.

PERSON BURIED. Abū Ḥafṣ ᶜUmar b. al-Ḥusayn b. ᶜAlī b. al-Ašᶜaṯ al-Baṣrī (d. around the middle of the third cent. H): MuwMuršid I pp. 467f. (see also **40**).

SOURCE. IZayKawākib p. 77.

DESCRIPTION. In the cemetery of the Banū l-Ašᶜaṯ there is the tomb of "a famous scholar" (*mina l-ʾaʾimmati l-mašhūrīn*), and "on his tomb was written: [...]".

hāḏā qabru ʾAbī Ḥafṣin ʿUmara bni l-Ḥusayni bni ʿAlīyi bni l-Ašʿaṯi bni Muḥammadini l-Baṣrīyi kāna bi-llāhi muʾminan / wa-li-rasūlihī muṣaddiqan || *māta wa-huwa yašhadu ʾan lā ʾilāha ʾillā llāhu wa-ʾanna Muḥammadan rasūlu llāh – taṣliyah*

"This is the tomb of Abū Ḥafṣ ᶜUmar b. al-Ḥusayn b. ᶜAlī b. al-Ašᶜaṯ b. Muḥammad al-Baṣrī. In God he believed / and in His Messenger he trusted. || He died confessing that there is no god but God and that Muḥammad is the Messenger of God – *taṣliyah*".

39

LOCATION. Cairo. DATE. 270 H or after.

PERSON BURIED. The ruler of Egypt Abū l-ᶜAbbās Aḥmad b. Ṭūlūn (*c*.220–70 H, r. from 254 H): AFidāʾMuḫt II pp. 53f.; MaqrḪiṭaṭ I pp. 313-21; NZ II pp. 1-49; IIyāsBad I pp. 161-9; ŠḎ II pp. 157f.; ZA I p. 140; EI^2 I pp. 278f. (Z. M. Hassan); CHE I pp. 91-103. For his mausoleum, see MuwMuršid I pp. 649ff. and Leisten: *Architektur für Tote* p. 213 (no. 2).

SOURCE. MuwMuršid I p. 72.

DESCRIPTION. "Upon the tomb of Aḥmad b. Ṭūlūn was written (*kutiba*): [...]". – Three verses in the metre *ṭawīl*:

*ʿabartu ʿalā qabri bni Ṭūlūna marratan * fa-ʾankartu fīmā kāna min ʿuẓmi qadrihī*
*wa-lam ʾara mimmā kāna yamliku kullihī * tabaqqā lahū šayʾan* (!) *siwā lawḥi qabrihī*
*wa-mā yanfaʿu l-ʾinsāna mimmā yaḥūzuhū * ʾiḏā fāraqa d-dunyā siwā ṭībi ḏikrihī*

"Once I came across the tomb of Ibn Ṭūlūn, * but I could not recognise (in what consisted) his former grandeur:
I could not see of all he had once possessed * that anything was left to him except a tombstone.[279]
Indeed, nothing of what man attains will be of benefit to him * when he has departed from the (present) world except to be remembered well".

40

LOCATION. Cairo (southern Qarāfah cemetery). DATE. 296 H.
PERSON BURIED. ᶜAbd Allāh b. ᶜUmar Ibn al-Ašᶜaṯ al-Baṣrī (d. 296 H), or his father Abū Ḥafṣ ᶜUmar (see **38**).
SOURCES. MuwMuršid I p. 468; IZayKawākib p. 77.
DESCRIPTION. According to al-Muwaffaq Ibn ᶜUṯmān, this epitaph belongs to the tomb of Abū Ḥafṣ (see above). He describes it as follows: "Upon the tomb of the before-mentioned ᶜUmar there was a marble slab bearing the inscription: [...]". Ibn az-Zayyāt: Upon all graves in the cemetery of the Banū l-Ašᶜaṯ "there were marble slabs, and upon one of them was written: [...]".

hāḏā qabru man ʾakṯara qirāʾata l-qurʾāni fī d-dayāǧī wa-ʿamila ʿamala l-ʾabrāri raġbatan fī mā huwa ʾilayhi ṣāʾirun wa-lam yazal yataraqqā ḏurwata l-falāḥi ḥattā ʿudda mina l-ʾakābiri l-ʾabrāri wa-laqiya llāha liqāʾa mani ʿtamada baʿda t-tawḥīdi ʿalayhi [wa-huwa ʿAbdu llāhi bnu ʿUmara bni l-Ḥusayni bni ʿAlīyi bni l-Ašʿaṯi bni Muḥammadini l-Baṣrīyu][280]

ʾakṯara qirāʾata l-qurʾāni fī d-dayāǧī: *lāzama qirāʾata l-ʾāyāti fī l-ʾasḥār* (IZayKawākib); *raġbatan*: om. MuwMuršid; *ʿudda mina l-ʾakābiri l-ʾabrār*: *ḥusiba mina l-ʿulamāʾi l-ʾakābir* (IZayKawākib); *wa-laqiya llāha ... ʿalayhi*: om. MuwMuršid.

"This is the tomb of someone who frequently recited the Qurʾān in the dark of the night, who performed the work(s) of the pious longing for (the destiny) he is going towards (after death), who did not stop to ascend the summit of salvation (*or* prosperity) until he was reckoned among the most eminent of the pious, who presents himself to God with the attitude of those who (faithfully) rely on Him after the profession of (God's) oneness [and this person is ᶜAbd Allāh b. ᶜUmar b. al-Ḥusayn b. ᶜAlī b. al-Ašᶜaṯ b. Muḥammad al-Baṣrī]".

279 There is another poem dealing with the grandeur of Ibn Ṭūlūn and his mortal fate, the first line of which runs (*basīṭ*): *ʾayna bnu Ṭūlūna bānīhī wa-sākinuhū * ʾamātahū l-maliku l-ʾaʿlā fa-ʾaqbarahū* (cited in NZ III p. 142).

280 The part in square brackets only in IZayKawākib. It is not clear whether this was a part of the epitaph or a comment added by the author, though the latter seems more likely.

41

LOCATION. Cairo (southern Qarāfah cemetery).

DATE. Unknown (third cent. H?).

PERSON BURIED. The legal scholar Ḥasan Ibn Wahb "al-Faqīh" (not identified, probably a relative of the famous Malikite scholar Ibn Wahb).

SOURCES. IMandahFaw I p. 195 (first line only); TMD LXV p. 34 (two identical versions of both lines); IḪallWaf VI p. 141; IZayKawākib p. 46; ŠḎ II p. 79.

DESCRIPTION. It is only Ibn az-Zayyāt's account that mentions the lines cited below as being an epitaph-poem proper: "Ibn al-Ǧabbās[281] said, 'Together with them in the mausoleum (*turbah*)[282] we have Ḥasan b. Wahb, as I found written upon his tomb. Upon his tomb there is also a marble slab (*ruḫāmah*) indicating his name and genealogy. It also bears the verses: [...]'" (IZayKawākib). All other sources agree in attributing these verses to a poem composed (or related) by the famous traditionist and biographer Yaḥyā b. Maᶜīn (d. Medina 233 H). Ibn Maᶜīn's poem consists of four lines in all, of which the first two[283] are, with minor differences in wording, identical to Ibn Wahb's alleged epitaph-poem. It stands to reason, therefore, that the verses chosen for his epitaph were deliberately taken from Ibn Maᶜīn's poem. – Two verses in the metre *kāmil*:

*al-mālu yanfuḏu ḥilluhū wa-ḥarāmuhū * yawman wa-yabqā fī ġadin ʾāṯāmuhū*
*laysa t-taqīyu bi-muttaqin fī dīnihī * ḥattā yaṭība šarābuhū wa-ṭaᶜāmuhū*

1 *yanfuḏu*: *yaḏhabu* (IMandahFaw, TMD, IḪallWaf, ŠḎ); *yawman wa-yabqā*: *ṭarran wa-tabqā* (TMD, IḪallWaf), *ṭawᶜan wa-tabqā* (ŠḎ). – 2 *fī dīnihī*: *li-ʾilāhihī* (TMD, IḪallWaf), *li-ʾālihihī* (!, ŠḎ misprinted).

"Wealth (*or* money), lawfully earned or not, will be consumed * one day, and tomorrow only its sins remain.
The God-fearing is thus not devout in his creed * unless his drink and food are without blemish".[284]

281 Either ᶜAlī Ibn al-Ǧabbās (ᶜAlī b. A. b. M. al-Qurašī aš-Šāfiᶜī, 556–638 H) or his son Šaraf ad-Dīn Abū ᶜAbd Allāh Ibn al-Ǧabbās al-Qurašī (632–*c.*700 H?). The father was an active promoter of the custom of visiting the Qarāfah cemetery regularly during Friday night (MaqrḪiṭaṭ II p. 461), and Ibn az-Zayyāṭ described him as "šayḫ az-ziyārah" (IZayKawākib p. 305). Both are credited with a cemetery guide in the sources, see MunḏTakm III p. 551; MaqrMuq VI pp. 252f.; Rāġib: *Inventaire* pp. 270-5. The work by the son bore the title *Kitāb Muhaḏḏib aṭ-ṭālibīn ʾilā qubūr aṣ-ṣāliḥīn*, "The Educator of Those who Appeal to the Tombs of the Righteous", *cf.* also NZ I p. 129; IZayKawākib pp. 189f., 197f. and *passim*.

282 The so-called *Turbat Bint Ṭūlūn*, burial place of Ibn Wahb (the famous) and others.

283 The second line is missing from the account in IMandahFaw.

284 I.e., when he can enjoy his meal without fear of his sins; *or also* when his meal derives from a source that does not entail, *or* lead to, sinful behaviour (as implied in the first verse).

42

LOCATION. Cairo (southern Qarāfah cemetery). DATE. 303 H.

PERSONS BURIED. Umm Muḥammad and her son Muḥammad b. Aḥmad b. Hārūn al-Aswānī (d. 303 H).

SOURCE. SaḫTuḥfAḥbāb pp. 143f.

DESCRIPTION. Beside the mausoleum of Abū Bakr al-Udfuwī[285] "there is a disarranged tomb and a number of ruined sites. On the tomb there was a marble slab bearing the inscription: [...]".

hāḏā qabru ʾummi Muḥammadin wa-waladihā Muḥammadi bni ʾAḥmada bni Hārūna l-ʾAswānīyi māta fī sanati ṯalāṯin wa-ṯalāṯimiʾah

"This is the tomb of Umm Muḥammad and of her son Muḥammad b. Aḥmad b. Hārūn al-Aswānī. He died in the year 303".

NOTE. The fact that mother and child are buried in one tomb and that only the date of the son is indicated allows us to assume that both died during or shortly after the birth.

43

LOCATION. Cairo (southern Qarāfah cemetery, near the tomb of Ḏū n-Nūn al-Miṣrī). DATE. 320 / 322 H.

PERSON BURIED. The mystic and pupil of both al-Ǧunayd and an-Nūrī (**20**), Abū ʿAlī ar-Rūḏbārī (M. b. A.[286] b. al-Qāsim, Baghdad ? – Egypt 320 or 322 H): ANuḤilyah X pp. 356f.; IǦawzīṢafwah I p. 607; TB I pp. 329-33; MuwMuršid I pp. 374-7; MaqrMuq I pp. 625-7 and V pp. 246-8 (double entry);[287] NZ III p. 247; SuyḤusnMuḥ I p. 339; ŠaʿrṬab I pp. 106f.; MunKawākib II pp. 18-23; ŠḎ II pp. 296f.; ZA V pp. 308f.

SOURCES. IADunyāQubūr (K) p. 101; ĠazIḥyāʾ (B) IV p. 488 / (C) IV p. 414 = ZabīdīŠIḥyāʾ X pp. 356f.; ŠarŠMaq I p. 177 (lacking vv. 3 and 5); SaḫTuḥfAḥbāb p. 10; FanSirāǧ p. 185; ŠayMaǧānī IV p. 39 (lacking vv. 3 and 5); at-Talīdī: *Mašāhid al-mawt* p. 47.

DESCRIPTION. "Upon his tomb one could read inscribed: [...]" (SaḫTuḥfAḥbāb); Ibn Abī d-Dunyā, al-Ġazālī, aš-Šarīšī and al-Fanānī (as well as the modern authors Šayḫū and at-Talīdī) simply say, "On a tomb the following inscription was found" (or similar), without mentioning a name. – Six verses in the metre *basīṭ*:

285 For the tomb of al-Udfuwī, see also MuwMuršid I pp. 271-3.

286 In a number of biographical entries, his name his given as "Aḥmad b. Muḥammad".

287 In the first entry as "A. b. M.", in the second as "M. b. A.". Still others claimed that his name was al-Ḥasan b. Hammām.

*ʾinna l-ḥabība mina l-ʾaḥbābi muḫtalasū * lā yamnaʿu l-mawta ḥuǧǧābun wa-lā ḥarasū*
*wa-kayfa tafraḥu bi-d-dunyā wa-laḏḏatihā * yā-man yuʿaddu ʿalayhi l-lafẓu wa-n-nafasū*
*ʾaṣbaḥta yā-ġāfilan fī n-naqṣi munġamisan * wa-ʾanta dahraka fī l-laḏḏāti munġamisū*
*lā yarḥamu l-mawtu ḏā mālin li-ʿizzatihī * wa-lā llaḏī kāna minhu l-ʿilmu yuqtabasū*
*kam ʾaḫrasa l-mawtu fī qabrin waqaftu bihī * ʿani l-ǧawābi lisānan mā bihī ḫarasū*
*qad kāna qaṣruka maʿmūran bihī šarafun * wa-qabruka l-yawma fī l-ʾaǧdāṯi mundarisū*

1 *ḥaǧǧābun*: *bawwābun* (IADunyāQubūr, ĠazIḥyāʾ [both eds.] and ZabīdīŠIḥyāʾ, ŠarŠMaq, FanSirāǧ, ŠayMaǧānī, at-Talīdī). – **2** *wa-kayfa*: *fa-kayfa* (ŠarŠMaq, ŠayMaǧānī). – **3** في الذات: في اللذات (ĠazIḥyāʾ [C], misprint?); منغمس: تنغمس (SaḫTuḥfAḥbāb). – **4** *ḏā mālin li-ʿizzatihī*: *ḏā ǧahlin li-ġirratihī* (IADunyāQubūr, ĠazIḥyāʾ [both eds.] and ZabīdīŠIḥyāʾ, FanSirāǧ, at-Talīdī), *ḏā ǧāhin li-ʿizzatihī* (ŠarŠMaq, ŠayMaǧānī). – **6** *bihī*: *lahū* (IADunyāQubūr, ZabīdīŠIḥyāʾ, FanSirāǧ, ŠayMaǧānī); *wa-qabruka*: *fa-qabruka* (ŠarŠMaq, ZabīdīŠIḥyāʾ, ŠayMaǧānī).

"The beloved one is inadvertedly carried away (*or* stolen) from the loved ones * and neither guard nor escort can protect against death.[288]
How can you rejoice at the world and the delights it offers, * O you whose (every) word and breath is counted?[289]
You are, O ignorant fool, submerged in ongoing loss (*or* decay) * while you immersed in pleasures all the time.
Death has no mercy upon the wealthy, for (all) his might, * or upon the one whose knowledge was often sought after.
How many a tongue, which was anything but silent, * was silenced by death and barred from answering in tombs I stood at![290]
Lo! Once your palace was peopled, full of (outstanding) nobility, * and today your tomb is crumbling among the (other) graves".

NOTES.

1. "Ongoing loss (*or* decay)" (verse 3). The concept that life is nothing but a gradual loss or decrease (*naqṣ*, *nuqṣān*) that eventually is brought to an end by

288 The concept that guardians (*ḥāris*, pl. *ḥurrās*), or an escort (*ḥaras*), are not sufficient or capable to keep away the fate of death is a common image in Arabic mourning poetry and elegies; *cf.* MaʿarrīLuzūm II pp. 17, 22 and 53; BN X p. 218.

289 I.e. whose existence is totally in the hands of God. *Cf.* the beginning of a verse quoted in IADunyāQaṣr p. 132, BN X p. 143, al-Lawāsānī: *Kaškūl* p. 74 and al-ʿAffānī: *Sakb* II pp. 413, 461 and 526: *ḥayātuka ʾanfāsun tuʿaddu* ("Your life is nothing but breaths counted"). In another poem, we find the line (*ḫafīf*): *kullu yawmin yamūtu minnī ǧuzʾun * wa-ḥayātī tanaffusun maʿdūdū* ("Every day a part of me is dying, * and my life is but a breathing counted", see al-ʿAffānī: *Sakb* II p. 461).

290 The first and second hemistichs are reversed in the translation.

death often figures in Arabic literature and poetry (*cf.* **224**). We find it succinctly expressed in a verse by Muḥammad b. Ayyūb al-Iṣbahānī (*ṭawīl*):

رَأَيْتُكَ فِي النُّقْصَانِ مُذْ أَنْتَ فِي المَهْدِ * تُقَرِّبُكَ السَّاعَاتُ مِنْ سَاعَةِ اللَّحْدِ

"I saw you in decrease since you were in the cradle, * the hours bringing you closer and closer to the hour of (entering) the burial niche".[291]

The pair "cradle" / "burial niche", in Arabic *mahd* / *laḥd*, exhibit an assonance similar to the rhyming words *womb* / *tomb* often seen in English poetry, e.g. by Francis Bacon in his *The Life of Man* (1629): *The world's a bubble, and the life of man / Lesse then a span, / In his conception wretched, from the wombe, / So to the tombe*. *Cf.* also the note to epitaph **111**.

2. "Your palace was peopled ..." (verse 6). The opposition of life and death was often expressed by a wordplay on *qaṣr* and *qabr* ("palace" and "tomb"),[292] a good example is the following verse from a mourning poem, ascribed to Abū l-ʿAtāhiyah and others (*mutaqārib*):

لَقَدْ كُنْتُ أَغْدُو إِلَى قَصْرِهِ * فَقَدْ صِرْتُ أَغْدُو إِلَى قَبْرِهِ

"Once I used to come to his palace in the morning, * but now I have started to come to his tomb in the morning".[293]

In a sermon by Ibn al-Ǧawzī we read in much the same vein: "Where is the one who once was living in his palace (*fī qaṣrihī*) in luxury and now has descended into his tomb (*fī qabrihī qad nazal*)? / It were as if he never had inhabited the present world (*ad-dār*) and since stayed for ever in the burial niche (*fī l-laḥdi lam yazal*)!"[294] Similarly, the "wise fool" Buhlūl was invited to give counsel to Hārūn ar-Rāšid and had nothing to offer but "How shall I counsel you? There are their palaces (*quṣūruhum*), there are their tombs (*qubūruhum*)!",[295] or as Abū d-Dardāʾ put it: "Today in their homes, / tomorrow in their tombs" (*al-yawma fī d-dūr / wa-ġadan fī l-qubūr*).[296] In *The 1001 Nights*, death is called *muḫarribu l-quṣūr / wa-muʿammiru l-qubūr* ("the destroyer of palaces, / the peopler of tombs").[297]

291 Cited in IADunyāQaṣr p. 136; al-ʿAffānī: *Sakb* II pp. 412 and 462.

292 *Cf.* also Kennedy: *Wine Song* p. 121.

293 For the sources, see below pp. 572f. (Addendum).

294 IǦawzīTabṣ I p. 268.

295 ŠaʿrṬab I p. 68; Marzolph: *Buhlūl* p. 38 (no. 28). The same phrase is attributed to an unknown *maǧnūn* from Baṣrah in ĀbīNaṯr III p. 266. To this we might add that a consolation book by Abū ʿAbd Allāh Ibn ʿAskar, now lost, was fittingly called *Risālat iddiḫār aṣ-ṣabr wa-ftiḫār al-qaṣr wa-l-qabr*, "Epistle concerning the Supply of Composure and the Vainglories of the Palace and the Grave", see NubQuḍātAnd p. 159.

296 IRaǧLaṭāʾif p. 102; MunKawākib I p. 118.

297 ALL (B) II p. 695 (371st night). See also a verse by the Andalusian poet Abū Bakr al-Maġīlī

Usāmah b. Munqiḏ had the two following verses inscribed upon a marble slab when he saw the ruined palace of ʿAyn ad-Dawlah Ibn Abī ʿAqīl (the ruler of Sidon, d. 465 H) (*mağzūʾ al-kāmil*):

عَمَرُوا وَشَادُوا مَا تَرَا * هُ مِنَ المَنَازِلِ وَالقُصُورِ
وَتَحَوَّلُوا مِنْ بَعْدِ سُكْـ * ـنَاهَا إِلَى سُكْنَى القُبُورِ

من بعد سكانها : من بعد سكناها (AŠāmahRawḍ, does not fit the metre).

"They built and firmly constructed what is before your * eyes of dwellings and castles.
But after they had lodged in them they were * transferred to (their) lodging in the tombs".[298]

A preserved inscription (dated 617 H) on the wall of a madrasah in Sivas contains the passage: *laqad ʾaḫrağanā min saʿati l-quṣūr / ʾilā ḍīqati l-qubūr* (RCEA 3850), "He (i.e. God) has made us leave the spaciousness of the palaces / for the narrowness of the tombs".

The contrast between tomb (*qabr*) and palace (*qaṣr*) is thus threefold: (a) the juxtaposition of spaciousness and narrowness, (b) the juxtaposition of material luxury and poverty or nudity, and finally (c) the juxtaposition of being in company (in "peopled palaces") and being secluded in the tomb, as in a verse by Ibn al-Muʿtazz (*ḫafīf*):

سَاكِناً بَيْتَ وَحْدَةٍ قَدْ خَلَتْ مِنْـ * ـهُ قُصُورٌ مَأهُولَةٌ وَبُيُوتُ

"Someone who settled in a house of solitude, hence he left * peopled palaces and houses devoid of him".[299]

EXCURSUS

Apart from *qaṣr / qabr*, another thought-provoking wordplay of the same kind was possible with the root *ʿẓm*: *ʿiẓam (ʿuẓm)* and *ʿaẓamah*, "power, greatness", or also *ʿiẓām*, "the powerful, mighty" (pl.), as opposed to *ʿaẓm* (pl. *ʿiẓām*, *ʾaʿẓum*) and *ʿaẓmah*, "bone". This was exploited by an unknown poet as follows (*ramal*):

فَالعَظِيمُ القَدْرِ لَو شَاهَدْتَهُ * لَمْ تَجِدْ فِي قَبْرِهِ إلاَّ عِظَامَا

"If you look at someone (once) of great (*ʿaẓīm*) power * you do not find in his tomb but bones (*ʿiẓāman*)".[300]

(*mutaqārib*): *fa-hāḏī l-qubūru bihim ʿummirat * wa-tilka l-quṣūru ḫalat minhumū* (ḤumĞadwah p. 392).

298 IMunqiḏDīwān 481 v. 3-4 (p. 281); AŠāmahRawḍ I p. 127.

299 IMuʿtDīwān 1152 v. 12 (III p. 17). The latter part of the translation does not follow strictly the syntax of the original.

300 Quoted in TurkLumaʿ I p. 403.

Similarly in a line by Abū l-ᶜAtāhiyah, with a clear allusion to Q 17:49 and 98 (*ʾidā kunnā ʿiẓāman wa-rufātan*) (*ḫafīf*):

فَالسَّرَاةُ العِظَامُ مِنْهُمْ عِظَامٌ * فِي بُطُونِ الثَّرَى حُطَامٌ رُفَاتُ

"What is left of the mighty (*al-ʿiẓāmu*) chieftains are bones (*ʿiẓāmun*) * in the depths of the moist earth, (reduced to) rubble, mortal remains".[301]

Finally, Ibn al-Ḫaṭīb composed the following line shortly before his death during his imprisonment (*mutaqārib*):

وَكُنَّا عِظَاماً فَصِرْنَا عِظَاماً * وَكُنَّا نَقُوتُ فَهَا نَحْنُ قُوتْ

"Once we were mighty (*ʿiẓāman*), then we became (nothing but) bones (*ʿiẓāman*); * once we were nourished, but, look! now it is we who are nourishment (i.e. for the worms)".[302]

44

LOCATION. Cairo (southern Qarāfah cemetery). DATE. 359 H.
PERSON BURIED. Abū l-Ḥasan al-Ḫawlānī (M. b. M., 314–59 H).
SOURCES. MuwMuršid I p. 273 (version I); IZayKawākib p. 160 (version II).
DESCRIPTION. Located in the Ḫiṭṭat Banī Ḫawlān, near the Zahrūn-Mosque and the mausoleum of Abū Bakr al-Udfuwī. This epitaph is known from two citations which differ considerably; even the name of the buried person is at variance. Version I is reported by al-Muwaffaq from "an inscribed tombstone (viz. tablet: *lawḥ*)" which seems to have been affixed at some part of the mausoleum or tomb-mosque. Version II (in small print below) is cited by Ibn az-Zayyāt from Ibn al-Ǧabbās: "Ibn al-Ǧabbās[303] said, 'In that zone I saw a tomb bearing the inscription: [...]'".

Version I:

yaqūlu Muḥammadun ʾAbū l-Ḥasani bnu Muḥammadi bni ʿUṯmāna bni ʿImrāna bni Zakarīyāʾa l-Ḫawlānīyu ʾinnī ʿabdu llāhi muqirrun bi-waḥdānīyatih / muʿtarifun bi-rubūbīyatih ‖ *wa-ʾinnī ʾašhadu ʾan lā ʾilāha ʾillā llāhu – subḥānahū – wa-ʾanna Muḥammadan ʿabduhū wa-rasūluhū – taṣliyah – wa-ʾanna llāha taʿālā ḫalaqanī wa-ʾaḥyānī wa-yumītunī wa-yuḥyīnī wa-yuḥāsibunī llāhumma ġfir lī ḏunūbī wa-taǧāwaz ʿan sayyiʾātī wa-rḥam ḍuʿfī wa-ʿfu ʿannī wa-qinī ʿaḏāba*

301 AᶜAtāhDīwān p. 97; ḤurRawḍ p. 33 (anonymously cited).

302 Cited in IḪaldᶜIbar VII p. 342; MaqqNafḥ (C) VII p. 39; IQāḍīDurrah II p. 273. *Cf.* also the German rendering in Schack: *Poesie und Kunst* I p. 348: "Macht, wie sie Wen'gen ward, war einst die meine, doch nichts bleibt nun von mir, als die Gebeine; zu meiner Tafel lud ich einst die Gäste und diene jetzt für Andre selbst zum Feste".

303 See above n. 281.

n-nāri llāhumma ʾinnī mutawakkilun ʿalā ʾiḥsānika wa-faḍlika yā-malika d-dunyā wa-l-ʾāḫirati banaytu hāḏā l-qabra fī Šawwālin li-tisʿin wa-ḫamsīna wa-ṯalāṯimiʾatin wa-qad maḍā min ʿumrī ḫamsun wa-ʾarbaʿūna sanatan allāhumma wa-ʾanta ʾaʿlamu bi-ʿumrī fa-ǧʿal mā baqiya minhu fī ṭāʿatika wa-btiġāʾi marḍātika wa-ʾūṣīkum ʾiḫwānī ʾannī ʾiḏā mittu ʾan taǧʿalūnī fīhi wa-tuḥillūnī wa-tastaġfirū lī rabbī ʾinnahū kāna ġaffāran allāhumma wa-tub ʿalayya wa-tawaffanī musliman wa-ʾanta ʾarḥamu r-rāḥimīn

ʿabduhū wa-rasūluhū: *ʿabduhū wa-nabīyuhū wa-rasūluhū* (variant in one ms.); *ḫamsun wa-ʾarbaʿūna*: *ḫamsun wa-ʾarbaʿīna* (var. in ms.); *wa-tastaġfirū*: *wa-tastaġfirūna* (var. in ms.); *ġaffāran allāhumma*: om. *allāhumma* (var. in ms.).

"Muḥammad Abū l-Ḥasan b. Muḥammad b. ʿUṯmān b. ʿImrān b. Zakarīyāʾ al-Ḫawlānī says, I, the servant of God, affirm His oneness / and acknowledge His lordship. || Further, I confess that there is no god but God – praise to Him! – and that Muḥammad is His servant and His Messenger – *taṣliyah* –, (and) that God, the Exalted, did create me and call me into life, (then) He shall make me die, call me back to life (again, i.e. on the Last Day)[304] and hold me responsible (for my deeds). O my God, pardon my sins, pass over my evil deeds,[305] have mercy upon my frailty, forgive me and protect me against the Chastisement of the Fire![306] O my God, I entrust myself to Your beneficence and grace, O King of the present world and the hereafter! I built this tomb in Šawwāl 359, when 45 years of my life had already passed. O my God, You know best about my life (i.e. how long it will last), thus let me spend what remains of it in obedience towards You and striving for Your satisfaction. My brothers, I commend to you that, once I have died, you lay me to rest in it (i.e. the tomb), settle me (in it) and ask forgiveness from my Lord on my behalf, because He was (and always is) much-forgiving. O my God, make me receive Your grace and take me unto You as a Muslim,[307] for You are the most merciful of those who have mercy!"

Version II:

ʾAbū l-Ḥasani bnu ʿUmara bni ʿUṯmāna bni ʿUmara bni Zakarīyāʾa l-Ḫawlānīyu ʾašhadu ʾannī ʿabda llāhi muqirrun bi-waḥdānīyatihī wa-ʾannī ʾašhadu ʾan lā ʾilāha ʾillā llāhu wa-ʾanna Muḥammadan rasūlu llāhi – taṣliyah – wa-ʾanna llāha taʿālā ḫalaqa s-samāwāti wa-l-ʾarḍa wa-ḫalaqanī wa-yuḥyīnī wa-yumītunī wa-yuḥāsibunī llāhumma fa-ġfir lī ḏunūbī wa-taǧāwaz ʿan

304 *Cf.* Q 22:66: *wa-huwa llaḏī ʾaḥyākum ṯumma yumītukum ṯumma yuḥyīkum* ("It is He who gave you life, then He shall make you dead, then He shall give you life") and Q 30:40: *allāhu llaḏī ḫalaqakum ṯumma razaqakum ṯumma yumītukum ṯumma yuḥyīkum* ("God is He that created you, then He provided for you, then He shall make you dead, then He shall give you life"). *Cf.* also Welch: *Death in the Qurʾān* p. 184.

305 *Cf.* Q 46:16: *nataǧāwazu ʿan sayyiʾātihim* ("We shall pass over their evil deeds"). See also Volume I pp. 163ff.

306 *Cf.* Q 3:16: *fa-ġfir lanā ḏunūbanā wa-qinā ʿaḏāba n-nāri* ("forgive us our sins, and guard us against the Chastisement of the Fire").

307 *Cf.* Q 7:126: *wa-tawaffanā muslimīna* ("and gather us unto You surrendering", i.e. as Muslims); Q 12:101 has the expression in the singular.

sayyi'ātī wa-rḥam ḍuʿfī wa-ʿfu ʿannī wa-qinī ʿaḏāba n-nāri llāhumma 'innī mutawakkilun ʿalā faḍlika wa-'iḥsānika yā-malika d-dunyā wa-l-'āḫirati māta ṣāḥibu hāḏā l-qabri fī sanati tisʿin wa-ḫamsīna wa-ṯalāṯimi'ah

"Abū l-Ḥasan b. ʿUmar b. ʿUṯmān b. ʿUmar b. Zakarīyā' al-Ḫawlānī: I bear witness that I am the servant of God, affirming His oneness, further that I confess that there is no god but God and that Muḥammad is the Messenger of God – *taṣliyah* –, that God, the Exalted, did create the heavens and the earth, and that He did create me, He calls me into being, makes me die and holds me responsible (on Judgment Day). O my God, therefore pardon my sins, pass over my evil deeds, have mercy upon my frailty, forgive me and protect me against the Chastisement of Fire! O my God, I trust in Your grace and beneficence, O King of the present world and the hereafter! The occupant of this tomb died in the year 359".

45

LOCATION. Cairo (southern Qarāfah cemetery). DATE. 391 H or after.

PERSON BURIED. The Iḫšīdid vizier Abū l-Faḍl Ibn Ḥinzābah (Ǧaʿfar b. al-Faḍl ... b. al-Furāt, Baghdad 308 – Cairo 391 H): YāqIršād II pp. 405-12; IḪallWaf I pp. 346-50; BN XI p. 329; NZ IV p. 203; MaqrMuq III pp. 41-50; CIA Égypte II pp. 94-101; EI^2 III p. 768 (D. Sourdel); Leisten: *Architektur für Tote* pp. 213f.

SOURCE. IḪallWaf I pp. 349f. = CIA Égypte II p. 101.

DESCRIPTION. Though some reports say that Ibn Ḥinzābah was carried in a coffin to Medina and buried there (see above p. 232), Ibn Ḫallikān writes that "his mausoleum in the Lesser Qarāfah is a famous site"[308] and that "he himself visited this mausoleum in the Qarāfah and saw the inscription: [...] upon it".[309]

hāḏā turbatu 'Abī l-Faḍli Ǧaʿfara bni l-Furāt

"This is the mausoleum of Abū l-Faḍl Ǧaʿfar b. al-Furāt".

46

LOCATION. Cairo (southern Qarāfah cemetery). DATE. 444 H.

PERSON BURIED. Ibn Waǧīh (not identified).

SOURCE. IZayKawākib p. 114.

DESCRIPTION. A square tomb made of stone, located in a tomb-recinct (*ḥawš*) and bearing the inscription: [...].

aš-šayḫu l-maʿrūfu bi-bni Waǧīhini l-muḥaddiṯi ʿan rasūli llāhi – taṣliyah – tuwuffiya fī l-Muḥarrami sanata 'arbaʿin wa-'arbaʿīna wa-'arbaʿimi'ah

"The sheikh, known as Ibn Waǧīh, the transmitter from the Messenger of God – *taṣliyah*. – He was taken (to God) in Muḥarram of the year 444".

308 For the tomb, see also IZayKawākib p. 202 (= CIA Égypte II p. 101) who describes it as an old mausoleum consisting of several buildings (*wa-t-turbatu qadīmatun ḏātu l-'abniyah*).

309 The account in MaqrMuq, albeit also mentioning his transport to Medina, does largely support this version without, however, mentioning an epitaph.

47

LOCATION. Cairo (southern Qarāfah cemetery).
DATE. Unknown (Fatimid period, probably fourth or early fifth cent. H).
PERSON BURIED. Hilāl al-Anṣārī (not identified).
SOURCE. IZayKawākib p. 180.
DESCRIPTION. "He was mentioned by al-Qurašī,[310] saying that his tomb was in the Greater Qarāfah (cemetery). Upon his tomb is written: [...]". Ibn az-Zayyāt adds that by his time the tomb had fallen into ruins.

hāḏā qabru Hilāla l-ʾAnṣārīyi darasa fī l-ʿilmi wa-ʾadmana l-ʿilma ḫamsa ʿašrata sanatan

"This is the tomb of Hilāl al-Anṣārī. He was intensely occupied with seeking knowledge and remained devoted to (the study of) knowledge for 15 years".

48

LOCATION. Cairo (southern Qarāfah cemetery). DATE. 500 H.
PERSON BURIED. Anas an-Nāsiḫ ("the copyist", d. 500 H).
SOURCE. IZayKawākib p. 230.
DESCRIPTION. An inscribed column upon the grave (Ibn az-Zayyāt cites from an older cemetery guide).

hāḏā llaḏī ṭāla ʿumruhū fī ṭāʿati llāhi nasaḫa bi-yadihī miʾata ḫatmatin wa-ʾarbaʿīna wa-sittatan wa-ʿišrīna Muwaṭṭaʾan wa-māta yawma l-ḫamīsi l-ʿāširi min Ǧumādā l-ʾāḫirati sanata ḫamsimiʾatin wa-lahū mina l-ʿumri miʾatu sanatin

"He spent his long life obeying God (and) he copied with his own hand the complete Qurʾān 140 times and the *Muwaṭṭaʾ* 26 times.[311] He died on Thursday 10th Ǧumādā II of the year 500, at the age of 100".

310 This might refer either to Ibn al-Ǧabbās (both father and son, see above n. 281) or to another author of whom nothing further is known. In his cemetery guide, Ibn az-Zayyāt felt the need to explain to the reader to whom he is referring and writes on p. 103: "Everything which we transmit in this book (i.e. the *Kawākib*) from 'al-Qurašī' is meant to stem from Ibn al-Ǧabbās, because they are two 'al-Qurašīs', the said Ibn al-Ǧabbās and the other, namely the author (*ṣāḥib*) of the *Kitāb al-Mazārāt*". This information goes well with the fact that Ibn az-Zayyāt in his initial bibliography of *ziyārah*-authors (p. 4) lists "al-Qurašī" first as author (*ṣāḥib*) of *al-Mazārāt* and then mentions "Abū ʿAbdallāh al-Qurašī, known as Ibn al-Ǧabbās". That is, besides Ibn al-Ǧabbās there is another author called "al-Qurašī" whose work was entitled *Kitāb al-Mazārāt*, probably *Kitāb al-Mazārāt al-Miṣrīyah fī l-ḫiṭaṭ aṣ-ṣaḥābīyah* ("The Cairene Shrines in the Quarters of the [Prophet's] Companions"). The title *Kitāb al-Mazārāt* is never ascribed to "Ibn al-Ǧabbās" but only to "al-Qurašī", and thus we can be sure to be dealing with two different works viz. authors. There are good reasons to believe – on the basis of the content as known from citations – that the *Kitāb al-Mazārāt* was composed before 564 H (Rāġib: *Inventaire* pp. 261f., citing from IZayKawākib p. 174).

311 The principal compendium of the Malikite legal tradition, by Mālik b. Anas and his pupils.

49

LOCATION. Cairo (southern Qarāfah cemetery). DATE. 501 H.
PERSON BURIED. al-Wāʿiẓ al-Wāsiṭī (M. b. al-Ḥusayn, d. 501 H): MuwMuršid I p. 337.
SOURCE. IZayKawākib p. 118.
DESCRIPTION. An inscribed column (*ʿamūdun maktūbun ʿalayhi*) upon the tomb.

Muḥammadu bnu l-Ḥusayni l-wāʿiẓu l-Wāsiṭīyu māta sanata ʾiḥdā wa-ḫamsimiʾah

"Muḥammad b. al-Ḥusayn al-Wāsiṭī, the sermoniser.[312] He died in the year 501".

50

LOCATION. Cairo (southern Qarāfah cemetery). DATE. 554 H.
PERSON BURIED. ʿAbd al-Ǧabbār b. Muḥammad an-Naḥḥās (d. 554 H).
SOURCE. IZayKawākib p. 123.
DESCRIPTION. "A column near the prayer-niche in the *qiblah*-wall, bearing the inscription: [...]", in the mausoleum of as-Sayyid aš-Šarīf al-Ḫaššāb (Abū ʿAbd Allāh b. al-Ḥusayn al-ʿAlawī).

hāḏā qabru š-šayḫi ʿAbdi l-Ǧabbāri bni Muḥammadini l-maʿrūfi bi-n-Naḥḥāsi tuwuffiya sanata ʾarbaʿin wa-ḫamsīna wa-ḫamsimiʾah

"This is the tomb of the sheikh ʿAbd al-Ǧabbār b. Muḥammad, known as 'an-Naḥḥās'. He was taken (to God) in the year 554".

51

LOCATION. Cairo (southern Qarāfah cemetery). DATE. 586 H.
PERSON BURIED. The judge Ṣafīy ad-Dīn Ibn al-Furāt (Abū M. ʿAbd al-Wahhāb b. Abī ṭ-Ṭāhir Ismāʿīl b. Muẓaffar, d. Rabīʿ II 586 H).
SOURCE. IZayKawākib p. 246 = RCEA 3442.
DESCRIPTION. "I saw that upon the tomb was written: [...]".

hāḏā qabru l-qāḍī l-ʾamīni Ṣafīyi d-Dīni ʾAbī Muḥammadin ʿAbdi l-Wahhābi bni ʾAbī ṭ-Ṭāhiri ʾIsmāʿīla bni Muẓaffari bni l-Furāti wafātuhū mašhūratun fī šahri Rabīʿi l-ʾāḫiri sanata sittin wa-ṯamānīna wa-ḫamsimiʾah

"This is the tomb of the trustworthy judge Ṣafīy ad-Dīn Abū Muḥammad ʿAbd al-Wahhāb b. Abī ṭ-Ṭāhir Ismāʿīl b. Muẓaffar b. al-Furāt. His being taken (to God) is commonly said (= is widely known) to have occurred in the month of Rabīʿ II in the year 586 ".

312 *al-wāʿiẓ*, "sermoniser", contrasted with *al-ḫaṭīb*, "preacher".

52

LOCATION. Cairo (southern Qarāfah cemetery). DATE. Unknown.
PERSON BURIED. Maǧd ad-Dīn ᶜAbd al-Muḥsin aš-Šāfiᶜī (not identified).
SOURCE. IZayKawākib p. 258.
DESCRIPTION. "If you proceed towards the cemetery of Ibn ᶜAbd al-Ġanīy, you will find to your right a column (*ʿamūd*) that bears the inscription: [...]".

al-faqīhu l-ʾimāmu Maǧdu d-Dīni ʿAbdu l-Muḥsini bnu l-faqīhi ʾAbī ʿAbdi llāhi Muḥammadi bni Yaḥyā bni ḫāli š-Šāfiʿīyi l-mudarrisi bi-madrasati (!) *l-Fāṭimīyati*

"The jurist, the Imam Maǧd ad-Dīn ᶜAbd al-Muḥsin, son of the jurist Abū ᶜAbd Allāh Muḥammad b. Yaḥyā, son of the (maternal) uncle of aš-Šāfiᶜī, lecturer in the Fatimid madrasah".

53

LOCATION. Cairo (southern Qarāfah cemetery). DATE. 603 H.
PERSON BURIED. Abū Isḥāq Ibrāhīm b. Naṣr al-Kātib (d. 603 H).
SOURCE. IZayKawākib p. 123 = RCEA 3621.
DESCRIPTION. "A column (*ʿamūd*) upon which is written: [...]". This column was beside the tomb of ᶜAbd al-Ǧabbār b. Muḥammad an-Naḥḥās (see above **50**).

hāḏā qabru š-šayḫi ʾAbī ʾIsḥāqa ʾIbrāhīma bni Naṣrini l-kātibi tuwuffiya sanata ṯalāṯin wa-sittimiʾah

"This is the tomb of the sheikh Abū Isḥāq Ibrāhīm b. Naṣr, the scribe. He was taken (to God) in the year 603".

54

LOCATION. Cairo (southern Qarāfah cemetery). DATE. 603 H.
PERSON BURIED. Tāǧ ad-Dīn al-Balīnāʾī (d. 603 H).
SOURCES. IZayKawākib p. 97; SaḫTuḥfAḥbāb pp. 214f.
DESCRIPTION. "Then turn towards the west to the tomb-recinct (*ḥawš*) of al-Fāsī, the warden (in the mosque of) the Prophet's relics (*al-ʾāṯār an-nabawīyah*). In this recinct there is a column (*ʿamūd*) bearing the inscription: [...]".

Tāǧu d-Dīni l-Balīnāʾiyu[313] *ḫādimu l-ʾāṯāri n-nabawīyati tuwuffiya sābiʿa Šaʿbānin sanata ṯalāṯin wa-sittimiʾah*

"Tāǧ ad-Dīn al-Balīnāʾī, warden at (the mosque of?) the Prophet's relics. He was taken (to God) on 7th Šaᶜbān in the year 603".

NOTE. The famous site in Cairo known in Mamluk times as *al-ʾāṯār an-nabawīyah*, an ascetic lodge together with a madrasah and a mosque, was not founded until the beginning of the eighth century H

313 البليناى as corrected from the ms.: البكناى (IZayKawākib); البليناي (SaḫTuḥfAḥbāb).

near the Nile to the south of Old Cairo. The relics of the Prophet had been bought shortly before from a family in Yanbuᶜ, and they remained in the newly founded complex until they were transferred in 909 H to the mausoleum of Sultan al-Ġawrī.[314] Hence either there was a place called *al-ʾĀṯār an-Nabawīyah* before the end of the seventh century H, or the date as given in the inscription is wrong.

55

LOCATION. Cairo (southern Qarāfah). DATE. 649 / 650 H.

PERSON BURIED. The state official and poet Ǧamāl ad-Dīn Ibn Maṭrūḥ (Abū l-Ḥasan [Ḥusayn] Ya. b. ᶜĪsā, Asyūṭ 592 – Cairo 649 or 650 H): AŠāmahTar p. 187; IḪallWaf VI pp. 258-66; NZ VII pp. 27-9; SuyḤusnMuḥ I p. 412; ŠḎ V pp. 247-9; ZA VIII p. 162; EI² III pp. 875f. (J. Rikabi).

SOURCES. IḪallWaf VI p. 266 / (Slane) IV p. 150; NuwIlmām IV p. 206; ŠḎ V p. 249.

DESCRIPTION. "He stipulated in his last will that at the head (of his tomb) the following *dūbayt* (quatrain), which he composed during his (last) illness, be written: [...]" (IḪallWaf and ŠḎ); "Somebody saw upon a tombstone engraved: [...]" (NuwIlmām).

*ʾaṣbaḥtu bi-qaᶜri ḥufratin murtahanā * lā ʾamliku min dunyāya ʾillā kafanā*
*yā-man wasiᶜat ᶜibādahū raḥmatuhū * min baᶜḍi ᶜibādika l-musīʾīna ʾanā*

1 حفرة: حفرتي (ŠḎ). – **2** المسيئين : المسيكين (!, ŠḎ).

"In the abyss of a pit (i.e. the tomb) I was deposited as a pledge, * and from my (former) world I (now) possess only a shroud.
O You whose mercy suffices for (all) His servants: * one of Your servants, who did wrong, am I".

NOTE. The expression "I was deposited in the abyss of a pit" seems close to a line by Abū Nuwās, who says in one of his mourning poems: *wa-ʾannaka ġāʾibun fī qaᶜri laḥdin* ("that you have disappeared in the abyss of a burial niche"),[315] but the expression "abyss of the tomb" (*qaᶜru l-qabri* or the like) is rather common in mourning poetry.[316]

56

LOCATION. Cairo (southern Qarāfah cemetery). DATE. 655 H.

PERSON BURIED. Abū Ḥaydarah Sayyid al-Kull, Ibn ᶜAṭūš (ᶜAl., d. 655 H).

SOURCE. IZayKawākib p. 257.

DESCRIPTION. An inscribed column upon a tomb, bearing the inscription: [...].

314 See MaqrḪiṭaṭ II p. 429; SuyḤusnMuḥ II p. 235; IlyāsBad I p. 385.

315 ANuwDīwān I p. 308.

316 E.g. IᶜARabᶜIqd (Ǧ) II pp. 168 and 180 / (M) III pp. 258 and 280 = ŠayMaǧānī IV p. 41.

al-faqīhu ʾAbū Ḥaydarata Sayyidu l-Kulli ʿAbdu llāhi l-wāʿiẓu n-nāsiḫu l-maʿrūfu bi-bni ʿAṭūšin māta sanata ḫamsin wa-ḫamsīna wa-sittimiʾah

"The jurist Abū Ḥaydarah Sayyid al-Kull ᶜAbd Allāh, the sermoniser and copyist, known as 'Ibn ᶜAṭūš'. He died in the year 655".

57

LOCATION. Cairo (southern Qarāfah cemetery). DATE. 659 H.
PERSON BURIED. Yūsuf b. Ibrāhīm b. ᶜAbd Allāh aš-Šarīf al-Ḥusaynī (d. 659 H).
SOURCE. IZayKawākib p. 107.
DESCRIPTION. Inscription on a wooden panel (*ṭirāz al-ḫašab*) upon the tomb.[317]

hāḏā qabru s-sayyidi š-šarīfi Yūsufa bni ʾIbrāhīma bni ʿAbdi llāhi l-Ḥusaynīyi tuwuffiya sanata tisʿin wa-ḫamsīna wa-sittimiʾah

"This is the tomb of the noble sayyid Yūsuf b. Ibrāhīm b. ᶜAbd Allāh al-Ḥusaynī. He was taken (to God) in the year 659".

58

LOCATION. Cairo (southern Qarāfah cemetery). DATE. 695 H.
PERSON BURIED. Šaraf ad-Dīn Ibn Abī l-Ḥusayn (M. b. ᶜAlī, d. 695 H).
SOURCE. IZayKawākib p. 123.
DESCRIPTION. On the cemetery of the clan (*ʾawlād*) of Ibn Bint Abī Saᶜd al-Anṣārī, "there is a marble slab (*ruḫāmah*) bearing the inscription: [...]".

hāḏā qabru š-šayḫi l-ʾimāmi l-ʿālimi l-ʾawḥadi ʾafqahi l-fuqahāʾ / wa-ʾaǧalli l-ʿulamāʾ || Šarafi d-Dīni ʾAbī ʿAbdi llāhi Muḥammadi bni ʾAbī l-Ḥusayni ʿAlīyin tuwuffiya fī šahri llāhi l-Muḥarrami sanata ḫamsin wa-tisʿīna wa-sittimiʾah

"This is the tomb of the sheikh, the learned, the unique Imam, the most accomplished of jurists / and most eminent of scholars: || Šaraf ad-Dīn Abū ᶜAbd Allāh Muḥammad b. Abī l-Ḥusayn ᶜAlī. He was taken (to God) in the month of God Muḥarram, in the year 695".

59

LOCATION. Cairo (southern Qarāfah cemetery).
DATE. Unknown (seventh cent. H?).
PERSON BURIED. The jurist ᶜAbd Allāh b. Yūsuf (b. ᶜAlī b. ᶜAr., not identified).

317 As Ibn az-Zayyāt says some lines previously, the whole tomb (viz. cenotaph) was made of wood.

SOURCE. IZayKawākib p. 268.
DESCRIPTION. "Upon his tomb is written: [...]".

hāḏā qabru man ǧamaʿa llāhu lahū bayna l-ʿilmi wa-l-ʿamal / wa-kafāhu l-ḫaṭaʾa wa-l-ḫaṭal || fa-qadima ʿalā llāhi qudūma man waḥḥadah / baʿda ʾan salaka ṭarīqa man ʿabadah / wa-qtafā sabīla man maǧǧadah || tarabbā ʿalā t-taqwā wa-d-dīni mina ṣ-ṣiġari ʾilā ġāyah / wa-zahada ʾilā ʾan ṣāra mina l-waraʿi fī nihāyah || māta wa-huwa yašhadu ʾan lā ʾilāha ʾillā llāhu wa-ʾanna Muḥammadan rasūlu llāh

"This is the tomb of one in whom God has joined learning and doing (*or* knowledge and action),[318] / whom He did protect from error and idle talk; || he presented himself to God as one who declares Him to be One (i.e. who professes the *tawḥīd*), / after pursuing the way of those who worship Him / and following the path of those who extol Him. || He (i.e. the deceased) was brought up in godliness and creed from his youth until (he reached) perfection, / and he led an ascetic life until he possessed piety to the utmost degree. || He died confessing that there is no god but God and that Muḥammad is the Messenger of God".

60

LOCATION. Cairo (southern Qarāfah cemetery). DATE. Unknown.
PERSON BURIED. Abū ʿAbd Allāh al-Hāšimī al-Ḥanbalī (M. b. al-Ḥusayn).
SOURCE. IZayKawākib p. 231.
DESCRIPTION. The inscription upon his grave. Ibn az-Zayyāt, who cites the epitaph from al-Qurašī, adds that the tomb was no longer known in his own time.

hāḏā llaḏī ʾufniya ʿumruhū fī ṭāʿati llāh

"This is someone whose life was consumed with the obedience of God".

61

LOCATION. Cairo (southern Qarāfah cemetery).
DATE. Unknown (seventh cent. H?).
PERSON BURIED. Abū Muḥammad ʿAbd Allāh aš-Šāfiʿī al-Anṣārī (not identified).
SOURCE. IZayKawākib p. 197.
DESCRIPTION. "Near the mausoleum of the Ṣayrafī clan (*turbat ʾawlād aṣ-Ṣayrafī*) there is a tomb enclosure with a column bearing the inscription: [...]".

hāḏā qabru š-šayḫi l-faqīhi l-ʾimāmi l-ʿālimi l-ʿallāmati muftī l-muslimīn / šayḫi l-muḥaqqiqīn || ʾAbī Muḥammadin ʿAbdi llāhi š-Šāfiʿīyi l-ʾAnṣārīyi

318 العلم و العمل, viz. the seminal concept that pure knowledge is worthless unless it is put into practice; *cf.* Rosenthal: *Knowledge Triumphant* pp. 246-51.

"This is the tomb of the sheikh, the jurist, the learned Imam, the most erudite, mufti of the Muslims / and sheikh of the experts: || Abū Muḥammad ᶜAbd Allāh aš-Šāfiᶜī al-Anṣārī".

62

LOCATIONS. (a) Cairo (southern Qarāfah cemetery). – (b) al-Manīḥah (a village outside Damascus).

DATES. (a) Unknown. – (b) First century H (but almost certainly later).

PERSONS BURIED. (a) ᶜImrān b. Dāʾūd b. ᶜAlī al-Ġāfiqī (not identified). – (b) Saᶜd b. ᶜUbādah al-Ḫazraǧī, a companion of the Prophet (d. 15 or 16 H): ISaᶜdṬab III pp. 613-7; TMD XX pp. 237-70; IḤaǧIṣābah II p. 30; ZA III p. 85.

SOURCES. (a) IZayKawākib p. 251.[319] – (b) IǦubRiḥlah (B) p. 253 / (W) p. 282 (version II); IBaṭṭRiḥlah p. 117 (version II); MuwMuršid I p. 70 (version I).

DESCRIPTION. (a) "Upon his tomb two lines (*saṭrayn*) were written with ink (*midād*) at the base of the column". – (b) (Version I:) "In al-Manīḥah near Damascus, I saw written upon the grave (*ḍarīḥ*) of Saᶜd b. ᶜUbādah – may God the Exalted be pleased with him: [...]". (Version II:) A little mosque was erected around the tomb of Saᶜd in al-Manīḥah and "at the head (of his tomb) was the following inscription: [...]" (IǦubRiḥlah, IBaṭṭRiḥlah). Ibn Šaddād in his town history mentions the tomb of Saᶜd at al-Manīḥah, but adds that Saᶜd actually died at Medina.[320]

(a) Two verses in the metre *ṭawīl*:

*wa-lammā ʾataynā qabrahū li-nazūrahū * ᶜarafnāhu lammā fāḥa ṭību turābihī*
*saqā llāhu min māʾi l-ǧināni turābahū * wa-naǧǧā bihī man zārahū min ᶜiqābihī*

"After we had come to his tomb in order to visit it, * we recognised it when the pleasant fragrance of its earth emanated (from it).[321]
May God irrigate its earth with the water of Paradise * and save by it those, who visit it (*sc*. ᶜImrān's tomb), from His punishment!"

(b) Version I (*ṭawīl*):

*wa-lammā ʾataynā qabra Saᶜdin nazūruhū * ᶜarafnāhu lammā fāḥa ṭību turābihī*
*saqā llāhu min māʾi l-ǧināni turābahū * wa-naǧǧā bihī man zārahū min ᶜaḏābihī*

"After we had come to Saᶜd's tomb to visit it, * we recognised it when the pleasant fragrance of its earth emanated (from it).
May God irrigate its earth with the water of Paradise * and save by it those who visit it (*sc*. Saᶜd's tomb) from the Chastisement He inflicts!"

319 The deceased, if not the epitaph, was already mentioned by al-Qurašī.

320 IŠadAᶜlāq II (Damascus) p. 182.

321 *Cf.* above p. 90.

Version II:

hāḏā qabru Saʿdi bni ʿUbādata raʾsi l-Ḫazraǧi ṣāḥibi rasūli llāh

"This is the tomb of Saᶜd b. ᶜUbādah, the chief of the Ḫazraǧ, the companion of the Messenger of God".[322]

NOTES.

1. The first line of the distich has a parallel in an inscription at the wall of the mausoleum of Abū Yaḥyā al-Kawākibī in Aleppo (*ṭawīl*):

هُدِينَا إِلَى هَذَا المَقَامِ بِطِيبِهِ * كَمَا يَهْتَدِي الهَادِي بِنُورِ الكَوَاكِبِ

"We were rightly guided to this shrine by its fragrance, * quite like the guide who is led (the right way) by the light of the stars".[323]

The second line of the distich, on the other hand, is similar to a verse from a poem praising the merits of visiting the Qarāfah cemetery. In the introduction to his cemetery guide, al-Muwaffaq Ibn ᶜUṯmān cites the line in the following form (*ṭawīl*):

سَقَى اللَّهُ مِنْ مَاءِ الجِنَانِ تُرَابَهَا * وَنَجَّى بِهَا مَنْ جَاءَ قَصْداً يَزُورُهَا

"May God irrigate its earth with the water of Paradise * and save by it (i.e. its earth)[324] those, who come intending to visit it, (from His punishment)"![325]

2. That epitaph (b) (version I) is considerably later than the date of Saᶜd's death seems clear from its very wording and content. Most likely, a conventional poem that could be applied in a number of contexts – as with epitaph (a) and the verse extolling the merits of the Qarāfah – was here adapted to a burial place by inserting Saᶜd's name in the first verse. However, the shorter, traditional inscription *hāḏā qabru* ... (epitaph b, version II) might well go back to the early Islamic centuries.

63

LOCATION. Cairo (southern Qarāfah cemetery). DATE. 710 H.

PERSON BURIED. The Shafiite jurist Naǧm ad-Dīn Ibn ar-Rafᶜah (Abū l-ᶜAbbās A. b. M. b. ᶜAlī, Cairo 645–710 H), author of voluminous legal works: SubkīṬab IX pp. 24-7; DK I pp. 303-6; IsnṬab I pp. 601f.; ITaġrManh II pp. 82f. and NZ IX p. 213; ŠḎ VI pp. 22f.; ŠawkBadr I pp. 115-7; GAL II p. 133 and GALS II p. 164; ZA I p. 222.

Ibn ar-Rafᶜah was claimed by many contemporaries to be the worthy Shafiite peer of Ibn Taymīyah (a claim rejected as ridiculous by the Hanbalites). However, besides being market

322 Ibn Baṭṭūṭah with the addition: *taslīman*.

323 al-Ġazzī: *Nahr aḏ-ḏahab* II p. 40.

324 Implied reference of *bihā* is *turbah*.

325 MuwMuršid I p. 13.

inspector of Cairo and deputy judge he never reached important academic positions: "Ibn ᶜAmmār (...) said: 'For all his greatness, Ibn ar-Rafᶜah did not even become a tutor, let alone a professor. Ignorant persons become professors through money or by mixing with contemptible office seekers'" (Rosenthal's translation).[326]

SOURCE. IZayKawākib p. 265.
DESCRIPTION. "A single verse is written upon his tomb: [...]" (*basīṭ*):

*yā-qāhiran bi-l-manāyā kulla ǧabbārī * bi-nūri waǧhika ʾaᶜtiqnī mina n-nārī*

"O You who will overcome by the fate of death every Sire:[327] * by the light of your Face[328] set me free from the Fire!"

64

LOCATION. Cairo (southern Qarāfah cemetery). DATE. 771 H.
PERSON BURIED. Bahāʾ ad-Dīn al-Qurašī (M. b. ᶜAbd al-Ḥamīd, d. 771 H).
SOURCE. IZayKawākib pp. 91f. = RCEA 771 004 = Volume I p. 45.
DESCRIPTION. A tomb on the path leading to the cemetery of the Qurayšites, having a "column (*ᶜamūd*) (...) upon which is written: [...]".

hāḏā qabru l-faqīhi l-ʾimāmi l-muḥaddiṯi Bahāʾi d-Dīnī ʾAbī ᶜAbdi llāhi Muḥammadi bni ᶜAbdi l-Ḥamīdi bni ᶜAbdi r-Raḥmāni l-Qurašīyi kāna – raḍiya llāhu ᶜanhu – mudarrisan bi-n-Nāṣirīyati wa-tuwuffiya sanata ʾiḥdā wa-sabᶜīna wa-sabᶜimiʾah

"This is the tomb of the jurist, the Imam, the traditionist Bahāʾ ad-Dīn Abū ᶜAbd Allāh Muḥammad b. ᶜAbd al-Ḥamīd b. ᶜAbd ar-Raḥmān al-Qurašī. He was – may God be pleased with him! – lecturer in the Nāṣirīyah (college) and was taken (to God) in the year 771".

65

LOCATION. Cairo (Kōm ar-Rīš, to the north of the town). DATE. 776 H.
PERSON BURIED. The Hanafite chief-judge Ṣadr ad-Dīn Ibn at-Turkumānī (Abū ᶜAl. M. b. al-Ǧamāl ᶜAl. al-Māridīnī, *c.*743–76 H): IᶜIrāqīḎᶜIbar II pp. 383-5; MaqrSulūk III p. 246; DK IV pp. 96f., IḤaǧInbāʾ I p. 135 and IḤaǧRafᶜ p. 374; IQŠuhbTārīḫ III p. 468; NZ XI p. 130; SaḫWaǧīz I p. 208.
SOURCES. MaqrSulūk III p. 246; IḤaǧRafᶜ p. 374.
DESCRIPTION. "He decreed in his last will that on his tomb be written from his own

326 SaḫIᶜlān p. 34 = Rosenthal: *Historiography* p. 315.

327 Lit. "tyrant".

328 *Cf.* Q 55:26f. *kulla man ᶜalayhā fānin * wa-yabqā waǧhu rabbika ḏū l-ǧalāli wa-l-ʾikrām* ("All that dwells upon the earth is perishing, * yet still abides the Face of thy Lord, majestic, splendid") and Q 28:88: *kullu šayʾin hālikun ʾillā waǧhahū* ("All things perish, except his Face").

poetry: [...]" (MaqrSulūk); "When he was near his death, he decreed that on his tomb be written: [...]" (IḤağRafᶜ). – Two verses in the metre *basīṭ*:

*ʾinna l-faqīra llaḏī ʾaḍḥā bi-ḥufratihī * nazīlu rabbin kaṯīri l-ᶜafwi sattārī*
*yūṣīka bi-l-ʾahli wa-l-ʾawlādi taḥfaẓuhum * fa-hum ᶜiyālun ᶜalā maᶜrūfika s-sārī*

1 *ʾaḍḥā*: *ʾamsā* (IḤağRafᶜ).

"The poor one who was transferred into his (burial) hole * settles with a Lord whose mercy is great, a Veiler.[329]
He bequeathes to you (*or* recommends to you) to guard the family and the children, * because they depend on your continuing beneficence".

66

LOCATION. Cairo. DATE. 794 H.
PERSON BURIED. The poet and *munšiʾ* ᶜAlāʾ ad-Dīn ᶜAlī b. ᶜAbd Allāh al-Bīrī al-Ḥalabī (born in Aleppo in 743 H; he was strangled on the order of Barqūq in Rabīᶜ I 794 H): MaqrSulūk III p. 778; DK III pp. 147f. and IḤağInbāʾ III p. 134; IFurTārīḫ IX p. 324; NZ XII pp. 132f.; SaḫWağīz I p. 303; ZA IV p. 306.
SOURCES. IḤağInbāʾ III p. 134; ᶜĀmBahğNāẓ p. 195; SaḫWağīz I p. 303.
DESCRIPTION. He stipulated in his last will that upon his tomb be written: [...] (IḤağInbāʾ, SaḫWağīz); al-ᶜĀmirī al-Ġazzī presents these lines simply as poetry whose author he does not identify. – Two verses in the metre *wāfir*:

bi-qāriᶜati ṭ-ṭarīqi[330] *ğaᶜaltu qabrī * li-ʾaḥẓā bi-t-taraḥḥumi min ṣadīqi*
*fa-yā-mawlā l-mawālī ʾanta ʾawlā * bi-raḥmati man yamūtu ᶜalā ṭ-ṭarīqi*

1 IḤağInbāʾ and SaḫWağīz have من صديقِ, while ᶜĀmBahğNāẓ has من صديقي. The first variant seems preferable.

"On the wayside I made my tomb * in order to obtain prayers for mercy (upon me) from a friend (who passes by).
O Patron of the patrons: You are the most likely * to grant mercy to someone who died while he was on the (good) way!"[331]

67

LOCATION. Cairo (southern Qarāfah cemetery).
DATE. Unknown (before the ninth cent. H, probably much earlier).
PERSON BURIED. aš-Šarīf Ğaᶜfar (not identified).

329 الستّار, one of the 99 names of God.

330 For this expression, *cf.* Wellhausen: *Reste* p. 179 with note 3. *Cf.* also **72** and **175**.

331 There is a play on the word *ṭarīq*: the term signifies a real "way" or "path" in the first verse, while it refers to the "right path (of belief)" (e.g. *aṭ-ṭarīq al-mustaqīm*) in the second line.

SOURCE. IZayKawākib p. 97.
DESCRIPTION. Near the mašhad of as-Sayyidah Kulṯūm, there is "a great tomb of tuff stone (*kaddān*), bearing a marble column with the inscription: [...]".

aš-šarīfu Ǧaʿfaruni l-muʿtarifu bi-ḏanbihī

"aš-Šarīf[332] Ǧaʿfar who confesses his sin(s)".

68

LOCATION. Cairo (southern Qarāfah, to the north of the mausoleum of Ibn al-Fāriḍ).
DATE and PERSON BURIED. Unknown.
SOURCE. IZayKawākib p. 297.
DESCRIPTION. "In that cemetery (i.e. the *maqburat mašāyiḫ al-Ḥanafīyah*) there is a tomb upon which is written: [...]". – Three verses in the metre *mutaqārib*:

*ʾiḏā fāta mā kuntu ʾammaltuhū * ǧaziʿtu wa-māḏā yufīdu l-ǧazaʿ*
*fa-fawwaḍtu li-llāhi kulla l-ʾumūri * fa-laysa yakūnu siwā mā yaqaʿ*
*wa-lā yaḫdaʿannaka ṣarfu z-zamāni * fa-ʾinna z-zamāna kaṯīru l-ḫudaʿ*

"When what I had been hoping for had vanished * I became anxious, but what use is anxiety?
I committed all affairs to God[333] * since nothing comes into being except what simply occurs (according to His will).
Do not let the turns of time (i.e. fortune) deceive you, * for truly time is much-deceiving!"

69

LOCATION. Cairo (southern Qarāfah cemetery). DATE. 910 H.
PERSON BURIED. Ibn al-Ūǧāqī (Taqīy ad-Dīn Abū l-Faḍl ʿAbd ar-Raḥīm b. al-Muḥibb M. b. M. al-Qāhirī aš-Šāfiʿī, Cairo 825–910 H): ḌL IV pp. 188f.; ĠazKawākib I pp. 234-6; ŠḎ VIII pp. 45f.
SOURCES. ḌL IV p. 189; IŠamQabas I p. 388; ĠazKawākib I p. 236; ŠḎ VIII p. 46.
DESCRIPTION. Ibn al-Ūǧāqī wrote two verses to as-Saḫāwī in order to have them inscribed upon his tomb (ḌL); during his lifetime, Ibn al-Ūǧāqī had already built a mausoleum for himself in the vicinity of aš-Šāfiʿī's tomb (IŠamQabas). The other sources simply have "He composed fine poetry (*šiʿr laṭīf*), like the following: [...]" (ĠazKawākib), or "He composed the following poem: [...]" (ŠḎ). – Two verses in the metre *muǧtaṯṯ*:

*taqūlu nafsī ʾa-taḫšā * min hawli ḏanbin ʿaẓīmī*
*lā taḫtašī min ʿiqābin * fa-ʾanta ʿabdu r-raḥīmī*

332 I.e. "the noble", viz. a descendant from the Prophet.

333 *Cf.* Q 40:44: *wa-ʾufawwiḍu ʾamrī ʾilā llāh* ("I commit my affair to God").

2 *fa-ʾanta*: *wa-ʾanta* (ĠazKawākib).

"My soul says, 'Are you afraid * of the terror of (your) great sin(s)?
(But) be not afraid of punishment, * *for you are the servant of the Compassionate / for you are called ʿAbd ar-Raḥīm*!'"[334]

70

LOCATION. Cairo (southern Qarāfah cemetery). DATE. 947 H.

PERSON BURIED. Šams ad-Dīn at-Tūnisī al-Mālikī, Maġūš (Abū ʿAl. M. b. M. al-Maġūšī, d. Cairo 947 H): ĠazKawākib II pp. 15-9; IḤanbDurr II pp. 212-17; ŠD̲ VIII pp. 270f.; IADīnārMuʾnis p. 163; ŠN 273; ZA VII p. 57.

SOURCES. ĠazKawākib II p. 17; ŠD̲ VIII p. 271.

DESCRIPTION. "Our teacher (...) al-Muḥibb al-Ḥanafī (...) told me that he read on his tomb the following text: [...]" (ĠazKawākib); "He was buried in the vicinity of Imam aš-Šāfiʿī – may God be pleased with him! – and upon his tomb was put the inscription: [...]" (ŠD̲). – Two verses in the metre *wāfir*:

*ʾa-lā yā-Mālika l-ʿulamāʾi yā-man * bihī fī l-ʾarḍi ʾat̲mara kullu maġris*
*la-ʾin ʾawḥašta Tūnisa baʿda buʿdin * fa-ʾanta bi-Miṣra mulka l-ḥusni tuʾnis*

1 ألا يا مــالك: أيا ملك (ĠazKawākib, does not fit the metre). – **2** بمصر: لمصر (ĠazKawākib).

"Verily, O Mālik among the scholars, O you * by whose work on earth every plantation became fertile:
Even though you made Tunis become a desert after (your) absence[335] (from it), * you delight (now by your presence) in Egypt the dominion of goodness (?)".[336]

NOTES.

1. Compare with the wording of this epitaph two obviously related verses by the poet Muḥammad al-Fāriḍī (d. after 980 H), mourning the death of Maġūš (*wāfir*):

تَقَضَّى التُّونِسِيُّ فقُلْتُ بَيْتاً * يُرَوِّحُ كُلَّ ذِي شَجَنٍ ويُؤْنِسْ
أَتُوحِشُنَا وتُؤنِسُ بَطْنَ لحْدٍ * وَلَكِنْ مِثْلَ مَا أَوْحَشْتَ تُونِسْ

1 *taqaḍḍā*: *tuwuffiya* (ḪafRayḥ); *baytan*: *baynan* (?, ĠazKawākib II p. 17); *yurawwiḥu*: *yuʾarriqu* (ḪafRayḥ); شجن: شخص (ĠazKawākib III p. 77). – **2** *laḥdin*: *ʾarḍin* (ḪafRayḥ).

334 The second hemistich contains a wordplay (*tawriyah*) and might thus be understood in either way (the alternative renderings are in italics).

335 Or "remoteness".

336 For the understanding of these verses it is helpful to know that Maġūš was an influential scholar and state official under the Ḥafṣid ruler Abū ʿAbd Allāh al-Ḥasan b. Muḥammad V (r. 932–41 H), but was then exiled from Tunis after it had been sacked by the corsar Ḫayr ad-Dīn ("Barbarossa") in 941 H (*cf.* MaqdīšNuzhah I pp. 607-10; Abu n-Nasr: *History of the Maghrib* p. 151). He first went to Istanbul, later to Cairo, where he died.

"at-Tūnisī has passed away, so I said a line * which revives and delights (the spirit) of everybody filled with sorrow:
'Do you grieve us with your absence[337] while you keep the company of the belly of a burial niche? * Well, but in the like manner you did grieve Tunis (before that)!'"[338]

These verses as well as the above-cited epitaph play upon the Arabic root *ʾns*, especially as the verb *ʾns* IV yields forms almost equal to the name of the town of Tunis, viz. *Tūnis*/*tuʾnis(u)*, and *tuʾnis(u)* might be written (and pronounced) *tūnis(u)*.

2. Both poems – not without reference to the vicissitudes in the life of Maġūš – contain the binary opposition of *wḥš* IV ("to be, *or* become, deserted", "to make lonesome, *or* deserted", "to grieve somebody by one's absence") and *ʾns* IV ("to entertain, *or* to delight, somebody with one's presence", "to keep company with someone"). This opposition was already noted by the Arab lexicographers[339] and is often encountered in poetry: a mourning poem from the year 947 H (the very year when Maġūš died) begins with the words *mawlāya ʾawḥašta d-diyāra* ("My patron, you left the abodes deserted"),[340] and a particularly illustrative example presents an inscription which reportedly was found on a marble slab in the garden of a ruined castle (*basīṭ*):

فَاخْرُجْ إِلَى الْقَصْرِ وَانْظُرْ كَيْفَ أَوْحَشَهُ * فِقْدانُ أَرْبَابِهِ مِنْ بَعْدِ إِينَاسِهِ

"Thus go forth to the castle and behold how the loss * of its owners made it a deserted place after it had been peopled with cheerful company".[341]

In a mourning poem by Abū Bakr b. aṣ-Ṣāʾiġ Ibn Bāǧǧah as-Saraqusṭī (d. 533 H) we read (*ṭawīl*):

لَئِنْ أَنِسَتْ تِلْكَ الْقُبُورُ بِلَحْدِهِ * لَقَدْ أَوْحَشَتْ أَمْصَارُهُ وَقُصُورُهُ

"If indeed those tombs were delighted by (the presence) of his burial niche (amidst them), * his camps and palaces were left to utter desolation".[342]

Finally, and going back in time to the late second century H, we find the following line in a poem by Abū ʿUṯmān Saʿīd b. Wahb al-Kātib (d. 209 H), mourning his son Abū l-Ḫaṭṭāb, who died at the age of ten (*ḫafīf*):

إِنْ غَدَا مُوحِشاً لِدَارِي فَقَدْ أَصْـ * ـبَحَ أُنْسَ الثَّرَى وَزَيْنَ التُّرَابِ

337 Or also "make us lonesome (by your absence)".

338 ĠazKawākib II p. 17 and III p. 77; ŠḎ VIII pp. 394f.; ḪafRayḥ p. 284.

339 See Lane s.r. *ʾns* IV.

340 ʿAydNūr p. 205. *Cf.* Bauer: *Fremdheit* pp. 97f.

341 YāfRawḍ p. 400.

342 IḪāqQal p. 353 (var. *ʾamṣāruhū*: *ʾaqṭāruhū*).

"Though he made my house a lonely place (after his death), at least he * became good company for the moist soil and the earth's ornament".[343]

71

LOCATION. Cairo (?). DATE. 1149 H. PERSON BURIED. Unknown.
SOURCE. ŠubrDīwān p. 15.
DESCRIPTION. The following epitaph was composed by ʿAbd Allāh b. Muḥammad aš-Šubrāwī (Cairo, 1091–1171 H),[344] since 1137 head of the Shafiites at al-Azhar. As is typical for the period, the final line contains a chronogram. It is not known for whose tomb the epitaph was intended. The year "chronogrammed" in the last line adds up to 1149 H, but the name "Ismāʿīl" mentioned is not sufficient for identification. – Four verses in the metre *ṭawīl*:

*tafakkartu fī ğūdi l-ʾilāhi wa-ʿafwihī * ʿani l-mudnibi l-ʿāṣī wa-ʾin ʿaẓuma d-danbū*
*wa-ʾaḥsantu ẓannī bi-lladī lā taḍurrahū * ḏunūbī fa-hāna ṣ-ṣaʿbu wa-nkašafa l-karbū*
*wa-min ğūdihī ʾammaltu ʾamnan wa-raḥmatan * li-sākini hādā l-qabri ʾin massahū ruʿbū*
*wa-ʾarraḫtuhū yā-rabbu ğūduka wāsiʿun * wa-ʿabduka ʾIsmāʿīlu yarğūka yā-rabbī*
213 33 137 102 212 229 223
= 1149

"I reflected on the generosity of God and His forgiveness * for the recalcitrant sinner, even if (his) sin has become great,[345]
And I am confident about the One, whom my sins * do not harm, and so hardship became easy and grief disappeared,
And from His generosity I hope for protection and mercy * for the occupant of this tomb when terror overcomes him.
I dated his death (as follows): 'O Lord, Your generosity is abundant * and Your servant Ismāʿīl implores you, O my Lord!'".

72

LOCATION. Córdoba (ar. Qurṭubah). DATE. 356 H.
PERSON BURIED. The famous man of letters Abū ʿAlī al-Qālī, author of the *ʾAmālī* (Ism. b. al-Qāsim al-Baġdādī, Manāzğird *c.*288 – Córdoba 356 H): IFarTārīḫ I p. 69; ḤumĞadwah pp. 164-7; YāqIršād II pp. 351-4; QifṭīInbāh I pp. 204-9;

343 *Aġānī* XX p. 339.
344 For him, see MurSilk III p. 107; ĞabʿAğāʾib I p. 347; ZA IV p. 130; GAL II pp. 281f. and GALS II p. 390.
345 See above note 1 to epitaph **26**.

TI XXVI pp. 138-40; BN XI pp. 264f.; MaqrMuq II pp.107-10; SuyBuġ I p. 453; MaqqNafḥ (C) IV pp. 70-3; QālīAmālī I p. ر (editor's introduction); ŠḎ III p. 18; ZA I pp. 321f.; Arié: *España musulmana* pp. 362f.; EI² IV pp. 501f. (R. Sellheim); CHAL *Andalus* p. 109.

SOURCES. IAbbTakm III p. 231; MaqqNafḥ (B) III p. 72 / (C) IV p. 72.

DESCRIPTION. Ibn aṭ-Ṭaylasān[346] reported from Ibn Ǧābir that he read the following two verses "inscribed on a marble slab which fell from the mausoleum (*qubbah*) that was built upon the tomb of Abū ᶜAlī al-Baġdādī when it collapsed: [...]" (both sources). – This epitaph-poem is also found on extant tombstones, see Volume I pp. 90f. – Two verses in the metre *ṭawīl*:

*ṣilū laḥda qabrī bi-ṭ-ṭarīqi wa-waddiᶜū * fa-laysa li-man wārā t-turābu ḥabību*
*wa-lā tadfinūnī bi-l-ᶜarā'i fa-rubbamā * bakā 'in ra'ā qabra l-ġarībi ġarību*

"Adjoin the niche of my tomb to the roadside and then take your leave, * because someone hidden in the earth[347] has no friend!
Do not bury me in the open field, thus maybe * a stranger (who passes by on the way) will weep if he sees the tomb of the stranger".

NOTE. The topos that the deceased remains without friends and is soon forgotten appears frequently in epitaphs (see **30**, **85**, **213** and **221**) and mourning poetry. A good example in the literary tradition is two verses by the Syrian poet ᶜAbd al-Muḥsin b. Muḥammad aṣ-Ṣūrī (Ibn Ġalbūn, d. 419 H) which he composed when he came across the tomb of a friend (*ḫafīf*):

عَجَباً لِي وَقَدْ مَرَرْتُ بِآثَا * رِكَ أَنِّيَ اهْتَدَيْتُ قَصْدَ الطَّرِيقِ
أَتَرَانِي نَسِيتُ عَهْدَكَ يَوْماً * صَدَقُوا مَا لِمَيِّتٍ مِنْ صَدِيـــقِ

"It seems to me a wondrous thing that, when I had stumbled upon your * vestiges, I was led the right way towards them (i.e. quite as if I had had the intention to go there)!
Do you think that even for one day I forgot the bond that was between us? * (But lo!,) they are right (in saying): the deceased has no friend!"[348]

Equally important in the above epitaph is the concept that a stranger is more likely to bewail the deceased than members of his family or friends. This notion was often used to criticise the negligent attitude of the relatives towards the deceased or even

346 For him, see above p. 299.

347 Commonly expressed with *wārāhu t-turāb* (or *wārāhu ṯ-ṯarā, al-qabr*, etc), e.g. in a verse by al-Ḫansā': *wa-māḏā yuwārī l-qabru taḥta turābihī* (Ḫansā'Dīwān [B] p. 52 = IḤamdTaḏk IV p. 200 = IṬawSabk p. 138), with the variant *wa-māḏā ṯawā fī l-laḥdi taḥta turābihī* (Ḫansā'Dīwān [Š] p. 46). For this expression, see also ḤamTanzīl p. 63 (*mā tawārā ṣ-ṣafā'iḥu*).

348 Cited in ṮaᶜālYat I p. 314.

their joy at their death.[349] Thus we read in a widely-cited poem by an unknown poet of pre- or early Islamic times (*basīṭ*):

يَبْكِي الغَرِيبُ عَلَيْهِ لَيْسَ يَعْرِفُهُ * وَذُو قَرَابَتِهِ فِي الحَيِّ مَسْرُورُ

"The stranger weeps for him although he does not know him (*sc.* the deceased) * while his relatives in the living-quarter are filled with joy!"[350]

For the topos of a tomb at the roadside, see also above **66**.

73

LOCATION. Córdoba. DATE. 426 H.

PERSON BURIED. The poet and state official Abū ᶜĀmir Ibn Šuhayd (A. b. ᶜAbd al-Malik al-Ašǧaᶜī, Córdoba 382–426 H, buried in the Umm Salamah cemetery): T̲aᶜālYat II pp. 36-50; ḤumĞad̲wah pp. 133-6; ŠantD̲aḫ III pp. 191-336; YāqIršād I pp. 218f.; IDiḥMuṭrib pp. 158-64; MaqqNafḥ (C) II pp. 150-2; ṢD̲ III p. 230; Nykl: *Hispano-Arabic Poetry* pp. 103-5; ZA I p. 163; Dickie: *Ibn Šuhayd*; EI^2 III pp. 938-40 (Ch. Pellat); CHAL *Andalus* pp. 220-4.

SOURCES. IḪāqQal p. 174 (only the verses); ŠantD̲aḫ I pp. 333f. = WKAS II p. 1711 (*s.r. lwḥ*, only the description; the text of the epitaph is not cited); IḪarrāṭᶜĀqibah p. 117 (only the verses); QurṭTad̲k p. 107 (only the verses); MaqqNafḥ (B) I p. 636 / (C) II pp. 161f. (only the verses); Nykl: *Hispano-Arabic Poetry* p. 104 (in English translation, only the verses and lacking v. 4); Dickie: *Ibn Šuhayd* p. 296 (the prose and vv. 1f. and 8 in English translation).

DESCRIPTION. "He stipulated in his last will that he was to be buried at the side of his friend Abū l-Walīd[351] az-Zaǧǧālī,[352] and that the following prose and poetry be written upon a marble slab and put on his tomb" (ŠantD̲aḫ; almost verbatim the other sources);[353] "In Córdoba the following was found inscribed upon the tomb of (...) Ibn Šuhayd, and he was buried beside his friend, the vizier Abū l-Marwān az-Zaǧǧālī;[354] it is as if he was addressing him (in his epitaph) and both were buried in a garden in which they often used to stroll around together:

349 *Cf.* also below pp. 526f.

350 Quoted in IQutᶜUyūn II p. 328; QālīAmālī II p. 182; RāġibMuḥāḍ IV p. 535 (var. *al-ġarību*: *ġarībun*); YāqIršād V p. 12; IHud̲aylMaq p. 47. *Cf.* also epitaph **178**.

351 IḪāqQal p 174 and MaqqNafḥ (C) II p. 161, with a similar notice, call him "Abū Marwān"; *cf.* also Nykl: *Hispano-Arabic Poetry* p. 104 and Dickie: *Ibn Šuhayd* pp. 293f.

352 Also a famous garden in Córdoba, named after this person (who bequeathed the area to the public).

353 The burial of Ibn Šuhayd is portrayed in detail in Dickie: *Ibn Šuhayd* pp. 293-6. The verses of the epitaph were, however, not the last poem composed by Ibn Šuhayd, see MaqqNafḥ (C) IV pp. 334f. and Dickie: *ib*. p. 293.

354 In the ed. text الزجاجي (!).

[...]" (QurṭTaḏk, similarly IḪarrāṭᶜĀqibah). – Prose text and eight verses in the metre *maǧzūʾ al-basīṭ*:

*basmalah. qul huwa nabaʾun ʿaẓīmun * ʾantum ʿanhu muʿriḍūna hāḏā qabru ʾAḥmada bni ʿAbdi l-Maliki bni Šuhaydini l-muḏnibi māta wa-huwa yašhadu ʾan lā ʾilāha ʾillā llāhu waḥdahū lā šarīka lahū wa-ʾanna Muḥammadan ʿabduhū wa-rasūluhū wa-ʾanna l-ǧannata ḥaqqun wa-ʾanna n-nāra ḥaqqun wa-ʾanna l-baʿṯa ḥaqqun wa-ʾanna s-sāʿata ʾātiyatun lā rayba fīhā wa-ʾanna llāha yabʿaṯu man fī l-qubūri*[355] *māta fī šahri* kaḏā *min ʿāmi* kaḏā [wa-yuktabu taḥta hāḏā n-naṯri hāḏā n-naẓmu:]

*yā-ṣāḥibī qum fa-qad ʾaṭalnā * ʾa-naḥnu ṭūla l-madā huǧūdū*
*fa-qāla lī lan naqūma minhā * mā dāma min fawqinā ṣ-ṣaʿīdū*
*taḏkuru kam laylatin lahawnā * fī ẓillihā wa-z-zamānu ʿīdū*
*wa-kam surūrin hamā ʿalaynā * saḥābatan ṯarratan taǧūdū*
*kullun ka-ʾan lam yakun taqaḍḍā * wa-šuʾmuhū ḥāḍirun ʿatīdū*
*ḥaṣṣalahū kātibun ḥafīẓun * wa-ḍammahū ṣādiqun šahīdū*
*yā-waylanā ʾin tanakkabatnā * raḥmatu man baṭšuhū šadīdū*
*yā-rabbi ʿafwan fa-ʾanta mawlan * qaṣṣara fī ʾamrika l-ʿabīdū*

1 *ʾaṭalnā*: *ʾaṭalta* (IḪarrāṭᶜĀqibah). – 2 *lan naqūma*: *lan taqūma* (IḪarrāṭᶜĀqibah). – **3** *taḏkuru*: *naḏkuru* (QurṭTaḏk); *lahawnā*: *naʿimnā* (IḪāqQal, IḪarrāṭᶜĀqibah, MaqqNafḥ). – **4** *surūrin*: يـنـيـر (QurṭTaḏk); *hamā*: *maḍā* (IḪarrāṭĀqibah); *ṯarratan*: *narahū* (!, IḪarrāṭᶜĀqibah); *taǧūdū*: بـجـود (QurṭTaḏk). – **5** *kullun ka-ʾan lam yakun*: *fa-ḫayruhū musriʿan* (MaqqNafḥ, in one ms.). – **6** *ḥaṣṣalahū kātibun*: *ḥaṣṣalatun kānat* (!, IḪarrāṭᶜĀqibah); *šahīdū*: *šadīdū* (QurṭTaḏk). – **7** *yā-waylanā*: *yā-ḥasratā* (IḪarrāṭᶜĀqibah, QurṭTaḏk); *tanakkabatnā*: *tanakkabathā* (IḪarrāṭᶜĀqibah). – **8** *ʾamrika*: *šukrika* (IḪāqQal), *ḥaqqihī* (IḪarrāṭᶜĀqibah).

"*Basmalah*. 'Say: It is a mighty tiding * from which you are turning away' (= Q 38:67f.).[356] This is the tomb of Aḥmad b. ᶜAbd al-Malik b. Šuhayd, the sinner who died confessing that there is no god but God, He being unique without an associate, that Muḥammad is His servant and His Messenger, that Paradise truly exists, that the Fire truly exists, that resurrection will truly happen, that the Hour (of Judgment Day) will come, no doubt of it, and that God will raise up those who are in the graves. He died in the month *so-and-so* of the year *so-and-so*. [*Below that prose passage the following verses are written:*]

(I said) 'O companion of mine, rise, because we have spent a long time (together). * Shall we forever spend the night awake?'
And he said to me, 'We will not rise from it (i.e. the tomb) * as long as (the earth) is piled over us.

355 Q 22:7: *wa-ʾanna s-sāʿata ʾātiyatun lā rayba fīhā wa-ʾanna llāha yabʿaṯu man fī l-qubūr*. See also above **36**.

356 A Qurʾānic passage also inscribed upon a tomb in Tunis (RCEA 783 001). M. b. ᶜAbd al-Bāqī al-Anṣārī (d. Baghdad 535 H) stipulated in his will that this Qurʾānic verse be written upon his tomb (IǦawzīMunt X p. 94).

You remember how many a night we trifled away * in its shade and time was passing like a feast,
And how many a pleasure poured forth on us * a soaking cloud that did us well!
All (that) has ended as if it never had been, * yet its evil omen (i.e. coming death) was (always) present and prepared'.
A writer, a prodigious scholar attained it (i.e. death), * and a trustworthy witness (i.e. Ibn Šuhayd?) embraced him.[357]
Woe unto us if the mercy of Him, * whose power is mighty, shuns us!
O my Lord, I beg forgiveness, for You are a protector * to whom the servants fall short (in their duty)."[358]

NOTE. This epitaph is one of the few quoted in literary sources which contains the lengthy confession formula (*šahādah*) "... confessing that there is no God but God" until "and that God will raise up those who are in the graves" (*cf.* also **32**). It is significant, however, that only Ibn Bassām cites it, whereas in the other sources only the verses are reported. Such a "confessional" passage is commonly found in preserved epitaphs, in particular from Egypt and the western lands (esp. al-Andalus, Morocco, Tunisia, Sicily), with the same or a slightly different wording.[359] Moreover, this lengthy formula (as in the above-quoted epitaph) was in use both among the Sunnites and the Shiites.[360]

74

LOCATION. Ḏamār (Yemen). DATE. Unknown (third century H.?).
PERSON BURIED. Unknown.
SOURCES. IADunyāFarağ p. 90; TanFarağ V pp. 67f.; IBuḥtUns p. 119; QazwĀṯār p. 52; ḤurRawḍ p. 32.
DESCRIPTION. "Abū l-Ḥasan al-Ḥanẓalī [var. al-Ḥanṭabī] told me from ʿAbd Allāh b. Hišām aḏ-Ḏamārī that they came across a tomb in Ḏamār and found a stone upon which the following poetry was inscribed: [...]" (IADunyāFarağ, TanFarağ); "On a tomb was found inscribed: [...]" (ḤurRawḍ); Ibn al-Buḥturī has no further information, but quotes these verses simply (and anonymously) as poetry; al-Qazwīnī writes: "On the wall of the vaulted arch (*ʾīwān*) of the as-

357 The exact meaning of this line is not beyond doubt, however. Maybe *kātibun ḥafīẓun* refers to the "recording angel" reaching the deceased, who then embraces him as someone *ṣādiqun šahīdun*, "someone who tells the truth and confesses (the Oneness of God)", i.e. someone who meets the requirements of the devout Muslim when encountering the Angel of Death.

358 I took the translation of the second hemistich from Dickie: *Ibn Šuhayd* p. 296. The variant *qaṣṣara fī šukrika* (see above) would translate (following Nykl) as "Never well enough thanked by His servants".

359 See Volume I, Chapters 1 and 2.

360 *Cf.* KulKāfī III p. 201.

sembly hall of Tubba^c[361] was found inscribed: [...]". – Two verses in the metre *maǧzū' al-kāmil (muraffal)*:

*iṣbir li-dahrin nāla min- * ka fa-hākaḏā maḏati d-duhūrū*
*faraḥun wa-ḥuznun wāqi^cun * lā l-ḥuznu dāma wa-lā s-surūrū*

1 *iṣbir*: *ṣabran* (QazwĀṯār). – **2** *faraḥun wa-ḥuznun wāqi^cun*: *faraḥan wa-ḥuznan marratan* (TanFaraǧ, ḤurRawḍ); *wāqi^cun*: *ba^cdahū* (QazwĀṯār); *lā l-ḥuznu*: *lā l-ḫawfu* (TanFaraǧ).

"Withstand with composure a fate which did harm you, * for this is how the turns of fate pass by in time:
Joy and grief do (both) occur, * and neither grief nor happiness is everlasting".[362]

75

LOCATION. Damascus (near the shrine of al-Ḫiḍr).
DATE. Unknown (fourth to fifth cent. H?).
PERSON BURIED. Muḥammad b. ^cAbd Allāh b. al-Ḥusayn b. ... Ǧa^cfar aṣ-Ṣādiq.
SOURCES. HarIšārāt p. 14; IŠadA^clāq II (Damascus) p. 186.
DESCRIPTION. The passage cited was part of an inscription upon the tomb (*^calā ḍ-ḍarīḥ*). It contains nothing less than the report of a vision authenticated by an authentic chain of transmission (*'isnād*).[363] To judge from the content, though, the inscription must have been added at a much later time.

rawāhu l-qāḍī l-ḫaṭību 'Abū l-Ḥusayni bnu ^cAbdi r-Raḥmāni bni ^cAbdi llāhi bni l-Ḥusayni bni 'Aḥmada bni 'Abī l-Ḥadīdi wa-l-faqīhu 'Abū l-Ḥasani bnu ^cAlīyi bni 'Aḥmada bni l-Ḥusayni qālā 'aḫbaranā 'Abū l-Ḥasani bnu Māsā wa-š-šayḫu 'Abū l-Qāsimi l-Ḥusaynu bnu ^cAlīyi bni Ḥasanin wa-ġayruhumā 'aḫbarū ^cani š-šayḫi 'Abī l-Ḥasani bni Māsā l-^cadli 'annahū ra'ā n-nabīya – taṣliyah – šāmīya l-qubbati l-ḫaribati llatī bihā š-šarīfu l-^cābidu wa-huwa yaqūlu man 'arāda ziyāratī wa-lam yastaṭi^c fal-yazuri ḍ-ḍarīḥa min waladī Muḥammadi bni ^cAbdi llāhi l-maḏkūr

'Abū l-Ḥasani bnu ^cAlīyi: *'Abū l-Ḥasani ^cAlīyu* (IŠadA^clāq); *bni Ḥasanin*: om. IŠadA^clāq; *bihā š-šarīfu l-^cābidu*: *bihā qabru š-šarīfi l-^cābidi* (IŠadA^clāq).

"It was transmitted by the judge and preacher Abū l-Ḥusayn b. ^cAbd ar-Raḥmān b. ^cAbd Allāh b. al-Ḥusayn b. Aḥmad b. Abī l-Ḥadīd and the jurist Abū l-Ḥasan ^cAlī b. Aḥmad b. al-Ḥusayn, both saying 'We were told by Abū l-Ḥasan b. Māsā as well as the sheikh Abū l-Qāsim al-Ḥusayn b. ^cAlī b. Ḥasan and others who told from the

361 A pre-Islamic king of Yemen.

362 The last hemistich is almost verbatim – *fa-lā ḥuznun yadūmu wa-lā surūrun* – contained in a poem ascribed to aš-Šāfi^cī, see ^cŪfīTarāǧim p. 130.

363 The practice of reporting a chain of transmission as part of funeral inscriptions is reminiscent of the tombstone of the Andalusian mystic Ibn al-^cArīf aṣ-Ṣanhāǧī (481–536 H) whose epitaph quotes, among other things, the persons included in Ibn al-^cArīf's chain of mystic succession (*silsilah*). It has been preserved in Marrakech, see EI^2 III p. 712 (A. Faure).

honest[364] sheikh Abū l-Ḥasan b. Māsā that he saw the Prophet – *taṣliyah* – to the left of the ruined dome under which the noble worshipper (i.e. the deceased) is buried, and the Prophet said, 'He who intends to visit my tomb, but is not able to do so, shall visit the shrine of my descendant Muḥammad b. ᶜAbd Allāh', (that is,) the one mentioned before'".[365]

NOTE. Traditions similar to the one cited towards the end of the epitaph are known from both Sunnite and Shiite literary sources.

Reports of that kind were made about other tombs in Damascus, e.g. the shrine of Abū ᶜUmar Ibn Qudāmah al-Ḥanbalī (528–607 H): "If someone visits this sheikh in his tomb it is as if he had performed the pilgrimage, and according to another version: (...) as if he had visited me (i.e. the Prophet)".[366] Another version, referring to the deceased's appearance in a dream, says "If someone saw Abū ᶜUmar on Friday night it is as if he had seen the Kaᶜbah".[367] Similarly, about the tomb of Abū Muḥammad Ibn Ṭabāṭabā (d. 348 H) in the Qarāfah cemetery: "It was said that a man performed the pilgrimage but he did not have the opportunity to visit the sepulchre of the Prophet. So he felt very depressed until the Prophet appeared to him in a dream, saying 'If you did not have the opportunity to visit me, then visit the tomb of ᶜAbd Allāh b. Aḥmad b. Ṭabāṭabā!' The person who had this dream was from Cairo".[368]

Among the Shiites, we know of the utterance of ᶜAlī ar-Riḍā: "If someone visits the tomb of my father (i.e. Mūsa al-Kāẓim) in Baghdad it is as if he had visited the tomb of the Messenger of God",[369] which according to other sources holds true also for the visitation of al-Ḥusayn's tomb.[370] Comparable Traditions include the following: the visit to the tombs of the martyrs of Uḥud (in Medina) or the sepulchre of al-Ḥusayn (in Karbalāʾ) was said to equal one, three or 50 pilgimages in company of the Prophet, or 20 or even 80 "normal" pilgrimages[371] (and 100, 1000 or 100.000 pilgrimages if performed during feast days);[372] the visitation of ᶜAlī's tomb equals two pilgrimages,[373] and the visitation of the shrine of ᶜAlī ar-Riḍā (al-Mašhad) was

364 Or "the notary".

365 As in other cases, it remains unclear from the passage cited whether *al-maḏkūr* was a part of the epitaph or a comment added by the author.

366 IṬūlQal II p. 561.

367 IRağDayl II p. 60. *Cf.* also Chamberlain: *Knowledge and social practice* p. 119 note 81.

368 *Wāfī* XVII p. 43; MaqrMuq IV p. 448.

369 IQūlKāmil p. 300; KulKāfī IV p. 583; ṬūsīTahḏ VI p. 82; ᶜĀmilīWas III pp. 427f.

370 IQūlKāmil pp. 149f.

371 IQūlKāmil pp. 154-64 and 169-84; KulKāfī IV pp. 548 and 580f.; ṬūsīTahḏ VI pp. 47f.; ᶜĀmilīWas III pp. 255, 278, 326f. and 348-54; al-Amīn: *Miftāḥ* II pp. 106f.; ṬurayḥīMunt pp. 70f. (20 pilgrimages, 20 *ᶜumrah*-pilgrimages and 1000 raids with a Prophet or an Imam).

372 ṬūsīMiṣbāḥ pp. 497f. and ṬūsīTahḏ VI pp. 46 and 49; ᶜĀmilīWas III pp. 359-74. For the argument *cf.* Ayoub: *Redemptive Suffering* pp. 187f.

373 ᶜĀmilīWas III p. 297.

considered to equal 70, 90 or even 70,000 (!) pilgrimages.[374] It could even be formulated as succinctly as: "If someone visits one of the Imams it is as if he had visited the Prophet (in Medina)".[375]

76

LOCATION. Damascus. DATE. 589 / 592 H.[376]

PERSON BURIED. The Ayyubid sultan Ṣalāḥ ad-Dīn Yūsuf b. Ayyūb ("Saladin", Tikrīt 532 – Damascus 589 H): AŠāmahRawḍ I; IḪallWaf VII pp. 139-218; IWāṣilKurūb II; *Wāfī* XXIX pp. 103-54; ŠḎ IV pp. 298-300; ZA VIII p. 220; EI^2 VIII pp. 910-4 (D.S. Richards); Malcolm C. Lyons/David E.P. Jackson: *Saladin. The Politics of the Holy War*, Cambridge 1982.

SOURCES. AŠāmahRawḍ II p. 215; IḪallWaf VII p. 206 / (Slane) IV p. 547; *Wāfī* XXIX p. 136; INubMaṭlaᶜ p. 450.

DESCRIPTION. "I visited his tomb on the first Friday of Ramaḍān 680 and I read on the cenotaph (*ṣundūq*) of his tomb, after the date of his death, the following: [...]. The local custodian mentioned that these words were drafted by al-Qāḍī al-Fāḍil" (IḪallWaf); "These words by al-Qāḍī al-Fāḍil were engraved upon the cenotaph (*ṣundūq*) of his tomb: [...]" (*Wāfī*); "al-Qāḍī al-Fāḍil also said [...]" (INubMaṭlaᶜ, without reference to Ṣalāḥ ad-Dīn and his tomb). The earliest account, by Abū Šāmah, presents the following – in a slightly different wording (similar to that of Ibn Nubātah)[377] – as uttered by al-Qāḍī al-Fāḍil, but he does not mention that it was meant to be inscribed upon Saladin's tomb. – Rhymed prose (according to IḪallWaf and *Wāfī*):

allāhummā fa-rḍa ᶜan tilka r-rūḥ / wa-ftaḥ lahū ʾabwāba l-ǧannati fa-hiya ʾāḫiru mā kāna yarǧūhu mina l-futūḥ

"O our God, now be pleased with that soul / and open the gates of Paradise for him, because this was the last (place) he always desired for (his) conquests".

NOTE. The expression "open the gates of Paradise for him" is a common formula on preserved tombstones. However, in this case there is some subtlety: *ftḥ* I can

374 KulKāfī IV p. 585; ṬūsīTahḏ VI p. 85; al-Amīn: *Miftāḥ* II pp. 190-2; Halm: *Schia* p. 75. Moreover it was said, "If someone visits his tomb and stays for a night it is as if he had visited God Himself on His throne", a phrase that we also find said about the visit to al-Ḥusayn's tomb (IQūlKāmil p. 149; MağlBihār C p. 119) and the Prophet's sepulchre (KulKāfī IV pp. 585f.; ṬūsīTahḏ VI p. 4; ᶜĀmilīWas III p. 262; MağlBihār C p. 144).

375 IQūlKāmil p. 147; ṬūsīTahḏ VI pp. 79 and 93; ᶜĀmilīWas III p. 257; MağlBihār C pp. 117-24.

376 Ṣalaḥ ad-Dīn died in 589 but was transferred to his actual mausoleum north of the Umayyad Mosque only in 592 H.

377 AŠāmahRawḍ: *raḍiya llāhu ᶜan tilka r-rūḥ / wa-fataḥa lahū bāba l-ǧannati fa-huwa ʾāḫiru mā kāna yarǧūhu mina l-futūḥ*; INubMaṭlaᶜ has the following: *wa-rawwaḥa tilka r-rūḥ / wa-fataḥa lahā ʾabwāba l-ǧannati fa-hiya ʾāḫiru mā kānat taʾmaluhū mina l-futūḥ*.

mean either "to open" or "to conquer". The final word of the epitaph, *futūḥ* ("conquests"), is thus related to the preceding imperative "open!". The second part of the epitaph, on the other hand, seems to yield two different ways of reading which I tried to preserve in the translation: "because this was the last (place) he always desired for (his) conquests" might signify either "because this was the last (place) he always desired to conquer" – i.e. no conquest remained unfulfilled for him, being a mighty ruler, except the conquest of Paradise – or "because this was the utmost he always desired to gain from his conquests" – i.e. Paradise being the ultimate reward for the conquests he achieved during his life.

77

LOCATION. Damascus (aṣ-Ṣāliḥīyah?). DATE. 873 H.
PERSON BURIED. The scholar Muḥammad b. Ibrāhīm (b. M. b. ᶜAlī) Ibn al-Muᶜtamad ad-Dimašqī aṣ-Ṣāliḥī aš-Šāfiᶜī (814–73 H): ḌL I p. 124 and VI p. 276.
SOURCE. ḌL I pp. 124f.
DESCRIPTION. The son of Muḥammad, Ibrāhīm, had inscribed the following verses upon the tomb of his father (*mağzūʾ al-kāmil*):

*yā-rabbanā yā-man lahū * niᶜamun ġizārun lā tuᶜad(d)*
*yā-man yurağğā faḏluhū * yā-man huwa l-fardu ṣ-ṣamad*
*iġfir li-sākini ḏā ḍ-ḍarī- * -ḥi Muḥammadini l-Muᶜtamad*

"O our Lord, O who possesses * plenty of favours beyond counting,
O you whose benevolence is hoped for, * O you who is the Unique, the Everlasting:
Pardon the inhabitant of this * tomb: Muḥammad (Ibn) al-Muᶜtamad".[378]

78

LOCATION. Damascus. DATE. 980 H.
PERSON BURIED. The preacher of the Umayyad Mosque Tāğ ad-Dīn ᶜAbd al-Wahhāb b. Muḥammad al-Ḥanafī (d. 980 H): ĠazKawākib III p. 156.
SOURCE. ĠazKawākib III p. 156.
DESCRIPTION. "The poet Māmāya (M. b. A. ar-Rūmī, d. 987 or 988 H) dated his death with a chronogram, and he composed what was written upon his tomb: [...]". – Four verses in the metre *rağaz*:

*ḏā qabru ʾaᶜlami l-warā * baḥri l-ᶜulūmi l-wāḍiḥah*
bi-ᶜAbdi Wahhābin summā (!)* *wa-n-nafsu minhu ṣāliḥah*
kāna ʾimāma l-ʾUmawī (!) * *ḥāza l-maᶜānī* (!) *r-rāğiḥah*
*yā-qāriʾan taʾrīḫuhū * hallā hadayta l-Fātiḥah*

36 419 525 = 980

378 One could detect a wordplay here, for if we read, as is possible, *al-muᶜtamid (ᶜalayka)* we could translate "who relies on You".

"This is the tomb of the most learned of mankind, * the sea of lucid learning.
ᶜAbd al-Wahhāb was he called * and he possessed a virtuous soul.
He was the Imam of the Umayyad (Mosque), * he had the winning arguments.
O reader, his chronogram (is as follows): * 'Why don't you procure (him) the Fātiḥah?'"[379]

Personal observation. Though the author of these lines, of Turkish origin, is of some renown,[380] this epitaph is a deplorable piece of epitaph-poetry, both for its style and poor linguistic standard.

79

Location. Damascus. Date. 985 H.

Person buried. ᶜImād ad-Dīn al-Ḥanafī (M. b. M. ad-Dimašqī, d. 985 H): ĠazKawākib III pp. 35-7.

Source. ĠazKawākib III p. 79.

Description. His relative Ibrāhīm b. Muḥammad b. Muḥibb ad-Dīn al-Ḥanafī studied with him, "and after ᶜImād ad-Dīn's death that person wrote upon his cenotaph (*tābūt*): [...]". – Three verses in the metre *wāfir*:

*ʾa-taᶜlamu yā-ᶜImādī ʾanna ruknī * li-faqdika qad wahā wa-nḥalla ᶜazmī*
*wa-ʾanna surūra qalbī yā-surūrī * taraḥḥala musriᶜan wa-zdāda hammī*
*wa-baᶜdaka mā ʾaradtu baqāʾa rūḥī * wa-lākin laysa ḏālika taḥta ḥukmī*

"Do you know, O *my ᶜImād, / my supporting pillar* that *my strength / my cornerstone*[381] has * for your absence (i.e. death) become feeble, that my energy has slackened,
That the joy of my heart, O my joy, * has wandered quickly away and that my affliction has increased?
After your death I did not want my soul to exist any longer, * but this is not something I have in my power to decide".

80

Location. Damascus (Bāb al-Farādīs cemetery). Date. 1024 H.

Person buried. The man of letters and scholar Ḥasan al-Būrīnī (Badr ad-Dīn Ḥasan b. M. b. M. aš-Šāfiᶜī, Ṣaffūrīyah 963 – Damascus 1024 H): ĠazLuṭf I pp. 355-90; ḪafRayḥ pp. 21-7; MuḥḪul II pp. 51-62; EI^2 I p. 1332b; ZA II p. 219; EAL I p. 163; Abāẓah/Muṭīᶜ: *ᶜUlamāʾ Dimašq* (q. 11) I pp. 302-11.

Source. MuḥḪul II p. 60 = Abāẓah/Muṭīᶜ: *ᶜUlamāʾ Dimašq* (q. 11) I p. 309.

Description. "He composed this quatrain (*rubāᶜīyah*) before his death and determined in his last will that it be written upon his tomb" (MuḥḪul).

379 I.e. why haven't you recited the Fātiḥah at his tomb yet?
380 *Cf.* GAL II pp. 271f. and ZA VI p. 7.
381 The italics indicate alternative meanings due to wordplays.

*yā-rabbi tabiʿtu sayyida l-ʾabrārī * wa-ḫtartu sabīla ṣuḥbati l-ʾaḫyārī*
*wa-l-yawma fa-laysa lī siwā luṭfika bī * yā-rabbi fa-waqqinī ʿaḏāba n-nārī*

"O my Lord, I (always) followed the Master of the Pious (i.e. the Prophet) * and I chose the way of adhering to the good (among the believers).
Today I am left with nothing but Your benevolence towards me. * O my Lord, protect me from the Chastisement of the Fire!"

81

LOCATION. Damascus (aṣ-Ṣāliḥīyah). DATE. 1128 H.

PERSON BURIED. The vizier Yūsuf Pasha aṭ-Ṭawīl (d. Damascus, Šaʿbān 1128 H): MurSilk IV p. 265; Abāẓah/Muṭīʿ: *ʿUlamāʾ Dimašq* (q. 12) I p. 349.

SOURCE. MurSilk IV p. 265 = Abāẓah/Muṭīʿ: *ʿUlamāʾ Dimašq* (q. 12) I p. 349.

DESCRIPTION. "He was buried in the cemetery adjacent to the burial site of the professor aš-Šayḫ al-Akbar (...) Ibn ʿArabī (...). A dressed stone (*taḥǧīr*) was constructed on his tomb, and upon it a slab was put bearing the chronogram of the date of his death which was composed by the professor (ʿAbd al-Ġanīy Ibn) an-Nābulusī, as follows: [...]" (MurSilk). – Three verses in the metre *maǧzūʾ al-ḫafīf*:

*māta fī š-Šāmi ḥākimun * qadruhū fī l-warā kabīr*
*ǧāʾa taʾrīḫunā lahū * baytu šiʿrin lahū qaṣīr*
*raḥima llāh muḥibbanā * Yūsufa Bāša* (!) *ʾal-wazīr*[382]

248 66 101 156 303 254 = 1128

"In Damascus died a governor * whose rank among the mortals is eminent.
Here comes our chronogram which we composed for him. * It is *a line of poetry that falls short of expressing his rank adequately / a short line of poetry that is devoted to him*:[383]
'May God have mercy upon our friend: * Yūsuf Pasha the vizier!'"

82

LOCATION. Damascus. DATE. 1178 H.

PERSON BURIED. The scholar and poet Muṣṭafā al-Luqaymī (Asʿad b. A., Dimyāṭ 1105 – Damascus 1178 H): MurSilk IV pp. 154-66; ǦabʿAǧāʾib I p. 367-94; GAL II p. 363 and GALS II p. 490; ZA VII p. 230; Abāẓah/Muṭīʿ: *ʿUlamāʾ Dimašq* (q. 12) III pp. 212-32 (with further sources).

382 This last verse only fits the required metre with much effort; however, يوسفَ yields a final short syllable although the metre demands a long syllable. Maybe one has to read, notwithstanding the first hemistich, the nominative *Yūsufun*?

383 Both versions are, to my understanding, possible. The use of *qaṣīr* in this verse clearly is meant to allude to the *laqab* of Yūsuf Pasha, viz. "aṭ-Ṭawīl".

SOURCES. MurSilk IV p. 166 = Abāẓah/Muṭīᶜ: *ʿUlamāʾ Dimašq* (q. 12) III pp. 227f.; ŠayMağānī IV p. 40; ZA VII p. 230 note 2 (only the last verse).

DESCRIPTION. He "was buried (...) in the Ḏahabīyah cemetery, beside the tomb of the sheikh Abū Šāmah (the historian) – may God be pleased with him! Some hours before his death he composed a chronogram (*taʾrīḫ*), giving the date of his death, to be inscribed upon his tomb, as follows: [...]" (MurSilk). – Three verses in the metre *kāmil*:

*qabrun bihī man ʾawṯaqathu ḏunūbuhū * wa-ġadā li-sūʾi fiʿālihī mutaḫawwifā*
*qad ḍāʿa minhū ʿumruhū bi-baṭālatin * wa-l-ʿayšu minhū bi-t-takadduri mā ṣafā*
*māḏā ṭawā qabru l-Luqaymiyi ʾarriḫū * mustamniḥun li-l-ʿafwi ʾAsʿadu Muṣṭafā*

598 216 135 229
= 1178

2 *wa-l-ʿayšu minhu*: *wa-l-ʿayšu fīhī* (Abāẓah/Muṭīᶜ). – **3** *māḏā*: *fa-ʾiḏā* (Abāẓah/Muṭīᶜ); *ṭawā*:*ṯawā*: (MurSilk, ZA, Abāẓah/Muṭīᶜ).

"(This is) a tomb containing someone who is laid in fetters by his sins, * who became frightened because of the evil of his doings.
His life slipped through his fingers in idleness * and his existence was nothing but turbid muddiness.
What the tomb of al-Luqaymī has swallowed up, date it thus: * 'Seeking the favour of (God's) forgiveness is Asᶜad Muṣṭafā'".

83

LOCATION. Egypt. DATE. Unknown (before *c*.250 H).
PERSON BURIED. Unknown.
SOURCE. IZayKawākib pp. 296f.
DESCRIPTION. Ibn az-Zayyāt cites a passage from Ibn al-Kindī's (ᶜUmar b. M., d. second half of the fourth cent. H) *Faḍāʾil Miṣr*[384] which in its turn transmits a report from Aḥmad b. ᶜAbd al-Karīm, via Yaḥyā b. ᶜUṯmān al-Qurašī (d. 282 H).[385] In this report we read simply "I saw written upon a tomb: [...]" (The citation is not of the complete poem, as we learn from Ibn az-Zayyāt). – Two verses in the metre *basīṭ*:

*iʿmal li-nafsika qabla l-mawti wa-rḍa bi-mā * yaʾtīka wa-nẓur ʾilā qabrī li-taʿrifanī*
*laqad malaktu mina l-ʾamwāli ʾuhbata mā * yazīdu fawqa ʾulūfin fa-hya ḏī fitanī*

"Prepare well for your sake before death and be satisfied with what * comes to you. Look at my tomb that you may find out about me:

384 *Cf.* GAS I p. 358.

385 GAS I p. 356. He wrote a treatise about Egypt which was later relied upon by the historians Abū ᶜUmar al-Kindī (M. b. Yūsuf, d. Fusṭāṭ 360 H) and his son Ibn al-Kindī. The tomb of Yaḥyā b. ᶜUṯmān lies on the slopes of the Muqaṭṭam Hill, near the mausoleum of Ibn al-Fāriḍ.

I once owned of possessions a hoard (?) that * well went beyond the thousands (dinars?),[386] and these are (now the cause of) my trials".

84

LOCATION. Fez (ar. Fās) (?). DATE. Seventh century H.

PERSON BURIED. The man of letters Abū l-Ḥasan ar-Ribāṭī (az-Zanāṭī) al-Kātib (ᶜAlī b. Marwān, d. ?): MaqqNafḥ (B) II p. 301-3 / (C) III pp. 67-9 (citing from Ibn Saᶜīd al-Maġribī).

SOURCE. MaqqNafḥ (B) II p. 303 / (C) III p. 69.

DESCRIPTION. "When his illness became more serious on the way between Tilimsān and Fez, he composed these verses and instructed in his will that they be written upon his tomb: [...]". – Three verses in the metre *mutaqārib*:

*ʾa-lā raḥima llāhu ḥayyan daᶜā * li-maytin qaḍā bi-l-falā naḥbahū*
*tamurru s-sawāfī ᶜalā qabrihī * fa-tuhdī li-ʾaḥbābihī turbahū*
*wa-laysa lahū ᶜamalun yurtaǧā * wa-lākinnahū yartaǧī rabbahū*

"Verily, may God have mercy upon someone alive who invokes (mercy) * for a dead man whose lifetime expired in the desert.[387]
Dust-raising winds roam over his tomb * and blow the earth in which he is lying away towards his loved ones.
He has not performed desirable deeds, * but nevertheless he desires (to encounter) his Lord".

85

LOCATION. Fez. DATE. 699 H.

PERSON BURIED. The man of letters and judge Ibn al-Muraḥḥal (Abū l-Ḥakam Mālik b. ᶜAr. b. ᶜAlī, b. Málaga 604 – d. Fez or Sabtah 699 H): IZubṢilah III p. 65; ṢafAᶜyān II pp. 392f.; IḪaṭIḥāṭah III pp. 303-25; SuyBuġ II pp.271; GAL I p. 274 and GALS I p. 484; ZA V p. 263.

SOURCES. ṢafAᶜyān II p. 393; IḪaṭIḥāṭah III p. 324.

DESCRIPTION. "Before his death he ordered the following to be written upon his tomb: [...]" (ṢafAᶜyān); "he died on Raǧab 19th in the year 699 and was buried in the cemetery of Fez. He ordered that upon his tomb be written: [...]" (IḪaṭIḥāṭah). – Four verses in the metre *maǧzūʾ al-ḫafīf*:

zur ġarīban bi-maqarrihī[388] * *nāziḥan mā lahū walī*
*tarakūhu muwassadan * bayna turbin wa-ǧandalī*

386 More freely: "property worth more than thousands".

387 *Cf.* Volume I p. 238.

388 *bi-maqarrihī* does not fit the metre; possible emendations are *bi-qabrihī* or *bi-maqbarin*. The version in ṢafAᶜyān has *bi-maġrabin* / *bi-maġribin* instead.

*wa-l-taqul ʿinda qabrihī * bi-lisāni t-tadallulī*
*yarḥamu llāhu ʿabdahū * Mālika bna l-Muraḥḥalī*

3 *at-tadallulī*: *at-taḏallulī* (ṢafAʿyān). **4** *yarḥamu*: *raḥḥama* (ṢafAʿyān).

"Do visit a stranger who in his dwelling * is distant, without any helping friend.
They left him behind (his head) resting * between earth and stones.
Therefore you shall say at his tomb * with a cajoling voice:
'May God have mercy upon his servant: * Mālik b. al-Muraḥḥal!'"

86

LOCATIONS. (a) Ǧazīrat Sawākin (Red Sea port).[389] – (b, d) Almería. – (c) Kairouan. – (e) Dalías (some 50 km NW of Almería). – (f) Cairo (southern Qarāfah).

DATES. (a) Unknown. – (b) 410 H. – (c) 429 H. – (d) 435 H. – (e) 517 H. – (f) Unknown (fifth or sixth century H?).

PERSONS BURIED. (a) al-Malik ʿAzīz ad-Dawlah Rayḥān (not identified). – (b) Sulaymān b. Tammām b. Ḥassān al-Qazzāzī (or al-Fazārī, al-Fazāzī?) (d. 410 H). – (c) Abū l-Ḫayr Ibn Ismāʿīl at-Tamīmī. – (d) Unknown. – (e) The jurist Abū Bakr Ibn al-Baǧǧānī (or al-Ḥāǧǧ?) al-Qaysī (M. b. ʿAl. b. Ya., d. 517 H). – (f) Unknown.

SOURCES. (a) IADunyāQubūr (K) p. 103; IʿABarrBahǧah II p. 346 (only the first two verses); ĠazIḥyāʾ (B) IV p. 488 / (C) IV p. 414 = ZabīdīŠIḥyāʾ X p. 357; IḪarrāṭʿĀqibah p. 116; IḪallWaf V p. 173 / (Slane) III p. 326; MuwMuršid I p. 67; BN XIII p. 41; ḤurRawḍ p. 32; at-Talīdī: *Mašāhid al-mawt* p. 47. – (b) Arabic Inscriptions (Caskel) IV (the first two verses?) = Inscriptions Espagne 116 (no verses quoted) = Inscripciones Almería 11. – (c) Inscriptions Kairouan 333. – (d) Arabic Inscriptions (Caskel) VI = Inscripciones Almería 16 (only the first verse). – (e) Inscriptions Espagne 128 with plate XXVIIa (three verses) = Arabic Inscriptions (Caskel) p. 3 = Inscripciones Almería 117 (two verses, a third one fragmentarily). – (f) IZayKawākib p. 114. – See also Volume I pp. 281f.

DESCRIPTION. (a) "A friend of mine told me that he saw in Ǧazīrat Sawākin the mausoleum of the local ruler ʿAziz ad-Dawlah Rayḥān, on whose tomb was written: [...]" (IḪallWaf); "On another tomb there was the inscription: [...]" (IADunyāQubūr and ĠazIḥyāʾ; similarly IḪarrāṭʿĀqibah and MuwMuršid, with no further information); "Another poet said, [...]" (IʿABarrBahǧah). According to ḤurRawḍ, it was al-Aṣmaʿī who read these lines upon a tombstone. A completely different story is offered by Ibn Kaṯīr (BN): A man had drowned in the Tigris in 601 H and after he was fished out a sheet of paper was found in his turban which contained the verses. – (b) Written on the border of a marble slab, fragmentarily preserved. – (c) An inscription in Kufi characters on a tombstone. – (d) Written in the bottom lines of a marble slab. – (e) Written on

389 *Cf.* YāqBuldān III p. 276 and FāsīʿIqd IV p. 153.

the border fringes of a marble slab. – (f) The inscription as written on a column (*ʿamūd*). – Three verses in the metre *munsariḥ*:

Text of (a), (c) and (f):

*yā-ʾayyuhā n-nāsu kāna lī ʾamalū * qaṣṣara bī ʿan bulūġihī l-ʾaǧalū*
*fal-yattaqi llāha rabbahū raǧulun * ʾamkanahū fī ḥayātihī l-ʿamalū*
*mā ʾanā waḥdī nuqiltu ḥayṯu tarā * kullun ʾilā miṯlihī sa-yantaqilū*

1 أمل: املا (c); *qaṣṣara bī ʿan*: *ʾaʿǧalanī min* (IʿABarrBahǧah); بلوغه: بلوغة (ḤurRawḍ, misprint). – **2** فليتق: فليتقي (c); رجل: رجلا (c); *ʾamkanahū*: *ʾamkaṯahū* (!, IḪarrāṭʿĀqibah); *fī ḥayātihī*: *qabla mawtihī* (IḪallWaf). – **3** *mā ʾanā waḥdī*: ها أنا مثل (MuwMuršid), *hā ʾanā waḥdī* (IḪarrāṭʿĀqibah); *nuqiltu*: *ǧuʿiltu* (ḤurRawḍ), *baqītu* (c); *nuqiltu ḥayṯu tarā*: *bi-fināʾi baytin yarā/yurā* (!, BN); إلى مثله: إلى مثقله (ĠazIḥyāʾ [B], does not fit the metre); *ʾilā miṯlihī sayantaqilū*: *ʾilā mā nuqiltu yantaqilu* (IḪallWaf, ḤurRawḍ), … سينقل (IḪarrāṭʿĀqibah and c).

"O you people (standing before my tomb), I used to harbour hope * but the term (of death) made me fall short of achieving it.
A man whose works have given him power in his life * should fear God, his Lord.[390]
I am not the only one brought to where you see (me now): * everybody will be brought to a similar place (i.e. the tomb)".

NOTE. The first verse refers to the well-known concept of *ṭūl al-ʾamal* ("harbouring over-reaching hope") which was meant to describe the condition of someone craving the things of the present world (*ṭalab ad-dunyā*) and following his passions, but disregarding his spiritual needs and neglecting the ever-present possibility of death.

This concept is treated at length in much theological and paraenetical literature, e. g. in works by al-Ġazālī[391] and al-Maʿbarī,[392] but above all in Ibn Abī d-Dunyā's *Qaṣr al-ʾamal*. As is apparent from the title of this monograph, the antithesis of *ṭūl al-ʾamal* is called *qaṣr al-ʾamal* or *taqṣīr al-ʾāmāl*[393] ("the shortening of hopes", i.e. not having over-reaching hopes) which basically stands for trust in God (*tawakkul*) and renunciation of this world (*az-zuhd fī d-dunyā*);[394] or in the words of Ḥātim al-Aṣamm: "Everything has a certain ornament and the ornament of worship is fear. The sign of fear is 'the shortness of hope' (*qaṣr al-ʾamal*)".[395] What the closely related, albeit opposite, concept of *ṭūl al-ʾamal* was understood to mean might be gleaned from what ʿAmmār b. Yāsir told Ibn Masʿūd after the latter had built a house for himself, "You built firmly / and you harboured over-reaching hope / but

390 The hemistichs are exchanged in the above translation. Caskel's translation of line 2 according to the versions (b-d): "Let any one among you fear God to whom in his life a delay has been granted" (Arabic Inscriptions [Caskel] IV = p. 4).

391 ĠazIḥyāʾ [B] IV pp. 452-61; *cf.* also IḪarrāṭʿĀqibah pp. 96f. and al-ʿAffānī: *Sakb* II pp. 433ff.

392 MaʿbIstiʿdād pp. 14-6 (*ḏamm ṭūl al-ʾamal*).

393 *Cf.* al-Qināwī: *Fatḥ ar-raḥīm* pp. 174f.

394 IQutʿUyūn II p. 357.

395 MaʿbIstiʿdād p. 6.

you will die soon" (*banayta šadīdan / wa-ʾammalta baʿīdan / wa-tamūtu qarīban*).[396] In an epitaph from Almería, we read the line: *wa-t-turbu* [*qa*]*ṣṣara bī ʿan kulli mā kuntu ʾāmilan*, "and the earth (of the tomb) cut me off from everything I hoped to attain" (Inscripciones Almería 10). An anonymous (?) ascetic poem renders the concepts involved here as follows (*rağaz*):

يَا مَنْ بِدُنْيَاهُ اشْتَغَلْ * قَدْ غَرَّهُ طُولُ الأَمَلْ
المَوْتُ يَأْتِي بَغْتَةً * وَالقَبْرُ صُنْدُوقُ العَمَلْ
وَلَمْ تَزَلْ فِي غَفْلَةٍ * حَتَّى دَنَا مِنْكَ الأَجَلْ

"O you who are only beset by your affairs in the present world: * over-reaching hope has deceived you!
Death comes suddenly, * and the tomb is but the box where (your) doings (in the present world) are stored.
(Thus) you remain in (blissful) ignorance * until the appointed time (of death) approaches you".[397]

In epitaph **86**, the concept of *qaṣr al-ʾamal* is clearly implied when we read in the first line that the hope of the deceased "failed to be fulfilled", that is, it "was shortened (*qṣr* II)" or "cut off" by destiny (the "appointed time of death") before it reached fulfilment. This notion does not necessarily refer to someone having died as a child or at young age because every human being, whatever his age, is mortal and thus will never be able to see all the hopes fulfilled which he entertained while alive. This was expressed by ʿAlī ar-Riḍā in the lines (*ramal*):

كُلُّنَا يَأْمُلُ مَدّاً فِي الأَجَلْ * وَالمَنَايَا هُنَّ آفَاتُ الأَمَلْ
لاَ تَغُرَّنْكَ أَبَاطِيلُ المُنَى * وَالْزَمِ القَصْدَ وَدَعْ عَنْكَ العِلَلْ
إِنَّمَا الدُّنْيَا كَظِلٍّ زَائِلٍ * حَلَّ فِيهِ رَاكِبٌ ثُمَّ ارْتَحَلْ

"Everyone of us hopes for a deferment of the appointed time * yet the forces of death are the ruin of hope!
May idle desires not deceive you, * but keep the right measure (i.e. do not transgress the proper limits) and avoid making excuses (for not behaving properly)!
The world is merely like a transitory shadow * under which a traveller rests before he proceeds with his journey".[398]

396 Quoted in MunKawākib I p. 185.

397 Cited in ʿĀmKaškūl II p. 271 and al-Lawāsānī: *Kaškūl* p. 153 (only lines 1-2).

398 Cited in BN X p. 250. For the metaphor of life as a shadow, see also below **219**.

87

LOCATION. Granada (?). DATE. After 480 H.

PERSON BURIED. The man of letters and author of a famous treatise on agriculture, Muḥammad b. Mālik al-Murrī aṭ-Ṭiġnarī (d. after 480 H): IḪaṭIḥāṭah II pp. 282-4.

SOURCE. IḪaṭIḥāṭah II p. 284.

DESCRIPTION. "He ordered that the following verses be written upon his tomb: [...]". – Three verses in the metre *ḫafīf*:

*yā-ḫalīlī ʿarriǧ ʿalā qabrī taǧid * ʾaklata t-turbi bayna ǧanbay ḍarīḥī*
*ḫāfitu ṣ-ṣawti ʾin naṭaqtu wa-lākin * ʾayyu nuṭqin ʾini ʿtabarta faṣīḥī*
*ʾabṣarat ʿayniya l-ʿaǧāʾiba lākin * farraqa l-mawtu bayna ǧismī wa-rūḥī*

1 *taǧid ʾaklata*: *taǧid min ʾaklati* (IḪaṭIḥāṭah, does not fit the metre); the passage *qabrī taǧid* does not fit the metre. – **2** *farraqa*: *lammā farraqa* (IḪaṭIḥāṭah, does not fit the metre). – **3** *wa-rūḥī*: *wa-r-rūḥī* (IḪaṭIḥāṭah, var. in one ms.). – The verse endings of **1** and **3** might have been also written ضريحي ("my tomb") and روحي ("my soul") though the printed edition shows ضريح and روح.

"O my dear friend, turn towards my tomb: then you will find * (but) the repast of the earth between two sides of a tomb!
My voice is silent if I were to speak, but * what speech (it would be) if you were to ponder my eloquence![399]
My eye has seen wondrous things, yet * (now) death has divided my body from soul".

88

LOCATION. Granada. DATE. 597 H.

PERSON BURIED. The philologist, poet and judge Ibn al-Faras al-Ġarnāṭī (Abū M. [ʿAl.] ʿAbd al-Munʿim b. M. al-Ḫazraǧī, Granada 524–97 H), teacher of al-Kalāʿī (d. 634 H): IAbbTakm III pp. 127f.; IḪaṭIḥāṭah III pp. 541-6; NubQuḍātAnd pp. 142f.; IFarDībāǧ pp. 312f.; SuyBuġ II p. 116; ZA IV p. 168.

SOURCE. IḪaṭIḥāṭah III pp. 546 = Casiri: *Bibliotheca* II p. 107 (with a free translation in Latin verse).

DESCRIPTION. "He ordered that upon his tomb be written: [...]" (IḪatIḥāṭah). – "He was buried outside Bāb Ilbīrah and his funeral was attended by a great multitude. The people tore his bier apart and divided it among themselves (IFarDībāǧ p. 313). – Four verses in the metre *ṭawīl*:

*ʿalayka salāmu llāhi yā-man yusallimū * wa-raḥmatuhū mā zurtanī tataraḥḥamū*
*ʾa-taḥsibunī waḥdī nuqiltu ʾilā hunā * sa-talḥaqu bī ʿammā qarībin fa-taʿlamū*
*ʾa-fayyā li-man yumsī li-dunyāhu muʾṯiran * wa-yuhmilu ʾuḫrāhū sa-tašqā wa-tandamū*
*fa-lā tafraḥan ʾillā bi-taqdīmi ṭāʿatin * fa-ḏāka llaḏī yunǧī ġadan wa-yusallimū*

399 I.e. there is nothing more eloquent than the lesson taught by the fate of someone deceased.

1 *mā*: om. Casiri. – **4** تفرحن: تبرحن (Casiri); غدا: غزا (Casiri, misprint).

"The peace of God be upon you, O you who greet (my tomb),[400] * and His mercy as long as you come to visit me praying for God's mercy (on my behalf)!
Do you suppose that I am the only one to have been carried to this place? * You will catch up with me after a little while, and then you will know!
O behold one who has come to prefer his (life in the) present world * and does not regard his (fate in the) hereafter: you will be wretched and you will repent!
You will certainly not rejoice unless you show obedience (towards God) before (your death), * for (only) this is which will make (you) safe tomorrow and protect (you from harm)".

89

LOCATION. Granada. DATE. 671 H.

PERSON BURIED. The Naṣrid ruler al-Ġālib bi-llāh Ibn al-Aḥmar (Abū ʿAl. Muḥammad I b. Yūsuf, Ibn Naṣr, born in 595, r. 629–71 H): IḪaṭIḥāṭah II pp. 92-101 and IḪaṭLamḥah pp. 42-9; ZA VII p. 151; Harvey: *Islamic Spain* pp. 20-40; Kennedy: *Muslim Spain* pp. 273-9; Arié: *Temps des Naṣrides* pp. 55-68.

SOURCES. IḪaṭIḥāṭah II pp. 100f. and IḪaṭLamḥah pp. 48f. = Casiri: *Bibliotheca* II pp. 265f. (only the prose); Inscripciones Granada pp. 166f. (poetry)[401] and 207f. (rhymed prose); Inscriptions Espagne 161 = RCEA 4658 (only the prose passage).

DESCRIPTION. "He was buried in the cemetery of the Old Mosque on the Sabīkah Hill (east of the Alhambra). Upon his tomb, on a marble slab (*ruḫām*), we find today engraved: [*rhymed prose*], and on the reverse side: [*poetry*]" (Ibn al-Ḫaṭīb). The quotation in IḪaṭIḥāṭah is longer than that in IḪaṭLamḥah and provides some additional material. – A passage in rhymed prose and 13 lines of poetry in the metre *basīṭ*:

hāḏā qabru s-sulṭāni l-ʾaʿlā ʿizzi l-ʾislām / ǧamāli l-ʾanām / faḫri l-layālī wa-l-ʾayyām || ġiyāṯi l-ʾummah / ġayṯi r-raḥmah / quṭbi l-millah / nūri š-šarīʿati ḥāmī s-sunnah || sayfi l-ḥaqq / kāfili l-ḫalq || ʾasadi l-hayǧāʾ / ḥimāmi l-ʾaʿdāʾ || qiwāmi l-ʾumūr / ḍābiṭi ṯ-ṯuġūr || kāsiri l-ǧuyūši qāmiʿi ṭ-ṭuġāh / qāhiri l-kafarati wa-l-buġāh || ʾamīri l-muʾminīn / ʿalami l-muhtadīn / qudwati l-muttaqīn / ʿiṣmati

400 This translates *man yusallimu* (as in the transcribed text) and thus takes up the inital *salāmu llāhi*, i.e. the buried person greets the one who salutes him. However, من يسلّم might also be read as *man yusallamu*, i.e. "O who you are (still) preserved from harm", that is, still alive. This would then correspond to the passage *fa-ḏāka llaḏī … yusallimu* in the last line.

401 In Inscripciones Granada, the authors claim, referring to earlier sources, that the verses do not belong to the epitaph of Muḥammad I, but rather to that of Muḥammad II (r. 671–701 H). However, as the verses in themselves do not indicate precisely the person deceased, Ibn al-Ḫaṭīb's account has been followed, which mentions these lines as part of the epitaph of Muḥammad I.

d-dīn / šarafi l-mulūki wa-s-salāṭīn || *al-Ġālibi bi-llāh / al-muǧāhidi fī sabīli llāh* || *ʾamīri l-muslimīna ʾAbū* (sic) *ʿAbdi llāhi Muḥammadi bni Yūsufa bni Naṣrini l-ʾAnṣārīyi – rafaʿahū llāhu ʾilā ʾaʿlā ʿIllīyīn / wa-ʾalḥaqahū bi-llaḏīna ʾanʿama llāhu ʿalayhim mina n-nabīyīna wa-ṣ-ṣādiqīn / wa-š-šuhadāʾi wa-ṣ-ṣāliḥīn – wulida – raḍiya llāhu ʿanhu / wa-ʾātāhu raḥmatan min ladunhu – ʿāma ʾaḥadin wa-tisʿīna wa-ḫamsimiʾatin wa-būyiʿa lahū yawma l-ǧumʿati s-sādisi wa-l-ʿišrīna* [lacuna][402] *wa-sittimiʾatin wa-kānat wafātuhū yawma l-ǧumʿati baʿda ṣalāti l-ʿaṣri t-tāsiʿi wa-l-ʿišrīna li-Ǧumādā l-ʾāḫiri ʿāma ʾaḥadin wa-sabʿīna wa-sittimiʾatin fa-subḥāna man lā yafnā sulṭānuh / wa-lā yabīdu mulkuhū wa-lā yanqaḍī zamānuh* || *lā ʾilāha ʾillā huwa r-raḥmānu r-raḥīm*

ʾamīri l-muʾminīn: *ʾamīri l-muslimīn* (Inscriptions Espagne, RCEA); *ʿalami l-muhtadīn*: *ʿalami l-muhtadīyīn* (!, Casiri); *ʾamīri l-muslimīn*: only in IḪaṭIḥāṭah, om. IḪaṭLamḥah, Casiri, Inscripciones Granada, Inscriptions Espagne, RCEA; *rafaʿahū llāhu ʾilā ʾaʿlā*: *rafaʿahū llāhu ʾaʿlā* (Casiri); *ʾanʿama llāhu ʿalayhim*: *ʾanʿama ʿalayhim* (Casiri); *wa-ṣ-ṣādiqīn*: *wa-ṣ-ṣiddīqīn* (Casiri); *wa-būyiʿa lahū* ... [lacuna] *wa-sittimiʾatin*: only in IḪaṭIḥāṭah, om. IḪaṭLamḥah, Casiri, Inscripciones Granada, Inscriptions Espagne, RCEA; *li-Ǧumādā*: *li-šahri Ǧumādā* (IḪaṭLamḥah, Casiri, Inscriptions Espagne, RCEA), *min Ǧumādā* (Inscripciones Granada).

"This is the tomb of the most exalted ruler, might of Islam, / beauty of mankind, / the pride of nights and days, || succour of the community, / (abundant) rain of compassion, / pole of the religious community, / light of the divine law, defender of the sunnah, || sword (in the service) of truth, / protector of the creation, || lion of combat, / death of the enemies, || support of the affairs of state, / upkeeper of the border castles, || crusher of armies, subduer of the tyrants, / victorious against the unbelievers and the oppressors, || the Prince of the Believers, / banner of the rightly guided, / example for the God-fearing, / protection of the creed, / glory of the kings and the rulers, || al-Ġālib bi-llāh,[403] / the one striving on the path of God,[404] || the leader of the Muslims Abū ʿAbd Allāh Muḥammad b. Yūsuf b. Naṣr al-Anṣārī – may God raise him to the highest of the High Heavens[405] and join him with those who enjoy the grace of God among the prophets and the truthful, / among the martyrs and the righteous![406] || He was born – may God be pleased with him and

402 The pledge of allegiance was in 635 H, so there is something missing in the text.

403 Lit. "gaining victory, *or* overcoming his enemies, (with the help) of God", used as a royal title by this and succeeding Naṣrid rulers.

404 That is, fighter for the cause of God, namely in the *ǧihād*. The expression recurs in other Naṣrid epitaphs.

405 *ʾaʿlā ʿIllīyīn*, for the term *cf.* Q 83:18-24: *The book of the pious is in ʿIllīyūn; (...) Surely the pious shall be in bliss, upon couches gazing; thou knowest in their faces the radiany of Bliss.* According to general belief, the souls of the believers, unlike those of the unbelievers, dwell in the ʿIllīyūn (IḤaǧǦawKāfī pp. 40f.; *cf.* also ʿĀmilīWas III pp. 324 and 326). However, only the souls of the prophets are said to dwell in "the highest of ʿIllīyūn" (HaytFatḤad p. 6), as also – according to Shiite belief – the souls of those who visited the tomb of al-Ḥusayn (IQūlKāmil pp.147f.).

406 For this expression, see Volume I p. 501.

bestow mercy upon him! – in the year 591[407] and allegiance was pledged to him on Friday 26th (of Ramaḍān in the year 35 and) 600. His death occurred after the afternoon prayer on Friday 29th Ǧumādā II in the year 671. Praise to the One whose might never ceases, / whose reign never perishes[408] and whose time never comes to an end. || There is no God but Him, the Merciful, the Compassionate".

*hāḏā maḥallu l-ʿulā wa-l-ḥilmi wa-l-karamī * qabru l-ʾimāmi l-humāmi ṭ-ṭāhirī l-ʿalamī*
*li-llāḥi mā ḍamma hāḏā l-laḥdu min šarafin * ǧammin wa-min šiyamin ʿulwīyati l-himamī*
*fa-l-baʾsu wa-l-ǧūdu mā taḥwī ṣafāʾiḥuhū * lā baʾsa ʿantaratin wa-lā nadā harimī*
*maġnā l-karāmati wa-r-riḍwāni yaʿmuruhū * faḫru l-mulūki l-karīmu ḏ-ḏāti wa-š-šiyamī*
*maqāmuhū fī kilā yawmay nadan wa-waġan * ka-l-ġayṯi fī l-maḥli ʾaw ka-l-layṯi fī ʾaǧamī*
*maʾāṯirun taliyat ʾāṯāruhā suwaran * tuqirru bi-l-ḥaqqi fīhā ǧumlatu l-ʾumamī*
*ka-ʾannahū lam yasir fī ǧaḥfalin laǧibin * taḍīqu ʿanhu bilādu l-ʿurbi wa-l-ʿaǧamī*
*wa-lam yuġādi l-ʿidā minhū bi-bādiratin * yaftarru minhā l-hudā ʿan ṯaġri mubtasimī*
*wa-lam yuǧahhiz lahum ḫaylan muḍammiratan * lā tašrabu l-māʾa ʾillā min qalībi damī*
*wa-lam yuqim ḥukma ʿadlin fī siyāsatihī * taʾwī raʿīyatuhū minhū ʾilā ḥaramī*
*man kāna yaǧhalu mā ʾawlāhu min niʿamin * wa-mā ḥamāhu li-dīni llāhi min ḥuramī*
*fa-tilka ʾāṯāruhū fī kulli makrumatin * ʾabdā wa-ʾawḍaḥu min nārin ʿalā ʿalamī*
*lā zāla yahmī ʿalā qabrin taḍammanahū * saḥāʾibu r-raḥmati l-wakkāfati d-diyamī*

[Final *ṣalwalah*:] *wa-ṣallā llāhu ʿalā sayyidinā wa-mawlānā Muḥammadin wa-ʿalā ʾālihī wa-ṣaḥbihī wa-sallama taslīman*

The text of the poem has been compared with plate XLa (showing the preserved tombstone) in Inscriptions Espagne. As can be seen from the variants listed in the following, the lines as quoted in IḪaṭLamḥah do faithfully, with two minor exceptions, reproduce the actual epitaph, whereas the citation in IḪaṭIḥāṭah gives a different wording in a sizable number of instances.

1 *wa-l-ḥilmi*: *wa-l-maǧdi* (IḪaṭIḥāṭah, IḪaṭLamḥah). – **2** *ǧammin ... al-himamī*: *wa-min šiyamin ʿulwīyati š-šiyami* (IḪaṭIḥāṭah). – **3** *fa-l-baʾsu wa-l-ǧūdu*: *bi-l-ǧūdi wa-l-baʾsi* (IḪaṭIḥāṭah). – **4** *yaʿmuruhū*: *yaʿhaduhū* (IḪaṭIḥāṭah). – **5** *fī l-maḥli*: *fī maǧdin* (IḪaṭIḥāṭah; does not fit the metre); *ʾaw ka-l-layṯi*: *wa-ka-l-layṯi* (IḪaṭIḥāṭah). – **6** *ǧumlatu l-ʾumamī*: *ḥamlatu l-ʾumamī* (sic, IḪaṭIḥāṭah). – **7** *fī ǧaḥfalin laǧibin*: *fī maḥfilin laǧibin* (IḪaṭIḥāṭah); *wa-l-ʿaǧamī*: *wa-l-ʿuǧmī* (sic, Inscriptions

407 In general, his year of birth is given as 595 H; see above.

408 The term *mulk* ("reign", "kingdom") was often, especially in the case of rulers, invoked to contrast the individual fate with the power of the Almighty. Thus the caliph Hārūn ar-Rašīd – or his son al-Maʾmūn – said shortly before his death and looking at his own tomb, "O You whose *mulk* never ceases, have mercy upon the one whose *mulk* has ceased" (IḪarrāṭʿĀqibah p. 68; IǦawzīTabṣ I p. 213).

Espagne, with plate XLa). – **8** *wa-lam yuġādi*: *wa-lam yubādi* (IḪaṭIḥāṭah). – **10** *fī siyāsatihī*: *fī musāyasatin* (IḪaṭLamḥah, Inscriptions Espagne). – **11** *ḥamāhu*: *ḥawāhu* (IḪaṭIḥāṭah). – *taṣliyah*: om. IḪaṭIḥāṭah and IḪaṭLamḥah.

"This is the dwelling place of the highest exaltedness, clemency and magnanimity: * the tomb of the Imam, the heroic, the pure, the banner.

By God, how much nobility does this (burial) niche contain * and (how many) high-aspiring traits of character,

For it is fortitude and generosity which are sheltered in its layers,[409] * but not the fortitude of the boastful nor the openhandedness of a decrepit!

A habitation of noble dignity and delight, peopled by * the pride of kings whose very being and whose traits are highly distinguished.

His stature on both the days of generosity and uproar * was like abundant rain on arid soil or like the (fierce) lion in the thicket.

(His are) glorious deeds of which vestiges[410] remain as signs, * a truth to which all peoples consent.

As if[411] he had not set out with a tumultuous army * such as cannot, for want of space, be arrayed in the countries of the Arabs and the (non-Arab) aliens,[412]

(As if) his enemies had not marched against him in the morning in a sudden attack * that had (his) right guidance reveal (only) a teeth-shimmering smile,

(As if) he had not provided for them (i.e. against his enemies) horses scantily fed for the assault * which had no sip of water except from wells of blood (in the battle),

(And as if) he had not established a rule of justice in his administration * in which his subjects seek refuge as if in a sacred precinct!

Who is unaware of the favours he displayed * and the inviolable obligations he protected for the sake of God's religion?

Those are his vestiges in every noble feature, * more resplendent and visible than a fire on the top of a hill.

409 The *ṣafā'iḥ* of a tomb might either be the "layers of earth" under which the deceased is buried (thus more or less synonymous with *turbah* and *ṯarā*), or, if there is stonework or a massive cenotaph, the "ledger stones" on a tomb; Homerin: *Death and Afterlife* pp. 182f. has "the earth and flag stones" for *turbatun wa-ṣafā'ihu*; Kennedy: *Wine Song* p. 121 translates the expression *bayna ṣ-ṣafā'iḥi wa-ṣ-ṣuḫūr* as "amongst tombstones and rocks", but I do not think that *ṣafā'iḥ* actually refers to tombstones. In any case, the term is much used in mourning poetry from the early Islamic period onwards, *cf.* MasMurūǧ (P) II p. 287 and III p. 348; SarrāǧMaṣ II p. 140; see also note 2 to epitaph **19**.

410 For this expression (*'āṯār – ma'āṯir*), *cf.* RCEA 6084 (750 AH) and below **170**.

411 For the style of this and the following verses, which exhibit a *figura repetitionis* (*ka-'annahū lam ... wa-lam ... wa-lam ... wa-lam*) also attested in early Arabic mourning poetry, see Goldziher: *Trauerpoesie* pp. 316-20.

412 I.e. his army was too numerous to find place in all the known countries.

May the clouds of mercy, trickling and continously showering, * never cease to pour forth upon a tomb which embraces him![413]
[Final *ṣalwalah*:] God bless our master and patron Muḥammad, his family and his company, and grant him salvation, farewell".

90

LOCATION. Granada. DATE. 725 H.

PERSON BURIED. The Naṣrid ruler Abū l-Walīd Ismāʿīl I b. al-Farağ (born 677,[414] r. 713–25): IḪaṭAʿmāl pp. 339-41, IḪaṭIḥāṭah I pp. 377-97 and IḪaṭLamḥah pp. 78-90; DK I pp. 401f.; ITaġrManh II pp. 416f. and NZ IX pp. 250f.; ZA I p. 321; Harvey: *Islamic Spain* pp. 180-87; Kennedy: *Muslim Spain* p. 287; Arié: *Temps des Naṣrides* pp. 93-8.

SOURCES. IḪaṭIḥāṭah I pp. 393f. and IḪaṭLamḥah pp. 87-9 = Casiri: *Bibliotheca* II p. 291 (only the prose); Inscripciones Granada pp. 217-21; Inscriptions Espagne 165 = RCEA 5498 (only the prose).

DESCRIPTION. According to Ibn al-Ḫaṭīb, a large marble slab (*lawḥ ar-ruḫām*) was put upon the tomb, facing the head of the deceased. The text of the inscription was composed by the famous court poet and man of letters Ibn al-Ğayyāb (d. 749 H);[415] it consisted of a passage in rhymed prose on one side, and of a poem of 15 verses length (in the metre *basīṭ*) on the other:

hāḏā qabru s-sulṭāni š-šahīdi fattāḥi l-ʾamṣār / wa-nāṣiri millati l-Muṣṭafā l-muḫtār / wa-muḥyī sabīli ʾābāʾihī l-ʾanṣār ‖ *al-ʾimāmī l-ʿādil / al-humāmi l-bāsil* ‖ *ṣāḥibi l-ḥarbi wa-l-miḥrāb / aṭ-ṭāhiri l-ʾansābi wa-l-ʾaṯwāb* ‖ *ʾasʿadi l-mulūki dawlah / wa-ʾamḏāhum fī ḏāti llāhi ṣawlah* ‖ *sayfi l-ğihād / wa-nūri l-bilād* ‖ *al-ḥusāmi l-maslūli fī nuṣrati l-ʾīmān / wa-l-fuʾādi l-maʿmūri bi-ḫašyati r-raḥmān* ‖ *al-muğāhidi fī sabīli llāh / al-manṣūri bi-faḍli llāh* ‖ *ʾamīri l-muslimīna ʾAbī l-Walīdi ʾIsmāʿīla bni l-humāmi l-ʾaʿlā ṭ-ṭāhiri ḏ-ḏāti wa-n-nuğār / al-karīmi l-maʾāṯiri wa-l-ʾāṯār* ‖ *kabīri l-ʾimāmati n-Naṣrīyah / wa-ʿimādi d-dawlati l-*

413 The first and second hemistich have been exchanged in the translation.

414 Not as late as 680 H (ITaġrManh II p. 416).

415 Ibn al-Ğayyāb (Abū l-Ḥasan ʿAlī b. M. al-Ġarnāṭī) was born in Granada in 673 H. A pupil of Ibn az-Zubayr and later the teacher of Ibn al-Ḫaṭīb, he became vizier and *Geheimsekretär* of the Naṣrid rulers. His poetry was widely celebrated, especially his verses in praise of the Prophet (see MN I p. 488, pp. 573f.; II pp. 296-8; III pp. 211-32); his *Dīwān* is extant, in the recension by Ibn al-Ḫaṭīb (*cf.* MaqqNafḥ [C] IX p. 307). He died of the plague in 749 H. For his biography, see IḪaṭIḥāṭah IV pp. 125-52 and IḪaṭKatībah pp. 183-93; IFarDībāğ p. 301; SuyBuġ II p.189; MaqqNafḥ (C) VII pp. 352-84; ŠN p. 214; GALS I p. 369; Arié: *España musulmana* p. 402; Serrano Ruano: *Los Banū ʿIyāḍ* p. 396 no. 212; María Jesús Rubiera de Epalza: *El medio literario en la Granada naṣrī en la primera mitad del siglo XIV (Ibn al-Jayyāb y su época)*, PhD thesis Madrid 1972; id.: *Ibn al-Jayyāb, el otro poeta de la Alhambra*, Granada 1982; ʿAlī M. an-Naqrāṭ: *Ibn al-Ğayyāb al-Ġarnāṭī (673–749h). Ḥayātuhū wa-šiʿruhū*, Binġāzī: Dār al-Kutub al-Waṭanīyah n.d.

Ġālibīyah ‖ *al-muqaddasi l-marḥūmi ʾAbī Saʿīda Farağı bni ʿalami l-ʾaʿlām / wa-ḥāmī ḥimā l-ʾislām* ‖ *ṣinwi l-ʾimāmi l-Ġālib / wa-ẓahīrihī l-ʿalīyi l-marātib* ‖ *al-muqaddasi l-marḥūmi ʾAbī l-Walīdi ʾIsmāʿīla bni Naṣrin – qaddasa llāhu rūḥahū ṭ-ṭayyib / wa-ʾafāḍa ʿalayhi ġayṯa raḥmatihī ṣ-ṣayyib –* ‖ *wa-nafaʿahū bi-l-ğihādi wa-š-šahādah / wa-ḥabāhu bi-l-ḥusnā wa-z-ziyādah* ‖ *ğāhada fī sabīli llāhi ḥaqqa l-ğihād / wa-ṣanaʿa llāhu lahū fī fatḥi l-bilād / wa-qatli kibāri mulūki l-ʾaʿād / mā yağiduhū maḏḫūran yawma t-tanād* ‖ *ʾilā ʾan qaḍā llāhu bi-ḥuḍūri ʾağalihī / fa-ḫatama ʿumrahū bi-ḫayri ʿamalihī* ‖ *wa-qabaḍahū ʾilā mā ʾaʿadda lahū min karāmatihī wa-ṯawābih / wa-ġubāru l-ğihādi ṭayyu ʾaṯwābih / fa-stušhida – raḥimahū llāhu – ġadratā / ʾaṯbatat lahū fī š-šuhadāʾi mina l-mulūki qadamā / wa-rafaʿat lahū fī ʾaʿlāmi s-saʿādati ʿalamā* ‖ *wulida – raḍiya llāhu ʿanhu – fī s-sāʿati l-mubārakati bayna yaday ṣ-ṣubḥi min yawmi l-ğumʿati sābiʿa ʿašara Šawwālin ʿāma sabʿatin wa-sabʿīna wa-sittimiʾatin wa-būyiʿa yawma l-ḫamīsi s-sābiʿi wa-l-ʿišrīna li-Šawwālin ʿāma ṯalāṯata ʿašara wa-sabʿimiʾatin wa-stušhida fī yawmi l-iṯnayni s-sādisi wa-l-ʿišrīna li-šahri Rağabi l-fardi ʿāma ḫamsatin wa-ʿišrīna wa-sabʿimiʾatin fa-subḥāna l-maliki l-ḥaqq / al-bāqī baʿda fanāʾi l-ḫalq*

wa-nūri l-bilād: *wa-sūri l-bilād* (Casiri, misprint?); *al-ḥusāmi l-maslūli*: *ḏī l-ḥusāmi l-maslūli* (IḪaṭIḥāṭah); *ʾamīri l-muslimīna ʾAbī l-Walīdi*: *ʾamīri l-muʾminīna ʾAbī l-Walīdi*: (IḪaṭIḥāṭah); *wa-n-nuğār*: *wa-l-faḫār* (IḪaṭIḥāṭah); *al-maʾāṯiri wa-l-ʾāṯār*: *al-maʾāṯiri l-ʾāṯār* (Casiri); *wa-ẓahīrihī l-ʿalīyi*: *wa-ẓahīrihī l-muqaddasi l-ʿalīyi* (IḪaṭIḥāṭah); *wa-ʾafāḍa ʿalayhi*: *wa-ʾafāḍa ʿalayhā* (IḪaṭIḥāṭah); *ġayṯa raḥmatihī ṣ-ṣayyibi wa-nafaʿahū*: *ġayṯa raḥmatihī ṭ-ṭayyibati wa-naqahū* (Casiri); *wa-ḥabāhu*: *wa-ḥayyāhu* (IḪaṭIḥāṭah); *ğāhada fī sabīli llāhi ḥaqqa l-ğihād*: only in IḪaṭIḥāṭah, om. IḪaṭLamḥah, Casiri, Inscripciones Granada, Inscriptions Espagne and RCEA; *wa-ṣanaʿa llāhu lahū*: *wa-ṣanaʿa lahū* (IḪaṭLamḥah, Casiri, Inscriptions Espagne, RCEA; for the expression see **91**); *wa-qatli kibāra mulūki l-ʾaʿād*: *wa-qatli kibāra l-ʾaʿād* (IḪaṭIḥāṭah); *yağiduhū maḏḫūran*: *yağiduhū mazḫūran* (Casiri, misprint); *fa-stušhida ... ġadratā*: *fa-stušhida ... šahādatā* (IḪaṭIḥāṭah), *ustušhida ...* (RCEA); *wa-l-ʿišrīna*: *wa-ʿišrīna* (Casiri); *li-šahri Rağabi l-fardi*: *li-šahri Rağabin* (IḪaṭIḥāṭah); *baʿda fanāʾi l-ḫalq*: *baʿda fāʾi l-ḫalq* (Casiri, misprint).

"This is the tomb of the ruler, the martyr, the conqueror of the cities, / who brought triumph to the religious community of the Chosen, the Elected (i.e. the Prophet), / and revived the path of his forefathers, the 'Helpers', ‖ the just Imam, / the heroic, the brave, / who was at home in the battlefield and the prayer-niche, / of pure ancestry and guise, ‖ the happiest king of a state / and the most energetic of them in waging war for the very cause of God, ‖ the sword of *ğihād* / and light of the countries, ‖ the drawn scimitar in defence of Faith, / one whose heart was filled with fear of the Merciful, ‖ striving in the path of God, / triumphant with the help of God, ‖ the leader of the Muslims Abū l-Walīd Ismāʿīl, son of the valiant, the most exalted, pure in his very being and his descent, / noble in (his) glorious deeds and their vestiges, ‖ the great (sovereign) of the Naṣrid Imamate / and the support of the dynasty of al-Ġālib bi-llāh, ‖ the sanctified, the late[416] Abū Saʿīd Farağ, son of the distinguished among the distinguished / and defender of the Islamic heartlands, ‖

416 Lit. "the one who is hoped to have gained the mercy (of God)"; *cf.* Volume I p. 19. However, the term is used in the sense of "the late, the deceased" here and in other epitaphs.

twin brother of the Imam al-Ġālib / and his most highly ranked supporter, || the sanctified, the late Abū l-Walīd Ismāᶜīl b. Naṣr – may God sanctify his noble soul / and pour forth upon him the heavy rain of His mercy || and make his *ğihād* and his martyrdom beneficial to him / and grant him the best outcome (in the hereafter) and even more than that![417] || – He strove in the path of God the veritable *ğihād*, / and by conquering the countries || and killing the greatest kings of his enemies / God made him perform deeds, which he will find stored up (for him) on Judgment Day, || until God decided that his time had come, / so He sealed his life with the best of his works || and took him away towards His favour and reward He had prepared for him, / while the dust of the *ğihād* still covered his garments. || He met his martyrdom – may God have mercy upon him! – through treachery[418] / which certainly brought him a foremost place among the martyr kings / and hoisted for him a banner among the banner-bearers of beatitude. || He was born – may God be pleased with him! – in the blessed hour of the morning rays on Friday 17th of Šawwāl in the year 677; he received the pledge of allegiance on Thursday 27th of Šawwāl in the year 713, and he met his martyrdom on Monday 26th of the month of Rağab, the separate, in the year 725.[419] Praise to the (eternal) king, the truthful, / who will not cease to exist after the extinction of creation".

*taḫuṣṣu qabraka yā-ḫayra s-salāṭīnī * taḥīyatun ka-ṣ-ṣabā marrat bi-Dārīnī*
*qabrun bihī min Banī Naṣrin ʾimāmu hudā * ᶜālī l-marātibi fī d-dunyā wa-fī d-dīnī*
*ʾAbū l-Walīdi wa-mā ʾadrāka min malikin * mustanṣirin wāṯiqin bi-llāhi maʾmūnī*
*sulṭānu ᶜadlin wa-baʾsin ġālibin wa-nadā * wa-faḍli taqwā wa-ʾaḫlāqin mayāmīnī*
*li-llāhi mā qad ṭawāhu l-mawtu min šarafin * wa-sirri mağdin bi-hāḏā l-laḥdi madfūnī*
*wa-min lisānin bi-ḏikri llāhi munṭaliqun * wa-min fuʾādin bi-ḥubbi llāhi maskūnī*
*ʾammā l-ğihādu fa-qad ʾaḥyā maᶜālimahū * wa-qāma minhu bi-mafrūḍin wa-masnūnī*
*fa-kam futūḥin lahū tazhū l-manābiru min * ᶜuğbin bihinna wa-ʾawrāqu d-dawāwīnī*
*muğāhidun nāla min faḍli š-šahādati mā * yuğbā ᶜalayhi bi-ʾağrin ġayri mamnūnī*
*qaḍā ka-ᶜUṯmāna fī š-šahri l-ḥarāmi ḍuḥan * wafāta mustašhidin fī d-dāri maṭᶜūnī*
*fī ᶜāriḍayhi ġubāru l-ġazwi tamsaḥuhū * fī ğannati l-ḫuldi ʾaydī ḥūrihā l-ᶜīnī*
*yusqā bihā ᶜayna Tasnīmin wa-qātiluhū * muraddadun bayna Zaqqūmin wa-Ġislīnī*
*tabkī l-bilādu ᶜalayhi wa-l-ᶜibādu maᶜan * fa-l-ḫalqu mā bayna ʾaḥzānin ʾafānīnī*
*lakinnahū ḥukmu rabbin lā maradda lahū * fa-ʾamruhū l-ğazmu bayna l-kāfi wa-n-nūnī*

417 *al-ḥusnā wa-z-ziyādah*: the expression is Qurʾānic: *al-ḥusnā wa-ziyādatun* ("the reward most fair and a surplus", Q 10:26). See also IĞawzīTabṣ I pp. 439f.

418 He was killed in the conflict with the Marīnid ruler Abū Saᶜīd (ᶜUṯmān II b. Yaᶜqūb, r. 710–730 H) and his confederates; *cf.* Thoden: *Merinidenpolitik* p. 81.

419 IḪaṭAᶜmāl p. 340: Sunday 24th of Rağab.

*fa-raḥmatu llāhi rabbi l-ʿālamīna ʿalā * sulṭāni ʿadlin bi-hāḏā l-qabri madfūnī*

3 *ʾadrāka*: *ʾadraka* (Inscripciones Granada; does not fit the metre). – **5** *wa-sirri*: *wa-sadda* (*sic*, Inscripciones Granada); *madfūnī*: *maknūnī* (Inscripciones Granada). – **7** *maʿālimahū*: *maʿlamahū* (Inscripciones Granada; does not fit the metre). – **8** om. Inscripciones Granada; *tazhū*: *tuzhī* (IḪaṭLamḥah). – **9** *yuğbā*: *yuḥyī* (Inscripciones Granada); *mamnūnī*: *masnūnī* (Inscripciones Granada). – **10** *qaḍā*: *qaṣā* (IḪaṭIḥāṭah). – **12** *Tasnīmin*: *taslīmin* (IḪaṭIḥāṭah); *muraddadun*: *mumarradun* (Inscripciones Granada). – **14** *al-ğazmu bayna l-kāfi wa-n-nūnī*: lac. Inscripciones Granada. – **15** *fa-raḥmatu*: *wa-raḥmatu* (Inscripciones Granada).

"A greeting exclusively distinguishes your tomb, O best of all rulers, * (perfumed) like the east wind that blows from Dārīn.[420]
A tomb which encloses an Imam of right guidance from the Naṣrid lineage, * of high rank in both the wordly and religious spheres.
(His name is) Abū l-Walīd. Do you realise what victorious * king he was, how confident in God, how trustworthy?
A ruler of justice and triumphant fortitude, of generosity, * of superior piety and fortunate traits of character!
By God, what nobility has death swallowed up, * what secret of glory is buried in this burial niche,
What tongue (he had) always swift to pronounce (the name) of God, * what heart inhabited by the love of God!
He revived the ways of the *ğihād* * and took part in it according to what was prescribed by duty and *sunnah*.
How many conquests did he perform, the pride of which * made the pulpits and the pages of the chancelleries gleam with delight![421]
(He was) a striver (in the path of God), who gained from the favour of the martyrdom what * will be collected for him as a reward beyond obligation.
Like ʿUṯmān on a morning of the sacred month he met * the death of a martyr, stabbed to death in his home,[422]
While on his cheeks still stuck the dust of (his last) military expedition * which in the garden of eternal bliss the hands of its dark-eyed virgins will wipe away.
There he is given to drink from the fountain of Tasnīm,[423] whereas his assassin * wavers between the Zaqqūm (tree) and the *ġislīn* meal.[424]

420 See YāqBuldān II p. 432: "a seaport in al-Baḥrayn where musk from India is imported", thus the connection between the winds blowing from there and the fragrance of musk is obvious.

421 For the pulpit as an element of the imagery in Arabic poetry and rhymed prose (*ʾinšāʾ*), see Diem: *Tašrīf* pp. 214ff. *Cf.* also pp. 342 and 370.

422 As is known, the third caliph ʿUṯmān was stabbed to death while performing the morning prayer in his house in Medina in Ḏū l-Ḥiğğah 35 H.

423 This hemistich takes up on Q 83:25-28 speaking about the pious in Paradise: *they are given to drink of a wine sealed whose seal is musk (...) and whose mixture is Tasnīm, a fountain at which do drink those brought nigh.* For the "drink of Tasnīm", see also ŠāmīSubul I pp. 71f.

424 az-Zaqqūm, a tree *that comes forth in the root of Hell* (Q 37:64) and being *the food of the guilty* (Q 44:44), and *ġislīn*, the foul nourishment of the infidels in Hell (see Q 69:36) and

The countries weep for him, together with their subjects, * and the (whole) creation shows the most diverse expressions of grief.
Yet (his death) is a decree of a Lord that cannot be rejected,[425] * for His command is the imperative that is composed of (the letters) *kāf* and *nūn*.[426]
So (I call) the mercy of God, Lord of the Worlds, upon * a ruler of justice who is buried in this tomb".

91

LOCATION. Granada. DATE. 730 H.

PERSON BURIED. Abū Saᶜīd b. Abī l-ᶜAlāʾ al-Marīnī (ᶜUṯmān b. Idrīs Ibn Maḥyū, before 650 – Málaga 730 H), representant of the "Andalusian Marīnids" and vizier to the Naṣrid ruler Abū l-Walīd Ismāᶜīl I (see **90**): IḪaṭIḥāṭah IV pp. 77-80; DK III pp. 50f.; IḪaldᶜIbar VII pp. 229f. and 263; Thoden: *Merinidenpolitik* pp. 81, 112f. and *passim*; ZA IV p. 203.

SOURCES. IḪaṭIḥāṭah IV pp. 79f.; an-Nāṣirī: *al-Istiqṣā* III p. 98 = RCEA 5576.

DESCRIPTION. "He died in Málaga on Sunday 2nd Ḏū Ḥiǧǧah of the year 730 in the advanced age of over 80 years. He was then brought to Granada and buried there. On his tomb a solid mausoleum (*bunyah*) was erected (...), and on his tomb there was a marble slab, with the inscription: [...]" (IḪaṭIḥāṭah). Without indicating his source, an-Nāṣirī writes: "After the death of ᶜUṯmān b. Abī l-ᶜAlāʾ – may God have mercy upon him! –, the following was written upon his tomb: [...]". On the basis of this passage, the epitaph is wrongly said in RCEA to be located in Morocco.

hāḏā qabru šayḫi l-ḥumāh / wa-ṣadri l-ʾabṭāli l-kumāh || wāḥidi l-ǧalālah / layṯi l-ʾiqdāmi wa-l-basālah || ᶜalami l-ʾaᶜlām / ḥāmī ḏimāri l-ʾislām || ṣāḥibi l-katāʾibi l-manṣūrah / wa-l-ʾafᶜāli l-mašhūrah / wa-l-maġāzī l-masṭūrah || wa-ʾimāmi ṣ-ṣufūf / al-qāʾimi bi-bābi l-ǧannati taḥta ẓilāli s-suyūf || sayfi l-ǧihād / wa-qāṣimi l-ʾaᶜād / wa-ʾasadi l-ʾāsād || al-ᶜālī l-himam / aṯ-ṯābiti l-qadam || al-ʾimāmi l-muǧāhidi l-ʾarḍā / al-baṭli l-bāsili l-ʾamḍā || al-muqaddami l-marḥūmi ʾAbī Saᶜīdin ᶜUṯmāna bni š-šayḫi l-ǧalīli l-ʾimāmi l-kabīr / al-ʾaṣīli š-šahīr || al-muqaddasi l-marḥūmi ʾAbī l-ᶜAlāʾi ʾIdrīsa bni ᶜAbdi llāhi bni ᶜAbdi l-Ḥaqqi kāna ᶜumruhū ṯamāniyan wa-ṯamānīna sanatan ʾanfaqahū mā bayna rawḥatin fī sabīli llāhi wa-ġadwah / ḥattā stawfā fī l-mašhūri sabᶜamiʾatin wa-ṯnatayni wa-ṯalāṯīna ġazwah || wa-qaṭaᶜa ᶜumrahū ǧāhidan muǧāhidan fī ṭāᶜati r-rabb / muḥtasiban fī ʾidārati l-ḥarb || māḍiya l-ᶜazāʾimi fī ǧihādi l-kuffār / muṣādiman man yadfiqu[427]

generally understood as meaning "what flows from the skins of the inmates of the Fire", or "what the Fire has cooked, of their flesh, and has fallen off, and is eaten by them" (Lane *s.r.*).

425 For the wording (*lā maradda lahū*), *cf.* Q 13:11, 30:43 and 42:47.

426 This refers to the imperative *kun*, "be!" – written with the Arabic letters *kāf* and *nūn*: كن – indicating the absolute creative power of God.

427 The edited texts have تدفق, see below n. 435.

t-tayyār / wa-ṣanaʿa llāhu lahū fīhim mina ṣ-ṣanāʾiʿi l-kibār / mā ṣāra ḏikruhū fī l-ʾaqṭār / ʾašhara mina l-maṯali s-sayyār ǁ ḥattā tuwuffiya – raḥimahū llāhu – wa-ġubāru l-ǧihādi ṭayya ʾaṯwābih / wa-huwa murāqibun li-ṭāġiyati l-kuffāri wa-ʾaḥzābih ǁ fa-māta ʿalā mā ʿāša ʿalayh / wa-fī malḥamati l-ǧihādi qabaḍahū llāhu ʾilayh ǁ wa-staʾṯara bihī saʿīdan murtaḍā / wa-sayfuhū ʿalā raʾsi maliki r-Rūmi muntaḍā ǁ muqaddimata qabūlin wa-ʾisʿād / wa-natīǧata ǧihādin wa-ǧilād ǁ wa-dalīlan ʿalā niyyatihī ṣ-ṣāliḥah / wa-tiǧāratihī r-rābiḥah ǁ fa-rtaǧǧati l-ʾAndalusu li-faqdih / ʾatḥafahū llāhu raḥmatan min ʿindih ǁ tuwuffiya yawma l-ʾaḥadi ṯ-ṯānī li-Ḏī l-Ḥiǧǧati min ʿāmi ṯalāṯīna wa-sabʿimiʾah

al-ʾimāmi l-muǧāhidi: *al-humāmi l-māǧidi* (an-Nāṣirī: *al-Istiqṣā*, RCEA); *al-muqaddami l-marḥūmi*: *al-muqaddasi l-marḥūmi* (an-Nāṣirī: *al-Istiqṣā*, RCEA); *ibni š-šayḫi l-ǧalīli l-ʾimāmi*: *ibni š-šayḫi l-ǧalīli l-humāmi* (an-Nāṣirī: *al-Istiqṣā*, RCEA); *wa-ṯamānīna*: *wa-sabʿīna*: (IḪaṭIḥāṭah); *ǧāhidan muǧāhidan*: *muǧāhidan muǧtahidan* (an-Nāṣirī: *al-Istiqṣā*, RCEA); *muḥtasiban*: *muḥtamiyan* (RCEA); *muṣādiman man*: *muṣādiman mā bayna ǧumūʿihim* (an-Nāṣirī: *al-Istiqṣā*, RCEA); *wa-ṣanaʿa llāhu*: *wa-ṣanaʿa llāhu taʿālā* (an-Nāṣirī: *al-Istiqṣā*, RCEA); *muntaḍā*: *munqaḍā* (RCEA); *wa-dalīlan ʿalā*: *wa-dalīlan ʿan* (IḪaṭIḥāṭah); *li-faqdih*: *li-buʿdih* (an-Nāṣirī: *al-Istiqṣā*, RCEA); *raḥmatan*: *bi-raḥmatin* (an-Nāṣirī: *al-Istiqṣā*, RCEA); *min ʿāmi*: *min sanati* (an-Nāṣirī: *al-Istiqṣā*, RCEA); *wa-sabʿimiʾah*: *wa-sabʿimiʾatin – raḥimahū llāhu* (an-Nāṣirī: *al-Istiqṣā*, RCEA).

"This is the tomb of the first among the protectors / and the very example of valiant heroes, ǁ the singular majesty, / lion of boldness and courage, ǁ the banner of the banners,[428] / defender of the inviolable possessions of Islam,[429] / commander of the victorious squadrons / (who carried out) famous deeds / and war campaigns which fill the history books, ǁ the first in line,[430] / standing at the gate of Paradise under the shadows of the swords,[431] ǁ the sword of *ǧihād* / and the crusher of the enemies, / the lion of lions, ǁ of high-aiming zeal / and firm step, ǁ the Imam, the *ǧihād*-warrior, the most agreeable, / the hero, the brave, the most effective, ǁ the advanced, the late Abū Saʿīd ʿUṯmān, son of the glorious sheikh, the great Imam / of noble origins, the famous, ǁ the sanctified, the late Abū l-ʿAlāʾ Idrīs b. ʿAbd Allāh b. ʿAbd al-Ḥaqq. His age was 88 years[432] which he consumed in journeying in the path of God (i.e. the *ǧihād*) and in mourning errands (attacking the foes), / until he completed, as is

428 Or "the most distinguished among the distinguished".

429 *Cf.* Lane s.r. *ḏmr*: *ḥāmī ḏ-ḏimār*, that is lit. "defender, *or* protector, of those things for which a man is to be blamed, and severely reproved, if he do not defend *or* protect them".

430 This expression is ambiguous: it might mean either "the Imam in leading the prayer, i.e. the one who stands before the rows (*ṣufūf*) of those praying", or "the one in front of the battle lines (*ṣufūf*) in combat".

431 An allusion to the Tradition: *wa-ʿlamū ʾanna l-ǧannata (*or *ʾabwāba l-ǧannati) taḥta ẓilāli s-suyūf*, see FB VI p. 41 (*ǧihād* 22) and p. 149 (*ǧihād* 112); Wensinck: *Concordance* s.r. *ẓll*. *Cf.* also above p. 49.

432 The variant "78 years" as in the wording cited in IḪaṭIḥāṭah does not seem convincing, the more so as Ibn al-Ḫaṭīb, in his introduction to the epitaph, explicitly mentions that Abū Saʿīd died at an age of over 80 years (see above).

known, 732 military expeditions.[433] || He passed his life striving as a *ǧihād*-warrior in obedience to the Lord, / as someone responsible[434] for the carrying out of war operations, || determined in fighting the *ǧihād* against the unbelievers, / opposing those who pour forth the flood (?).[435] / God made him perform against them (i.e. the enemies) memorable (lit. great) actions / so that the mentioning of his name in every place / became more famous than common proverbs, || until he was taken (to God) – may God have mercy upon him! – while the dust of the *ǧihād* still covered his garments / and while he was chasing (*or* controlling the moves of) the tyrant of the unbelievers and his troops. || Thus he died in the same manner as he was living / and in (the midst) of fierce battle God seized him || and took him unto Him in bliss and contentment, / his sword unsheathed against the head of the Christian king. || (He seized him) as a sign (*or* display) of (His) reception and support, / for what he had accomplished in *ǧihād* and combat || and as a proof of (?) his righteous intentions / and flourishing (*or* lucrative) affairs. || al-Andalus was shaken (with grief) at his loss / which God had donated as a mercy of His. || He was taken (to God) on Sunday, the second D̲ū l-Ḥiǧǧah of the year 730".

92 a-d

Like the epitaphs **89–91** above and **114** below, the following epitaphs of Naṣrid rulers, quoted in IḪaṭIḥāṭah and IḪaṭLamḥah, have been repeatedly edited and translated in Casiri: *Bibliotheca*, Inscripciones Granada, Inscriptions Espagne and RCEA. It was therefore considered unnecessary to provide another complete edition here.

92 a

LOCATION. Granada. – DATE. 713 H. – PERSON BURIED. The Naṣrid ruler Abū ʿAbd Allāh Muḥammad III b. Muḥammad II (r. 701–8, died 713 H). – SOURCES. IḪaṭIḥāṭah I pp. 554-6 and IḪaṭLamḥah pp. 68f. = Casiri: *Bibliotheca* II p. 277; Inscripciones Granada pp. 209-11; Inscriptions Espagne 162 = RCEA 5129. – DESCRIPTION. "He was buried in the Sabīkah cemetery, the burial place of his family, at the side of his grandfather al-Ġālib bi-llāh (see **89**). He was extolled by his tomb on which there is the following inscription: [*rhymed prose*]. And on the reverse side: [*poetry*]" (IḪaṭIḥāṭah). A passage in rhymed prose and 21 verses (*ṭawīl*).

433 Here, indeed, one might wonder whether, given the preceding text, the number originally referred to his date of death, viz. 730 H. In that case, the text as cited is corrupt.

434 Or maybe "looking for the reward (from God) by ..."; for *ḥsb* VIII, see Volume I pp. 310ff.

435 I.e. those who lead against him, and the Muslims, huge armies. However, the expression is not clear to me. The edited text has تدفق and the entire expression has been vowelled by the modern editor of IḪaṭIḥāṭah as *muṣādiman min tadaffuqi t-tayyār*, but I cannot see what this could possibly mean. To my mind, *ṣdm* III necessitates an object in this context and thus only *man* is possible; this, in turn, precludes the reading of تدفق as a verbal noun.

NOTE. The text as preserved in IḪaṭIḥāṭah leaves no doubt that the epitaph was that of the tomb of Muḥammad III. Lafuente y Alcántara and after him Lévi-Provençal, however, quote the epitaph as copied by Alonso del Castillo in the 16th century CE; here, the epitaph, whose wording diverges substantially from Ibn al-Ḫaṭīb's version, clearly refers to Muḥammad II b. Muḥammad I, yet Ibn al-Ḫaṭīb in his entries on Muḥammad II (r. 671–701) in both IḪaṭLamḥah pp. 50-60 and IḪaṭIḥāṭah I pp. 556-66 does not cite an epitaph. With the original epitaph lost today it seems impossible to decide which version reproduces the correct inscription, as it might have belonged to the tomb of either Muḥammad II or his son Muḥammad III; the fragment edited in RCEA 5316 corroborates, in my view, the version cited in IḪaṭIḥāṭah. However, as Muḥammad II – nicknamed *al-faqīh*, "the jurist" – was known for his learning in religious matters, the decidedly religious tone throughout much of the prose passage of the epitaph, setting it also apart from other funeral inscriptions of Naṣrid rulers, could point to Muḥammad II. The verses, on the other hand, contain explicit allusions to the forced abdication of the ruler as well as to his father and must therefore refer to Muḥammad III who was known as *al-maḫlūʿ*, "the one who was forced to resign".

92 b

LOCATION. Granada. – DATE. 720 H. – PERSON BURIED. Abū Saʿīd Farağ b. Ismāʿīl b. Naṣr (d. 720 H). – SOURCES. IḪaṭIḥāṭah IV pp. 244-6; Inscriptions Espagne 163 = RCEA 5423. – DESCRIPTION. "On the 14th of Rabīʿ I in the year 720 he died in Šalūbānīyah (sp. Salobrena) ... and was buried (in Granada) in the Sabīkah cemetery. (...) On his tomb there is today an inscription, engraved on a most beautifully executed marble slab". A passage in rhymed prose and 16 verses.

92 c

LOCATION. Granada. – DATE. 722 H. – PERSON BURIED. The Naṣrid ruler Abū l-Ğuyūš Naṣr b. Muḥammad II (686–722, r. 708–13 H) and brother of Muḥammad III (**92a**), after his demise governor of Guadix. – SOURCES. IḪaṭIḥāṭah III pp. 341f. and IḪaṭLamḥah pp. 76f. = Casiri: *Bibliotheca* II pp. 282f.; Inscripciones Granada pp. 213-6; Inscriptions Espagne 164 = RCEA 5467. – DESCRIPTION. "He was buried in the Qaṣbah Mosque of Wādī Āš (sp. Guadix), but was then transferred to Granada (...) and laid to rest in the mausoleum (*turbah*) of his grandfather (Muḥammad I) in the Sabīkah cemetery. (...) On his tomb was written on a marble slab (*fī r-ruḫām*): [...]" (Ibn al-Ḫaṭīb). A passage in rhymed prose and 12 verses in the metre *kāmil.*

92 d

LOCATION. Granada. – DATE. 755 H. – PERSON BURIED. The Naṣrid ruler al-Muʾayyad Abū l-Ḥağğāğ Yūsuf I b. Ismāʿīl I (r. 733–55 H). – SOURCES. IḪaṭIḥāṭah IV pp. 333-6 and IḪaṭLamḥah pp. 110-2 = Casiri: *Bibliotheca* II p. 306; Inscripciones Granada pp. 222-31; Inscriptions Espagne 174 = RCEA 6201; Schack: *Poesie und Kunst* I pp. 213-6 (only the epitaph-poem, in German translation). – DESCRIPTION. The inscription on the marble tombstone (preserved in part) of Abū l-Ḥağğāğ consists of a passage in rhymed prose and, on the other side, of 27 lines of poetry (in the metre *ṭawīl*). For the execution of the epitaph, liquid gold and powdered lapis lazuli (*ḏawb aḏ-ḏahab wa-saḥq al-lāzaward*) were used;[436] the text was drafted by Ibn al-Ḫaṭīb himself.

436 The same is noted for inscriptions in the Meccan Kaʿbah complex (IĞubRiḥlah [B] p. 72: *ḏahabun marsūmun fī l-lāzawardi qad ḫuṭṭa fīhi ḫaṭṭun badīʿun*).

93

LOCATION. Ǧundīsābūr. DATE. 265 H.

PERSON BURIED. Yaᶜqūb aṣ-Ṣaffār (Abū Yūsuf b. al-Layṯ al-Ḫāriǧī, d. Ahwāz 265 H): MasMurūǧ (P) V pp. 108-14; IḪallWaf VI pp. 402-32; AFidā᾽Muḫt II pp. 52f.; NZ III p. 40; ŠḎ II pp. 150f.; ZA VIII pp. 201f.

SOURCES. TawḥBaṣā᾽ir VIII p. 141 (a different version of version II see below); ṬurṭSirāǧ p. 7 (version I, only the verses); IBuḥtUns p. 245 (version I, only the verses); IḪallWaf VI p. 420 / (Slane) IV pp. 320f. (versions I and II, missing the first verse); ZawzḤam I p. 195 (version II, three verses); BaybZubdah p. 275 (version I); ḤurRawḍ pp. 27f. (a different version of version II, see below); ALL (B) I p. 147 (33rd night) / (C) I p. 186 (35th night) = Littmann I p. 419 = Mahdī p. 446 (version I, only the verses); *ib.* (B) II p. 467 / (C) II p. 248 (192nd night) = Littmann II p. 407 = Mahdī p. 561 (version I, three verses); *ib.* (B) IV p. 1336 / (C) VI p. 163 (824th night) = Littmann V p. 480 (version I); *ib.* (B) IV p. 1418 (876th night) / (C) VI p. 222 (871st night) = Littmann V p. 680 (version I, five verses); ALL Littmann I p. 33 (1st night) = Mahdī p. 73; ALL Mahdī p. 283; IbšīhīMust II p. 463 (ch. 83) (version I, only the verses); ᶜAyniᶜIqd III p. 27 (version I, vv. 1–2); NZ III p. 257 (version I, only the verses); ᶜĀmKaškūl II pp. 393 and 507 (version I, only the verses); MunKawākib II p. 180 (version I, only the verses); ŠḎ II p. 151 (version I, only the prose line).

DESCRIPTION. Yaᶜqūb aṣ-Ṣaffār's epitaph is somewhat of a mystery, as two completely different epitaphs are quoted in the sources. The first – version I – is known (as an epitaph) from the citation in IḪallWaf, while the other – version II – is also quoted (with an additional line) in ZawzḤam. – (Version I:) "He was carried in his coffin (*tābūt*) to Ǧundīsābūr and buried there. Upon his tomb was written: [...]" (IḪallWaf); aṭ-Ṭurṭūšī, Ibn al-Buḥturī, al-ᶜAynī and al-Ibšīhī do not describe these lines as an epitaph. Similarly, in *The 1001 Nights* the verses of version I (plus some additional lines, see above) are very frequently quoted in a number of contexts, in one case recited by the girl Anīs al-Ǧalīs. According to MunKawākib, these verses were often recited by Abū ᶜAlī al-Ḥasan b. ᶜAlī ad-Daqqāq an-Nīsābūrī (d. 405/6 H). Bahā᾽ ad-Dīn al-ᶜĀmilī offers two reports: "It was found inscribed on the top of the palace of the vizier Abū ᶜAlī Ibn Muqlah[437] after it had been burned and his possessions confiscated: [...]" (ᶜĀmKaškūl II p. 393, somewhat differently in NZ) and "al-Aṣmaᶜī heard an Arab bedouin recite: [...]. He then said, This seems inspired by the word of the Exalted: *Until, when they rejoiced in what they were given, We seized them suddenly, and behold, they were sore confounded*"[438] (*ib.* II p. 507). – (Version II:) "Abū l-Wafā᾽ al-Fārisī told me that he saw a sheet (!, *ṣaḥīfah*) upon his

437 For Ibn Muqlah, see above p. 207.

438 Q 6:44 (*ḥattā ᵓiḏā fariḥū bimā ᵓūtū ᵓaḫaḏnāhum baġtatan fa-ᵓiḏā hum mublisūna*).

tomb, and someone had written on it: [...]" (IḪallWaf); "Isḥāq b. Aḥmad az-Zawzanī told me that he read on the tomb of Yaʿqūb b. al-Layṯ in Ǧundīsābūr: [...]" (ZawzḤam); "Upon a tomb was found inscribed: [...]" (ḤurRawḍ).

Version I:
The name of the deceased, followed by two verses in the metre *basīṭ*:

hāḏā qabru Yaʿqūba l-miskīn

*ʾaḥsanta ẓannaka bi-l-ʾayyāmi ʾiḏ ḥasunat * wa-lam taḫaf sūʾa mā yaʾtī bihī l-qadarū*
*wa-sālamatka l-layālī fa-ġtararta bihā * wa-ʿinda ṣafwi l-layālī yaḥduṯu l-kadarū*

1 *ʾaḥsanta*: *ḥassanta* (ʿAynīʿIqd, IbšīhīMust); *ʾiḏ*: *ʾiḏā* (ʿAynīʿIqd, IbšīhīMust, does not fit the metre); *sūʾa*: *šarra* (MunKawākib; ʿĀmKaškūl, both cit.); *yaʾtī*: *yaǧrī* (NZ). – **2** *wa-sālamatka*: *wa-sāʿadatka* (BaybZubdah, IBuḥtUns); *yaḥduṯu*: *tūǧadu* (ALL Mahdī p. 561).

"This is the tomb of the miserable Yaʿqūb.

You were confiding in (*or* thought well of) the days when they were bright, * and you did not fear calamity which Fate brings on.
The nights made their peace with you, so you were deluded by them, * but it is in clear nights[439] that gloom appears".[440]

Version II:
Three verses in the metre *ṭawīl*:

*tafakkar binā yā-zāʾira l-qabri wa-ʿtabir * wa-lā taku fī d-dunyā hudīta bi-ʾānisī*
malaktu[441] *Ḫurāsānan wa-ʾaknāfa Fārisin * wa-mā kuntu ʿan mulki l-ʿIrāqi bi-ʾāyisī*
*salāmun ʿalā d-dunyā wa-ṭībi nasīmihā * ka-ʾan lam yakun Yaʿqūbu fīhā bi-ǧālisī*

"Ponder our fate, O visitor of the tomb, and reflect! * Do not stay in the world as if guided (?) by a friendly mate!
I ruled over Ḫurāsān and the lands of Fārs,[442] * and I did not despair of ruling Iraq.
Farewell to the world and the fragrance of its breeze! * It is as if Yaʿqūb did never dwell in it!"

NOTE. The first version of this epitaph-poem ranks among the most famous and often-cited poetic pieces in *The 1001 Nights* and texts of the Mamluk period, whereas the second version and related lines are mainly found in sources up to the seventh century H. The second hemistich of the second verse (version II) is also quoted by Ibn Ḫallikān, together with a six-line poem by the Umayyad caliph Muʿāwiyah b. Abī Sufyān which is different in content, but close in wording and

439 Nights of glittering stars, devoid of calamity.

440 That is, it is in the serenity of the nights that grief appears.

441 Some editions vowel *malakta* ... *kunta*.

442 Yaʿqūb aṣ-Ṣaffār conquered the province of Fars in 262 H.

the rhymes used.[443] In addition, at-Tawḥīdī, al-Ḥurayfīš and modern editors of other texts also quote other versions as being the epitaph of Yaᶜqūb, composed by himself; according to al-Ḥurayfīš, whose verses 3-6 differ completely, these lines "were found inscribed upon a tomb". This variant of the epitaph consists of two lines (vv. 1f.) which are also ascribed to Abū l-ᶜAtāhiyah,[444] whereas the last three lines (vv. 4-6) take up the above-cited version II (*ṭawīl*).[445] The confusion inherent in the transmission history of these lines is further increased by variant verses (*ṭawīl*) quoted by al-Masᶜūdī as being from the poetry of Yaᶜqūb b. al-Layṯ himself; the first line of these verses mirrors the verse known from his epitaph (version II).[446]

94

LOCATION. Ǧurǧānīyat Ḫwārazm. DATE. 538 H.

PERSON BURIED. The famous scholar, man of letters and exegete az-Zamaḫšarī (Abū l-Qāsim Maḥmūd b. ᶜUmar al-Makkī, Ǧārullāh, Zamaḫšar 467 – Ǧurǧānīyat Ḫwārazm 538 H): AnbNuzhah pp. 391-3; IṣfḪar (I) II pp. 167-72; IǦawzīMunt X p. 112; YāqIršād VII pp. 147-51; IḪallWaf V pp. 168-74; QifṭīInbāh III pp. 265-72; *Wāfī* XXV pp. 247-56; FāsīᶜIqd VI pp. 37-44; NZ V p. 274; SuyBuġ II pp. 279f.; DāʾūdīṬab II pp. 314-6; ŠḎ IV pp. 118-21.

SOURCES. ZamKaššāf I p. 47 (*ad* Q 2:26); IḪallWaf V p. 173 / (Slane) III p. 326 = FāsīᶜIqd VI p. 43; QurṭTaḏk p. 162 (only the verses 1-2);[447] ŠḎ IV p. 121; ḤamTanzīl p. 215.

DESCRIPTION. "In his book *al-Kaššāf* ("The Uncoverer"), a famous Qurʾān commentary, az-Zamaḫšarī recited some verses composed by somebody else in connection with his interpretation of God's speech in the surah 'The Cow' *God is not ashamed to strike a similitude even of a gnat, or aught above it* (Q 2:26), because he said 'I was told the following verses that someone composed: [...]'. A distinguished person recited these verses to me in Aleppo and added that the before-mentioned az-Zamaḫšarī stipulated in his last will that those verses be written on the slab of his tomb (*ᶜalā lawḥ qabrihī*)" (IḪallWaf); according to Muḥibb ad-Dīn al-Ḥamawī, the verses were composed by az-Zamaḫšarī himself although he frequently attributed his own compositions to others in his *Kaššāf*. Ibn al-ᶜImād (ŠḎ) quotes these lines without mentioning an epitaph, and according to al-Qurṭubī they were composed by Abū l-ᶜAlāʾ b. Sulaymān al-Maġribī

443 IḪallWaf VI pp. 431f. Muᶜāwiyah's poem is also cited in MubKāmil (C) I pp. 325f.

444 AᶜAtāhAnwār pp. 129f. and AᶜAtāhDīwān p. 225 (*salāmun ᶜalā ʾahli l-qubūri ... fī l-maǧālisī / wa-lam ... wa-yābisī*) = ZawzḤam I p. 195 note = ŠayMaǧānī II p. 26.

445 ḤurRawḍ pp. 27f. (the first two lines; vv. 3-6 differ from the version cited above); AᶜAtāhAnwār p. 129 note; ZawzḤam I p. 195 note.

446 MasMurūǧ (P) V p. 110.

447 Plus an additional three lines which are nowhere else reported to have been part of az-Zamaḫšarī's epitaph.

(without reference to any funerary inscription). – Three verses in the metre *kāmil*:

*yā-man yarā madda l-baʿūḍi ǧanāḥahā * fī ẓulmati l-layli l-bahīmi l-ʾalyalī*
*wa-yarā ʿurūqa niyāṭihā fī naḥrihā * wa-l-muḫḫa fī tilka l-ʿiẓāmi n-nuḥḥalī*
*iġfir li-ʿabdin tāba min faraṭātihī * mā kāna minhū fī z-zamāni l-ʾawwalī*

2 *ʿurūqa niyāṭihā*: *manāṭa ʿurūqihā* (ŠD), *manāṭa ʿurūqihā fī laḥmihā* (QurṭTaḏk).

"O You (i.e. God) seeing the gnats spreading their wings * in the darkness of the gloomy, jet-black night
And observing the veins (of the aorta) in their upper chest * and the marrow in those slender bones:
Pardon a servant who has repented of his transgressions * which he committed in the first time (of his life)!"

95

LOCATION. Ǧurǧānīyat Ḫwārazm (?). DATE. 538 H.
PERSON BURIED. az-Zamaḫšarī (see preceding entry) (?).
SOURCES. IḪallWaf V p. 173 / (Slane) III p. 326; DāʾūdīṬab II p. 316; ʿĀmKaškūl II p. 535. – The first verse has a parallel in an extant epitaph, see Vol. I pp. 199f.
DESCRIPTION. "He instructed in his last will that upon the slab of his tomb be written: [...]" (DāʾūdīṬab); "in the *History* of Ibn Ḫallikān we find that ... az-Zamaḫšarī, when his death approached, stipulated by will that these two verses be written upon his tomb; and I (*sc*. al-ʿĀmilī) may add that they were obviously of his own composition: [...]" (ʿĀmKaškūl). However, in the source quoted by al-ʿĀmilī we merely read that Ibn Ḫallikān was told by someone in Aleppo that somebody else – without indication of a person or his whereabouts – had stipulated in his last will that the following verses be written on his tomb. – Two verses in the metre *ṭawīl*:

*ʾilāhī laqad ʾaṣbaḥtu ḍayfaka fī ṯ-ṯarā * wa-li-ḍ-ḍayfi ḥaqqun ʿinda kulli karīmī*
*fa-hab lī ḏunūbī fī qirāya fa-ʾinnahū * ʿaẓīmun wa-lā yuqrā li-ġayri ʿaẓīmī*

2 *fa-ʾinnahū*: *fa-ʾinnahā* (all sources); *yuqrā li-*: *yufrā bi-* (IḪallWaf); *li-ġayri*: *bi-ġayri* (DāʾūdīṬab).

"(O) my God, I have become Your guest in the moist earth, * and the guest has a right with every noble (host)!
Thus forgive me my sins as a gift of hospitality for me, for it (i.e. the gift) is * great and as such it will not be expected except from a Great One".[448]

NOTE. For the motif of the deceased person enjoying the hospitality of God, see notes to epitaphs **5** and **26**.

448 *Cf.* Slane's translation of the last verse: "As a gift of Thy hospitality, bestow on me the pardon of my sins; the gift is great, but great is Thy hospitality". See also **226**, first verse.

96

LOCATION. Ǧūzağān (in Ḫurāsān). DATE. 125 H.

PERSON BURIED. Yaḥyā b. Zayd b. ᶜAlī b. al-Ḥusayn b. ᶜAlī (98–125 H): YāqBuldān II p. 182; ZA IX p. 146.

SOURCE. ZawzḤam I p. 219.

DESCRIPTION. "ᶜAlī b. Aḥmad al-Wāṣilī told me that on the tomb of Yaḥyā b. Zayd b. ᶜAlī al-ᶜAlawī was written: [...]". – One verse in the metre *wāfir*:

*ʾilayhim kullu makrumatin taʾūlū * ʾiḏā mā qīla ğadduhumu r-rasūlū*

"Every noble deed is attributed to them * whenever it is said: their ancestor is the Messenger (of God)".

NOTE. This inscription is obviously a sarcastic graffito which was scribbled upon the tomb by some visitor. As such, it is comparable to the inscription upon the grave of Ibn Ṭūlūn (**35**); for insults written upon tombs, see also above page 321.

97

LOCATION. al-Ḫalīl (Hebron, near the mausoleum of Lūṭ).

DATE. 110 H or later.

PERSON BURIED. Umm Salamah Fāṭimah bt. Ḥusayn b. ᶜAlī (40–110 H): ŠḎ I p. 139; ZA V p. 130.

SOURCES. IBaṭṭRiḥlah pp. 77f.; ᶜUlaymīUns I p. 72 (only the verses 1-2); RCEA 2151 (only the prose passage, on the first piece of marble, and the signature of the sculptor, on the second).

DESCRIPTION. "In the vicinity of the mosque[449] there is a cave which contains the tomb of Fāṭimah bt. al-Ḥusayn b. ᶜAlī – peace be upon them both! (*sic*) On the upper and on the lower side of the tomb there are two marble slabs, the first of which bears an engraved writing in marvellous letters: [I], and upon the second is engraved: [II]" (IBaṭṭRiḥlah); "At her tomb there is a marble slab (*ruḫāmah*) bearing an inscription in Kufic letters: [...]" (ᶜUlaymīUns); "huit lignes en coufique simple, la dernière, en haut de la stèle en marbre, sur le cadre. Petits caractères, en relief, sauf ceux de la dernière ligne, gravés en creux" (RCEA). – The version is cited according to Ibn Baṭṭūṭah:

I. First marble:

basmalah. lahū l-ʿizzatu wa-l-baqāʾu wa-lahū mā ḏarā wa-barā wa-ʿalā ḫalqihī kataba l-fanāʾa wa-fī rasūli llāhi ʾuswatun ḥasanatun hāḏā qabru ʾUmmi Salamata Fāṭimata binti l-Ḥusayni – raḍiya llāhu ʿanhu

lahū: *li-llāhi* (RCEA); *wa-fī rasūli llāhi ʾuswatun ḥasanah*: *wa-fī rasūlihī ʾuswatun wa-ʿazāʾ* (RCEA); *binti l-Ḥusayni*: *binti l-Ḥusayni bni [ʿAlīyi bni ʾAbī Ṭālibin]* (RCEA).

449 I.e. the *masǧid al-yaqīn*, erected in Šaᶜbān 352 H at the spot where Abraham reportedly thanked God for the destruction of Lot and his people.

"In the Name of God, the Merciful, the Compassionate. His is the might and eternal existence, and His is what He formed (from dust) and created. He decreed that His creation (i.e. mankind) would perish (*or* pass away),[450] and the Messenger of God provides a beautiful example. This is the tomb of Umm Salamah Fāṭimah bt. al-Ḥusayn – may God be pleased with him!"

II. Second marble, exhibiting the signature of the sculptor and followed by three verses in the metre *basīṭ*:

ṣanaʿahū Muḥammadu bnu ʾAbī Sahlini n-naqqāšu bi-Miṣr

*ʾaskanta man kāna fī l-ʾaḥyāʾi maskanuhū * bi-r-raġmi minniya bayna t-turbi wa-l-ḥaǧarī*
*yā-qabra Fāṭimatin binti bni Fāṭimatin * binti l-ʾaʾimmati binti l-ʾanǧumi z-zuharī*
*yā-qabru mā fīka min dīnin wa-min waraʿin * wa-min ʿafāfin wa-min ṣawnin wa-min ḫafarī*

1 في الأحياء: the texts of Ibn Baṭṭūṭah and al-ʿUlaymī have في الأحشاء ("in the innermost parts") which likewise fits the metre, but makes here little sense if compared to the common and idiomatic في الأحياء – **2** ياقبر: أفديك (ʿUlaymīUns).

"This (inscription) was made by Muḥammad b. Abī Sahl the sculptor in Egypt.[451]
You (i.e. addressing the tomb) lodge a person, whose dwelling place was among the living, * against my will between earth and stones.
O tomb of Fāṭimah, daughter of Fāṭimah's son (i.e. al-Ḥusayn b. ʿAlī), * daughter of the Imams, daughter of the brightest shining stars.
O tomb, how much creed you contain, how much piety, * how much chastity, how much respectability, how much shyness!"

NOTES.

1. The central passage of the first inscription – "His is the might and eternal existence, and His is what He formed (from dust) and created", etc. – is also found on a number of extant tombstones. All of these are of western (Andalusian), South Italian or Egyptian origin. Strangely enough, the epitaph of Umm Salamah as quoted above from Ibn Baṭṭūṭah (and RCEA) seems to be the only known example from a site east of Egypt which contains the formula *li-llāhi l-ʿizzatu wa-l-baqāʾ* etc. At the same time, the substitution of the expression *ʾuswatun wa-ʿazāʾ* (common on preserved tombstones) with *ʾuswah ḥasanah* (which exactly parallels the Qurʾānic

450 One could also read: ... *kutiba l-fanāʾu*, "Perishing was decreed ...", but a number of variant wordings and related versions suggest the active form, e.g. from various third-century Egyptian epitaphs: *al-ḥamdu li-llāhi llaḏī kataba r-raḥmata ʿalā nafsihī wa-l-mawta ʿalā ḫalqihī* (RCEA 305f.: 230 H, 317: 232 H, 333f.: 234 H, 353: 237 H, 397: 243 H, 400: 243 H and 872: 295 H); RCEA 343 (235 H) with the significant addition: ... *wa-l-mawta wa-l-baʿṯa ʿalā ḫalqihī*; see also IʿABarrBahǧah II p. 356: *ʾinna llāha kataba l-mawta ʿalā ḫalqihī*. *Cf.* also Volume I pp. 561ff.

451 In a number of cases, preserved epitaphs from all over the Muslim world contain either the signature of the sculptor or the writer or the person who commissioned the epitaph.

wording, see the following) in Ibn Baṭṭūṭah's version seems to be a slip of the author and was therefore not retained in RCEA. There is only one parallel that I know of, in an epitaph from Almería: ... *wa-ʿalā*] *ḫalqihī kataba l-fanāʾa wa-fī rasūli llāhi ʾuswatun ḥasanatun* (Inscripciones Almería 47, sixth cent. H).[452]

In addition, Ibn Baṭṭūṭah skipped the familiar genealogy of al-Ḥusayn as reported in the epitaph, probably because of its familiarity. Nonetheless, since the preserved inscription is upon a marble stele, while Ibn Baṭṭūṭah explicitly mentions "two marble slabs" (*lawḥāni mina r-ruḫām*), it might still be the case that he indeed saw an epitaph different from that cited in RCEA; epitaphs were sometimes renewed and in that process some of the wording could have been changed.

2. The expression *ʾuswah ḥasanah* ("a beautiful example") is taken from Q 33:21, and thus al-Ġazālī closes his chapter on the death of the Prophet with the words "In his death we have a perfect admonition and the Muslims find in it a beautiful example",[453] while the large section dealing with the death of the Prophet in IĞawzīṮabāt commences with the words *iʿlam ʾanna fī rasūli llāhi ʾuswatun ḥasanatun.*[454] In other cases, the Prophet himself was depicted as comforting the believers shortly before or during their death: al-Muḥibbī relates that Ibrāhīm Ibn Bīrī al-Ḥanafī (d. Mecca 1099 H) "was anxious about death and so in the night before he died he saw the Prophet in a dream, saying 'O Ibrāhīm, die, because in me you have a beautiful example!'"[455] In a more general sense, the expression *ʾuswah ḥasanah* is used by Ibn Isḥāq in the context of the Banū Qurayẓah episode.[456]

3. Muḥammad's death was seen as "the worst calamity (*muṣībah*) which ever befell the Islamic community of believers" – a phrase also often cited in Egyptian epitaphs[457] and even inscribed as a graffito on a pharaonic building (RCEA 137) –, and the believers were exhorted to think of this calamity when something comparable happened to them.[458] In an epitaph from Egypt (285 H) we read the outstanding passage: "Those who fear God and are exhorted by the exhortations of God (*bi-*

452 In other contexts, however, we find the term *ʾuswah ḥasanah* more regularly on extant tombstones, e.g. from the Meccan Maʿlāh cemetery: *li-llāhi mā ʾaḫaḏa wa-li-llāhi mā ʾaʿṭā wa-fī rasūli llāhi ʾuswatun ḥasanatun li-mani stasā wa-hidāyatun li-mani htadā wa-ʿiẓatun li-man waʿā* (RCEA 2972: 511 H); from a tombstone near aṭ-Ṭāʾif: *laqad kāna lakum fī rasūli llāhi ʾuswatun ḥasanatun li-man kāna yarǧū llāha* ... (Arabic Inscriptions [Grohmann] Z 30: 518 H = Q 33:21). See also Amari: *Musulmani di Sicilia* II p. 519 note 1.

453 ĠazIḥyāʾ IV (B) p. 476; *cf.* also IʿARabʿIqd (Ğ) II p. 157 / (M) III p. 242; *cf.* also RāġibMuḥāḍ IV p. 513 and ZamRabīʿ IV p. 194.

454 IĞawzīṮabāt p. 74.

455 MuḥḪul I p. 20; *cf.* also Schöller: *Exegetisches Denken* p. 26.

456 IHišSīrah III p. 259 = IHišLife p. 467.

457 From Fusṭāṭ between 186 H (RCEA 67) and 240 H (RCEA 368), from Aswān between 205 H (RCEA 124) and 364 H (RCEA 1834), from Alexandria (RCEA 216: 217 H), from other parts in Egypt or of unknown origin between 193 H (RCEA 86) and 348 H (RCEA 1496).

458 *Muwaṭṭaʾ* I p. 236 (*ǧanāʾiz* 14); ṬabMiškāh p. 279; ZawzḤam I p. 263; INāṣMağlis p. 24; SaffĠiḏāʾ II p. 261.

mawāʿiẓi llāhi), if a calamity befalls them, they pray to be taken back (to Him) and consider the reward (they receive) from God, and then they find patience and are consoled by the calamity which had befallen the Messenger of God – *taṣliyah* –, thus finding composure".[459]

In their cemetery guides, al-Muwaffaq Ibn ʿUṯmān and Ibn az-Zayyāt quote four verses as recited by the mystic Sulaymān b. ʿAbd as-Samīʿ al-Qūṣī (d. 380 H) dealing with composure in calamity. As it is, these lines are – with some variants in wording – from the many "wandering" verses of Abū l-ʿAtāhiyah; they are contained in his *Dīwān* and cited in a number of later sources (*kāmil*):

اصْبِرْ لِكُلِّ مُصِيبَةٍ وَتَجَلَّدِ * وَاعْلَمْ بِأَنَّ المَرْءَ غَيْرُ مُخَلَّدِ
أَوَمَا تَرَى أَنَّ المَصَائِبَ رَحْمَةٌ * وَتَرَى المَنِيَّةَ لِلعِبَادِ بِمَرْصَدِ (...)
وَإِذَا أَتَتْكَ مُصِيبَةٌ فَاصْبِرْ لَهَا * وَاذْكُرْ مُصَابَكَ بِالنَبِيِّ مُحَمَّدِ

"Show composure in every calamity (that befalls you) and bear it with patience, * and know that man is not immortal!
How? Do you not see that the calamities are a mercy? * Do you (not) see that death is lying in wait for the servants (of God)?[460] (...)
If a calamity has befallen you then bear it with patience * and reconsider the disaster brought about you by (the death of) the Prophet Muḥammad!"[461]

The death of the Prophet understood as an example and hence as a consolation for the believers is a common motif in Islamic literature[462] and appears in other epitaphs as well (**206**).

The greater third-century Ḥadīṯ anthologies sometimes contain whole chapters on the last illness and the death of the Prophet, e.g. al-Buḫārī's *Ṣaḥīḥ* (in the chapter on the Prophet's raids, *maġāzī*)[463] or at-Tirmiḏī's *Ǧāmiʿ* (in the chapter on the virtues of the Prophet, *manāqib*).[464] In a number of *sīrah*

459 RCEA 803. For a shorter, though similar passage see also RCEA 896 (298 H, Upper Egypt), 1381 (332 H, Egypt) and 1439 (338 H, Egypt). *Cf.* also IʿABarrBahǧah II p. 348.

460 So that they cannot escape it, see Lane s.r. *rṣd*.

461 MuwMuršid I p. 601; IZayKawākib p. 290 (only lines 1-2); AʿAtāhDīwān p. 129 (4 vv.) = IʿABarrBahǧah II pp. 348f. = ManbTasl (C) p. 18 / (M) p. 20; IRaǧLaṭāʾif p. 114; ʿŪfīTarāǧim p. 137 (only lines 1 and 3, cited anonymously); SaffĠiḏāʾ II p. 262 (with the last verse changed in the later sources into a reference to the Prophet's calamity which might not have been part of what Abū l-ʿAtāhiyah originally composed (see what follows; *kāmil*): *wa-ʾiḏā ḏakarta l-ʿābidīna wa-ḏullahum * fa-ǧʿal malāḏaka bi-l-ʾilāhi l-ʾawḥadī* is in other sources (including the cemetery guides with the var. *iṣbir lahā*: *tašǧā bihā*) cited as *wa-ʾiḏā ʾatatka muṣībatun tašǧā bihā * fa-ḏkur muṣābaka bi-n-nabīyi Muḥammadī* (IʿABarrBahǧah, IRaǧLaṭāʾif) or as *fa-ʾiḏā ḏakarta Muḥammadan wa-muṣābahū * fa-ḏkur muṣābaka bi-n-nabīyi Muḥammadī* (SaffĠiḏāʾ; ManbTasl, with the additional variant *fa-ḏkur*: *fa-ǧʿal*). However, the version in as-Saffārīnī's text introduces these verses saying that Abū l-ʿAtāhiyah wrote these lines to comfort one of his friends who had lost a son called Muḥammad.

462 *Cf.* also Haja: *Mort et Jugement Dernier* pp. 19-21.

463 FB VIII pp. 163-91; KirmŠBuḫ XVI pp. 233-51; QasṭIršād VI pp. 374-85.

464 TirǦāmiʿ IV pp. 265-7.

works, the death of the Prophet is treated separately and in considerable detail. The topic was first made the subject of a monograph by the Syrian Hanbalite traditionist ᶜAbd al-Ġanīy al-Maqdisī (Ǧammāᶜīl 544 – Cairo 600 H) in his small work – a fascicle, *ǧuzʾ* – entitled *Wafāt an-nabī*, "The Death of the Prophet".[465] Later works include the extant treatise by ᶜIzz ad-Dīn Ibn ᶜAbd as-Salām (d. 660 H), simply known as *Qiṣṣat wafāt an-nabī*,[466] a work entitled *al-ʾInḏār bi-wafāt al-Muṣṭafā al-Muḫtār* ("The Admonition through the Death of the Chosen, the Selected [Prophet]") by the Damascene mystic Abū Bakr b. Dāʾūd (782/3–806 H),[467] and Ibn Nāṣir ad-Dīn al-Qaysī's *Maǧlis* (written in 818 H, = INāṣMaǧlis) which almost exclusively deals with the Prophet's death. The last pre-modern work on the subject that I know of – if it is not identical with the work mentioned already – was likewise composed by Ibn Nāṣir ad-Dīn and bears the title *Kitāb al-ʾAḫbār bi-wafāt al-Muḫtār* ("Treatise Concerning the Reports about the Death of the Selected [Prophet]").[468] During the Mamluk period, the topic also entered *ʾadab* anthologies,[469] and celebrated men of letters composed poems mourning the death of the Prophet.[470]

4. "He decreed that His creation would perish". This echoes the Qurʾānic passage *All that dwells upon earth is perishing* (Q 55:26, *kullu man ᶜalayhā fānin*), which is often found in preserved epitaphs.[471] The related expression "He decreed that His creation etc." not only recurs in epitaphs (see above), but frequently appears in poetry, for example in a verse by Abū Nuwās (*maǧzūʾ al-kāmil*):

كُتِبَ الفَنَاءُ عَلَى العِبَـا * دِ فَكُلُّ نَفْسٍ ذَاهِبَهْ

"Perishing (*or* extinction) has been decreed for the servants * (of God), and every soul (i.e. human being) is bound to perish".[472]

According to Ibn ᶜAbd al-Ḥakam (d. Egypt 268/9 H), the phrase should be used by a Muslim condoling with a Christian relative, by saying "God has decreed death for His creation, and the entire creation is signed for death".[473]

98

LOCATION. Ḥamāh. DATE. 598 H.

PERSON BURIED. The traditionist Abū Muḥammad Ǧaᶜfar b. Abī l-Ḥasan Muḥammad al-ᶜAbbāsī al-Makkī (572–98 H): IDimMustafād pp. 95f.

465 IRaǧḎayl II p. 18; IṬūlQal p. 320. He also wrote a work dealing with the prayer for the deceased, entitled *Ṣalāt al-ʾaḥyāʾ ʾilā l-ʾamwāt* (ḎahTaḏk IV p. 1374).

466 GAL I p. 431.

467 IṬūlQal p. 203.

468 IFahdLaḥẓ p. 320; ŠḎ VII p. 244; for the ms., see Chester Beatty 3295 (5) (= II p. 20).

469 E.g. ḤurRawḍ pp. 301-10.

470 E.g. Ibn Abī Ḥaǧalah, see IAḤaǧSulwah pp. 159-63 (62 lines, *ṭawīl*, rhyme -*ᶜā*).

471 Arabic Inscriptions (Grohmann) Z 5 (537 H) and Z 8 (718 H), both near aṭ-Ṭāʾif; Arabic Inscriptions (Caskel) LIII (604 H, al-Andalus). Many further examples are found in RCEA.

472 ANuwDīwān I p. 309. *Cf.* Q 3:185 and 29:57: *kullu nafsin ḏāʾiqatu l-mawt.*

473 DāʾūdīṬab II p. 180.

SOURCE. IDimMustafād p. 96.

DESCRIPTION. "Ǧaᶜfar b. Muḥammad al-ᶜAbbāsī stipulated before his death that the following be written upon his tomb: [...]".

ḥawāʾiğu lam tuqḍa wa-ʾāmālun lam tunal wa-ʾanfusun mātat bi-ḥasarātihā

"Desires unfulfilled, hopes deluded, souls that died of grief".

99

LOCATION. al-Ḥīrah, Dayr Hind al-Kubrā. – DATE. Pre-Islamic, fifth cent. CE (?). – PERSON BURIED. Unknown (but see below). – SOURCES. YaᶜqTārīḫ II pp. 422f.; IṣfDayrāt pp. 168f.; TawḥBaṣāʾir VIII p. 53; IᶜARabᶜIqd (Ǧ) II p. 161 / (M) III pp. 249f.; BakrīMuᶜǧam II p. 607; YāqBuldān II pp. 542f. – DESCRIPTION. In a village in Iraq, in the church of the monastery Dayr al-ᶜAmr,[474] the tomb of its founder from pre-Islamic times (YaᶜqTārīḫ); the philologist al-Aṣmaᶜī (d. 213 H) said, "Yaḥyā b. Ḫālid the Barmakid (120 – ar-Raqqah 190 H) took me by the hand and and led me to a tomb in al-Ḥirah[475] which bore the inscription: [...]" (IᶜARabᶜIqd, TawḥBaṣāʾir). According to Yāqūt and al-Iṣfahānī, however, the inscription was found in the Dayr Hind al-Kubrā in al-Ḥīrah: ᶜAbd Allāh b. Mālik al-Ḫuzāᶜī went together with Yaḥyā b. Ḫālid and the caliph ar-Rašīd to that place, and they saw "something inscribed on the wall, so he (i.e. Yaḥyā) called for a ladder and ordered the inscription to be read out, and the following appeared to be written: [...]" (YāqBuldān, very similar already IṣfDayrāt and BakrīMuᶜǧam). Eight verses (in some sources also less) in the metre *sarīᶜ*, beginning with *ʾinna banī l-Munḏiri ᶜāma nqaḍaw*. This inscription, cited in a number of sources and with considerable variants, was in all probability not a funerary inscription. Reportedly and according to the majority of sources, it was found inscribed on the wall of a monastery in al-Ḥīrah and dates back to pre-Islamic times. – Another pre-Islamic epitaph, reportedly found at al-Ḥīrah, is quoted verbatim in IḪarrāṭᶜĀqibah p. 116, on the authority of al-Aṣmaᶜī. The deceased's name is given as ᶜAbd al-Masīḥ, and the inscription is said to have been found on a tombstone (*lawḥ*); three verses (rhyme *-īdī/-ūdī*).

100

LOCATION. Ḥiṣn al-Ward (near Munti Mayūr, sp. Monte Mayor).

DATE. 465 H.

PERSON BURIED. Abū Ǧaᶜfar al-Lamāʾī al-Mālaqī (Aḥmad b. Ayyūb, d. Málaga 465 H): IḪaṭIḥāṭah I pp. 232-5; Nykl: *Hispano-Arabic Poetry* p. 122.

SOURCE. IḪaṭIḥāṭah I p. 235.

DESCRIPTION. "From Málaga his body was carried to Ḥiṣn al-Ward, near the Ḥiṣn of Monte Mayor ... There he was buried, according to his last will. He had also

474 I presume this is a mistake for "Dayr (Hind Umm) al-ᶜAmr (b. Hind)", *cf.* YāqBuldān II p. 542 (*s.v.*) and what follows above.

475 al-Ḥīrah was in general, as also Persepolis and other ruined places of pre-Islamic rulers, a site which evoked a strong sentiment of *vanitas* and the transitoriness of earthly things (the motif known as *ubi sunt qui ante nos*). Hence many Arabic sources report inscriptions or graffiti from these sites which mourn their former glory; especially noteworthy in regard to al-Ḥīrah is a nostalgic poem by aš-Šarīf ar-Raḍīy (ŠarīfRaḍDīwān I pp. 509f.).

ordered that the following verses be written on his tomb: [...]". – Four verses in the metre *ṭawīl*:

*banaytu wa-lam ʾaskun wa-ḥaṣṣantu ǧāhidan * fa-lammā ʾatā l-maqdūru ṣayyarahū qabrī*
*wa-lam yakun ḥaẓẓī ġayra mā ʾanta mubṣirun * bi-ʿaynika mā bayna ḏ-ḏirāʿi ʾilā š-šibrī*
*fa-yā-zāʾiran qabrī ʾuwaṣṣīka ǧāhidan * ʿalayka bi-taqwā llāhi fī s-sirri wa-l-ǧahrī*
*fa-lā tuḥsinan bi-d-dahri ẓannan fa-ʾinnamā * mina l-ḥazmi ʾallā yustanāma ʾilā d-dahrī*

"I built (a house, *or* a castle)[476] but I did not settle (in it), although I fortified (it) as much as I could, * because when what had been decreed (i.e. Death) had come, it turned it into my tomb.
My lot was nothing but what you are looking at now * with your (own) eye(s), (a tomb that measures) between a cubit and the span of a hand.[477]
O visitor to my tomb, I charge to you with all (my) might:[478] * to fear God in (all) secret and public affairs![479]
Do not trust in (*or* think well of) Fate, because it is merely * a sign of prudence simply not to rely upon Fate!"

101

LOCATIONS. (a) Hīt (Iraq). – (b) Kairouan. – (c) al-Aylah (al-Ubullah?).

DATES. (a) 281 H. – (b) Between 427 and 432 H. – (c) Unknown.

PERSONS BURIED. (a) The jurist and traditionist ʿAbd Allāh b. al-Mubārak al-Ḥanẓalī, d. 181 H or after: TMD XXXII pp. 396-484; IĞawzīṢafwah II pp. 330-8; NZ II pp. 103f.; MunKawākib I pp. 350-4; ŠḎ I p. 295-7; GALS I p. 256; GAS I p. 95; ZA IV p. 115. – (b) The scholar Abū Ḥafṣ al-ʿAttār (ʿUmar b. M. at-Tamīmī, d. between 427 and 432 H): DabMaʿālim III pp. 164f.; ŠN p. 107. – (c) Unknown.

SOURCES. (a) TMD XXXII p. 480 (only vv. 1 and 3). – (b) DabMaʿālim III p. 165. – (c) TMD LIV p. 57; QurṭTaḏk p. 88; IRaǧAhwāl p. 190.

DESCRIPTION. (a) "ʿAbd Allāh b. Rustam said that on the tomb of ʿAbd Allāh b. al-Mubārak could be seen inscribed: [...]" (TMD XXXII p. 480). – (b) "He was buried in the Bāb Salm (cemetery), and his tomb is widely known and venerated. On his tombstone (*mašhad*)[480] is inscribed: [...]". – (c) "On another

476 I presume this refers to Ḥiṣn al-Ward where he was buried, or to his home there.

477 This might refer to the breadth of the tomb and the height of its mound.

478 Again *ǧāhidan*, taken up from verse 1 ("as much as I could").

479 Or "inwardly and outwardly".

480 In the usage of DabMaʿālim, the term *mašhad* often denotes the tombstone itself, not a larger building around it or a shrine in the proper sense. In other cases, the term is used to refer to the cenotaph.

tomb in Aylah (?) one could read: [...]" (IRağAhwāl); "al-ᶜAbbās b. Mūsā said, 'I read on a tomb: [...]" (TMD LIV p. 57); al-Qurṭubī presents these lines as "regular" poetry, anonymously and without reference to an epitaph. – Three verses in the metre *sarīʿ*:

*al-mawtu baḥrun ʿāmiqun mawǧuhū * taḥāru fīhi ḥīlatu s-sābiḥī*
*yā-nafsu ʾinnī wāʿiẓun fa-smaʿī * maqālatan min mušfiqin nāṣiḥī*
*mā yaṣḥabu l-mayyita fī qabrihī * ġayru t-tuqā wa-l-ʿamali ṣ-ṣāliḥī*

1 *ʿāmiqun*: *ṭāfiḥun* (QurṭTaḏk), *ġālibun* (TMD, IRağAhwāl); *taḥāru*: *taḏhabu* (TMD LIV p. 57, QurṭTaḏk), *taḏhalu* (TMD XXXII p. 480), *taḍullu* (IRağAhwāl); *ḥīlatu*: *ḥiyalu* (TMD XXXII p. 480). – **2** *wāʿiẓun fa-smaʿī*: *qāʾilun* ... (TMD LIV p. 57, QurṭTaḏk), *qāʾilun fa-stamiʿī* (IRağAhwāl, does not fit the metre). – **3** *mā yaṣḥabu l-mayyita*: *lā yaṣḥabu l-ʾinsāna* (TMD LIV p. 57), *lā yaṣḥābu l-marʾa ʾilā qabrihī* (TMD XXXII p. 480), *lā yanfaʿu l-ʾinsāna* (QurṭTaḏk), *mā ṣāḥaba l-ʾinsāna* (IRağAhwāl); *ġayru*: *miṯlu* (IRağAhwāl).

"Death is an ocean with deep waves[481] * in which the tricks of the swimmer are of little avail.
O soul, I am truly an (exhorting) sermoniser, so listen * to the discourse of someone full of tenderness who gives good advice:
The deceased in his tomb is accompanied * only by godliness and righteous deeds!"

102

LOCATION. Ḫurāsān. DATE. Unknown.
PERSON BURIED. The father of ᶜAlī Šār, Maǧd ad-Dīn (no historical figure).
SOURCE. ALL (B) II p. 621 (= 310th night) = Littmann III p. 210 (309th night, in German translation).
DESCRIPTION. "They put him into the ground (*wa-wārūhu fī t-turāb*) and inscribed upon his tomb the following two verses: [...]". – Two verses in the metre *wāfir*:

*ḫuliqta mina t-turābi fa-ṣirta ḥayyan * wa-ʿullimta l-faṣāḥata fī l-ḫiṭābī*
*wa-ʿudta ʾilā t-turābi fa-ṣirta maytan * ka-ʾannaka mā bariḥta mina t-turābī*

"You were created from earth and began to live, * and then you were taught to express yourself eloquently in speech,
And then you returned to the earth and became dead, * just as if you had never left the earth!"

NOTE. Man's being created from earth, and his eventually being returned to earth, is a frequent topos in Arabic mourning poetry; it is as well a concept familiar to the Western reader from the Christian tradition. The author of the *Sirāǧ al-mulūk*, aṭ-Ṭurṭūšī, relates the following in the hortatory section of his book:

481 The same is said of the present world in a poem cited in ṬurṭSirāǧ p. 12 (*ʾayyuhā l-marʾu ʾinna dunyāka baḥrun * ṭāfiḥun mawǧuhū ...*).

"One day I stayed in Iraq, and when I took a sip of water a companion of mine, who was a person of sound understanding, told me, 'My fellow, the mug from which you are drinking was perhaps a man some day in the past. Since after his death he turned into earth, it may have happened that the potter took the earth of the tomb, moulded earthenware from it and heated it in the fire, so he (*sc.* the deceased) became the mug, which you are holding now![482] And he was moulded into vessels that are employed and used in daily service, after having been a well-proportioned human being who ate and drank, who prospered (in life), who cheered and sang'. Indeed, my companion's words are not far from the truth, because man turns into earth after his death, as he had been before his initial coming into being. Then it may happen that his burial niche is dug open and its earth soaked with water, then someone produces vessels from it for domestic use or as a brick. As a consequence, he (i.e. the former human being) is put in a wall (as a brick); or he tiles a roof as clay; or he covers the street in a village, where he is trampled upon by many feet; or he is smeared on a wall as clay. It is even possible that a tree is planted at his tomb, and thus the earth of a man will change into a tree and leaves and fruits. The beasts will then pasture the leaves and the men eat the fruits, from which their flesh will grow and their bones stretch".[483]

103

LOCATION. Játiva (ar. Šāṭibah). DATE. 587 H.

PERSON BURIED. The man of letters and traditionist Abū Bakr Ibn Muġāwir (ʿAr. b. M. as-Sulamī, Šāṭibah 502–87 H): IAbbTakm III pp. 39-41, ŠḎ IV p. 289.

SOURCES. IAbbTakm III p. 40; QurṭTaḏk p. 106; MaqqNafḥ (B) III p. 331 (only verses 1-3) and IV p. 342 / (C) VI pp. 74f.; IDiḥMuṭrib p. *ش (editor's introduction).

DESCRIPTION. Various scholars reported that "Abū Bakr as-Sulamī (Ibn Muġāwir) directed that there should be inscribed upon his tomb (*ḫṭṭ* I): [...]" (IAbbTakm); "He ordered that these verses, composed by him, be written upon his tomb: [...]" (MaqqNafḥ); "Abū Bakr (...) Ibn Muġāwir as-Sulamī al-Kātib, an eloquent scholar from eastern al-Andalus, excelled in his saying [...]" (QurṭTaḏk). – Four verses in the metre *ḫafīf*:

*ʾayyuhā l-wāqifu ʿtibāran bi-qabrī * stamiʿ fīhi qawla ʿaẓmī r-ramīmī*
*ʾawdaʿūnī baṭna ḍ-ḍarīḥi wa-ḫāfū * min ḏunūbin kulūmuhā bi-ʾadīmī*
*qultu lā taǧziʿū ʿalayya fa-ʾinnī * ḥasanu ẓ-ẓanni bi-r-raʾūfi r-raḥīmī*
*wa-trukūnī bi-mā ktasabtu rahīnan * ġaliqa r-rahnu ʿinda mawlan karīmī*

2 *ḏunūbin ... bi-ʾadīmī*: *ḏunūbī wa-ʾāyasū min naʿīmī* (QurṭTaḏk); بأديمي: بأديم (IAbbTakm, var. in ms.). – **3** om. MaqqNafḥ (B) III p. 331, IDiḥMuṭrib (introd.). – **4** *wa-trukūnī*: *wa-daʿūnī* (QurṭTaḏk, MaqqNafḥ, both citations; IDiḥMuṭrib); *bimā ktasabtu*: *bimā katabtu* (IDiḥMuṭrib).

482 This motif is also elaborated in several poems by the sixth-century poet ʿUmar Ḫayyām, see Arberry: *Omar Khayyám* pp. 54 (no. 17), 58 (no. 29), 78 (no. 89), 83 (no. 105) and *passim*.

483 ṬurṭSirāǧ p. 26.

"O you standing before my tomb and reflecting: * lend your ear to what my decaying bones are saying in it (i.e. the tomb)!
They deposited me in the belly of the grave and were afraid * of sins whose scars were on my skin.
I said, 'Do not grieve over me, because I am * full of confidence in (*or* I think well of) the Merciful, the Compassionate!
Leave me alone with what I have acquired as a pledge (in the tomb): * the pledge can only be redeemed with a noble patron (i.e. God)'".

104

LOCATION. Kairouan (ar. Qayrawān). DATE. 270 / 277 H.

PERSON BURIED. The Hanafite judge Abū r-Rabīᶜ Sulaymān b. ᶜImrān (183–270 or 277 H): ḪušṬab pp. 49-51 and 89; MālRiyāḍ I p. 514; DabMaᶜālim II pp. 151-8; ŠN pp. 70f.

SOURCES. DabMaᶜālim II pp. 157f. (version I), III p. 96 (version II); ŠN p. 71 (version II).

DESCRIPTION. "His tomb is a place of frequent visiting (*mazār*), and at its head there is a tombstone (*lawḥ*) upon which is written: [...], followed by the date of his death, as usual (*kamā huwa l-ᶜādah*)" (version I);[484] "When I looked at his tombstone (*mašhaduhū*),[485] I noticed that upon it was inscribed: [...]" (version II).

Version I:

hāḏā qabru l-qāḍī Sulaymāna bni ᶜImrān

"This is the tomb of the judge Sulaymān b. ᶜImrān".

Version II:

hāḏā qabru Sulaymāna bni ᶜImrāna l-qāḍī tuwuffiya laylata s-sabti li-sabᶜin baqīna min Ṣafarin sanata sabᶜin wa-sabᶜīna wa-miʾatayn

"This is the tomb of Sulaymān b. ᶜImrān the judge. He died during the night to Saturday, seven nights before the end of Ṣafar of the year 277".[486]

484 Ibn Nāǧī at-Tanūḫī makes a similar comment about the tomb of Abū Bakr Ibn Abī Ṭāᶜah (d. Ḏū l-Ḥiǧǧah 438 H): "On the tombstone his name, his father's name and the date of his death are inscribed, as is usually done in those cases (*ᶜalā ǧaryi l-ᶜādati fī ḏālika*).

485 For the term *mašhad*, "tombstone", see also DabMaᶜālim III p. 174 (addition of Ibn Nāǧī at-Tanūḫī) and above n. 480.

486 In DabMaᶜālim II p. 156, the date of Sulaymān's death is correctly given in one ms. according to what we read in version II (see p. 156 notes 1f.), whereas the ms. chosen by the modern editor for the main text is corrupt and makes the time of his death appear to be the time of his birth. However, the year 270 is there adduced in both mss., in obvious disagreement with the information provided in version II.

105

Location. Kairouan.

Date. Unknown (before the middle of the fifth century H).

Person buried. The reciter and poet ᶜAbd Allāh b. Falāḥ: IRašUnmūḏağ pp. 196f.; *Wāfī* XVII pp. 403f.

Sources. IRašUnmūḏağ p. 197; *Wāfī* XVII p. 403 (var. *rasmuhū*: *ramsuhū*).

Description. "The following is what he had written on a marble slab under his head upon his tomb" (?, *wa-minhu mā katabahū fī ruḫāmatin taḥta raʾsihī fī qabrihī*: IRašUnmūḏağ); "(...) what was written on a marble slab at the head of his tomb" (... *mā kutiba fī ruḫāmatin ᶜinda raʾsihī fī qabrihī*: *Wāfī*). – Three verses in the metre *ṭawīl*:

*ʾa-yā-man raʾā qabran taḍammana rasmuhū * ʾaḫā sakratin mā ʾin yufīqu ʾilā l-ḥašri*
*wa-mā sāʾanī l-ʾaḥbābu fī barzaḫi l-bilā * fa-ʾaṣbaḥtu lā ʾazdādu ʾillā ᶜalā ᶜuqrī*
wa-ʾaṣbaḥa waǧhī baᶜda ʾāyi[487] *naḍāratin * kasāhu l-bilā ṯawban yuǧaddu maᶜa d-dahrī*

"O you who saw a tomb whose shape encloses * a brother given to inebriety[488] who will certainly not get up again[489] until the (Day of the) Gathering.
The loved ones do not vex me in the limbo of decay * since I came to grow only in sterility.[490]
And my face was, after signs of freshness (in life), * clothed by decay as with a garment that is (always) renewed in the course of time".

106

Location. al-Karmīnīyah (near Buḫārā). Date. Fourth century H (?).

Person buried. The poet Abū l-Ḥusayn Muḥammad b. Muḥammad al-Murādī.

Sources. ṮaᶜālYat IV p. 76; ZawzḤam I p. 218.

Description. "Abū l-Ǧadd al-Ḫuzāᶜī told me that he read on the tomb of Abū l-Ḥusayn al-Murādī in Karmīnīyah the following two verses, and he (i.e. the deceased) had ordered them to be inscribed (*ʾamara bi-katbihimā*): [...]" (ZawzḤam); aṯ-Ṯaᶜālibī does not describe these lines as an epitaph. – Two verses in the metre *sarīᶜ*:

487 Both editions of the poem vowel *ʾayyi naḍāratin*, but I think *ʾāy* fits the present context much better.

488 I wonder whether a wordplay is intended here: *sakratun*, "intoxication, inebriety", or also "the agony, *or* pain of death" (*sakratu l-mawt*).

489 Or "regain his sobriety"?

490 I.e. he left no offspring, because he grew more and more sterile, due to drinking. Thus there are no loved children whose grief would vex the deceased in his tomb.

*ʿāša l-Murādīyu li-ʾaḍyāfihī * wa-māta ḍayfan li-ʾilāhi s-samā*
*wa-llāhu ʾawlā bi-qirā ḍayfihī * fal-yadaʿi n-nāsu ʿalayhi l-bukā*

1 *wa-māta*: *fa-ṣāra* (ṮaʿālYat). – 2 *an-nāsu*: *al-bākī* (ṮaʿālYat).

"al-Murādī used to live for his guests * and he died as a guest of the God of Heaven.
God is the most likely to receive his guest hospitably, * so let the people stop weeping for him (i.e. the deceased)!"

107

LOCATION. Konya (ar. Qunyah). DATE. 1054 H.
PERSON BURIED. The Turkish scholar and mystic ʿAbd Allāh b. ʿAbdī ar-Rūmī al-Būsnawī (992–1054 H): MuḥḪul III p. 86.
SOURCE. MuḥḪul III p. 86.
DESCRIPTION. "He was buried near the mausoleum (*qubbah*) of the mystic Ṣadr ad-Dīn al-Qūnawī. Upon his tomb a mausoleum was constructed and on his tomb was written: [...]".

hāḏā qabru ġarībi llāhi fī ʾarḍihī wa-smuhū ʿAbdu llāh

"This is the tomb of a stranger of God in *his land* / *His land*, and his name is ʿAbd Allāh".

NOTE. The message of this epitaph is not wholly clear to me. However, there is a saying by the mystic Abū l-ʿAbbās al-Mursī which might shed some light on it: "The ascetic (*zāhid*) is a stranger in the present world, because his homeland (*waṭan*) is the hereafter and the gnostic (*ʿārif*) is a stranger in the hereafter, because he stays with God".[491]

108

LOCATION. Kūfah. DATE. *c.*154 H.
PERSON BURIED. The philologist Abū ʿAmr b. al-ʿAlāʾ b. ʿAmmār (al-Māzinī at-Tamīmī, born in Mecca between 65 and 70, d. Kūfah *c.*154 H): MarzNūr pp. 25-37; AnbNuzhah pp. 24-9; ŠarŠMaq II pp. 276-9; IḪallWaf III pp. 466-70; SuyBuġ II pp. 231f.; GAS IX pp. 40-2.
SOURCES. ŠarŠMaq II p. 278; IḪallWaf III p. 469 / (Slane) II p 402.
DESCRIPTION. "On his tomb is written: [...]" (ŠarŠMaq); "A traditionist mentioned that he saw the tomb of Abū ʿAmr in Kūfah bearing the inscription: [...]" (IḪallWaf).

491 Quoted in ŠaʿrṬab II p. 17. *Cf.* also Bauer: *Fremdheit* pp. 99-101.

hāḏā qabru ʾAbī ʿAmri bni l-ʿAlāʾi mawlā banī Ḥanīfah

hāḏā qabru ʾAbī: *hāḏā ʾAbū* (ŠarŠMaq); *mawlā banī Ḥanīfah*: om. IḪallWaf.

"This is the tomb of Abū ʿAmr b. al-ʿAlāʾ, the client of the Banū Ḥanīfah".

109

LOCATION. Kūfah (an-Naǧaf). DATE. 418 (or 428 H).

PERSON BURIED. The Shiite man of letters, scholar and state official al-Wazīr al-Maġribī (Abū l-Qāsim al-Ḥusayn b. ʿAlī b. al-Ḥusayn,[492] Cairo or Aleppo 370 – Mayyāfāriqīn 418 or, less probable, 428 H): IṢayrIšārah pp. 48f.; IǦawzīMunt VIII pp. 32f.; YāqIršād IV pp. 60-4; IḪallWaf II pp. 172-7; *Wāfī* XII pp.440-6; BN XII p. 23; MaqrMuq III pp. 536-60; DāʾūdīṬab I pp. 155-8; ŠḎ III p. 210; ZA II p. 245.[493]

SOURCES. IǦawzīMunt VIII p. 33; YāqIršād IV p. 61; IḪallWaf II p. 176 / (Slane) I p. 454; *Wāfī* XII p. 443; BN XII p. 23; MaqrMuq III p. 554; NZ IV p. 266; DāʾūdīṬab I pp. 157.

DESCRIPTION. After his death in Mayyāfāriqīn, al-Wazīr al-Maġribī "was brought to Kūfah, according to his last will (...) There he was buried in a mausoleum (*turbah*) in the vicinity of the shrine of ʿAlī b. Abī Ṭālib,[494] and he had instructed that on his tomb be inscribed: [...]" (IḪallWaf, almost verbatim also YāqIršād);[495] "He composed a *Dīwān* of poetry, and from his poetry are the following verses: [...]" (MaqrMuq); IǦawzīMunt and BN do not mention an epitaph. – Three verses in the metre *ḫafīf*:

*kuntu fī safrati l-ġawāyati wa-l-ǧah- * li muqīman fa-ḥāna minnī qudūmū*
*tubtu min kulli maʾṯamin fa-ʿasā yum- * ḥā bi-hāḏā l-ḥadīṯi ḏāka l-qadīmū*
*baʿda ḫamsin wa-ʾarbaʿīna laqad mā * ṭultu ʾillā ʾanna l-ġarīma karīmū*

1 *al-ġawāyati*: *al-biṭālati* (IǦawzīMunt); *muqīman*: *zamānan* (IǦawzīMunt, MaqrMuq); *minnī qudūmū*: *minnī l-qudūmu* (BN, MaqrMuq). – **3** *baʿda*: *ibnu* (MaqrMuq). The first and third lines in BN are corrupt.

"I was heading out on a journey of error and igno- * rance steadily, then it was time for my arrival (to God):
I repented for every sin, and maybe this new (change of mind) will wipe * out all that (had taken place) of old.

492 *Cf.* IʿAdīmBuġyah VI pp. 241ff.

493 See also the editor's introduction in MaġrSīrah I pp. س – ن.

494 Until here, the notice is corroborated by MaqrMuq III p. 553.

495 For the mausoleum, see Leisten: *Architektur für Tote* p. 207 (no. 3). The mausoleum of a certain al-Wazīr Abū l-Qāsim b. al-Maġribī in Cairo (see IZayKawākib p. 165, SaḫTuḥfAḥbāb p. 140) must therefore belong to somebody else, possibly to the vizier Abū l-Faraǧ Ibn al-Maġribī (M. b. Ǧaʿfar, d. Cairo 478 H), see MaqrMuq V pp. 502f.

After five and forty (years of my life), I did not stay * (on earth any longer) except (trusting) that my debtor (i.e. God) is noble-minded".[496]

Note. These verses, especially the last line, obviously refer to the biography of al-Wazīr al-Maġribī. Since the story of his life is, notwithstanding the richness of the sources, not satisfactorily known till now, the exact meaning of the verses cited above is difficult to determine. However, in 415 H – i.e. at the age of 45, which matches the date given in the third line of the epitaph – he was dismissed from his post as vizier under the Būyid ruler Abū ᶜAlī Mušarrif ad-Dawlah (r. 412–16 H) in Baghdad and afterwards did not, it seems, take up another official position.

110

Location. Lebanon (on the top of a hill). Date. Second century H (?).
Person buried. Unknown.
Source. IADunyāQubūr (A) p. 161.
Description. "I read on a tomb: [...]". The chain of transmission mentions Aḥmad b. Sahl al-Azdī who read the inscription and afterwards commented, "By God, whenever this verse comes to my mind, I start trembling". – One verse in the metre *maǧzūᵓ al-ḫafīf*:

*kariha l-mawta man ᶜaraf * kuraba l-mawti wa-l-ġuṣaṣ*

"Everyone hates death who experienced (*or* knows) * the torments of death and mortal agony".[497]

111

Location. Maᶜarrat an-Nuᶜmān. Date. 449 H.
Person buried. The acclaimed poet Abū l-ᶜAlāᵓ al-Maᶜarrī (A. b. ᶜAl. b. Sulaymān at-Tanūḫī, Maᶜarrat an-Nuᶜmān 363–449 H): TB IV pp. 240f.; YāqIršād I pp. 162-216; IḪallWaf I pp. 113-6; QifṭīInbāh I pp. 46-83; *Wāfī* VII pp. 94-111; NZ V pp. 61f.; SuyBuġ I pp. 315-7; GAL I pp. 254f.; ZA I p. 157; EAL I pp. 24f.
Sources. IḪallWaf I p. 115 / (Slane) I p. 96; ṢafĠayṯ II p. 338; BN XII p. 75; SuyBuġ I p. 317; BaḥrKaškūl III p. 198; al-Ġazzī: *Nahr aḏ-ḏahab* I p. 323; Ǧarǧūr: *Taslīṭ an-nūr* p. 47; Khawam: *Poésie arabe* p. 266 (in French translation); Reynold A. Nicholson: *A Literary History of the Arabs*, London 1907, p. 317; Nicholson: *Studies* p. 140 (both in English translation).
Description. al-Maᶜarrī instructed in his will that the line quoted below be written on his tomb. For all we know, the epitaph was never part of al-Maᶜarrī's tomb.

496 *Cf.* Slane's translation: "I had hoped for a longer respite, did I not know that my ...".

497 On the throes of death and the agony of dying, as well as the various terms for this in Arabic, see the detailed survey in IǦawzīṮabāt pp. 61-70.

Parts of al-Maᶜarrī's cenotaph as well as his epitaph, on a fragment of a stone stele (reconstructed in the early 20th century CE), can still be seen in Maᶜarrat an-Nuᶜmān,[498] but his mausoleum has largely vanished (see above p. 292). However, the partially effaced tombstone as visible today does not bear the line cited below: the conserved part of the inscription, in florial Kufic letters, contains on one side of the stele the name of the poet ([...] *al-ʿAlāʾi bni ʿAbdi / llāhi bni Sulaymāna*), while on the other it simply says *raḍiya llāhu ʿanhu* ("may God be pleased with him").[499] According to al-Ġazzī, on the other hand, the verses actually inscribed upon the tomb of al-Maᶜarrī were those of the epitaph of Šihāb ad-Dīn as-Suhrawardī (**5**). In any case it seems that, as far as we can say today, the verse quoted below was never actually written on the tomb of al-Maᶜarrī. This is supported by the fact that in the literary sources at our disposal nobody claims to have read the verse on this tomb, and even the Aleppine philologist Ibn al-Qifṭī, who visited al-Maᶜarrī's tomb and "walked around his cenotaph", mentions neither this nor another inscription on the tomb or an affixed tombstone (see above p. 292). The most explicit reference for this, however, is provided by aṣ-Ṣafadī who in his commentary on the *Lāmīyat al-ʿağam* cites the following passage from ᶜAlāʾ ad-Dīn al-Wadāᶜī: "I visited his tomb – may God the Exalted have mercy upon him! – in al-Maᶜarrah in Rabīᶜ I of the year 679 and I did not see inscribed upon it what is said to be his epitaph. The tomb was ruined and thickly covered by earth. I composed the following verses (*kāmil*):

قَدْ زُرْتُ قَبْرَ أَبِي العَلَاءِ المُرْتَضَى * لَمَّا أَتَيْتُ مَعَرَّةَ النُّعْمَانِ
وَسَأَلْتُ مَنْ غَفَرَ الخَطَايَا أَنَّهُ * يُهْدِي إِلَيْهِ رِسَالَةَ الغُفْرَانِ

"I visited the tomb of Abū l-ᶜAlāʾ, the satisfying one (in the eyes of God), * when I came to Maᶜarrat an-Nuᶜmān,
And I asked the Pardoner of sins that He * may bring him 'The Epistle of Pardoning'".[500]

One verse in the metre *mağzūʾ al-kāmil*:

*hāḏā ğanāhu ʾabī ʿalay- * ya wa-mā ğanaytu ʿalā ʾaḥad*

"This wrong was by my father done * to me, but ne'er by me to one" (Nicholson's translation).[501]

Note. The second hemistich implies (correctly) that al-Maᶜarrī himself did not produce any offspring. The tone of al-Maᶜarrī's epitaph has the pessimistic ring to it for which much of the poet's work has become famous,[502] yet it seems that Reynold

498 Mausolée Abū l-ᶜAlāʾ plates V-VIII. *Cf.* also EI² V p. 926.

499 RCEA 2592; Mausolée Abū l-ᶜAlāʾ p. 290 (with plate VI).

500 ṢafĠayṯ II p. 339. As is obvious, the last verse contains a wordplay (*tawriyah*) upon the title of one of al-Maᶜarrī's most famous works, entitled *Risālat al-ġufrān*.

501 In his *Studies*, Nicholson translates: "My sire brought this on me, but I on none". The first hemistich is obviously rather ironical, for the expression *hāḏā ğanāhu* ... mirrors the common formula *hāḏā qabru* ... ("This is the tomb of ...") and the continuation ... *ʾabī ʿalayya* clearly plays with the poet's name, viz. Abū l-ᶜAlāʾ, as if one would expect the line to run: *hāḏā qabru ʾAbī l-ʿAlāʾi.*

502 This, on the other hand, sheds some doubt upon the veracity of the line, especially as it does not seem to have ever been inscribed on the poet's tomb. For his pessimism as well as his other views pertaining to religion and belief, al-Maᶜarrī was by many dubbed a "heretic", a fact that was also seen to influence the poet's destiny after his death and "we find a description of two snakes hanging down a blind man's chest biting his flesh, while he is calling for help.

Nicholson's assessment of the epitaph overemphasises its actual message: "Here we face pessimism as a practical creed remorselessly pointing to the extinction of mankind".[503]

Begetting a child was often, at least among ascetics and the pious, labelled "committing an offense against someone" or "bringing wrong upon someone", because birth was seen as the initial stage of the tormented process eventually leading to death and decay. Ibn Ḫallikān explicitly mentions this concept after citing al-Maᶜarrī's epitaph, and the Western reader will be reminded of what Rousseau wrote in the first chapter of his *Confessions*: "ma naissance fut le premier de mes malheurs".[504] However, in Arabic mourning poetry we also find the concept of "bringing injury upon someone" (*ǧny* I *ᶜalā*) connected with the early death of children, for example in verses by al-Qāḍī al-Fāḍil.[505] In this case, the injury was seen as that of death cruelly and undeservedly shortening life and thus "bringing an injury upon someone".

The connection between birth and death was well expressed by Hilāl b. Isāf who said, "No new-born enters the world without some dust in his navel of the earth in which he will die".[506] The following utterance is ascribed to Ḥasan al-Baṣrī: "O Child of Man (*ibn ʾĀdam*), tread the earth with your feet because soon it will be your grave, and you have not ceased losing your life since you left the womb of your mother".[507] In a similar vein, Abū Ḥafṣ ᶜUmar b. al-Ḥasan Ibn al-Fūnī (or al-Qaranī?) said in a verse of his, "To death belongs what is born, not to life" (*li-l-mawti mā yūlad lā li-l-ḥayāti*),[508] and this takes up an old topos which already appears in a line by al-Ḥāriṯ b. ᶜAmr: *fa-li-l-mawti mā talidu l-wālidah*.[509] From the modern account of an Arab Jew from Mosul, Otto Jastrow recorded the following: "Please, I want to ask you a favour. I am seventy years old, I am ailing, and tomorrow or the day after tomorrow I am going to die. My name is Ǧabr. When I die – and I am going to die here, he told him –, write on my tombstone: This man was called Ǧabr. From his mother's womb (lit. vagina) he went directly to the grave".[510]

The motiv of birth as the prelude to death (or the begin of dying), not of life, was commonly employed in the so-called *ḏamm ad-dunyā* poetry which deals with the hardships of life and the concept of *vanitas mundi*. As might be expected,

Along with this sight, a voice is heard: 'This is al-Maᶜarrī the heretic'" (cited from Ibn Kaṯīr in Kinberg: *Interaction* p. 294).

503 Nicholson: *Studies* p. 140f.

504 Jean-Jacques Rousseau: *Œuvres complètes I: Les confessions. Autres textes autobiographiques*, edd. B. Gagnebin et al., Paris 1959 (and repr.), p. 7.

505 QFāḍilDīwān pp. 394 and 407.

506 Quoted in IQutᶜUyūn II pp. 331f. and (ascribed to others) KU 42766 (XC p. 692). Interestingly, there are some very similar Traditions in KulKāfī III pp. 202, attributed to Ǧaᶜfar aṣ-Ṣādiq.

507 Quoted in ANuḤilyah II p. 155 and TawḥBaṣāʾir IX p. 182.

508 IṣfḪar (M) I p. 103 and IQaṭṭāᶜDurrah p. 146.

509 Cited in WriǦurzah p. 106.

510 The implication being that the man had reached the age of seventy, yet he had lived a bitter life and thus did not really live it. See Jastrow: *Three Anecdotes* pp. 62f.

though, equating birth with death was not convincing in the eyes of the Sunnite theologians and they preferred to view it the other way round, death as a "second birth" or a rebirth.[511]

112

LOCATION. Málaga (ar. Mālaqah). DATE. 652 H.

PERSON BURIED. The man of letters Ibn Bāq al-Umawī (Abū ᶜAbd Allāh Muḥammad. b. Ibrāhīm b. ᶜAlī, d. 652 H): IḪaṭIḥāṭah II pp. 338-41; MaqqNafḥ (C) VIII pp. 370-2.

SOURCES. IḪaṭIḥāṭah II pp. 340f.; MaqqNafḥ (B) VI p. 265 / (C) VIII p. 372.

DESCRIPTION. "He had directed in his last will (...) that the following verses be written upon his tomb: [...]" (IḪaṭIḥāṭah); "He directed by will, after his tomb had been dug between his two teachers al-Ḫaṭīb Abū ᶜAbd Allāh aṭ-Ṭanǧālī and al-Ḫaṭīb Abū ᶜUṯmān b. ᶜĪsā, that he be buried in it and that the following verses be written upon it: [...]" (MaqqNafḥ). – Five verses in the metre *ṭawīl*:

*taraḥḥam ᶜalā qabri bni Bāqin wa-ḥayyihī * fa-min ḥaqqi mayti l-ḥayyi taslīmu ḥayyihī*
wa-qul ᵓammana[512] *r-raḥmānu rawᶜata ḫāᵓifin * li-tafrīṭihī fī l-wāǧibāti wa-ġīyihī*
*qadi ḫtāra hāḏā l-qabra fī l-ᵓarḍi rāǧiyan * mina llāhi taḫfīfan bi-qurbi*[513] *walīyihī*
*fa-qad yašfaᶜu l-ǧāru l-karīmu li-ǧārihī * wa-yašmalu bi-l-maᶜrūfi ᵓahla nadīyihī*
*wa-ᵓinnī bi-faḍli llāhi ᵓawṯaqu wāṯiqin * wa-ḥasbī wa-ᵓin ᵓaḏnabtu ḥubbu nabīyihī*

"Invoke mercy upon the tomb of Ibn Bāq and greet him, * for the dead of the quarter[514] are entitled to receive the greeting of those who are (still) alive in it!
And say: 'May the Merciful take away the fear of someone who is frightened * because of his negligence in the (religious) duties and (of) his transgression!'
He (i.e. the deceased) chose this tomb in the earth hoping * from God for an easing (of his fate) by being near to His close associate.[515]
For it happens that the Noble Neighbour intercedes on behalf of his protégé * and bestows favours upon the people of His assembly (i.e. community).
I am most firmly confident about the grace of God * and, although I did wrong (in life), the love of His Prophet will suffice for me".

511 HarMirqātMaf I p. 176.

512 Or *ᵓāmana*, as in MaqqNafḥ (B).

513 MaqqNafḥ: *bi-qadri*.

514 I.e. of his living quarter (*al-ḥayy*). The term *ḥayy* – which might also mean "living" or "alive" – was coupled here with *mayt* by the poet on purpose.

515 Here: the Prophet.

113

LOCATION. Málaga. DATE. Second half of the 7th or early 8th century H.

PERSON BURIED. The state official Yūsuf b. Ridwān al-Anṣārī an-Naǧǧārī (d. Málaga ?), father of the judge Abū l-Qāsim.

SOURCE. IḪaṭIḥāṭah IV pp. 426f.

DESCRIPTION. "Upon his tomb is inscribed from the poetry of his son: [...]". – Eight verses in the metre *ṭawīl*:

*ʾilāhiya ḫaddī fī t-turābi taḏallulan * busiṭtu ʿasā ruḥmāka yuḥyā bihā r-rūḥū*
*wa-ǧāwaztu ʾaǧdāṯa l-mamāliki ḫāḏiʿan * wa-qalbiya maṣdūʿun wa-damʿiya masfūḥū*
*wa-waǧǧahtu waǧhī naḥwa ǧūdika ḍāriʿan * laʿalla r-riḍā min ǧanbi ḥilmika mamnūḥū*
*ʾataytu faqīran wa-ḏ-ḏunūbu taʾudduni * wa-fī l-qalbi min ḫawfi l-ǧarāʾimi tabrīḥū*
*wa-lam ʾaʿtamid ʾillā r-raǧāʾa wasīlatan * wa-ʾiḫlāṣa ʾīmānin bihī ṣ-ṣadru mašrūḥū*
*wa-ʾanta ġanīyun ʿan ʿaḏābī wa-ʿālimun * bi-faqrī wa-bābu l-ʿafwi ʿindaka maftūḥū*
*fa-hab liya ʿafwan min ladunka wa-raḥmatan * yakūnu bihā min riqbati ḏ-ḏanbi tasrīḥū*
*wa-ṣalli ʿalā l-muḫtāri mā hamaʿa l-ḥayā * wa-mā ṭalaʿat šamsun wa-mā habbati r-rīḥū*

"O my God, my cheek lies in the earth! In humble abasement * I was stretched out, yet perhaps by your saying 'May God have mercy upon you!' my soul will be revived!
I have been past by the tombs of royal powers (lit. kingdoms) in submissiveness[516] * while my heart was broken and my tears kept pouring,
And I turned my face towards Your generosity in frailty, * perhaps the satisfaction (with me) on part of Your clemency will be granted.
I came (to You) destitute, sins afflicting me * and in the heart agony caused by the fear of the offenses (I committed).
I did not rely upon anything as a means (of securing Your mercy) except the hope * and the sincerity of faith that gladdens the heart.
You are in no need of my Chastisement and You know * that I am in need (of You), the door of forgiveness being open with You.
Thus bestow on me Your forgiveness and mercy * that will release (me) from the bond of sinful behaviour
And invoke blessings upon the Chosen (Prophet) as long as the rain pours forth * and as long as the sun rises and as long as the wind blows!

516 The significance of this hemistich is not altogether clear to me. Perhaps the tombs reminded him of death and so created the feeling of submissiveness.

114

LOCATION. Málaga. DATE. 733 H.

PERSONS BURIED. The Naṣrid ruler Abū ᶜAbd Allāh Muḥammad IV b. Ismāᶜīl I, Ibn Abī l-Walīd (born 715, r. 725–33 H): IḪaṭIḥāṭah I pp. 532-44 and IḪaṭLamḥah pp. 90-102; DK IV pp. 9f.; ZA VI p. 36; Harvey: *Islamic Spain* pp. 187-9; Kennedy: *Muslim Spain* pp. 287f.; Arié: *Temps des Naṣrides* pp. 98-101.

SOURCES. IḪaṭIḥāṭah I pp. 541f. and IḪaṭLamḥah pp. 97f. = Casiri: *Bibliotheca* II p. 297 (only the prose); Inscriptions Espagne 167 (only the passage in prose).

DESCRIPTION. "On a marble slab (*lawḥ ar-ruḫām*) at the head (of the tomb) there is the inscription: [...]". From the description given by Ibn al-Ḫaṭīb it appears that Muḥammad IV was not, as the other ruling members of his family, buried in Granada, but in Málaga (where later a mausoleum, *qubbah*, was constructed over his tomb). The epitaph cited, no longer extant, contains a passage in rhymed prose and a poem of 11 verses (*kāmil*). – The wording edited in the following, especially the poetry, is largely based on IḪaṭLamḥah:

hāḏā qabru s-sulṭāni l-ʾaǧalli l-maliki l-humāmi l-ʾamḍā l-bāsili l-ǧawādi ḏī l-maǧdi l-ʾaṯīl / wa-l-mulki l-ʾaṣīl || al-muqaddasi l-marḥūmi ʾAbī ᶜAbdi llāhi Muḥammadi bni s-sulṭāni l-ǧalīli l-kabīri r-rafīᶜi l-ʾawḥadi l-muǧāhidi l-humāmi ṣāḥibi l-futūḥi l-masṭūrah / wa-l-maġāzī l-mašhūrah || sulālati ʾanṣāri n-nabīyi – taṣliyah – ʾamīri l-muʾminīn / wa-nāṣiri d-dīn || aš-šahīdi l-muqaddasi l-marḥūmi ʾAbī l-Walīdi bni Faraǧi bni Naṣrin – qaddasa llāhu rūḥahū wa-barrada ḍarīḥahū – kāna mawliduhū fī ṯ-ṯāmini li-Muḥarramin ᶜāma ḫamsata ᶜašara wa-sabᶜimiʾatin wa-būyiᶜa fī l-yawmi llaḏī stušhida fīhi wāliduhū – raḍiya llāhu ᶜanhu – s-sādisi wa-l-ᶜišrīna li-Raǧabin ᶜāma ḫamsatin wa-ᶜišrīna wa-sabᶜimiʾatin wa-tuwuffiya – raḥimahū llāhu – fī ṯ-ṯāliṯi ᶜašara li-Ḏī l-Ḥiǧǧatin min ᶜāmi ṯalāṯatin wa-ṯalāṯīna wa-sabᶜimiʾatin fa-subḥāna man lā yamūt[517]

al-masṭūrah: *al-mastūrah* (IḪaṭLamḥah, Inscriptions Espagne); *ʾamīri l-muʾminīn*: *ʾamīri l-muslimīn* (IḪaṭLamḥah, Casiri, Inscriptions Espagne); *aṯ-ṯāmini li-Muḥarramin*: *aṯ-ṯānī li-Muḥarramin* (IḪaṭIḥāṭah; Ibn al-Ḫaṭīb himself states shortly before on p. 540 of IḪaṭIḥāṭah that Muḥammad's birth took place on Muḥarram 8th);[518] *raḥimahū llāhu*: om. IḪaṭLamḥah and Casiri; the passage *fa-subḥāna man lā yamūt* is inserted before *tuwuffiya* etc. in Casiri.

"This is the tomb of the most sublime ruler, the heroic king, the most effective, the brave, the most generous, the one possessing the glory of noble ancestry / and a kingdom of majestic origins, || the sanctified, the late Abū ᶜAbd Allāh Muḥammad, the son of the sublime ruler, the great, the high-ranking, the unequalled, the heroic striver (on the path of God, i.e. the *ǧihād*), the one in charge of conquests (whose descriptions) fill the chronicles / and of famous campaigns, || the descendant of the 'Helpers' of the Prophet – *taṣliyah* –, the Prince of the Believers, / protector of the creed, || the martyr, the sanctified, the late Abū l-Walīd b. Faraǧ b. Naṣr – may God sanctify his soul and cool his tomb! – His (*sc*. Muḥammad's) birth was on Muḥarram

517 For this closing formula in epitaphs, *cf*. also RCEA 3712 (610 H, Tilimsān).

518 This is further confirmed in DK IV pp. 9f.

8th of the year 715, and allegiance was pledged to him the day his father met his martyrdom – may God be pleased with him –, on Rağab 26th of the year 725. He was taken (to God) – may God have mercy upon him! – on D̲ū l-Ḥiğğah 13th in the year 733. Praise to the One who never dies!”

*yā-qabra sulṭāni š-šuğāʿati wa-n-nadā * farʿi l-mulūki ṣ-ṣīdi ʾaʿlāmi l-hudā*
*wa-sulālati s-salafi llad̲ī ʾāṯāruhū * waḍḍāḥatun li-mani qtadā wa-mani htadā*
*salafun li-ʾanṣāri n-nabīyi nuğāruhū * qad ḥalla minhū fī l-makārimi maḥtidā*
*mutawassiṭu l-bayti llad̲ī qad ʾassasat- * hū sādatu l-ʾamlāki ʾawḥada ʾawḥadā*
*baytun banāhu Muḥammadūna ṯalāṯatun * min ʾāli Naṣrin ʾawraṯūhu Muḥammadā*
*ʾūdiʿta wağhan qad tahallala ḥusnuhū * badran bi-ʾāfāqi l-ğalālati qad badā*
*wa-nadan yasuḥḥu ʿalā l-ʿufāti mawāhiban * maṯnā l-ʾayādī s-sābiġāti wa-mawḥadā*
*yabkīka mad̲ʿūrun bika staʿdā ʿalā * ʾaʿdāʾihī fa-saqaytahum kaʾsa r-radā*
*yabkīka muḥtāğun ʾatāka muʾammilan * fa-ġadā wa-qad šafaʿat yadāka lahū l-yadā*
*ʾammā samāḥuka fa-hwa ʾahmā dīmatan * ʾammā ğalāluka fa-hwa ʾasmā maṣʿadā*
*ğādat ṯarāka mina l-ʾilāhi saḥāʾibun * li-riḍāhu ʿanka tağūdu hād̲ā l-maʿhadā*

2 *waḍḍāḥatun*: *wāḍiḥatun* (IḪaṭIḥāṭah). – **4** *allad̲ī*: om. IḪaṭIḥāṭah; *al-ʾamlāki*: *ʾamlākin* (IḪaṭIḥāṭah). – **5** *banāhu*: *banūhu* (IḪaṭLamḥah). – **6** *qad badā*: *mubradā* (IḪaṭIḥāṭah). – **9** om. IḪaṭIḥāṭah. – **10** *ʾahmā dīmatan*: *ʾasnā dīyatan* (IḪaṭIḥāṭah). – **11** *saḥāʾibun*: *saḥābatun* (IḪaṭIḥāṭah).

“O tomb of the ruler of courage and generosity, * offspring of proud kings, the banners of right guidance,
Descendant of forefathers whose vestiges * are brilliantly clear to those who follow (their) example and are rightly guided,
Ancestors whose descent goes back to the Prophet’s ‘Helpers’ * are the origin of his noble deeds.
(He was) at the centre of a (royal) dynasty which had been foun- * ded by the overlords of the kings, unequalled one after another.
The dynasty was build by three Muḥammads * from the family of Naṣr, and they bequeathed it to Muḥammad (the fourth).
A face was entrusted to you (*sc*. the grave) whose beauty had been radiant * like a full moon that appeared on the horizons of majesty,
And a generosity which on the seekers of favours pours gifts, * conferring liberal benefactions twice and once (more).
A terrified person weeps for you, one who (once) asked your aid * against his enemies, and (then) you served them the cup of destruction (i.e. death).
A needy person weeps for you, one who (once) turned to you full of hope, * he came and your hands had already granted assistance.
As to your magnanimity, it is the most down-pouring of continuous rain, * your sublimity is the loftiest summit!
May clouds (sent) from God shower the moist earth in which you lie, * clouds which pour upon this place (i.e. the tomb) because He has found satisfaction with you!”

115 a–c

al-Maqqarī and al-Yafrānī cite in full three epitaphs and a commemorative tablet, belonging to members of the Moroccan Saᶜdid dynasty. All epitaphs are extant and have been photographed, transcribed and translated repeatedly. It was thus considered unnecessary to edit them again in the present catalogue. However, the fact that they were reproduced in literary sources is interesting in itself, and for that reason I decided to provide at least some basic information about them.

115 a

Location. Marrakech (ar. Marrākuš). – Date. between 964 and 1012 H.[519] – Person buried. The Saᶜdid ruler Muḥammad [Maḥammad] aš-Šayḫ al-Mahdī bi-llāh (r. in Marrakech from 951, in Fez from 956, d. 964 H): Terrasse: *Histoire du Maroc* II pp. 162-78; Abun-Nasr: *History of the Maghrib* pp. 211-3; ZA VII p. 58. – Sources. (Poem:) MaqqRawḍah p. 150; YafrNuzhah p. 37; al-Marrākušī: *Iᶜlām* IV p. 169; Mausolée Saᶜdiens 41; Inscriptions Marrakech 123 (with further modern literary sources). – (Prose:) MaqqRawḍah pp. 151-3; Mausolée Saᶜdiens 26; Inscriptions Marrakech 85 (with plate X). – Description. (Poem:) Abū Firās ᶜAbd al-ᶜAzīz al-Fištālī (957–1030 H or the year after) "recited to me this poem (*qiṭᶜah*), which he had composed to be written upon the tomb (i.e. cenotaph) of the Prince of the Believers al-Mahdī bi-llāh – may God be pleased with him! –, the father of the Prince of the Believers al-Manṣūr bi-llāh[520] – may God support his power and prolong his life for the people in East and West (*li-ʾahli l-ḫāfiqayni*)! –, and I also saw this poem inscribed upon the afore-said tomb: [...]" (MaqqRawḍah); "Upon the marble slab (*ruḫāmah*) of his tomb was engraved: [...]" (YafrNuzhah). The epitaph, the upper sides of a marble *mqābrīyah*, is extant and has been published repeatedly; Deverdun describes it as follows: "caractères élégants entrelacés de rinceaux, assez difficile à lire". – (Prose:) al-Fištālī composed the prose passage "which was written in golden letters upon marble (*marmar*),[521] beside the tomb of the Prince of the Believers al-Mahdī bi-llāh – may God be pleased with him! The text is as follows: [...]" (MaqqRawḍah).

115 b

Location. Marrakech. Date. Between 981 and 1012 H. – Person buried. The Saᶜdid ruler Abū Muḥammad al-Ġālib ᶜAbd Allāh b. Muḥammad [Maḥammad] aš-Šayḫ (r. in Fez 964–81 H), son of al-Mahdī (**115a**): Terrasse: *Histoire du Maroc* II pp. 179-83. – Sources. (Poem:) MaqqRawḍah pp. 154f.; YafrNuzhah p. 47; Mausolée Saᶜdiens 40; Inscriptions Marrakech 125. – (Prose:) MaqqRawḍah pp. 153f.; Mausolée Saᶜdiens 29; Inscriptions Marrakech 82. – Description. (Poem:) The poem is said by al-Maqqarī "to have been composed not by the above-mentioned secretary al-Fištālī (see

519 Considering the fact that the epitaph was composed by the poet al-Fištālī (born in 957 H) it must have been done considerable time after the death of al-Mahdī; al-Fištālī was ordered by al-Manṣūr (see following note) to compose the epitaph, yet we do not know exactly at which point during the reign of al-Manṣūr this happened.

520 al-Manṣūr (r. 986–1012 H), who commissioned the new palace al-Badīᶜ in the Qaṣbah of Marrakech, also had the mausoleum constructed which contains the tomb of al-Mahdī, and commissioned this epitaph from al-Fištālī; see the detailed description of al-Maqqarī's visit to that site in MaqqRawḍah p. 153.

521 For the marble imported from Italy under al-Manṣūr, see Terrasse: *Histoire du Maroc* II pp. 195f.

115a), but by a secretary of al-Mawlā ᶜAbd Allāh";[522] al-Maqqarī quotes the wording "according to what I read inscribed upon the tomb". al-Yafranī, who quotes the verses (but not the commemorative tablet), simply has "His tomb is well-known, and the following was engraved on the marble slab (*ruḫāmah*) on his tomb". The verses are inscribed on the upper sides of the cenotaph, three verses on each side. – (Prose:) Following al-Maqqarī, the prose passage was drafted by al-Fištālī on order of the Saᶜdid ruler al-Manṣūr. As already in the case of **115a**, al-Maqqarī describes its execution as of "golden letters on marble". This prose inscription is engraved separately on a marble slab (praised by Deverdun as "très belle", see also Inscriptions Marrakech IXb).

115 c

LOCATION. Marrakech. DATE. 1000 H (or some time after). – PERSON BURIED. Masᶜūdah, mother of the Saᶜdid ruler Abū l-ᶜAbbās al-Manṣūr Aḥmad b. Maḥammad aš-Šayḫ (r. in Fez 986–1012 H), son of al-Mahdī (**115a**). She died in 1000 H. – SOURCES. MaqqRawḍah p. 155; Mausolée Saᶜdiens 38; Inscriptions Marrakech 127. – DESCRIPTION. According to al-Maqqarī, this epitaph was like the preceding one, written in golden letters on marble, and composed by the same secretary of Mawlā ᶜAbd Allāh (see **115b**). The inscription was engraved on a marble slab which is extant and in good condition ("magnifique plaque de marbre", see also Inscriptions Marrakech plate XIV).

116

LOCATION. Mecca (ar. Makkah). DATE. After 187 H.

PERSONS BURIED. The famous ascetic al-Fuḍayl b. ᶜIyāḍ (Abū ᶜAlī at-Tamīmī, Samarqand *c.*110 – Mecca 187 H), his son ᶜAlī and his grandson ᶜUmar: NasQand pp. 647ff.; IĞawzīṢafwah I pp. 476-81; ŠaybīŠaraf ff. 15b-16a; IFahdItḥāf II p. 245 (short notice); ŠaᶜrṬab I pp. 68f.; MunKawākib I pp. 395-403; Knysh: *Mysticism* pp. 23f. (with further literature). His son Abū ᶜUbaydah ᶜAlī died before his father; he had become famous as an example of piety.[523]

SOURCE. ŠaybīŠaraf ff. 15b-16a.

DESCRIPTION. "On his tombstone is written after the *basmalah*: [...]".

allāhumma nūra s-samāwāti wa-l-ʾarḍi nawwir li-ᶜabdika l-Fuḍayli bni ᶜIyāḍa wa-li-waladihī ʾAbī ᶜUbaydata wa-li-waladi waladihī ᶜUmara bni ᶜUbaydata nawwir lahum fī qubūrihim wa-ʾalḥiqhum bi-nabīyihim Muḥammadin – taṣliyah – wa-ʾānis waḥdatahum wa-rḥam ṣarᶜatahum wa-ǧᶜalhum mina l-ʾāminīna yawma l-fazaᶜi l-ʾakbari yā-ʾarḥama r-rāḥimīn

522 The ruler referred to was either Abū Fāris ᶜAbd Allāh (r. 1012–18 H), a son of al-Manṣūr, or ᶜAbd Allāh b. Maḥammad (!) aš-Šayḫ al-Maʾmūn (r. 1015–32 H).

523 See IĞawzīAᶜmār p. 17 and IĞawzīṢafwah I pp. 481f. According to some, ᶜAlī was found dead in the prayer-niche after having spent the night awake reciting the Qurʾān (IĞawzīAᶜmār p. 17; NasQand p. 649), whereas according to aṯ-Ṯaᶜlabī he died as a result of listening to a Qurʾān recitation (ṮaᶜlQatlā pp. 129f.). Reportedly, his father al-Fuḍayl – who laughed little, or never, in his life – burst out into laughter when sitting at the grave of his recently buried son ᶜAlī, in order to despise the power of Satan (cited in al-Munayyar: *Tasliyah* pp. 29f.; the same story is told of ᶜAl. b. ᶜUmar in IbšīhīMust II p. 449 [ch. 81]). The tomb of al-Fuḍayl b. ᶜIyāḍ is also mentioned in HarIšārāt p. 88.

"O (our) God, Light of the heavens and the earth, enlighten Your servant al-Fuḍayl b. ᶜIyāḍ, his son Abū ᶜUbaydah and the son of his son ᶜUmar b. [Abī] ᶜUbaydah! Illuminate (*or* light) them in their tombs and join them with their Prophet Muḥammad – *taṣliyah* –, ease their solitude, have mercy upon their (miserable) condition and make them part of those safe on the Day of the Greatest Terror (i.e. Judgment Day), O you most merciful of those who have mercy!"

NOTE. al-Fāsī[524] mentions the following in the biography of al-Fuḍayl's grandson ᶜUmar: "I know nothing about him except the fact that he was buried in the tomb of his grandfather al-Fuḍayl b. ᶜIyāḍ in the Maᶜlāh (cemetery), because on his tombstone is written *hāḏā qabru l-Fuḍayli bni ʿIyāḍa wa-waladihī ʾAbī ʿUbaydata wa-waladi waladihī ʿUmara bni ʾAbī ʿUbaydata* ('This is the tomb of al-Fuḍayl b. ᶜIyāḍ, his son Abū ᶜUbaydah and his grandchild ᶜUmar b. Abī ᶜUbaydah')". Scholars of later times desired to be buried beside al-Fuḍayl, e.g. the Hanbalite scholar Abū Bakr az-Zāhid (A. b. ᶜAlī b. A., d. 503 H): "When he performed the pilgrimage, he visited the tombs in Mecca and went to the tomb of al-Fuḍayl, traced the soil with his walking stick and said, 'O my Lord! Here, here (*yā-rabbi hāhunā*)!'"[525]

117

LOCATION. Mecca. DATE. 291 H.

PERSON BURIED. The man of letters, poet and mystic Abū ᶜIqāl (b.?) Ġalbūn [ᶜAlwān] b. al-Ḥasan (Kairouan ? – d. Mecca 291 H), belonging to the Aġlabid clan and for his piety nick-named "the dove of the Sacrosanct Recinct" (*ḥamāmat al-Ḥaram*):[526] MālRiyāḍ I pp. 527-45; ṬurṭSirāǧ p. 22; DabMaᶜālim II pp. 214-31; SaḫTuḥfLaṭ II p. 271; ŠN p. 73;[527] ZA V p. 121.

SOURCES. MālRiyāḍ I p. 538; ṬurṭSirāǧ p. 22; DabMaᶜālim II pp. 217f.

DESCRIPTION. "Abū Bakr b. Saᶜdūn said, 'I saw on the tomb of Abū ᶜIqāl verses which his sister composed when she mourned him. They run as follows: [...]'" (MālRiyāḍ); "He had a devoted sister and when he died she came to visit his tomb in Mecca. She wept at it and wrote these verses upon it: [...]" (ṬurṭSirāǧ); "After his sister had heard of his death, she travelled to Mecca and visited his tomb. She wrote these verses upon the tomb: [...], and his sister was a poetess" (DabMaᶜālim). – Four verses in the metre *ramal*:

*layta šiʿrī mā llaḏī ʿāyantahū * baʿda dawmi ṣ-ṣawmi maʿ nafyi l-wasan*
*maʿ nuzūḥi n-nafsi ʿan ʾawṭānihā * wa-t-taḫallī ʿan ḥabībin wa-sakan*

524 FāsīᶜIqd V p. 358.

525 IĞawzīManIḤanbal p. 526 and IĞawzīṢafwah I p. 632; IRağḎayl II p. 105; FāsīᶜIqd III p. 64; al-ᶜAffānī: *Sakb* I p. 290.

526 He does not seem to be identical to the man of letters Abū ᶜIqāl Saᶜīd b. M. b. Ğurayḥ al-Qayrawānī (second half of the third cent. H) who is mentioned in YāqIršād IV p. 242.

527 This is the only source to give the year of Abū ᶜIqāl's death as 296 H.

*yā-waḥīdan laysa min waǧdī bihī * lawʿatun tamnaʿunī min ʾan ʾuǧan(n)*
*fa-kamā tablā wuǧūhun fī t̠-t̠arā * fa-kad̠ā yablā ʿalayhinna l-ḥazan*

1 *baʿda dawmi*: *baʿda ṭūli* (DabMaᶜālim). – **2** *nuzūḥi*: *ʿuzūbi* (DabMaᶜālim), *ʿuzūfi* (ṬurṭSirāǧ); *ʾawṭānihā*: *ʾawṭārihā* (ṬurṭSirāǧ); *wa-t-taḫallī ʿan ḥabībin*: *min naʿīmin wa-ḥamīmin* (MālRiyāḍ). – **3** *yā-waḥīdan*: *yā-šaqīqa* (ṬurṭSirāǧ, DabMaᶜālim); *min*: *fī* (ṬurṭSirāǧ, DabMaᶜālim); *lawʿatun*: *ʿillatun* (ṬurṭSirāǧ, DabMaᶜālim). – **4** *fa-kamā*: *wa-kamā* (ṬurṭSirāǧ, DabMaᶜālim).

"If I only knew what you saw * after the long, continuous fasting and the refusal of shelter,
The emigration of the soul from its homeland * and the abandonement of a beloved and a dwelling place!?
O you (resting) in solitude! (Yet) there is no grief resulting from my passion (*or* longing) for him * that would prevent me from becoming insane (from love)
Because as certain faces decay in the moist earth * so decays the grief (*or* sorrow) over them!"

NOTE. The sister of Abū ᶜIqāl might have been less of a gifted poetess than these verses suggest because the last line has also been ascribed to Abū l-ᶜAtāhiyah.[528]

118

LOCATION. Mecca (al-Maᶜlāh cemetery). DATE. 470 H.
PERSON BURIED. Yaḥyā b. ᶜAbd ar-Raḥmān aš-Šaybī (d. 470 H): FāsīᶜIqd VI p. 223; IFahdItḥāf II p. 480.
SOURCE. FāsīᶜIqd VI p. 223.
DESCRIPTION. "[...]. He was one of the wardens of the Kaᶜbah, and I know nothing about him besides that (...). He was buried in the Maᶜlāh (cemetery), and I copied the date of his death and his genealogy from his tombstone". (Reconstructed from the account of al-Fāsī):

[hād̠ā qabru] Yaḥyā bni ʿAbdi r-Raḥmāni bni Barakāta š-Šaybīyi l-ʿAbdarīyi + tuwuffiya yawma s-sabti n-niṣfi min Ramaḍāna sanata sabʿīna wa-ʾarbaʿimiʾah

"[This is the tomb of] Yaḥyā b. ᶜAbd ar-Raḥmān b. Barakāt aš-Šaybī al-ᶜAbdarī + He was taken (to God) on Saturday, the middle of Ramaḍān in the year 470".

119

LOCATION. Mecca (al-Maᶜlāh cemetery). DATE. 482 H.
PERSON BURIED. Abū Manṣūr al-Qušayrī (ᶜAbd ar-Raḥmān b. Abī l-Qāsim ᶜAbd al-Karīm b. Hawāzin b. ᶜAbd al-Malik, d. 482 H), the third of the four sons of the famous mystic al-Qušayrī (author of the *Risālah fī t-taṣawwuf*, d. Nīsābūr 465

528 IQutᶜUyūn III p. 66 (with the var. *wa-kamā* ...); the verse is not contained in the various editions of the *Dīwān* of Abū l-ᶜAtāhiyah.

H). He had studied in Nīsābūr and Baghdad and performed the pilgrimage after the death of his mother Fāṭimah in 480 H: NawMuḫt pp. 456f.; FāsīᶜIqd V p. 38; ŠaybīŠaraf ff. 14a-b.

SOURCE. ŠaybīŠaraf f. 14a = RCEA 2779.

DESCRIPTION. "An inscribed tombstone, with writing in old Kufic script. After the *basmalah* and the word of God the Exalted *Every soul shall taste of death* etc. (Q 3:185) is written: [...]" (ŠaybīŠaraf). His tomb is in the vicinity of the grave of al-Fuḍayl b. ᶜIyāḍ.[529]

hāḏā qabru š-šayḫi l-ʾimāmi z-zāhidi ʾAbū (sic) *Manṣūri bni ʿAbdi l-Karīmi bni Hawāzina l-Qušayrīyi – nawwara llāhu ḥufratahū – tuwuffiya s-sādisa min Šaʿbāna sanata ṯnayni wa-ṯamānīna wa-ʾarbaʿimiʾatin – ṣalwalah*

"This is the tomb of the sheikh, the Imam, the ascetic Abū Manṣūr b. ᶜAbd al-Karīm b. Hawāzin al-Qušayrī – may God illuminate his (burial) pit![530] – He was taken (to God) on 6th Šaᶜbān in the year 482 – *ṣalwalah*".

120

LOCATION. Mecca (al-Maᶜlāh cemetery). DATE. 519 H.

PERSON BURIED. The Meccan judge ᶜAbd al-Malik b. Abī Muslim an-Nahāwandī (d. 519 H): FāsīᶜIqd V p. 133; IFahdItḥāf II p. 499.

SOURCE. FāsīᶜIqd V p. 133.

DESCRIPTION. "[...] I copied this entry from his tombstone".

[hāḏā qabru] ʾimāmi maqāmi ʾIbrāhīma l-Ḫalīli – ʿalayhi s-salām – ʿAbdi l-Maliki bni ʾAbī Muslimini l-Hāwandīyi (sic) *tuwuffiya yawma l-iṯnayni sābiʿi Ḏī l-Ḥiǧǧati sanata tisʿa ʿašrata wa-ḫamsimiʾah*

"[This is the tomb of] the Imam of the *maqām* of Abraham 'the intimate Friend (of God)' – peace be upon him! – ᶜAbd al-Malik b. Abī Muslim an-[Na]hāwandī. He was taken (to God) on Monday 7th Ḏū l-Ḥiǧǧah in the year 519'".

121

LOCATION. Mecca (al-Maᶜlāh cemetery). DATE. 519 H.

PERSON BURIED. al-Karīmah Balṭūn al-Ǧamālīyah.

SOURCE. ŠaybīŠaraf f. 27b = RCEA 3017.

529 FāsīᶜIqd V p. 38. He also mentions that he read the date of his death, viz. 6th Šaᶜbān 482 H, on his tombstone.

530 A prayer frequently expressed in epitaphs, see e.g. above **116**; for further details, see Volume I, pp. 136ff. In literary sources, we often find it as part of eulogies, e.g. TawḥImtāᶜ III p. 127 (*nawwara llāhu qabrahū wa-ḍarīḥahū*); IŠadMalẒāhir p. 230 (*qaddasa llāhu rūḥahū wa-nawwara ḍarīḥahū*); IḤiǧṮam pp. 191 and 193 (*nawwara llāhu ḍarīḥahū*); IIyāsBad I p. 363 (*qaddasa llāhu rūḥahū wa-nawwara ḍarīḥahū*).

DESCRIPTION. "There is a tombstone which bears the writing, after the *basmalah* and after the word of God *yubašširuhum rabbuhum* ("Their Lord gives them good tidings") until the end of the verse (Q 9:21): [...]".

hāḏā qabru l-ǧihati l-karīmati [one word][531] *l-Ǧamālīyati Balṭūna binti ʿAbdi llāhi l-ḥurrati*[532] *l-mawsūmati bi-riḍāʿi l-ʾimāmi l-Mustaẓhiri bi-llāhi ʾamīri l-muʾminīna – qaddasa llāhu rūḥahū wa-nawwara ḍarīḥahū wa-ǧaʿala l-ʾimāmata bāqiyatan fī ʿuqbihī ʾilā yawmi d-dīni – raḥimahā llāhu taʿālā wa-ʾalḥaqahā bi-nabīyihā Muḥammadin – taṣliyah – tuwuffiyat laylata l-ʾarbaʿāʾi li-ṯalāṯata ʿašara min Raǧabin sanata tisʿa ʿašrata wa-ḫamsimiʾah wa-ṣallā llāhu ʿalā Muḥammadin*

"This is the tomb of the grande dame,[533] the noble [*lacuna*] al-Ǧamālīyah, Balṭūn, daughter of ʿAbd Allāh, the free woman distinguished by foster-relationship with the Imam al-Mustaẓhir bi-llāh (r. 487–512 H), the Prince of the Believers – may God sanctify his soul and illuminate his tomb, may He preserve the existence of the Imamate among his offspring until the Day of Judgment! – May God the Exalted have mercy upon her and join her with her Prophet Muḥammad! – *taṣliyah* –. She died in the night to Wednesday 13th Raǧab of the year 519. May God bless Muḥammad!"

122

LOCATION. Mecca (al-Maʿlāh cemetery). DATE. 524 H.

PERSON BURIED. Rukn ad-Dīn aṭ-Ṭabarī (Abū Ǧaʿfar M. b. al-Ḥasan, d. Minā 524 H): FāsīʿIqd II p. 163; IFahdItḥāf II p. 501.

SOURCE. FāsīʿIqd II p. 163.

DESCRIPTION. "[...]. He was buried in the Maʿlāh cemetery, and what I said about him I took from his tombstone. There he was given the titles: *al-ġarīb* ...". (Reconstructed from the account of al-Fāsī):

[*hāḏā qabru*] *l-ġarībi š-šahīdi š-šayḫi l-ʾimāmi* + *Rukni d-Dīni ʾAbī Ǧaʿfara Muḥammadi bni l-Ḥasani n-Nāṣiḥi l-Ḥanafīyi ṭ-Ṭabarīyi tuwuffiya yawma l-ǧumʿati ʿāširi Ḏī l-Ḥiǧǧati sanata ʾarbaʿin wa-ʿišrīna wa-ḫamsimiʾatin bi-Minā*

"[This is the tomb of] the stranger, the martyr, the sheikh, the Imam + Rukn ad-Dīn Abū Ǧaʿfar Muḥammad b. al-Ḥasan an-Nāṣiḥ al-Ḥanafī aṭ-Ṭabarī who was taken (to God) on Friday 10th of Ḏū l-Ḥiǧǧah in the year 524 in Minā".

531 Lacuna in the ms. here.

532 RCEA: الحرمة.

533 For the term *al-ǧihah*, see CIA Égypte II pp. 200f.

123

LOCATION. Mecca (al-Maᶜlāh cemetery). DATE. 528 H.

PERSON BURIED. Abū Ṭāhir aḍ-Ḍabbī al-Maḥāmilī (Yaḥyā b. M. al-Baġdādī, died 528 H during a heavy rainfall that lasted for seven days and caused many houses to collapse; he thus died a martyr, as al-Fāsī explains): FāsīᶜIqd VI p. 228; IFahdItḥāf II p. 504.

SOURCE. ŠaybīŠaraf f. 24b = RCEA 3064.

DESCRIPTION. A tombstone, bearing the following inscription after the *šahādah*, the *basmalah* and the word of God *wa-ʾan laysa li-l-ʾinsāni ʾillā mā saʿā* ("And that a man shall have to his account only as he has laboured") to the words *al-ǧazāʾa l-ʾawfā* ("the fullest recompense") (= Q 53:39-41): [...], executed in Kufic letters.

hāḏa qabru l-ʾimāmi s-saʿīdi faḫri l-ʿulamāʾi muftī l-ḥaramayni Yaḥyā bni Muḥammadi bni ʾAḥmada bni Muḥammadi bni ʾAḥmada bni l-Qāsimi bni ʾIsmāʿīla bni Saʿīdi bni ʾAbāna l-Maḥāmilīyi ḍ-Ḍabbīyi – riḍwānu llāhi ʿalayhi – tuwuffiya fī yawmi l-ǧumʿati li-ṯalāṯin baqīna min Rabīʿi l-ʾawwali sanata ṯamānin wa-ʿišrīna wa-ḫamsimiʾah

"This is the tomb of the Imam, the blissful, the pride of the scholars, muftī of the two Sacrosanct Recincts (i.e. of Mecca and Medina), Yaḥyā b. Muḥammad b. Aḥmad b. Muḥammad b. Aḥmad b. al-Qāsim b. Ismāᶜīl b. Saᶜīd b. Abān al-Maḥāmilī aḍ-Ḍabbī – may he find the approval of God! – He was taken (to God) on Friday, three nights before the end of Rabīᶜ I in the year 528".

124

LOCATION. Mecca (al-Maᶜlāh cemetery). DATE. 534 H

PERSON BURIED. Ibrāhīm Rāmušt (Abū l-Qāsim b. al-Ḥusayn b. Šīrawayh al-Fārisī, d. 534 H), founder of a famous Meccan Sufi hospice (*ribāṭ*) in 529 H. He was brought for his burial to Mecca only in 537 H, carried in a coffin by the Iraqi pilgrimage caravan.[534]

SOURCE. ŠaybīŠaraf ff. 27a-b = RCEA 3099.

DESCRIPTION. A tombstone, bearing the following inscription after the *basmalah* and the word of God the Exalted *kullu nafsin ḏāʾiqatu l-mawt* ("Every soul shall taste of death", Q 3:185): [...].

hāḏā qabru š-šayḫi š-šahīdi ġiyāṯi l-ḥaramayni n-nāḫuḏahi[535] *ʾIbrāhīma Rāmušta bni l-Ḥusayni bni Šīrawayha bni l-Ḥusayni bni Ǧaʿfarini l-Fārisīyi tuwuffiya fī šahri Šaʿbāna sanata ʾarbaʾin wa-ṯalāṯīna wa-ḫamsimiʾatin – raḥimahū llāhu taʿālā wa-raḥima man taraḥḥama ʿalayhi – ṣalwalah*

534 IFahdItḥāf II pp. 504 and 508.

535 RCEA: الناخذاه.

"This is the tomb of the sheikh, the martyr, the succour of the two Sacrosanct Recincts (i.e. Mecca and Medina), the naval captain, Ibrāhīm Rāmušt b. al-Ḥusayn b. Šīrawayh b. al-Ḥusayn b. Ǧaᶜfar al-Fārisī. He was taken to God in the month of Šaᶜbān in the year 534 – may God the Exalted have mercy upon him and upon those who invoke mercy upon him (i.e. the deceased)! – *ṣalwalah*".

125

LOCATION. Mecca (al-Maᶜlāh cemetery). DATE. 546 H.

PERSON BURIED. The Fatimid emir Abū Isḥāq al-Miṣrī (Ibr. b. Walaḫšī [?], d. 546 H): FāsīᶜIqd III p. 170; IFahdItḥāf II p. 513.

SOURCE. FāsīᶜIqd III p. 170.

DESCRIPTION. "On his tombstone in the Maᶜlāh (cemetery) I read the following: *hāḏā qabru* (...) *as-salāṭīna*. Then comes his name as I cited it, and finally: *tuwuffiya* (...)". (Reconstructed from the account of al-Fāsī):

hāḏā qabru l-ʾamīri l-ʾaǧalli l-ʾawḥadi l-ʾamīri Nāṣiri d-Dīn / ʿumdati l-muslimīn // šarafi l-ḫilāfah / ʿumdati l-ʾimāmah // muqaddami l-ʾumarāʾi ʿaḍudi l-mulūki wa-s-salāṭīn || + *ʾAbī ʾIsḥāqa ʾIbrāhīma bni Walaḫšīyini* [?] *l-Miṣrīyi* + *tuwuffiya bi-l-ḥarami š-šarīfi yamwa l-ǧumʿati li-tisʿin baqīna min Ṣafarin min sanati sittin wa-ʾarbaʿīna wa-ḫamsimiʾah*

"This is the tomb of the most mighty and unique emir, the emir Nāṣir ad-Dīn, / supporter of the Muslims, / the glory of the caliphate // and supporter of the Imamate, // the foremost among the emirs, the helper of kings and rulers, || + Abū Isḥāq Ibrāhīm b. Walaḫšī [?] al-Miṣrī. + He was taken (to God) in the Noble Recinct (of Mecca) on Friday, nine nights before the end of Ṣafar of the year 546".

126

LOCATION. Mecca (al-Maᶜlāh cemetery). DATE. 547 H.

PERSON BURIED. ᶜAlam Umm Manṣūr b. Fātik b. Ǧayyāš, al-Malikah al-Ḥurrah (d. Zabīd 546):[536] ŠaybīŠaraf ff. 13a-b; IDaybaᶜBuġ pp. 59-65; ZA IV p. 248.[537]

SOURCE. ŠaybīŠaraf f. 13a = RCEA 3156.

DESCRIPTION. "An inscribed tombstone, with beautifully executed writing resembling that of the first (afore-mentioned) tombstone, and I think – God knows best – that it is actually the same (writing). After the *basmalah* and the verse beginning with *Their Lord gives them good tidings of mercy from him* (Q 9:21) is written:

536 Maybe she had died in 545 H, as also aš-Šaybī notes with regard to the date given in her epitaph. On her husband and son, see IDaybaᶜBuġ pp. 54-8.

537 She is, of course, not the same as the famous Ṣulayḥid queen Arwā bt. Aḥmad, known as as-Sayyidah al-Ḥurrah (444 – Ḏū Ǧiblah 532 H). One her, see ZA I pp. 289f. and Daftary: *Sayyida Ḥurra* (with further literature).

[...]. On the lateral parts of the tombstone there are verses from the surah *Has there come* (Q 76)".

hāḏā qabru l-ḥurrati l-fāḍilati z-zakīyati r-raḍīyati waḥīdati z-zaman / sayyidati mulūki l-Yaman || kāfilati l-ʿarab wa-l-ʿağam / wālidati l-maliki l-muntaḫabi l-musammāti ʿAlam || – qaddasa llāhu rūḥahā wa-raḥimahā – tuwuffiyat bi-ʾarḍi l-Ḥuṣaybi[538] *yawma l-iṯnayni ṯāliṯi ʿišrīna šahri Ramaḍāna sanata sittin wa-ʾarbaʿīna wa-ḫamsimiʾatin wa-nuqilat ʾilā Makkata l-mušarrafati fī Ḏī l-Ḥiğğati sanata sabʿin wa-ʾarbaʿīna wa-ḫamsimiʾatin – raḥimahā llāhu wa-raḥima man taraḥḥama ʿalayhā – ṣalwalah*

kāfilati: *kāmilati* (RCEA); *sanata sittin*: *sanata sittatin* (ŠaybīŠaraf).

"This is the tomb of the free (woman), the distinguished, the chaste, the satisfactory (to God), the unique of her time, / the Lady of the kings of Yemen, || the guarantor of Arabs and non-Arabs, / mother of the chosen (i.e. distinguished) king, called ʿAlam by name || – may God sanctify her soul and have mercy upon her! – She died in al-Ḥuṣayb on Monday 23rd of the month of Ramaḍān in the year 546 and was carried to Mecca 'the illustrious' in Ḏū l-Ḥiğğah of the year 547 – may God have mercy upon her and upon those who invoke mercy upon her! – *ṣalwalah*".

127

LOCATION. Mecca (al-Maʿlāh cemetery). DATE. 554 H.

PERSON BURIED. ʿAbd ar-Raḥmān b. ʿAlī aš-Šaybānī aṭ-Ṭabarī al-Makkī (Mecca, 492–554 H): FāsīʿIqd V pp. 47f.; IFahdItḥāf II p. 522.

SOURCE. FāsīʿIqd V pp. 47f.

DESCRIPTION. "On his tombstone in the Maʿlāh (cemetery) I found: *tuwuffiya (...)*; he was buried together with his father and given the titles: *qāḍī l-ḥaramayn* (...). The tombstone also contains some verses mourning him, as follows: [...]". Six verses in the metre *kāmil* (reconstructed from the account of al-Fāsī):

[*hāḏā qabru*] *qāḍī l-ḥaramayni wa-muftīhimā* (!) + *tuwuffiya yawma ṯ-ṯalāṯāʾi li-sabʿin baqīna min Rabīʿi l-ʾawwali sanata ʾarbaʿin wa-ḫamsīna wa-ḫamsimiʾatin*

"[This is the tomb of] the judge of the two Sacrosanct Recincts and their muftī + He died on Tuesday, seven nights before the end of Rabīʿ I in the year 545".

*ʾinnī ʾarā l-ʾislāma baʿda ʾimāmihī * yarnū bi-ṭarafi murawwaʿin ḥayrānī*
*ḫallafta fī l-ʾislāmi baʿdaka ṯulmatan * tabqā ʿalā marri z-zamāni l-fānī*
*man li-l-fatāwā wa-s-suʾālāti llatī * mā zāla yakšifuhā bi-ḥusni bayānī*
*man li-š-šarīʿati ʾin taṭāwala mulḥidun * li-ʿinādihā bi-z-zūri wa-l-buhtānī*
*man li-l-yatāmā wa-l-ʾarāmili baʿdahū * yarʿāhumū bi-l-birri wa-l-ʾiḥsānī*
*fa-saqā ḍarīḥaka musbilun min ʿanwatin * wa-ḥabāka bi-l-ġufrāni wa-r-riḍwānī*

538 I presume that this is the correct name of the place, near Zabīd in Yemen. However, the texts have الخضيب (aš-Šaybī) and الخصيب (RCEA).

"Truly I see Islam after the death of its Imam * looking with the glance of someone terrified and dismayed.
You did leave in Islam after your death a gap * which will remain (open) over the course of vanishing time!
Who[539] shall now deal with fatwas and inquiries which * he examined ceaselessly and with beautiful clearness?
Who shall now defend the religious law if a heretic dares * to oppose it with falsehood and untruth?
Who shall after his death take care of the orphans and the widows * to protect them with kindness and beneficence?
Thus may a downpour flow forth upon your tomb – and heavily so! – * and may it award you pardoning and (divine) approval!"

128

LOCATION. Mecca (al-Maᶜlāh cemetery). DATE. 557 H.
PERSON BURIED. The judge ᶜIzz ad-Dīn aš-Šaybānī aṭ-Ṭabarī (A. b. ᶜAr., d. Mecca 557 H): FāsīᶜIqd III p. 49; IFahdItḥāf II p. 526.
SOURCE. FāsīᶜIqd III p. 49.
DESCRIPTION. "On his tombstone in the Maᶜlāh (cemetery) he is given the following titles: *al-qāḍī* (...) *ᶜIzzi d-Dīn*, and after "aṭ-Ṭabarī" we read: *qāḍī l-ḥaramayni š-šarīfayni*". (Reconstructed from the account of al-Fāsī):

[hāḏā qabru] l-qāḍī s-saᶜīdi l-ᶜālimi ᶜIzzi d-Dīni + ᵓAḥmada bni ᶜAbdi r-Raḥmāni bni ᶜAlīyi bni l-Ḥusayni š-Šaybānīyi ṭ-Ṭabarīyi + qāḍī l-ḥaramayni š-šarīfayni + tuwuffiya fī Ǧumādā l-ᵓūlā sanata sabᶜin wa-ḫamsīna wa-ḫamsimiᵓah

"[This is the tomb of] the judge, the blissful, the learned, ᶜIzz ad-Dīn + Aḥmad b. ᶜAbd ar-Raḥmān b. ᶜAlī b. al-Ḥusayn aš-Šaybānī aṭ-Ṭabarī, + the judge of both noble Sacrosanct Recincts (i.e. of Mecca and Medina). + He was taken (to God) in Ǧumādā I in the year 557".

129

LOCATION. Mecca (al-Maᶜlāh cemetery). DATE. 564 H.
PERSON BURIED. The warden of the Kaᶜbah ᶜAbd ar-Raḥmān b. Daylam aš-Šaybī (d. 564 H): IFahdItḥāf II p. 531.[540]

539 For another poem, not dissimilar in content, using *man li-*, see below **158**.

540 Strangely enough al-Fāsī, who in general refers to extant epitaphs, has an entry on ᶜAbd ar-Raḥmān b. Daylam aš-Šaybī (FāsīᶜIqd V p. 20), but he neither cites from the tombstone nor gives the date of his death. This omission is probably the reason why Ibn Fahd (who in general does *not* refer to epitaphs) quotes in this case from a tombstone, thus supplementing the account of al-Fāsī.

SOURCE. IFahdItḥāf II p. 531.
DESCRIPTION. "[...] I copied it so from his tombstone in the Maᶜlāh (cemetery)". (Reconstructed from the account of Ibn Fahd):

[hāḏā qabru] fātiḥi bayti llāhi l-ḥarāmi ʿAbdi r-Raḥmāni bni Daylama bni Muḥammadi bni ʾIbrāhīma bni Šaybata bni ʾIbrāhīma bni ʿAbdi llāhi bni Šaybata bni Muḥammadi bni Šaybata bni ʿUmara bni Ṭalḥata bni ʾAbī Ṭalḥata l-Qurašīyi l-ʿAbdarīyi š-Šaybīyi + tuwuffiya yawma s-sabti li-ḫamsin baqīna min šahri Ramaḍān

"[This is the tomb of] the opener of the Sacrosanct House of God (i.e. the Kaᶜbah) ᶜAbd ar-Raḥmān b. Daylam b. Muḥammad b. Ibrāhīm b. Šaybah b. Ibrāhīm b. ᶜAbd Allāh b. Šaybah b. Muḥammad b. Šaybah b. ᶜUmar b. Ṭalḥah b. Abī Ṭalḥah al-Qurašī al-ᶜAbdarī aš-Šaybī. + He was taken (to God) five nights before the end of the month of Ramaḍān".

130

LOCATION. Mecca (al-Maᶜlāh cemetery). DATE. 569 H.
PERSON BURIED. Ismāᶜīl aš-Šaybī (Ism. b. M., d. 569 H): FāsīᶜIqd III p. 192; IFahdItḥāf II p. 535.
SOURCE. FāsīᶜIqd III p. 192.
DESCRIPTION. "I compiled this entry from his tombstone in the Maᶜlāh (cemetery), and there he is styled: *aš-šābb*". (Reconstructed from the account of al-Fāsī):

[hāḏā qabru] š-šābbi + ʾIsmāʿīla bni Muḥammadi bni ʾIsmāʿīla bni ʿAbdi r-Raḥmāni bni Daylama bni Muḥammadi bni Šuyūḫini š-Šaybīyi l-ḥağabīyi fātiḥi bayti llāhi l-ḥarāmi tuwuffiya fī Rağabin sanata tisʿin wa-sittīna wa-ḫamsimiʾah

"[This is the tomb of] the youth + Ismāᶜīl b. Muḥammad b. Ismāᶜīl b. ᶜAbd ar-Raḥmān[541] b. Daylam b. Muḥammad b. Šuyūḫ aš-Šaybī, gatekeeper (of the Kaᶜbah),[542] opener (i.e. warden, *or* key-holder) of the Sacrosanct House of God. He was taken (to God) in Rağab in the year 569".

131

LOCATION. Mecca (al-Maᶜlāh cemetery). DATE. 571 H.
PERSON BURIED. ᶜUmar b. al-Ḥusayn an-Nasawī (d. 571 H): FāsīᶜIqd V p. 329; IFahdItḥāf II p. 538.
SOURCE. FāsīᶜIqd V p. 329.
DESCRIPTION. "[...] I found (his name) thus mentioned on his tombstone in the Maᶜlāh

541 See also above **129**.

542 "al-Ḥağabī" refers to the office of gatekeeper (*ḥiğābah*).

(cemetery), and he was given the title: *aš-šayḫ* (...) It also said: *tuwuffiya* (...)". (Reconstructed from the account of al-Fāsī):

[hāḏā qabru] š-šayḫi z-zāhidi l-ʿābidi š-šahīdi l-ġarībi šayḫi š-šuyūḫi + ʿUmara bni l-Ḥusayni n-Nawawīyi + tuwuffiya fī mustahalli l-Muḥarrami sanata ʾiḥdā wa-sabʿīna wa-ḫamsimiʾah

"[This is the tomb of] the sheikh, the ascetic, the worshipper, the martyr, the stranger,[543] the most important sheikh + ʿUmar b. al-Ḥusayn an-Nasawī. + He was taken (to God) at the beginning of Muḥarram in the year 571".

132

LOCATION. Mecca (al-Maʿlāh cemetery). DATE. 572 H.

PERSON BURIED. The commander ʿUmārah b. Ǧayyāš al-Qāsimī[544] (Ibn Abī Ṯāmir[545] al-Mubārak, d. 572 H), the brother of Abū l-Ḥasan (**133**): FāsīʿIqd V p. 323; IFahdItḥāf II p. 540.

SOURCE. FāsīʿIqd V p. 323.

DESCRIPTION. "[...] He was buried in the Maʿlāh (cemetery), and I copied this entry from his tombstone. There he was given the title *al-qāʾid.* The *nisbah* 'al-Qāsimī' refers to the emir of Mecca Abū l-Qāsim M. b. Ǧaʿfar Ibn Abī Hāšim al-Ḥasanī". (Reconstructed from the account of al-Fāsī):

[hāḏā qabru] l-qāʾidi + ʿUmārata bni Ǧayyāša bni ʾAbī Ṯāmirini l-Mubāraki l-Qāsimīyi + tuwuffiya fī yawmi l-ʾarbaʿāʾi ṯānī Raǧabin sanata ṯnatayni wa-sabʿīna wa-ḫamsimiʾah

"[This is the tomb of] the commander + ʿUmārah b. Ǧayyāš b. Abī Ṯāmir al-Mubārak al-Qāsimī. + He was taken (to God) on Wednesday 2nd Raǧab in the year 572".

543 The *nisbah* refers to Nasā (in Ḫurāsān), thus he was a stranger to Mecca; his death as a martyr indicates that he probably died during the pilgrimage (*cf.* below **138** and **153**), though he might also have been killed under other circumstances.

544 al-Fāsī explains this *nisbah* as referring to his being a retainer of Qāsim b. M. al-Ḥasanī, the emir of Mecca (FāsīʿIqd III p. 203) or to Abū l-Qāsim M. (*sic*) b. Ǧaʿfar b. M. b. ʿAl. Ibn Abī Hāšim al-Ḥasanī (*ib.* V p. 323). This would refer to the Hāšimid emir Abū M. Qāsim b. M. b. Ǧaʿfar (in power 487–517 or 518 H), father of Fulaytah, see FāsīZuhūr p. 230; IFahdItḥāf II p. 498; SinǧManāʾiḥ II pp. 238 and 243; De Gaury: *Rulers of Mecca* p. 62; az-Zaylaʿī: *Amirate of Mecca* pp. 63-5. However, it could also refer, given the advanced age of ʿUmārah at his death, to the later emir al-Qāsim b. Hāšim b. Fulaytah (r. and d. 557 H), but he remained only briefly in power and was killed shortly after, see FāsīZuhūr p. 230; SinǧManāʾiḥ II pp. 249f.; De Gaury: *Rulers of Mecca* p. 62; az-Zaylaʿī: *Amirate of Mecca* pp. 67f.

545 "Tāmir" in Ibn Fahd's account.

133

LOCATION. Mecca (al-Muzdalifah). DATE. 575 H.

PERSON BURIED. The commander Abū Ḥasan al-Qāsimī (Ṯāmir[546] b. Ǧayyāš, d. 575 H), brother of al-ʿUmārah (**132**):[547] FāsīʿIqd III pp. 256; IFahdItḥāf II p. 543.

SOURCE. FāsīʿIqd III p. 203.

DESCRIPTION. "I copied this entry (*tarǧamah*) from his tombstone".

[hāḏā qabru] l-qāʾidi ʾAbī Ḥasanin Ṯāmiri bni Ǧayyāša bni ʾAbī Ṯāmirini l-Mubāraki l-Qāsimīyi tuwuffiya yawma s-sabti tāsiʿi šahri Ramaḍāna sanata ḫamsin wa-sabʿīna wa-ḫamsimiʾah

"[This is the tomb of] the commander Abū Ḥasan Ṯāmir b. Ǧayyāš b. Abī Ṯāmir al-Mubārak al-Qāsimī who was taken (to God) on Saturday 9th of the month of Ramaḍān in the year 575".

134

LOCATION. Mecca. DATE. *c.*580 / 600 H.

PERSON BURIED. Aḥmad, son of the Hāšimid emir of Mecca Dāʾūd[548] b. ʿĪsā b. Fulaytah Ibn Abī Hāšim: FāsīʿIqd IV p. 69.

SOURCE. FāsīʿIqd IV p. 69.

DESCRIPTION. "On his tombstone I saw him styled: *aš-šābb* (...) *as-saʿīd*, but the stone does not show the year of his death and I do not know anything about him besides that". (Reconstructed from the account of al-Fāsī):

[hāḏā qabru] š-šābbi š-šarīfi l-ʾamīri s-saʿīdi + ʾAḥmada bni [l-ʾamīri s-saʿīdi š-šarīfi Dāʾūda bni ʿĪsā bni (...) ʾAbī Hāšimini l-Ḥasanīyi l-Makkī][549]

"[This is the tomb of] the noble youth, the blissful emir + Aḥmad, son [of the blissful emir, the noble Dāʾūd b. ʿĪsā b. (...) Abī Hāšim al-Ḥasanī al-Makkī]".

135

LOCATION. Mecca (al-Maʿlāh cemetery). DATE. 588 H.

PERSON BURIED. Naǧm ad-Dīn al-ʿAsqalānī (M. b. M., d. 588 H): FāsīʿIqd II p. 363; IFahdItḥāf II p. 560.

SOURCE. FāsīʿIqd II p. 363.

546 Ibn Fahd has "Tāmir".

547 Their other brothers Maʿmar and Yaḥyā died in 588 H (IFahdItḥāf II p. 560).

548 He became emir of Mecca in 570 H, then jointly with his brother Mukṯir till 586 H when he was deposed because he had confiscated property of the Kaʿbah estate; he died in either 589 or 590 H in Naḫlah, see FāsīZuhūr p. 231; IFahdItḥāf II pp. 536ff., esp. pp. 559f.; SinǧManāʾiḥ II pp. 256ff.; De Gaury: *Rulers of Mecca* p. 63; az-Zaylaʿī: *Amirate of Mecca* p. 70.

549 The latter part of the epitaph marked [ ] is not quoted by al-Fāsī.

DESCRIPTION. "I copied his genealogy and the date of his death from his tombstone, which is in the writing (*bi-ḫaṭṭ*) of Muḥammad b. Barakāt b. Abī Ḥaramī". (Reconstructed from the account of al-Fāsī):

[hāḏā qabru] s-saʿīdi š-šahīdi + Naǧmi d-Dīni ʾAbī ʿAbdi llāhi Muḥammadi bni + l-faqīhi š-šahīdi + Raḍīyi d-Dīni Muḥammadi bni ʿAbdi llāhi bni ʿUṯmāna l-ʿAsqalānīyi l-Makkīyi + tuwuffiya yawma l-iṯnayni ṯ-ṯānī min Ḏī l-Qaʿdati sanata ṯamānin wa-ṯamānīna wa-ḫamsimiʾah

"[This is the tomb of] the blissful, the martyr + Naǧm ad-Dīn Abū ʿAbd Allāh Muḥammad, son of + the jurist, the martyr + Raḍīy ad-Dīn Muḥammad b. ʿAbd Allāh b. ʿUṯmān al-ʿAsqalānī al-Makkī. + He was taken (to God) on Monday 2nd Ḏū l-Qaʿdah in the year 588".

136

LOCATION. Mecca (al-Maʿlāh cemetery). DATE. 589 H.
PERSON BURIED. Ṣubayḥ (d. 589 H): FāsīʿIqd IV p. 273; IFahdItḥāf II pp. 560f.
SOURCE. FāsīʿIqd IV p. 273.
DESCRIPTION. "I copied this entry (*tarǧamah*) from his tombstone, and (the *nisbah*) 'aṯ-Ṯaġrī' was here made explicit with ث and غ".

[hāḏā qabru] Ṣubayḥi mawlā s-sulṭāni ʾAbī s-Saddādi Yaḥyā bni ʾAbī s-Saddādi l-Muwaffaqi ṯ-Ṯaġrīyi l-ʾIslāmīyi tuwuffiya fī yawmi l-iṯnayni ṯāliṯa ʿašara Ḏī l-Ḥiǧǧati sanata tisʿin wa-ṯamānīna wa-ḫamsimiʾah

"[This is the tomb of] of Ṣubayḥ, client (i.e. freedman) of sultan Abū s-Saddād Yaḥyā b. Abī s-Saddād al-Muwaffaq aṯ-Ṯaġrī al-Islāmī. He was taken (to God) on Monday 13th Ḏū l-Ḥiǧǧah in the year 589".[550]

137

LOCATION. Mecca (al-Maʿlāh cemetery). DATE. 591 H.
PERSON BURIED. Šihāb ad-Dīn al-ʿAsqalānī al-Makkī (Abū l-Ḥasan ʿAlī b. ʿAl. b. ʿUṯmān, d. 591 H), possibly the nephew of Ḥusayn b. ʿUṯmān al-ʿAsqalānī (d. 593 H):[551] FāsīʿIqd V p. 266; IFahdItḥāf II p. 562.
SOURCE. FāsīʿIqd V p. 266.
DESCRIPTION. "[...] He was buried in the Maʿlāh (cemetery), and I compiled the information concerning him from his tombstone. It is written upon it: *hāḏā qabru* (...), and there are also (these verses): [...]". (Reconstructed from the account of al-Fāsī). – A passage in prose and five lines in the metre *basīṭ*:

550 He was possibly an Ethiopian, because there is another Ṣubayḥ (d. 584 H) listed as "Ḥabašī" in MundTakm I p. 81, viz. a *mawlā* of Abū l-Qāsim Naṣr b. al-ʿAṭṭār al-Ḥarrānī (d. 553 H).

551 FāsīʿIqd III p. 420; IFahdItḥāf II p. 564.

hāḏā qabru š-šābbi Šihābi d-Dīni + ʾAbī l-Ḥasani ʿAlīyi bni ʿAbdi llāhi bni ʿUṯmāna l-ʿAsqalānīyi l-Makkīyi + tuwuffiya yamwa s-sabti s-sādisi wa-ʿišrīna min Šaʿbāna sanata ʾiḥdā wa-tisʿīna wa-ḫamsimiʾah

"This is the tomb of the youth, Šihāb ad-Dīn + Abū l-Ḥasan ᶜAlī b. ᶜAbd Allāh b. ᶜUṯmān al-ᶜAsqalānī al-Makkī. + He was taken (to God) on Saturday 26th Šaᶜbān in the year 591".

*ʾinna l-ʿazā bi-Šihābi d-Dīni qad manaʿat * minhu l-qulūbu wa-qad ʾawdā bihā t-talafū*
*našʾun takāmala fīhi ẓ-ẓarfu wa-ğtamaʿat * fīhi šamāʾilu lā tanfakku taʾtalifū*
*wa-manẓaru muḫğilin li-š-šamsi ʾin ṭalaʿat * yā-laytahū lam yakun bi-l-bayni yankasifū*
*ʾiḏā badā nāṭiqan fī wasṭi muḥtafalin * fa-d-durru muntaẓimun wa-š-šuhdu muqtaṭafū*
*maḥāsinun naẓẓama l-ʾiğmāʿu ṣiḥḥatahā * ka-l-luʾluʾi ntaqabat ʿan ḥusnihī ṣadafū*[552]

"The consolation (for the death) of Šihāb ad-Dīn has been prevented * by the hearts since the harm (*or* loss) has destroyed them.
A youth in whom grace reached perfection and in whom were combined * traits of nature that always were in harmony.
(He had) the (radiant) appearance of someone who would put the sun to shame when it rises! * O if only he had not been eclipsed in the meantime!
When he appeared as a speaker in the midst of an assembly * then the pearls (i.e. his words) were well-strung (i.e. well-chosen and ordered) and the honey (i.e. his sweetness of expression) was of the first choice.
(His) beautiful qualities, whose soundness has been settled by universal agreement (?) (lit. put on a string *or* put into verse), * are like pearls whose beauty is (now) veiled by a shell".[553]

138

LOCATION. Mecca (al-Maᶜlāh cemetery). DATE. 599 H.
PERSON BURIED. Muḥammad b. Ṣāliḥ al-ᶜAṭṭār (al-Makkī, d. 599 H): FāsīᶜIqd II p. 182; IFahdItḥāf II p. 570.
SOURCE. FāsīᶜIqd II p. 182.
DESCRIPTION. "This (biographical) entry I put together from his tombstone, and there we also read: *dufina* (...)". (Reconstructed from the account of al-Fāsī):

[*hāḏā qabru*] *Muḥammadi bni Ṣāliḥi bni ʾAbī Ḥaramīna*[554] *Futūḥa bni Banīnini l-Makkīyi l-ʿAṭṭāri tuwuffiya šahīdan muḥriman yawma l-iṯnayni ṯāniya ʿašara Ğu-*

552 The edition has صدق (misprint).
553 The shell being a metaphor for the tomb, see above pp. 349ff.
554 Or *Ḥaramayni*?

mādā l-ʾūlā sanata tisʿin wa-tisʿīna wa-ḫamsimiʾatin + dufina yawma l-ḫāmisi ʿašara mina š-šahri l-maḏkūr

"[This is the tomb] of Muḥammad b. Ṣāliḥ b. Abī Ḥaramī [Ḥurmā?] Futūḥ b. Banīn al-Makkī al-ʿAṭṭār. He was taken (to God) as a martyr, while in the (sacred) state of pilgrimage, on Monday 12th Ǧumādā I in the year 599. + He was buried on Thursday 10th of the same month".

139

LOCATION. Mecca (al-Maʿlāh cemetery). DATE. 614 H.

PERSON BURIED. The Shafiite judge Muḥyī d-Dīn aṭ-Ṭabarī (Abū Ǧaʿfar A. b. Abī Bakr al-Makkī, Mecca 573–614 H): FāsīʿIqd III p. 12; IFahdItḥāf III p. 25; SaḫTuḥfLaṭ I p. 105.

SOURCES. ŠaybīŠaraf ff. 22a-b; FāsīʿIqd III p. 12 (only the prose); RCEA 3808 (only the prose).

DESCRIPTION. Here we have an interesting case of being able to compare two literary quotations of a single epitaph with the text of the preserved epitaph (*cf.* above p. 336). – (I) The version by aš-Šaybī: A prose passage followed by poetry. – (II) (Reconstructed from the account of al-Fāsī): "I found the date of his death upon his tombstone in the Maʿlāh (cemetery), in the writing (*bi-ḫaṭṭ*) of ʿAbd ar-Raḥmān b. Abī Ḥaramī, and he gave him the following titles: *al-qāḍī l-ʾimām* (...)". – (III) The prose wording of the preserved epitaph (as cited in RCEA). The poetry will be cited after the versions of the prose passage.

(I) *hāḏā qabru l-faqīhi l-qāḍī l-ʾimāmi l-ʿālimi z-zāhidi l-mudarrisi bi-l-ḥarami š-šarīfi faḫri d-dīni nāṣiri š-šarʿi šarafi l-quḍāti qāḍī l-ḥaramayni š-šarīfayni wa-l-muftī bihimā ʾAbī Ǧaʿfara ʾAḥmada bni š-šayḫi ṣ-ṣāliḥi s-saʿīdi ʾAbī Bakrini bni Muḥammadi bni ʾIbrāhīma ṭ-Ṭabarīyi tuwuffiya fī yawmi ṯ-ṯulāṯāʾi r-rābiʿi Rabīʿi l-ʾāḫiri sanata ʾarbaʿa ʿašrata wa-sittimiʾatin – raḥimahū llāhu taʿālā raḥmatan wāsiʿatan wa-ǧamīʿa l-muslimīn*

(II) [*hāḏā qabru*] *l-qāḍī l-ʾimāmi l-ʿālimi z-zāhidi l-mudarrisi bi-l-ḥarami š-šarīfi muḥyī s-sunnati nāṣiri š-šarʿi šarafi l-quḍāti qāḍī l-ḥaramayni š-šarīfayni wa-l-muftī bihimā Muḥyī d-Dīni ʾAbī Ǧaʿfarin ʾAḥmada bni ʾAbī Bakrini bni Muḥammadi bni ʾIbrāhīma ṭ-Ṭabarīyi l-Makkīyi š-Šāfiʿīyi tuwuffiya fī yawmi ṯ-ṯulāṯāʾi rābiʿi Rabīʿi l-ʾāḫiri sanata ʾarbaʿa ʿašrata wa-sittimiʾah*

(III) *basmalah* – Q 39:73f. – *hāḏā qabru l-faqīhi l-qāḍī l-ʾimāmi l-ʿālimi z-zāhidi l-mudarrisi bi-l-ḥarami š-šarīfi muḥyī d-dīni nāṣiri š-šarʿi šarafi l-quḍāti qāḍī l-ḥarami š-šarīfi wa-l-muftī bihā* (sic) *ʾAbī Ǧaʿfarin ʾAḥmada bni š-šayḫi ṣ-ṣāliḥi s-saʿīdi ʾAbī Bakrini bni Muḥammadi bni ʾIbrāhīma ṭ-Ṭabarīyi tuwuffiya yawma ṯ-ṯulāṯāʾi r-rābiʿi Rabīʿi l-ʾāḫiri sanata ʾarbaʿa ʿašrata wa-sittimiʾatin – raḥimahū llāhu taʿālā raḥmatan wāsiʿatan wa-ǧamīʿa l-muslimīn*

(III) "*Basmalah.* – 'Then those that feared their Lord shall be driven in companies into Paradise, till, when they have come thither, and its gates are opened, and its keepers will say to them, 'Peace be upon you! Well you have fared; enter in, to dwell forever. * And they shall say: Praise belongs to God, who has been true in His promise to us, and has bequeathed upon us the earth, for us to make our dwelling wheresoever we will in Paradise. How excellent is the wage of those that labour!' (= Q 39:73f.) – This is the tomb of the judge, the learned Imam, the ascetic, the lecturer in the Noble Recinct (of Mecca, i.e. at the Kaᶜbah), who revived the creed and helped the law to triumph, the glory of (all) judges, the judge and muftī at the noble Sacrosanct Recinct (i.e. Mecca)[555] Abū Ǧaᶜfar Aḥmad, son of the righteous sheikh, the blissful Abū Bakr b. Muḥammad b. Ibrāhīm aṭ-Ṭabarī. He was taken (to God) on Tuesday 4th Rabīᶜ II in the year 614. – May God the Exalted grant his all-embracing mercy to him and to all Muslims!"

NOTE. Comparing both literary citations we observe some differences in wording, yet the main bulk of al-Fāsī's text agrees with that of aš-Šaybī; however, no citation is perfectly correct as to the actual wording on the preserved tombstone, nor is the Qurʾānic passage mentioned. al-Fāsī adds the nisbahs "al-Makkī aš-Šāfiᶜī", but he omits the titles of his father (*aš-šayḫ aṣ-ṣāliḥ as-saʿīd*). The poetry reported by aš-Šaybī (*Šaraf* 22a-b), edited below, was likewise not taken into consideration by al-Fāsī and in RCEA.

Poetry: The epitaph-poem is only in part quoted by aš-Šaybī. This becomes clear from his remark after the seventh line: "These are many verses", which means in fact that he omitted some of them. However, after quoting the last line he adds, "These are most of the verses, with only about six or seven missing whose decipherment was difficult for me, so out of caution I left them out, given the uncertainty in deciphering them". – 15 verses in the metre *mutaqārib*:

ʾa-yā-ʿaynu ğūdī wa-lā tanfurī[556] * *bi-damʿin madā l-ʿumri mustaġfirī*
*ʿalā l-ʾaryaḥīyi r-riḍā l-lawḏaʿīyi * karīmi l-ġarīzati wa-l-ʿunṣurī*
*muʿizzi š-šarīʿati ḫalfi t-tuqā * ʾAbī Ǧaʿfarin ʾAḥmada ṭ-Ṭabarī*
sa-ʾufnī d-dumūʿa wa-ʾuğrī[557] *n-nağīʿa * wa-ʾaslū*[558] *ʿani l-ʾahli wa-l-matğarī*
*wa-lastu bi-nāsīka waqta ṭ-ṭawāfi * wa-yawma*[559] *ṣ-ṣuʿūdi wa-fī l-mašʿarī*
*wa-ʾinniya ʾarğūka yawma l-wuqū- * fī bayna yaday rabbika l-ʾakbarī*
*kasāka l-ʾilāhu mina stabraqi l- * ğināni wa-min sundusin ʾaḫḍarī*

[Here aš-Šaybī interrupts the quotation of the poem but goes on to cite:]

555 He had become judge of Mecca only shortly before his death in 614 H.

556 Ms. تنقرى.

557 Ms. ادري, but what could this mean?

558 Written اسلوا in the ms.

559 The ms. has, if I read it correctly, ويدم.

{ʾiḏ}[560] *yaqūlu ʾiḏā mā ʾatayta l-ḥaǧūfa* (?) * *ʿalayka s-salāmu ʾAbā Ǧaʿfarī*
ʾanā muḥyiyu (sic) *d-dīni yā-ḫayra man * tawallā l-ḥukūmata fī l-ʾaʿṣurī*
*saqā qabraka l-ǧūdu ǧamma l-ʿitāqi * wa-ḥuyyīta bi-l-wardi wa-{bi}-l-ʿabharī*
*wa-ṭayyaba laḥdaka rūḥu l-ʾilāhi * fa-yazrī ʿalā l-miski wa-l-ʿanbarī*
*ḥaḍarta s-samāʿa wa-ḥuzta l-ʿulūma * wa-ḫalladta ḏikraka li-l-ʾaʿṣurī*
*kafalta l-yatāmā wa-ʿulta l-ʾayāmā * wa-kunta lahum ka-ʾabin ḫayyirī*
*wa-ʾaṯnaw ʿalayka ladā l-mawti ḫayran * wa-hāḏī s-siyādatu min maʿšarī*
*tazawwadtahā yawma faṣli l-qaḍāʾi * wa-ḥašri l-ḫalāʾiqi fī l-maḥšarī*

"Lo, O eye, pour forth – and do not recoil! – * a tear that asks for (the deceased's) being pardoned the whole life long!
On the generous, the approved, the sagacious, * (on) one of noble nature and stock,
(On) the fortifier of the Divine Law, the last bearer of godliness,[561] * (on) Abū Ǧaʿfar Aḥmad aṭ-Ṭabarī
Will I use up my tears and let the blood flow, * and think no more of family and business.
I will not forget you at the time of circumambulation, * on the day of the ascent[562] and at the pilgrims' station.
I will hope for you (i.e. for meeting you) on the Day of (your) standing * before your Lord, who is greater (than everything).
May God cover you with the brocade of the * Gardens (i.e. Paradise) and green silk!

[Interruption of the quotation.]

He (*sc.* the Prophet) will say (to you) when you will have arrived at the bucket (?)[563] * 'Peace be upon you, O Abū Ǧaʿfar!'
(You answer,) 'I am the Reviver of the Creed, O best of those who * took charge of governing (the people) in all times!'
May the abundant rain water your tomb with plentiful release[564] * and may you be saluted by the rose and the scented storax-tree!
May the spirit of God perfume your burial niche * so that it scorns the musk and the amber!
You were present at the *samāʿ*[565] and obtained all kinds of knowledge, * and (thus) you made the mention of your name eternal for all time to come!
Your cared for the orphans and sustained the widows, * and you were to them like a benevolent father.

560 Does not fit the metre.

561 Or maybe *ḥilf at-tuqā*, "the sworn confederate of godliness"?

562 Given the context, this must refer to some activity connected with the pilgrimage.

563 Does this refer to the Basin (*al-ḥawḍ*) in Paradise, or to the fountain of Tasnīm?

564 From sorrow, *or also* from the Chastisement of the Grave.

565 Either a Ḥadīṯ lecture or a mystical session.

And they said in praise of you, when death had come, nothing but good * and with this lord-like dominion of the people
You supplied yourself (as provisions) for the Day of the Final Judgment * and for the Gathering of the Creation at the Place of Gathering".

140

LOCATION. Mecca (al-Maᶜlāh cemetery). DATE. 623 H.
PERSON BURIED. Kuš Isfahsalār Waḫš (M. b. M., d. 623 H): FāsīᶜIqd II pp. 379f.; IFahdItḥāf III p. 42.
SOURCE. FāsīᶜIqd II pp. 379f.
DESCRIPTION. "On his tombstone in the Maᶜlāh cemetery he is given various titles (*or* titles), including: *al-ġarīb* (...) *al-ʿālamīn*, and on his tombstone we also read: *tuwuffiya* (...)". (Reconstructed from the account of al-Fāsī):

[hāḏā qabru] l-ġarībi s-saʿīdi š-šahīdi l-Malakīyi l-ʿālimī l-ʿādili l-Muʾayyadīyi l-Muẓaffari l-Manṣūri Tāǧi d-Dawlati wa-d-Dīn / iḫtiyāri l-mulūki wa-s-salāṭīn / maliki l-ʾumarāʾ fī l-ʿālamīn || *Muḥammadi bni Muḥammadi bni ʿAlīyini l-Waḫšīyi l-maʿrūfi bi-Kuš Isfahsalār Waḫš + tuwuffiya fī l-ʿašari l-ʾawwali min Rabīʿi l-ʾawwali sanata ṯalāṯin wa-ʿišrīna wa-sittimiʾah*

"[This is the tomb of] the stranger, the blissful, the martyr, the learned, the just, the retainer of al-Malik al-Muʾayyad, the triumphant, the victorious, Diadem of the Dynasty and the Creed, / best choice of the kings and rulers, / king of the emirs of the worlds, || Muḥammad b. Muḥammad b. ᶜAlī al-Waḫšī known as Kuš Isfahsalār Waḫš. + He was taken (to God) during the first ten days of Rabīᶜ I in the year 623".

141

LOCATION. Mecca (al-Maᶜlāh cemetery). DATE. 625 H.
PERSON BURIED. Šaraf ad-Dīn aš-Šāmī (ᶜAdīy b. Abī l-Barakāt b. Ṣaḫr, d. 625 H): FāsīᶜIqd V p. 199; IFahdItḥāf III p. 45.
SOURCE. FāsīᶜIqd V p. 199.
DESCRIPTION. "[...] So runs his genealogy on his tombstone in the Maᶜlāh (cemetery), and he was given the titles: *al-ʾimām* (...). It further said: *tuwuffiya* (...), and that is all the information I have about him". (Reconstructed from al-Fāsī):

[hāḏā qabru] l-ʾimāmi l-ʿālimi l-ʿābidi l-wariʿi Šarafi d-Dīni ǧalāli l-ʾislāmi qudwati l-mašāyiḫi + ʿAdīyi bni ʾAbī l-Barakāti bni Ṣaḫrini š-Šāmīyi + tuwuffiya yamwa ṯ-ṯalāṯāʾi s-sābiʿi min Ḏī l-Ḥiǧǧati sanata ḫamsin wa-ʿišrīna wa-sittimiʾah

"[This is the tomb of] the Imam, the learned, the worshipper, the pious, Šaraf ad-Dīn, the splendour of Islam, the exemplary sheikh + ᶜAdīy b. Abī l-Barakāt b. Ṣaḫr aš-Šāmī. + He was taken (to God) on Tuesday 7th Ḏū l-Ḥiǧǧah in the year 625".

142

LOCATION. Mecca (al-Maᶜlāh cemetery). DATE. 626 H.

PERSON BURIED. Abū l-Muẓaffar al-Malik al-Masᶜūd Yūsuf (597–626 H), the Ayyubid governor and Rasūlid ruler of Yemen, the son of al-Malik al-Kāmil. He died in Mecca after a heavy stroke: IWāṣilKurūb IV p. 259f.; IFuwaṭīḪaw pp. 12f.; ḪazrᶜUqūd I pp. 34-46; IFahdItḥāf III p. 45; SinǧManāʾiḥ II pp. 295f.

SOURCE. IḪallWaf V p. 84 / (Slane) III pp. 245f.

DESCRIPTION. A pious man of Kurdish origin called Ṣiddīq b. Badr b. Ǧanāḥ (d. 639 H) was to supervise his burial in Mecca and take care of his possessions. Moreover, al-Malik al-Masᶜūd had directed in his last will that there should be no building upon his grave; rather, he ordered that he should be buried beside the Maᶜlāh cemetery in Mecca and that on his tomb be inscribed: [...], "and all this was duly executed" (IḪallWaf); "He stipulated in his last will (...) to be buried among the strangers (*ġurabāʾ*) in the cemetery of the people of Mecca. Thus he was buried in the Maᶜlāh cemetery, and afterwards a mausoleum (*qubbah*), which is famous until this very day, was erected over his tomb" (ḪazrᶜUqūd, IFahdItḥāf).

hāḏā qabru l-faqīri ʾilā raḥmati llāhi taᶜālā Yūsufa bni Muḥammadi bni ʾAbī Bakri bni ʾAyyūb

raḥmati llāhi taᶜālā: *raḥmati rabbihī* (IḪallWaf, a variant in the mss.).

"This is the tomb of one who is in need of the mercy of God the Exalted: Yūsuf b. Muḥammad b. Abī Bakr b. Ayyūb".

143

LOCATION. Mecca. DATE. 627 H.

PERSON BURIED. Sirāǧ ad-Dīn al-Ḫūzī (Abū Ǧaᶜfar ᶜUmar b. Makkī, d. 627 H): IFahdItḥāf III p. 48.

SOURCE. ŠaybīŠaraf f. 27a = RCEA 4017.

DESCRIPTION. A tombstone, bearing the following inscription after the *basmalah* and the word of God the Exalted *riǧālun lā tulhīhim tiǧāratun wa-lā bayᶜun ᶜan ḏikri llāhi* ("Men whom neither commerce nor trafficking diverts from the remembrance of God") until the words *wa-llāhu yarzuqu man yašāʾu bi-ġayri ḥisāb* ("and God provides whomsoever He will, without accounting") (Q 24:37f.): [...], (...) and on the upper fringe of the tombstone the blessing upon the Prophet (*taṣliyah*) and two *šahādah*s are inscribed, as also the following: *raḥima llāhu man qaraʾa "qul huwa llāhu ʾaḥad" wa-daᶜā lī bi-raḥmatihī*, 'May God have mercy upon those who recite: *Say*: *He is God, One* (Q 112:1) and invoke His mercy on my behalf'".

hāḏā qabru l-faqīri ʾilā llāhi taᶜālā š-šayḫi l-faqīhi l-ʾimāmi l-ᶜālimi l-ᶜābidi z-zāhidi l-wariᶜi šayḫi ṭ-ṭarīqah / wa-maᶜdini l-ḥaqīqah || qudwati s-sālikīn / kahfi l-fuqarāʾī wa-masākīn || *Sirāği d-Dīni Šamsi š-šarīʿati muftī l-farīqayni ʾAbī Ǧaʿfara ʿUmara bni Makkīyi bni ʿAlīyi l-Ḫūzīyi – qaddasa rūḥahū wa-nawwara ḍarīhahū – tuwuffiya laylata l-ʾarbaʿāʾi s-sādisa ʿašara min šahri l-Muḥarrami sanata sabʿin wa-ʿišrīna wa-sittimiʾah*

"This is the tomb of one who is in need of God the Exalted, the sheikh, the jurist, the Imam, the learned, the worshipper, the ascetic, the pious, sheikh of the (mystic) path / and mine of true wisdom, || the example for the mystics, / the cavern (i.e. the refuge) for the poor and the destitute, || Sirāğ ad-Dīn, the sun of the religious law, muftī of both parties,[566] Abū Ǧaʿfar ʿUmar b. Makkī b. ʿAlī al-Ḫūzī – may (God) sanctify his soul and illuminate his tomb! – He was taken (to God) in the night to Wednesday 16th of the month of Muḥarram in the year 627".

144

LOCATION. Mecca (al-Maʿlāh cemetery). DATE. 633 H or after.

PERSON BURIED. Abū n-Nuʿmān Bašīr b. Abī Bakr b. Sulaymān al-Ǧaʿfarī at-Tabrīzī (Ardabīl 570 – Mecca 633 H or after),[567] Shafiite jurist and the teacher of Quṭb ad-Dīn al-Qasṭallānī (d. Mecca 686 H): FāsīʿIqd III pp. 240-2; IFahdItḥāf III p. 68.

SOURCE. ŠaybīŠaraf f. 20b = RCEA 4088.

DESCRIPTION. A tombstone that, after the *basmalah* and the word of God the Exalted *kullu man ʿalayhi fānin* ("All that dwells upon the earth is perishing" = Q 55:26) until the end of the verse, bears the following inscription: [...]. aš-Šaybī ends the quotation of the epitaph by saying:

"This is all that I was able to read on the tombstone. The inscription upon it was not obliterated by the long course of time, but by the softness of the stone and its lack of hardness.[568] The word following 'He was taken away' is not clear to me, thus I do not know whether it is 'day' or 'night'.[569] As to the date of death, it surely is written as I have transcribed it, no doubt of it, yet this is strange because I took the information from the hand-writing of sheikh Abū l-ʿAbbās al-Mayūrqī who says that he (*sc.* at-Tabrīzī) died in the month of Ṣafar in the year 646".[570]

566 This does not refer to *al-ḥaramayn* of Mecca and Medina, but rather to the fact that he was muftī according to both the Malikite and Shafiite schools of law.

567 His name and date of death are not known with certainty. In the epitaph cited by aš-Šaybī, his name runs "Abū n-Nuʿmān Bašīr b. Abī Bakr b. Sulaymān b. Yūsuf", while al-Fāsī lists him as "Naǧm ad-Dīn Abū n-Nuʿmān Bašīr b. *Ḥāmid* b. Sulaymān b. Yūsuf" and Ibn Fahd as "Zayn ad-Dīn Abū n-Nuʿmān Bašīr b. Sulaymān". His date of death, on the other hand, is given in the epitaph as 633, whereas several literary sources – as stated by al-Fāsī, aš-Šaybī and Ibn Fahd – unanimously report that he died only in Ṣafar 646 H.

568 *ʿadam ṣalābatihī*, the latter word being mistakenly written صلاينه.

569 Ms. *fa-lā ʾadrī hal hiya yawmun* {*wa-laylatun*} *ʾaw laylatun.*

570 *Cf.* above pp. 330f.

hāḏā qabru l-ʿālimi muftī l-muslimīna ʾAbī n-Nuʿmāni Bašīri bni ʾAbī Bakri bni Sulaymāna bni Yūsufa l-Ǧaʿfarīyi t-Tabrīzīyi qubiḍa yawma (?) *l-iṯnayni ṯ-ṯāmini ʿašara min šahri llāhi Raǧabin sanata ṯalāṯin wa-ṯalāṯīna wa-sittimiʾatin – ǧaʿalahū llāhu šafīʿan li-wālidayhi ʾāmīn*

"This is the tomb of the learned, the Mufti of the Muslims Abū n-Nuʿmān Bašīr b. Abī Bakr b. Sulaymān b. Yūsuf al-Ǧaʿfarī at-Tabrīzī. He was taken away on Monday, the 18th of the month of God Raǧab in the year 633. – May God make him an intercessor for his parents![571] Amen".

145

LOCATION. Mecca (al-Maʿlāh cemetery). DATE. 634 H.

PERSON BURIED. Abū Muḥammad an-Nahāwandī (ʿAbd al-Ġaffār b. ʿAbd al-Karīm, d. 634 H): FāsīʿIqd V p. 100; IFahdItḥāf III p. 52.

SOURCE. FāsīʿIqd V p. 100.

DESCRIPTION. "[...] On his tombstone were also the titles: *aš-šayḫ al-marḥūm* (...), and further (we read): *tuwuffiya* (...)":

[*hāḏā qabru*] *š-šayḫi l-marḥūmi ṣ-ṣāliḥi z-zāhidi l-ʿābidi zayni l-ḥāǧǧi wa-l-ḥaramayni ʾabī l-yatāmā wa-l-masākīn* / *kahfi l-fuqarāʾi wa-l-munqaṭiʿīn* || + *al-qāḍī ʾAbī Muḥammadin ʿAbdi l-Ġaffāri bni ʿAbdi l-Karīmi bni ʿAbdi r-Raḥmāni n-Nahāwandīyi* + *tuwuffiya yawma ṯ-ṯalāṯāʾi t-tāsiʿi ʿašara min Ǧumādā l-ʾūlā sanata ʾarbaʿin* [lacuna] *wa-sittimiʾah*

"[This is the tomb of] the late sheikh, the righteous, the ascetic, the worshipper, ornament of the pilgrims and the two Sacrosanct Recincts (of Mecca and Medina), father to the orphans and the needy, / (sheltering) cave (i.e. refuge) for the poor and the unattached (lit. those cut off from their relatives, *or* home towns), || the judge Abū Muḥammad ʿAbd al-Ġaffār b. ʿAbd al-Karīm b. ʿAbd ar-Raḥmān an-Nahāwandī. + He was taken (to God) on Tuesday 19th[572] Ǧumādā I in the year 4 [*lacuna*][573] and 600".

146

LOCATION. Mecca (al-Maʿlāh cemetery). DATE. 643 H.

PERSON BURIED. A pious woman called (al-)Muwaffaqah (d. 643 H). She had been lame but was then approached by the Prophet (in a dream?) who took her by the hand and made her walk: MarǧBahǧah II p. 405; FāsīʿIqd VI pp. 438f.; IFahdItḥāf III p. 63.

571 For this prayer, see Volume I pp. 304f.

572 Ibn Fahd has *tāsiʿ*, "9th".

573 According to Ibn Fahd, an-Nahāwandī died in 634 H, so *wa-ṯalāṯīna* is missing from the quotation ofthe epitaph.

SOURCES. MarǧBahǧah II p. 405 = FāsīᶜIqd III p. 439 (incomplete).
DESCRIPTION. "My mother showed me her tomb in the Maᶜlāh cemetery (...). Upon it was a tombstone bearing the inscription: [...]".

hāḏā qabru l-faqīrati ʾilā llāhi taʿālā ʿatīqati rasūli llāhi – taṣliyah – mina z-zamani l-Muwaffaqati Kulṯūma [*binti*] *Ḫalīli bni ʾIbrāhīma l-ʾAnṣārīyi tuwuffiyat laylata t-tāsiʿi ʿašara min Ramaḍāna sanata ṯalāṯin wa-ʾarbaʿīna wa-sittimiʾah*

"This is the tomb of a woman in need of God the Exalted, freedwoman of the Messenger of God – *taṣliyah* –, (freed) from chronic illness, al-Muwaffaqah Kulṯūm bint[574] Ḫalīl b. Ibrāhīm al-Anṣārī. She died in the night of the 19th Ramaḍān in the year 634".

147

LOCATION. Mecca. DATE. 647 H.
PERSON BURIED. Abū Aḥmad Ibn Ẓuhayrah (ᶜAṭīyah b. Ẓuhayrah al-Makkī al-Maḫzūmī, d. Muḥarram 647 H), founding father of the later important Ibn Ẓuhayrah clan and the first of them to settle in Mecca: FāsīᶜIqd V pp. 220f.; ITaġrManh VIII pp. 18-20; IFahdItḥāf III p. 69.
SOURCES. FāsīᶜIqd V pp. 220f. = ITaġrManh VIII p. 19.
DESCRIPTION. "On his tombstone is written: *hāḏā qabru* (...)". The epitaph is quoted only in part, because later al-Fāsī adds regarding Ibn Ẓuhayrah's date of death: "I found written on his tombstone: *wa-tuwuffiya* (...)".

hāḏā qabru š-šayḫi l-ʾaǧall / kabīri l-qadri wa-l-maḥall / kaṯīri n-nafʿi li-man ʾaqall || + *tuwuffiya – raḥimahū llāhu – yawma l-ʾarbaʿāʾi s-sādisi mina l-Muḥarrami sanata sabʿin wa-ʾarbaʿīna wa-sittimiʾah*

"This is the tomb of the most sublime sheikh, / of great distinction and rank, / of much benefit to those of lesser (rank *or* possession). || + He was taken (to God) – may God have mercy upon him! – on Wednesday 6th Muḥarram in the year 647".

148

LOCATION. Mecca (al-Maᶜlāh cemetery). DATE. 652 H.
PERSON BURIED. The emir Muḫtār ad-Dīn al-Muẓaffarī (Ḥamd b. Muḥammad, d. 652 H): FāsīᶜIqd III p. 440; IFahdItḥāf III p. 76.
SOURCE. FāsīᶜIqd III p. 440.
DESCRIPTION. "I compiled the major part of this entry (*tarǧamah*) from his tombstone".

574 The addition *bint*, not present in the wording of MarǧBahǧah, is necessitated by the context and confirmed by FāsīᶜIqd and IFahdItḥāf.

Although it is difficult, in this case, to separate the comment by al-Fāsī from the wording of the original epitaph, it can be reconstructed from his account:

[*hāḏā qabru*] *Muḫtāri d-Dīni Ḥamdi bni l-ʾamīri Šamsi d-Dīni Muḥammadi bni ʾAḥmada bni l-Musayyabi l-Muẓaffarīyi qutila – raḥimahū llāhu – bayna ṣ-ṣaffayni fī l-ḥarbi llaḏī kāna* (!) *bayna bni Barṭāsa wa-ʾahli Makkata wa-ḏālika fī yawmi ṯ-ṯulāṯāʾi r-rābiʿi wa-l-ʿišrīna min Ḏī l-Qaʿdati l-harāmi sanata ṯnayni wa-ḫamsīna wa-sittimiʾah*

"[This is the tomb of] Muḫtār ad-Dīn Ḥamd, son of the emir Šams ad-Dīn Muḥammad b. Aḥmad b. al-Musayyab al-Muẓaffarī.[575] He was killed – may God have mercy upon him! – in the lines of battle in the conflict between Ibn Barṭās[576] and the Meccans, on Tuesday 24th of the sacred (month) Ḏū l-Qaʿdah in the year 652".

149

LOCATION. Mecca. DATE. 663 H.

PERSON BURIED. Ḍiyāʾ ad-Dīn al-Qasṭallānī (Abū ʿAl. M. b. Abī l-Barakāt ʿUmar b. M. b. al-Ḥasan), great uncle of the more famous Quṭb ad-Dīn al-Qasṭallānī (d. Mecca 686 H): ŠaybīŠaraf ff. 23a-24b; IFahdItḥāf III p. 89. The Qasṭallānī-clan possessed an area of the Maʿlāh cemetery which was called by their name.[577]

SOURCE. ŠaybīŠaraf ff. 23a-b = RCEA 4538 (only the prose).

DESCRIPTION. A tombstone, bearing the following inscription after the *basmalah* and the word of God *ʾinna l-muttaqīna fī ǧannātin wa-naharin * fī maqʿadi ṣidqin ʿinda malīkin muqtadirin* ("Surely the godfearing shall dwell amid gardens and a river * in a sure abode, in the presence of a King Omnipotent", Q 54:54f.): [...]. This is followed by two poems and a passage in prose; aš-Šaybī adds that between the 7 lines of the first poem and the 12 lines of the second no division had been made to separate them.

First poem (*ṭawīl*):

*ʾanā la-musīʾun sayyidī min taǧāwuzī * ʾatāka bi-lā zādin li-qaṭʿi l-ma*[*f*]*āwizī*
*wa-ʿafwuka maʾmūlun li-kulli muʾammilin * wa-birruka mawǧūdun li-kulli munāhizī*
*wa-bābuka maftūḥun wa-faḍluka šāmilun * wa-mā ʾanā ʾin ʾaǧramtu*[578] *hāḏā bi-fāʾizī*

575 The deputy governor of Mecca from 646 H, by the order of the Rasūlid ruler al-Malik al-Manṣūr (r. 626–47 H), see SinǧManāʾiḥ II p. 307 and az-Zaylaʿī: *Amirate of Mecca* p. 183.

576 The commander Mubāriz ad-Dīn al-Ḥusayn b. ʿAlī Ibn Barṭās [Birṭās] was sent to Mecca in 652 H by the Rasūlid ruler al-Malik al-Muẓaffar Yūsuf I b. ʿUmar (r. 647–94 H) in order to take control of the town (*cf.* also ḪazrʿUqūd I p. 115; SinǧManāʾiḥ II pp. 316f.; az-Zaylaʿī: *Amirate of Mecca* p. 166); the *nisbah* "al-Muẓaffarī" refers to that ruler.

577 *Cf.* FāsīʿIqd II p.11 and IV p. 316.

578 Ms. اخرمت.

wa-qad ǧiʾtu ʾarǧū l-ʿafwa bi-ġāyati l-munā[579] * *muqirran ʿalā nafsī bi-ǧurmi l-mubārizī*
ʾusawwifu bi-ṭ-ṭāʿāti taswīfa musrifin * *wa-ʾafqidu fī l-ʿiṣyāni naqḏa*[580] *l-munāǧizī*
fa-ʾin taʿfu ʿan ǧurmī fa-ʾinnaka ʾahluhū * *wa-ʾillā fa-mā šayʾun ʿani n-nāri ḥāǧizī*
wa-ʿādātu sādāti l-warā ʾan yuʿāmilū * *mufirran ʾatāhum bi-r-riḍā wa-t-taǧāwuzī*

"I am, O my Master, an evildoer by transgressing (Your bounds) * who came to You without provisions to traverse the deserts!
Your forgiveness is hoped for by everyone who is hopeful * and Your kindness is available for everyone who is near (to You).
Your gate (of mercy) is open and Your grace is total, * and if I committed this (sin) I will not attain success (i.e. on the Last Day).
I came (to You) imploring forgiveness as the greatest of (my) desires * although I confess unto myself the sin of one who contends (Your will).
I put off my obedience recklessly * and I lose in disobedience the rescue of those who strive (for obedience).
If You forgive my sins then You are most suitable for doing so, * and if not so, then nothing will shield (me) from the Fire!
The customs of the lords of mankind are such that they deal gently with * a fugitive, that escapes to them, through approval and passing over (his misdeeds)".

Second poem (*wāfir*):

wa-ḥaqqika mā ʿaṣaytuka mustahīnan * *bi-ʾamrika yā-malāḏī wa-ʿtimādī*
wa-lākin ġarra bī karamun wa-ḥulmun * *wa-taʾmīlun li-qawlika: ʿyā-ʿibādīʾ*
fa-ʿāmaltu l-ʾayādiya bi-l-maʿāṣī * *wa-ṣāḥabtu l-maʾātima bi-t-tamādī*
fa-yā-[ ][581] *wa-yā-ḥayātī* * *ʾiḏā nūdītu bi-smī fī l-maʿādī*
wa-ʾutītu l-kitāba wa-qīla lī qraʾ * *wa-ʿāyantu l-musaṭṭara fīhi bādī*
wa-mā qaddamtu min ʾaʿmāli sūʾin * *kafā ʾannī qadimtu bi-ġayri zādī*
fa-law ʾannī ʾanūḥu bi-qadri ǧurmī * *labistu mina l-ʾasā ṯawba l-ḥidādī*
wa-ʾaǧraytu l-madāmiʿa min ǧufūnī * *wa-himtu maʿa l-wuḥūši bi-kulli wādī*[582]
wa-tiḥta mina l-ḫaṭā yā-nawḥa ṯaklā * *wa-ʾaʿzabta l-maḥāǧira bi-s-suhādī*
wa-mā lī lā ʾanūḥu ʿalā ḏunūbin * *bihā bāraztu ḫallāqa l-ʿibādī*
wa-mā lī šāfiʿun ʾillā raǧāʾī * *wa-ḥusnu ẓ-ẓanni bi-l-maliki l-ǧawādī*
fa-ʾin taʿfū fa-ʾanta li-ḏāka[583] *ʾahlun* * *wa-ʿabdu s-sūʾi ʾahlun li-l-biʿādī*

"By your right! I did not contradict You, thereby showing disdain * towards your command, O my refuge and my support (*or* strength)!

579 The last two words do not fit the metre; ms. باغاية المنى (?).

580 Ms. نقد.

581 The bracketed part is illegible in the ms.; it seems to contain two words.

582 Written مراد in the ms.

583 Ms. *fa-ḏāka*.

But (Your) munificence and clemency beguiled me * as well as the hopeful expectation (*or* confidence) caused by You saying 'O my servants!',[584]

Thus I exchanged Your favours with sins * and kept company with misdeeds persistently.

O [ ], O my life * when I am called by my name in the hereafter,

(When) I am given the book[585] and am told: 'Read!' * and (when) I see the writing in it plainly!

And all the evil deeds I had done (before in life), * then – it is enough for me to present myself (to You) without any provisions (*sc.* of good deeds).

If I wailed as much as my sins necessitate, * (then) I would put on garments of mourning for such grief

And I would make the tears flow down from my eyelids * and I would roam with wild beasts every valley

And, given my fault, you would come easy (?), O lament of a woman bereaved of her child, * and would make the eyes hollow from sleeplessness!

But why do I not bewail sins * by which I challenged the Creator of Mankind?

(It is because) I have no intercessor apart from my hope * and my confidence in (*or* having a good opinion of) the Magnanimous King (i.e. God).

If You forgive (me) You are surely best suited (*or* apt) to that * as the servant of evil doings is best suited for (*or* deserves) remoteness (from You)!"

The passage in prose:

hāḏā qabru l-faqīhi l-ʾimāmi Ḍiyāʾi d-Dīni ʾAbū (sic) *ʿAbdi llāhi Muḥammadi bni l-faqīhi l-marḥūmi ʾAbī l-Barakāti ʿUmara bni Muḥammadi bni ʿUmara bni l-Ḥasani l-Qasṭallānīyi ʾimāmi l-Mālikīyati bi-l-ḥarami š-šarīfi māta yawma l-iṯnayni ṯāmini ʿišrīna Šawwālin sanata ṯalāṯin wa-sittīna wa-sittimiʾatin raḥimahū llāhu taʿālā*

"This is the tomb of the jurist, the Imam Ḍiyāʾ ad-Dīn Abū ʿAbd Allāh Muḥammad, son of the late jurist Abū l-Barakāt ʿUmar b. Muḥammad b. ʿUmar b. al-Ḥasan al-Qasṭallānī, Imam of the Malikites in the Sacrosanct Recinct (of Mecca). He died on Monday 28 Šawwāl in the year 663. – May God the Exalted have mercy upon him!"

150

LOCATION. Mecca (al-Maʿlāh cemetery). DATE. 663 H.

PERSON BURIED. The emir ʿAlam ad-Dīn Qayṣar (d. 663 H), freedman of the Ayyubid

584 This obviously refers to Q 39:53: *qul yā-ʿibādiya llaḏīna ʾasrafū ʿalā ʾanfusihim lā taqnaṭū min raḥmati llāhi ʾinna llāha yaġfiru ḏ-ḏunūba ǧamīʿan* (Arberry translates "Say: 'O my people who have been prodigal against yourselves, do not despair of God's mercy: surely God forgives sins altogether'").

585 The book or "Document" in which his good and evil deeds are registered.

emir Īldukuz: Fāsīᶜİqd V pp. 488f.; MaqrSulūk II pp. 109, 189, 301, 406 and 532 (?); IFahdItḥāf III p. 89.

SOURCE. Fāsīᶜİqd V pp. 488f.

DESCRIPTION. "On his tombstone in the Maᶜlāh (cemetery) I found (written): [...]":

hāḏā qabru l-ʾamīri l-ʾağalli l-ʾisfahsalāri l-muḥtarami l-kabīri l-ġarībi š-šahīdī ʿAlami d-Dīni Qayṣar ʾamīri l-ḥāğği l-miṣrīyi ʾilā l-ḥaramayni l-Malakīyi l-Kāmilīyi ʿatīqi l-ʾamīri l-ʾağalli l-ʾisfahsalāri l-kabīri Šamsi d-Dīni ʾĪldukuza ʾustāḏ-dāri (sic) *l-Maliki l-ʿĀdili tuwuffīya yawma ṯ-ṯalāṯāʾi ḫāmisi ʿišrī Rabīʿi l-ʾāḫiri sanata ṯalāṯin wa-sittīna wa-sittimiʾah*

"This is the tomb of the most sublime emir, the honoured Isfahsalār, the great, the stranger, the martyr ᶜAlam ad-Dīn Qayṣar, leader of the Egyptian pilgrim caravan to the Sacrosanct Recincts (of Mecca and Medina) of al-Malik al-Kāmil, freedman of the most sublime emir, the great general Šams ad-Dīn Īldukuz,[586] majordomo to al-Malik al-ᶜĀdil. He was taken (to God) on Tuesday 25th[587] Rabīᶜ II in the year 663".

151

LOCATION. Mecca. DATE. 664 H.

PERSON BURIED. ᶜAfīf ad-Dīn az-Zaᶜfarānī (Abū l-Muẓaffar Manṣūr b. Abī l-Faḍl M. b. Saᶜd [Manᶜah], d. 664 H): ŠaybīŠaraf f. 17b; IFahdItḥāf III p. 90.

SOURCE. ŠaybīŠaraf f. 17b = RCEA 4558.

DESCRIPTION. "Beside the former two tombs (i.e. of al-Fuḍayl, **116**, and al-ᶜIzz Ibn Ğamāᶜah, **158**) there is a tombstone which bears, after the *basmalah* and (the word of God) *li-miṯli hāḏā fal-yaʿmali l-ʿāmilūna* ("For the like of it let the workers work", Q 37:61), the inscription: [...]".

hāḏā qabru l-ʿabdi l-faqīri ʾilā llāhi taʿālā l-lāʾiḏi bi-ʿaẓīmi ğanābih / al-ʿāʾiḏi min ʾalīmī ʿiqābih ‖ *al-mutawakkili ʿalayh / wa-l-muqaddimi ḫidmata ḥaramihī wa-ḥarami nabīyihī (wa-)*[588]*wasīlihī bayna yadayh* ‖ *ʿAfīfi d-dīni ʾAbī l-Muẓaffari Manṣūri bni ʾAbī l-Faḍli bni Saʿdi l-Baġdādīyi šayḫi l-ḥaramayni š-šarīfayni – taġammadahū llāhu bi-riḍwānih / wa-ʾaskanahū bi-karamihī bi-buḥbūḥati ğinānih* ‖ – *qullida*[589] *ʾamrahumā sanata ʾarbaʿin wa-ʿišrīna wa-sittimiʾatin ʾilā ḥīni wafātihī mina l-ḫāmisi wa-l-ʿišrīna min Ḏī l-Qaʿdati min sanati ʾarbaʿa wa-sittīna wa-sittimiʾatin – ʿafā llāhu taʿālā ʿanhu wa-ʾaḥsana ʾilayhī wa-taʿaṭṭafa ʿalayhī – ṣalwalah*

586 His name is rendered as الدقز by Ibn Fahd.

587 Ibn Fahd in his entry has *ḫāmisa ʿašara*, "15th".

588 Add. RCEA; haplography in the ms.

589 The respective word in ŠaybīŠaraf seems to be written (mistakenly) تلد, not قلد (as in RCEA).

"This is the tomb of the servant who is in need of God the Exalted, who seeks shelter with His Most Sublime Majesty / and asks for protection from His painful punishment, || who relies upon Him / and offers the service of His Sacrosanct Recinct and the Sacrosanct Recinct of His Prophet, his means (of intercession), before Him, || ᶜAfīf ad-Dīn Abū l-Muẓaffar Manṣūr b. Abī l-Faḍl b. Saᶜd al-Baġdādī, sheikh of both noble Sacrosanct Recincts. – May God cover him with His satisfaction and may He, as a sign of His generosity, make him dwell in the centre of His Gardens (of Paradise)! – He was invested with their affairs in the year 624 and (held them) until the time of his death on Ḏū l-Qaᶜdah 25th in the year 664. – May God the Exalted forgive him, treat him kindly and be clement to him! – *ṣalwalah*".

152

LOCATION. Mecca (al-Maᶜlāh cemetery). DATE. 718 H.

PERSON BURIED. Ǧamāl ad-Dīn aṭ-Ṭabarī al-Makkī (M. b. ᶜAlī b. ᶜAl. aš-Šaybānī, d. Mecca 718 H): FāsīᶜIqd II p. 180; IFahdItḥāf III p. 161.

SOURCE. FāsīᶜIqd II p. 180.

DESCRIPTION. "I copied all this from his tombstone".

[hāḏā qabru] š-šābbi l-maqtūli ẓulman Ǧamāli d-Dīni Muḥammadi bni l-Qāḍī Bahāʾ ad-Dīni ʾAbī Saʿdin ʿAlīyi bni ʿAbdi llāhi bni ʿUmara bni ʾAbī l-Maʿālī Yaḥyā bni ʿAbdi r-Raḥmāni bni l-Ḥusayni bni ʿAlīyi š-Šaybānīyi ṭ-Ṭabarīyi l-Makkīyi tuwuffiya laylata l-iṯnayni sādisi Muḥarramin sanata ṯamāniya ʿašrata wa-sabʿimiʾatin bi-Makkah

"[This is the tomb] of the youth, wrongfully killed, Ǧamāl ad-Dīn Muḥammad, son of the judge Bahāʾ ad-Dīn Abū Saᶜd ᶜAlī b. ᶜAbd Allāh b. ᶜUmar b. Abī l-Maᶜālī Yaḥyā b. ᶜAbd ar-Raḥmān b. al-Ḥusayn b. ᶜAlī aš-Šaybānī aṭ-Ṭabarī al-Makkī. He was taken (to God) in the night of Monday 6th Muḥarram in the year 718 in Mecca".

153

LOCATION. Mecca (al-Maᶜlāh cemetery). DATE. 727 H.

PERSON BURIED. Afḍal b. Maḥmūd as-Sarwī (d. Minā 727 H): FāsīᶜIqd III pp. 203; IFahdItḥāf III p. 186.

SOURCE. FāsīᶜIqd III p. 203.

DESCRIPTION. "[...] I found it mentioned so on his tombstone in the Maᶜlāh (cemetery), and he was given the titles: *aš-šayḫ* (...) *al-ʿārif bi-llāh*". (Reconstructed from the account of al-Fāsī):

[hāḏā qabru] š-šayḫi ṣ-ṣāliḥi l-ʿābidi z-zāhidi l-ʿālimi l-kāmili l-ʿārifi bi-llāhi + ʾAfḍala bni Maḥmūdi bni Maḥmudini s-Sarwīyi tuwuffiya bi-Minā fī ʾayyāmi t-tašrīqi sanata sabʿin wa-ʿišrīna wa-sabʿimiʾah

"[This is the tomb of] the righteous sheikh, the worshipper, the ascetic, the learned, the perfect, who had gained the acquaintance of God, + Afḍal b. Maḥmūd b. Maḥmūd as-Sarwī.[590] He was taken (to God) in Minā in the (three) days (of festivity) after the Day of Immolation (during the pilgrimage) in the year 727".

154

Location. Mecca (al-Maᶜlāh cemetery). Date. 728 H.

Person buried. The mystic and scholar Muwaffaq ad-Dīn az-Zaylaᶜī (Abū l-Ḥasan ᶜAlī b. Abī Bakr M. al-ᶜAqīlī, d. 728 H): FāsīᶜIqd V pp. 243-5; ITaġrManh VIII p. 30; IFahdItḥāf III p. 188.

Source. FāsīᶜIqd V p. 243.

Description. After quoting the complete name, al-Fāsī adds "I found it so written upon his tombstone in the Maᶜlāh (cemetery)". He then says that "he was styled: *al-faqīh* (...) *al-quṭb*, and the date of his death is mentioned: *tuwuffiya* (...)". According to al-Fāsī, the tomb of az-Zaylaᶜī "is a famous grave in the Maᶜlāh cemetery, and the people come to visit it".[591] (Reconstructed from the account of al-Fāsī):

[hāḏā qabru] l-faqīhi ṣ-ṣāliḥi l-ʿābidi n-nāsiki l-quṭbi + Muwaffaqi d-Dīni ʾAbī l-Ḥasanī ʿAlīyi bni ʾAbī Bakrin Muḥammadini z-Zaylaʿīyi l-ʿAqīlīyi nasaban + tuwuffiya yamwa ṯ-ṯalāṯāʾi s-sābiʿi wa-l-ʿišrīna min Ḏī l-Ḥiǧǧati sanata ṯamānin wa-ʿišrīna wa-sabʿimiʾah

"[This is the tomb of] the jurist, the righteous, the worshipping, the devout, the pole + Muwaffaq ad-Dīn Abū l-Ḥasan ᶜAlī b. Abī Bakr M. the Zaylaᶜid, the ᶜAqīlid of descent. + He was taken (to God) on Tuesday 27th Ḏū l-Ḥiǧǧah of the year 728".

155

Location. Mecca (al-Maᶜlāh cemetery). Date. 742 H.

Person buried. Umm al-Faḍl Ṣafīyah bt. Ibrāhīm (d. 742 H): FāsīᶜIqd VI p. 410.

Source. FāsīᶜIqd VI p. 410.

Description. "Her death occurred in Mecca, according to what I found on her tombstone in the Maᶜlāh (cemetery) (...), and there she was given various titles, among them: *as-sitt* (...). It also contained her *kunyah*". (Reconstructed from the account of al-Fāsī):

[hāḏā qabru] s-sitti š-šayḫati l-ʿālimati l-ʿāmilah / z-zāhidati l-fāḍilah || l-wariʿīyati s-saʿīdati š-šahīdati šayḫati ṣ-ṣūfīyāti ḫādimati l-fuqarāʾ bi-l-ḥaramayni š-šarīfayni + ʾUmmi l-Faḍli + tuwuffiyat fī sanati ṯnatayni wa-ʾarbaʿīna wa-sabʿimiʾah

590 His *nisbah* might refer to the people called *as-sarwu l-Yamanīyūn*, see IFahdItḥāf II p. 548 and the editor's note.

591 *Cf.* also ITaġrManh VIII p. 30 (*qabruhū mašhūrun bi-l-Maʿlāh*).

"[This is the tomb of] the sister, the sheikhah, the learned, the effective,[592] / the ascetic, the distinguished, || the blissful, the martyress, sheikhah of the (female) Sufis, servant to the poor in the noble (Sacrosanct) Recincts (of Mecca and Medina) + Umm al-Faḍl + She was taken (to God) in the year 742".

156

LOCATION. Mecca (al-Maᶜlāh cemetery). DATE. 749 H.

PERSON BURIED. Mūsā b. ᶜUmar al-Ǧaᶜbarī (d. 749 H): FāsīᶜIqd VI p. 140; IFahdItḥāf III p. 239.

SOURCE. FāsīᶜIqd VI p. 140.

DESCRIPTION. "[...] Both their (names and) *laqab*s (i.e. of father and son) I copied from his tombstone, and there it is further said: *tuwuffiya* (...)". (Reconstructed from the account of al-Fāsī):

[hāḏā qabru] l-ʾimāmi l-qudwati l-ʿārifi bi-llāhi Muḥibbi d-Dīni Mūsā bni š-šayḫi ṣ-ṣāliḥi ʾawḥadi zamānihī Rukni d-Dīni ʿUmara l-Ǧaʿbarīyi + tuwuffiya fī ḥādiya ʿašara Ramaḍāna sanata tisʿin wa-ʾarbaʿīna wa-sabʿimiʾah

"[This is the tomb of] the Imam, the exemplum, 'the knower of God' (i.e. the gnostic), Muḥibb ad-Dīn Mūsā, son of the righteous sheikh, the unique of his time, Rukn ad-Dīn ᶜUmar al-Ǧaᶜbarī. + He was taken (to God) on Ramaḍān 11th in the year 749".

157

LOCATION. Mecca (al-Maᶜlāh cemetery). DATE. 764 H.

PERSON BURIED. The judge Abū l-Ḥasan at-Tilimsānī (ᶜAlī b. ᶜAl. b. M., d. 764 H): FāsīᶜIqd V pp. 266f.; IFahdItḥāf III p. 299.[593]

SOURCE. FāsīᶜIqd V pp. 266f.

DESCRIPTION. "[...] He was buried in the Maᶜlāh (cemetery), and I copied all that I mention about him from his tombstone. There he was given the titles: *aš-šayḫ* (...)". (Reconstructed from the account of al-Fāsī):

[hāḏā qabru] š-šayḫi ṣ-ṣāliḥi z-zakīyi l-faqīhi l-ʿālimi l-muftī l-mudarrisi l-ʾafḍali l-ʾakmali + l-qāḍī ʾAbī l-Ḥasani ʿAlīyi bni ʾAbī Muḥammadin ʿAbdi llāhi bni Muḥammadi bni ʿAbdi n-Nūri t-Tilimsānīyi qadima ʾilā Makkata ḥāǧǧan fī sanati ʾarbaʿin wa-sittīna wa-sabʿimiʾatin wa-ṭāfa bi-l-bayti l-ḥarāmi wa-saʿā fī yawmi qudūmihī wa-tuwuffiya ʾiṯra ḏālika wa-ḏālika fī yawmi l-iṯnayni ṯāliṯi šahri Ḏī l-Ḥiǧǧati mina s-sanati l-maḏkūrah

592 I.e. putting her knowledge (*ʿilm*) into practice (*ʿamal*).

593 Ibn Fahd gives his name as "ᶜAlī b. ᶜAwn Allāh Muḥammad b. ᶜAbd an-Nūr".

"[This is the tomb of] the righteous sheikh, the chaste, the jurist, the learned, the muftī, the lecturer, the most distinguished, the most perfect + the judge Abū l-Ḥasan ᶜAlī b. Abī Muḥammad ᶜAbd Allāh b. Muḥammad b. ᶜAbd an-Nūr at-Tilimsānī. He arrived in Mecca as a pilgrim in the year 764. He circumambulated the Sacrosanct House (i.e. the Kaᶜbah) and performed the 'running' (between aṣ-Ṣafā and al-Marwah) on the (very) day of his arrival and was taken (to God) immediately after that, on Monday 3rd of the month of D̲ū l-Ḥiǧǧah in the before-mentioned year".

158

LOCATION. Mecca. DATE. 767 H.

PERSON BURIED. ᶜIzz ad-Dīn Ibn Ǧamāᶜah (Abū ᶜUmar ᶜAbd al-ᶜAzīz b. al-Badr M. b. Ibr. b. Saᶜd Allāh al-Kinānī al-Ḥamawī al-Miṣrī aš-Šāfiᶜī, Damascus 694 – Mecca 767 H):[594] ḤusD̲ayl pp. 41-3; SubkīṬab X pp. 79-81; BN XIV p. 319; IMulᶜIqd p. 411; ŠaybīŠaraf ff. 16a-17b; IᶜIrāqīD̲ᶜIbar I pp. 200-7; MaqrSulūk III p. 125; IḤağRafᶜ pp. 243-6 and DK II pp. 489-91; IsnṬab I pp. 388-90; IQŠuhbTārīḫ III pp. 284-6; ITaġrManh VII pp. 300-2; IFahdItḥāf III p. 306; ŠD̲ VI pp. 208f.; GAL II p. 72; Salibi: *Banū Jamāᶜa* pp. 101f.; ZA IV pp. 15f.; Escovitz: *Office of Qāḍī* pp. 62 and 72f.

SOURCE. ŠaybīŠaraf ff. 16a-b = RCEA 767 004.

DESCRIPTION. "Beside the former tomb (of al-Fuḍayl, see above **116**) there is a tombstone which bears, after the *basmalah* and the word of God the Exalted *wa-man yaḫruǧ min baytihī muhāǧiran* ("Whoso goes forth from his house an emigrant", Q 4:100), the following inscription: [*prose*]. On the sides of the aforesaid tombstone the following (verses) are inscribed: [*poetry*], and I copied it here as I found it written".[595] – A passage in prose and six verses in the metre *basīṭ*:

hād̲ā qabru l-ᶜabdi l-faqīri ʾilā llāhi taᶜālā qāḍī l-muslimīna ᶜIzzi d-Dīni ʾAbī[596] *ᶜUmara ᶜAbdi l-ᶜAzīzi bni l-ᶜabdi l-faqīri ʾilā llāhi taᶜālā l-qāḍī Badri d-Dīni ʾAbī ᶜAbdi llāhi Muḥammadi bni š-šayḫi l-ʾislāmi Burhāni d-Dīni ʾIbrāhīma bni ᶜAbdi llāhi bni Ǧamāᶜata l-Kinānīyi š-Šāfiᶜīyi qāḍī l-quḍāti bi-d-diyāri l-Miṣrīyati – taġammadahū llāhu bi-raḥmatih / wa-ʾaskanahū bi-buḥbūḥati ǧannatih* || –

594 For reasons of devotion and a dream telling him to do so Ibn Ǧamāᶜah moved to the Ḥiǧāz and died in Mecca in Ǧumādā II 767 H, only a few days after having visited the Prophet's sepulchre in Medina. Ibn Ǧamāᶜah had already participated in the famous pilgrimage of the year 732 H, and in 735 H he had sojourned for a whole year in the Ḥiǧāz. From that time onwards, his hope had been to die in the Prophet's home town and his wish was granted.

595 "He was buried in the Maᶜlāh cemetery, beside the tomb of al-Fuḍayl b. ᶜIyāḍ, between it and the tomb of Abū l-Qāsim (*sic*) al-Qušayrī" (IḤağRafᶜ p. 246 note 1; similar IQŠuhbTārīḫ III p. 286, IᶜIrāqīD̲ᶜIbar I p. 201 and ITaġrManh VII p. 302).

596 RCEA: بن.

tuwuffiya ʾilā raḥmati llāhi taʿālā bi-Makkata l-mušarrafati yawma l-iṯnayni ḥādiya ʿašara Ǧumādā l-ʾāḫiri sanata sabʿin wa-sittīna wa-sabʿimiʾah

"This is the tomb of the servant who is in need of God the Exalted, the judge of the Muslims ʿIzz ad-Dīn Abū ʿUmar ʿAbd al-ʿAzīz, son of the servant who is in need of God the Exalted, the judge Badr ad-Dīn Abū Abd Allāh Muḥammad,[597] son of the Sheikh of Islam Burhān ad-Dīn Ibrāhīm b. ʿAbd Allāh b. Ǧamāʿah al-Kinānī aš-Šāfiʿī, chief-judge in Egypt. – May God cover him with His mercy / and make him dwell in the centre of His Garden! || – He was taken to the mercy of God the Exalted in Mecca 'the illustrious' on Monday 11th Ǧumādā II in the year 767".

ʾaḍḥā li-faqdika ruknu l-maǧdi munhadimū (!) * *wa-l-ʿilmu baʿdaka ʿIzzi d-Dīni munṯalimū*
*wa-l-faḍlu wa-l-ǧūdu wa-l-maʿrūfu kulluhumū * mātū li-mawtika wa-l-ʾiḥsānu wa-l-karamū*
*man li-š-šarīʿati wa-l-fatwā ʾiḏā ʿaǧizat * ʾūlū l-ʿulūmi wa-ʿan ʾidrākihā faḥamū*[598]
*man li-l-qaḍāʾi wa-man li-l-ḥukmi baʿdaka yā- * qāḍī l-quḍāti wa-man li-l-ḥaqqi multazimū*
*man li-l-masākīni wa-l-ʾaytāmi yakfuluhum * man li-l-muqillī ʾiḏā ʾawdā bihī l-ʿadamū*
*saqā ḍarīḥaka rabbu l-ʿarši ġādiyatan * mina l-ġamāmi wa-riḍwānan*[599] *lahū diyamū*

"The cornerstone of fame has become destroyed for the loss of you[600] * and knowledge is after your death, O ʿIzz ad-Dīn, nothing but bits and pieces.
Kindness, generosity, the knowledge of what is just: they all * died with you, and with them died beneficence and noble-mindedness.
Who[601] shall deal with the religious Law and the fatwas if the foremost scholars * are unable to do it and cannot live up to accomplish that?
Who shall after your death perform judging and sentence, O * chief-judge, and who will be committed to the truth?
Who will there be to sustain the needy and the widows, * who shall care for the destitute when he is annihilated by indigence?
May the Lord of the Throne pour upon your tomb a mourning shower * from the clouds and (His) satisfaction which continuously pours down!"

597 Badr ad-Dīn Ibn Ǧamāʿah (Ḥamāh, Rabīʿ II 639 – Cairo, Ǧumādā I 733 H) had been Shafiite chief-judge in Jerusalem (687–90), then three times Egyptian chief-judge during the years 690–93, 702–10 and 711–27. For his biography, see: IĞazḪaw III pp. 620-7; BN XIV p. 163; IṬūlṮaġr pp. 80-2; ʿUlaymīUns II pp. 136f.; *cf.* also Escovitz: *Office of Qāḍī* pp. 62 and 70f.

598 The paper to the margin of lines 3–5 is somewhat torn but it seems that there are no words or letters missing; at least, in the given form, the required metre turns out.

599 Ms. *riḍwānun*.

600 *Cf.* above epitaph **79**.

601 For another poem with a series of verses beginning *man li-*, see above **127**.

159

LOCATION. Mecca. DATE. 768 H.

PERSON BURIED. The Yemenite Shafiite scholar and mystic ʿAfīf ad-Dīn al-Yāfiʿī (Abū M. ʿAl. b. Asʿad, Aden 698 H or shortly before – Mecca 768 H), author of important treatises in defense of asceticism and Sufism:[602] ŠaybīŠaraf ff. 17b-20a; IQŠuhbTārīḫ III pp. 299f.; IsnṬab II pp. 579-3; IʿIrāqīḎʿIbar I pp. 225-7; ITaġrManh VII pp. 74-9 and NZ XI pp. 93f.; IFahdItḥāf III p. 307; MunKawākib III pp. 35-8; ŠḎ VI pp. 210-2; GAL II pp. 176f.; ZA IV p. 72; Knysh: *Mysticism* pp. 239f.

SOURCE. ŠaybīŠaraf f. 17b = RCEA 768 005.

DESCRIPTION. "Near the aforesaid tomb of al-Fuḍayl b. ʿIyāḍ there is a tombstone[603] which bears, after the *basmalah* and the word of God the Exalted *yubašširuhum rabbuhum bi-raḥmatin minhu* ("Their Lord gives them good tidings of mercy from Him", Q 9:21), the inscription: [...]".

hāḏā qabru š-šayḫi l-ʾimāmi l-ʿālimi l-ʿallāmati l-muḥaqqiqi l-ʿārifi l-qudwati šayḫi ṭ-ṭarīqah / wa-l-ǧāmiʿi bayna š-šarīʿati wa-l-ḥaqīqah ‖ *muršidi s-sālikīn / wa-murabbī l-murīdīn* ‖ *quṭbi z-zamān / wa-baḥri l-ʿirfān* ‖ *muftī l-farīqatayn / wa-ʾimāmi ṭ-ṭarīqayn / nazīli l-ḥaramayni š-šarīfayn* ‖ *baqīyati s-salafi ṣ-ṣāliḥi ʿAfīfi d-Dīni ʾAbī Muḥammadin ʿAbdi llāhi bni ʾAsʿada l-Yāfiʿīyi – qaddasa llāhu rūḥahū wa-nawwara ḍarīḥahū – tuwuffiya laylata l-ʾaḥadi l-ʿišrīna min Ǧumādā l-ʾuḫrā* (sic) *sanata ṯamānin wa-sittīna wa-sabʿimiʾatin – barrada llāhu ṯarāh / wa-ǧaʿala l-ǧannata maʾwāh* ‖ *wa-ġafara li-man taraḥḥama ʿalayh / wa-qaraʾa l-Qurʾāna l-ʿaẓīma wa-ʾahdāhu ʾilayh* ‖ *– ṣalwalah*

"This is the tomb of the sheikh, the Imam, the learned, the foremost scholar, the diligent, who had gained the acquaintance (of God), the exemplum, the sheikh of the (mystic) path, / who joined the religious law and the (mystic experience of) truth together, ‖ the leader of those on the (spiritual) path, / tutor of the novices, ‖ the pole of (his) time, / the ocean of gnostic wisdom, ‖ muftī of both parties / and Imam of both ways,[604] / who had settled in the noble Sacrosanct Recincts, ‖ who descends from righteous ancestors: ʿAfīf ad-Dīn Abū Muḥammad ʿAbd Allāh b. Asʿad al-Yāfiʿī – may God sanctify his soul and illuminate his tomb! – He was taken (to God) in the night to Sunday 20th Ǧumādā II in the year 768 – may God

602 Ibn Baṭṭūṭah seems to have seen al-Yāfiʿī in Mecca and stresses his religious fervour and unremitting energy in performing rituals at the Kaʿbah day and night. In that context Ibn Baṭṭūṭah relates, among other things, the following: "He was married to the daughter of the jurist Šihāb ad-Dīn b. al-Burhān. She was young and always complained about her fate with her father who commanded her patience. Indeed, she went on living with al-Yāfiʿī for a number of years before she finally left him" (IBaṭṭRiḥlah p. 171).

603 *Cf.* also IQŠuhbTārīḫ III p. 300; ITaġrManh VII p. 78, MunKawākib III p. 38 and ŠḎ VI p. 212 (*dufina ... bi-ǧanbi / bi-ǧiwāri l-Fuḍayla bni ʿIyāḍ*).

604 I.e. of the religious law and the mystic path.

cool the moist earth of his tomb / and make Paradise his dwelling! || May He forgive those who invoke mercy upon him / and recite the eminent Qurʾān and dedicate this to him! || – *ṣalwalah*."

160

LOCATION. Mecca. DATE. 773 H.

PERSON BURIED. Bahāʾ ad-Dīn as-Subkī (Abū Ḥāmid [not: Abū l-Baqāʾ][605] Aḥmad [formerly Tammām] b. Taqīy ad-Dīn ʿAlī, Cairo 719 – Mecca 773 H): ḎahMuʿǧam pp. 28f.; BN XIV p. 296; ŠaybīŠaraf ff. 14b-15b; MaqrSulūk III p. 200; DK I pp. 224-29; IQŠuhbTārīḫ III pp. 401f.; IʿIrāqīḎʿIbar II pp. 334-6; ITaġrManh I pp. 408-14 and NZ XI pp. 121f.; IFahdItḥāf III p. 317; SaḫTuḥfLaṭ I pp. 224f.; SuyBuġ I pp. 342f. and SuyḤusnMuḥ I pp. 364f.; IṬūlṮaġr p. 108; ŠḎ VI pp. 226f.; ZA I p. 171; EI² IX p. 744 (J. Schacht / C. E. Bosworth); Escovitz: *Office of Qāḍī* pp. 62 and 73f.

Son of the Shafiite jurist Taqīy ad-Dīn (d. 756 H) and brother of Tāǧ ad-Dīn as-Subkī (d. 771 H), al-Bahāʾ became *mudarris* in 739 H, but was later given the most prestigious posts of Cairene scholarship. He continued teaching until he left for Mecca, where he died in Raǧab 773 H. He was buried near the tombs of Ḫadīǧah (the Prophet's first wife) and Fuḍayl b. ʿIyāḍ.

SOURCE. ŠaybīŠaraf f. 14b = RCEA 773 008.

DESCRIPTION. "Beside the former tomb (of al-Fuḍayl, **116**)[606] there is an inscribed tombstone that bears, after the *basmalah* and the word of God the Exalted *Whoso goes forth from his house an emigrant* (Q 4:100), the following inscription: [...]".

hāḏā qabru l-faqīri ʾilā llāhi taʿālā š-šayḫi l-ʾimāmi l-ʿālimi l-ʿallāmati šayḫi l-ʾislāmi Bahāʾi d-Dīni ʾAḥmada bni š-šayḫi l-ʾimāmi l-ʿālimi l-ʿallāmati Taqīyi d-Dīni ʿAlīyi bni š-šayḫi l-ʾimāmi l-ʿālimi l-ʿallāmati Zayni d-Dīni ʿAbdi l-Ġanīyi s-Subkīyi š-Šāfiʿīyi – taġammadahumu llāhu bi-raḥmatih / wa-ʾaskanahum fasīḥa ǧannatih[607] || – *tuwuffiya ʾilā raḥmati llāhi taʿālā yawma l-ḫamīsi sābiʿi šahri Raǧabi l-fardi sanata ṯalāṯin wa-sabʿīna wa-sabʿimiʾatin – wa-l-ḥamdu li-llāhi waḥdah*

"This is the tomb of the one who is in need of God the Exalted, the sheikh, the Imam, the learned, the foremost scholar, Sheikh of Islam Bahāʾ ad-Dīn Aḥmad, son of the sheikh, the Imam, the learned, the foremost scholar Taqīy ad-Dīn ʿAlī, son of

605 This occasional mistake is probably due to the confusion of A. b. ʿAlī with his relative and near-namesake Bahāʾ ad-Dīn Abū l-Baqāʾ as-Subkī (M. b. ʿAbd al-Barr, 707–77 H); for him, see IḤaǧRafʿ pp. 360-4.

606 al-Bahāʾ as-Subkī "is buried in the Maʿlāh cemetery close to al-Fuḍayl b. ʿIyāḍ", see IʿIrāqīḎʿIbar II p. 334 and SaḫTuḥfLaṭ I p. 225.

607 This and similar expressions are also attested in epitaphs preserved *in situ*, e.g. in the epitaph of al-Qāḍī ʿIyāḍ (d. 544) in Marrakech: *wa-sakanahū bi-raḥmatihī fasīḥa l-ǧinān* (RCEA 3141). For further examples, see Volume I, esp. pp. 172ff.

the sheikh, the Imam, the learned, the foremost scholar Zayn ad-Dīn ᶜAbd al-Ġanīy as-Subkī aš-Šāfiᶜī – may God cover them with His mercy / and make them dwell in His wide Garden (of Paradise)! || – He was taken to the mercy of God the Exalted on Thursday 7th Raǧab 'the unique' in the year 773 – Praise be to God alone!"

161

LOCATION. Mecca (al-Maᶜlāh cemetery). DATE. 773 H.

PERSON BURIED. The traditionist Badr ad-Dīn al-Āqṣarāʾī (Abū ᶜAl. Muḥammad b. M. b. ᶜĪsā al-Ḥanafī, 724–73 H), a pupil of al-Mizzī: IᶜIrāqīḎᶜIbar II pp. 339f.; FāsīᶜIqd II p. 385; IFahdItḥāf III p. 317; IQŠuhbTārīḫ III p. 408; ŠḎ VI p. 229.

SOURCE. FāsīᶜIqd II p. 385.

DESCRIPTION. "I put this (biographical) entry (entirely) together from his tombstone":

[hāḏā qabru] š-šayḫi l-ᶜallāmati muftī l-muslimīna wa-ḫaṭībihim Badri d-Dīni ʾAbī ᶜAbdi llāhi Muḥammadi bni l-ᶜallāmati ᶜAlāʾi d-Dīni ʾAbī ᶜAbdi llāhi Muḥammadini l-ʾĀqṣarāʾīyi l-Ḥanafīyi tuwuffiya yawma l-ǧumᶜati ṯāliṯi ᶜišrī Ḏī l-Qaᶜdati sanata[608] *ṯalāṯin wa-sabᶜīna wa-sabᶜimiʾah*

"[This is the tomb] of the learned sheikh, mufti and preacher of the Muslims, Badr ad-Dīn Abū ᶜAbd Allāh Muḥammad, son of the learned ᶜAlāʾ ad-Dīn Abū ᶜAbd Allāh Muḥammad al-Āqṣarāʾī al-Ḥanafī. He was taken (to God) on Friday 23th Ḏū l-Qaᶜdah in the year 773".

162

LOCATION. Mecca (al-Maᶜlāh cemetery). DATE. 783 H.

PERSON BURIED. Ǧamāl ad-Dīn Ibn Abī Ǧarrādah al-ᶜAdīmī (ᶜAl. b. an-Naǧm ᶜUmar, Ibn al-ᶜAdīm al-Ḥalabī al-Ḥanafī, d. Mecca 783 H):[609] FāsīᶜIqd IV p. 394; ŠaybīŠaraf ff. 20a-b; ITaġrManh VII p. 110; IFahdItḥāf III p. 203.

SOURCES. ŠaybīŠaraf f. 20a = RCEA 783 010 (version I); FāsīᶜIqd IV p. 394 (version II).

DESCRIPTION. (Version I:) "On a tombstone there is, after the *basmalah* and the word of God the Exalted *Whoso goes forth from his house* (Q 4:100), the following inscription: [...]" (ŠaybīŠaraf). – (Version II:) "[...] I found it mentioned so on his tombstone in the Maᶜlāh (cemetery). It also said: *tuwuffiya* (...), and I know nothing about him except that. The clan of Ibn al-ᶜAdīm is famous in Aleppo, and a number of them were judges in that town" (FāsīᶜIqd).

608 سنة: سن (FāsīᶜIqd, misprint).

609 He must not be confused with his contemporary (and possibly his nephew) Ǧamāl ad-Dīn Ibn Abī Ǧarrādah (Ibr. b. M. b. ᶜUmar, d. Aleppo 787 H), see IQŠuhbTārīḫ I pp. 166f. and ITaġr-Manh I p. 171.

(I) *hāḏā qabru l-ʿabdi l-faqīri ʾilā llāhi taʿālā qāḍī l-quḍāti Ğamāli d-Dīni ḫādimi ʾamīri l-muʾminīna ʾAbī Muḥammadin ʿAbdi llāhi bni l-qāḍī Nağmi d-Dīni ʿUmara bni ʾAbī Ğarrādata l-Ḥanafīyi l-ʿAdīmīyi l-ḥākimi bi-Ḥamāta wa-ʾaʿmālihā – taġammadahū llāhu taʿālā bi-raḥmatihī wa-riḍwānihī – tuwuffiya bi-taʾrīḫi rābiʿi Ḏī l-Ḥiğğati l-ḥarāmi sanata ṯalāṯin wa-ṯamānīna wa-sabʿimiʾatin – ṣalwalah*

(II) [*hāḏā qabru*] *Ğamāli d-Dīni ʿAbdi llāhi bni ʿAmri* [*sic*] *bni ʾAbī Ğarrādata l-ʿAdīmīyi l-Ḥanafīyi qāḍī l-quḍāti bi-Ḥamāta wa-ʾaʿmālihā + tuwuffiya rābiʿa ʿašara l-Ḥiğğati* [sic] *sanata ṯalāṯin wa-ṯamānīna wa-sabʿimiʾah*

Translation of I:

"This is the tomb of the servant who is in need of God the Exalted, the chief-judge Ğamāl ad-Dīn, servant of the Prince of the Believers, Abū Muḥammad ᶜAbd Allāh, son of the judge Nağm ad-Dīn ᶜUmar b. Abī Ğarrādah al-Ḥanafī al-ᶜAdīmī, who was active as a judge in Ḥamāh and its province – may God the Exalted cover him with His mercy and His satisfaction! – He died on the date of 4th Ḏū l-Ḥiğğah 'the sacrosanct (month)' in the year 783 – *ṣalwalah*".

NOTE. Ibn Fahd, who in general depends much on al-Fāsī's work, has the same information as version II in his entry, although he included the notice about Ibn Abī Ğarrādah in the necrologies of the year 733 H. Thus, in the manuscript(s) he used there might have been *ṯalāṯīna* instead of *ṯamānīna*.

163

LOCATION. Medina (Baqīᶜ cemetery). DATE. 59 / 62 H.

PERSON BURIED. Umm Salamah Hind bt. Abī Umayyah (d. Medina 59, 60 or Šawwāl 62 H),[610] she – or Maymūnah bt. al-Ḥariṯ al-Hilālīyah (famed for her beauty) – was allegedly the last of the Prophet's wives to die; he had married her in 2 or 4 H: ISaᶜdṬab VIII pp. 86-96; ṬabSimṭ pp. 146-61 and 356-8; BN VIII pp. 214f.; FāsīᶜIqd VI pp. 444f.; IḤağIṣābah IV pp. 458-60; ZA VIII pp. 97f.

SOURCES. IŠabAḫbār I pp. 79f. = SamWafāʾ III p. 912; INağDurrah pp. 403f.; MarğBahğah II p. 431 (= SamWafāʾ III p. 912, from Ibn Zabālah).

DESCRIPTION. "When Muḥammad b. Zayd b. ᶜAlī[611] had excavations made near the tomb of Fāṭimah, the daughter of the Prophet, they found a broken stone eight yards deep, part of which bore the inscription: [...]. And this is how the tomb of Umm Salamah became known. Muḥammad b. Zayd b. ᶜAlī ordered his family to bury him in this very grave, at a depth of eight yards. (After his death), his will was executed and he was buried there" (IŠabAḫbār); "Ibrāhīm b. ᶜAlī ar-Rāfiᶜī said that people were digging the grave of Sālim al-Bānikī, the *mawlā* of Muḥammad b. ᶜAlī, when they found a long stone bearing the in-

610 *Cf.* also IŠadAᶜlāq II (Damascus) p. 185.

611 For his house in the Baqīᶜ area, *cf.* SamWafāʾ III p. 893.

scription: [...]. The earth was put back on it and the grave of Sālim was dug elsewhere". The tomb of Umm Salamah was reportedly opposite the *ḫawḫah* (passage-way) of Nubayh b. Wahb[612] (INağDurrah, MarğBaḥğah). The accounts of Ibn an-Naǧǧār and al-Marǧānī go back to the early historian Ibn Zabālah (M. b. al-Ḥasan, d. end of the second cent. H) as becomes clear from the citation in the book of as-Samhūdī.[613]

hāḏā qabru ʾUmmi Salamata zawǧi n-nabīyi [– *taṣliyah*][614]

hāḏā qabru: om. IŠabAḫbār (and the citation in SamWafāʾ).

"This is the tomb of Umm Salamah, the wife of the Prophet [– *taṣliyah*]".

164

LOCATION. Medina (Baqīᶜ cemetery). DATE. First century H.

PERSON BURIED. Fāṭimah bt. Asad al-Hāšimīyah, the mother of ᶜAlī b. Abī Ṭālib (d. *c*.5 H):[615] ISaᶜdṬab VIII p. 222; FāsīᶜIqd VI p. 431; IḤağIṣābah IV p. 380; ZA V p. 130.

SOURCE. IǦubRiḥlah (B) p. 174 / (W) p. 199.

DESCRIPTION. The epitaph as written on her tomb.[616]

mā ḍamma qabrun ʾaḥad / ka-Fāṭimata binti ʾAsad

"No grave ever contained a person / like Fāṭimah bt. Asad".

165

LOCATION. Medina (Baqīᶜ cemetery).

DATE. First century H (epitaph I); late second century or after (epitaph II).

PERSON BURIED. Fāṭimah bt. Muḥammad (the daughter of the Prophet): FāsīᶜIqd VI pp. 423-5; IḤağIṣābah IV pp. 377-80; Beinhauer-Köhler: *Fāṭima*.

SOURCES. (Epitaph I:) INağDurrah p. 401; MarğBahğah II p. 426. – (Epitaph II:) MasMurūğ (P) IV p. 133 and MasTanbīh p. 260; SamWafāʾ III p. 905.

DESCRIPTION. (Epitaph I:) "Some gravediggers said that when preparing a grave they found another grave, seven yards away from the *ḫawḫah* of Nubayh[617] (b.

612 Located to the west of the place known as "the tombs of the Prophet's wives" (*qubūr ʾazwāǧ an-nabī*), see SamWafāʾ III p. 911.

613 SamWafāʾ III p. 912.

614 Perhaps a part of the epitaph, but probably not.

615 Some, however, maintain that she died in Mecca before the Hiğrah.

616 For her tomb and mausoleum (contained in the larger shrine of the caliph ᶜUṯmān), see ṬabQirā p. 685; SaḫTuḥfLaṭ I p. 42; SamWafāʾ III pp. 895-9 and p. 919; MağlBihār C pp. 219f.; for the visitation of her tomb: al-Amīn: *Miftāḥ* II pp. 32f.

617 His name is variously misprinted, most unfortunately in INağDurrah p. 403 as بيته.

Wahb). Upon its surface was a tombstone (*lawḥ*) bearing the inscription: [...]" (MarǧBahǧah). – (Epitaph II:) "On their tombs[618] in that area of the Baqīᶜ (cemetery) is a marble slab (*ruḫāmah*) bearing the inscription: [...]" (MasMurūǧ, MasTanbīh, SamWafāʾ). Clearly, the second epitaph cannot have been inscribed before the later second cent. H.

Epitaph I:

hāḏā qabru Fāṭimata binti rasūli llāh [– *taṣliyah*]

"This is the tomb of Fāṭimah, daughter of the Messenger of God [– *taṣliyah*]".[619]

NOTE. The exact location of Fāṭimah's tomb is uncertain.[620] Some maintain that she was buried in her house which was later made part of the larger Prophet's mosque by the caliph ᶜUmar b. ᶜAbd al-ᶜAzīz – thus ultimately becoming part of the *rawḍah* (see above pp. 48f.) – and which included the tomb of her son Ḥasan (*qubbat Ḥasan*).[621] This place was said to lie between the house of Nubayh b. Wahb and the house of ᶜAqīl b. Abī Ṭālib (the brother of ᶜAlī).[622] Others held the opinion that Fāṭimah's tomb – in a building known as *bayt al-ḥuzn*, "the house of sorrow *or* grief" – was inside the mausoleum of al-ᶜAbbās (*qubbat al-ᶜAbbās*) in the Baqīᶜ cemetery,[623] as claimed by Abū l-ᶜAbbās al-Mursī. The Shiites, for whom the veneration of Fāṭimah has been especially important, thus thought it best to visit all the places which were said to contain her tomb, in order not to miss the right one.[624]

Epitaph II:

basmalah. al-ḥamdu li-llāhi mubīdi l-ʾumam / muḥyī r-rimam || hāḏā qabru Fāṭimata binti rasūli llāhi – taṣliyah – sayyidati nisāʾi l-ᶜālamīn / wa-qabru l-Ḥasani bni ᶜAlīyi bni ʾAbī Ṭālibin wa-ᶜAlīyi bni l-Ḥusayni bni ᶜAlīyin wa-qabru Muḥammadi bni ᶜAlīyin wa-Ǧaᶜfari bni Muḥammadin – raḍiya llāhu ᶜanhum ʾaǧmaᶜīn

618 I.e. of Fāṭimah and some children and grandchildren of ᶜAlī, see below.

619 As it is usual in literary sources, we do not know for sure whether the final *taṣliyah* was part of the epitaph or added by the author.

620 See also ṬūsīMiṣbāḥ p. 494; ᶜĀmilīWas III p. 288; SamWafāʾ III pp. 901-8; al-Amīn: *Miftāḥ* II pp. 20f.; MaǧlBihār XLIII pp. 180 and 185, C pp. 191-3; Beinhauer-Köhler: *Fāṭima* pp. 269-75.

621 al-Ḥasan directed in his last will that he be buried beside the Prophet (*fī ḥuǧrati n-nabī*), but this was refused by Muᶜāwiyah, who had him buried beside his mother (*Wāfī* XII p. 110). *Cf.* also IǦubRiḥlah (B) p. 170; ṬabQirā p. 685; SamWafāʾ III pp. 908f.

622 ISaᶜdṬab VIII p. 30; IḤaǧIṣābah IV p. 380; SamWafāʾ III p. 901. *Cf.* Grütter: *Bestattungsbräuche* p. 184.

623 IǦubRiḥlah (B) p. 174; SamWafāʾ III pp. 907 and 918. For the mausoleum, see also MunKawākib I p. 376.

624 ṬūsīMiṣbāḥ p. 494.

basmalah: om. MasTanbīh. – *mubīdi l-ʾumam*: *mubdiʾi l-ʾumam* (MasMurūǧ, in some mss.);[625] *ibni ʾAbī Ṭālibin*: om. SamWafāʾ; *wa-qabru Muḥammadi bni ʿAlīyin*: *wa-qabru* om. MasMurūǧ and MasTanbīh; *raḍiya llāhu ʿanhum ʾaǧmaʿīn*: *ʿalayhimi s-salām* (SamWafāʾ), *riḍwānu llāhi ʿalayhim ʾaǧmaʿīn* (MasTanbīh).

"*Basmalah*. Praise to God, the destroyer of nations, / the reviver of decayed bones. || This is the tomb of Fāṭimah, daughter of the Messenger of God – *taṣliyah* –, the mistress of the women of the worlds, / and the tomb of al-Ḥasan b. ʿAlī, of (Zayn al-ʿĀbidīn) ʿAlī b. al-Ḥusayn b. ʿAlī, the tomb of (Abū Ǧaʿfar al-Bāqir) Muḥammad b. ʿAlī and of Ǧaʿfar (aṣ-Ṣādiq) b. Muḥammad – may God be pleased with them all!"[626]

166

LOCATION. Medina (?). DATE. *c*.80 H or after.

PERSON BURIED. ʿAbd Allāh b. Ǧaʿfar b. Abī Ṭālib al-Hāšimī (aṭ-Ṭayyār, d. in Medina 80 H or after): TMD XXVII pp. 248-98; IAṯīrUsd III pp. 133-5; *Wāfī* XVII pp. 107-9; BN IX pp. 33f.; IḤaǧIṣābah II pp. 289f. and IḤaǧTahḏ V pp. 170f.; SaḫTuḥfAḥbāb II pp. 25f.; ŠḎ I p. 87; ZA IV p. 76.

SOURCES. IṣfStrangers pp. 52f. (in English translation only); ZamRabīʿ IV p. 180; TMD XXVII p. 298; IǦawzīṢafwah II pp. 78f.; IAṯīrUsd III p. 135; QazwĀṯār p. 75; YāfRawḍ pp. 187 and 401; IRaǧLaṭāʾif p. 351; WKAS II p. 1711 (s.r. *lwḥ*; only the first hemistich of v. 1). See also Volume I p. 268.

DESCRIPTION. "On the tomb of ʿAbd Allāh b. Ǧaʿfar was written (*kutiba*): [...]" (ZamRabīʿ, similarly IAṯīrUsd); "The people of the Ḥiǧāz, of Baṣrah and of Kūfah agree that there never were heard more beautiful verses than those they had seen on the tomb of Abū Ǧaʿfar (...): [...]" (TMD); "Abū ʿUmar Yaḥyā b. ʿUmar told me that his father told him that Abū Muslim heard al-Aṣmaʿī say, 'I used to read what is written on gravestones, and I never saw anything like these two verses, which I deciphered from one of them: [...]'" (IṣfStrangers); "They recited what they had found inscribed on a tomb: [...]" (YāfRawḍ p. 187, similarly on p. 401); "An Arab woman recited at a tomb: [...]" (QazwĀṯār); "ad-Dāʾūd aṭ-Ṭāʾī heard these two verses from a woman in a cemetery when she was bewailing a dead relative" (IǦawzīṢafwah, IRaǧLaṭāʾif). – Two verses in the metre *ṭawīl*:

*muqīmun ʾilā ʾan yabʿaṯa llāhu ḫalqahū * liqāʾuka lā yurǧā wa-ʾanta qarībū*
*tazīdu bilan fī kulli yawmin wa-laylatin * wa-tunsā ka-mā tablā wa-ʾanta ḥabībū*

2 *tazīdu*: *yazīdu* (QazwAṯār); تنسى: تبقى (QazwĀṯār), تبلى (YāfRawḍ pp. 187 and 401), *tuslā* (IǦawzīṢafwah).

625 As the editor remarks, the term *mubdiʾi* (or contracted *mubdī*) *al-ʾumam* could well be an allusion to Q 29:19: *ʾaw lam yaraw kayfa yubdiʾu llāhu l-ḫalqa ṯumma yuʿīduhū* ("or have they not seen how God originates creation, then brings it back again?").

626 *Cf.* also SamWafāʾ III p. 909.

"(You are) staying (in your tomb) until God resurrects His creation: * one cannot hope to meet you though you are near!
You are decaying steadily every day and night, * and you are forgotten as you rot away though you are (still) a beloved!"

NOTE. The translation renders the double sense of these lines only very sketchily. To my understanding, the second hemistichs of both verses bear a double meaning, namely: (verse 1) "To meet you is not desired though you are near" means either "To come to your tomb and visit it is not desired by the living though are buried near to where they are living", or "The living do not desire to die, that is, to meet with you in the hereafter, though you are near, i.e. you have preceded them only by a short time"; (verse 2) "You are forgotten (by the living) as you rot away though you are a beloved" means either "... though you are a former friend, i.e. beloved, of them", or "... though you are now a God-lover, as the dead are" (for the term *ḥabību llāh* said of a deceased, see above p. 133).

Longer epitaphs which contain these two lines have been found on extant tombstones, see Volume I pp. 268f.

167

LOCATION. Medina (Baqīᶜ cemetery). DATE. 179 H.
PERSON BURIED. The Medinan legal authority Mālik b. Anas (Medina, 93/5–179 H): IḪallWaf IV pp. 135-9; *Wāfī* XXV pp. 39-43; ZA V pp. 257f.
SOURCES. (Version I:) HarIšārāt pp. 93f. – (Version II:) al-Marrākušī: *Iᶜlām* III pp. 227f. (quoting from al-ᶜAbdarī's *Riḥlah*).
DESCRIPTION. (Version I:) "I read on his tomb the following inscription: [...]" (HarIšārāt). – (Version II:) "On the wall facing the head (of his tomb) was written in stone, *or* upon a stone (*fī ḥağar*): [...]" (al-ᶜAbdarī).

Version I:

basmalah. kullu nafsin ḏāʾiqatu l-mawti [wa-ʾinnamā tuwaffawna ʾuǧūrakum yawma l-qiyāmati fa-man zuḥziḥa ᶜani n-nāri wa-ʾudḫila l-ǧannata fa-qad fāza wa-mā l-ḥayātu d-dunyā ʾillā matāᶜu l-ġurūr][627] *hāḏā qabru Māliki bni ʾAnasa bni ᶜĀmirini l-ʾAṣbaḥīyi min banī Tamīmi bni Murrata min Qurayšin ᶜāša ḫamsan wa-ṯamānīna sanatan tuwuffiya sanata tisᶜin wa-sabᶜīna wa-miʾatin wa-dufina bi-l-Baqīᶜ*

"*Basmalah*. 'Every soul shall taste of death; [you shall surely be paid in your full wages on the Day of Resurrection. Whosoever is removed from the Fire and admitted to Paradise, shall win the triumph. The present life is but the joy of delusion]' (= Q 3:185).[628] This is the tomb of Mālik b. Anas b. ᶜĀmir al-Aṣbaḥī, from the Banū

627 al-Harawī does not quote the whole verse, but only the initial words.

628 This Qurʾānic passage is found frequently on preserved tombstones and is one of the most common Qurʾānic citations in funerary inscriptions.

Tamīm b. Murrah of the Qurayš, he lived 85 years. He was taken (to God) in the year 179 and was buried in the Baqīᶜ (cemetery)".[629]

Version II:

tuwuffiya l-imāmu Māliku bnu ʾAnasa – raḍiya llāhu ʿanhū – fī Rabīʿi l-ʾawwali sanata tisʿin wa-sabʿīna wa-miʾatin wa-mawliduhū fī Rabīʿi l-ʾāḫiri sanata ṯalāṯin wa-tisʿīna

"The Imam Mālik b. Anas – may God be satisfied with him! – was taken to God in Rabīᶜ I in the year 179, and his birth occurred in Rabīᶜ II in the year 93".

168

LOCATION. Medina. DATE. 580 H.

PERSON BURIED. Ḥamzah b. ᶜAbd al-Muṭṭalib (d. 3 H), the (paternal) uncle of the Prophet, killed during the battle of Uḥud:[630] FāsīᶜIqd III pp. 441f.; SamWafāʾ III pp. 935f. For his mausoleum, see Leisten: *Architektur für Tote* p. 194 (no. 1).

SOURCE. SamWafāʾ III p. 922 = RCEA 3395.

DESCRIPTION. "The tomb of Ḥamzah is today a structure, plastered with gypsum (*qaṣṣah*),[631] but without any wooden parts. On top of it, towards the head of it, there is a stone upon which (is written) after the *basmalah*: [...]" (SamWafāʾ).[632]

ʾinnamā yaʿmuru masāǧida llāhi man ʾāmana bi-llāhi wa-l-yawmi l-ʾāḫiri hāḏā maṣraʿu Ḥamzata bni ʿAbdi l-Muṭṭalibi – ʿalayhi s-salāmu – wa-muṣallā n-nabīyi – taṣliyah – ʿamarahū l-ʿabdu l-faqīru ʾilā raḥmati rabbihī Ḥusaynu bnu ʾAbī l-Ḥayǧāʾi – ġafara llāhu lahū wa-li-wālidayhī – sanata ṯamānīna wa-ḫamsimiʾatin

muṣallā n-nabīyi: om. RCEA.

"'Only he shall maintain[633] God's places of worship who believes in God and the Last Day' (= Q 9:18). This is the place where Ḥamzah b. ᶜAbd al-Muṭṭalib – peace be upon him! – met his cruel fate and the Prophet's place of prayer – *taṣliyah* –. It

629 For Mālik's mausoleum, a small domed structure no longer extant, see INaǧDurrah p. 404; SaḫTuḥfLaṭ I p. 42; SamWafāʾ III p. 920. The final words "and was buried in the Baqīᶜ (cemetery)", taken by J. Sourdel-Thomine to be an integral part of the epitaph, are probably al-Harawī's own comment, especially because this information makes little sense as part of the epitaph and because the following passage seems to be corrupt as the divergences between the manuscripts of al-Harawī's text show.

630 *Cf.* also TirĠāmiᶜ II p. 41.

631 For that usage, see above pp. 258ff.

632 However, the architectural history of the mausoleum of Ḥamzah is complex and can be reconstructed only in part, see SamWafāʾ II pp. 921-3.

633 The exact meaning of *ʿmr* I in this verse is disputed, see also Arberry's translation: "Only he shall inhabit God's places of worship ...".

was restored by the servant (of God), who is in need of the mercy of his Lord, Ḥusayn b. Abī l-Hayǧāʾ[634] – may God forgive him and his parents! – in the year 580".

NOTE. The tomb of Ḥamzah is one of the famous burial sites outside the Medinan Baqīʿ cemetery.[635] Its significance might be illustrated by the following anecdote about the Libyan mystic Abū l-ʿAbbās Aḥmad b. Muḥammad (d. after 1060 H): "It is counted among his miracle-like blessings (*karāmāt*) that he performed the pilgrimage and then went (to Medina) where he stood before the Prophet's sepulchre, saying to himself 'I will not visit the tomb of Ḥamzah nor any other tomb, because the Prophet suffices for me'. When a year had passed after that, he saw the Prophet in a dream telling him, 'O Aḥmad, O my dear friend (*ḥabībī*): know that a man's uncle equals his father!' Immediately he set out to visit the tomb of our master Ḥamzah".[636]

169

LOCATION. Medina. DATE. Eighth century H.

According to as-Saḫāwī, Ayman b. Muḥammad (d. 734 H), an encomiast of the Prophet and thus called *ʿāšiq an-nabī*, "Lover of the Prophet",[637] composed the following verses which "are written on a number of tombs in the (Medinan) Baqīʿ cemetery" (*ṭawīl*):

*ʾiḏā kāna qabrī fī l-Baqīʿi bi-Ṭaybatin * fa-lā šakka ʾannī fī ḥimā ṣāḥibi l-qabrī*
*nabīyi l-hudā l-mabʿūṯi min ʾāli Hāšimin * ʿalayhi ṣalātu llāhi fī s-sirri wa-l-ǧahrī*

"If my tomb is in the Baqīʿ (cemetery) in Medina,[638] * then there is no doubt that I am under the protection of the inhabitant of the Sepulchre:

634 He is very probably identical with the Fatimid vizier Ibn Abī l-Hayǧāʾ whose mausoleum is likewise located in the Baqīʿ cemetery, see SamWafāʾ III p. 917.

635 *Cf.* Rāġib: *Premiers monuments* p. 31.

636 al-Anṣārī: *Nafaḥāt* p. 127.

637 Abū l-Barakāt al-Amīn Ayman b. Muḥammad b. M. b. M. b. M. b. M. ... (actually 14 of his forefathers were called "Muḥammad") al-Andalusī al-Ġarnāṭī al-Buzūlī at-Tūnisī: ṢafAʿyān I pp. 221f. and *Wāfī* X pp. 33-5; BN XIV pp. 168f.; DK I pp. 461-3; SaḫTuḥfLaṭ I pp. 203-7 (important entry). Born in Tunis, Ayman came first to live in Cairo, then in Medina. He was known for his satirical spirit, though the stay in Medina changed his mind and he became a pious man. He set himself the task of composing every day a qaṣīdah-poem in praise of the Prophet which he did. His wish to leave Medina for his home town was not granted by the Prophet himself who appeared to Ayman in a dream, gave him three morsels of porridge to eat and asked him whether he would be content if separated from him. Ayman denied this and thus remained in Medina until his death in Rabīʿ I 734 H. He was buried in the Baqīʿ cemetery. Some of his verses are also quoted in SamWafāʾ III p. 797.

638 Lit. "a certain pleasant place", or "a scented place" (Ṭaybah).

The Prophet of right guidance, sent (by God) from among the Hāšimites * – the blessing of God be upon him, in secret and openly".[639]

170

LOCATION. Medinaceli (ar. Madīnat Sālim, northeast of Madrid).

DATE. 392 H or after.

PERSON BURIED. The chamberlain (*ḥāǧib*) of the Umayyad boy-caliph Hišām II, as well as *de facto* ruler, al-Manṣūr Ibn Abī ᶜĀmir ("Almanzor", Abū ᶜĀmir M. b. ᶜAl.: b. 326 – d. Madīnat Sālim 392 or 394 H): IᶜIḏBayān III p. 301; ḤumĞaḏwah pp. 78f.; IAbbḤullah I pp. 268-77; ISaᶜidMuġrib I pp. 194-8; IḪaṭIḥāṭah II pp. 102-8; MaqqNafḥ (C) I pp. 372-99 and IV pp. 84-93; Lévi-Provençal: *Espagne musulmane*, passim; ZA VI p. 226; Makki: *History of al-Andalus* pp. 41-5; EI² VI pp. 430-2 (P. Chalmeta).

SOURCES. IᶜIḏBayān II p. 301; IAbbḤullah I p. 273 = Casiri: *Bibliotheca* II p. 50 (with a translation in Latin verse); ISaᶜīdMuġrib I p. 197; IḪaṭIḥāṭah II p. 108; NubQuḍātAnd p. 109; MaqqNafḥ (B) I p. 398 and III p. 189 / (C) I p. 375 and IV p. 179; al-ᶜAffānī: *Sakb* I p. 364.

DESCRIPTION. "On his tomb the following poem was written (*kutiba*, or *ᶜalayhi maktūban*): [...]" (IAbbḤullah, IḪaṭIḥāṭah); "He had ordered his trusted companions to bury him wherever his death occurred and not to take him away in a coffin, so his tomb is there (i.e. in Madīnat Sālim).[640] On his mausoleum or tomb (*mašhad*) there is the following inscription: [...]" (NubQuḍātAnd; similarly ISaᶜīdMuġrib); "This is what reportedly was written upon the tomb of al-Manṣūr – may God the Exalted have mercy upon him! –: [...]" (MaqqNafḥ [C] I p. 375); "When he had passed away (*qaḍā naḥbahū*), it was written upon his tomb: [...]" (*ib*. IV p. 179). The earliest source, IᶜIḏBayān, has: "How well-done are the following verses a poet composed about him: [...]. It was said that these two verses were engraved on a marble slab (*ruḫāmah*) on his tomb". – al-Ḥumaydī writes about Ibn Abī ᶜĀmir's preparations for death: "Every time he returned to his camp from fighting the enemy, he ordered the dust to be shaken out from his clothes which he had worn during the battle, collected and conserved it. When his death (*manīyah*) was near, he ordered that the dust which had been gathered should be strewn over his shroud after he was laid in the grave".[641] – Two verses in the metre *kāmil*:

639 SaḫTuḥfLaṭ I p. 206.

640 Thus he was not transferred to Córdoba but buried in his local palace in Madīnat Sālim; *cf.* ISaᶜīdMuġrib I p. 197 and MaqqNafḥ (C) IV p. 93.

641 ḤumĞaḏwah p. 79. A similar custon was followed by the Ḥamdānid ruler Sayf ad-Dawlah who "collected the dust which gathered on him during battles he fought, from which he had made a brick (*labinah*) which was the size of a hand. He then stipulated in his will that the same brick be placed under his head in the burial niche" (NZ IV p. 18).

*ʾāṯāruhū tunbīka ʿan ʾawṣāfihī * ḥattā ka-ʾannaka bi-l-ʿiyāni tarāhū*
*tā-llāhi lā yaʾtī z-zamānu bi-miṯlihī * ʾabadan wa-lā yaḥmī ṯ-ṯuġūra siwāhū*

1 *ʾawṣāfihī*: *ʾaḫbārihī* (IᶜIḏBayān, IAbbḤullah, IḪaṭIḥāṭah, NubQuḍātAnd, MaqqNafḥ [B] I p. 398 and [C] I p. 375, Casiri);[642] *bi-l-ʿiyāni*: *bi-l-ʿuyūni* (IᶜIḏBayān, al-ᶜAffānī). – **2** *tā-llāhi lā*: *wa-llāhi mā* (NubQuḍātAnd); *az-zamānu*: *az-zamanu* (Casiri). The whole verse runs in IᶜIḏBayān: *tā-llāhi mā malaka l-ǧazīrata miṯluhū * ḥaqqan wa-lā qāda l-ǧuyūša siwāhū.*

"His vestiges tell you of his qualities * until you almost seem to see him with your own eyes.
By God, time will never bring his like (again), * and nobody will (ever) guard the frontier regions[643] as he did!"

NOTES.

1. The expression "time will never bring his like again" or similar wordings are commonly used in eulogies and mourning poetry, and there is at least one famous verse which should not be passed over in that context, especially as its first hemistich is remarkably similar to the second line of the epitaph. Composed by Abū Tammām, it has been applied to a number of outstanding personalities, e.g. to the Abbasid governor ᶜAbd Allāh b. Ṭāhir al-Ḫuzāᶜī (182–230 H), to Ibn Ḥaǧar al-ᶜAsqalānī and to ᶜAbd al-Ġanīy (Ibn) an-Nābulusī (*kāmil*):

هَيْهَاتَ لاَ يَأْتِي الزَّمَانُ بِمِثْلِهِ * إِنَّ الزَّمَانَ بِمِثْلِهِ لَبَخِيلُ

"But O! time will never bring his like (again), * for time with his like is a miser!"[644]

A similar line was also produced, or so we are told, by Abū Nuwās (*munsariḥ*):

لَمْ يَخْلُقِ الدَّهْرُ مِثْلَهُ أَبَداً * هَيْهَاتَ هَيْهَاتَ شَأْنُهُ عَجَبُ

"Time did never bring forward (*or* create) his like! * But O, but O! The matter with him is wondrous!"[645]

2. The epitaph of Ibn Abī ᶜĀmir – authentic or not – is very much the epitome of a soldier's boastful pride.[646] As such, it is remarkable for its succinct brevity, but less

642 In view of the transmission of that verse, the mainstream variant *ʾaḫbārihī* should have been the first choice of the editor. However, for the general meaning, I preferred the version as cited by al-Maqqarī.

643 *aṯ-ṯuġūr*, "the Marches" in Central Spain, being "zones de guerre, où l'on se tient toujours sur le qui-vive et dont les limites, dans la direction du pays ennemi, varient au cours des années et suivant les circonstances politiques. La soumission des populations qui y vivent n'est jamais sans doute que passegère: elle a besoin d'être régulièrement confirmée par des expéditions de plus ou moins grande envergure" (Lévi-Provençal: *Espagne musulman* p. 118).

644 ATamDīwān IV p. 102 = MurSilk III p. 30; TMD XXIX p. 242; ŠTalḫīṣ IV p. 487 = MehrenRhetorik p. 150; NuwNih V p. 210; IṬūlQal p. 333 (var. *hayhātu ʾan* ...).

645 Cited in NZ III p. 163. I was unable to find that line in ANuwDīwān.

646 In order to assess Ibn Abī ᶜĀmir's proud epitaph rightly, we might consult modern summaries of his achievements: he "led 52 raids against the three Christian Spanish states: the kingdom

original as regards its content. I presume Ibn Abī ᶜĀmir would have been also pleased with the following line found upon the tomb of a Roman soldier (2nd cent. CE): *Viderit anne aliquis post me mea gesta sequatur: exemplo mihi sum, primus qui talia gessi* ("It remains to be seen whether anyone will equal my deeds after my death: I am my own exemplum, the first to perform such deeds").[647]

3. The notion that somebody's posthumous fame rests upon the record of his achievements is trivial and needs no further explanation. This concept is conventionally, but forcefully rendered in the following anonymous lines (*sarīᶜ*):

المَرءُ بَعْدَ المَـوْتِ أُحْدُوثَةٌ * يَفْنَى وَتَبْقَى مِنْهُ آثَـارُهُ
فَأَحْسَنُ الحَالاَتِ حَالُ امْرِئٍ * تَطِيبُ بَعْدَ المَوْتِ أَخْبَارُهُ

"Man is after death a rumour: * he vanishes, yet his vestiges remain.
Thus the best of all states is the state of a man * of whom, after death, nothing but good is told".[648]

Incidentally, the tomb of the Abbasid state official ᶜAbd Allāh b. Ṭāhir – to whom Abū Tammām's verse "But O! time will never bring (again) his like" was also applied (see above) – features as a symbol for the "vestiges" (*ʾāṯār*) of its occupant in a story told in Ibn ᶜAsākir's *History of Damascus*:

> "Zakarīyāʾ b. Dulawayh used to visit the tomb of ᶜAbd Allāh b. Ṭāhir every Friday.[649] On his way there, he passed the markets and the tomb of Aḥmad b. Ḥarb, his former teacher, but he would not stop at his tomb. When he was reproached for this, he said 'The asceticism (*zuhd*) of Aḥmad b. Ḥarb and of others among the scholars and the rightcous passed away with them, yet the vestiges (*ʾāṯār*) of ᶜAbd Allāh b. Ṭāhir will remain as long as the heavens and the earth remain!'"[650]

of Navarre, the kingdom of León and the county of Castile. These forays were made both in winter and in summer, and he carried them to a point attained by no previous Muslim general, inflicting on the states such humiliation and destruction as they had never seen throughout their history. (...) Yet, for all that, his politics were totally amoral, being directed solely towards serving his own personal interests (...), his military expeditions accomplished little, since their goal was speedy victories which would dazzle the eyes of the people, but whose traces vanished as quickly" (Makki: *History of al-Andalus* pp. 42 and 45); "[T]he ᶜĀmirid raids were not responses, but attacks, and thus difficult to foresee. They were conducted with a ferocity unprecedented in the Spanish context, and left behind a long trail of destruction, of death and of rancour" (EI² VI p. 432).

647 Geist: *Grabinschriften* 327 (lines 10f.).

648 Cited in IHuḏaylMaq p. 73.

649 *Cf.* above pp. 33f.

650 TMD XXIX p. 241.

171

LOCATION. al-Munastīr (Monastir, modern Tunisia).

DATE. 528/9 or 546 H.

PERSON BURIED. The man of letters, scholar and physician Abū ṣ-Ṣalt al-Andalusī (Umayyah b. ᶜAbd al-ᶜAzīz ad-Dānī, born in Dāniyah [sp. Denia] or Seville 460 – d. in al-Mahdīyah in 528 or 529, or as late as 546 H, buried in al-Munastīr): IAbbTakm I pp. 168f.; IAUṣaybᶜUyūn pp. 501-15; ISaᶜīdMuġrib I pp. 256f.; IṣfḪar (M) I pp. 189-270; IḪallWaf I pp. 243-7; YāqIršād II pp. 361-5; MaqrMuq II pp. 297f.; MaqqNafḥ (C) II pp. 307-11; ŠḎ IV pp. 83f. and 144 (double entry); Nykl: *Hispano-Arabic Poetry* pp. 238-40; ZA II p. 23; CHAL *Andalus* pp. 73 and 117; EI^2 I p. 149.

SOURCES. IAUṣaybᶜUyūn pp. 503f.; IṣfḪar (M) I pp. 269f.; IḪallWaf I p. 246 / (Slane) I p. 230 = Schack: *Poesie und Kunst* I p. 219 (in German translation, see below); TI XXXVI p. 165; MaqqNafḥ (B) II p. 108 and (repeated) III pp. 297f. / (C) II p. 310; ŠḎ IV p. 84; ŠayMaǧānī IV p. 39; Nykl: *Hispano-Arabic Poetry* p. 239 (in English translation); Bahǧat: *Ittiǧāh* p. 259.

DESCRIPTION. "Shortly before his death he recited some verses and ordered that they be engraved upon his tomb, and the verses are: [...]" (IAUṣaybᶜUyūn); "Abū ṣ-Ṣalt died in al-Mahdīyah, but was buried in al-Munastīr (...). He composed some verses and instructed in his last will that they shall be written upon his tomb" (IḪallWaf, similarly ŠḎ); "The following is from his poetry and he had directed that they should be inscribed upon his tomb; it also shows that he possessed a flawless faith: [...]" (TI); "Abū ṣ-Ṣalt decreed by will that on his tomb shall be written what he composed before his death: [...]" (MaqqNafḥ; similarly ŠayMaǧānī and Bahǧat); "The last words which he spoke in his life were the following: [...]" (IṣfḪar, no epitaph mentioned). – Five verses in the metre *ṭawīl*:

*sakantuki yā-dāra l-fanāʾi muṣaddiqan * bi-ʾannī ʾilā dāri l-baqāʾi ʾaṣīrū*
*wa-ʾaᶜẓamu mā fī l-ʾamri ʾanniya ṣāʾirun * ʾilā ᶜādilin fī l-ḥukmi laysa yaǧūrū*
*fa-yā-layta šiᶜrī kayfa ʾalqāhu ᶜindahā * wa-zādī qalīlun wa-ḏ-ḏunūbu kaṯīrū*
*fa-ʾin ʾaku maǧzīyan bi-ḏanbī fa-ʾinnanī * bi-šarri ᶜiqābi l-muḏnibīna ǧadīrū*
*wa-ʾin yaku ᶜafwun minhu ᶜannī wa-raḥmatun * fa-ṯamma naᶜīmun dāʾimun wa-surūrū*

3 *ᶜindahā*: *baᶜdahā* (IṣfḪar). – **4** *bi-šarri ᶜiqābi*: *bi-ḥarri ᶜaḏābi* (IṣfḪar). – **5** *minhu ... fa-ṯamma*: *ṯamma ... fa-ṯamma* (IAUṣaybᶜUyūn, IṣfḪar, MaqqNafḥ [B] II p. 108 and [C] II p. 310; ŠayMaǧānī, Bahǧat: *Ittiǧāh*), *min ǧanīyin wa-mufḏilin* (MaqqNafḥ [B] III p. 298); *dāʾimun*: *zāʾidun* (ŠayMaǧānī).

"I came to dwell in you, O house of transience, trusting * that towards the house of (eternal) permanence I travel,
And what is most serious in that matter is that I am heading * towards someone just in (His) verdict and never acting unjustly.
I wish I knew what course my encounter with Him will take, * given that my provisions are little, but the sins are many.

If I am found guilty for my sinful behaviour, then I * truly deserve the awful punishment of the sinners,
Yet if He bestows forgiveness upon me and mercy, * then there will be everlasting bliss and joy".

Schack's translation:

"So lang auf dieser flücht'gen Welt ich weilte, / Wußt' ich, daß ich dem Tod entgegeneilte;
Doch nun beim Scheiden bangt mir vor dem Einen: / Am Thron des höchsten Richters zu erscheinen.
O wüßt' ich, was mich drüben für ein Loos / Erwartet! Meiner Sünden Zahl ist groß,
Und wenn mich Gott bestraft für meine Schuld, / So[651] ist sein Spruch gerecht; doch wenn mit Huld
Er mir vergibt, dann werd' ich – o der Wonnen! – / In ew'ger Lust und Seligkeit mich sonnen".

Notes. This widely-quoted epitaph presents a typical example of Arabic "grave poetry", centred on eschatological themes and the fate of the deceased after his death. Many are known from other epitaphs, mourning poetry or also ascetic poetry (*zuhdīyāt*).

1. "House of transience" (*dār al-fanāʾ*). This expression normally indicates the present world, whereas "house of (eternal) permanence" (*dār al-baqāʾ*) signifies the hereafter, a combination of terms used in many other epitaphs from the seventh century H onwards.

For examples, see RCEA 4863 (684 H), 5814 (740 H), 5965 (743 H), 6130 (750 H), 6333 (761 H), 785 005, 787 004, 789 005, 796 013, 797 018, 800 032 (all without exception from Anatolian epitaphs). In an Iranian epitaph we find: ... *min dāri l-fanāʾi ʾilā ʿālami l-baqāʾi* (RCEA 6188, 753 H), and in another epitaph : ... *mina d-dāri l-fāniyati ʾilā d-dāri l-bāqiyati* (RCEA 5596, 730 H). In poetry and in sermons we sometimes encounter the contrasting terms *dār mafarr* ("the house of escape" or "the fugitive abode", i.e. the present world) and *dār maqarr* ("the house of permanent settlement" or "the permanent abode", i.e. the hereafter), e.g. ḤuṣZahr (M) II p. 456 / (Ṭ) I p. 388; this is similar to the wording of a preserved inscription on the ruins of the palace of Darius in Persepolis: *ad-dunyā dāru mamarrin lā dāra maqarrin* (RCEA 773 012). On extant tombstones, the antithesis *fanāʾ – baqāʾ* is, above all, present in the common formula *li-llāhi l-ʿizzatu wa-l-baqāʾu wa-ʿalā ḫalqihī kataba l-fanāʾa* (see above note to **97**); in another, early fourth-century epitaph (dated 313 H) we find: *li-llāhi l-baqāʾu wa-lanā l-fanāʾu wa-huwa l-ġanīyu wa-naḥnu l-fuqarāʾu wa-kullu l-ḫalqi yafnā wa-yabqā waǧhu rabbinā l-ʾaʿlā*, "God possesses (eternal) permanence and we are subject to transience, He is the rich and we are the poor, the whole creation vanishes and the most exalted Face of our Lord remains" (RCEA 1091, Fusṭāṭ), partly an adaption of Q 55:26f.: *All that dwells upon the earth is perishing, * yet still abides the Face of thy Lord, majestic, splendid* (see also above **144**).

651 *Sic*, instead of "... Schuld. So ..." in the printed text.

Both expressions ("house of transience / house of [eternal] permanence") are commonly used in Arabic poetry.[652] One of the more typical verses includes a line in a poem by Abū l-Ḥasan Ibn Ḥamdūn al-Marīnī, mourning the Shafiite scholar ᶜIzz ad-Dīn Ibn ᶜAbd as-Salām (d. 660 H) (*kāmil*):

عَجَباً لِمُغْتَرٍّ بِدَارِ فَنَائِهِ * وَلَهُ إِلَى دَارِ البَقَاءِ مَصِيرُ

"A wondrous thing that someone is beguiled by the house of his transience (*or* of his perdition, i.e. the present world) * while his way leads him towards the house of (eternal) permanence".[653]

Somewhat more pathetic – as required by the occasion – is a verse in a poem by ᶜImād ad-Dīn (al-Kātib al-Iṣfahānī, d. 597 H) mourning the death of the Zangīd ruler Nūr ad-Dīn (d. 569 H) (*kāmil*):

أَزْهَدْتَ فِي دَارِ الفَنَاءِ وَأَهْلِهَا * وَرَغِبْتَ فِي الخُلْدِ المُقِيمِ وَحُورِهِ

"You did renounce the house of transience and its inhabitants * and yearned for the enduring perpetuity (i.e. Paradise) and its dark-eyed virgins".[654]

The famous mystic Abū Yazīd al-Bisṭāmī (d. 261 H) saw ᶜAlī appear to him in a dream, and when he woke up he found the following lines written in golden letters on his palm (*basīṭ*):

قَدْ كُنْتَ مَيْتاً فَصِرْتَ حَيّاً * وَعَنْ قَلِيلٍ تَكُونُ مَيْتَا
فَابْنِ بِدَارِ البَقَاءِ بَيْتاً * وَاهْدِمْ بِدَارِ الفَنَاءِ بَيْتَا

"You were dead (i.e. before your birth) and then given life, * and after a little while you will again be dead:
Thus build in the house of permanence a house * and destroy one in the house of transience!"[655]

In a poem by Abū Ǧaᶜfar Ibn al-Badūḫ (d. Damascus 575 or 576 H), the tomb is called "a door to the house of permanence" (*al-qabru bābun ʾilā dāri l-baqāʾ*);[656]

652 E.g. in IḪafDīwān p. 210 (*ṭawīl*): *fa-hal ʾanta fī dāri l-fanāʾi mumahhadun * maḥalluka fī dāri l-baqāʾi wa-manziluk*, "Did you settle at ease in the house of transience? * Your (true) place is in the house of permanence, and your dwelling place". For the life in the present world depicted as being ultimately nothing but *fanāʾ*, see also a verse by Maḥmūd al-Warrāq cited in ANuwDīwān I p. 305 (with further examples on the following pages).

653 Quoted in SuyBuġ II p. 142.

654 Cited in AŠāmahRawḍ I p. 245; for *zhd* I as an antithesis to *rġb* I, see Lane *s.r.* In other mourning poetry, we also find the expression *dār al-ḫuld* ("house of perpetuity") indicating the hereafter, see Ṯaᶜāl Yat II p. 72.

655 Quoted in TMD XLIII p. 562 (var. *takūnu*: *taᶜūdu* and *wa-hdim*: *wa-daᶜ*); SuyŠṢudūr p. 387; MunKawākib I p. 113 (quoted from TMD, but not showing the wording of TMD).

656 Cited in IAUṣaybᶜUyūn p. 629.

the Seljuq ruler Sanǧar b. Malik-Šāh (r. 511–52 H) had his mausoleum fittingly called *dār al-ʾāḫirah*, "house of the hereafter".[657]

2. "Journey" and "provisions". Both the notions that the deceased undertakes his "journey to the hereafter" with little or no provisions (*zād*) and that his final destiny in the other world is unknown to him are important motifs in Islamic piety and religious literature.

From the Prophet's companion Abū Hurayrah was reported: "During his last illness he started to cry and said, 'But I tell you, I do not cry for our world (which I am about to leave), but I cry for the distance of my journey (to the hereafter) and the scarceness of my provisions, and because I started an ascent (*ṣuʿūd*) that will bring me either into the Garden or the Fire, yet I do not know into which I will be cast'".[658] When the second-century ascetic ʿAbd al-ʿAzīz b. Abī Rawwād – who was blind for 20 years without his family and friends realising this – was asked about his gloomy spirit, he replied, "How else would be the state of a man who is left in utter ignorance as to death, in view of his many sins which surround him (...) and without knowing whether his way leads into the Garden or the Fire?",[659] and another early ascetic replied to the same question: "How is the state of someone who wishes to undertake a long journey without provisions (*bi-lā zād*), who enters the tomb in solitariness without company, who rushes to a Lord, a King, without an argument (*ḥuǧǧah*) (to defend his cause)?"[660] The Persian mystic Abū Ḥamzah al-Ḫurāsānī (d. 290 H) replied to someone who asked him for spiritual advice: "Prepare your provisions (*zād*) for the journey which is right before you!"[661] However, in the view of the pious, God himself was to substitute for the provisions if needs be, a concept for which Abū ʿAbd Allāh Muḥammad b. Yaḥyā Ibn al-Ǧalāʾ (d. 306 H) has found the most surprising expression: "He was asked, 'What do you say about a man who enters the desert without provisions (*bi-lā zād*)?', and he replied, 'This is the way of men who confide in God (*hāḏā min fiʿli riǧāli llāh*)'. 'But what if the man dies?' 'The murderer has to pay blood-money (*ad-diyatu ʿalā l-qātil*)'",[662] that is, God will (and even is obliged to) compensate him for that.

172

LOCATION. Nīsābūr. DATE. 258 H.

PERSON BURIED. Abū Zakarīyāʾ ar-Rāzī al-Wāʿiẓ (Ya. b. Muʿāḏ, d. Nīsābūr 258 H), one of the "weeping ascetics" (*al-bakkāʾūn*): TB XIV pp. 208-12; IḪallWaf VI pp. 165-8; MunKawākib I pp. 726-30; ZA VIII p. 172; EI^2 I p. 959 and VI p. 570 (where his death is given as in 248 H).

657 IǦawzīMunt X p. 178.

658 Cited in IQutʿUyūn II p. 333; similar in meaning, but different in wording in IǦawzīTabṣ I p. 213; IbšīhīMust II p. 443 (ch. 81); *cf.* also Gramlich: *Vorbilder* I p. 74. Almost verbatim, this dictum has also been attributed to Ibrāhīm b. ʿAbd al-Malik in IBuḥtUns p. 83; similarly, but much shorter, attributed to al-Fuḍayl b. ʿIyāḍ in IḪarrāṭʿĀqibah p. 70.

659 Cited in ŠaʿrṬab I p. 61. Similar reports from ʿAṭāʾ as-Salīmī in Gramlich: *Vorbilder* I p. 126; from Ibn Sīrīn in MubKāmil (C) IV p. 82; from aš-Šāfiʿī in IBuḥtUns p. 62; from Muʿāḏ b. Ǧabal: *ib.* pp. 82f.; from Saʿdūn al-Maǧnūn in YāfRawḍ p. 67; from Ibrāhīm an-Naḫaʿī (d. 95 H) in BN IX p. 140.

660 Quoted in IʿABarrBahǧah II p. 368.

661 Cited in MunKawākib I p. 551.

662 ŠaʿrṬab I p. 88.

SOURCES. TB XIV p. 212; IḪallWaf VI p. 168 / (Slane) IV p. 54.
DESCRIPTION. "Muḥammad b. ʿAbd Allāh said, 'I read on the tombstone of Yaḥyā b. Muʿāḏ ar-Rāzī: [...]'" (TB and IḪallWaf).

māta ḥakīmu z-zamāni Yaḥyā bnu Muʿāḏini r-Rāzīyu – raḥimahū llāhu taʿālā wa-bayyaḍa waǧhahū wa-ʾalḥaqahū bi-nabīyihī Muḥammadin – taṣliyah – yawma l-iṯnayni li-sitta ʿašrata laylatan ḫalat min Ǧumādā l-ʾūlā sanata ṯamānin wa-ḫamsīna wa-miʾatayn

taʿālā: om. TB; *laylatan*: om. TB. One of the mss. of the IḪallWaf has *yaʿnī* ("that is") before the name of the deceased. The translated version in Slane includes at the end of the epitaph "at Nīsābūr", though this is unlikely to have been part of the epitaph.

"The sage of the age, Yaḥyā b. Muʿāḏ ar-Rāzī – may God, the Exalted, have mercy upon him, may He whiten his face[663] and join him with his Prophet Muḥammad![664] – *taṣlīyah* – died on Monday, the 16th Ǧumādā I of the year 258".

173

LOCATION. Qaṣr Kutāmah (al-Qaṣr al-Kabīr or "Alcazarquivir", Northern Morocco).
DATE. 695 H.
PERSON BURIED. Abū Muḥammad Ibn Ašqīlūlah (sp. Escayola or Escayuela) (ʿAl. b. Ibr. b. ʿAlī b. M. at-Tuǧībī, d. 695 H): IḪaṭIḥāṭah III pp. 376-9.
SOURCES. IḪāṭIḥāṭah III p. 378 (complete); TMD XLV p. 319 (only the verses); MuwMuršid p. 72 and INāṣBard (A) p. 44 / (C) p. 39 = SuyBard p. 123 (only the verses); RCEA 4998 (only the prose passage).[665]
DESCRIPTION. "When I entered Qaṣr Kutāmah[666] on Tuesday 22nd Ḏū Qaʿdah in the year 755 (...), I visited at its outskirts the cemetery of the chieftains (*ruʾasāʾ*) of the Banū Ašqīlūlah. In a mausoleum (*qubbah*), firmly built and with a wide courtyard, (...) there is the tomb of the aforesaid chieftain (*raʾīs*) Abū Muḥammad, on the left upon entering. Between it and between the *qiblah*-wall there is (another) tomb. Its enclosure (*or* cenotaph?)[667] is made of marble and bears the inscription: [*poetry*]. At the top of the marble enclosure there is an inclined

663 A common formula on preserved tombstones, sometimes also rendered as *naḍḍara waǧhahū* or *nawwara waǧhahū* ("may He brighten his face"). *Cf.* above p. 357.

664 For this eulogy, see Volume I, Chapter 2.

665 *Cf.* also the note in Inscriptions Espagne I p. 142.

666 Ibn al-Ḫaṭīb gives a short (poetic) description of Qaṣr Kutāmah in IḪaṭRayḥ II pp. 306f. (which is preceded by the description of Ṭanǧah [Tanger] and followed by those of Aṣīlā and Salé); *cf.* also EI^2 I p. 496 and IV p. 729. However, YāqBuldān IV p. 362 (*s.v.*) locates Qaṣr Kutāmah mistakenly in al-Andalus, near al-Ǧazīrat al-Ḫaḍrāʾ (sp. Algeciras, west of Gibraltar). See also below n. 682.

667 *sanām*, literally "hump". This term was used by legal scholars in order to describe the mound, see above p. 171, n. 7. Here it might indicate the prismatic upper part of the *mqābriyah*, typical of many tombs in the Islamic West and often inscribed.

slab likewise made of marble, upon which (is written): [*prose*]" (IḪaṭIḥāṭah). According to Ibn ᶜAsākir (TMD), the inscription was found on a tomb. The verses are cited by al-Muwaffaq Ibn ᶜUṯmān without further comment, except: "Upon another (tomb) was written"; Ibn Nāṣir ad-Dīn quotes from al-Aṣmaᶜī who "saw an Arab woman in the wilderness at the tomb of her daughter, reciting the verses: [...]".[668]

The versions of the poetry and the prose passage are given according to Ibn al-Ḫaṭīb, the first because it is said, in this form, to have been part of an epitaph (while the other literary sources are less explicit), the latter because it is considerably longer than that cited in RCEA (which lacks, apart from most eulogies, some important passages or words).

Poetry. Four verses in the metre *muǧtaṯṯ*:

*qabrun ʿazīzun ʿalaynā * law ʾanna man fīhi yufdā*
*ʾaskantu qurrata ʿaynī * wa-qiṭʿata l-qalbi laḥdā*
*mā zāla ḥukmun ʿalayhī * wa-mā l-qaḍāʾu taʿaddā*
*fa-ṣ-ṣabru ʾaḥsanu ṯawbin * bihī l-ʿazīzu taraddā*

1 *man fīhi yufdā*: *mā fīhi yuhdā* (MuwMuršid), *mā fīhi yufdā* (SuyBard). – **2** *wa-qiṭʿata l-qalbi*: *wa-munyata n-nafsi* (TMD, MuwMuršid), *wa-yuʾnisu n-nafsu* (INāṣBard), *wa-muʾnisa n-nafsi* (SuyBard), *wa-munyata l-qalbi* (b). – **3** *mā zāla ḥukmun ʿalayhī*: *mā ǧāra ḫalqun ʿalaynā* (TMD, MuwMuršid, INāṣBard = SuyBard); *wa-mā*: *wa-lā* (TMD, al-Muwaffaq, INāṣBard = SuyBard). – **4** *fa-ṣ-ṣabru*: *fa-li-ṣ-ṣabri* (IḪaṭIḥāṭah, does not fit the metre), *wa-l-mawtu* (!, MuwMuršid), *wa-ṣ-ṣabru* (INāṣBard = SuyBard); *ṯawbin*: *šayʾin* (INāṣBard = SuyBard); *al-ʿazīzu*: *al-fatā* (TMD, MuwMuršid), *al-karīmu* (INāṣBard = SuyBard). – The first two lines of that poem are also inscribed on a number of extant fifth-century tombstones in Kairouan, see Volume I pp. 228, 246f. and 265f.

"(This is) a grave dear to us, * if only who dwells in it could be ransomed!
I lodged the delight of my eye[669] * and a piece of the heart in (its) burial niche,
There is still a judgment on him (to be passed) * and the (divine) decree is inviolable.[670]
So composure is the best garment * which the beloved can put on".

Prose passage:

ʾaʿūḏu bi-llāhi mina š-šayṭāni r-raǧīm / basmalah – ṣalwalah

hāḏā qabru r-raʾīsi l-ǧalīli l-ʾaʿlā al-humāmi l-ʾawḥadi l-ʾasʿadi l-mubāraki l-ʾasnā[671] *l-ʾasmā l-ʾaḥfali l-ʾakmali l-muǧāhidi l-muqaddasi l-marḥūmi ʾAbī Muḥammadin ʿAbdi llāhi bni r-raʾīsi l-ǧalīli l-humāmi l-ʾawḥadi l-ʾasʿadi l-mubāraki l-ʾamḍā l-ʾasnā l-ʾasmā l-muʿaẓẓami l-muraffaʿi l-muǧāhidi l-ʾarḍā l-muqaddasi l-marḥūmi ʾAbī ʾIsḥāqa Ibrāhīma bni ʾAšqīlūlata – raḥimahū llāhu*

668 al-Aṣmaᶜī seems to have frequented cemeteries regularly. He not only transmitted several other poems recited at tombs (see, e.g., IǦawzīḪaṯṯ pp. 48f.), but also a number of epitaphs (see **166**, **173**, **197**, **210**, **211** and **213**); once in a cemetery, he met Buhlūl (Marzolph: *Buhlūl* p. 41, no. 46).

669 For this very common term of affection for deceased infants, see Gilᶜadi: *Consolation Treatise* p. 375 and Volume I p. 371.

670 *Cf.* Volume I pp. 246f.

671 For this term, typical of North African usage, see CIA Égypte II p. 198.

wa-ʿafā ʿanhu wa-ʾaskanahū ǧannatahū – ẓahara – ʿafā llāhu ʿanhu – bi-Wādī ʾĀša – ʾammanahā llāhu – qāʿidatin min qawāʿidi l-ʾAndalusi wa-tasalṭana wa-nuširat ʿalāmātu salṭanatihī wa-ḍuribati ṭ-ṭubūlu wa-ǧāhada minhā l-ʿadūwa – qaṣamahū llāhu – wa-ẓahara ʿalā ḫālihī sulṭāni l-ʾAndalusi wa-ʾaqāma fī salṭanatihī naḥwan min ṯalāṯatin (!) *wa-ʿišrīna sanatan ṯumma qāma bi-daʿwati l-maliki l-ʾaʿlā s-sulṭāni l-muʾayyadi l-Manṣūri ʾamīri l-muslimīna l-Muʾayyadi bi-llāhi ʾAbī Yaʿqūba – ʾayyadahū llāhu bi-naṣrih / wa-ʾamaddahū bi-maʿūnatihī wa-yusrih* || *– wa-ʾamarahū – ʾayyadahū llāhu – ʾan yataḫallā ʿan Wādī ʾĀša l-maḏkūrati wa-yaṣila li-l-Maġribi fa-tanaḫḫā ʿani l-ʾAndalusi li-l-Maġribi – ʾānasahū llāhu – fī Ǧumādā l-ʾūlā min ʿāmi sittatin wa-ṯamānīna wa-sittimiʾatin fa-ʾaʿṭāhu – ʾayyadahū llāhu – Qaṣra ʿAbdi l-Karīmi – ʾammanahū llāhu wa-ʾanʿama ʿalayhi – fa-ʾaqāma bihī muddatan min ṯamāniyati ʾaʿwāmin wa-ǧāza minhu ʾilā l-ʾAndalusi – ʾammanahā llāhu – wa-ǧāhada bihā marratayni ṯumma raǧaʿa ʾilā Qaṣri ʿAbdi l-Karīmi l-maḏkuri wa-tuwuffiya – šarrafa llāhu rūḥahū ṭ-ṭayyibata l-muǧāhidata – ʿašīya yawmi s-sabti l-ʿāširi min šahri Muḥarramin sanata ḫamsin wa-tisʿīna wa-sittimiʾah*

ʾaʿūḏu bi-llāhi ... taslīman: *basmalah*. *ṣallā llāhu ʿalā Muḥammadin wa-ʾālihī* (RCEA); *al-humāmi*: om. RCEA; *al-ʾasʿadi*: om. RCEA; *al-marḥūmi*: om. RCEA; *ʾAbī Muḥammadin ʿAbdi llāhi bni r-raʾīsi l-ǧalīli ... al-ʾasnā l-ʾasmā*: *ʾAbī ʿAbdi llāhi Muḥammadi* [sic] *bni r-raʾīsi l-ǧalīli l-ʾasnā* (RCEA); *al-muǧāhidi*: om. RCEA; *al-muqaddasi*: om. RCEA; *Ibrāhīma bni ʾAšqīlūlata*: RCEA om. *bni*; *ẓahara ʿafā llāhu ʿanhu*: om. RCEA; *ʾammanahā llāhu*: *ʾāmanahū llāhu* (RCEA); *wa-nuširat ... qaṣamahū llāhu*: om. RCEA; *sulṭāni l-ʾAndalusi*: *sulṭāni l-ʾAndalusi l-ġālibi* (RCEA); *naḥwan min*: om. RCEA; *al-maliki l-ʾaʿlā s-sulṭāni ... al-muʾayyadi bi-llāhi*: *al-maliki s-sulṭāni l-muʾayyadi bi-llāhi l-manṣūri* (RCEA); *bi-naṣrihī*: om. RCEA; *wa-yusrihī wa-ʾamarahū ʾayyadahū llāhu ʾan*: *wa-ʾamarahū ʾan* (RCEA); *al-maḏkūrati*: om. RCEA; *li-l-Maġribi fa-tanaḫḫā ʿani l-ʾAndalusi li-l-Maġribi*: *li-l-ġarbi ... li-l-ġarbi* (RCEA; according to the editor of the IḫaṭIḥāṭah, the Escorial ms. of the text has likewise *li-l-ġarbi*); *Ǧumādā l-ʾūlā*: *Ǧumādā l-ʾawwali* (*sic*, RCEA); *fa-ʾaʿṭāhu ʾayyadahū llāhu*: *fa-ʾaʿṭāhu* (RCEA); *ʾammanahū llāhu wa-ʾanʿama ʿalayhi*: om. RCEA; *ʾaʿwāmin*: *ʾayyāmin* (RCEA); *ʾilā l-ʾAndalusi ʾammanahā llāhu*: *ʾilā l-ʾAndalusi* (RCEA); *ṯumma raǧaʿa ʾilā Qaṣri ʿAbdi l-Karīmi l-maḏkuri wa-*: om. RCEA; *šarrafa llāhu rūḥahū ṭ-ṭayyibata l-muǧāhidata ʿašīya*: om. RCEA; *yawmi s-sabti*: *yawma l-ǧumʿati* (RCEA).

"I take refuge with God from the cursed[672] Devil! / *Basmalah – ṣalwalah*.[673]

This is the tomb of the glorious, the most exalted, the heroic, the most unique (!), the happiest, the blessed, the most brilliant, the most eminent, the most diligent, the most perfect chieftain, the *ǧihād*-fighter, the sanctified, the late Abū Muḥammad ʿAbd Allāh, son of the glorious, the heroic, the most unique, the happiest, the blessed, the most accomplishing, the most brilliant, the most eminent, the august, the sublime chieftain, the *ǧihād*-fighter, the most agreeable, the sanctified, the late

672 Literally "stoned" (in the classical sense).

673 For this beginning, especially the *taʿawwuḏ*-formula (*ʾaʿūḏu bi-llāhi mina š-šayṭāni r-raǧīm*, *cf.* Q 114), see also Inscriptions Espagne 24 (= RCEA 2884: 496 H, Córdoba), RCEA 3141 (544 H, Marrakech, in the epitaph of al-Qāḍī ʿIyāḍ), 4500 (661 H, Jaén, the epitaph on the tomb of Abū l-Ḥasan b. Abī M. b. Abī l-Ḥasan Ibn Ašqīlūlah at-Tuǧībī) and 5201 (706 H). Sometimes, the *taʿawwuḏ*-formula was put at the end of an epitaph, see Inscriptions Espagne 28 = RCEA 3445 (Córdoba 587 H).

Abū Isḥāq Ibrāhīm son of Ašqīlūlah – may God have mercy upon him, may He forgive him and make him dwell in His Garden! –. He appeared – may God forgive him! – in Wādī Āš[674] – may God protect it! –, one of the fortresses of al-Andalus. He took power,[675] the signs of his dominion spread and the drums were beaten, from there he waged the *ǧihād* against the enemy – may God shatter them! He triumphed over his uncle,[676] the ruler of al-Andalus,[677] and remained in power for about 23 years,[678] then he promoted the cause[679] of the most exalted king, the ruler supported (by God), al-Manṣūr, Prince of the Believers, al-Muʾayyad bi-llāh Abū Yaʿqūb[680] — may God support him with His help, / may He aid him with His backing and his abundance! || – who – may God support him! – gave him the order to abandon the afore-said Wādī Āš and to come to the Maghrib, so he retreated from al-Andalus to the Maghrib – may God make it an enjoyable place! – in Ǧumādā I of the year 686.[681] Then he (*sc.* Abū Yaʿqūb) – may God support him! – handed over to him Qaṣr ʿAbd al-Karīm[682] – may God protect it and bestow His favours upon it! – where he stayed for a period of eight years.[683] From there he crossed into al-Andalus – may God protect it! – and twice waged the *ǧihād*, then he returned to the afore-said Qaṣr ʿAbd al-Karīm and was taken away – may God raise his good and striving soul

674 Sp. Guadix.

675 Initially as Naṣrid governour of Wādī Āš.

676 Becoming quasi-independent ruler of Wādī Āš, in the same manner like other members of his family who held power in Málaga and Comaraes, *cf.* IḪaṭIḥāṭah I pp. 564f.

677 The first Naṣrid ruler Abū ʿAl. al-Ġālib Ibn al-Aḥmar (d. 671 H), for him see above **89**.

678 This date is seemingly correct if we assume, as told further below in the epitaph, that Abū Muḥammad left al-Andalus for the Maghrib in 686 H and that the conflict between the Naṣrid ruler and the various members of the Banū Ašqīlūlah, his former supporters, broke out during the years 662–64 H (see Kennedy: *Muslim Spain* p. 279; EI² VII p. 1021).

679 This is corroborated in IḪaṭIḥāṭah III p. 377 and IḪaṭLamḥah p. 57. *Cf.* also Arié: *España musulmana* pp. 38f.; Makki: *History of al-Andalus* pp. 78f.

680 The Marīnid ruler an-Nāṣir (al-Manṣūr) Yūsuf b. Yaʿqūb (r. 685–706 H).

681 IḪaṭIḥāṭah III p. 377 mentions the year 689, but تسعة may have been written instead of ستة (or *vice versa*). Guadix was the last base for the Banū Ašqīlūlah on Andalusian soil after they had surrendered Málaga to the Naṣrids eight years before; *cf.* also Kennedy: *Muslim Spain* p. 284; EI² VII p. 1022.

682 Qaṣr ʿAbd al-Karīm is said in YāqBuldān IV p. 360 (*s.v.*) to be on the Moroccan coast near Sabtah (sp. Ceuta); IḪaṭIḥāṭah I p. 565, III p. 377 and IḪaṭLamḥah p. 57 mentions (describing the same event as reported in the epitaph) Qaṣr Kutāmah. In fact, Qaṣr Kutāmah has alternatively been called "Qaṣr ʿAbd al-Karīm", referring to the emir ʿAbd al-Karīm al-Kutāmī who built the local fortress as early as 102 H, see the relevant entry in EI² IV p. 792. There we also read that in 687 H – the above-cited epitaph has 686 – the Marīnid ruler Yūsuf al-Manṣūr (see above n. 680) "appointed as its governor the Raʾīs Abū l-Ḥasan [*sic*] b. Ashkīlūla, whose descendants for long remained lords of the town".

683 RCEA has "days", but in view of the biographical information this does not seem correct.

to distinction! – on the evening of Saturday,[684] the tenth of the month Muḥarram in the year 695".

174

LOCATION. ar-Ramlah. DATE. 1007 H.

PERSON BURIED. The mystic Mūsā al-Qubbī (?) ar-Ramlī (d. 1007 H): MuḥḪul IV p. 435.

SOURCES. BN XIII p. 46; MuḥḪul IV p. 435; ᶜĀmKaškūl II p. 162.

DESCRIPTION. "I saw in the material about him (*fī ʾaḫbārihī*) that upon his tomb is inscribed: [*prose*]", followed by these two verses: [*poetry*]" (MuḥḪul). According to Ibn Kaṯīr and Bahāʾ ad-Dīn al-ᶜĀmilī, who quote only the verses, these are no epitaph-poem but something which was composed by a young lad in Baghdad in 603 H as he was about to be executed because he had killed another boy. – Prose and two lines in the metre *wāfir*:

hāḏā qabru šayḫi ṭ-ṭarīqati wa-l-ḥaqīqah

*qadimtu ʿalā l-karīmi bi-ġayri zādin * mina l-ḥasanāti wa-l-ʿamali s-saqīmī*
*wa-ḥamlu z-zādi ʾaqbaḥu mā tarāhū * ʾiḏā kāna l-qudūmu ʿalā karīmī*

1 *qadimtu*: *wafadtu* (ᶜĀmKaškūl); *wa-l-ʿamali*: *wa-l-qalbi* (BN, ᶜĀmKaškūl). – 2 The first hemistich runs in BN and ᶜĀmKaškūl: *wa-sūʾu ẓ-ẓanni ʾan yuʿtadda zādun.*

"This is the tomb of the sheikh of the (mystic) path and of truthful wisdom.

I came to the Generous without any provisions * of good deeds and (with) evil work(s),
But to carry provisions is very disgraceful indeed * when you come to someone generous!"

175

LOCATION. Ronda (ar. Rundah) (?). DATE. 684 H.

PERSON BURIED. The poet and man of letters Abū ṭ-Ṭayyib Ibn Šarīf ar-Rundī (Ṣāliḥ b. Yazīd b. Ṣāliḥ, 601–84 H): IḪaṭIḥāṭah III pp. 360-76; Nykl: *Hispano-Arabic Poetry* pp. 337-9; ZA III p. 198.

SOURCE. IḪaṭIḥāṭah III pp. 375f.

DESCRIPTION. "The man of letters (*ʾadīb*) Abū ṭ-Ṭayyib Ṣāliḥ (...) b. Šarīf ar-Rundī recited the following verses of his own composition, in order that they be written upon his tomb: [...]". – Two verses in the metre *ṭawīl*:

684 The version of RCEA has "Friday", although the 10th Muḥarram was a Saturday (as reported in the epitaph).

*ḫalīlayya bi-l-waddi llaḏī baynanā ǧʿalā * ʾiḏā mittu qabrī ʿurḍatan li-t-taraḥḥumī*
*ʿasā muslimun yadnū fa-yadʿū bi-raḥmatin * fa-ʾinniya muḥtāǧun li-daʿwati musallimī*

"(O) my two friends, for the love that is between us, do make, * once I have died, my tomb a place exposed to the prayer for mercy!
It may be that a Muslim will come near (my tomb) and invoke mercy * for I am in need of the invocation of someone (passing by and) greeting (me)".

176

LOCATION. Sabtah (sp. Ceuta). DATE. *c.*605 H.

PERSON BURIED. The mystic Abū l-Ḥaǧǧāǧ Yūsuf b. Aḥmad al-Manṣafī al-Balansī (d. Sabtah *c.*605 H): IAbbTakm IV p. 220.

SOURCES. MuwMuršid I p. 67; IAbbTakm IV p. 220; MaqqNafḥ (B) I p. 181, III p. 595 (B) = (C) V p. 132, (B) IV p. 336.

DESCRIPTION. "On a tomb was found written: [...]" (MuwMuršid); Ibn al-Abbār quotes these verses simply as from al-Manṣafī's poetry; al-Maqqarī cites the epitaph three times in his *Nafḥ*, not once with the same wording (though the variations are minor). Abū l-Ḥaǧǧāǧ al-Manṣafī ordered that these lines be written upon his tomb in Sabtah. – Two verses in the metre *sarīʿ*:

*qālat liya n-nafsu ʾatāka r-radā * wa-ʾanta fī baḥri l-ḫaṭāyā muqīm*
*hallā ddaḫarta z-zāda qultu qṣirī * lā yuḥmalu z-zādu li-dāri l-karīm*

2 *hallā ttaḫaḏta* (IAbbTakm, MaqqNafḥ IV p. 336); *lā*: *hal* (IAbbTakm, MaqqNafḥ I p. 181 and IV p. 336). The second verse runs in the version of MuwMuršid: *fa-ʾayna ḥusnu z-zādi qultu qṣirī * fa-hal yaʿuddu z-zāda ḍayfu l-karīm.*

"The soul told me, 'Destruction (i.e. death) has come upon you * and you are still stuck in the sea of sins?
Did you not gather provisions?' I said, 'Shut up! * You should not bring provisions to the abode of the Generous!'"

NOTE. The important concept of provisions for the "travel to the hereafter" and ultimately before the eyes of God is present in a number of epitaphs (*cf.* above page ---). Yet the notion not only that the believer may not, but also must not carry provisions with him – given that he steers towards the house of God, the most generous host – makes this epitaph-poem very similar to what we read in the verses of **174**.

177

LOCATIONS. (a) Seville (ar. Išbīlīyah). – (b, d) Dahlak. – (c) Marrakech.

DATES. (a) 525 H. – (b) 588 H. – (c) 595 or 596 H. – (d) 607 H.

PERSONS BURIED. (a) The traditionist and physician Abū l-ʿAlāʾ Zuhr b. ʿAbd al-Malik al-Išbīlī al-Iyādī ("Abulelizor", d. Córdoba 525 H, buried in Seville): IAbbTakm I p. 267-9; IAUṣaybʿUyūn pp. 517-9; ŠḎ IV pp. 74f.; ŠN p. 131; GAL I p. 486 and GALS I p. 889; Arié: *España musulmana* p. 419; ZA III p. 50; EI^2 III pp. 976f.; CHAL *Andalus* p. 117. – (b, d) N. N. – (c) The philologist and physician, grandson of Abū l-ʿAlāʾ Zuhr and therefore known as "al-Ḥafīd" Ibn Zuhr ("Avenzoar", Abū Bakr M. b. Abī Marwān ʿAbd al-Malik b. Zuhr al-Išbīlī, Seville 504 or 507 – Marrakech 595 or 596 H): IDiḥMuṭrib pp. 203-9; IAbbTakm II p. 75; IAUṣaybʿUyūn pp. 521-8; IḪallWaf IV pp. 434-7; MaqqNafḥ (C) III pp. 16-20; ŠN pp. 160f.; al-Marrākušī: *Iʿlām* III pp. 50-64; GAL I p. 489; Nykl: *Hispano-Arabic Poetry* pp. 248-51; ZA VI p. 250; EI^2 III pp. 978f.

SOURCES. (a) IḪarrāṭʿĀqibah p. 118; IAbbTakm I pp. 268f.; ŠN p. 131. – (b) Stèles Dahlak 229 (only the first two lines). – (c) YāqIršād VII p. 25 (only lines 1 and 3); IḪallWaf IV p. 436 / (Slane) III p. 436 = Schack: *Poesie und Kunst* I p. 238 (in German translation, see below); MaqqNafḥ (B) III p. 434 / (C) IV p. 399; al-Marrākušī: *Iʿlām* III pp. 62f.; Nykl: *Hispano-Arabic Poetry* p. 249 (in English translation). – (d) Stèles Dahlak 237 (only the first two lines).

DESCRIPTION. (a) "A piece of ascetic poetry was reported to me which Abū l-ʿAlāʾ composed and had ordered to be written upon his tomb: [...]" (IAbbTakm); "He ordered that on his tomb be written: [...]" (ŠN, similarly IḪarrāṭʿĀqibah). – (b, d) See Stèles Dahlak 229 and 237. – (c) "He directed in his last will that after his death the following verses be written on his tomb. In these verses he refers to his knowledge of medicine and his curing the people: [...]" (IḪallWaf, almost verbatim also MaqqNafḥ and al-Marrākušī: *Iʿlām*); "He also composed the following and ordered it to be written upon his tomb" (YāqIršād). – Three verses in the metre *mutaqārib*:

*taraḥḥam bi-faḍlika yā-wāqifan * wa-lāḥiẓ makānan dufiʿnā ʾilayhī*
*turābu ḍ-ḍarīḥi ʿalā wağnatī * ka-ʾanniya lam ʾamši yawman ʿalayhī*
*ʾudāwī l-ʾanāma ḥaḏāri l-manūna * wa-hā ʾanā qad ṣirtu rahnan ladayhī*

1 *taraḥḥam*: *taʾammal* (MaqqNafḥ), *taraḥḥam bi-faḍlika*: *taʾammal bi-ḥaqqika* (YāqIršād, IḪallWaf, al-Marrākušī: *Iʿlām*); *wa-lāḥiẓ*: *wa-ʾabṣir* (a, b); *dufiʿnā*: *dufiʿtu* (YāqIršād; b). – **2** *ʿalā wağnatī*: *ʿalā ṣafḥatī* (a and b; MaqqNafḥ). – **3** The first hemistich runs in YāqIršād: *fa-ʾanniya ḥaḏḏartu minhu l-ʾanāma*; *wa-hā*: *fa-hā* (a; MaqqNafḥ).

"Have mercy if you please,[685] O you standing (before my tomb), * and notice which place we have been cast in!
The earth of the grave (now) covers my cheek * as if I never walked upon it (i.e. the earth, *or* ground) on any day.

685 Ibn Ḫallikān's and Yāqūt's version (*taʾammal bi-ḥaqqika*) would translate as "Ponder your true fate, *or* what you are obliged to do ...!"

(Now) I cure the men (by saying), 'Beware of death!'[686] * and – look here! I have become a pledge in his hands!"

Schack's translation:

"Steh und erwäge![687] Eine von den Stätten / Ist dies, wo wir zuletzt uns Alle betten.
Die Erde deckt mein Antlitz nun, als ob sie meine Füße nie betreten hätten.
Gar Viele heilt' ich, sie dem Tod entreißend, und konnte doch mich selbst vor ihm nicht retten".

NOTES.

1. The wanderings of an epitaph. From the description in some literary sources we may gain the impression that Abū l-ᶜAlāʾ Zuhr had composed these verses himself, especially as he implies that he is a physician in the last line. Later on, the very personal third verse, which could only be applied to a physician, could have been omitted and the remaining lines re-used in other epitaphs, e.g. in those of Dahlak (which are lacking the third line). If that is indeed the case, it would demonstrate the gradual "wandering" of this epitaph towards the East during the sixth cent. H. Still it would be difficult to explain, according to this hypothesis, why his grandson should have wanted to have the same verses inscribed on his own tomb.

On the other hand, it might well have been the other way round and the epitaph "made its way" from the East towards the West. We know that Abū l-ᶜAlāʾ's father Abū Marwān ᶜAbd al-Malik (d. *c.*470 H), likewise a physician, had travelled to Egypt before he later settled at Denia where he died.[688] So he might have come across the two lines (as preserved in the epitaphs from Dahlak) somewhere in Egypt and then taken them to al-Andalus; his son Zuhr would in that case have only added the personal third verse for his own epitaph. Yet there is still another possibility, because it seems rather improbable that both grandfather and grandson would have liked to have identical verses written on their tombs (though they were buried in different towns). On the basis of the extant sources it is impossible to decide whether Zuhr or his grandson actually devised this epitaph for their respective tombstones, but if the notice in IAbbTakm (and ŠN) is wrong and the epitaph was indeed composed by the grandson, it is rather likely that he had heard these verses from somebody, maybe of his own family, who had read them on a grave in the East; al-Ḥafīd Ibn Zuhr would then have added only the third line. This seems just as plausible given the fact that at least one epitaph from Dahlak predates the decease of Ibn Zuhr (the grandson).

686 This refers to his medical skill, the twist here being that he does still "cure" the people (by making them reconsider) although he is dead and no longer able to practice his skills as he used to do.

687 This translates *taʾammal bi-ḥaqqika* of the version in IḪallWaf.

688 IDiḥMuṭrib p. 203; MaqqNafḥ (C) III pp. 13f. See also EI^2 III p. 976 and Vernet: *Natural Sciences* p. 944.

2. "The earth covers my cheek". This expression is known only from Ibn Ḫallikān's citation, while the extant epitaphs as well as other literary sources have *ʿalā ṣafḥatī* ("... covers my face"). Nonetheless this variant need not be a simple transmission mistake or a *lapsus calami*, but could well have been part of the original wording as composed by Abū l-ʿAlāʾ or his grandson. In any case, the motif is not uncommon in epitaphs (see **34**, **113**, **177**, **184** and **213**) and in "regular" mourning poetry. Of particular interest in that regard are also the verses ascribed to Abū ʿAbd Allāh Ibn at-Tabbān (d. Kairouan 397 H) (*basīṭ*):

المَوْتُ لاَ بُدَّ آتٍ فَاسْتَعِدَّ لَهُ * إنَّ اللَّبِيبَ بِذِكْرِ المَوْتِ مَشْغُولُ
وَكَيْفَ يَلْهُو بِعَيْشٍ أَوْ يَلَذُّ بِهِ * مَنِ التُّرَابُ عَلَى خَدَّيْهِ مَجْبُولُ

"Death is inevitably coming, so (better) prepare for it! * The man of reason is (always) busy reflecting upon death!
How can someone enjoy life or find it pleasant * who was created with his cheeks that turn again to earth?"[689]

Above on p. 164, we also encountered the Kūfan ascetic Dāʾūd b. Nuṣayr aṭ-Ṭāʾī who once strolled around between the tombs and fainted when he heard a woman say "O my love! If I only knew which of your cheeks will be the first to decay? The right or the left?"[690]

3. "Beware of death!" (verse 3). The use of the root *ḥḏr* in connection with the mention of death is also encountered in mourning poetry. Although not exactly identical to the wording of epitaph **177**, the following line ascribed to Abū Nuwās illustrates this fact (*ṭawīl*):

وَكُنْتُ عَلَيْهِ أَحْذَرُ المَوْتَ وَحْدَهُ * فَلَمْ يَبْقَ لِي شَيءٌ عَلَيْهِ أُحَاذِرُ

"I did fear nothing for him but death alone, * for now (after his death) nothing is left for me to fear for!"[691]

In the same vein, Abū Isḥāq aṣ-Ṣūlī (Ibr. b. al-ʿAbbās, d. 243 H) wrote in a poem mourning the death of one of his sons (*maǧzūʾ al-kāmil*):

مَنْ شَاءَ بَعْدَكَ فَلْيَمُتْ * فَعَلَيْكَ كُنْتُ أُحَاذِرُ

689 Cited in DabMaʿālim III p. 130 and (anonymously) al-Qināwī: *Fatḥ ar-raḥīm* p. 177 (var. *ʾātin*: *minhū* and *maǧbulū*: *maǧʿūlū*).

690 This drastic image, contrasting former beauty with present decay, reminds one much of a verse in the poem by aš-Šarīf ar-Raḍīy mourning his mother Fāṭimah (d. 385 H): *wa-nawāẓirun kaḥala t-turābu ǧufūnahā*, "(her) eyes whose lids are (now) coloured (as if by antimony) by the earth (of the tomb)" (ŠarīfRaḍDīwān I p. 30).

691 Cited in IQutʿUyūn III p. 65 and IQutŠiʿr p. 517; IDāʾūdZahrah p. 366; IḤamdTaḏk IV p. 241; BaṣrīḤam (C) II p. 187; IBuḥtUns p. 93; NuwNih V p. 164; IAḤaǧSulwah p. 53.

"Whosoever wishes to die after you have (now) died may do so! * It was only you that I feared for!"[692]

178

Location. Silves (ar. Šilb, modern Portugal). Date. 532 H.

Person buried. The man of letters, preacher and traditionist Abū Bakr al-Qurašī [al-Qaršī?] aš-Šilbī (M. b. Ibr. al-ʿĀmirī, Bāǧah [port. Beja] 446 – Šilb 532 H): IBaškṢilah II p. 582; SuyBuġ I p. 17; Casiri: *Bibliotheca* I p. 95 (as cited from the ms. of *Zād al-musāfir* by Ṣafwān b. Idrīs at-Tuǧībī, d. 598 H).[693]

Sources. YāqBuldān III p. 358 (*s.v.* Šilb) = al-Ǧubūrī: *Muʿǧam* p. 652; SuyBuġ I p. 17; Bahǧat: *Ittiǧāh* pp. 261f.

Description. "From his poetry (are the following verses), and he ordered that they be written on his tomb: [...]" (SuyBuġ); "He ordered to be inscribed upon his tomb: [...]" (YāqBuldān). – Four verses in the metre *mutaqārib*:

*la-ʾin nuffiḏa l-qadaru s-sābiqū * bi-mawtī kamā ḥakama l-ḫāliqū*
*fa-qad māta wāliдunā ʾĀdamun * wa-māta Muḥammaduni ṣ-ṣādiqū*
*wa-māta l-mulūku wa-ʾašyāʿuhum * wa-lam yabqa min ǧamʿihim nāṭiqū*
*fa-qul li-llaḏī sarrahū maṣraʿī * taʾahhab fa-ʾinnaka bī lāḥiqū*

1 لئن: لين (Casiri). – 4 سرّه: سرّ (Casiri, does not fit the metre); *maṣraʿī*: *mahlakī* (SuyBuġ).

"If it so happens that the predestined Fate is carried out * with my death, according to what the Creator has decreed,
Well, our father Adam also met his death, * and death took away Muḥammad, the sincere,
And the sovereigns and (all) their partisans died, * and not (a single one) is left from among their crowd (who still opens his mouth) to speak.
So say to someone rejoicing at my having been thrown down (by death): * 'Make yourself ready, for you will (certainly) join me!'"

Note. The topos that malicious people, or somebody's enemies, express joy or satisfaction about the death of a person is not infrequently mentioned or alluded to in epitaphs (**231**) and mourning poetry. An example is a line from a poem by Lisān ad-Dīn Ibn al-Ḫaṭīb who, while imprisoned, mourned his bitter fate and towards the end of the poem addresses his enemies with the words (*mutaqārib*):

فَمَنْ كَانَ يَفْرَحُ مِنْهُمْ لَهُ * فَقُلْ يَفْرَحُ اليَوْمَ مَنْ لاَ يَمُوتُ

692 Quoted in TawḥBaṣāʾir VIII p. 142; YāqIršād I p. 266; IbšīhīMust II p. 456 (anon.). See also the lines (second hemistich each) cited in BaṣrīḤam (B) I p. 220: *wa-mā kuntu ʾiyyāhum ʿalayhi ʾuḥāḏirū*; *ib.* p. 248: *li-kulli mriʾin min yawmihī mā yuḥāḏirū*.

693 *Cf.* GALS I pp. 482 and 963.

"To those among them, who rejoiced for his (i.e. Ibn al-Ḫaṭīb's) death, * say 'Is anyone rejoicing today who is *not* going to die!?'"[694]

Many centuries before that, the famous jurist aš-Šāfiᶜī – and others as well – recited the following lines expressing the same thought; though the wording was changed somewhat, they belonged originally to a qaṣīdah by the pre-Islamic poet ᶜAbīd b. al-Abraṣ (*ṭawīl*):

تَمَنَّى رِجَالٌ أَنْ أَمُوتَ وَإِنْ أَمُتْ * فَتِلْكَ سَبِيلٌ لَسْتُ فِيهَا بِأَوْحَدِ
فَقُلْ لِلَّذِي يَبْغِي مَمَاتِيَ عَاجِلاً * تَأَهَّبْ لأُخْرَى بَعْدَهَا وكَأَنْ قَدِ

"Some men wish that I may die! Yet if I die, * I am not the only one to take that way![695]

Thus say to someone who covets my speedy death: * 'Prepare for another (death) after that,[696] and it is (so near) as if it had already happened!'"[697]

179

LOCATION. Šīrāz. DATE. 180 H or after.

PERSON BURIED (?). The famous grammarian Sībawayh (ᶜAmr b. ᶜUṯmān, d. 180 H. or after): AnbNuzhah pp. 60-6; MarzNūr pp. 95-7; TB XII pp. 195-9; IḪallWaf III pp. 463-5 / (Slane) II pp. 396-9; QifṭīInbāh II pp. 346-60; ŠīrŠadd pp. 95-99; SuyBuġ II pp. 229f.; MaqqNafḥ (C) V pp. 224f.; ZA V p. 81.

SOURCES. IADunyāQubūr (A) p. 174 = IRaǧAhwāl p. 189; IsfStrangers p. 31 (only verses 1-2, in English translation); IǦawzīTabṣ II pp. 64 and 206f.; IḪallWaf III pp. 464f. / (Slane) II p. 398; QifṭīInbāh II p. 360; ŠarŠMaq II p. 19; al-ᶜAffānī: *Sakb* II pp. 393 and 398 (quoted anonymously).

DESCRIPTION. "Ibrāhīm b. Yaᶜqūb told me that Yaḥyā b. Yūnus told him in Šīrāz that he had read on a tomb in Šīrāz: [...]" (IADunyāQubūr); "A teacher of ours told

694 IḪaldᶜIbar VII p. 342 (var. *minhum*: *minkum*) = MaqqNafḥ (C) VII p. 39.

695 For this expression – *fa-tilka sabīlun lastu fīhā bi-ʾawḥadī* –, see also *ʾAmālī l-Marzūqī*, ed. Yaḥyā Wuhayb al-Ǧubūrī, Beirut: Dār al-Ġarb al-Islāmī 1995, pp. 88f.

696 I.e. your own death after mine.

697 Cited in HamTanzīl p. 209; TMD LI p. 428; IḤaǧTawālī pp. 178f.; MaqrMuq II p. 406 (the second verse in the latter three: *fa-qul li-llaḏī yabġī* [TMD: *yabqā*] *ḫilāfa llaḏī maḍā* * *tahayyaʾ* [TMD: *taǧahhaza*] *li-ʾuḫrā miṯlihā wa-kaʾan* [MaqrMuq: *fa-kaʾan*] *qadī*). In TawḥBaṣāʾir VIII p. 64, TMD LXI pp. 306f. (only v. 1) and BN IX p. 232, these verses are said to have been recited by an Umayyad caliph (second verse as in IḤaǧTawālī). The lines are not contained in *Dīwān al-ʾImām aš-Šāfiᶜī*, ed. Ī. Badīᶜ Yaᶜqūb, Beirut: Dār al-Kitāb al-ᶜArabī ²1414/²1994. – The verses as composed by ᶜAbīd: *tamannā mruʾu l-Qaysi mawtī wa-ʾin ʾamut* * *fa-tilka sabīlun lastu fīhā bi-ʾawḥadī* // *laᶜalla llaḏī yarǧū radāya wa-mītatī* * *safāhan wa-ǧubnan ʾan yakūna huwa r-radī*, see *The Dīwāns of ᶜAbīd ibn al-Abraṣ, of Asad, and ᶜĀmir ibn aṭ-Ṭufail* etc., ed. Charles Lyall, Leiden: Brill / London: Luzac 1913, p. ٨٠ (no. XXX, vv. 29f.).

us that he read this, which someone had written on the wall of Sībawayh's tomb: [...]" (IṣfStrangers); "On a tomb in Šīrāz, the following verses could be read: [...]" (IRaġAhwāl); "Abū Saᶜīd aṭ-Ṭawwāl[698] said, 'I saw upon the tomb of Sībawayh – may God have mercy upon him! – the following verses inscribed, and they were composed by Sulaymān b. Yazīd al-ᶜAdawī: [...]'" (IḪallWaf and QifṭīInbāh, almost verbatim also ŠarŠMaq). Interestingly, in IĞawzīTabṣ, the verses are quoted twice and not presented as an epitaph at all, but rather as verses of Ibn al-Ğawzī's own (!) composition in the middle of sermons in rhymed prose (as the variants show, he either took the verses from Ibn Abī d-Dunyā or a common source). In ŠīrŠadd pp. 98f., a reliable (though relatively late) source for the local burial sites, we learn that the author "could not identify Sībawayh's tomb with certainty", nor does he mention (or even cite) any epitaph.[699] – Three verses in the metre *kāmil*:

*ḏahaba l-ʾaḥibbatu baʿda ṭūli tawaddudin * wa-naʾā l-mazāru fa-ʾaslamūka wa-ʾaqšaʿū*
*tarakūka ʾawḥaša mā takūnu bi-qafratin * lam yuʾnisūka wa-kurbatin lam yadfaʿū*
*quḍiya l-qaḍāʾu wa-ṣirta ṣāḥiba ḥufratin * ʿanka l-ʾaḥibbatu ʾaʿraḍū wa-taṣaddaʿū*

1 *ḏahaba*: *ḏahala* (IADunyāQubūr); *tawaddudin*: *tazāwurin* (Ibn Ḫallikān, QifṭīInbāh, ŠarŠMaq); *wa-ʾaqšaʿū*: *wa-ʾasraʿū* (ŠarŠMaq). – **2** *tarakūka ʾawḥaša mā takūnu bi-qafratin*: *ḫaḏalūka ʾafqara mā takūnu bi-qaryatin* (IADunyāQubūr), *ḫaḏalūka ʾafqara mā takūnu bi-ġurbatin* (IRaġAhwāl), *mā takūnu*: *mā yakūnu* (ŠarŠMaq), *ḫaḏalūka ... li-ġurbatin* (IĞawzīTabṣ; al-ᶜAffānī). – **3** *quḍiya*: *fa-qaḍā* (IADunyāQubūr); *ʿanka*: *ʿinda* (IADunyāQubūr, IRaġAhwāl); *ʾaʿraḍū*: اعضوا (IADunyāQubūr).

"The loved ones departed after a long time (that there had been bonds) of affection * and the visitation-site has become distant, they have deserted you and dispersed!
They left you behind in a state of solitude worse than in a desert[700] * without keeping you company and not chasing away (your) grief.
Fate has been carried out and you became the inhabitant of a (burial) hole * from whom the loved ones turned away and departed".

180

LOCATION. Šīrāz. DATE. 732 H.

PERSON BURIED. The reciter Faḫr ad-Dīn aš-Šīrāzī (Abū M. A. b. Maḥmūd), also known as *al-ʿAšarah* ("the Ten-Man") for his mastership of the ten common

698 ŠarŠMaq II p. 19 has "aṣ-Ṣūlī".

699 (Ibn) al-Anbārī, who likewise does not quote the epitaph, quotes Ibn Durayd (via al-Marzubānī) with the information that Sībawayh died in Šīrāz and was buried there (AnbNuzhah p. 66). Ibn ᶜAbd al-Barr quotes a line which was reportedly uttered by Sībawayh before his death (IᶜABarrBahğah II p. 374); others say that he died in Baṣrah.

700 Perhaps one has to read *bi-qaʿratin* instead of *bi-qafratin*. The first hemistich would then translate as "They left you behind in a most solitary state in a deep pit (i.e. the tomb)".

ways of reciting the Qurʾānic wording (d. 732 H): ŠīrŠadd p. 145; ĞazṬab I p. 138.

SOURCES. TMD LXVI p. 75; ŠīrŠadd p. 145.

DESCRIPTION. "On his tomb is inscribed: [...]" (ŠīrŠadd). As is apparent from the quotation in TMD, aš-Šīrāzī's epitaph-poem was adapted from two lines composed originally by Abū Bakr aš-Šiblī (d. 334 or 335 H) in occasion of the death of one of his brothers. – Two verses in the metre *kāmil*:

*sa-ʾuwaddiʿu l-qurrāʾa baʿdaka wa-l-warā * ʾiḏ ḥāna minka l-baynu wa-t-tawdīʿū*
*wa-la-ʾasfikanna laka d-dimāʾa taʾassufan * law kāna Diğlatu lī ʿalayka dumūʿū*

1 *sa-ʾuwaddiʿu l-qurrāʾa baʿdaka wa-l-warā*: *sa-ʾuwaddiʿu l-ʾiḥsāna baʿdaka wa-n-nuhā* (TMD). – **2** *wa-la-ʾasfikanna laka d-dimāʾa taʾassufan * law kāna ...*: *wa-la-ʾastaqillu laka d-dumūʿa ṣabābatan * wa-law ʾanna ...* (TMD).

"I will say farewell to the reciters after your death and to mankind (as well), * since the time of seperation and farewell has come for you!
Truly, I swear to shed streams of tears out of regret (for you): * had I but the (waters of the) Tigris they would be tears shed for you!"[701]

181

LOCATION. Syria (*fī ṭarīq aš-Šām*). DATE. Second century H (?).

PERSON BURIED. Unknown.

SOURCES. IADunyāQubūr (A) p. 159 = ZabīdīŠIḥyāʾ X p. 357; ANuḤilyah II pp. 383f. = Gramlich: *Vorbilder* I p. 76 (in German translation); IʿABarrBahğah II p. 329; TMD XL p. 123; al-ʿAffānī: *Sakb* I p. 662 and II p. 523.

DESCRIPTION. The chains of transmission given by Ibn Abī d-Dunyā and Abū Nuʿaym mention the Baṣran Mālik b. Dīnār as the one who read the following verses as "inscribed on a tomb" and subsequently transmitted them; "A stone (*ḥağar*) was found in the Yamāmah region in a well, namely the well of Ṭasm and Ğadīs [?] in a village called Muʿtaq. Upon it was written: [...]" (IʿABarrBahğah); al-ʿAffānī quotes the lines not as an epitaph, but as verses uttered by the dead, probably following the account in TMD: "It is believed that an-Nuʿmān b. al-Munḏir once went to a cemetery outside Kūfah in the company of ʿAmr b. ʿAdīy. There an-Nuʿmān said, 'If the dead could speak, what would they say? They would say: [...]'". – Three verses in the metre *basīṭ*:

*yā-ʾayyuhā r-rakbu sīrū ʾinna ġāyatakum * ʾan tuṣbiḥū ḏāta yawmin lā tasīrūnā*
*ḥuṯṯū l-maṭāyā wa-ʾarḫū min ʾazimmatihā * qabla l-mamāti wa-qaḍḍū mā tuqaḍḍūnā*
*kunnā ʾunāsan kamā kuntum fa-ġayyaranā * dahrun fa-sawfa kamā ṣirnā taṣīrūnā*

1 *ar-rakbu*: *an-nāsu* (IʿABarrBahğah, al-ʿAffānī: *Sakb* II p. 523); *ʾinna ġāyatakum*: *ʾin maṣīrukumū* (IADunyāQubūr); *ʾinna qaṣrakumū* (!, IʿABarrBahğah, ZabīdīŠIḥyāʾ, al-ʿAffānī: *Sakb* II p. 523), *ʾin*

701 Alternatively also: *law kāna Diğlata lī ʿalayka dumūʿū*, "If my tears (shed) about you were only (as many as the waters of) the Tigris!"

qaṣadtum (TMD, does not fit the metre); *ʾan tuṣbiḥū*: om. TMD. – **2** *ḥuṯṯū l-maṭāyā*: *ḥillū r-rikāba* (TMD); *al-maṭāyā*: *al-maṭīyah* (IᶜABarrBahǧah, al-ᶜAffānī: *Sakb* II p. 523); من: في (IᶜABarrBahǧah); *wa-qaḍḍū mā tuqiḍḍūna*: *wa-nuṣṣū mā yanuṣṣūna* (ZabīdīŠIḥyāʾ), *wa-faḍḍū wa-tufaḍḍūna* (!, TMD). – **3** *fa-sawfa*: *wa-ᶜan qalīlin* (IADunyāQubūr, does not fit the metre), *fa-ʾantum* (IᶜABarrBahǧah, al-ᶜAffānī: *Sakb* II p. 523); *ṣirnā taṣīrūnā*: *kunnā takūnūnā* (ANuḪilyah, IᶜABarrBahǧah, ZabīdīŠIḥyāʾ, al-ᶜAffānī: *Sakb* I p. 662 and II p. 523). Line 3 is corrupt in TMD.

"O you riders-by, move on! Your end will be * that one day you will not be moving on any longer,
Thus stir up your riding animals and let their bridles go * before death befalls you, and carry out what you are about to carry out!
Once we were people like you, but Time has changed * us, and you will certainly become what we already came to be!"

NOTE. For the last verse *cf.* the beginning of a (fragmentarily) preserved epitaph from Jerusalem: *lā tuᶜaǧǧibka nafsuka miṯlaka kuntu wa-miṯlī takūn* ("Do not be surprised: I was like you, and like me you will be!", RCEA 1876); almost the same wording (*lā tuᶜaǧǧibannaka* etc.) appears also in another epitaph from Jerusalem (RCEA 1272, dated 325 H). As a variant of what we find in TMD, we read in other literary sources that ᶜAdīy b. Zayd walked in a cemetery with the Ġassānid ruler of al-Ḥīrah, an-Nuᶜmān b. al-Munḏir. The latter said, "Do you know what this cemetery is saying? (...) Its words are: 'O you riders trotting * upon the earth assiduously: // Like you we were, * and like us you will be" (*kamā ʾantumū kaḏā kunnā * wa-kamā naḥnu takūnūnā*).[702] *Cf.* also epitaph **183**.

The following, concerning the tomb of a Turkish official (10th c. H) in Istanbul, is taken from the English translation of al-Ayvānsarāyī's eleventh-century treatise *The Garden of the Mosques*; the original was not available to me. "These couplets in Turkish and Arabic are written on his gravestone:

> The world is a guest-house.
> Foolish are those who make not provision for death.
>> O visitor to my grave, think about my condition:
>> I was yesterday like you and you shall be tomorrow like me".[703]

182

LOCATION. Syria (*bi-š-Šām*). DATE. Unknown (third century H?).
PERSON BURIED. Unknown.
SOURCES. IQutᶜUyūn II p. 326; TawḥBaṣāʾir IV p. 198; IᶜABarrBahǧah II p. 322

702 Quoted in IᶜABarrBahǧah II pp. 325f.; ṬurṭSirāǧ p. 15; IBuḥtUns p. 64; ŠayMaǧānī III p. 18. The same story is retold in IᶜABarrBahǧah II p. 340, although the reported text is different. Almost verbatim, we find this thought expressed in Latin epitaphs belonging to the ancient Mediterranean culture: *quod tu es, ego fui; quod nunc sum, et tu eris* ("What you are, I was; what I am now, you will also be"), and in later Christian medieval epitaphs: *Sum quod eris fueramque quod es* ("I am what you will be and I was what you are"), see Geist: *Grabinschriften* 503; Houlbrooke: *Death in England* p. 347.

703 AyvānGarden p. 260.

(only verse 1); ṬurṭSirāǧ p. 10; ŠarŠMaq I p. 175; IḪallWaf III pp. 272f.; AFidāʾMuḫt II pp. 44f.; BN XI p. 15; ʿIṣāmīSimṭ III p. 339; BaḥrKaškūl I p. 353 and III p. 186; al-Lawāsānī: *Kaškūl* p. 20; al-ʿAffānī: *Sakb* II p. 518 (vv. 1-4 and 15f. of a much longer poem, cited anonymously).

DESCRIPTION. "I gathered the information that one could read on a tomb in Syria: [...]" (IQutʿUyūn: it remains unclear from the context whether this sentence is still part of a report mentioned before and having a chain of transmission, or whether the wording is due to Ibn Qutaybah himself); at-Tawḥīdī and others present these verses simply as poetry, without reference to an epitaph. According to Abū l-Fidāʾ, Ibn Kaṯīr, al-ʿIṣāmī and al-Lawāsānī, these verses were recited (if not composed?) by Abū l-Ḥasan ʿAlī b. Muḥammad al-Hādī (d. 254 H), the tenth Imam of the Twelver-Šiʿites, at the court of the caliph al-Mutawakkil in Sāmarrāʾ; aṭ-Ṭurṭūšī and Yūsuf al-Baḥrānī (d. 1186 H) present these verses as being an inscription of the pre-Islamic Yemenite king Sayf b. Ḏī Yazan (I p. 353);[704] al-Baḥrānī quotes them again as part of a longer poem by ʿAlī (III p. 186); the first version gives, albeit with variants, the six lines of the epitaph. – Six verses in the metre *basīṭ*:

*bātū ʿalā qulali l-ʾaǧbāli taḥrusuhum * ġulbu r-riǧāli fa-lam tanfaʿhumu l-qulalū*
*wa-stunzilū baʿda ʿizzin min maʿāqilihim * fa-ʾuskinū ḥufratan yā-biʾsa mā nazalū*
*nādāhumū ṣāriḫun min baʿdi mā dufinū * ʾayna l-ʾasirratu wa-t-tīǧānu wa-l-ḥulalū*
*ʾayna l-wuǧūhu llatī kānat muḥaǧǧabatan * min dūnihā tuḍrabu l-ʾastāru wa-l-kilalū*
*fa-ʾafṣaḥa l-qabru ʿanhum ḥīna sāʾalahum * tilka l-wuǧūhu ʿalayhā d-dūdu taqtatilū*
*qad ṭāla mā ʾakalū dahran wa-mā naʿimū * fa-ʾaṣbaḥū baʿda ṭūli l-ʾakli qad ʾukilū*

1 *fa-lam*: *fa-mā* (BaḥrKaškūl I p. 353); *tanfaʿhumu*: *tamnaʿhumu* (TawḥBaṣāʾir, IʿABarrBahǧah), *ʾaġnathumu* (IḪallWaf, AFidāʾMuḫt, BN). – 2 *min*: *ʿan* (al-Lawāsānī: *Kaškūl*, al-ʿAffānī: *Sakb*); *min maʿāqilihim*: *min manāzilihim* (BaḥrKaškūl III p. 186); *fa-ʾūdiʿū ḥufaran* (ŠarŠMaq, IḪallWaf, AFidāʾMuḫt, BN, ʿIṣāmīSimṭ), *ʾilā maqābirihim* (BaḥrKaškūl III p. 186, al-Lawāsānī: *Kaškūl*, al-ʿAffānī: *Sakb*). *fa-ʾuskinū ḥufratan*: *wa-ʾunzilū* ... (TawḥBaṣāʾir), *fa-ʾuskinū ḥufaran* (ṬurṭSirāǧ), *fa-stawṭanū ḥufaran* (BaḥrKaškūl I p. 353). – 3 *nādāhumū*: *nādā bihim* (BN); *mā dufinū*: *dafnihimū* (TawḥBaṣāʾir), *mā qubirū* (IḪallWaf, AFidāʾMuḫt, BN, ʿIṣāmīSimṭ), *min baʿdi dafnihim* (BaḥrKaškūl, both versions). – 4 *muḥaǧǧabatan*: *munaʿʿamatan* (ŠarŠMaq, IḪallWaf, AFidāʾMuḫt, BN). – 5 *fa-ʾafṣaḥa*: *fa-ʾaṣbaḥa* (al-Lawāsānī: *Kaškūl*, does not make sense); *sāʾalahum*: سيل بهم (ŠarŠMaq); *taqtatilu*: *tantaqilu* (BaḥrKaškūl III p. 186, misprint?). – 6 *dahran*: *fīhā* (TawḥBaṣāʾir, BaḥrKaškūl III p. 186, al-ʿAffānī: *Sakb*), *yawman* (ṬurṭSirāǧ); *naʿimū*: *šaribū* (ṬurṭSirāǧ, ŠarŠMaq, IḪallWaf, AFidāʾMuḫt, ʿIṣāmīSimṭ, BaḥrKaškūl I p. 353, al-Lawāsānī: *Kaškūl*, al-ʿAffānī: *Sakb*), *labisū* (BN); *ṭūli*: *ḏāka* (ṬurṭSirāǧ, BaḥrKaškūl I p. 353).

704 at-Ṭurṭūšī remarks that the poem was found by Wahb b. Munabbih in the Yemenite palace of Sayf, inscribed in Sabaen letters and then translated by Wahb, yet al-Baḥrānī's quotation is introduced with the words: "Upon his tomb was *also* found written ..." (*wa-wuǧida maktūban ʿalā qabrihī ʾayḍan*).

"They passed the nights upon the summits of the mountains[705] guarded * by thick-necked men, but the summits were of no help to them.
And they were brought down, after having been powerful, from their strongholds, * then they were made to dwell in a (burial) hole. Into what a miserable place they descended!
A caller cried to them after they had been buried, * 'Where are (now) the reclining seats (*or* thrones), the crown and the festive dresses?
Where are (now) the faces that were veiled from sight, * (shielded) from others by drawing up screens and lofty veils?'
And the tomb spoke flawlessly on their behalf at the moment when he (i.e. the caller) asked them, * 'Upon those faces the worms are fighting each other!
The time when they were consuming and living in luxury lasted an eternity, * but after their long consumation they (now) came themselves to be consumed!'"

NOTE. Whether these popular lines were ever inscribed upon a tomb is doubtful though not impossible. They exhibit a decidedly hortatory character that is commonly known from ascetic poetry, playing on the current motif that death supersedes all, the mighty and the lowly (*cf.* above pp. 175f.); in diction and style they resemble an inscription found in al-Ḥīrah (**99**). A very close parallel to the above-cited epitaph presents an inscription on the wall of a palace which, according to al-Maqqarī, consisted of the following lines (*basīṭ*):

قَدْ كَانَ صَاحِبُ هَذَا القَصْرِ مُغْتَبِطاً * فِي ظِلِّ عَيْشٍ يَخَافُ النَّاسُ مِنْ بَأْسِهِ
فَبَيْنَمَا هُوَ مَسْرُورٌ بِلَذَّتِهِ * فِي مَجْلِسِ اللَهْوِ مَغْبُوطٌ بِجُلاَّسِهِ
إِذْ جَاءَهُ بَغْتَةً مَا لاَ مَرَدَّ لَهُ * فَخَرَّ مَيْتاً وَزَالَ التَّاجُ عَنْ رَأْسِهِ

"The inhabitant of this palace[706] had been happy * in a protected life, the people being in fear of his might.
Yet while he was delighted by its pleasure, * enjoying the company of his entourage in entertaining gatherings,
Suddenly something which cannot be averted (i.e. Fate) came upon him, * and he fell down dead, the crown sliding from his head".[707]

183

LOCATION. Ṭabaristān.
DATE and PERSON BURIED. Unknown.
SOURCE. IRaǧAhwāl p. 191.

705 I.e. at the height of power.

706 This poem would make for a perfect epitaph if it was to start with the words *qad kāna ṣāḥibu hāḏā l-qabri* ... instead.

707 MaqqNafḥ VII p. 83.

DESCRIPTION. "From the *Kitāb al-ʿAǧāʾib* of Yaškūr al-Ḥāfiẓ: 'On a tomb in Ṭabaristān could be read inscribed: [...]'". – Three verses in the metre *muǧtaṯṯ*:

*ʾa-mā tarawna maḥallī * ġadan taṣīrūna miṯlī*
*ʾablā t-turābu šabābī * wa-kullakum sawfa tublī*
*sabīlukum ka-sabīlī * sabīlu man kāna qablī*

"Don't you see my place (of rest)? * Tomorrow you will become like me!
The earth has made my youth decay, * and surely it will make decay all of you!
Your way is like my way, * the way of those who came before me".

NOTE. The text as printed in IRaǧAhwāl is corrupt in various places and has been tacitly corrected in the quotation above. The ideas conveyed in this epitaph are familiar enough also to the Western reader; a number of other epitaphs play with the same theme (see **181** and **213**).[708]

184

LOCATION. Near aṭ-Ṭāʾif. DATE. Second century H (?).
PERSON BURIED. Unknown.
SOURCES. IADunyāQubūr (A) p. 163; IRaǧAhwāl p. 190.
DESCRIPTION. ʿAmr b. Sayf al-Makkī was on his way to aṭ-Ṭāʾif when his camel went astray. Having reached a well in the wilderness, "far from any human presence and only rarely visited by herdsmen or errants", he found a tomb bearing the cited epitaph.[709] After having quoted the line, ʿAmr added, "By God, I wept that day till I vomited". – Two verses in the metre *maǧzūʾ al-ḫafīf*:

*raḥima llāhu man bakā * li-ġarībin wa-qad ʿafā*
*ġabara l-qabru waǧhahū * fa-maḥā l-ḥusna wa-ṣ-ṣafā*

1 *wa-qad*: *fa-qad* (IRaǧAhwāl). – **2** *waǧhahū*: om. IRaǧAhwāl.

"May God have mercy upon someone weeping * for a stranger who has been wiped out long ago.
The grave has covered his face by dust * and effaced beauty and candour".

708 *Cf.* also a line in an anonymous poem cited in TawḥBaṣāʾir VIII p. 117 (*maǧzūʾ al-kāmil*): *wa-ʿalimtu ʾanniya hālikun * wa-sabīlu man wallā sabīlī.*

709 Maybe, the area indicated lies close to the Wādī Waǧǧ, to the south-west of aṭ-Ṭāʾif, where today one finds the vestiges of former settlements as well as two old cemeteries, with tombs covered by stone slabs and having one stele each at the foot and at the head, without inscriptions (see Gaube: *Taif* p. 30).

185

LOCATION. aṯ-Ṯaᶜlabīyah (on the way from Kūfah to Mecca).
DATE. 240 H.
PERSON BURIED. The traditionist Abū ᶜAlī al-Māsarǧisī (al-Ḥasan b. ᶜĪsā b. Māsarǧis an-Nīsābūrī, d. 240 H); a former Christian, he had become a Muslim on the instigation of Ibn al-Mubārak (see **101**): TB VII pp. 351-4; TI XVII pp. 134-7; *Wāfī* XII p. 199; NZ II p. 303; IḤaǧTahḏ II pp. 313-5; ŠḎ II p. 94.
SOURCES. TB VII pp. 353f. = Rāġib: *Premiers monuments* p. 32; TI XVII p. 136; IḤaǧTahḏ II p. 314 (incomplete).
DESCRIPTION. Ibn Yaᶜqūb, who was on his way to Mecca with the two sons of al-Muʾammil b. al-Ḥasan in order to perform the pilgrimage, visited the tomb of al-Māsarǧisī and there, he reports, "I read the following upon his tombstone (*ʿalā lawḥi qabrihī*): [...]" (TB); al-Ḥākim (an-Nīsābūrī) said that he performed the pilgrimage with the two sons of al-Muʾammil b. al-Ḥasan. When he visited the tomb of their grandfather in aṯ-Ṯaᶜlabīyah, he read on a tombstone: [...] (TI, similarly IḤaǧTahḏ).

basmalah – wa-man yaḫruǧ min baytihī muhāǧiran ʾilā llāhi wa-rasūlihī ṯumma yudrikhu l-mawtu fa-qad waqaʿa ʾaǧruhū ʿalā llāhi – hāḏā qabru l-Ḥasani bni ʿĪsā bni Māsarǧisa mawlā ʿAbdi llāhi bni l-Mubāraki tuwuffiya fī Ṣafarin sanata ʾarbaʿīna wa-miʾatayn[710]

"*Basmalah.* – 'Whoso goes forth from his house an emigrant to God and His Messenger, and then death overtakes him, his wage shall have fallen on God' (= Q 4:100). – This is the tomb of al-Ḥasan b. ᶜĪsā b. Māsarǧis, client of ᶜAbd Allāh b. al-Mubārak. He died in Ṣafar in the year 240".

186

LOCATION. Toledo (ar. Ṭulayṭilah). DATE. 447 / 449 H.
PERSON BURIED. The Imam Muḥammad b. Aḥmad b. M. b. Muġīṯ (d. 447 or 449 H).
SOURCE. ĠazNatīǧah p. 167 = Inscriptions Espagne 65 = RCEA 2574.
DESCRIPTION. "On the cemetery of the Muslims – may God have mercy upon them! – there was a marble column (*sāriyah mina r-ruḫām*) upon which was inscribed in Kufic letters (*bi-ḫaṭṭ kūfī*): [...]" (ĠazNatīǧah); for the description of the extant tombstone, see Inscriptions Espagne I p. 71 (with plate XVIIc). The literary source yields the following wording:

basmalah. "yā-ʾayyuhā n-nāsu ʾinna waʿda llāhi ḥaqqun fa-lā taġurrannakumu l-ḥayātu d-dunyā wa-lā yaġurrannakum bi-llāhi l-ġarūr" hāḏā qabru l-ʾimāmi ʾAḥmada bni ʾAḥmada bni Muġīṯin kāna yašhadu ʾallā ʾilāha ʾillā llāhu waḥdahū lā šarīka lahū wa-ʾanna Muḥammadan ʿabduhū wa-rasūluhū ʾarsalahū bi-l-hudā

710 The citation in IḤaǧTahḏ is very faulty. He merely reports: "(...) I read on a tombstone: *hāḏā qabru l-Ḥasani bni ʿĪsā tuwuffiya fī Ṣafarin sanata 240*".

wa-dīni l-ḥaqqi "li-yuẓhirahū ʿalā d-dīni kullihī wa-law kariha l-mušrikūna" tuwuffiya – raḥimahū llāhu – laylata l-ʾaḥadi li-ṯamānin baqīna min Rabīʿi ṯ-ṯānī sanata tisʿin wa-ʾarbaʿīna wa-ʾarbaʿimiʾah

"*Basmalah.* 'O men, God's promise is true; so let not the present life delude you, and let not the Deluder delude you concerning God' (= Q 35:5). This is the tomb of the Imam Aḥmad b. Aḥmad b. Muġīṯ who used to confess that there is no god but God, He is unique and without an associate, and that Muḥammad is His servant and His Messenger whom He sent with the right guidance and the creed of truth 'that he may uplift it above every creed, though the unbelievers be averse' (= Q 9:33, 61:9). He was taken (to God) – may God have mercy upon him! – in the night to Sunday eight nights before the end of Rabīʿ II in the year 449".

NOTE. If confronted with the wording of the extant (and edited) epitaph the citation in ĠazNatīǧah shows serious errors. Especially the name of the deceased is completely miswritten; it runs in the original: (*hāḏā qabru*) *Muḥammadi bni ʾAḥmada bni Muḥammadi bni Muġīṯ*. Further below, regarding the date of death, the extant tombstone has: *tuwuffiya – raḥimahū llāhu – laylata l-ʾaḥadi li-ṯamānin baqīna min Rabīʿi l-ʾāḫiri sanata sabʿin wa-ʾarbaʿīna wa-ʾarbaʿimiʾah.*

187

LOCATION. Toledo. DATE. 472 H.

PERSON BURIED. The judge Abū ṭ-Ṭayyib al-Ḥadīdī (Saʿīd b. Yaḥyā b. Saʿīd at-Tuǧībī, d. Toledo 472 H): IBaškṢilah I p. 223.

SOURCE. IBaškṢilah I p. 223.

DESCRIPTION. "Abū ṭ-Ṭayyib underwent trial, his father had been killed and he himself was put in prison (...) until he died. Before that, he had stipulated (*ʿahida*) that he be buried in iron fetters and that the following should be written upon a (tomb)stone (*ḥaǧar*) and put on his grave: [...]. This was then carried out (*fa-mtuṯila ḏālika*)".

ʾin yamsaskum qarḥun fa-qad massa l-qawma qarḥun miṯluhū wa-tilka l-ʾayyāmu nudāwiluhā bayna n-nās

"If a wound touches you, a like wound has already touched the (heathen) folk; such days we deal out in turn among men" (= Q 3:140).

188

LOCATION. Valencia (ar. Balansiyah) (?). DATE. *c*.530 H.

PERSON BURIED. The Andalusian poet and panegyrist Ibn az-Zaqqāq (Abū l-Ḥasan ʿAlī b. ʿAṭīyah al-Balansī, i.e. from Valencia, d. *c*.530 H), nephew of the poet Ibn Ḫafāǧah and pupil of Ibn Sīd al-Baṭalyawsī (d. 521 H): IDiḥMuṭrib p. 100; *Wāfī* XXI pp. 316-26; KutFawāt III pp. 47-51; Nykl: *Hispano-Arabic Poetry* pp. 231-3; CHAL *Andalus* pp. 224-7; EI² III p. 971 (F. de la Granja); ZA IV p. 312. "His life was short but very happy, to judge by his epitaph, which he wrote himself" (EI²).

SOURCES. IZaqqāqDīwān no. 70 (pp. 44 and 205) = Poesías no. 29 (pp. 94f., with Spanish translation); *Wāfī* XXI p. 324; KutFawāt III p. 51; MaqqNafḥ (B) IV p. 340 / (C) VI pp. 72f.; ŠayMaǧānī IV p. 39; Bahǧat: *Ittiǧāh* p. 261.

DESCRIPTION. : "He – may God have mercy upon him! – composed the following, and I think it was written upon his tomb: [...]" (*Wāfī*); "He directed in his will that the following be written upon his tomb, and it was the last poem he composed: [...]" (KutFawāt); "Ibn az-Zaqqāq composed the following, and it is said that it is inscribed upon his tomb: [...]" (MaqqNafḥ); "Ibn az-Zaqqāq recited the following verses and directed in his last will that they be written upon his tomb: [...]" (ŠayMaǧānī, similarly Bahǧat). – Four verses in the metre *ṭawīl*:

*ʾa-ʾiḫwānanā wa-l-mawtu qad ḥāla dūnanā * wa-li-l-mawti ḥukmun nāfiḏun fī l-ḫalāʾiqī*
*sabaqtukumū li-l-mawti wa-l-ʿumru ṭayyahū * wa-ʾaʿlamu ʾanna l-kulla lā budda lāḥiqī*
*bi-ʿayšikumū ʾaw bi-ḍṭiǧāʿiya fī ṯ-ṯarā * ʾa-lam naku fī ṣafwin mina l-ʿayši rāʾiqī*
*fa-man marra bī fa-l-yamḏi bī mutaraḥḥiman * wa-lā yaku mansīyan wafāʾu l-ʾaṣādiqī*

1 *dūnanā*: *baynanā* (Bahǧat). – 2 *ṭayyahū*: طيّة (Poesías, *Wāfī*, MaqqNafḥ); *.ẓinnatun* (IZaqqāqDīwān). – 3 *mina l-ʿayši*: *mina l-waddi* (IZaqqāqDīwān).

"My brothers, death has intervened between us, * but death's is a sentence that is carried out among (all) the creatures!
I preceded you in death and life is herein enclosed,[711] * but I know that everybody is bound to join me (i.e. in death).
By your life, or by my reclining in moist earth (I ask you now), * Were we not (then) in pure, delightful serenity of life!?
So whoever passes by, let him do so with prayers for mercy (for me), * and let not the loyalty of friends be forgotten!"

NOTE. The concept that death will come upon all, poor and rich alike, is widely known and frequent in Arabic poetry (*cf.* above p. 173). For the present purposes, therefore, it must suffice to give just two further illustrations, viz. a line composed by the mystic Ḏū n-Nūn al-Miṣrī (*basīṭ*):

المَوْتُ فِيهِ جَمِيعُ الخَلْقِ مُشْتَرِكُ * لَا سُوقَةٌ مِنْهُمُ يَبْقَى وَلَا مَلِكُ

711 I.e. life is limited from both sides – before and after – by death or non-existence.

"In death all creation has its share: * of them neither a mob nor a king will remain (for ever)!"[712]

Ibn-i Zarkūb Šīrāzī in his town history of Šīrāz quotes the following line anonymously (*ṭawīl*):

تَأَمَّلْ إِلَى مَنْ مَاتَ قَبْلَكَ وَاعْتَبِرْ * فَلَمْ يَبْقَ مَمْلُوكٌ وَلَمْ يَبْقَ مَالِكُ

"Think about those who died before you, and reflect: * No slave has ever remained (alive on earth) and no employer of slaves!"[713]

189

Location. Unknown (Egypt?). Date. First century H.

Person buried. The Ḥiǧāzī poet and ʿUḏrite lover Ǧamīl b. ʿAbd Allāh b. Maʿmar (*c.*40 – Egypt 82 H): *Aġānī* VIII pp. 90-154; TMD XI pp. 255-81; IḪallWaf I pp. 366-71; EI² II pp. 427f. (F. Gabrieli).

Sources. ALL (B) III p. 1115 / (C) V p. 178 (691st night); (Ps.) ǦāḥMaḥ pp. 106f. = Rescher: *Gesammelte Werke* II.3 p. 93 (in German translation); IǦawzīNisāʾ p. 60.

Description. The poet Ǧamīl desired to be buried together, in one shroud and one tomb, with the mortal remains of his beloved, his cousin Buṯaynah.[714] He composed the following verses, which were to be inscribed upon his tomb (*basīṭ*):

*kunnā ʿalā ẓahrihā wa-l-ʿayšu fī raġadin * wa-š-šamlu muǧtamiʿun wa-d-dāru wa-l-waṭanū*
*fa-farraqa d-dahru wa-t-taṣrīfu ʾulfatanā * wa-ṣāra yaǧmaʿunā fī baṭnihā l-kafanū*

1 *fī raġadin*: *fī mahalin* (ǦāḥMaḥ, IǦawzīNisāʾ); *wa-š-šamlu muǧtamiʿun*: *wa-d-dahru yaǧmaʿunā* (ǦāḥMaḥ), *wa-š-šamlu yaǧmaʿunā* (IǦawzīNisāʾ). – **2** *fa-farraqa*: *fa-ḫānanā* (ǦāḥMaḥ); *wa-t-taṣrīfu*: *fī tafrīqi* (ǦāḥMaḥ), *bi-t-taṣrīfi* (IǦawzīNisāʾ); *wa-ṣāra*: *wa-l-yawma* (ǦāḥMaḥ).

"We were (living) upon the back (of the earth) and life was pleasant; * we were joined together, united by household and homeland.
But Destiny and the turning (of Fate) did separate[715] our loving union, * and the shroud has come to join us again in its belly (i.e. of the earth)".

712 Cited in BN X p. 347. In ʿIṣāmīSimṭ III p. 334 the verses are presented as composed by the caliph al-Wāṯiq (var. *al-ḫalqi muštarikū*: *an-nāsi taštarikū*).

713 IZarkŠīrāz p. 101.

714 The accompanying story in ǦāḥMaḥ also retells the story of Ǧamīl, although without mentioning his name; the verses cited in ǦāḥMaḥ are rather different from those quoted in *The 1001 Nights*.

715 *frq* II, *cf.* below n. 766.

190

LOCATION, DATE and PERSON BURIED. Unknown.

SOURCES. WriĠurzah p. 115 (the first line only); IQutᶜUyūn III p. 76; IḤamdTaḏk IV p. 205; MuwMuršid I p. 73; BaṣrīḤam (C) II p. 101 (only v. 1); NuwNih V p. 178 (the first verse only); *cf.* also Volume I p. 253.

DESCRIPTION. "On a tomb was written: [...]" (MuwMuršid). According to all other sources, these lines were merely part of a mourning poem (without reference to an epitaph), possibly composed by Šamardal al-Layṯī (2nd cent. H); Ibn Ḥamdūn has these verses in a poem by ᶜAbd Allāh b. Ayyūb at-Taymī (d. 209 H) mourning Manṣūr b. Ziyād. – Three verses in the metre *kāmil*:

*ʾammā l-qubūru fa-ʾinnahunna ʾawānisun * bi-ğiwāri qabrika wa-d-diyāru qubūrū*
*ᶜammat fawāḍiluhū fa-ᶜamma muṣābuhū * fa-n-nāsu fīhi kulluhum maʾğūrū*
*raddat ṣanāʾiᶜuhū ʾilayhi ḥayātahū * fa-ka-ʾannahū min našrihā manšūrū*

1 *bi-ğiwāri*: *bi-fināʾi* (WriĠurzah, IḤamdTaḏk, NuwNih). – 2 *fawāḍiluhū*: *muṣībatuhū* (MuwMuršid); *muṣābuhū*: *halākuhū* (IQutᶜUyūn), *halākuhā* (MuwMuršid). – **3** *fa-kaʾannahū*: *fa-kaʾannahā* (MuwMuršid).

"Truly the tombs were delighted by * the neighbourhood of your tomb (amidst them), and the houses have become graves now!

His merits embraced all, so now his calamity (i.e. death) touches all, * and there is no one among all people who is not indebted towards him.

His deeds (performed in life) gave him back his life (i.e. rendered his fame immortal) * and it is as if he was resurrected by their being sent forth."[716]

191

LOCATION. Unknown.

DATE and PERSON BURIED. Unknown (but see below).

SOURCES. AᶜAtāhDīwān p. 411; IADunyāQubūr (K) p. 102; *Aġānī* XVIII p. 151; ĠazIḥyāʾ (B) IV p. 488 / (C) IV p. 414 and ZabīdīŠIḥyāʾ X p. 356; IḪallWaf III p. 354 / (Slane) II p. 293; *Wāfī* XIII p. 197; BN X p. 268; NuwIlmām IV p. 203 (anonymous, only v. 1).

DESCRIPTION. "On another tomb there was the inscription: [...]" (ĠazIḥyāʾ, without further details). Nevertheless, it is quite unlikely that the verses cited below were ever written on an actual epitaph. The reason is, according to Ibn Ḫallikān, aṣ-Ṣafadī and Ibn Kaṯīr, that these verses were composed by Abū l-ᶜAtāhiyah, mourning the death of Abū Ġānim Ḥumayd b. ᶜAbd al-Ḥamīd aṭ-Ṭūsī (d. 220 H), and thus certainly not intended as a funeral inscription; according to al-Iṣfahānī, it was Musāwir (b. Sawwār, d. *c.*150 H) al-Warrāq who recited these lines at the tomb of his friend Ḥumayd aṭ-Ṭūsī. This makes sense, and the

716 I.e. with all people talking about what he had done in life, he returned to life. There is a word-play here with *našr* which means either "diffusion, sending forth" or also "resurrection, sending out (of the tomb)".

corruption of *ʾAbā Ġānimin* (ابا غانم) into *ʾa-yā-ġānimu* (ايا غانم) in the "epitaph"-version in ĠazIḥyāʾ neither fits the metre, nor does it provide meaningful wording. – Two verses in the metre *ṭawīl*:

*ʾAbā Ġānimin ʾammā ḏarāka fa-wāsiʿun * wa-qabruka maʿmūru l-ǧawānibi muḥkamū*
*wa-mā yanfaʿu l-maqbūra ʿumrānu qabrihī * ʾiḏā kāna fīhi ǧismuhū yatahaddamū*

1 *ʾAbā Ġānimin*: *ʾa-yā-ġānimu* (ĠazIḥyāʾ, both eds.).

"O Abū Ġānim, vast (i.e. hospitable) was your court, * and the sides of your tomb are peopled (with visitors), (its stones are) neatly set.
But of no use to the buried one is the gathering of people at his tomb * if in it his body disintegrates (more and more)".

NOTE. The "peopling" of the tomb – i.e. large numbers of visitors – is a frequent topos in mourning poetry. Interesting in this regard are the verses by Abū Tammām in which he mourns the death of Muḥammad b. al-Faḍl al-Ḥimyarī (*ḫafīf*):

وَتَبَدَّلْتَ مَنْزِلاً ظَاهِرَ الجَد * بِ يُسَمَّى مُقَطِّعَ الأَسْبَابِ
مَنْزِلاً مُوحِشاً وَإِنْ كَانَ مَعْ * مُوراً بِجُلِّ الصَّدِيقِ وَالأَحْبَابِ

"You took in exchange a dwelling of outer barren- * ness called 'the cutter of ties (*or* relations)',[717]
A desolate dwelling even though peopled * by a mass of (mourning) friends and loved ones".[718]

The notion of "peopling" or "inhabiting" a place (*ʿmr* I/II) is similarly employed in a famous line by Abū Nuwās, from a poem of his mourning the death of the caliph al-Amīn (or, according to others, of Muḥammad b. Zubaydah). Ṭāhā Ḥusayn remarked when quoting the poem, "I believe that Abū Nuwās was never sincere in his mourning poetry except in one case, namely when he mourned al-Amīn"[719] (*ṭawīl*):

لَئِنْ عُمِّرَتْ دُورٌ بِمَنْ لاَ أَوَدُّهُ * لَقَدْ عُمِّرَتْ مِمَّنْ أُحِبُّ المَقَابِرُ

"Even if houses are peopled[720] with those whom I do not like, * (at least) the cemeteries have been peopled with those whom I love".[721]

717 *Cf.* Q 2:166: *wa-raʾaw l-ʿaḏāba wa-taqaṭṭaʿat bihimu l-ʾasbāb* ("And they see the chastisement, and their cords are cut asunder").

718 ATamDīwān IV p. 45 (var. *bi-ǧulli*: *bi-ḥilli*); NuwNih V p. 200; ŠayMaǧānī VI p. 226. See also *The Diwan of Abū Tammām Habīb ibn Aus al Tāi from the text of Abū Zakarīya Yahya ibn ʿAli al-Khatīb al- Tibrīzi (d. 512 a.h.), translated by Arthur Wormhoudt*, William Penn College 1974, p. 56.

719 Ḥusayn: *al-Adab al-ʿarabī* II p. 229.

720 Another possible reading is *ʿamirat*, "are peopled".

721 ANuwDīwān I p. 299; IDāʾūdZahrah p. 366 (var. *ʾawadduhū*: *ʾuḥibbuhū*); ZawzḤam I p. 194

192

LOCATION, DATE and PERSON BURIED. Unknown.

SOURCES. AᶜAtāhDīwān p. 96; IADunyāQubūr (K) p. 102; ĠazIḥyāʾ (B) IV pp. 487f. / (C) IV p. 414 = ZabīdīŠIḥyāʾ X p. 356; IḪarrāṭᶜĀqibah p. 116; ŠarŠMaq I p. 177; MuwMuršid I p. 70; ḤurRawḍ p. 26; ŠayMağānī II p. 37; al-Amīn: *Aʿyān aš-Šīʿah* XIV p. 159; al-Lawāsānī: *Kaškūl* p. 239 = Marzolph: *Buhlūl* p. 63 (no. 108, in German translation); al-ᶜAffānī: *Sakb* II p. 531.

DESCRIPTION. "On a tomb was written: [...]" (ĠazIḥyāʾ and ŠarŠMaq, similarly al-MuwMuršid and ŠayMağānī); without further comment IḪarrāṭᶜĀqibah and ḤurRawḍ, but with a third line[722] added in the latter citation; the lines are also recorded as being by Abū l-ᶜAtāhiyah. In some further sources (al-Amīn: *Aʿyān aš-Šīʿah*; al-Lawāsānī: *Kaškūl*), the distich is recorded as poetry recited by Buhlūl when he visited a cemetery in Kūfah. – Two verses in the metre *ṭawīl*:

*tunāğīka ʾağdāṯun wa-hunna ṣumūtū * wa-sukkānuhā taḥta t-turābi ḫufūtū*
*ʾa-yā-ğāmiʿa d-dunyā li-ġayri balāġihī * li-man tağmaʿu d-dunyā wa-ʾanta tamūtū*

1 *tunāğīka*: *tunādīka* (al-Amīn: *Aʿyān aš-Šīʿah*, al-Lawāsānī: *Kaškūl*); *ʾağdāṯun*: *ʾaḥdāṯun* (ĠazIḥyāʾ [C], al-Amīn: *Aʿyān aš-Šīʿah*; makes little sense), *ʾamwātun* (ḤurRawḍ); *ṣumūtū*: *ṣuʿūtū* (misprint, IḪarrāṭᶜĀqibah); *sukūtū* (ŠarŠMaq, MuwMuršid, ḤurRawḍ, ŠayMağānī, al-ᶜAffānī); *wa-sukkānuhā*: *wa-ʾarbābuhā* (al-Amīn: *Aʿyān aš-Šīʿah*, al-Lawāsānī: *Kaškūl*). – **2** *ʾa-yā*: *fa-yā* (al-Amīn: *Aʿyān aš-Šīʿah*, al-Lawāsānī: *Kaškūl*); *li-ġayri balāġihī*: *ḥarīṣan li-ġayrihī* (al-Amīn: *Aʿyān aš-Šīʿah*, al-Lawāsānī: *Kaškūl*); *balāġihī*: *balāġatin* (ŠarŠMaq, MuwMuršid, ḤurRawḍ, ŠayMağānī, al-ᶜAffānī).

"Tombs confide to you (a message), though they are silent * and their occupants under the earth haved ceased to speak:[723]
O you accumulating wordly goods beyond your needs: * for whom do you accumulate worldly goods when you are going to die (anyway)?"

193

LOCATION. Unknown (Ḫurāsān, maybe Marw, or Siğistān?).

DATE. *c.*180 H.

PERSON BURIED. The poet Abū l-Hindī Ġālib b. ᶜAbd al-Quddūs [or b. Ribᶜī] (d. *c.*180 H), allegedly the first among the Muslim poets to have composed a certain kind of wine poetry (*waṣf al-ḫamr*): IMuᶜtṬab pp. 136-43; *Aġānī* XX pp. 329-34; KutFawāt III pp. 169-71; GAS II p. 473; ZA V p. 114.

SOURCES. IMuᶜtṬab p. 138; *Aġānī* XX p. 332 (only v. 1 and 3); KutFawāt III p. 171 = al-ᶜAffānī: *Sakb* I p. 517 (only vv. 1 and 3); ZA V p. 114 note 1 (central column, only verse 1); *cf.* also Heine: *Wein und Tod* p 120.

(var. *ʾawadduhū*: *ʾuḥibbuhū*); NuwNih V p. 164 (var. *ʾawadduhū*: *nuḥibbuhū* and *ʾuḥibbuhū*: *nuḥibbuhū*).

722 Namely *wa-ʾannakumū ʾiḏ mā ʿalaynā tusallimū * naruddu ʿalaykum wa-l-lisānu ṣamūtū*, "And you, if you greet us, * we reply to you though our tongue is silent".

723 *Cf.* note to epitaph **14**.

DESCRIPTION. Ṣadaqah b. Ibrāhīm al-Bakrī, a companion of Abū l-Hindī (who accidentally strangled himself after a night of wine-drinking), went to the latter's tomb and found the following verses inscribed. In spite of Ġālib's drunken death, young men would gather at his tomb, drink together and pour a cup on his grave.[724] – Three verses in the metre *ramal*:

*iǧʿalū ʾin mittu yawman kafanī * waraqa l-karmi wa-qabrī l-miʿṣarah*
*wa-dfinūnī wa-dfinū r-rāḥa maʿī * wa-ǧʿalū l-ʾaqdāḥa ḥawla l-maqburah*
*ʾinnanī ʾarǧū mina llāhi ġadan * baʿda šurbi r-rāḥi ḥusna l-maġfirah*

1 *al-miʿṣarah*: *miʿṣarah* (IMuʿtṬab and ZA).

"When I am dead one day, do make my shroud * from the leaves of the vine and my tomb the wine press!
Bury me and bury the wine with me, * put the (drinking) cups around the tomb!
Tomorrow I hope from God – * after drinking wine (today) – the benefaction of pardon".

NOTE. Peter Heine in his study of the role of death and dying in wine-poetry cites, in German translation, three lines composed by Abū ʿAlī Bakr b. Ḫāriǧah al-Warrāq from Kūfah (d. during the caliphate of al-Maʾmūn), who in his short poem asks to be washed with wine after his death and to be interred in the courtyard of an inn.[725] Moreover, the epitaph of Abū l-Hindī recalls several well-known verses in which poets of the early Abbasid period expressed their desire to be buried by or under a grapevine. The verse by Abū l-Miḥǧan (already cited above p. 185) runs:

"After my death bury me by a grapevine * whose roots after my death may slake (the thirst of) my bones".

This line was, apparently, imitated a little later by Abū Nuwās. His verses show some similarity to the line by Abū Miḥǧan and the epitaph of Abū l-Hindī (*mutaqārib*):

خَلِيلَيَّ بِاللّٰهِ لاَ تَحْفِرَا * لِي القَبْرَ إلاَّ بِقُطْرَبُّلِ
خِلاَلَ المَعَاصِرِ بَيْنَ الكُرُومِ * وَلاَ تُدْنِيَانِي مِنَ السُّنْبُلِ
لَعَلِّيَ أَسْمَعُ فِي حُفْرَتِي * إذَا عُصِرَتْ ضَجَّةَ الأَرْجَلِ

"O my two friends, by God, do not dig * a tomb for me except in Quṭrabbul![726]
(Dig it) between the wine presses among the grapevines * but don't put me near the corn;
Perhaps, I will hear in my (burial) pit * the stamping of the feet when the grapes are pressed!"[727]

724 For this usage, see also above p. 191f.

725 Heine: *Wein und Tod* p. 119. In *Wāfī* X p. 204, aṣ-Ṣafadī describes Bakr b. Ḫāriǧah as an "obscene poet, (...) whose mind was weakened by wine towards the end of his life".

726 A known resort near Baghdad famous for its wine-cellars.

727 ANuwDīwān III p. 265 (no. 230, 3-6); Heine: *Wein und Tod* p. 122 (in German translation).

194

LOCATION. Unknown.

DATE and PERSON BURIED. Unknown (a young man and his female cousin).

SOURCES. ĞāḥBayān I p. 147; IQutᶜUyūn II p. 177 and IQutŠiᶜr p. 492; *Aġānī* XVII p. 236 (only v. 2); TB XIV p. 214 (only v. 2); SarrāğMaṣ II p. 68 = WKAS II p. 478 and p. 1711 (only the beginning of the description); TMD LVI p. 358; YāqIršād VI p. 65 (only v. 2).

DESCRIPTION. Both lines were composed by the Kūfan poet Mālik b. Asmāʾ b. Ḫāriğah (d. *c.*100 H), probably about his wife (or concubine) Ḥabībah bt. Abī Ğundub al-Anṣārī. Apart from SarrāğMaṣ and TMD, the remaining sources do not describe these lines as an epitaph but simply quote them as being from Mālik's poetry.[728] Preceded by a complete chain of transmission, as-Sarrāğ and Ibn ᶜAsākir report from Muṣᶜab: "I read (inscribed) upon two tombstones on two graves (*ᶜalā lawḥayni ᶜalā qabrayni*): [...]". As Muṣᶜab is further quoted, he found a woman sitting at both tombs and learns that buried there were her son and his female cousin who both died young of broken hearts. The woman, like Mālik b. Asmāʾ of the Banū Fazārah, had these verses written upon both tombs, because her son had often recited them while alive. – Two verses in the metre *ḫafīf*:

*ʾa-muġaṭṭan minnī ᶜalā baṣarī li-l-ḥub- * -bi ʾam ʾanti ʾakmalu n-nāsi ḥusnā*
*wa-ḥadīṯin ʾaladduhū huwa mimmā * yanᶜatu n-nāᶜitūna yūzanu waznā*

1 *li-l-ḥubbi*: *fī l-ḥubbi* (SarrāğMaṣ, TMD), *bi-l-ḥubbi* (IQutŠiᶜr). – 2 *yanᶜatu*: *yaštahī* (IQutᶜUyūn, IQutŠiᶜr; TMD in one version: *taštahīhi n-nufūsu*).

"Is it that my perception is covered (i.e. distorted) for the * love (I bear) or are you (truly) the most beautiful creation of mankind?
Of many an utterance the most enjoyable is that which * 'those that describe' (i.e. the grammarians) describe as being patterned according to pattern".

195

LOCATIONS. (a, b) Unknown (probably Iraq). – (c) al-Fusṭāṭ.

DATES. (a) Third century H. – (b) Before 228 H (?). – (c) 259 H.

PERSONS BURIED. (a) Unknown (a male child). – (b) A small child, son of Abū ᶜAr. M. b. ᶜUbayd Allāh al-ᶜUtbī (d. 228 H, see below). – (c) Abū ᶜUmar b. Isḥāq b. Ibrāhīm b. Ayyūb al-Ḫawlānī (d. 259 H; not identified).

SOURCES. (a) IADunyāQubūr (A) p. 166; TawḥBaṣāʾir VIII p. 117 (only v. 1-2). – (b) ḤuṣZahr (M) III p. 852 / (Ṭ) II p. 191; ŠayMağānī III pp. 43f. – (c) Stèles

728 All sources which have these verses only as from the poetry of Mālik also add another line – *manṭiqun ṣāʾibun wa-talḥanu ʾaḥyā- * -nan wa-ʾaḥlā* (var. *ḫayru*) *l-ḥadīṯi mā kāna laḥnā* – and state that the poet composed these lines about the peculiar speech of one of his slave-girls or wives. *Cf.* also Fück: *Arabiya* pp. 131-4 and Charles Pellat: *Note sur un contresens de Ǧāḥiẓ*, in: Arabica 21 (1974), pp. 183f.

Musée arabe du Caire 989 = RCEA 631 = Taylor: *Vicinity of the Righteous* pp. 39f. (English translation) = Volume I pp. 229ff.

DESCRIPTION. (a) Ibn Abī d-Dunyā describes these lines as found on a tombstone; at-Tawḥīdī cites the first two lines as anonymous poetry. – (b) According to al-Ḥuṣrī, the verses were composed by the poet and man of letters Abū ʿAbd ar-Raḥmān Muḥammad b. ʿUbayd Allāh al-Baṣrī al-ʿUtbī (d. 228 H)[729] when a son of his died at an early age. – (c) Preserved as part of a funerary inscription. – Four verses in the metre *maǧzūʾ ar-ramal*:

*ʾin yakun māta ṣaġīran * fa-l-ʾasā ġayru ṣaġīrī*
*kāna rayḥānī fa-ṣāra l- * yawma rayḥāna l-qubūrī*
*ʾayya ʾaġṣānin malīḥā- * tin badīʿātin bi-nūrī*
*ġarasathā fī basātī- * ni l-bilā ʾaydī d-duhūrī*

1 *ʾin yakun māta*: *ʾin taku<n> mitta* (RCEA); *fa-l-ʾasā ġayru*: *fa-lā šayʾun ʿan* (!, IADunyāQubūr). This wording is without doubt a misreading by the editor or already wrong in the manuscript. Apart from making little sense, it does not fit the metre, and the emended reading is supported by the remaining versions as well as by a verse by al-Mutanabbī (see ch. 5). – **2** *kāna rayḥānī fa-ṣāra l-yawma rayḥāna*: *kunta rayḥānatī fa-qad ʾaṣbaḥta rayḥānata* (RCEA, does not fit the metre); *fa-ṣāra l-yawma rayḥāna*: *fa-ʾamsā wa-hwa rayḥānu* (ḤuṣZahr). – **3** om. ḤuṣZahr; *malīḥātin badīʿātin*: *badīʿātin malīḥātin* (RCEA). – **4** *ġarasathā*: *ġarasathū* (ḤuṣZahr); *fī basātīni l-bilā*: *fī basātīni ṯ-ṯarā* (RCEA).

"Even though he died as a little boy, * the grief is not little.
He was my fragrant plant, and * today he has become the fragrant plant of the graves,
What beautiful twigs (it has), * shimmering with light!
They were planted in the gardens * of decay by the hands of Fate".

NOTE. In the literary sources only these four verses are cited while other parts of the epitaph (name of the deceased, blessings and eulogies, dates of death, etc.) have been left out. Nevertheless, this is arguably the most famous and influential Arabic epitaph for a deceased child, and a touching example of piety as well. The wording of this epitaph-poem, its wider significance and impact are analysed in detail in Chapter 5 below.

196

LOCATION, DATE and PERSON BURIED. Unknown.
SOURCES. IADunyāQubūr (K) pp. 102f.; ĠazIḥyāʾ (B) IV p. 488 / (C) IV p. 414 =

729 Both editions of ḤuṣZahr have "Abū ʿAbd Allāh al-ʿUtbī" whom I could not identify. However, there are good reasons to believe that he is identical with Abū ʿAbd ar-Raḥmān al-ʿUtbī (for his biography, see *Fihrist* p. 135; TB II pp. 324-6; GAS II pp. 371f. with further sources; Rosenthal: *Historiography* p. 509). Especially the entries in MubKāmil (C) II p. 41, IBuḥtUns p. 91, NZ II p. 253, IbšīhīMust II p. 458 (ch. 82) and ŠḎ II p. 65 (here corrupted into "ʿUbayd Allāh b. M. al-ʿAyšī"!) support this hypothesis, because several other verses are cited there from al-ʿUtbī which he is said to have composed when one of his sons died prematurely.

ZabīdīŠIḥyāʾ X p. 356; MuwMuršid I p. 68. The first line is also quoted in DabMaʿālim I p. 307, yet as an "ordinary" verse often recited by Yaḥyā b. Muʿāḏ ar-Rāzī and without reference to an epitaph.

DESCRIPTION. "Ibn as-Simāk (Muḥammad b. Ṣubayḥ al-Baġdādī, al-Wāʿiẓ) said, 'I went around in the cemeteries, and there I found a tomb bearing the inscription: [...]'" (IADunyāQubūr, ĠazIḥyāʾ and ZabīdīŠIḥyāʾ); "On a tomb was found (written): [...]" (MuwMuršid). – Three verses in the metre *wāfir*:

*yamurru ʾaqāribī ǧanabāti qabrī * ka-ʾanna ʾaqāribī lam yaʿrifūnī*
*ḏawū l-mīrāṯi yaqtasimūna mālī * wa-mā yaʾlūna ʾan ǧaḥadū duyūnī*
*wa-qad ʾaḫaḏū sihāmahumū wa-ʿāšū * fa-yā-li-llāhi ʾasraʿa mā nasūnī*

1 *ǧanabāti*: *bi-ǧanābi* (MuwMuršid, in one ms.), *bi-ʾizāʾi* (DabMaʿālim). – **2** *ḏawū*: *ḏawī* (ĠazIḥyāʾ, both eds.), *wa-ḏū* (MuwMuršid, in two mss.); *yaqtasimūna*: *yaqtassūna* (ĠazIḥyāʾ [C]); *ʾan ǧaḥadū duyūnī*: *ʾallā yaḏkurūnī* (MuwMuršid).

"My relatives walk around the sides of my tomb, * as if my relatives had never known me!
Those entitled to inheritance divide my possessions among themselves * and lose no time in denying my debts (i.e. they left them unpaid),
They took their shares (of the heritage) and went on living. * Indeed, by God, how quickly they forgot me!"[730]

NOTE. This epitaph yields one of the relatively few examples of biting irony in pre-modern Arabic funerary poetry. To pay the debts of a deceased was in general seen as an important obligation for his relatives; of course, as in every society, this was not always carried out to the satisfaction of the interested parties. The dead sometimes appeared in dreams either asking their relatives to settle their debts or giving hints to them of how to raise the sum necessary.[731] That the relatives do not care for the deceased and merely enjoy the inherited possessions is not without parallel in Arabic epitaphs, *cf.* **166**, **179**, **202**, **212** and **215**.

197

LOCATION, DATE and PERSON BURIED. Unknown.

SOURCES. IADunyāQubūr (K) p. 102; ĠazIḥyāʾ (B) IV p. 488 / (C) IV p. 414 = ZabīdīŠIḥyāʾ X p. 357; IḪarrāṭʿĀqibah p. 117; ŠarŠMaq I p. 177; MuwMuršid I p. 71; ŠīrŠadd p. 178; IRaǧAhwāl p. 191; IZayKawākib p. 251; ḤurRawḍ p. 32.

DESCRIPTION. "On another tomb there was the inscription: [...]" (IADunyāQubūr and ĠazIḥyāʾ, almost verbatim ŠarŠMaq and IRaǧAhwāl); "On a tomb was found written: [...]" (IḪarrāṭʿĀqibah); MuwMuršid adds the detail: "in *nasḫ* script".

730 For these verses *cf.* also ZamRabīʿ IV pp. 179f.

731 Kinberg: *Interaction* p. 306.

According to ḪurRawḍ, it was al-Aṣmaʿī who read these lines upon a tombstone. – Differently ŠīrŠadd p. 178: "I read in his hand-writing: [...]", referring to the traditionist and mystic Ḍiyāʾ ad-Dīn Muḥammad as-Salmānī (d. 745 H) and thus presenting the following lines rather as being the latter's poetry, with no connection whatsoever with an epitaph. Yet another version is given by Ibn az-Zayyāt, according to whom these verses were recited by ʿImrān b. Dāʾūd b. ʿAlī al-Ġāfiqī (d. Cairo, see **62**) shortly before his death. – Two verses in the metre *wāfir*:

*waqaftu ʿalā l-ʾaḥibbati ḥīna ṣuffat * qubūruhumū ka-ʾafrāsi r-rihānī*
*fa-lammā ʾan bakaytu wa-fāḍa damʿī * raʾat ʿaynāya baynahumū makānī*

1 *waqaftu*: *marartu* (ŠīrŠadd); *ʿalā l-ʾaḥibbati*: *ʿalā l-ʾaǧinnati* (IḪarrāṭʿĀqibah); *ḥīna*: *ḥayṯu* (ŠīrŠadd). – 2 *ʿaynāyā*: *ʿaynānī* (!, IḪarrāṭʿĀqibah).

"I stood before the loved ones when their tombs were * lined up like the horses running for the wager,
And after I had wept and my tears had poured forth, * my eyes saw among them my (own future) place".

NOTE. The expression "like the horses running for the wager" refers to a saying "applied to (...) persons running a race to a goal, *and being equal*: the comparison relating to the beginning (of a contest)" (Lane s.r. *frs*; my italics), hence it is also said "placed in a row" or "lined up". The comparison refers in the first place to the tombstones which stand in straight lines and "lined up like thoroughbreds". But the comparison is also meant to indicate the equality of all men in the face of death and as such prepares for the message which is conveyed in the second hemistich of the next line.

198

LOCATION and DATE. Unknown.
PERSON BURIED. Unknown (a physician, and see below).
SOURCES. IADunyāQubūr (K) p. 102; ĠazIḥyāʾ (B) IV p. 488 / (C) IV p. 414 = ZabīdīŠIḥyāʾ X p. 357; IlyāsBad I p. 32.
DESCRIPTION. "On the tomb of a physician there was the inscription: [...]". Ibn Iyās describes this inscription as the epitaph of Ibn Sīnā (Abū ʿAlī Ḥusayn b. ʿAlī, "Avicenna", d. 428 H) who was mainly known for his medical works in the Islamic lands; in Ibn Iyās's citation the name of the deceased is inserted in the first line. – Three verses in the metre *sarīʿ*:

*qad qultu lammā qāla lī qāʾilun * qad ṣāra Luqmānu ʾilā ramsihī*
*fa-ʾayna mā yūṣafu min ṭibbihī * wa-ḥiḏqihī fī l-māʾi maʿ ǧassihī*
*hayhātu lā yadfaʿu ʿan ġayrihī * man kāna lā yadfaʿu ʿan nafsihī*

1 *qad ṣāra*: *ṣāra* (both editions of ĠazIḥyāʾ: a short or long syllable before *ṣāra* is required by the metre); *qad ṣāra Luqmānu*: *ṣāra bnu Sīnāʾi* (IlyāsBad). – **2** The second hemistich runs in IlyāṣBad:

وحدّثه بالماء مع جنسه – **3** *man kāna lā yadfaʿu*: *man kāna lā yadaʿu* (ĠazIḥyāʾ [C]; does not fit the metre), *kayfa ʾan yadfaʿu* (IlyāsBad).

"I said when somebody told me, * 'Even (the wise) Luqmān had (eventually) to go to his tomb':
'But where is all that medical knowledge he was praised to have * and his skill with water, his ability to feel with the hand?
Far from it! (Death) cannot keep away from others * who is not even able to keep it away from himself!'"

Note. Luqmān was known for wisdom and longevity, having "the life of seven vultures".[732] For his title *al-ḥakīm* ("the wise, the sage" or "the physician") he was frequently depicted as a physician in later Arabic (and also Turkish) tradition.

The topos of the physician who saves others from death but cannot save himself appears also in Arabic poetry (see **177**). There, it has been expressed in an almost classical mode by Abū l-ʿAtāhiyah (*kāmil*):

إِنَّ الطَّبِيبَ بِطِبِّهِ وَدَوَائِهِ * لَا يَسْتَطِيعُ دِفَاعَ مَكْرُوهٍ أَتَى
مَا لِلطَّبِيبِ يَمُوتُ بِدَاءِ الَّذِي * قَدْ كَانَ يُبْرِئُ مِنْهُ فِيمَا قَدْ مَضَى

"Verily, the doctor, with (all) his medical knowledge and remedies, * is not able to repel something hateful (i.e. an illness, or death) that (suddenly) appears!
How is it that the doctor dies of the very disease * of which he used to cure in the past?"[733]

This motif is also known from other cultures, e.g. in the following ancient Latin epitaph: *Aegros multorum potui relevare dolores / morbum non potui vincere ab arte meum* ("The pains of many a diseased person I was able to relieve; / my own illness I was unable to cure").[734]

In the discourse of the Islamic mystics, the topos of the physician who brings about, or is not able to prevent, death is changed into a completely different image. Thus we read that as-Sarī as-Saqaṭī, the famous third-century mystic and teacher of al-Ǧunayd, when asked how he was, just before he died, exclaimed (*ḫafīf*):

كَيْفَ أَشْكُو إِلَى طَبِيبِي مَا بِي * وَالَّذِي بِي أَصَابَنِي مِنْ طَبِيبِي

732 *Cf.* EI² V pp. 811a-3b.

733 AʿAtāhDīwān p. 29 = ŠayMaǧānī II p. 34; MasMurūǧ (P) IV p. 230 (no. 2554, var. *makrūhin ʾatā*: *maḥḏūri l-qaḍā*; *minhu fīmā qad*: *miṯlahū fīmā*); IḪarrāṭʿĀqibah p. 68 (both lines are completely corrupt there); QurṭTaḏk p. 26 (var. *makrūhin*: *naḥbin qad* and in the second verse: *qad kāna ʾabraʾa miṯlahū fīmā maḍā*); IBuḥtUns p. 77 (var. *qad kāna yubriʾu miṯlahū fīmā maḍā*). According to al-Masʿūdī, Ibn al-Ḫarrāṭ, al-Qurṭubī and Ibn al-Buḥturī, the caliph Hārūn ar-Rašīd recited these verses during his last illness. For other verses of that sort, see MarzMuw p. 532.

734 Geist: *Grabinschriften* 286.

"How can I complain to my doctor about my illness * since my illness befell me thanks to my doctor (i.e. God)!?"[735]

199

LOCATION. Unknown. DATE. Third century H (?).
PERSON BURIED. Unknown.
SOURCE. IADunyāQubūr (A) p. 166.
DESCRIPTION. An inscription as found on a tomb. – Three verses in the metre *ḫafīf*:

*ḏā ʿazīzī daʿāhu rabbun raḥīmū * ġāfiru ḏ-ḏanbi bi-l-ʿibādi ʿalīmū*
*qad ḫalā fī t-turābi fardan waḥīdan * fa-ġfiri l-yawma ḏanbahū yā-ʿalīmū*
*wa-tafaḍḍal bi-ʿafwika l-yawma yā-rab- * bi ʿalayhi fa-ʾanta rabbun karīmū*

1 *ḏā*: the edited text has *hāḏā*, but this does not fit the metre.

"Here is my dearest one who was called by a merciful Lord, * the Pardoner of the sins and of (His) servants all-knowing.
He has been left in the earth, all on his own and lonely, * so today pardon his sinful behaviour, O all-knowing (Lord),
And today bestow upon him Your forgiveness, O * my Lord, for You are a generous Lord!"

200

LOCATION. Unknown (*fī ṭarīqi baʿḍi s-sawāḥil*).
DATE. Second century H (?).
PERSON BURIED. Unknown ("I was told that this was the tomb of a sheikh who died at the age of 120 and instructed in his last will that this line should be written upon his tomb").
SOURCE. IADunyāQubūr (A) p. 162.
DESCRIPTION. "I read upon a tomb: [...]". The chain of transmission mentions ʿAbd al-ʿAzīz b. Salmān[736] "the worshipper" to have reported the inscription. – One line in the metre *sarīʿ*:

*ʾalḥaqanā l-mawtu bi-ʾābāʾinā * wa-kullu man ʿāša fa-yawman yamūt*

"Death joined us with our forefathers,[737] * and everyone alive is bound one day to die".

735 Quoted in ĠazIḥyāʾ (B) IV p. 483; IḪarrāṭʿĀqibah p. 90; ḤurRawḍ p. 138.

736 A Baṣran ascetic, see IĞawzīṢafwah II pp. 229f. and MunKawākib I p. 359.

737 Or "May death join us ...", though the optative seems not intended here. For this and similar expressions based on *lḥq* IV, see Volume I, Chapter 4.

201

LOCATION. Unknown. DATE and PERSON BURIED. Unknown.

SOURCES. IDāʾūdZahrah p. 366; MuwMuršid I pp. 72f.; IbšīhīMust II p. 459 (ch. 82; only verse 3).

DESCRIPTION. "On another tomb was written: [...]" (MuwMuršid); "Aḥmad b. Ṭāhir recited to me these verses by Abū Tammām: [...]" (IDāʾūdZahrah). Ibn Dāʾūd quotes a poem of seven lines, the verses 2-3 and 6-7 constitute the text of the presumed epitaph cited by al-Muwaffaq Ibn ʿUṯmān, with some differences in wording. However, the verses cited in IDāʾūdZahrah are not contained in ATamDīwān. In IbšīhīMust, the third verse is quoted as anonymous poetry. – Four verses in the metre *ṭawīl*:

*wa-qultu ʾaḫī qālū ʾaḫun min qarābatin * fa-qultu naʿam ʾinna š-šukūla ʾaqāribū*
*nasībiya fī ʿizzī wa-raʾyī wa-manṣibī * wa-ʾin bāʿadatnā fī d-diyāri l-manāsibū*
*ʿaǧībun li-ṣabrī baʿdahū wa-hwa mayyitun * wa-qad kuntu ʾabkīhi daman wa-hwa ġāʾibū*
*ʿalā ʾannamā l-ʾayyāmu qad ṣirna kulluhā * ʿaǧāʾiba ḥattā laysa fīhā ʿaǧāʾibū*

2 *fī ʿizzī wa-raʾyī wa-manṣibī*: *fī raʾyin wa-ʿazmin wa-maḏhabin* (IDāʾūdZahrah); *fī d-diyāri*: *fī l-ʾuṣūli* (IDāʾūdZahrah). – **3** *ʿaǧībun*: *ʿaǧibtu* (IDāʾūdZahrah, IbšīhīMust); *wa-qad kuntu ʾabkīhi*: *wa-kuntu mraʾan ʾabkī* (IDāʾūdZahrah). – *ʾannamā*: *ʾannahā* (IDāʾūdZahrah).

"I said, '(He is) my brother', whereupon they said 'A brother of kinship?', * thus I rejoiced 'Truly so (because) those that resemble each other are akin!'
(He was) my relative in power, judgment and dignity, * even if (different) parentage separated us in our (respective) homes.
I marvel at my composure now that he is dead, * given that I used to shed tears of blood when he was absent (from me while still alive)!
However, the days have all become * marvels, to the point where there is nothing marvellous about them any longer."

NOTE. In the absence of biographical information about the dead man and his mourner we can only surmise that the mourner is lamenting the death of somebody who was neither related to him by kinship nor considered a suitable companion in the eyes of others, yet who was "his brother in spirit"; most probably, the dead man belonged to a tribe, or a family, hostile to that of the mourner.

202

LOCATIONS. (a) Unknown. – (b) Kairouan.

DATES. (a) Third century H. – (b) 374 H.

PERSONS BURIED. (a) Unknown. – (b) ʿAbd Allāh b. Aḥmad al-Muʾaddib.

SOURCES. (a) IʿARabʿIqd (Ǧ) II p. 162 / (M) III p. 250; al-Amīn: *Aʿyān aš-Šīʿah* XIV p. 159; al-Lawāsānī: *Kaškūl* p. 239 (vv. 1-2, with the second verse much differing) = Marzolph: *Buhlūl* p. 63 (no. 108; verses 1-2 in German translation). (b) Inscriptions Kairouan 155 = Volume I p. 569 (vv. 2-3, in reversed order).

DESCRIPTION. (a) The philologist aš-Šaybānī "said that on a tomb was found inscribed: [...]" (IᶜARabᶜIqd). According to the other sources, the first two lines of this poem, spoken by an unseen caller, were heard by al-Fuḍayl b. ᶜIyāḍ (**116**) and Buhlūl when they passed some time among the tombs in a cemetery of Kūfah. – (b) Preserved inscription upon a tombstone. – Four verses in the metre *kāmil*:

*malla l-ʾaḥibbatu zawratī fa-ğufītū * wa-sakantu fī dāri l-bilā fa-nusītū*
*al-ḥayyu yakḏibu lā ṣadīqa li-mayyitin * law kāna yaṣduqu māta ḥīna yamūtū*
*yā-muʾnisan sakana ṯ-ṯarā wa-baqītū * law kuntu ʾaṣduqu ʾiḏ bulīta bulītū*
*ʾaw kāna yaᶜmā li-l-bukāʾi mufağğaᶜun * min ṭūli mā ʾabkī ᶜalayka ᶜamītū*

1 *malla*: *mallū* (al-Lawāsānī: *Kaškūl*). – **2** صديق: صدق (IᶜARabᶜIqd [Ğ]), صديقي (b); *yaṣduqu*: يصدقي (b) This line runs so in those sources that speak of al-Fuḍayl and Buhlūl: *wa-kaḏāka yunsā kullu man sakana ṯ-ṯarā * wa-tamalluhū z-zuwwāru ḥīna yamūtū*. – **3** *yā-muʾnisan*: *yā-mufradan* (b); *ʾaṣduqu*: أصدقي (b).

"[The buried person says,] The loved ones were tired of with visiting me so I was shunned; * I came to dwell in the house of decay and was forgotten!
The living one lies: there is no friend for a dead person! * If (the living one) was honest he would die when he (i.e. his friend) dies.
[The visitor says,] O man of cheerful company who now dwells in moist earth while I remain (alive): * if I was honest (I would say), 'When you were afflicted I was afflicted!
Or someone grieved was blinded by weeping (says): * I became blind from the long time that I wept for you!'"

NOTE. The expression "house of decay" (*dār al-bilā*) is sometimes encountered in mourning poetry, e.g. in a verse by Ibn Ḫafāğah describing the condition of Man and his fugitive soul (*ṭawīl*):

يَخُبُّ بِهَا فِي كُلِّ يَومٍ وَلَيْلَةٍ * مَطَايَا إلَى دَارِ البِلَى وَرِكَابُ

"With it (i.e. the soul) riding animals and camels * trott along, every day and night, towards the house of decay".[738]

And in a verse by Abū Hurayrah Aḥmad b. ᶜAbd Allāh b. Abī l-ᶜIṣām (*sarīᶜ*):

خَلَّوهُ فِي دَارِ البِلَى مُفْرَداً * وَنَاحَ فِي أَوْطَانِهِ النَّائِحُ

"They left him behind in the house of decay, alone, * and the mourner wept (for him, *or* announced his death) in his (former) homeland".[739]

738 IḪafDīwān p. 53 = al-Nowaihi: *Ibn Khafājah* p. 38 (var. *min kulli yawmin*); the hemistichs are partly reversed in translation. The verse by Ibn Ḫafāğah is much reminiscent of comparable lines by Muḥammad b. Masarrah (*ḫafīf*): *ʾinnamā l-mawtu ġāyatun naḥnu nasᶜā * ḫababan naḥwahā ᶜalā l-ʾaqdāmī / ʾinnamā l-laylu wa-n-nahāru maṭāyā * li-banī l-ʾarḍi naḥwa dāri ḥimāmī* (IKattTašb p. 271 = IKattVergleiche p. 224).

739 Cited in ṮaᶜālYat I p. 419.

203

LOCATION. Unknown (Baṣrah?). DATE. 270 H.

PERSON BURIED. ʿAlī b. Muḥammad "Ṣāḥib az-Zanǧ" (d. 270 H): NZ III p. 48; ZA IV p. 324. The famous story of his revolt against the Abbasids is told in all major history books.

SOURCE. TawḥBaṣāʾir VIII p. 141.

DESCRIPTION. "Upon the tomb of al-Baṣrī al-ʿAlawī Ṣāḥib az-Zanǧ could be read: [...]". – Two verses in the metre *ṭawīl*:

*ʿalayka salāmu llāhi yā-ḫayra munzilin * raḥalnā wa-ḫallafnāka ġayra ḏamīmī*
*fa-ʾin takuni l-ʾayyāmu ʾaḥdaṯna furqatan * fa-man ḏā llaḏī min ramyihā bi-salīmī*

"The peace of God be upon you, O best of hosts![740] * We rode off and left you behind (in the earth) as someone who cannot be blamed.

Even if the days (i.e. Time, *or* Destiny) have brought about separation (from you, by your death), * who is there who is safe from their shooting?"[741]

204

LOCATION, DATE and PERSON BURIED. Unknown.

SOURCE. TawḥBaṣāʾir VIII p. 45 = WKAS II p. 1704a (verse 1 and the major part of verse 3, up to *li-Laylā*).

DESCRIPTION. at-Tawḥīdī quotes a story from al-Mufarraǧ (Abū ʿAl. M. b. A. al-Baṣrī, a Shiite poet, d. 320 H), from a number of earlier authorities, according to which an Arab woman searched for her brother who had disappeared – or died – and finally was shown his tomb when she came to a certain tribe. This tomb bore the inscription: [...]. – Three verses in the metre *ṭawīl*:

*ʾalīḥā li-Laylā qabra man law raʾaytahū * yaǧūdu wa-taʾbā nafsuhū wa-hwa ḍāʾiʿū*
*saqīṭun ka-ǧuṯmāni l-ḫalā lam yaṭuf bihī * ḥamīmun wa-lam taḏrif ʿalayhi l-madāmiʿū*
*ʾiḏan la-raʾayta ḏ-ḏulla wa-ḍ-ḍayma qad badā * li-Laylā wa-lam yadfaʿ laka ḍ-ḍayma dāfiʿū*

"Show Laylā the grave of someone who, if you could see him, * (you would find to be) noble, whose heart is obstinate while he is forlorn.

Fallen (to the ground) like a body of herbage freshly cut,[742] no friend walks round him (i.e. his grave) and no tear-ducts flood over him.

So you saw that shame and injury have appeared * with Laylā, while no-one has put shame on you".

740 *Cf.* Q 12:59.

741 Viz. safe from "the arrows of death".

742 *Cf.* epitaph **222** (verse 3).

NOTE. Without further information, and with the hardly adequate notice provided by at-Tawḥīdī, it is unlikely that we will be able to understand the meaning of these verses properly. However, it seems that Laylā is the beloved who did not care for the tomb of her lover.[743] This brings shame on her, whereas other visitors do not incur shame as they are not, like the deceased's beloved, "obliged" to visit his tomb.

205

LOCATION, DATE and PERSON BURIED. Unknown.

SOURCES. MāwAdab (B) p. 142 / (C) p. 107 = (in German translation) Rescher: *Gesammelte Werke* II.3 p. 200; IBuḥtUns p. 64.

DESCRIPTION. "It was reported that upon a tomb was found inscribed: [...]" (IBuḫtUns, similarly though shorter MawAdab). The line does not follow any of the Arabic metres exactly, yet it resembles, but for a few syllables, the *sarīʿ*:

man ʾam(m)ala l-baqāʾa wa-qad raʾā maṣāriʿanā fa-huwa maġrūrū

"He who entertains hope for (eternal) permanence, although he has seen our (state of) perdition, is (certainly) deceived".

NOTE. Compare with that what Abū d-Dardāʾ told the people of Ḥimṣ, "Their dwellings became tombs / and their hope deception" (*ṣārat masākinuhum qubūrā / wa-ʾamaluhum ġurūrā*).[744] See also **29** and **171**.

206

LOCATION. Unknown.

DATE and PERSON BURIED. Unknown (most probably a Shiite).

SOURCES. RāġibMuḥāḍ IV p. 513; ZawzḤam I pp. 225f.; NuwIlmām III p. 170; ʿŪfī-Tarāǧim p. 137.

DESCRIPTION. "On a tomb could be seen (*ruʾiya*): [...]" (RāġibMuḥāḍ); "Some poet said, [...]" (ZawzḤam); an-Nuwayrī quotes these verses as poetry mourning the death of al-Ḥasan b. ʿAlī, whereas al-ʿŪfī cites them as anonymous poetry. – Two verses in the metre *mutaqārib*:

*taʿazza fa-kam laka min ʾuswatin * tubarridu ʿanka ġalīla l-ḥazanī*
*bi-mawti n-nabīyi wa-qatli l-waṣīyi * wa-ḏabḥi l-Ḥusayni wa-sammi l-Ḥasanī*

1 *taʿazza*: *tasallā* (sic, ʿŪfīTarāǧim); *ʾuswatin*: *salwatin* (NuwIlmām); *tubarridu*: *tusakkinu* (Zawz-

743 There seems to be no discernible connection between the woman referred to in the epitaph-poem and the famous poetess and beloved of Tawbah b. al-Ḥumayyir, Laylā al-Aḫyalīyah; the above-cited verses are not in LaylāDīwān and related sources.

744 Cited in IQutʿUyūn II p. 357.

Ḥam), *tufarriğu* (NuwIlmām); second hemistich: *tuğalliya ʿanka humūma l-ḥazanī* (ʿŪfīTarāğim). – **2** *al-waṣīyi*: *ar-raḍīyi* (ʿŪfīTarāğim); *wa-ḏabḥi*: *wa-qatli* (NuwIlmām).

"Take comfort because how many examples * – that chill the burning sentiment of your grief – do you possess
In the death of the Prophet,[745] the killing of the trustee (i.e. ʿAlī), * the slaughter of al-Ḥusayn and the poisoning of al-Ḥasan!"[746]

207

Location, Date and Person buried. Unknown.

Sources. ṬurṭSirāğ p. 26; MuwMuršid I p. 68; YāqBuldān III p. 288 = al-Ğubūrī: *Muʿğam* p. 838; al-ʿAffānī: *Sakb* II p. 487.

Description. "Upon another tomb was found written: [...]" (MuwMuršid). Following aṭ-Ṭurṭūšī, this distich was inscribed in a royal palace, and according to Yāqūt, these lines were found inscribed upon a ruined house in the Suwayqat ʿAbd al-Wahhāb in Baghdad. The modern author al-ʿAffānī mentions both verses as a distich composed by Maḥmūd al-Warrāq. – Two verses in the metre *basīṭ*:

*hāḏī manāzilu ʾaqwāmin ʿahidtuhumū * fī ẓilli ʿayšin ʿağībin mā lahū ḫaṭarū*
*ṣāḥat bihim ḥādiṯātu d-dahri fa-rtaḥalū * ʾilā l-qubūri fa-lā ʿaynun wa-lā ʾaṯarū*

1 *fī ẓilli ʿayšin ʿağībin*: *fī ḫafḍi ʿayšin nafīsin* (ṬurṭSirāğ), *fī raġdi ʿayšin raġībin* (YāqBuldān, al-ʿAffānī). – **2** *ḥādiṯātu*: *nāʾibātu* (ṬurṭSirāğ, YāqBuldān, al-ʿAffānī); *fa-rtaḥalū*: *fa-nqalabū* (ṬurṭSirāğ, al-ʿAffānī).

"These are dwellings of kinsfolk that I knew well (*or* frequented) * under the protection of (lit. in the shadow of) a life of marvels without any peril.[747]
Then the accidents of Time called them and they departed * for the tombs (leaving behind) neither substance nor trace (i.e. nothing at all)".

Note. The meaning of the term *ʿayn* in the expression *lā ʿaynun wa-lā ʾaṯarun* is not easy to determine. Although it might mean "property" or "material wealth" – if we disallow the literal meaning "eye" in this context –, it probably refers here to the substance or essence of a thing, or a person. There is parallel use of that expression in YāqBuldān III p. 284 (*s.v.* "Sūq al-ʿAṭš) which points in that direction: *wa-hāḏā kulluhū l-ʾāna ḫarābun lā ʿaynun wa-lā ʾaṯarun wa-lā ʾaḥadun min ʾahli Baġdāda yaʿrifu mawḍiʿahū* ("Today, this is all destroyed, with none [of its] substance [left] and without trace, and no inhabitant of Baghdad knows its location"). The expression

745 *Cf.* note to epitaph **97**.

746 al-Ḥasan was purportedly poisoned by his wife Ğaʿdah bt. al-Ašʿaṯ b. Qays al-Kindī, on the instigation of the Umayyad Yazīd b. Muʿāwiyah, see ZamRabīʿ IV pp. 208f.; IĞawzīṢafwah I p. 329; NuwIlmām VI p. 169; MunKawākib I p. 139.

747 Or maybe "a life of marvels which they thought little of".

is also common in poetry.[748] Especially a line by aš-Šarīf ar-Raḍīy is important in our context (*ramal*):

أَيْنَ مَنْ كَانَ قَبْلَنَا * ذَهَبَ الشَّخْصُ وَالأَثَرْ

"Where are those who were before us? * The person has gone and the trace".[749]

Here, it seems, *šaḫṣ* is used as a synonym for *ʿayn* which would then refer to a person's "inner" substance or also to his personality. Thus *ʿayn*, "substance, essence", might mean "personality" or "individual" if applied to a person. The term *ʾaṯar*, on the other hand, contrasts with *ʿayn* as does outer form with inner substance. In some mystical poems by ᶜAbd al-Ġanīy (Ibn) an-Nābulusī, *ʿayn* stands for the eternal essence of Being and the Divine reality, whereas the opposed term *ʾaṯar* stands for matter and the ephimeral universe of created things.[750]

208

Location, Date and Person buried. Unknown.
Source. ṬurṭSirāğ p. 14.
Description. "At the top of a tomb was found inscribed: [...]".

qaharanā man qaharanā fa-ṣirnā li-n-nāẓirīna ʿibratan

"He that subdued us subdued us, thus we became a warning lesson for the onlookers".

Cf. also above **14** and **31**.

209

Location and Date. Unknown.
Person buried. Unknown.
Sources. TMD VI p. 347 (vv. 1 and 3-4); BN X p. 144; IRağLaṭāʾif p. 315.
Description. "On a tomb was found inscribed of poetry: [...]" (IRağLaṭāʾif). According to Ibn ᶜAsākir (TMD) and Ibn Kaṯīr (BN), these lines were recited, or composed, by Ibrāhīm b. Adham (see **233**). – Four verses in the metre *ṭawīl*:

748 *Cf.* the lines cited in al-Ğubūrī: *Muʿğam* p. 837 and YāqBuldān II p. 276 (*wa-lā lahū fīhi ʿaynun wa-lā ʾaṯarun*).

749 Cited in NZ III p. 272 (not in ŠarīfRaḍDīwān). The poetry of ar-Raḍīy is conspicuously replete with the expression *lā ʿaynun wa-lā ʾaṯarun*, e.g. in one of his mourning poems: *wa-lam yabqa ʿaynun li-l-liqāʾi wa-lā ʾaṯrū* (ŠarīfRaḍDīwān I p. 498); *cf.* also: *fa-lam yabqa li-l-ʾiṯrābi ʿaynun wa-lā ʾaṯrū* (*ib.* II p. 514); *mā fīhi li-l-ḥubbi lā ʿaynun wa-lā ʾaṯarū* (*ib.* I p. 525). *Cf.* also MubTaᶜāzī p. 270 (in a poem: *lā ʿaynun minhu wa-lā ʾaṯarun*).

750 NābDīwān p. 219 (*basīṭ*: *wa-ʿlam bi-ʾanna ğamīʿa l-kawni maġlaṭatun * wa-abil* (!) *ʿalā l-ʿayni lā tuqbil ʿalā l-ʾaṯarī*) and p. 255 (*basīṭ*: *wa-l-ḥaqqu ḥaqqun qadīmun fī marātibihī * ʿaynu l-marātibi wa-l-fānī huwa l-ʾaṯarū*).

*nadimtu ʿalā mā kāna minnī nadāmatan * wa-man yattabiʿ* [!] *mā taštahī n-nafsu yandamū*
*ʾa-lam taʿlamū ʾanna l-ḥisāba ʾamāmakum * wa-ʾanna warākum ṭāliban laysa yuslimū*
*fa-ḫāfū li-kay-mā taʾmanū baʿda mawtikum * sa-talqawna rabban ʿādilan laysa yaẓlimū*
*fa-laysa li-maġrūrin bi-dunyāhu rāḥatun * sa-yandamu ʾin zallat bihī n-naʿlu fa-ʿlamū*

3 *sa-talqawna*: *sa-yalqawna* (TMD). – **4** *li-maġrūrin*: *bi-maġrūrin* (TMD); *rāḥatun*: *zāǧirun* (TMD, BN); فاعلموا: فاعلم (TMD).

"I repented that what I wrought (in life) strongly, * and (everyone) who follows the appetite of the soul will repent.
Do you not know that the Accounting is before you, * and behind you is a Pursuer (i.e. death) that does not spare (you)?
So have fear in order to be safe after your death, * (yet) you will encounter a just Lord who does not ill-treat (you).
The one who is deceived by his world (in the present life) will find no rest. * Know that he will surely repent if his sandal makes him slip (on the Bridge)!"

NOTE. The expression in the last verse – "if his sandal makes him slip" – refers to the calamity which befalls the unbeliever, or the negligent Muslim, on the Last Day when crossing the Bridge. A poem in praise of the Prophet, composed by al-Witrī (d. 663 H), exhibits this concept in the very first line (*ṭawīl*):

تَكَاثَرَتِ المَدَّاحُ فِي مَدْحِ أَحْمَدِ * عَسَاهُ يُنَجِّيهِمْ إِذَا النَّعْلُ زَلَّتِ

"The encomiasts rallied to the praise of Aḥmad (i.e. the Prophet); * perhaps he will save them (for that) when the sandal slips (on the Bridge)".[751]

210

LOCATION, DATE and PERSON BURIED. Unknown.
SOURCES. IḪarrāṭʿĀqibah p. 116; ḤurRawḍ p. 32; al-Qināwī: *Fatḥ ar-raḥīm* p. 177:
DESCRIPTION. al-Aṣmaʿī said that he used to reflect much about the tombs and found comfort in reading the inscriptions (*kitābah*) upon them. Once he saw three tombs in a row, upon one of which there was an inscribed tombstone (*lawḥ*) bearing the following epitaph: [...]. – Two verses in the metre *mutaqārib*:

*ʾa-qalla li-māšin ʿalā qabrinā * ġufūlun bi-ʾašyāʾa ḥallat binā*
*sa-yandamu yawman li-tafrīṭihī * ka-mā qad nadimnā li-tafrīṭinā*

1 *ʾa-qalla*: *ʾa-lā qalla* (all sources, does not fit the metre); *bi-ʾašyāʾa*: *ʿan ʾašyāʾa* (IḪarrāṭʿĀqibah); *li-ʾašyāʾa* (ḤurRawḍ).

751 Quoted in MN I p. 510.

"Has the carelessness of those who pass by our tomb * diminished by (looking at) the things which did befall us (i.e. death and decay)?
He will repent one day of his negligence * as we have repented of our negligence".

211

LOCATION, DATE and PERSON BURIED. Unknown.

SOURCES. IḪarrāṭ'Āqibah p. 115f.; ḤurRawḍ pp. 32f.; FanSirāǧ pp. 71f.

DESCRIPTION. al-Aṣmaʿī said that he strolled around in a cemetery and found the following verses inscribed upon a tombstone (*lawḥ*): [...]; quoted as an anonymous epitaph-poem, without mentioning al-Aṣmaʿī, in IḪarrāṭ'Āqibah. The version cited in IḪarrāṭ'Āqibah in some points differs greatly from that reported in the other sources. – Six verses in the metre *ḫafīf*:

*ʾayyuhā l-māšī bayna hāḏī l-qubūrī * ġāfilan ʿan muʿaqqibāti l-ʾumūrī*
udnu minnī ʾunbīka[752] *ʿannī wa-lā yun- * bīka ʿannī yā-ṣāḥi miṯlu ḫabīrī*
*ʾana maytun kamā tarānī ṭarīḥun * bayna ʾaṭbāqi ǧandalin wa-ṣuḫūrī*
*ʾana fī bayti ġurbatin wa-nfirādin * maʿa qurbī min ǧīratī wa-ʿašīrī*
*laysa lī fīhi muʾnisun ġayru saʿyin * min ṣalāḥin saʿaytuhū ʾaw fuǧūrī*
*fa-kaḏā ʾanta fa-ttaʿiẓ bī wa-ʾillā * ṣirta miṯlī rahīna yawmi n-nušūrī*

1 *al-māšī*: *al-mārru* (IḪarrāṭ'Āqibah); *hāḏī*: *hāḏihī* (IḪarrāṭ'Āqibah, does not fit the metre); *ʿan muʿaqqibāti l-ʾumūrī*: *ʿan ḥaqīqati l-maqbūrī* (IḪarrāṭ'Āqibah). – **2** *ʿannī yā-ṣāḥi*: *al-yawma ʿannī* (IḪarrāṭ'Āqibah). – *ǧandalin*: رضمة (?, IḪarrāṭ'Āqibah). – **4** *maʿa qurbī min*: *maʿa ʾannī bayna* (FanSirāǧ, does not fit the metre). – **5** *saʿyin*: *saʿyī* (IḪarrāṭ'Āqibah). – **6** *fa-kaḏā*: *wa-kaḏā* (IḪarrāṭ'Āqibah); *fa-ttaʿiẓ bī*: *fa-ʿtabir* (ḤurRawḍ, does not fit the metre); *ṣirta miṯlī rahīna yawmi n-nušūrī*: *fa-qad yurā minka l-ġadāta naḏīrī* (IḪarrāṭ'Āqibah).

"O wanderer among these tombs, * heedless of how matters will turn out in the end (*or* of the unending change of matters in time),
Come near me, so that I can tell you about me (i.e. about my condition), and there is no * other comparably expert, O my friend, to tell you about me:
I am dead, as you see me now, thrown down * between layers of stones and rocks.
I am in an abode (lit. house) of estrangement and loneliness * although I am near to my neighbours and fellows.
In that abode I have nothing to keep me company except the deeds (I have wrought in life), * no matter whether my acts resulted in righteousness or iniquity.
You are in the same condition, thus be warned by me (i.e. my example)! And if you are not – * (nevertheless), like me you are a pledge of the Day of Resuscitation!"

NOTE. The topos that the dead is only "accompanied" by the deeds or the "works" (*al-ʿamal*) he performed during his life (verse 5), and will be judged according to their value on Judgment Day, is common in epitaphs (see **101**, **211** and **233**) and mourning poetry. However, the wording found here certainly echoes two Qurʾānic

752 In all printed eds. أنبئك, but this falls short of the required metre.

verses: *That a man shall have to his account only as he has laboured * and that his labouring shall surely be seen* (Q 53:39f.: *wa-ʾanna laysa li-l-ʾinsāni ʾillā mā saʿā * wa-ʾanna saʿyahū sawfa yurā*). The concept is also expressed in a number of Prophetical Traditions, e.g. the following: "The dead man is followed (to his grave) by three things, viz. his family, his possessions and his works. Yet two (of these) return and only one remains then (with the deceased), for his family and his possessions return and his works remain (with him)".[753]

212

LOCATION, DATE and PERSON BURIED. Unknown.

SOURCES. IḪarrāṭʿĀqibah p. 50; QurṭTaḏk p. 88; FanSirāǧ pp. 189f.

DESCRIPTION. "On a tomb was found inscribed: [...]" (FanSirāǧ). In IḪarrāṭʿĀqibah and QurṭTaḏk, these lines are cited as a poem by an unknown author, without reference to an epitaph. – Six verses in the metre *sarīʿ*:

*ʾaslamanī l-ʾahlu bi-baṭni ṯ-ṯarā * wa-nṣarafū ʿannī fa-yā-waḥšatā*
*wa-ġādarūnī muʿdiman bāʾisan * fa-mā yubaddā*[754] *l-yawma ʾillā l-bukā*
*wa-kullu mā kāna ka-ʾan lam yakun * wa-kullu mā ḥaḏartuhū qad ʾatā*
*wa-ḏākumu l-maǧmūʿu wa-l-muqtanā * qad ṣāra fī kaffī ka-miṯli l-habā*
*wa-lam ʾaǧid lī muʾnisan hāhunā * ġayra fuǧūrin kāna lī ʾaw ḫanā*
*fa-law tarānī ʾaw tarā ḥālatī * bakayta lī yā-ṣāḥi mimmā tarā*

2 The first hemistich is corrupt in IḪarrāṭʿĀqibah; ما يبدى: see note 757; *al-yawma*: *al-qawmu* (IḪarrāṭʿĀqibah). – **5** *fuǧūrin kāna lī ʾaw ḫanā*: *fuǧūrin mawbiqin ʾaw baqā* (QurṭTaḏk). – **6** *ʾaw tarā*: *wa-tarā* (QurṭTaḏk); يا صاح: يا صاح (FanSirāǧ, misprint); *mimmā tarā*: *mustaʿlinā* (FanSirāǧ).

"The family deposited me in the belly of moist earth * and turned their backs on me, O what loneliness!
They left me behind destitute, wretched, * thus today only weeping is manifested.
Everything which ever was is now as if it had never been * and everything I did beware of (*or* feared)[755] has come.
O you goods gathered and things acquired, * you have in my hand become like dust floating in the air!
I did not find company for myself in here * except the iniquities I wrought (in life) or indecent acts (*or* words).[756]
If you could see me then, or see my condition, * you would weep over me, O my friend, for what you are seeing!"

753 FB 6514 (XI p. 440 = *riqāq* 42); KU 42687 (XV p. 675) and 42761 (p. 690).

754 The edited texts at the beginning of the second hemistich have ما يبدى which is irreconcilable with the metre, whatever the vowels. Perhaps it is *fa-mā yubaddā*, as above, substituting *bdy* II for *bdy* IV.

755 *Cf.* above note 3 to epitaph **177**.

756 The deceased in his tomb is only accompanied by the deeds he wrought in life, see **101**, **211** and **233**.

213

LOCATION, DATE and PERSON BURIED. Unknown.
SOURCES. IḪarrāṭʿĀqibah p. 117; ḤurRawḍ p. 32.
DESCRIPTION. "On another tomb was found inscribed: [...]" (IḪarrāṭʿĀqibah); "al-Aṣmaʿī said that he found inscribed upon a tomb: [...]" (ḤurRawḍ, only lines 1-2). – Four verses in the metre *muǧtaṯṯ*:

*qif wa-ʿtabir fa-qarīban * taḥillu hāḏā l-maḥallā*
*hāḏā makānun yusāwī * fīhi l-ʾaʿazzu l-ʾaḏallā*
*mā kāna lī min ṣadīqin * ʾillā ǧafānī wa-mallā*
*wa-mā ǧafānī wa-lākin * ṭāla l-madā fa-tasallā*

1 *fa-qarīban taḥillu*: *fa-kuntu* (printed: *fa-kāna*) *qad ḥalaltu* (IḪarrāṭʿĀqibah).

"Halt and reflect, for soon * you will settle in a place like this!
This is a place in which the * mightiest equals the humblest.
All friends of mine * shunned me and became bored (*sc.* of visiting my tomb),
Nay, they did not shun me, but * time grew long and thus (their grief) was dispelled!"

NOTE. The concept of death as the force which does away with earthly differences of power, wealth and status among men is a common topos in Arabic funerary and mourning poetry as well as in homilies and hortatory preaching (*waʿẓ*); *cf.* **218** and above page 173. – A closely related epitaph is cited in ŠayMağānī which, however, I could not verify in a pre-modern literary source (*mağzūʾ al-kāmil*):

قِفْ وَاعْتَبِرْ يَا مَنْ تَرَى * قَبْرِي وَمَا بِي قَدْ جَرَى
بِالأَمْسِ كُنْتُ نَظِيرَكُمْ * وَاليَوْمَ أَبْرَانِي البَرَى
قُلْ رَبَّنَا أَلْطِفْ بِنَا * وَارْحَمْ عِظَاماً فِي الثَّرَى

"Halt and reflect, O you who seest * my tomb and what has happened to me!
Yesterday I was your like * and today the dust has covered me.
Say: 'O our Lord, do treat us gently * and have mercy upon bones in the moist earth!'"[757]

214

LOCATION, DATE and PERSON BURIED. Unknown.
SOURCE. IḪarrāṭʿĀqibah p. 85.
DESCRIPTION. Ḏū n-Nūn al-Miṣrī said, "In my neighbourhood, a young man was living who was immoderate with himself and beset by many sins. When once he had fallen ill I went to restore him (to vigour), but I found him already a dead man. He had stipulated that something be written upon his tomb, and afterwards I saw him in sleep and asked him, 'What did God do to you?'. He

757 ŠayMağānī II p. 34.

replied, 'He forgave me'. 'For what reason?' 'I reflected upon my wrongdoing and upon His forgiveness, and I found His forgiveness greater than my wrongdoing!'[758] After waking up, I went to his tomb and I noticed the following inscription: [...]" (IḪarrāṭʿĀqibah). – Two verses in the metre *ramal*:

*ḥusnu ẓannī bika kāna * minnī ğirānī ʿalaykā*
*fa-rḥami llāhumma ʿabdan * ṣāra ramsan* (?) *fī yadaykā*

1 *al-ʾaḥibbatu*: *al-ʾağinnatu* (IḪarrāṭʿĀqibah). The second hemistich does not fit the metre.

"My confidence in (*or* good opinion of) You was * to be my protection from You (i.e. shielding me against Your power).
O my God, have mercy upon a servant * who has become a corpse (lit. a grave)[759] in Your hands!"

NOTE. Ibn Rağab in one of his works quotes a hortatory poem, or rather a rhymed prayer, which also exhibits the connection between the notions of *ḥusn aẓ-ẓann*[760] and the imploration of divine forgiveness (see **15** and **26**) and mercy (*muğtaṯṯ*):

يَارَبِّ أَنْتَ رَجَائِي * وَفِيكَ حَسَّنْتُ ظَنِّي
يَارَبِّ فَاغْفِرْ ذُنُوبِي * وَعَافِنِي وَاعْفُ عَنِّي
اَلْعَفْوُ مِنْكَ إِلَهِي * وَالذَّنْبُ قَدْ جَاءَ مِنِّي
وَالظَّنُّ فِيكَ جَمِيلٌ * حَقِّقْ بِحَقِّكَ ظَنِّي

"O (my) Lord, You are my hope * and in You I put my confidence!
O (my) Lord, pardon my sins then, * and protect me and forgive me!
Forgiveness is Yours, my God, * as the sins are mine;
I think only good of You: * make my thought of you come true!"[761]

215

LOCATION, DATE and PERSON BURIED. Unknown.
SOURCE. IḪarrāṭʿĀqibah p. 117.
DESCRIPTION. "al-Qāsim b. Saʿd said, 'I saw a tomb in a garden full of palms, pomegranates and other types of trees, bearing the inscription: [...]'" (IḪarrāṭʿĀqibah). – One verse in the metre *kāmil*:

kām sākinin (!) *fī ḥufratin tublī ḥadīda* (?) *ğamālihī * taraka l-ʾaḥibbatu baʿdahū yataladdadūna bi-mālihī*

1 *al-ʾaḥibbatu*: *al-ʾağinnatu* (IḪarrāṭʿĀqibah).

758 For this reasoning, see above **26** with note.
759 I wonder whether this is misread, or misprinted, for *rahnan*, i.e. "a pledge (in Your hands)".
760 *Cf.* Vol. I pp. 204ff.
761 IRağLaṭāʾif p. 19.

"How many an occupant in a (grave-)hole, which makes the iron (?)[762] of his beauty decay, * was left behind by (his) loved ones who, after his passing away, are enjoying his possessions!"[763]

216

LOCATION. Unknown.

DATE and PERSON BURIED. Unknown (but see below).

SOURCES. IĞawzīMunt IX p. 69 = Kilito: *Letter* pp. 81f. (in English translation); MuwMuršid I p. 67; QifṭīInbāh II p. 157; *Wāfī* XVIII pp. 20f.; BN XII p. 141; SuyBuġ II p. 67; ᶜĀmKaškūl II p. 162.

DESCRIPTION. "On a tomb there was the inscription: [...]" (MuwMuršid). Substantially different, though, is the information we find in the remaining sources. There we read about the poet ᶜAbd Allāh (or ᶜAbd al-Bāqī) b. Muḥammad Ibn Nāqiyā (410 – Baghdad 485)[764] who not only harboured some unorthodox theological opinions, but had also composed much obscene poetry (*muğūn*). When his corpse was washed after his death, two verses were found scribbled on his left hand, or perhaps on his shroud,[765] beginning with the words *nazaltu bi-ğārin lā yuḥayyabu ḍayfuhū* etc. (as cited below). But there is more: in one of the next entries in *Wāfī* (XVIII p. 21) both verses turn up again, this time with regard to the man of letters and poet Abū Muḥammad ᶜAbd al-Bāqī b. Muḥammad al-ᶜAbartānī (fifth century H) and with the explanation added: "from his poetry we know what was found written on his shroud after his death: [...]". This "epitaph" is therefore a telling example of how uncertain the evidence of literary sources with regard to actual epitaphs is in fact; yet of course, verses could be applied to more than one occasion. The story of Ibn Nāqiyā is amply analysed, and with interesting insights, in Kilito: *Letter*. – Two verses in the metre *ṭawīl*:

*nazaltu bi-ğārin lā yuḥayyibu ḍayfahū * ʾuraǧǧī naǧātī min ʿaḏābi ǧahannamī*
*wa-ʾinnī ʿalā ḫawfin mina llāhi wāṯiqun * bi-ʾinʿāmihī wa-llāhu ʾakramu munʿimī*

762 The word "iron" in this context seems certainly strange, but I cannot think of an alternative based on this root or of another term similarly written in Arabic.

763 The second hemistich could also be read as *taraka l-ʾaḥibbata yataladdadūna* etc., i.e. "(How many an occupant ...) left the loved ones behind who enjoy ...", or as "(How many an occupant ...) let the loved ones enjoy ...". However, for idiomatic reasons and the fact that it is normally the relatives who leave the deceased behind (and not *vice versa*), the reading *taraka l-ʾaḥibbatu* (with *kam sākinin* being the object) seems preferable.

764 On him see IĞawzīMunt IX pp. 68f.; QifṭīInbāh II pp. 156f.; *Wāfī* XVIII pp. 16-20; SuyBuġ II p. 67; GALS I p. 486.

765 The Arabic words "palm of the hand" (*kaff*) and "shroud" (*kafan*) being very similar in writing, it is indeed probable that we are dealing here with a copyist's mistake or a typographical error, see also Kilito: *Letter* p. 89f.

2خوفٍ: خوفي (*Wāfī* XVIII p. 20, on p. 21: خوفٍ; BN, ʿĀmKaškūl).

"I came to lodge with a Protector who will not disappoint his guest, * hoping for my salvation from the Chastisement of Hell.
Despite my fear of God, I trust * in His kindness because God is the most generous of those who bestow kindness".

217

Location and Date. Unknown.
Persons buried. Asmāʾ bt. ʿAbd Allāh aṯ-Ṯaqafīyah and her cousin Kāmil b. ar-Raḏīn, both tragically in love with each other and married only shortly before their death.
Source. IĞawzīNisāʾ p. 54.
Description. Kāmil and Asmāʾ were buried in one tomb (*fī qabr wāḥid*, see above pp. 137f.), and "upon their joint tomb was inscribed: [...]". – Three verses in the metre *ṭawīl*:

*bi-nafsī humā mā muttiʿā bi-hawāhumā * ʿalā d-dahri ḥattā ġuyyibā fī l-maqābirī*
*ʾaqāmā ʿalā ġayri t-tazāwuri burhatan * fa-lammā ʾuṣībā qurribā bi-t-tazāwurī*
*fa-yā-ḥusna qabrin zāra qabran yuḥibbuhū * wa-yā-zawratan ǧāʾat bi-raybi l-maqādirī*

"By my soul! These two were not made enjoy their love * for the work of Fate (*or* for ever) until they were concealed in the cemetery!
They could not meet each other for a little while, * but after they both were struck (by Fate) they were brought near by visiting each other (in the grave).
O for the beauty of a tomb that visits a beloved tomb! * O for a visit that (only) came about through the turns of Destiny!"

218

Location, Date and Person buried. Unknown.
Sources. MuwMuršid p. 83; IbšīhīMust II p. 463 (ch. 83); ŠayMağānī IV p. 38
Description. "A man of some village (*min baldatin*) died, and upon his tomb was written (*kutiba*): [...]" (MuwMuršid); "A man of the Banū Kindah had died, and on his tomb the following verses were written: [...]" (IbšīhīMust, ŠayMağānī). – Four verses in the metre *kāmil*:

yā-wāqifīna ʾa-lam takūnū taʿlamū (!) * *ʾanna l-ḥimāma bikum ʿalaynā qādimū*
*lā tastaʿizzū bi-l-ḥayāti fa-ʾinnakum * tabnūna wa-l-mawtu l-mufarriqu hādimū*

*law tanzilūna bi-šiʿbinā la-ʿaraftumū * ʾanna l-mufarriṭa fī t-tazawwudi nādimū*
*sāwā r-radā mā baynanā fa-ʾaḥallanā * ḥayṯu l-muḫaddamu wāḥidun wa-l-ḫādimū*

2 لا تستعزّوا: لا تستغرّوا (ŠayMaǧānī). – **2-3** Verses 2 and 3 are exchanged in IbšīhīMust and ŠayMaǧānī. – **4** *fa-ʾaḥallanā*: *fī ḥufratin* (IbšīhīMust, ŠayMaǧānī).

"O you (people) standing (at my tomb): do you not know * that the fate of death will bring you to us?
Do not glorify what you reach in life, because what you * build, death, the separator,[766] will tear down!
If you descended into our abyss (i.e. the tomb) you would know * that the one who falls short in storing up supplies (for the next life) will repent.
Destruction (i.e. death) has made us all equal, for it made us settle * where there is no difference between the served and the servant".[767]

219

LOCATION, DATE and PERSON BURIED. Unknown.
SOURCES. MuwMuršid I pp. 68f.; IWāṣilKurūb III pp. 231f.
DESCRIPTION. "Upon the tomb of some distinguished person was found written: [...]" (MuwMuršid). In the account of Ibn Wāṣil, we find these verses – not all of them and partly in reversed order – as part of a poem by Ibn an-Nabīh (al-Kamāl ʿAlī b. M., d. 619 H) mourning al-Malik al-ʿĀdil (d. 615 H). – Seven verses in the metre *sarīʿ*:

*an-nāsu li-l-mawti ka-ḫayli ṭ-ṭirād * fa-s-sābiqu s-sābiqu minhā l-ǧiyād*
*wa-llāhu lā yadʿū ʾilā dārihī * ʾillā mani staṣlaḥa min ḏī l-ʿibād*
*al-ʿumrū ka-ẓ-ẓilli wa-lā budda ʾan * yazūla ḏāka ẓ-ẓillu baʿda mtidād*
*wa-l-mawtu naqqādun ʿalā kaffihī * ǧawāhiru yaḫtāru minhā l-ǧiyād*
*ʾarġamta yā-mawtu ʾunūfa r-radā * ka-ʾannamā fī kulli qalbin ramād*
*ṭaraqta yā-mawtu karīman fa-lam * yaqnaʿ bi-ġayri n-nafsi li-ḍ-ḍayfi zād*
*qaṣiftahū min sidrati l-muntahā * ġuṣnan fa-šullat yadu ʾahli l-ʿinād*

1 *al-ǧiyād*: *al-ǧawād* (IWāṣilKurūb). – **2** *ḏī*: *ḏā* (IWāṣilKurūb). – **3** *al-ʿumru*: *wal-marʾu* (IWāṣilKurūb); *wa-*: om. MuwMuršid. – **4** Lines 3 and 4 are exchanged in IWāṣīlKurūb. – 5 In IWāṣilKurūb: *ʾarġamta yā-mawtu ʾunūfa l-qanā * wa-dusta ʾaʿnāqa s-suyūfi l-ḥadād*. – **6–7** om. IWāṣilKurūb.

"The people are for death like hunting horses: * those that come first and are in front[768] are the thoroughbreds,
While God does not invite to His abode * except those among his servants whom He deems suitable!

766 Death as "separator" (*mufarriq*) is a common concept. There exist various expressions in this regard, e.g. death as *mufarriq al-ʾaḥibbah*, that is, death envisaged as separating the loved ones from each other. See also Abu-Zahrah: *Pure and Powerful* p. 59 and above p. 537.

767 *Cf.* **188** (note), **197** and **213**.

768 I.e. the winners and champions, or maybe the first to the quarry.

Life is like shadow, and inevitably * this shadow will recede after it has spread.
Death is a good judge of value in whose palm * jewels (*or* pearls) lie the best of which he selects.
You abased, O Death, the forces of destruction * just as if there were ashes in every heart.[769]
You came (by night), O Death, to a certain noble person, and * he was not satisfied with anything but the soul as provisions for the guest.
You broke him away like a branch of the Lote-Tree in the Farthest Heaven[770] * and the hand of his enemies[771] was dried up (*or* paralysed)".

220

LOCATION. Unknown (Cairo or Iraq?).
DATE and PERSON BURIED. Unknown.
SOURCES. MuwMuršid I p. 68 note 1 and p. 495; IZayKawākib p. 212.
DESCRIPTION. "A man from Iraq had made the vow to visit the tomb of aš-Šāfiᶜī in Egypt and to recite the complete Qurʾān (*ḫatmah*) forty times at his tomb. He fulfilled that vow, came (to Cairo) and performed the recitation at the tomb. The following two verses speak about that (vow), and it is said that they were written upon his tomb: [...]". However, it remains unclear from this description whether they were written upon the man's tomb or that of aš-Šāfiᶜī. The first possibility seems more likely, given the context, but al-Muwaffaq (MuwMuršid p. 495, citing from Abū ᶜAbd Allāh al-Ḥasan b. Ǧaᶜfar al-Warrāq) explicitly states that the verses could be read "on a stone" at the head of the tomb of aš-Šāfiᶜī; the notice in IZayKawākib is short and yields no details. – Two verses in the metre *ḫafīf*:

*qad wafaynā bi-naḏrinā yā-bna ʾIdrī- * sa wa-ǧiʾnāka min bilādi l-ᶜIrāqī*
*wa-qaraʾnā ᶜalayka mā qad naḏarnā * min kalāmi l-muhaymini l-ḫallāqī*

1 *qad*: om. MuwMuršid (both versions); *wa-ǧiʾnāka*: *wa-zurnāka* (MuwMuršid p. 495). – **2** *naḏarnā*: *ḥafiẓnā* (MuwMuršid p. 495), *talawnā* (Ibn az-Zayyāt).

"We have fulfilled the vow we made, O son of Idrī- * -s (= aš-Šāfiᶜī), and came to visit you from the lands of Iraq!
We recited to you what we had vowed (before) * from the speech of the Protector, the Creator (i.e. the Qurʾān)".

NOTE. The importance of the visitation of aš-Šāfiᶜī's mausoleum prompted many visitors to compose verses to commemorate the occasion. Particularly noteworthy in this respect are the lines composed by the encomiast of the Prophet, Šaraf ad-Dīn

769 A hemistich in another verse in IWāṣilKurūb has instead: *ka-ʾannahā fī kulli qalbin zinād.* But what does this line of the epitaph mean?

770 *Cf.* Q 53:14. This hemistich stresses that the buried person belongs rightfully to Paradise.

771 Literally "obstinate people, people that opposed (him, *or* God)".

al-Būṣīrī (d. *c.*696 H), when he went to aš-Šāfiʿī's tomb and met there the vizier Faḫr ad-Dīn ᶜUmar b. ᶜAbd al-ᶜAzīz al-Ḫalīlī ad-Dārī (d. 711 H aged 72).[772] Two verses in the metre *kāmil*:

زُرْتُ الإمَـامَ الشَّافِعِيَّ وَلَمْ أَكُنْ * لِزِيَارَتِي أَبَداً لَهُ بِالتَّـارِكْ
فَوَجَدْتُ مَوْلاَنَا الوَزِيرَ يَزُورُهُ * فَظَفِرْتُ عِنْدَ الشَّافِعِيِّ بِمَالِكْ

"I came to visit Imam aš-Šāfiᶜī – and I have never * ever stopped paying him my visits –
And there I met our patron, the vizier, paying his visit, * and at aš-Šāfiᶜī's place *I gained the better of Mālik / I found a holder of power*".[773]

221

Location, Date and Person buried. Unknown.
Source. MuwMuršid I p. 71.
Description. "Upon another tomb was found (written): [...]". – Four verses in the metre *kāmil*:

*yā-hāǧirī ʾiḏ ǧiʾtanī zāʾiran * mā kāna min ʿādātika l-haǧrū*
*yā-ṣāḥiba l-qabri l-ǧadīdi wa-man * qad ḥāla dūna liqāʾihī l-qabrū*
*daʿnī ʾuʿallilu fīka ǧāriḥatan * taklā wa-qalban massahū ḍ-ḍurrū*
ǧurnā[774] *ʿalayka fa-ʾin taṭāwala bī * mannu l-firāqi fa-ḥālatī nukrū*

"[The deceased says,] O my friend who abandoned me! Now that you have come to visit me (I tell you), * Abandoning (the beloved) was not a habit of yours!
[The visitor says,] O occupant of the new grave[775] and whom * the grave prevents (me) from meeting:
Let me justify myself with regard to you as (if I were) a woman hurt, * bereft of her beloved (child), and a heart that was touched by the hurt (of loss).[776]

772 *Cf. Wāfī* XXII p. 514.

773 Quoted in ṢafAyᶜān II p. 293 (the lines are not in BūṣDīwān). In my view, the last verse contains a wordplay (*tawriyah*) on the name of the jurist Mālik b. Anas (see **167**). The exact intention of the poet, however, remains unclear to me. The visitation of aš-Šāfiᶜī's mausoleum caused many scholars to compose poems which often show wordplays on aš-Šāfiᶜī's name. See e.g. the verses by Ibn al-Ǧazarī (d. 833 H) containing the words *aš-Šāfiᶜī*, *nāfiᶜ*, *šafāᶜah* and *šāfiᶜ* (IǦazṬab II p. 97).

774 The edited text in MuwMuršid has *ǧuznā*.

775 I.e. newly dug?

776 I.e. "I was too sad to come".

[The deceased replies,] I was unjust to you (by wrongly blaming you for not visiting me), but if the 'gift of separation' * lasts long with me (in the future), my attitude will be one of disapproval!"[777]

222

LOCATION, DATE and PERSON BURIED. Unknown.
SOURCE. MuwMuršid I p. 69.
DESCRIPTION. "Upon a tomb was found (written): [...]". – Three verses in the metre *kāmil*:

*ḏahaba llaḏīna takammalū ʾāǧāluhum * wa-maḍaw wa-ḥāna li-ʾāḫarīna wurūdū*
*yamḍī ṣ-ṣaġīru ʾiḏā nqaḍat ʾayyāmuhū * ʾiṯra l-kabīri wa-yūladu l-mawlūdū*
*wa-n-nāsu fī qasmi l-manīyati baynahum * ka-z-zarʿi minhū qāʾimun wa-ḥaṣīdū*

"Gone are those whose appointed time was consummated * and they passed away, yet for others came the time of their arrival:
The little one passes away when his days are over, * following the older one, and a newborn is given life.
People are in their share of mortal destiny * like the crop (in the fields): part of it is (still) standing, part of it is harvested!"[778]

223

LOCATION, DATE and PERSON BURIED. Unknown.
SOURCE. MuwMuršid I p. 70.
DESCRIPTION. "Upon a tomb was found written: [...]". – Three verses in the metre *ḫafīf*:

*ḥammalūhu ʿalā r-riqābi btidāran * ṯumma wārawhū fī t-turābi dafīnā*
*ʾayyu naǧmin hawā ʾaṣāba bihī d-dah- * ru qulūban mankūbatan wa-ʿuyūnā*
*kam raʾaynāhū muʿṭiyan wa-munīlan * ṯumma ʾaḍḥā min baʿdi ḏāka rahīnā*

"They carried him swiftly upon the necks,[779] * then they concealed him buried in the earth.
What a star has tumbled (with him)! Fate has afflicted * by his death unhappy hearts and eyes.

777 There is some irony here. The last line intends to say that for the moment the visitor is excused for not having visited the tomb but if this should remain so in the future then the occupant of the tomb will revoke the loving bond between them. The topoi of this epitaph are taken over from love poetry that deals with the bond between lovers and the pain (and consequences) of separation if one of them does not care for or deliberately leaves the other.

778 For this expression, see also epitaph **204** (verse 2).

779 I.e. on the bier, born on the shoulders during the funeral procession; *cf.* above **1** (note 4).

How often did we see him as donor and benefactor, * then he became after that himself a pledge (*sc.* of the grave)".

224

LOCATION, DATE and PERSON BURIED. Unknown.
SOURCE. MuwMuršid I p. 71.
DESCRIPTION. "Upon another tomb (was found written): [...]". – Three verses in the metre *wāfir*:

*wa-ʿumrī kulla yawmin fī ntiqāṣin * wa-ḏāka n-naqṣu luqqiba bi-zdiyādī*
*wa-lī ḥaẓẓun wa-li-l-ʾayyāmi ḥaẓẓun * wa-baynahumā mubāyanatu l-midādī*
*fa-ʾaktubuhū sawādan fī bayāḍin * wa-taktubuhū bayāḍan fī sawādī*

"My life is diminishing every day, * and this decrease is commonly called 'increase' (*or* growth)![780]
I am allotted a share and Time (i.e. Destiny) is (allotted) a share, * and between both there is the difference of ink:
I write my share black on white[781] * and (Time) writes its share white on black".[782]

225

LOCATION, DATE and PERSON BURIED. Unknown.
SOURCES. MuwMuršid I p. 80; IḪaṭIḥāṭah III p. 440.
DESCRIPTION. "On a tomb, burial site of a female person, was found written: [...]" (MuwMuršid). According to Ibn al-Ḫaṭīb, these verses were composed by ʿAbd Allāh b. Muḥammad b. Sārah al-Bakrī (d. 519 H) mourning his deceased daughter. – Three verses in the metre *wāfir*:

*ʾa-lā yā-mawtu kunta binā ḥafīyan * fa-ǧaddadta s-surūra lanā bi-zawrah*
*ḥamidtu li-saʿyika l-maškūri lammā * kafayta maʾūnatan wa-satarta ʿawrah*
*fa-ʾankaḥnā ḍ-ḍarīḥa[783] bi-lā ṣadāqin * wa-ǧahhaznā l-ʿarūsa bi-ġayri šawrah*

"Indeed, O Death, you received us kindly * and restored our joy by your calling!
I praise your labour, to be thanked, since * you were sufficient as a succour and you have 'veiled shameful parts'.[784]

780 For the notion of life as a "decrease" or "continuous loss", see above pp. 396f.

781 I.e. my deeds are registered with God in black and white.

782 The obvious implication being that time is whitening the hair during the process of ageing, thus bringing the person nearer to death.

783 Printed in MuwMuršid الصريح.

784 As far as I am aware, this is often, as probably here, a metaphorical expression for a woman being married. However, apart from the literal meaning "to veil the *pudendum*" viz. "to protect the virtue of a woman", the expression *str* I *al-ʿawrah* might also be applied generally,

Thus we gave (her) in marriage to the grave without having received a nuptial gift * and we did not give the bride a beautiful garb as a dowry".

NOTE. This is obviously the epitaph of a woman who died before being married, thus she "was wedded to death" and not clad in her marriage dress but rather in a shroud. See also Volume I pp. 435f.

226

LOCATION, DATE and PERSON BURIED. Unknown.
SOURCE. MuwMuršid I p. 70; see also Volume I p. 202.
DESCRIPTION. "Upon another tomb (was found written): [...]". – Two verses in the metre *ramal*:

*qad ʾanāẖat bika rūḥī * fa-ǧʿali l-ʿafwa qirāhā*
*hiya tarǧūka wa-taẖšā- * ka fa-lā taqṭaʿ raǧāhā*

"My soul has come to stay with You,[785] * thus make forgiveness a gift for it (as a sign of Your hospitality)![786]
It (i.e. the soul) has set hope in You and fears * You (at the same time), thus do not disappoint its expectation!"

227

LOCATION, DATE and PERSON BURIED. Unknown.
SOURCE. MuwMuršid I p. 71.
DESCRIPTION. "Upon the tomb of a jurist was found (written): [...]". – Two verses in the metre *ṭawīl*:

*ʾa-yā-ḥuǧǧata l-ʾislāmi muḏ ġibta baġtatan * ġadat li-l-ʾaʿādī ḥuǧǧatun wa-manāqibū*
*ʾa-lam tara ʾanna š-šamsa ʾin ġāba ḍawʾuhā * talaʾlaʾu fī ǧawwi s-samāʾi l-kawākibū*

"O Proof of Islam![787] Since you suddenly disappeared * the proof (i.e. the winning argument) and the virtues were handed over to the enemies:

to men and women alike, to signify "protecting s.o." or also "supporting s.o.", that is, to ease the hardships of life of someone in need. There are several reports using the expression in this sense, see IMandahFaw II p. 228; KU 16487 (VI p. 449) and 43043 (XV p. 774); see also TMD LI p. 167 (in a spurious Tradition: *qāla: li-l-marʾati sitrāni l-qabru wa-z-zawǧu qāla fa-ʾayyuhumā ʾafḍalu qāla l-qabru*). Interestingly, the concept of *sitr al-ʿawrah* was also attributed to the tomb itself, as becomes apparent from a verse quoted in MubTaʿāzī p. 301, the second hemistich of which reads (*wāfir*): *ka-ʿawrati muslimin sutirat bi-qabrī*.

785 Addressing God.

786 *Cf.* above epitaph **95** (verse 2).

787 A honorific title awarded to outstanding scholars.

Don't you see that when the brightness of the sun disappears[788] * the stars in heaven's firmament sparkle?"[789]

228

LOCATION, DATE and PERSON BURIED. Unknown.
SOURCE. MuwMuršid I p. 72.
DESCRIPTION. "On a tomb was found (written): [...]". – Two verses in the metre *ṭawīl*:

*wa-mā d-dahru wa-l-ʾayyāmu ʾillā kamā tarā * razīyatu mālin ʾaw firāqu ḥabībī*
*wa-ʾinna mraʾan qad ǧarraba d-dahra lam yaḫaf * taqalluba ʿaṣrayhī la-ġayru labībī*

2 The ed. text has *wa-ʾinna mraʾan*, but this makes little sense with regard to what follows.

"Fate and Time (i.e. Destiny) are nothing, as you see, * but a (great) loss of possessions or a lover's parting.
A man, who has experienced Fate (and) who does not fear * the turning upside down of his nights and days,[790] is without discernment!"

229

LOCATION, DATE and PERSON BURIED. Unknown.
SOURCES. MuwMuršid I p. 72; ŠayMaǧānī II p. 25 (with considerable variation).
DESCRIPTION. "On another (tomb) was written: [...]" (MuwMuršid); according to ŠayMaǧānī, the verses were composed by ʿAlī. – Two verses in the metre *ṭawīl*:

*ʾa-yā-mawtu mā hāḏā t-tafarruqu ʿanwatan * ruwaydaka lā tusriʿ li-kulli ḫalīlī*
*ʾarāka baṣīran bi-llaḏīna ʾuḥibbuhum * ʾaẓunnuka tamḍī naḥwahum bi-dalīlī*

1 *ʾa-lā ʾayyuhā l-mawtu llaḏī laysa tārikī * ʾariḥnī fa-qad ʾafnayta kulla ḫalīlī* (ŠayMaǧānī). – **2** *ʾaẓunnuka tamḍī*: *ka-ʾannaka tanḥū* (ŠayMaǧānī).

"O death, why this forced separation? * Slow down! Do not rush to each friend (of mine)!
I see you very informed about those I love; * I even think you are led to them (as if) by a guide!"

788 The jurist bemourned probably bore the honorific title "Šams ad-Dīn".

789 I.e. only after the death of the jurist will his adversaries come to the fore and gain attention.

790 *al-ʿaṣrāni*, "night and day " or also "morning and evening" (*cf.* Lane *s.r.*); often used to indicate "all the time" or "every moment".

230

LOCATION, DATE and PERSON BURIED. Unknown.
SOURCES. MuwMuršid I p. 69; IbšīhīMust II p. 453 (only verse 1).
DESCRIPTION. "Upon the tomb of another (was found written): [...]" (MuwMuršid). The first verse is quoted in IbšīhīMust as anonymous poetry. – Two verses in the metre *sarīʿ*:

*lā budda min faqdin wa-min fāqidin * hayhātu mā fī n-nāsi min ḫālidī*
*kuni l-muʿazzī lā l-muʿazzā bihī * ʾin kāna lā budda mina l-wāḥidī*

"Inevitably there is bereavement and someone bereft, * and Lo!, nobody among men is living for eternity!
Be the condoler, not the one condoled with, * if you must choose (to be) one (or the other)!"

I clearly remember having read these verses in a number of other sources as well but I did not take note. However, they were said to have been inscribed or found inscribed upon a tomb nowhere else.

231

LOCATION and DATE. Unknown.
PERSON BURIED. The emir Abū Isḥāq (not identified).
SOURCE. ZawzḤam I p. 195.
DESCRIPTION. "It is written upon the tomb of emir Abū Isḥāq: [...]". According to the modern editor, these two verses are from the poetry of ʿAlī (*wāfir*):

*ǧamīʿu fawāʾidi d-dunyā ġurūrū * wa-lā yabqā li-masrūrin surūrū*
*fa-qul li-š-šāmitīna binā staʿiddū * fa-ʾinna nawāʾiba d-dunyā tadūrū*

"All the benefits of the present world are an illusion * and no joy endures for the joyful.
So say to those who rejoice at our misfortune: 'Prepare yourselves, * because the calamities of the (present) world circulate (among the people)!'"

232

LOCATION, DATE and PERSON BURIED. Unknown.
SOURCE. YāfRawḍ p. 400.
DESCRIPTION. Some people strolling around in a deserted palace came across a mausoleum (*qubbah*) in its precinct "and in the centre there was a tomb, at the head of which was a slab of white marble (*lawḥun min ruḫāmin ʾabyaḍ*) bearing the inscription: [...]". – One verse in the metre *ḫafīf*:

*ʾana rahnu t-turābi fī l-laḥdi waḥdī * wāḍiʿan taḥta libnati t-turbi ḫaddī*

"I am the pledge of the earth in a burial niche all alone, * under a brick of clay I laid my cheek".

233

LOCATION. Unknown (Syria?). DATE. Second century H.
PERSON BURIED. Unknown.
SOURCE. IRaǧAhwāl p. 205.
DESCRIPTION. "It is related from Ibrāhīm b. Adham (d. 161 H or after)[791] that he read on a tomb: [...]". – Two verses in the metre *sarīʿ*:

*mā ʾaḥadun ʾakrama min mufradin * fī qabrihī ʾaʿmāluhū tuʾnisuh*
*munaʿʿamun yaltaḏḏu fī rawḍatin * zayyanahā llāhu fa-hya maǧlisuh*

2 The printed text has يلثد (?).

"No one is more distinguished than a person alone * in his grave, (a person) whose (good) deeds (which he wrought in life) keep him company:
Leisure is bestowed upon him and he finds delight in a garden[792] * which God has made beautiful, and it is his place".

234

LOCATION, DATE and PERSON BURIED. Unknown.
SOURCE. FanSirāǧ p. 38.
DESCRIPTION. "On a tomb was found inscribed: [...]". – 14 verses in the metre *ramal*:

*ʾana mašġūlun bi-ḏanbī * ʿan ḏunūbi l-ʿālamīnā*
*wa-ḫaṭāyā ʾaṯqalatnī * tarakat qalbī ḥazīnā*
*ṣirtu fī l-ʾarḍi waḥīdan * fī ǧiwāri l-hālikīnā*
*baʿdamā kuntu ǧalīlan * fī ʿuyūni n-nāẓirīnā*
*ṣirtu fī ẓulmati qabrī * ṯāwiyan fīhā rahīnā*
*wa-taraktu l-māla wa-l-ʾah- * la la-ʿamrī wa-l-banīnā*
*wa-laqad ʿummirtu dahran * wa-šuhūran wa-sinīnā*
*fī naʿīmin wa-surūrin * fawqa waṣfi l-wāṣifīnā*
*wa-malaktu š-šarqa wa-l-ġar- * ba wa-kāna l-mulku fīnā*
wa-fataḥtu l-mudna (sic) *qahran * wa-ġalabtu l-ġālibīnā*
*fa-ʾatā l-mawtu ʿalaynā * baʿda hāḏā fa-fanīnā*

791 A Kūfan ascetic who later settled in Syria and was buried somewhere on the Levantine coast, see MaqrMuq I p. 45-90. Interestingly, al-Maqrīzī reports from Ibn Adham other inscriptions he had read in the Syrian hill country, one of these engraved on "a stone" and others on a "great rock which resembled a prayer-niche" (MaqrMuq I p. 88).

792 Either the tomb (*cf.* above p. 50), or also Paradise.

*ʾayyuhā l-maġrūru bādir * li-ṯawābi ṣ-ṣāliḥīnā*
*wa-llaḏī ṣaḥḥa ladaynā * wa-ʿalimnāhu yaqīnā*
*ʾanna ḥayyan laysa yabqā * ġayra rabbi l-ʿālamīnā*

"I am distracted by my sin(s) * from the sins of mankind[793]
And sinful lapses which weigh heavily on me * left my heart in grief.
I became a loner in the earth, * in the neighbourhood of the dying,
After I had been exalted * in the eyes of those who looked (at me).
In the darkness of my tomb * I came to settle in it, being pledged (to it),
And I left possessions and fami- * ly, upon my life!, and the children.
I had prospered (in life) for a long while, * for months and for years,
Enjoying bliss and merriness * beyond imagination.[794]
I reigned over East and West, * the power (of rule) was ours,
I conquered cities by force * and I conquered the conquerors.
Then death came upon us * after that, and I vanished into nothing.
O you deceived (by the world), hurry up to * prepare for yourself the reward of the righteous!
There is one thing we deem true * and know for certain:
No living being lasts forever * except the Lord of the Worlds!"

235

LOCATION. Unknown (perhaps Cairo).
DATE and PERSON BURIED. Unknown.
SOURCE. ZabīdīŠIḥyāʾ X p. 357, citing from ʿAfīf ad-Dīn Abū Sālim Muḥammad b. Aḥmad al-Maġribī al-ʿAyyāšī's (d. 1091 H) *Kitāb ar-Riḥlah* (*al-ʿAyyāšīyah*).
DESCRIPTION. "In the *Travel-(book)* of Abū Sālim al-ʿAyyāšī I found that somebody had ordered the following to be written upon his tomb: [...]. I (*sc.* az-Zabīdī) had them inscribed upon the grave of my wife Umm al-Faḍl Zubaydah, the daughter of the late Ḏū l-Fiqār ad-Dimyāṭī – may God the Exalted have mercy upon them both!" – Two verses in the metre *wāfir*:

*ʾiḏā ʾamsā firāšī min turābin * wa-ṣirtu muǧāwira r-rabbi r-raḥīmī*
*fa-hannūnī bi-ʾiḫlāʾī wa-qūlū * hanīʾan qad qadimta*[795] *ʿalā karīmī*

2 *bi-ʾiḫlāʾī*: *ʾaḫlāʾī* (as in the printed text, does not fit the metre).

"Now that the earth has become my bed * and I will have become the (protected) neighbour of the Merciful Lord,

793 I.e., the sinful behaviour of the deceased precludes taking over sins of others and making them easier to bear. This interpretation can be deduced from what the author says before quoting this epitaph.

794 Lit. "beyond the description by those who describe (it)", i.e. "impossible to describe".

795 If taken as epitaph of az-Zabīdī's wife, read: *qadimti*. However, the masculine term *muǧāwir* in the first verse would not fit a woman, and f. *muǧāwirah* does not fit the metre.

Then congratulate me for my leaving (this world) and say (to me): * 'Be glad! You came to a Generous (Lord)!'"

NOTE. For the expression of the last hemistich – *qad qadimta ʿalā karīmin* –, see also **95**, **103** and **174**.

236

LOCATION, DATE and PERSON BURIED. Unknown.
SOURCE. ZabīdīŠIḥyāʾ X p. 357.
DESCRIPTION. "Somebody else ordered to be written upon his tomb: [...]". – One verse in the metre *wāfir*:

*wa-lam ʾağzaʿ li-hawli l-mawti lākin * bakaytu li-qillati l-bākī ʿalayyā*

"I was not anxious for the dread that death brings, but * I wept for the scarseness of weeping (that would be done) for me".

NOTE. For the motif that the buried person is not, or only slightly, grieved over, see **30** and **72**.

237

LOCATION and DATE. Unknown.
ANIMAL BURIED. A dog.
SOURCES. IMarzFaḍlKilāb p. ٢٣ (p. 18 of the translation); IḤiğṮam p. 127 (citing from Ibn al-Ğawzī's *Kitāb al-ʾAḏkiyāʾ*).
DESCRIPTION. Someone found a tomb in a cemetery which was covered by a dome that bore the inscription (*fa-ʾiḏā qabrun ʿalayhi qubbatun maktūbun ʿalayhā*):

hāḏā qabru l-kalbi fa-man ʾaḥabba ʾan yaʿlama ḫabarahū fa-l-yamḍi ʾilā qaryatin kaḏā wa-kaḏā *fa-ʾinna fīhā man yuḫbiruhū*

"This is the tomb of the dog. Whosoever wants to know what its story was should go to the village *so-and-so* where there is somebody to tell him about it".

NOTE. Unfortunately the dog's story is too long to be retold here fully. However, the gist of the story is that the dog had saved his owner's life, but was killed in doing so: he was quicker than his master in eating a milk pudding which had been poisoned by a snake without anybody having noticed. Although such stories can happen in reality, the motif itself (including the setting up of a tombstone upon the dog's burial place) is a *Wandermotiv* and also attested outside Arabo-Islamic literature, e.g. in Jewish tales. As part of the Talmudic lore it appears as follows (in the translation of Emanuel bin Gorion):

> "*Des Hundes Mal.* Hirten hatten Milch gemolken; da kam eine Schlange herzu und trank davon, und einzig der Hund hatte dem zugesehen. Als hernach die Hirten von der Milch trinken wollten, bellte der Hund sie an, sie aber achteten nicht auf ihn. Da stellte

sich der Hund auf seine Hinterbeine, trank als erster von der Milch und verendete. Die Hirten begruben den Hund und setzten ihm einen Denkstein; den nennt man bis zum heutigen Tag: des Hundes Mal".[796]

Poems mourning the death of animals, or at least verses alluding to their death, are not uncommon in Arabic poetry.[797] A famous example is the verses written by Abū l-Ḥusayn Ibn al-Ǧazzār on the occasion of the death of his donkey.[798] In a similar manner, Abū Muḥammad al-Qāsim, the brother of Abū Ǧaᶜfar Aḥmad b. Yūsuf b. Ṣubayḥ al-Kātib al-Kūfī, secretary to al-Maʾmūn, was a prolific poet and "he had made it his prime occupation to compose adulatory verses about cattle and poems mourning them, and most of his poetry consists of that".[799] A mourning poem for a cat, composed by Ibn al-ᶜAllāf (Husayn b. ᶜAlī, d. 318 or 319 H), is mentioned in GAL I p. 81.

A curious story is the following, related in the *Book of Strangers* attributed to al-Iṣfahānī. It concerns the mausoleum of a donkey:

> "They say that Abū so-and-so al-Madanī was a miser. He would recite, *Say, He is God, one* (Q 112:1) seven times in his donkey's nosebag when it was time to fill it and hang it on the donkey (without putting any food in it), so the donkey soon died. He then buried it and built a dome over it, writing the following on the wall:
>
> O donkey who outstripped all other donkeys and who is now left alone by the flowing water in the grave.
>
> May God recompense you with well-sieved barley fodder and make you dwell in the paradise of donkeys.
>
> When he was asked where the paradise of donkeys was, he said that it was a meadow of clover".[800]

Addendum

A mourning poem of up to 19 verses,[801] ascribed to Abū l-ᶜAtāhiyah and others, is in a single literary source, viz. a fourth-century *ʾadab* anthology, presented as an epitaph (*qaraʾtu ᶜalā qabrin*: [...]). The exceptional length of the poem as well as the fact that almost all sources do not describe it as an epitaph, render the possibility of it ever having been inscribed upon a tomb highly unlikely.

The poem commences with the following two verses, the second already having been cited above p. 397 (*mutaqārib*):

796 *Geschichten aus dem Talmud. Herausgegeben und übersetzt von Emanuel bin Gorion*, Frankfurt 1966, pp. 393f.

797 *Cf.* the editor's note in TanFarağ III pp. 111f. and Wagner: *Dichtung* I pp. 133f.

798 See ᶜĀmKaškūl I p. 38. *Cf.* also ṢafĠayṯ II p. 234 and TanFarağ III p. 111.

799 *Aġānī* XXIII p. 118. For a letter of condolence for a deceased ape, see ḤuṣZahr (M) IV p. 1032.

800 IṣfStrangers pp. 42f.

801 The length of the poem varies a great deal in the sources; see what follows below.

*ʾaḫun ṭālamā sarranī ḏikruhū * fa-qad ṣirtu ʾašǧā ladā ḏikrihī*
*wa-qad kuntu ʾaġdū ʾilā qaṣrihī * fa-qad ṣirtu ʾaġdū ʾilā qabrihī*

"A friend (lit. brother) whom to think of often cheered me, * but now I become sad when thinking of him.
Once I used to come to his palace in the morning, * but now I have to come to his tomb in the morning".

SOURCES. (Cited as epitaph:) MuᶜāfāĞalīs III p. 276 (17 Verses). – (Cited from Abū l-ᶜAtāhiyah, as a mourning poem about one of his brethren or companions:) AᶜAtāhAnwār pp. 124f. and AᶜAtāhDīwān pp. 206f. (18 Verses; with variants and additional lines); QālīAmālī I pp. 276f. (19 Verses; some variants and a different sequence of the lines). – (Cited as distich by an Arab woman:) RāġibMuḥāḍ IV p. 519 (Verses 2-3, with variants). – (Cited as verses by Ibr. b. Muḥammad al-Muʾaddib:) ZawzḤam I p. 213 (Verses 1-2; var. *ʾaġdū*: *ʾarūḥu*). – (Cited from an anonymous poet:) IQutᶜUyūn III p. 10 (Verses 1-4; var. *fa-qad ṣirtu*: *fa-ʾaṣbaḥtu*); IᶜARabᶜIqd (Ğ) II p. 175 / (M) III pp. 269f. (Verses 1-4; var. *ladā*: *ʾilā*); ŠayMaġānī III p. 41 (Verses 1-2; var. *ladā*: *ʾilā*). – (German translation:) Rescher: *Gesammelte Werke* V.1 pp. 109f.

5 "He was My Fragrant Plant ..." *An Arabic Epitaph-Poem and its Intertextuality*

1. *Introduction*

One of the most remarkable Arabic epitaphs in verse, apart from being a touching example of piety and arguably the most beautiful Arabic epitaph for a child which has been passed down to us, contains a poem which the reader, ancient or modern, is unlikely to forget. This epitaph-poem has already been edited in Volume I pp. 229ff. as well as in Chapter 4 of the present book (**195**). The far-reaching implications and intertextual relations of this epitaph-poem are the subject of the present chapter.[1]

In order to facilitate the reading of what follows, I would like to repeat here the text of the epitaph-poem **195** in the form in which we know it from literary sources, without philological notes (*maǧzūʾ ar-ramal*):

إنْ يَكُنْ مَاتَ صَغِيراً * فَالأَسَى غَيْرُ صَغِيرِ
كَانَ رَيْحَانِي فَصَارَ الـ * ـيَوْمَ رَيْحَانَ القُبُورِ
أَيَّ أَغْصَانٍ مَلِيحًا * تٍ بَدِيعَاتٍ بِنُورِ
غَرَسَتْهَا فِي بَسَاتِيـ * ـنِ البِلَى أَيْدِي الدُّهُورِ

"Even though he died as a little boy, * the grief is not little.
He was my fragrant plant, and * today he has become the fragrant plant of the graves,
What beautiful twigs (it has), * shimmering with light!
They were planted in the gardens * of decay by the hands of Fate".

Both the first literary attestations of this epitaph-poem and the extant tombstone stem from the third century H. Unfortunately, the literary sources do not indicate the place(s) of origin, while the tombstone has been found in al-Fusṭāṭ (Cairo). In the literary sources, only these four verses are cited, while other parts of the epitaph – viz. name of the deceased, blessings and eulogies, dates of death, etc. –, also pre-

1 The question of how people coped with the death of children in the culture of Islam, and how this is reflected in Arabic epitaphs and mourning poetry, is dealt with in Volume I, Chapter 3, and hence will not be taken into consideration on the following pages.

served on the extant tombstone, have been left out.[2] Clearly, the Arabic authors were only interested in the epitaph-poem and its message.

2. *Intertextuality, first mode: single verses*

The first line has a close parallel in a widely-quoted verse by al-Mutanabbī, who may have taken his inspiration from this or a similar epitaph; at least this is explicitly said so by al-Ḥuṣrī (*ṭawīl*):

فَإِنْ تَكُ فِي قَبْرٍ فَإِنَّكَ فِي الحَشَى * وَإِنْ تَكُ طِفْلاً فَالأَسَى لَيْسَ بِالطِّفْلِ

"Even though you are in a tomb, you are still in the innermost,[3] * and even though you are a child, the grief (about your death) is not a child then".[4]

Some four centuries later, this motif was also taken up in a poem by Ibn Nubātah in which he mourns the death of one of his children (*kāmil*):

قَالُوا صَغِيراً قُلْتُ إِنَّ وَرُبَّمَا * كانَتْ بِهِ الحَسَرَاتُ غَيْرَ صِغَارِ

"They told me, '(Your child) was only a little boy', and I said, 'Truly, but perhaps * the grief for him was anything but little'".[5]

The second line of the epitaph ("He was my fragrant plant ...") has a parallel in a poem by Sahl b. Ibrāhīm al-Warrāq,[6] a fourth-century poet of the Fatimid period who was active in al-Mahdīyah and Kairouan (*ṭawīl*):

2 The most obvious difference between the verses quoted in literary sources and those found on the extant tombstone is the change from the third to the second person: on the preserved tombstone, the deceased child is addressed directly (*kunta*, "you were", instead of *kāna*, "he was"), thus giving to the whole a more personal note. The use of the second person is somewhat more typical of epitaph-poetry, while the third person is often preferred in mourning poetry.

3 I.e. in my heart *or* inside me.

4 MutanDīwān (W) p. 409 (v. 5) = ṮaᶜālYat I p. 230 = RāġibMuḥāḍ IV p. 529 = ḤuṣZahr (M) III p. 853 / (Ṭ) II p. 192 = ŠSiqṭZand II p. 937 = IḤamdTaḏk IV p. 279; also cited in IAṯīrMaṯal p. 486 and IAḤaǧSulwah p. 128 (anon.) and 140. Cited in English translation in Smoor: *Poems on Death* p. 58 note 24; *cf.* also Ashtiany: *Mutanabbī's Elegy* p. 367. The verse is not discussed in Winter: *al-Mutanabbī's Elegies*.

5 INubDīwān p. 218 = IAḤaǧSulwah p. 138 (with the var. *ṣaġīran*: *tuṣabbir*, which, however, destroys the pun). The line is also quoted in translation, via as-Saḫāwī, in Gilᶜadi: *Consolation Treatise* p. 373 and, from Ibn Nubātah's *Dīwān*, in Bauer: *Kindertotenlieder* p. 92.

6 His identity is difficult to establish, see MālRiyāḍ II p. 112 note 654; *cf.* also YāqBuldān III p. 282 (*s.v.* Sūsah), where he appears as "Sahm b. Ibrāhīm al-Warrāq". He might have been included in Ibn Rašīq's lost *Kitāb ar-Rawḍah al-muwaššīyah fī šuᶜarāᵓ al-Mahdīyah*, and we find two verses of his quoted in BakrīMas II p. 690 (no. 1157, about the city of Sousse).

أَرَيْحَانَةٌ قَدْ صِرْتَ رَيّحَانَةَ الثَرَى * فَأَضْحَى البِلَى فِي جِسْمِكَ الغَضِّ يَسْرُعُ
أَلا بِأَبِي الغُصْنُ النَّضِيرُ الَّذِي ذَوَى * فَعَيْنِي عَلَى تِلْكَ النِّظارَةِ تَدْمَعُ

"O fragrant plant, you became[7] a fragrant plant in the moist earth, * and decay has entered your tender body quickly.
Lo!, dearer than my father is to me this radiant twig that withered away (*or* that dried up)! * My eye sheds tears for that sight".[8]

These verses are particularly interesting in our context not only because they exhibit the image of the "shimmering twig" which already occurs in our epitaph-poem, but also because here – if we are to believe what the sources tell us – the *rayḥān(ah)*-metaphor is not applied to a deceased child but to an adult person who died at the age of 83.[9] More exactly, these lines are said to belong to a poem mourning the death of Ibn al-Ḥaddād al-Ġassānī, a scholar and philologist from Kairouan.[10]

However, it is improbable that al-Warrāq's mourning poem relates to the death of Abū ᶜUṯmān Ibn al-Ḥaddād. After all, the deceased person is addressed three times as "ᶜUṯmān" – not as "Abū ᶜUṯmān", something which the modern editor explains as poetic licence[11] –, and many lines of the poem, including the above-quoted verses, do not convey the impression that the person mourned was an adult. On the contrary, the perspective of the mourner seems to be that of the father or of someone condoling with the father. The poem may thus either mourn a deceased son of the poet himself or a son of Ibn al-Ḥaddād; the latter is known to have lost a young child, on the occasion of which he composed several mourning poems.[12] Still, there is at least one example of *rayḥānah* said of a male adult person, viz. in a mourning poem upon the death of the Hanafite jurist ᶜAbd al-Wahhāb b. Aḥmad al-Farfūrī ad-Dimašqī (1012–73 H), beginning with the words: *rayḥānatu l-ᵓafḍāli ᶜāǧalahā r-radā* ("the fragrant plant of merits, to whom death came too swiftly!").[13] In any case, *rayḥānah* is here not used literally, but in the sense of "the best example of" or "the first choice of" (see below pp. 590f.).

Without having recourse to the *rayḥānah*-metaphor, but still close in meaning to epitaph-poem **195** is a verse by aš-Šarīf ar-Raḍīy, from a poem mourning the death of his niece who had died as a child (*sarīᶜ*):

يَا غُصُناً طَالَ وَفَرْعاً طَابَا * لَمَّا ذَوَى أَودَعْتَهُ التُّرَابَا

7 One could also vocalise *ṣirti* (f.), in line with the preceding *rayḥānah*, but very probably a male person is referred to.

8 MālRiyāḍ II p. 114. For the wording of the second line, see also a verse by the sixth-century poet Ibn Sanāᵓ al-Mulk (*kāmil*): *yā-turbu mā ᵓanṣafta nuḍrata ġuṣnihī * ᵓa-kaḏā ṣanīᶜu t-turbi bi-l-ᵓaġṣānī* (cited in INubMaṭlaᶜ p. 348).

9 The use of feminine *rayḥānah* would not be unusual if applied to a male person (see below).

10 Abū ᶜUṯmān Saᶜīd b. M. (219–302 H): MālRiyāḍ II pp. 57-115; IDabMaᶜālim II pp. 295-315; SuyBuġ I p. 589; ZA III p. 100.

11 In a second mourning poem by al-Warrāq, Abū ᶜUṯmān is called by this very *kunyah*, see MālRiyāḍ II p. 115.

12 ZA III p. 100.

13 MuḥḪul III p. 101.

"O long-grown twig, O scented bough! * When it had withered, you[14] entrusted it to the earth (of the grave)".[15]

The expression "hands of Fate" (line 4, *ʾaydī d-duhūr*) or similar wordings, being primarily a euphemism for "death", are not uncommon in Arabic mourning poetry. It was aṣ-Ṣafadī who remarked that the plural form *ʾaydin* ("hands") bears a negative connotation, hence its being fittingly applied to Fate or Death, whereas the other plural *ʾayādin* ("hands") stood for a positive concept, e.g. in the expression "the generous hands" (*al-ʾayādī al-karīmah*) when said of the liberality of a person, especially a secular ruler.[16]

In the poetry of Kušāǧim (d. *c*.360 H) we find *ʾaydī l-bilā* ("the hands of decay"), *ʾaydī l-manūn* ("the hands of death") and *ʾaydī l-manāyā* ("the hands of Fate").[17] This last expression seems to have been especially common in Arabic mourning poetry,[18] while in some other poems we also encounter *ʾaydī ṭ-ṭawāʾiḥ* ("the hands of adversities"),[19] (*ʾaṣābathum*) *ʾaydī l-maṣāʾib* ("they were struck by the hands of disasters"),[20] or *ʾaydī n-nawāʾib* ("the hands of calamities").[21]

3. *Intertextuality, second mode: "my fragrant plant"*

The most striking line of the poem presently under discussion is undoubtedly the second verse where the deceased child is likened to *rayḥān*. As will be seen in the following, the *rayḥān*(*ah*)-metaphor is the central element of the entire poem. Its significance can be discovered by analysing the intertextual relations of this metaphor.

3.1. General meaning

The word *rayḥān* (sg. *rayḥān*[*ah*], pl. *rayāḥīn*) denotes in modern Arabic the sweet basil (*ocimum basilicum*, also ar. *ḥabaq*, pl. *ʾaḥbāq*, and *ḥamāḥim*).[22] In classical and middle Arabic use, however, *rayḥān* signifies generically "a plant of sweet

14 The edited text has *ʾawdaʿtuhū* ("I entrusted it"), but this makes little sense since one would expect that the father of the deceased girl – aš-Šarīf's brother – is addressed in this line.

15 ŠarīfRaḍDīwān I p. 156 (v. 31).

16 Cited in BahrKaškūl III p. 356.

17 KušDīwān 282 v. 23 (p. 245), 200 v. 12 (p. 199) and 226 v. 2 (p. 203); *cf*. also IAṯīrMaṯal p. 444 (*ʾaydī l-manīyah*).

18 *Cf*. also IṣfḪar (Š) I p. 526.

19 INubDīwān p. 99.

20 ṬurayḥīMunt p. 203.

21 ŠarīfRaḍDīwān I p. 34 (v. 3).

22 For special kinds, e.g. the "fox's basilicum" (*rayḥān aṯ-ṯaʿālib*), see EI[2] IX p. 435. More examples are listed in Lane s.r. *ḥbq* and Dozy: *Supplément* s.r. *rayḥān*. *Cf*. also MuḥḪul IV p. 286; Spitaler: *Philologica* p. 314; Schönig: *Jemenitinnen* pp. 230-2.

odour",[23] hence simply "fragrant plant" and also "perfume". The Syrian poet Kušāǧim, describing the amenities of a drinking-bout, mentions in a verse that there were "different kinds of aromatic plants" (*ṣunūfun mina r-rayāḥīn*),[24] thus referring to various herbs possessing the same characteristics.

Similarly, we read that the Andalusian poet Ibn Ḫafāǧah (d. 533 H) was famous for "describing rivulets, flowers, meadows, fragrant plants (*rayāḥīn*) and gardens",[25] where *rayāḥīn* is likewise used generically;[26] the various poems on a wide range of flowers by aṭ-Ṭuġrāʾī have been catalogued by al-Iṣfahānī generically under the heading *waṣf ar-rayāḥīn*.[27] As is well-known, there is a chapter in the Ḥadīṯ-anthology of Muslim about the use of musk and fragrant plants (*Bāb istiʿmāl al-misk* [...] *wa-karāhat radd ar-rayḥān wa-ṭ-ṭīb*), which basically deals with a famous Tradition, saying "Whosoever is offered *rayḥān* shall not refuse it for it is light to bear and of pleasant smell".[28]

Often, *rayḥān* was applied in particular to the myrtle (*marsīn* or *ʾās*), especially in Egypt or when used, as in epitaph **195**, in the specific expression *rayḥān al-qubūr*.[29] The myrtle was called, by some men of letters, "the prince of fragrant plants" (*ʾamīr ar-rayāḥīn*),[30] and the Prophet referred to it in a Tradition as *sayyidatu rayḥāni d-dunyā*.[31] As a plant partially associated with tombs and cemeteries, the *rayḥān* in Arabo-Islamic culture bears some of the connotations of the cypress in Mediterranean countries. The placing of palm leaves and myrtles upon the tombs, much discussed among Muslim scholars (see above Chapter 2), has even become a hallmark of Islamic cemeteries in the Western perception, maybe also because this is reminiscent of the Christian practice. A Western nineteenth-century author wrote accordingly: "In the 'Cities of Silence' of Turkey, the graves are adorned with leaves of the palm tree, and marked by boughs of myrtle and cypress".[32]

23 FīrūzQāmūs I p. 222 (*rwḥ*). *Cf.* also AnṭTaḏk I p. 172. as-Suyūṭī quotes al-Ǧamāl al-Waṭwāṭ (d. 718 H) with the words that "the Arabs apply the term *rayḥān* to every plant of pleasant fragrance" (SuyḤusnMuḥ II p. 352).

24 KušDīwān 64 v. 11 (p. 66). Comparable expressions, linking the fragrant plants with the presence of fruit, recur in IRūmīDīwān VI p. 2420 (no. 1302 l. 6) and MarzMuw p. 546 (*fa-hunna fākihatun šattā wa-rayḥānun*); in a verse by Tamīm b. al-Muʿizz (IṣfḪar (M) I p. 153: *wa-maǧlisin fīhi rayḥānun wa-fākihatun*, this line is not in the *Dīwān* of Tamīm, printed Cairo: Maṭb. Dār al-Kutub 1376/1957); in ŠarŠMaq II p. 247 (*wa-fī l-maǧlisi ṣunūfu r-rayāḥīni wa-ġarāʾibu l-fawākihi*); in IIyāsBad I p. 39 (*ʾin kāna fī ṣ-ṣayfi rayḥānun wa-fākihatun*).

25 MaqqNafḥ (C) II p. 199 (*fī waṣfi l-ʾanhāri wa-l-ʾazhāri wa-r-riyāḍi wa-r-rayāḥīni wa-l-basātīn*).

26 Another example of the generic use of *rayḥān* would be a verse by Abū Nuwās, who says that the fragrant of *rayḥān* emanates from pomegranates, myrtles, roses and lilies (ANuwDīwān III p. 325 = Kennedy: *Wine Song* pp. 66f.).

27 IṣfḪar (M) I pp. 109ff.

28 NawŠMuslim XV pp. 8f.; *cf.* also IʿASalāmŠaǧarah p. 262.

29 SuyḤusnMuḥ II p. 351; AnṭTaḏk I p. 172; Lane s.r. *rwḥ*.

30 *Nūr an-nahār* p. 83. *Cf.* also Dozy: *Supplément* s.r. *rayḥānī*.

31 SuyḤusnMuḥ II p. 351.

32 Kippax: *Churchyard Literature* p. 22.

3.2. Planting or placing *rayḥān* upon the tomb

The *rayḥān(ah)*-metaphor as well as the related expressions "beautiful twigs" (verse 3) and "planted in the gardens (of decay)" (verse 4) refer, in the first place, to the practice of placing *rayḥān* branches upon a tomb or even of planting flowers upon or around the grave. This custom also left its mark in early Arabic mourning poetry.[33]

The growth of plants upon (or around) graves was in general seen as a way of procuring divine blessing and thus tolerated or even encouraged by many Sunnite scholars. Branches of *rayḥān* were set upon the tomb, as we understand from the treatise of the Hanbalite al-Manbiǧī (d. 785 H) who condemned the planting of "different kinds of fragrant plants" (*ʾanwāʿ ar-rayāḥīn*) on tombs as "disapproved innovation".[34] The popularity of this custom is demonstrated by a fatwa drafted by Ibn Ḥaǧar al-ʿAsqalānī; this fatwa has been quoted in full above on pp. 253f. The Sevillan poet Ibn Šiblāq (d. 413 H) saw in a dream "a tomb surrounded by much *rayḥān*, and people had gathered around it for a bacchanal".[35]

For further details concerning the growth of *rayḥān* and other plants on graves, the reader is asked to return to the relevant section in Chapter 2 (pp. 180ff).

3.3. Shape and perfume of the *rayḥān(ah)*

The third verse of the epitaph-poem (*ʾayya ʾaġṣānin malīḥātin* etc.), which further develops the *rayḥān(ah)*-metaphor, might be compared with the related expression *malīḥun ka-ġuṣni rayḥānin* ("beautiful as a myrtle twig") that appears in a verse by Ibn al-Muʿtazz.[36] Similarly, in a story told by Abū l-Faraǧ al-Iṣfahānī (d. *c.*363 H) we read: "We saw a young woman with a face like an inscribed dinar, as the saying goes, who was swaying and swinging like a branch of basil in the breeze of the north wind" (... *tatamāyalu wa-tanṯanī ka-ġuṣni r-rayḥāni fī nasīmi š-šimāli*).[37]

The obvious analogies with a *rayḥān* twig moved by the wind, when applied to persons, are slenderness as well as elegant movements, or even softness and "ela-

33 See *Aġānī* IX p. 51.

34 ManbTasl (C) p. 203 / (M) p. 197.

35 Cited above on p. 182.

36 IMuʿtDīwān 341 v. 1 (I p. 399); *cf.* also *ib.* 816 v. 5 (II p. 234). See also IṣfḪar (Š) II p. 403 (*ʾalwī mina r-rayḥāni ġuṣnan ʾahyafā*); MaqqNafḥ (C) IV p. 127 (*rayḥānatun hayfāʾu ʿāṭiratun naḍīratun*).

37 Cited in YāqIršād V p. 158 = IṣfStrangers pp. 32f. *Cf.* a verse by Ibn ʿAbd Rabbih (*ṭawīl*): *wa-sāḥibatin faḍli ḏ-ḏuyūli ka-ʾannahā * qaḍībun mina r-rayḥāni fawqa kaṯībī* (cited in ṮaʿālYat II p. 7); said about a slave-girl in a red gown: *qaḍībun mina r-rayḥāni fī waraqin ḥumrin* (IAbbḤullah II p. 158); applied to a man (*kāmil*): *wa-ʾaḫin tahuzzu l-ʿulā ʾaʿṭāfahū * fa-ka-ʾannahū rayḥānatun wa-šamūlū* (IḪafDīwān p. 207); *cf.* also *ib.* p. 9 (*kāmil*): *wa-tamīsu fī ʾaṯwābihī rayḥānatun * karaʿat ʿalā ẓamaʾin bi-ǧadwali māʾī*; MaqqNafḥ (C) IV p. 205 (*wa-nṯanā qaḍībun mina r-rayḥāni min fawqi ǧadwalin*). See also the following note.

sticity".[38] Often, this was combined with the perfume of the twig which emanates the stronger when the twig is moved (see below). The comparison of bodily features with twigs or branches is a commonplace in Arabic love poetry, though it was seldom the *rayḥān* – and rather the moringa-tree, *bān* – which was taken for comparison.[39] Possibly both the shape and the perfume of the beloved are referred to in another verse by Ibn al-Muᶜtazz, describing the lovers' union (*sarīᶜ*):

كَأَنَّنِي عَانَقْتُ رَيْحَانَةً * تَنَفَّسَتْ فِي لَيْلِهَا البَارِدِ

"As if I embraced a *rayḥānah* * which draw breath in the cool night".[40]

In another context, the shape of the *rayḥān* leaves gave origin to the current name of a style of slender writing called *rayḥānī*.[41] This obviously refers to the curly shape of that plant, and in poetry it was the shape of the *rayḥān* leaves which served as comparison for the hair of black persons.[42] However, the name "Rayḥān", common among slaves or eunuchs[43] of black complexion, fits the widespread use of calling black persons by names of aromatic plants or fragrances (*ᶜanbar*, "ambcr", *kāfūr*, "camphor", *misk*, "musk", *ṣandal*, "sandalwood"); the curly hair does not seem to have been the main reason for calling black persons by that name.

Throughout the centuries of pre-modern Islamic culture, *Rayḥān* (m.)[44] or *Rayḥānah* (f.) have been common as personal names. More rarely, they were used in the form of a male *kunyah*, that is "Abū Rayḥān(ah)". In addition, the *rayḥān* trade gave origin to the respective nisbah "ar-Rayḥānī",[45] which in the later Mamluk period could be also used for retainers of persons called "Rayḥān". As a male name, Rayḥān became common from the second half of the sixth century H onwards, though the first attestations reach back to the second century H: Rayḥān b. Yazīd al-ᶜĀmirī al-Badawī, who appears as a traditionist in legal literature;[46] Abū ᶜIṣmah Rayḥān b. Saᶜīd b. al-Muṯannā b. Maᶜadd

38 *Cf.* IḪafDīwān p. 97 (*kamā hazza našru r-rīḥi rayḥānatan sakrā*); IKattTašb p. 144 = IKatt-Vergleiche p. 137 (*qaḍībun mina r-rayḥāni qad māla wa-nṯanā*); Nykl: *Hispano-Arabic Poetry* p. 27 (the poem by Ziryāb), p. 31 (the verse by Ibn Ǧūdī) and p. 120 (a verse by Ibn Zaydūn: *qaḍībun mina r-rayḥāni ᵓaṯmara bi-l-badri*); MaqqNafḥ (C) IV p. 149 (*qaḍībun mina r-rayḥāni ladnun munᶜamun*); *hiya rayḥānatun ᵓiḏā mā taṯannat * wa-šaqīqun wa-mā lahā min šaqīqī* (Ottoman poetry, cited by Thomas Bauer in: Zeitschrift für arabische Linguistik 41 [2002], p. 94).

39 For this topic in general, see Bauer: *Liebesdichtung* pp. 314-8, *cf.* also Kennedy: *Wine Song* p. 80. Young men were also compared, as to their shape and perfume, to a myrtle branch (*qaḍību ᵓāsin*), see MaqqNafḥ (C) II p. 111.

40 IMuᶜtDīwān 145 v. 3 (I p. 268) = Bauer: *Liebesdichtung* p. 511; IḤamdTaḏk VI p. 98.

41 *Cf.* EI² IV p. 1123; Dozy: *Supplément* s.r. *rayḥān*.

42 For examples, see Ullmann: *Neger in der Bildersprache* pp. 198-200 (nos. 289-92).

43 For general observations on the names of these groups, see Ayalon: *Eunuchs* pp. 289-95.

44 In modern Turkey, however, this is a female name.

45 *Cf.* SamAnsāb VI p. 213.

46 AᶜUbAmwāl 1728 (p. 221); IZanǧAmwāl 2071 (III p. 1118); see also MizTuḥfah 1944 (IX pp. 261f., with further sources p. 261 n. 7); IḤaǧTahḏ III p. 302.

as-Sāmī an-Nāǧī (al-Qurašī?) al-Baṣrī (d. Baṣrah 203 or 204 H), again a traditionist.[47] The fact that "Rayḥān" was, from a certain point in time, seen as a typical name of non-Arabs and chiefly black persons becomes clear from the remark in two later sources that Rayḥān b. Yazīd al-ᶜĀmirī (mentioned above) was "a true Arab" (*kāna ᶜarabīyan ṣadūqan*),[48] as though this was belied by his name. The frequent filiation of persons called "Rayḥān" as "son of ᶜAbd Allāh" might indicate in most cases that their father had not been a Muslim or originally bore some indigenous name which was then dropped in favour of "ᶜAbd Allāh".[49] As a female name, Rayḥānah is frequent during the first three centuries H, yet after that there is little evidence that the name was still in use in the Arabic-speaking world (in contrast with the Islamic East); the only later example that I know of from the Arabic world is a woman called Rayḥānah attested in an epitaph from Évora (dated 525 H).[50] In Arabic *belles lettres*, a girl called Rayḥānah appears as a beloved and heroine of a book by an unknown author, entitled *Kitāb Rayḥānah wa-Qaranful* ("The Story of Myrtle and Clove"),[51] and Rayḥānah is also the name of several women in *The Thousand and One Nights*, viz. a (probably black) slave-girl (93rd and 143rd nights) and a cunning prostitute in Cairo (719th night).[52]

More important for the poetical imagery than the shape of the *rayḥān* was, however, its perfume. Thus we find *rayḥānatī* ("my perfume, my fragrant plant") applied to a beloved woman[53] and said of a male lover, e.g. by Abū Nuwās;[54] *rayḥān* was employed for a beautiful girl (possibly referring to her perfume: *ġuṣnun wa-rayḥān*),[55] or for the poet himself (who takes up the lover's role), e.g. by Baššār b. Burd.[56] Women as such were often compared to *rayḥān*. Ibn Ḥazm writes that "women are like *rayḥān* plants: if they are not taken care of they wither away",[57] and a Yemenite proverb says that "the woman is like the smell of *rayḥān*", meaning that you may enjoy her fragrance but you must not treat her roughly.[58]

In poems which describe the faces of male persons, *rayḥān* is part of the metaphorical imagery for the first growth of the beard[59] or the fragrance (and the curly or curved shape) of the earlock

47 TB VIII p. 427; MizTuḥfah 1943 (IX pp. 260f., with further sources p. 260 note 1); IḤaǧTahḏ III p. 301.

48 MizTuḥfah IX p. 262 and IḤaǧTahḏ III p. 302.

49 *Cf.* also Ayalon: *Eunuchs* pp. 294f.

50 RCEA 3039.

51 INadFihrist p. 366.

52 *Cf.* also Spitaler: *Philologica* p. 472.

53 See below pp. 586f.

54 ANuwDīwān IV p. 175 (*muḏakkarāt* 42 l. 2, metre *basīṭ*: *qurratu ᶜaynī wa-bardu ᶜayšī * bāna wa-rayḥānatī wa-ṭībī*) = Bauer: *Liebesdichtung* p. 83.

55 ISaᶜīdMuġrib II p. 291. *Cf.* also MuḥNafḥah II p. 171 (*lā ᵓarā fī siwāki mā fīki min ṭī- * bin wa-min bahǧatin wa-min rayḥānī*).

56 BaššārDīwān 343 v. 10 (p. 224) = IMuᶜtṬab p. 429 = Kennedy: *Wine Song* p. 58 (*ᵓaw kuntu min quḍubi r-rayḥāni rayḥānā*).

57 IḤazmṬawq p. 105.

58 Goitein: *Jemenica* p. 151 = Schönig: *Jemenitinnen* p. 231.

59 IṣfḪar (Š) I p. 269 (*ramal*): *wa-mina r-rayḥāni fī ᶜāriḍihī * ᵓarǧulu n-namli bi-miskin taktubū*, *cf.* also Bauer: *Liebesdichtung* pp. 264f. and 279f.; INubDīwān p. 447 (*ḫaṭṭu rayḥānihī ᶜalā māᵓi ḫaddin*); Dozy: *Supplément* s.r. *rayḥān*. See also MaqqRawḍah p. 44 (*kāmil / basīṭ*):

(*ṣudġ*).[60] This last motif also entered panegyric poetry in praise of secular rulers,[61] but both the shape and the perfume of the *rayḥān* were dominant mainly in love poetry (when describing the beauty of the beloved), as well as in wine and garden poetry (see below).

On the other hand, the pleasant odour of a tomb (or the earth thereof), often likened to musk and other fragrances, was a common motif in verses in praise of the Prophet. The fragrance emanating from the earth of his sepulchre (*ṭību turābi l-qabri*), or from the soil of Medina, was metaphorically said to guide the visitors towards it, for example in a verse by Aḥmad b. Muḥammad al-ᶜĀrif (*ṭawīl*):

فَمَا عَبِقَ الرَّيْحَانُ إلاَّ وَتُرْبُهَا * أَجَلُّ مِنَ الرَّيْحَانِ طِيباً وَأَعْبَقُ

"Never did a fragrant plant exhale fragrance but that its earth[62] * proved more scented and more perfumed than a fragrant plant".[63]

In the epitaph of the Naṣrid ruler Yūsuf III (d. 820 H), the buried person is likened to *rayḥān*.[64] The obvious reason for this is, however, not only the fragrance of *rayḥān*, but also the metaphorical connection of that plant with Paradise (see below).

By Ibn ar-Rūmī (d. 283 H) and Abū Manṣūr Baḫtiyār (d. *c*.385 H) *rayḥān* is used, generically, for the comparison with the pleasant smell of the narcissus,[65] while other poets compared it to the

*min ᶜanbari š-Šaḥrāmi ᵓam min miski Dārīni * balī wa-minhu nasīmātu r-rayāḥīnī*; YāqIršād VI p. 488 (*rayḥānatun ḍumiḫat bi-l-miski*); MuḥNafḥah II p. 497 (*rayḥānu ḫaddika*).

60 See IḪafDīwān p. 265 = MaqqNafḥ (C) II p. 206 (*ṭawīl*): *ka-ᵓan lam yaṣilnī fīhi ẓabyun yaqūmu lī * lamāhu wa-ṣudġāhū bi-rāḥī wa-rayḥānī*; in a verse by Ibn an-Nabīh: *ruḍābuka rāḥī ᵓāsu ṣudġika rayḥānī* (cited in ṢafĠayṯ I p. 444); in a verse by ᶜAwn ad-Dīn Ibn al- ᶜAǧamī, cited MaqqNafḥ (C) III p. 167 (*wa-min ṣudġihī ᵓāsī wa-rayḥānī*); two verses by Ibn Ǧābir al-Andalusī (d. 779 H), cited *ib*. III p. 435 (*wa-ḫaṭṭa fī ṣ-ṣudġi wāwa rayḥānin*; *wa-fī ḥawāšīhi li-ṣ-ṣudġayni rayḥānun*); MuḥNafḥah II p. 170 (*wa-bi-ṣudġihī la-l-ᵓāsi wa- r-rayḥāni*); also playing on this motif: *wuqūfu rayḥānatin ᶜalā ᵓuḏunin* (ANuwDīwān III p. 105 = *ḫamrīyāt* no. 81) = Kennedy: *Wine Song* p. 44.

61 In a verse by Ibn Qusaym al-Ḥamawī (Muslim b. al-Ḫiḍr, d. 541 H or after) in praise of the Zangid ruler Nūr ad-Dīn Maḥmūd (r. 541–69 H) (*wāfir*): *mudāmī min muqabbalihī * wa-min ṣudġayhi rayḥānī* (cited in IṣfḪar [Š] I p. 476); a verse by as-Sarīy ar-Raffāᵓ (*kāmil*): *ḥattā ḥasabtu l-warda min ᵓašǧārihī * yuǧnā ᵓawi r-rayḥāna min ᵓāṣālihī* (cited in ṮaᶜālYat II p. 162); a verse by Ibn an-Nabīh in praise of al-Malik al-Ašraf (*munsariḥ*): *wa-niltu min rīqihī wa-ᶜāriḍihī * ᵓaṭyaba min rāḥihī wa-rayḥānihī* (cited in IWāṣilKurūb III p. 157); a verse by aš-Šihāb A. Ibn al-Qāḍī (960–1025 H) (*basīṭ*): *rīqun wa-ḫālun wa-ḫaddun wa-l-ᶜiḏāru bihī * ḫamrun wa-miskun wa-kāfūrun wa-rayḥānū* (cited in MaqqRawḍah p. 241).

62 I.e. the earth of Medina.

63 Cited in QasṭMaw III p. 417.

64 Inscripciones Granada p. 159 = Inscriptions Espagne 182.

65 IRūmīDīwān I p. 147 (no. 104 v. 6, var. *durarun*: *durrun*) = ᶜAskMaᶜānī II p. 373 = ḤuṣZahr (M) II p. 565 / (Ṭ) I p. 463 = IRašᶜUmdah I p. 564 = IAṯīrMaṯal p. 242 (*kāmil*): *rayḥānuhum ḏahabun ᶜalā durarin * wa-šarābuhum durarun ᶜalā ḏahabī*; the verse by Baḫtiyār (*mutaqārib*): *fa-yā-ḥabbaḏā rawḍatā narǧisin * tuḥayyā n-nudāmā bi-rayḥānihā* (ṮaᶜālYat II p. 219); *cf*. also Schoeler: *Naturdichtung* p. 75.

scent of the lemon (*ʾutruǧǧ*)[66] or referred to the fruit of the quince (*safarǧal*) as *rayḥānah*;[67] likewise due to the fragrance, *rayḥānī* was the name for a sort of figs in Córdoba.[68] Ibn al-Muʿtazz describes the locality of Quṭrabbul (near Baghdad) as "full of fragrant plants and meadows",[69] a conventional image which also appears in poems praising the beauties of major cities, e.g. Damascus[70] or Baghdad.[71]

In another context the Sunnite scholars discussed whether the pilgrim in the state of *ʾiḥrām* might use the perfume of the *rayḥān* plant. The Shafiites considered this to be prohibited while the other legal traditions merely judged it to be disapproved of.[72] It seems peculiar to the religious discourse, with no evidence from poetry that I know of, that the perfume of *rayḥān* was contrasted with the actual bitter taste of the plant, viz. in this Tradition: "The heretic (*al-munāfiq*, in other versions *al-fāǧir*) who recites the Qurʾān is like the *rayḥānah*: its fragrance is pleasant, but its taste is bitter".[73] This means that the recitation of the Qurʾān is still pleasant, even if pronounced by a heretic whose deviant creed smacks bitterly to the righteous believers.

3.4. The further role of *rayḥān* in poetry and rhymed prose

In wine songs, either the perfume of the wine or the pleasant odour at the scene was often described with reference to the *rayḥān* plant.[74] Entertainment, as seen with the poets' eyes, was thus (*ḫafīf*)

زَمَنُ الخَمْرِ وَالمُسَاوِرِ وَالجَشْـ * نِ وَوَرْدِ الخِلَافِ وَالرَّيْحَانِ

"The time of wine, of the intoxicated (?), of cheerful * company, of the bloom of the salix-tree and of the *rayḥān*".[75]

66 ʿAskMaʿānī II p. 386.

67 IAbbḪullah I p. 262.

68 IBaškṢilah I p. 38; Dozy: *Supplément* s.r. *rayḥānī*.

69 IMuʿtDīwān 690 v. 1 (II p. 99: *ḏātu r-rayāḥīni wa-l-ḫuḍar*); *cf.* also *ib.* 838 v. 9 (II p. 260: *rawḍan mina r-rayḥāni* = ʿAskMaʿānī II p. 396) and 1006 v. 6 (II p. 514).

70 A verse by Ibn aẓ-Ẓāhir al-Irbilī (d. 677 H) (*ṭawīl*): *wa-min kulli rayḥānin muqīmin wa-zāʾirin * yuṣāfiḥu rayyāhu r-riyāḍa fa-taʿbaqū* (MaqqNafḥ (C) III p. 153).

71 In a verse by Manṣūr an-Namirī (*basīṭ*): *ʾiḏā ṣ-ṣabā nafaḥat wa-l-laylu muʿtakirun * fa-ḥarrašat bayna ʾaġṣāni r-rayāḥīnī* (IMuʿtṬab p. 246); *cf.* also the following verse (*basīṭ*): *nādaytuhū wa-ẓilālu l-layli muʿtakirun * taḥta r-ruwāqi dafīnan fī r-rayāḥīnī* (*ib.* p. 369).

72 FB III pp. 505f. (*ḥaǧǧ* 18).

73 FB IX p. 81 and 123 (*faḍāʾil al-Qurʾān* 17 and 36), IX p. 693 (*ʾaṭʿimah* 30), XIII p. 655 (*tawḥīd* 57); NawŠMuslim VI p. 84 (*musāfirīn* 243).

74 KušDīwān 64 v. 11 (p. 66: *rayāḥīn*); IMuʿtDīwān 638 v. 20 (II p. 56: *wa-tanaffasa r-rayḥānu fī l-ǧannāt*) and 713 v. 2 (II p. 130: *šamimnā r-rayḥāna bi-l-kāfūr*); ANuwDīwān III p. 132 = IQutŠiʿr p. 504 (*ʾaʿṭatka rayḥānahā l-ʿuqāru*); ʿAskMaʿānī I p. 311; ṮaʿālYat II p. 172 (ar-Raffāʾ: *wa-ʾahdat laka r-rāḥu rayḥānahā*); ḪafDīwān p. 124 (*taḥta rayḥānati l-faǧri*); *cf.* also Schoeler: *Naturdichtung* p. 33f. (with numerous examples in German translation).

75 Cited in TawḥImtāʿ III p. 74. In a mock wine song, ʿAntara called his spear his *rayḥānah*: *wa-rayḥānatī rumḥī* (cited in Kennedy: *Wine Song* p. 153).

It seems very fitting, therefore, that the greatest inner courtyard of the Alhambra in Granada is to this day known as *patio de los arrayanes*, "the Court of the Myrtles",[76] as the Naṣrid palace was seen as a place of entertainment and luxurious life. However, there might be also an allusion to Paradise in that name (see below).

In general, the combination of wine and *rayḥān* had some currency in the imagery of Arabic poetry, especially as one of the common terms for "wine", *ar-rāḥ*, gave ample opportunity to apply the stylistic device of *tağnīs* – i.e. playing on the related words *rīḥ* ("wind, breeze"), *rāḥah* ("leisure, repose" or "palm of the hand") and *rayḥān*.[77] A typical expression, in a verse by Ismāᶜīl b. Badr, runs *taᶜāṭaynā ᶜalā r-rayḥāni rāḥan*, "we consumed wine on (a bed of) myrtles".[78] Of the morning draught, following a pleasant night of carousing, Ibn al-Muᶜtazz wrote in a *rağaz* poem (though avoiding the coupling of *rāḥ* and *rayḥān*):

وَرُفِعَ الرَّيْحَـــــــانُ وَالنَّبِيذُ * وَزَالَ عَنَّا عَيْشُـــنَا اللَّـــذِيذُ
وَلَسْتَ فِي طُولِ النَّهَارِ آمِنَا * مِنْ حَدِيثٍ لَمْ يَكُ قَبْلُ كائِنَا
أَو خَبَرٍ يُكْرَهُ أَوْ كِتَـــــــابِ * يَقْطَعُ طِيـبَ اللَّهْوِ وَالشَّـرَابِ

"Now *rayḥān* and wine are gone and do no longer last, * our enjoyable life is merely past!
For the whole day long you won't be protected * from new things happening, not existing before and freshly projected,
And from hateful news or letters * that tie the pleasure of joking and drinking in fetters!"[79]

In garden poetry,[80] the aromatic *rayḥān* is often the natural complement to coloured

76 *arrayán* means "myrtle" in present-day Spanish, and there are still place names like *Arrayanal*, "place where myrtles grow" (Asín Palacios: *Toponimia árabe* p. 77). The place name (*Ḥiṣn*) *ar-Rayāḥīn* is attested for al-Andalus, see IdrīsīDescr pp. ١٩١ and 233; IKardHistoria p. 139.

77 IMuᶜtṬab p. 238 (Muslim b. al-Walīd: *ᶜaynāka rāḥī wa-rayḥānī*); *ib.* p. 307 (Aḥmad al-Ḫārakī: *marḥaban bi-r-rāḥi wa-rā- * ᵓiḥin min rayḥānataynī*); IRūmīDīwān VI p. 2469 (no. 1348 l. 22: *tağidu r-rāḥa fīhi wa-r-rayḥānā*); ᶜAskMaᶜānī I p. 306 (*ar-rayḥānu wa-r-rāḥu*) and 311 (*qad ḫalaṭnā bi-nasīmi ṣ-ṣabā * nasīma rāḥin wa-rayāḥīnā*); TawḥBaṣāᵓir III p. 80 (Abū Dulaf: *lastu li-rayḥānin wa-lā rāḥin*); ṮaᶜālYat II p. 151 (*mina r-rāḥi wa-r-rayḥān*) and 152 (*rayḥānun wa-nuqlun*, "fragrant plants and candy sweets", fitting requisites for a wine-bout); MaqqNafḥ (C) IV p. 371 (*bi-r-rāḥi wa-r-rayḥāni wa-l-yāsmīni*) and MaqqRawḍah p. 12 (*ḥadīṯu r-rakbi rayḥānī wa-rāḥī*); *cf.* also Schoeler: *Naturdichtung* pp. 46 and 49; Wagner: *Dichtung* II p. 141; Kennedy: *Wine Song* p. 99. See also IKattTašb p. 57 = IKattVergleiche pp. 56 and 86.

78 IKattTašb p. 93 = IKattVergleiche pp. 88f.

79 IMuᶜtDīwān 996 vv. 86-8 (II p. 501) = *Wāfī* XVII pp. 461f.

80 For examples, see Wagner: *Dichtung* II pp. 140f.

flowers[81] or it is seen in connection with a refreshing breeze;[82] flowers and *rayḥān* could also be sent as a present, if possible accompanied by an appropriate verse or two.[83] In a poem praising al-Andalus we read (*kāmil*):

يَاحُسْنَهَا وَالطَّلُّ يَنْثُرُ فَوْقَهَا * دُرَراً خِلالَ الوَرْدِ وَالرَّيْحَانِ

"O for her[84] beauty when the dew spreads over her * pearls between the roses and the fragrant plants!"[85]

In the Arabic poetical genres known as spring-, garden- and flower-poems (*rabīʿīyāt*, *rawḍīyāt* and *zahrīyāt*), the *rayḥān* is omnipresent, especially in the Islamic West. There are also poems which describe the beautiful features of the *rayḥān* plant as it exists in reality,[86] and several verses describing the *rayḥān* plant – its shape, colours and pleasant odour – were collected by aṣ-Ṣafadī (d. 764 H),[87] al-Ibšīhī (d. 850 H)[88] and as-Suyūṭī.[89] The Arabic lexicographers took great interest in the names and shapes of plants,[90] though the only monograph dealing with *rayḥān* and its like seems to have been the (lost) *Kitāb ar-Rayāḥīn* by Abū ʿAbd Allāh Yūsuf b. ʿAbd Allāh az-Zuǧāǧī (Hamdān *c.*352 – Astarābād in 415 H).[91]

In addition, we know of dispute poems (sg. *munāẓarah*) between flowers, most famous those between the rose and the narcissus,[92] but also between various other plants and the *rayḥān*, e.g. the *munāẓarah* from *Kašf al-ʾasrār ʿan ḥukm aṭ-ṭuyūr wa-l-ʾazhār* by Ibn Ġānim al-Maqdisī[93] or the

81 IMuʿtDīwān 399 v. 12 (*ar-rayāḥīnu wa-z-zahr*); ʿAskMaʿānī II p. 381 (*az-zahru wa-r-rayḥān*); Ṯaʿālyat II pp. 84, 138 (*min zahri r-rayāḥīn*) and 323 (description of a garden by ʿAlī b. al-Qāsim al-Qāšānī, *munsariḥ*: *ǧāwara ḥawḏānuhā banafsaǧahā * wa-zāna rayḥānuhā šaqāʾiqahā*); Nykl: *Hispano-Arabic Poetry* p. 232 (Ibn az-Zaqqāq).

82 MaqqNafḥ (C) II p. 117 (*wa-rāḥatu r-rīḥi tamtā- * ru nafḥata r-rayḥānī*).

83 See e.g. MarzMuw p. 534 (*qad baʿaṯnā bi-ṭībi r-rayhāni* etc.).

84 I.e. of al-Andalus.

85 Quoted in MaqqNafḥ (C) I p. 212. In another poem, praising the beauties of Córdoba, we read of the *ʿarfu r-rayāḥīn* (*ib.* II p. 81).

86 E.g. two verses cited in IḪaṭIḥāṭah III p. 369f. or three verses (about a *rayḥān* garden) by Abū l-Faḍl al-Mīkālī, see ḤuṣZahr (M) II p. 571 / (Ṭ) I p. 468; there is also a distich by as-Sarīy ar-Raffāʾ describing the *rayḥān* (*fī waṣfi r-rayḥān*), cited in Ṯaʿālyat II p. 178 and SuyḤusnMuḥ II pp. 352f. Several poems employ the *rayḥān*-metaphor in IḪafDīwān pp. 148f.

87 ṢafKašf pp. 296-9. These specimens also include the metaphorical use of the *rayḥān*.

88 IbšīhiMust II pp. 321f. (chapter 72).

89 SuyḤusnMuḥ II pp. 352-4.

90 *Cf.* Bauer: *Pflanzensystematik*.

91 YāqIršād VII p. 308; GAS VIII p. 228 (no. 8).

92 *Cf. Nūr an-nahār* pp. 8-26 and 41-50; Wagner: *Dichtung* II pp. 148-50; EAL II p. 186; Wolfhart Heinrichs: *Rose Versus Narcissus. Observations on an Arabic Literary Debate*, in: Reinink/ Vanstiphout: *Dispute Poems* pp. 179-98.

93 Cited in *Nūr an-nahār* pp. 81-4.

Maqāmah al-wardīyah fī r-rayāḥīn wa-z-zuhūr by the ninth-century polymath as-Suyūṭī.[94] One of the earliest dispute poems between the rose and narcissus, composed by aṣ-Ṣanawbarī (d. 334 H), opens with an invocation of all kinds of flowers and *rayḥān* (*ḫafīf*):

زَعَمَ الوَرْدُ أَنَّهُ هُوَ أَزْهَى * مِنْ جَمِيعِ الأَزْهَارِ وَالرَّيْحَانِ

"Die Rose behauptete, daß sie schöner sei * als alle Blumen und Duftkräuter" (Schoeler's translation).[95]

Quite outstanding, and leading away from garden poetry and related genres, is a verse by Kušāǧim who uses the *rayḥān*-metaphor in describing the licking flames of a fire-place.[96] Ibn Nubātah likened the language of a famous poet to *rayḥān*,[97] and some literary critic described certain verses as "more odoriferous than the myrtle".[98] However, comparing poetry to *rayḥān* was not always meant as a compliment, e.g. in the following dictum by Ibn al-Anbārī: "The poems of those 'modern' poets – such as Abū Nuwās and his peers – are merely like *rayḥān*: you enjoy its fragrance for one day, then it withers and is thrown away".[99]

In official documents and letters, good news are likened to fragrant plants, e.g. in a letter by Ibn Ḥiǧǧah al-Ḥamawī (d. 837 H) edited and translated by Werner Diem: *wa-lā zāla samʿuhū l-karīmu mušannafan min ʿuqūdi masarratinā bi-kulli durrah / wa-rayāḥīnu bašāʾirinā tutḥifuhū bi-mā yaḍūʿu našruhū mina l-ḥaḍrah* ("Möge sein edles Ohr weiterhin jede Perle aus unseren Freudenkolliers als Ohrring entgegennehmen, / und mögen die Duftpflanzen unserer Frohbotschaften ihn auch fürderhin mit Nachrichten beschenken, die bei ihrer Verbreitung der Residenzstadt wohlriechend entströmen!").[100]

Likewise unique – but unfortunately too long to be related here – is the story of why *rayḥān* occurs as a metaphor in the foundation inscription on the royal horse stables in Fez.[101] Yet notwithstanding all these examples, *rayḥān* was not among the truly common themes and images of Arabic poetry and rhymed prose.

3.5. *Rayḥān*(*ah*) said of deceased women (slave-girls)

In a long poem mourning the death of his slave-girl, the pre-Islamic poet al-Muʿallā aṭ-Ṭāʾī has the following verses (*kāmil*):

94 *Nūr an-nahār* pp. 52-69 and John Mattock: *The Arabic Tradition: Origin and Developments*, in: Reinink/Vanstiphout: *Dispute Poems*, esp. pp. 160f. *Cf.* also IKattTašb pp. 51f. = IKatt-Vergleiche p. 53.

95 ṢafĠayṯ II p. 268; Schoeler: *Naturdichtung* p. 313.

96 KušDīwān 47 v. 5 (p. 51).

97 INubDīwān p. 221 (*fa-l-lafẓu wa-l-ʿarḍu rayḥānun wa-kāfūrū*).

98 Cited in Nykl: *Hispano-Arabic Poetry* p. 128.

99 Cited in MarzMuw p. 384.

100 Diem: *Tašrīf* pp. 163f.

101 MaqqRawḍah p. 79.

فَكَأَنَّهَا وَالنَّفْسُ زَاهِقَةٌ * غُصْنٌ مِنَ الرَّيْحَانِ قَدْ جَفَّا
يَاقَبْرُ أَبْقِ عَلَى مَحَاسِنِهَا * فَلَقَدْ حَوَيْتَ النُّورَ وَالظَّرْفَا

"It is, when the soul had left (her), as if she were * a twig of *rayḥān* that had dried up.
O tomb, preserve her charms, * for you have come to embrace light and gracefulness!"[102]

Here, we have an example of an effective combination of the motifs discussed above. On the one hand, the girl is compared to a *rayḥān* twig, a comparison playing on the shape of the plant (*qua* slenderness). On the other hand, the fragrance of the girl is alluded to. A new motif in these verses appears to be the comparison between the death of the girl and the drying up of a fragrant plant.[103]

This motif, in inverted form, is attested in a story where we read that *rayḥān* taken from a tomb remained miraculously fresh for 70 days, viz. in the story about the burial of the Kūfan ascetic Muḥammad b. an-Naḍr al-Ḥāriṯī (d. 174 H): there, myrtles (or fragrant plants, *rayḥān*) were found spread out in his burial niche (meaning that the deceased had been rewarded by God with the bliss of Paradise, see below), and so someone had descended into the tomb and collected a part of them. He kept them at his home where the *rayḥān* remained fresh for 70 days and "the people gathered in great numbers in order to see this, that the local emir was afraid of unrest and took the myrtles away from the man".[104]

Moreover, the above-quoted verses of aṭ-Ṭāʾī also combine the metaphor of the fragrant plant with the metaphor of "light" or "illumination", not dissimilar to the third line of our epitaph-poem (... *badīʿātin bi-nūrī*).

The related concept that a tomb "illuminates" the surrounding tombs (or a whole cemetery) is likewise attested in poetry and of some interest in this context. Thus, a tomb could "make a cemetery radiate", and in a verse we read (*ṭawīl*):

لَئِنْ أَظْلَمَتْ مِنْ بَعْدِكَ الأَرْضُ وَحْشَةً * لَقَدْ أَشْرَقَتْ أُنْساً إِلَيْكَ الْمَقَابِرُ

"Though after your passing away the world grew dark through desolation, * the cemetery radiated with light, out of joy in your company".[105]

In a poem mourning the death of Ibn Šuǧāʿ aṣ-Ṣūfī (Abū ʿAl. al-Ḥusayn, d. 423 H), aš-Šarīf ar-Raḍīy has the following lines (*mutaqārib*):

مُجَاوِرَ قَوْمٍ بِأَيْدِي الْبِلَى * تُمَزِّقُهُمْ يَرْقُبُونَ النُّشُورَا

102 Cited in IʿARabʿIqd (Ǧ) II p. 180 / (M) III p. 280.

103 In a poem describing a bout of wine-drinking on a rainy day, Ibn al-Muʿtazz sadly mentions the dryness (*ǧafāf*) of the *rayḥān* because it had been plucked by his companions and brought into the house where it soon dried up, see IMuʿtDīwān 961 v. 15 (II p. 455); the same motif, again in wine poetry, in ANuwDīwān III p. 183 (*ḫamrīyāt* no. 157): *wa-ʾaḍġāṯu rayḥānin ǧanīyun wa-yābisū* (= IMuʿtṬab p. 206 and MubKāmil [C] III p. 144).

104 MunKawākib I p. 438.

105 Cited in RāġibMuḥāḍ IV p. 528.

وَلاَ زَالَ قَبْرُكَ مِنْ نُورِهِ * بِجُنْحِ الظَّلاَمِ يُضِيءُ القُبُورَا

“O neighbour of people in the hands of decay, * torn to pieces by them, who anxiously look forward to the Resuscitation.
May your tomb by its light not cease to * illuminate, in the gloom of darkness, the (other) tombs!”[106]

There is another Arabic mourning poem about a slave-girl which contains the *rayḥānah*-metaphor, coupled with the image of the garden (*rawḍah*). According to some, this four-line-poem was composed by Hārūn ar-Rašīd (who had fallen much in love with that girl), while others attribute it – probably incorrectly – to his court poet al-ᶜAbbās b. al-Aḥnaf (d. 192 H) (*sarīᶜ*):

أُخْتُلِسَتْ رَيْحَانَتِي مِنْ يَدِي * أَبْكِي عَلَيْهَا آخَرَ المُسْنَدِ
كانَتْ هِيَ الأُنْسَ إذا اسْتَوْحَشَتْ * نَفْسِي مِنَ الأقْرَبِ وَالأَبْعَدِ
وَرَوْضَةً لِي لَمْ تَزَلْ مَرْتَعِي * وَمَنْهَلاً كَانَ بِهِ مَوْرِدِي
كَانَتْ يَدِي كانَتْ بِهَا قُوَّتِي * فَاخْتَلَسَ الدَّهْرُ يَدِي مِنْ يَدِي

“My fragrant plant was snatched away from my hand, * (and) I will weep for her until the end of time.
She was my (comforting) company whenever my soul * was deserted by the nearest and the farthest (i.e. by all),
(And she was) a garden for me that always was my pasture ground * and a water place I went to to quench my thirst.
She was my hand,[107] she provided for my strength, * but destiny has snatched ‘my hand’ from my hand”.[108]

3.6. *Rayḥān*(*ah*) said of children

In a poem by Yaḥyā aṣ-Ṣarṣarī (d. 656 H), one of the foremost eastern encomiasts of the Prophet (see above pp. 57f.), the expression *rayḥānu qalbī*, “myrtle of my heart”, is used as “children dear to my heart” or simply “my dear children”.[109] Already the caliph ᶜUmar had called one of his sons (who died at a young age) “a fragrant plant whose scent I smell” (*rayḥānatun ʾašammuhā*).[110] In a poem by Abū

106 ŠarīfRaḍDīwān II p. 30 (no. 188 v. 27-8).

107 “My hand” is metaphorically said for “my force”, but the following paradoxical image necessitates the literal translation.

108 Quoted in RāġibMuḥāḍ IV p. 531 (only vv. 1 and 4, with the variants *rayḥānatī wa-ḫtulisat min* etc. and *kānat yadan* etc.) and IBuḫtUns p. 88. The lines are not contained in IAḥnafDīwān.

109 MN II p. 19 (v. 17).

110 IAḤaǧSulwah p. 118. The same notion appears in a verse by Abū Farᶜūn (?!) al-Aᶜrābī: *bunayyatī rayḥānatī ʾašammuhā* (TawḥBaṣāʾir VI, p. 233).

Ḥayyān (d. 745 H), congratulating Badr ad-Dīn Ibn Ǧamāᶜah on the birth of his son ᶜUmar whose birth was preceded by that of two daughters, we read (*mutaqārib*):

هُبِيتَ بِرَيْحَانَتَي رَوْضَةٍ * وَبَعْدَهُمَا جَاءَ نَجْلٌ أَجَرْ

"You were given as a gift two fragrant plants of a garden, * and after them came a beautiful son".[111]

A similar use of *rayḥānah* – the feminine form was also applied to male children – is attributed to the Prophet who called his grandsons al-Ḥasan and al-Ḥusayn, the sons of ᶜAlī, "my two fragrant plants" (*rayḥānatāya*),[112] more exactly "my two fragrant plants in the present world" (*rayḥānatāya mina d-dunyā*)[113] or also "from the *rayḥān* of Paradise" (*min rayḥāni l-ǧannah*).[114]

In Shiite and Sunnite sources alike we therefore find either al-Ḥusayn or al-Ḥasan referred to as "the grandson of the Prophet and his *rayḥānah*",[115] and their father ᶜAlī accordingly as *ʾAbū r-Rayḥānatayn.*[116] The traditionist and poet Ibn Ḫallād ar-Rāmhurmuzī (Abū M. al-Ḥasan b. ᶜAr., d. *c.*360 H) even wrote a monograph entitled *Kitāb ar-Rayḥānatayni l-Ḥasan wa-l-Ḥusayn.*[117] In the famous poem in praise of the Prophet by al-Būṣīrī, called *al-Hamzīyah*, al-Ḥasan and al-Ḥusayn are mentioned as *rayḥānatayni*, and "their perfume" (*ṭībuhumā*) is explained by their belonging to the Prophet's offspring who was famous for the sweet smell of his body and sweat.[118]

In this sense, *rayḥān* (or *rayḥānah*) often meant "offspring" or "child" in general,[119] as also in epitaph **195**. Ibn Ḥağar al-ᶜAsqalānī explains this use of *rayḥānah* either with the fact that one likes to kiss a child and smell his perfume, similar to the real *rayḥān* plant, or because *rayḥān* stands for "subsistence" (*rizq*),[120] i.e. the "bounty of God" (*rayḥānu llāh*) which provides for someone's well-being, quite as in the saying *subḥāna llāh wa-rayḥānahū* ("Praise God and His bounty!").[121] al-Qāḍī ᶜIyāḍ and others, sticking closer to the eschatological imagery, quote the Tradition:

111 Cited in MaqqNafḥ (C) III p. 325.

112 In some versions mistakenly *rayḥānatī* or *rayḥānī*.

113 FB VII p. 119 (*faḍāʾil aṣ-ṣaḥābah* 22) and X pp. 522f. (*ʾadab* 18); ᶜIyāḍMaš I p. 377 (*rwḥ*); IǦawzīṢafwah I p. 330 and IǦawzīTabṣ I p. 453; FāsīᶜIqd III p. 395; MağlBihār XLIII pp. 180 and 264; Lane s.r. *rwḥ*. See also an extended version of this report in DaylFird II p. 407: *al-waladu rayḥānatu ǧaddihī wa-rayḥānatī* (sic) *Ḥasanun wa-Ḥusayn.*

114 ṮaᶜālṮimār p. 696.

115 NZ I p. 154 (al-Ḥusayn); SaḫWağīz III p. 1167 (al-Ḥasan); MunKawākib I pp. 134 (al-Ḥasan) and 142 (al-Ḥusayn); al-Amīn: *Miftāḥ* II p. 353 (al-Ḥusayn). See also IDaqŠArbaᶜīn p. 61 (al-Ḥasan).

116 MağlBihār XLIII p. 180.

117 Quoted by title in INadFihrist p. 172.

118 Verse 331 of the *Hamzīyah*, as commented upon in HaytMinaḥ III pp. 1116f.

119 *Cf.* also ᶜIyāḍMaš I p. 377 (*rwḥ*); FīrūzQāmūs I p. 222 (*rwḥ*); Lane s.r. *rwḥ*.

120 *Cf.* FīrūzQāmūs I p. 222 (*rwḥ*); Lane s.r. *rwḥ*.

121 FB VII p. 124 and X p. 524. *Cf.* also FīrūzQāmūs I p. 223 (*rwḥ*); HarMirqātMaf IV p. 22; Lane s.r. *rwḥ*: *al-waladu min rayḥāni llāhi*, "Offspring are of the bounty of God".

"The good child is a fragrant plant from the fragrant plants of Paradise" (*al-waladu ṣ-ṣāliḥu rayḥānatun min rayāḥīni l-ğannati*),[122] or in a shorter form: "The child is a fragrant plant from Paradise" (*al-waladu rayḥānun mina l-ğannati*).[123]

Apart from the epitaph presently under discussion, it is worth mentioning that in two preserved epitaphs deceased children are spoken of as *rayḥānat al-ğannah*, "the fragrant plant of Paradise", and *rayḥānat al-ʾakbād*, "the fragrant plant of the hearts (lit. livers)".[124]

3.7. *Rayḥān(ah)* said of pious or otherwise outstanding persons

In a broader sense and applied to adults, *rayḥānah* could be said of persons of outstanding qualities and/or piety. At least two Syrian ascetics were called *rayḥānat aš-Šām*, namely Abū Muslim ᶜAbd Allāh b. Ṯawb[125] al-Ḫawlānī (d. *c.*62 H)[126] and Abū l-Ḥusayn (or Ḥasan) Aḥmad b. Abī l-Ḥiwārī Maymūn from Damascus (d. in the first half of the third century, probably in 230 H) – reportedly, the latter was called so by the mystic al-Ğunayd.[127] Literally, this epithet means "the fragrant plant of Syria", but it clearly denotes an outstanding person who "fills Syria with perfume", perhaps more freely rendered as "the pride, *or* the glory, of Syria".[128] A fourth-century mystic who died in 382 H is praised by Ibn Taġrī Birdī with the words, "As a lord, he was like a fragrant plant among the Sufis" (*kāna ka-r-rayḥānati bayna ṣ-ṣūfiyati sayyidan*).[129]

As can be seen from the last example, *rayḥānah* + genitive was often intended to mean "the first choice of" or "the most eminent, *or* outstanding, person among ...". We encounter this use of *rayḥānah* also without a religious connotation, e.g. in the story of the love-affair between the caliph Abū l-ᶜAbbās as-Saffāḥ (r. 132–36 H) and Umm Salamah bt. Yaᶜqūb al-Maḫzūmī: according to this story, the caliph was told that Umm Salamah's tribe, the Banū Maḫzūm, were "the fragrant plant (i.e. the best) of Qurayš" (*rayḥānatu Qurayš*) and she herself "the choicest of all fragrant plants" (*rayḥānatu r-rayāḥīn*);[130] in another context, ᶜAlī described the Banū l-

122 ᶜIyāḍMaš I p. 377 (*rwḥ*); DaylFird II p. 407.

123 TawḥBaṣāʾir VII p. 250.

124 See Volume I p. 327.

125 His name is not certain, see NZ I p. 156.

126 *Wāfī* XVII pp. 99f.; MunKawākib I p. 224; ZA IV p. 75.

127 QušRis p. 410; IĞawzīṢafwah II p. 404; ŠaᶜrṬab I p. 82; MunKawākib I p. 534 (here: *rayḥānatu ʾahli š-Šām*).

128 In a mourning poem by Ibn al-Muᶜtazz we also find the comparable expression *rayḥānat an-nadāmā*, see IMuᶜtDīwān 1200 v. 5 (III p. 86) = ḤuṣZahr (M) III p. 724 / (Ṭ) II p. 77.

129 NZ IV p. 163. *Cf.* also FīrūzQāmūs II p. 224 s.r. *fḫr*: *al-fāḫūr* explained as *rayḥānu š-šuyūḫi*.

130 IḤiğṮam p. 412. The term *rayḥānatu Qurayš* also appears in a letter quoted in MaqqNafḥ (C) VI p. 237.

Muġīrah as "the *rayḥānah* of Qurayš".[131] Some 900 years later, the sheikh Abū l-Mawāhib al-Bakrī was praised by a contemporary as "the fragrant plant in the gardens of the progeny of (Abū Bakr) aṣ-Ṣiddīq" (*rayḥānatu rawḍi banī ṣ-Ṣiddīqi*).[132] A Moroccan poet and Saᶜdid vizier from Fez is praised by al-Ḫafāǧī as *rayḥānatu fuḍalāʾihā*, "the fragrant plant of the excellent (of that town)".[133] In this vein, somebody could boast by saying of himself *laqad kuntu rayḥānatan fī n-nadā*, "I have been the best example of generosity",[134] and this use of *rayḥānah* also crept into academic prose, for example into a Sudanese biographical dictionary, with *rayḥānah* meaning there "an exquisite choice of" in expressions such as *rayḥānatun min ʾaḫbārihī* and used interchangeably with *nubḏatun min ʾaḫbārihī*, "a condensed notion, *or* a piece, of what is known of him".[135]

Most importantly in our context, and leading us on to the next section – *rayḥān* as symbolic representation of Paradise –, the expression *rayḥānatu* + gen. appears in the following dictum ascribed to the Prophet and Shiite circles: *al-mawtu rayḥānatu l-muʾmini*,[136] "Death is the fragrant plant of the believer", that is, "Death" – and hence Paradise – "is the best thing which awaits, *or* happens to, the believer".

3.8. *Rayḥān* as symbolic representation of Paradise

More than anything else, *rayḥān* was made into a symbol for the pleasure of life in the hereafter viz. Paradise. As such, *rayḥān* is part of the vast Islamic eschatological imagery:[137] Ṣadaqah al-Maqāburī told a dream of his in which he saw Maᶜrūf al-Karḫī (d. 200 H or after) "and it was as if the dead were sitting upright in their tombs and he was going to and fro among them with *rayḥān*".[138]

In a report from ᶜUṯmān b. Sawdah, who saw his pious mother in a dream, we read the following: When he asked her, "O my mother, how are you doing?", she replied "My child, verily death is an awful pain, but I praise God that I am in the praiseworthy *barzaḫ* (i.e. limbo) where we lie down on *rayḥān* and put our heads on silk brocade" (see below).[139] A Tradition from the Prophet, via Abū Hurayrah, says that "when the believer dies, angels will bring him a silken garment,

131 ĀbīNaṯr I p. 270.

132 DarwSāniḥāt II p. 21.

133 ḪafRayḥ p. 148.

134 *Aġānī* VII p. 198.

135 IḌayfṬab pp. 46f., 74 and 206.

136 DaylFird II p. 363 = SuyBušrā p. 5; KU 42136 (XV p. 551).

137 Interestingly, the *rayḥān* also ranks among the fragrant plants of the Zoroastrian Paradise, see EI² II p. 1035 (A. Bausani).

138 IAYaṬab I p. 387. The same story, with different wording and ascribed to Abū Bakr al-Ḫayyāṭ, is also cited in ḤurRawḍ p. 221 (*fa-ʾiḏā ʾahlu l-qubūri ǧulūsun ᶜalā qubūrihim wa-bayna ʾaydīhimu r-rayāḥīnu* etc.).

139 IRaǧAhwāl p. 113; with a similar wording in MuwMuršid I p. 53; *cf.* also SuyBušrā p. 44 and al-ᶜAffānī: *Sakb* I p. 219. Another report (giving no names) with the same passage in ŠīrŠadd p. 34.

perfumed with musk, and bundles of *rayḥān*".[140] From another Tradition we learn that "God the Exalted, after He had created Paradise, surrounded it with *rayḥān*".[141]

The similarly frequent expression *rawḥ wa-rayḥān* goes back to the Qurʾānic *fa-rawḥun wa-rayḥānun wa-ǧannatu naʿīmin* (Q 56:89), rather loosely rendered by Arberry as "there shall be repose and ease (*rayḥān*) and a Garden of Delight".[142] To stay in *rawḥ wa-rayḥān*[143] or to go to *rawḥi llāhi wa-rayḥānihī*[144] was thus often understood to mean "staying in, *or* entering, Paradise", and in some Traditions we find that the soul of a believer who had died is taken to Paradise wrapped in *rayḥān*.[145] Paradise was depicted by the Prophet himself, according to some Traditions, as "a *rayḥānah* which quivers (in the wind) and a light which pearl-like shimmers".[146] This was taken up in a mourning poem by Ibn al-Muʿtazz, who wrote about the grave of a friend (*maǧzūʾ al-kāmil*):

طَافَتْ بِقَبْرِكَ رَحْمَةٌ * وَبِشَارَةٌ وَنَعِيمُ
وَاهْتَزَّ رَيْحَانٌ بِهِ * وَجَرَى عَلَيْهِ نَسِيمُ

"May mercy, good tidings and * bliss go around your tomb,
May *rayḥān* quiver upon it, * and may blow over it a perfumed breeze!"[147]

Older examples of the formula *rawḥ wa-rayḥān* – rendered in the following by "repose and ease" or the like for lack of a better term – are two verses by Ibn ar-Rūmī. The first describes a garden, and it seems that the poet is playing with the double meaning of *ǧannah*, "garden" or, more specifically, "the Garden of Paradise" (*basīṭ*):

حَيَّتْكَ عَنَّا شِمَالٌ طَافَ طَائِفُهَا * بِجَنَّةٍ فَجَرَتْ رَوْحاً وَرَيْحَانَا

140 ANuḤilyah III p. 104; SuyBušrā p. 19.

141 MālRiyāḍ I p. 248; *cf.* also Lane s.r. *ḥff*.

142 In Q 55:12, Arberry translates *rayḥān* as "fragrant herbs". For the exegesis of Q 56:89, see al-ʿAffānī: *Sakb* I pp. 606-8. Some second-century reciters (e.g. Qatādah and al-Ḥasan al-Baṣrī) read, as is tempting, *fa-rūḥun* instead of *fa-rawḥun*, and *rawḥ* was understood as "ease" or "mercy" (*raḥmah*), see SuyInbāʾAḏk p. 59 and Lane s.r. *rwḥ*. In preserved epitaphs we find the expressions *raḥmatun wa-rayḥānun* (RCEA 797 017) and *bi-r-rayḥāni wa-r-rawḥ*; in a verse we read *rayḥānuhū wa-raḥmatuhū*, "His bounty and His mercy", said of God (Lane s.r. *drr*), *cf.* also FB VI p. 518 (*ʾanbiyāʾ* 19): *min rawḥi llāhi ʾay min raḥmati llāh*.

143 As more or less synonymous expressions we sometimes find *rawḥ wa-ṭīb* (e.g. HarMirqātMaf I p. 206) or *rawḥ wa-rāḥah* (e.g. ŠīrŠadd p. 33); *cf.* also Dozy: *Supplément* s.v. *rawḥ*.

144 HarMirqātMaf IV p. 21.

145 SuyBušrā pp. 23f.

146 IMāǧah II p. 1448 (*zuhd* 39) = IǦawzīTabṣ I p. 436.

147 IMuʿtDīwān 1199 vv. 8f. (III p. 82). The word order of the first verse is changed in the translation.

"May a north wind greet you from us whose breeze has made its way * through a garden and so become 'refreshment and fragrance' (i.e. repose and ease)".[148]

The second verse belongs to a mourning poem of his (*ṭawīl*):

سَلَامٌ وَرَيْحَانٌ وَرَوْحٌ وَرَحْمَةٌ * عَلَيْكَ وَمَمْدُودٌ مِنَ الظِلِّ سَجْسَجُ

"Peace and ease and repose and mercy * be upon you, and outstretched shade, temperate!"[149]

The brother of Ribʿī b. Ḫirāš al-ʿAbsī spoke after his death and told the people around his bier that God "has received me *bi-rawḥin wa-rayḥānin* and silk brocade", or according to another version: "I met my Lord after departing from you and He received me *bi-rawḥin wa-rayḥān*".[150] In a number of Shiite Traditions we find the Qurʾānic expression *rawḥun wa-rayḥānun wa-ǧannatu naʿīm* denoting the stay in Paradise,[151] and in other Traditions we read the following: "He who replies correctly (during the Interrogation in the tomb) will be *bi-rawḥin wa-rayḥānin* in his tomb and in a Garden of Bliss (*ǧannatu naʿīm*) in the hereafter".[152] What is more, the angels themselves will shroud those who die on their way to the tomb of al-Ḥusayn and they will "make a bed of *rayḥān* for them".[153]

In a poem by Ibn Qayyim al-Ǧawzīyah, describing the beauties of the Virgins of Paradise (*al-ḥūr*), the Qurʾānic expression *rawḥ wa-rayḥān* clearly left its imprint in the following line (*kāmil*):

وَسَلِ الْمُتَيَّمَ كَيْفَ مَجْلِسُهُ مَعَ الْـ * ـمَحْبُوبِ فِي رَوْحٍ وَفِي رَيْحَانِ

"And ask the infatuated how he finds his stay with the * Beloved *in repose and in ease / in the Bliss of Paradise*".[154]

As said above, the terms *rawḥ wa-rayḥān* do appear in early Arabic mourning poetry, yet they were not commonly used before the sixth century H. Some examples for their later conventional use are provided in the following verses:

(a) In a sixth-century (?) mourning poem quoted by Ibn Kaṯīr (*basīṭ*):

سَقَى ثَرًى أَوْدَعُوهُ رَحْمَةً مَلَأَتْ * مَثْوَى قُبُورِهِمِ رَوْحاً وَرَيْحَانَا

"May (God) irrigate a certain moist earth, to which they consigned him, with mercy that fills * the abodes of their tombs with repose and ease!"[155]

148 IRūmīDīwān VI p. 2460 (no. 1338 l. 1) = Schoeler: *Naturdichtung* pp. 224f. Of interest is also another line by Ibn ar-Rūmī (*sarīʿ*): *wa-kāna lī ʾunsan laday waḥšatī * wa-kāna lī rawḥan wa-rayḥānā* (IRūmīDīwān IV p. 2590 = no. 1473 v. 3).

149 IRūmīDīwān II p. 494 (no. 366 v. 26) = IṬiqFaḫrī p. 241.

150 ANuḤilyah IV pp. 367f.; IǦawzīṢafwah II p. 21; BN VI p. 158; also quoted (from Abū Nuʿaym's version) in ŠirŠadd pp. 18f.

151 KulKāfī III p. 232; MaǧlBiḥār VI pp. 207, 222 and 225.

152 MaǧlBiḥār VI p. 279.

153 IQūlKāmil p. 123.

154 IQaylthāf p. 265.

155 Quoted in BN XII p. 279 (*ad* 569 H).

(b) In a poem mourning the death of the grammarian Ibn Mālik (d. Damascus 672 H), by his pupil Ibn an-Naḥḥās (d. 698 H) (*kāmil*):

فَسَقَى ضَرِيحاً ضَمَّهُ صَوْبُ الحَيَا * يَهْمِي بِهِ بِالرَّوْحِ وَالرَّيْحَانِ

"May the abundant rain irrigate a grave that encloses him (i.e. the deceased person), * pouring forth upon him[156] repose and ease!"[157]

(c) In a poem mourning Ǧamāl ad-Dīn Ibrāhīm aṭ-Ṭībī (d. 706 H) (*mutaqārib*):

سَأَلْتُ إلهِيَ إكْرَامَهُ * بِنُزْلٍ وَرَوْحٍ وَرَيْحَانِهِ

"I asked my God to treat him hospitably * by (rewarding him with) nourishment,[158] repose and His ease".[159]

(d) In a mourning poem by Ibn Nubātah, the line being certainly an imitation of the verse by Ibn ar-Rūmī cited above page 593 (*ṭawīl*):

سَلامٌ وَرِضْوانٌ عَلَيْهِ وَرَحْمَةٌ * وَرَوْحٌ وَرَيْحَانٌ وَخَمْرٌ مُنَوَّعُ

"Peace be with him and (God's) satisfaction and mercy * and repose and ease and various sorts of wine".[160]

(e) In a poem mourning the death of Taqīy ad-Dīn aš-Šumunnī (d. 872 H), by his pupil as-Suyūṭī (*basīṭ*):

أَبْصِرْ بِرَوْحٍ وَرَيْحَانٍ وَدَارِ رِضًى * وَرَحْمَةٍ وَصَفَاءٍ مَا بِهِ كَدَرُ

"Ponder repose and ease, and an Abode of Satisfaction, * and mercy and pure happiness, untroubled!"[161]

(f) In a mourning poem from Mauritania, composed by ʿAbd Allāh b. Muḥammad al-ʿAlawī (*fl.* eleventh century H) (*ṭawīl*):

سَقَى اللّهُ قَبْراً ضَمَّهُ وَبْلَ رَحْمَةٍ * مِنَ الرَّوْحِ وَالرَّيْحَانِ تَهْمِي سَحَائِبُهُ

"May God irrigate a tomb that encloses him with a downpour of mercy * (consisting) of repose and ease, (a downpour) whose clouds are filled with rain!"[162]

156 *Cf.* Dozy: *Supplément* II p. 765 (s.r. *hmy*).

157 Quoted in MaqqNafḥ (C) II p. 426.

158 I wonder whether the reading *bi-nazlin*, i.e. "with lodging (in Paradise)", is preferable.

159 ŠīrŠadd p. 344.

160 INubDīwān p. 307.

161 SuyBuġ I p. 381.

162 ŠinqWasīṭ p. 17. See also the first lines from the epitaph-poem of the Naṣrid ruler al-Muʾayyad Abū l-Ḥaǧǧāǧ Yūsuf I b. Ismāʿīl I (r. 733–55 H): *yuḥyīka bi-r-rayḥāni wa-r-rawḥi min qabrī * raḍiya llāhu ʿamman ḥalla fīka madā d-dahrī* (**92d**).

Not surprisingly, the Qurʾānic expression *rawḥ wa-rayḥān* also occurs in poetry in praise of the Prophet. In a poem celebrating the Prophet's birthday (*mawlid an-nabī*) by the Moroccan poet ʿAbd al-ʿAzīz b. Muḥammad al-Fištālī (d. 1030 H) we find a late, but illustrative example of this (*ṭawīl*):

أَحِنُّ إِلَى تِلْكَ الْمَعَاهِدِ إِنَّهَا * مَعَاهِدُ رَاحَاتِي وَرَوْحِي وَرَيْحَانِي

"I yearn for those places[163] for they are * the places where I find my comfort, my repose and my ease".[164]

When put in this way, using the expression *rawḥ wa-rayḥān*, the places where the Prophet used to live are here equaled with Paradise, since it is there that "repose and ease" are found. In the same way, *rawḥ wa-rayḥān* could occur in the openings and eulogies of official letters, e.g. in a letter from the Marīnid ruler Abū l-Ḥasan addressing the Mamluk ruler an-Nāṣir Muḥammad b. Qalāwūn: *yatawallāhu rawḥun wa-rayḥānun*, "May he be cared for by repose and ease!"[165]

The appearance of the eschatologically flavoured expression *rawḥ wa-rayḥān* in wine songs seems exceptional. Here, it stands metaphorically for a "the Paradise-like mood" caused by the joys of the event and refers also to the probable real scene of the drinking bout.[166] In a poem by Baššār b. Burd, an encounter with a girl is depicted as an encounter with *rawḥ wa-rayḥān*, namely when the poet is kissing her.[167]

In some cases, the symbolic value of the *rayḥān* plant and its importance in the eschatological context gave rise to reports about the presence of *rayḥān* in somebody's tomb. Thus Ibn al-Ǧawzī relates that beside the shrine of Ibn Ḥanbal (in Baghdad) another tomb was opened and a *rayḥānah* was found on the breast of the corpse.[168] Similarly, when the people buried the Kūfan ascetic Muḥammad b. an-Naḍr al-Ḥāriṯī, they found *rayḥān* spread out in his burial niche (see also above p. 92). Finally, we know the following anecdote about the ascetic Harim b. Ḥayyān (*cf.* p. 187): on some days, he would go with a companion to the market where *rayḥān* was sold, and they would ask God for Paradise and utter pious invocations. Afterwards, they would continue on to the blacksmiths' quarter to seek protection from Hell-fire.[169]

3.9. *Rayḥān* in two anecdotes

Anas b. Mālik said, "When I stayed once with al-Ḥusayn, a slave-girl entered with a *rayḥān* (branch *or* plant) in her hand. She gave it to him as a greeting, and he said,

163 I.e. the Ḥiǧāz, or Medina in particular.

164 MaqqNafḥ (C) VI p. 328 (read "al-Fištālī" instead of "al-Qaštālī") and MaqqRawḍah p. 121; MN IV p. 243 (v. 20).

165 As cited in MaqqNafḥ (C) VI p. 122.

166 See the verse by Abū ʿĀmir b. al-Ḥammārah in IDiḥMuṭrib p. 109.

167 BaššārDīwān 344 l. 2 (p. 226).

168 Quoted in IRaǧAhwāl p. 92.

169 ANuḤilyah II p. 119.

'You are free, for the sake of God!' I asked him, 'How? A simple slave-girl, of no standing whatsoever, greets you with a bunch of *rayḥān* and you set her free?' He replied, 'This is how God the Exalted instructed us, for He said, *And when you are greeted with a greeting greet with a fairer than it, or return it* (Q 4:86), and to free her was fairer (than her greeting me with a *rayḥān* branch)'".[170]

The following is told of ᶜĪsā b. Ḥaǧǧāǧ al-Yamanī al-ᶜĀmirī (d. 664 H), a saintly man: "Everybody who entered to him or left him kissed his hand. When he was criticised for this by someone, he replied, 'The believer (*al-ʿabd al-muʾmin*) is the fragrant plant of God (*rayḥānat allāh*) on His earth, so there is nothing wrong with enjoying the scent of fragrant plants in coming and going!'"[171]

4. *Conclusion*

The essential key-term *rayḥān*, "myrtle" or "fragrant plant", as it appears in several examples of funerary epigraphy, can now, after its numerous significations have been explored, be connected with the following notions:

(a) A deceased child could be likened to *rayḥān*, because *rayḥān* was in general said of small children and used metaphorically for beautiful and sweet-smelling persons in general. In addition, *rayḥān(ah)* was also said of distinguished persons and this might indicate the high esteem the parents must have felt for their child.

(b) A child could be likened to *rayḥān* for its slender body. This is, in the present context, confirmed by the metaphorical mentioning of the twigs in the third line of epitaph-poem **195**. Still, the metaphor of *rayḥān* and its twigs includes two more concepts. First, the custom of placing plants upon tombs, and second, the fact that the death of a person could be described as "the withering away" of a fragrant plant. The first concept is expressed clearly in the epitaph-poem in the second verse: "He has become the fragrant plant of the graves". Of course, this also takes up the notion that the earth of a tomb, or a cemetery, was often thought to be perfumed, and it is here that the element "fragrance, perfume" of the *rayḥān*-metaphor, complex as it is, plays its part: the child was a *rayḥān* in life, but it also emanates the scent of *rayḥān* after death and perfumes the other tombs by being buried amidst them.

(c) That a deceased child was "planted in the gardens", as said in the epitaph-poem (line 4), plays again on the *rayḥān*-metaphor. Additionally, I presume that the Qurʾānic concept of life in Paradise as being "in repose and ease" (*bi-rawḥin wa-rayḥānin*) is present in the epitaph-poem at least implicitly. In any case, every

170 TawḥBaṣāʾir VII p. 137.

171 MunKawākib II pp. 511f.; MuḥḪul I p. 339. The eleventh-century philologist and poet Šihāb ad-Dīn al-Ḫafāǧī also composed a little poem about this anecdote.

Muslim reader in some ways familiar with the Qurʾānic wording will easily make this association.

These numerous implications of the key-term *rayḥān* taken together constitute the strong intertextual character of the epitaph-poem we have been analysing. Admittedly, the main features of this intertextuality might have been demonstrated using a lesser array of sources and material than has been done in this chapter, but as the proverb says:

مَنْ يَزْرَعِ الثُومَ لَمْ يَقْلَعْهُ رَيْحَانَا

"He who sows garlic won't pluck *rayḥān*".[172]

172 Ṯaʿāl*Tamṯīl* p. 274 (lit. "... won't pluck it as *rayḥān*").

Arabic Appendix
Epitaph-Poetry Cited in Literary Sources

NOTE. The following pages contain the Arabic texts of all the epitaph-poems edited in the preceding catalogue of epitaphs (Chapter 4, pp. 337–573); the bold numbers refer to the respective entries. It is important to bear in mind that almost all the epitaph-poems quoted in the following are part of epitaphs which are known exclusively from literary sources. In general, we have no means to ascertain whether the epitaph-poems were in fact ever inscribed upon a particular grave.

1 (p. 340)

قبرَ الغريبِ سقاك الرائحُ الغادِي * حقّاً ظفِرتَ بأشلاءِ ابنِ عبَّادِ
بالحلمِ بالعلم بالنُعْمَى إذا اتّصلتْ * بالخِصْب إنْ أجدبوا بالرِيِّ للصادي
بالطاعن الضارب الرامي إذا اقتتلوا * بالموت أحمرَ بالضِرغامة العادي
بالدهر في نِقَمٍ بالبحر في نِعَمٍ * بالبدر في ظُلَم بالصدر في النادي
نعم هو الحقّ حاباني به قدرٌ * من السماء فوافاني لميعادِ
ولم أكن قبل ذاك النعْش أعلمُه * أنّ الجبالَ تُهادَى فوق أعْوادِ
كفاك فارْفُقْ بما استُودِعْتَ من كرمٍ * روّاك كلّ قطوب البرق رعّادِ
يبكي أخاه الّذي غيّبْتَ وابلَهُ * تحت الصفيح بدمع رائحٍ غادي
حتّى يجودَك دمع الطلّ مُنْهَمِراً * من أعيُن الزُهر لم تبخل بإسْعادِ
ولا تزل صلوات اللّه دائمةً * على دفينك لا تحصَى بتعْدادِ

2 (p. 345)

الموت أخرجَني من دار مملكتي * فالتُرْب مضطجعي من بعد تشريفِي
لِله عبدٌ رأى قبري فأحزنَه * وخاف من دهره ريبَ التصاريفِ
هذا مصير بني الدنيا وإنْ عَمَرُوا * فيها وغرّهمُ طول التساويفِ
أستغفر الله من عَمْدِي ومن حَنَقِي * وأسأل الله فوزاً يومَ توقيفي

3 (p. 347)

مَن زارَ قبري فَليكُنْ مُوقِناً * أنَّ الّذي ألقاهُ يلقاهُ
فيرحم الله امرأ زارَنِـي * وقالَ لي يرحمكَ اللــهُ

4 (p. 349)

قد كان صاحبُ هذا القبر جَوْهرةً * مكنُونةً قد بَراها الله من شَرَفِ
فلم تكنْ تعرفِ الأيامُ قِـــيمتَهُ * فردَّها غَيْرةً مِنه إلى الــصَدَفِ

6 (p. 354)

مات الإمــامُ الخالديُّ فساءنا * يوم النـوَى والحُزن عادَ مُخَلَّــدَا
وأصيب في العام الّذي تأريخُه * قد طاب مثواه الرحيب وَوُطِّدَا

7 (p. 355)

في الخدّ أُخدودٌ به جرتِ الدِما * من فقدِ من قد حاز طيبَ مقام
ولدي الّذي تأريخ عــام وفـاته * كم نــال محمودٌ ثواب مقـــام

8 (p. 356)

ذا ضريحٌ حلّ فيه فاضــلٌ * طاب من ريّا أياديــه النسيــمْ
مات في العام الّذي تأريخه * كم لصدر الدين من أربى نعيمْ

9 (p. 356)

أبو بكرٍ النقّاش أحْوَجُ سائلٍ * إلى رحمةٍ تُقصيه عن مُوجِب الوَزْرِ
فيا أيــها المجــتاز نحو ضريحه * تمهَّل قليــلاً داعـــياً لأبي بكرِ

11 (pp. 357f.)

وكيف يلذّ العيشَ من هو عالمٌ * بأنّ إلهَ الخلق لا بدّ سائلُه
فيأخذ منه ظُلمَه لعباده * ويَجزيه بالخير الّذي هو فاعــلُه

وكيف يلذّ العيشَ من كان مُوقِناً * بأنّ المنايا بغتةً سَتُعَاجِلُه
فتسلبه ملكاً عظيماً وبهجةً * وتُسكنه البيت الّذي هو آهِــلُه

وكيف يلذّ العيشَ من كان صائراً * إلى جدثٍ تُبلي الشبابَ منازِلُه
ويَذهب وسمُ الوجه من بعد ضوءه * سريعاً ويَبلى جسمه ومفاصِلُه

12 (p. 359)

ليس للميّت في قبرهِ * فطرٌ ولا أضحىً ولا عشْرُ
ناءَ عن الأهل على قربهِ * كذاك من مسكنهُ القبْرُ

13 (p. 360)

أنا البعيد القريب الدار منظرهُ * بين الجنادل والأحجار مرموسُ

14 (p. 362)

وعظتْك واعظةٌ صمتْ * ونعتك ناعيةٌ خفتْ
وتكلّمت عن أعظمٍ * تَبلى وعن صورٍ سبتْ
وأرتْك وجهَك في الترا * ب وأنت حيٌّ لم تمتْ

وعظتك أجداثٌ صمتْ * ونعتك أزمنةٌ خفتْ
وتكلّمت عن أوجهٍ * تبلى وعن صورٍ شتتْ
وأرتك قبرَك في القبو * ر وأنت حيٌّ لم تمتْ

15 (p. 364)

يا غافرَ الذنبِ العظيمِ بجُودِهِ * اغفرْ لعبدِكَ ذنبَهُ مُتفضِّلاَ

يا نُوَاسِيُّ توقّرْ * وتعزّى وتصبّرْ
ساءك الدهر بشيءٍ * وبما سرّك أكثرْ
يا كبيرَ الذنب عفو الـ * ـله من دنبك أكبرْ

16 (p. 365)

كابَرَنيك الزمانُ يا حَسَنُ * فخاب سهمي وأفلح الزمنُ
ليتك إذ لم تكن بقيتَ لنا * لم تبقَ روحٌ يحوطها بدنُ

17 (p. 366)

أذنَ حيٍ تَسمَّعي * اسمعي ثمّ عِي وَعِي
أنا رهنٌ بمضجعي * فاحذري مثلَ مصرَعي
عِشْتُ تسعين حجّةً * في ديار التزعزُعي
ليس زادٌ سوى التُقَى * فخذي منه أو دَعي

18 (p. 369)

إنّ عيشاً يكون آخره المو * ت لَعَيْشٌ مُعجّل التنغيصِ

19 (p. 370)

أقول لقبرٍ زرتُه مُتلثّماً * سقى الله بردَ العفو صاحبةَ القبرِ
لقد غيَّبوا تحت الثرى قمر الدُجَى * وشمس الضُحَى بين الصفائح والعفرِ
عجبتُ لعينٍ بعدها ملّت البكى * وقلبٍ عليها يَرْتَجِي راحة الصبرِ

21 (p. 374)

رُبّ ميتٍ قد صار بالعلم حياً * ومُبقٍّ قد مات جهلاً وعَيَا
فاقتنوا العلم كي تنالوا خلوداً * لا تعدُّوا الحياةَ في الجهل شيَا

23 (pp. 376f.)

نفس يا نفس كم تُمادِينَ في الغَيِّ * وتأتِينَ بالفعال المَعيبِ
راقبي الله واحذري موضع الأر * ض وخافي يوم الحساب العَصيبِ
لا تغرنّنّكِ السلامة في العيـ * ـش فإنّ السليم رهن الخُطوبِ
كلّ حيّ فللمنون ولا يد * فع كأس المنون كيد الأريبِ
واعلمي أنّ للمنية وقتا * سوف يأتي عجلانَ غير هَيُوبِ
فأعدّي لذلك اليوم زاداً * وجواباً لله غير كَذُوبِ
إنّ حبَّ الصدِّيق في موقف الحشـ * ـر أمانٌ للخائف الطلوبِ

26 (p. 379)

يا كثيرَ العفو عمّن * كثُر الذنب لَدَيْهِ
جاءك المذنب يرجو الصـ * ـفح عن جُرْم يديهِ
أنا ضيفٌ وجزاء الضـ * ـيف إحسانٌ إليهِ

29 (p. 383)

يا غافلَ القلب عن ذكر المنيات * عمّا قليلٍ ستثوي بين أمواتِ
فاذكُر محلَّك من قبل الحُلول به * وتُب إلى الله من لهوٍ ولذّاتِ
إنّ الحمامَ له وقتٌ إلى أجلٍ * فاذكر مصائب أيّامٍ وساعاتِ
لا تطمئِنَّ إلى الدنيا وزِينتها * قد حان للموت يا ذا اللُبِّ أنْ يأتِ

30 (p. 384)

ستُعرض عن ذكري وتَنْسَى مَودّتي * ويُحْدَثُ بعدي للخليل خليلُ
إذا انقطعت يوماً من العيش مُدّتي * فإنّ غِناءَ الباكيات قليلُ

31 (p. 385)

ما بال قبرك يا كافور مُنفرداً * بالصَحْصَح المَرْت بعد العسكر اللَجِبِ
يدوس قبرَك آحاد الرجال وقد * كانت أُسود الشَرَى تخشاك في الكُبَبِ

32 (p. 386)

رحم الله فقيراً * زار قبري وقرَا لي
سورةَ السبع المثاني * بخشوعٍ ودعَا لي

33 (p. 387)

أيها الواقفَ هَوْناً فاعتبرْ * إنّ في الموت لَشُغلاً فادّكرْ

34 (p. 387)

أتيتُ إلى خالقي خاضعاً * ومن خدّه في الثرى يخضعُ
وإن كنتُ وافيته مُجْرِماً * فإنّيَ في عفوه أطمعُ
وكيف أخاف ذنوباً مضَتْ * وأحمد في زَلَّتي يشفعُ
فأخلِص دُعاءك يا زائري * لعلّ الإله به ينفعُ

35 (p. 388)

يا أيها الغافل جدَّ الرحيلْ * وأنت في اللهو وزادكْ قليلْ
لو كنتَ تدري ما تُلاقي غداً * لَذُبْتَ من فَطْرِ البُكا والعويلْ

فأخلص التوبة تحظى بها * فما بقَى (!) في العمر إلاّ القليلْ
ولا تَنَمْ إنْ كنتَ ذا فِطنةٍ * فإنّ قُدّامك نومٌ طويلْ

39 (p. 392)

عبرتُ على قبر ابن طولونَ مرّةً * فأنكرت فيما كان من عظم قدرهِ
ولم أرَ ممّا كان يملك كلّه * تبقّى له شيئاً (!) سوى لوح قبرهِ
وما ينفع الإنسان ممّا يحوزه * إذا فارق الدنيا سوى طِيب ذكرهِ

41 (p. 394)

المال ينفذ حلّه وحرامه * يوماً ويبقى في غدٍ أثامهُ
ليس التقيُ بمتقٍ في دينه * حتّى يطيبَ شرابه وطعامهُ

43 (p. 396)

إنّ الحبيبَ من الأحباب مُختَلَسُ * لا يمنع الموتَ حُجّابٌ ولا حَرَسُ
وكيف تفرح بالدنيا ولذّتها * يامن يُعَدّ عليه اللفظ والنَفَسُ
أصبحتَ يا غافلاً في النقص مُنغَمِساً * وأنتَ دهرك في اللذّات مُنغَمِسُ
لا يرحم الموتَ ذا مالٍ لعزّته * ولا الّذي كان منه العلم يُقتَبَسُ
كم أخرس الموت في قبرٍ وقفتُ به * عنِ الجواب لساناً ما به خَرَسُ
قد كان قصرُك معموراً به شرفٌ * وقبرك اليومَ في الأجداث مُندَرِسُ

55 (p. 405)

أصبحتُ بقعر حفرةٍ مُرتهَنَا * لا أملك من دنيايَ إلاّ كفنَا
يا من وسِعتْ عبادَه رحمتهُ * من بعضِ عِبادك المُسيئين أنَا

62 (p. 408)

ولمّا أتينا قبره لنزورَهُ * عرفناه لما فاح طيبُ ترابهِ
سقى الله من ماء الجنان ترابَه * ونجّى به من زاره من عقابهِ

ولمّا أتينا قبر سعد نزورُهُ * عرفناه لما فاح طيبُ ترابهِ
سقى الله من ماء الجنان ترابَه * ونجّى به من زاره من عذابهِ

63 (p. 410)

يا قاهراً بالمنايا كلَّ جبّارِ * بنور وجهِك أعْتِقني منَ النارِ

65 (p. 411)

إنّ الفقيرَ الّذي أضْحَى بحفرته * نزيلُ ربّ كثيرِ العفو ستّـــارِ
يوصيك بالأهل والأولاد تحفظهم * فهم عيال على معروفك الساري

66 (p. 411)

بقارعةِ الطريقِ جعلْتُ قبري * لأحْظَى بالترحُّمِ مِن صديـــقِ
فيا مولى الموالي أنت أولَى * برحمةِ مَن يموت على الطريقِ

68 (p. 412)

إذا فات ما كنتُ أمّلته * جَزِعْتُ وماذا يُفـــيد الجَزَعْ
ففوّضْتُ لله كلَّ الأمور * فليس يكون سِوى ما يَقَــعْ
ولا يخدعنّك صرف الزمان * فإنّ الزمانَ كثير الخُدَعْ

69 (p. 412)

تقول نفسي أتخشَى * من هول ذنبٍ عظيمِ
لا تختشي من عقابٍ * فأنت عبد الرحـــيمِ

70 (p. 413)

ألا يا مـــالكَ العلمـــاء يا من * به في الأرض أثمر كلّ مَغْرِسْ
لئن أوحشتَ تونسَ بعد بُعدٍ * فأنت بمصرَ ملك الحُسن تُؤْنِسْ

71 (p. 415)

تفكّرتُ في جود الإله وعفوه * عنِ المُذنب العاصي وإنْ عظُم الذَنْـــبُ
وأحسنتُ ظنّي بالذي لا تضُرّه * ذنوبي فهان الصَعْب وانكشف الكَرْبُ
ومِن جوده أمّلـت أمناً ورحمةً * لســاكن هذا القبر إنْ مسّــه رُعْـــبُ
وأرّخته يا ربّ جودُك واســـعٌ * وعبدُك اسمـــاعيل يرجـــوك يا ربِّي

72 (p. 416)

صِلوا لحدَ قبري بالطريق وودِّعوا * فليس لمن وارى التراب حبيبُ
ولا تدفنوني بالعراء فربّمـــا * بكى إنْ رأى قبر الغريبِ غريبُ

73 (p. 418)

ياصاحبِي قُمْ فقد أطلنا * أنحن طولَ المدى هُجُـودُ
فقال لي لن نقومَ منها * ما دام من فوقنا الصَعِيدُ
تذكر كَم ليــلةٍ لَهَوْنا * في ظلّها والزمان عِيــدُ
وكم سرورٍ هما علينا * ســحابةً ثرَّةً تَجُــودُ
كلٌّ كأنْ لم يكن تقضَّى * وشؤمــه حاضرٌ عَتِــيدُ
حصّله كاتبٌ حفيــظٌ * وضمّه صــادقٌ شَهِــيدُ
يا ويلنا إن تنكّبتْــنا * رحمةُ من بطشه شَدِيــدُ
ياربّ عفواً فأنت مولًى * قصَّر في أمرك العَبِــيدُ

74 (p. 420)

اصبر لدهرٍ نال منـ * ـك فهكذا مَضَتِ الدهورُ
فرحٌ وحزنٌ واقعٌ * لا الحُزْنُ دام ولا الســرورُ

77 (p. 423)

يا ربّنا يا من لـــه * نِعَـــمٌ غِزارٌ لا تُعَدْ
يا من يُرَجَّى فضلُه * يا من هو الفرد الصَمَدْ
اغفر لساكن ذا الضريـ * ـح محمّدٍ المُعْتَـمَدْ

78 (p. 423)

ذا قبرُ أعلم الوَرَى * بحر العلوم الواضحهْ
بعبد وهابٍ سُمَّى (!) * والنفس منه صالحهْ
كان إمــام الأموي * حاز المعاني الراجحـهْ
يا قارئــاً تأريخه * هلاّ هدَيْـتَ الفاتحـــهْ

79 (p. 424)

أتعلم يا عمادي أنّ ركني * لفقدك قد وهــى وانحَلَّ عَزْمِــي

وأنّ سرورَ قلبي يا سروري * ترحَّل مُسْرِعاً وازداد هَمِّي
وبعدك ما أرَدْتُ بقاء روحي * ولكن ليس ذلك تحت حُكْمِي

80 (p. 425)

يا ربّ تبعتُ سيّد الأبرار * واختَرْتُ سبيل صُحبة الأخيارِ
واليومَ فليس لي سوى لطفك بي * يا ربّ فَوَقِّنِي عذابَ النارِ

81 (p. 425)

مات في الشام حاكمٌ * قدرهُ في الورى كبيرْ
جاء تأريخنا له * بيت شعرٍ له قصيرْ
رحم اللهْ مُحِبَّنا * يوسفَ باشَ ألوزيرْ

82 (p. 426)

قبرٌ به من أوثقته ذنوبه * وغدا لسوء فعاله مُتَخَوِّفَا
قد ضاع منه عمره ببطالةٍ * والعيش منه بالتكدّر ما صَفَا
ماذا طوى قبر اللُقَيْمي أرِّخُوا * مُسْتَمْنِحُ للعفو أسعد مصطفى

83 (p. 426)

اِعمل لنفسك قبل الموت وَارْضَ بما * يأتيك وَانْظر إلى قبري لتعرفَنِي
لقد ملكتُ من الأموال أُهْبَةَ ما * يزيد فوق ألوفٍ فَهْيَ ذي فِتَنِي

84 (p. 427)

ألا رحم الله حيّاً دعا * لميْتٍ قَضَى بالفلا نَحْبَهُ
تمرّ السوافي على قبره * فتُهدي لأحبابه تُرْبَهُ
وليس له عملٌ يُرْتَجَى * ولكنّه يَرْتَجِي رَبَّهُ

85 (pp. 427f.)

زُر غريباً بمقرّه * نازحاً ما له وليِ
تركوه مُوَسَّداً * بين تُربٍ وجندلِ
وَلْتَقُلْ عند قبره * بلسان التدلُّلِ
يرحم الله عبدَه * مالِكَ بن المُرَحَّلِ

86 (p. 429)

يا أيها الناس كان لي أملُ * قصّر بي عن بلوغه الأجلُ
فَلْيَتَّقِ اللهَ ربَّه رجلٌ * أمكنه في حياته العملُ
ما أنا وحدي نُقِلتُ حيث تَرَى * كلٌّ إلى مثله سَيَنْتَقِلُ

87 (p. 431)

ياخليلِي عَرِّجْ على قبري تَجِدْ * أكلة الترب بين جنبَيْ ضريحِ
خافِتُ الصوتِ إن نطقتُ ولكن * أيّ نطقٍ إن اعتبرتَ فصيحِ
أبصرتْ عينِيَ العجائبَ لكن * فرَّق الموت بين جسمي وروحِ

88 (p. 431)

عليك سلام الله يا من يسلّمُ * ورحمته ما زُرتني تترحّمُ
أتحسبني وحدي نُقِلْتُ إلى هنا * ستلحق بي عمّا قريبٍ فتعلمُ
أفيّا لمن يُمْسِي لدنياه مُؤثِراً * ويُحْمِلُ أُخراه ستشقى وتندمُ
فلا تفرحَنْ إلاّ بتقديم طاعةٍ * فذاك الّذي يُنجِي غداً ويسلّمُ

89 (p. 434)

هذا محلّ العُلى والحلم الكَرَمِ * قبر الإمام الهُمام الطاهر العَلَمِ
للّه ما ضمّ هذا اللحد من شرفٍ * جمٍّ ومن شِيَمٍ عُلوية الهِمَمِ
فالبأس والجود ما تَحوي صفائحه * لا بأس عنترةٍ ولا ندى هَرِمِ
مغنَى الكرامة والرضوان يعمره * فخر الملوك الكريم الذات والشِيَمِ
مقامه في كلا يومَيْ ندىً ووغىً * كالغيث في المحل أو كالليث في أجم
مآثرٌ تليتْ آثارها سُوَراً * تُقرّ بالحقّ فيها جملة الأُمَمِ
كأنّه لم يَسِرْ في جحفلٍ لجِبٍ * تضيق عنه بلاد العُرْب والعَجَمِ
ولم يُغادِ العِدا منه ببادرةٍ * يفترّ منها الهدى عن ثغر مبتسم
ولم يُجهّز لهم خيلاً مُضمّرةً * لا تشرب الماءَ إلاّ من قليب دم
ولم يُقِم حكم عدلٍ في سياسته * تأوي رعيته منه إلى حَرم
من كان يجهل ما أولاه من نِعَمٍ * وما حماه لدين الله من حُرم
فتلك آثاره في كلّ مكرُمةٍ * أبدى وأوضحُ من نارٍ على عَلَمِ
لا زال يهمي على قبرٍ تضمّنه * سحائب الرحمة الوكّافة الدِيَمِ

90 (pp. 438f.)

تَخُصّ قبرك يا خير السلاطين * تحيةٌ كالصبا مرّت بدارينِ
قبرٌ به من بني نَصْرٍ أمام هدى * عالي المراتب في الدنيا وفي الدين
أبو الوليد وما أدراك من ملكٍ * مُستنصرٍ واثقٍ بالله مأمون
سلطان عدلٍ وبأسٍ غالبٍ وندى * وفضل تقوى وأخلاقٍ مَيامين
لله ما قد طواه الموت من شرفٍ * وسرّ مجدٍ بهذا اللحد مدفون
ومن لسانٍ بذكر الله منطلقٌ * ومن فؤادٍ بحبّ الله مسكون
أما الجهاد فقد أحيا معالمه * وقام منه بمفروضٍ ومسنون
فكم فتوحٍ له تَزهُو المنابر من * عُجْبٍ بهنّ وأوراق الدواوين
مجاهدٌ نال من فضل الشهادة ما * يُجْبَى عليه بأجرٍ غير ممنون
قضى كعثمانَ في الشهر الحرام ضُحىً * وفاةَ مستشهدٍ في الدار مطعون
في عارضَيْهِ غبار الغزو تمسحه * في جنّةَ الخلد أيدي حورها العِين
يُسقى بها عينَ تسنيمٍ وقاتله * مردّدٌ بين زَقُّومٍ وغِسْلين
تبكي البلاد عليه والعباد معاً * فالخلق ما بين أحزانٍ أفانين
لكنّه حكم ربٍّ لا مَرَدَّ له * فأمره الجزم بين الكاف والنون
فرحمة الله ربّ العالمين على * سلطان عدلٍ بهذا القبر مدفون

93 (p. 445)

أحسنتَ ظنّك بالأيّام إذْ حسُنتْ * ولم تخَف سُوءَ ما يأتي به القَدَرُ
وسالَمَتْك الليالي فاغترَرْتَ بها * وعند صفوِ الليالي يحدث الكَدَرُ

تفكَّرْ بنا يا زائرَ القبر واعتبرْ * ولا تكُ في الدنيا هُدِيتَ بآنسِ
ملكت خراساناً وأكناف فارسٍ * وما كنت عن ملك العراق بآيسِ
سلامٌ على الدنيا وطيبِ نسيمها * كأنْ لم يكن يعقوبُ فيها بجالسِ

94 (p. 447)

يا من يرى مَدَّ البَعوض جَناحها * في ظلمة الليل البَهيم الألْيَلِ
ويرى عروقَ نِياطها في نَحْرِها * والمُخَّ في تلك العظام النُحَّلِ
اغفرْ لعبدٍ تاب من فَرَطاته * ما كان منه في الزمان الأوَّلِ

95 (p. 447)

إلهي لقد أصبحتُ ضيفك في الثرى * وللضيف حقٌّ عند كلّ كريمِ
فهَب لي ذنوبـي في قِرايَ فإنّه * عظيـمٌ ولا يُقرَى لغير عظيـمِ

96 (p. 448)

إليهم كلّ مكرُمةٍ تَؤولُ * إذا ما قيل جدّهمُ الرسولُ

97 (p. 449)

أسكنتَ من كان في الأحياء مسكنُه * بالرغم منِّيَ بين التُرب والحجرِ
يا قبرَ فاطمةٍ بنت ابن فاطمـــةٍ * بنت الأئمّة بنت الأنجُـــم الزُهَرِ
يا قبرُ ما فيك من دينٍ ومن وَرَعٍ * ومن عفافٍ ومن صَوْنٍ ومن خَفَرِ

100 (p. 454)

بنيـتُ ولم أسكن وحصَّنـتُ جاهداً * فلمّا أتى المقـدور صيَّره قبْــري
ولم يكن حظّي غير ما أنت مُبْصِرٌ * بعينك ما بين الذراع إلى الشبْرِ
فيا زائراً قبري أُوَصِّيـك جـاهداً * عليك بتقـوى الله في السرّ والجهْرِ
فلا تُحْسِـنْ بالدهر ظنّاً فإنّـما * من الحَزم ألاّ يُستنــام إلى الدهْـــرِ

101 (p. 455)

الموت بحرٌ عـامقٌ مَوْجُه * تَحــار فيه حِيــلة الســابحِ
يا نفسُ إنّي واعظٌ فاسمعي * مقــالةً من مُشْفِقٍ ناصــحِ
ما يصحب الميِّتَ في قبره * غير التقى والعمل الصالحِ

102 (p. 455)

خُلقتَ من التراب فصرتَ حيّاً * وعُلِّمْتَ الفصاحة في الخطابِ
وعُدْتَ إلى التراب فصرتَ مَيْتاً * كأنّك ما بَرِحْتَ من الترابِ

103 (p. 456)

أيّها الواقفُ اعتباراً بقبري * استمعْ فيه قول عَظمي الرميمِ
أوْدَعُوني بطن الضريح وخـافوا * من ذنوبٍ كلومُها بأديمـــي

قلـتُ لا تَجْزِعُوا عليّ فإنّي * حسن الظنّ بالرؤوف الرحيـمِ
وَاتركوني بما اكتسبتُ رَهيـناً * غلِق الرهنُ عند مولًى كريـمِ

105 (p. 458)

أيامن رأى قبراً تضمّن رسمهُ * أخا سَكرةٍ ما إن يُفِيقُ إلى الحَشْـرِ
وما ساءني الأحباب في برزخ البلى * فأصبحت لا أزداد إلاّ على عُقرِ
وأصبح وجهي بعد اَي نضـارةٍ * كسـاه البلى ثوباً يُجَدُّ مع الدَهـرِ

106 (p. 459)

عاش المراديُّ لأضيـافه * ومـات ضيفاً لإله السمَا
والله أولى بقِرى ضيفه * فالْيَدَعِ الناس عليه البكَا

109 (p. 460)

كنتُ في سفرة الغواية والجهـ * ـل مُقيـماً فحـان منّي قُدومُ
تبتُ من كلّ مأثمٍ فعسى يُمْـ * ـحَى بهذا الحديث ذاك القديمُ
بعد خمسٍ وأربعـين لقد ما * طلـتُ إلاّ أنّ الغـريمَ كريـمُ

110 (p. 461)

كَرِهَ الموتَ من عَرَفْ * كُرَبَ الموتِ والغُصَصْ

111 (p. 462)

هذا جناه أبي عليٍّ * وما جنَيْت على أحدْ

112 (p. 464)

ترحّـم على قبر ابن باقٍ وحيّه * فمن حقّ مَيْت الحيّ تسلـيم حيّهِ
وقل أمّن الرحمن رَوْعَة خائفٍ * لتفريـطه في الواجبـات وَغيِّهِ
قدِ اختار هذا القبر في الأرض راجياً * منَ الله تخفيفاً بقرب وليهِ
فقد يشـفع الجـار الكريم لجـاره * ويشمل بالمعـروف أهل نديـهِ
وإنّي بفضـل الله أوثق واثقٍ * وحسبـي وإن أذنبـتُ حبّ نبـيـهِ

113 (p. 465)

إلهِيَ خدّي في التـراب تذلّلاً * بُسِطْتُ عسى رُحمـاك يُحْيَى بها الروحُ
وجاوزتُ أجداث المـــالك خاضعاً * وقلبِيَ مصـدوعٌ ودمعِيَ مسفــــوحُ
ووجّهتُ وجهي نحو جودك ضارعاً * لعلّ الرضى من جنب حلمك ممنوحُ
أتيت فقيراً والذنـــوب تأدّني * وفي القلــب من خوف الجـرائم تبريحُ
ولم اعتمد إلاّ الرجـاءَ وسيلةً * وإخـــلاصَ إيمانٍ به الصدر مشـــروحُ
وأنتُ غنـــيٌ عن عذابي وعـــالمٌ * بفقري وبـاب العفو عنـدك مفتوحُ
فهَبْ لي عفواً من لدُنك ورحـــمةً * يكون بها من رقبة الذنـب تسريحُ
وصلِّ على المختـــار ما همع الحيا * وما طلعتْ شمسٌ وما هبّتِ الريـحُ

114 (p. 467)

يا قبرَ سلطان الشجاعة والندى * فرع الملوك الصيْد أعلام الهدَى
وسُلالةِ السـلف الذي آثـاره * وضّـاحةٌ لمن اقتدى ومنِ اهتدَى
سلفٌ لأنصـار النبيّ نُجاره * قد حلّ منه في المكـارم مَحْتِدا
متوسِّط البيـت الذي قد أسّستْ * ـه سادة الأمـلاك أوحدَ أوْحَدا
بيتٌ بنـاه محمّـدون ثلاثةٌ * من آل نَصْرٍ أورثـوه مُحمّـــدا
أُودِعْـتَ وجهاً قد تهلّل حسنـه * بدراً بآفـاق الجلالة قد بَـدا
وندىً يسحّ على عُفـاة مواهباً * مثنى الأيادي السابغات ومَوْحَدا
يبكيـك مذعورٌ بك استعدَى على * أعدائه فسقيتـهم كأس الردَى
يبكيك محتـاجٌ أتاك مؤمّلاً * فغدا وقد شفعت يداك له اليــدا
أما سمـاحك فَهْوَ أهْمَـى دِيمةً * أما جلالك فَهْوَ أسمى مصْـعَدا
جادَت ثراك من الإله سحـائبٌ * لرضاه عنك تجود هذا المعْهَدا

117 (pp. 470f.)

ليت شعري ما الّذي عايَنتَه * بعد دَوم الصَوم معْ نفْيِ الوَسَنْ
معْ نزوح النفـس عن أوطـانها * والتخلِّي عن حبيـبٍ وسكَـنْ
يا وحيـداً ليـس من وجدي به * لَوْعَةٌ تمنعـني من أنْ أُجَــنْ
فكـما تَبْـلَى وجــوهٌ في الثـرى * فكذا يبلى عليـهنّ الحَزَنْ

127 (p. 476)

إنّي أرى الإسلام بعد إمـــامه * يَرْنُو بطرَفِ مُروَّعٍ حَيْــرانِ

خلّفتَ في الإسلام بعدك ثُلمةً * تبقى على مَرِّ الزمان الفانـي
من للفتـاوى والسؤالات التي * ما زال يكشفها بحسن بَيـانِ
من للشريعة إن تطاول مُلحِدٌ * لعِنادها بالزُور والبُهْتـانِ
من لليتـامى والأرامِل بعده * يرعـاهمُ بالبرّ والإحسـانِ
فسقى ضريحك مُسبِلٌ من عنوةٍ * وحبّاك بالغُفران والرضوانِ

137 (p. 482)

إنّ العزا بشهاب الدين قد منعتْ * منه القلوب وقد أوْدَى بها التَلَفُ
نَشْؤٌ تكـامل فيه الظرف واجتمعت * فيه شمـائلُ لا تنفكّ تأتَلِـفُ
ومنظر مُخجلٍ للشمس إن طلعـت * ياليته لم يكن بالبَيْن ينكَسِـفُ
إذا بدا نـاطقاً في وسْط مُحْتَـفَلٍ * فالدرّ مُنتـظمٌ والشُهد مُقتطَـفُ
محـاسنٌ نظّم الإجمـاع صحّتَها * كاللؤلؤ انتقبـت عن حسنه صَدَفُ

139 (pp. 484f.)

أياعينُ جـودي ولا تَنْفُرِي * بدمـعٍ مدى العُمر مُستـغفِرِ
على الأرْيَحـي الرضى اللّوذَعـي * كريم الغريزة والعُنصُـرِ
معزّ الشـريعة خلْف التـقى * أبي جعـفرٍ أحمدَ الطبـري
سأفني الدموع وأجري النجيع * وأسلو عن الأهل والمتجَري
ولست بناسيـك وقتَ الطواف * ويومَ الصعود وفي المشعَرِ
وإنّيَ أرجـوك يومَ الوقـو * ف بين يَـدَيْ ربّـك الأكبـرِ
كسـاك الإله منَ استبرق الـ * جنـان ومن سُندُسٍ أخضرِ

يقـول إذا ما أتيتَ الحَجُـوفَ * عليك السـلام أبا جعـفرِ
أنا محيي الديـن ياخيرَ من * تولّى الحكومةَ في الأعصُـرِ
سقى قبرك الجـود جمّ العتـاق * وحُيِّيتَ بالورد والعبـهَرِ
وطيّـب لحدك روح الإله * فَيَزْرِي على المسـك والعنـبَرِ
حضرْتَ السمـاع وحُزتَ العلـوم * وخلّدتَ ذكرك للأعصُـرِ
كفلـتَ اليتامى وعُلْتَ الأيـامى * وكنـت لهم كأبٍ خيِّـرِ
وأثنوا عليك لدى الموت خيـراً * وهذي السيادة من معشَرِ
تزوَّدتَها يومَ فصـل القضاء * وحشر الخـلائق في المحشَرِ

149 (pp. 491f.)

أنا لَمسيءُ سيّدي من تجــاوز * أتـــاك بلا زادٍ لقطع الم[فـ]ـاوزِ
وعفـــوك مأمـــولٌ لكلّ مُؤمِّلٍ * وبرّك موجـــودٌ لكلّ مُنـــاهزِ
وبابك مفتـــوحٌ وفضلك شامـــلٌ * وما أنا إن أجرمْتُ هذا بِفـــائزِ
وقد جئت أرجو العفو بغاية المنى * مقرّاً على نفسي بجرم المبارزِ
أسوّف بالطاعـات تسويف مفسرٍ * وأفقد في العصيان نقذ المناجزِ
فإنْ تَعْفُ عن جُرْمي فإنّك أهله * وإلاّ فما شيءٌ عن النـــار حـــاجزِ
وعادات سادات الورى أن يُعاملوا * مُقِرّاً أتاهم بالرضى والتجـــاوزِ

وحقِّك ما عَصَيْتُك مُستهـــيناً * بأمرك يامـلاذي واعتمــــادي
ولكن غرَّ بي كـــــرمٌ وحلـــمٌ * وتأميـــلٌ لقولك يا عبـــادي
فعاملتُ الأيـــادِيَ بالمعـــاصي * وصاحبت المـــآتم بالتمـــادي
فيا [ ] وياحيـــاتي * إذا نُودِيـــتُ باسمي في المعادِ
وأُتيتُ الكتـــاب وقيل لي اقرأ * وعاينت المسطّر فيه بـــادي
وما قدَّمـــتُ من أعمـــال سوءٍ * كفى أني قدمْـــت بغير زادي
فلو أني أنوح بقدر جرمي * لبستُ من الأسى ثوب الحِـــدادِ
وأجريت المدامع من جفوني * وهِمتُ مع الوحـــوش بكلّ وادِ
وتِحْتَ من الخطا يا نوحَ ثكلـــى * وأعزبتَ المحـــاجر بالسُهـــادِ
وما لي لا أنـــوح على ذنـــوبٍ * بها بارزتُ خـــلاّق العبـــادِ
وما لي شافـــعٌ إلاّ رجـــائي * وحســـن الظنّ بالملك الجوادِ
فإن تعفو فأنـــت لـــذاك أهلٌ * وعبد الســـوء أهل للبِعـــادِ

158 (p. 499)

أضحـــى لفقدك ركن المجد مُنهَدِمٌ * والعلم بعدك عزّ الديـــن مُنثَلِـــمُ
والفضل والجود والمعـروف كلّـهمُ * مـــاتوا لموتك والإحســـان والكرمُ
من للشريعة والفتوى إذا عَجِزَتْ * أولو العلوم وعن إدراكها فَحَمُوا
من للقضـــاء ومن للحكم بعدك يا * قاضي القضـــاة ومن للحقّ مُلتَزِمُ
من للمســـاكيـــن والأيتـــام يكفلـــهم * من للمُقـــلّ إذا أودَى به العَدَمُ
سقـــى ضريحك ربّ العرش غـــاديةً * من الغمـــام ورضواناً له دِيَمُ

166 (p. 506)

مقيمٌ إلى أن يبعثَ الله خلقه * لقاؤك لا يُرجَى وأنت قريبُ
تَزيد بِلىً في كلّ يومٍ وليلةٍ * وتُنْسى كما تَبلى وأنت حبيبُ

169 (p. 509)

إذا كان قبري في البقيع بطَيْبَةٍ * فلا شكّ أنّي في حِمَى صاحب القبرِ
نبيٍّ الهدى المبعوث من آل هاشمٍ * عليه صلاة الله في السرّ والجهرِ

170 (p. 511)

آثاره تُنبيك عن أوصافِه * حتّى كأنّك بالعِيان تَراهُ
تالله لا يأتي الزمان بمثلِه * أبداً ولا يَحْمِي الثغورَ سِواهُ

171 (p. 513)

سكنتُكِ يا دار الفناء مُصدِّقاً * بأنّي إلى دار البقاء أصيرُ
وأعظم ما في الأمر أنّيَ صائرٌ * إلى عادلٍ في الحكم ليس يَجورُ
فياليت شعري كيف ألقاه عندها * وزادي قليلٌ والذنوب كثيرُ
فإن أكُ مَجْزياً بذنب فإنّني * بشرِّ عقابِ المذنبين جديرُ
وإن يكُ عفوٌ منه عنّي ورحمةٌ * فثَمَّ نعيمٌ دائمٌ وسرورُ

[1]**173** (p. 518)

قبرٌ عزيزٌ علينا * لو أنّ من فيه يُفدَى
أسكنتَ قرّة عيني * وقِطعة القلب لحْدَا
ما زال حكمٌ عليه * وما القضاء تَعَدَّى
فالصبر أحسنُ ثوبٍ * به العزيز تَرَدَّى

174 (p. 521)

قَدِمْتُ على الكريم بغير زادٍ * من الحسنات والعمل السقيمِ
وحمْلُ الزاد أقبحُ ما تراه * إذا كان القُدوم على كريمِ

1 The variants of these lines are considerable. See the entry in Chapter 4.

175 (p. 522)

خليليَّ بالودّ الّذي بيننا اجعلا * إذا مِتُّ قبري عُرْضةً للتَرَحُّمِ
عسى مسلمٌ يَدنو فيدعو برحمةٍ * فإنِّيَ محتاجٌ لدعوة مُسَلِّمِ

176 (p. 522)

قالت لِيَ النفس أتاك الرَدَى * وأنت في بحر الخطايا مقيمْ
هلاّ ادّخَرْتَ الزاد قلتُ اقْصِرِي * لا يُحمل الزادُ لدار الكريمْ

177 (p. 523)

ترحّمْ بفضلك يا واقفاً * ولاحِظ مكاناً دُفِعْنا إليهِ
تراب الضريح على وجْنَتي * كأنِّيَ لم أمشِ يوماً عليهِ
أداوِي الأنام حَذارِ المنونَ * وها أنا قد صرت رَهْناً لديهِ

178 (p. 526)

لئن نُفِّذَ القدر السابق * بموتي كما حكَم الخالقُ
فقد مات والدنا آدمٌ * ومات محمّدٌ الصادقُ
ومات الملوك وأشياعهم * ولم يبقَ من جَمْعهم ناطقُ
فقل للّذي سرَّه مهلكي * تأهّبْ فإنّك بي لاحقُ

179 (p. 528)

ذهب الأحبّةُ بعد طول تودُّدٍ * ونأى المزار فأسلموك وأقشعُوا
تركوك أوحشَ ما تكون بقفرةٍ * لم يؤنسوك وكُربةٍ لم يدفعوا
قُضِيَ القضاء وصرت صاحب حفرةٍ * عنك الأحبّة أعرضوا وتصدّعوا

180 (p. 529)

سأُوَدِّعُ القرّاءَ بعدك والورى * إذ حان منك البَيْنُ والتوديعُ
ولا أسفِكنَّ لك الدِماء تأسّفاً * لو كان دِجلةُ لي عليك دموعُ

181 (p. 529)

ياأيّها الركْب سِيروا إنّ غايتكم * أنْ تُصبحوا ذات يومٍ لا تَسيرونَ

حُثّوا المطايا وأرْخوا عن أزِمَّتها * قبل الممات وقضُّوا ما تقضّونَ
كنّا أناساً كما كنتم فغيَّرنا * دهرٌ فسوف كما صرنا تصيرونَ

182 (p. 531)

باتوا على قُلل الأجْبال تحرسهم * غُلب الرجال فلم تنفعهمُ القُلَلُ
واستُنْزِلوا بعد عزٍّ من معاقِلهم * فأُسْكِنوا حفرةً يا بِئسَ ما نَزَلُوا
ناداهمُو صارخٌ من بعد ما دُفِنوا * أين الأسرَّة والتيجان والحُلَلُ
أين الوجوه التي كانت محجّبةً * من دونها تضرب الأستار والكِلَلُ
فأفصح القبرُ عنهم حين ساءَلهم * تلك الوجوه عليها الدود تقتَتِلُ
قد طال ما أكلوا دهراً وما نعِموا * فأصبحوا بعد طول الأكل قد أُكِلوا

183 (p. 533)

أما ترَون محلّي * غداً تصيرون مثلي
أبلى التراب شبابي * وكلّكم سوف تُبلي
سبيلكم كسبيلي * سبيلُ من كان قبلي

184 (p. 533)

رحم اللّه من بكى * لغريبٍ وقد عفَا
غبر القبر وجهَه * فمحى الحسنَ والصفَا

188 (p. 536)

أ إخواننا والموت قد حال دوننا * وللموت حكمٌ نافذٌ في الخلائقِ
سبقتكمُ للموت والعمر طَيَّهُ * وأعلم أنّ الكلّ لا بدّ لاحقي
بعيشكمُ أو باضطجاعِيَ في الثرى * ألم نكُ في صفوٍ من العيش رائقِ
فمن مرّ بي فاليَمْضِ لي مُترحِّماً * ولا يكُ مَنْسياً وفاء الأصادقِ

189 (p. 537)

كنّا على ظهرها والعيش في رَغَدٍ * والشمْل مُجتمعٌ والدار والوَطَنُ
ففرَّق الدهر والتصريف أُلفتَنا * وصار يجمعنا في بطنها الكَفَنُ

190 (p. 538)

أما القبور فإنّهنّ أوانسٌ * بجوار قبرك والديار قبورُ
عمّت فواضِله فعمّ مُصابه * فالناس فيه كلّهم مأجورُ
ردَّتْ صنائعه أليه حياتَه * فكأنّه من نشْرها مَنشورُ

191 (p. 539)

أبا غانمٍ أما ذراك فواسعٌ * وقبرك معمور الجوانب مُحْكَمُ
وما ينفع المقبورَ عُمرانُ قبره * إذا كان فيه جسمه يتهدَّمُ

192 (p. 540)

تُناجِيك أجداثٌ وهنّ صموتٌ * وسكّانها تحت التراب خفوتُ
أيا جامعَ الدنيا لغير بلاغه * لمن تجمع الدنيا وأنت تموتُ

193 (p. 541)

اِجعلوا إنْ مِتّ يوماً كفني * ورق الكرْم وقبري المِعْصَرَه
وادفنوني وادفنوا الراحَ معي * واجعلوا الأقداح حول المقْبُرَه
إنّني أرْجو من اللّه غداً * بعد شرْب الراح حسْن المَغْفِرَه

194 (p. 542)

أمُغَطّىً منّي على بصري للحبْ * بِ أم أنتِ أكملُ الناس حُسْنَا
وحديثٍ ألذّهُ هو ممّا * ينعتُ الناعتون يُوزَنُ وَزْنَا

195 (pp. 543, 574)

إن يكُنْ مات صغيراً * فالأسى غيرُ صغيرِ
كان رَيْحاني فصار الـ * ـيومَ ريحانَ القبورِ
أيَّ أغصانٍ مليحا * تٍ بديعاتٍ بنورِ
غرستْها في بساتيـ * ـن البِلَى أيْدي الدهورِ

196 (p. 544)

يمرّ أقاربي جنَبات قبري * كأنّ أقاربي لم يعرفونِي

ذَوو الميراث يقتسمون مالي * وما يألُون أنْ جحَدوا دُيوني
وقد أخذوا سِهامهمُ وعاشوا * فيا لله أسرعَ ما نَسُوني

197 (p. 545)

وقفتُ على الأحبّة حين صُفَّت * قبورهمُ كأفراس الرِهانِ
فلمّا أن بكيتُ وفاض دمعي * رأتْ عَيْنَايَ بينهمُ مكانِي

198 (p. 545)

قد قلتُ لمّا قال لي قائلٌ * قد صار لُقْمانُ إلى رمْسِهِ
فأين ما يوصَف من طبِّه * وحِذقه في الماء معْ جسِّهِ
هيهاتُ لا يدفع عن غيره * من كان لا يدفع عن نفسِهِ

199 (p. 547)

ذا عزيزي دعاه ربٌّ رحيمُ * غافر الذنب بالعباد عليمُ
قد خلا في التراب فرداً وحيداً * فاغفرِ اليوم ذنبه يا عليمُ
وتفضَّلْ بعفوك اليوم يا ر * بّ عليه فأنت ربٌّ كريمُ

200 (p. 547)

ألحقَنا الموت بآبائنا * وكلّ من عاش فيوماً يموتْ

201 (p. 548)

وقلتُ أخي قالوا أخٌ من قرابةٍ * فقلت نَعَمْ إنّ الشُكُول أقاربُ
نسيبِيَ في عزّي ورأيي ومَنْصِبِي * وإن باعدتنا في الديار المناسبُ
عجيبٌ لصبري بعده وَهْوَ ميِّتٌ * وقد كنت أبكيه دَماً وَهْوَ غائبُ
على أنّما الأيام قد صرْنَ كلّها * عجائبَ حتّى ليس فيها عجائبُ

202 (p. 549)

ملّ الأحبّة زَوْرَتي فجُفِيتُ * وسكنتُ في دار البلى فنُسِيتُ
الحيّ يكذب لا صديق لميّتٍ * لو كان يصْدُق مات حين يموتُ
يا مُؤنِساً سكن الثرى وبَقِيتُ * لو كنت أصدق إذ بُلِيتَ بُلِيتُ
أو كان يَعْمَى للبكاء مُفجَّعٌ * من طول ما أبكي عليك عَمِيتُ

203 (p. 550)

عليك سلام الله يا خير مُنزلٍ * رحلنا وخلّفناك غير ذَميمِ
فإن تكنِ الأيام أحدثْنَ فُرقةً * فمن ذا الّذي من رميها بسَليمِ

204 (p. 550)

ألِيحا لِلَيْلَى قبر من لو رأيته * يجود وتَأبَى نفسه وَهْوَ ضائعُ
سقيطُ كجُثمان الخلا لم يَطُفْ به * حَميمُ ولم تذْرفْ عليه المدامعُ
إذا لَرأيتَ الذلّ والضَيْم قد بدا * للَيْلَى ولم يدفع لك الضَيْم دافعُ

206 (p. 551)

تعزَّ فكم لك من أسوةٍ * تُبرِّد عنك غليل الحَزَنِ
بموت النبيّ وقتل الوصيّ * وذبح الحسين وسمّ الحَسَنِ

207 (p. 552)

هذي منازلُ أقوامٍ عهدتهمُ * في ظلِّ عيشٍ عجيبٍ ما له خَطَرُ
صاحتْ بهم حادثات الدهر فارتحلوا * إلى القبور فلا عينٌ ولا أثَرُ

209 (p. 554)

ندمتُ على ما كان منّي ندامةً * ومن يتّبع ما تشتهي النفسُ يَنْدَمُ
ألم تعلموا أنَّ الحسابَ أمامكم * وأنَّ وراكم طالِباً ليس يُسْلِمُ
فخافوا لكيما تأمنوا بعد موتكم * ستلقَوْن ربّاً عادلاً ليس يظلِمُ
فليس لمغرورٍ بدنياه راحةٌ * سيندم إنْ زلَّتْ به النعل فاعلمُوا

210 (p. 554)

أقلّ لماشٍ على قبرنا * غفولٌ بأشياءَ حلَّتْ بنَا
سيندَم يوماً لتفريطه * كما قد ندِمنا لتفريطنَا

211 (p. 555)

أيها الماشي بين القبور * غافلاً عن مُعقّبات الأمورِ
أُدْنُ منّي أُنْبِيك عنّي ولا يُنـ * ـبيك عنّي ياصاحِ مثل خبيرِ
أنا مَيْتٌ كما تراني طريحٌ * بين أطباق جندلٍ وصخورِ

أنا في بيت غُربةٍ وانفـرادٍ * مع قُربي من جيرتي وعشيرِي
ليس لي فيه مُؤنسٌ غير سعْيٍ * من صلاحٍ سعَيته أو فجورِ
فكذا أنت فاتّعِظْ بي وإلاّ * صرتَ مثلي رهينَ يوم النُشـورِ

212 (p. 556)

أسلمني الأهل ببطن الثرى * وانصرفوا عنّي فيا وحشتَا
وغادروني مُعْـدِماً بائسـاً * فما يُبدّى اليوم إلاّ البكَا
وكلّ ما كان كأنْ لم يكُـنْ * وكلّ ما حـذرته قد أتَـى
وذاكمُ المجموع والمقتنى * قد صار في كفّي كمثل الهبَا
ولم أجِد لي مؤنساً هاهنا * غير فجورٍ كان لي أو خنَا
فلو تراني أو ترى حالتي * بكَيْتَ لي يا صاحِ مِمًّا تَرَى

213 (p. 557)

قِفْ واعتبرْ فقريباً * تَحلُّ هذا المحلاَّ
هذا مكانٌ يُساوي * فيه الأعزّ الأذلاَّ
ما كان لي من صديقٍ * إلاّ جَفاني ومَلاَّ
وما جفاني ولكن * طال المَدَى فتسلاَّ

214 (p. 558)

حسن ظنّي بك كان * منّي جراني عليكَا
فارحمِ اللهمَّ عبداً * صار رمساً في يدَيْكَا

215 (p. 558)

كم ساكنٍ(!) في حفرةٍ تُبلِي حديدَ جمالهِ * ترك الأحِبّةُ بعده يتلذّذون بمالهِ

216 (p. 559)

نزلتُ بجارٍ لا يخيِّب ضيفَه * أُرَجِّي نجاتي من عذاب جَهنَّمِ
وإنّي على خوفٍ من اللّه واثقٌ * بإنعامه واللّه أكرم مُنعِمِ

217 (p. 560)

بنفسي هُما ما مُتِّعا بهواهُما * على الدهر حتّى غُيِّبَا في المقابرِ
أقام على غير التزاوُر بُرْهَةً * فلمّا أُصيبا قُرِّبا بالتزاورِ
فيا حسنَ قبرٍ زار قبراً يُحبّه * ويا زَورةً جاءتْ بريْب المقادرِ

218 (pp. 560f.)

يا واقفينَ ألم تكونوا تعلموا * أنّ الحِمام بكم علينا قادمُ
لا تستعزّوا بالحياة فإنّكم * تبنون والموت المُفرِّق هادمُ
لو تنزلون بشِعْبنا لعرفتمُ * أنّ المفرّط في التزوّد نادمُ
ساوى الردى ما بيننا فأحلّنا * حيث المخدّم واحدٌ والخادمُ

219 (p. 561)

الناس للموت كخيل الطِرادْ * فالسابقُ السابق منها الجِيَادْ
واللهُ لا يدعو إلى داره * إلاّ منِ استصلح من ذي العِبَادْ
العمر كالظلّ ولا بدّ أنْ * يزولَ ذاك الظلّ بعدَ امْتِدادْ
والموت نقّادٌ على كفّه * جواهرُ يختار منها الجِيَادْ
أرغمْتَ ياموتُ أنوف الردى * كأنّما في كلّ قلبٍ رَمَادْ
طرقتَ ياموت كريماً فلم * يقنعْ بغير النفس للضيف زادْ
قصفتَهُ من سِدرة المنتهى * غَصناً فشُلّتْ يد أهل العِنَادْ

220 (p. 562)

قد وفَينا بنذْرنا يا ابن إدريـ * ـسَ وجئناك من بلاد العراقِ
وقرأنا عليك ما قد نذرْنا * من كلام المُهَيْمِن الخلّاقِ

221 (p. 563)

يا هاجري إذ جئتني زائراً * ما كان من عاداتك الهَجْرُ
يا صاحبَ القبر الجديد ومن * قد حال دون لقائه القبرُ
دَعْني أعلّل فيك جارحةً * ثَكْلَى وقلباً مسَّه الضرُّ
جُرْنا عليك فإن تطاول بي * منٌّ الفراق فحالتي نُكْرُ

222 (p. 564)

ذهب الّذين تكمّلوا آجـــالهم * ومضـَوا وحان لآخرين وُرُودُ
يمضي الصغير إذا انقضتْ أيّامه * عثرَ الكبير ويُولد المولودُ
والنـــاس في قسم المنية بينهم * كالزرع منه قائمٌ وحَصِـيدُ

223 (p. 564)

حمّلوه على الرقاب ابتداراً * ثمّ واروه في التراب دفينَا
أيُّ نجمٍ هوى أصاب به الدهـ * ـر قلـوباً منكـوبةً وعيـونَا
كم رأيناه مُعطياً ومُنيلاً * ثمّ أضحى من بعد ذاك رهينَا

224 (p. 565)

وعمري كلّ يومٍ في انتقاصٍ * وذاك النقص لُقِّبَ بازديادِ
ولي حظٌّ وللأيّـــام حظٌّ * وبينـــهما مُبـــايَنة المِـــدادِ
فأكتبه ســـواداً في بيـاضٍ * وتكتبه بيـــاضاً في سَوادِ

225 (p. 565)

ألا يا موتُ كنت بنا حفيـاً * فجدَّدْتَ الســـرور لنا بزَوْرَهْ
حمدتُ لسَعْيك المشكـور لمّا * كفيتَ مؤونةً وسـترت عَوْرَهْ
فأنكحْنا الضريحَ بلا صداقٍ * وجهَّزنا العروس بغير شَوْرَهْ

226 (p. 566)

قد أناخَتْ بك روحي * فاجعلِ العفو قِراها
هي ترجـوك وتخشا * ك فلا تقطعْ رَجاها

227 (p. 566)

أيا حُجَّة الإســـلام مُذ غِبْـتَ بغتةً * غدتْ للأعـــادي حجّةٌ ومنـــاقبُ
ألم ترى أنّ الشمسَ إنْ غاب ضووُها * تلألأ في جَوِّ السماء الكواكبُ

228 (p. 567)

وما الدهر والأيّـــام إلاّ كما ترى * رَزِيَة مـالٍ أو فراق حبـيبِ
وإنّ امرءً قد جرَّب الدهر لم يَخَفْ * تقلّب عصرَيْه لغير لبيبِ

229 (p. 567)

أيا موتُ ما هذا التفرّق عنوةً * رُوَيدك لا تُسرعْ لكلّ خليلِ
أراك بصيــراً بالّدين أحبّهم * أظنّك تمضي نحوهم بدليـلِ

230 (p. 568)

لا بدّ من فقدٍ ومن فاقدٍ * هيهات ما في الناس من خالدِ
كُنِ المُعَــزِّي لا المُعَــزَّى به * إنْ كان لا بدّ من الواحـــدِ

231 (p. 568)

جميع فـوائد الدنيا غرورُ * ولا يبقى لمسرورٍ سرورُ
فقُل للشامِتين بنا استعِدُّوا * فإنّ نوائبَ الدنيا تدورُ

232 (p. 569)

أنا رهن التراب في اللحد وحْدِي * واضعاً تحت لِبْنة الترب خدِّي

233 (p. 569)

ما أحدٌ أكرم من مُفردٍ * في قبره أعماله تُؤنسُهْ
مُنَعَّمٌ يلتذّ في روضةٍ * زيَّنها الله فَهْيَ مجلِسُهْ

234 (pp. 569f.)

أنا مشغـولٌ بذنبي * عن ذنــوب العــالمينَا
وخطـــايا أثقلتني * تركـــتْ قلبي حزيـنَا
صرتُ في الأرض وحيداً * في جوار الهالكينَا
بعدما كنـــت جليـلاً * في عيــون الناظرينَا
صرت في ظلمة قبري * ثــاوياً فيها رهينَا
وتركـتُ المــال والأهـ * ـل لعمــري والبنـينَا
ولقد عمّـــرت دهــراً * وشهـــوراً وسنـــينَا
في نِعَمٍ وســـرورٍ * فـوق وصف الواصفينَا
وملكــتُ الشرق والغر * بَ وكان الملك فيـنَا
وفتحـــتُ المُدْنَ قهراً * وغلبـــتُ الغالبيـــنَا
فأتى الموت علـيـــنا * بعد هذا فَـــفنـــينَا

أيّها المغـــرور بادرْ * لثـــواب الصالحـــينَا
والّذي صحّ لدَيْـــنا * وعلمـــناه يقيـــنَا
أنّ حيّاً ليـــس يبقى * غير ربٍّ العالمـــينَا

235 (p. 570)

إذا أمسى فراشي من ترابٍ * وصرتُ مُجاوِرَ الربّ الرحيمِ
فهـنّوني بإخـلائي وقولـوا * هَنـيأ قد قَدِمْـت على كريمِ

236 (p. 571)

ولم أجزعْ لهول الموت لكن * بكيتُ لقِلّة الباكي عليَّا

تـــمـت

Bibliography*

1. *Sources*

1.1. Epigraphic sources

Arabic Inscriptions (Caskel) = W. Caskel: *Arabic Inscriptions in the Collection of the Hispanic Society of America*, New York 1956 (Hispanic Notes and Monographs).

Arabic Inscriptions (Grohmann) = A. Grohmann: *Expédition Philby-Ryckmans-Lippens en Arabie. IIe Partie. Textes épigraphiques, tome 1: Arabic Inscriptions*, Louvain 1962 (Bibliothèque du Muséon 50).

CIA Alep = E. Herzfeld: *Matériaux pour un Corpus Inscriptionum Arabicarum, deuxième partie: Syrie du Nord. Inscriptions et monuments d'Alep*, vols. I (text) and II (plates), Cairo 1954–56.

CIA Égypte I = M. van Berchem: *Matériaux pour un Corpus Inscriptionum Arabicarum, première partie: Égypte*, Paris 1903.

CIA Égypte II = G. Wiet: *Matériaux pour un Corpus Inscriptionum Arabicarum, première partie: Égypt II*, 2 vols., Cairo 1929f.

Inschriften Syrien = H. Gaube: *Arabische Inschriften aus Syrien*, Beirut – Wiesbaden 1978 (Beiruter Texte und Studien 17).

Inscripciones Almería = M. Ocaña Jiménez: *Repertorio de inscripciones árabes de Almería*, Madrid – Granada 1964.

Inscripciones Granada = D. E. Lafuente y Alcántara: *Inscripciones árabes de Granada*, Madrid 1860.

Inscriptions Espagne = É. Lévi-Provençal: *Inscriptions arabes d'Espagne*, vols. I (text) and II (plates), Leiden – Paris 1931.

Inscriptions Ḥawrān = S. Ory: *Cimetières et inscriptions du Ḥawrān et du Ǧabal ad-durūz*, Paris 1989.

Inscriptions Kairouan = B. Roy and P. Poinssot: *Inscriptions arabes de Kairouan*, Fasc. 1–2, Paris 1950–58.

Inscriptions Marrakech = G. Deverdun: *Inscriptions arabes de Marrakech*, Rabat 1956 (Publications de l'Institut des hautes-études marocaines 60).

Iscrizioni arabe Napoli = V. Grassi: *Iscrizioni funerarie arabe nel Napoletano*, in: A. Cilardo (ed.): *Presenza araba e islamica in Campania (Atti del convegno 1989)*, Naples 1992, pp. 337–64.

Mausolée Abū l-ʿAlāʾ = J. Sourdel-Thomine: *Inscriptions du mausolée d'Abū l-ʿAlāʾ à Maʿarrat al-Nuʿmān*, in: Arabica 2 (1955), pp. 289–94.

* This short-title bibliography contains all seminal writings as well as books and articles which are cited *more than once* in this volume. References of further items which are quoted once only are given in the respective footnotes. The abbreviation of Arabic names follows the usage of GAL.

Mausolée Saʿdiens = G. Rousseau: *Le mausolée des princes saʿdiens à Marrakech. Préface par Edmond Doutté, texte arabe et traduction des inscriptions par Félix Arin* [...]. *Aquarelles, dessins et relevés de l'auteur*, Paris 1925.

Pierres tombales Ẓafār-ḏī Bīn = M. Schneider: *Pierres tombales des cimètieres arabes de Ẓafār-ḏī Bīn*, Istanbul 1988 (Uitgaven van het Nederlands Historisch-Archaeologisch Instituut te Istanbul 62).

RCEA = *Répertoire chronologique d'épigraphie arabe*, edd. É. Combe, J. Sauvaget, G. Wiet *et al.*, vols. I–XVIII, Cairo 1931–91 (Publications de l'institut français d'archéologie orientale).

Stèles Dahlak = M. Schneider: *Stèles funéraires musulmanes des îles Dahlak (Mer Rouge)*, 2 vols., Cairo 1983.

Stèles Damas = K. Moaz and S. Ory: *Inscriptions arabes de Damas. Les stèles funéraires I: Cimetière d'al-Bāb al-Ṣaġīr*, Damascus 1977.

Stèles Musée arabe du Caire = *Musée national de l'art arabe. Catalogue général du Musée arabe du Caire: Stèles funéraires*, 10 vols., Cairo 1932–42.

1.2. Bibliographies and manuscript catalogues

Ahlwardt = W. Ahlwardt: *Verzeichniss der arabischen Handschriften der Königlichen Bibliothek zu Berlin*, 10 vols., Berlin 1887–99 (repr. Cairo n.d.).

Aumer: *Staatsbibliothek* = J. Aumer: *Die arabischen Handschriften der Kgl. Hof- und Staatsbibliothek in Muenchen (Catalogus codicorum manu scriptorum bibliothecae regiae Monacensis, Tomus I, pars II: Codices arabicos complectens)*, [1]1866 (repr. Wiesbaden 1970).

Casiri: *Bibliotheca* = Michael [Miguel] Casiri: *Bibliotheca Arabico-Hispana Escurialensis (sive Librorum omnium Mss. quos Arabicè ab auctoribus magnam partem Arabo-Hispanis compositos Bibliotheca Cúnobii Escurialensis complectitur, Recensio & Explanatio)*, 2 vols., Madrid 1760–70 (repr. Osnabrück 1969).

Chester Beatty = A. J. Arberry: *The Chester Beatty Library. A Handlist of the Arabic Mansucripts*, 8 vols., Dublin 1955–66 and 1973.

Ḏayl ḤḪ = Ismāʿīl Pasha b. M. al-Baġdādī: *ʾĪḍāḥ al-maknūn fī ḏ-ḏayl ʿalā Kašf aẓ-ẓunūn (li-Ḥāǧǧī Ḫalīfah)*, edd. M. Šaraf ad-Dīn Yāltiqāyā and Rifʿat Bīlgeh al-Kilīsī, 2 vols., Istanbul: Millî Eğitim Basımevi 1364–66 / 1945–47.

GAL(S) = C. Brockelmann: *Geschichte der arabischen Litteratur*, 5 vols. (including the three-volume *Supplement*), Leiden 1937–49 (repr. with a new introduction 1996).

GAS = F. Sezgin: *Geschichte des arabischen Schrifttums*, vols. Iff., Leiden 1967ff.

ḤḪ = Muṣṭafā b. ʿAl. Kātib Çelebi Ḥāǧǧī Ḫalīfah: *Kašf aẓ-ẓunūn fī ʾasāmī l-kutub wa-l-funūn*, edd. M. Šaraf ad-Dīn Yāltiqāyā and Rifʿat Bīlgeh al-Kilīsī, 2 vols., Istanbul: Maarıf Matbaası 1360–66 / 1941–47.

Loth: *Indian Office* = O. Loth: *A Catalogue of the Arabic Manuscripts in the Library of the India Office*, repr. Osnabrück 1975 ([1]1877).

Maḫṭūṭāt Dār al-Kutub = F. Sayyid (ed.): *Fihrist al-maḫṭūṭāt našratan bi-l-maḫṭūṭāt allatī qtanathā d-Dār min sanat 1936–1955*, 3 vols., Cairo 1380–83 / 1962–63.

Mingana Collection = D. Hopwood *et al.*: *Catalogue of the Mingana Collection of Manuscripts (Selly Oak Colleges Library), volume IV: Arabic Manuscripts*, Birmingham 1963.

as-Sunaydī: *Muʿǧam* = ʿAbd al-ʿAzīz b. Rāšid b. ʿAbd al-Karīm as-Sunaydī: *Muʿǧam mā ʾullifa ʿan Makkah*, ar-Riyāḍ 1420/1999.

1.3. Primary literary sources[1]

AʿArabṬab	Abū l-ʿArab M. b. A. b. Tamīm al-Qayrawānī: *Ṭabaqāt ʿulamāʾ ʾIfrīqīyah wa-Tūnis*, edd. ʿAlī aš-Šābbī and Nuʿaym Ḥ. al-Yāfī, Tunis: ad-Dār at-Tūnisīyah li-n-Našr / Algiers: al-Muʾassasah al-Waṭanīyah li-l-Kitāb ^{2}1985.
AʿAtāhAnwār	Abū l-ʿAtāhiyah Ismāʿīl b. al-Qāsim b. Suwayd: *al-ʾAnwār az-zāhiyah fī dīwān ʾAbī l-ʿAtāhiyah*, Beirut: Maṭbaʿat al-Ābāʾ al-Yasūʿīyīn 1887.
AʿAtāhDīwān	Id.: *Dīwān ʾAbī l-ʿAtāhiyah*, ed. N. N. (K. al-Bustānī), Beirut: Dār Ṣādir 1384/1964 (repr. 1418/1998).
ĀbīNaṯr	Abū Saʿd Manṣūr b. al-Ḥusayn al-Ābī: *Naṯr ad-durr*, edd. M. ʿAlī Qarnah and M. ʿAlī al-Biǧāwī, vols. I–IV, Cairo: al-Hayʾah al-Miṣrīyah al-ʿĀmmah li-l-Kitāb 1980–85.
Adab al-mulūk	*Adab al-mulūk. Ein Handbuch der islamischen Mystik aus dem 4./10. Jahrhundert*, ed. B. Radtke, Beirut – Stuttgart: F. Steiner 1991 (Beiruter Texte und Studien 37); *see also below* GramlLebensweise.
ADāʾūd	Abū Dāʾūd Sul. b. al-Ašʿaṯ as-Siǧistānī: *Kitāb as-Sunan*, ed. M. Muḥyī d-Dīn ʿAbd al-Ḥamīd, 4 vols., Cairo: al-Maktabah at-Tiǧārīyah al-Kubrā ^{2}1369/^{2}1950.
ʿAdīDīwān	ʿAdīy b. Zayd: *Dīwān ʿAdīy b. Zayd al-ʿIbādī*, ed. M. Ǧabbār al-Muʿaybad, Baghdad 1385/1965.
Aġānī	Abū l-Faraǧ al-Iṣfahānī: *Kitāb al-ʾAġānī*, 24 vols., Cairo: Dār al-Kutub al-Miṣrīyah 1345–94 / 1927–74.
AFidāʾMuḫt	ʿImād ad-Dīn Ism. Abū l-Fidāʾ: *al-Muḫtaṣar fī ʾaḫbār al-bašar*, 4 vols. in 2, repr. Beirut n.d.
AfricDescr (fr.)	Leo Africanus (al-Ḥasan b. M. al-Wazzān al-Ġarnāṭī az-Zayyātī): *Description de l'Afrique*, tr. by A. Épaulard, 2 vols., Paris 1980f.
AfricDescr (it.)	Id.: *Descrittione dell'Africa*, in: *Letteratura Italiana Zanichelli (CD-Rom LIZ 3.0)*, edd. P. Stoppelli and E. Picchi, vol. III (1998).[2]
AḫfIḫt	ʿAlī b. Sul. al-Aḫfaš al-Aṣġar: *Kitāb al-Iḫtiyārayn al-Mufaḍḍalīyāt wa-l-ʾAṣmaʿīyāt*, ed. Faḫr ad-Dīn Qabāwah, Beirut: Dār al-Fikr al-Muʿāṣir / Damascus: Dār al-Fikr 1999.
ALL (B)	*Kitāb ʾAlf laylah wa-laylah*, 4 vols., Beirut: al-Maṭbaʿah al-Adabīyah 1880–1882. (This edition follows the influential Būlāq edition).
ALL (C)	*ʾAlf laylah wa-laylah*, 7 vols., Beirut: al-Maṭbaʿah al-Kāṯūlīkīyah 1957–58 (this edition follows the Calcutta edition, as also ALL Littmann).
ALL (Littmann)	*Die Erzählungen aus den tausendundein Nächten. Vollständige deutsche Ausgabe in zwölf Bänden, zum ersten Mal nach dem arabischen Urtext der Calcuttaer Ausgabe aus dem Jahre 1839 übertragen von Enno Littmann*, 6 vols. in 12, Wiesbaden: Insel ^{1}1953 (repr. Frankfurt 1976).

1 This section lists writings *originally composed in oriental languages until the middle of the thirteenth century (c.1250 H)*, including *later anthologies* – e.g. MN, *Nūr an-nahār*, ŠayMaǧānī, WriǦurzah – and *modern translations of pre-modern literature and poetry*, e.g. ALL (Littmann), IḪallWaf (Slane), IṣfStrangers and ṬabHistory. The definite article *al-* and the diacritical signs have not been considered in the alphabetical order of items.

2 The text reproduces the version of G.B. Ramusio: *Navigationi et viaggi* (Venice 1550–56), ed. M. Milanesi, Turin: Einaudi 1978–88.

ALL (Mahdī) — *Kitāb ʾAlf laylah wa-laylah min ʾuṣūlihī l-ʿarabīyah l-ʾūlā*, ed. M. Mahdi, Leiden: Brill 1984.

ᶜĀmBahǧah — ᶜImād ad-Dīn Ya. b. Abī Bakr al-ᶜĀmirī: *Bahǧat al-maḥāfil wa-buġyat al-ʾamāṯil fī talḫīṣ al-muʿǧizāt wa-s-siyar wa-š-šamāʾil*, 2 vols., Cairo 1331 (repr. Beirut: Dār Ṣādir n.d.).

ᶜĀmBahǧNāẓ — Abū l-Barakāt M. b. Amīn al-Ġazzī al-ᶜĀmirī: *Kitāb Bahǧat an-nāẓirīn ʾilā tarāǧim al-mutaʾaḫḫirīn min aš-Šāfiʿiyah al-bāriʿīn*, ed. Abū Ya. ᶜAl. al-Kindī, Beirut: Dār Ibn Ḥazm 1421/2000.

ᶜĀmilīWas — M. b. al-Ḥusayn al-ᶜĀmilī: *Wasāʾil aš-šīʿah ʾilā taḥṣīl masāʾil aš-šarīʿah*, 20 vols., ed. al-Aġā al-Mayrazā ᶜAbd ar-Raḥīm ar-Rabbānī, Tehran: Maktabah Islāmīyah 1381.

ᶜĀmKaškūl — Bahāʾ ad-Dīn M. b. al-Ḥusayn al-ᶜĀmilī: *al-Kaškūl*, 2 vols., Qum *c.*1378/1958.

AnbNuzhah — Abū l-Barakāt al-Kamāl ᶜAr. b. M. (Ibn) al-Anbārī: *Nuzhat al-ʾalibbāʾ fī ṭabaqāt al-ʾudabāʾ*, ed. M. Abū l-Faḍl Ibrāhīm, Cairo: Dār Nahḍat Miṣr 1386/1967.

AnbŠQaṣ — Abū Bakr M. b. al-Qāsim al-Anbārī: *Šarḥ al-qaṣāʾid as-sabʿ aṭ-ṭiwāl al-ǧāhilīyāt*, ed. ᶜAbd as-Salām M. Hārūn, Cairo: Dār al-Maᶜārif 1963 (Ḏaḫāʾir al-ᶜArab 35).

AnṣTuḥfah — Zak. b. M. al-Anṣārī al-Šāfiᶜī: *Tuḥfat al-ṭullāb bi-šarḥ matn Taḥrīr Tanqīḥ al-lubāb*, ed. Abū ᶜAr. Ṣalāḥ b. M. b. ᶜUwayḍah, Beirut: Dār al-Kutub al-ᶜIlmīyah 1418/1997.

AnṭTaḏk — Dāʾūd b. ᶜUmar al-Anṭākī: *Taḏkirat ʾūlī l-ʾalbāb wa-l-ǧāmiʿ li-l-ʿaǧab al-ʿuǧǧāb*, 2 vols., Cairo 1309 (repr. Beirut: al-Maktabah aṯ-Ṯaqāfīyah n.d.).

ANuAḫbIṣf — Abū Nuᶜaym A. b. ᶜAl. al-Iṣfahānī: *Kitāb Ḏikr ʾaḫbār ʾIṣfahān*, ed. S. Dedering, 2 vols., repr. Cairo: Dār al-Kitāb al-Islāmī 1411/1991.

ANuḤilyah — Id.: *Ḥilyat al-ʾawliyāʾ wa-ṭabaqāt al-ʾaṣfiyāʾ*, 4 vols., Cairo: Maktabat al-Ḫānǧī / Maṭbaᶜat as-Saᶜādah 1351–54 / 1932–35.

ANuwDīwān — Abu Nuwās al-Ḥasan b. Hāniʾ: *Dīwān ʾAbī Nuwās (Der Dīwān des Abū Nuwās)*, ed. E. Wagner, 4 vols., Wiesbaden: F. Steiner 1958–88 (Bibliotheca Islamica 20a–b).

ᶜARazMuṣ — ᶜAbd ar-Razzāq b. Hammām aṣ-Ṣanᶜānī: *al-Muṣannaf*, ed. Ḥabīb ar-Raḥmān al-Aᶜẓamī, 12 vols., Beirut: al-Maktab al-Islāmī 1403/1983.

ArdAnwār — Yūsuf b. Ibr. al-Ardabīlī aš-Šāfiᶜī: *al-ʾAnwār li-ʾaʿmāl al-ʾabrār (fī fiqh al-ʾImām aš-Šāfiʿī)*, 2 vols., Cairo: al-Maktabah at-Tiǧārīyah al-Kubrā n.d. (1328).

AŠāmahBāᶜiṯ — Šihāb ad-Dīn Abū Šāmah ᶜAr. b. Ism.: *al-Bāʿiṯ ʿalā ʾinkār al-bidaʿ wa-l-ḥawādiṯ*, Cairo: al-Maktabah al-Maḥmūdīyah n.d.

AŠāmahRawḍ — Id.: *Kitāb ar-Rawḍatayn fī ʾaḫbār ad-dawlatayn an-Nūrīyah wa-ṣ-Ṣalāḥīyah*, 2 vols., Cairo: Maṭbaᶜat Wādī n-Nīl 1287f.

AŠāmahTar — Id.: *Tarāǧim riǧāl al-qarnayn as-sādis wa-s-sābiʿ (= aḏ-Ḏayl ʿalā Kitāb ar-Rawḍatayn)*, ed. M. Zāhid al-Kawṯarī, Beirut: Dār al-Ǧīl 2 1974 (1 1947).

AŠayḫAḫlāq — Abū M. ᶜAl. b. M. b. Ǧaᶜfar al-Iṣbahānī, Abū š-Šayḫ: *ʾAḫlāq an-nabī wa-ʾādābuhū*, ed. ᶜIṣām ad-Dīn Sayyid aṣ-Ṣabābiṭī, Cairo: ad-Dār al-Miṣrīyah al-Lubnānīyah 2 1413/2 1993.

AšḫŠBahǧah — Ǧamāl ad-Dīn M. al-Ašḫar al-Yamanī: *Šarḥ Bahǧat al-maḥāfil*, printed in: ᶜĀmBahǧah.

ᶜAskMaᶜānī — Abū Hilāl Ḥasan b. ᶜAl. al-ᶜAskarī: *Dīwān al-maʿānī*, ed. A. Ḥasan Basağ, 2 vols. in 1, Beirut: Dār al-Kutub al-ᶜIlmīyah 1414/1994.

AṬālibAmālī — al-Imām Abū Ṭālib Ya. b. al-Ḥusayn: *Taysīr al-maṭālib fī ʾamālī l-ʾimām ʾAbī Ṭālib*, ed. Ya. ᶜAbd al-Karīm al-Faḍīl, Beirut: Muʾassasat al-Aᶜlamī li-l-Maṭbūᶜāt 1395/1975.

ATamDīwān — Abū Tammām Ḥabīb b. Aws aṭ-Ṭāʾī: *Dīwān ʾAbī Tammām bi-šarḥ al-Ḫaṭīb at-Tabrīzī*, ed. M. ᶜAbduh ᶜAzzām, 4 vols., Cairo: Dār al-Maᶜārif 1951–57 (vols. I–III) and [3]1983 (vol. IV) (Ḏaḫāʾir al-ᶜArab 5).

AᶜUbAmwāl — Abū ᶜUbayd al-Qāsim b. Sallām: *Kitāb al-ʾAmwāl*, Beirut: Muʾassasat Nāṣir li-ṯ-Ṯaqāfah 1981.

AwsDīwān (G) — Aws b. Ḥağar at-Tamīmī: *ad-Dīwān (Gedichte und Fragmente des ʾAus ibn Ḥajar)*, ed. R. Geyer, Vienna 1892.

AwsDīwān (N) — Id.: *Dīwān ʾAws b. Ḥağar*, ed. M. Yūsuf Nağm, Beirut: Dār Ṣādir / Dār Bayrūt 1380/1960.

ᶜAydNūr — ᶜAbd al-Qādir b. Šayḫ b. ᶜAl. al-ᶜAydarūsī: *an-Nūr as-sāfir ʿan ʾaḫbār al-qarn al-ʿāšir*, repr. Beirut: Dār al-Kutub al-ᶜIlmīyah 1405/1985.

ᶜAynīᶜIqd — Badr ad-Dīn Maḥmūd b. A. al-ᶜAynī al-Ḥanafī: *ʿIqd al-ğumān fī tārīḫ ʾahl az-zamān*, ed. M. M. Amīn, 4 vols., Cairo: al-Hayʾah al-Miṣrīyah al-ᶜĀmmah li-l-Kitāb 1409/1989.

ᶜAynīᶜUmdah — Id.: *ʿUmdat al-qārī šarḥ Ṣaḥīḥ al-Buḫārī*, 20 vols., Cairo: Muṣṭafā al-Bābī al-Ḥalabī 1392/1972.

AYūsĀṯār — Abū Yūsuf Yaᶜqūb b. Ibr. al-Anṣārī al-Ḥanafī: *Kitāb al-ʾĀṯār*, ed. Abū l-Wafā, Beirut: Dār al-Kutub al-ᶜIlmīyah n.d.

AyvānGarden — *The Garden of the Mosques. Hafiz Hüseyin al-Ayvansarayî's Guide to the Muslim Monuments of Ottoman Istanbul. Translated and Annotated by Howard Crane*, Leiden 2000 (Studies in Islamic Art and Architecture VIII), a translation of al-Ayvānsarāyī's *Hadikat al-Cevami (Ḥadīqat al-ğawāmiʿ)*, 2 vols., Istanbul: Matbaa-i Amire 1281.

AzdīTārMawṣil — Abū Zak. Yazīd b. M. al-Azdī: *Tārīḫ al-Mawṣil*, ed. ᶜAlī Ḥabībah, Cairo: Muʾassasat Dār at-Taḥrīr li-ṭ-Ṭabᶜ wa-n-Našr 1387/1967.

AzrMakkah — Abū l-Walīd M. b. ᶜAl. al-Azraqī: *Tārīḫ Makkah (Kitāb ʾAḫbār Makkah)*, ed. Rušdī aṣ-Ṣāliḥ Malḥas, 2 vols., Beirut: Dār al-Andalus [3]1389/[3]1969.

Bā-FaqīhŠiḥr — Bā-Faqīh M. b. ᶜUmar aṭ-Ṭayyib: *Tārīḫ aš-Šiḥr wa-ʾaḫbār al-qarn al-ʿāšir*, ed. ᶜAl. M. al-Ḥabašī, Beirut: ᶜĀlam al-Kutub 1419/1999.

BaġAnwār — al-Ḥusayn b. Masᶜūd al-Baġawī: *al-ʾAnwār fī šamāʾil an-nabī al-muḫtār*, edd. Ibr. and M. al-Yaᶜqūbī, 2 vols., Damascus: Dār al-Maktabī 1416/1995.

BaġdḪizānah — ᶜAbd al-Qādir b. ᶜUmar al-Baġdādī: *Ḫizānat al-ʾadab wa-lubb lubāb lisān al-ʿarab*, 4 vols., Cairo: al-Maṭbaᶜah as-Salafīyah 1347–51.

BāğīMunt — Abū l-Walīd Sulaymān b. Ḫalaf al-Bāğī al-Mālikī: *Kitāb al-Muntaqā (šarḥ Muwaṭṭaʾ Mālik)*, 7 vols., Cairo: Maṭbaᶜat as-Saᶜādah 1331f.

BaḥrKaškūl — Yūsuf al-Baḥrānī: *al-Kaškūl*, 3 vols., an-Nağaf: Maṭb. an-Nuᶜmān 1381/1961.

BakrīAnwār — Abū l-Ḥasan A. b. ᶜAl. al-Bakrī: *al-ʾAnwār (wa-miftāḥ as-surūr wa-l-ʾafkār) fī mawlid an-nabī al-muḫtār*, ed. Niḍāl M. ᶜAlī, Beirut: Muʾassasat al-Aᶜlamī li-l-Maṭbūᶜāt 1420/1999.

BakrīMas — Abū ᶜUbayd ᶜAl. b. ᶜAbd al-ᶜAzīz al-Bakrī: *Kitāb al-Masālik wa-l-mamālik*, edd. A. P. Van Leeuwen and A. Ferré, 2 vols., Beirut: Dār al-Ġarb al-Islāmī / Tunis: ad-Dār al-ᶜArabīyah li-l-Kitāb 1992.

BakrīMuᶜǧam — Id.: *Muᶜǧam mā staᶜǧam min ᵓasmāᵓ al-bilād wa-l-mawāḍiᶜ*, ed. Muṣṭafā as-Saqqā, 4 vols. in 2, Cairo: Maṭbaᶜat Laǧnat at-Taᵓlīf wa-t-Tarǧamah wa-n-Našr 1364–68 / 1945–49.

BalFutūḥ — Abū l-ᶜAbbās A. b. Ya. al-Balāḏurī: *Kitāb Futūḥ al-buldān*, ed. ᶜAl. Anīs aṭ-Ṭabbāᶜ, Beirut: Muᵓassasat al-Maᶜārif 1407/1987.

BaṣrīḤam (B) — Ṣadr ad-Dīn ᶜAlī b. Abī l-Faraǧ al-Baṣrī: *Kitāb al-Ḥamāsah al-Baṣrīyah*, 2 vols., ed. Muḫtār ad-Dīn Aḥmad, Hyderabad: Dāᵓirat al-Maᶜārif al-ᶜUṯmānīyah 1964 (repr. Beirut: ᶜĀlam al-Kutub 1403/1983).

BaṣrīḤam (C) — Id.: *Kitāb al-Ḥamāsah al-Baṣrīyah*, 2 vols., ed. ᶜĀdil Sul. Ǧamāl, Cairo: Wizārat al-Awqāf 1408/1987.[3]

BaššārDīwān — Baššār b. Burd: *ad-Dīwān*, ed. M. Badr ad-Dīn al-ᶜAlawī, Beirut: Dār aṯ-Ṯaqāfah 1963.

BaṭalMuḫt — Abū M. ᶜAl. b. M. al-Baṭalyawsī: *Šarḥ al-Muḫtār min Luzūmīyāt ᵓAbī l-ᶜAlāᵓ (al-Maᶜarrī)*, 2 vols. in 1, ed. Ḥāmid ᶜAbd al-Maǧīd, Cairo: Dār al-Kutub al-Miṣrīyah 1970.

BaybZubdah — Rukn ad-Dīn Baybars al-Manṣūrī ad-Dawādār: *Zubdat al-fikrah fī tārīḫ al-hiǧrah*, ed. D. S. Richards, Beirut – Berlin: Das Arabische Buch 1998 (Bibliotheca Islamica 42).

BayDal — Abū Bakr A. b. al-Ḥusayn al-Bayhaqī aš-Šāfiᶜī: *Dalāᵓil an-nubūwah wa-maᶜrifat ᵓaḥwāl ṣāḥib aš-šarīᶜah*, ed. ᶜAbd al-Muᶜṭī Qalᶜaǧī, 7 vols., Cairo: Dār ad-Dayān li-t-Turāṯ / Beirut: Dār al-Kutub al-ᶜIlmīyah 1985 (repr. 1408/1988).

BayḍTafsīr — Nāṣir ad-Dīn ᶜAl. b. ᶜUmar al-Bayḍāwī aš-Šīrāzī: *Tafsīr al-Bayḍāwī (ᵓAnwār at-tanzīl wa-ᵓasrār at-taᵓwīl)*, 5 vols. in 2, Cairo 1306 (repr. Beirut: Dār Ṣādir n.d.).

BayḤayātAnb — Abū Bakr A. b. al-Ḥusayn al-Bayhaqī aš-Šāfiᶜī: *Ḥayāt al-ᵓanbiyāᵓ (fī qubūrihim)*, ed. Abū Sahl Naǧāḥ Ṣiyam and Šaᶜbān M. Ismāᶜīl, al-Manṣūrah: Maktabat al-Īmān 1993.

BayManŠāf — Id.: *Manāqib aš-Šāfiᶜī*, ed. as-Sayyid A. Ṣaqr, 2 vols., Cairo: Dār at-Turāṯ 1390/1970.

BaySunan — Id.: *Kitāb as-Sunan al-kubrā*, 10 vols., Hyderabad 1344–55 (repr. Beirut n.d.).

BišrDīwān — Bišr b. Abī Ḫāzim al-Asadī: *ad-Dīwān*, ed Ṣalāḥ ad-Dīn al-Hawwārī, Beirut: Dār al-Hilāl 1997.

BN — ᶜImād ad-Dīn Ism. b. ᶜUmar Ibn Kaṯīr aš-Šāfiᶜī: al-*Bidāyah wa-n-nihāyah*, 14 vols., Beirut: Maktabat al-Maᶜārif / ar-Riyāḍ: Maktabat an-Naṣr 1388/1966f.

Buḫārī — *See* ᶜAynīᶜUmdah; FB; KirmŠBuḫ; QasṭIršād.

BūṣDīwān — Šaraf ad-Dīn Abū ᶜAl. M. b. Saᶜīd: *Dīwān al-Būṣīrī*, ed. M. Sayyid Kīlānī, Cairo: Muṣṭafā al-Bābī al-Ḥalabī 1374/1955.

BustīSīrah — Abū Ḥātim M. b. Ḥibbān al-Bustī: *as-Sīrah an-nabawīyah wa-ᵓaḫbār al-ḫulafāᵓ (min Kitāb aṯ-Ṯiqāt)*, edd. as-Sayyid ᶜAzīzbak *et al.*, Beirut: Muᵓassasat al-Kutub aṯ-Ṯaqāfīyah 1407/1987.

ḌabbīBuġ — A. b. Ya. aḍ-Ḍabbī: *Buġyat al-multamis fī tārīḫ riǧāl ᵓahl al-ᵓAndalus*, ed. F. Codera, Madrid 1883 (Bibliotheca Arabico-Hispana III).

3 This edition has also been published in a new print in 4 vols. including numerous indices, Cairo: Maktabat al-Ḫānǧī 1420/1999.

DabMaᶜālim — Abū Zayd ᶜAr. b. M. al-Anṣārī al-Usaydī: *Maᶜālim al-ʾaymān fī maᶜrifat ʾahl al-Qayrawān*, completed and annotated by Abū l-Faḍl Ibn Nāǧī at-Tanūḫī, edd. Ibrāhīm Šabbūḥ, M. al- Aḥmadī Abū n-Nūr and M. Māḍūr, 3 vols., Cairo: Maktabat al-Ḫānǧī / Tunis: al-Maktabah al-ᶜAtīqah 1968–78.

ḎahᶜIbar — Šams ad-Dīn M. b. A. aḏ-Ḏahabī aš-Šāfiᶜī: *al-ᶜIbar fī ḫabar man ᶜabar*, 5 vols., edd. Ṣalāḥ ad-Dīn al-Munaǧǧid and Fuʾād Sayyid, al-Kuwayt: Dāʾirat al-Maṭbūᶜāt wa-n-Našr 1960–66 (at-Turāṯ al-ᶜArabī nos. 4–5, 7, 10 and 15).

ḎahMuᶜǧam — Id.: *Muᶜǧam muḥaddiṯī ḏ-Ḏahabī*, ed. Rūḥīyah ᶜAr. as-Suyūfī, Beirut: Dār al-Kutub al-ᶜIlmīyah 1413/1993.

ḎahMuᶜǧŠuyūḫ — Id.: *Muᶜǧam šuyūḫ aḏ-Ḏahabī*, ed. Rūḥīyah ᶜAr. as-Suyūfī, Beirut: Dār al-Kutub al-ᶜIlmīyah 1410/1990.

ḎahMuḫtDub — Id.: *al-Muḫtaṣar al-muḥtāǧ ilayhi min Tārīḫ al-ḥāfiẓ ʾAbī ᶜAbd ʾAllāh (ad-Dubayṯī)*, edited as vol. XV of TB (*see below*).

ḎahTaḏk — Id.: *Kitāb Taḏkirat al-ḥuffāẓ*, 4 vols., Hyderabad: Maṭbaᶜat Maǧlis Dāʾirat al-Maᶜārif al-ᶜUthmānīyah [4]1390/[4]1970.

ḎahTalḫ — Id.: *Talḫīṣ al-Mustadrak*, printed on the margins of: HākMust.

DarwSāniḥāt — Darwīš M. b. A. aṭ-Ṭālawī al-Urtuqī: *Sāniḥāt dumā l-qaṣr fī muṭāraḥāt banī l-ᶜaṣr*, ed. M. Mursī al-Ḫawlī, 2 vols., Beirut: ᶜĀlam al-Kutub 1403/1983.

DāʾūdīṬab — Šams ad-Dīn M. b. ᶜAlī ad-Dāʾūdī: *Ṭabaqāt al-mufassirīn*, 2 vols., Beirut: Dār al-Kutub al-ᶜIlmīyah n.d.

DaylFird — Abū Šuǧāᶜ Šīrawayh b. Šahridār ad-Daylamī: *Musnad al-firdaws (Firdaws al-ʾaḫbār)*, 2 vols., Beirut: Dār al-Fikr 1418/1997.

DiᶜbilDīwān — Diᶜbil b. ᶜAlī al-Ḫuzāᶜī: *Dīwān Diᶜbil b. ᶜAlī al-Ḫuzāᶜī*, ed. ᶜAbd aṣ-Ṣāḥib ad-Daǧīlī, an-Naǧaf: Maṭbaᶜat al-Ādāb 1382/1962.

DimSīrah — Šaraf ad-Dīn ᶜAbd al-Muʾmin b. Ḫalaf ad-Dimyāṭī: *as-Sīrah an-nabawīyah*, ed. Asᶜad M. aṭ-Ṭayyib, Aleppo: Dār aṣ-Ṣābūnī 1416/1996.

DīnMuǧāl — Abū Bakr A. b. Marwān ad-Dīnawarī al-Mālikī: *al-Muǧālasah wa-ǧawāhir al-ᶜilm*, ed. Abū ᶜUbaydah Mašhūr b. Ḥasan Āl Salmān, 10 vols., Beirut: Dār Ibn Ḥazm 1419/1998.

DiyTārḪamīs — Ḥusayn b. M. ad-Diyārbakrī al-Ḥanafī: *Tārīḫ al-ḫamīs fī ʾaḥwāl ʾanfas nafīs*, 2 vols., Cairo 1266 (repr. Beirut: Dār al-Kutub al-ᶜIlmīyah n.d.).

DK — Šihāb ad-Dīn A. b. ᶜAlī Ibn Ḥaǧar al-ᶜAsqalānī aš-Šafiᶜī: *ad-Durar al-kāminah fī ʾaᶜyān al-miʾah aṯ-ṯāminah*, ed. M. Sayyid Ǧād al-Ḥaqq, 5 vols., Cairo: Dār al-Kutub al-Ḥadīṯah 1385/1966.

ḌL — Šams ad-Dīn M. b. ᶜAr. as-Saḫāwī: *aḍ-Ḍawʾ al-lāmiᶜ fī ʾahl al-qarn at-tāsiᶜ*, 12 vols. in 6, Cairo: Maktabat al-Quds 1354 (repr. Cairo: Dār al-Kitāb al-Islāmī n.d.).

FākAḫbMakkah — Abū ᶜAl. M. b. Isḥāq al-Fākihī al-Makkī: *Kitāb ʾAḫbār Makkah*, ed. ᶜAbd al-Malik b. ᶜAl. b. Dahiš, 6 vols. in 3, Mecca: Maktabat an-Nahḍah al-Ḥadīṯah / Beirut: Dār Ḫiḍr [3]1419/[3]1998.

FanSirāǧ — Abū ᶜAlī Zayn ad-Dīn ᶜAlī al-Muᶜīrī (?) al-Fanānī:[4] *Kitāb Sirāǧ al-qulūb wa-ᶜilāǧ aḏ-ḏunūb*, printed on the margins of: MakkīQūt I pp. 2–256.

4 This is the author's name as given on the title-page of the printed edition: المعيري الفناني GALS II p. 607f. ascribes the work to a well-known tenth-century Shiite author (Nūr Allāh al-Marᶜašī aš-Šuštarī); *cf.* also ḪḪ II p. 983. The *incipit* reported in ḪḪ, however, does not fit the actual text, nor does the description of its content or the name of its author.

FāsīʿIqd	Taqīy ad-Dīn M. b. A. al-Fāsī al-Mālikī: *al-ʿIqd aṯ-ṯamīn fī tārīḫ al-balad al-ʾamīn*, 7 vols., ed. M. ʿAbd al-Qādir A. ʿAṭā, Beirut: Dār al-Kutub al-ʿIlmīyah 1419/1998.
FāsīŠifāʾ	Id.: *Šifāʾ al-ġarām bi-ʾaḫbār al-balad al-ḥarām*, edd. M. Mabrūk Nāfiʿ *et al.*, 2 vols., repr. Beirut: Dār al-Kutub al-ʿIlmīyah / Mecca: Dār al-Bāz n.d.
FāsīZuhūr	Id.: *az-Zuhūr al-muqtaṭafah min tārīḫ Makkah al-mušarrafah* (an abridgement of his *Šifāʾ al-ġarām*), edd. Adīb M. al-Ġazzāwī and Maḥmūd al-Arnāʾūṭ, Beirut: Dār Ṣādir 2000.
FāzĀṯār	Abū Zayd ʿAr. b. Yaḫlaftan al-Fāzāzī: *ʾĀṯār ʾAbī Zayd al-Fāzāzī al-ʾAndalusī (nuṣūṣ ʾadabīyah min al-qarn al-hiǧrī as-sābiʿ ǧamaʿahā baʿḍ talāmīḏihī fī ḥayātih)*, ed. ʿAbd al-Ḥamīd ʿAl. al-Harāmah, Beirut – Damascus: Dār Qutaybah 1412/1991.
FB	Šihāb ad-Dīn A. b. ʿAlī Ibn Ḥaǧar al-ʿAsqalānī: *Fatḥ al-bārī bi-šarḥ (Ṣaḥīḥ) al-Buḫārī*, edd. ʿAbd al-ʿAzīz b. ʿAl. b. Bāz and M. Fuʾād ʿAbd al-Bāqī, 16 vols. (including the unnumbered vols. containing the *Muqaddimah* and the indices), Beirut: Dār al-Kutub al-ʿIlmīyah ²1418/²1997.
FīrūzQāmūs	Maǧd ad-Dīn M. b. Yaʿqūb aš-Šīrāzī al-Fīrūzābādī: *al-Qāmūs al-muḥīṭ*, 4 vols. in 2, Cairo: al-Maṭbaʿah al-Amīrīyah ³1301 (repr. Cairo: al-Hayʾah al-Miṣrīyah al-ʿĀmmah li-l-Kitāb 1397/1977).
ĞabʿAǧāʾib	ʿAr. b. Ḥasan al-Ǧabartī: *ʿAǧāʾib al-ʾāṯār fī t-tarāǧim wa-l-ʾaḫbār*, edd. ʿAbd ar-Raḥīm ʿAr. ʿAbd ar-Raḥīm, vols. I–II, Cairo: Maṭbaʿat Dār al-Kutub al-Miṣrīyah 1997f.
ĞāḥBayān	Abū ʿUṯmān ʿUmar b Baḥr al-Ǧāḥiẓ: *Kitāb al-Bayān wa-t-tabyīn*, ed. ʿAbd as-Salām M. Hārūn, 4 vols., Cairo: Maṭbaʿat Laǧnat at-Taʾlīf 1367/1948.
ĞāḥḤay	Id.: *Kitāb al-Ḥayawān*, ed. ʿAbd as-Salām M. Hārūn, 8 vols., Cairo: Muṣṭafā al-Bābī al-Ḥalabī ²1386–89 / ²1967–69.
ĞāḥMaḥ	Id. (wrong ascription): *Kitāb al-Maḥāsin wa-l-ʾaḍdād*, ed. G. von Vloten, Leiden 1898 (repr. Amsterdam: Oriental Press 1974).
ĠazDurrah	Abū Ḥāmid M. b. M. al-Ġazālī: *Kitab ad-Durrah al-fāḫirah fī kašf ʿulūm al-ʾāḫirah*, ed. L. Gautier, Geneva 1878 (repr. Beirut 1417/1997).
ĠazIḥyāʾ (B)	Id.: *ʾIḥyāʾ ʿulūm ad-dīn* (with az-Zayn al-ʿIrāqī's gloss on the margin and appendices), 5 vols., repr. Beirut: Dār Iḥyāʾ at-Turāṯ al-ʿArabī n.d.
ĠazIḥyāʾ (C)	Id.: *ʾIḥyāʾ ʿulūm ad-dīn* (with several glosses on the margins), 4 vols. in 2, Cairo: al-Maṭbaʿah al-ʿUṯmānīyah 1352/1933.
ĠazKawākib	Naǧm ad-Dīn M. b. M. al-Ġazzī: *al-Kawākib ad-durrīyah bi-ʾaʿyān al-miʾah al-ʿāširah*, ed. Ḫalīl al-Manṣūr, 3 vols. in 2, Beirut: Dār al-Kutub al-ʿIlmīyah 1418/1997.
ĠazLuṭf	Id.: *Luṭf as-samar wa-qaṭf aṯ-ṯamar min tarāǧim ʾaʿyān* (...) *al-qarn al-ḥādī ʿašar*, ed. Maḥmūd aš-Šayḫ, 2 vols., Damascus: Wiz. aṯ-Ṯaqāfah n.d.
ĠazNatīǧah	A. b. al-Mahdī al-Ġazzāl: *Natīǧat al-iǧtihād fī l-muhādanah wa-l-ǧihād (Riḥlat al-Ġazzāl wa-safāratuh ʾilā l-ʾAndalus)*, ed. Ism. al-ʿArabī, Beirut: Dār al-Ġarb al-Islāmī 1980.
ĞazṬab	Šams ad-Dīn Abū l-Ḫayr M. b. M. (Ibn) al-Ǧazarī: *Ṭabaqāt al-qurrāʾ (Ġāyat an-nihāyah fī ṭabaqāt al-qurrāʾ)*, edd. G. Bergsträsser and O. Pretzl, 3 vols., Cairo: Maṭb. as-Saʿādah 1933–35 (Bibliotheca Islamica 8a-c).
GramlLebensweise	R. Gramlich: *Die Lebensweise der Könige: Adab al-mulūk. Ein Handbuch zur islamischen Mystik*, Stuttgart 1993 (Abhandlungen für die Kunde des Morgenlandes 50, 3), see also above *Adab al-mulūk*.

ĠubrᶜUnwān — Abū l-ᶜAbbās A. b. A. al-Ġubrīnī: *ᶜUnwān ad-dirāyah fī man ᶜurifa min al-ᶜulamāʾ fī l-miʾah as-sābiᶜah bi-Biǧāyah*, ed. ᶜĀdil Nuwayhiḍ, Beirut: Laǧnat at-Taʾlīf wa-t-Tarǧamah wa-n-Našr 1969.

HadjIbnLabb — H. Hadjadji: *Ibn al-Labbāna. Le poète d'al-Muᶜtamid, Prince de Séville, ou Le symbole de l'amitié*, Paris: éd. El-Ouns 1997.[5]

ḤaḍrMuq — ᶜAl. b. ᶜAr. Bā-Faḍl al-Ḥaḍramī: *al-Muqaddimah al-Ḥaḍramīyah fī fiqh as-sādah aš-Šāfiᶜīyah*, printed on the margins of: HaytMinhāǧ.

ḪafRayḥ — Šihāb ad-Dīn Maḥmūd al-Ḫafāǧī: *Rayḥānat al-ʾalibbā wa zahrat al-ḥayāh ad-dunyā*, Cairo: al-Maṭbaᶜah al-ᶜĀmirīyah al-ᶜUṯmānīyah 1306.

ḤākMust — al-Ḥākim an-Nīsābūrī, M. b. ᶜAl.: *al-Mustadrak ᶜalā ṣ-Ṣaḥīḥayn fī l-ḥadīṯ*, 4 vols., repr. ar-Riyāḍ: Maktabat an-Naṣr al-Ḥadīṯah 1968.

ḤalInsān — Nūr ad-Dīn ᶜAlī al-Ḥalabī: *ʾInsān al-ᶜuyūn fī sīrat al-ʾamīn al-maʾmūn (as-Sīrah al-Ḥalabīyah)*, 3 vols., Cairo 1320 (repr. Beirut: al-Maktabah al-Islāmīyah n.d.).

HamdIklīl — Abū M. al-Ḥasan b. A. Ibn al-Ḥāʾik al-Hamdānī: *al-ʾIklīl – al-ǧuzʾ aṯ-ṯāmin*, ed. N. A. Fāris, Princeton: UP 1940 (Princeton Oriental Texts VII).

HamdTakm — M. b. ᶜAbd al-Malik al-Hamdānī: *Takmilat Tārīḫ aṭ-Ṭabarī*, ed. A. Yūsuf Kanᶜān, vol. I, Beirut: al-Maṭbaᶜah al-Kāṯūlīkīyah 1961.

ḤamTanzīl — Muḥibb ad-Dīn Efendi al-Ḥamawī: *Tanzīl al-ʾāyāt ᶜalā š-šawāhid al-ʾabyāt šarḥ šawāhid al-Kaššāf (li-z-Zamaḫšarī)*, Būlāq 1281.

ḪansāʾDīwān (B) — Tumāḍir bint ᶜAmr al-Ḫansāʾ: *ad-Dīwān*, ed. Karam al-Bustānī, Beirut: Dār Ṣādir / Dār Beirut 1379/1960.

ḪansāʾDīwān (Š) — Id.: *ʾAnīs al-ǧulasāʾ fī mulaḫḫaṣ šarḥ Dīwān al-Ḫansāʾ*, ed. L. Šayḫū, Beirut: al-Maṭbaᶜah al-Kāṯūlīkīyah 1895.

HarǦamᶜWas — al-Mullā ᶜAlī b. Sulṭān al-Qārīʾ al-Harawī al-Makkī: *Ǧamᶜ al-wasāʾil fī šarḥ aš-Šamāʾil (li-t-Tirmiḏī)*, 2 vols., Cairo 1318 (repr. Beirut: Dār al-Maᶜrifah n.d.).

HarIšārāt — Abū l-Ḥasan ᶜAlī b. Abī Bakr al-Harawī: *Kitāb al-ʾIšārāt ʾilā maᶜrifat az-ziyārāt*, ed. J. Sourdel-Thomine, Damascus: Institut français de Damas 1953; *see also below* SourdelLieux.

ḤarMaq (Chenery) — *The Assemblies of al Ḥarīri*, 2 vols., tr. by T. Chenery, London – Edinburgh 1867 (repr. Westmead, Farnborough 1969); *see also below* ŠarŠMaq.

HarMawrid — al-Mullā ᶜAlī b. Sulṭān al-Qārīʾ al-Harawī al-Makkī al-Ḥanafī: *al-Mawrid ar-rawī fī mawlid an-nabī*, ed. Mabrūk Ism. Mabrūk, Cairo: Maktabat al-Qurʾān 1992.

HarMirqātMaf — al-Mullā ᶜAlī b. Sulṭān al-Qārīʾ al-Harawī al-Makkī: *Mirqāt al-mafātīḥ šarḥ Miškāt al-maṣābīḥ (li-l-Ḫaṭīb at-Tabrīzī)*, 8 vols. in 4, Multān: Maktabah Amdādīyah / Maǧlis Išāᶜat al-Maᶜārif 1386f./1966f.

HarŠŠifāʾ — Id.: *Šarḥ Kitāb aš-Šifā bi-taᶜrīf ḥuqūq al-Muṣṭafā (li-l-Qāḍī ᶜIyāḍ)*, 2 vols., Istanbul: al-Maṭbaᶜah al-ᶜUṯmānīyah 1319 (repr. Beirut: Dār al-Kutub al-ᶜIlmīyah n.d.).

ḤassānDīwān — Ḥassān b. Ṯābit al-Anṣārī: *ad-Dīwān*, ed. W. ᶜArafāt, 2 vols., London: Luzac & Co. 1971 (E. J. W. Gibb Memorial Series N. S. 25).

5 This book contains a selection of Ibn al-Labbānah's poetry in Arabic and French relating to al-Muᶜtamid Ibn ᶜAbbād.

ḪaydLafẓ	Quṭb ad-Dīn M. b. M. al-Ḫaydarī aš-Šāfiʿī: *al-Lafẓ al-mukarram bi-ḫaṣāʾiṣ an-nabī al-muʿaẓẓam*, ed. Muṣṭafā Ṣamīdah, Beirut: Dār al-Kutub al-ʿIlmīyah 1417/1997.
HaytFatḤad	A. b. M. Ibn Ḥağar al-Haytamī al-Makkī: *al-Fatāwā al-ḥadīṯīyah*, Cairo: Muṣṭafā al-Bābī al-Ḥalabī ³1409/³1989.
HaytFatFiqh	Id.: *al-Fatāwā al-kubrā al-fiqhīyah*, 4 vols. in 2, Cairo: Maktabat ʿAbd al-Ḥamīd A. Ḥanafī 1357/1938 (also repr. Cairo: Maktabat al-Mašhad al-Ḥusaynī n.d.).
HaytĞawhar	Id.: *Kitāb al-Ğawhar al-munaẓẓam fī ziyārat al-qabr aš-šarīf an-nabawī al-mukarram*, ed. M. Zaynuhum M. ʿAzab, Cairo: Maktabat al-Madbūlī 2000 (Mawsūʿat Makkah wa-l-Madīnah 1).
HaytMinaḥ	Id.: *al-Minaḥ al-Makkīyah fī šarḥ al-Hamzīyah (li-l-Būṣīrī)*, ed. Bassām M. Bārūd, 3 vols., Abu Dhabi: al-Mağmaʿ aṯ-Ṯaqāfī / Beirut: Dār al-Ḥāwī 1418/1998.
HaytMinhāğ	Id.: *al-Minhāğ al-qawīm šarḥ ʿalā l-Muqaddimah al-Ḥaḍramīyah fī fiqh as-sādah aš-Šāfiʿīyah (li-l-Ḥaḍramī)*, Cairo: Muṣṭafā al-Bābī al-Ḥalabī 1358/1939.
HaytTuḥfMuḥt	Id.: *Tuḥfat al-muḥtāğ bi-šarḥ al-Minhāğ (li-n-Nawawī)*, printed on the margins of: ŠirwḤāš.
HaytTuḥfZuw	Id.: *Tuḥfat az-zuwwār ʾilā qabr an-nabī al-muḫtār*, ed. as-Sayyid Abū ʿAmmih, Ṭanṭā: Dār aṣ-Ṣaḥābah li-t-Turāṯ 1412/1992.
ḤāzIʿtibār	Abū Bakr M. b. Mūsā al-Ḥāzimī: *al-Iʿtibār fī n-nāsiḫ wa-l-mansūḫ min al-ʾāṯār*, ed. Zak. ʿUmayrāt, Beirut: Dār al-Kutub al-ʿIlmīyah 1416/1996.
ḪazrʿUqūd	ʿAlī b. al-Ḥasan al-Ḫazrağī: *al-ʿUqūd al-lūlūwīyah fī tārīḫ ad-dawlah ar-Rasūlīyah*, 2 vols., ed. M. Vasyūnī ʿAsal, Leiden: Brill / Cairo: Maṭbaʿat al-Hilāl 1329–32 / 1911–14 (repr. n.d.) (E. J. W. Gibb Mem. Series III, 4–5).
ḤillīRiğāl	Taqīy ad-Dīn al-Ḥasan b. ʿAlī Ibn Dāʾūd al-Ḥillī: *Kitāb ar-Riğāl*, ed. Ğalāl ad-Dīn al-Ḥusaynī, Tehran: Intišārat-i Dānišgāh-i Tihrān 1383/1963.
ḤumĞuḏwah	Abū ʿAl. M. b. Abī Naṣr al-Azdī al-Ḥumaydī: *Ğaḏwat al-muqtabis fī ḏikr wulāt al-ʾAndalus*, Cairo: ad-Dār al-Miṣrīyah li-t-Taʾlīf wa-t-Tarğamah 1966.
ḤurRawḍ	Šuʿayb b. Saʿd al-Miṣrī al-Makkī al-Ḥurayfīš: *ar-Rawḍ al-fāʾiq fī l-mawāʿiẓ wa-r-raqāʾiq*, ed. Ḫalīl al-Manṣūr, Beirut: Dār al-Kutub al-ʿIlmīyah 1417/1997.
ḤusḎayl	Šams ad-Dīn Abū l-Maḥāsin M. b. ʿAlī al-Ḥusaynī ad-Dimašqī: *Ḏayl Taḏkirat al-ḥuffāẓ li-ḏ-Ḏahabī*, ed. Ḥusām ad-Dīn al-Qudsī, Beirut: Dār Iḥyāʾ at-Turāṯ al-ʿArabī n.d.
ḪušṬab	Abū ʿAl. M. b. ʿAbd as-Salām al-Ḫušanī: *Ṭabaqāt ʿulamāʾ ʾIfrīqīyah*, ed. M. Zaynuhum M. ʿAzab, Cairo: Maktabat al-Madbūlī 1413/1993.
ḤuṣZahr (M)	Abū Isḥāq Ibr. b. ʿAlī al-Qayrawānī al-Ḥuṣrī: *Zahr al-ʾādāb wa-ṯamr al-ʾalbāb*, ed. M. Zakīy Mubārak, 4 vols. in 2, Beirut: Dār al-Ğīl ⁴1972.
ḤuṣZahr (Ṭ)	Id.: *Zahr al-ʾādāb wa-ṯamr al-ʾalbāb*, ed. Yūsuf ʿAlī Ṭawīl, 2 vols., Beirut: Dār al-Kutub al-ʿIlmīyah 1417/1997.
IʿABarrBahğah	Abū ʿUmar Ibn ʿAbd al-Barr an-Namirī al-Mālikī: *Bahğat al-mağālis wa-ʾuns al-muğālis wa-šaḥḏ aḏ-ḏāhin wa-l-hāğis*, edd. M. Mursī al-Ḫawlī and ʿAbd al-Qādir al-Qiṭṭ, 2 vols., Cairo: Dār al-Kitāb al-ʿArabī (1969).
IʿABarrDurar	Id.: *ad-Durar fī ḫtiṣār al-maġāzī wa-s-siyar*, Beirut: Dār al-Kutub al-ʿIlmīyah 1404/1984.

IᶜABarrIst — Id.: *al-Istīʿāb fī ʾasmāʾ al-ʾaṣḥāb*, printed on the margins of: IḤağIṣābah (Cairo 1328).

IAbbDīwān — Abū ᶜAl. M. b. ᶜAl. Ibn al-Abbār al-Quḍāᶜī: *Dīwān Ibn al-ʾAbbār*, ed. ᶜAbd as-Salām al-Harrās, Tunis: ad-Dār at-Tūnisīyah li-n-Našr 1405/1985.

IAbbḤullah — Id.: *al-Ḥullah as-siyarāʾ*, ed. Ḥusayn Muʾnis, Cairo: aš-Šarikah al-ᶜArabīyah li-ṭ-Ṭibāᶜah wa-n-Našr 1963.

IAbbMuᶜǧṢadafī — Id.: *al-Muʿǧam fī ʾaṣḥāb ʾAbī ʿAlī aṣ-Ṣadafī*, ed. F. Codera, Madrid 1886 (Bibliotheca Arabico-Hispana IV).

IAbbMuqt — Id. / Ibr. b. M. al-Balfīqī: *al-Muqtaḍab min Kitāb Tuḥfat al-qādim*, ed. Ibr. al-Ibyārī, Cairo: Dār al-Kitāb al-Miṣrī / Beirut: Dār al-Kitāb al-Lubnānī ²1402/²1982.

IAbbTakm — Abū ᶜAl. M. b. ᶜAl. Ibn al-Abbār al-Quḍāᶜī: *at-Takmilah li-Kitāb aṣ-Ṣilah (li-bn Baškuwāl)*, ed. ᶜAbd as-Salām al-Harrās, 4 vols., Beirut: Dār al-Fikr 1415/1995.

IᶜAbdūnTraité — É. Lévi-Provençal: *Séville musulmane au début du XIIᵉ siècle. Le Traitè d'Ibn ʿAbdun* (sic) *sur la vie urbaine et les corps de métiers. Traduit avec une introduction et notes*, Paris 1947 (repr. 2001).

IᶜAdīmBuġyah — Kamāl ad-Dīn ᶜUmar b. A. Ibn al-ᶜAdīm al-Ḥalabī al-Ḥanafī: *Buġyat aṭ-ṭalab fī tārīḫ Ḥalab*, 10 vols., Frankfurt/M. 1986–89 (Publ. of the Institute for the History of Arabic-Islamic Science, Ser. C: Facsimile editions 33).

IᶜAdīmZubdah — Id.: *Zubdat al-ḥalab min tārīḫ Ḥalab*, ed. Ḫalīl al-Manṣūr, Beirut: Dār al-Kutub al-ᶜIlmīyah 1417/1996.

IADīnārMūnis — Abū ᶜAl. M. b. Abī l-Qāsim ar-Ruᶜaynī, Ibn Abī Dīnār: *al-Mūnis fī ʾaḫbār ʾIfrīqiyā wa-Tūnis*, ed. M. Šammām, Tunis: al-Maktabah al-ᶜAtīqah ³1387/³1967 (Min Turāṯinā al-Islāmī 3).

IADunyāFarağ — Abū Bakr ᶜAl. b. M. Ibn Abī d-Dunyā al-Qurašī: *Kitāb al-Farağ baʿd aš-šiddah*, ed. Abū Ḥuḏayfah ᶜUbayd Allāh b. ᶜĀliyah, Cairo: Dār al-Mašriq al-ᶜArabī 1407/1987.

IADunyāMawt — *Kitāb al-mawt (The Book of Death) & Kitāb al-qubūr (The Book of Graves) by Ibn Abī ad-Dunyā (d. 280/892) reconstructed with an introduction by Leah Kinberg*, Haifa: Qism al-Luġah al-ᶜArabīyah wa-Ādābihā (Haifa University) 1983.

IADunyāQaṣr — Id.: *Kitāb Qaṣr al-ʾamal*, ed. M. Ḫayr Ramaḍān Yūsuf, Beirut: Dār Ibn Ḥazm ²1417/²1997.

IADunyāQubūr (A) — Id.: *Kitāb al-Qubūr*, ed. Ṭāriq M. Suklūᶜ al-ᶜAmūdī, Medina: Maktabat al-Ġurabāʾ al-Aṯarīyah 1420/2000.

IADunyāQubūr (K) — Id.: *Kitāb al-Qubūr*, ed. L. Kinberg, printed in: IADunyāMawt pp. 71–103.

IAĞamrBahğah — Abū M. ᶜAl. b. Saᶜd Ibn Abī Ğamrah al-Azdī al-Andalusī: *Bahğat an-nufūs wa-taḥallīhā bi-maʿrifat mā lahā wa-ʿalayhā*, ed. Bakrī Šayḫ Amīn, 2 vols., Beirut: Dār al-ᶜIlm li-l-Malāyīn 1997.

IᶜAHādīṢārim — Abū ᶜAl. M. b. A. Ibn ᶜAbd al-Hādī aṣ-Ṣāliḥī al-Ḥanbalī: *aṣ-Ṣārim al-munkī fī r-radd ʿalā s-Subkī*, ed. M. Rašād Ġānim, Beirut: Dār al-Kutub al-ᶜIlmīyah 1405/1985.

IᶜAHādīṬab — Id.: *Ṭabaqāt ʿulamāʾ al-ḥadīṯ*, edd. Akram al-Būšī and Ibr. az-Zaybaq, 4 vols., Beirut: Muʾassasat ar-Risālah ²1417/²1996.

IAḤağSulwah — Šihāb ad-Dīn A. b. Ya., Ibn Abī Ḥağalah at-Tilimsānī: *Sulwat al-ḥazīn fī mawt al-banīn*, ed. Muḫayyar Ṣāliḥ, Amman: Dār al-Fayḥāʾ n.d. (*c.*1995).

IAHawlFaḍ — Abū l-Ḥasan ʿAlī b. M. Ibn Abī l-Hawl ar-Rabaʿī al-Mālikī: *Faḍāʾil aš-Šām wa-Dimašq*, ed. Ṣalāḥ ad-Dīn al-Munağğid, Damascus: al-Majmaʿ al-ʿIlmi al-ʿArabī 1950.

IAḪiṣālRas — Abū ʿAl. M. Ibn Abī l-Ḫiṣāl al-Ġāfiqī: *Rasāʾil Ibn ʾAbī l-Ḫiṣāl*, ed. M. Riḍwān ad-Dāyah, Beirut: Dār al-Fikr 1408/1987.

IAḥnafDīwān — al-ʿAbbās b. al-Aḥnaf: *Dīwān al-ʿAbbās b. al-ʾAḥnaf*, ed. Karam al-Bustānī, Beirut: Dār Ṣādir 1398/1978.

IʿARabʿIqd (Ğ) — Abū ʿUmar A. b. M. Ibn ʿAbd Rabbih al-Andalusī: *Kitāb al-ʿIqd al-farīd*, 4 vols. in 2, Cairo: al-Maṭbaʿah al-Ğamālīyah 1331/1913.

IʿARabʿIqd (M) — Id.: *Kitāb al-ʿIqd al-farīd*, edd. A. Amīn, A. az-Zayn and Ibr. al-Ibyārī, 7 vols., Cairo: Maṭbaʿat Lağnat at-Taʾlīf wa-t-Tarğamah wa-n-Našr ²1948–67.

IʿArabŠFākihah — A. b. M. Ibn ʿArab-Šāh al-Ḥanafī: *Fākihat al-ḫulafāʾ wa-mufākahat aẓ-ẓurafāʾ*, Cairo 1325.

IʿASalāmFat — ʿIzz ad-Dīn ʿAbd al-ʿAzīz Ibn ʿAbd as-Salām aš-Šāfiʿī: *al-Fatāwā al-Mawṣilīyah*, ed. Iyād Ḫ. aṭ-Ṭabbāʿ, Damascus: Dār al-Fikr / Beirut: Dār al-Fikr al-Muʿāṣir 1999.

IʿASalāmQaw — Id.: *al-Qawāʿid al-kubrā (Qawāʿid al-ʾaḥkām fī ʾiṣlāḥ al-ʾanām)*, ed. Nazīyah K. Ḥammād and ʿUṯmān Ğ. Ḍamīrīyah, 2 vols., Damascus: Dār al-Qalam 1421/2000.

IʿASalāmŠağarah — Id.: *Šağarat al-maʿārif wa-l-ʾaḥwāl wa-ṣāliḥ al-ʾaqwāl wa-l-ʾaʿmāl*, ed. Abū ʿAl. Ḥusayn b. ʿAkāšah, Jeddah: Dār Māğid ʿAsīrī 1421/2000.

IAŠayMuṣ — ʿAl. b. M. Ibn Abī Šaybah al-Kūfī: *al-Muṣannaf (fī l-ʾaḥādīṯ wa-l-ʾāṯār)*, ed. Saʿīd al-Laḥḥām, 9 vols., Beirut: Dār al-Fikr 1409/1989.

IʿAṭāʾḤikam — Ibn ʿAṭāʾ Allāh as-Sikandarī: *Kitāb al-Ḥikam (Ibn ʿAṭāʾ Allāh (m. 709/1309) et la naissance de la confrérie Šāḏilite)*, ed. P. Nwyia, Beirut: Dār al-Mašriq ²1990 (Recherches N. S. A. II).

IAṯīrKāmil — ʿIzz ad-Dīn Abū l-Ḥasan ʿAlī b. M. Ibn al-Aṯīr: *al-Kāmil fī t-tārīḫ*, 13 vols., Beirut: Dār Ṣādir / Dār Bayrūt 1385–87 / 1965–67.

IAṯīrMaṯal — Ḍiyāʾ ad-Dīn Naṣr Allāh b. M. Ibn al-Aṯīr al-Mawṣilī: *al-Maṯal as-sāʾir fī ʾadab al-kātib wa-š-šāʿir*, Būlāq: al-Maṭbaʿah al-ʿĀmirah 1282.

IAṯīrNih — Mağd ad-Dīn al-Mubārak b. M. Ibn al-Aṯīr: *an-Nihāyah fī ġarīb al-ḥadīṯ wa-l-ʾaṯar*, 4 vols. in 2, Cairo: al-Maṭbaʿah al-Ḫayrīyah 1318–22.

IAṯīrUsd — ʿIzz ad-Dīn Abū l-Ḥasan ʿAlī b. M. Ibn al-Aṯīr: *ʾUsd al-ġābah fī maʿrifat aṣ-ṣaḥābah*, 5 vols., Cairo 1280–86.

IAUṣaybʿUyūn — Muwaffaq ad-Dīn Abū l-ʿAbbās A. b. al-Qāsim Ibn Abī Uṣaybiʿah: *ʿUyūn al-ʾanbāʾ fī ṭabaqāt al-ʾaṭibbāʾ*, ed. Nizār Riḍā, Beirut: Dār Maktabat al-Ḥayāh n.d.

IAYaṬab — Abū l-Husayn M. Ibn Abī Yaʿlā: *Ṭabaqāt al-Ḥanābilah*, ed. M. Ḥāmid al-Fiqī, 2 vols., Cairo: Maṭbaʿat as-Sunnah al-Muḥammadīyah 1371/1952.

IʿAẒāhirTašrīf — Muḥyī d-Dīn ʿAl. b. ʿAbd aẓ-Ẓāhir as-Saʿdī: *Tašrīf al-ʾayyām wa-l-ʿuṣūr fī sīrat al-Malik al-Manṣūr*, edd. Murād Kāmil and M. ʿAlī an-Naǧǧār, Cairo: Wizārat aṯ-Ṯaqāfah 1961.

IBābManLā — Abū Ğaʿfar M. b. ʿAlī Ibn Bābawayh [Bābūyah]: *Man lā yaḥḍuruhū l-faqīh*, 4 vols., ed. Ḥasan al-Mūsawī al-Ḫarsān, an-Nağaf: Dār al-Kutub al-Islāmīyah ⁴1377f. / ⁴1957–59.

IBaškQurbah — Abū l-Qāsim Ḫalaf b. ʿAbd al-Malik Ibn Baškuwāl: *al-Qurbah ʾilā rabb al-ʿālamīn bi-ṣ-ṣalāh ʿalā Muḥammad Sayyid al-mursalīn*, edd. Sayyid M.

Sayyid and Ḫilāf Maḥmūd ᶜAbd as-Samīᶜ, Beirut: Dār al-Kutub al-ᶜIlmīyah 1420/1999.

IBaškṢilah — Id.: *Kitāb aṣ-Ṣilah*, 2 vols., Cairo: ad-Dār al-Miṣrīyah li-t-Taʾlīf wa-t-Tarǧamah 1966 (al-Maktabah al-Andalusīyah 4–5).

IBaṭṭRiḥlah — Abū ᶜAl. M. b. ᶜAl. Ibn Baṭṭūṭah: *Riḥlat Ibn Baṭṭūṭah (al-musammāh Tuḥfat an-naẓẓār fī ġarāʾib al-ʾamṣār)*, ed. Ṭalāl Ḥarb, Beirut: Dār al-Kutub al-ᶜIlmīyah 1407/1987.

IbšīhīMust — Šihāb ad-Dīn al-Ibšīhī: *al-Mustaṭraf fī kull fann mustaẓraf*, ed. Darwīš al-Ǧuwaydī, 2 vols. in 1, Ṣaydā – Beirut: al-Maktabah al-ᶜAṣrīyah 1416/1996.

IBuḥtUns — Ṣafīy ad-Dīn Abū l-Fatḥ ᶜĪsā b. al-Buḥturī al-Ḥalabī: *ʾUns al-masǧūn wa-rāḥat al-maḥzūn*, ed. M. Adīb al-Ǧādir, Beirut: Dār Ṣādir 1997.

IDaqŠArbaᶜīn — Taqīy ad-Dīn M. b. ᶜAlī Ibn Daqīq al-ᶜĪd al-Miṣrī: *Šarḥ al-ʾArbaᶜīn an-Nawawīyah*, Beirut: Muʾassasat ar-Rayyān ^{4}1417/^{4}1997.

IDāʾūdZahrah — Abū Bakr M. b. Dāʾūd al-Iṣfahānī: *an-Niṣf al-ʾawwal min Kitāb az-Zahrah*, edd. A. R. Nykl and Ibr. Ṭūqān, Chicago: UP / Beirut: Maṭbaᶜat al-Ābāʾ al-Yasūᶜīyīn 1351/1932.

IDawKanz — Abū Bakr b. ᶜAl. Ibn ad-Dawādārī: *Kanz ad-durar wa-ǧāmiᶜ al-ġurar*, ed. D. Krawulsky, vol. V, Wiesbaden: F. Steiner 1413/1992 (Quellen zur Geschichte des islamischen Ägyptens 1e).

IDaybaᶜBuġ — Waǧīh ad-Dīn ᶜAr. b. ᶜAlī az-Zabīdī aš-Šaybānī, Ibn ad-Daybaᶜ: *Buġyat al-mustafīd fī ʾaḫbār madīnat Zabīd*, ed. ᶜAl. M. al-Ḥabašī, Ṣanᶜāʾ: Markaz ad-Dirāsāt wa-l-Buḥūṯ al-Yamanī 1979.

IDaybaᶜFaḍl — Id.: *al-Faḍl al-mazīd ᶜalā Buġyat al-mustafīd fī ʾaḫbār (madīnat) Zabīd*, ed. M. ᶜĪsā Ṣāliḥīyah, Kuwait: al-Maǧlis al-Waṭanī 1403/1982 (as-Silsilah at-Turāṯīyah 3).

IDaybaᶜḤad — Id.: *Ḥadāʾiq al-ʾanwār wa-maṭāliᶜ al-ʾasrār fī sīrat an-nabī al-muḫtār*, ed. ᶜAl. Ibr. al-Anṣārī, 3 vols., Mecca: al-Maktabah al-Makkīyah ^{2}1413/^{2}1993.

IDaybaᶜḤisbah — Id.: *Kitāb Buġyat al-ʾirbah fī maᶜrifat ʾaḥkām al-ḥisbah*, ed. Ṭalāl b. Ǧamīl ar-Rifāᶜī, Mecca: Ǧāmiᶜat Umm al-Qurā 1423/2002.

IḌayfṬab — M. an-Nūr Ḍayf Allāh: *Kitāb aṭ-Ṭabaqāt ʾaw Ḫuṣūṣ al-ʾawliyāʾ wa-ṣ-ṣāliḥīn wa-l-ᶜulamāʾ wa-š-šuᶜarāʾ fī s-Sūdān*, ed. Yūsuf Faḍl Ḥasan, Khartoum: Dār at-Taʾlīf wa-t-Tarǧamah wa-n-Našr ^{2}1974.

IDiḥIbtihāǧ — Abū l-Ḫaṭṭāb ᶜUmar Ibn Diḥyah al-Kalbī: *al-Ibtihāǧ fī ʾaḥādīṯ al-Miᶜrāǧ*, ed. Rifᶜat Fawzī ᶜAbd al-Muṭṭalib, Cairo: Maktabat al-Ḫānǧī 1417/1996.

IDiḥMuṭrib — Id.: *al-Muṭrib min ʾašᶜār ʾahl al-Maġrib*, edd. Ibr. al-Ibyārī, Ḥāmid ᶜAbd al-Maǧīd and A. A. Badawī, Cairo 1955 (repr. Cairo: Maṭbaᶜat Dār al-Kutub al-Miṣrīyah 1997).

IDimMustafād — A. b. Aybak Ibn ad-Dimyāṭī al-Ḥusaynī: *al-Mustafād min ḏayl Tārīḫ Baġdād*, ed. C. Faraḥ, repr. Beirut: Dār al-Kutub al-ᶜIlmīyah n.d.

IdrīsīDescr — Abū ᶜAl. M. b. M. al-Idrīsī: *Description de l'Afrique et de l'Espagne*, edd. R. Dozy and M. J. de Goeje, Leiden: Brill ^{2}1968 (^{1}1866).

IFahdItḥāf — Naǧm ad-Dīn M. (ᶜUmar) b. M. Ibn Fahd al-Makkī: *Itḥāf al-warā bi-ʾaḫbār ʾUmm al-qurā*, edd. Fahīm M. Šaltūt, ᶜAbd al-Karīm ᶜAlī Bāz *et al.*, 5 vols., Mecca: Ǧāmiᶜat Umm al-Qurā / Jeddah: Dār al-Madanī 1983–90 / 1404–10 (partially repr. Cairo: Maktabat al-Ḫānǧī n.d.).

IFahdLaḥẓ — Taqīy ad-Dīn Ǧār Allāh M. b. M. Ibn Fahd al-Makkī: *Laḥẓ al-ʾalḥāẓ bi-ḏayl Ṭabaqāt al-ḥuffāẓ (li-ḏ-Ḏahabī)*, ed. Ḥusām ad-Dīn al-Qudsī, printed in: ḤusḎayl.

IFarDībāǧ	Nūr ad-Dīn Ibr. b. ʿAlī Ibn Farḥūn al-Mālikī: *ad-Dībāǧ al-mudhab fī maʿrifat ʾaʿyān ʿulamāʾ al-maḏhab*, ed. Maʾmūn b. Muḥyī d-Dīn al-Ǧinān, Beirut: Dār al-Kutub al-ʿIlmīyah 1417/1996.
IFāriḍDīwān	Rušayd b. Ġālib ad-Daḥdāḥ: *Šarḥ Dīwān Ibn al-Fāriḍ min šarḥ Ḥasan al-Būrīnī wa-ʿAbd al-Ġanīy an-Nābulusī*, 2 vols. in 1, Būlāq 1289 (repr. Cairo: Dār Iḥyāʾ al-Kutub al-ʿArabīyah / Maktabat al-Kullīyāt al-Azharīyah n.d.).
IFarTārīḫ	Abū l-Walīd ʿAl. b. M. b. Yūsuf Ibn al-Faraḍī al-Azdī: *Tārīḫ ʿulamāʾ al-ʾAndalus*, 2 vols. in 1, Cairo: ad-Dār al-Miṣrīyah li-t-Taʾlīf wa-t-Tarǧamah 1966 (al-Maktabah al-Andalusīyah 2).
IFūdīBayān	M. b. ʿUṯmān b. M. Ibn Fūdī (Usuman dan Fodio): *Kitāb Bayān al-bidaʿ aš-šayṭānīyah allatī ʾaḥdaṯahā n-nās fī ʾabwāb al-millah al-Muḥammadīyah*, Max Freiherr von Oppenheim Foundation (Oriental Institute of Cologne University) manuscript no. 50 (8 fols.).
IFurTārīḫ	Nāṣir ad-Dīn M. b. ʿAbd ar-Raḥīm Ibn al-Furāt: *Tārīḫ Ibn al-Furāt*, ed. C. K. Zurayk, vol. VII, Beirut: AUB Press 1942 (al-ʿUlūm aš-Šarqīyah 17).
IFuwaṭīḤaw	Kamāl ad-Dīn ʿAbd ar-Razzāq b. al-Fuwaṭī al-Baġdādī: *al-Ḥawādiṯ al-ǧāmiʿah wa-t-taǧārib an-nāfiʿah fī l-miʾah as-sābiʿah*, ed. Muṣṭafā Ǧawād, Baghdad: al-Maktabah al-ʿArabīyah 1351.
IĠalbTiḏkār	Abū ʿAl. M. b. Ḫalīl Ġalbūn aṭ-Ṭarābulusī: *at-Tiḏkār fī man malaka Ṭarābulus wa-mā kāna bihā min al-ʾaḫyār*, ed. aṭ-Ṭāhir A. az-Zāwī, Tripoli: Maktabat an-Nūr 1386/1967.
IĞamMuḫt	ʿIzz ad-Dīn Abū ʿUmar ʿAbd al-ʿAzīz b. M. Ibn Ǧamāʿah al-Kinānī aš-Šāfiʿī: *al-Muḫtaṣar al-kabīr fī sīrat ar-rasūl*, ed. S. Makkī al-ʿĀnī, Beirut: Muʾassasat ar-Risālah / Amman: Dār al-Bašīr 1413/1993.
IǦawzīAʿmār	Abū l-Faraǧ ʿAr. b. ʿAlī Ibn al-Ǧawzī al-Ḥanbalī: *(Kitāb) ʾAʿmār al-ʾaʿyān*, ed. Maḥmūd M. aṭ-Ṭunāḥī, Cairo: Maktabat al-Ḫānǧī 1414/1994.
IǦawzīḤaṯṯ	Id.: *(Kitāb) al-Ḥaṯṯ ʿalā ḥifẓ al-ʿilm wa-ḏikr kibār al-ḥuffāẓ*, Beirut: Dār al-Kutub al-ʿIlmīyah ²1406/²1986.
IǦawzīManIḤanbal	Id.: *Manāqib al-ʾimām ʾAḥmad b. Ḥanbal*, Beirut: Dār al-Āfāq al-Ǧadīdah ³1402/³1982.
IǦawzīMawḍ	Id.: *Kitāb al-Mawḍūʿāt*, ed. ʿAr. M. ʿUṯmān, 3 vols., Medina: al-Maktabah as-Salafīyah 1386–88 / 1966– 68.
IǦawzīMunt	Id.: *al-Muntaẓam fī tārīḫ al-mulūk wa-l-ʾumam*, vols. 5–10, Hyderabad: Maṭbaʿat Dāʾirat al-Maʿārif al-ʿUṯmānīyah 1358–59 (repr. Beirut: Dār aṯ-Ṯaqāfah n.d.).
IǦawzīNisāʾ	Id.: *ʾAḫbār an-nisāʾ*, ed. Barakāt Yūsuf Habbūd, Ṣaydā - Beirut: al-Maktabah al-ʿAṣrīyah 1421/2000.
IǦawzīṢafwah	Id.: *Ṣifat aṣ-ṣafwah*, ed. M. b. ʿAbbās al-Ḫaṭīb, 2 vols., Beirut: Dār al-Ǧīl 1412/1992.
IǦawzīṮabāt	Id.: *aṯ-Ṯabāt ʿinda l-mamāt*, ed. M. ʿAbd al-Qādir A. ʿAṭā, Beirut: Dār al-Kutub al-ʿIlmīyah 1406/1986.
IǦawzīTabṣ	Id.: *Kitāb at-Tabṣirah*, ed. Muṣṭafā ʿAbd al-Wāḥid, 2 vols., Cairo: ʿĪsā al-Bābī al-Ḥalabī 1390/1970.
IǦawzīWafā	Id.: *al-Wafā bi-ʾaḥwāl al-Muṣṭafā*, ed. Muṣṭafā ʿAbd al-Qādir ʿAtā, Beirut: Dār al-Kutub al-ʿIlmīyah 1408/1988.
IǦazḤaw	Šams ad-Dīn Abū ʿAl. M. b. Ibr. Ibn al-Ǧazarī al-Qurašī: *Ḥawādiṯ az-zamān wa-ʾanbāʾihī wa-wafayāt al-ʾakābir wa-l-ʾaʿyān min ʾabnāʾihī (= Tārīḫ*

Ibn al-Ğazarī), ed. ᶜUmar ᶜAbd as-Salām Tadmurī, 3 vols., Ṣaydā – Beirut: al-Maktabah al-ᶜAṣrīyah 1419/1998.

IĞubRiḥlah (B) — Abū l-Ḥusayn M. b. A. Ibn Ğubayr al-Balansī aš-Šāṭibī: *Riḥlat Ibn Ğubayr*, Beirut: Dār Ṣādir n.d.

IĞubRiḥlah (W) — Id.: *Riḥlat Ibn Ğubayr*, ed. W. Wright, Leiden: Brill 1852.

IĞuzQaw — Abū l-Qāsim M. b. A. Ibn Ğuzayy al-Kalbī al-Mālikī: *Qawānīn al-ʾaḥkām aš-šarᶜīyah wa-masāʾil al-furūᶜ al-fiqhīyah*, Beirut: Dār al-ᶜIlm li-l-Malāyīn 1968.

IĞuzTashīl — Id.: *at-Tashīl li-ᶜulūm at-tanzīl*, ed. M. Sālim Hāšim, 2 vols., Beirut: Dār al-Kutub al-ᶜIlmīyah 1415/1995.

IḤaddDurr — ᶜAl. b. ᶜAlawī al-Ḥaddād al-Ḥaḍramī: *ad-Durr al-manẓūm li-ḏawī l-ᶜuqūl wa-l-fuhūm*, ed. as-Sayyid ᶜAlī b. ᶜĪsā al-Ḥaddād, Cairo: ᶜĪsā al-Bābī al-Ḥalabī, 1400/1980.

IḪafDīwān — Abū Isḥāq Ibr. b. Abī l-Fatḥ Ibn Ḫafāğah: *Dīwān Ibn Ḫafāğah*, Beirut: Dār Ṣādir n.d.

IḤağAḥwāl — Šihāb ad-Dīn A. b. ᶜAlī Ibn Ḥağar al-ᶜAsqalānī: *ʾAḥwāl al-mayyit min ḥīn al-iḥtiḍār ʾilā l-ḥašr*, ed. Yusrī ᶜAbd al-Ġanīy al-Bišrī (al-Bašarī), Cairo: Maktabat Ibn Sīnā n.d. (*c.* 1989).

IḤağḎaylDK — Id.: *Ḏayl ad-Durar al-kāminah*, ed. ᶜAdnān Darwīš, Cairo: Maᶜhad al-Maḫṭūṭāt al-ᶜArabīyah 1412/1992.

IḤağĞawKāfī — Id.: *al-Ğawāb al-kāfī ᶜan as-suʾāl al-ḫāfī*, printed as appendix to *Fatāwā Ibn aṣ-Ṣalāḥ*, Cairo: aṭ-Ṭibāᶜah al-Munīrīyah 1348 (repr. Cairo: Dār al-Kalimah aṭ-Ṭayyibah / ar-Riyāḍ: Maktabah Ṭayyibah 1404/1984).

IḤāğğMadḫ — M. b. M. Ibn al-Ḥāğğ al-Fāsī al-Mālikī: *al-Madḫal (ʾilā tanmiyat al-ʾaᶜmāl* etc.*)*, 4 vols. in 2, repr. Cairo: Maktabat Dār at-Turāṯ n.d.

IḤağInbāʾ — Šihāb ad-Dīn A. b. ᶜAlī Ibn Ḥağar al-ᶜAsqalānī: *ʾInbāʾ al-ġumr bi-ʾabnāʾ al-ᶜumr fī t-tārīḫ*, 9 vols. in 5, ed. M. ᶜAbd al-Ḥamīd Ḫān, Hyderabad 1387/1967 (repr. Beirut: Dār al-Kutub al-ᶜIlmīyah 1406/1986).

IḤağIṣābah — Id.: *al-ʾIṣābah fī tamyīz aṣ-ṣaḥābah*, 4 vols., Cairo 1328 (repr. Beirut: Dār al-Fikr n.d.).

IḤağLisān — Id.: *Lisān al-mīzān*, 7 vols., Hyderabad 1329–31 (repr. Beirut: Muʾassasat al-Aᶜlamī li-l-Maṭbūᶜāt 1390/1971).

IḤağMağmaᶜ — Id.: *al-Mağmaᶜ al-muʾassas li-l-Muᶜğam al-mufahras*, ed. M. Maḥmūd Šakūr al-Mayādīnī, Beirut: Muʾassasat ar-Risālah 1417/1996.

IḤağMuᶜğam — Id.: *al-Muᶜğam al-mufahras ʾaw Tağrīd ʾasānīd al-kutub al-mašhūrah wa-l-ʾağzāʾ al-manṯūrah*, ed. M. Šakūr Maḥmūd al-Mayādīnī, Beirut: Muʾassasat ar-Risālah 1418/1998.

IḤağRafᶜ — Id.: *Rafᶜ al-ᶜiṣr ᶜan quḍāt Miṣr*, ed. ᶜAlī M. ᶜUmar, Cairo: Makt. al-Ḫānğī 1418/1998.

IḤağTahḏ — Id.: *Tahḏīb at-Tahḏīb*, 12 vols., Hyderabad: Mağlis Dāʾirat al-Maᶜārif al-ᶜUṯmānīyah 1325–27 (repr. Beirut n.d.).

IḤağTarğITay — Id.: *Tarğamat Šayḫ al-ʾislām Ibn Taymīyah*, ed. Abū ᶜAr. Saᶜīd Maᶜšāšah, Beirut: Dār Ibn Ḥazm 1419/1998.

IḤağTawālī — Id.: *Tawālī t-taʾsīs li-maᶜālī Muḥammad b. ʾIdrīs (aš-Šāfiᶜī)*, ed. Abū l-Fidāʾ ᶜAl. al-Qāḍī, Beirut: Dār al-Kutub al-ᶜIlmīyah 1406/1986.

IḪaldᶜIbar — ᶜAr. Ibn Ḫaldūn al-Maġribī: *Kitāb al-ᶜIbar wa-dīwān al-mubtadaʾ wa-l-ḫabar fī ʾayyām al-ᶜarab wa-l-ᶜağam wa-l-barbar wa-man ᶜāṣarahum min ḏawī s-sulṭān al-ʾakbar*, vols. II–VII, Būlāq: al-Maṭbaᶜah al-Kubrā al-Miṣrīyah 1284.

IḪallWaf — Abū l-ᶜAbbās Šams ad-Dīn A. b. M. Ibn Ḫallikān: *Wafayāt al-ʾaᶜyān wa-ʾanbāʾ ʾabnāʾ az-zamān*, 8 vols., ed. Iḥsān ᶜAbbās, Beirut: Dār Ṣādir n.d. (1968ff.).

IḪallWaf (Slane) — Id.: *Ibn Khallikan's Biographical Dictionary*, 4 vols., tr. B. Mac Guckin de Slane, Paris 1842–43 (repr. Beirut: Librairie du Liban 1970).

IḤamdīsDīwān — ᶜAbd al-Ǧabbār Ibn Ḥamdīs: *Dīwān*, ed. I. ᶜAbbās, Beirut: Dār Ṣādir n.d.

IḤamdTaḏk — M. b. al-Ḥasan Ibn Ḥamdūn: *at-Taḏkirah al-Ḥamdūnīyah*, edd. Iḥsān and Bakr ᶜAbbās, 9 vols., Beirut: Dār Ṣādir 1996.

IḤanbDurr — Raḍīy ad-Dīn M. b. Ibr. al-Ḥalabī Ibn al-Ḥanbalī: *Durr al-ḥabab fī tārīḫ ʾaᶜyān al-Ḥalab*, edd. M. A. al-Fāḫūrī and Yaḥyā Zak. ᶜAbbārah, 2 vols. in 4, Damascus: Wizārat aṯ-Ṯaqāfah 1973.

IḤanbMusnad — Aḥmad b. M. b. Ḥanbal: *al-Musnad*, ed. Aḥmad M. Šākir, vols. I–XV, Cairo: Dār al-Maᶜārif 1368–75 / 1949–56.

IHāniʾDīwān — M. Ibn Hāniʾ al-Andalusī: *ad-Dīwān*, ed. M. al-Yaᶜlāwī, Beirut: Dār al-Ġarb al-Islāmī 1995.

IḪāqQal — Abū Naṣr al-Fatḥ b. M. Ibn Ḫāqān: *Qalāʾid al-ᶜiqyān fī maḥāsin al-ʾaᶜyān*, Paris 1277/1860 (repr. Tunis: al-Maktabah al-ᶜAtīqah 1966).

IḪarrāṭᶜĀqibah — ᶜAbd al-Ḥaqq b. ᶜAr. al-Azdī al-Išbīlī, Ibn al-Ḫarrāṭ: *Kitāb al-ᶜĀqibah (fī ʾaḥwāl al-ʾāḫirah)*, ed. Abū ᶜAl. M. Ḥasan Ismāᶜīl, Beirut: Dār al-Kutub al-ᶜIlmīyah 1415/1995.

IḪaṭAᶜmāl — Lisān ad-Dīn M. b. ᶜAl. Ibn al-Ḫaṭīb al-Ġarnāṭī: *Kitāb ʾAᶜmāl al-ʾaᶜlām fī-man būyiᶜa qabla l-iḥtilām min mulūki l-ʾislām* (second part), ed. É. Lévi-Provençal, Rabat: Éd. F. Moncho 1353/1934; *see also* Hoenerbach: *Islamische Geschichte Spaniens*.

IḪaṭDīwān — Id.: *Dīwān Lisān ad-Dīn Ibn al-Ḫaṭīb (aṣ-Ṣayb wa-l-ǧahām wa-l-māḍī wa-l-kahām)*, ed. M. Miftāḥ, 2 vols., Casablanca: Dār aṯ-Ṯaqāfah 1409/1989.

IḪaṭIḥāṭah — Id.: *al-ʾIḥāṭah fī ʾaḫbār Ġarnāṭah*, ed. M. ᶜAl. ᶜInān, 4 vols., Cairo: Maktabat al-Ḫānǧī 1393–97 / 1973–77.

IḪaṭKatībah — Id.: *al-Katībah al-kāminah fī man laqaynāhu bi-l-ʾAndalus min šuᶜaraʾ al-miʾah aṯ-ṯāminah*, ed. Iḥsān ᶜAbbās, Beirut: Dār aṯ-Ṯaqāfah 1983.

IḪaṭLamḥah — Id.: *al-Lamḥah al-badrīyah fī d-dawlah an-Naṣrīyah*, Beirut: Dār al-Āfāq al-Ǧadīdah ³1400/³1980.

IḪaṭRayḥ — Id.: *Rayḥānat al-kuttāb wa-nuǧᶜat (tuḥfat) al-muntāb*, ed. M. ᶜAl. ᶜInān, 2 vols., Cairo: Maktabat al-Ḫānǧī 1401/1980f.

IḤazmǦaw — Abū M. ᶜAlī b. A. Ibn Ḥazm al-Andalusī: *Ǧawāmiᶜ as-sīrah an-nabawīyah*, Beirut: Dār al-Ǧīl / Cairo: Maktabat at-Turāṯ al-Islāmī ³1404/³1984.

IḤazmMuḥ — Id.: *Kitāb al-Muḥallā*, ed. A. M. Šākir, 11 vols. in 8, Cairo: Idārat aṭ-Ṭibāᶜah al-Munīrīyah 1347–52.

IḤazmṬawq — Id.: *Ṭawq al-ḥamāmah*, ed. D. K. Pétrof, St. Petersburg – Leiden: Brill 1914 (Mém. de la fac. des lettres de l'Univ. impér. de St. Pétersbourg 119).

IḤiǧṮam — Taqīy ad-Dīn Abū Bakr ᶜAlī b. M. Ibn Ḥiǧǧah al-Ḥamawī: *Ṯamarāt al-ʾawrāq fī l-muḥāḍarāt*, ed. Mufīd M. Qumayḥah, Beirut: Dār al-Kutub al-ᶜIlmīyah 1403/1983.

IHišLife — *The Life of Muhammad. A Translation of Isḥāq's* [sic] Sīrat Rasūl Allāḥ, *with introduction and notes by A. Guillaume*, Oxford 1955.

IHišSīrah — ᶜAbd al-Malik b. Hišām al-Ḥimyarī / M. Ibn Isḥāq: *as-Sīrah an-nabawīyah*, edd. as-Saqqā, al-Ibyārī and Šalabī, 4 vols., repr. Beirut: Dār Iḥyāʾ at-Turāṯ al-ᶜArabī 1985.

IHuḏaylMaq — ᶜAlī b. ᶜAr. Ibn Huḏayl al-Fazārī al-Ġarnāṭī: *Maqālāt al-ʾudabāʾ wa-munāẓarāt an-nuǧabāʾ*, ed. M. Adīb al-Ǧādir, Damascus: Dār al-Bašāʾir 1423/2002.

IᶜIbrīMuḫt — Gregorius al-Malaṭī Ibn al-ᶜIbrī (Bar Hebraeus): *Tārīḫ muḫtaṣar ad-duwal*, Beirut: al-Maṭbaᶜah al-Kāṯūlīkīyah 1958.

IᶜIḏBayān — Ibn ᶜIḏārī al-Marrākušī: *al-Bayān al-muġrib fī ʾaḫbār al-ʾAndalus wa-l-Maġrib*, edd. G. S. Colin and É. Lévi-Provençal (I–III: *Histoire de l'Afrique du Nord et de l'Espagne musulmane intitulée Kitāb al-Bayān al-mughrib par Ibn ʿIdhārī al-Marrākushī*), I. ᶜAbbās (IV), 4 vols., Beirut: Dār aṯ-Ṯaqāfah (partially repr.) ³1983.

IᶜIrāqīḎᶜIbar — Walīy ad-Dīn Abū Zurᶜah A. b. ᶜAbd ar-Raḥīm (Ibn) al-ᶜIrāqī: *aḏ-Ḏayl ʿalā l-ʿIbar fī ḫabar man ʿabar (li-ḏ-Ḏahabī)*, ed. Ṣāliḥ Mahdī ᶜAbbās, 3 vols., Beirut: Muʾassasat ar-Risālah 1409/1989.

IIyāsBad — M. b. A. Ibn Iyās al-Ḥanafī: *Badāʾiʿ az-zuhūr fī waqāʾiʿ ad- duhūr*, ed. M. Muṣṭafā, 5 in 6 vols., Wiesbaden: F. Steiner 1961–84 (Bibl. Islamica 5).

IKardHistoria — Ibn al-Kardabūs: *Historia de al-Andalus (Kitāb al-Iktifāʾ)*, tr. by F. Maíllo Salgado, Madrid 1986.

IKattTašb — Abū ᶜAl. M. Ibn al-Kattānī: *Kitāb at-Tašbīhāt min ʾašʿār ʾahl al-ʾAndalus*, ed. Iḥsān ᶜAbbās, Beirut: Dār aṯ-Ṯaqāfah n.d. (1966) (al-Maktabah al-Andalusīyah 15); *see also* IKattVergleiche.

IKattVergleiche — W. Hoenerbach: *Dichterische Vergleiche der Andalus-Araber I und II*, Bonn 1973 (Bonner Orientalistische Studien 26).

ᶜImādīRawḍah — ᶜAr. b. Muḥammad al-ᶜImādī: *Rawḍat ar-rayyā fī man dufina bi-Dārayyā*, ed. ᶜAbduh ᶜAlī al-Kūšak, Damascus: Dār al-Maʾmūn li-t-Turāṯ 1408/1988.

IMāǧah — Abū ᶜAl. M. b. Yazīd Ibn Māǧah: *Kitāb as-Sunan*, ed. M. Fuʾād ᶜAbd al-Bāqī, 2 vols., Cairo: Dār Iḥyāʾ al-Kutub al-ᶜArabīyah 1372f./1952f.

IMaʾmūnAḫbār — Ǧamāl ad-Dīn Abū ᶜAlī Mūsā b. al-Maʾmūn al-Baṭāʾiḥī: *Nuṣūṣ min ʾAḫbār Miṣr li-bn Maʾmūn*, ed. A. F. Sayyid, Cairo: Institut français d'archéologie orientale 1983.

IMandahFaw — ᶜAbd al-Wahhāb b. M. Ibn Mandah al-Iṣfahānī: *(Kitāb) al-Fawāʾid*, ed. Ḫ. Maḥmūd ᶜAbd as-Samīᶜ, 2 vols., Beirut: Dār al-Kutub al-ᶜIlmīyah 1423/2002.

IMarzFaḍlKilāb — Abū Bakr M. b. Ḫalaf Ibn al-Marzubān: *Kitāb Faḍl al-kilāb ʿalā kaṯīr mimman labisa ṯ-ṯiyāb (The Book of the Superiority of Dogs over many of Those who wear Clothes)*, edd. M. A. S. Abdel Haleem and G. R. Smith, Warminster: Aris & Phillips 1978.

IMaᶜṣDīwān — Ṣadr ad-Dīn ᶜAlī b. A. Ibn Maᶜṣūm: *Dīwān Ibn Maʿṣūm*, ed. Šākir Hādī Šukr, Beirut: ᶜĀlam al-Kutub 1408/1988.

IMaymMunt — M. b. al-Mubārak b. M. Ibn Maymūn: *Muntahā ṭ-ṭalab min ʾašʿār al-ʿarab*, ed. M. Nabīl Ṭarīfī, 9 vols., Beirut: Dār Ṣādir 1999.

IMibrḎayl — Yūsuf b. Ḥasan b. ᶜAbd al-Hādī, Ibn al-Mibrad: *Ḏayl Ibn ʿAbd al-Hādī ʿalā Ṭabaqāt Ibn Raǧab*, ed. Abū ᶜAl. Maḥmūd b. M. al-Ḥaddād, ar-Riyāḍ: Dār al-ᶜĀṣimah 1408 (Ṭabaqāt al-Ḥanabilah 1).

IMuflĀdāb — Šams ad-Dīn Abū ᶜAl. M. Ibn Mufliḥ al-Maqdisī al-Ḥanbalī: *al-ʾĀdāb aš-šarʿīyah wa-l-minaḥ al-marʿīyah*, edd. ᶜĀmir al-Ǧazzār and Anwar al-Bāz, 3 vols., al-Manṣūrah: Dār al-Wafāʾ 1419/1999.

IMuflFurūᶜ Id.: *Kitāb al-Furūᶜ*, ed. ᶜAbd as-Sattār A. Farrāḫ, 6 vols., Beirut: ᶜĀlam al-Kutub 1405/1985.

IMuḥKunūz A. b. Ibr. Ibn al-Muḥaddiṯ, Sibṭ b. al-ᶜAǧamī al-Ḥalabī: *Kunūz aḏ-ḏahab fī tārīḫ Ḥalab*, edd. Šawqī Šawṯ and Fāliḥ al-Bakkūr, 2 vols., Aleppo: Dār al-Qalam al-ᶜArabī 1417/1996.

IMulᶜIqd Sirāǧ ad-Dīn Abū Ḥafṣ ᶜUmar b. ᶜAlī Ibn al-Mulaqqin aš-Šāfiᶜī: *al-ᶜIqd al-muḏhab fī ṭabaqāt ḥamalat al-maḏhab*, edd. Ayman N. al-Azharī and Sayyid Muhannā, Beirut: Dār al-Kutub al-ᶜIlmīyah 1417/1997.

IMunḏIǧmāᶜ Abū Bakr M. b. Ibr. b. al-Munḏir an-Nīsābūrī: *Kitāb al-ᵓIǧmāᶜ*, ed. ᶜAl. ᶜUmar al-Bārūdī, Beirut: Dār al-Ǧinān 1406/1986.

IMunlāMutᶜah A. b. M. b. ᶜAlī Ibn al-Munlā al-Ḥaṣkafī aš-Šāfiᶜī: *Mutᶜat al-ᵓaḏhān min at-Tamattuᶜ bi-l-ᵓiqrān (li-bn Ṭūlūn) bayna tarāǧim aš-šuyūḫ wa-l-ᵓaqrān*, ed. Ṣalāḥ ad-Dīn Ḫalīl aš-Šaybānī al-Mawṣilī, 2 vols., Beirut: Dār Ṣādir 1999.

IMunqiḏDīwān Usāmah b. Munqiḏ aš-Šayzarī: *Dīwān ᵓUsāmah b. Munqiḏ*, edd. A. A. Badawī and Ḥāmid ᶜAbd al-Maǧīd, Beirut: ᶜĀlam al-Kutub n.d.

IMunqiḏManāzil Id.: *al-Manāzil wa-d-diyār*, ed. Muṣṭafā Ḥiǧāzī, Cairo: Laǧnat Iḥyāᵓ at-Turāṯ al-Islāmī 1415/1994.

IMuᶜtBadīᶜ ᶜAl. b. al-Muᶜtazz al-ᶜAbbāsī: *Kitāb al-Badīᶜ*, ed. I. Kratchkovsky, London 1935 (E. J. W. Gibb Mem. Ser. N.S. 10).

IMuᶜtDīwān Id.: *Dīwān šiᶜr Ibn al-Muᶜtazz (ṣanᶜat ᵓAbī Bakr Muḥammad b. Yaḥyā aṣ-Ṣūlī)*, ed. Yūnus A. as-Sāmarrāᵓī, 3 vols., Beirut: ᶜĀlam al-Kutub 1417/1997.

IMuᶜtṬab Id.: *Ṭabaqāt aš-šuᶜarāᵓ*, ed. ᶜAbd as-Sattār A. Farāǧ, Cairo: Dār al-Maᶜārif 1375/1956.

IMuyassarAḫbār Tāǧ ad-Dīn M. b. ᶜAlī Ibn Muyassar: *al-Muntaqā min ᵓAḫbār Miṣr li-bn Muyassar intaqāhu Taqīy ad-Dīn ᵓAḥmad b. ᶜAlī al-Maqrīzī*, ed. A. F. Sayyid, Cairo: Institut français d'archéologie orientale 1981.

INadFihrist Abū l-Faraǧ M. b. Isḥaq (Ibn) an-Nadīm: *Kitāb al-Fihrist*, ed. Riḍā Taǧaddud al-Māzandarānī, Beirut: Dār al-Masīrah [3]1988 ([1]1973).

INaǧDurrah M. b. Maḥmūd Ibn an-Naǧǧār: *ad-Durrah aṯ-ṯamīnah fī tārīḫ al-Madīnah*, printed in: FāsīŠifāᵓ II pp. 317–406.

INāṣBard (A) M. b. ᶜAl. Ibn Nāṣir ad-Dīn al-Qaysī ad-Dimašqī: *Bard al-ᵓakbād ᶜinda faqd al-ᵓawlād*, ed. ᶜAbd al-Qādir A. ᶜAbd al-Qādir, Amman: Dār an-Nafāᵓis [3]1413/[3]1993.

INāṣBard (C) Id.: *Bard al-ᵓakbād ᶜinda faqd al-ᵓawlād*, ed. ᶜAbd al-Qādir b. Šaybah al-Ḥamd, Cairo: Maṭbaᶜat al-Madanī n.d. (*c.* 1979).

INāṣMaǧlis Id.: *al-Maǧlis fī ḫaṭm as-Sīrah an-nabawīyah*, ed. Ibr. Ṣāliḥ, Damascus: Dār al-Bašāᵓir 1419/1999.

INāṣRadd Id.: *ar-Radd al-wāfir ᶜalā man zaᶜama bi-ᵓanna man sammā bn Taymīyah šayḫ al-ᵓIslām kāfir*, ed. Zuhayr aš-Šāwīš, Beirut: al-Maktab al-Islāmī 1411/1991.

INaqᶜUmdah A. Ibn Naqīb al-Miṣrī aš-Šāfiᶜī: *ᶜUmdat as-sālik wa-ᶜuddat an-nāsik (The Reliance of the Traveller)*, ed. and translated by N. H. M. Keller, Beltsville [2]1994.

INubDīwān Ǧamāl ad-Dīn M. b. M. Ibn Nubātah al-Miṣrī: *Dīwān Ibn Nubātah*, Cairo 1905 (repr. Beirut: Dār Iḥyāᵓ at-Turāṯ al-ᶜArabī n.d.).

INubMaṭlaᶜ — Id.: *Maṭlaᶜ al-fawāʾid wa-maǧmaᶜ al-farāʾid*, ed. ᶜUmar Mūsā Bāšā, Damascus: Maǧmaᶜ al-Luġah al-ᶜArabīyah 1392/1972.

INuǧBaḥr — Zayn ad-Dīn Ibn Nuǧaym al-Ḥanafī: *al-Baḥr ar-rāʾiq šarḥ Kanz ad-daqāʾiq*, 8 vols., Cairo: al-Maṭbaᶜah al-ᶜIlmīyah 1311/1893.

IQāḍīDurrah — Abū l-ᶜAbbās A. b. M. Ibn al-Qāḍī al-Miknāsī: *Durrat al-ḥiǧāl fī (ġurrat) ʾasmāʾ ar-riǧāl*, ed. M. al-Aḥmadī Abū n-Nūr, 3 vols. in 2, Cairo: Dār at-Turāṯ / Tunis: al-Maktabah al-ᶜAtīqah 1390–92 / 1970–72.

IQāsimFatḥ — aš-Šams Abū ᶜAl. M. Ibn Qāsim al-Ġazzī aš-Šāfiᶜī: *Fatḥ al-qarīb al-muǧīb fī šarḥ at-Taqrīb (al-Muḫtaṣar li-ʾAbī Šuǧāᶜ)*, ed. L. W. C. van den Berg, Leiden: E. J. Brill 1894.

IQaṭṭāᶜDurrah — Abū l-Qāsim ᶜAlī b. Ǧaᶜfar as-Saᶜdī, Ibn al-Qaṭṭāᶜ aṣ-Ṣiqillī: *ad-Durrah al-ḫaṭīrah fī šuᶜarāʾ al-ǧazīrah*, ed. Bašīr al-Bakkūš, Beirut: Dār al-Ġarb al-Islāmī 1995.

IQayIġāṯah — Šams ad-Dīn M. b. Abī Bakr Ibn Qayyim al-Ǧawzīyah al-Ḥanbalī: *ʾIġāṯat al-lahfān min maṣāyid aš-šayṭān*, ed. M. Ḥāmid al-Fiqī, 2 vols., rev. repr. Beirut: Dār al-Kutub al-ᶜIlmīyah 1420/1999.

IQayItḥāf — Id.: *ʾItḥāf al-ᶜāšiqīn bi-tahḏīb Rawḍat al-muḥibbīn*, ed. Rāʾid b. Ṣabrī b. Abī ᶜAlafah, Amman: Bayt al-Afkār ad-Duwalīyah n.d.

IQayMuʾallIbnTaym — Id.: *ʾAsmāʾ muʾallafāt Ibn Taymīyah*, ed. Ṣalāḥ ad-Dīn al-Munaǧǧid, Damascus 1953.

IQayZād — Id.: *Zād al-maᶜād fī hady ḫayr al-ᶜibād*, edd. Šuᶜayb and ᶜAbd al-Qādir al-Arnāʾūṭ, 6 vols., Beirut: Muʾassasat ar-Risālah / Maktabat al-Manār al-Islāmīyah 1414/1994.

IQŠuhbMaġMūsā — Yūsuf b. M. Ibn Qāḍī Šuhbah: *ʾAḥādīṯ muntaḫabah min Maġāzī Mūsā b. ᶜUqbah*, ed. Mašhūr Ḥasan Salmān, Beirut: Muʾassasat ar-Rayyān / Dār Ibn Ḥazm 1412/1991.

IQŠuhbTārīḫ — Taqīy ad-Dīn Abū Bakr b. A. Ibn Qāḍī Šuhbah ad-Dimašqī: *at-Tārīḫ*, ed. ᶜAdnān Darwīš, 4 vols., Damascus: Institut français de Damas 1977–94.

IQudMuġnī — Abū M. ᶜAl. Ibn Qudāmah al-Ḥanbalī: *al-Muġnī fī l-fiqh*, 9 vols., Cairo: Dār al-Manār ³1367/³1947.

IQudᶜUmdah — Id.: *al-ᶜUmdah fī fiqh ʾImām as-sunnah ʾAḥmad b. Ḥanbal*, Beirut: Dār Iḥyāʾ al-Kutub al-ᶜArabīyah n.d.

IQūlKāmil — Abū l-Qāsim Ǧaᶜfar Ibn Qūlūyah: *Kāmil az-ziyārāt*, ed. Mīrzā ᶜAbd al-Ḥusayn al-Amīnī at-Tabrīzī, an-Naǧaf: al-Maṭbaᶜah al-Murtaḍawīyah 1356 (1937).

IQutŠiᶜr — Abū M. ᶜAl. b. Muslim Ibn Qutaybah: *Kitāb aš-Šiᶜr wa-š-šuᶜarāʾ*, ed. M. J. de Goeje, Leiden: Brill 1904.

IQutTaʾwīl — Id.: *Kitāb Taʾwīl muḫtalif al-ḥadīṯ*, Beirut: Dār al-Kitāb al-ᶜArabī n.d.

IQutᶜUyūn — Id.: *ᶜUyūn al-ʾaḫbār*, ed. Yūsuf ᶜAlī Ṭawīl, 4 vols. in 2, Beirut: Dār al-Kutub al-ᶜIlmīyah 1985.

IRaǧAhwāl — Zayn ad-Dīn ᶜAr. b. A. Ibn Raǧab al-Ḥanbalī: *ʾAhwāl al-qubūr wa-ʾaḥwāl ʾahlihā ʾilā n-nušūr*, ed. Bašīr M. ᶜUyūn, Damascus: Dār al-Bayān / ar-Riyāḍ: Maktabat al-Mu'ayyad ²1414/²1994.

IRaǧḎayl — Id.: *Ḏayl Ṭabaqāt al-Ḥanābilah (li-bn ʾAbī Yaᶜlā)*, ed. M. Ḥāmid al-Fiqī, 2 vols., Cairo: Maṭbaᶜat as-Sunnah al-Muḥammadīyah 1372/1952f.

IRaǧLaṭāʾif — Id.: *Kitāb Laṭāʾif al-maᶜārif fīmā li-mawāsim al-ᶜām min al-waẓāʾif*, ed. Muḥammad al-Ġamrāwī, Cairo: Dār Iḥyāʾ al-Kutub al-ᶜArabīyah 1343 (repr. Beirut: Dār al-Ǧīl 1975).

IRašᶜUmdah — Abū ᶜAlī al-Ḥasan b. Rašīq al-Qayrawānī: *al-ʿUmdah fī ṣināʿat aš-šiʿr wa-naqdih*, ed. ᶜAbd al-Wāḥid Šaᶜlān, 2 vols., Cairo: Maktabat al-Ḫānǧī 1420/2000.

IRašUnmūḏaǧ — Id.: *ʾUnmūḏaǧ az-zamān fī šuʿarāʾ al-Qayrawān*, edd. M. al-ᶜArūsī al-Maṭwī and Bašīr al-Bakkūš, Algiers: al-Muʾassasat al-Waṭanīyah li-l-Kitāb / Tunis: ad-Dār at-Tūnisīyah li-n-Našr 1406/1986.

IRūmīDīwān — Abū l-Ḥasan ᶜAlī b. al-ᶜAbbās Ibn ar-Rūmī: *Dīwān Ibn ar-Rūmī*, ed. Ḥusayn Naṣṣār, 6 vols., Cairo 1973–81.

IRušdBid — Abū l-Walīd M. b. A. Ibn Rušd al-Qurṭubī al-Mālikī: *Bidāyat al-muǧtahid wa-nihāyat al-muqtaṣid*, 2 vols., Beirut: Dār al-Maᶜrifah [8]1406/[8]1986.

IŠabAḫbār — Abū Zayd ᶜUmar Ibn Šabbah al-Baṣrī: *ʾAḫbār al-Madīnah (Kitāb Tārīḫ al-Madīnah)*, edd. ᶜAlī M. Dandal and Yāsīn Saᶜd ad-Dīn Bayān, 2 vols., Beirut: Dār al-Kutub al-ᶜIlmīyah 1417/1996.

IŠadAᶜlāq — al-ᶜIzz Abū ᶜAl. M. b. ᶜAlī Ibn Šaddād: *al-ʾAʿlāq al-ḫaṭīrah fī ḏikr ʾumarāʾ aš-Šām wa-l-Ǧazīrah*, edd. D. Sourdel and S. ad-Dahhān, 3 vols., Damascus: Institut français de Damas 1953–63.

IŠadMalẒāhir — Id.: *Tārīḫ al-Malik aẓ-Ẓāhir (Baybars)*, ed. A. Ḥuṭayṭ, Wiesbaden: F. Steiner Verlag 1403/1983 (Bibliotheca Islamica 31).

ISaᶜdṬab — Muḥammad b. Saᶜd: *(Kitāb) aṭ-Ṭabaqāt al-kubrā*, ed. Iḥsān ᶜAbbās, 8 vols. and index, Beirut: Dār Ṣādir 1376–88 / 1957–68.

ISahlDīwān — Abū Isḥāq Ibr. b. Sahl al-Isrāʾīlī al-Išbīlī: *Dīwān ʾIbrāhīm b. Sahl al-ʾIšbīlī*, ed. M. F. Duġaym, Beirut: Dār al-Ġarb al-Islāmī 1998.

IŠāhNāsiḫ — Abū Ḥafṣ ᶜUmar b. A. Ibn Šāhīn al-Baġdādī: *Kitāb Nāsiḫ al-ḥadīṯ wa-mansūḫih*, ed. Karīmah bt. ᶜAlī, Beirut: Dār al-Kutub al-ᶜIlmīyah 1420/1999.

ISaᶜīdMuġrib — A. b. Mūsā Ibn Saᶜīd al-Maġribī: *al-Muġrib fī ḥulā l-Maġrib*, ed. Rušqā Ḍayf, 2 vols., Cairo: Dār al-Maᶜārif 1953.

ᶜIṣāmīSimṭ — ᶜAbd al-Malik b. al-Ḥusayn al-ᶜIṣāmī al-Makkī: *Simṭ an-nuǧūm al-ʿawālī fī ʾanbāʾ al-ʾawāʾil wa-t-tawālī*, 4 vols., Cairo: al-Maktabah as-Salafīyah 1380.

IŠamQabas — Zayn ad-Dīn ᶜUmar b. A. Ibn aš-Šammāᶜ al-Ḥalabī: *al-Qabas al-ḥāwī li-ġurar Ḍawʾ as-Saḫāwī*, edd. Maḥmūd al-Arnāʾūṭ *et al.*, 2 vols., Beirut: Dār Ṣādir 1998.

ISayNāsMinaḥ — Fatḥ ad-Dīn M. b. M. Ibn Sayyid an-Nās aš-Šāfiᶜī: *Minaḥ al-madḥ (ʾaw Šuʿarāʾ aṣ-ṣaḥābah mimman madaḥa r-rasūl ʾaw raṯāh)*, ed. ᶜIffat Wiṣāl Ḥamzah, Damascus – Beirut: Dār al-Fikr 1407/1987.

ISayNāsᶜUyūn — Id.: *ʿUyūn al-ʾaṯar fī funūn al-maġāzī wa-š-šamāʾil wa-s-siyar*, ed. Ibr. M. Ramaḍān, 2 vols., Beirut: Dār al-Qalam 1414/1993.

IṢayrIšārah — Amīn ad-Dīn Abū l-Qāsim ᶜAlī b. Munǧab Ibn aṣ-Ṣayrafī: *al-ʾIšārah ʾilā man nāla l-wizārah*, ed. ᶜAbd Allāh Muḫliṣ, Cairo: Maṭbaᶜat al-Maᶜhad al-ᶜIlmī al-Faransī 1924.

IṣfDayrāt — Abū l-Faraǧ al-Iṣfahānī: *Kitāb ad-Dayrāt*, ed. Ḫalīl al-ᶜAṭīyah, London – Cyprus: Riyāḍ ar-Raʾīs li-l-Kutub wa-n-Našr 1991.

IṣfĠurabāʾ — Id. (wrongly attributed?): *Kitāb (ʾUdabāʾ) al-ġurabāʾ*, *see* IṣfStrangers.

IṣfḪar (I) — al-ᶜImād al-Iṣfahānī: *Ḫarīdat al-qaṣr wa-ǧarīdat al-ʿaṣr fī ḏikr fuḍalāʾ ʾahl al-ʾIṣfahān*, ed. ᶜAdnān M. Āl Ṭuᶜmah, 2 vols., Tehran 1999.

IṣfḪar (M) — Id.: *Ḫarīdat al-qaṣr wa-ǧarīdat al-ʿaṣr: qism šuʿarāʾ al-Maġrib*, edd. *M.* al-Marzūqī *et al.*, 2 vols., Tunis: ad-Dār at-Tūnisīyah li-n-Našr 1966–71.

IṣfḪar (Š) — Id.: *Ḫarīdat al-qaṣr wa-ǧarīdat al-ʿaṣr: qism šuʿarāʾ aš-Šām*, ed. Šukrī Fayṣal, 2 vols., Damascus: al-Maṭbaʿah al-Hāšimīyah 1375–78 / 1955–59.

IṣfRiyāḍ — ʿAl. b. ʿĪsā Efendi al-Iṣfahānī: *Riyāḍ al-ʿulamāʾ wa-ḥiyād al-fuḍalāʾ*, 6 vols., ed. Aḥmad al-Ḥusaynī, Qum: Maṭbaʿat al-Ḫayyām 1401/1980.

IṣfStrangers — P. Crone and S. Moreh: *The Book of Strangers. Mediaeval Arabic Graffiti on the Theme of Nostalgia (Attributed to Abu 'l-Faraj al-Iṣfahānī)*, Princeton 1999 (Princeton Series on the Middle East).

ISīrīnMunt — Muḥammad b. Sīrīn: *Muntaḫab al-kalām fī tafsīr al-ʾaḥlām*, printed in: NābTaʿṭīr, volume I.[6]

IsnṬab — Ǧamāl ad-Dīn ʿAbd ar-Raḥīm al-Isnawī: *Ṭabaqāt aš-Šāfiʿīyah*, ed. ʿAl. al-Ǧabbūrī, 2 vols., Baghdad: Maṭbaʿat al-Iršād 1390f./1970f.

IṢuqTālīWaf — Faḍl Allāh b. Abī l-Faḫr Ibn aṣ-Ṣuqāʿī: *Tālī Kitāb Wafayāt al-ʾaʿyān (li-bn Ḫallikān)*, ed. J. Sublet, Damascus: Institut français de Damas 1974.

ITaġrManh — Ǧamāl ad-Dīn Abū l-Maḥāsin Yūsuf Ibn Taġrī Birdī al-Atābakī: *al-Manhal aṣ-ṣāfī wa-l-mustawfā baʿd al-Wāfī*, edd. Muḥammad M. Amīn and Nabīl M. ʿAbd al-ʿAzīz, vols. I–VIII, Cairo: al-Hayʾah al-Miṣrīyah al-ʿĀmmah li-l-Kitāb (I–VII) / Dār al-Kutub al-Miṣrīyah (VIII) 1984–99.

IṬawSabk — ʿAbd al-Wāḥid b. M. Ibn aṭ-Ṭawwāḥ at-Tūnisī: *Sabk al-maqāl li-fakk al-ʿiqāl*, ed. M. Masʿūd Ǧubrān, Beirut: Dār al-Ġarb al-Islāmī 1995.

ITayʿIlmḤadīṯ — Taqīy ad-Dīn Abū l-ʿAbbās A. b. ʿAbd al-Ḥalīm Ibn Taymīyah ad-Dimašqī al-Ḥanbalī: *(Kitāb) ʿIlm al-ḥadīṯ*, ed. Mūsā A. ʿAlī, Beirut: ʿĀlam al-Kutub ²1405/²1985.

ITayIqtiḍāʾ — Id.: *Kitāb Iqtiḍāʾ aṣ-ṣirāṭ al-mustaqīm muḫālafat ʾaṣḥāb al-ǧaḥīm*; for the abridged English translation, *see* Memon: *Ibn Taimīya's Struggle*.

ITayIstiġ — Id.: *al-Istiġāṯah fī r-radd ʿalā l-Bakrī*, ed. ʿAl. b. Duġayn as-Sahlī, 2 vols., ar-Riyāḍ: Dār al-Waṭan 1417/1997.

ITayMaǧm — Id.: *Maǧmūʿ fatāwā šayḫ al-ʾislām ʾAḥmad Ibn Taymīyah (bi-tartīb ʿAr. b. M. al-ʿĀṣimī an-Naǧdī)*, 37 vols., Cairo: Maktabat Ibn Taymīyah n.d.

ITayMinhāǧ — Id.: *Kitāb Minhāǧ as-sunnah an-nabawīyah fī naqḍ kalām aš-šīʿah wa-l-qadarīyah*, 4 vols. in 2, Būlāq: al-Maṭbaʿah al-Kubrā al-Amīrīyah 1321f. (repr. Cairo n.d.).

ITayZiy — Id.: *Kitāb az-Ziyārah*, ed. Ǧamāl ʿAbd ar-Rāfiʿ, Cairo: Dār al-Bayān 1415/1995.

IṬiqFaḫrī — M. b. ʿAlī Ibn Ṭiqṭiqā: *Kitāb al-Faḫrī fī l-ʾādāb as-sulṭānīyah wa-d-duwal al-ʾislāmīyah*, Beirut: Dār Beirut 1385/1966.

IṬūlFulk — Šams ad-Dīn M. b. ʿAlī Ibn Ṭūlūn aṣ-Ṣāliḥī: *al-Fulk al-mašḥūn fī ʾaḥwāl Muḥammad b. Ṭūlūn*, ed. M. Ḫayr Ramaḍān Yūsuf, Beirut: Dār Ibn Ḥazm 1416/1996.

IṬūlIʿlām — Id.: *ʾIʿlām al-warā bi-man wulliya nāʾiban min al-ʾatrāk bi-Dimašq aš-Šām al-kubrā*, ed. M. A. Dahmān, Damascus: al-Maṭbaʿah wa-l-Ǧarīdah ar-Rasmīyah 1383/1964.

IṬūlMufāk — Id.: *Mufākahat al-ḫillān fī ḥawādiṯ az-zamān*, ed. Ḫalīl al-Manṣūr, Beirut: Dār al-Kutub al-ʿIlmīyah 1418/1998.

6 This work was actually neither written by Ibn Sīrīn (d. 110 H) nor, for that matter, during his lifetime, but stems from a certain ad-Dārī (ninth cent. H), see van Gelder: *God's Banquet* p. 119 and GALS II p. 1039.

ITūlQal — Id.: *al-Qalāʾid al-ǧawharīyah fī tārīḫ aṣ-Ṣāliḥīyah*, edd. M. A. Dahmān *et al.*, 2 vols. in 1, Damascus: al-Maǧmaᶜ al-Luġah al-ᶜArabīyah 1401/1980.

ITūlṮaġr — Id.: *al-Ṯaġr al-bassām fī ḏikr man wulliya qaḍāʾ aš-Šām (Quḍāt Dimašq)*, ed. Ṣalāḥ ad-Dīn al-Munaǧǧid, Damascus: Maǧmaᶜ al-ᶜIlmī al-ᶜArabī 1956.

ITuwNuzhah — Abū M. ᶜAbd as-Salām b. al-Ḥasan al-Qaysarānī Ibn aṭ-Ṭuwayr: *Nuzhat al-muqlatayn fī ʾaḫbār ad-dawlatayn*, ed. A. Fuʾād Sayyid, Beirut – Stuttgart: F. Steiner 1992 (Bibliotheca Islamica 39).

IWakīᶜMunṣif — Abū M. al-Ḥasan b. ᶜAlī b. Wakīᶜ: *Kitāb al-Munṣif li-s-sāriq wa-l-masrūq minhu fī ʾiẓhār sariqāt ʾAbī ṭ-Ṭayyib al-Mutanabbī*, ed. M. Yūsuf Naǧm, 2 vols., Beirut: Dār Ṣādir 1412/1992.

IWardīNaṣIḫwān — Abū Ḥafṣ ᶜUmar b. al-Muẓaffar, Ibn al-Wardī: *Naṣīḥat al-ʾiḫwān wa-muršidat al-ḫillān, see below* al-Qināwī: *Fatḥ ar-raḥīm*

IWāṣilKurūb — Ǧamāl ad-Dīn M. b. Sālim Ibn Wāṣil: *Mufarriǧ al-kurūb fī ʾaḫbār Banī ʾAyyūb*, edd. Ǧamāl ad-Dīn aš-Šayyāl *et al.*, 5 vols., Cairo: al-Maṭbaᶜah al-Amīrīyah / Maṭbaᶜat Dār al-Kutub 1953–77.

ᶜIyāḍMaḏ — al-Qāḍī ᶜIyāḍ b. Mūsā al-Yaḥṣubī al-Mālikī: *Maḏāhib al-ḥukkām fī nawādir al-ʾaḥkām*, ed. M. b. Šarīfah, Beirut: Dār al-Ġarb al-Islāmī 1990.

ᶜIyāḍMaš — Id.: *Mašāriq al-ʾanwār ʿalā ṣiḥāḥ al-ʾāṯār*, 2 vols., Beirut: Dār al-Fikr 1418/1997.

ᶜIyāḍŠifāʾ (B) — Id.: *aš-Šifā bi-taʿrīf ḥuqūq al-Muṣṭafā*, ed. Kamāl Basyūnī Zaġlūl al-Miṣrī, 2 vols., Beirut: Muʾassasat al-Kutub aṯ-Ṯaqāfīyah 1416/1995.

ᶜIyāḍŠifāʾ (Š) — Id.: *aš-Šifā bi-taʿrīf ḥuqūq al-Muṣṭafā* (with aš-Šumunnī's commentary *Muzīl al-ḫafāʾ ʿan ʾalfāẓ aš-Šifāʾ* on the margins), 2 vols., repr. Beirut: Dār al-Kutub al-ᶜIlmīyah n.d.; *see also* HarŠŠifāʾ.

ᶜIyāḍTartīb — Id.: *Tartīb al-madārik wa-taqrīb al-masālik li-maʿrifat ʾaʿlām maḏhab Mālik*, ed. A. Bakīr Maḥmūd, 4 vols. in 2, Beirut: al-Ḥayyāṭ 1387f./1967f.

IZanǧAmwāl — Abū A. Ḥumayd b. Maḫlad Ibn Zanǧawayh: *Kitāb al-ʾAmwāl*, ed. Šākir Ḏīb Fayyāḍ, 3 vols., ar-Riyāḍ: Markaz al-Malik Fayṣal li-l-Buḥūṯ wa-d-Dirāsāt al-Islāmīyah 1406/1986.

IZaqqāqDīwān — ᶜAlī Ibn az-Zaqqāq al-Balansī: *Dīwān Ibn az-Zaqqāq*, ed. ᶜAfīfah Maḥmūd Dayrānī, Beirut: Dār aṯ-Ṯaqāfah 1964 (al-Maktabah al-Andalusīyah 13).

IZaqqāqPoesías — Id.: *Ibn az-Zaqqāq: Poesías. Edición y traducción en verso de Emilio García Gómez*, Madrid 1956.

IZarkŠīrāz — Muᶜīn ad-Dīn Abūl-ᶜAbbās b. Abī l-Ḫayr Zarkūb Šīrāzī: *Šīrāz-nāmah*, ed. Ism. Wāᶜiẓ Ǧawādī, Tehran n.d.

IZawlFaḍMiṣr — al-Ḥasan b. Ibr. Ibn Zawlāq al-Layṯī: *Faḍāʾil Miṣr wa-ʾaḫbāruhā wa-ḫawāṣṣuhā*, ed. ᶜAlī M. ᶜUmar, Cairo: Maktabat al-Ḫānǧī ²1420/²2000.

IZayKawākib — Šams ad-Dīn Abū ᶜAl. M. b. M. Ibn az-Zayyāt as-Suᶜūdī: *al-Kawākib as-sayyārah fī tartīb az-ziyārah*, ed. A. Taymūr, Būlāq 1325/1907 (repr. Baghdad: Maktabat al-Muṯannā n.d.).

IẒuhFaḍMiṣr — Ǧamāl ad-Dīn M. b. M. Ibn Ẓuhayrah: *al-Faḍāʾil al-bāhirah fī maḥāsin Miṣr wa-l-Qāhirah*, edd. Muṣṭafā as-Saqqā and Kāmil al-Muhandis, Cairo: Maṭbaᶜat Dār al-Kutub 1969.

IZumrDīwān — M. b. Yūsuf Ibn Zumruk al-Ġarnāṭī: *ad-Dīwān*, ed. A. Salīm al-Ḥamdī, Ṣaydā – Beirut: al-Maktabah al-ᶜAṣrīyah 1418/1998.

Jahangirnama — *The Jahangirnama [Ǧahāngir-nāmah]. Memoirs of Jahangir, Emperor of India*, tr. and annotated by W. M. Thackston, Washington – Oxford 1999.

KalIktifāʾ — Abū r-Rabīʿ Sulaymān b. Mūsā al-Kalāʿī: *al-Iktifāʾ bi-mā taḍammanahū min maġāzī rasūl Allāh wa-ṯalāṯat al-ḫulafāʾ*, ed. M. Kamāl ad-Dīn ʿIzz ad-Dīn ʿAlī, 4 vols., Beirut: ʿĀlam al-Kutub 1417/1997.

KarKawākib — Marīy b. Yūsuf al-Karmī al-Ḥanbalī: *al-Kawākib ad-durrīyah fī manāqib al-muǧtahid Ibn Taymīyah*, ed. Naǧm ʿAr. Ḫalaf, Beirut: Dār al-Ġarb al-Islāmī 1406/1986.

KirmŠBuḫ — al-Kirmānī: *Šarḥ Ṣaḥīḥ al-Buḫārī*, 25 vols. in 12, Cairo 1937.

KU — ʿAlāʾ ad-Dīn ʿAlī al-Hindī: *Kanz al-ʿummāl fī sunan al-ʾaqwāl wa-l-ʾafʿāl*, edd. Bakrī Ḥayyānī and Ṣafwah as-Saqqā, 18 vols., repr. Beirut: Muʾassasat ar-Risālah 1409/1989.

KulKāfī — Abū Ǧaʿfar M. b. Yaʿqūb al-Kulaynī ar-Rāzī: *al-Furūʿ min al-Kāfī*, 7 vols., ed. M. al-Āḫawandī, Tehran: Dār al-Kutub al-Islāmīyah 1377–79.

KušDīwān — Maḥmūd b. al-Ḥusayn Kušāǧim: *Dīwān Kušāǧim*, ed. Maǧīd Ṭarrād, Beirut: Dār Ṣādir 1997.

KutFawāt — M. b. Šākir al-Kutubī: *Fawāt al-Wafayāt wa-ḏ-ḏayl ʿalayhā*, ed. Iḥsān ʿAbbās, 4 vols. and index, Beirut: Dār Ṣādir 1973f.

LA — Ǧamāl ad-Dīn M. b. Makram Ibn Manẓūr al-Ḫazraǧī: *Lisān al-ʿArab*, 15 vols., Beirut: Dār Ṣādir / Dār Bayrūt 1388/1968.

LaylāDīwān — *Šarḥ dīwānay Laylā l-ʾAḫyalīyah wa-Tawbah ibn al-Ḥumayyir wa-qiṣṣat ḥubbihimā*, ed. Anṭwān al-Qawwāl, Beirut: Dār al-Fikr al-ʿArabī 2003.

MaʿarrīLuzūm — Abū l-ʿAlāʾ A. b. ʿAl. b. Sul. al-Maʿarrī: *Luzūm mā lā yalzam (al-Luzūmīyāt)*, 2 vols., Beirut: Dār Ṣādir 1381/1961.

MaʿarrīŠḤam — Id.: *Šarḥ Dīwān Ḥamāsat ʾAbī Tammām al-mansūb li-ʾAbī l-ʿAlāʾ al-Maʿarrī*, ed. Ḥusayn M. Naqšah, 2 vols., Beirut: Dār al-Ġarb al-Islāmī 1411/1991.

MaʿbIstiʿdād — Zayn ad-Dīn b. ʿAlī al-Maʿbarī: *al-Istiʿdād li-l-mawt wa-suʾāl al-qabr*, Cairo: Maktabat at-Turāṯ al-Islāmī n.d.

MaǧlBiḥār — Muḥammad Bāqir al-Maǧlisī: *Biḥār al-ʾanwār*, 110 vols., Tehran: Šarikat Ṭabʿ Biḥār al-Anwār / Dār al-Kutub al-Islāmīyah 1376ff.

MaǧmRasMun — *Maǧmūʿat ar-rasāʾil al-Munīrīyah*, 3 vols. in 2, Cairo: aṭ-Ṭibāʿah al-Munīrīyah 1343–46 (repr. Cairo: Dār al-Kalimah aṭ-Ṭayyibah / ar-Riyāḍ: Maktabat Ṭayyibah 1404/1984).

MaġrSīrah — Abū l-Qāsim al-Ḥusayn b. ʿAlī al-Wazīr al-Maġribī: *as-Sīrah an-nabawīyah li-bn Hišām bi-šarḥ al-Wazīr al-Maġribī*, ed. Suhayl Zakkār, 2 vols., Beirut: Dār al-Fikr 1412/1992.

MakkīQūt — Abū Ṭālib M. b. ʿAlī al-Makkī: *Kitāb Qūt al-qulūb fī muʿāmalat al-maḥbūb*, Cairo 1310.

MālRiyāḍ — Abū Bakr ʿAl. b. M. al-Mālikī: *Riyāḍ an-nufūs fī ṭabaqāt ʿulamāʾ al-Qayrawān wa-ʾIfrīqīyah wa-zuhhādihim wa-nussākihim wa-siyar min ʾaḫbārihim wa-faḍāʾilihim wa-ʾawṣāfihim*, edd. Bašīr al-Bakkūš and M. al-ʿArūsī al-Maṭwī, 3 vols., Beirut: Dār al-Ġarb al-Islāmī 1401–03 / 1981–84.

ManbTasl (C) — Abū ʿAl. M. b. M. al-Manbiǧī al-Ḥanbalī: *Tasliyat ʾahl al-maṣāʾib*, Cairo: Maktabat al-Furqān 1403.

ManbTasl (M) — Id.: *Tasliyat ʾahl al-maṣāʾib*, ed. as-Saʿīd al-Mandūh, Cairo: Dār al-Kutubī 1411/1991.

MaqdīšNuzhah — Maḥmūd Maqdīš: *Nuzhat al-ʾanẓār fī ʿaǧāʾib at-tawārīḫ wa-l-ʾaḫbār*, ed. ʿAlī az-Zawārī, 2 vols., Beirut: Dār al-Ġarb al-Islāmī 1988.

MaqdMuṯīr — Šihāb ad-Dīn Abū Maḥmūd A. b. M. b. Tamīm al-Maqdisī: *Muṯīr al-ġarām ʾilā ziyārat al-Quds wa-š-Šām*, ed. A. al- Ḫuṭaymī, Beirut: Dār al-Ǧīl 1415/1994.

MaqdᶜUddah — Bahāʾ ad-Dīn Abū M. ᶜAr. b. Ibr. al-Maqdisī: *al-ʿUddah šarḥ al-ʿUmdah (li-bn Qudāmah)*, printed in: IQudᶜUmdah.

MaqqAzhār — Šihāb ad-Dīn Aḥmad b. M. al-Maqqarī at-Tilimsānī: *ʾAzhār ar-riyāḍ fī ʾaḫbār ʿIyāḍ*, edd. Muṣṭafā as-Saqqā, Ibr. al-Ibyārī, ᶜAbd al-Ḥafīẓ Šalabī, 3 vols., Cairo: Maṭbaᶜat Lağnat at-Taʾlīf wa-t-Tarğamah wa-n-Našr 1358–61 / 1939–42.

MaqqNafḥ (B) — Id.: *Nafḥ aṭ-ṭīb min ġuṣn al-ʾAndalus ar-raṭīb*, ed. Iḥsān ᶜAbbās, 8 vols., Beirut: Dār Ṣādir 1388/1968.

MaqqNafḥ (C) — Id.: *Nafḥ aṭ-ṭīb min ġuṣn al-ʾAndalus ar-raṭīb wa-ḏikr wazīrihā Lisān ad-Dīn Ibn al-Ḫaṭīb*, ed. Muḥyī d-Dīn ᶜAbd al-Ḥamīd, 10 vols. in 5, Cairo: al-Maktabah at-Tiğārīyah al-Kubrā 1367–69 / 1949f.

MaqqRawḍah — Id.: *Rawḍat al-ʾās al-ʿāṭirat al-ʾanfās fī ḏikr man laqaytuhū min ʾaʿlām al-ḥaḍratayn Marrākuš wa-Fās*, ed. ᶜAbd al-Wahhāb b. Manṣūr, Rabat: al-Maṭbaᶜah al-Malakīyah 1383/1964.

MaqrDurar — Abū M. Taqīy ad-Dīn A. b. ᶜAlī al-Maqrīzī: *Durar al-ʿuqūd al-farīdah fī tarāğim al-ʾaʿyān al-mufīdah*, ed. M. Kamāl ad-Dīn ᶜIzz ad-Dīn ᶜAlī, 2 vols., Beirut: ᶜĀlam al-Kutub 1412/1992.

MaqrḪiṭaṭ — Id.: *Kitāb al-Mawāʿiẓ wa-l-iʿtibār bi-ḏikr al-ḫiṭaṭ wa-l-ʾāṯār*, 2 vols., Būlāq 1270 (repr. Cairo: Maktabat aṯ-Ṯaqāfah ad-Dīnīyah n.d.).

MaqrMuq — Id.: *Kitāb al-Muqaffā*, ed. M. al-Yaᶜlāwī, 7 vols. and index, Beirut: Dār al-Ġarb al-Islāmī 1411/1991.

MaqrSulūk — Id.: *Kitāb as-Sulūk li-maʿrifat duwal al-mulūk*, edd. M. Muṣṭafā Ziyādah and Saᶜīd ᶜAbd al-Fattāḥ ᶜĀšūr, 4 in 11 vols., Cairo: Maṭbaᶜat Dār al-Kutub 1956–72.

MarğBahğah — ᶜAl. b. M. al-Marğānī al-Makkī: *Bahğat an-nufūs wa-l-ʾasrār fī tārīḫ dār hiğrat an-nabī al-muḫtār*, 2 vols., ar-Riyāḍ – Mecca: Maktabat Nizār Muṣṭafā al-Bāz 1418/1998.

MarġBid — Burhān ad-Dīn Abū l-Ḥasan ᶜAlī b. Abī Bakr al-Marġīnānī: *al-Hidāyah šarḥ Bidāyat al-mubtadiʾ*, ed. M. ᶜAdnān Darwīš, 4 vols. in 2, Beirut: Dār al-Arqam b. Abī l-Arqam n.d.

MarrḎayl — Abū ᶜAl. M. b. M. al-Marrākušī al-Awsī: *as-Sifr as-sādis min aḏ-ḏayl wa-t-takmilah li-Kitābay al-Mawṣūl wa-ṣ-Ṣilah*, ed. Iḥsān ᶜAbbās, Beirut: Dār aṯ-Ṯaqāfah 1973 (al-Maktabah al-Andalusīyah).

MarrMuᶜğib — ᶜAbd al-Wāḥid al-Marrākušī: *al-Muʿğib fī talḫīṣ ʾaḫbār al-Maġrib*, ed. M. Saᶜīd al-ᶜUryān, Cairo: al-Mağlis al-Aᶜlā li-š-Šuʾūn al-Islāmīyah 1383/1963.

MarzḤam — Abū ᶜAlī A. b. M. al-Marzūqī: *Šarḥ Dīwān al-Ḥamāsah*, edd. A. Amīn and ᶜAbd as-Salām Hārūn, 4 vols., Cairo: Maṭbaᶜat Lağnat at-Taʾlīf 1371/1951.

MarzMuw — M. b. ᶜImrān al-Marzubānī: *Kitāb al-Muwaššaḥ*, ed. ᶜAlī M. al-Bağāwī, Cairo: Dār Nahḍat Miṣr 1965.

MarzNūr — Id.: *Nūr al-qabas al-muḫtaṣar min al-Muqtabas*, ed. R. Sellheim, Wiesbaden: F. Steiner 1964 (Bibliotheca Islamica 23).

MasMurūğ (B) — Abū l-Ḥasan ᶜAlī b. al-Ḥusayn al-Masᶜūdī: *Les Prairies d'Or. Texte et Traduction*, ed. C. Barbier de Meynard, 9 vols., Paris 1871.

MasMurūğ (P) — Id.: *Murūğ aḏ-ḏahab wa-maʿādin al-ğawhar*, edd. Charles Pellat *et al.*, 7 vols., Beirut: al-Ğāmiᶜah al-Lubnānīyah 1966–79.

MasTanbīh	Id.: *at-Tanbīh wa-l-ʾišrāf*, ed. ʿAl. Ism. aṣ-Ṣāwī, repr. Cairo: al-Maktabah at-Tiǧārīyah 1357/1938.
MaṭTārMad	Ǧamāl ad-Dīn M. b. A. al-Maṭarī: *Tārīḫ al-Madīnah aš-šarīfah*, ed. Saʿīd ʿAbd al-Fattāḥ, ar-Riyāḍ – Mecca: Maktabat al-Bāz 1417/1997.
MāwAdab (B)	Abū l-Ḥusayn ʿAlī b. M. al-Māwardī: *(Kitāb) ʾAdab ad-dunyā wa-d-dīn*, ed. M. Karīm Rāǧiḥ, Beirut: Dār Iqrāʾ 1404/1984.
MāwAdab (C)	Id.: *Kitāb ʾAdab ad-dunyā wa-d-dīn*, Cairo: al-Maṭbaʿah al-Amīrīyah ^{16}1343/^{16}1925.
MāwAḥkām	Id.: *Kitāb al-ʾAḥkām as-sulṭānīyah wa-l-wilāyāt ad-dīnīyah*, ed. Aḥmad Mubārak al-Baġdādī, Kuwait: Dār Ibn Qutaybah 1409/1989.
MehrenRhetorik	August F. M. (von) Mehren: *Die Rhetorik der Araber nach den wichtigsten Quellen dargestellt*, Copenhague – Vienna 1853 (repr. Hildesheim 1970); *see also below* ŠTalḫīṣ.
MiknāsīIḥrāz	M. b. ʿAbd al-Wahhāb al-Miknāsī, Ibn ʿUṯmān: *ʾIḥrāz al-muʿallā wa-r-raqīb fī ḥaǧǧ bayt Allāh al-ḥarām wa-ziyārat al-Quds aš-šarīf wa-l-Ḫalīl wa-t-tabarruk bi-qabr al-ḥabīb (Riḥlat al-Miknāsī)*, ed. M. Bū-Kabūṭ, Beirut: al-Muʾassasah al-ʿArabīyah li-d-Dirāsāt wa-n-Našr / Abu Dhabi: Dār as-Suwaydī li-n-Našr wa-t-Tawzīʿ 2003.
MizTuḥfah	Ǧamāl ad-Dīn Abū l-Ḥaǧǧāǧ Yūsuf b. ʿAr. al-Mizzī: *Tuḥfat al-ʾašrāf bi-maʿrifat al-ʾaṭrāf*, Bombay: ad-Dār al-Qayyimah 1384–1403 / 1965–82.
MN	Yūsuf an-Nabhānī: *al-Maǧmūʿah an-Nabhānīyah fī l-madāʾiḥ an-naba-wīyah*, 4 vols., Beirut 1903 (repr. Beirut: Dār al-Fikr n.d.).
MuʿāfāǦalīs	Abū l-Faraǧ al-Muʿāfā b. Zak. al-Ǧarīrī an-Nahrawānī: *(Kitāb) al-Ǧalīs aṣ-ṣāliḥ al-kāfī wa-l-ʾanīs an-nāṣiḥ aš-šāfī*, ed. Iḥsān ʿAbbās, 4 vols., Beirut: ʿĀlam al-Kutub 1413/1993.
MubKāmil (C)	Abū l-ʿAbbās M. b. Yazīd al-Mubarrad: *(Kitāb) al-Kāmil*, edd. M. Abū l-Faḍl Ibrāhīm and as-Sayyid Šiḥātah, 4 vols, Cairo: Dār Nahḍat Miṣr n.d.
MubKāmil (W)	*Kitāb al-Kāmil (li-Muḥammad b. Yazīd al-Mubarrad)*, ed. W. Wright, 2 vols., Leipzig 1864–92.
MubTaʿāzī	Id.: *Kitāb at-Taʿāzī wa-l-marāṯī*, ed. M. ad-Dībāǧī, Damascus: Maṭbaʿat Zayd b. Ṯābit 1396/1976.
MuġulṭāyWāḍiḥ	ʿAlāʾ ad-Dīn Abū ʿAl. Muġulṭāy: *Kitāb al-Wāḍiḥ al-mubīn fī ḏikr man ustušhida min al-muḥibbīn*, ed. O. Spies, Stuttgart: W. Kohlhammer 1936 (Bonner Orientalistische Studien 18).
MuḥḪul	M. Amīn b M. al-Muḥibbī ad-Dimašqī: *Ḫulāṣat al-aṯar fī ʾaʿyān al-qarn al-hādī ʿašar*, ed. Muṣṭafā Wahbī, 4 vols., Cairo: al-Maṭbaʿah al-Wahbīyah 1284 (repr. Cairo: Dār al-Kitāb al-Islāmī n.d.).
MuḥNafḥah	Id.: *Nafḥat ar-Rayḥānah wa-rašḥat ṭilāʾi l-ḥānah*, ed. ʿAbd al-Fattāḥ M. al-Ḥulw, 6 vols. (including the *ḏayl*), Cairo: ʿĪsā al-Bābī al-Ḥalabī 1387–91 / 1967–71.
MunḏTakm	Abū M. ʿAbd al-ʿAẓīm al-Munḏirī: *at-Takmilah li-wafayāt an-naqalah*, ed. Baššār ʿAwwād Maʿrūf, 4 vols. (including the index), Beirut: Muʾassasat ar-Risālah 1401/1981.
MunḏTarġīb	Id.: *at-Tarġīb wa-t-tarhīb min al-ḥadīṯ aš-šarīf*, ed. Muṣṭafā M. ʿAmārah, 4 vols., repr. Beirut: Dār al-Kutub al-ʿIlmīyah 1406/1986.
MunKawākib	Zayn ad-Dīn ʿAbd ar-Raʾūf al-Munāwī al-Miṣrī: *al-Kawākib ad-durrīyah fī tarāǧim as-sādah aṣ-ṣūfīyah*, ed. M. Adīb al- Ǧādir, 5 vols. in 6, Beirut: Dār Ṣādir 1999.

MunŠŠam — Id.: *Šarḥ aš-Šamāʾil (li-t-Tirmiḏī)*, printed on the margins of: HarĞamᶜWas.

MurSilk — Abū l-Faḍl M. Ḫalīl b. ᶜAlī al-Murādī: *Silk ad-durar fī ʾaʿyān al-qarn aṯ-ṯānī ʿašar*, 4 vols. in 2, Būlāq: al-Maṭbaᶜah al-Mīrīyah 1301 (repr. Beirut: Dār Ibn Ḥazm / Dār al-Bašāʾir al-Islāmīyah ³1408/³1988).

Muslim — *See* NawŠMuslim

MuᶜtamidDīwān — Abū l-Qāsim M. al-Muᶜtamid Ibn ᶜAbbād al-Išbīlī: *Dīwān al-Muʿtamid Ibn ʿAbbād*, edd. Ḥāmid ᶜAbd al-Mağīd and A. Badawī, Cairo: Maṭbaᶜat Dār al-Kutub al-Miṣrīyah ²1997 (¹1951).

MutanDīwān (M) — Abū ṭ-Ṭayyib A. b al-Ḥusayn al-Mutanabbī: *Šarḥ Dīwān ʾAbī ṭ-Ṭayyib al-Mutanabbī li-ʾAbī l-ʿAlāʾ al-Maʿarrī (Muʿğiz aḥmad* etc.*)*, ed. ᶜAbd al-Mağīd Diyāb, 4 vols., Cairo: Dār al-Maᶜārif ²1413/²1992 (Ḏaḫāʾir al-ᶜArab 65).

MutanDīwān (U) — Id.: *Dīwān ʾAbī ṭ-Ṭayyib al-Mutanabbī bi-šarḥ ʾAbī l-Baqāʾ al-ʿUkbarī (al-musammā at-Tibyān fī šarḥ ad-Dīwān)*, ed. Kamāl Ṭālib, 4 vols., Beirut: Dār al-Kutub al-ᶜIlmīyah 1418/1997.

MutanDīwān (W) — Id.: *Dīwān al-Mutanabbī bi-šarḥ al-Wāḥidī*, ed. F. Dieterici, Berlin 1861.

Muwaṭṭaʾ — Mālik b. Anas al-Madanī: *Kitāb al-Muwaṭṭaʾ (ʿan Ya. b. Ya.)*, ed. M. Fuʾād ᶜAbd al-Bāqī, 2 vols., repr. Beirut: Dār Iḥyāʾ at-Turāṯ al-ᶜArabī 1406/1985; *see also* BāğīMunt; SuyTanwīr; ZurqŠMuw.

MuwMuršid — Muwaffaq ad-Dīn Ibn ᶜUṯmān: *Muršid az-zuwwār ʾilā qubūr al-ʾabrār al-musammā ad-Durr al-munaẓẓam fī ziyārat al-ğabal al-Muqaṭṭam*, ed. M. Fatḥī Abū Bakr, 2 vols., Cairo – Beirut: ad-Dār al-Miṣrīyah al-Lubnānīyah 1415/1995.

NābDīwān — ᶜAbd al-Ġanīy b. Ism. (Ibn) an-Nābulusī: *Dīwān al-ḥaqāʾiq wa-mağmaʿ ar-raqāʾiq*, ed. M. ᶜAbd al-Ḫāliq az-Zanātī, Beirut: Dār al-Kutub al-ᶜIlmīyah 1421/2001.

NābḤaqīqah (C) — Id.: *al-Ḥaqīqah wa-l-mağāz fī riḥlah ʾilā bilād aš-Šām wa-Miṣr wa-l-Ḥiğāz*, ed. A. ᶜAbd al-Mağīd Huraydī, Cairo: al-Hayʾah al-Miṣrīyah al-ᶜĀmmah li-l-Kitāb 1986.[7]

NābḤaqīqah (D) — Id.: *al-Ḥaqīqah wa-l-mağāz fī riḥlat bilād aš-Šām wa-Miṣr wa-l-Ḥiğāz*, ed. Riyāḍ ᶜAbd al-Ḥamīd Murād, Damascus: Dār al-Maᶜrifah 1410/1989 (incomplete edition).

NābiġahDīwān — an-Nābiġah aḏ-Ḏubyānī: *ad-Dīwān*, ed. H. Derenbourg, Paris 1869.

NābNisyān — ᶜAbd al-Ġanīy b. Ism. (Ibn) an-Nābulusī: *(Risālat) al-Kašf wa-l-bayān fī-mā yataʿallaq bi-n-nisyān*, ed. Ḫālid M. Maḥmūd, Cairo: Maktabat al-Qāhirah 1421/2000.

NābTaᶜṭīr — Id.: *Taʿṭīr al-ʾanām fī taʿbīr al-manām*. 2 vols., Cairo: Maktabat al-Mašhad al-Ḥusaynī n.d.

NābTuḥfah — Id.: *at-Tuḥfah an-Nābulusīyah fī r-riḥlah aṭ-Ṭarābulusīyah*, ed. H. Busse, (repr.) Cairo: Maktabat aṯ-Ṯaqāfah ad-Dīnīyah n.d.

NasQand — Nağm ad-Dīn ᶜUmar b. M. an-Nasafī: *al-Qand fī ḏikr ʿulamāʾ Samarqand*, ed. Yūsuf al-Hādī, Tehran: Markaz-i Našr at-Turāṯ al-Maḫṭūṭ 1420/1999.

NasSunan — Abū ᶜAr. b. Šuᶜayb an-Nasāʾī: *Kitāb as-Sunan al-muğtabā*, 8 vols., Cairo: Muṣṭafā al-Bābī al-Ḥalabī 1383/1964; *see also* SuyZahr.

7 This is the photomechanical reprint of a manuscript copied in 1231 AH by a great-grandson of the author.

NawāǧīMaṭāliʿ — Šams ad-Dīn M. b. al-Ḥasan an-Nawāǧī: *Maṭāliʿ aš-Šamsīyah fī l-madāʾiḥ an-nabawīyah*, ed. Ḥasan M. ʿAbd al-Hādī, Amman: Dār al-Yanābīʿ li-n-Našr wa-t-Tawzīʿ 1999.

NawFat — Abū Zak. Ya. b. Šaraf an-Nawawī aš-Šāfiʿī: *Fatāwā l-ʾImām an-Nawawī rattabahā wa-ḥarrara ʾalfāẓahā l-ʾImām (...) ʿAlāʾ ad-Dīn ʿAlī b. Ibr. b. al-ʿAṭṭār ad-Dimašqī*, ed. Maḥmūd al-Arnāʾūṭ, Damascus: Dār al-Fikr 1419/1999.

NawMuḫt — Id.: *Muḫtaṣar ṭabaqāt al-fuqahāʾ*, edd. ʿĀdil ʿAbd al-Mawǧūd and ʿAlī Muʿawwaḍ, Beirut: Muʾassasat al-Kutub aṯ-Ṯaqāfīyah 1416/1995.

NawRawḍah — Id.: *Rawḍat aṭ-ṭālibīn*, 8 vols., Amman: al-Maktab al-Islāmī 1386/1966.

NawRiyāḍ — Id.: *Riyāḍ aṣ-ṣāliḥīn*, ed. Ḥ. Šukr, Beirut: Dār al-Kutub al-ʿIlmīyah 1405/1985.

NawŠMuslim — Id.: *Šarḥ Ṣaḥīḥ Muslim*, 18 vols. in 6, Cairo: al-Maṭbaʿah al-Miṣrīyah 1349f./1930.

NB (B) — Kamāl ad-Dīn Maytam b. ʿAlī al-Baḥrānī: *Šarḥ Nahǧ al-balāġah*, 5 vols., Beirut: Manšūrāt Dār aṯ-Ṯaqalayn 1420/1999.

NB (Ḥ) — Ibn Abī l-Ḥadīd: *Šarḥ Nahǧ al-balāġah (al-ǧāmiʿ li-ḫuṭab wa-rasāʾil wa-ḥikam ʾamīr al-muʾminīn ʾAbī l-Ḥasan ʿAlī b. ʾAbī Ṭālib)*, 4 vols., Cairo 1328 (repr. Beirut: Dār al-Andalus n.d.).

NubQuḍātAnd — Abū l-Ḥasan ʿAlī b. ʿAl. an-Nubāhī al-Mālaqī al-Mālikī: *Tārīḫ Quḍāt al-ʾAndalus (= al-Marqabah al-ʿulyā fī-man yastaḥiqqu l-qaḍāʾ wa-l-futyā)*, ed. Maryam Qāsim Ṭawīl, Beirut: Dār al-Kutub al-ʿIlmīyah 1415/1995.

Nūr an-nahār — *Nūr an-nahār min munāẓarāt al-ward wa-r-rayāḥīn wa-l-ʾazhār*,[8] ed. M. aš-Šištāwī, Cairo: Dār al-Āfāq al-ʿArabīyah 1419/1999.

NuwIlmām — M. b. Qāsim b. M. an-Nuwayrī al-Mālikī: *Kitāb al-ʾIlmām bi-l-ʾiʿlām fī mā ǧarat bihī l-ʾaḥkām wa-l-ʾumūr al-maqḍīyah fī waqʿat al-ʾIskandarīyah*, edd. É. Combe and ʿA. S. ʿAṭīyah, 7 vols., Hyderabad: Dāʾirat al-Maʿārif al-ʿUṯmānīyah 1389–93 / 1969–73.

NuwNih — Šihāb ad-Dīn A. b. ʿAbd al-Wahhāb an-Nuwayrī: *Nihāyat al-ʾarab fī funūn ʾal-adab*, vols. I–XXXI, Cairo 1342–1412 / 1923–92.

NZ — Ǧamāl ad-Dīn Abū l-Maḥāsin Yūsuf Ibn Taġrī Birdī al-Atābakī: *an-Nuǧūm az-zāhirah fī mulūk Miṣr wa-l-Qāhirah*, edd. Fahīm M. Šaltūt and Ǧamāl M. Mahraz, 15 vols., Cairo: al-Hayʾah al-Miṣrīyah al-ʿĀmmah li-t-Taʾlīf etc. n.d. (1383–92 / 1963–72).

Q — Text of the Qurʾān in the edition Cairo 1337 H; English translation: *The Koran Interpreted. Translated with an Introduction by Arthur J. Arberry*, Oxford 1964 (repr. 1998).

QālīAmālī — Abū ʿAlī Ism. b. al-Qāsim al-Qālī: *Kitāb al-ʾAmālī*, ed. M. ʿAbd al-Ǧawād al-Aṣmaʿī, 2 vols., repr. Beirut: al-Maktab at-Tiǧārī n.d.

QalNawādir — Šihāb ad-Dīn A. b. A. b. Salāmah al-Qalyūbī: *(Kitāb) an-Nawādir*, Cairo: Muṣṭafā al-Bābī al-Ḥalabī ^{3}1374/^{3}1955; for the German translation, *see* O. Rescher: *Gesammelte Werke. Abteilung II: Schriften zur Adab-Literatur, Band 2*, Osnabrück 1980.

QasṭIršād — Šihāb ad-Dīn A. al-Qasṭallānī aš-Šāfiʿī: *ʾIršād as-sārī ʾilā šarḥ (Ṣaḥīḥ) al-Buḫārī*, 10 vols. in 5, Būlāq 1276.

8 A modern collection of pre-modern Arabic dispute-poems.

QasṭMaw — Id.: *al-Mawāhib al-ladunīyah bi-l-minaḥ al-Muḥammadīyah*, ed. Maʾmūn b. Muḥyī d-Dīn al-Ǧinān, 3 vols., Beirut: Dār al-Kutub al-ᶜIlmīyah 1416/1996.

QazwĀṯār — Zak. b. M. al-Qazwīnī: *Kitāb ʾĀṯār al-bilād wa-ʾaḫbār al-ʿibād*, Beirut: Dār Ṣādir 1389/1969.

QFāḍilDīwān — ᶜAbd ar-Raḥīm b. ᶜAlī al-Qāḍī al-Fāḍil: *ad-Dīwān*, edd. A. A. al-Badawī and Ibr. al-Ibyārī, 2 vols., Cairo: Wizārat aṯ-Ṯaqāfah 1961.

QifṭīInbāh — Ǧamāl ad-Dīn ᶜAlī b. Yūsuf (Ibn) al-Qifṭī: *ʾInbāh ar-ruwāh ʿalā ʾanbāh an-nuḥāh*, ed. M. Abū l-Faḍl Ibrāhīm, 3 vols., Cairo: Dār al-Kutub al-Miṣrīyah 1369–74 / 1950–55.

QifṭīTārīḫ — Id.: *Tārīḫ al-ḥukamāʾ wa-huwa Muḫtaṣar az-Zawzanī*, ed. J. Lippert, Leipzig: Dieterich'sche Verlagsbuchhandlung 1903.

QNuᶜmDaᶜāʾim — al-Qāḍī Abū Ḥanīfah an-Nuᶜmān b. M. al-Maġribī al-Ismāᶜīlī: *Daʿāʾim al-ʾislām wa-ḏikr al-ḥalāl wa-ḥarām wa-l-qaḍāyā wa-l-ʾaḥkām ʿan ʾahl bayt rasūl Allāh ʿalayhi wa-ʿalayhim ʾafḍal as-salām*, ed. Āṣif b. ᶜAlī Aṣġar Fayḍī (Fyzee), 2 vols., Cairo: Dār al-Maᶜārif 1383/1963.

QurṭTaḏk — Šamṣ ad-Dīn Abū ᶜAl. M. b. A. al-Qurṭubī: *at-Taḏkirah fī ʾaḥwāl al-mawtā wa-ʾumūr al-ʾāḫirah*, edd. ᶜAl. al-Minšāwī and M. Bayyūmī, al-Manṣūrah: Maktabat al-Īmān 1416/1995.

QušRis — Abū l-Qāsim ᶜAbd al-Karīm b. Hawāzin al-Qušayrī: *ar-Risālah (fī ʿilm at-taṣawwuf)*, edd. Maᶜrūf Zurayq and ᶜAlī Abū l-Ḫayr, Damascus – Beirut: Dār al-Ḫayr 1418/1997.

RāġibMuḥāḍ — Abū l-Qāsim Ḥusayn b. M. ar-Rāġib al-Iṣfahānī: *Muḥāḍarāt al-ʾudabāʾ wa-muḥāwarāt aš-šuʿarāʾ wa-l-bulaġāʾ*, 4 vols., Beirut: Dār Maktabat al-Ḥayāh 1961.

RamlīFat — Šams ad-Dīn M. b. A. ar-Ramlī aš-Šāfiᶜī: *Fatāwā r-Ramlī*, printed on the margins of: HaytFatFiqh.

RamlīNih — Id.: *Nihāyat al-muḥtāǧ ʾilā šarḥ al-Minhāǧ (li-n-Nawawī)*, 8 vols., Cairo: Muṣṭafā al-Babı al-Ḥalabī 1357/1938.

RašīdīḤusn — aš-Šayḫ Aḥmad ar-Rašīdī: *Ḥusn aṣ-ṣafāʾ wa-l-ibtihāǧ bi-ḏikr man wulliya ʾimārata l-ḥāǧǧ*, ed. L. ᶜAbd al-Laṭīf Aḥmad, Cairo: Makt. al-Ḫānǧī 1980.

RundīŠḤikam — M. b. Ibr. Ibn ᶜAbbād ar-Rundī: *Šarḥ ʿalā Kitāb al-Ḥikam (li-bn ʿAṭāʾ Allāh)*, ed. A. Saᶜd ᶜAlī, 2 vols., Cairo: Muṣṭafā al-Bābī al-Ḥalabī 1358/1939.

ṢafAᶜyān — Ṣalāḥ ad-Dīn Ḫalīl b. Aybak aṣ-Ṣafadī: *ʾAʿyān al-ʿaṣr wa-ʾaʿwān an-naṣr*, 3 vols., Frankfurt/M.: Institute for the History of Arabic-Islamic Science 1410/1990 (Ms. 1809 Atif Collection, Süleymaniye Library Istanbul) (Publ. of the Institute for the History of Arabic-Islamic Science, Ser. C: Facsimile editions 50).

SaffĠiḏāʾ — M. b. A. b. Sālim as-Saffārīnī al-Ḥanbalī: *Ġiḏāʾ al-ʾalbāb šarḥ Manẓūmat al-ʾādāb (li-l-Mardāwī)*, ed. M. ᶜAbd al-ᶜAzīz al-Ḫālidī, 2 vols., Beirut: Dār al-Kutub al-ᶜIlmīyah 1417/1996.

ṢafĠayṯ — Ṣalāḥ ad-Dīn Ḫalīl b. Aybak aṣ-Ṣafadī: *al-Ġayṯ al-musaǧǧam fī šarḥ Lāmīyat al-ʿaǧam (li-ṭ-Ṭuġrāʾī)*, 2 vols., Beirut: Dār al-Kutub al-ᶜIlmīyah ²1411/²1990.

ṢafKašf — Id.: *al-Kašf wa-t-tanbīh ʿalā l-waṣf wa-t-tašbīh*, edd. Hilāl Nāǧī and Walīd b. A. al-Ḥusayn, Leeds – Medina: Maǧallat al-Ḥikmah 1420/1999.

ṢafNakt — Id.: *Nakt al-himyān fī nukat al-ʿumyān*, ed. Aḥmad Zakīy Bey, Cairo: al-Maṭbaᶜah al-Ǧamālīyah 1329/1911.

ŠāfUmm — M. b. Idrīs al-Imām aš-Šāfiᶜī: *Kitāb al-ʾUmm*, ed. Maḥmūd Maṭarǧī, 9 vols. in 8, Beirut: Dār al-Kutub al-ᶜIlmīyah 1413/1993.

SaḫḎRafᶜ — Šams ad-Dīn M. b. ᶜAr. as-Saḫāwī: *aḏ-Ḏayl ʿalā Rafʿ al-ʿiṣr (ʿan quḍāt Miṣr li-bn Ḥağar) ʾaw Buġyat al-ʿulamāʾ wa-r-ruwāh*, edd. Ǧūdah Hilāl and M. Maḥmūd Ṣubḥ, Cairo: ad-Dār al-Miṣrīyah li-t-Taʾlīf wa-t-Tarǧamah n.d.

SaḫĞawāhir — Id.: *al-Ğawāhir wa-d-durar fī tarğamat Šayḫ al-ʾislām Ibn Ḥağar*, ed. Ibr. Bāğis ᶜAbd al-Mağīd, 3 vols., Beirut: Dār Ibn Ḥazm 1419/1999.

SaḫIᶜlān — Id.: *al-ʾIʿlān bi-t-tawbīḫ li-man ḏamma t-tārīḫ*, Damascus 1349 (repr. Beirut: Dār al-Kitāb al-ᶜArabī 1403/1983); English translation in Rosenthal: *Historiography* pp. 269–539.

SaḥnūnMud — Saḥnūn b. Saᶜīd al-Mālikī: *al-Mudawwanah al-kubrā*, 14 vols. in 7, Cairo Maṭbaᶜat as-Saᶜādah 1323.

SaḫQaṣāʾid — ᶜAlam ad-Dīn Abū l-Ḥasan ᶜAlī b. M. al-Hamdānī as-Saḫāwī: *al-Qaṣāʾid as-sabʿ (fī madḥ sayyid al-ḫalq Muḥammad) bi-šarḥ ʾAbī Šāmah*, Ms. Berlin We I 56 (= Ahlwardt No. 7752), ff. 69b-76a.

SaḫTibr — Šams ad-Dīn M. b. ᶜAr. as-Saḫāwī: *Kitāb at-Tibr al-masbūk fī ḏayl as-Sulūk*, Cairo: Maktabat al-Kullīyāt al-Azharīyah n.d.

SaḫTuḥfAḥbāb — Nūr ad-Dīn Abū l-Hasan ᶜAlī b. A. as-Saḫāwī al-Ḥanafī: *Tuḥfat al-ʾaḥbāb wa-buġyat aṭ-ṭullāb fī l-ḫiṭaṭ wa-l-mazārāt wa-t-tarāğim wa-l-biqāʿ al-mubārakāt*, Cairo: Maktabat al-Kullīyāt al-Azharīyah ²1406/²1986.

SaḫTuḥfLaṭ — Šams ad-Dīn M. b. ᶜAr. as-Saḫāwī: *at-Tuḥfah al-laṭīfah fī tārīḫ al-Madīnah aš-šarīfah*, 2 vols., Beirut: Dār al-Kutub al-ᶜIlmīyah 1414/1993.

SaḫWağīz — Id.: *Wağīz al-kalām fī ḏ-ḏayl ʿalā Duwal al-ʾislām (li-ḏ-Ḏahabī)*, edd. Baššār ᶜAwwād Maᶜrūf, ᶜIṣām ad-Dīn Fāris al-Ḥarastānī and A. al-Ḫuṭaymī, 4 vols., Beirut: Muʾassasat ar-Risālah 1416/1995.

SamAnsāb — Abū Saᶜd ᶜAbd al-Karīm b. M. as-Samᶜānī: *Kitāb al-ʾAnsāb*, ed. ᶜAr. b. Ya. al-Muᶜallimī al-Yamānī, 13 vols., Hyderabad 1382–1402 / 1962–82.

SamḪizānah — Abū l-Layṯ Naṣr b. M. as-Samarqandī al-Ḥanafī: *Ḫizānat al-fiqh wa-ʿuyūn al-masāʾil*, ed. Ṣāliḥ ad-Dīn an-Nāhī, 2 vols., Baghdad: Šarikat aṭ-Ṭabᶜ wa-n-Našr al-Ahlīyah 1385/1965.

ŠāmīSubul — Šams ad-Dīn M. b. M. aš-Šāmī: *Subul al-hudā fī sīrat ḫayr al-warā*, 12 vols., Beirut: Dār al-Kutub al-ᶜIlmīyah 1416/1996.

SamTafsīr — Abū l-Layṯ Naṣr b. M. as-Samarqandī al-Ḥanafī: *Tafsīr as-Samarqandī (Baḥr al-ʿulūm)*, ed. Maḥmūd Maṭarğī, 3 vols., Beirut: Dār al-Fikr 1418/1997.

SamWafāʾ — Nūr ad-Dīn ᶜAlī as-Samhūdī: *Wafāʾ al-wafā bi-ʾāḫbār dār al-Muṣṭafā*, ed. M. Muḥyī d-Dīn ᶜAbd al-Ḥamīd, 4 vols. in 3, Cairo: 1374/1955 (repr. Beirut: Dār al-Kutub al-ᶜIlmīyah 1404/1984).

ŠantḎaḫ — Abū l-Ḥasan ᶜAlī b. Bassām aš-Šantarīnī: *aḏ-Ḏaḫīrah fī maḥāsin ʾahl al-ğazīrah*, ed. Iḥsān ᶜAbbās, 4 vols. in 8, Beirut: Dār aṯ-Ṯaqāfah 1399/1979.

ŠantŠḤam — Abū l-Ḥağğāğ Yūsuf al-Aᶜlam aš-Šantamarī: *Šarḥ Ḥamāsat ʾAbī Tammām (Tağallī ġurar al-maʿānī* etc.*)*, ed. ᶜAlī al-Mufaḍḍal Ḥammūdān, 2 vols., Beirut: Dār ar-Fikr al-Muᶜāṣir 1413/1992.

SaqaṭīḤisbah — Abū ᶜAl. M. b. Abī M. as-Saqaṭī al-Mālaqī: *Kitāb fī ʾādāb al-ḥisbah*, edd. G.-S. Colin and É. Lévi-Provençal, Paris: Librairie E. Leroux 1931.

ŠaᶜrAnwārQudsīyah — ᶜAbd al-Wahhāb b. A. aš-Šaᶜrānī: *Lawāqiḥ al-ʾanwār al-qudsīyah fī bayān al-ʿuhūd al-Muḥammadīyah.* Cairo: Muṣṭafā al-Bābī al-Ḥalabī 1381/1961.

ŠaᶜrDurar — Id.: *Durar al-ġawāṣṣ ʿalā fatāwā sayyidī ʿAlī al-Ḫawāṣṣ*, ed. ᶜAbd al-Wāriṯ M. ᶜAlī, Beirut: Dār al-Kutub al-ᶜIlmīyah 1420/1999.

SarrāğMaṣ — Abū M. Ğaᶜfar b. Aḥmad as-Sarrāğ al-Qāriʾ: *Maṣāriᶜ al-ᶜuššāq*, ed. Karam al-Bustānī, 2 vols., Beirut: Dār Ṣādir n.d.

ŠaᶜrṬab — ᶜAbd al-Wahhāb aš-Šaᶜrānī: *aṭ-Ṭabaqāt al-kubrā (Lawāqiḥ al-ʾanwār fī ṭabaqāt al-ʾaḫyār)*, 2 vols., Cairo 1374/1954 (repr. Beirut n.d.).

ŠarīfMurtRas — aš-Šarīf al-Murtaḍā Abū l-Qāsim ᶜAlī b. al-Ḥusayn (...) b. al-Imām Mūsā al-Kāẓim: *Rasāʾil aš-Šarīf al-Murtaḍā*, edd. A. al-Ḥusaynī and Mahdī Rağāʾī, 3 vols., Qum: Dār al-Qurʾān al-Karīm 1405.

ŠarīfRaḍDīwān — aš-Šarīf ar-Raḍīy M. b. al-Ḥusayn: *ad-Dīwān*, ed. Iḥsān ᶜAbbās, 2 vols., repr. Beirut: Dār Ṣādir 1994.

ŠarŠMaq — Abū l-ᶜAbbās A. b. ᶜAbd al-Muʾmin al-Qaysī aš-Šarīšī: *Šarḥ Maqāmāt al-Ḥarīrī*, 2 vols., Būlāq: al-Maṭbaᶜah al-Kubrā al-Mīrīyah ^{2}1300 (^{1}1284).

ŠawkBadr — M. b. ᶜAlī aš-Šawkānī: *al-Badr aṭ-ṭāliᶜ fī maḥāsin man baᶜd al-qarn as-sābiᶜ*, 2 vols., Cairo 1332–48 (repr. Cairo: Dār al-Kitāb al-Islāmī n.d.).

ŠawkDurr — Id.: *Kitāb ad-Durr an-naḍīd fī ʾiḫlāṣ kalimat at-tawḥīd*, in: *ar-Rasāʾil as-salafīyah fī ʾiḥyāʾ sunnat Ḫayr al-barīyah*, repr. Beirut: Dār al-Kutub al-ᶜIlmīyah n.d. (1340–50 / 1923–32), no. 8.

ŠawkŠṢudūr — Id.: *Šarḥ aṣ-ṣudūr fī taḥrīm rafᶜ al-qubūr*, in: MağmRasMun I pp. 62–76 (the treatise is also reprinted in his *Rasāʾil as-salafīyah* no. 1, *see the preceding entry*).

ŠaybīŠaraf — Ğamāl ad-Dīn M. b. ᶜAlī b. M. al-Makkī aš-Šaybī: *aš-Šaraf al-ʾaᶜlā fī ḏikr qubūr maqburat al-Maᶜlā*,[9] Ms. Berlin 6124, ff. 1–28.

ŠayMağānī — Lūyis Šayḫū [Louis Cheikho]: *Mağānī l-ʾadab fī ḥadāʾiq al-ᶜarab*, Beirut: Maṭbaᶜat al-Ābāʾ al-Yasūᶜīyīn 1914 (vol. IV), al-Maṭbaᶜah al-Kāṯūlīkīyah 1954 (vol. III) and 1957 (vol. VI).

ŠayŠuᶜarāʾNaṣr — Id.: *Šuᶜarāʾ an-naṣrānīyah baᶜd al-ʾislām*, Beirut: al-Maṭbaᶜah al-Kāṯūlīkīyah 1967.

ŠayzḤisba — ᶜAbd ar-Raḥmān b. Naṣr aš-Šayzarī: *The Book of the Islamic Market Inspector. Nihāyat al-Rutba fī Ṭalab al-Ḥisba (The Utmost Authority in the Pursuit of Ḥisba)*, tr. R. P. Buckley, Oxford 1999 (Journal of Semitic Studies Suppl. 9).

ŠḎ — ᶜAbd al-Ḥayy b. A. b. al-ᶜImād: *Šaḏarāt aḏ-ḏahab fī ʾaḫbār man ḏahab*, 8 vols. in 4, Cairo 1350f./1932 (repr. Beirut: al-Maktab at-Tiğārī li-ṭ-Ṭibāᶜah wa-n-Našr n.d.).

SiggelGifte — A. Siggel: *Das Buch der Gifte (Kitāb as-sumūm, arab.-dt.) des Ğābir Ibn-Ḥayyān*, Wiesbaden: F. Steiner 1958.

SiğNaḫlah — Abū Ḥātim Sahl b. M. as-Siğistānī: *Kitāb an-Naḫlah*, ed. Ḥātim Ṣ. aḍ-Ḍāmin, in: al-Mawrid 14 (1985), pp. 107–58.

SinğManāʾiḥ — ᶜAlī b. Tāğ ad-Dīn as-Sinğārī: *Manāʾiḥ al-karam fī ʾaḫbār Makkah wa-l-bayt wa-wulāt al-ḥaram*, ed. Ğamīl ᶜAl. M. al-Miṣrī, 5 vols. and index, Mecca: Ğāmiᶜat Umm al-Qurā 1419/1998.

ŠinqWasīṭ — A. b. al-Amīn aš-Šinqīṭī: *al-Wasīṭ fī tarāğim ʾudabāʾ Šinqīṭ*, ed. Fuʾād Sayyid, Cairo: Maktabat al-Ḫānğī ^{2}1390/^{2}1961 (repr. 1409/1989).

ŠīrMuhaḏ — Abū Isḥāq Ibr. b. ᶜAlī aš-Šīrāzī: *Kitāb al-Muhaḏḏab fī l-fiqh ᶜalā maḏhab aš-Šāfiᶜī*, 2 vols., Cairo: ᶜĪsā al-Bābī al-Ḥalabī n.d.

ŠīrŠadd — Muᶜīn ad-Dīn Abū l-Qāsim Ğunayd aš-Šīrāzī: *Šadd al-ʾizār fī ḥaṭṭ al-ʾawzār ᶜan zuwwār al-mazār*, edd. M. Qazwīnī and ᶜAbbās Iqbāl, Tehran 1328š.

9 The title is not given as such in the manuscript.

ŠirwḤāš	ᶜAbd al-Ḥamīd aš-Širwānī al-Makkī: *Ḥāšiyah ʿalā Tuḥfat al-muḥtāǧ (li-bn Ḥaǧar al-Haytamī)*, 10 vols., Cairo 1315 (repr. Beirut: Dār Ṣādir n.d.).
SourdelLieux	J. Sourdel-Thomine: *Guide des lieux de pèlerinage de Abū l-Ḥasan ʿAlī b. Abī Bakr al-Harawī*, Damascus 1957; *see also* HarIšārāt.
ŠSiqṭZand	*Šurūḥ Siqṭ az-zand li-l-Maʿarrī (li-t-Tabrīzī, al-Baṭalyawsī, al-Ḫwārazmī)*, ed. Muṣṭafā as-Saqqā *et al.*, 5 vols., Cairo: al-Hayʾah al-Miṣrīyah al-ᶜĀmmah li-l-Kitāb 1406–8 / 1986f.
ŠTalḫīṣ	The commentaries by Saᶜd ad-Dīn at-Taftāzānī (*Šarḥ at-Talḫīṣ*), Ibn Yaᶜqūb al-Maġribī (*Mawāhib al-fattāḥ*) and as-Subkī (*ʿArūs al-ʾafrāḥ*) to the *Talḫīṣ al-Miftāḥ (fī ʿilm al-balāġah)* by al-Qazwīnī, 4 vols., Būlāq 1317–19 (repr. Beirut: Dār al-Kutub al-ᶜIlmīyah n.d.); *see also above* MehrenRhetorik.
SubkīFat	Taqīy ad-Dīn Abū l-Ḥasan ᶜAlī b. ᶜAbd al-Kāfī as-Subkī aš-Šāfiᶜī: *Fatāwā s-Subkī*, 2 vols., repr. Beirut: Dār al-Maᶜrifah n.d.
SubkīŠifāʾ	Id.: *Šifāʾ as-siqām fī ziyārat Ḫayr al-ʾanām*, Beirut: Dār al-Ǧīl 1411/1991.
SubkīṬab	Tāǧ ad-Dīn ᶜAbd al-Wahhāb b. ᶜAlī as-Subkī: *Ṭabaqāt aš-Šāfiʿīyah al-kubrā*, edd. ᶜAbd al-Fattāḥ M. al-Ḥulw and Maḥmūd M. aṭ-Ṭunāḥī, 10 vols., Cairo: ᶜĪsā al-Bābī al-Ḥalabī 1964–76.
ŠubrḤāš	Nūr ad-Dīn ᶜAlī b. ᶜAlī aš-Šubrāmallīsī: *Ḥāšiyah ʿalā Nihāyat al-muḥtāǧ (li-r-Ramlī)*, printed on the margins of: RamlīNih.
SuhrᶜAwārif	Abū n-Naǧīb ᶜAbd al-Qāhir b. ᶜAl. as-Suhrawardī: *Kitāb ʿAwārif al-maʿārif*, Beirut: Dār al-Kitāb al-ᶜArabī ^{2}1403/^{2}1983.
SuyBard	Ǧalāl ad-Dīn ᶜAr. b. Abī Bakr as-Suyūṭī:[10] *Bard al-ʾakbād ʿinda faqd al-ʾawlād*, in: *al-Ǧannah wa-n-nār wa-Faqd al-ʾawlād*, ed. M. Zaynuhum M. ᶜAzab, Cairo: Dār al-Amīn 1414/1993, pp. 79–145.
SuyBuġ	Id.: *Buġyat al-wuʿāh fī ṭabaqāt al-luġawīyīn wa-n-nuḥāh*, ed. M. Abū l-Faḍl Ibrāhīm, 2 vols., Cairo: ᶜĪsā al-Bābī al-Ḥalabī 1384/1964–65.
SuyBušrā	Id.: *Bušrā al-kaʾīb bi-liqāʾ al-ḥabīb*, Cairo: Muṣṭafā al-Bābī al-Ḥalabī ^{2}1389/^{2}1969.[11]
SuyǦal	Id. / al-Ǧalāl al-Maḥallī: *Tafsīr al-Ǧalālayn*, ed. Marwān Sawār, Damascus: 1407 / 1987.
SuyḪaṣ	Id.: *al-Ḫaṣāʾiṣ al-kubrā (Kifāyat aṭ-ṭālib al-labīb fī ḫaṣāʾiṣ al-ḥabīb)*, 2 vols., Beirut: Dār al-Kutub al-ᶜIlmīyah 1405/1985.
SuyḤāwī	Id.: *al-Ḥāwī li-l-fatāwī*, 2 vols. in 1, repr. Beirut: Dār al-Ǧīl 1412/1992.
SuyḤusnMuḥ	Id.: *Ḥusn al-muḥāḍarah fī ʾaḫbār Miṣr wa-l-Qāhirah*, ed. Ḫalīl al-Manṣūr, 2 vols., Beirut: Dār al-Kutub al-ᶜIlmīyah 1418/1997.
SuyInbāʾAḏk	Id.: *ʾInbāʾ al-ʾaḏkiyāʾ bi-ḥayāt al-ʾanbiyāʾ (fī qubūrihim)*, printed in: BayḤayātAnb pp. 43–65 (also printed in: SuyRas pp. 197–211).
SuyMasālik	Id.: *Masālik al-ḥunafāʾ fī (ʾislām) wāliday al-Muṣṭafā*, printed in: SuyḤāwī II pp. 202–33 (also printed in: SuyRas pp. 44–101).
SuyMunǧam	Id.: *al-Munǧam fī l-muʿǧam*, ed. Ibr. Bāǧis ᶜAbd al-Maǧīd, Beirut: Dār Ibn Ḥazm 1995/1415.

10 This treatise is wrongly ascribed to as-Suyūṭī, as already observed in GAL II p. 148, n. 1. For the author, see INāṣBard.

11 As as-Suyūṭī himself states in the preface, this treatise is basically an abbreviation of his larger monograph *Šarḥ aṣ-ṣudūr* (= SuyŠṢudūr).

SuyNašr — Id.: *Našr al-ʿalamayn al-munīfayn fī ʾiḥyāʾ al-ʾabawayn aš-šarīfayn*, printed in: SuyRas pp.103–18.

SuyNaẓmʿIqyān — Id.: *Naẓm al-ʿiqyān fī ʾaʿyān ʾal-ʾaʿyān*, ed. Ph. Hitti, New York: Syrian-American Press 1927 (repr. Beirut: al-Maktabah al-ʿIlmīyah n.d.).

SuyNūrLum — Id.: *Nūr al-lumʿah fī ḫaṣāʾiṣ al-ǧumʿah*, in: MaǧmRasMun I pp. 188–223.

SuyRas — Id.: *ar-Rasāʾil al-ʿašrah*, ed. Beirut: Dār al-Kutub al-ʿIlmīyah 1409/1989.

SuyŠṢudūr — Id.: *Šarḥ aṣ-ṣudūr bi-šarḥ ḥāl al-mawtā wa-l-qubūr*, ed. M. Ḥasan al-Ḥimṣī, Damascus: Dār ar-Rašīd / Beirut: Muʾassasat al-Īmān [3]1407/[3]1986.

SuySubul — Id.: *Subul al-ǧalīyah fī l-ʾābāʾ al-ʿalīyah*, printed in: SuyRas pp. 165–79.

SuyTanwīr — Id.: *Tanwīr al-ḥawālik šarḥ ʿalā Muwaṭṭaʾ Mālik*, ed. M. ʿAbd al-ʿAzīz al-Ḫālidī, Beirut: Dār al-Kutub al-ʿIlmīyah 1418/1997.

SuyZahr — Id.: *Zahr ar-rubā ʿalā l-Muǧtabā (Sunan an-Nasāʾī)*, printed in: NasSunan.

ṮaʿālLaṭāʾif — Abū Manṣūr ʿAbd al-Malik b. M. aṯ-Ṯaʿālibī: *The Book of Curious and Entertaining Information. The Laṭāʾif al-maʿārif of Thaʿālibī*, tr. by C. E. Bosworth, Edinburgh: UP 1968.

ṮaʿālTafsīr — Abū Zayd ʿAr. b. M. aṯ-Ṯaʿālibī: *al-Ǧawāhir al-ḥisān fī tafsīr al-qurʾān*, ed. Abū M. al-Ġumārī al-Idrīsī, 3 vols., Beirut: Dār al-Kutub al-ʿIlmīyah 1416/1996.

ṮaʿālTamṯīl — Abū Manṣūr ʿAbd al-Malik aṯ-Ṯaʿālibī: *at-Tamṯīl wa-l-muḥāḍarah*, ed. ʿAbd al-Fattāḥ M. al-Ḥulw, Cairo: ʿĪsā al-Bābī al-Ḥalabī 1381/1961.

ṮaʿālṮimār — Id.: *Ṯimār al-qulūb fī l-muḍāf wa-l-mansūb*, ed. M. Abū l-Faḍl Ibrāhīm, Cairo: Dār Nahḍat Miṣr 1384/1965.

ṮaʿālYat — Id.: *Yatīmat ad-dahr fī maḥāsin ʾahl al-ʿaṣr*, ed. M. Muḥyī d-Dīn ʿAbd al-Ḥamīd, 4 vols., Cairo: Maṭbaʿat as-Saʿādah [2]1375–77 / [2]1956–57.

ṬabHistory — Abū Ǧaʿfar M. b. Ǧarīr aṭ-Ṭabarī: *The History of al-Ṭabarī (An Annotated Translation)*, ed. E. Yar-Shater *et al.*, vols. 1ff., New York: SU Press 1989ff. (Bibliotheca Persica).

ṬabMiškāh — Abū l-Faḍl ʿAlī aṭ-Ṭabarsī: *Miškāt al-ʾanwār fī ġurar al-ʾaḫbar*, Beirut: Dār al-Kutub al-Islāmīyah 1385/1965.

ṬabQirā — Muḥibb ad-Dīn A. b. ʿAl. aṭ-Ṭabarī al-Makkī: *al-Qirā li-qāṣid ʾUmm al-Qurā*, ed. Muṣṭafā as-Saqqā, Cairo 1367/1948 (repr. Beirut: Dār al-Fikr [3]1403/[3]1983).

ṬabSimṭ — Id.: *as-Simṭ aṯ-ṯamīn fī manāqib ʾummahāt al-muʾminīn*, edd. Ḥamzah an-Našartī and ʿAbd al-Ḥāfiẓ Farġalī, Cairo: al-Maktabah al-Qayyimah 1996.

ṮaʿlQatlā — Abū Isḥāq A. b. Ibr. an-Nīsābūrī aṯ-Ṯaʿlabī: *Kitāb fīhi qatlā l-qurʾān (Die vom Koran Getöteten. Aṯ-Ṯaʿlabīs* Qatlā l-Qurʾān *nach der Istanbuler und den Leidener Handschriften. Edition und Kommentar)*, ed. B. Wiesmüller, Würzburg: Ergon Verlag 2002 (Arbeitsmaterialien zum Orient 12).

TanFarağ — Abū ʿAlī al-Muḥassan b. ʿAlī at-Tanūḫī: *Kitāb al-Faraǧ baʿd aš-šiddah*, ed. ʿAbbūd aš-Šāliǧī, 5 vols. , Beirut: Dār Ṣādir 1398/1978.

ṬarafDīwān (B) — Ṭarafah b. al-ʿAbd al-Bakrī: *Dīwān Ṭarafah b. al-ʿAbd, šarḥ al-ʾAʿlam aš-Šantamarī*, edd. D. al-Ḫaṭīb and L. aṣ-Ṣaqqāl, al-Baḥrayn: Dāʾirat aṯ-Ṯaqāfah wa-l-Funūn / Beirut: al-Muʾassasah al-ʿArabīyah [2]2000.

ṬarafDīwān (P) — Id.: *Dīwān Ṭarafah b. al-ʿAbd al-Bakrī maʿa šarḥ al-ʾadīb Yūsuf al-ʾAʿlam aš-Šantamarī*, ed. M. Seligsohn, Paris: Librairie É. Bouillon 1901.

TawḥBaṣāʾir — Abū Ḥayyān at-Tawḥīdī: *Kitāb al-Baṣāʾir wa-ḏ-ḏaḫāʾir*, ed. Wadād al-Qāḍī, 9 vols. in 8, Beirut: Dār Ṣādir [4]1419/[4]1999.

TawḥImtāʿ — Id.: *Kitāb al-ʾImtāʿ wa-l-muʾānasah*, edd. A. Amīn and A. az-Zayn, 3 vols. in 1, repr. Beirut: Dār Maktabat al-Ḥayāh n.d.

TB — Abū Bakr A. b. ʿAlī al-Ḫaṭīb al-Baġdādī: *Tārīḫ Baġdād*, 19 vols., repr. Beirut: Dār al-Kutub al-ʿIlmīyah 1405–8 / 1983–87.

TI — Šams ad-Dīn M. b. A. aḏ-Ḏahabī aš-Šāfiʿī: *Tārīḫ al-ʾislām wa-wafayāt al-mašāhir wa-l-ʾaʿlām*, ed. ʿUmar ʿAbd as-Salām Tadmurī, 38 vols., Beirut: Dār al-Kitāb al-ʿArabī 1987–99.

TiǧRiḥlah — Abū M. ʿAl. b. M. at-Tiǧānī: *Riḥlat at-Tiǧānī*, ed. Ḥasan ʿAbd al-Wahhāb, Tunis: al-Maṭbaʿah ar-Rasmīyah 1377/1958.

Tir(m)Ǧāmiʿ — Abū ʿĪsā M. b. ʿĪsā at-Tirmiḏī: *al-Ǧāmiʿ aṣ-ṣaḥīḥ*, ed. ʿAr. M. ʿUṯmān, 5 vols., Medina: al-Maktabah as-Salafīyah 1384–87 / 1964–67.

TMD — Abū l-Qāsim ʿAlī b. al-Ḥasan b. Hibat Allāh Ibn ʿAsākir: *Tārīḫ madīnat Dimašq*, edd. ʿAlī Šīrī and Muḥibb ad-Dīn Ibn Ġarāmah, 80 vols., Beirut: Dār al-Fikr 1415–19 / 1995–98.

ṬurayḥīMunt — Faḫr ad-Dīn b. M. aṭ-Ṭurayḥī an-Naǧafī: *al-Muntaḫab fī ǧamʿ al-marāṯī wa-l-ḫuṭab*, Beirut: Muʾassasat al-Aʿlamī li-l-Maṭbūʿāt n.d. (*c.*1980).

TurkLumaʿ — Idrīs b. Baydakīn (Ibn) at-Turkumānī al-Ḥanafī: *Kitāb al-Lumaʿ fī l-ḥawādiṯ wa-l-bidaʿ*, ed. Ṣubḥī Labīb, 2 vols., Cairo: Dār Iḥyāʾ al-Kutub al-ʿArabīyah 1406/1986 (Quellen zur Geschichte des islamischen Ägyptens 3 a-b).

ṬurṭSirāǧ — Abū Bakr M. b. M. b. al-Walīd aṭ-Ṭurṭūšī al-Mālikī: *(Kitāb) Sirāǧ al-mulūk*, ed. Ṭāhā Maḥmūd Quṭrīyah, Cairo 1289.

ṬūsīMabsūṭ — Abū Ǧaʿfar M. b. al-Ḥasan aṭ-Ṭūsī: *al-Mabsūṭ fī fiqh al-ʾimāmīyah*, 8 vols., edd. M. Taqīy al-Kašfī and M. al-Bāqir al-Bihbūdī, Tehran: al-Maktabah al-Murtaḍawīyah 1967–72.

ṬūsīMiṣbāḥ — Id.: *Miṣbāḥ al-mutahaǧǧid*, ed. Faḍīlah Ḥusayn al-Aʿlamī, Beirut: Muʾassasat al-Aʿlamī li-l-Maṭbūʿāt 1418/1998.

ṬūsīTahḏ — Id.: *Tahḏīb al-ʾaḥkām fī šarḥ al-Muqtaniʿah li-š-šayḫ al-Mufīd Riḍwān*, 10 vols., ed. as-Sayyid Ḥasan al-Mūsawī al-Ḫarsān, an-Naǧaf: Maṭbaʿat an-Nuʿmān 1380/1961.

UdfṬāliʿ — Abū l-Faḍl Kamāl ad-Dīn Ǧaʿfar b. Ṯaʿlab al-Udfuwī: *aṭ-Ṭāliʿ as-saʿīd al-ǧāmiʿ ʾasmāʾ nuǧabāʾ aṣ-Ṣaʿīd*, edd. Saʿd M. Ḥasan and Ṭāhā al-Ḥāǧirī, Cairo: ad-Dār al-Miṣrīyah li-t-Taʾlīf wa-t-Tarǧamah 1966.

ʿŪfīTarāǧim — Ibr. b. ʿAbī Bakr aṣ-Ṣawāliḥī al-ʿŪfī al-Ḥanbalī: *Tarāǧim aṣ-ṣawāʿiq fī wāqiʿat aṣ-ṣanāǧiq*, ed. ʿAr. ʿAbd ar-Raḥīm, Cairo: Institut français d'archéologie orientale 1986.

ʿUǧIhdāʾ — Ḥasan b. ʿAlī al-ʿUǧaymī: *ʾIhdāʾ al-laṭāʾif min ʾaḫbār aṭ-Ṭāʾif*, ed. Ya. Maḥmūd Ǧunayd Sāʿātī, aṭ-Ṭāʾif: Dār Ṯaqīf li-n-Našr wa-t-Taʾlīf ^{2}1400/ ^{2}1980.

ʿUlaymīManh — Muǧīr ad-Dīn Abū l-Yumn ʿAr. b. M. al-ʿUlaymī al-Maqdisī al-Ḥanbalī: *al-Manhaǧ al-ʾaḥmad fī tarāǧim ʾaṣḥāb al-ʾImām ʾAḥmad*, ed. Muṣṭafā ʿAbd al-Qādir A. ʿAṭā, 3 vols., Beirut: Dār al-Kutub al-ʿIlmīyah 1420/1999.

ʿUlaymīUns — Id.: *al-ʾUns al-ǧalīl bi-tārīḫ al-Quds wa-l-Ḫalīl*, 2 vols., repr. an-Naǧaf: al-Maktabah al-Ḥaydarīyah 1386/1966.

ʿUmMas — Šihāb ad-Dīn Ibn Faḍl Allāh al-ʿUmarī: *Masālik al-ʾabṣār fī mamālik al-ʾamṣār*, 27 fascicles, Frankfurt/M. 1988 (Publications of the Institute for the History of Arabic-Islamic Science, Ser. C: Facsimile editions 46).

ʿUrḍīMaʿādin — Abū l-Wafāʾ al-Ḥalabī al-ʿUrḍī: *Maʿādin aḏ-ḏahab fī l-ʾaʿyān al-mušarrafah bihim Ḥalab*, ed. M. at-Tūnǧī, Aleppo: Dār al-Maṣlaḥ 1407/1987.

WāḥAsbāb — Abū l-Ḥasan ᶜAlī b. A. al-Wāḥidī: *ʾAsbāb nuzūl al-qurʾān*, ed. Kamāl Basyūnī Zaġlūl, Beirut: Dār al-Kutub al-ᶜIlmīyah 1411/1991.

WanšMiᶜyār — Abū l-ᶜAbbās A. b. Ya. al-Wanšarīsī al-Mālikī: *al-Miʿyār al-muʿrib wa-l-ǧāmiʿ al-muġrib ʿan fatāwā ʾahl ʾIfrīqiyā wa-l-ʾAndalus wa-l-Maġrib*, edd. M. Ḥaǧǧī *et al.*, 13 vols., Beirut – Rabat: Wizārat al-Awqāf 1401/1981.

WāqMaġ — M. b. ᶜUmar al-Wāqidī: *Kitāb al-Maġāzī*, ed. M. Jones, 3 vols., Oxford – London 1966 (also repr. Beirut: Muʾassasat al-Aᶜlamī li-l-Maṭbūᶜāt ^{3}1409/^{3}1989).

Wāfī — Ṣalāḥ ad-Dīn Ḫalīl b. Aybak aṣ-Ṣafadī: *al-Wāfī bi-l-wafayāt*, numerous editors, vols. 1ff., Beirut – Wiesbaden: F. Steiner / Beirut – Berlin: Das Arabische Buch 1931ff. (Bibliotheca Islamica 6).

WāsTārīḫ — Aslam b. Sahl ar-Razzāz al-Wāsiṭī: *Tārīḫ Wāsiṭ*, ed. Kūrkīš ᶜAwwād, Beirut: ᶜĀlam al-Kutub 1406/1986.

WaṭwāṭĠurar — Abū Isḥāq Burhān ad-Dīn al-Kutubī al-Waṭwāṭ: *Ġurar al-ḫaṣāʾiṣ al-wāḍīḥah wa-ʿurar an-naqāʾiṣ al-fāḍīḥah*, repr. Beirut: Dār Ṣaᶜb n.d.

WriǦurzah — W. Wright: *Ǧurzat al-ḥāṭib wa-tuḥfat aṭ-ṭālib (Opuscula Arabica)*, Leiden: Brill 1859.

YāfNašr — Abū M. ᶜAl. b. Asᶜad al-Yāfiᶜī: *Našr al-maḥāsin al-ġāliyah fī faḍl al-mašāyiḫ aṣ-ṣūfīyah ʾaṣḥāb al-maqāmāt al-ʿāliyah*, ed. Ibr. ᶜAṭwah ᶜIwaḍ, Cairo: Muṣṭafā al-Bābī al-Ḥalabī ^{2}1410/^{2}1990.

YāfRawḍ — Id.: *Rawḍ ar-rayāḥīn fī ḥikāyāt aṣ-ṣāliḥīn*, ed. Ḫalīl ᶜImrān al-Manṣūr, Beirut: Dār al-Kutub al-ᶜIlmīyah 1421/2000.

YafrNuzhah — Abū ᶜAbd Allāh M. b. M. al-Yafranī (Yufrānī): *Nuzhat al-hādī bi-ʾaḫbār mulūk al-qarn al-ḥādī*, lithography Fās n.d.

YaᶜqTārīḫ — Aḥmad b. Abī Yaᶜqūb al-Yaᶜqūbī: *Tārīḫ al-Yaʿqūbī*, 2 vols., Beirut: Dār Ṣādir / Dār Bayrūt 1379/1960.

YāqBuldān — Yāqūt b. ᶜAl. al-Ḥamawī ar-Rūmī: *Kitāb al-Buldān*, 5 vols., repr. Beirut: Dār Ṣādir n.d.

YāqIršad — Id.: *ʾIršād al-ʾarīb ʾilā maʿrifat al-ʾadīb (al-maʿrūf bi-Muʿǧam al-ʾudabāʾ)*, ed. D. S. Margoliouth, 7 vols., Cairo: Maṭbaᶜah Hindīyah / London: Luzac ^{2}1923–31.

ZabīdīŠIḥyāʾ — M. b. M. al-Ḥusaynī az-Zabīdī, Murtaḍā: *Kitāb ʾItḥāf as-sādah al-muttaqīn bi-šarḥ ʾasrār ʾIḥyāʾ ʿulūm ad-dīn taṣnīf ḫātimat al-muḥaqqiqīn wa-ʿumdat ḏawī l-faḍāʾil min al-mudaqqiqīn*, 10 vols., Cairo 1311 (repr. Beirut: Iḥyāʾ at-Turāṯ al- ᶜArabī n.d.).

ẒāhirḤukamāʾ — Ẓāhir ad-Dīn Abū l-Ḥasan ᶜAlī b. Zayd al-Bayhaqī: *Tārīḫ ḥukamāʾ al-ʾislām*, ed. M. Kurd ᶜAlī, Damascus: Maṭbaᶜat at-Taraqqī 1365/1946 (also repr. Damascus: Dār al-Fikr 1409/1988).

ẒāhIšārāt — Ġars ad-Dīn Ḫalīl b. Šāhīn aẓ-Ẓāhirī: *al-ʾIšārāt fī ʿilm al-ʿibārāt*, ed. Sayyid Kisrawī Ḥasan, Beirut: Dār al-Kutub al-ᶜIlmīyah 1413/1993.[12]

ZamAsās — Maḥmūd b. ᶜUmar az-Zamaḫšarī: *ʾAsās al-balāġah*, Beirut: Dār Ṣādir / Dār Bayrūt 1385/1965.

ZamKaššāf — Id.: *al-Kaššāf ʿan ḥaqāʾiq ġawāmiḍ at-tanzīl*, 2 vols., Cairo: al-Maṭbaᶜah al-Bahīyah al-Miṣrīyah 1343f./1924f.

12 The text is also printed in NābTaᶜṭīr volume II (see above), but this edition has not been taken into consideration.

ZamRabī^c Id.: *Rabī^c al-ʾabrār wa-nuṣūṣ al-ʾaḫbār*, ed. Salīm an-Nu^caymī, 4 vols., Baghdad: Maṭba^cat al-^cĀnī 1375–81 / 1976–82.

ZarkAḥkām M. b. ^cAl. az-Zarkašī: *ʾI^clām as-sāǧid bi-ʾaḥkām al-masāǧid*, ed. Abū l-Wafā Muṣṭafā al-Marāġī, Cairo: al-Maǧlis al-A^clā li-š-Šuʾūn al-Islāmīyah 1384.

ZawzḤam Abū M. ^cAl. b. M. az-Zawzanī: *Ḥamāsat aẓ-ẓurafāʾ min ʾaš^cār al-muḥdaṯīn wa-l-qudamāʾ*, ed. M. Sālim, 2 vols., Beirut: Dār al-Kitāb al-Lubnānī / Cairo: Dār al-Kitāb al-Miṣrī 1420/1999.

ZawzŠMu^call al-Ḥusayn b. A. az-Zawzanī: *Šarḥ al-Mu^callaqāt as-sab^c*, Beirut: Dār al-Kutub al-^cIlmīyah 1405/1985.

ZurqŠMuw M. az-Zurqānī al-Mālikī: *Šarḥ ^calā Muwaṭṭaʾ Mālik*, 4 vols., Cairo: Maṭba^cat al-Istiqāmah 1373/1954.

2. *Secondary literature*

Abāẓah/Muṭī^c: *^cUlamāʾ Dimašq* (q. 11) = Nazār Abāẓah / M. Muṭī^c al-Ḥāfiẓ: *^cUlamāʾ Dimašq wa-ʾa^cyānuhā fī l-qarn al-ḥādī ^cašar al-hiǧrī*, 2 vols., Damascus / Beirut 2000.

—: *^cUlamāʾ Dimašq* (q. 12) = Nazār Abāẓah / M. Muṭī^c al-Ḥāfiẓ: *^cUlamāʾ Dimašq wa-ʾa^cyānuhā fī l-qarn aṯ-ṯānī ^cašar al-hiǧrī*, 3 vols., Damascus / Beirut 2000.

Abdesselem: *Thème de la mort* = M. Abdesselem: *Le thème de la mort dans la poésie arabe des origines à la fin du IIIe/IXe siècle*, Tunis 1977.

Abu Zahra: *Pure and Powerful* = N. Abu-Zahra: *The Pure and Powerful. Studies in Contemporary Muslim Society*, Reading 1997.

Abun-Nasr: *History of the Maghrib* = J. M. Abun-Nasr: *A history of the Maghrib in the Islamic period*, Cambridge 1987.

Acién Almansa/Torres Palomo: *Cementerios* = M. Acién Almansa / P. Torres Palomo (eds.): *Estudios sobre cementerios islámicos andalusíes*, Málaga 1995.

Adang: *Women's Access* = C. Adang: *Women's Access to Public Space According to* al-Muḥallā bi-l-Āthār, in: M. Marín / R. Deguilhem (eds.): *Writing the Feminine. Women in Arab Sources*, London – New York 2002, pp. 75–94.

al-^cAffānī: *Sakb* = Sayyid b. Ḥusayn al-^cAffānī: *Sakb al-^cabarāt li-l-mawt wa-l-qabr wa-s-sakarāt*, 3 vols., Banī Suwayf 1420/2000.

Āl Salmān/aš-Šuqayrāt: *Muʾallafāt as-Saḫāwī* = Abū ^cUbaydah Mašhūr Āl Salmān / Abū Ḥuḏayfah A. aš-Šuqayrāt: *Muʾallafāt as-Saḫāwī*, Beirut 1419/1998.

al-Albānī: *Aḥkām al-ǧanāʾiz* = M. Nāṣir ad-Dīn al-Albānī: *ʾAḥkām al-ǧanāʾiz wa-bida^cuhā*, Beirut – Damascus 1388/1969 (also repr. 1406/1986).

Amari: *Musulmani di Sicilia* = M. Amari: *Storia dei Musulmani di Sicilia. Seconda edizione modificata e accresciuta dall'autore*, ed. C. A. Nallino, 3 vols. in 5, Catania 1933–39 (repr. Catania 1986).

al-Amīn: *A^cyān aš-Šī^cah* = as-Sayyid al-Amīn Muḥsin al-^cĀmilī al-Ḥusaynī: *ʾA^cyān aš-Šī^cah*, 56 vols., various publishing houses in Beirut, Damascus etc., 1946–75 (partially second edition).

—: *Miftāḥ* = Id.: *Miftāḥ al-ǧannāt fī l-ʾad^ciyah wa-l-ʾa^cmāl wa-ṣ-ṣalawāt wa-z-ziyārāt*, 3 vols., Beirut n.d. (repr. *c.* 1985).

Anawati: *Mort en Islam* = G. C. Anawati: *La mort en Islam*, in: Studia missionalia 31 (1982) (= *Sens de la mort dans le Christianisme et les autres religions. Meaning of Death in Christianity and other Religions*, Rome 1982), pp. 187–210.

Andezian: *Maghreb* = S. Andezian: *Le culte des saints musulmans au Maghreb*, in: Chambert-Loir/Guillot: *Culte des saints* pp. 97–114.

al-ᶜAnqāwī: *al-Fāsī* = ᶜAl. ᶜAqīl al-ᶜAnqāwī: *al-Muʾarriḫ Taqīy ad-Dīn al-Fāsī wa-kitābuhū 'Šifāʾ al-ġarām bi-ʾaḫbār al-balad al-ḥarām'*, in: *Sources for the History of Arabia* I, 2 pp. ٦١–٦٧.

al-Anṣārī: *Nafaḥāt* = A. b. al-Ḥusayn an-Nāʾib al-Anṣārī: *Nafaḥāt an-nasrīn wa-r-rayḥān fī man kāna bi-Ṭarābulus min al-ʾaᶜyān*, ed. ᶜAlī Muṣṭafā al-Miṣrātī, Beirut 1963.

Arberry: *Omar Khayyám* = A. J. Arberry: *Omar Khayyám. A New Version Based upon Recent Discoveries*, London 1952.

—: Sîra *in Verse* = Id.: *The* Sîra *in Verse*, in: G. Makdisi (ed.): *Arabic and Islamic Studies in Honor of Hamilton A. R. Gibb*, Leiden 1965, pp. 64–72.

—: *Sufism* = Id.: *Sufism. An Account of the Mystics of Islam*, London 1950 (and repr.).

Arié: *España musulmana* = R. Arié: *España musulmana (siglos VIII–XV)*, Barcelona ²1984.

—: *Ibn al-Khaṭīb* = Id.: *Lisān al-dīn b. al-Khaṭīb: quelques aspects de son œuvre*, in: *Atti del terzo congresso di studi arabi e islamici (Ravello 1966)*, Naples 1967, pp. 69–81.

—: *Temps des Naṣrides* = Id.: *L'Espagne musulmane au temps des Naṣrides (1232–1492)*, Paris 1990.

Ariès: *Essais* = P. Ariès: *Essais sur l'histoire de la mort en Occident du Moyen Age à nos jours*, Paris 1975.

—: *Western Attitudes* = Id.: *Western Attitudes towards Death: From the Middle Ages to the Present*, tr. by P. M. Ranum, London – New York 1976.

Arkoun: *Pensée arabe* = M. Arkoun: *La pensée arabe*, Paris ⁵1996 (¹1975).

Ashtiany: *Mutanabbī's Elegy* = J. Ashtiany: *Mutanabbī's Elegy on Sayf al-Dawla's Son*, in: W. Heinrichs / G. Schoeler (eds.): *Festschrift Ewald Wagner II: Studien zur arabischen Dichtung*, Beirut 1994, pp. 362–72.

Asín Palacios: *Toponimia árabe* = M. Asín Palacios: *Contribución a la toponimia árabe de España*, Madrid ²1944 (Publicaciones de las escuelas de estudios árabes de Madrid y Granada B, 4).

al-Ašraf: *al-Qabr* = Ašraf b. ᶜAbd al-Maqṣūd b. ᶜAbd ar-Raḥīm: *al-Qabr: al-ʾasbāb allatī yuᶜaḏḏabu bihā ʾaṣḥāb al-qubūr wa-l-ʾasbāb al-munǧiyah min ᶜaḏāb al-qabr*, ed. Rabīᶜ b. Hārī ᶜUmayr al-Madḫalī, Cairo / al-ᶜIsmāᶜīlīyah 1407.

Assmann: *Ägypten* = J. Assmann: *Ägypten. Eine Sinngeschichte*, Darmstadt 1996.

—: *Der literarische Aspekt* = Id.: *Der literarische Aspekt des ägyptischen Grabes und seine Funktion im Rahmen des "Monumentalen Diskurses"*, in: A. Loprieno (ed.): *Ancient Egyptian Literature. History and Forms*, Leiden 1996, pp. 97–104.

—: *Tod als Thema* = Id.: *Der Tod als Thema der Kulturtheorie. Totenbilder und Totenriten im Alten Ägypten*, Frankfurt/M. 2000.

—: *Tod und Jenseits* = Id.: *Tod und Jenseits im Alten Ägypten*, Munich 2001.

Ayalon: *Eunuchs* = D. Ayalon: *Eunuchs, Caliphs and Sultans. A Study in Power Relationships*, Jerusalem 1999.

Ayoub: *Cult and culture* = M. Ayoub: *Cult and culture: common saints and shrines in Middle Eastern popular piety*, in: R. G. Hovannisian / G. Sabagh (eds.): *Religion and culture in Medieval Islam*, Cambridge 1999 (Giorgio Levi Della Vida Conferences XIV), pp. 103–15.

—: *Redemptive Suffering* = Id.: *Redemptive Suffering in Islām. A Study of the Devotional Aspects of ᶜĀshūrāʾ in Twelver Shīᶜism*, The Hague 1978 (Religion and Society 10).

ᶜAzzām: *Ibn ᶜAbbād* = ᶜAbd al-Wahhāb ᶜAzzām: *al-Muᶜtamid Ibn ᶜAbbād, al-malik al-ǧawād aš-šuǧāᶜ, aš-šāᶜir al-murazzaʾ*, Cairo 1959.

Bacqué-Grammont/Laquer: *Stelae Turcicae* II = J.-L. Bacqué-Grammont, H.-P. Laquer and N. Vatin: *Stelae Turcicae II. Cimetières de la mosquée de Ṣokollu Meḥmed Paşa à Kadırga Limanı, de*

Bostanci Ali et du türbe de Şokollu Meḥmed Paşa à Eyüp avec la contribution du Prof. Dr. Mustafa Cezar, Tübingen 1990 (Istanbuler Mitteilungen Beiheft 36).

Bacqué-Grammont/Tibet: *Cimetières et traditions funéraires* = J.-L. Bacqué-Grammont / A. Tibet (eds.): *Cimetières et traditions funéraires dans le monde islamique – İslam dünyasında mezarlıklar ve defin gelenekleri (Actes du colloque international, Istanbul 1991)*, 2 vols., Ankara 1996 (Türk Tarih Kurumu Yayınları XXVI, 6–6a).

Badr: *Styles of Tombs* = A. Badr: *Styles of Tombs and Mausoleums in Ottoman Cairo*, in: Bacqué-Grammont/Tibet: *Cimetières et traditions funéraires* I pp. 349–84.

Baffioni: *Filosofia islamica* = C. Baffioni: *Storia della filosofia islamica*, Milan 1991.

Bağçi: *Mavi, mor ve siyah* = S. Bağçi: *İslam toplumlarında matemi simgeleyen renkler: Mavi, mor ve siyah*, in: Bacqué-Grammont/Tibet: *Cimetières et traditions funéraires* II pp. 163–8.

Bahğat: *Ittiğāh* = Munğid M. Bahğat: *al-Ittiğāh al-ʾislāmī fī š-šiʿr al-ʾAndalusī fī ʿahday mulūk aṭ-ṭawāʾif wa-l-murābiṭīn*, Beirut 1407/1986.

Baldick: *Imaginary Muslims* = J. Baldick: *Imaginary Muslims. The Uwaysi Sufis of Central Asia*, London – New York 1993.

Bannerth: *Wallfahrtsstätten Kairos* = E. Bannerth: *Islamische Wallfahrtsstätten Kairos*, Cairo 1973 (Schriften des Österreichischen Kulturinstituts Kairo 2).

Barrucand: *L'Égypte fatimide* = M. Barrucand (ed.): *L'Égypte fatimide. Son art et son histoire (Actes du colloque organisé à Paris mai 1998)*, Paris 1999.

Basset: *Contes* III = R. Basset: *Mille et un contes, récits & légendes arabes, tome III: Légendes religieuses*, Paris 1926.

Bauden: *Ṭabariyya* = F. Bauden: *Les Ṭabariyya. Histoire d'une importante famille de la Mecque (fin XIIe à fin XVe s.)*, in: U. Vermeulen / D. De Smet (eds.): *Egypt and Syria in the Fatimid, Ayyubid and Mamluk Eras*, Leuven 1995, pp. 253–66.

Bauer: *Fremdheit* = T. Bauer: *Fremdheit in der klassischen arabischen Kultur und Sprache*, in: B. Jostes / J. Trabant (eds.): *Fremdes in fremden Sprachen*, Munich 2001, pp. 85–105.

—: *Kindertotenlieder* = Id.: *Communication and Emotion: The Case of Ibn Nubāta's* Kindertotenlieder, in: Mamlūk Studies Review VII (2003), pp. 49–95.

—: *Liebesdichtung* = Id.: *Liebe und Liebesdichtung in der arabischen Welt des 9. und 10. Jahrhunderts. Eine literatur- und mentalitätsgeschichtliche Studie des arabischen Ġazal*, Wiesbaden 1998 (Diskurse der Arabistik 2).

—: *Pflanzensystematik* = Id.: *Die Pflanzensystematik der Araber*, in: C. Wunsch (ed.): *XXI. Deutscher Orientalistentag: Vorträge*, Stuttgart 1994 (Suppl. der Zeitschrift der Deutschen Morgenländischen Gesellschaft X), pp. 108–17.

—: *Todesdiskurse* = Id.: *Todesdiskurse im Islam*, in: Asiatische Studien 53 (1999), pp. 5–16.

Behrens-Abouseif: *Cairo Heritage* = D. Behrens-Abouseif (ed.): *The Cairo Heritage. Essays in Honor of Laila Ali Ibrahim*, Cairo 2000.

—: *Islamic Architecture in Cairo* = Id.: *Islamic Architecture in Cairo. An Introduction*, Cairo 1989.

—: *Ottoman Rule* = Id.: *Egypt's Adjustment to Ottoman Rule. Institutions, Waqf and Architecture in Cairo (16th and 17th Centuries)*, Leiden 1994 (Islamic History and Civilization. Studies and Texts 7).

—: *Qubba* = Id.: *The Qubba, an aristocratic type of zāwiya*, in: Annales Islamologiques 19 (1983), pp. 1–7.

Beinhauer-Köhler: *Fāṭima* = B. Beinhauer-Köhler: *Fāṭima bint Muḥammad. Metamorphosen einer frühislamischen Frauengestalt*, Wiesbaden 2002.

Berkey: *Culture and society* = J. Berkey: *Culture and society during the late Middle Ages*, in: CHE I pp. 375–411.

Berkey: *Transmission of Knowledge* = J. Berkey: *The Transmission of Knowledge in Medieval Cairo. A Social History of Islamic Education*, Princeton 1992 (Princeton Studies on the Near East).

Betteridge: *Shrines in Shiraz* = A. H. Betteridge: *Muslim Women and Shrines in Shiraz*, in: D. Lee Bowen / E. A. Early (eds.): *Everyday Life in the Muslim Middle East*, Bloomington ²2002, pp. 276–89.

Biegman: *Egypt* = N. H. Biegman: *Egypt: Moulids, Saints, Sufis*, The Hague – London 1990.

Bierman: *Writing Signs* = I. A. Bierman.: *Writing Signs. The Fatimid Public Text*, Berkeley – London 1998.

Binski: *Medieval Death* = P. Binski: *Medieval Death. Ritual and Representation*, London 2001 (¹1996).

Biografías almohades I = *Biografías almohades I*, edd. M. Fierro and M. L. Ávila, Madrid – Granada 1999 (Estudios onomástico-biográficos de al-Andalus IX).

Blair: *Inscriptions* = Sh. S. Blair: *Islamic Inscriptions*, Edinburgh 1998.

—: *Sufi Saints and Shrine Architecture* = Id.: *Sufi Saints and Shrine Architecture in the Early Fourteenth Century*, in: Muqarnas 7 (1990), pp. 35–49.

Borst/Graevenitz: *Tod im Mittelalter* = A. Borst / G. von Graevenitz *et al.* (eds.): *Tod im Mittelalter*, Konstanz 1993 (Konstanzer Bibliothek 20).

Bosworth: *Dynasties* = C. E. Bosworth: *The New Islamic Dynasties. A chronological and genealogical manual*, Edinburgh 1996.

—: *Ṣanawbarī's Elegy* = Id.: *Ṣanawbarī's Elegy on the Pilgrims Slain in the Carmathian Attack on Mecca (317/930): A Literary-Historical Study*, in: Arabica 19 (1972), pp. 222–39.

Braet/Verbeke: *Death in the Middle Ages* = H. Braet / W. Verbeke (eds.): *Death in the Middle Ages*, Leiden 1983 (Mediaevalia Lovaniensia I, 9).

Bravmann: *Spiritual Background* = M. M. Bravmann: *The Spiritual Background of Early Islam. Studies in Ancient Arabic Concepts*, Leiden 1972.

Bresciani: *Antico Egitto* = E. Bresciani: *Letteratura e poesia dell'antico Egitto. Cultura e società attraverso i testi. Nuova edizione*, Milan 1999.

Casey: *Early Modern Spain* = J. Casey: *Early Modern Spain. A social history*, London – New York 1999.

Cervantes: *Don Quijote* = M. de Cervantes: *Don Quijote de la Mancha*, ed. Francisco Rico, 2 vols., Barcelona ³1999.

CHAL *Andalus* = *The Cambridge History of Arabic Literature: The Literature of al-Andalus*, edd. M. R. Menocal, R. P. Scheindlin and M. Sells, Cambridge 2000.

Chamberlain: *Knowledge and social practice* = M. Chamberlain: *Knowledge and social practice in medieval Damascus, 1190–1350*, Cambridge 1994 (Cambridge Studies in Islamic Civilization).

Chambert-Loir/Guillot: *Culte des saints* = H. Chambert-Loir / Cl. Guillot (eds.): *Le culte des saints dans le monde musulman*, Paris 1995 (École Française d'Extrème-Orient: Études Thématiques 4).

—: *Indonésie* = Id.: *Le culte des saints musulmans en Indonésie*, in: Chambert-Loir/Guillot: *Culte des saints* pp. 235–54.

CHE = *The Cambridge History of Egypt*, edd. M. W. Daly and Carl F. Petry, 2 vols., Cambridge 1998.

Chih: *Rawda* = R. Chih: *Zâwiya, Sâha et Rawda* (sic) *: Développement et rôle de quelques institutions soufies en Égypte*, in: Annales Islamologiques 31 (1997), pp. 49–60.

Chodkiewicz: *Sainteté et les saints* = M. Chodkiewicz: *La sainteté et les saints en islam*, in: Chambert-Loir/Guillot: *Culte des saints* pp. 13–32.

Colloque Caire = *Colloque international sur l'histoire du Caire (1969)*, Cairo 1972.

Cornell: *Abū Madyan* = V. J. Cornell: *The Way of Abū Madyan. Doctrinal and Poetic Works of Abū Madyan Shuʿayb ibn al-Ḥusayn al-Anṣārī*, Cambridge 1996.

Currie: *Muʿīn al-Dīn Chishtī* = P. M. Currie: *The Shrine and Cult of Muʿīn al-Dīn Chishtī of Ajmer*, Delhi 1989 (Oxford University South Asian Studies Series).

Daʿdūr: *Ġurbah* = Ašraf ʿAlī Daʿdūr: *al-Ġurbah fī š-šiʿr al-ʾAndalusī ʿaqb suqūṭ al-ḫilāfah*, Cairo 1966.

Daftary: *Sayyida Ḥurra* = F. Daftary: *Sayyida Ḥurra: The Ismāʿīlī Ṣulayḥid Queen of Yemen*, in: Hambly: *Women in the Islamic World* pp. 117–30.

Davidson: *Lamentations* = O. M. Davidson: *Women's Lamentations as Protest in the 'Shāhnāma'*, in: Hambly: *Women in the Islamic World* pp. 131–46.

D'Avray: *Memorial Preaching* = D. L. D'Avray: *Death and the Prince. Memorial Preaching before 1350*, Oxford 1994.

De Gaury: *Rulers of Mecca* = G. de Gaury: *Rulers of Mecca*, repr. New York 1980 ([1]1954).

De Haas: *Moisture* = W. P. de Haas: *The Semantic Spectrum of Moisture in Arabic with Some Indonesian Analogies*, 'S-Gravenhage 1954.

Dermenghem: *Culte des saints* = É. Dermenghem: *Le culte des saints dans l'Islam maghrébin*, Paris [3]1954.

Desai: *Major Dargahs* = Ziyauddin E. Desai: *The Major Dargahs of Ahmadabad*, in: Troll: *Muslim Shrines* pp. 76–97.

Dickie: *Ibn Šuhayd* = J. Dickie: *Ibn Šuhayd. A Biographical and Critical Study*, in: al-Andalus 29 (1964), pp. 243–310.

Diem: *Amtliche Briefe* = W. Diem: *Arabische amtliche Briefe des 10. bis 16. Jahrhunderts aus der Österreichischen Nationalbibliothek. Textband, Tafelband,* Wiesbaden 1996 (Documenta Arabica Antiqua 3).

—: *Arabische Briefe* = Id.: *Arabische Briefe des 7. bis 13. Jahrhunderts aus den Staatlichen Museen Berlin. Textband*, Wiesbaden 1997 (Documenta Arabica Antiqua 4).

—: *Tašrīf* = Id.: *Ehrendes Kleid und ehrendes Wort. Studien zu* Tašrīf *in mamlūkischer und vormamlūkischer Zeit*, Würzburg 2002 (Abh. f. d. Kunde d. Morgenlandes 54, 2).

Donaldson: *Shiʾite Religion* = D. M. Donaldson: *Shiʾite Religion. A History of Islam in Persia and Irak*, London 1933.

Dozy: *Historia de los Musulmanes* = R. P. Dozy: *Historia de los Musulmanes de España (hasta la conquista de Andalucía por los Almorávides)*, 4 vols., Madrid 1877 (rev. ed. Madrid 1984).

—: *Loci de Abbadidis* = Id.: *Scriptorum Arabum loci de Abbadidis nunc primum editi*, 3 vols., Leiden 1846–63 (repr. in one vol. Hildesheim 1992).

—: *Recherches* II = Id.: *Recherches sur l'histoire et la littérature de l'Espagne pendant le moyen âge II*, Leiden [2]1881.

—: *Supplément* = Id.: *Supplément aux dictionnaires arabes*, 2 vols., Leiden [2]1881.

EAL = *The Routledge Encyclopaedia of Arabic Literature*, edd. J. Scott Meisami and P. Starkey, 2 vols., London – New York 1998.

EI[2] = *Encyclopaedia of Islam (second edition)*, vols. 1ff., Leiden: 1960ff.; CD-Rom edition (Leiden 2002).

Einzmann: *Volksbrauchtum* = H. Einzmann: *Religiöses Volksbrauchtum in Afghanistan. Islamische Heiligenverehrung und Wallfahrtswesen im Raum Kabul*, Wiesbaden 1977.

—: *Ziarat und Pir-e-Muridi* = Id.: *Ziarat und Pir-e-Muridi. Golra Sharif, Nurpur Shahan und Pir Baba: Drei Muslimische Wallfahrtsstätten in Nordpakistan*, Wiesbaden 1988 (Beiträge zur Südasienforschung Heidelberg 120).

Eklund: *Death and Resurrection* = R. Eklund: *Life between death and resurrection according to Islam*, PhD thesis Uppsala 1941.

El Cheikh: *Mourning* = N. M. El Cheikh: *Mourning and the Role of the* nāʾiḥa, in: C. de la Puente (ed.): *Identidades marginales*, Madrid 2003 (Est. onom.-biogr. de al-Andalus XIII), pp. 395–412.

EQ = *Encyclopaedia of the Qurʾān. Volume One: A–D*, ed. J. Dammen McAuliffe, Leiden 2001.

Escovitz: *Office of Qāḍī* = J. H. Escovitz: *The Office of Qāḍī al-Quḍāt in Cairo under the Baḥrī Mamlūks*, Berlin 1984 (Islamkundliche Untersuchungen 100).

Esin: *Qubbah Turkiyyah* = E. Esin: *'al-Qubbah al-Turkiyyah'. An Essay on the Origins of the Architectonic Form of the Islamic Turkish Funerary Monument*, in: *Atti del terzo congresso di studi arabi e islamici (Ravello 1966)*, Naples 1967, pp. 281–313.

Falaturi: *Zwölfer-Schia* = A. Falaturi: *Die Zwölfer-Schia aus der Sicht eines Schiiten: Probleme ihrer Untersuchung*, in: Gräf: *Festschrift Caskel* pp. 62–95.

Finster: *Islamic Religious Architecture* = B. Finster: *An Outline of the History of Islamic Religious Architecture in Yemen*, in: Muqarnas 9 (1992), pp. 124–47.

Franke: *Vers-Epitaph* = W. W. Franke: *Gattungskonstanten des englischen Vers-Epitaphs von Ben Jonson zu Alexander Pope*, PhD thesis Erlangen 1964.

Frenkel: *Baybars* = Y. Frenkel: *Baybars and the Sacred Geography of* Bilād al-Shām*: A Chapter in the Islamization of Syria's Landscape*, in: Jerusalem Studies in Arabic and Islam 25 (2001), pp. 153–70.

Fück: *Arabiya* = J. Fück: *Arabiya. Untersuchungen zur arabischen Sprach- und Stilgeschichte*, Berlin 1950.

Gaborieau: *Cult of Muslim Saints* = M. A. Gaborieau: *A Nineteenth-Century Indian 'Wahhabi' Tract Against the Cult of Muslim Saints: Al-Balagh al-Mubin*, in: Troll: *Muslim Shrines* pp. 198–239.

Ǧād: *Suknā l-maqābir* = Maḥmūd M. Ǧād: *Suknā l-maqābir fī l-Qāhirah. ʾIṭlālah tārīḫīyah wa-bānūrāmā maydānīyah*, Cairo 1992.

al-Ǧalālī: *Mazārāt ahl al-bayt* = M. al-Ḥusaynī al-Ǧalālī: *Mazārāt ʾahl al-bayt wa-tārīḫuhā*, Beirut ^{3}1415/^{3}1995.

Ġarǧūr: *Taslīṭ an-nūr* = Maṭānis Ġarǧūr: *Taslīṭ an-nūr ʿalā ṣafāʾiḥ al-qubūr*, Damascus 1995.

Gaube: *Taif* = H. Gaube *et al.*: *Taif. Entwicklung, Struktur und traditionelle Architektur einer arabischen Stadt im Umbruch*, Wiesbaden 1993 (Beihefte zum TAVO B, 86).

Gayraud: *Qarāfa al-Kubrā* = R.-P. Gayraud: *Le Qarāfa al-Kubrā, dernière demeure des Fatimides*, in: Barrucand: *L'Égypte fatimide* 443–64.

al-Ġazzī: *Nahr aḏ-ḏahab* = Kāmil al-Bālī al-Ḥalabī al-Ġazzī: *Nahr aḏ-ḏahab fī tārīḫ Ḥalab*, edd. Šawqī Šaʿṯ and Maḥmūd Fāḫūrī, 3 vols., Aleppo ^{2}1412f. / ^{2}1991–93.

Geary: *Living with the Dead* = P. J. Geary: *Living with the Dead in the Middle Ages*, Ithaca – London 1994.

—: *Phantoms of Remembrance* = Id.: *Phantoms of Remembrance. Memory and Oblivion at the End of the First Millennium*, Princeton 1994.

Geist: *Grabinschriften* = H. Geist: *Römische Grabinschriften. Gesammelt und ins Deutsche übertragen (...), betreut von Gerhard Pfohl*, Munich ^{2}1976.

Geoffroy: *Proche-Orient* = E. Geoffroy: *Le culte des saints musulmans au Proche-Orient*, in: Chambert-Loir/Guillot: *Culte des saints* pp. 33–56.

—: *Le Mausolée de ʿAbd al-Qādir* = Id.: *Le mausolée de ʿAbd al-Qādir al-Ǧīlānī à Bagdad*, in: Chambert-Loir/Guillot: *Culte des saints* pp. 57–60.

Gierlichs: *Imāmzādagan* = J. Gierlichs: Imāmzādagan *in Iran: Überlegungen zur Entwicklung und Ausstattung*, in: H. Schild / S. Wild (eds.): *Akten des 27. Deutschen Orientalistentages. Norm und Abweichung*, Würzburg 2001, pp . 555–65.

Gil: *History of Palestine* = M. Gil: *A History of Palestine, 634–1099*, tr. from the Hebrew by E. Broido, Cambridge 1992.

Gilᶜadi: *Consolation Treatise* = A. Gilᶜadi: *"The child was small ... not so the grief for him": Sources, Structure, and Content of al-Sakhāwī's Consolation Treatise for Bereaved Parents*, in: Poetics Today 14 (1993), pp. 367–86.

—: *Consolation Treatises* = Id.: *Islamic Consolation Treatises for Bereaved Parents: Some Bibliographical Notes*, in: Studia Islamica 81 (1995), 197–202.

Goitein: *Jemenica* = S. D. Goitein: *Jemenica. Sprichwörter und Redensarten aus Zentral-Jemen, mit zahlreichen Sach- und Worterklärungen*, repr. Leiden 1970 ([1]1934).

—: *Mediterranean Society* = Id.: *A Mediterranean Society. The Jewish Communities of the Arab World as Portrayed in the Documents of the Cairo Geniza*, 6 vols., Berkeley – London 1967–93.

Goldziher: *Culte des ancètres* = I. Goldziher: *Le culte des ancètres et le culte des morts chez les Arabes*, in: *Gesammelte Schriften* VI pp. 157–84.

—: *Culte des saints* = Id.: *Le culte des saints chez les musulmans*, in: *Gesammelte Schriften* VI pp. 62–156.

—: *Gesammelte Schriften* = Id.: *Gesammelte Schriften*, ed. J. Desomogyi, 6 vols., Hildesheim 1967–73.

—: *Trauerpoesie* = Id.: *Bemerkungen zur arabischen Trauerpoesie*, in: Wiener Zeitschrift für die Kunde des Morgenlandes 16 (1902), pp. 307–39.

Gonnella: *Heiligenverehrung* = J. Gonnella: *Islamische Heiligenverehrung im urbanen Kontext am Beispiel von Aleppo (Syrien)*, Berlin 1995 (Islamkundliche Untersuchungen 190).

Gordon/Marshall: *Place of the Dead* = B. Gordon / P. Marshall (eds.): *The Place of the Dead. Death and Remembrance in Late Medieval and Early Modern Europe*, Cambridge 2000.

Grabar: *Commemorative Structures* = O. Grabar: *The earliest Islamic commemorative structures: Notes and documents*, in: Ars Orientalis VI (1966), pp. 7–46.

—: *Graffiti* = Id.: *Graffiti or Proclamations: Why Write on Buildings?*, in: Behrens-Abouseif: *Cairo Heritage*, pp. 69–76.

Gräf: *Auffassungen vom Tod* = E. Gräf: *Auffassungen vom Tod im Rahmen islamischer Anthropologie*, in: J. Schwartländer (ed.): *Der Mensch und sein Tod*, Göttingen 1976, pp. 126–45.

—: *Festschrift Caskel* = Id. (ed.): *Festschrift Werner Caskel*, Leiden 1968.

Gramlich: *Vorbilder* I = R. Gramlich: *Alte Vorbilder des Sufitums. Erster Teil: Scheiche des Westens*, Wiesbaden 1995 (Akad. d. Wiss. u. d. Lit. Mainz: Veröffentl. d. Oriental. Komm. 42, 1).

—: *Vorbilder* II = Id.: *Alte Vorbilder des Sufitums. Zweiter Teil: Scheiche des Ostens*, Wiesbaden 1996 (Akad. d. Wiss. u. d. Lit. Mainz: Veröffentl. d. Oriental. Komm. 42, 2).

—: *Wunder* = Id.: *Die Wunder der Freunde Gottes. Theologien und Erscheinungsformen des islamischen Heiligenwunders*, Wiesbaden 1987 (Freiburger Islamstudien XI).

Grandin: *Nord-Soudan oriental* = N. Grandin: *Le culte des saints musulmans au Nord-Soudan oriental*, in: Chambert-Loir/Guillot: *Culte des saints* pp. 81–95.

Gronke: *Derwische* = M. Gronke: *Derwische im Vorhof der Macht. Sozial- und Wirtschaftsgeschichte Nordwestirans im 13. und 14. Jahrhundert*, Stuttgart 1993 (Freiburger Islamstudien 15).

—: *Missbräuche* = Id.: *»Alles Neue ist ein Irrweg«. Zum mittelalterlichen arabischen Schrifttum über religiöse Missbräuche*, in: M. Gronke *et al.* (eds.): *Islamstudien ohne Ende. Festschrift für Werner Ende*, Würzburg 2002, pp. 127–38.

Grunebaum: *Islam im Mittelalter* = G. E. von Grunebaum: *Der Islam im Mittelalter*, Zurich – Stuttgart 1963 (Bibliothek des Morgenlandes).

—: *Muhammadan Festivals* = Id.: *Muhammadan Festivals*, London – New York 1958.

Grütter: *Bestattungsbräuche* = I. Grütter: *Arabische Bestattungsbräuche in frühislamischer Zeit (nach Ibn Saʿd und Buḫārī)*, in: Der Islam 31 (1954), pp. 147–73; 32 (1957), pp. 79–104 and pp. 168–94.

al-Ǧubūrī: *Muʿǧam* = K. Salmān al-Ǧubūrī (*sic*): *Muʿǧam aš-šuʿarāʾ fī Muʿǧam al-buldān (li-Yāqūt)*, Beirut 2002.

Güngör: *Stèles figurées* = H. Güngör: *Stèles funéraires figurées de la vallée de Zamanti, Kayseri*, in: Bacqué-Grammont/Tibet: *Cimetières et traditions funéraires* II pp. 185–7.

Haja: *Mort et Jugement Dernier* = F. Haja: *La mort et le Jugement Dernier selon les enseignements de l'Islam*, traduction par Ch. Mohamed, Paris 1991.

al-Ḫalīlī: *Mawsūʿat al-ʿatabāt* I = Ǧ. al-Ḫalīlī (ed.): *Mawsūʿat al-ʿatabāt al-muqaddasah I: Qism an-Naǧaf*, Baghdad – Beirut 1965.

Halm: *Fatimids* = H. Halm: *The Fatimids and their Traditions of Learning*, London – New York 1997 (Ismaili Heritage Series 2).

—: *Naql al-ǧanāʾiz* = Id.: *Eine schiitische Kontroverse über* naql al-ǧanāʾiz, in: Zeitschrift der Deutschen Morgenländischen Gesellschaft Suppl. IV (Wiesbaden 1980), *XX. Deutscher Orientalistentag 1977: Vorträge*, pp. 217f.

—: *Schia* = Id.: *Die Schia*, Darmstadt 1988.

Hambly: *Women in the Islamic World* = G. R. G. Hambly (ed.): *Women in the Medieval Islamic World. Power, Patronage, and Piety*, New York 1998 (The New Middle Ages 6).

Harvey: *Islamic Spain* = L. P. Harvey: *Islamic Spain, 1250 to 1500*, Chicago – London 1990.

al-Ḫašrūm: *Ġurbah* = ʿAbd ar-Razzāq al-Ḫašrūm: *al-Ġurbah fī š-šiʿr al-ǧāhilī*, Damascus 1982.

Heine: *Wein und Tod* = P. Heine: *Wein und Tod. Überlegungen zu einem Motiv der arabischen Dichtung*, in: Die Welt des Orients 13 (1982), pp. 114–26.

Hillenbrand: *Islamic Architecture* = R. Hillenbrand: *Islamic Architecture. Form, Function and Meaning*, Edinburgh 1994.

—: *Turco-Iranian Elements* = Id.: *Turco-Iranian Elements in the Medieval Architecture of Pakistan: The Case of the Tomb of Rukn-i ʿAlam at Multan*, in: Muqarnas 9 (1992), pp. 148–74.

Hoenerbach: *Islamische Geschichte Spaniens* = W. Hoenerbach: *Islamische Geschichte Spaniens. Übersetzung der Aʿmāl al-Aʿlām und ergänzender Texte*, Zurich – Stuttgart 1970; *see also above* IḪaṭAʿmāl.

Hoffmann: *Das Mausoleum Khomeinis* = B. Hoffmann: *Das Mausoleum Khomeinis in Teheran. Überlegungen zur persisch-islamischen Gedächtnisarchitektur*, in: Die Welt des Islams 39 (1999), pp. 1–30.

Homerin: *Death and Afterlife* = Th. E. Homerin: *Echoes of a Thirsty Owl: Death and Afterlife in Pre-Islamic Arabic Poetry*, in: Journal of Near Eastern Studies 44 (1985), pp. 165–84.

—: *Domed Shrine* = Id.: *The Domed Shrine of Ibn al-Fāriḍ*, in: Annales Islamologiques 25 (1991), pp. 133–8.

—: *Ibn al-Fāriḍ* = Id.: *From Arab Poet to Muslim Saint. Ibn al-Fāriḍ, his Verse, and his Shrine*, Columbia 1994 (Studies in Comparative Religion).

Horten: *Gedankenwelt* = M. Horten: *Die religiöse Gedankenwelt des Volkes im heutigen Islam*, Halle 1917f.

Houlbrooke: *Death in England* = R. Houlbrooke: *Death, Religion and the Family in England, 1480–1750*, Oxford 1998.

Hoyland: *Arabia* = R. Hoyland: *Arabia and the Arabs: From the Bronze Age to the Coming of Islam*, London 2001.

Ḥusayn: *al-Adab al-ʿarabī* = Ṭāhā Ḥusayn: *Min tārīḫ al-ʾadab al-ʿarabī*, 2 vols., Beirut 1971.

—: *Burdah* = Ḥasan Ḥusayn: *Ṯulāṯīyat al-Burdah*, Cairo 1987.

—: *Subkī* = M. Ṣādiq Ḥusayn: *al-Bayt as-Subkī: Bayt ʿilmin fī dawlatay al-mamālīk*, Cairo 1948.

Ibn Zaydān: *Itḥāf* = ʿAr. b. M. Ibn Zaydān al-Ḥasanī: *ʾItḥāf ʾiʿlām an-nās bi-ǧamāl ʾaḫbār ḥāḍirat Miknās (aw ʿAbīr al-ʾās min rawḍat tārīḫ Miknās, ʾaw Ḥusn al-Iqtibās min mufāḫarat ad-dawlah al-ʿAlawīyah wa-tārīḫ Miknās)*, 4 vols. (incomplete), Rabat 1347–50.

Illi: *Begräbnis und Kirchhof* = M. Illi: *Wohin die Toten gingen. Begräbnis und Kirchhof in der vorindustriellen Stadt*, Zurich 1992.

Insoll: *Archaeology of Islam* = T. Insoll: *The Archaeology of Islam*, Oxford 1999.

Irwin: *Mamluk Sultanate* = R. Irwin: *The Middle East in the middle ages. The Early Mamluk Sultanate 1250–1382*, Carbondale 1986.

Ivanow: *Ismaili Literature* = W. Ivanow: *Ismaili Literature. A Bibliographical Survey*, Tehran 1963.

Jackson: *Tomb of Bābā Ṭāhir* = A. V. Williams Jackson: *A Visit to the Tomb of Bābā Ṭāhir at Hamadān*, in: T. W. Arnold / R. A. Nicholson (eds.): *A Volume of Oriental Studies Presented to Edward G. Browne*, Cambridge 1922, pp. 257–60.

Jackson: *Two-Tiered Orthodoxy* = S. A. Jackson: *In Defense of Two-Tiered Orthodoxy: a Study of Shihāb al-Dīn al-Qarāfī's* Kitāb al-Iḥkām fī Tamyīz al-Fatāwā, PhD thesis Univ. of Pennsylvania 1991.

Jacobi: *Camel-Section* = R. Jacobi: *The Camel-Section of the Panegyrical Ode*, in: The Journal of Arabic Literature 13 (1982), pp. 1–22.

Jafri: *Origins and Early Development* = S. H. M. Jafri: *Origins and Early Development of Shiʿa Islam*, London – New York 1979 (Arab Background Series).

Jarrar: *Al-Maqrizi's Reinvention* = S. Jarrar: *Al-Maqrizi's Reinvention of Egyptian Historiography through Architectural History*, in: Behrens-Abouseif: *Cairo Heritage* pp. 31–53.

Jastrow: *Three Anecdotes* = O. Jastrow: *Three Anecdotes in Jewish Maslawi*, in: J. Rosenhouse / A. Elad-Bouskila (eds.): *Linguistic and Cultural Studies on Arabic and Hebrew. Essays Presented to Professor Moshe Piamenta for his Eightieth Birthday*, Wiesbaden 2001, pp. 61–70.

Jayyusi: *Muslim Spain* = S. Kh. Jayyusi (ed.): *The Legacy of Muslim Spain*, 2 vols., Leiden 1992.

Jong: *Cairene Ziyâra-Days* = F. de Jong: *Cairene* Ziyâra-*Days. A Contribution to the Study of Saint Veneration in Islam*, in: Die Welt des Islams 17 (1976–77), pp. 26–43.

Jonker: *Topography of Remembrance* = G. Jonker: *The Topography of Remembrance. The Dead, Tradition and Collective Memory in Mesopotamia*, Leiden 1995 (Studies in the History of Religions LXVIII).

Jupp/Howarth: *Changing Face of Death* = P. C. Jupp / G. Howarth (eds.): *The Changing Face of Death. Historical Accounts of Death and Disposal*, Basingstoke – London 1997.

Kabbani: *Heiligenverehrung* = M. Kabbani: *Die Heiligenverehrung im Urteil Ibn Taimiyas und seiner Zeitgenossen*, PhD thesis Bonn 1979.

Karaman: *Ölüm* = H. Karaman: *Ölüm, ölü, defin ve merasimler*, in: Bacqué-Grammont/Tibet: *Cimetières et traditions funéraires* I pp. 3–15.

al-Kattānī: *Fahras* = ʿAbd al-Ḥayy b. ʿAbd al-Kabīr al-Kattānī: *Fahras al-fahāris wa-l-ʾaṯbāt*, ed. Iḥsān ʿAbbās, 3 vols., Beirut ^{2}1402/^{2}1982.

Katz: *Dreams and Sainthood* = J. G. Katz: *Dreams, Sufism and Sainthood. The Visionary Career of Muhammad al-Zawâwî*, Leiden 1996 (Studies in the History of Religions 71).

Kemp: *Ancient Egypt* = B. J. Kemp: *Ancient Egypt. Anatomy of a Civilization*, London – New York 1989 (repr. 1991).

Kennedy: *Historiography* = H. Kennedy (ed.): *The Historiography of Islamic Egypt (c.950–1800)*, Leiden 2001 (The Medieval Mediterranean 31).

—: *Muslim Spain* = Id.: *Muslim Spain and Portugal. A Political History of al-Andalus*, London – New York 1996.

Kennedy: *Wine Song* = Ph. F. Kennedy: *The Wine Song in Classical Arabic Poetry. Abū Nuwās and the Literary Tradition*, Oxford 1997 (Oxford Oriental Monographs).

Kervran: *Cimetières islamiques* = M. Kervran: *Cimetières islamiques de Bahrain (Ier–Xe siècles de l'Hégire / VIIe ou VIIIe–XVIe siècles de l'ère chrétienne)*, in: Bacqué-Grammont/Tibet: *Cimetières et traditions funéraires* I pp. 57–78.

Kessler: *Funerary Architecture* = C. Kessler: *Funerary Architecture within the City*, in: *Colloque Caire* pp. 257–67.

Khalis: *Vie litteraire* = Salah Khalis (Ṣalāḥ Ḫāliṣ): *La vie litteraire à Seville au XIe siècle*, Algiers 1966.

Khawam: *Poésie arabe* = *La poésie arabe des origines à nos jours. Anthologie établie, traduite et présentée par René R. Khawam*, Paris 1995.

Kilito: *Letter* = A. Kilito: *A Letter from Beyond the Grave*, in: Id.: *The Author and His Doubles. Essays on Classical Arabic Culture. Translated by M. Cooperson, with a Foreword by R. Allen*, Syracuse 2001, pp. 78–90.

al-Kinānī: *Takmīl* = M. b. Ṣāliḥ al-Kinānī al-Qayrawānī: *Takmīl aṣ-ṣulaḥāʾ wa-l-ʾaʿyān li-Maʿālim al-ʾaymān fī ʾawliyāʾ al-Qayrawān*, ed. M. al-ʿInābī, Tunis 1970.

Kinberg: *Interaction* = L. Kinberg: *Interaction between this World and the Afterworld in Early Islamic Tradition*, in: Oriens 29–30 (1986), pp. 285–308.

Kippax: *Churchyard Literature* = J. R. Kippax: *Churchyard Literature: A Choice Collection of American Epitaphs, with Remarks on Monumental Inscriptions and the Obsequies of Various Nations*, Chicago 1877 (repr. Detroit 1969).

Kister: *Three Mosques* = M. J. Kister: *«You Shall only Set Out for Three Mosques». A Study of an Early Tradition*, in: Id.: *Studies in Jāhiliyya and Early Islam*, London 1980, ch. XIII.

KM = ʿUmar Riḍā Kaḥḥālah: *Muʿǧam al-muʾallifīn. Tarāǧim muṣannifī l-kutub al-ʿarabīyah*, 15 vols. in 8, Damascus 1376–81 / 1957–61.

Knysh: *Ibn ʿArabi* = A. D. Knysh: *Ibn ʿArabi in the Later Islamic Tradition. The Making of a Polemical Image in Medieval Islam*, Albany 1999.

—: *Mysticism* = Id.: *Islamic Mysticism. A Short Introduction*, Leiden 2000.

Krawietz: *Ḥurma* = B. Krawietz: *Die Ḥurma. Schariatrechtlicher Schutz vor Eingriffen in die körperliche Unversehrtheit nach arabischen Fatwas des 20. Jahrhunderts*, Berlin 1991 (Schriften zur Rechtstheorie 145).

Kriss: *Volksglaube* I = R. Kriss / H. Kriss-Heinrich: *Volksglaube im Bereich des Islam, Band I: Wallfahrtswesen und Heiligenverehrung*, Wiesbaden 1960.

Labes: *Mémoire des tombes* = B. Labes: *La mémoire des tombes. Les épitaphes en France*, Paris 1996.

Lane = E. W. Lane: *An Arabic-English Lexicon*, 8 parts, London 1863–93 (repr. Cambridge 1984).

—: *Manners and Customs* = Id.: *An Account of the Manners and Customs of the Modern Egyptians*, Cairo – London 1895 (repr. 1989).

Langner: *Historische Volkskunde* = B. Langner: *Untersuchungen zur historischen Volkskunde Ägyptens nach mamlukischen Quellen*, Berlin 1983 (Islamkundliche Untersuchungen 74).

Laoust: *Schismes* = H. Laoust: *Les schismes dans l'Islam. Introduction à une étude de la religion musulmane*, Paris 1965 (Bibliothèque historique).

Lapidus: *Ayyūbid Religious Policy* = I. M. Lapidus: *Ayyūbid Religious Policy and the Development of the Schools of Law in Cairo*, in: *Colloque Caire* pp. 279–86.

Laqueur: *Cemeteries in Orient and Occident* = H.-P. Laqueur: *Cemeteries in Orient and Occident. The Historical Development*, in: Bacqué-Grammont/Tibet: *Cimetières et traditions funéraires* II pp. 3–7.

Laquer: *Friedhöfe Istanbul* = H.-P. Laqueur: *Osmanische Friedhöfe und Grabsteine in Istanbul*, Tübingen 1993 (Istanbuler Mitteilungen Beiheft 38).

Lassner: *Topography of Baghdad* = J. Lassner: *The Topography of Baghdad in the Early Middle Ages. Text and Studies*, Detroit 1970.

al-Lawāsānī: *Kaškūl* = Ḥasan b. M. al-Ḥusaynī al-Lawāsānī an-Nağafī: *Kaškūl laṭīf wa-ta'līf ẓarīf*, Tehran 1388/1968.

Lawrence: *Medieval Monasticism* = C. H. Lawrence: *Medieval Monasticism. Forms of Religious Life in Western Europe in the Middle Ages. Third Edition*, London – New York 2001.

Lecker: *Burial of Martyrs* = M. Lecker: *On the Burial of Martyrs in Islam*, in: Yanagihashi Hiroyuki (ed.): *The Concept of Territory in Islamic Law and Thought*, London – New York 2000, pp. 37–49.

Le Goff: *Naissance du Purgatoire* = J. Le Goff: *La naissance du Purgatoire*, Paris 1981 (repr. 1998).

Leisten: *Architektur für Tote* = T. Leisten: *Architektur für Tote. Bestattung in architektonischem Kontext in den Kernländern der islamischen Welt zwischen 3./9. und 6./12. Jahrhundert* (sic), Berlin 1998 (Materialien zur iranischen Archäologie 4).

—: *Attitudes* = Id.: *Between Orthodoxy and Exegesis: Some Aspects of Attitudes in the Shariʿa towards Funerary Architecture*, in: Muqarnas 7 (1990), pp. 12–22.

—: *Funerary Structures* = Id.: *Dynastic Tomb or Private Mausolea: Observations on the Concept of Funerary Structures of the Fāṭimid and ʿAbbāsid Caliphs*, in: Barrucand: *L'Égypte fatimide* pp. 465–79.

Lemaitre: *Mémoire des morts* = J.-L. Lemaitre (ed.): *L'Église et la mémoire des morts dans la France médiévale*, Paris 1986.

Lev: *Saladin* = Y. Lev: *Saladin in Egypt*, Leiden 1999 (The Medieval Mediterranean 21).

Lévi-Provençal: *Espagne musulmane* = É. Lévi-Provençal: *L'Espagne musulmane au Xe siècle*, Paris 1932 (repr. 2002).

Little: *Detention of Ibn Taymiyya* = D. P. Little: *The Historical and Historiographical Significance of the Detention of Ibn Taymiyya*, in: Id.: *History and Historiography of the Mamlūks*, London 1986, ch. VII.

—: *Mamluk Madrasahs* = Id.: *Notes on Mamluk Madrasahs*, in: Mamlūk Studies Review 6 (2002), pp. 9–20.

—: *Religion under the Mamluks* = Id.: *Religion under the Mamluks*, in: Id.: *History and Historiography of the Mamlūks*, London 1986, ch. X (first published in: The Muslim World 73, 1983, pp. 165–81).

Mabrūk: *Bidaʿ* = M. Ismāʿīl Mabrūk: *Bidaʿ wa-munkarāt ʿinda l-qubūr*, Cairo 1996.

MacKenzie: *Ayyubid Cairo* = N. D. MacKenzie: *Ayyubid Cairo. A Topographical Study*, Cairo 1992.

Madelung: *Succession* = W. Madelung: *The succession to Muḥammad. A study of the early Caliphate*, Cambridge 1977.

Mahdawī: *Taḏkirah* = S. Muṣliḥ ad-Dīn Mahdawī: *Taḏkirat al-qubūr yā Dānišmandān u buzurgān-i Iṣfahān*, Iṣfahān 1348š.

Mahjoub: *Pérennité des structures* = N. Mahjoub: *Pérennité des structures architecturales de l'espace sépulcral – espace-sacré*, in: Bacqué-Grammont/Tibet: *Cimetières et traditions funéraires* II pp. 151–61.

Makki: *History of al-Andalus* = M. Makki: *The Political History of al-Andalus (92/711–897/1492)*, in: Jayyusi: *Muslim Spain* I pp. 3–87.

al-Makkī: *Madā'iḥ* = M. ʿAlī (al-)Makkī: *al-Madā'iḥ an-nabawīyah*, Cairo – al-Ğīzah 1991.

Marcus: *Funerary and Burial Practices* = A. Marcus: *Funerary and Burial Practices in Syria, 1700–1920*, in: Bacqué-Grammont/Tibet: *Cimetières et traditions funéraires* II pp. 97–104.

al-Marrākušī: *Iʿlām* = ʿAbbās b. Ibr. al-Marrākušī: *al-ʾIʿlām bi-man ḥalla Marrākuš wa-ʾAġmāt min al-ʾaʿlām*, vols. I–V, Fās 1355–57 / 1936–38; vol. X, ed. ʿAbd al-Wahhāb Ibn Manṣūr, Rabat 1403/1983.

Marzolph: *Buhlūl* = U. Marzolph: *Der weise Narr Buhlūl*, Wiesbaden 1983 (Abhandlungen für die Kunde des Morgenlandes XLVI, 4).

Massignon: *Cité des morts* = L. Massignon: *La cité des morts au Caire (Qarāfa – Darb al-Aḥmar)*, in: *Opera* III pp. 233–85.

—: *Opera* III = Id.: *Opera Minora* III, ed. Y. Moubarac, Beirut 1963 (Recherches et Documents).

—: *Rawda* = Id.: *La Rawda de Médine: Cadre de la meditation musulmane sur la destine du Prophète*, in: *Opera* III pp. 286–315.

—: *Saints musulmans* = Id.: *Les saints musulmans enterrés à Bagdad*, in: *Opera* III pp. 94–101.

Masud: *Definition of Bidʿa* = M. Kh. Masud: *The definition of Bidʿa in the South Asian Fatāwā literature*, in: Annales Islamologiques 27 (1993), pp. 55–75.

Matringe: *Pakistan* = D. Matringe: *Le culte des saints musulmans au Pakistan*, in: Chambert-Loir/Guillot: *Culte des saints* pp. 167–91.

Mayeur-Jaouen: *Égypte* = C. Mayeur-Jaouen: *Le culte des saints musulmans en Égypte*, in: Chambert-Loir/Guillot: *Culte des saints* pp. 61–73.

Mayeur[-Jaouen]: *Intercession* = Id.: *L'intercession des saints en Islam égyptien: Autour de Sayyid al-Badawī*, in: Annales Islamologiques 25 (1991), pp. 363–88.

McManamon: *Funeral Oratory* = J. M. McManamon: *Funeral Oratory and the Cultural Ideals of Italian Humanism*, Chapel Hill – London 1989.

Memon: *Ibn Taimīya's Struggle* = M. Umar Memon: *Ibn Taimīya's Struggle against Popular Religion. With an Annotated Translation of his Kitāb iqtiḍāʾ aṣ-ṣirāṭ al-mustaqīm mukhālafat aṣḥāb al-jaḥīm*, The Hague 1976 (Religion and Society 1).

Merklinger: *Tombs at Holkonda* = E. I. Merklinger: *Seven Tombs at Holkonda: A Preliminary Survey*, in: Kunst des Orients 10 (1975), pp. 187–97.

MF = *al-Mawsūʿah al-fiqhīyah*, vols. 1ff., Kuwayt: Wizārat al-Awqāf wa-š-Šuʾūn al-Islāmīyah 1414 ff./1993ff.

Millward: *al-Fāsī's Sources* = W. G. Millward: *Taqī al-Dīn al-Fāsī's Sources for the History of Mecca from the Fourth to the Ninth Centuries A. H.*, in: *Sources for the History of Arabia* I, 2 pp. 37–49.

Milstein: *Kitāb Shawq-Nāma* = R. Milstein: *Kitāb Shawq-Nāma – An Illustrated Tour of Holy Arabia*, in: Jerusalem Studies in Arabic and Islam 25 (2001), pp. 275–345.

Moazz: *Cimetières Damas* = A. Moazz: *Cimetières et mausolées à Damas du XIIe au début du XVIe siècle. Le cas du quartier de Suwayqat Ṣārūjā*, in: Bacqué-Grammont/Tibet: *Cimetières et traditions funéraires* I pp. 79–98.

Moini: *Rituals and Customary Practices* = S. Liyaqat Hussain Moini: *Rituals and Customary Practices at the Dargah of Ajmer*, in: Troll: *Muslim Shrines* pp. 60–75.

Mokri: *Pleureuses professionelles* = M. Mokri: *Pleureuses professionnelles et lamentations funéraires en Iran occidental. La mort de Chîrîn*, in: Bacqué-Grammont/Tibet: *Cimetières et traditions funéraires* II pp. 73–96.

Morris: *Burial and ancient society* = I. Morris: *Burial and ancient society. The rise of the Greek city-state*, Cambridge 1987.

Mortensen: *Cemeteries Luristan* = I. Demant Mortensen: *Nomadic Cemeteries and Tombstones from Luristan, Iran*, in: Bacqué-Grammont/Tibet: *Cimetières et traditions funéraires* II pp. 175–83.

Motzki: *Biography of Muḥammad* = H. Motzki (ed.): *The Biography of Muḥammad. The Issue of the Sources*, Leiden 2000 (Islamic History and Civilization. Studies and Texts 32).

al-Muᶜallimī: *ᶜImārat al-qubūr* = ᶜAr. b. Ya. al-Muᶜallimī al-Makkī: *ᶜImārat al-qubūr*, ed. Māǧid ᶜAbd al-ᶜAzīz az-Ziyādī, Mecca 1418/1998 (Silsilat Rasāʾil al-Muᶜallimī 7–9).

Mubārak: *Ḫiṭaṭ* = ᶜAlī Pasha Mubārak: *al-Ḫiṭaṭ at-tawfīqīyah al-ǧadīdah li-Miṣr al-Qāhirah wa-mudunihā al-qadīmah wa-š-šahīrah*, 20 parts in 4 vols., Būlāq 1304–06 / 1886–89.

al-Munayyar: *Tasliyah* = M. al-Munayyar: *Tasliyat al-muṣāb ᶜinda faqd al-ʾaḥbāb*, Cairo 1988.

Nagel: *Heilszusage* = T. Nagel: *Im Offenkundigen das Verborgene. Die Heilszusage des sunnitischen Islams*, Göttingen 2002.

Nakash: *Shiᶜis of Iraq* = Y. Nakash: *The Shiᶜis of Iraq. With a New Introduction by the Author*, Princeton – Oxford 2003.

—: *Visitation of the Shrines* = Id.: *The Visitation of the Shrines of the Imams and the Shiᶜi Mujtahids in the Early Twentieth Century*, in: Studia Islamica 81 (1995), pp. 153–64.

an-Nāṣirī: *al-Istiqṣā* = Abū l-ᶜAbbās A. b. Ḫālid an-Nāṣirī as-Salāwī: *Kitāb al-Istiqṣā li-ʾaḫbār duwal al-maġrib al-ʾaqṣā*, vols. I–IV, edd. Ǧaᶜfar and M. an-Nāṣirī, Casablanca 1954f.

Nedoroscik: *City of the Dead* = J. A. Nedoroscik: *The City of the Dead. A History of Cairo's Cemetery Communities*, Westport – London 1997.

Nicholson: *Studies* = R. A. Nicholson: *Studies in Islamic Poetry*, Cambridge 1921.

Niebuhr: *Reisebeschreibung* = C. Niebuhr: *Reisebeschreibung nach Arabien und andern umliegenden Ländern. Mit einem Vorwort von Stig Rasmussen und einem biographischen Porträt von Barthold Georg Niebuhr*, Zurich 1997 (Abridged from the three-volume edition of the same title published between 1774 and 1837).

Northrup: *Mamlūk sultanate* = L. S. Northrup: *The Baḥrī Mamlūk sultanate, 1250–1390*, in: CHE I pp. 242–89.

al-Nowaihi: *Ibn Khafājah* = M. M. al-Nowaihi: *The Poetry of Ibn Khafājah. A Literary Analysis*, Leiden – New York 1993 (Studies in Arabic Literature 16).

Nykl: *Hispano-Arabic Poetry* = A. R. Nykl: *Hispano-Arabic Poetry and its Relations with the Old Provençal Troubadours*, Baltimore 1946.

Ohler: *Sterben und Tod im Mittelalter* = N. Ohler: *Sterben und Tod im Mittelalter*, Munich 1990.

Olesen: *Culte des saints* = N. H. Olesen: *Culte des saints et pèlerinages chez Ibn Taymiyya (661/1263–728/1328)*, Paris 1991 (Bibliothèque d'Études Islamiques 16).

Padwick: *Muslim Devotions* = C. E. Padwick: *Muslim Devotions. A Study of Prayer-Manuals in Common Use*, Oxford 1961 (repr. 1997).

Parkinson: *Voices from Ancient Egypt* = R. B. Parkinson: *Voices from Ancient Egypt. An Anthology of Middle Kingdom Writings*, London – Norman 1991 (Oklahoma Series in Classical Culture 9).

Penelas/Zanón: *Nómina de ulemas andalusíes* = M. Penelas / J. Zanón: *Nómina de ulemas andalusíes de época almohade*, in: *Biografías almohades* I pp. 11–222.

Peral Bejarano: *Excavación y estudio* = C. Peral Bejarano: *Excavación y estudio de los cementerios urbanos andalusíes. Estado de la cuestión*, in: Acién Almansa/Torres Palomo: *Cementerios islámicos* pp. 11–36.

Peters: *Mecca* = F. E. Peters: *Mecca. A Literary History of the Muslim Holy Land*, Princeton 1994.

Petrucci: *Writing the Dead* = A. Petrucci: *Writing the Dead. Death and Writing Strategies in the Western Tradition*, tr. by M. Sullivan, Stanford 1998 (= *Le scritture ultime: Ideologia della morte e strategie dello scrivere nella tradizione occidentale*, Turin 1995).

Pinault: *Zaynab bt. ᶜAlī* = D. Pinault: *Zaynab bt. ᶜAlī and the Place of the Women of the Households of the First Imāms in Shīᶜite Devotional Literature*, in: Hambly: *Women in the Islamic World* pp. 69–98.

Prinz: *Epitaphios Logos* = K. Prinz: *Epitaphios Logos. Struktur, Funktion und Bedeutung der Bestattungsreden im Athen des 5. und 4. Jahrhunderts*, Frankfurt/M. 1997 (Europäische Hochschulschriften III, 747).

al-Qināwī: *Fatḥ ar-raḥīm* = aš-Šarīf Masʿūd b. Ḥasan al-Qināwī: *Fatḥ ar-raḥīm ar-raḥmān fī šarḥ Naṣīḥat al-ʾiḫwān wa-muršidat al-ḫullān (li-bn al-Wardī)*, Cairo 1390/1970.

Qummī: *Mafātīḥ al-ǧinān* = ʿAbbās Qummī: *Kullīyāt (Mafātīḥ al-ǧinān)*, Tehran 1345š/1967.

Rabbat: *Architecture in Mamluk Sources* = N. Rabbat: *Perception of Architecture in Mamluk Sources*, in: Mamlūk Studies Review VI (2002), pp. 155–76.

Rāġib: *Deux monuments* = Y. Rāġib: *Sur deux monuments funéraires du cimetière d'al-Qarāfa al-Kubrā au Caire*, in: Annales Islamologiques 12 (1974), pp. 67–83.

—: *Faux morts* = Id.: *Faux morts*, in: Studia Islamica 57 (1983), pp. 5–30 (in Turkish translation also in Bacqué-Grammont/Tibet: *Cimetières et traditions funéraires* II pp. 59–71).

—: *Inventaire* = Id.: *Essai d'inventaire chronologique des guides à l'usage des pèlerins du Caire*, in: Revue des Études Islamiques 41 (1973), pp. 259–80.

—: *Mausolées Fatimides* = Id.: *Les mausolées fatimides du Quartier d'al-Mašāhid*, in: Annales Islamologiques 17 (1981), pp. 1–30.

—: *Premiers monuments* = Id.: *Les premiers monuments funéraires de l'Islam*, in: Annales Islamologiques 9 (1970), pp. 21–36.

—: *Sanctuaires* = Id.: *Les sanctuaires des Gens de la Famille dans la cité des morts au Caire*, in: Rivista di Studi Orientali 51 (1977), pp. 47–76.

—: *Structure de la tombe* = Id.: *Structure de la tombe d'après le droit musulman*, in: Arabica 39 (1992), pp. 393–403 (in Turkish translation also in Bacqué-Grammont/Tibet: *Cimetières et traditions funéraires* I pp. 17–23).

ar-Rašīd: *Banū Fahd* = Nāṣir b. Saʿd ar-Rašīd: *Banū Fahd: Muʾarriḫū Makkah al-Mukarramah wa-t-taʿrīf bi-maḫṭūṭ an-Naǧm Ibn Fahd 'ʾItḥāf al-warā bi-ʾaḫbār ʾUmm al-Qurā'*, in: *Sources for the History of Arabia* I, 2 pp. ٩٠–١٦٩.

Reinink/Vanstiphout: *Dispute Poems* = G. J. Reinink / H. L. Vanstiphout (eds.): *Dispute Poems and Dialogues in the Ancient and Mediaeval Near East. Forms and Types of Literary Debates in Semitic and Related Literatures*, Leuven 1991.

Reintjens-Anwari: *Tod aus islamischer Sicht* = H. Reintjens-Anwari: *Der Tod aus islamischer Sicht*, in: C. von Barloewen (ed.): *Der Tod in den Weltkulturen und Weltreligionen*, Munich 1996, pp. 169–200.

Rescher: *Gesammelte Werke* = O. Rescher: *Gesammelte Werke in fünf Abteilungen*, Osnabrück 1983.

Reynolds/Waugh: *Encounters with Death* = F. E. Reynolds / E. H. Waugh (eds.): *Religious Encounters with Death. Insights from the History and Anthropology of Religions*, University Park – London 1977.

Rhodokanakis: *Trauerlieder* = N. Rhodokanakis: *al-Ḫansāʾ und ihre Trauerlieder. Ein literarhistorischer Essay mit textkritischen Exkursen*, Vienna 1904 (Sitzungsber. d. kgl. Akad. d. Wiss., phil.-hist. Kl. 147, 4).

Richard: *Iran* = Y. Richard: *Le culte des saints musulmans en Iran*, in: Chambert-Loir/Guillot: *Culte des saints* pp. 147–57.

—: *Shiʾite Islam* = Id.: *Shiʾite Islam. Polity, Ideology, and Creed*, translated by A. Nevill, Oxford – Cambridge (Mass.) 1995.

Rippin: *Muslims* I = A. Rippin: *Muslims. Their Religious Beliefs and Practices, Volume I: The Formative Period*, London – New York 1990.

Rosenthal: *Historiography* = F. Rosenthal: *A History of Muslim Historiography*, Leiden ²1968.

Rosenthal: *Knowledge Triumphant* = F. Rosenthal: *Knowledge Triumphant. The Concept of Knowledge in Medieval Islam*, Leiden 1970.

—: *Stranger* = Id.: *The Stranger in Medieval Islam*, in: Arabica 44 (1997), pp. 35–75.

Rosiny: *Pakistan* = T. Rosiny: *Pakistan. Drei Hochkulturen am Indus: Harappa – Gandhara – Die Moguln*, Köln [4]1990 (DuMont Kunst-Reiseführer).

Rubin: *Seven Mathānī* = U. Rubin: *Exegesis and Ḥadīth: The case of the seven Mathānī*, in: G. R. Hawting / A. A. Shareef (eds.): *Approaches to the Qur'ān*, London – New York 1993, pp. 141–56.

Rypka: *Iranian Literature* = J. Rypka: *History of Iranian Literature*, ed. K. Jahn, Dordrecht 1968.

Saǧǧādī: *Surḫāb* = Sayyid Ḍiyāʾ ad-Dīn Saǧǧādī: *Kū-yi Surḫāb-i Tabrīz wa-maqbarat aš-šuʿarāʾ*, Tehran 1375š ([1]1356š/[1]1397 H).

Salibi: *Banū Jamāʿa* = K. S. Salibi: *The Banū Jamāʿa. A Dynasty of Shāfiʿite Jurists in the Mamluk Period*, in: Studia Islamica 9 (1958), pp. 97–109 (and genealogical tables).

Sayyid: *Genre de Khiṭaṭ* = A. F. Sayyid: *L'évolution de la composition du genre de Khiṭaṭ en Égypte musulmane*, in: Kennedy: *Historiography* pp. 77–92.

—: *Maṣādir tārīḫ al-Yaman* = Id.: *Maṣādir tārīḫ al-Yaman fī l-ʿaṣr al-ʾislāmī*, Cairo 1974.

—: *al-Qāhira et al-Fusṭāṭ* = Id.: *La capitale de l'Égypte jusqu'à l'époque fatimide al-Qāhira et al-Fusṭāṭ. Essai de reconstruction topographique*, Beirut 1998 (Beiruter Texte und Studien 48).

Schacht: *Revaluation* = J. Schacht: *A Revaluation of Islamic Tradition*, in: Journal of the Royal Asiatic Society 3–4 (1949), pp. 143–54.

Schack: *Poesie und Kunst* I = A. Freiherr von Schack: *Poesie und Kunst der Araber in Spanien und Sizilien. Erster Band*, Berlin 1865 (repr. Hildesheim 1979).

Schimmel: *Ausdrucksformen* = A. Schimmel: *Künstlerische Ausdrucksformen des Islams*, in: A Schimmel *et al.* (eds.): *Der Islam III: Islamische Kultur – Zeitgenössische Strömungen – Volksfrömmigkeit*, Stuttgart 1990 (Religionen der Menschheit 25, 3), pp. 267–99.

—: *Messenger* = Id.: *And Muhammad is His Messenger. The Veneration of the Prophet in Islamic Piety*, Chapel Hill – London 1985.

—: *Sufismus* = Id.: *Sufismus und Heiligenverehrung im spätmittelalterlichen Ägypten*, in: Gräf: *Festschrift Caskel* pp. 274–89.

—: *Träume* = Id.: *Die Träume des Kalifen. Träume und ihre Deutung in der islamischen Kultur*, Munich 1998.

Schober: *Heiligtum ʿAlīs* = I. Schober: *Das Heiligtum ʿAlī b. Abī Ṭālibs in Naǧaf. Grabstätte und Wallfahrt*, Bern – Frankfurt/M. 1991 (Europäische Hochschulschriften XIX: A 36).

Schoeler: *Der Fremde im Islam* = G. Schoeler: *Der Fremde im Islam*, in: M. Schuster (ed.): *Die Begegnung mit dem Fremden. Wertungen und Wirkungen in Hochkulturen vom Altertum bis zur Gegenwart*, Stuttgart – Leipzig 1996, pp. 117–30.

—: *Naturdichtung* = Id.: *Arabische Naturdichtung. Die Zahrīyāt, Rabīʿīyāt und Rauḍīyāt von ihren Anfängen bis aṣ-Ṣanaubarī. Eine gattungs-, motiv- und stilgeschichtliche Untersuchung*, Beirut 1974 (Beiruter Texte und Studien 15).

Schöller: *Anfänge* = M. Schöller: *Anfänge und »erste Male«, gesehen mit den Augen der Araber*, in: K. Röttgers / M. Schmitz-Emans (eds.): *Anfänge und Übergänge*, Essen 2003 (Philosophisch-literarische Reflexionen 5), pp. 28–48.

—: *Exegetisches Denken* = Id.: *Exegetisches Denken und Prophetenbiographie. Eine quellenkritische Analyse der Sīra-Überlieferung zu Muḥammads Konflikt mit den Juden*, Wiesbaden 1998 (Diskurse der Arabistik 3).

—: *Methode und Wahrheit* = Id.: *Methode und Wahrheit in der Islamwissenschaft. Prolegomena*, Wiesbaden 2000.

Schöller: *Palmen* = M. Schöller: *Die Palmen (*līna*) der Banū n-Naḍīr und die Interpretation von Koran 59:9*, in: Zeitschrift der Deutschen Morgenländischen Gesellschaft 146 (1996), pp. 317–80.

—: *Sīra and Tafsīr* = Id.: *Sīra and Tafsīr: Muḥammad al-Kalbī on the Jews of Medina*, in: Motzki: *Biography of Muḥammad* pp. 18–48.

Schönig: *Jemenitinnen* = H. Schönig: *Schminken, Düfte und Räucherwerk der Jeminitinnen. Lexikon der Substanzen, Utensilien und Techniken*, Beirut 2002 (Beiruter Texte und Studien 91).

Schuman: *History of the Yemen* = L. O. Schuman: *Political History of the Yemen at the Beginning of the 16th Century. Abu Makhrama's Account of the Years 906–927 H. (1500–1521 A. D.) with Annotations*, PhD thesis Groningen 1960.

Scodel: *Poetic Epitaph* = J. Scodel: *The English Poetic Epitaph. Commemoration and Conflict from Jonson to Wordsworth*, Ithaca – London 1991.

Seidensticker: *Rūḥ* = T. Seidensticker: *Der rūḥ der Toten*, in: *Kaškūl. Festschrift zum 25. Jahrestag der Wiederbegründung des Instituts für Orientalistik an der Justus-Liebig-Universität Giessen*, edd. E. Wagner and K. Röhrborn (Wiesbaden 1989), pp. 141–56.

Serrano Ruano: *Los Banū ʿIyāḍ* = D. Serrano Ruano: *Los Banū ʿIyāḍ, de la caída del imperio almorávid a la instauración de la dinastia nazarí*, in: *Biografías almohades* I pp. 351–406.

Shoshan: *Popular culture* = B. Shoshan: *Popular culture in medieval Cairo*, Cambridge 1993 (Cambridge Studies in Islamic Civilization).

Sirriyeh: *Sufis and Anti-Sufis* = E. Sirriyeh: *Sufis and Anti-Sufis. The Defence, Rethinking and Rejection of Sufism in the Modern World*, Richmond 1999.

Smith/Haddad: *Islamic Understanding of Death* = J. I. Smith / Y. Haddad: *The Islamic Understanding of Death and Resurrection*, Albany 1981.

Smoor: *Poems on Death* = P. Smoor: *Elegies and Other Poems on Death by Ibn al-Rūmī*, in: Journal of Arabic Literature 27 (1996), pp. 49–85.

ŠN = M. b. M. Maḫlūf: *Šağarat an-nūr az-zakīyah fī ṭabaqāt al-Mālikīyah*, repr. Beirut n. d. ([1]1349).

Sobhani: *Doctrines of Shiʿi Islam* = Ayatollah Jaʿfar Sobhani: *Doctrines of Shiʿi Islam. A Compendium of Imami Beliefs and Practices*. Translated and edited by Reza Shah-Kazemi, London – New York 2001.

Sources for the History of Arabia I, 2 = ʿAr. aṭ-Ṭayyib al-Anṣārī [Abd al-Rahman Al-Ansary] (ed.): *Studies in the History of Arabia, Volume I: Sources for the History of Arabia, Part Two*, ar-Riyāḍ 1379/1979.

Sourvinou-Inwood: *'Reading' Greek Death* = C. Sourvinou-Inwood: *'Reading' Greek Death. To the End of the Classical Period*, Oxford 1995.

Spitaler: *Philologica* = A. Spitaler: *Philologica. Beiträge zur Arabistik und Semitistik*, herausgegeben von H. Bobzin und mit Indices versehen von S. Weninger, Wiesbaden 1998 (Diskurse der Arabistik 1).

Stern: *Ismāʿīlī Movement* = S. Stern: *Cairo as the Centre of the Ismāʿīlī Movement*, in: *Colloque Caire* pp. 437–50.

Storey: *Persian Literature* I, 2 = C. A. Storey: *Persian Literature. A Bio-bibliographical Survey, Vol. I, Part Two: Biography. Additions and Corrections. Indexes*, London 1953.

Ström: *Funeral Poetry* = A. Ström: *Lachrymae Catharinae. Five Collections of Funeral Poetry from 1628*, Stockholm 1994 (Acta Universitatis Stockholmiensis: Studia Latina Stockholmiensia XXXVIII).

Subtelny: *Cult of Anṣārī* = M. E. Subtelny: *The Cult of ʿAbdullāh Anṣārī under the Timurids*, in: A. Giese / J. Chr. Bürgel (eds.): *Gott ist schön und Er liebt die Schönheit (Festschrift Annemarie Schimmel)*, Bern – Frankfurt/M. 1994, pp. 377–406.

as-Suṭūḥī: *Maqābir al-Hū* = Maḥmūd as-Suṭūḥī: *az-Zaḫārif aš-šaʿbīyah ʿalā maqābir al-Hū*, Cairo 1388/1968.

Tabbaa: *Transformation* = Y. Tabbaa: *The Transformation of Islamic Art during the Sunni Revival*, London – New York 2002.

at-Talīdī: *Mašāhid* = ʿAl. at-Talīdī: *Mašāhid al-mawt wa-ʾahwāl al-barzaḫ wa-l-qubūr*, Beirut 1414/1993.

Taylor: *Reevaluating the Shiʿi Role* = C. S. Taylor: *Reevaluating the Shiʿi Role in the Development of Monumental Islamic Funerary Architecture: The Case of Egypt*, in: Muqarnas 9 (1992), pp 1–10.

—: *Vicinity of the Righteous* = Id.: *In the Vicinity of the Righteous.* Ziyāra *and the Veneration of Muslim Saints in late Medieval Egypt*, Leiden 1999 (Islamic History and Civilization. Studies and Texts 22).

Terrasse: *Histoire du Maroc* = H. Terrasse: *Histoire du Maroc des origines à l'établissement du Protectorat français*, 2 vols., Casablanca 1949–50 (also repr. New York 1975).

Thoden: *Merinidenpolitik* = R. Thoden: *Abū l-Ḥasan ʿAlī. Merinidenpolitik zwischen Nordafrika und Spanien in den Jahren 710–752 H. / 1310–1351*, Freiburg i. Br. 1973 (Islamkundliche Untersuchungen 21).

Torres Balbás: *Cementerios* = L. Torres Balbás: *Cementerios hispanomusulmanes*, in: al-Andalus 22 (1957), pp. 131–91.

Troll: *Muslim Shrines* = C. W. Troll (ed.): *Muslim Shrines in India. Their Character, History and Significance*, Delhi 1989 (repr. 1992).

Ullmann: *Neger in der Bildersprache* = M. Ullmann: *Der Neger in der Bildersprache der arabischen Dichtung*, Wiesbaden 1998.

al-ʿUmarī: *al-Qāḍī ʿIyāḍ* = A. Ǧamāl al-ʿUmarī: *as-Sīrah an-nabawīyah fī mafhūm al-Qāḍī ʿIyāḍ*, Cairo 1988.

Vadet: *Bestattungsbräuche* = J.-Cl. Vadet: *Review of Irene Grütter: Arabische Bestattungsbräuche* [see above], in: Arabica 4 (1957), p. 201f.

van Ess: *Prémices* = J. van Ess: *Les prémices de la théologie musulmane*, Paris 2002 (Collection «La Chaire de l'IMA» de l'Institut du monde arabe).

van Gelder: *God's Banquet* = G. J. van Gelder: *God's Banquet. Food in Classical Arabic Literature*, New York 2000.

Vatin/Yerasimos: *Cimetières Istanbul* = N. Vatin / S. Yerasimos: *L'implantation des cimetières musulmans intra muros à Istanbul*, in: Bacqué-Grammont/Tibet: *Cimetières et traditions funéraires* II pp. 37–56.

Vernet: *Natural Sciences* = J. Vernet: *Natural and Technical Sciences in al-Andalus*, in: Jayyusi: *Muslim Spain* II pp. 937–51.

Vizcaíno: *Vida y obra de Ibn Jayr* = J. M. Vizcaíno: *Vida y obra de Ibn Jayr (m. 575/1179)*, in: *Biografías almohades* I pp. 307–49.

Wafā: *Aḥkām al-ǧanāʾiz* = M. Wafā: *ʾAḥkām al-ǧanāʾiz fī l-fiqh al-ʾislāmī. Dirāsah muqāranah bayn al-maḏāhib al-ʾislāmīyah*, Asyūṭ 1413/1993.

Wagner: *Dichtung* I = E. Wagner: *Grundzüge der klassischen arabischen Dichtung. Band I: Die altarabische Dichtung*, Darmstadt 1987 (Grundzüge 68).

—: *Dichtung* II = Id.: *Grundzüge der klassischen arabischen Dichtung. Band II: Die arabische Dichtung in islamischer Zeit*, Darmstadt 1988 (Grundzüge 70).

Wali Songo Pilgrimage = *Wali Songo Pilgrimage* [The "Nine Saints of Islam" Pilgrimage], Surabaya: Regional Government of East Java 1992.

Watt: *Islamic Creeds* = W. M. Watt: *Islamic Creeds. A Selection*, Edinburgh 1994.

Waugh: *Muḥarram Rites* = E. H. Waugh: *Muḥarram Rites: Community Death and Rebirth*, in: Reynolds/Waugh: *Encounters with Death* pp. 200–13.

Weipert/Weninger: *Ibn Abī d-Dunyā* = R. Weipert / S. Weninger: *Die erhaltenen Werke des Ibn Abī d-Dunyā. Eine vorläufige Bestandsaufnahme*, in: Zeitschrift der Deutschen Morgenländischen Gesellschaft 146 (1996), pp. 415–55.

Welch: *Death in the Qurʾān* = A. T. Welch: *Death and Dying in the Qurʾān*, in: Reynolds/Waugh: *Encounters with Death*, pp. 183–99.

Wellhausen: *Reste* = J. Wellhausen: *Reste arabischen Heidentums. Gesammelt und erläutert*, Berlin [3]1961.

Wensinck: *Concordance* = A. J. Wensinck: *Concordance et Indices de la Tradition Musulmane*, augmented by W. Raven and J. Witkam, 8 vols., Leiden [2]1992.

—: *Weinen* = Id.: *Über das Weinen in den monotheistischen Religionen Vorderasiens*, in: G. Weil (ed.): *Festschrift Eduard Sachau zum siebzigsten Geburtstag*, Berlin 1915, pp. 26–35.

Wha: *Baraka* = M. Byung Wha: Baraka, *as Motif and Motive, in the* Riḥla *of Ibn Baṭṭūṭa (1304–1369)*, PhD thesis Univ. of Utah 1991.

Williams: *Islamic Monuments* = Id.: *Islamic Monuments in Cairo*, Cairo [4]1993 (repr. 1999).

—: *The Cult of ʿAlid Saints* = C. Williams: *The Cult of ʿAlid Saints in the Fatimid Monuments of Cairo*, in: Muqarnas 1 (1983), pp. 37–52 and Muqarnas 3 (1985), pp. 38–60.

Winkler: *Volkskunde* = H. A. Winkler: *Ägyptische Volkskunde*, Stuttgart 1936.

Winter: *al-Mutanabbī's Elegies* = M. Winter: *Content and Form in the Elegies of al-Mutanabbī*, in: *Studia Orientalia Memoriae D. H. Baneth Dedicata*, Jerusalem 1979, pp. 327–45.

Wirth: *Orientalische Stadt* = E. Wirth: *Die orientalische Stadt im islamischen Vorderasien und Nordafrika. Städtische Bausubstanz und räumliche Ordnung, Wirtschaftsleben und soziale Organisation. Band I: Text*, Mainz 2000.

WKAS = *Wörterbuch der klassischen arabischen Sprache*, vols. 1f., edd. A. Spitaler and M. Ullmann, Wiesbaden 1972ff.

Woodward: *Islam in Java* = M. R. Woodward: *Islam in Java. Normative Piety and Mysticism in the Sultanate of Yogyakarta*, Tucson 1989 (The Association for Asian Studies Monographs 45).

Wright: *Grammar* = W. Wright: *A Grammar of the Arabic Language, 3rd revised edition*, 2 vols., Cambridge 1951.

ZA = Ḫayr ad-Dīn az-Ziriklī: *al-ʾAʿlām. Qāmūs tarāǧim li-ʾašhar ar-riǧāl wa-n-nisāʾ* etc., 8 vols., Beirut [14]1999.

Zajadacz-Hastenrath: *Chaukhandigräber* = S. Zajadacz-Hastenrath: *Chaukhandigräber. Studien zur Grabkunst in Sind und Baluchistan*, Wiesbaden 1978.

Zaman: *Funeral processions* = M. Q. Zaman: *Death, funeral processions, and the articulation of religious authority in early Islam*, in: Studia Islamica 93 (2001), pp. 27–58.

az-Zaylaʿī: *Amirate of Mecca* = A. ʿUmar az-Zaylaʿī: *The Southern Area of the Amirate of Mecca (3rd–7th/9th–13th Centuries), its History, Archaeology and Epigraphy*, PhD thesis Durham 1983.

Zepter: *Friedhöfe* = J. Zepter: *Friedhöfe als Gegenstand der bidʿa-Literatur anhand ausgewählter Quellen*, unpublished M. A. thesis Cologne 1996.

Arabic-English Glossary

al-ʾāḫirah[1]	the hereafter
iḥtisāb	debiting (of a deceased person to God's accounts)
ʾamīr al-muʾminīn	the Prince of the Believers
al-ʾinǧīl	the Gospel
al-baʿṯ	the Raising (of the dead)
al-bayt al-ḥarām	the Sacred House (i.e. the Kaʿbah)
taʿziyah pl. *taʿāzī*	condolence(s)
at-tawrāh	the Torah
tawaffāhu llāhu	God took him unto Him (i.e. he died)
tuwuffiya	he was taken (by God unto Him) *or* he was taken (unto God), i.e. he died
ǧannāt al-firdaws	the Gardens of Paradise
ǧannāt an-naʿīm	the Gardens of Bliss (i.e. Paradise)
al-ǧannah	the Garden (i.e. Paradise)
ǧihād	fight for Islam *or* in the cause of Islam; Holy War
ǧiwār Allāh	the neighbourhood of God (with the connotation of protection)
al-ḥāǧǧ	the pilgrim
al-ḥaǧǧ	the pilgrimage
al-ḥuǧǧah	the Argument (of man after death)
ḥadīṯ pl. *ʾaḥādīṯ*	Tradition(s)
al-ḥisāb	the Accounting *or* the Settlement of Accounts (at the Last Judgment)
al-ḥašr	the Gathering (of men after the Resurrection)
ḥufrah	pit (i.e. the grave)
al-ḥawḍ	the Basin (of the Prophet Muḥammad from which the Muslims will drink)
dār al-baqāʾ	the House of Permanence (i.e. the hereafter)
dār al-bilā	the House of Decay (i.e. the grave)
dār al-ġurūr	the House of Delusion (i.e. this world)
dār al-fanāʾ	the House of Transience *or* Extinction (i.e. this world)
duʿāʾ pl. *ʾadʿiyah*	prayer (for someone)

1 In this glossary, important terms occurring in both volumes are given in order of the Arabic alphabet. The Arabic definite article is not taken account of in the arrangement of the items.

ad-dunyā	this world
ad-dawāwīn	the Registers (containing men's deeds)
rawḍah	garden (as a designation of graves or cemeteries)
rayḥān	fragrant plant (as an affectionate designation of persons)
zād	provisions (of man, consisting of good deeds for the hereafter)
as-sāʿah	the Hour (i.e. the Last Judgment)
as-saʿīd	the blissful (one)
as-sūr	the Wall (separating Paradise and Hell)
šafāʿah	intercession
šahādah	testimony *or* profession of the creed (esp. of a person at death, as attributed to him in his epitaph)
aš-šahīd	the martyr
aṣ-ṣāliḥūn	the righteous
ṣabr	composure
aṣ-ṣuḥuf	the Leaves (which men will receive at the Last Judgment)
aṣ-ṣiddīqūn	the veracious
aṣ-ṣirāṭ	the Bridge (over Hell)
ʿaḏāb al-qabr	the Chastisement of the Grave
ʿaḏāb an-nār	the Chastisement of the Fire (i.e. Hell)
ʿĪd al-ʾAḍḥā	the Feast of Sacrifice
ʿĪd al-Fiṭr	the Feast of the Breaking of the Fast
al-ʿĪd al-Kabīr	the Great Feast
al-ġarīb	the stranger (in a foreign country *or* in the grave)
fitnat al-qabr	the Trial of the Grave
qabr	grave, tomb
qurrat ʿaynī	the delight (lit. coolness) of my eye (affectionate designation of children)
al-qiyāmah	the Resurrection
kitāb pl. *kutub*	the Document (which man will receive at the Last Judgment)
al-kitāb	the Book (i.e. the Qurʾān)
kitāb Allāh	God's Book (i.e. the Qurʾān)
laḥd	burial niche
al-muttaqūn	the God-fearing
marṯiyah pl. *marāṯī*	mourning poem(s)
al-masʾalah (or *al-musāʾalah*)	the Interrogation (of man after death by the angels Munkar and Nakīr)
al-maẓlūm	the wronged one (designation of persons in epitaphs who probably suffered a violent death)
millat ʾIbrāhīm	the creed *or* community of Ibrāhīm (i.e. Abraham)

al-munaġġaṣ (*bi-šabābihi* etc.)	the one prevented from enjoying (his youth etc.)
al-mawlā	the Patron (*sc*. God)
al-mīzān	the Balance (of the Last Judgment)
an-nār	the Fire (i.e. Hell)
an-nušūr	the Resuscitation
yawm ad-dīn	the Day of Judgment
yawm al-qiyāmah	the Day of the Resurrection